About the Author

Alan Brinkley is the Allan Nevins Professor of History at Columbia University in New York. He is the author of *Voices of Protest: Huey Long, Father Coughlin, and the Great Depression* (which won the 1983 American Book Award); *American History: A Survey; The End of Reform: New Deal Liberalism in Recession and War*; and *Liberalism and Its Discontents*. He was educated at Princeton and Harvard and has been a member of the faculties at M.I.T., Harvard (where he received the Joseph R. Levenson Memorial Teaching Prize), and the City University of New York Graduate School. He was the Harmsworth Professor of American History at Oxford University in 1998–1999, and has been a visiting professor at Princeton University, the Ecole des Haute Etudes en Sciences Sociales in Paris, and the University of Torino. His articles, essays, and reviews appear frequently in both scholarly and non-scholarly journals.

Brief Contents

Contents

List of Illustrations

List of Maps

Preface

T HE STORY OF the American past, which is the subject of this book, has undergone many transformations in recent decades. The past itself has not changed, of course, but the way Americans understand it has changed dramatically. And in the wake of those changes have come both new forms of presentation and bitter controversies.

In one sense, American history is thriving as almost never before through the workings of American popular culture. Historical museums and exhibitions have multiplied and have attracted large audiences. Popular writing on history—both nonfiction and novels—has grown in popularity. History is a continuing presence on television, in films, and increasingly on the Internet. The popular appetite for American history seems to be almost boundless. At the same time, however, historical scholarship has become the source of increasing debate—among historians themselves, among the various publics historians try to reach, and even among politicians, some of whom attack the historical profession for what they claim is an excessively critical view of the past.

Both the growing popularity of history and the growing controversies surrounding it reflect the character of our time. It is an era of rapid and bewildering change, which encourages people to look to the past for guidance and reassurance—for reminders of what many believe were simpler, stabler times. But the turbulence of our age has also encouraged historians to ask new questions of the past—and thus to reinterpret it—in an effort to understand the tensions and contests that preoccupy us today. As the population of the United States has become more diverse and as groups that once stood outside the view of scholarship have thrust themselves into its center, historians have labored to reveal the immense complexity of their country's past.

Historical narratives once recounted little beyond the experiences of great men and the unfolding of great public events. Today, they attempt to tell a more complicated story—one that includes private as well as public lives, ordinary people as well as celebrated ones, difference as well as unity. This newer history seems fragmented at times, because it attempts to embrace so many more areas of human experience than the older narratives. It is often disturbing, because it reveals failures and injustices as well as triumphs. But it is also richer, fuller, and better suited to helping us understand our own diverse and contentious world.

Threading one's way through the many, conflicting demands of contemporary scholars and contemporary readers is no easy task. But I have tried in this book to consider both the diversity and the unity that have characterized the American experience. The United States is, and has always been, a nation of many cultures. To understand its history, we must understand the experiences of the many groups who have shaped American society—the many worlds that have developed within it based on region, religion, class, ideology, race, gender, and ethnicity.

But the United States is not simply a collection of different cultures. It is also a great nation. And as important as understanding its diversity is understanding the forces that have drawn it together and allowed it to survive and flourish despite division. The United States has constructed a remarkably stable and enduring political system, which touches the lives of all Americans. It has developed an immense and highly productive national economy that affects the working and consuming lives of virtually everyone. It has created a mass popular culture that colors the experiences and assumptions of almost all Americans, and of the people of much of the rest of the world as well. One can admire these unifying forces for their contributions to America's considerable success as a nation, or condemn them for creating or failing to address injustices. But no one proposing to understand the history of the United States can afford to ignore them.

This third edition of *The Unfinished Nation*, like its predecessors, tries to tell the complicated and endlessly fascinating story of America for students of history and for general readers. Those familiar with earlier editions will notice some significant changes. Perhaps the most important is considerably expanded attention throughout the book to the history of science and technology, whose importance to American history has been incalculable. For example, chapter 1 contains new material on military technology to accompany the discussion of King Philip's War; a new section on medical science, which discusses the discovery of anaesthesia and early steps toward the germ theory of disease has been added to chapter 12; and chapter 34 offers a substantial new section on science and technology, examining the digital revolution and new genetic research. I want to express my appreciation to the scholarly reviewers who helped to determine which science and technology topics the book should include: Edward J. Larson, University of Georgia; Sarah K.A. Pfatteicher, University of Wisconsin; Carroll Pursell, Case Western Reserve University; Bruce E. Seely, Michigan Technological University; Howard Segal, University of Maine; and Steven W. Usselman, Georgia Institute of Technology. There is also a great deal of new material on the history of American culture, and on popular culture in particular. There are four new "Debating the Past" essays, exploring significant controversies among scholars; they appear in chapters 1, 25, 28, and 32. There is a substantially revised and expanded final chapter, which recounts very recent events and examines recent social, economic, and cultural trends. There is a new summary conclusion at the end of each chapter, and new annotated bibliographies, which include references to relevant films and Internet sites.

The result of these and many other changes is, I hope, a book that will introduce readers to enough different aspects of American history to make them aware of its extraordinary richness and complexity. But I hope, too, that it will give readers some sense of the shared experiences of Americans and of the forces that have sustained the United States as a nation.

***

I am grateful to many people for their help on this book: Lyn Uhl, Kristen Mellitt, Suzanne Daghlian, and Jayne Klein at McGraw-Hill; Deborah Bull, for her expert photo research and John Stoner and Thad Russell for their indispensable help with research. I also want to thank the various scholars who reviewed the second edition and its supplements, and offered suggestions and comments: Guy Alchon, *University of Delaware*; Paul Bethel, *American River College*; Thomas J. Brown, *University of South Carolina*; William R. Cario, *Concordia University Wisconsin*; Paul N. Chardoul, *Grand Rapids Community College*; J.H. DeBerry, *Somerset Community College*; David DiLeo, *Saddleback Community College*; William Dofflemyer, *San Joaquin Delta College*; Don Fisher, *Niagra County Community College*; Stephen E. Gooch, *Richland College*; Elizabeth A. Hachten, *University of Wisconsin-Whitewater*; Roger H. Hall, *Allan Hancock College*; Michael Haridopolos, *Brevard Community College*; Michael Mini, *Montgomery County Community College*; Ronald Petrin, *Oklahoma State University*; Jody Suhanek,

Lane Community College; Roger Tate, *Somerset Community College;* Michael Welsh, *University of Northern Colorado;* and Nelson E. Woodard, *California State University-Fullerton.* I am also grateful to those readers of the book who have offered me unsolicited comments, criticisms, and corrections. I hope they will continue to do so. Suggestions can be sent to me at the Department of History, Columbia University, New York, NY 10027, or by E-mail at ab65@columbia.edu.

Alan Brinkley

CHAPTER ONE

The Meeting of Cultures

America Before Columbus ～ *Europe Looks Westward*
The Arrival of the English

T HE DISCOVERY OF America did not begin with Christopher Columbus. It started many thousands of years earlier when human beings first crossed an ancient land bridge—over the Bering Strait into what is now Alaska—and almost certainly without realizing it began to people a new continent.

AMERICA BEFORE COLUMBUS

No one is certain when these migrations began; recent estimates suggest that they started between 14,000 and 16,000 years ago. They were probably a result of the development of stone-tipped spears and other hunting implements that made it possible for humans to pursue large animals from Asia into North America. Year after year, a few at a time, these nomadic peoples—probably drawn from a Mongolian stock similar to that of modern-day eastern Siberia—entered the new continent and moved deeper into its heart. Perhaps as early as 8,000 B.C., the migrations reached the southern tip of South America. By the end of the fifteenth century A.D., when the first important contact with Europeans occurred, America was the home of many millions of men and women. Scholars estimate that well over 50 million people—and perhaps as many as 75 million—lived in the Americas by 1500 and that perhaps 10 million lived in the territory that now constitutes the United States.

1

TIME LINE			
16,000-14,000 B.C.	**1492**	**1497**	**1502**
Asians migrate to North America	Columbus discovers America	Cabot explores North America	African slaves arrive in Spanish America

1518–1530	**1519–1522**	**1558**	**1565**	**1587**
Smallpox ravages Indians	Magellan circumnavigates globe	Elizabeth I becomes English queen	St Augustine, Florida founded	"Lost Colony" established on Roanoke Island

1603	**1607**	**1608**	**1609**	
James I becomes English king	Jamestown founded	French establish Quebec	Spanish found Santa Fe	

The Civilizations of the South

The most elaborate of these societies emerged in South and Central America and in Mexico. In Peru, the Incas created a powerful empire of perhaps 6 million people. They developed a complex political system and a large network of paved roads that welded together the populations of many tribes under a single government. In Central America and on the Yucatan Peninsula of Mexico, the Mayas built a sophisticated culture with a written language, a numerical system similar to the Arabic, an accurate calendar, and an advanced agricultural system. They were succeeded by the Aztecs, a once-nomadic warrior tribe from the north. In the late thirteenth century, the Aztecs established a precarious rule over much of central and southern Mexico and built elaborate administrative, educational, and medical systems comparable to the most advanced in Europe at the time. The Aztecs also developed a harsh religion that required human sacrifice. Their Spanish conquerors discovered the skulls of 100,000 victims in one location when they arrived in 1519.

The economies of these societies were based primarily on agriculture, but there were also substantial cities. Tenochtitlán, the Aztec capital built on the site of present-day Mexico City, had a population of over 100,000 in 1500, which was comparable to some of the largest European cities of the time. The Mayas (at Mayapan and elsewhere) and the Incas (in such cities as Cuzco and Machu Picchu) produced elaborate settlements with striking religious and ceremonial structures. These civilizations accomplished all this without some of the important technologies that Asian and European civilizations possessed. As late as the sixteenth century, no American society had yet developed wheeled vehicles.

The Civilizations of the North

The peoples north of Mexico—in the lands that became the United States and Canada—developed less elaborate but still substantial civilizations. Inhabitants of the northern regions of the continent subsisted on some combination of hunting, gathering, and fishing. They included the Eskimos of the Arctic Circle, who fished and hunted seals and whose civilization spanned thousands of miles of largely frozen land; the big-game hunters of the northern forests, who led nomadic lives based on pursuit of moose and caribou; the tribes of the Pacific Northwest, whose principal occupation was salmon fishing and who created substantial permanent settlements along the coast; and a group of tribes spread through relatively arid regions of the Far West, who developed successful communities based on fishing, hunting small game, and gathering edible plants.

Other societies in North America were primarily agricultural. Among the most developed were those in the Southwest. The people of that arid region built large irrigation systems, and they constructed substantial towns of stone and adobe structures. In the Great Plains region, too, most tribes were engaged in sedentary farming (corn and other grains) and lived in large permanent settlements, although some small nomadic tribes subsisted by hunting buffalo.

The eastern third of what is now the United States—much of it covered with forests and inhabited by the Woodland Indians—had the greatest food resources of any area of the continent. Most of the many tribes of the region engaged in farming, hunting, gathering, and fishing simultaneously. In the South there were substantial permanent settlements and large trading networks based on the corn and other grains grown in the rich lands of the Mississippi River valley. Cahokia, a trading center located near present-day St. Louis, had a population of 40,000 at its peak in A.D. 1200.

The agricultural societies of the Northeast were less stationary. Farming techniques there were designed to exploit the land quickly rather than to develop permanent settlements. Many of the tribes living east of the Mississippi River were linked together loosely by common linguistic roots. The largest of these language groups consisted of the Algonquin tribes, which

INDIANS FISHING The English explorer John White visited areas of the Atlantic coast in the 1580s and created a series of watercolors of native life there—among them this scene of Woodland Indians fishing from a canoe.

lived along the Atlantic seaboard from Canada to Virginia; the Iroquois Confederacy, which was centered in what is now upstate New York; and the Muskogean tribes, which consisted of the tribes in the southernmost region of the eastern seaboard. Alliances among the various Indian societies (even among those with common languages) were fragile, since the peoples of the Americas did not think of themselves as members of a single civilization.

Religion was as important to Indian society as it was to most other cultures, and it was usually closely linked with the natural world on which the tribes depended. Native Americans worshipped many gods, whom they associated variously with crops, game, forests, rivers, and other elements of nature.

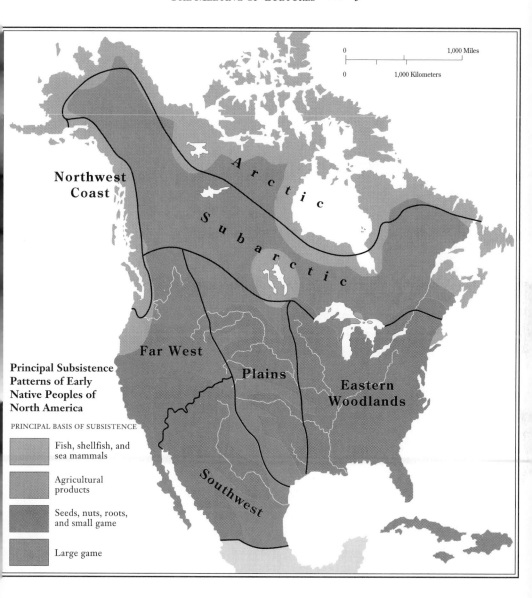

Principal Subsistence Patterns of Early Native Peoples of North America

PRINCIPAL BASIS OF SUBSISTENCE

- Fish, shellfish, and sea mammals
- Agricultural products
- Seeds, nuts, roots, and small game
- Large game

Northwest Coast

Arctic

Subarctic

Far West

Plains

Eastern Woodlands

Southwest

0   1,000 Miles

0   1,000 Kilometers

All tribes assigned women the jobs of caring for children, preparing meals, and gathering certain foods. But the allocation of other tasks varied from one society to another. Some tribal groups (notably the Pueblos of the Southwest) reserved farming tasks almost entirely for men. Among other groups (including the Algonquins, the Iroquois, and the Muskogean), women tended the fields, while men engaged in hunting, warfare, or clearing land. Because women and children were often left alone for extended

DEBATING THE PAST

The American Population Before Columbus

N O ONE knows how many people lived in the Americas in the centuries before Columbus. But scholars, and others, have spent more than a century, and have written many thousands of pages, debating the question nevertheless. Interest in this question survives, despite the near impossibility of answering it, because the debate over the pre-Columbian population is closely connected to the much larger debate over the consequences of European settlement of the Western Hemisphere.

Throughout the nineteenth century, Native Americans—drawing from their own rich tradition of oral history—spoke often of the great days before Columbus when there were many more people in their tribes. The painter and ethnographer George Catlin, who spent much time among the tribes in the 1830s, listened to these oral legends and estimated that there had been 16 million Indians in North America before the Europeans came. Other white Americans dismissed such claims as preposterous, insisting that Indian civilization was far too primitive ever to have sustained a population even as large as a million.

In 1928, James Mooney, an ethnologist at the Smithsonian Institution, drawing from early accounts of soldiers and missionaries in the sixteenth century, came up with the implausibly precise figure of 1.15 million natives who lived north of Mexico in the early sixteenth century. That was a larger figure than nineteenth-century writers had suggested, but still much smaller than the Indians themselves claimed. A few years later, the anthropologist Alfred Kroeber used some of Mooney's methods to come up with an estimate considerably larger than Mooney's, but much lower than Catlin's. He concluded in 1934 that there were 8.4 million people in the Americas in 1492, half in North America and half in the Caribbean and South America. His conclusions remained largely uncontested until the 1960s.

These low early estimates reflected an assumption that the arrival of the Europeans did not much reduce the native population. But in the 1960s and 1970s, scholars discovered that the early tribes had been cata-strophically decimated by European plagues not long after the arrival of Columbus—that the numbers Europeans observed even in the late 1500s were already dramatically smaller than the numbers in 1492. Drawing on early work by anthropologists and others who discovered evidence of widespread deaths by disease, historians such as William McNeill in 1976 and Alfred Crosby a decade later produced powerful accounts of the near extinction of some tribes and the dramatic depopulation of others in a pestilential holocaust with few parallels in history.

The belief that the native population was much larger in 1492 than it was a few decades later has helped spur much larger estimates of how many people were in America before Columbus. Henry Dobyns, an anthropologist, claimed in 1966 that there were between 10 and 12 million people north of Mexico in 1492, and between 90 and 112 million in all of the Americas. No subsequent scholar has made so high a claim, but most subsequent estimates have been much closer to Dobyns's than to Kroeber's. The geographer William M. Denevan, for example, argued in 1976 that the American population in 1492 was around 55 million and that the population north of Mexico was under 4 million. These are among the lowest of modern estimates, but still dramatically higher than the nineteenth-century numbers.

The vehemence with which scholars, and at times the larger public, have debated these figures does not stem solely from the difficulty inherent in the effort to determine population size. It is also because the debate over the population is part of the debate over whether the arrival of Columbus—and the millions of Europeans who followed him—was a great advance in the history of civilization (as most Americans believed in 1892 when they ebulliently celebrated the 400th anniversary of Columbus's voyage) or an unparalleled catastrophe that virtually exterminated a large and flourishing native population (as some Americans and Europeans argued during the far more somber commemoration of the 500th anniversary in 1992). How to balance the many achievements of European civilization in the New World after 1492 against the terrible destruction of native peoples that accompanied it is, in the end, less a historical question, perhaps, than a moral one.

periods while men were away hunting or fighting, women in some tribes tended to control the social and economic organization of the settlements.

EUROPE LOOKS WESTWARD

Europeans were almost entirely unaware of the existence of the Americas before the fifteenth century. A few early wanderers—Leif Eriksson, an eleventh-century Norse seaman, and perhaps others—had glimpsed parts of the New World on their voyages. But even if their discoveries had become common knowledge (and they did not), there would have been little incentive for others to follow. Europe in the Middle Ages (roughly A.D. 500–1500) was too divided and decentralized, too limited in its commerce, and too lacking in powerful political leaders to inspire many great ventures. By the end of the fifteenth century, however, conditions in Europe had changed, and the incentive for overseas exploration had grown.

Commerce and Nationalism

Two changes in particular encouraged Europeans to look toward new lands. One was a result of the significant growth in Europe's population in the fifteenth century. The Black Death, a catastrophic epidemic of the bubonic plague that began in Constantinople in 1347, had killed (according to some estimates) as many as half the people of the continent. But a century and a half later, the population had rebounded. With that growth came a reawakening of commerce and a general increase in prosperity. A new merchant class was emerging to meet the rising demand for goods from abroad. As trade increased, and as advances in navigation and shipbuilding made long-distance sea travel more feasible, interest in expanding trade even further grew quickly.

The second change was the emergence of new governments that were more united and powerful than the feeble political entities of the feudal past. In the western areas of Europe in particular, strong new monarchs were emerging, creating centralized nation-states and growing eager to enhance the commercial development of their nations.

Ever since the early fourteenth century, when Marco Polo and other adventurers had returned from Asia bearing exotic spices, cloths, and dyes, and even more exotic tales, Europeans who craved commercial glory had dreamed above all of trade with the East. For two centuries, that trade had been limited by the difficulties of the long overland journey to the Asian courts. But in the fourteenth century, as the maritime talents of several western European societies increased, talk of finding a faster, safer sea route to East Asia began. In the late fifteenth century, some of the new monarchs were ready to finance daring voyages to find it.

The Portuguese were the preeminent maritime power in the fifteenth century largely because of Prince Henry the Navigator, who devoted much of his life to the promotion of exploration. In 1486, after Henry's death, the Portuguese explorer Bartholomeu Dias rounded the southern tip of Africa (the Cape of Good Hope); and in 1497–1498, Vasco da Gama proceeded all the way around the cape to India. But the Portuguese were not the first to encounter the New World.

Christopher Columbus

Christopher Columbus was born and reared in Genoa, Italy, and spent his early seafaring years in the service of the Portuguese. By the time he was a young man, he had developed great ambitions. He believed he could reach East Asia by sailing west, across the Atlantic, rather than east, around Africa. Columbus's optimism rested on several basic misconceptions. He thought the world was far smaller than it actually is. He also believed that the Asian continent extended farther eastward than it actually does. Most important, he did not realize that anything lay to the west between Europe and the lands of Asia.

Columbus failed to enlist the leaders of Portugal behind his plan, so he turned instead to Spain. The marriage of Spain's two most powerful regional rulers, Ferdinand of Aragon and Isabella of Castile, had produced the strongest monarchy in Europe, one that was eager to demonstrate its strength by sponsoring new commercial ventures. Columbus appealed to Queen Isabella for support for his proposed westward voyage, and in 1492, she agreed. Commanding ninety men and three ships—the *Niña*, the *Pinta*, and the *Santa María*—Columbus left Spain in August 1492 and sailed west into the Atlantic. Ten weeks later, he sighted land and assumed he had reached an island off Asia. In fact, he had landed in the Bahamas. When he pushed on and encountered Cuba, he assumed he had reached China. He returned to Spain, bringing with him several captured natives as evidence of his achievement. (He called the natives "Indians" because he believed they were from the East Indies in the Pacific.)

But Columbus did not, of course, bring back news of the great khan's court in China or any samples of the fabled wealth of the Indies. And so a year later, he tried again, this time with a much larger expedition. As before, he headed into the Caribbean, discovering several other islands and leaving a small and short-lived colony on Hispaniola. On a third voyage,

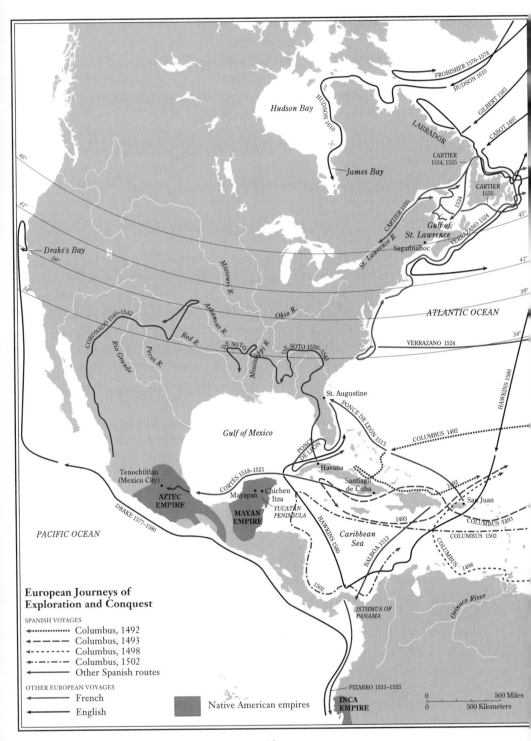

FROBISHER 1576–1578
HUDSON 1610
GILBERT 1583
CABOT 1497

Hudson Bay
HUDSON 1610
LABRADOR
CARTIER 1534, 1535
CARTIER 1535
CARTIER 1535
1534
James Bay
VERRAZANO 1524

45°
41°

Drake's Bay
36°
34°

Missouri R.

St. Lawrence R.
Gulf of St. Lawrence
Sagadahoc
VERRAZANO 1524

45°
41°

Arkansas R.
Ohio R.
ATLANTIC OCEAN

38°

CORONADO 1540–1542
Red R.
DE SOTO
Mississippi R.
DE SOTO 1539–1542
VERRAZANO 1524

34°

Rio Grande
Pecos R.

St. Augustine
PONCE DE LEÓN 1513
COLUMBUS 1492
HAWKINS 1580

Gulf of Mexico
PONCE DE LEÓN
Havana
COLUMBUS 1492

Tenochtitlan (Mexico City)
CORTÉS 1518–1521
Mayapan
Chichen Itza
YUCATÁN PENINSULA
Santiago de Cuba
1492
San Juan

AZTEC EMPIRE
DRAKE 1577–1580
MAYAN EMPIRE
1493
COLUMBUS 1493
COLUMBUS 1502
COLUMBUS 1498

PACIFIC OCEAN
HAWKINS 1580
Caribbean Sea
BALBOA 1513
1502

Orinoco River

ISTHMUS OF PANAMA

European Journeys of Exploration and Conquest

SPANISH VOYAGES
••••••••••• Columbus, 1492
– – – – – Columbus, 1493
- - - - - - Columbus, 1498
–·–·–·– Columbus, 1502
——→ Other Spanish routes

OTHER EUROPEAN VOYAGES
——→ French
——→ English

Native American empires

PIZARRO 1531–1533
INCA EMPIRE

0   500 Miles
0   500 Kilometers

10

in 1498, he finally reached the mainland and cruised along the northern coast of South America. He then realized, for the first time, that he had encountered not a part of Asia but a separate continent. Still, he remained convinced that Asia was only a short distance away.

Columbus's celebrated accomplishments made him a popular hero for a time, but he ended his life in obscurity. Ultimately, he was even unable to give his name to the land he had revealed to the Europeans. That distinction went instead to a Florentine merchant, Amerigo Vespucci, a passenger on a later Portuguese expedition to the New World, who wrote a series of vivid descriptions of the lands he visited and helped popularize the idea that the Americas were new continents.

Partly as a result of Columbus's initiative, Spain began to devote greater resources and energy to maritime exploration and gradually replaced Portugal as the foremost seafaring nation. In 1513 the Spaniard Vasco de Balboa crossed the Isthmus of Panama and became the first known European to gaze westward upon the great ocean that separated America from China. Seeking access to that ocean, Ferdinand Magellan, a Portuguese in Spanish employ, found the strait that now bears his name at the southern end of South America, struggled through the stormy narrows and into the ocean (so calm by contrast that he christened it the *Pacific*), and then proceeded to the Philippines. There Magellan died in a conflict with the natives, but his expedition went on to complete the first known circumnavigation of the globe (1519–1522). By 1550, Spaniards had explored the coasts of North America as far north as Oregon in the west and Labrador in the east.

The Spanish Empire

In time, Spanish explorers in the New World stopped thinking of America simply as an obstacle to their search for a route to the East and began instead to consider it a possible source of wealth in itself. The Spanish claimed for themselves the whole of the New World, except for a piece of it (today's Brazil) that was reserved by a papal decree for the Portuguese; and by the mid-sixteenth century, they were establishing a substantial American empire.

The early Spanish colonists, beginning with those Columbus brought on his second voyage, settled on the islands of the Caribbean. But then, in 1518, Hernando Cortés, who had been an unsuccessful Spanish government official in Cuba for fourteen years, decided to lead a small military expedition (about 600 men) against the Aztecs in Mexico and their powerful emperor, Montezuma, after hearing stories of great treasures there. His

San Francisco (1776)
Monterey (1770)
San Luis Obispo (1772)
Los Angeles (1781)
San Juan Capistrano (1776)
San Diego de Alcala (1769)
Tucson (1709)

LOUISIANA
(Spanish 1763-1800)

Taos (1609)
Santa Fe (1607)
Red R.

UNITED STATES
(from 1783)

Mississippi R.

Rio Grande

Culiacán (1531)

Tampico

VICEROYALTY OF

Mexico City (Tenochtitlán) (1325)
Veracruz (1519)

Yucatan Peninsula

NEW SPAIN

Guatemala (1519)

Gulf of Mexico

SPANISH FLORIDA (to 1819)

St. Augustine (1565)

La Habana (1515)

Cuba (1492)
Santiago (1514)

Jamaica (to Britain 1655)

Bahamas (to Britain 1646)

ATLANTIC OCEAN

Española (1492)

Espanola (1492)

Puerto Rico (1502)

HAITI (French after 1697)

Santo Domingo (1496)

Caribbean Sea

Trinidad (1498)

Panama (1519)

Caracas (1567)

Orinoco R.

FRENCH GUIANA (1626)

VICEROYALTY OF

Santa Fe de Bogotá (1538)

NEW GRANADA

SURINAM (Dutch) (1625)

PACIFIC OCEAN

Quito (1534)

Amazon River

Guayaquil (1535)

Ciudad de los Reyes (Lima) (1535)

Cuzco (1535)

VICEROYALTY OF
NEW CASTILIA (Peru)

La Paz (1548)

VICEROYALTY OF
LA PLATA

Rio de Janeiro (1567)

São Paulo (1554)

Paraná R.

Valparaiso (1544)

Santiago (1541)

Spanish America

Colonial boundaries and provincial names are for the late 18th century

Aztec Empire at the time of Spanish conquest

Inca Empire at the time of Spanish conquest

OUTPOSTS ON THE NORTHERN FRONTIER OF NEW SPAIN
(Not simultaneous; through the 18th century)

• Missions

○ Forts (sometimes with missions)

• Settlements

Buenos Aires (1580)

Montevideo (1724)

Rio de la Plata

World divided into Spanish and Portuguese hemispheres: Treaty of Tordesillas (1494)

PORTUGUESE BRAZIL

Straits of Magellan
Tierra del Fuego

0   1,000 Miles
0   1,000 Kilometers

12

THE MEXICANS STRIKE BACK In this vivid scene from the Duran Codex, Mexican artists illustrate a rare moment in which Mexican warriors gained the upper hand over the Spanish invaders. Driven back by native fighters, the Spanish have taken refuge in a room in the royal palace in Tenochtitlán while brightly attired Mexican warriors besiege them. Although the Mexicans gained a temporary advantage in this battle, the drawing illustrates one of the reasons for their inability to withstand the Spanish in the longer term. The Spanish soldiers are armed with rifles and crossbows, while the Indians carry only spears and shields.

first assault on Tenochtitlán, the Aztec capital, failed. But Cortés and his army had, unknowingly, unleashed an assault on the Aztecs far more devastating than military attack: they had exposed the natives to smallpox. An epidemic of that deadly disease decimated the Aztec population and made it possible for the Spanish to triumph in their second attempt at conquest. Through his ruthless suppression of the surviving natives, Cortés established himself as one of the most brutal of the Spanish "conquistadores" (conquerors). Twenty years later, Francisco Pizarro conquered the Incas in Peru and opened the way for other advances into South America.

The conquistadores—through their daring and their terrible brutality—had cleared the way for the first Spanish settlers in America. They were interested only in exploiting the American stores of gold and silver, and they were fabulously successful. For 300 years, beginning in the sixteenth century, the mines of Spanish America yielded more than ten times as much gold and silver as the rest of the world's mines together. After the first wave of conquest, however, most Spanish settlers in America traveled to the New World for other reasons. Many went in hopes of profiting from agriculture, and they helped establish elements of European civilization permanently in America. Other Spaniards—priests, friars, and other missionaries—went to America to spread the Christian religion; through their efforts, the influence of the Catholic Church ultimately extended throughout South and Central America and Mexico.

By the end of the sixteenth century, the Spanish Empire had become one of the largest in the history of the world. It included the Caribbean islands, Mexico, and southern North America. The Spanish Empire also spread into South America and included what is now Chile, Argentina, and Peru. In 1580, when the Spanish and Portuguese monarchies temporarily united, Brazil came under Spanish jurisdiction as well.

Northern Outposts

The Spanish fort of St. Augustine, established in Florida in 1565, became the first permanent European settlement in the present-day United States. But it was little more than a small military outpost. A more substantial colonizing venture began in the Southwest in 1598, when Don Juan de Onate traveled north from Mexico with a party of 500, claimed for Spain some of the lands of the Pueblo Indians in what is now New Mexico, and began to establish a colony. Onate granted *encomiendas* (the right to exact tribute and labor from the natives on large tracts of land) to favored Spaniards. In 1609, Spanish colonists founded Santa Fe. By 1680, there were over 2,000 Spanish colonists living among about 30,000 Pueblos. The economic heart of the colony was cattle and sheep, raised on the *ranchos* that stretched out around the small towns Spanish settlers established.

In 1680, the colony was nearly destroyed when the Pueblos rose in revolt. Despite widespread conversions to Catholicism, most natives (including the converts) continued also to practice their own religious rituals. In 1680, Spanish priests and the colonial government were trying to suppress these rituals. In response, Pope, an Indian religious leader, led an uprising that killed hundreds of European settlers (including twenty-one priests), captured Santa Fe, and drove the Spanish temporarily from the region. Twelve years later the Spanish returned, resumed seizing Pueblo lands, and crushed a last revolt in 1696.

After the revolts, many Spanish colonists seemed to understand that they could not hope to prosper in New Mexico in constant conflict with a native population that greatly outnumbered them. On the one hand, the Spanish intensified their efforts to assimilate the Indians—baptizing Indian children at birth and enforcing observance of Catholic rituals. On the other hand, they now permitted the Pueblos to own land; they stopped commandeering Indian labor; and they tacitly tolerated the survival of tribal religious rituals. There was significant intermarriage between Europeans and Indians. And increasingly, the Pueblos came to consider the Spanish their allies in the continuing battles with the Apaches and Navajos. By 1750, the Spanish population had grown modestly to about 4,000. The Pueblo population had declined (through disease, war, and migration) to about 13,000—less than half what it had been in 1680. New Mexico had by then become a reasonably stable but still weak and isolated outpost of the Spanish Empire.

Biological and Cultural Exchanges

European and native cultures never entirely merged in the Spanish Empire. Indeed, significant differences remain today between European and Indian cultures throughout South and Central America. Nevertheless, the arrival of whites launched a process of interaction between different peoples that left no one unchanged.

That Europeans were exploring the Americas at all was a result of their early contacts with the natives, from whom they had learned of the rich deposits of gold and silver. From then on, the history of the Americas became one of increasing levels of exchanges—some beneficial, some catastrophic—among different peoples and cultures. The first and perhaps most profound result of this exchange was the importation of European diseases to the New World. It would be difficult to exaggerate the consequences of the exposure of Native Americans to such illnesses as influenza, measles, typhus, and above all smallpox—diseases to which Europeans had, over time, developed at least a partial immunity but to which Americans were tragically vulnerable. Millions died. In some areas, native populations were virtually wiped out within a few decades of their first contact with whites. On Hispaniola—where the Dominican Republic and Haiti are today, and where Columbus landed and established a small, short-lived colony in the 1490s—the native population quickly declined from approximately 1 million to about 500. In the Mayan areas of Mexico, as much as 95 percent of the population perished within a few years of the natives' first contact with the Spanish. Many (although not all) of the tribes north of Mexico, whose contact with European settlers came later and was often less intimate, were spared the worst of the epidemics. But for other areas of the New World, this was a catastrophe at least as grave as, and in some places far worse than, the Black Death that had killed as much as half the population of Europe two centuries before.

The decimation of native populations in the southern regions of the Americas was not, however, purely a result of exposure to infection. It was also a result of the conquistadores' deliberate policy of subjugation and extermination. Their brutality was in part a reflection of the ruthlessness with which Europeans waged war in all parts of the world. It was also a result of their conviction that the natives were "savages"—uncivilized peoples who could be treated as somehow not fully human. By the 1540s, the combined effects of European diseases and European military brutality had all but destroyed the empires of Mexico and South America and allowed the Spanish to exert their authority with few organized challenges from the natives.

Not all aspects of the exchange were so disastrous to the Indians. The Europeans introduced to America important new crops (among them sugar and bananas), domestic livestock (cattle, pigs, and sheep), and, perhaps most significant, the horse, which gradually became central to the lives of many natives and transformed their societies.

The exchange was at least as important (and more beneficial) to the Europeans. In both North and South America, the arriving white peoples learned from the natives new agricultural techniques appropriate to the demands of the new land. They discovered new crops—above all maize (corn), which Columbus took back to Europe from his first trip to America. Such foods as squash, pumpkins, beans, sweet potatoes, tomatoes, peppers, and potatoes all found their way into European diets by way of the natives of the Americas.

In South America, Central America, and Mexico, a society in which Europeans and natives lived in intimate, if unequal, contact with one another emerged. Many natives gradually came to speak Spanish or Portuguese, but they created a range of dialects fusing the European languages with elements of their own. Gradually, Europeans spread Catholicism through most areas of the Spanish Empire. But native Christians combined the new religion with features of their old religions. European men outnumbered European women by at least ten to one. As a result, male Spanish immigrants had substantial sexual contact with native women. Intermarriage—often forcible—became frequent. Before long, the population of the colonies came to be dominated (numerically, at least) by people of mixed race, or mestizos.

Virtually all the enterprises of the Spanish and Portuguese colonists depended on an Indian work force. In some places, Indians were sold into slavery. More often, colonists used a coercive (or "indentured") wage system, under which Indians worked in the mines and on the plantations under duress for fixed periods. That was not, in the end, enough to meet the labor needs of the colonists—particularly since the native population had declined (and in some places virtually vanished) because of disease and war. As early as 1502, therefore, European settlers began importing slaves from Africa.

Africa and America

Over half of all the immigrants to the New World between 1500 and 1800 were Africans, virtually all of them sent to America against their will. Most came from a large region in west Africa below the Sahara Desert, known as Guinea.

Europeans and white Americans came to portray African society as primitive and uncivilized (in part to justify the enslavement of Africa's people). But most Africans were, in fact, civilized peoples with well-developed economies and political systems. The residents of upper Guinea had substantial commercial contact with the Mediterranean world—trading ivory, gold, and slaves for finished goods—and, largely as a result, became early converts to Islam. After the collapse of the ancient kingdom of Ghana around A.D. 1100, they created the even larger empire of Mali, which survived into the fifteenth century and whose trading center at Timbuktu became fabled as a center of education and a meeting place of the peoples of many lands.

Farther south, Africans were more isolated from Europe and the Mediterranean and were more politically fragmented. The central social unit was the village, which usually consisted of members of an extended family group. Some groups of villages united in small kingdoms. But no large empires emerged in the south. Nevertheless, these southern societies developed extensive trade—in woven fabrics, ceramics, wooden and iron goods, as well as crops and livestock—both among themselves and, to a lesser degree, with the outside world.

African civilizations developed economies that reflected the climates and resources of their lands. In upper Guinea, fishing and rice cultivation, supplemented by the extensive trade with Mediterranean lands, were the foundation of the economy. Farther south, Africans grew wheat and other food crops, raised livestock, and fished. There were some more nomadic tribes in the interior, who subsisted largely on hunting and gathering and had less elaborate social systems. But most Africans were sedentary, farming people.

As in many Indian societies in America, but unlike societies in Europe, African families tended to be matrilineal. This means that people traced their heredity through and inherited property from their mothers. Women played a major role, often the dominant role, in trade. In many areas, they were the principal farmers (while the men hunted, fished, and raised livestock), and everywhere, they managed child care and food preparation. Most tribes also divided political power by gender, with men choosing leaders and systems for managing male affairs and women choosing parallel leaders to handle female matters.

In those areas of west Africa where indigenous religions had survived the spread of Islam (which included most of the lands south of the empire of Mali), people worshiped many gods, whom they associated with various aspects of the natural world and whose spirits they believed lived in trees, rocks, forests, and streams. Most Africans also developed forms of ancestor worship and took great care in tracing family lineage; the most revered priests were generally the oldest people.

Small elites of priests and nobles stood at the top of many African societies. Most people belonged to a large middle group of farmers, traders, crafts workers, and others. At the bottom of society were slaves—men and women who were put into bondage after being captured in wars, because of criminal behavior, or as a result of unpaid debts. Slavery was not usually permanent; African people were generally in bondage for a fixed term, and in the meantime retained certain legal protections (including the right to marry). Children did not inherit their parents' condition of bondage.

The African slave trade long preceded European settlement in the New World. As early as the eighth century, west Africans began selling small numbers of slaves to traders from the Mediterranean and later to the Portuguese. In the sixteenth century, however, the market for slaves increased dramatically as a result of the growing European demand for sugar cane. The small areas of sugar cultivation in the Mediterranean could not meet the demand, and production soon spread to new areas: to the island of Madeira off the African coast, which became a Portuguese colony, and not long thereafter (still in the sixteenth century) to the Caribbean islands and Brazil. Sugar was a labor-intensive crop, and the demand for African workers in these new areas of cultivation was high. At first the slave traders were overwhelmingly Portuguese and, to a lesser extent, Spanish. By the seventeenth century, the Dutch had won control of most of the market. In the eighteenth century, the English dominated it. By then, slavery had spread well beyond its original locations in the Caribbean and South America and into the English colonies to the north.

THE ARRIVAL OF THE ENGLISH

England's first documented contact with the New World came only five years after Spain's. In 1497, John Cabot (like Columbus, a native of Genoa) sailed to the northeastern coast of North America on an expedition sponsored by King Henry VII, in an unsuccessful search for a northwest passage through the New World to the Orient. But nearly a century passed before the English made any serious efforts to establish colonies in America. Like other European nations, England had to experience an internal transformation before it could begin settling new lands.

Incentives for Colonization

Interest in colonization grew in part as a response to social and economic problems in sixteenth-century England. The English people suffered from frequent and costly European wars, and they suffered from almost constant religious strife within their own land. Many suffered, too, from harsh economic changes in their countryside. Because the worldwide demand for wool was growing rapidly, landowners were converting their land from fields for crops to pastures for sheep. The result was a significant growth in the wool trade but a reduction in the amount of land available for growing food. Many of the displaced farmers became beggars or criminals. England's food supply declined at the same time that the English population was growing—from 3 million in 1485 to 4 million in 1603. To some of the English, the New World began to seem attractive because it offered something that was growing scarce in England: land.

At the same time, new merchant capitalists were prospering by selling the products of England's growing wool-cloth industry abroad. At first, most exporters did business almost entirely as individuals. In time, however, merchants formed companies, whose charters from the king gave them monopolies for trading in particular regions. Investors in these companies often made fantastic profits, and they were eager to expand their trade.

Central to this trading drive was the emergence of a new concept of economic life known as mercantilism. Mercantilism rested on the belief that the world's wealth was finite, that one person or nation could grow rich only at the expense of another, and that a nation's economic health depended, therefore, on selling as much as possible to foreign lands and buying as little as possible from them. The principles of mercantilism spread throughout Europe in the sixteenth and seventeenth centuries and increased the competition among nations. One result was the increased attractiveness of acquiring colonies, which could become the source of raw materials and a market for the colonizing power's goods.

In England, the mercantilistic program thrived at first on the basis of the flourishing wool trade with the European continent, and particularly with the great cloth market in Antwerp. In the 1550s, however, that glutted market began to collapse, and English merchants had to look elsewhere for overseas trade. The establishment of colonies seemed to be an answer to their problems. Some English also believed colonies would help alleviate poverty and unemployment by siphoning off the surplus population. Perhaps most important, colonial commerce would allow England to acquire products for which the nation had previously been dependent on foreigners—products such as lumber, naval stores, and silver and gold.

There were also religious motives for colonization. The Protestant Reformation began in Germany in 1517, when Martin Luther challenged some of the basic practices and beliefs of the Roman Catholic Church, which had been, until then, the supreme religious authority. Luther quickly won a wide following among ordinary men and women in northern Europe. When the pope excommunicated him in 1520, Luther began leading his followers out of the Catholic Church entirely.

As the spirit of the Reformation spread rapidly throughout Europe, other dissidents began offering other alternatives to Catholicism. The Swiss theologian John Calvin went even further than Luther had in rejecting the Catholic belief that human behavior could affect an individual's prospects for salvation. Calvin introduced the doctrine of predestination. God "elected" some people to be saved and condemned others to damnation; each person's destiny was determined before birth, and no one could change that predetermined fate. But those who accepted Calvin's teachings came to believe that the way they led their lives might reveal to them their chances of salvation. A wicked or useless existence would be a sign of damnation; saintliness, diligence, and success could be signs of grace. Calvinism created anxieties among its followers, but it also produced a strong incentive to lead virtuous, productive lives. The new creed spread rapidly throughout northern Europe and produced (among other groups) the Huguenots in France and the Puritans in England.

The English Reformation, however, was more a result of a political dispute between the king and the pope than of these doctrinal revolts. In 1529 King Henry VIII, angered by the refusal of the pope to grant him a divorce from his Spanish wife, broke England's ties with the Catholic

Church and established himself as the head of the Christian faith in his country. After Henry's death, his Catholic daughter, Queen Mary, restored England's allegiance to Rome and persecuted those who resisted. But when Mary died in 1558, her half-sister, Elizabeth I, became England's sovereign and once again severed the nation's connection with the Catholic Church, this time for good.

To many English people, however, the new Church of England—which differed little at first from the Catholic Church—was not reformed enough. Some had been affected by the teachings of the European Reformation, and they complained that theirs was a church that had abandoned Rome without abandoning Rome's offensive beliefs and practices. They clamored for reforms that would "purify" the church, and thus they became known as Puritans.

The most radical Puritans, known as Separatists, were determined to worship as they pleased in their own independent congregations, despite English laws that required all subjects to attend regular Anglican services. But most Puritans did not wish to leave the Church of England. They wanted, rather, to simplify Anglican forms of worship and reform the leadership of the church. Like the Separatists, they grew increasingly frustrated by the refusal of political and ecclesiastical authorities to respond to their demands.

Puritan discontent grew rapidly after the death of Elizabeth, the last of the Tudors, and the accession of James I, the first of the Stuarts, in 1603. Convinced that kings ruled by divine right, James quickly antagonized the Puritans, a group that included most of the rising businessmen, by resorting to illegal and arbitrary taxation, by favoring English Catholics in the granting of charters and other favors, and by supporting "high-church" forms of ceremony. By the early seventeenth century, some religious nonconformists were beginning to look for places of refuge outside the kingdom.

England's first experience with colonization came not in the New World but in neighboring Ireland. The English had long laid claim to the island, but only in the late sixteenth century did serious efforts at colonization begin. The long, brutal process by which the English attempted (never entirely successfully) to subdue the Irish led to an important assumption about colonization that the English would take with them to America: the belief that settlements in foreign lands must retain a rigid separation from the native populations. Unlike the Spanish in America, the English in Ireland tried to build a separate society of their own, peopled with emigrants from England itself. They would take that concept with them to the New World.

The French and the Dutch in America

English settlers in North America were to encounter not only natives but also other Europeans who were, like them, driven by mercantilist ideas. There were scattered North American outposts of the Spanish Empire, whose residents looked on the English as intruders. And, more important, there were French and Dutch settlers who were also vying for a stake in the New World.

France founded its first permanent settlement in America at Quebec in 1608, less than a year after the English started their first at Jamestown. The colony's population grew very slowly, but the French exercised an influence in the New World disproportionate to their numbers, because of their relationships with Native Americans. Unlike the early English settlers, who hugged the coastline and traded with the Indians of the interior mostly through intermediaries, the French forged close ties with natives deep inside the continent. French Jesuit missionaries established some of the first contacts between the two peoples. More important were the *coureurs de bois*—adventurous fur traders and trappers—who also penetrated far into the wilderness and developed an extensive trade that became one of the underpinnings of the French colonial economy. The French traders formed partnerships with the Indians and often became virtually a part of native society, living among the natives and at times marrying Indian women. The fur trade helped open the way for French agricultural estates (or *seigneuries*) along the St. Lawrence River and for the development of trade and military centers at Quebec and Montreal.

The English also faced competition from the Dutch in North America. Holland in the early seventeenth century was one of the leading trading nations of the world. In 1609 an English explorer in the employ of the Dutch, Henry Hudson, sailed up the river that was to be named for him in what is now New York State. His explorations led to a Dutch claim on that territory. In 1624, not long after the first two permanent English colonies took root in Jamestown and Plymouth, the Dutch created a wedge between them when the Dutch West India Company established a series of permanent trading posts on the Hudson, Delaware, and Connecticut Rivers that soon became the colony of New Netherland. Its principal town, New Amsterdam, was on Manhattan Island. The Dutch population remained relatively small.

The First English Settlements

The first permanent English settlement in the New World was established at Jamestown, in Virginia, in 1607. But for nearly thirty years before that, English merchants and adventurers had been engaged in a series of failed efforts to create colonies in America.

Through much of the sixteenth century, the English had harbored mixed feelings about the New World. They were intrigued by its possibilities, but they were also leery of Spain, which remained the dominant force in America and the dominant naval power in Europe. In 1588, however, King Philip II of Spain sent one of the largest military fleets in the history of warfare—the Spanish Armada—across the English Channel to attack England itself. The smaller English fleet, taking advantage of its greater maneuverability, defeated the armada and, in a single stroke, ended Spain's domination of the Atlantic. This great shift in naval power caused interest in colonizing the New World to grow quickly.

The pioneers of English colonization were Sir Humphrey Gilbert and his half-brother Sir Walter Raleigh—both friends of Queen Elizabeth, and both veterans of earlier colonial efforts in Ireland. In 1578 Gilbert obtained from Elizabeth a six-year patent granting him the exclusive right "to inhabit and possess any remote and heathen lands not already in the possession of any Christian prince." Five years later, after several setbacks, he led an expedition to Newfoundland and proceeded south looking for a good place to build a profitable colony. But a storm sank his ship, and he was lost at sea. The next year, Sir Walter Raleigh secured his own six-year grant from the queen and sent a small group of men on an expedition to explore the North American coast. When they returned, Raleigh named the region they had explored Virginia, in honor of Elizabeth, who was unmarried and was known as the "Virgin Queen."

In 1585 Raleigh recruited his cousin, Sir Richard Grenville, to lead a group of men to the island of Roanoke, off the coast of what is now North Carolina, to establish a colony. Grenville deposited the settlers on the island, antagonized the natives by destroying an Indian village as retaliation for a minor theft, and returned to England. The following spring, with expected supplies and reinforcements from England long overdue, Sir Francis Drake unexpectedly arrived in Roanoke. The dispirited colonists boarded his ships and left.

Raleigh tried again in 1587, sending an expedition to Roanoke carrying ninety-one men, seventeen women (two of them pregnant), and nine children. The settlers attempted to take up where the first group of colonists

ROANOKE A drawing by one of the English colonists in the ill-fated Roanoke expedition of 1585 became the basis for this engraving by Theodore DeBry, published in England in 1590. A small European ship carrying settlers approaches the island of Roanoke, at left. The wreckage of several larger vessels farther out to sea and the presence of Indian settlements on the mainland and on Roanoke itself suggest some of the perils the settlers encountered.

had left off. (Shortly after arriving, one of the women—the daughter of the commander of the expedition, John White—gave birth to a daughter, Virginia Dare, the first American-born child of English parents.) White returned to England after several weeks, in search of supplies and additional settlers, leaving his daughter and granddaughter behind. Because of a war with Spain, he was unable to return to Roanoke for three years. When he did, in 1590, he found the island utterly deserted, with no clue to the fate of the settlers other than the cryptic inscription "Croatoan" carved on a post. No solution to the mystery of the "Lost Colony" has ever been found.

The Roanoke disaster marked the end of Sir Walter Raleigh's involvement in English colonization of the New World. No later colonizer would receive grants of land in America as vast or undefined as those Raleigh and Gilbert had acquired. But despite the discouraging example of these first experiences, the colonizing impulse remained very much alive. In the early years of the seventeenth century, a group of London merchants to whom Raleigh had assigned his charter rights decided to renew the attempt at colonization in Virginia. A rival group of merchants, from the area around Plymouth, was also interested in American ventures and was sponsoring voyages of exploration farther north. In 1606 James I issued a new charter, which divided North America between the two groups. The London group got the exclusive right to colonize in the south, and the Plymouth merchants received the same right in the north. Through the efforts of these and other companies, the first enduring English colonies would be established in America.

CONCLUSION

The lands that Europeans eventually named the Americas were the home of many millions of people before the arrival of Columbus. Having migrated from Asia thousands of years earlier, the pre-Columbian Americans spread throughout the Western Hemisphere and eventually created great civilizations. Among the most notable of them were the Incas in Peru, and the Mayas and Aztecs in Mexico. In the regions north of what was later named the Rio Grande, the human population was smaller and the civilizations less advanced than they were further south. Even so, North American natives created a cluster of civilizations that thrived and expanded. There may have been as many as 10 million people living north of Mexico by the time Columbus arrived.

In the century after European contact, these native populations suffered a series of catastrophes that all but destroyed the civilizations they had built: brutal invasions by Spanish and Portuguese conquistadore and, even more devastating, a series of plagues inadvertently imported by Europeans that decimated native populations. By the middle of the sixteenth century, the Spanish and Portuguese—no longer faced with effective resistance from the native populations—had established colonial control over all of South America and much of North America, creating one of the largest empires in the world.

In the parts of North America that would eventually become the United States, the European presence was for a time much less powerful. The Spanish established an important northern outpost in what is now New Mexico, a society in which Europeans and Indians lived together intimately, if unequally. They created a fort at St. Augustine, Florida. On the whole, however, the North American Indians remained largely undisturbed by Europeans until the English, French, and Dutch migrations began in the early seventeenth century.

FOR FURTHER REFERENCE

Suggested Readings

Alvin M. Josephy, ed., *America in 1492: The World of the Indian Peoples Before the Arrival of Columbus* (1993) provides a strong introduction to pre-Columbian history. Francis Jennings, *The Founders of America* (1993) and *The Invasion of America: Indians, Colonialism, and the Cant of Conquest* (1975) are important histories of the native populations both before and after European contact. William M. Denevan, ed., *The Native Population of the Americas in 1492* (1976) is an important contribution to the debate over the size and character of the American population before Columbus. Alfred Crosby, *The Columbian Exchange: Biological and Cultural Consequences of 1492* (1972) explores the results of European-Indian contact both in the Americas and Europe. D. W. Meinig, *The Shaping of America, Vol I: Atlantic America, 1492–1800* (1986) is an account of the early contacts between Europeans and the New World. James H. Merrell, *The Indians' New World* (1989) is an excellent social history of native adaptation to the arrival of Europeans. James Axtell, *Beyond 1492: Encounters in Colonial North America* (1992) examines the early interaction between Europeans and Indians. Patrick Manning, *Slavery and African Life* (1990) is a good introduction to the early slave trade with the New World. Peter Laslett, *The World We Have Lost* (1965) is a classic study of Britain around the time of colonization. Karen Kupperman, *Roanoke: The Abandoned Colony* (1984) is a fine study of the first English settlement in the New World.

Films

(The best source for information on how to find these and other films is *Bowker's Complete Video Directory*—three volumes.)

Columbus & the Age of Discovery (1991) is a seven-volume documentary series on Christopher Columbus, his era, and his legacy. *Native American History, Pt. 1: Wilderness* (1993) explores the history of pre-Columbian American peoples, based on recent assessments by historians and archaeologists, and reveals the extent to which the European arrival altered life for Native Americans. *Early American Civilizations* (1988) documents the story of the Olmecs, Mayas, Toltecs, Aztecs, and Incas. *Slavery in the Americas & the Triangular Trade* (1992) looks at the Africans, Europeans, and Americans who participated in the Atlantic slave trade. *Roanoke* (1986) recreates the dress and setting for both settlers and Indians in the doomed English settlement.

Internet Resources

Internet websites containing historical material relevant to the subjects discussed in this chapter can be reached through the McGraw-Hill history site at www.mhhe.com/socscience/history/usa/link/linktop.htm.

CHAPTER TWO

The English "Transplantations"

The Early Chesapeake ∿ *Caribbean Colonization*
The Growth of New England ∿ *The Restoration Colonies*
The Development of Empire

T HE ROANOKE FIASCO dampened colonization enthusiasm in England for a time. But the lures of the New World—the presumably vast riches, the abundant land, the promise of religious freedom, the chance to begin anew—were too strong to be suppressed for very long. By the early seventeenth century, the effort to establish permanent English colonies in the New World had resumed.

The new efforts were much like the earlier, failed ones: private ventures, with little planning or direction from the English government; small, fragile enterprises led by people unprepared for the hardships they were to face. Unlike the Roanoke experiment, they survived, but not before experiencing a series of disastrous setbacks.

Four things in particular shaped the character of these English settlements. First, the colonies were business enterprises, and one of their principal concerns was to produce a profit for their corporate sponsors. Second, because the colonies were tied only indirectly to the crown, they began from the start to develop their own political and social institutions. Third, as in Ireland, there were few efforts to blend English society with the society of the natives. The Europeans tried to isolate themselves from the Indians and created communities that would be entirely their own: "transplantations" of societies from the Old World to the New. And fourth, almost nothing worked out as they had planned.

27

TIME LINE					
1607	**1619**	**1620**	**1622**	**1624**	**1630**
Jamestown founded	First African workers in Virginia Virginia House of Burgesses meets	Pilgrims found Plymouth Colony	Powhatan Indians attack Virginia	Dutch settle Manhattan	Puritans establish Massachusetts Bay Colony

1634	**1636**	**1637**		**1663**	**1664**
Maryland founded	Roger Williams founds Rhode Island	Anne Hutchinson expelled from Massachusetts Bay Colony Pequot War		Carolina chartered	English capture New Netherlands

1675	**1676**	**1681**	**1686**	**1689**	**1732**
King Philip's War	Bacon's Rebellion	Pennsylvania chartered	Dominion of New England	Glorious Revolution in America	Georgia chartered

THE EARLY CHESAPEAKE

Once James I had issued his 1606 charters to the London and Plymouth Companies, the Plymouth group floundered and largely abandoned its efforts at settling the northern regions of British America. But the London Company moved quickly and decisively to launch a colonizing expedition headed for Virginia—a party of 144 men aboard three ships, the *Godspeed*, the *Discovery*, and the *Susan Constant*, which set sail for America early in 1607.

The Founding of Jamestown

Only 104 men survived the journey. They reached the American coast in the spring of 1607, sailed into Chesapeake Bay and up a river they named the James, and established their colony on a peninsula. They called it Jamestown.

They chose an inland setting that they believed would offer them security from the natives. But they chose poorly. The site was low and

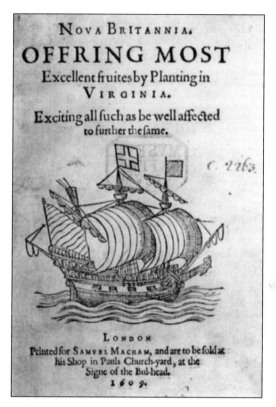

RECRUITING FOR THE COLONIES, 1609 This is the title page for a pamphlet that describes the attractions of settlement in the New World. Most accounts of the "excellent fruites" of life in Virginia were, like this one, written by people who had never seen America but who shared the excitement that the colonies inspired among the early-seventeenth-century English.

swampy and subject to outbreaks of malaria. It was surrounded by thick woods, which were difficult to clear for cultivation. And it bordered the territories of powerful local Indians. The result could hardly have been more disastrous. For seventeen years, one wave of settlers after another attempted to make Jamestown a habitable and profitable colony. Every effort failed. The town became instead a place of misery and death, and the London Company found itself saddled with endless losses. All that could be said of Jamestown at the end of this first period of its existence was that it had survived.

The initial colonists ran into serious difficulties from the moment they landed. They had no prior exposure to the infections of the new land and were highly vulnerable to local diseases, particularly malaria. The promoters in London demanded a quick return on their investment and diverted the colonists' energies into futile searches for gold and only slightly more successful efforts to pile up lumber, tar, pitch, and iron for export. These energies would have been better spent on growing food. The promoters also had little interest in creating a family-centered community, and they sent virtually no women to Jamestown. Hence, settlers could not establish real households and had difficulty feeling any sense of a permanent stake in the community.

By January 1608, when ships appeared with additional men and supplies, all but 38 of the first 104 colonists were dead. Jamestown, now facing extinction, survived largely as a result of the efforts of Captain John Smith, who at age twenty-seven was already a famous world traveler. Leadership in the colony had been bitterly divided until the fall of 1608, when Smith took control. He imposed work and order on the community. He also organized raids on neighboring Indian villages to steal food and kidnap natives. During the colony's second winter, fewer than a dozen (in a population of about 200) died. By the summer of 1609, when Smith returned to England, the colony was showing promise of survival. But Jamestown's ordeal was not over yet.

Reorganization and Expansion

As Jamestown struggled to survive, the London Company (now renamed the Virginia Company) was already dreaming of bigger things. In 1609, it obtained a new charter from the king, which increased its power and enlarged its territory; and it sent Lord De La Warr to be the colony's first governor. The company raised money by selling additional stock. It offered stock in the company to planters who were willing to migrate at their own expense. And it provided free passage to Virginia for poorer people who would agree to serve the company for seven years. In the spring of 1609, confident that it was now poised to transform Jamestown into a vibrant, successful venture, the Virginia Company dispatched a fleet of nine vessels with about 600 people aboard (including some women and children) to Virginia.

Disaster followed. One of the Virginia-bound ships was lost at sea in a hurricane. Another ran aground on one of the Bermuda islands and was unable to free itself for months. Many of those who reached Jamestown, still weak from their long and stormy voyage, succumbed to fevers before winter came. The winter of 1609–1610 became known as the "starving time," a period worse than anything before. The local Indians, antagonized by hostile actions by the early English settlers, killed off the livestock in the woods and kept the colonists barricaded within their palisade. The Europeans lived on what they could find: "dogs, cats, rats, snakes, toadstools, horsehides," and even the "corpses of dead men," as one survivor recalled. When the migrants who had run aground in Bermuda finally arrived in Jamestown the following May, they found only about 60 emaciated people (out of 500 residents the previous summer) still alive. The new arrivals took the survivors onto their ship, abandoned the settlement, and sailed for home. But as the refugees proceeded down the James, they met an English ship coming up the river—part of a fleet bringing supplies and the colony's first governor, Lord De La Warr. The departing settlers agreed to return to Jamestown. New relief expeditions with hundreds of colonists soon began to arrive, and the effort to turn a profit in Jamestown resumed.

Under the leadership of its first governors, Virginia survived and even expanded. New settlements began lining the river above and below Jamestown. That was partly because of the order and discipline the governors at times managed to impose and because of increased military assaults on the local Indian tribes to protect the new settlements. But it was also because the colonists had at last discovered a marketable crop: tobacco.

Europeans had become aware of tobacco soon after Columbus's first return from the West Indies, where he had seen the Cuban natives smoking small cigars (tabacos), which they inserted in the nostril. By the early seventeenth century, tobacco from the Spanish colonies was already in wide use in Europe. Then in 1612, the Jamestown planter John Rolfe, noting that local Indians were growing a strain of tobacco, began trying to cultivate the crop in Virginia. Tobacco planting soon spread up and down the James.

Almost immediately, tobacco cultivation created great pressure for territorial expansion. Tobacco growers needed large areas of farmland to grow their profitable crops; and because tobacco exhausted the soil very quickly, the demand for land increased rapidly. As a result, English farmers began establishing plantations deeper and deeper in the interior, isolating themselves from the center of European settlement, Jamestown, and penetrating farther into the territory of the native tribes.

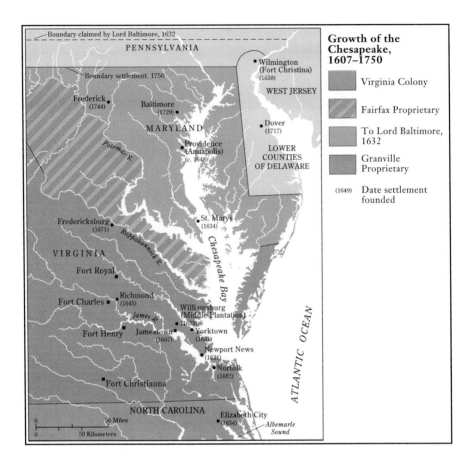

Growth of the
Chesapeake,
1607–1750

Virginia Colony

Fairfax Proprietary

To Lord Baltimore,
1632

Granville
Proprietary

(1649) Date settlement
founded

The tobacco economy also created a heavy demand for labor. To entice new workers to the colony, the Virginia Company established what it called the "headright" system. Headrights were fifty-acre grants of land. Those who already lived in the colony received two headrights (100 acres) apiece. Each new settler received a single headright for himself or herself. This system encouraged family groups to migrate together, since the more family members who traveled to America, the more land the family would receive. In addition, anyone who paid for the passage of immigrants to Virginia would receive an extra headright for each arrival, an encouragement to the prosperous to import new laborers. As a result, some colonists were able to assemble large plantations.

The company also transported ironworkers and other skilled craftsmen to Virginia to diversify the economy. In 1619, it sent 100 Englishwomen to the colony (which was still overwhelmingly male) to become the wives of male colonists. It promised the male colonists the full rights of Englishmen (as provided in the original charter of 1606), an end to strict and arbitrary rule, and even a share in self-government. On July 30, 1619, delegates from the various communities met as the House of Burgesses. It was the first meeting of an elected legislature within what was to become the United States.

A month later, Virginia established another important precedent. As John Rolfe recorded, "about the latter end of August" a Dutch ship brought in "20 and odd Negroes." There is some reason to believe that the colonists did not consider these first Africans in Virginia slaves, that they thought of them rather as servants to be held for a term of years and then freed, like the white servants with whom the planters were already familiar. For a time, moreover, the use of black labor remained limited. Although Africans trickled steadily into the colony, planters continued to prefer European indentured servants until at least the 1670s, when white servants began to become scarce and expensive. But the small group of blacks who arrived in 1619 marked the first step toward the enslavement of Africans within what was to be the American republic.

The European settlers in Virginia built their society not only on the coerced labor of imported Africans but also on the effective suppression of the local Indians. For two years in the 1610s, Sir Thomas Dale, De La Warr's successor as governor, led unrelenting assaults against the Powhatan Indians, led by (and named for) their formidable chief, Powhatan. In the process, Dale kidnapped Powhatan's young daughter Pocahontas. Several years earlier, Pocahontas had played a role in mediating differences between her people and the Europeans and, according to legend, once intervened with her father to spare John Smith from execution. But now, Powhatan refused to ransom her. Living among the English, Pocahontas gradually adapted to many of their ways. She converted to Christianity and in 1614 married John Rolfe and visited England with him. As a Christian convert and a gracious woman, she stirred interest among many English in projects to "civilize" the Indians. She died shortly before her planned return to Virginia.

By the time of Pocahontas's marriage, Powhatan had ceased his attacks on the English in the face of overwhelming odds. But after his death several years later, his brother, Opechancanough began secretly to plan the elimination of the English intruders. On a March morning in 1622, tribesmen called on the white settlements as if to offer goods for sale; then they suddenly attacked. Not until 347 whites of both sexes and all ages (including

John Rolfe) lay dead were the Indian warriors finally forced to retreat. And not until over twenty years later were the Powhatans finally defeated.

By then, however, the Virginia Company in London was defunct. The company had poured virtually all its funds into its profitless Jamestown venture and in the aftermath of the 1622 Indian uprising faced imminent bankruptcy. In 1624, James I revoked the company's charter, and the colony at last came under the control of the crown where it would remain until 1776. The colony, if not the company, had survived—but at a terrible cost. In Virginia's first seventeen years, more than 8,500 white settlers had arrived in the colony, and nearly eighty percent of them had died.

Exchanges of Agricultural Technology

The hostility the early English settlers expressed toward their Indian neighbors was in part a result of their conviction that their own civilization was greatly superior to that of the natives—and perhaps above all that they were more technologically advanced. The English, after all, had great ocean-going vessels, muskets and other advanced implements of weaponry, and many other tools that the Indians had not developed. Indeed, when John Smith and other early Jamestown residents grew frustrated at their inability to find gold and other precious commodities, they often blamed the backwardness of the natives. The Spanish in South America, Smith once wrote, had grown rich because the natives there had built advanced civilizations and mined much gold and silver. If Mexico and Peru had been as "ill peopled, as little planted, laboured and manured as Virginia," he added, the Spanish would have found no more wealth than the English did.

Yet the survival of Jamestown was, in the end, largely a result of agricultural technologies developed by Indians and borrowed by the English. Native agriculture was far better adapted to the soil and climate of Virginia than the agricultural traditions the English settlers brought with them. The Indians of Virginia were not nomadic hunters, but settled farmers whose villages were surrounded by neatly ordered fields in which grew a variety of crops—beans, pumpkins, vegetables, and above all maize (known to us as corn), which had been previously unknown to the English. Some of the Indian farmlands stretched over hundreds of acres and supported substantial populations.

The English settlers did not adopt all the Indian agricultural techniques. Natives cleared fields not, as the English did, by cutting down and uprooting all the trees. Instead they killed trees in place by "girdling" them (that is, making deep incisions around the base) in the areas in which they planted or setting fire to their roots; and they planted crops not in long, straight rows, but in curving patterns around the dead tree trunks. But in other respects, the English learned a great deal from the Indians about how to grow food in the New World. In particular, they quickly recognized the great value of corn, which proved to be easier to cultivate and to produce much greater yields than any of the European grains the English had known at home. Corn was also attractive to the settlers because its stalks could be a source of sugar and it spoiled less easily than other grains. The English also learned the advantages of growing beans alongside corn to enrich the soil. An early settler in New England (where the English also learned how to cultivate corn from the natives) wrote that the Indians had taught the settlers "to cull out the finest seede, to observe the fittest season, to keepe distance for holes, and fit measure for hills, to worme it, and weede it; to prune it, and dresse it as occasion shall require."

Like the natives, the English quickly learned to combine the foods they grew with food for which they hunted and fished, and here, too, Indian techniques proved of great value. Particularly valuable was the canoe, which was much better at navigating the rivers and streams of Virginia (and later New England) than were any English vessels, and which proved especially useful for fishing and for reaching hunting areas as agricultural cultivation of the coastal region drove many animals inland. Canoes could be made by hollowing them out from a single log (dugouts) or sewing birchbark around a simple frame and sealing it with resin (birchbark canoes, some of which could hold as many as eighty people). John Smith was a particular admirer of the Indian canoes, and compared them unfavorably to the large and cumbersome river vessels that the Virginia Company sent to Jamestown from England. The "primitive" civilizations of the natives in fact provided the early settlers with some of their most vital agricultural techniques and technologies.

Maryland and the Calverts

The Maryland colony ultimately came to look much like Virginia, but its origins were very different from those of its southern neighbor. George Calvert, the first Lord Baltimore, was a recent convert to Catholicism and a shrewd businessman, and he envisioned establishing a colony in America both as a great speculative venture in real estate and as a retreat for English Catholics oppressed by the Anglican establishment at home. Calvert died while still negotiating with the king for a charter to establish a colony in the Chesapeake region. But in 1632 his son Cecilius, the second Lord Baltimore, finally received the charter.

Lord Baltimore named his brother, Leonard Calvert, as governor of the colony. In March 1634, two ships—the *Ark* and the *Dove*—bearing Calvert along with 200 or 300 other colonists, entered the Potomac River, turned into one of its eastern tributaries, and established the village of St. Mary's on a high, dry bluff. Neighboring Indians befriended the settlers and provided them with temporary shelter and with stocks of corn. The early Marylanders experienced no Indian assaults, no plagues, no starving time.

The Calverts needed to attract thousands of settlers to Maryland if their expensive colonial venture was to pay. As a result, they had to encourage the immigration of Protestants as well as their fellow English Catholics. The Calverts soon realized that Catholics would always be a minority in the colony, and so they adopted a policy of religious toleration, embodied in the 1649 "Act Concerning Religion," which ensured freedom of worship for all Christians. Nevertheless, politics in Maryland remained plagued for years by tensions, and at times violence, between the Catholic minority and the Protestant majority.

At the insistence of the first settlers, the Calverts agreed in 1635 to the calling of a representative assembly—the House of Delegates—whose proceedings were based on the rules of Parliament. But the proprietor retained absolute authority to distribute land as he wished; and since Lord Baltimore granted large estates to his relatives and to other English aristocrats, a distinct upper class soon established itself. By 1640, a severe labor shortage forced a modification of the land-grant procedure; and Maryland, like Virginia, adopted a headright system—a grant of 100 acres to each male settler, another 100 for his wife and each servant, and 50 for each of his children. But the great landlords of the colony's earliest years remained powerful even as the population grew larger and more diverse. Like Virginia, Maryland became a center of tobacco cultivation; and as in Virginia, planters worked their land with the aid, first, of indentured servants imported from England and then, beginning late in the seventeenth century, of slaves imported from Africa.

Bacon's Rebellion

For more than thirty years, one man—Sir William Berkeley, the royal governor of Virginia—dominated the politics of the colony. He took office in 1642 at the age of thirty-six and with but one brief interruption remained in control of the government until the 1670s. In his first years as governor, he helped open up the interior of Virginia by sending explorers across the Blue Ridge Mountains and crushing a 1644 Indian uprising. The defeated Indians agreed to a treaty ceding to England most of the territory east of the mountains and establishing a boundary west of which white settlement would be prohibited. But the rapid growth of the Virginia population made this agreement difficult to sustain. Between 1640 and 1660, Virginia's population rose from 8,000 to over 40,000. By 1652, English settlers had established three counties in the territory set aside by the treaty for the Indians. Unsurprisingly, there were frequent clashes between natives and whites.

In the meantime, Berkeley was expanding his own powers. By 1670, the vote for delegates to the House of Burgesses, once open to all white men, was restricted to landowners. Elections were rare, and the same burgesses, representing the established planters of the eastern (or tidewater) region of the colony and subservient to the governor, remained in office year after year. The more recent settlers on the frontier were underrepresented in the assembly or not represented at all.

Resentment of the power of the governor and the tidewater aristocrats grew steadily in the newly settled lands of the west (often known as the "backcountry"). In 1676, this resentment helped create a major conflict, led by Nathaniel Bacon, a young, handsome aristocrat who had arrived in Virginia in 1673. Bacon had a good farm in the west and a seat on the governor's council. But like other members of the new backcountry gentry, he chafed at the governor's attempts to hold the line of settlement steady so as to avoid antagonizing the Indians. Bacon's rift with Berkeley was also a result of resentment that he was not part of the inner circle of the governor's council and that Berkeley refused to allow him a piece of the Indian fur trade, which the governor himself controlled.

In 1675, a major conflict erupted in the west between whites and natives. As the fighting escalated, Bacon and other concerned landholders demanded that the governor send the militia. When Berkeley refused, Bacon responded by offering to organize a volunteer army of backcountry men who would do their own fighting. Berkeley, who saw Bacon as a potential rival and feared a needless slaughter of the natives, rejected the offer. Bacon ignored him and launched a series of vicious but unsuccessful pursuits of the Indian challengers. When Berkeley heard of the unauthorized military effort, he dismissed Bacon from the governor's council and proclaimed him and his men to be rebels. Bacon now turned his army against the governor and, in what became known as Bacon's Rebellion, twice led his troops east to Jamestown. The first time he won a temporary pardon from the governor; the second time, after the governor repudiated the agreement, Bacon burned much of the city and drove the governor into exile. But then Bacon died suddenly of dysentery; and Berkeley, his position bolstered by the arrival of British troops, soon regained control. In 1677, the Indians (aware of their inability to defeat the white forces militarily) reluctantly signed a new treaty that opened new lands to white settlement.

Bacon's Rebellion was evidence of the continuing struggle to define the Indian and white spheres of influence in Virginia. It also revealed the bitterness of the competition among rival elites and between easterners and westerners in particular, and it demonstrated the potential for instability in the colony's large population of free, landless men. One result was that landed elites in both eastern and western Virginia began to recognize a common interest in quelling social unrest from below. That was among the reasons that they turned increasingly to the African slave trade to fulfill their need for labor. African slaves, unlike white indentured servants, did not need to be released after a fixed term and hence did not threaten to become an unstable, landless class.

CARIBBEAN COLONIZATION

The Chesapeake was the site of the first permanent English settlements in the New World. But throughout the first half of the seventeenth century, the most important destinations for English immigrants were the islands of the Caribbean and the northern way station of Bermuda. These Caribbean societies had close ties to English North America and influenced the development of the mainland colonies in many ways.

The West Indies

Before the arrival of the Europeans, most of the Caribbean islands had substantial native populations. But beginning with Christopher Columbus's first visit in 1492, and accelerating after 1496, when the Spanish established their first colony on Hispaniola, the native population was all but wiped out by European epidemics.

The Spanish claimed all the Caribbean islands, but they created substantial settlements only on the largest of them: Cuba, Hispaniola, and Puerto Rico. English, French, and Dutch traders began settling on some of the smaller islands early in the sixteenth century, despite the Spanish

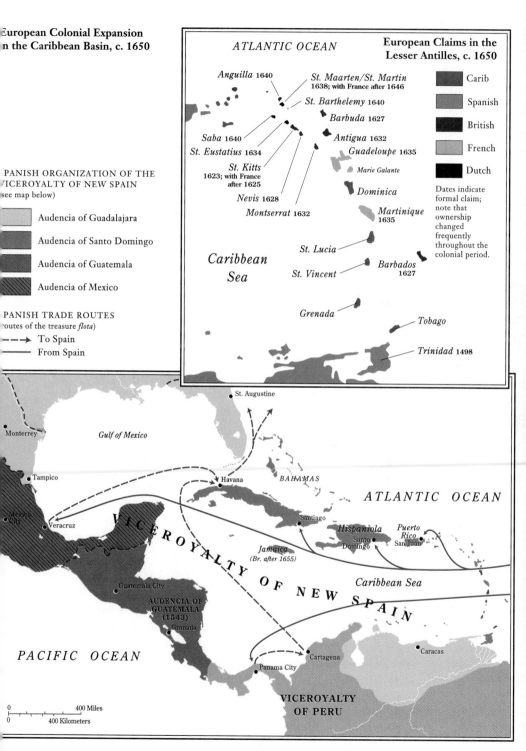

European Colonial Expansion in the Caribbean Basin, c. 1650

European Claims in the Lesser Antilles, c. 1650

ATLANTIC OCEAN

Anguilla 1640

St. Maarten/St. Martin 1638; with France after 1646

St. Barthelemy 1640

Barbuda 1627

Saba 1640

Antigua 1632

St. Eustatius 1634

Guadeloupe 1635

St. Kitts 1623; with France after 1625

Marie Galante

Nevis 1628

Dominica

Montserrat 1632

Martinique 1635

Caribbean Sea

St. Lucia

St. Vincent

Barbados 1627

Grenada

Tobago

Trinidad 1498

Carib

Spanish

British

French

Dutch

Dates indicate formal claim; note that ownership changed frequently throughout the colonial period.

PANISH ORGANIZATION OF THE VICEROYALTY OF NEW SPAIN
(see map below)

Audencia of Guadalajara

Audencia of Santo Domingo

Audencia of Guatemala

Audencia of Mexico

PANISH TRADE ROUTES
routes of the treasure *flota*)

→ To Spain

— From Spain

St. Augustine

Monterrey

Gulf of Mexico

Tampico

Havana

BAHAMAS

ATLANTIC OCEAN

Mexico City

Veracruz

Santiago

Hispaniola

Puerto Rico

Jamaica (Br. after 1655)

Santo Domingo

San Juan

VICEROYALTY OF NEW SPAIN

Guatemala City

Caribbean Sea

AUDENCIA OF GUATEMALA (1543)

Granada

PACIFIC OCEAN

Cartagena

Caracas

Panama City

VICEROYALTY OF PERU

0   400 Miles

0   400 Kilometers

claim to them. These fledgling colonies were always vulnerable to Spanish attack. But after Spain and the Netherlands went to war in 1621 (distracting the Spanish navy and leaving the English in the Caribbean relatively unmolested), the pace of English colonization increased. By midcentury, there were several important English settlements on the islands, the most important of them on Antigua, St. Kitts, Jamaica, and Barbados.

In their first years in the Caribbean, English settlers experimented unsuccessfully with tobacco and cotton. But they soon discovered that the most lucrative export crop was sugar, for which there was a substantial and growing market in Europe. Because raising sugar required a great deal of labor, and because the native population was too small to provide a work force, English planters quickly found it necessary to import laborers. As in the Chesapeake, they began by bringing indentured servants from England. But the arduous work and the tropical climate discouraged white laborers. By midcentury, therefore, the English planters in the Caribbean (like the Spanish colonists) were relying more and more heavily on an enslaved African work force, which soon substantially outnumbered them.

On Barbados and other islands where a flourishing sugar economy developed, the English planters were a tough, aggressive, and ambitious breed. Some of them grew enormously wealthy; and since their livelihoods depended on their work forces, they created a rigid slave system remarkably quickly. By the late seventeenth century, African slaves outnumbered white settlers by better than four to one.

Masters and Slaves

A small white population, much of it enjoying great economic success, and a large African population, all of it in bondage, were a potentially explosive combination. Fearful of slave revolts, whites in the Caribbean monitored their labor forces closely and often harshly, and the English West Indians devised a rigid set of laws and practices to ensure control over their black laborers. Planters paid little attention to the welfare of their workers. Many concluded it was cheaper to buy new slaves periodically than to protect the well-being of those they already owned, and it was not uncommon for masters literally to work their slaves to death. Few African workers survived more than a decade in the brutal Caribbean working environment. Even whites, who worked far less strenuously, often succumbed to the harsh climate and the local diseases; most died before the age of forty.

Establishing a stable society and culture was extremely difficult for people living in such harsh and even deadly conditions. Those whites who could returned to England with their fortunes and left their estates in the hands of overseers, and the white population remained a distinct minority on the islands. The society of Europeans in the Caribbean lacked many of the institutions that gave stability to the North American settlements: church, family, community.

Africans in the Caribbean faced much greater difficulties than the white settlers, but because they had no chance of leaving, they created what was in many ways a more elaborate culture than did the white settlers. They started families (although many of them were broken up by death or the slave trade); they sustained African religious and social traditions (and resisted Christianity); and within the rigidly controlled world of the sugar plantations, they established patterns of resistance.

The Caribbean settlements became an important part of the Atlantic trading nexus in which many Americans became involved. They were the principal source of African slaves for the mainland colonies. And because Caribbean planters established an elaborate plantation system earlier than planters in North America, they provided models that many mainland people emulated.

THE GROWTH OF NEW ENGLAND

The northern regions of British North America were slow to attract settlers, in part because the Plymouth Company was never able to mount a successful colonizing expedition after receiving its charter in 1606. It did, however, sponsor explorations of the region. Captain John Smith, after his departure from Jamestown, made an exploratory journey for the Plymouth merchants, wrote an enthusiastic pamphlet about the lands he had seen, and called them New England.

Plymouth Plantation

A discontented congregation of Puritan Separatists in England, not the Plymouth Company, established the first enduring European settlement in New England. In 1608, after years of persecution for attempting to practice their own religion, a congregation of Separatists from the hamlet of Scrooby began emigrating quietly (and illegally), a few at a time, to

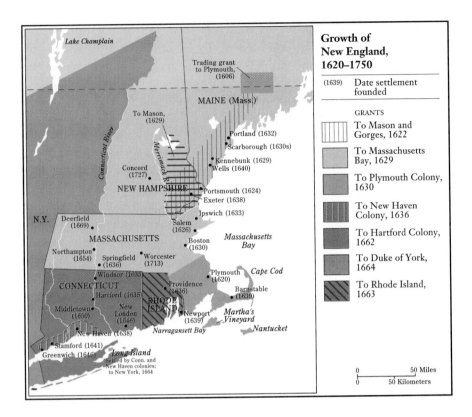

Growth of New England, 1620–1750

(1639) Date settlement founded

GRANTS

To Mason and Gorges, 1622

To Massachusetts Bay, 1629

To Plymouth Colony, 1630

To New Haven Colony, 1636

To Hartford Colony, 1662

To Duke of York, 1664

To Rhode Island, 1663

Lake Champlain

Trading grant to Plymouth, (1606)

MAINE (Mass.)

To Mason, (1629)

Portland (1632)

Scarborough (1630s)

Kennebunk (1629)

Wells (1640)

Concord (1727)

NEW HAMPSHIRE

Portsmouth (1624)

Exeter (1638)

Ipswich (1633)

N.Y. Deerfield (1669)

Salem (1626)

MASSACHUSETTS

Boston (1630)

Massachusetts Bay

Northampton (1654)

Springfield (1636)

Worcester (1713)

Windsor (1635)

CONNECTICUT

Providence (1636)

Plymouth (1620) *Cape Cod*

Barnstable (1639)

Hartford (1635)

RHODE ISLAND

Middletown (1650)

New London (1646)

Newport (1639)

Martha's Vineyard

New Haven (1638) *Narragansett Bay* *Nantucket*

Stamford (1641)

Greenwich (1646) *Long Island*

Settled by Conn. and New Haven colonies; to New York, 1664

0   50 Miles

0   50 Kilometers

Leyden, Holland, where they could enjoy freedom of worship. But as foreigners in Holland, they had to work at unskilled and poorly paid jobs. They also watched with alarm as their children began to adapt to Dutch society and drift away from their church. Finally, some of the Separatists decided to move again, across the Atlantic, where they hoped to create a stable, protected community where they could spread "the gospel of the Kingdom of Christ in those remote parts of the world."

In 1620, leaders of the Scrooby group obtained permission from the Virginia Company to settle in Virginia. Several English merchants advanced the necessary funds for the venture. The "Pilgrims," as they saw themselves, sailed from Plymouth, England, in September 1620 on the *Mayflower*; thirty-five "saints" (Puritan Separatists) and sixty-seven "strangers" (people who were not part of the congregation) were aboard. In November, after a long and difficult voyage, they sighted land—the shore of what is now known as Cape Cod. That had not been their destination, but it was too late in the year to sail farther south. So the Pilgrims chose a site for their settlement in the area just north of the cape, a place John Smith had labeled "Plymouth" on a map he had drawn during an earlier exploration of New England. Because Plymouth lay outside the London Company's territory, the settlers were not bound by the company's rules. While still aboard ship, the "saints" in the group drew up an agreement, the Mayflower Compact, to establish a government for themselves. Then, on December 21, 1620, they stepped ashore at Plymouth Rock.

The Pilgrims' first winter was a difficult one. Half the colonists perished from malnutrition, disease, and exposure. But the colony survived, in large part because of crucial assistance from local Indians, who showed them how to gather seafood and cultivate corn. Trade and other exchanges with the Indians were critical to the settlers and attractive to the natives. The tribes provided the colonists with furs (contributing to a rapid depletion of the fur-bearing animal population of the region). They also showed the settlers how to cultivate corn and how to hunt wild animals for meat. After the first autumn harvest, the settlers invited the natives to join them in a festival, the original Thanksgiving. But the relationship between the settlers and the local Indians was not a happy one for long. Thirteen years after the Pilgrims arrived, a devastating smallpox epidemic—a result of natives' exposure to Europeans carrying the disease—wiped out much of the Indian population around Plymouth.

The Pilgrims could not create rich farms on the sandy and marshy soil around Plymouth, but they developed a profitable trade in fish and furs. New colonists arrived from England, and in a decade the population reached 300. The people of Plymouth Plantation chose as their governor the remarkable William Bradford, who governed successfully for many years without any serious interference from London. The Pilgrims were always poor. As late as the 1640s, they had only one plow among them. But they were, on the whole, content to be left alone to live their lives in what they considered godly ways.

The Massachusetts Bay Experiment

Events in England encouraged other Puritans to migrate to the New World. King James I had pursued harsh, repressive policies toward Puritans for years. When he died in 1653, his son and successor, Charles I, was even more hostile to Puritans than his father had been and imprisoned many of them for their beliefs. The king dissolved Parliament in 1629 (it was not to be recalled until 1640), ensuring that there would be no one in a position to oppose him.

In the midst of this turmoil, a group of Puritan merchants began organizing a new colonial venture in America. They obtained a grant of land in New England for most of the area now comprising Massachusetts and New Hampshire, and they acquired a charter from the king (who was evidently unaware of their religious inclinations) allowing them to create the Massachusetts Bay Company and to establish a colony in the New World. Some members of the Massachusetts Bay Company saw the enterprise as more than a business venture. They wanted to create a refuge in New England for Puritans. They bought out the interests of company members who preferred to stay in England, and owners elected a governor, John Winthrop. They then sailed for New England in 1630. With 17 ships and 1,000 people, mostly family groups, it was the largest single migration of its kind in the seventeenth century. Winthrop carried with him the charter of the Massachusetts Bay Company, which meant that the colonists would be responsible to no company officials in England.

The Massachusetts migration quickly produced several settlements. The port of Boston, at the mouth of the Charles River, became the capital, but in the course of the next decade colonists established several other towns in eastern Massachusetts: Charlestown, Newtown (later renamed Cambridge), Roxbury, Dorchester, Watertown, Ipswich, Concord, Sudbury, and others.

The Massachusetts Puritans were not grim or joyless, as many critics would later come to believe, but they were serious and pious. They strove to lead useful, conscientious lives of thrift and hard work, and they honored material success as evidence of God's favor. Winthrop and the other founders of Massachusetts believed they were founding a holy commonwealth, a model—a "city upon a hill"—for the corrupt world to see and emulate. To that end, the ministers and the officers of the government worked closely together. Colonial Massachusetts was a "theocracy," a society in which the church was almost indistinguishable from the state. Residents had no more freedom of worship than the Puritans themselves had had in England.

Like other new settlements, the Massachusetts Bay colony had early difficulties. During the first winter (1629–1630), nearly 200 people died and many others decided to leave. But, more rapidly than Jamestown, the colony grew and prospered. The nearby Pilgrims and neighboring Indians helped with food and advice. Incoming settlers, many of them affluent, brought needed tools and other goods. The dominance of families in the colony (a sharp contrast to the early years at Jamestown) helped ensure a feeling of commitment to the community and a sense of order among the settlers, and it also ensured that the population would reproduce itself.

The Expansion of New England

It did not take long for English settlement to begin moving outward from Massachusetts Bay to other parts of New England and beyond. Some people migrated in search of soil more productive than that the stony land around Boston provided. Others left because of the oppressiveness of the church-dominated government of Massachusetts.

The Connecticut River valley, about 100 miles west of Boston, began attracting English families as early as the 1630s—despite the presence of powerful native tribes and despite claims to those lands by the Dutch—because of the valley's fertile lands and its isolation from Massachusetts Bay. In 1635, Thomas Hooker, a minister of Newtown (Cambridge), defied the Massachusetts government, led his congregation west, and established the town of Hartford. Four years later, the people of Hartford and of two other newly founded towns nearby established a colonial government of their own and adopted a constitution known as the Fundamental Orders of Connecticut, which created a government similar to that of Massachusetts Bay but gave a larger proportion of the men the right to vote and hold office. (Women were barred from voting virtually everywhere.)

Another Connecticut colony grew up around New Haven on the Connecticut coast. Unlike Hartford, it reflected unhappiness with what its founders considered the increasing religious laxity in Boston. The Fundamental Articles of New Haven (1639) established a Bible-based government even stricter than that of Massachusetts Bay. New Haven remained independent until 1662, when a royal charter officially gave the Hartford colony jurisdiction over the New Haven settlements.

European settlement in what is now Rhode Island was a result of the religious and political dissent of Roger Williams, an engaging but controversial young minister who lived for a time in Salem, Massachusetts. Williams was a confirmed Separatist who argued that the Massachusetts church should abandon all allegiance to the Church of England. He was also friendly with the neighboring Indians and proclaimed that the land the colonists were occupying belonged to the natives and not to the king or to the Massachusetts Bay Company. The colonial government voted to deport him, but he escaped before they could do so. During the winter of 1635–1636, he took refuge with Narragansett tribesmen; the following spring he bought a tract of land from them, and with a few followers, created the town of Providence. In 1644, after obtaining a charter from Parliament, he established a government for Providence and the surrounding settlements—a government similar to that of Massachusetts but without any ties to the church. For a time, Rhode Island was the only colony in which all faiths (including Judaism) could worship without interference.

Another challenge to the established religious order in Massachusetts Bay came from Anne Hutchinson, an intelligent and charismatic woman from a substantial Boston family. She argued that many clergy (including her own uninspiring minister) were not among the "elect" and were, therefore, entitled to no spiritual authority. Such teachings (known as the Antinomian heresy) were a serious threat to the spiritual authority of the established clergy. Hutchinson also challenged prevailing assumptions about the proper role of women in Puritan society. She was not a retiring, deferential wife and mother but a powerful religious figure in her own right. As Hutchinson's influence grew, and as she began to deliver open attacks on members of the clergy, the Massachusetts hierarchy mobilized to stop her. In 1638, she was convicted of heresy and sedition and was banished. With her family and some of her followers, she moved to a point on Narragansett Bay not far from Providence. Later she moved south into New York, where in 1643 she and her family died during an Indian uprising.

The Hutchinson affair had an important impact on the settlement of the areas north of Massachusetts Bay. New Hampshire and Maine were established in 1629 by two English proprietors. But few settlers moved into these northern regions until the religious disruptions in Massachusetts Bay. In 1639, John Wheelwright, a disciple of Anne Hutchinson, led some of his fellow dissenters to Exeter, New Hampshire. Others soon followed. The Massachusetts Bay Company tried to extend its authority over this entire northern territory, but with only partial success. New Hampshire became a separate colony in 1679. Maine remained a part of Massachusetts until 1820.

Settlers and Natives

The first white settlers in New England had generally friendly relations with the natives. Indians taught whites how to grow vital food crops such as corn, beans, pumpkins, and potatoes; they also taught them new agricultural techniques, such as annual burning for fertilization and planting beans to replenish exhausted soil. European farmers also benefited from the extensive lands Indians had already cleared (and either abandoned or sold). White traders used Indians as partners in some of their most important trading activities (and particularly in the creation of the thriving North American fur trade). Indeed, commerce with the Indians was responsible for the creation of some of the first great fortunes in British North America.

Other white settlers attempted to educate the Indians in European religion and culture. Protestant missionaries converted some natives to Christianity, and a few Indians became at least partially assimilated into white society.

But as in other areas of white settlement, tensions soon developed—primarily as a result of the white colonists' insatiable appetite for land. The particular character of those conflicts—and the brutality with which whites assaulted their Indian foes—emerged as well out of Puritan attitudes toward the natives. The religious leaders of New England came to consider the tribes a threat to their hopes of creating a godly community in the New World. Gradually, the image of Indians as helpful neighbors came to be replaced by the image of Indians as "heathens" and barbarians.

The Pequot War and the Technology of Battle

In 1637, hostilities broke out between English settlers in the Connecticut Valley and the Pequot Indians of the region, a conflict (known as the Pequot War) that ended disastrously for the natives. The Pequot tribe was almost wiped out. But the bloodiest and most prolonged encounter between whites and Indians in the seventeenth century began in 1675, a conflict that whites called King Philip's War. As in the Pequot War, an Indian tribe—the Wampanoags, under the leadership of a chieftain known to the white settlers as King Philip and among his own people as Metacomet—rose up to resist the English. For three years, the natives inflicted terror on a string of Massachusetts towns, killing over a thousand people. But beginning in 1676, the white settlers gradually prevailed, and with the help of a group of Mohawk allies who ambushed Metacomet, shot and killed him. Without Metacomet, the fragile alliance among the tribes collapsed, and the white settlers were soon able to crush the uprising.

The character of the Pequot War, King Philip's War, and many other conflicts between natives and settlers in the years that followed was crucially affected by earlier exchanges of technology between the English and the tribes. In particular, the Indians made effective use of a relatively new weapon introduced to New England by Myles Standish and others: the flintlock rifle. It replaced the earlier staple of colonial musketry; the matchlock rifle, which proved too heavy, cumbersome, and inaccurate to be useful in the kind of combat characteristic of Anglo-Indian struggles. The matchlock had to be steadied on a fixed object and ignited with a match before firing; the flintlock could be held up without support and fired without a match. (Indians using bows and arrows often outmatched settlers using the clumsy matchlocks.)

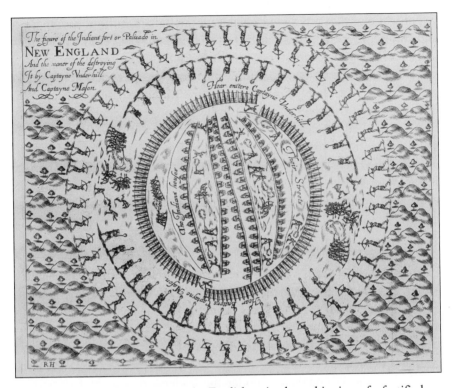

A PEQUOT VILLAGE DESTROYED An English artist drew this view of a fortified Pequot village in Connecticut surrounded by English soldiers and their allies from other tribes during the Pequot War in 1637. The invaders massacred more than 600 residents of the settlement.

Many English settlers were slow to give up their cumbersome matchlocks for the lighter flintlocks. But the Indians recognized the advantages of the newer rifles right away and began purchasing them in large quantities as part of their regular trade with the colonists. Despite rules forbidding colonists to instruct natives on how to use and repair the weapons, the natives learned to handle the rifles, and even to repair them, very effectively on their own. They even built a substantial forge for shaping and repairing rifle parts. In King Philip's War, the very high casualties on both sides were a result of the use of these more advanced rifles.

Indians also used more traditional military technologies in their conflicts with the English—especially the construction of forts. The Narragansetts, allies of the Wampanoags in King Philip's War, built an enormous fort in the Great Swamp of Rhode Island in 1675, which became the site of one of the bloodiest battles of the war before English attackers burned it down. After that, a band of Narragansetts set out to build a large stone fort, with the help of a member of the tribe who had learned masonry while working with the English. When English soldiers discovered the stone fort in 1676, after the end of King Philip's War, they killed most of its occupants and destroyed it. In the end, the technological skills of the Indians (both those they borrowed from the English and those they drew from their own traditions) were no match for the overwhelming advantages of the English settlers in both numbers and firepower.

THE RESTORATION COLONIES

For nearly thirty years after Lord Baltimore received the charter for Maryland in 1632, no new English colonies were established in America. England had to deal with troubles of its own at home before it could resume its colonizing ventures.

The English Civil War

After Charles I dissolved Parliament in 1629 and began ruling as an absolute monarch, he steadily alienated a growing number of his subjects— and the members of the powerful Puritan community, above all. Finally, desperately in need of money, Charles called Parliament back into session in 1640 and asked it to levy new taxes. But he antagonized the members by dismissing them twice in two years; and in 1642, they organized a military force, thus beginning the English Civil War.

The conflict between the Cavaliers (the supporters of the king) and the Roundheads (the forces of Parliament, who were largely Puritans) lasted seven years. In 1649, the Roundheads defeated the king's forces, captured Charles himself, and beheaded the monarch. The stern Roundhead leader Oliver Cromwell replaced the king and assumed the position of "protector." But when Cromwell died in 1658, his son and heir proved unable to maintain his authority. Two years later, King Charles II, son of the beheaded monarch, returned from exile and seized the throne, in what became known as the Restoration.

Among the results of the Restoration was the resumption of colonization in America. Charles II rewarded faithful courtiers with grants of land in the New World, and in the twenty-five years of his reign he issued charters for four additional colonies: Carolina, New York, New Jersey, and Pennsylvania.

The Carolinas

In successive charters issued in 1663 and 1665, Charles II awarded eight proprietors joint title to a vast territory stretching south from Virginia to the Florida peninsula and west to the Pacific Ocean. Like Lord Baltimore, they received almost kingly powers over their grant, which they prudently called Carolina (a name derived from the Latin word for "Charles"). They reserved tremendous estates for themselves and distributed the rest through a headright system similar to those in Virginia and Maryland, after which they collected annual payments from the settlers. Although committed Anglicans themselves, the proprietors guaranteed religious freedom to all Christian faiths. They also created a representative assembly to make laws. They hoped to attract settlers from the existing American colonies and to avoid the expense of financing expeditions from England.

But their initial efforts to profit from settlement in Carolina failed dismally. A few early attempts at colonization were quickly abandoned, and most of the original proprietors soon gave up the project. Anthony Ashley Cooper, however, persisted. He convinced the other proprietors to give up on attracting settlers from other colonies and to finance expeditions to Carolina from England, the first of which set sail with 300 people in the spring of 1670. Only 100 people survived the difficult voyage; those who did established a settlement at Port Royal on the Carolina coast. Ten years later they founded a city at the junction of the Ashley and Cooper Rivers, which in 1690 became the colonial capital. They called it Charles Town (it was later renamed Charleston).

With the aid of the English philosopher John Locke, Cooper (now the earl of Shaftesbury) drew up the Fundamental Constitution for Carolina in 1669 in an attempt to create a highly ordered society. It divided the colony into counties of equal size and divided each county into equal parcels. It also envisioned an elaborate social hierarchy of the proprietors themselves (who were to be known as "seigneurs"), a local aristocracy (consisting of lesser nobles known as "landgraves" or "caciques"), and ordinary settlers ("leet-men"). At the bottom of this stratified society would be poor whites, who would have few political rights, and African slaves, whose subjection would be complete. Proprietors, nobles, and other landholders would have a voice in the colonial parliament in proportion to the size of their landholdings.

In reality, Carolina developed along lines quite different from the carefully ordered vision of Shaftesbury and Locke. For one thing, the colony was never really united in anything more than name. The northern and southern regions of settlement were widely separated and socially and economically distinct from one another. The northern settlers were mainly backwoods farmers, scratching out a meager existence at subsistence agriculture. In the south, fertile lands and the good harbor at Charles Town promoted a more prosperous economy and a more stratified, aristocratic society. Settlements grew up rapidly along the Ashley and Cooper Rivers, and colonists established a flourishing trade, particularly (beginning in the 1660s) in rice—which was to become the colony's principal commercial crop.

Southern Carolina very early developed close commercial ties to the large (and overpopulated) European colony on the Caribbean island of Barbados (see pp. 38–41). During the first ten years of settlement, in fact, most of the new residents in Carolina were Barbadians, some of whom arrived with large groups of black workers and established themselves as substantial landlords. African slavery had taken root on Barbados earlier than in any of the mainland colonies, and the white Caribbean migrants—tough, uncompromising profit seekers—established a similar slave-based plantation society in Carolina.

Carolina was one of the most divided English colonies in America. There were tensions between the small farmers of the Albemarle region in the north and the wealthy planters in the south. And there were conflicts between the rich Barbadians in southern Carolina and the smaller landowners around them. After Lord Shaftesbury's death, the proprietors proved unable to establish order. In 1719, the colonists seized control of the colony from them. Ten years later, the king divided the region into two royal colonies, North Carolina and South Carolina.

New Netherland, New York, and New Jersey

In 1664, Charles II granted his brother James, the duke of York, all the territory lying between the Connecticut and Delaware Rivers. But the grant faced a major challenge from the Dutch, who claimed the entire area and controlled settlements at New Amsterdam and other strategic points.

England and the Netherlands were already commercial rivals in Europe, and that rivalry now extended to America, where the Dutch served as a wedge between the northern and southern English colonies. In 1664, vessels of the English navy, under the command of Richard Nicolls, put in at New Amsterdam, the capital of the Dutch colony of New Netherland, and extracted a surrender from the arbitrary and unpopular Dutch governor, Peter Stuyvesant. Several years later, in 1673, the Dutch reconquered and briefly held their old provincial capital. But they lost it again, this time for good, in 1674.

The duke of York, now firmly in possession of his territory, renamed it New York and set out to govern the diverse region. New York contained not only Dutch and English but Scandinavians, Germans, French, and a large number of Africans (imported as slaves by the Dutch West India Company), as well as members of several different Indian tribes. James wisely made no effort to impose his own Roman Catholicism on the colony. He delegated powers to a governor and a council but made no provision for representative assemblies.

Property holding and political power remained highly divided and highly unequal in New York. In addition to confirming the great Dutch "patroonships" already in existence, James granted large estates to some of his own political supporters. Power in the colony thus remained widely dispersed among wealthy English landlords, Dutch patroons, fur traders, and the duke's political appointees. By 1685, when the duke of York ascended the English throne as James II, New York contained about four times as many people (around 30,000) as it had twenty years before, and it was one of the most turbulent colonies in America.

Shortly after James received his charter, he gave a large part of the land south of New York to a pair of political allies, both Carolina proprietors, Sir John Berkeley and Sir George Carteret. Carteret named the territory New Jersey, after the island in the English Channel on which he had been born. But the venture in New Jersey generated few profits, and in 1674, Berkeley sold his half interest. The colony was divided into two jurisdictions, East Jersey and West Jersey, which squabbled with one another until 1702, when the two halves of the colony were again joined and became a single royal colony. New Jersey, like New York (from which much of its population came), was a colony of enormous ethnic and religious diversity, and the weak colonial government made few efforts to impose strict control over the fragmented society. But unlike New York, New Jersey developed no important class of large landowners (most of its residents remained small farmers) and nor did New Jersey produce any single important city.

The Quaker Colonies

Pennsylvania was born out of the efforts of a dissenting English Protestant sect, the Society of Friends, to find a home for their own distinctive social order. The society began in the mid-seventeenth century under the leadership of George Fox, a Nottingham shoemaker, and Margaret Fell. Their followers came to be known as Quakers (from Fox's instruction to them to "tremble at the name of the Lord"). Unlike the Puritans, Quakers rejected the concept of predestination and original sin. All people, they believed, had divinity within themselves and need only learn to cultivate it; all could attain salvation. Also unlike the Puritans, Quakers granted women a position within the church generally equal to that of men.

The Quakers had no formal church government and no traditional church buildings, only meetinghouses. They had no paid clergy, and in their worship they spoke up one by one as the spirit moved them. Disregarding distinctions of gender and class, they addressed one another with the terms "thee" and "thou," words commonly used in other parts of English society only in speaking to servants and social inferiors. As confirmed pacifists, they would not take part in wars. Unpopular in England both with the government and with members of other religious orders (whose services Quakers occasionally disrupted), the Quakers began looking to America for asylum. A few migrated to New England or Carolina, but most Quakers wanted a colony of their own. As members of a despised sect, however, they could not get the necessary royal grant without the aid of someone influential at the court.

Fortunately for the Quaker cause, a number of wealthy and prominent men had converted to the faith. One of them was William Penn, son of an admiral in the Royal Navy who was also a landlord of valuable Irish estates. Over his father's objections, the younger Penn converted to Quakerism, took up evangelism, and was sent repeatedly to prison. He soon began working with George Fox to create a Quaker colony in America. When his father died in 1681, Charles II paid a large debt he had owed to the older Penn with an enormous grant to the son of territory between New York and Maryland. Penn was to control it as both landlord and ruler. At the king's insistence, the territory was to be named Pennsylvania, after Penn's late father.

Through his informative and honest advertising, Penn soon made Pennsylvania the best-known and most cosmopolitan of all the English colonies in America, a place to which settlers flocked from England and the Continent. More than any other English colony, Pennsylvania prospered from the outset, because of Penn's successful recruiting, his careful planning, and the region's mild climate and fertile soil. Penn sailed to Pennsylvania in 1682 to oversee the laying out, between the Delaware and Schuylkill Rivers, of the city he named Philadelphia ("Brotherly Love"), which, with its rectangular streets, helped set the pattern for most later cities in America. Penn recognized Indians' claims to the land in the province, and he was scrupulous about reimbursing them for it. The Indians generally respected Penn, and during his lifetime the colony had no major battles with the natives.

But the colony was not without conflict. By the late 1690s, some residents of Pennsylvania were beginning to resist the nearly absolute power of the proprietor. Residents of the southern areas of the colony, in particular, complained that the government in Philadelphia was unresponsive to their needs. Pressure from these groups grew to the point that in 1701, shortly before he departed for England for the last time, Penn agreed to a Charter of Liberties for the colony. The charter established a representative assembly (consisting, alone among the English colonies, of only one house) that greatly limited the authority of the proprietor. The charter also permitted "the lower counties" of the colony to establish their own representative assembly. The three counties did so in 1703 and as a result became, in effect, a separate colony—Delaware—although until the American Revolution it continued to have the same governor as Pennsylvania.

The Founding of Georgia

Not until 1733, decades after the founding of the Restoration colonies, did another new English settlement emerge in America: Georgia, the last English colony to be established in what would become the United States. Georgia was unlike any other colony. It was founded neither by a corporation nor by a wealthy proprietor. Its guiding purpose was neither the pursuit of profit nor the desire for a religious refuge. The founders of Georgia, led by General James Oglethorpe, were driven primarily by military and philanthropic motives. They wanted to erect a military barrier between the Spanish lands to the south and the established English colonies to the north, and they wanted to provide a refuge for the impoverished, a place where English men and women without prospects at home could begin a new life.

The need for a military buffer between South Carolina and the Spanish settlements in Florida seemed urgent in the 1730s because of tense relations between England and Spain that made new wars between them seem imminent. Oglethorpe, a hero of Queen Anne's War (a conflict between England and Spain that lasted from 1701 to 1713), was aware of the military advantages of the new colony. But his own interests were primarily philanthropic. As head of a parliamentary committee investigating English prisons, he was moved by the plight of honest debtors rotting in confinement. Such prisoners, and other poor people in danger of succumbing to a similar fate, could, he believed, become the farmer-soldiers of the new colony in America.

In 1732, a charter from King George II transferred the land between the Savannah and Altamaha Rivers to Oglethorpe and his fellow trustees. Oglethorpe himself led the first colonial expedition to Georgia, which built a fortified town at the mouth of the Savannah River in 1733 and later constructed additional forts south of the Altamaha. The trustees organized the colony in part to make it militarily defensible. They limited the size of landholdings to make the settlement compact and easily defended against Spanish and Indian attacks. Blacks—free or slave—and Roman Catholics were excluded; rum was prohibited; trade with the Indians was strictly regulated—all to limit the possibility of wartime insurrection or collusion with future enemies. Only a few debtors were released from jail and sent to Georgia, but the trustees brought hundreds of needy tradesmen and artisans from England and Scotland and many religious refugees from Switzerland and Germany.

The strict rules governing life in the new colony stifled its development and created dissent in its early years. Settlers in Georgia needed a work force and almost from the start demanded the right to buy slaves. Some opposed the restrictions on the size of individual property holdings. Many resented the nearly absolute political power of Oglethorpe and the trustees. As a result, newcomers to the region generally preferred to settle in South Carolina, where there were fewer restrictive laws. Eventually, the trustees removed the limitation on individual landholdings and later the ban on slavery and the prohibition of rum. In 1751, they returned control of the colony to the king, who permitted the election of a representative assembly. Georgia continued to grow more slowly than the other southern colonies, but it now developed along lines roughly similar to those of South Carolina.

THE DEVELOPMENT OF EMPIRE

The English colonies in America had begun as separate projects, and for the most part they grew up independent of one another and subject to little more than nominal control from London. Yet by the mid-seventeenth century, the growing commercial success of the colonial ventures was producing pressure in England for a more rational, uniform structure to the empire.

The English government began trying to regulate colonial trade in the 1650s, when Parliament passed laws to keep Dutch ships out of the English colonies. Later, Parliament passed three important Navigation Acts. The first of them, in 1660, closed the colonies to all trade except that carried by English ships, and it required that tobacco and other items be exported from the colonies only to England or to English possessions. The second act, in 1663, required that all goods sent from Europe to the colonies pass through England on the way, where they would be subject to English taxation. The third act, in 1673, imposed duties on the coastal trade among the English colonies, and it provided for the appointment of customs officials to enforce the Navigation Acts. These acts, and later additions to them, formed the legal basis of England's regulation of the colonies for a century.

The Dominion of New England

Before the Navigation Acts, all the colonial governments (except that of Virginia, a royal colony with a governor appointed by the king) had operated largely independently of the crown, with governors chosen by the proprietors or by the colonists themselves and with powerful representative assemblies. Officials in London recognized that to increase their control over their colonies they would have to create a center of authority less tied to the independent-minded colonial governments, which were unlikely to enforce the new laws.

In 1675, the king created a new body, the Lords of Trade, to make recommendations for imperial reform. In 1679, following their advice, he moved to increase his control over Massachusetts, the most defiant of the colonies. He stripped it of its authority over New Hampshire and chartered a separate, royal colony there whose governor he would himself appoint. And in 1684, citing the colonial assembly's defiance of the Navigation Acts, he revoked the Massachusetts charter.

Charles II's brother James II, who succeeded him to the throne in 1685, went further. He created a single Dominion of New England, which combined the government of Massachusetts with the governments of the rest of the New England colonies and later with those of New York and New Jersey as well. He eliminated the existing assemblies within the new Dominion and appointed a single governor, Sir Edmund Andros, to supervise the entire region from Boston. Andros's rigid enforcement of the Navigation Acts and his brusque dismissal of the colonists' claims to the "rights of Englishmen" made him quickly and thoroughly unpopular.

The "Glorious Revolution"

James II was not only losing friends in America; he was making powerful enemies in England by attempting to control Parliament and the courts and by appointing his fellow Catholics to high office. By 1688, his popular support had all but vanished, and Parliament invited his Protestant daughter Mary and her husband, William of Orange, ruler of the Netherlands, to assume the throne. James II (perhaps remembering what had happened to his father, Charles I) offered no resistance and fled to France. As a result of this bloodless coup, which the English called the "Glorious Revolution," William and Mary became joint sovereigns.

When Bostonians heard of the overthrow of James II, they arrested and imprisoned the unpopular Andros. The new sovereigns in England accepted the toppling of Andros, abolished the Dominion of New England, and restored separate colonial governments. They did not, however, re-create them as they had been. In 1691, they combined Massachusetts with Plymouth and made it a single, royal colony. The new charter restored the General Court, but it gave the crown the right to appoint the governor. It also replaced church membership with property ownership as the basis for voting and officeholding.

Andros had been governing New York through a lieutenant governor, Captain Francis Nicholson, who enjoyed the support of the wealthy merchants and fur traders of the province. Other, less favored colonists—farmers, mechanics, small traders, and shopkeepers—had a long accumulation of grievances against Nicholson and his allies. The leader of the New York dissidents was Jacob Leisler, a German immigrant and a prosperous merchant who had never won acceptance as one of the colony's ruling class. In May 1689, when news of the Glorious Revolution in England and the fall of Andros in Boston reached New York, Leisler raised a militia, captured the city fort, drove Nicholson into exile, and proclaimed himself the new head of government in New York. For two years, he tried in vain to stabilize his power in the colony amid fierce factional rivalry. In 1691, when William and Mary appointed a new governor, Leisler briefly resisted. He was convicted of treason and executed. Fierce rivalry between what became known as the "Leislerians" and the "anti-Leislerians" dominated the politics of the colony for many years thereafter.

In Maryland, many people erroneously assumed when they heard news of the Glorious Revolution that their proprietor, the Catholic Lord Baltimore, who was living in England, had sided with the Catholic James II and opposed William and Mary. So in 1689, an old opponent of the proprietor's government, the Protestant John Coode, led a revolt that drove out Lord Baltimore's officials and led to Maryland's establishment as a royal colony in 1691. The colonial assembly then established the Church of England as the colony's official religion and excluded Catholics from public office. Maryland became a proprietary colony again in 1715, after the fifth Lord Baltimore joined the Anglican Church.

The Glorious Revolution of 1688 in England touched off revolutions, mostly bloodless ones, in several colonies. Under the new king and queen, the representative assemblies that had been abolished were revived, and the scheme for colonial unification from above was abandoned. But the Glorious Revolution in America did not stop the reorganization of the empire. Its ultimate results, in fact, were governments that actually increased the crown's potential authority. As the first century of English settlement in America came to its end, the colonists were becoming more a part of the imperial system than ever before.

CONCLUSION

The English colonization of North America—which began with several unsuccessful attempts at settlement in the late sixteenth century and started its permanent life in Virginia in 1607—was part of a larger effort by England and other European nations to expand the reach of their increasingly commercial societies. Although some English settlers came to the New World to escape religious or political persecution, most came in hopes of finding opportunities to prosper by serving the needs of the emerging market economies of Europe.

In the South, civilization grew rapidly once the settlers discovered a European market for tobacco. Land was plentiful and cheap, but labor was scarce. So the early settlers relied heavily on indentured white laborers from England. Gradually, however, they turned instead to another source of labor: men and women captured in Africa, carried forcibly to the Americas, and sold into bondage. The white recruitment of African labor gradually evolved into a rigid system of absolute white ownership of blacks—slavery.

In the northern colonies, the economies and the European populations were more diverse—and composed in much greater numbers of religious refugees from England and of immigrants from other European nations as well. There an even more vigorously commercial economy developed that relied heavily on trade with Europe and the Caribbean.

By the early eighteenth century, English settlement had spread from northern New England (in what is now Maine) south into Georgia, while a substantial French empire had developed to the north in Canada. Most of the colonists considered themselves English subjects, with the same rights and privileges as those who lived in England itself. But as time went on, they began to develop social and political traditions very different from those in England—traditions that led to increasing of tension and conflict.

FOR FURTHER REFERENCE

Suggested Readings

William Cronon, *Changes in the Land: Indians, Colonists, and the Ecology of New England* (1983) examines the social and environmental effects of English settlement in colonial America. Perry Miller, *The New England Mind: From Colony to Province* (1953) and Edmund Morgan, *The Puritan Dilemma: The Story of John Winthrop* (1958) are classic expositions of the Puritan intellectual milieu. David Hall, *Worlds of Wonder, Days of Judgment* (1989) is a reconsideration of Puritan theology. Michael Kammen, *Colonial New York* (1975) illuminates the diversity and pluralism of New York under the Dutch and the English. Edmund Morgan, *American Slavery, American Freedom* (1975) is an excellent narrative of political and social development in early Virginia, as is T. H. Breen, *Tobacco Culture* (1985). Peter H. Wood, *Black Majority* (1974) describes the early importance of slavery in the founding of South Carolina. Richard S. Dunn, *Sugar and Slaves: The Rise of the Planter Class in the English West Indies, 1624–1713* (1972) is important for understanding the origins of British colonial slavery. Gary Nash, *Red, White and Black: The Peoples of Early America* (1982) provides a brief survey of the cultural and racial mixture of peoples in early America. Philip Curtin, *The Atlantic Slave Trade: A Census* (1969) has become the indispensable starting point for understanding African forced migration to the Americas. An outstanding collection of essays that summarizes recent scholarship on colonial America is Jack P. Greene and J. R. Pole, eds., *Colonial British America: Essays in the New History of the Early Modern Era* (1984).

Films

(The best source for information on how to find these and other films is *Bowker's Complete Video Directory*—three volumes.) *The Era of Colonization*, Vol. 2 (1996) explores European settlement from New England to Virginia, and relations between Europeans and Indians from the late sixteenth century through the Seven Years' War. *The Puritan Experience: Forsaking England*, and *The Puritan Experience: Making of a New World* (1975) follow the Higgins family from England to Massachusetts in the 1630s. *Jamestown: The Beginning* (1992) tells the story of Virginia's first permanent English settlement from the viewpoint of John Leydon, one of the few settlers who managed to survive the first few decades of settlement. *Slavery & Freedom*, Vol. 3 (1996) examines the rise of slavery in the New World. *The Southern Colonies* (1987) analyzes the origins of slavery in colonial Virginia.

Internet Resources

Internet websites containing historical material relevant to the subjects discussed in this chapter can be reached through the McGraw-Hill history site at www.mhhe.com/socscience/history/usa/link/linktop.htm.

CHAPTER THREE

Society and Culture in Provincial America

The Colonial Population ∼ *The Colonial Economies*
Patterns of Society ∼ *The Colonial Mind*

A S THE EXTENT of settlement in North America grew, and as the economies of the colonies began to flourish, several distinctive ways of life emerged. The new American societies differed considerably from the society that most had attempted to re-create in the New World—the society of England. They differed as well from one another. Indeed, the pattern of society in some areas of North America seemed to resemble that of others scarcely at all. Americans would eventually decide that they had enough in common to enable them to join together and form a single nation. But regional differences would continue to shape their society throughout their history.

THE COLONIAL POPULATION

After uncertain beginnings at Jamestown and Plymouth, the non-Indian population of English North America grew rapidly and substantially, through continued immigration and through natural increase. By the late seventeenth century European and African immigrants outnumbered the natives along the Atlantic coast.

A few of the early settlers were members of the English upper classes, but the dominant element was English laborers. Some came independently, such as the religious dissenters in early New England, who paid their own way and settled on their own land. But in the Chesapeake, at

TIME LINE				
1636	**1662**	**1685**	**1692**	**1697**
Harvard founded	Halfway Covenant	Huguenots migrate to America	Salem witchcraft trials	Slave importations increase

1720	**1734**	**1739**	**1740s**	
Cotton Mather starts smallpox inoculations	Great Awakening begins Zenger Trial	George Whitefield arrives in America Great Awakening intensifies Stono Slave rebellion	Indigo production begins	

least three-fourths of the immigrants in the seventeenth century arrived as indentured servants.

Indentured Servitude

The system of temporary servitude developed out of practices in England. Young men and women bound themselves to masters for fixed terms of servitude (usually four to five years) in exchange for passage to America, food, and shelter. Male indentures were supposed to receive clothing, tools, and occasionally land upon completion of their service. In reality, however, many left service with nothing. Most women indentures—who constituted roughly one-fourth of the total in the Chesapeake—worked as domestic servants and were expected to marry when their terms of servitude expired. Since men greatly outnumbered women in the region, most of them did.

By the late seventeenth century, the indentured servant population had become one of the largest elements of the colonial population and was creating serious social problems. Some former indentures managed to establish themselves successfully as farmers, tradespeople, or artisans, and some of the women married propertied men. Others (mostly males) found themselves without land, without employment, without families, and without prospects; and there grew up in some areas, particularly the Chesapeake, a large floating population of young single men—such as those who supported Bacon's Rebellion—who served as a potential (and at times actual) source of social unrest.

Beginning in the 1670s, a decrease in the birth rate in England and an improvement in economic conditions there reduced the pressures on laboring men and women to emigrate, and the flow of indentured servants declined. Those who did travel to America as indentures now generally avoided the southern colonies, where working conditions were arduous and prospects for advancement were slim. In the Chesapeake, therefore, landowners began to rely much more heavily on African slavery as their principal source of labor.

Birth and Death

Although immigration remained for a time the greatest source of population growth, the most important long-range factor in the increase of the colonial population was its ability to reproduce itself. Marked improvement in the reproduction rate began in New England and the mid-Atlantic colonies in the second half of the seventeenth century, and after the 1650s natural increase became the most important source of population growth in those areas. The New England population more than quadrupled through reproduction alone in the second half of the seventeenth century. This rise was a result not only of families having large numbers of children. It was also because life expectancy in New England was unusually high, both in comparison to that of other colonies and in comparison to that of England.

Conditions improved much more slowly in the South. The high death rates in the Chesapeake region did not begin to decline to the levels of those elsewhere until the mid-eighteenth century. Throughout the seventeenth century, the average life expectancy for European men in the region was just over forty years, and for women slightly less. (In New England, life expectancy was up to thirty years longer.) One in four white children died in infancy, and half died before the age of twenty. Children who survived infancy often lost one or both of their parents before reaching maturity. Widows, widowers, and orphans thus formed a substantial proportion of the white Chesapeake population. Only after settlers developed immunity to local diseases (particularly malaria) did life expectancy increase significantly. Population growth was substantial in the region, but it was largely a result of immigration.

The natural increases in the population in the seventeenth century were in large part a result of steady improvement in the balance between men and women in the colonies. In the early years of settlement, more than three-quarters of the white population of the Chesapeake consisted of men. And even in New England, which from the beginning had attracted more families (and thus more women) than the southern colonies, 60 percent of the inhabitants were male in 1650. Gradually, however, more women began to arrive in the colonies; and increasing birth rates, which of course produced roughly equal numbers of males and females, contributed to shifting the sex ratio (the balance between men and women) as well. Throughout the colonial period, the population almost doubled every twenty-five years. By 1775, the non-Indian population of the colonies was over 2 million—a nearly tenfold increase since the beginning of the century.

Medicine in the Colonies

The very high death rates of women who bore children illustrate the primitive nature of medical knowledge and practice in the colonies. Seventeenth- and eighteenth-century physicians had little or no understanding of infection and sterilization. As a result, many people died from infections contracted during childbirth or surgery. Because communities were unaware of bacteria, many were plagued with infectious diseases transmitted by garbage or unclean water.

One result of the limited extent of medical knowledge was that it was relatively easy for people to enter the field, even without any professional training. The biggest beneficiaries of this ease of access were women, who established themselves in considerable numbers as midwives. Midwives assisted women in childbirth, but they also dispensed other medical advice—usually urging their patients to use herbs or other natural remedies. Midwives were popular because they were usually friends and neighbors of the people they treated, unlike physicians, who were few and therefore not often well known to their patients. Male doctors felt threatened by the midwives and struggled continually to drive them from the field, although they did not make substantial progress in doing so until the nineteenth century.

Midwives and doctors alike practiced medicine on the basis of the prevailing assumptions of their time, most of them derived from the theory of "humoralism" popularized by the great second-century Roman physician Galen. Galen argued that the human body was governed by four "humors" that were lodged in four bodily fluids: yellow bile (or "choler"), black bile ("melancholy"), blood, and phlegm. In a healthy body, the four humors existed in balance. Illness represented an imbalance and suggested the need for removing from the body the excesses of whatever fluid was causing the imbalance. That was the rationale that lay behind the principal medical techniques of the seventeenth century: purging, expulsion, and bleeding. Bleeding was the most extreme of the treatments (and the most destructive), and it was practiced mostly by male physicians. Midwives preferred more homeopathic treatments and favored "pukes" and laxatives. The great majority of early Americans, however, had little contact with physicians, or even midwives, and sought instead to deal with illness on their own, confident that their own abilities were equal to those of educated physicians. The assumption that treating illness was the exclusive province of trained professionals, so much a part of the twentieth century, lay far in the distance in the colonial era.

That seventeenth-century medicine rested so much on ideas produced 1,400 years before is evidence of how little support there was for the scientific method—which rests on experimentation and observation rather than on inherited faiths—in England and America at the time. Bleeding, for example, had been in use for hundreds of years, during which time there had been no evidence at all that it helped people recover from illness; indeed, if anyone had chosen to look for it, there was considerable evidence that bleeding could do great harm. But what would seem in later eras to be the simple process of testing scientific assumptions was not yet a common part of Western thought. That was one reason that the birth of the Enlightenment in the late seventeenth century—with its faith in human reason and its belief in the capacity of individuals and societies to create better lives— was important not just to politics but to science.

Women and Families in the Colonies

Because there were many more men than women in colonial America, few women remained unmarried for long. The average European woman in America married for the first time at twenty or twenty-one years of age, considerably earlier than in England. Because of the large numbers of indentured servants who were forbidden to marry until their terms of service expired, premarital sexual relationships were frequent. Over a third of Chesapeake marriages occurred with the bride already pregnant. Children born out of wedlock to indentured women were often taken from their mothers at a young age and themselves bound out as indentured servants.

Women in the Chesapeake could anticipate a life consumed with childbearing. The average wife experienced pregnancies every two years. Those who lived long enough bore an average of eight children apiece (up to five of whom typically died in infancy or early childhood). Since childbirth was one of the most frequent causes of female death, many women did not survive to see their children grow to maturity. Those who did, however, were often widowed, since they were usually much younger than their husbands. By the early eighteenth century, however, the demographic character of the Chesapeake was beginning to change, and with it the nature and structure of the typical family. Life expectancy was increasing, and indentured servitude was in decline. Natural reproduction was becoming the principal source of white population growth.

In New England, where many more immigrants arrived with family members and where death rates declined far more quickly, family structure was much more stable than in the Chesapeake and hence more traditional. The sex ratio was more balanced than in the Chesapeake, so most men could expect to marry. As in the Chesapeake, women married young, began producing children early, and continued to do so well into their thirties. In contrast to the situation in the South, however, northern children were more likely to survive (the average family raised six to eight children to maturity), and their families were more likely to remain intact. Fewer New England women became widows, and those who did generally lost their husbands later in life. Hence women were less often cast in roles independent of their husbands. Young women, moreover, had less control over the conditions of marriage, both because there were fewer unmarried men vying for them than in the South and because their fathers were more likely to be alive and able to exercise control over their choices.

The longer lives in New England meant that parents continued to control their children longer than did parents in the South. Few sons and daughters could choose a spouse entirely independently of their parents' wishes. Men tended to rely on their fathers for land to cultivate—generally a prerequisite for beginning families of their own. Women needed dowries from their parents if they were to attract desirable husbands. Stricter parental supervision of children meant, too, that fewer women became pregnant before marriage than was the case in the South (although even in Puritan New England the premarital pregnancy rate was as high as 20 percent in some communities).

Puritanism placed a high value on the family, and the position of wife and mother was highly valued in Puritan culture. At the same time, however, Puritanism served to reinforce the idea of nearly absolute male authority and the assumption of female weakness and inferiority. Women were expected to be modest and submissive. A wife was expected to devote herself almost entirely to serving the needs of her husband. Women were vital to the family economy, and they continuously engaged in tasks crucial to the functioning of the farm—gardening, raising poultry, tending cattle, spinning, and weaving, as well as cooking, cleaning, and washing.

The Beginnings of Slavery in English North America

The demand for African servants to supplement the scarce southern labor force existed almost from the first moments of settlement. For a time, however, black workers were hard to find. Not until the mid-seventeenth century, when a substantial commerce in slaves grew up between the Caribbean islands and the southern colonies, did black workers become generally available in North America.

The demand for slaves in North America helped expand the transatlantic slave trade. And as slave trading grew more extensive and more sophisticated, it also grew more horrible. Before it ended in the nineteenth century, it was responsible for the forced immigration of as many as 11 million Africans to North and South America and the Caribbean. Indeed, through much of the eighteenth century, the number of African immigrants to the Americas was higher than that of Europeans. In the flourishing slave marts

AFRICANS BOUND FOR AMERICA Shown here are the below-deck slave quarters of a Spanish vessel en route to the West Indies. A British warship captured the slaver, and a young English naval officer (Lt. Francis Meynell) made this watercolor sketch on the spot. The Africans seen in this picture appear somewhat more comfortable than prisoners on other slave ships, some of whom were chained and packed together so tightly that they had no room to stand or even sit.

on the African coast, native chieftains brought captured members of rival tribes to the ports. The terrified victims were then packed into the dark, filthy holds of ships for the horrors of the "middle passage"—the long journey to the Americas, during which the prisoners were usually kept chained in the bowels of the slave ships and supplied with only minimal food and water. Women were often victims of rape and other sexual abuse. Many slave traders tried to cram as many Africans as possible into their ships to ensure that enough would survive to yield a profit at journey's end. Those who died en route, and many did, were simply thrown overboard. Upon arrival in the New World, slaves were auctioned off to white landowners and transported, frightened and bewildered, to their new homes.

North America was a less important direct destination for African slaves than were such other parts of the New World as the Caribbean islands and Brazil; fewer than 5 percent of the Africans imported to the Americas arrived first in the English colonies. Through most of the seventeenth century, those blacks who were transported to what became the United States came not directly from Africa but from the West Indies. Not until the 1670s did traders start importing blacks directly from Africa to North America. Even then the flow remained small for a time, mainly because a single group, the Royal African Company of England, monopolized the trade and kept prices high and supplies low.

A turning point in the history of the black population in North America was 1697, the year rival traders broke the Royal African Company's monopoly. With the trade now open to competition, prices fell and the number of Africans greatly increased. By 1700, about 25,000 African slaves lived in English North America. That was only 10 percent of the total non-Indian population, but because blacks were so heavily concentrated in a few southern colonies, they were already beginning to outnumber whites in some areas. There were perhaps twice as many black men as black women in most areas, but in some places the African-American population grew by natural increase nevertheless. In the Chesapeake more new slaves were being born than were being imported from Africa. In South Carolina, by contrast, the arduous conditions of rice cultivation ensured that the black population would barely be able to sustain itself through natural increase until much later. By 1760, the number of Africans in the colonies had increased to approximately a quarter of a million. A few (16,000 in 1763) lived in New England; slightly more (29,000) lived in the middle colonies. The vast majority, however, lived in the South. By then blacks had almost wholly replaced white indentured servants as the basis of the southern work force.

DEBATING THE PAST

The Origins of Slavery

HE DEBATE among historians over how and why white Americans created a system of slave labor in the seventeenth century—and how and why they determined that African Americans and no others should populate that system—has been an unusually lively one. At its center is a debate over whether slavery was a result of white racism, or whether racism was a result of slavery.

In 1950, Oscar and Mary Handlin published an influential article comparing slavery to other systems of "unfreedom" in the colonies. What separated slavery from other conditions of servitude, they argued, was that it was restricted to people of African descent, that it was permanent, and that it passed from one generation to the next. The unique characteristics of slavery, the Handlins argued, were part of an effort by colonial legislatures to increase the available labor force. White laborers needed an incentive to come to America; black laborers, forcibly imported from Africa, did not. The distinction between the conditions of white workers and the conditions of black workers was, therefore, based on legal and economic motives, not on racism.

Winthrop Jordan was one of a number of historians who later challenged the Handlins' thesis and argued that white racism, more than economic interests, produced African slavery. In *White Over Black* (1968) and other works, Jordan argued that Europeans had long viewed people of color—and black Africans in particular—as inferior beings appropriate for serving whites. Those attitudes migrated with white Europeans to the New World, and white racism shaped the treatment of Africans in America—and the nature of the slave labor system—from the beginning. Even without the economic incentives the Handlins described, in other words, whites would have been likely to oppress blacks in the New World.

Peter Wood's *Black Majority* (1974), a study of seventeenth-century South Carolina, was one of a number of works that moved the debate back toward social and economic conditions. Wood demonstrated that blacks and whites often worked together on relatively equal terms in the early years of settlement; that racism, in other words, did not inevitably shape the relationships between the blacks and whites. But as rice cultivation expanded, it became more difficult to find white laborers willing to do the arduous work. The increase in the forcible importation of African workers, and the creation of a system of permanent bondage, was a response to this growing demand for labor. It was also a response to fears among whites that without slavery it would be difficult to control a labor force brought to America against its will. Edmund Morgan's *American Slavery, American Freedom* (1975) argued similarly that the southern labor system was at first relatively flexible and later grew more rigid. In colonial Virginia, he claimed, white settlers did not at first intend to create a system of permanent bondage for blacks or whites. But as the tobacco economy grew and created a high demand for cheap labor, white landowners began to feel uneasy about their dependence on a large group of dependent white workers. Such workers were difficult to recruit and control. Slavery, therefore, was less a result of racism than of the desire for whites to find a reliable and stable labor force.

Robin Blackburn's *The Making of New World Slavery* (1996) argues particularly strenuously that, while race was a factor in making the enslavement of Africans easier for whites to justify to themselves, the real reasons for the emergence of slavery were hardheaded economic decisions by ambitious entrepreneurs who realized very early that a slave-labor system in the labor-intensive agricultural world of the American South and the Caribbean was more profitable than a free-labor system. Slavery served the interests of a powerful combination of groups: planters, merchants, industrialists, and consumers. The most important reason for the creation and continuation of the system, therefore, was not racism, but the pursuit of profit—and the success of the system in producing it. Slavery was not, Blackburn concludes, an antiquated remnant of an older world. It was a recognizably modern labor system that, however horrible, served the needs of an emerging market economy.

For a time, the legal and social status of the African laborers remained somewhat fluid. In some areas—South Carolina, for example, where the number of black arrivals grew more quickly than anywhere else—white and black laborers worked together at first on terms of relative equality. Some blacks were treated much like white hired servants, and some were freed after a fixed term of servitude. By the late seventeenth century, however, a rigid distinction was emerging between blacks and whites. Gradually, the assumption spread that blacks would remain in service permanently and that black children would inherit their parents' bondage. White beliefs about the inferiority of the black race reinforced the growing rigidity of the system. Whites had long ago defined themselves as a superior race in their relations with the native Indian population; the idea of subordinating an "inferior" race was, therefore, already part of European thinking by the time substantial numbers of Africans appeared in their midst.

The system of permanent servitude—American slavery—became legal in the early eighteenth century when colonial assemblies began to pass "slave codes" granting white masters almost absolute authority over their slaves. Only one factor determined whether a person was subject to the slave codes: color. In the colonial societies of Spanish America, people of mixed race were granted a different (and higher) status than pure Africans. English America recognized no such distinctions. Any African ancestry was enough to classify a person as black.

Changing Sources of European Immigration

The most distinctive and enduring feature of the American population was that it brought together peoples of many different races, ethnic groups, and nationalities. North America was home to a substantial population of natives, to a growing number of English immigrants, to forcibly imported Africans, and to substantial non-English groups from Europe.

The earliest of these non-English European immigrants were about 300,000 French Calvinists, or Huguenots, who left Roman Catholic France for the English colonies of North America after the Edict of Nantes, which had guaranteed them substantial liberties, was revoked in 1685. Many German Protestants emigrated to America to escape similarly arbitrary religious policies and the frequent wars between their principalities and France. The Rhineland of southwestern Germany, known as the Palatinate, was exposed to frequent invasion; more than 12,000 Palatinate Germans fled to England early in the eighteenth century, and approximately 3,000 of them found their way to America. Most settled in Pennsylvania, where they ultimately became known to English settlers as the "Pennsylvania Dutch" (a corruption of the German term for their nationality, *Deutsch*). Other, later German immigrants headed to Pennsylvania as well, among them the Moravians and Mennonites, whose religious views were similar to those of the Quakers.

The most numerous of the newcomers were the so-called Scotch-Irish—Scotch Presbyterians who had settled in northern Ireland (in the province of Ulster) in the early seventeenth century. Most of the Scotch-Irish in America pushed out to the edges of European settlement and occupied land without much regard for who actually claimed to own it. They were as ruthless in their displacement and suppression of the Indians as they had been with the native Irish Catholics in Ireland.

There were also immigrants from Scotland itself and from southern Ireland. Scottish Highlanders, some of them Roman Catholics, mainly immigrated into North Carolina. Scottish Presbyterian Lowlanders, fleeing high rents and unemployment, left for America in large numbers shortly before the American Revolution. The Irish migrated steadily over a long period and by the time of the Revolution were almost as numerous as the Scots. Many of them abandoned their Roman Catholic religion and much of their ethnic identity after they arrived in America.

THE COLONIAL ECONOMIES

Farming dominated almost all areas of European and African settlement in North America throughout the seventeenth and eighteenth centuries. Even so, the economies of the different regions varied markedly from one another.

The Southern Economy

A strong European demand for tobacco enabled some planters in the Chesapeake (Maryland and Virginia) to become enormously wealthy and at times allowed the region as a whole to prosper. But throughout the seventeenth and eighteenth centuries, production of tobacco frequently exceeded demand, and as a result the price of the crop sometimes suffered severe declines. The result was a boom-and-bust cycle in the Chesapeake economy, with the first major bust occurring in 1640.

South Carolina and Georgia relied on rice production, since the low-lying coastline with its many tidal rivers made it possible to create rice

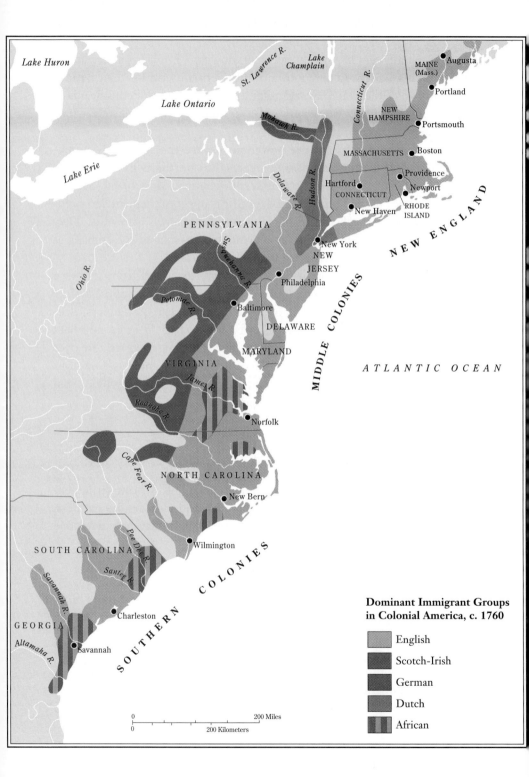

Lake Huron

Lake Ontario

Lake Erie

St. Lawrence R.

Lake Champlain

Connecticut R.

MAINE (Mass.) ● Augusta

● Portland

NEW HAMPSHIRE

● Portsmouth

MASSACHUSETTS ● Boston

Mohawk R.

Delaware R.

Hudson R.

Hartford ● ● Providence
CONNECTICUT ● Newport

● New Haven RHODE ISLAND

PENNSYLVANIA

Susquehanna R.

● New York
NEW JERSEY

● Philadelphia

Ohio R.

Potomac R.

● Baltimore

DELAWARE

MARYLAND

VIRGINIA

James R.

Roanoke R.

● Norfolk

Cape Fear R.

NORTH CAROLINA

● New Bern

MIDDLE COLONIES

NEW ENGLAND

ATLANTIC OCEAN

SOUTH CAROLINA

Pee Dee R.

● Wilmington

SOUTHERN COLONIES

Santee R.

Savannah R.

GEORGIA

Altamaha R.

● Charleston

● Savannah

**Dominant Immigrant Groups
in Colonial America, c. 1760**

English

Scotch-Irish

German

Dutch

African

0   200 Miles
0   200 Kilometers

SELLING TOBACCO This late-seventeenth-century label was used in the sale of American tobacco in England. The drawing depicts Virginia as a land of bright sunshine, energetic slaves, and prosperous, pipe-smoking planters.

paddies that could be flooded and drained. Rice cultivation was arduous work performed standing knee-deep in malarial swamps—a task so difficult and unhealthy that white laborers generally refused to perform it. Hence planters in South Carolina and Georgia were much more dependent on slaves than were their northern counterparts. African workers were adept at rice cultivation, in part because some of them had come from rice-producing regions of west Africa and in part because they were generally more accustomed to the hot, humid climate than were Europeans.

Because of their dependence on large-scale cash crops, the southern colonies developed less of a commercial or industrial economy than the colonies of the North. The trading in tobacco and rice was handled largely by merchants based in London and, later, in the northern colonies. Few cities of more than modest size developed in the South.

Northern Economic and Technological Life

In the North, as in the South, agriculture continued to dominate, but it was agriculture of a more diverse kind. Agriculture, however, did not remain the only major economic activity in the North because conditions for farming were less favorable there than in the South. In northern New England, in particular, colder weather and hard, rocky soil made it difficult for colonists to develop the kind of large-scale commercial farming system that southerners were creating. Conditions for agriculture were better in southern New England and the middle colonies, where the soil was fertile and the weather more temperate. New York, Pennsylvania, and the Connecticut River valley were the chief suppliers of wheat to much of New England and to parts of the South. Even there, however, a substantial commercial economy emerged alongside the agricultural one.

Almost every colonist engaged in a certain amount of industry at home. Occasionally these home industries provided families with surplus goods they could trade or sell. Beyond these domestic efforts, craftsmen and artisans established themselves in colonial towns as cobblers, blacksmiths, riflemakers, cabinetmakers, silversmiths, and printers. In some areas, entrepreneurs harnessed water power to run small mills for grinding grain, processing cloth, or milling lumber. And in several places, large-scale shipbuilding operations began to flourish.

The first effort to establish a significant metals industry in the colonies was an ironworks established in Saugus, Massachusetts, in the 1640s after iron ore deposits had been discovered in the region. Iron technology was already advancing rapidly in England, and the colonists attempted to transfer those skills to America. The Saugus works used water power to drive a bellows, which controlled the heat in a charcoal furnace. The carbon from the burning charcoal helped remove the oxygen from the ore and thus reduced its melting temperature. As the ore melted, it trickled down into molds or was taken in the form of simple "sow bars" to a nearby forge to be shaped into iron objects such as pots and anvils. There was also a mill suitable for turning the "sow bars" into narrow rods that blacksmiths could cut into nails. The Saugus works was a technological success; indeed, it could boast technological capabilities equal to any ironworks in Europe at the time. But it was a financial failure. It began operations in 1646; in 1668, its financial problems forced it to close its doors.

Metal works, however, gradually became an important part of the colonial economy. The largest industrial enterprise anywhere in English North America was the ironworks of the German ironmaster Peter

Hasenclever in northern New Jersey. Founded in 1764 with British capital, it employed several hundred laborers, many of them imported from ironworks in Germany. There were other, smaller ironmaking enterprises in every northern colony (with particular concentrations in Massachusetts, New Jersey, and Pennsylvania), and there were ironworks as well in several of the southern colonies. Even so, these and other growing industries did not become the basis for the kind of explosive industrial growth that Great Britain experienced in the late eighteenth century—in part because English parliamentary regulations such as the Iron Act of 1750 restricted metal processing in the colonies. Similar prohibitions limited the manufacture of woolens, hats, and other goods. But the biggest obstacles to industrialization in America were an inadequate labor supply, a small domestic market, and inadequate transportation facilities and energy supplies.

More important than manufacturing were industries that exploited the natural resources of the continent. By the mid-seventeenth century, the flourishing fur trade of earlier years was in decline. Taking its place were lumbering, mining, and fishing, particularly in the waters off the New England coast. These industries provided commodities that could be exported to England in exchange for manufactured goods. And they helped produce the most distinctive feature of the northern economy: a thriving commercial class.

The Extent and Limits of Technology

Despite the technological progress that was occurring in some parts of America in the seventeenth and eighteenth centuries, much of colonial society was conspicuously lacking in even very basic technological capacities. Up to half the farmers in the colonies were so primitively equipped that they did not even own a plow. Substantial numbers of households owned no pots or kettles for cooking. And only about half the households in the colonies owned guns or rifles—with rural people almost as unlikely to have firearms as urban people. The relatively low levels of ownership of these and other elementary tools was not because such things were difficult to make, but because most Americans remained too poor or too isolated to be able to afford them. Many households had few if any candles, because they were unable to afford candle molds or tallow (wax), or because they had no access to commercially produced candles. In the early eighteenth century, very few farmers owned wagons. Most made do with two-wheeled carts, which could be hauled by hand (or by horse) around the farm but which were not very efficient for transporting crops to market. The most commonly-owned tool on American farms was the axe, which suggests how much time most farmers had to spend clearing land.

Even so, few colonists were self-sufficient in the late seventeenth and early eighteenth centuries. The popular image of early American households is of people who had little connection to the market, who grew their own food, made their own clothes, and bought little from anyone else. In fact, relatively few colonial families owned spinning wheels or looms, which suggests that most people purchased whatever yarn and cloth they needed, or could afford, from merchants. Most farmers who grew grain took it to centralized facilities for processing.

In general, unsurprisingly, people who lived in isolated or poor areas owned fewer tools and had less access to advanced technologies than did those in more populous or affluent areas. But throughout the colonies, the ability of people to acquire manufactured implements lagged far behind the economy's capacity to produce them.

The Rise of Colonial Commerce

Perhaps the most remarkable feature of colonial commerce in the seventeenth century was that it was able to survive at all. American merchants faced such bewildering and intimidating obstacles, and lacked so many of the basic institutions of trade, that they managed to stay afloat only with great difficulty. The colonies had almost no gold or silver, and their paper currency was not acceptable as payment for goods from abroad. For many years, colonial merchants had to rely on barter or on money substitutes such as beaver skins.

A second obstacle was lack of information about supply and demand. Traders had no way of knowing what they would find in foreign ports; vessels sometimes stayed at sea for years, journeying from one port to another, trading one commodity for another, attempting to find some way to turn a profit. There was also an enormous number of small, fiercely competitive companies, which made the problem of rationalizing the system even more acute.

Nevertheless, commerce in the colonies survived and grew. There was elaborate trade among the colonies themselves and with the West Indies. The mainland colonies offered their Caribbean trading partners rum, agricultural products, meat, and fish. The islands offered sugar, molasses, and at times slaves in return. There was also trade with England, continental Europe, and the west coast of Africa. This commerce has often

Overseas Trade During the Colonial Period

From Northern colonies to Britain:
Furs, fish, fruit
From Britain to Northern colonies:
Manufactured goods

From Northern colonies to Europe:
Fish, fruit, meat
From Southern colonies to Britain:
Rice, indigo, tobacco, furs,
naval stores (pitch, tar, masts)
From Britain to Southern colonies:
Manufactured goods

From West Indies
to Northern colonies
and Britain:
Sugar, molasses
From Northern colonies
to West Indies:
Flour, fish, lumber,
manufactured goods

From Northern colonies
to West Africa:
Rum

From West Africa
to West Indies:
Slaves, golddust

been described, somewhat inaccurately, as the "triangular trade," suggesting a neat process by which merchants carried rum and other goods from New England to Africa, exchanged their merchandise for slaves, whom they then transported to the West Indies (hence the term "middle passage" for the dreaded journey—it was the second of the three legs of the voyage), and then exchanged the slaves for sugar and molasses, which they shipped back to New England to be distilled into rum. In reality, the so-called triangular trade in rum, slaves, and sugar was a complicated maze of highly diverse trade routes. Out of this risky trade emerged a group of adventurous entrepreneurs who by the mid-eighteenth century were beginning to constitute a distinct merchant class concentrated in the port cities of the North. The British Navigation Acts protected them from foreign competition in the colonies. They had ready access to the market in England for such colonial products as furs, timber, and American-built ships. But they also developed markets illegally outside the British Empire—in the French, Spanish, and Dutch West Indies—where they could often get higher prices for their goods than in the British colonies.

PATTERNS OF SOCIETY

Although there were sharp social distinctions in the colonies, the well-defined and deeply entrenched class system of England failed to reproduce itself in America. In England, land was scarce and the population large, and the relatively few landowners had enormous power over the landless. In colonial America, in contrast, land was abundant and people were scarce. Aristocracies emerged there, to be sure; but they tended to rely less on landownership than on control of a substantial work force, and they were generally less secure and less powerful than their English counterparts. More than in England, white people in America faced opportunities for social mobility—both up and down. There were also new forms of community in America, and they varied greatly from one region to another.

Masters and Slaves on the Plantation

The plantation system of the American South produced one form of community. The first plantations emerged in the tobacco-growing areas of Virginia and Maryland. Some of the early planters became established aristocrats with vast estates. On the whole, however, seventeenth-century colonial plantations were rough and relatively small. In the early days in Virginia, they were little more than crude clearings where landowners and indentured servants worked side by side in conditions so harsh that death was an everyday occurrence. Even in later years, when the death rate declined and the landholdings became more established, plantation work forces seldom exceeded thirty people. Most landowners lived in rough cabins or houses, with their servants or slaves nearby. The economy of the plantation was a precarious one. Planters could not control their markets, so even the largest of them were constantly at risk. When prices fell—as tobacco prices did, for example, in the 1660s—planters faced the prospect of ruin. The plantation economy created many new wealthy landowners, but it also destroyed many.

The enslaved African Americans, of course, lived very differently. On the smaller farms with only a handful of slaves, it was not always possible for a rigid separation to develop between whites and blacks. But by the early eighteenth century, over three-fourths of all blacks lived on plantations of at least ten slaves, and nearly half lived in communities of fifty slaves or more. In those settings, they were able to develop a society and culture of their own. Although whites seldom encouraged formal marriages among slaves, blacks themselves developed a strong and elaborate family structure, even though slave families were always precarious because any member could be sold at any time to another planter, even to one in another colony. There was also a distinctive slave religion, which blended Christianity with African folklore and which became a central element in the emergence of an independent black culture.

Nevertheless, black society was subject to constant intrusions from and interaction with white society. Black house servants, for example, were isolated from their own community and were under constant surveillance from whites. Black women were subject to usually unwanted sexual advances from owners and overseers and hence to bearing mulatto children, who were rarely recognized by their white fathers but were generally accepted as members of the slave community. On some plantations, black workers were treated with kindness and sometimes responded to their owners with genuine devotion. On others, they encountered physical brutality and occasionally even sadism, against which they were virtually powerless.

Slaves often resisted their masters, in large ways and small. The most serious example in the colonial period was the Stono Rebellion in South Carolina in 1739, during which about 100 blacks rose up, seized weapons, killed several whites, and attempted to escape south to Florida. The uprising was quickly crushed, and most participants were executed. A more frequent form of resistance was simply running away, but that provided no real solution either. There was nowhere to go. So for most slaves, resistance took the form of subtle, and often undetected, defiance or evasion of their masters' wishes.

Most slaves, male and female, worked as field hands (with the women shouldering the additional burdens of cooking and child rearing). But on the larger plantations that aspired to genuine self-sufficiency, some slaves learned trades and crafts: blacksmithing, carpentry, shoemaking, spinning, weaving, sewing, midwifery, and others. These skilled crafts workers were at times hired out to other planters. Some set up their own establishments in towns or cities and shared their profits with their owners. A few were able to buy their freedom. There was a small free black population living in southern cities by the time of the Revolution.

The Puritan Community

The characteristic social unit in New England was not the isolated farm but the Puritan town, which was both an economic and a religious unit. In the early years of colonization, each new settlement drew up a "covenant" binding all residents tightly together both religiously and socially.

Colonists laid out a village, with houses and a meetinghouse arranged around a central pasture, or "common." Thus families generally lived with their neighbors close by, reinforcing a strong sense of community. They divided up the outlying fields and woodlands among the residents; the size and location of a family's field depended on the family's numbers, wealth, and social station.

Once a town was established, residents held a yearly "town meeting" to decide important questions and to choose a group of "selectmen," who ran the town's affairs. Participation in the meeting was generally restricted to adult males who were members of the church. Only those who could give evidence of being among the elect assured of salvation (the "visible saints") were admitted to full church membership, although other residents of the town were required to attend church services.

New Englanders did not adopt the English system of primogeniture—the passing of all property to the firstborn son. Instead, a father divided up his land among all his sons. His control of this inheritance gave him great power over the family. Often a son would reach his late twenties before his father would allow him to move into his own household and work his own land. Even then, sons would usually continue to live in close proximity to their fathers. Young women were generally more mobile than their brothers, since they did not stand to inherit land.

The early Puritan community was a tightly knit organism. Yet as the years passed and the communities grew, this communal structure experienced strains. This was partly because of the increasing commercialization of New England society, which introduced new forces and new tensions into the communities of the region. It was also partly because of population growth. As towns grew larger, residents tended to cultivate lands farther and farther from the community center and, by necessity, to live at increasing distances from the church. The control of land by fathers also created strains. In the first generations, fathers generally controlled enough land to satisfy the needs of all their sons. After several generations, however, when such lands were being subdivided for the third or fourth time, there was often too little to go around, particularly in communities surrounded by other towns, with no room to expand outward. The result was that in many communities, groups of younger residents broke off and moved elsewhere—at times far away—to form towns of their own.

The tensions building in Puritan communities could produce bizarre and disastrous events. One example was the widespread hysteria in the 1680s and 1690s over accusations of witchcraft (the human exercise of satanic powers) in New England. The most famous outbreak (although by no means the only one) was in Salem, Massachusetts, where adolescent girls began to exhibit strange behavior and leveled charges of witchcraft against several West Indian servants steeped in voodoo lore. Hysteria spread throughout the town, and hundreds of people (most of them women) were accused of witchcraft. Nineteen residents of Salem were put to death before the trials finally ended in 1692; the girls who had been the original accusers later recanted and admitted that their story had been fabricated.

The Salem experience was not unique. Accusations of witchcraft spread through many New England towns in the early 1690s (and indeed had emerged regularly in Puritan society for many years before) and centered

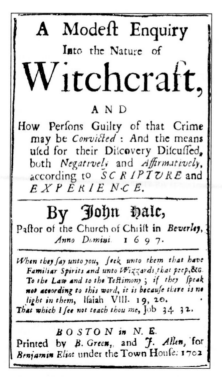

A STUDY OF WITCHCRAFT This pamphlet, originally written in 1697 near the height of the witchcraft phenomenon in New England, was one of many contemporary studies to take the idea of witchcraft seriously. Belief in witches was widespread in early New England society, and many of the charges that seem preposterous to twentieth-century eyes appeared entirely plausible even to educated people of the time.

mostly on women. Research into the background of accused witches reveals that most were middle-aged women, often widowed, with few or no children. Many accused witches were of low social position, were often involved in domestic conflicts, had frequently been accused of other crimes, and were considered abrasive by their neighbors. Others were women who, through inheritance or hard work, had come into possession of substantial property of their own and thus challenged the gender norms of the community.

The witchcraft controversies were also a reflection of the highly religious character of New England societies. New Englanders believed in the power of Satan and his ability to assert his power in the world. Belief in witchcraft was not a marginal superstition rejected by the mainstream. It was a common feature of Puritan religious conviction.

Cities

In the 1770s the two largest colonial ports—Philadelphia and New York— had populations of 28,000 and 25,000, respectively, which made them larger than most English urban centers of their time. Boston (16,000), Charles Town (later Charleston), South Carolina (12,000), and Newport, Rhode Island (11,000), were also substantial communities by the standards of the day.

Colonial cities served as trading centers for the farmers of their regions and as marts for international commerce. Their leaders were generally merchants who had acquired substantial wealth. Class divisions in American cities were not as sharp as those in Europe. But more than in any other area of colonial life (except, of course, in the relationship between masters and slaves), social distinctions were real and visible in urban areas.

Cities were the centers of much of what industry there was in the colonies, such as distilleries for turning imported molasses into exportable rum. They were the locations of the most advanced schools and sophisticated cultural activities and of shops where imported goods could be bought. In addition, they were communities with urban social problems: crime, vice, pollution, traffic. Unlike smaller towns, cities needed to set up constables' offices and fire departments and develop systems for supporting the urban poor, whose numbers became especially large in times of economic crisis—to which cities were particularly vulnerable.

Finally, cities were places where new ideas could circulate and be discussed. There were newspapers, books, and other publications from abroad, and hence new intellectual influences. The taverns and coffee-houses of cities provided forums in which people could gather and debate the issues of the day. That is one reason why the Revolutionary crisis, when it began to build in the 1760s and 1770s, began first in the cities.

THE COLONIAL MIND

Intellectual life in colonial America revolved around the conflict between the traditional outlook of the sixteenth and seventeenth centuries, with its emphasis on a personal God deeply involved in individual lives, and the new spirit of the Enlightenment, which was sweeping both Europe and America and which stressed the importance of science and human reason. The old views placed a high value on a stern moral code in which intellect was less important than faith. The Enlightenment suggested that people had substantial control over their own lives and societies.

The Pattern of Religions

Religious toleration flourished in America to a degree unmatched in any European nation, not because Americans deliberately sought to produce it but because conditions virtually required it. Settlers in America brought with them so many different religious practices that it proved impossible to impose a single religious code on any large area.

The Church of England was established as the official faith in Virginia, Maryland, New York, the Carolinas, and Georgia. Except in Virginia and Maryland, however, the laws establishing the Church of England as the official colonial religion were largely ignored. Even in New England, where the Puritans had originally believed that they were all part of a single faith, there was a growing tendency in the eighteenth century for different congregations to affiliate with different denominations, especially Congregationalism and Presbyterianism. In parts of New York and New Jersey, Dutch settlers had established their own Calvinist denomination, Dutch Reformed, which survived after the colonies became part of the British Empire. American Baptists (of whom Roger Williams is considered the first) developed a great variety of sects. All Baptists shared the belief that rebaptism, usually by total immersion, was necessary when believers reached maturity. But while some Baptists remained Calvinists (believers in predestination) others came to believe in salvation by free will.

Protestants extended toleration to one another more readily than they did to Roman Catholics. Many Protestants in America, like many in England, feared and hated the pope. New Englanders, in particular, viewed their Catholic neighbors in New France (Canada) not only as commercial and military rivals but also as dangerous agents of Rome. In most of the English colonies, however, Roman Catholics were too few to cause serious conflict. They were most numerous in Maryland, and even there they numbered no more than 3,000. Perhaps for that reason they suffered their worst persecution in that colony. After the overthrow of the original proprietors in 1691, Catholics in Maryland not only lost their political rights but also were forbidden to hold religious services except in private houses.

Jews in provincial America totaled no more than about 2,000 at any time. The largest community lived in New York City. Smaller groups settled in Newport and Charleston, and there were scattered Jewish families in all the colonies. Nowhere could they vote or hold office. Only in Rhode Island could they practice their religion openly.

By the beginning of the eighteenth century, some Americans were growing troubled by the apparent decline in religious piety in their society. The movement of the population westward and the wide scattering of settlements had caused many communities to lose touch with organized religion. The rise of commercial prosperity created a more secular outlook in urban areas. The progress of science and free thought in Europe—and the importation of Enlightenment ideas to America—caused at least some colonists to doubt traditional religious beliefs.

Concerns about weakening piety surfaced as early as the 1660s in New England, where the Puritan oligarchy warned of a decline in the power of the church. Sabbath after Sabbath, ministers preached sermons of despair (known as "jeremiads"), deploring the signs of waning piety. By the standards of other societies or other eras, the Puritan faith remained remarkably strong. But New Englanders measured their faith by their own standards, and to them the "declension" of religious piety seemed a serious problem.

The Great Awakening

By the early eighteenth century, similar concerns were emerging in other regions and among members of other faiths. Everywhere, colonists were coming to believe, religious piety was in decline and opportunities for spiritual regeneration were dwindling. The result was the first great American revival: the Great Awakening.

The Great Awakening began in earnest in the 1730s, reached its climax in the 1740s, and brought a new spirit of religious fervor that many Americans believed was reversing the trend away from piety. The revival had particular appeal to women (who constituted the majority of converts) and to younger sons of the third or fourth generation of settlers—those who stood to inherit the least land and who faced the most uncertain futures. The rhetoric of the revival emphasized the potential for every person to break away from the constraints of the past and start anew in his or her relationship with God. Such beliefs may have reflected the desires of many people to break away from their families or communities and start a new life.

Powerful evangelists from England helped spread the revival. John and Charles Wesley, the founders of Methodism, visited Georgia and other colonies in the 1730s. George Whitefield, a powerful open-air preacher and for a time an associate of the Wesleys', made several evangelizing tours through the colonies and drew tremendous crowds. But the outstanding preacher of the Great Awakening was the New England Congregationalist Jonathan Edwards, a deeply orthodox Puritan but a highly original theologian. From his pulpit in Northampton, Massachusetts, Edwards attacked the new doctrines of easy salvation for all. He preached anew the traditional Puritan ideas of the absolute sovereignty of God, predestination, and salvation by God's grace alone. His vivid descriptions of hell could terrify his listeners.

The Great Awakening led to the division of existing congregations (between "New Light" revivalists and "Old Light" traditionalists) and to the founding of new ones. It also affected areas of society outside the churches. Some of the revivalists denounced book learning as a hindrance to salvation, and some communities repudiated secular education altogether. But other evangelists saw education as a means of furthering religion, and they founded or led schools for the training of New Light ministers.

The Enlightenment

The Great Awakening caused one great cultural upheaval in the colonies. The Enlightenment caused another, very different one. The Enlightenment was the product of some of the great scientific and intellectual discoveries in Europe in the seventeenth century—discoveries that revealed what scientists and others considered the "natural laws" that regulated the workings of nature. The new scientific knowledge encouraged many thinkers to begin celebrating the power of human reason and scientific inquiry, and to argue that rational thought, not just religious faith, could create progress and advance knowledge in the world.

In celebrating reason, the Enlightenment slowly undermined the power of traditional religious authority. It encouraged men and women to look to themselves and their own intellect—not just to God—for guidance as to how to live their lives and shape their societies. It helped produce a growing interest in education and a heightened concern with politics and government.

In the early seventeenth century, Enlightenment ideas in America were largely borrowed from Europe—from such great thinkers as Francis Bacon and John Locke of England, Baruch Spinoza of Amsterdam, and René Descartes of France. Later, however, such Americans as Benjamin Franklin, Thomas Paine, Thomas Jefferson, and James Madison made their own important contributions to Enlightenment thought.

Literacy and Technology

White male Americans achieved a high degree of literacy in the eighteenth century. By the time of the Revolution, well over half of all white men could read and write, a rate substantially higher than that in most European countries. The literacy rate for women lagged behind the rate for men until the nineteenth century. While opportunities for education beyond the primary level were scarce for men, they were almost nonexistent for women. Nevertheless, the literacy rate for American females was also substantially higher than that of their European counterparts.

The large number of colonists who could read created a market for the first widely circulated publications in America other than the Bible: almanacs. They appeared first in the 1630s in Massachusetts. By 1700, there were dozens, perhaps hundreds, of almanacs circulating throughout the colonies and even in the sparsely settled lands to the west. Most families had at least one, and they appeared in many languages to serve the various ethnic communities in the colonies. Almanacs provided medical advice, navigational and agricultural information, practical wisdom, humor, and predictions about the future—most famously, predictions about weather patterns for the coming year, which many farmers used as the basis of decisions about crops even though the predictions were notoriously unreliable. The most famous almanac in eighteenth-century America was *Poor Richard's Almanac*, published by Benjamin Franklin in Philadelphia.

The wide availability of reading material in colonial America by the eighteenth century was a result of both improvements in and the spread of printing technology. The first printing press began operating in the colonies in 1639, and by 1695 there were more towns in America with printers than there were in England. At first, many of these presses did not get very much use. Over time, however, the rising literacy of the society created a demand for books, pamphlets, and almanacs that the presses rushed to fill.

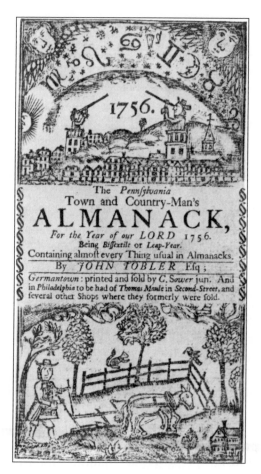

TOWN AND COUNTRY-MAN'S ALMANACK As the population of colonial cities and towns grew, almanacs—originally targeted mainly at farmers—began to appeal to townspeople as well.

The first newspaper in the colonies, *Publick Occurrences*, was published in Boston in 1690 using a relatively advanced printing facility there. It lasted only one issue, but it was the first step toward what would eventually become a large newspaper industry in America. One reason the Stamp Act of 1765, which imposed a tax on printed materials, created such a furor in the colonies (see pp. 107–108) was because printing technology—and thus print itself—had by then become central to colonial life.

Education

Even before Enlightenment ideas penetrated America, colonists placed a high value on formal education, despite the difficulties they confronted in gaining access to it. Some families tried to teach their children to read and write at home, although the heavy burden of work in most agricultural households limited the time available for schooling. In Massachusetts, a 1647 law required that every town support a school; and even though many communities failed to comply, a modest network of public schools emerged as a result. The Quakers and other sects operated church schools, and in some communities widows or unmarried women conducted "dame schools" by holding private classes in their homes. In cities, master craftsmen set up evening schools for their apprentices.

African Americans, most of whom were enslaved, had virtually no access to education. Occasionally a master or mistress would teach slave children to read and write; but as the slave system became more firmly entrenched, strong social (and ultimately legal) sanctions developed to discourage such efforts because of fears that literacy might encourage slaves to question their stations. Indians, too, remained largely outside the white educational system—to a large degree by choice: most tribes preferred to educate their children in their own way. Some white missionaries and philanthropists established schools for Native Americans and helped create a small population of Indians literate in spoken and written English.

Harvard, the first American college, was established in 1636 by Puritan theologians who wanted to create a training center for ministers. (The college was named for a Charlestown minister, John Harvard, who had left it his library and half his estate). In 1693, William and Mary College (named for the English king and queen) was established in Williamsburg, Virginia, by Anglicans; like Harvard, it was conceived as an academy to train clergymen. And in 1701, conservative Congregationalists, dissatisfied with the growing religious liberalism of Harvard, founded Yale (named for one of its first benefactors, Elihu Yale) in New Haven, Connecticut. Out of the Great Awakening emerged the College of New Jersey, founded in 1746 and known later as Princeton (after the town in which it was located); one of its first presidents was Jonathan Edwards. Despite the religious basis of these colleges, most of them offered curricula that included not only theology but logic, ethics, physics, geometry, astronomy, rhetoric, Latin, Hebrew, and Greek. King's College, founded in New York in 1754 and later renamed Columbia, was specifically devoted to the spread of secular knowledge; it had no theological faculty and was interdenominational from the start. The Academy and College of Philadelphia, founded in 1755 and later renamed the University of Pennsylvania, was also a completely secular institution, established by a group of laymen under the inspiration of Benjamin Franklin.

After 1700, most colonial leaders received their entire educations in America (rather than attending university in England, as had once been the case). But higher education remained available only to relatively afflu-ent white men.

The Spread of Science

The clearest indication of the spreading influence of the Enlightenment in America was an increasing interest in scientific knowledge. Most of the early colleges established chairs in the natural sciences and introduced some of the advanced scientific theories of Europe, including Copernican astron-omy and Newtonian physics, to their students. But the most vigorous pro-motion of science in these years occurred outside the colleges, through the private efforts of amateurs and the activities of scientific societies. Leading merchants, planters, and even theologians became corresponding members of the Royal Society of London, the leading English scientific organization. Benjamin Franklin, the most celebrated amateur scientist in America, won international fame through his experiments with electricity. Particularly no-table was his 1747 theory and his 1752 demonstration, using a kite, that lightning and electricity were the same. Previously, most scientists had be-lieved that there were several distinct types of electricity; Franklin's discov-ery that there was only one represented a major advance in knowledge about electricity. His research on the way in which electricity could be "grounded" led to the development of the lightning rod, which greatly re-duced fires and other damage to buildings during thunderstorms.

The high value that influential Americans were beginning to place on scientific knowledge was clearly demonstrated by the most daring and controversial scientific experiment of the eighteenth century: inoculation against smallpox. The Puritan theologian Cotton Mather had learned of experiments in England by which people had been deliberately infected with mild cases of smallpox in order to immunize them against the deadly disease. Despite strong opposition from many of his neighbors, he urged inoculation on his fellow Bostonians during an epidemic in the 1720s. The results confirmed the effectiveness of the technique. Other theolo-gians (including Jonathan Edwards) took up the cause, along with many physicians. By the mid-eighteenth century, inoculation had become a common medical procedure in America.

THE MAGNETIC DISPENSARY In this 1790 painting, artist Samuel Collings caricatured the popular enthusiasm that Benjamin Franklin and others had produced for scientific experiments. The men and women shown here are rubbing iron rods with silk cloth to produce static electricity. A popular pastime was to place the charged rods over people's heads to watch their hair stand on end.

Concepts of Law and Politics

In law and politics, as in other parts of their lives, Americans in the seventeenth and eighteenth centuries believed that they were re-creating in the New World the practices and institutions of the Old. But as in other areas, they in fact created something very different.

Changes in the law in America resulted in part from the scarcity of English-trained lawyers, who were almost unknown in the colonies until after 1700. Although the American legal system adopted most of the essential elements of the English system, including such ancient rights as trial by jury, significant differences developed in court procedures, punishments, and the definition of crimes. In England, for example, a printed attack on a public official, whether true or false, was considered libelous. At the 1734 trial of the New York publisher John Peter Zenger, who was powerfully defended by the Philadelphia lawyer Andrew Hamilton, the courts ruled that criticisms of the government were not libelous if factually true—a verdict that removed some colonial restrictions on the freedom of the press.

More significant for the future of the relationship between the colonies and England were differences emerging between the American and British political systems. Because the royal government—in theory the ultimate authority over the colonies—was so far away, Americans created a group of institutions of their own that gave them a large measure of self-government. In most colonies, local communities grew accustomed to running their own affairs with minimal interference from higher authorities. The colonial assemblies came to exercise many of the powers that Parliament exercised in England. Provincial governors (appointed by the king after the 1690s) had broad powers on paper, but their actual influence was limited. Control over appointments and contracts resided largely in England or with local colonial leaders.

The result of all this was that colonial politics had a largely local focus. The provincial governments became accustomed to acting more or less independently of Parliament, and a set of assumptions and expectations about the rights of the colonists took hold in America that was not shared by policymakers in England. These differences caused few problems before the 1760s, because the British did little to exert the authority they believed they possessed. But when, beginning in 1763, the English government began attempting to tighten its control over the American colonies, a historic crisis resulted.

CONCLUSION

What began as a few small, isolated, precarious settlements in the wilderness had evolved by the mid-eighteenth century into a large and complex society. The English colonies in America grew steadily between the 1650s and the 1750s: in population, in the size of their economies, and in the sophistication—and diversity—of their cultures. Although most white Americans in the 1750s still believed that they were fully a part of the British Empire, they were in fact living in a world that had become very different from that of England.

Many distinct societies developed in the colonies, but the greatest distinction was between the colonies of the North and those of the South. In the North, society was dominated by relatively small family farms and by towns and cities of growing size. A thriving commercial class was developing, and with it an increasingly elaborate urban culture. In the South, there were many family farms as well. But there were also large plantations cultivating tobacco, rice, indigo, and cotton for export. By the late seventeenth century, these plantations were relying heavily on African workers who had been brought to the colonies forcibly as slaves. There were few significant towns and cities in the South, and little commerce other than the marketing of crops.

The colonies did, however, also have much in common. Most white Americans accepted common assumptions about racial inequality. That enabled them to tolerate (and at times celebrate) the enslavement of African men and women and to justify a campaign of displacement and often violence against Native Americans that would continue for two centuries. Most white Americans (and, in different ways, most nonwhite Americans as well) were deeply religious. The Great Awakening, therefore, had a powerful impact throughout the colonies, North and South. And most white colonists shared a belief in certain basic principles of law and politics, which they considered embedded in the English constitution, and which in the years after the 1750s would lead to a great imperial crisis.

FOR FURTHER REFERENCE

Suggested Readings

Bernard Bailyn, *Voyagers to the West: A Passage in the Peopling of America on the Eve of the Revolution* (1986) reveals the complexity and scope of European emigration to North America. Bailyn's *The Origin of American Politics* (1968) remains an excellent introduction to colonial politics. David Hackett Fischer, *Albion's Seed* (1989) offers a provocative argument that four major folkways shaped English settlement in America. Laurel Thatcher Ulrich, *Good Wives: Image and Reality in the Lives of Women in Northern New England, 1650–1750* (1982) offers a typology of women's roles in colonial New England. Kathleen M. Brown, *Good Wives, Nasty Wenches, and Anxious Patriarchs: Gender, Race and Power in Colonial Virginia* (1996) places gender at the center of the development of slavery in the Chesapeake. Rhys Isaac, *The Transformation of Virginia, 1740–1790* (1982) uses the methods of cultural anthropology in an influential study of the world of the colonial Virginia gentry. Richard Bushman, *The Refinement of America: Persons, Houses, Cities* (1992) traces the growing interest of Americans in material comfort and display. John Putnam Demos, *Entertaining Satan: Witchcraft and the Culture of Early New England* (1982); Paul Boyer and Stephen Nissenbaum, *Salem Possessed* (1974); and Carol Karlsen, *The Devil in the Shape of a Woman: Witchcraft in Colonial New England* (1987) are three important studies of witchcraft in New England.

Films

(The best source for information on how to find these and other films is *Bowker's Complete Video Directory*—3 volumes.) *The Roots of Democracy: The 1700s* studies the economic forces and political beliefs that shaped the British colonies. *Colonial America: Life in the Maturing Colonies* (1991) looks at the lives of New World settlers and explores their attitudes toward Indians, slaves, and women. *Benjamin Franklin* (1987) looks at the life of one of the leading figures of American colonial history. *Religion in the Colonies* (1994) explores the diversity of religious sects transported from Europe to the American colonies. *Anne Hutchinson* (1983) narrates the life and struggles of an important dissident woman in the Massachusetts Bay colony. *The Salem Witch Trials* introduces the accused "witches," judges, and girls involved in a tragic episode in the history of colonial Massachusetts.

Internet Resources

Internet websites containing historical material relevant to the subjects discussed in this chapter can be reached through the McGraw-Hill history site at www.mhhe.com/socscience/history/usa/link/linktop.htm.

CHAPTER FOUR

The Empire Under Strain

Loosening Ties ～ *The Struggle for the Continent*
The New Imperialism ～ *Stirrings of Revolt*
Cooperation and War

A s LATE AS the 1750s, few Americans objected to their membership in the British Empire. The imperial system provided many
commercial and political benefits to the Americans, and it had few costs,
because for the most part the English government left the colonies alone.
By the mid-1770s, however, the relationship between the American
colonies and their British rulers had become so strained, so poisoned, so
characterized by suspicion and resentment that the empire was on the
verge of unraveling. And in the spring of 1775, the first shots were fired in
a war that would ultimately win America its independence. How had it
happened? And why so quickly?

LOOSENING TIES

In one sense, it had not happened quickly at all. Ever since the first days of
English settlement in North America, the ideas and institutions of the
colonies had been diverging from those in Britain in countless ways. In
another sense, however, the Revolutionary crisis emerged in response to
important and relatively sudden changes in the administration of the empire. In 1763 the English government began to enforce a series of policies
toward its colonies that brought the differences between the two societies
into sharp focus.

TIME LINE				
1754	**1756**	**1760**	**1763**	**1764**
Beginning of French and Indian War	Seven Years' War begins	George III becomes king	Peace of Paris Proclamation of 1763	Sugar Act
1765	**1766**	**1767**	**1770**	
Stamp Act	Stamp Act repealed Declaratory Act	Townshend Duties	Boston Massacre Most Townshend Duties repealed	
1771	**1772**	**1773**	**1774**	**1775**
Regulator movement in North Carolina	Committees of correspondence in Boston Gaspée incident	Tea Act, Boston Tea Party	Intolerable Acts First Continental Congress in Philadelphia	Battles of Lexingon and Concord American Revolution begins

A Decentralized Empire

In the fifty years after the Glorious Revolution, the English Parliament (which became the British Parliament after the union of England and Scotland in 1707) established a growing supremacy over the king. Under Kings George I (1714–1727) and George II (1727–1760), both of whom were German-born and unaccustomed to English ways, the prime minister and his cabinet became the nation's real executives. Because they depended politically on the great merchants and landholders of England, who had a great stake in the colonial trade, they were less inclined than the seventeenth-century monarchs had been to try to tighten control over the empire, which many merchants feared would disrupt the profitable commerce with the colonies. As a result, administration of the colonies remained loose, decentralized, and inefficient, with no single office or agency responsible for colonial affairs.

The character of the royal officials in America—the governors and other officers of the royal colonies and (in all the colonies) the naval officers and collectors of customs—contributed further to the looseness of the imperial system. Few governors were able men. Many, perhaps most, had used bribery to obtain their offices and continued to accept bribes once they assumed their offices. Some appointees remained in England and hired substitutes to take their places in America.

The colonial assemblies, taking advantage of the weak imperial administration, had asserted their own authority to levy taxes, make appropriations, approve appointments, and pass laws for their respective colonies. The assemblies came to look upon themselves as little parliaments, each practically as sovereign within its colony as Parliament itself was in England.

The Colonies Divided

Even so, the colonists continued to think of themselves as loyal English subjects. Many felt stronger ties to England than they did to the other American colonies because the differences among the colonial societies were so great. Although the colonies had slowly learned to cooperate with one another on such practical matters as intercolonial trade, road construction, and the creation of a colonial postal service, they remained reluctant to cooperate in larger ways, even when, in 1754, they faced a common threat from their old rivals, the French, and France's Indian allies. Delegates from Pennsylvania, Maryland, New York, and New England met in Albany in that year to negotiate a treaty with the Iroquois and tentatively approved a proposal by Benjamin Franklin to set up a "general government" in America to manage relations with the Indians on behalf of all the colonies. War with the French and Indians was already beginning when the Albany Plan was presented to the colonial assemblies. None approved it.

THE STRUGGLE FOR THE CONTINENT

The war that raged in North America through the late 1750s and early 1760s was part of a larger struggle between England and France for dominance in world trade and naval power. The British victory in that struggle, known in Europe as the Seven Years' War, confirmed England's commercial supremacy and cemented its control of the settled regions of North America. In America, however, the conflict was also the final stage in a long struggle among the three principal powers in northeastern North America: the English, the French, and the Iroquois.

New France and the Iroquois Nation

By the end of the seventeenth century, the French Empire in America had come to possess a vast territory: the whole length of the Mississippi River and its delta (which they named Louisiana, after their king), and the continental interior as far west as the Rocky Mountains and as far south as the Rio Grande. France claimed, in effect, the entire interior of the continent.

To secure their hold on these enormous claims, they founded a string of widely separated communities, strategically located fortresses, and far-flung missions and trading posts. Would-be feudal lords established large estates (*seigneuries*) along the banks of the St. Lawrence River. On a high bluff above the river stood the fortified city of Quebec, the center of the French Empire in America. Montreal to the south and Sault Sainte Marie and Detroit to the west marked the northern boundaries of French settlement. On the lower Mississippi emerged plantations much like those in the southern colonies of English America, worked by black slaves and owned by "Creoles" (white immigrants of French descent). New Orleans, founded in 1718 to service the French plantation economy, was soon as big as some of the larger cities of the Atlantic seaboard; Biloxi and Mobile to the east completed the string of French settlement.

But the French shared the continental interior with a large and powerful Indian population. Both the French and the English were aware that the battle for control of North America would be determined in part by which group could best win the allegiance of native tribes—as trading partners and, at times, as military allies. The English—with their more advanced commercial economy—could usually offer the Indians better and more plentiful goods. But the French offered tolerance. Unlike the English, the French settlers in the interior generally adjusted their own behavior to Indian patterns. French fur traders frequently married Indian women and adopted tribal ways; Jesuit missionaries interacted comfortably with the natives and converted them to Catholicism by the thousands without challenging most of their social customs. By the mid-eighteenth century, therefore, the French had better and closer relations with most of the Indians of the interior than did the English.

The most powerful native group, however, had remained aloof from both the British and the French. The Iroquois Confederacy—five Indian nations (Mohawk, Seneca, Cayuga, Onondaga, and Oneida) that had formed a defensive alliance in the fifteenth century—had been the most powerful native presence in the Ohio Valley and a large surrounding region since the 1640s, unchallenged by either the French or the English. The Iroquois maintained their autonomy by avoiding too close a relationship with either group. They traded successfully with both the English and the French and astutely played the two groups against each other. As a result, they maintained an uneasy balance of power in the Great Lakes region.

Anglo-French Conflicts

As long as England and France remained at peace and as long as the precarious balance in the North American interior survived, English and French colonists coexisted without serious difficulty. But after the Glorious Revolution in England, a series of Anglo-French wars erupted in Europe and continued intermittently for nearly eighty years, creating important repercussions in America.

King William's War (1689–1697) produced only a few, indecisive clashes between the English and the French in northern New England. Queen Anne's War, which began in 1701 and continued for nearly twelve years, generated more substantial conflicts: border fighting with the Spaniards in the South as well as with the French and their Indian allies in the North. The Treaty of Utrecht, which brought the conflict to a close in 1713, transferred substantial territory from the French to the English in North America, including Acadia (Nova Scotia) and Newfoundland. Two decades later, disputes over British trading rights in the Spanish colonies produced a conflict between England and Spain that soon grew into a much larger European war, in which England and France lined up on opposite sides. The English colonists in America were drawn into the struggle, which they called King George's War; and between 1744 and 1748 they engaged in a series of conflicts with the French. New Englanders captured the French bastion at Louisbourg on Cape Breton Island, but the peace treaty that finally ended the conflict forced them to abandon it.

In the aftermath of King George's War, relations among the English, French, and Iroquois in North America quickly deteriorated. The Iroquois (in what appears to have been a major blunder) granted trading concessions in the interior to English merchants for the first time. The French, fearful (probably correctly) that the English were using the concessions as a first step toward expansion into French lands, began in 1749 to construct new fortresses in the Ohio Valley. The English interpreted the French activity as a threat to their western settlements, protested, and began building up their military forces and building fortresses of their

own. The balance of power that the Iroquois had carefully and successfully maintained for so long rapidly disintegrated.

For the next five years, tensions between the English and the French increased. In the summer of 1754 the governor of Virginia sent a militia force
(under the command of an inexperienced young colonel, George Washington) into the Ohio Valley to challenge French expansion. Washington built
a crude stockade (Fort Necessity) not far from Fort Duquesne, the larger
outpost the French were building on the site of what is now Pittsburgh.
After the Virginians staged an unsuccessful attack on a French detachment,
the French countered with an assault on Fort Necessity, trapping Washington and his soldiers inside. After a third of them died in the fighting, Washington surrendered. The clash marked the beginning of the French and Indian War.

The Great War for the Empire

The French and Indian War lasted nearly nine years, and it moved through
three distinct phases. During the first of these phases, from the Fort Necessity debacle in 1754 until the expansion of the war to Europe in 1756, it
was primarily a local, North American conflict. Virtually all the tribes except the Iroquois were now allied with the French; they had interpreted
the defeat of the Virginians at Fort Duquesne as evidence of British weakness and launched a series of raids on western English settlements. The
English colonists fought largely alone to defend themselves against those
raids. The Iroquois, although nominally allied with the British, feared antagonizing the French and remained largely passive in the conflict. By late
1755, many English settlers along the frontier had withdrawn to the east of
the Allegheny Mountains to escape the hostilities.

The second phase of the struggle began in 1756, when the governments of France and England formally opened hostilities and a truly international conflict (the Seven Years' War) began. The fighting now spread to
the West Indies, India, and Europe itself. But the principal struggle remained the one in North America, where so far England had suffered
nothing but frustration and defeat. Beginning in 1757, William Pitt, the
English secretary of state (and future prime minister), brought the war for
the first time fully under British control. Pitt himself planned military
strategy, appointed commanders, and issued orders to the colonists. Military recruitment had slowed dramatically in America, and to replenish the
army British commanders began forcibly enlisting colonists (a practice
known as "impressment"). Officers also seized supplies from local farmers

RECUITING FOR THE FRENCH AND INDIAN WAR The extravagant promises in this recruiting poster, distributed to colonists during the French and Indian War, suggest how difficult it sometimes was to persuade Americans to fight in the British army.

and tradesmen and compelled colonists to offer shelter to British troops— all generally without compensation. The Americans resented these new impositions and firmly resisted them—at times, as in a 1757 riot in New York City, violently. By early 1758, the friction between the British authorities and the colonists was threatening to bring the war effort to a halt.

Beginning in 1758, therefore, Pitt initiated the third and final phase of the war by relaxing many of the policies that Americans had found obnoxious. He agreed to reimburse the colonists for all supplies requisitioned by the army. He returned control over recruitment to the colonial assemblies (which resulted in an immediate and dramatic increase in enlistments). And he dispatched large numbers of additional British troops to America. Finally, the tide of battle began to turn in England's favor. The French had always been outnumbered by the British colonists. After 1756, moreover, they suffered from a series of poor harvests. As a result, they were unable to sustain their early military successes. By mid-1758, the British regulars in America (who did the bulk of the actual fighting) and the colonial militias were seizing one French stronghold after another. Two brilliant English generals, Jeffrey Amherst and James Wolfe, captured the fortress at Louisbourg in July 1758; a few months later Fort Duquesne fell without a fight. The next year, at the end of a siege of Quebec, supposedly impregnable atop its towering cliff, the army of General Wolfe struggled up a hidden ravine under cover of darkness, surprised the larger forces of the Marquis de Montcalm, and defeated them in a battle in which both commanders were killed. The dramatic fall of Quebec on September 13, 1759, marked the beginning of the end of the American phase of the war. A year later, in September 1760, the French army formally surrendered to Amherst in Montreal. Peace finally came in 1763, with the Peace of Paris, by which the French ceded to Great Britain some of their West Indian islands, most of their colonies in India and Canada, and all other French territory in North America east of the Mississippi. They ceded New Orleans and their claims west of the Mississippi to Spain, thus surrendering all title to the mainland of North America.

The French and Indian War had profound effects on the British Empire and the American colonies. It greatly expanded England's territorial claims in the New World. At the same time, the cost of the war greatly enlarged Britain's debt and substantially increased British resentment of the Americans. English leaders were contemptuous of the colonists for what they considered American military ineptitude during the war; they were angry that the colonists had made so few financial contributions to a struggle waged, they believed, largely for American benefit; they were particularly bitter that some colonial merchants had been selling food and other goods to the French in the West Indies throughout the conflict. All these factors combined to persuade many English leaders that a major reorganization of the empire giving London increased authority over the colonies would be necessary in the aftermath of the war.

The war had an equally profound but very different effect on the American colonists. It was an experience that forced them, for the first time, to act in concert against a common foe. And the friction of 1756–1757 over British requisition and impressment policies and the 1758 return of authority to the colonial assemblies seemed to many Americans to confirm the illegitimacy of English interference in local affairs.

For the Indians of the Ohio Valley, the third major party in the French and Indian War, the British victory was disastrous. Those tribes that had allied themselves with the French had earned the enmity of the victorious English. The Iroquois Confederacy, which had allied itself with Britain, fared only slightly better. English officials saw the passivity of the Iroquois during the war (a result of their effort to hedge their bets and avoid antagonizing the French) as evidence of duplicity. In the aftermath of the peace settlement, the Iroquois alliance with the British quickly unraveled, and the Iroquois Confederacy itself began to crumble from within. The tribes would continue to contest the English for control of the Ohio Valley for another fifty years; but increasingly divided and increasingly outnumbered, they would seldom again be in a position to deal with their European rivals on terms of military or political equality.

THE NEW IMPERIALISM

With the treaty of 1763, England found itself truly at peace for the first time in more than fifty years. As a result, the British government could now turn its attention to the organization of its empire. Saddled with enormous debts from the many years of fighting, England was desperately in need of new revenues from its empire. Responsible for vast new lands in the New World that had doubled the size of the British Empire, the imperial government believed it must increase its administrative capacities in America. The result was a dramatic and, for England, disastrous redefinition of the colonial relationship.

Burdens of Empire

The experience of the French and Indian War should have suggested that increasing imperial control over the colonies would not be easy. Not only had the colonists proved so resistant to British control that Pitt had been forced to relax his policies in 1758, but the colonial assemblies had continued after that to chart a course different from, and often in conflict with, the desires of the government in London. Defiance of imperial trade regulations and other British demands continued. The American colonial governments were already claiming jurisdiction over much of the western territories, although many officials in London wanted authority over the new lands to remain in England. But the most immediate problem for London was its staggering war debt. Landlords and merchants in England were objecting strenuously to any further tax increases, and the colonial assemblies had repeatedly demonstrated their unwillingness to pay for the war effort. Many officials in England believed that only by taxing the Americans directly from London could the empire effectively meet its financial needs.

At this crucial moment in Anglo-American relations, with the imperial system in need of redefinition, the government of England was thrown into turmoil by the accession to the throne of a new king, George III, who assumed power in 1760. He brought two particularly unfortunate qualities to the office. First, he was determined, unlike his two predecessors, to reassert the authority of the monarchy. He removed from power the relatively stable coalition of Whigs that had governed the empire for much of the century and replaced it with a new and very unstable coalition of his own, assembled through patronage and bribes. The new ministries that emerged as a result of this change each lasted in office an average of only about two years.

The king also had serious intellectual and psychological limitations. He suffered, apparently, from a rare mental disease that produced intermittent bouts of insanity. (Indeed, in the last years of his long reign he was, according to most accounts, a virtual lunatic, confined to the palace and unable to perform any official functions.) Yet even when George III was lucid and rational, which was most of the time in the 1760s and 1770s, he was painfully immature (he was only twenty-two when he ascended the throne) and insecure. The king's personality, therefore, contributed both to the instability and to the rigidity of the British government during these critical years.

More directly responsible for the problems that soon emerged with the colonies, however, was George Grenville, whom the king made prime minister in 1763. Grenville shared the prevailing opinion within Britain that the colonists had been too long indulged and that they should be compelled to obey the laws and to pay a part of the cost of defending and administering the empire.

The British and the Tribes

With the defeat of the French, frontiersmen from the English colonies had begun immediately to move over the mountains and into tribal lands in the upper Ohio Valley. An alliance of Indian tribes, under the Ottawa chieftain Pontiac, struck back. Fearing that an escalation of the fighting might threaten western trade, the British government—in the Proclamation of

1763—forbade settlers to advance beyond the mountains that divided the Atlantic coast from the interior. Slower western settlement, London believed, would limit costly wars with the Indians.

Although Native Americans had few illusions about the Proclamation, many Indian groups supported the agreement as the best bargain available to them. The Cherokee, in particular, worked actively to hasten the drawing of the boundary, hoping finally to put an end to white movements into their lands. Relations between the western tribes and the British improved for a time in at least some areas after the Proclamation, partly as a result of the work of the Indian superintendents the British appointed, who were sympathetic to tribal needs.

In the end, however, the Proclamation of 1763 failed to meet even the modest expectations of the Indians, because on the crucial point of the line of settlement it was almost completely ineffective. White settlers continued to swarm across the boundary and continued to claim lands farther and farther into the Ohio Valley. The British authorities failed repeatedly to enforce limits to the expansion. In 1768, new agreements with the western tribes pushed the boundary further west in another effort to create a permanent western boundary for European settlement. But these treaties (signed respectively at Hard Labor Creek, South Carolina, and Fort Stanwix, New York) also failed to stop the white advance. Within a few years, the 1768 agreements were replaced with new ones, which pushed the line of settlement still farther west.

Battles over Trade and Taxes

The Grenville ministry increased its authority in the colonies in other ways as well. Regular British troops were stationed permanently in America, and under the Mutiny Act of 1765 the colonists were required to help provision and maintain the army. Ships of the British navy patrolled American waters to search for smugglers. The customs service was reorganized and enlarged. Royal officials were required to take up their colonial posts in person instead of sending substitutes. Colonial manufacturing was restricted, so that it would not compete with rapidly expanding industries in Great Britain.

The Sugar Act of 1764, designed in part to eliminate the illegal sugar trade between the continental colonies and the French and Spanish West Indies, raised the duty on sugar (while lowering the duty on molasses, further damaging the market for sugar grown in the colonies). It also established new vice-admiralty courts in America to try accused smugglers—thus

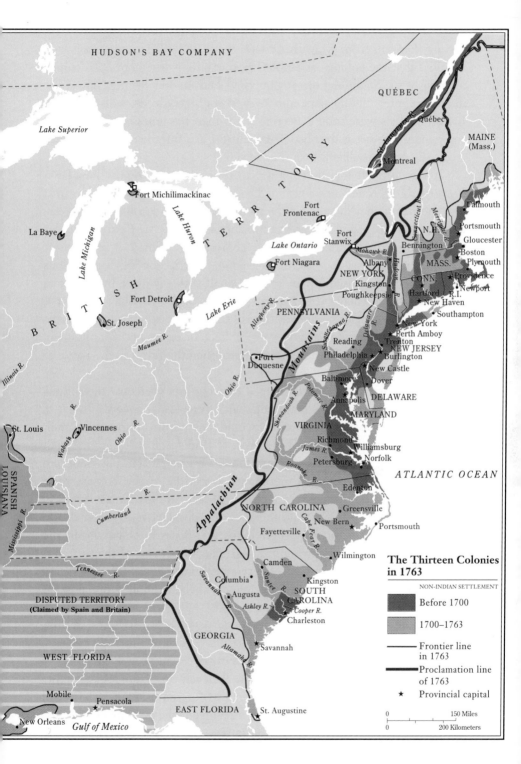

HUDSON'S BAY COMPANY

Lake Superior

QUÉBEC

St. Lawrence R.

Québec

MAINE
(Mass.)

Fort Michilimackinac

Fort
Frontenac

Montreal

La Baye

Lake Michigan

Lake Huron

B R I T I S H   T E R R I T O R Y

Lake Ontario

Fort
Stanwix

Fort Niagara

Mohawk R.

Albany

NEW YORK

Kingston

Poughkeepsie

N.H.

Bennington

Falmouth

Portsmouth

Gloucester

Boston

Plymouth

MASS.

Merrimac R.

Connecticut R.

CONN.

Hartford

New Haven

Providence

Newport

R.I.

Southampton

New York

Fort Detroit

Lake Erie

St. Joseph

Maumee R.

PENNSYLVANIA

Allegheny R.

Appalachian Mountains

Susquehanna R.

Reading

Philadelphia

NEW JERSEY

Perth Amboy

Trenton

Burlington

New Castle

Delaware R.

Fort
Duquesne

Ohio R.

Baltimore

Dover

DELAWARE

Annapolis

MARYLAND

Potomac R.

Illinois R.

St. Louis

Vincennes

Wabash R.

Ohio R.

VIRGINIA

Richmond

Shenandoah R.

James R.

Williamsburg

Norfolk

Petersburg

Roanoke R.

ATLANTIC OCEAN

SPANISH LOUISIANA

Mississippi R.

Cumberland R.

R.

Edenton

NORTH CAROLINA

Greensville

New Bern

Portsmouth

DISPUTED TERRITORY
(Claimed by Spain and Britain)

Tennessee R.

Fayetteville

Cape Fear R.

Wilmington

Camden

Kingston

Columbia

Augusta

Savannah R.

Santee R.

SOUTH
CAROLINA

Ashley R.

Cooper R.

Charleston

GEORGIA

Altamaha R.

Savannah

**The Thirteen Colonies
in 1763**

NON-INDIAN SETTLEMENT

Before 1700

1700–1763

Frontier line
in 1763

Proclamation line
of 1763

★ Provincial capital

WEST FLORIDA

Mobile

Pensacola

EAST FLORIDA

St. Augustine

New Orleans

Gulf of Mexico

| 0 | | 150 Miles |
| 0 | | 200 Kilometers |

cutting them off from sympathetic local juries. The Currency Act of 1764 required that the colonial assemblies stop issuing paper money. Most momentously, the Stamp Act of 1765 imposed a tax on every printed document in the colonies: newspapers, almanacs, pamphlets, deeds, wills, licenses. British officials were soon collecting more than ten times as much annual revenue in America as they had been before 1763. But the new policies created many more problems than they solved.

It was difficult for the colonists to resist these unpopular new laws. For one thing, Americans continued to harbor as many grievances against one another as they did against the authorities in London. In 1763, for example, a band of Pennsylvania frontiersmen known as the Paxton Boys descended on Philadelphia to demand tax relief and financial support for their defense against Indians. Bloodshed was averted only by concessions from the colonial assembly. In 1771, a small-scale civil war broke out in North Carolina when the Regulators, farmers of the Carolina upcountry, organized and armed themselves to resist the high taxes that local sheriffs (appointed by the colonial governor) collected. An army of militiamen, most of them from the eastern counties, crushed the revolt in the Battle of Alamance.

But the Grenville program helped the colonists overcome their internal conflicts and recognize that the policies from London were a threat to all Americans. Northern merchants would suffer from restraints on their commerce, from the closing of the West to land speculation and fur trading, and from the restriction of opportunities for manufacturing. Southern planters, in debt to English merchants, would be unable to ease their debts by speculating in western land. Small farmers, the largest group in the colonies, would suffer from the abolition of paper money, which had been the source of most of their loans. Workers in towns faced the prospect of narrowing opportunities, particularly because of the restraints on manufacturing and currency. Everyone stood to suffer from increased taxes. The new restrictions came, moreover, at the beginning of a postwar economic depression in America.

In reality, most Americans soon found ways to live with (or circumvent) the new British laws without terrible hardship. But their political grievances remained. Americans were accustomed (and deeply attached) to wide latitude in self-government. They believed that colonial assemblies had the sole right to control appropriations for the costs of government within the colonies. By attempting to circumvent the assemblies and raise extensive revenues directly from the public, the British government was challenging the basis of colonial political power.

STIRRINGS OF REVOLT

By the mid-1760s, a hardening of positions had begun in both England and America that would bring the colonies into increasing conflict with the mother country. The result was a progression of events that, more rapidly than imagined, destroyed the British Empire in America.

The Stamp Act Crisis

Grenville could not have devised a better method for antagonizing and unifying the colonies than the Stamp Act of 1765 if he had tried. Unlike the Sugar Act of a year earlier, which affected only a few New England merchants, the tax on printed documents fell on everyone. More alarming than the relatively light taxes, however, was the precedent they seemed to create. In the past, taxes and duties on colonial trade had always been designed to regulate commerce, not raise money. The Stamp Act, however, was clearly an attempt by England to raise revenue in the colonies without the consent of the colonial assemblies.

Few colonists believed that they could do anything more than grumble until the Virginia House of Burgesses aroused Americans to action. Patrick Henry made a dramatic speech to the House in May 1765, concluding with a vague prediction that if present policies were not revised, George III, like earlier tyrants, might lose his head. There were shocked cries of "Treason!" and, according to one witness, an immediate apology from Henry (although many years later he was quoted as having made the defiant reply: "If this be treason, make the most of it"). But Henry introduced a set of resolutions (only some of which the assembly passed) declaring that Americans possessed the same rights as the English, especially the right to be taxed only by their own representatives; that Virginians should pay no taxes except those voted by the Virginia assembly; and that anyone advocating the right of Parliament to tax Virginians should be deemed an enemy of the colony. Henry's resolutions were printed and circulated as the "Virginia Resolves."

In Massachusetts at about the same time, James Otis persuaded his fellow members of the colonial assembly to call an intercolonial congress to take action against the new tax. And in October 1765, the Stamp Act Congress, as it was called, met in New York with delegates from nine colonies. In a petition to the British government, the congress denied that the colonies could rightfully be taxed except through their own provincial assemblies.

In the summer of 1765, meanwhile, mobs were rising up in several colonial cities against the Stamp Act. The largest of them was in Boston, where men belonging to the newly organized Sons of Liberty terrorized stamp agents and burned stamps. The agents, themselves Americans, hastily resigned. In Boston, the mob also attacked such supposedly pro-British "aristocrats" as the lieutenant governor, Thomas Hutchinson (who had privately opposed passage of the Stamp Act but who felt obliged to support it once it became law). Hutchinson's elegant house was pillaged and virtually destroyed.

The crisis finally subsided largely because England backed down. The authorities in London were less affected by the political protests than by economic pressure. Many New Englanders had stopped buying English goods to protest the Sugar Act of 1764, and the Stamp Act caused the boycott to spread, particularly once the Sons of Liberty intimidated reluctant colonists into participating in it. Under pressure from English merchants concerned about the loss of much of their colonial market, Parliament—under a new prime minister, the Marquis of Rockingham—repealed the unpopular law on March 18, 1766. To satisfy his strong and vociferous opponents, Rockingham also pushed through the Declaratory Act, which confirmed parliamentary authority over the colonies "in all cases whatsoever." In their rejoicing over the Stamp Act repeal, most Americans paid little attention to this ominous declaration of Parliament's power.

The Townshend Program

When the Rockingham government's policy of appeasement met substantial opposition in England, the king dismissed the Rockingham ministry and replaced it with a new government led by the aging but still powerful William Pitt, who was now Lord Chatham. Chatham had been a critic of the Stamp Act and had in the past been sympathetic toward American interests. Once in office, however, he was so hobbled by gout and at times so incapacitated by mental illness that the actual leadership of his administration fell to the chancellor of the exchequer, Charles Townshend.

Townshend had to deal with colonial grievances left over from the Grenville ministry. With the Stamp Act repealed, the greatest American grievance involved the Mutiny (or Quartering) Act of 1765, which required the colonists to provide shelter and supplies for British troops in America. The colonists objected not so much to quartering or supplying the troops but to being required by London to do so. It was, they believed, another form of taxation without their consent. The Massachusetts and New York assemblies went so far as to refuse to vote the mandated supplies to the troops.

Townshend responded in 1767 by disbanding the New York Assembly until the colonists agreed to obey the Mutiny Act. By singling out New York, he believed, he would avoid antagonizing all the colonies at once. He also imposed new taxes (known as the Townshend Duties) on various goods imported to the colonies from England—lead, paint, paper, and tea. Townshend assumed that since these were taxes purely on "external" transactions (imports from overseas), as opposed to the internal transactions the Stamp Act had taxed, the colonists would not object. But all the colonies resented the suspension of the New York Assembly, believing it to be a threat to every colonial government. And all the colonies rejected Townshend's careful distinction between external and internal taxation. The purpose of the new duties, they claimed, was the same as that of the Stamp Act: to raise revenue from the colonists without their consent.

Townshend also established a board of customs commissioners in America to stop the rampant corruption in the colonial customs houses. To some extent the plan worked. The new commissioners virtually ended smuggling in Boston, where they established their headquarters, although smugglers continued to carry on a busy trade in other colonial seaports. The Boston merchants—accustomed to loose enforcement of the Navigation Acts and angry that the new commission was diverting the lucrative smuggling trade elsewhere—helped organize a boycott of British goods that were subject to the Townshend Duties. Merchants in Philadelphia and New York joined them in a nonimportation agreement in 1768, and later some southern merchants and planters also agreed to cooperate. Throughout the colonies, American homespun and other domestic products became suddenly fashionable, while English luxuries fell from favor.

Late in 1767, Charles Townshend died—before the consequences of his ill-conceived program had become fully apparent. In March 1770, the new prime minister, Lord North, hoping to end the American boycott, repealed all the Townshend Duties except the tea tax.

The Boston Massacre

Before news of the repeal reached America, an event in Massachusetts electrified colonial opinion. The harassment of the new customs commissioners in Boston had grown so intense that the British government had placed four regiments of regular troops in the city—a constant affront to the colonists' sense of independence. Many of the poorly paid British soldiers looked for

THE BOSTON MASSACRE (1770), BY PAUL REVERE This is one of many engravings, by Revere and others, of the conflict between British troops and Boston laborers that became important as propaganda for the Patriot cause in the 1770s. Among the victims of the massacre listed by Revere was Crispus Attucks, probably the first black man to die in the struggle for American independence.

jobs in their off-duty hours and thus competed with local workers in an already difficult labor market. Clashes between the two groups were frequent.

On the night of March 5, 1770, a few days after a particularly intense skirmish between workers at a ship-rigging factory and British soldiers who were trying to find jobs there, a mob of dockworkers, "liberty boys," and others began pelting the sentries at the customs house with rocks and snowballs. Hastily, Captain Thomas Preston of the British regiment lined up several of his men in front of the building to protect it. There was some scuffling; one of the soldiers was knocked down; and in the midst of it all, apparently, several British soldiers fired into the crowd, killing five people (among them a mulatto sailor, Crispus Attucks).

This murky incident, almost certainly the result of panic and confusion, was quickly transformed by local resistance leaders into the "Boston Massacre"—a graphic symbol of British oppression and brutality. The victims became popular martyrs; the event became the subject of such lurid (and inaccurate) accounts as the widely circulated pamphlet *Innocent Blood Crying to God from the Streets of Boston*. A famous engraving by Paul Revere portrayed the massacre as a calculated assault on a peaceful crowd. The British soldiers, tried before a jury of Bostonians, were found guilty only of manslaughter and given token punishment. But colonial pamphlets and newspapers convinced many Americans that the soldiers were guilty of official murder. Year after year, resistance leaders marked the anniversary of the massacre with demonstrations and speeches.

The leading figure in fomenting public outrage over the Boston Massacre was Samuel Adams, the most effective radical in the colonies. England, he argued, had become a morass of sin and corruption; only in America did public virtue survive. In 1772, he proposed the creation of a "committee of correspondence" in Boston to publicize the grievances against England throughout the colony. Other colonies followed Massachusetts's lead, and a loose intercolonial network of political organizations was soon established that kept the spirit of dissent alive through the 1770s.

The Philosophy of Revolt

Although a superficial calm settled on the colonies for approximately three years after the Boston Massacre, the crises of the 1760s had helped arouse enduring ideological challenges to England and had produced powerful instruments for publicizing colonial grievances. Gradually a political outlook gained a following in America that would ultimately serve to justify revolt.

The ideas that would support the Revolution emerged from many sources. Some were drawn from religious (particularly Puritan) sources or from the political experiences of the colonies. Others came from abroad. Most important, perhaps, were the "radical" ideas of those in Great Britain who stood in opposition to their government. Some were Scots, who considered the English state tyrannical. Others were embittered "country Whigs," who felt excluded from power and considered the existing system corrupt and oppressive. Drawing from some of the great philosophical minds of earlier generations—most notably John Locke—these English dissidents framed a powerful argument against their government.

Central to this emerging ideology was a new concept of what government should be. Because humans were inherently corrupt and selfish, government was necessary to protect individuals from the evil in one another. But because any government was run by corruptible people, the people needed safeguards against its possible abuses of power. Most people in both England and America considered the English constitution the best system ever devised to meet these necessities. By distributing power among the three elements of society—the monarchy, the aristocracy, and the common people—the English political system ensured that no individual or group could exercise authority unchecked by another. Yet by the mid-seventeenth century, dissidents in both England and America had become convinced that the constitution was in danger. A single center of power—the king and his ministers—was becoming so powerful that it could not be effectively checked, and the system was becoming a corrupt and dangerous tyranny.

Such arguments found little sympathy in most of England. The English constitution was not a written document or a fixed set of unchangeable rules. It was a general sense of the "way things are done," and most people in England were willing to accept changes in it. Americans, by contrast, drew from their experience with colonial charters, in which the shape and powers of government were permanently inscribed on paper. They resisted the idea of a flexible, changing set of basic principles.

One basic principle, Americans believed, was the right of people to be taxed only with their own consent—a belief that gradually took shape in the widely repeated slogan, "No taxation without representation." Whatever the nature of a tax—whether internal or external, whether designed to raise revenue or to control trade—it could not be levied without the consent of the colonists themselves.

This clamor about "representation" made little sense to the English. According to English constitutional theory, members of Parliament did not represent individuals or particular geographical areas. Instead, each member represented the interests of the whole nation and indeed the whole empire, no matter where the member happened to come from. The many boroughs of England that had no representative in Parliament, the whole of Ireland, and the colonies thousands of miles away—all were thus represented in the Parliament at London, even though they elected no representatives of their own. This was the theory of "virtual" representation. But Americans, drawing from their experiences with their town meetings and their colonial assemblies, believed in "actual" representation. Every community was entitled to its own representative, elected by the people of that community and directly responsible to them. Since the colonists had none of their own representatives in Parliament, it followed that they were not represented there. Americans believed that the colonial assemblies played the same role within the colonies that Parliament did within England. The empire, the Americans argued, was a sort of federation of commonwealths, each with its own legislative body, all tied together by common loyalty to the king.

Such ideas illustrated a fundamental difference of opinion between England and America over the nature of sovereignty—over the question of where ultimate power lay. By arguing that Parliament had the right to legislate for England and for the empire as a whole, but that only the provincial assemblies could legislate for the individual colonies, Americans were in effect arguing for a division of sovereignty. Parliament would be sovereign in some matters; the assemblies would be sovereign in others. To the British, such an argument was absurd. In any system of government there must be a single, ultimate authority. And since the empire was, in their view, a single, undivided unit, there could be only one authority within it: the English government of king and Parliament.

Sites of Resistance

The apparent calm in America in the first years of the 1770s hid a growing sense of frustration and resentment about the continued and increasingly heavy-handed enforcement of the Navigation Acts. Popular anger was visible in occasional acts of rebellion. At one point, colonists seized a British revenue ship on the lower Delaware River. In 1772, angry residents of Rhode Island boarded the British schooner *Gaspée*, set it afire, and sank it in Narragansett Bay.

Colonists kept the growing spirit of resistance alive in many ways, but most of all through writing and talking. Dissenting leaflets, pamphlets, and books circulated widely through the colonies. In towns and cities, men gathered in churches, schools, town squares, and above all in taverns to discuss politics. Indeed, the tavern culture of the colonies was crucial to the growth of Revolutionary sentiment. Taverns were appealing, of course, because they provided alcoholic drinks in a culture where the craving for alcohol—and the extent of drunkenness—was very high. But taverns were also among the few public spaces were people could meet and talk openly, and to many colonists the life of the tavern was the only vaguely democratic experience open to them. The tavern was a mostly male institution, just as politics was considered a mostly male concern. The combination of male companionship and political conversation emerged naturally out of the tavern culture.

THE SCALES OF JUSTIS This sign for a Hartford tavern promises hospitality (from "the charming Patroness") and "entertainment" as well as food and drink.

As the Revolutionary crisis deepened, taverns and pubs became the central meeting places for discussions of ideas about resistance—and the sites of elaborate celebrations of the anniversaries of resistance to the Stamp Act. Taverns were also places were resistance pamphlets and leaflets could be distributed, and the settings for meetings for the planning of protests and demonstrations. Massachusetts had the most elaborately developed tavern culture, which was perhaps one reason why the spirit of resistance grew more quickly there than anywhere else. Almost all politicians in Boston found it necessary to visit taverns if they wanted any real contact with the public.

The Tea Excitement

The Revolutionary fervor of the 1760s revived, finally, as a result of a new act of Parliament—one that the English government had expected to be relatively uncontroversial. It involved the business of selling tea. In 1773, Britain's East India Company (which possessed an official monopoly on trade with the Far East) was sitting on large stocks of tea that it could not sell in England. It was on the verge of bankruptcy. In an effort to save it, the government passed the Tea Act of 1773, which gave the company the right to export its merchandise directly to the colonies without paying any of the regular taxes that were imposed on the colonial merchants, who had traditionally served as the middlemen in such transactions. With these privileges, the company could undersell American merchants and monopolize the colonial tea trade.

The act proved inflammatory for several reasons. First, it angered influential colonial merchants, who feared being replaced and bankrupted by a powerful monopoly. More important, however, the Tea Act revived American passions about the issue of taxation without representation. The law provided no new tax on tea. But the original Townshend duty on the commodity—the only one of the original duties that had not been repealed—survived; and the East India Company was now exempt from paying it. Lord North had assumed that most colonists would welcome the new law because it would reduce the price of tea to consumers by removing the middlemen. But resistance leaders in America argued that the law, in effect, represented an unconstitutional tax. The colonists responded by boycotting tea.

Unlike earlier protests, most of which had involved relatively small numbers of people, the tea boycott mobilized large segments of the population. It also helped link the colonies together in a common experience of mass popular protest. Particularly important to the movement were the activities of colonial women, who were among the principal consumers of tea and who became the leaders of the effort to boycott it. The Daughters of Liberty—a women's patriotic organization which, like the Sons of Liberty, was committed to agitating against British policies—proclaimed, "rather than Freedom, we'll part with our Tea."

In the last weeks of 1773, with strong popular support, leaders in various colonies made plans to prevent the East India Company from landing its cargoes in colonial ports. In Philadelphia and New York, determined colonists kept the tea from leaving the company's ships, and in

Charleston, they stored it away in a public warehouse. In Boston, after failing to turn three ships away from the harbor, local patriots staged a spectacular drama. On the evening of December 16, 1773, three companies of fifty men each, masquerading as Mohawk Indians, passed through a crowd of spectators, went aboard the three ships, broke open the tea chests, and heaved them into the harbor. As the electrifying news of the Boston "tea party" spread, colonists in other seaports staged similar acts of resistance.

Parliament retaliated in four acts of 1774: closing the port of Boston, drastically reducing the powers of self-government in Massachusetts, permitting royal officers in America to be tried in other colonies or in England when accused of crimes, and providing for the quartering of troops by the colonists. These Coercive Acts—or, as they were more widely known in America, "Intolerable Acts"—were followed by the Quebec Act, which was unrelated to them but also provocative to English Americans. The law extended the boundaries of Quebec to include the French communities between the Ohio and Mississippi Rivers. It also granted political rights to Roman Catholics and recognized the legality of the Roman Catholic Church within the enlarged province. Many colonists feared that a plot was afoot in London to subject Americans to the authority of the pope. Those interested in western lands, moreover, believed that the act would hinder westward expansion.

The Coercive Acts, far from isolating Massachusetts, made it a martyr in the eyes of residents of other colonies and sparked new resistance up and down the coast. Colonial legislatures passed a series of resolves supporting Massachusetts. Women's groups throughout the colonies mobilized to extend the boycotts of British goods and to create substitutes for the tea, textiles, and other commodities they were shunning. In Edenton, North Carolina, fifty-one women signed an agreement in October 1774 declaring their "sincere adherence" to the anti-British resolutions of their provincial assembly and proclaiming their duty to do "every thing as far as lies in our power" to support the "publick good."

COOPERATION AND WAR

Beginning in 1765, colonial leaders developed a variety of organizations for converting popular discontent into action—organizations that in time formed the basis for an independent government.

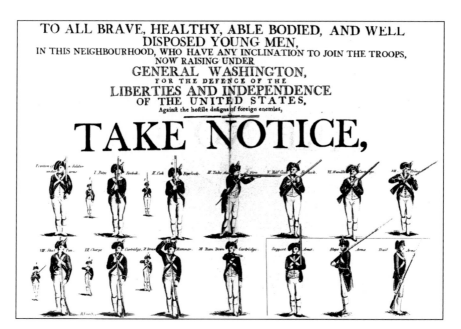

RECRUITING PATRIOTS This Revolutionary War recruiting poster tries to attract recruits by appealing to their patriotism (asking them to defend "the liberties and independence of the United States"), their vanity (by showing the "handsome clothing" and impressive bearing of soldiers), and their greed (by offering them "a bounty of twelve dollars" and "sixty dollars a year").

New Sources of Authority

The passage of authority from the royal government to the colonists themselves began on the local level. In colony after colony, local institutions responded to the resistance movement by simply seizing authority on their own. At times, entirely new institutions emerged and began to perform some of the functions of government.

The most effective of these new groups were the committees of correspondence that Samuel Adams had inaugurated in Massachusetts in 1772. Virginia later established the first intercolonial committees of correspondence, which helped make possible continuous cooperation among the colonies, and later took the greatest step of all toward united action. After the royal governor dissolved the assembly in 1774, a rump session met in the Raleigh Tavern at Williamsburg, declared that the Intolerable Acts menaced the liberties of every colony, and issued a call for a Continental Congress.

Delegates from all thirteen colonies except Georgia were present when, in September 1774, the First Continental Congress convened in Philadelphia. They made five major decisions. First, they rejected a plan for a colonial union under British authority. Second, they endorsed a relatively moderate statement of grievances, which seemed to concede Parliament's right to regulate colonial trade by addressing the king as "Most Gracious Sovereign," but which also included a demand for the repeal of all oppressive legislation passed since 1763. Third, they approved a series of resolutions from a Massachusetts convention recommending that military preparations be made for defense against possible attack by the British troops in Boston. Fourth, they agreed to a series of boycotts that they hoped would stop all trade with Great Britain, and they formed a "Continental Association" to see that these agreements were enforced. Finally, the delegates agreed to meet again the following spring, evidence that they saw the Continental Congress as a continuing organization.

During the winter, the Parliament in London debated proposals for conciliating the colonists, and early in 1775 Lord North finally won approval for a series of measures known as the Conciliatory Propositions. Parliament proposed that the colonies, instead of being taxed directly by Parliament, would tax themselves at Parliament's demand. With this offer, Lord North hoped to separate the American moderates, whom he believed represented the views of the majority, from the extremist minority. But his offer was too little and too late. It did not reach America until after the first shots of war had been fired.

Lexington and Concord

For months, the farmers and townspeople of Massachusetts had been gathering arms and ammunition and training as "minutemen," preparing to fight on a minute's notice. The Continental Congress had approved preparations for a defensive war, and the citizen-soldiers waited only for an aggressive move by the British regulars in Boston.

In Boston, General Thomas Gage, commanding the British garrison, considered his army too small to do anything without reinforcements. He resisted the advice of less cautious officers, who assured him that the Americans would never dare actually to fight, that they would back down quickly before any show of British force. When General Gage received orders to arrest the rebel leaders Sam Adams and John Hancock, known to be in the vicinity of Lexington, he still hesitated. But when he heard that the minutemen had stored a large supply of gunpowder in Concord

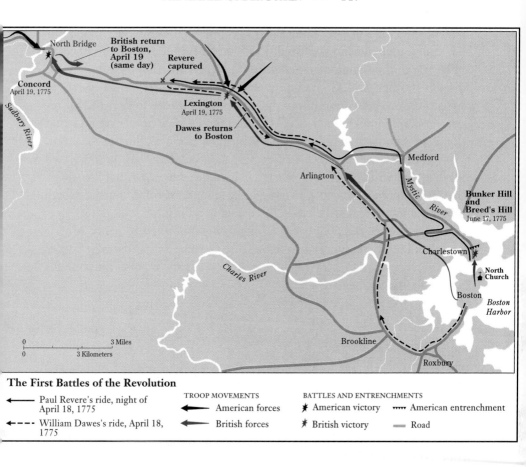

The First Battles of the Revolution

—— Paul Revere's ride, night of April 18, 1775		
◄- - - William Dawes's ride, April 18, 1775		

TROOP MOVEMENTS

◄—— American forces

◄—— British forces

BATTLES AND ENTRENCHMENTS

✶ American victory   ⁓⁓⁓ American entrenchment

✶ British victory   —— Road

(eighteen miles from Boston), he decided to act. On the night of April 18, 1775, he sent a detachment of about 1,000 men out from Boston on the road to Lexington and Concord. He hoped to surprise the colonials and seize the illegal supplies without bloodshed.

But patriots in Boston were watching the British movements closely, and during the night two horsemen, William Dawes and Paul Revere, rode out to warn the villages and farms. When the redcoats arrived in Lexington the next day, several dozen minutemen awaited them on the town common. Shots were fired and minutemen fell; eight of them were killed and ten more were wounded. Advancing to Concord, the British discovered that the Americans had hastily removed most of the powder supply, but the redcoats burned what was left of it. All along the road from Concord back to Boston, the British were harassed by the gunfire of farmers hiding behind trees, rocks, and stone walls. By the end of the day, the British had lost almost three times as many men as the Americans.

The first shots—the "shots heard 'round the world," as Americans later called them—had been fired. But who had fired them first? According to one of the minutemen at Lexington, the British commander, Major Thomas Pitcairn, had shouted to the colonists on his arrival, "Disperse, ye rebels!" When they ignored him, he ordered his troops to fire. British officers and soldiers claimed that the minutemen had fired first and that only after seeing the flash of American guns had they begun to shoot. Whatever the truth, the rebels succeeded in circulating their account well ahead of the British version, adorning it with tales of British atrocities. The effect was to rally to the rebel cause thousands of colonists, North and South, who previously had little enthusiasm for it.

It was not immediately clear to the British, or even to many Americans, that the skirmishes at Lexington and Concord were the first battles of a war. But whether they recognized it at the time or not, the War for Independence had begun.

CONCLUSION

When the French and Indian War ended in 1763, it might have seemed reasonable to expect that relations between the English colonists in America and Great Britain itself would have been cemented more firmly than ever. America and Britain had fought together in a great war against the French and their Indian allies. They had won impressive victories. They had vastly expanded the size of the British Empire.

But in fact the end of the French and Indian War altered the imperial relationship forever, in ways that ultimately drove Americans to rebel against English rule and begin a war for independence. To the British, the lesson of the war was that the colonies in America needed firmer control from London. The empire was now much bigger, and it needed better administration. The war had produced great debts, and the Americans—among the principal beneficiaries of the war—should help pay them. And so for more than a decade after the end of the fighting, the British tried one strategy after another to tighten control over and extract money from the colonies, all of them in the end failures.

To the colonists, this effort to tighten imperial rule appeared both a betrayal of the sacrifices they had made in the war and a challenge to their long-developing assumptions about the rights of English people to rule themselves. Gradually, white Americans came to see in the British policies evidence of a conspiracy to establish tyranny in the New World. And so throughout the 1760s and 1770s, the colonists developed ever more overt and effective forms of resistance. By the time the first shots were fired in the American Revolution in 1775, Britain and America—not long before bonded so closely to one another that most white Americans considered themselves as English as any resident of London—had come to view each other as two very different societies. Their differences, which came to seem irreconcilable, propelled them into a war that would change the course of both countries' history.

FOR FURTHER REFERENCE

Suggested Readings

Richard White, *The Middle Ground: Indians, Empires, and Republics in the Great Lakes Region, 1650–1815* (1991) argues that Indians in the Great Lakes region were able to take advantage of European rivalries for much of the eighteenth century. Francis Jennings, *The Ambiguous Iroquois Empire* (1984) makes a similar point. Richard Bushman, *King and People in Colonial Massachusetts* (1987) traces the fracture between Massachusetts colonists and the imperial government. Fred Anderson, *A People's Army: Massachusetts Soldiers and Society in the Seven Years' War* (1984) describes the ideological impact of the French and Indian War on the colonists who fought in it. Gary Nash, *The Urban Crucible: The Northern Seaports and the Origins of the American Revolution* (1979) argues that increasing class stratification in northern cities contributed to the coming of the American Revolution. Robert R. Palmer, *The Age of Democratic Revolution: Vol. 1, The Challenge* (1959) and J. G. A. Pocock, *The Machiavellian Moment* (1975) both place the American Revolution in the context of a transatlantic political culture. Bernard Bailyn, *The Ideological Origins of the American Revolution* (1967) was one of the first works by an American historian to emphasize the importance of English republican political thought to the Revolutionary ideology of the American colonists.

Films

(The best source for information on how to find these and other films is *Bowker's Complete Video Directory*—3 volumes.)*The American Story, No. 1: Road to Revolution* (1985) reviews the events, beginning with the Stamp Act crisis, that led the American colonies to the brink of open rebellion. *Colonial America in the Seventeen Sixties* (1967) examines the conflicts between the colonies and Britain in the crucial years after 1763. *Colonial America: The Roots of Revolution, 1607–1775* (1979) uses full-costume re-creations to help explain the economic, cultural, and religious reasons for revolution. *Paul Revere* (1996) is a biography of one of America's most celebrated patriots. *Lexington, Concord, & Independence* (1967) narrates the first battles of the American Revolution. *Patrick Henry: Virginia Patriot* (1990) documents the life and achievements of the man whose words "Give Me Liberty or Give Me Death" became a rallying cry of the Revolution.

Internet Resources

Internet websites containing historical material relevant to the subjects discussed in this chapter can be reached through the McGraw-Hill history site at www.mhhe.com/socscience/history/usa/link/linktop.htm.

CHAPTER FIVE

The American Revolution

The States United ～ *The War for Independence*
War and Society ～ *The Creation of State Governments*
The Search for a National Government

WO STRUGGLES OCCURRED simultaneously during the seven years of war that began in April of 1775. One was the military conflict with Great Britain. The second was a political conflict within America.

The military conflict was, by the standards of later wars, a relatively modest one. By the standards of its own day, however, it was an unusually savage conflict, pitting not only army against army but the civilian population against a powerful external force. The shift of the war from a traditional, conventional struggle to a new kind of conflict—a revolutionary war for liberation—is what made it possible for the United States to defeat the more powerful British.

At the same time, Americans were wrestling with the great political questions that the conflict necessarily produced: first, whether to demand independence from Britain; then, how to structure the new nation they had proclaimed. Only the first of these questions had been resolved by the time of the British surrender at Yorktown in 1781.

THE STATES UNITED

Although many Americans had been expecting a military conflict with Britain for months, even years, the actual beginning of hostilities in 1775 found the colonies generally unprepared for war against the world's greatest armed power.

TIME LINE				
1775	**1776**	**1777**	**1778**	**1781**
Second Continental Congress	Paine's *Common Sense*	Articles of Confederation adopted	French-America alliance	Articles of Confederation ratified
Washigton commands American forces	Declaration of Independence Battle of Trenton	British defeat at Saratoga		Cornwallis surrenders at Yorktown

1783	**1784**		**1786**	**1787**
Treaty of Paris	Postwar depression begins		Shays's Rebellion	Northwest Ordinance

Defining American War Aims

Three weeks after the battles of Lexington and Concord, when the Second Continental Congress met in Philadelphia, delegates from every colony (except Georgia, which had not yet sent a representative) agreed to support the war. But they disagreed about its purpose. At one extreme was a group led by the Adams cousins (John and Samuel), Richard Henry Lee of Virginia, and others, who already favored independence; at the other extreme was a group led by such moderates as John Dickinson of Pennsylvania, who hoped for a quick reconciliation with Great Britain. Most of the delegates tried to find some middle ground between these positions.

Like the moderates in Congress, most Americans believed at first that they were fighting not for independence but for a redress of grievances within the British Empire. During the first year of fighting, however, many of them began to change their minds. The costs of the war—human and financial—were so high that the original war aims began to seem too modest to justify them. Many colonists were enraged when the British began trying to recruit Indians, African slaves, and German mercenaries (the hated "Hessians") against them. When the British government blockaded the colonial ports to cut off overseas trade and rejected all efforts at conciliation, many colonists concluded that independence was the only remaining option.

An impassioned pamphlet crystallized these feelings in January 1776: Thomas Paine's *Common Sense*. Paine, who had emigrated from England to

America less than two years before, wanted to turn the anger of Americans away from particular parliamentary measures and toward what he considered the root of the problem—the English constitution itself. It was simple common sense, he wrote, for Americans to break completely with a political system that could produce so corrupt a monarch as George III and could inflict such brutality on its own people. *Common Sense* sold more than 100,000 copies (an astonishing number given the size of the colonial population) in only a few months. It helped create a rapid growth of support for the idea of independence in the early months of 1776.

The Declaration of Independence

In the meantime, the Continental Congress in Philadelphia was moving toward a complete break with England. At the beginning of the summer, it appointed a committee to draft a formal declaration of independence; and on July 2, 1776, it adopted a resolution: "That these United Colonies are, and, of right, ought to be, free and independent states; that they are absolved from all allegiance to the British crown, and that all political connexion between them and the state of Great Britain is, and ought to be, totally dissolved." Two days later, on July 4, Congress approved the Declaration of Independence itself, which provided formal justifications for the actions the delegates had taken two days earlier.

Thomas Jefferson, a thirty-three-year-old Virginian, wrote most of the Declaration, with help from Benjamin Franklin and John Adams. As Adams later observed, Jefferson said little in the document that was new, but brought to its familiar ideas a compelling eloquence. The Declaration expressed concepts that had been circulating throughout the colonies over the previous few months in the form of at least ninety other, local "declarations of independence"—declarations drafted up and down the coast by town meetings, artisan and militia organizations, county officials, grand juries, Sons of Liberty, and colonial assemblies. Jefferson borrowed heavily from these texts, both for the ideas he expressed and even, to some extent, for the precise language he used.

The final document was in two parts. In the first, the Declaration restated the familiar contract theory of John Locke: the theory that governments were formed to protect what Jefferson called "life, liberty and the pursuit of happiness." In the second part, it listed the alleged crimes of the king, who, with the backing of Parliament, had violated his contract with the colonists and thus had forfeited all claim to their loyalty.

The Declaration launched a period of energetic political innovation, as one colony after another reconstituted itself as a "state." By 1781, most states had produced written constitutions for themselves that established republican governments. At the national level, however, the process was more uncertain. In November 1777, finally, Congress adopted a plan for union, the Articles of Confederation. The document confirmed the existing weak, decentralized system, which proved ill-suited for managing a continental war.

Mobilizing for War

Financing the war was particularly difficult, because Congress lacked the authority and the states generally lacked the inclination to impose taxes on the public. Congress had no authority to levy taxes on its own, and when it requisitioned money from the state governments, none contributed more than a small part of its expected share. Congress had little success borrowing from the public, since few Americans could afford to buy bonds and those who could preferred to invest in more profitable ventures, such as privateering. In the end, there was no alternative but to issue paper money. Printing presses turned out enormous amounts of "Continental currency," and the states printed currencies of their own. The result, predictably, was soaring inflation. Unable to stop the inflation, Congress soon found that the Continental currency was virtually worthless. Ultimately, it financed the war mostly by borrowing from other nations.

After a first surge of patriotism in 1775, volunteer soldiers were scarce. States had to pay bounties or use a draft to recruit the needed men. At first, the militiamen remained under the control of their respective states. But Congress recognized the need for a centralized military command, and it created a Continental army with a single commander in chief: George Washington. A forty-three-year-old Virginia planter-aristocrat who had commanded colonial forces during the French and Indian War, Washington had considerable military experience and was an early advocate of independence; he was admired, respected, and trusted by nearly all Patriots. He took command of the new army in June 1775. With the aid of foreign military experts such as the Marquis de Lafayette from France and the Baron von Steuben from Prussia, he built a force that prevailed against the mightiest power in the world. Even more important, perhaps, Washington's steadiness, courage, and dedication to his cause provided the army—and the people—with a symbol of stability around which they could rally.

D E B A T I N G   T H E   P A S T

The American Revolution

T HE LONGSTANDING debate over the origins of the American Revolution has intended to reflect two broad schools of interpretation. One sees the Revolution largely as a political and intellectual event and argues that the revolt against Britain was part of a defence of ideals and principles. The other views the Revolution as a social and economic phenomenon and contends that material interests were at the heart of the rebellion.

The Revolutionary generation itself portrayed the conflict as a struggle over ideals, and this interpretation prevailed through most of the nineteenth century. But in the early twentieth century, historians influenced by the reform currents of the progressive era began to identify social and economic forces that they believed had contributed to the rebellion. Carl Becker, for example, wrote in a 1909 study of New York that two questions had shaped the Revolution: "The first was the question of home rule; the second was the question . . . of who should rule at home." The colonists were not only fighting the British; they were also engaged in a kind of civil war, a contest between radicals and conservatives that led to the "democratization of American politics and society."

Other "progressive" historians elaborated on Becker's thesis. J. Franklin Jameson, writing in 1926, argued, "Many economic desires, many social aspirations, were set free by the political struggle, many aspects of society profoundly altered by the forces thus let loose." Arthur M. Schlesinger maintained a 1917 book that colonial merchants, motivated by their own interest in escaping the restrictive policies of Bitish mercantilism, aroused American resistance in the 1760s and 1770s.

Beginning in the 1950s, a new generation of scholars began to reemphasize the role of ideology and de-emphasize the role of economic interests. Robert E. Brown (in 1955) and Edmund S. Morgan (in 1956) both argued that most eighteenth-century Americans shared common political principles and that the social and economic conflicts the progressives had identified were not severe. The rhetoric of the Revolution, they suggested, was not propaganda but a real reflection of the ideas of the colonists. Bernard Bailyn, in *The Ideological Origins of the American Revolution* (1967), demonstrated the complex roots of the ideas behind the Revolution and argued that this carefully constructed political stance was not a disguise for economic interests but a genuine ideology, rooted in deeply held convictions about rights and power, that itself motivated the colonists to act. The Revolution, he exclaimed, "was above all an ideological, constitutional, political struggle and not primarily a controversy between social groups undertaken to force changes in the organization of the society or the economy."

By the late 1960s, a new generation of historians—many influenced by the New Left—were reviving economic interpretations of the Revolution by exploring the social and economic tensions that they claimed shaped the Revolutionary struggle. Historians cited the actions of mobs in colonial cities, the economic pressures on colonial merchants, the growing climate of economic distress in colonial cities, and other changes in the character of American culture and society as critical prerequisites for the growth of the Revolutionary movement. Gary Nash, attempting to reconcile the emphasis on economic interests with the role of ideology, argued that the two things were not incompatible. "Everyone has economic interests," he claimed, "and everyone . . . has an ideology." Exploring the relationship between the two, he argues, is critical to historians' ability to understand either. Also, as Linda Kerber and others have argued, the newer social interpretations have raised increasing interest in the experience of workers, slaves, women, Native Americans, and other groups previously considered marginal to public life as part of the explanation of the Revolutionary struggle.

Finally, Gordon Wood, in *The Radicalism of the American Revolution* (1992) revived an idea once popular and recently unfashionable: that the Revolution was a genuinely radical event that led to the breakdown of such longstanding characteristics of society as deference, patriarchy, and traditional gender relations. Class conflict may not have caused the Revolution, he argues, but the Revolution had a profound, even radical, effect on society nevertheless.

REVOLUTIONARY SOLDIERS Jean Baptist de Verger, a French officer serving in America during the Revolution, kept an illustrated journal of his experiences. Here he portrays four American soldiers carrying different kinds of arms: a black infantryman with a light rifle, a musketman, a rifleman, and an artilleryman.

THE WAR FOR INDEPENDENCE

The British seemed to have overwhelming advantages as the War for Independence began: the greatest navy and the best-equipped army in the world, the resources of an empire, a coherent structure of command. Yet the United States had advantages, too. Americans were fighting on their own ground. They were more committed to the conflict than were the British. And, beginning in 1777, they received substantial aid from abroad.

But the American victory was also a result of a series of blunders and miscalculations by the British in the early stages of the fighting, when England could (and probably should) have won. And it was, finally, a result of the transformation of the war—through three distinct phases—into a new kind of conflict that the British military, for all its strength, was unable to win.

The First Phase: New England

For the first year of the conflict—from the spring of 1775 to the spring of 1776—many English authorities thought that British forces were not fighting a real war, but simply quelling pockets of rebellion in the contentious area around Boston. After the redcoats withdrew from Lexington and Concord in

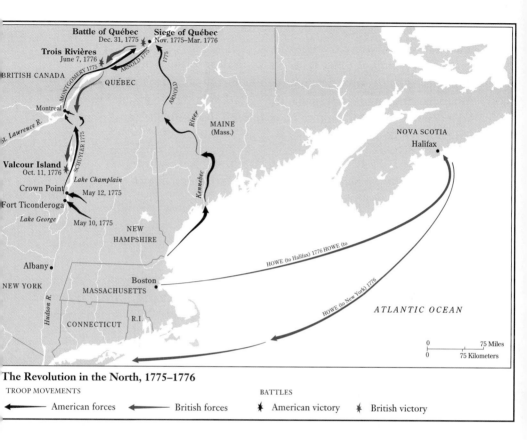

Battle of Québec
Dec. 31, 1775

Siege of Québec
Nov. 1775–Mar. 1776

Trois Rivières
June 7, 1776

BRITISH CANADA

QUÉBEC

Montreal

St. Lawrence R.

Valcour Island
Oct. 11, 1776

Lake Champlain

Crown Point
May 12, 1775

Fort Ticonderoga

Lake George   May 10, 1775

NEW HAMPSHIRE

Albany

NEW YORK

Boston

MASSACHUSETTS

Hudson R.

CONNECTICUT   R.I.

MAINE
(Mass.)

Kennebec

River

NOVA SCOTIA
Halifax

HOWE (to Halifax) 1776 HOWE (to

HOWE (to New York) 1776

ATLANTIC OCEAN

0   75 Miles
0   75 Kilometers

The Revolution in the North, 1775–1776

TROOP MOVEMENTS   BATTLES

⬅— American forces   ⬅— British forces   ✸ American victory   ✸ British victory

April, American forces besieged them in Boston. In the Battle of Bunker Hill (actually fought on Breed's Hill) on June 17, 1775, the Patriots suffered severe casualties and withdrew. But they inflicted even greater losses on the enemy (indeed, the heaviest casualties the British were to suffer in the entire war). The siege continued. Early in 1776, finally, the British decided that Boston was a poor place from which to fight. It was in the center of the most anti-British part of America and tactically difficult to defend because it was easily isolated and surrounded. And so, on March 17, 1776, the redcoats evacuated Boston for Halifax, Nova Scotia, with hundreds of Loyalist refugees.

In the meantime, a band of southern Patriots, at Moore's Creek Bridge in North Carolina, crushed an uprising of Loyalists (Americans still loyal to England and its king) on February 27, 1776, and discouraged a British plan to invade the southern states. And to the north, the Americans began an invasion of Canada. Generals Benedict Arnold and Richard Montgomery unsuccessfully threatened Quebec in late 1775 and early 1776 in a battle in which Montgomery was killed and Arnold wounded.

With the defeat at Quebec died any American hopes that Canada would join the Revolution.

By the spring of 1776, it had become clear to the British that the conflict was not just a local phenomenon in the area around Boston. The American campaigns in Canada, the agitation in the South, and the growing evidence of colonial unity all suggested that England must prepare to fight a much larger conflict.

The Second Phase: The Mid-Atlantic Region

During the next phase of the war, which lasted from 1776 until early 1778, the British were in a good position to win. Indeed, had it not been for a series of blunders and misfortunes, they probably would have crushed the rebellion.

The British regrouped quickly after their retreat from Boston. During the summer of 1776, hundreds of British ships and 32,000 British soldiers arrived in New York, under the command of General William Howe, who hoped simply to awe the Americans into submission. He offered Congress a choice between surrender with royal pardon and a battle against apparently overwhelming odds. To oppose Howe's great force, Washington could muster only about 19,000 inadequately armed and poorly trained soldiers; he had no navy at all. Even so, the Americans rejected Howe's offer and suffered a succession of major defeats. The British pushed the Patriot forces off Long Island, forced them to abandon Manhattan, and then drove them in slow retreat over the plains of New Jersey, across the Delaware River, and into Pennsylvania.

The British settled down for the winter in northern and central New Jersey, with an outpost of Hessians at Trenton, on the Delaware River. But Washington did not sit still. On Christmas night 1776, he daringly recrossed the icy Delaware River, surprised and scattered the Hessians, and occupied Trenton. Then he advanced to Princeton and drove a force of redcoats from their base in the college there. But Washington was unable to hold either Princeton or Trenton and finally took refuge for the rest of the winter in the hills around Morristown. The campaign of 1776 came to an end with the Americans having triumphed in two minor battles and with their main army still intact. The British were no nearer than before to a decisive triumph.

For the campaigns of 1777 the British devised a strategy to divide the United States in two. Howe would move from New York up the Hudson to Albany, while another force would come down from Canada to meet

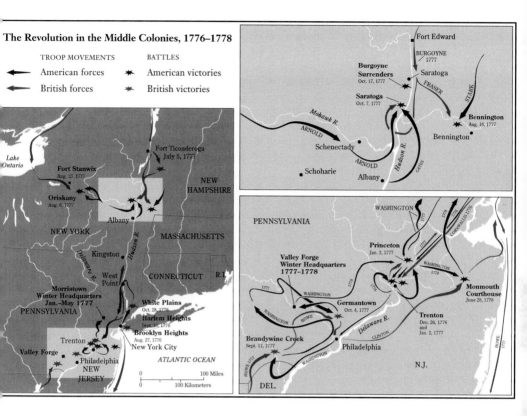

The Revolution in the Middle Colonies, 1776–1778

him. John Burgoyne, commander of the northern force, began a two-pronged attack to the south along both the Mohawk and the upper Hudson approaches to Albany. But having set the plan in motion, Howe abandoned his part of it. Instead of moving north to meet Burgoyne, he went south and captured Philadelphia, hoping that his seizure of the rebel capital would discourage the Patriots, rally the Loyalists, and bring the war to a speedy conclusion. Philadelphia fell with little resistance—and the Continental Congress moved into exile in York, Pennsylvania. After launching an unsuccessful Patriot attack against the British on October 4 at Germantown (just outside Philadelphia), Washington went into winter quarters at Valley Forge.

Howe's move to Philadelphia left Burgoyne to carry out the campaign in the north alone. He sent Colonel Barry St. Leger up the St. Lawrence River toward Lake Ontario. Burgoyne himself advanced directly down the upper Hudson Valley and easily seized Fort Ticonderoga, with its large store of powder and supplies. But Burgoyne soon experienced two staggering defeats.

In one of them—at Oriskany, New York, on August 6—Patriots held off a force of Indians and Tories commanded by St. Leger. That allowed Benedict Arnold to close off the Mohawk Valley to St. Leger's advance. In the other battle—at Bennington, Vermont, on August 16—New England militiamen mauled a detachment that Burgoyne had sent to seek supplies. Short of materials, with all help cut off, Burgoyne fought several costly engagements and then withdrew to Saratoga, where General Horatio Gates surrounded him. On October 17, 1777, Burgoyne surrendered—an event that became a major turning point in the war.

The campaign in upstate New York was not just a British defeat. It was a setback for the ambitious efforts of several Iroquois leaders. Although the Iroquois Confederacy had declared its neutrality in the Revolutionary War in 1776, some of its members allied themselves with the British, among them a Mohawk brother and sister, Joseph and Mary Brant. This ill-fated alliance further divided the already weakened Iroquois Confederacy, because only three of the Iroquois nations (the Mohawk, the Seneca, and the Cayuga) followed the Brants in support of the British. A year after the defeat at Oriskany, Iroquois forces joined British troops in a series of raids on white settlements in upstate New York. Patriot forces under the command of General John Sullivan harshly retaliated, wreaking such destruction on Indian settlements that large groups of Iroquois fled north into Canada to seek refuge. Many never returned.

Securing Aid from Abroad

The leaders of the American effort knew that victory would not be likely without aid from abroad. And their most promising allies, they realized, were the French, who believed they had much to gain from seeing Britain lose a crucial part of its empire. At first, France provided the United States with badly needed supplies but remained reluctant to grant formal diplomatic recognition to the United States. After the Declaration of Independence, Benjamin Franklin himself went to France to lobby for aid and diplomatic recognition. Franklin quickly became a hero to the French, but France's foreign minister, the Count de Vergennes, wanted evidence that the Americans had a real chance of winning before supporting open French intervention. The British defeat at Saratoga, he believed, offered that evidence.

When the news from Saratoga arrived in London and Paris in early December 1777, a shaken Lord North made a new peace offer: complete home rule within the empire for Americans if they would quit the war.

Vergennes feared the Americans might accept the offer and thus destroy France's opportunity to weaken Britain. Encouraged by Franklin, he agreed on February 6, 1778, to give formal recognition to the United States as a sovereign nation and to provide it with greatly expanded military assistance.

France's entry into the war made it an international conflict, which over the year pitted France, Spain, and the Netherlands against Great Britain. That helped reduce the resources available for the English effort in America. All three of Britain's foes offered assistance to the Patriots, but France was always America's most important ally. It furnished the new nation with most of its money and munitions, and it provided a navy and an expeditionary force that were vital to the final, successful phase of the Revolutionary conflict.

The Final Phase: The South

The American victory at Saratoga and the intervention of the French transformed the war and began its final phase. Instead of mounting a full-scale military struggle against the American army, the British now tried to enlist the support of those elements of the American population—a majority, they continued to believe—who were still loyal to the crown. And since Loyalist sentiment was thought to be strongest in the South, and since the English also hoped slaves would rally to their cause, the main focus of the British effort shifted there.

The new strategy was a dismal failure. British forces spent three years (from 1778 to 1781) moving through the South, fighting small battles and large. But they had badly overestimated the extent of Loyalist sentiment. And they had underestimated the logistical problems they would face. Patriot forces could move at will throughout the region, living off the resources of the countryside, blending in with the civilian population, and leaving the British unable to distinguish friend from foe. The British, by contrast, suffered all the disadvantages of an army in hostile territory.

It was this phase of the conflict that made the war "revolutionary"— not only because it introduced a new kind of warfare, but because it had the effect of mobilizing and politicizing large groups of the population who had until then remained aloof from the struggle. With the war expanding into previously isolated communities, with many civilians forced to involve themselves whether they liked it or not, the political climate of the United States grew more heated than ever. And support for independence, far from being crushed as the British had hoped, greatly increased.

In the North, where significant numbers of British troops remained, the fighting settled into a stalemate. Sir Henry Clinton replaced the unsuccessful William Howe in May 1778 and moved what had been Howe's army from Philadelphia back to New York. There the British troops stayed for more than a year, with Washington and his army keeping watch around them. In the meantime, George Rogers Clark led a Patriot expedition over the Green Mountains and captured settlements in the Illinois country from the British and their Indian allies. On the whole, however, there was relatively little military activity in the North after 1778. There was, however, considerable intrigue. In the fall of 1789, American forces were shocked by the exposure of treason on the part of General Benedict Arnold. Arnold had been one of the early heroes of the war, but now, convinced that the American cause was hopeless, he conspired with British agents to betray the Patriot stronghold at West Point on the Hudson River. When the scheme was exposed and foiled, Arnold fled to the safety of the British camp, where he spent the rest of the war.

The British did have some significant military successes during this period. On December 29, 1778, they captured Savannah, Georgia. On May 12, 1780, they took the port of Charleston, South Carolina, and inspired some Loyalists to take up arms and advance with them into the interior. But although the British were able to win conventional battles, they were constantly harassed as they moved through the countryside by Patriot guerrillas led by such resourceful fighters as Thomas Sumter, Andrew Pickens, and Francis Marion, the "Swamp Fox." Penetrating to Camden, South Carolina, Lord Cornwallis (whom Clinton named British commander in the South) met and crushed a Patriot force under Horatio Gates on August 16, 1780. Congress recalled Gates, and Washington replaced him with Nathanael Greene, one of the ablest of all the American generals of the time.

Even before Greene arrived in the South, the tide of battle had begun to turn against Cornwallis. At King's Mountain (near the North Carolina–South Carolina border) on October 7, 1780, a band of Patriot riflemen from the backwoods killed, wounded, or captured every man in a force of 1,100 New York and South Carolina Tories, upon whom Cornwallis had depended as auxiliaries. Once Greene arrived, he confused and exasperated Cornwallis by dividing the American forces into fast-moving contingents while avoiding open, conventional battles. One of the contingents inflicted what Cornwallis admitted was "a very unexpected and severe blow" at Cowpens on January 17, 1781. Finally, after receiving reinforcements, Greene combined all his forces and maneuvered to meet the British at Guilford Court House, North

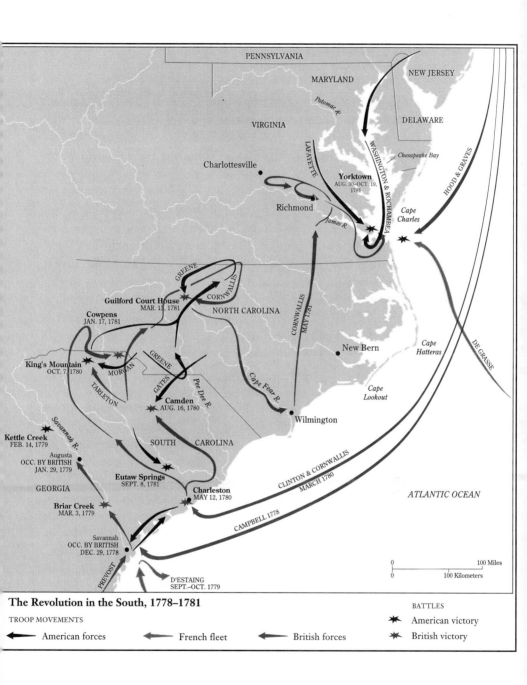

The Revolution in the South, 1778–1781

PENNSYLVANIA

MARYLAND

NEW JERSEY

DELAWARE

VIRGINIA

Potomac R.

Charlottesville

LAFAYETTE

Richmond

James R.

Yorktown
AUG. 30–OCT. 19, 1781

WASHINGTON & ROCHAMBEAU

Chesapeake Bay

HOOD & GRAVES

Cape Charles

GREENE

CORNWALLIS

Guilford Court House
MAR. 15, 1781

NORTH CAROLINA

CORNWALLIS MAY 1781

New Bern

Cape Hatteras

DE GRASSE

Cowpens
JAN. 17, 1781

GREENE

MORGAN

GATES

Pee Dee R.

Cape Fear R.

King's Mountain
OCT. 7, 1780

TARLETON

Camden
AUG. 16, 1780

Cape Lookout

Wilmington

Kettle Creek
FEB. 14, 1779

Savannah R.

SOUTH CAROLINA

Augusta
OCC. BY BRITISH
JAN. 29, 1779

GEORGIA

Eutaw Springs
SEPT. 8, 1781

Charleston
MAY 12, 1780

CLINTON & CORNWALLIS
MARCH 1780

ATLANTIC OCEAN

Briar Creek
MAR. 3, 1779

Savannah
OCC. BY BRITISH
DEC. 29, 1778

CAMPBELL 1778

PREVOST

D'ESTAING
SEPT.–OCT. 1779

0   100 Miles

0   100 Kilometers

BATTLES

TROOP MOVEMENTS

American forces

French fleet

British forces

✳ American victory

✳ British victory

135

Carolina. After a hard-fought battle there on March 15, 1781, Greene was driven from the field; but Cornwallis had lost so many men that he decided to abandon the Carolina campaign. Instead, he moved north, hoping to carry on raids in the interior of Virginia. But Clinton, fearful that the southern army might be destroyed, ordered him to take up a defensive position on the peninsula between the York and James Rivers and wait for transport to New York or Charleston. Cornwallis retreated to Yorktown and began to build fortifications there.

At that point, American and French forces descended on Yorktown in an effort to trap Cornwallis. Washington and the Count de Rochambeau marched a French-American army from New York to join the Marquis de Lafayette in Virginia, while Admiral de Grasse took a French fleet with additional troops up Chesapeake Bay to the York River. These joint operations caught Cornwallis between land and sea. After a few shows of resistance, he surrendered on October 17, 1781. Two days later, as a military band played the old tune "The World Turn'd Upside Down," he surrendered his whole army of more than 7,000.

Winning the Peace

Cornwallis's defeat provoked outcries in England against continuing the war. Lord North resigned as prime minister; Lord Shelburne emerged from the political wreckage to succeed him; and British emissaries appeared in France to talk informally with the American diplomats there, of whom the three principals were Benjamin Franklin, John Adams, and John Jay.

The Americans were under instructions to cooperate with France in their negotiations with England. But Vergennes, the French foreign minister, insisted that France could not agree to any settlement of the war with England until its ally Spain had achieved its principal war aim: winning back Gibraltar from the British. There was no real prospect of that happening soon, and the Americans began to fear that the alliance with France might keep them at war indefinitely. As a result, Franklin, Jay, and Adams began proceeding on their own, without informing Vergennes, and soon drew up a preliminary treaty with Great Britain, which was signed on November 30, 1782. Franklin, in the meantime, skillfully pacified Vergennes and avoided an immediate rift in the French-American alliance.

The final treaty was signed September 3, 1783, after both Spain and France agreed to end hostilities against Britain. The agreement was, on the whole, remarkably favorable to the United States. It provided a clear-cut recognition of independence and a large, though ambiguous, cession of territory to the new nation—from the southern boundary of Canada to the northern boundary of Florida and from the Atlantic to the Mississippi. The American people had good reason to celebrate as the last of the British occupation forces embarked from New York and General Washington, at the head of his troops, rode triumphantly into the city.

WAR AND SOCIETY

Historians have long debated whether the American Revolution was a social as well as a political revolution. But whatever the intention of those who launched and fought the war, the conflict had important effects on the nature of American society.

Loyalists and Minorities

Estimates differ as to how many Americans remained loyal to England during the Revolution, but it is clear that there were many—at least a fifth (and some estimate as much as a third) of the white population. Some were officeholders in the imperial government. Others were merchants whose trade was closely tied to the imperial system (although most merchants supported the Revolution). Still others were people who lived in relative isolation and had simply retained their traditional loyalties. And there were those who, expecting the British to win the war, were simply currying favor with the anticipated victors.

Many of these Loyalists were hounded by Patriots in their communities and harassed by legislative and judicial actions. Up to 100,000 fled the country. Those who could afford to—for example, the hated Tory governor of Massachusetts, Thomas Hutchinson—fled to England. Others of more modest means moved to Canada, establishing the first English-speaking community in the province of Quebec. Some returned to America after the war and gradually managed to reenter the life of the nation. Others remained abroad for the rest of their lives.

The war weakened other groups as well. The Anglican Church, many of whose members were Loyalist, lost its status as the official religion of Virginia and Maryland, as well as the economic aid they were accustomed to receiving from Britain. By the time the fighting ended, many Anglican parishes could no longer even afford clergymen. Also weakened were the Quakers, whose pacifism won them widespread unpopularity when they refused to support the war.

Other Protestant denominations, however, grew stronger as a result of their enthusiastic support for the war. Presbyterian, Congregational, and Baptist churches successfully tied themselves to the Patriot cause. And most American Catholics also supported the Patriots during the war and won increased (although far from universal) popularity as a result. Shortly after the peace treaty was signed, the Vatican provided the United States with its own hierarchy and, in 1789, its first bishop.

For the largest of America's minorities—the African-American population—the war had limited effects. For some, the Revolution meant freedom. Because so much of the fighting occurred in the South during the last years of the war, many slaves came into contact with the British army, which—in the interests of disrupting and weakening the American cause—emancipated thousands of them and took them out of the country. For most African Americans, however, the Revolution meant exposure to the idea, although not the reality, of liberty.

Native Americans and the Revolution

Indians viewed the American Revolution with considerable uncertainty. Most tribes ultimately chose to stay out of the war. But many Indians feared that the Revolution would replace a ruling group in which they had developed at least some measure of trust (the British, who had tried to limit the expansion of white settlement into tribal land) with one they considered generally hostile to them (the Patriots, who had spearheaded the expansion). Thus some Indians, among them the Iroquois who participated in the Burgoyne campaign in upper New York, chose to join the English cause. Still others took advantage of the conflict to launch attacks of their own.

In the western Carolinas and Virginia, Cherokee led by Chief Dragging Canoe launched a series of attacks on outlying white settlements in the summer of 1776. Patriot militias responded in great force, ravaging Cherokee lands and forcing the chief and many of his followers to flee west across the Tennessee River. Those Cherokee who remained behind agreed to a new treaty by which they gave up still more land. Some Iroquois, despite the setbacks at Oriskany, continued to wage war against Americans in the West and caused widespread destruction in agricultural areas of New York and Pennsylvania whose crops were of crucial importance to the Patriot cause. The retaliating American armies inflicted heavy losses on the Indians, but the attacks continued throughout the war.

In the end, the Revolution generally weakened the position of Native Americans in several ways. The Patriot victory increased white demand for western lands. Many whites resented the assistance such nations as the Mohawk had given the British and insisted on treating them as conquered people. Others drew from the Revolution a paternalistic view of the tribes that was only slightly less dangerous to the Native Americans than open hostility. Thomas Jefferson, for example, came to view the Indians as "noble savages," uncivilized in their present state but redeemable if they were willing to adapt to the norms of white society.

Women's Rights and Women's Roles

The long Revolutionary War had a profound effect on American women. The departure of so many men to fight in the Patriot armies left wives, mothers, sisters, and daughters in charge of farms and businesses. Often, women handled these tasks with great success. But in other cases, inexperience, inflation, the unavailability of male labor, or the threat of enemy troops led to failure. Some women whose husbands or fathers were called away to war did not have even a farm or shop to fall back on. Cities and towns had significant populations of impoverished women, who on occasion led protests against price increases or rioted and looted for food. On several other occasions (in New Jersey and Staten Island), women launched attacks on occupying British troops, whom they were required to house and feed at considerable expense.

Not all women stayed behind when the men went off to war. Sometimes by choice, more often by necessity, women flocked to the camps of the Patriot armies to join their male relatives. These female "camp followers" increased army morale and provided a ready source of volunteers to do cooking, laundry, nursing, and other necessary tasks. In the rough environment of the camps, traditional gender distinctions proved difficult to maintain. Considerable numbers of women became involved, at least intermittently, in combat—including the legendary "Molly Pitcher" (so named because she carried pitchers of water to soldiers on the battlefield), who watched her husband fall during one encounter and immediately took his place at a gun. A few women even disguised themselves as men so as to be able to fight.

The emphasis on liberty and the "rights of man" led some women to begin to question their own position in society. "By the way," Abigail Adams wrote to her husband John Adams in 1776, "in the new code of laws which I suppose it will be necessary for you to make, I desire you would remember the ladies and be more generous and favorable to them than your ancestors. Do not put such unlimited power into the hands of the Husbands." Adams was calling for a relatively modest expansion of women's rights: for new protections against abusive and tyrannical men. A few women, however, went further. Judith Sargent Murray, one of the leading essayists of the late eighteenth century, wrote in 1779 that women's minds were as good as those of men and that girls as well as boys therefore deserved access to education.

But little changed as a result. Under English common law, an unmarried woman had some legal rights, but a married woman had virtually no rights at all. Everything she owned and everything she earned belonged to her husband. Because she had no property rights, she could not engage in any legal transactions on her own (buying or selling, suing or being sued, writing wills). She could not vote. She had no legal authority over her children. Nor could she initiate a divorce; that, too, was a right reserved almost exclusively to men. After the Revolution, it did become easier for women to obtain divorces in a few states. In New Jersey, women obtained the right to vote (although that right was repealed in 1807). Otherwise, there were few advances and some setbacks—including the loss of the right of widows to regain their dowries from their husbands' estates. The Revolution, in other words, did not really challenge, but actually confirmed and strengthened, the patriarchal legal system. Abigail Adams, in the same letter in which she asked her husband to "remember the ladies," also urged him to "regard us then as Beings placed by providence under your protection and in imitation of the Supreme Being make use of that power only for our happiness."

But the Revolution did encourage people of both sexes to reevaluate the contribution of women to the family and society. As the new republic searched for a cultural identity for itself, it attributed a higher value to the role of women as mothers. The new nation was, many Americans liked to believe, producing a new kind of citizen, steeped in the principles of liberty. Mothers had a particularly important task, therefore, in instructing their children in the virtues that the republican citizenry now was expected to possess.

The War Economy

The Revolution also produced important changes in the structure of the American economy. After more than a century of dependence on the British imperial system, American commerce suddenly found itself on its own. English ships no longer protected American vessels, but tried to drive them from the seas. British imperial ports—including those in England itself—were closed to American trade. But this disruption in traditional economic patterns served in the long run to strengthen the American economy. The restrictive rules of empire had inhibited American exploration of many markets. Now, enterprising merchants in New England and elsewhere began to develop new commerce in the Caribbean and South America. By the mid-1780s, American merchants were also developing an important trade with Asia. There was also a substantial increase in trade among the American states.

When English imports to America were cut off—first by the prewar boycott, then by the war itself—there were desperate efforts throughout the states to stimulate domestic manufacturing of certain necessities. No great industrial expansion resulted, but there was a modest increase in production and an even greater increase in expectations.

THE CREATION OF STATE GOVERNMENTS

At the same time that Americans were struggling to win their independence on the battlefield, they were also struggling to create new institutions of government to replace the British system they had repudiated. That struggle continued for more than fifteen years, but its most important phase occurred during the war itself, at the state level.

The Assumptions of Republicanism

If Americans agreed on nothing else when they began to build new governments for themselves, they agreed that those governments would be republican. To them, that meant a political system in which all power came from the people, rather than from some supreme authority (such as a king). The success of such a government depended on the nature of its citizenry. If the population consisted of sturdy, independent property owners imbued with civic virtue, then the republic could survive. If it consisted of a few powerful aristocrats and a great mass of dependent workers, then it would be in danger. From the beginning, therefore, the ideal of the small freeholder (the independent landowner) was basic to American political ideology.

Another crucial part of that ideology was the concept of equality. The Declaration of Independence had given voice to that idea in its most ringing phrase: "All men are created equal." It was a belief that stood in direct contrast to the old European assumption of an inherited aristocracy. The innate talents and energies of individuals, not their positions at birth, would determine their roles in society. Some people would inevitably be wealthier and more powerful than others. But all people would have to earn their success. There would be no equality of condition, but there would be equality of opportunity.

In reality, of course, the United States was never a nation in which all citizens were independent property holders. From the beginning, there was a sizable dependent labor force—the white members of which were allowed many of the privileges of citizenship, the black members of which were allowed virtually none. American women remained both politically and economically subordinate. Native Americans were systematically exploited and displaced. Nor was there ever full equality of opportunity. American society was more open and more fluid than that of most European nations, but the condition of a person's birth was almost always a crucial determinant of success.

Nevertheless, in embracing the assumptions of republicanism, Americans were adopting a powerful, even revolutionary, ideology, and their experiment in statecraft became a model for many other countries. It made the United States for a time the most admired and studied nation on earth.

The First State Constitutions

Two states—Connecticut and Rhode Island—already had governments that were republican in all but name even before the Revolution. They simply deleted references to England and the king from their charters and adopted them as constitutions. The other eleven states, however, produced new documents.

The first and perhaps most basic decision was that the constitutions were to be written down, because Americans believed the vagueness of England's unwritten constitution had produced corruption. The second decision was that the power of the executive, which Americans believed had grown too great in England, must be limited. Pennsylvania eliminated the executive altogether. Most other states inserted provisions limiting the power of governors over appointments, reducing or eliminating their right to veto bills, and preventing them from dismissing the legislature. Most important, every state forbade the governor or any other executive officer from holding a seat in the legislature, thus ensuring that, unlike in England, the two branches of government would remain wholly separate.

But the new constitutions did not embrace direct popular rule. In Georgia and Pennsylvania, the legislature consisted of one popularly elected house. But in every other state, there was an upper and a lower chamber, and in most cases, the upper chamber was designed to represent the "higher orders" of society. There were property requirements for voters—some modest, some substantial—in all states.

Revising State Governments

By the late 1770s, Americans were growing concerned about the apparent divisiveness and instability of their new state governments, which were having trouble accomplishing anything at all. Many believed the problem was one of too much democracy. As a result, most of the states began to revise their constitutions to limit popular power. Massachusetts was the first to act on the new concerns. By waiting until 1780 to ratify its first constitution, Massachusetts allowed these changing ideas to shape its government, and the state produced a constitution that served as a model for others.

Two changes in particular differentiated the Massachusetts and later constitutions from the earlier ones. The first was a change in the process of constitution writing itself. Most of the first documents had been written by state legislatures and thus could easily be amended (or violated) by them. Massachusetts, and later other states, sought a way to protect the constitutions from ordinary politics and created the constitutional convention: a special assembly of the people that would meet only for the purpose of writing the constitution and that would never (except under extraordinary circumstances) meet again.

The second change was a significant strengthening of the executive, a reaction to what many believed was the instability of the original state governments that had weak governors. The 1780 Massachusetts constitution made the governor one of the strongest in any state. He was to be elected directly by the people; he was to have a fixed salary (in other words, he would not be dependent on the good will of the legislature each year for his wages); he would have significant appointment powers and a veto over legislation. Other states followed. Those with weak or nonexistent upper houses strengthened or created them. Most increased the powers of the governor. Pennsylvania, which had no executive at all at first, now produced a strong one. By the late 1780s, almost every state had either revised its constitution or drawn up an entirely new one in an effort to produce stability in government.

Toleration and Slavery

The new states moved far in the direction of complete religious freedom. Most Americans continued to believe that religion should play some role in government, but they did not wish to give special privileges to any particular denomination. The privileges that churches had once enjoyed were now largely stripped away. In 1786, Virginia enacted the Statute of Religious Liberty, written by Thomas Jefferson, which called for the complete separation of church and state.

More difficult to resolve was the question of slavery. In areas where slavery was already weak—in New England, where there had never been many slaves, and in Pennsylvania, where the Quakers opposed slavery—it was abolished. Even in the South, there were some pressures to amend or even eliminate the institution; every state but South Carolina and Georgia prohibited further importation of slaves from abroad, and South Carolina banned the slave trade during the war. Virginia passed a law encouraging manumission (the freeing of slaves).

Nevertheless, slavery survived in all the southern and border states. There were several reasons: racist assumptions among whites about the inferiority of blacks; the enormous economic investments many white southerners had in their slaves; and the inability of even such men as Washington and Jefferson, who had moral misgivings about slavery, to envision any alternative to it. If slavery were abolished, what would happen to the black people in America? Few whites believed blacks could be integrated into American society as equals. In maintaining slavery, Jefferson once remarked, Americans were holding a "wolf by the ears." However unappealing it was to hold on to it, letting go would be even worse.

THE SEARCH FOR A NATIONAL GOVERNMENT

Americans were much quicker to agree on state institutions than they were on the structure of their national government. At first, most believed that the central government should remain a relatively weak and unimportant force and that each state would be virtually a sovereign nation. It was in response to such ideas that the Articles of Confederation emerged.

The Confederation

The Articles of Confederation, which the Continental Congress had adopted in 1777, provided for a national government much like the one already in place. Congress remained the central—indeed the only—institution of national authority. Its powers expanded to give it authority to conduct wars and foreign relations and to appropriate, borrow, and issue money. But it did not have power to regulate trade, draft troops, or levy taxes directly on the people. For troops and taxes it had to make

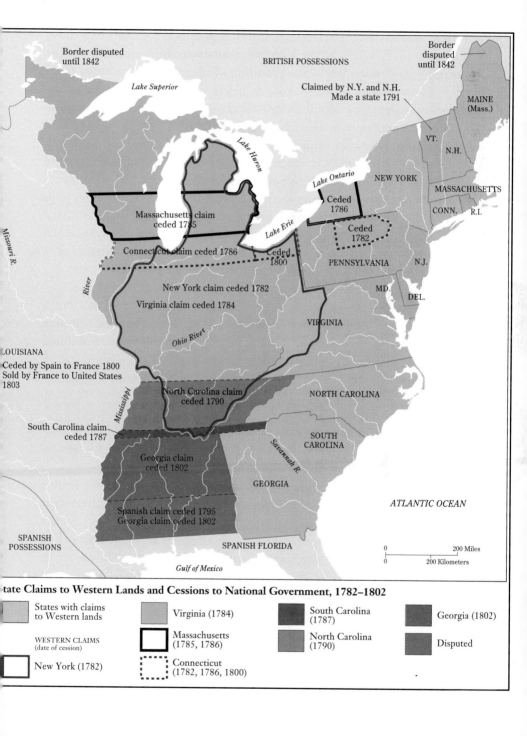

Border disputed until 1842

BRITISH POSSESSIONS

Border disputed until 1842

Lake Superior

Lake Huron

Lake Ontario

Claimed by N.Y. and N.H. Made a state 1791

MAINE (Mass.)

VT.

N.H.

NEW YORK

MASSACHUSETTS

Ceded 1786

Massachusetts claim ceded 1785

CONN.

R.I.

Lake Erie

Connecticut claim ceded 1786

Ceded 1782

Ceded 1800

PENNSYLVANIA

N.J.

New York claim ceded 1782

MD.

DEL.

Virginia claim ceded 1784

Ohio River

VIRGINIA

Missouri R.

River

LOUISIANA
Ceded by Spain to France 1800
Sold by France to United States
1803

North Carolina claim ceded 1790

NORTH CAROLINA

Mississippi

South Carolina claim ceded 1787

SOUTH CAROLINA

Savannah R.

Georgia claim ceded 1802

GEORGIA

ATLANTIC OCEAN

Spanish claim ceded 1795
Georgia claim ceded 1802

SPANISH POSSESSIONS

SPANISH FLORIDA

| 0 | | 200 Miles |
| 0 | | 200 Kilometers |

Gulf of Mexico

tate Claims to Western Lands and Cessions to National Government, 1782–1802

States with claims to Western lands

WESTERN CLAIMS
(date of cession)

New York (1782)

Virginia (1784)

Massachusetts (1785, 1786)

Connecticut (1782, 1786, 1800)

South Carolina (1787)

North Carolina (1790)

Georgia (1802)

Disputed

formal requests to the state legislatures, which could—and often did—refuse them. There was no separate executive; the "president of the United States" was merely the presiding officer at the sessions of Congress. Each state had a single vote in Congress, and at least nine of the states had to approve any important measure. All thirteen state legislatures had to approve any amendment of the Articles.

During the process of ratifying the Articles of Confederation (which required approval by all thirteen states), broad disagreements over the plan became evident. The small states had insisted on equal state representation, but the larger states wanted representation to be based on population. The smaller states prevailed on that issue. More important, the states claiming western lands wished to keep them, but the rest of the states demanded that all such territory be turned over to the national government. New York and Virginia had to give up their western claims before the Articles were finally approved. They went into effect in 1781.

The Confederation, which existed from 1781 until 1789, was not a complete failure, but it was far from a success. It lacked adequate powers to deal with interstate issues or to enforce its will on the states, and it had little stature in the eyes of the world.

Diplomatic Failures

Evidence of the low esteem in which the rest of the world held the Confederation was its difficulty in persuading Great Britain (and to a lesser extent Spain) to live up to the terms of the peace treaty of 1783.

The British had promised to evacuate American territory, but British forces continued to occupy a string of frontier posts along the Great Lakes within the United States. Nor did the British honor their agreement to make restitution to slaveowners whose slaves the British army had confiscated. There were also disputes over the northeastern boundary of the new nation and over the border between the United States and Florida, which Britain had ceded back to Spain in the treaty. Most American trade remained within the British Empire, and Americans wanted full access to British markets; England, however, placed sharp restrictions on that access.

In 1784, Congress sent John Adams as minister to London to resolve these differences, but Adams made no headway with the English, who were never sure whether he represented a single nation or thirteen different ones. Throughout the 1780s, the British government refused even to send a diplomatic minister to the American capital.

Confederation diplomats agreed to a treaty with Spain in 1786. The Spanish accepted the American interpretation of the Florida boundary. In return the Americans recognized the Spanish possessions in North America and accepted limits on the right of United States vessels to navigate the Mississippi for twenty years. Southern states, incensed at the idea of giving up their access to the Mississippi, blocked ratification, further weakening the government's standing in world diplomacy.

The Confederation and the Northwest

The Confederation's most important accomplishment was its resolution of some of the controversies involving the western lands. When the Revolution began, only a few thousand whites lived west of the Appalachian divide; by 1790 their numbers had increased to 120,000. The Confederation had to find a way to include these new settlements in the political structure of the new nation. The landed states began to yield their claims to the national government in 1781, and by 1784 the Confederation controlled enough land to permit Congress to begin making policy for the national domain.

The Ordinance of 1784, based on a proposal by Thomas Jefferson, divided the western territory into ten self-governing districts, each of which could petition Congress for statehood when its population equaled the number of free inhabitants of the smallest existing state. Then, in the Ordinance of 1785, Congress created a system for surveying and selling the western lands. The territory north of the Ohio River was to be surveyed and marked off into neat rectangular townships, each divided into thirty-six identical sections. In every township four sections were to be set aside for the United States; the revenue from the sale of one of the other sections was to support creation of a public school. Sections were to be sold at auction for no less than one dollar an acre.

The organization of the western territories established a pattern that would dominate much of the landscape of the United States for centuries to come: the grid. The precise rectangular pattern imposed on the Northwest Territory became a model for all subsequent land policies of the federal government and for many other planning decisions in states and localities. The grid also became characteristic of the layout of many American cities, among them New York and Philadelphia. The grid had many advantages. It eliminated the uncertainty about property borders that earlier, more informal land systems had produced. It sped the development of the western lands by making land ownership simple and

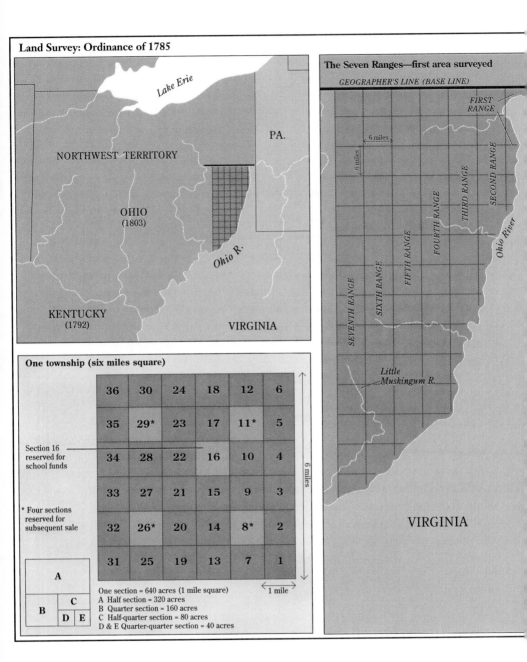

Land Survey: Ordinance of 1785

NORTHWEST TERRITORY

OHIO (1803)

PA.

KENTUCKY (1792)

VIRGINIA

Lake Erie

Ohio R.

One township (six miles square)

36	30	24	18	12	6
35	29*	23	17	11*	5
34	28	22	16	10	4
33	27	21	15	9	3
32	26*	20	14	8*	2
31	25	19	13	7	1

Section 16 reserved for school funds

* Four sections reserved for subsequent sale

6 miles

1 mile

A		
B	C	
	D	E

One section = 640 acres (1 mile square)
A Half section = 320 acres
B Quarter section = 160 acres
C Half-quarter section = 80 acres
D & E Quarter-quarter section = 40 acres

The Seven Ranges—first area surveyed

GEOGRAPHER'S LINE (BASE LINE)

FIRST RANGE

SECOND RANGE

THIRD RANGE

FOURTH RANGE

FIFTH RANGE

SIXTH RANGE

SEVENTH RANGE

6 miles

6 miles

Ohio River

Little Muskingum R.

VIRGINIA

understandable. But it also encouraged a dispersed form of settlement—with each farm family separated from its neighbors—that made the formation of community more difficult; and it led farmers to arrange their fields in ways that did not necessarily make the best use of the local topography. Whatever its consequences, however, the 1785 Ordinance made a dramatic and indelible mark on the American landscape.

The original ordinances proved highly favorable to land speculators and less so to ordinary settlers, many of whom could not afford the price of the land. Congress compounded the problem by selling much of the best land to the Ohio and Scioto Companies before making it available to anyone else. Criticism of these policies led to the passage in 1787 of another law governing western settlement—legislation that became known as the "Northwest Ordinance." The 1787 Ordinance abandoned the ten districts established in 1784 and created a single Northwest Territory out of the lands north of the Ohio; the territory could be divided subsequently into between three and five territories. It also specified a population of 60,000 as a minimum for statehood, guaranteed freedom of religion and the right to trial by jury to residents of the Northwest, and prohibited slavery throughout the territory.

The western lands south of the Ohio River received less attention from Congress, and development was more chaotic there. The region that became Kentucky and Tennessee developed rapidly in the late 1770s, and in the 1780s speculators and settlers began setting up governments and asking for recognition as states. The Confederation Congress was never able to resolve the conflicting claims in that region successfully.

Indians and the Western Lands

On paper at least, the western land policies of the Confederation created a system that brought order and stability to the process of white settlement in the Northwest. But in reality, order and stability came slowly and at great cost, because much of the land the Confederation was neatly subdividing and offering for sale consisted of territory claimed by the Indians of the region. Congress tried to resolve that problem in 1784, 1785, and 1786 by persuading Iroquois, Choctaw, Chickasaw, and Cherokee leaders to sign treaties ceding substantial western lands in the North and South to the United States. But those agreements proved ineffective. In 1786, the leadership of the Iroquois Confederacy repudiated the treaty it had signed two years earlier and threatened to attack white settlements in the disputed lands. Other tribes had never really accepted the treaties affecting them and continued to resist white movement into their lands.

Violence between whites and Indians on the Northwest frontier reached a crescendo in the early 1790s. In 1790 and again in 1791, the Miami, led by the famed warrior Little Turtle, defeated United States forces in two major battles near what is now the western border of Ohio; in the second of those battles, on November 4, 1791, 630 white Americans died in fighting at the Wabash River (the greatest military victory Indians had ever or would ever achieve in their battles with whites). Efforts to negotiate a settlement failed because of the Miami's insistence that no treaty was possible unless it forbade white settlement west of the Ohio River. Negotiations did not resume until after General Anthony Wayne led 4,000 soldiers into the Ohio Valley in 1794 and defeated the Indians in the Battle of Fallen Timbers.

A year later, the Miami signed the Treaty of Greenville, ceding substantial new lands to the United States (which was now operating under the Constitution of 1789) in exchange for a formal acknowledgment of their claim to the territory they had managed to retain. This was the first time the new federal government recognized the sovereignty of Indian nations; in doing so, the United States was affirming that Indian lands could be ceded only by the tribes themselves. That hard-won assurance, however, proved a frail protection against the pressure of white expansion westward in later years.

Debts, Taxes, and Daniel Shays

The postwar depression, which lasted from 1784 to 1787, increased the perennial American problem of an inadequate money supply, a problem that weighed particularly heavily on debtors. In dealing with this problem, Congress most clearly demonstrated its weakness.

The Confederation itself had an enormous outstanding debt that it had accumulated during the Revolutionary War, and few means with which to pay it. It had sold war bonds that were now due to be repaid; it owed money to its soldiers; it had substantial debts abroad. But it had no power to tax. It could only make requisitions of the states, and it received only about one-sixth of the money it requisitioned. The fragile new nation was faced with the grim prospect of defaulting on its obligations.

This alarming possibility brought to the fore a group of leaders who would play a crucial role in the shaping of the republic for several decades. Committed nationalists, they sought ways to increase the powers of the central government and to meet its financial obligations. Robert Morris, the head of the Confederation's treasury; Alexander Hamilton, his young

DANIEL SHAYS AND JOB SHATTUCK Shays and Shattuck were the principal leaders of the 1786 uprising of poor Massachusetts farmers demanding relief from their indebtedness. Shattuck led an insurrection in the east, which collapsed when he was captured on November 30. Shays organized the rebellion in the west, which continued until it was finally dispersed by state militia in late February 1787. The following year, state authorities pardoned Shays; even before that, the legislature responded to the rebellion by providing some relief to the impoverished farmers. This drawing is part of a hostile account of the rebellion published in 1787 in a Boston almanac.

protégé; James Madison of Virginia; and others called for a "continental impost"—a 5 percent duty on imported goods to be levied by Congress and used to fund the debt. Many Americans, however, feared that the impost plan would concentrate too much financial power in the hands of Morris and his allies in Philadelphia. Congress failed to approve the impost in 1781 and again in 1783. Angry and discouraged, the nationalists largely withdrew from any active involvement in the Confederation.

The states had war debts, too, and they generally relied on increased taxation to pay them. But poor farmers, already burdened by debt and now burdened again by new taxes, considered such policies unfair, even tyrannical. They demanded that the state governments issue paper currency to increase the money supply and make it easier for them to meet their obligations. Resentment was especially high among farmers in New England, who felt that the states were squeezing them to enrich already wealthy bondholders in Boston and other towns.

Throughout the late 1780s, therefore, mobs of distressed farmers rioted periodically in various parts of New England. Dissidents in the Connecticut Valley and the Berkshire Hills of Massachusetts, many of them Revolutionary veterans, rallied behind Daniel Shays, a former captain in the Continental army. Shays issued a set of demands that included paper

money, tax relief, a moratorium on debts, the relocation of the state capital from Boston to the interior, and the abolition of imprisonment for
debt. During the summer of 1786, the Shaysites concentrated on preventing the collection of debts, private or public, and used force to keep courts
from sitting and sheriffs from selling confiscated property. In Boston,
members of the legislature, including Samuel Adams, denounced Shays
and his men as rebels and traitors. When winter came, the rebels advanced on Springfield, hoping to seize weapons from the arsenal there. An
army of state militiamen, financed by a loan from wealthy merchants, set
out from Boston to confront them. In January 1787, this army met Shays's
band and dispersed his ragged troops.

As a military enterprise, Shays's Rebellion was a failure, although it
produced some concessions to the aggrieved farmers. Shays and his lieu-
tenants, at first sentenced to death, were later pardoned, and Massachusetts offered the protesters some tax relief and a postponement of debt
payments. The rebellion had more important consequences for the future
of the United States, for it added urgency to a movement already gathering support throughout the new nation—the movement to produce a new,
national constitution.

CONCLUSION

Between a small, inconclusive battle on a village green in New England in
1775 and a momentous surrender at Yorktown in 1781, the American people fought a great and terrible war against the mightiest military nation in
the world. No one outside America, and few within it, would have predicted in 1775 that the makeshift armies of the colonies could withstand
the armies and navies of the British empire. But a combination of luck,
brilliance, determination, and timely aid from abroad allowed the patriots,
as they began to call themselves, to make full use of the advantages of
fighting on their home soil and to frustrate British designs time and again.

The war was not just a historic military event. It was also a great political one, for it propelled the colonies to unite, to organize, and—in July
1776—to declare their independence. Having done so, they fought with
even greater determination, defending now not just a set of principles, but
an actual, fledgling nation. By the end of the war, they had created new
governments at both the state and national level and had begun experimenting with new political forms that would distinguish the United States
from any previous nation in history.

The war was also important for its effects on American society—for the way it shook (although never overturned) the existing social order; for the way it caused women to question (although seldom openly to challenge) their place in society; and for the way it spread notions of liberty and freedom throughout a society that in the past had often been rigidly hierarchiacal and highly deferential. Even African-American slaves absorbed some of the ideas of the Revolution, although it would be many years before they would be in any position to make very much use of them.

Victory in the American Revolution solved many of the problems of the new nation, but it also produced others. What should the United States do about its relations with the Indians and with its neighbors to the north and south? What should it do about the distribution of western lands? What should it do about slavery? How should it balance its commitment to liberty with its need for order? These questions bedeviled the new national government in its first years of existence and ultimately led Americans to create a new polical order.

FOR FURTHER REFERENCE

Suggested Readings

Robert Middlekauff, *The Glorious Cause: The American Revolution, 1763-1789* (1985) and Edward Countryman, *The American Revolution* (1985) are useful overviews. Gordon Wood, *The Radicalism of the American Revolution* (1992) emphasizes the profound political change that the Revolution entailed. Charles Royster, *A Revolutionary People at War: The Continental Army and American Character* (1979) suggests the importance of the military service for American men. Mary Beth Norton, *Libertys Daughters: The Revolutionary Experience of American Women, 1750–1800* (1980) demonstrates that the Revolution had a significant impact on the lives of American women as well, and Linda K. Kerber, *Women of the Republic: Intellect and Ideology in Revolutionary America* (1980) shows the impact of the Revolutionary era on the assumptions and roles of women. Eric Foner, *Tom Paine and Revolutionary America* (1976) connects the leading pamphleteer of the Revolution with urban radicalism in Philadelphia. Pauline Maier, *American Scripture* (1997) is a penetratng study of the making of the Declaration of Independence, and of its impact on subsequent generations of Americans. Collin Calloway, *The American Revolution in Indian Country* (1995) is a new and important study on an often neglected aspect of the war. Sylvia R. Frey, *Water from the Rock: Black Resistance in a Revolutionary Age* (1991) argues that the American Revolution was a major turning point in the history of slavery in the American South. John Shy, *A People Numerous and Armed* (1976) and *The American Revolution* (1973) are excellent military histories. Bernard Bailyn, *The Ordeal of Thomas Hutchinson* (1974) is a classic study of a Loyalist before and during the Revolution. Jack N. Rakove, *The Beginning of National Politics* (1979) is a fine study of the United States before the Constitution.

Films

(The best source for information on how to find these and other films is *Bowker's Complete Video Directory*—3 volumes.) *Liberty* (1997) is a compelling six-hour documentary history of the American Revolution from its early origins in the 1760s. *The American Revolution Collector's Edition* is a comprehensive (300 minutes) and riveting documentary produced by the Art & Entertainment Network. *The American Story, No. 2: Declaring Independence* (1985) features the writing, consequences, and significance of the Declaration of Independence. *The Early Campaigns of Francis Marion and the Loyalists in the South* explores key battles of the American Revolution in the southern colonies. *Thomas Jefferson: Philosopher of Freedom* (1996) is a biography of America's leading Revolutionary from the Arts & Entertainment Network. *The Battle of Yorktown* (1983) examines the climactic battles of the American Revolution.

Internet Resources

Internet websites containing historical material relevant to the subjects discussed in this chapter can be reached through the McGraw-Hill history site at www.mhhe.com/socscience/history/usa/link/linktop.htm.

CHAPTER SIX

The Constitution and the New Republic

Framing a New Government ～ *Adoption and Adaptation*
Federalists and Republicans ～ *Establishing National Sovereignty*
The Downfall of the Federalists

B Y THE LATE 1780s, many Americans had grown dissatisfied with the Confederation. It was ridden with factions, unable to deal effectively with economic problems, and frighteningly powerless in the face of Shays's Rebellion. A decade earlier, Americans had deliberately avoided creating a strong national government. Now they reconsidered. In 1787, in a burst of great political creativity, the nation produced a new constitution and a new, much more powerful government with three independent branches. The government the Constitution produced has survived for more than two centuries as one of the stablest and most successful in the world. Yet the adoption of the Constitution did not complete the creation of the republic. For, while most Americans agreed that the Constitution was a nearly perfect document, they disagreed—at times fundamentally—on what that document meant.

FRAMING A NEW GOVERNMENT

The Confederation Congress had become so unpopular and ineffectual by the mid-1780s that it began to lead an almost waiflike existence. In 1783, its members timidly withdrew from Philadelphia to escape army veterans demanding their back pay. They took refuge for a while in Princeton, New Jersey, then moved on to Annapolis, and in 1785 settled in New York. Delegates were often scarce. Only with great difficulty could Congress produce a quorum to ratify the treaty with Great Britain ending the Revolutionary

155

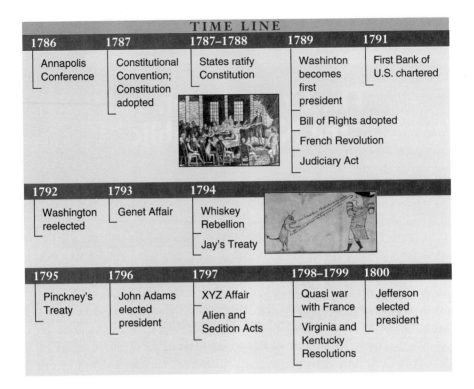

TIME LINE

1786	1787	1787–1788	1789	1791
Annapolis Conference	Constitutional Convention; Constitution adopted	States ratify Constitution	Washinton becomes first president Bill of Rights adopted French Revolution Judiciary Act	First Bank of U.S. chartered

1792	1793	1794
Washington reelected	Genet Affair	Whiskey Rebellion Jay's Treaty

1795	1796	1797	1798–1799	1800
Pinckney's Treaty	John Adams elected president	XYZ Affair Alien and Sedition Acts	Quasi war with France Virginia and Kentucky Resolutions	Jefferson elected president

War. Only eight state delegations voted on the Confederation's most important piece of legislation, the Northwest Ordinance.

Advocates of Reform

In the 1780s, some of the wealthiest and most powerful groups in the population began to clamor for a genuinely national government capable of dealing more effectively with the country's problems. By 1786, such demands had grown so intense that even defenders of the existing system reluctantly agreed that the government needed strengthening at its weakest point—its lack of power to tax.

The most resourceful advocate of a stronger national government was Alexander Hamilton, the illegitimate son of a Scottish merchant in the West Indies, who had become a successful New York lawyer and had once served as an aide to George Washington. Hamilton now called for a national convention to overhaul the Articles of Confederation. He found an important ally in James Madison of Virginia, who persuaded the Virginia legislature to convene an interstate conference on commercial questions.

Only five states sent delegates to the meeting, which took place at Annapolis, Maryland, in 1786; but the conference approved a proposal drafted by Hamilton for a convention of special delegates from all the states to meet in Philadelphia the next year and consider ways to "render the constitution of the Federal government adequate to the exigencies of the union."

At first there seemed little reason to believe the Philadelphia convention would attract any more delegates than had the Annapolis meeting. Then, early in 1787, the news of Shays's Rebellion spread throughout the nation, alarming many previously apathetic leaders. Most important of all, the rebellion aroused George Washington, who promptly made plans to travel to Philadelphia for the Constitutional Convention. His support gave the meeting wide credibility.

A Divided Convention

Fifty-five men, representing all the states except Rhode Island, attended one or more sessions of the convention that sat in the Philadelphia State House from May to September 1787. These "Founding Fathers," as they became known much later, were relatively young men; the average age was forty-four, and only one delegate (Benjamin Franklin, then eighty-one) was genuinely aged. They were well educated by the standards of their time. Most were relatively wealthy property owners, and many feared what one of them called the "turbulence and follies" of democracy. Yet all were also products of the American Revolution and retained the Revolutionary suspicion of concentrated power.

The convention unanimously chose Washington to preside over its sessions and then closed its business to the public and the press. (If James Madison had not kept a private diary chronicling the proceedings, historians might know little about what happened in Philadelphia.) It then ruled that each state delegation would have a single vote and that major decisions would require not unanimity, as they did in Congress, but a simple majority. Almost all the delegates agreed that the United States needed a stronger central government. But there agreement ended.

Virginia, the largest state in population, sent a well-prepared delegation to Philadelphia led by James Madison (thirty-six years old), who had devised in some detail a plan for a new "national" government. The Virginia Plan shaped the agenda of the convention from the moment Edmund Randolph of Virginia opened the debate by proposing "a national government ought to be established, consisting of a supreme Legislative, Executive, and Judiciary." Even that brief description outlined a government very

THE CONVENTION AT PHILADELPHIA This engraving of delegates at work, created in 1823, is one of countless efforts in the early nineteenth century to imaginatively re-create the great Constitutional Convention in Philadelphia in 1787. It appeared in an early *History of the United States of America* by Rev. Charles A. Goodrich.

different from the Confederation, which had no executive and no independent judiciary. But the delegates were so committed to fundamental reform that they approved the resolution after only brief debate.

There was less agreement about the details of Madison's Virginia Plan. It called for a national legislature of two houses. In the lower house, states would be represented in proportion to their population; thus the largest state (Virginia) would have about ten times as many representatives as the smallest (Delaware). Members of the upper house were to be elected by the lower house under no rigid system of representation; thus some of the smaller states might at times have no members at all in the upper house.

The proposal aroused immediate opposition among delegates from the smaller states. William Paterson of New Jersey offered an alternative (the New Jersey Plan) that would have retained the essence of the existing system with its one-house legislature in which all states had equal representation, but which would have given Congress expanded powers to tax and to regulate commerce. The convention rejected Paterson's proposal, but supporters of the Virginia Plan now realized they would have to make concessions to the small states if the delegations were ever to agree. They agreed to permit members of the upper house to be elected by the state legislatures, ensuring that every state would be represented.

Many questions remained unresolved. Among the most important was the question of slavery. There was no serious discussion of abolishing slavery during the convention. But other issues were debated heatedly. Would slaves be counted as part of the population in determining representation in Congress? Or would they be considered property, not entitled to representation? Delegates from the states with large slave populations wanted to have it both ways. They argued that slaves should be considered persons in determining representation but as property if the new government levied taxes on the states on the basis of population. Representatives from states where slavery had disappeared or was expected soon to disappear argued that slaves should be included in calculating taxation but not representation.

Compromise

The delegates argued for weeks. By the end of June, as both temperature and tempers rose to uncomfortable heights, the convention seemed in danger of collapsing. But the delegates refused to give up (partly because of the patient urging of Benjamin Franklin). Finally, on July 2, the convention created a "grand committee," chaired by Franklin and with one delegate from each state, which produced a proposal that became the basis of the "Great Compromise." It called for a two-house legislature. In the lower house, the states would be represented on the basis of population; each slave would be counted as three-fifths of a free person in determining the basis for both representation and direct taxation. In the upper house, the states would be represented equally with two members apiece. On July 16, 1787, the convention voted to accept the compromise.

In the next few weeks, the convention agreed to another important compromise on the explosive issue of slavery. To placate southern delegates, who feared the new government would interfere with slavery, the convention agreed to bar the new government from stopping the slave trade for twenty years.

Some significant issues remained unaddressed. Most important was the absence of a list of individual rights, which would restrain the powers of the national government in the way that bills of rights restrained the state governments. Madison opposed the idea, arguing that specifying rights that were reserved to the people would, in effect, limit those rights. Others, however, feared that without such protections the national government might abuse its new authority.

The Constitution of 1787

Many people contributed to the creation of the American Constitution, but the most important person in the process was James Madison. Madison had devised the Virginia Plan, from which the final document ultimately emerged, and he did most of the drafting of the Constitution itself. Madison's most important achievement, however, was in helping resolve two important philosophical questions that had served as obstacles to the creation of an effective national government: the question of sovereignty and the question of limiting power.

How could a national government exercise sovereignty concurrently with state governments? Where did ultimate sovereignty lie? The answer, Madison and his contemporaries decided, was that all power, at all levels of government, flowed ultimately from the people. Thus neither the federal government nor the state governments were truly sovereign. All of them derived their authority from below. The opening phrase of the Constitution—"We the people of the United States of America"—is an expression of that belief. The resolution of the problem of sovereignty made possible one of the distinctive features of the Constitution—its division of powers between the national and state governments. The Constitution and the government it created were to be the "supreme law" of the land; no state would have the authority to defy it. At the same time, however, the Constitution left important powers in the hands of the states.

In addition to solving the question of sovereignty, the Constitution produced a distinctive solution to the problem of concentrated authority, which many Americans feared would produce tyranny. Drawing from the ideas of the French philosopher Baron de Montesquieu, most Americans had long believed that the best way to avoid tyranny was to keep government close to the people. A republic must remain confined to a relatively small area; a large nation would breed corruption and despotism because the rulers would be so distant from most of the people that there would be no way to control them.

Madison, however, helped break the grip of these assumptions by arguing that a large republic would be less, not more, likely to produce tyranny because it would contain so many different factions that no single group would ever be able to dominate it. This idea of many centers of power "checking each other" and preventing any single, despotic authority from emerging also helped shape the internal structure of the federal government. The Constitution's most distinctive feature was its "separation of powers" within the government, its creation of "checks and balances" among the legislative, executive, and judicial branches. The forces within the government would constantly compete with (and often frustrate) one another. Congress would have two chambers, each checking the other, since both would have to agree before any law could be passed. The president would have the power to veto acts of Congress. The federal courts would be protected from both the executive and the legislature, because judges, once appointed by the president and confirmed by the Senate, would serve for life.

The "federal" structure of the government was designed to protect the United States from the kind of despotism that Americans believed had emerged in England. But it was also designed to protect the nation from another kind of despotism: the tyranny of the people. Shays's Rebellion, most of the founders believed, had been only one example of what could happen if a nation did not defend itself against the unchecked exercise of popular will. Thus in the new government, only the members of the House of Representatives would be elected directly by the people. Senators, the president, federal judges—all would be insulated in varying degrees from the public.

On September 17, 1787, thirty-nine delegates signed the Constitution. Benjamin Franklin expressed the feelings of many of them at the end when he said: "Thus I consent, Sir, to this Constitution, because I expect no better, and because I am not sure that it is not the best."

ADOPTION AND ADAPTATION

The delegates at Philadelphia had greatly exceeded their instructions from Congress and the states. Instead of making simple revisions in the Articles of Confederation, they had produced a plan for a completely different form of government. They feared that the Constitution would not be ratified under the rules of the Articles of Confederation, which required unanimous approval by the state legislatures. So the convention changed the rules, proposing that the new government come into being when nine of the thirteen states ratified the Constitution and recommending that state conventions, not state legislatures, be called to ratify it.

Federalists and Antifederalists

The Congress in New York, demoralized and overshadowed by the events in Philadelphia, passively accepted the convention's work and submitted it to the states for approval. All the state legislatures except Rhode Island elected delegates to ratifying conventions, most of which began meeting in early 1788. Even before the ratifying conventions adjourned, however, a

great national debate on the new Constitution had begun—in the state legislatures, in public meetings, in newspapers, and in ordinary conversations.

Supporters of the Constitution had a number of advantages. They
were better organized. They had the support of the two most eminent men
in America, Franklin and Washington. And they seized an appealing label
for themselves: "Federalists"—a term that opponents of centralization had
once used to describe themselves—thus implying that they were less committed to a "nationalist" government than in fact they were. The Federalists also had the support of the ablest political philosophers of their time:
Alexander Hamilton, James Madison, and John Jay. Those three men,
under the joint pseudonym "Publius," wrote a series of essays—widely
published in newspapers throughout the nation—explaining the meaning
and virtues of the Constitution. The essays were later issued as a book, and
they are known today as *The Federalist Papers*. They are among the greatest
American contributions to political theory.

The Federalists called their critics "Antifederalists," which suggested
that their rivals had nothing to offer except opposition. But the Antifederalists, too, were represented by distinguished leaders of the Revolution,
among them Patrick Henry and Samuel Adams. And they had serious and
intelligent arguments of their own. They saw themselves as the defenders of
the true principles of the Revolution. The Constitution, they believed,
would betray those principles by establishing a strong, potentially tyrannical, center of power in the new national government. The new government,
they claimed, would increase taxes, weaken the states, wield dictatorial powers, favor the "well-born" over the common people, and abolish individual
liberty. But their biggest complaint was that the Constitution lacked a bill of
rights. No government could be trusted to protect the liberties of its citizens, they argued. Only by enumerating the natural rights of the people
could there be any certainty that those rights would be protected.

Despite the efforts of the Antifederalists, ratification proceeded
quickly during the winter of 1787–1788. The Delaware convention was
the first to act. It ratified the Constitution unanimously, as did New Jersey
and Georgia. New Hampshire ratified the document in June 1788—the
ninth state to do so. It was now theoretically possible for the Constitution
to go into effect. A new government could not hope to succeed, however,
without Virginia and New York, whose conventions remained closely divided. But by the end of June, first Virginia and then New York had consented to the Constitution by narrow margins—on the assumption that a
bill of rights would be added in the form of amendments to the Constitu-

CELEBRATING THE CONSTITUTION Perhaps because opposition to the Constitution had been so intense, its champions staged elaborate celebrations at the time of ratification in an effort to enhance its legitimacy. In 1788, supporters of the constitution organized an elaborate parade down Wall Street, which included the ship on wheels (representing the "ship of state") pictured here. Alexander Hamilton, whose name is emblazoned on the ship's banners, was New York's leading advocate of the Constitution.

tion. North Carolina's convention adjourned without taking action, waiting to see what happened to the amendments. Rhode Island did not even consider ratification.

Completing the Structure

The first elections under the Constitution were held in the early months of 1789. Almost all the newly elected members of Congress had favored ratification, and many had served as delegates to the Philadelphia convention. There was never any doubt about who would be the first president. George Washington had presided at the Constitutional Convention, and many who had favored ratification did so only because they expected him to preside over the new government as well. Washington received the votes of all the presidential electors. John Adams, a leading Federalist, became vice president. After a journey from his estate at Mount Vernon, Virginia, marked by elaborate celebrations along the way, Washington was inaugurated in New York on April 30, 1789.

The first Congress served in many ways as a continuation of the Constitutional Convention, because its principal responsibility was filling in the various gaps in the Constitution. Its most important task was drafting a bill of rights. By early 1789, even Madison had come to agree that some sort of bill of rights would be essential to legitimize the new government in the eyes of its opponents. On September 25, 1789, Congress approved twelve amendments, ten of which were ratified by the states by the end of 1791. These first ten amendments to the Constitution comprise what we know as the Bill of Rights. Nine of them placed limitations on Congress by forbidding it to infringe on certain fundamental rights: freedom of religion, speech, and the press; immunity from arbitrary arrest; trial by jury; and others. The Tenth Amendment reserved to the states all powers except those specifically withheld from them or delegated to the federal government.

On the subject of federal courts, the Constitution said only: "The judicial power of the United States shall be vested in one Supreme Court, and in such inferior courts as the Congress may from time to time ordain and establish." It was left to Congress to determine the number of Supreme Court judges to be appointed and the kinds of lower courts to be organized. In the Judiciary Act of 1789, Congress provided for a Supreme Court of six members and a system of lower district courts and courts of appeal. In the same act, Congress gave the Supreme Court the power to make the final decision in cases involving the constitutionality of state laws.

The Constitution referred indirectly to executive departments but did not specify which ones or how many there should be. The first Congress created three such departments—state, treasury, and war—and also established the offices of the attorney general and postmaster general. To the office of secretary of the treasury Washington appointed Alexander Hamilton of New York, who at age thirty-two was an acknowledged expert in public finance. For secretary of war he chose a Massachusetts Federalist, General Henry Knox. As attorney general he named Edmund Randolph of Virginia, sponsor of the plan on which the Constitution had been based. As secretary of state he chose another Virginian, Thomas Jefferson.

FEDERALISTS AND REPUBLICANS

The resolution of these initial issues, however, did not resolve the disagreements about the nature of the new government. The framers of the Constitution had dealt with many controversies not by solving them but by papering them over with a series of vague compromises; as a result, the disagreements survived to plague the new government, and the first twelve years under the Constitution produced a politics of unusual acrimony.

At the heart of the controversies of the 1790s was the same basic difference in philosophy that had been at the heart of the debate over the Constitution. On one side stood a powerful group who believed that America required a strong, national government. They envisioned that the country's mission was to become a genuine nation-state, with centralized authority, a complex commercial economy, and a proud standing in world affairs. On the other side stood another group—a minority at first, but one that gained strength during the decade—whose members envisioned a more modest national government. The United States should not, this group believed, aspire to be a highly commercial or urban nation. It should remain predominantly rural and agrarian. The centralizers became known as the Federalists and gravitated to the leadership of Alexander Hamilton. Their opponents acquired the name Republicans and gathered under the leadership of Thomas Jefferson and James Madison.

Hamilton and the Federalists

For twelve years, the Federalists retained firm control of the new government. That was in part because George Washington had always envisioned a strong national government and as president did little to stop those attempting to create one. But the president, Washington believed, should stand above political controversies, and so he avoided personal involvement in the deliberations of Congress. As a result, the dominant figure in his administration became Alexander Hamilton, who exerted more influence than anyone else on domestic and foreign policy. Of all the national leaders of his time, Hamilton was one of the most aristocratic in personal tastes and political philosophy; he believed that a stable and effective government required an elite ruling class. Thus the new government needed the support of the wealthy and powerful; and to get that, it needed to give elites a stake in its success. Hamilton proposed, therefore, that the existing public debt be "funded": that the various certificates of indebtedness that the old Congress had issued during and after the Revolution—many of them now in the possession of wealthy speculators—be called in and exchanged for interest-bearing bonds. He also recommended that the States' Revolutionary debts be "assumed" (taken over by the federal government) to cause state bondholders also to look to the central government for eventual payment. Hamilton did not envision paying off and thus eliminating the debt; he wanted to create a permanent national debt, with new bonds being issued as old ones were paid off. The result, he believed, would be that the wealthy classes, who were the most likely to lend money to the government, would always have a reason to want the government to survive.

Hamilton also wanted to create a national bank. It would provide loans and currency to businesses. It would give the government a safe place for the deposit of federal funds. It would facilitate the collection of taxes and the disbursement of the government's expenditures. And it would provide a stable center to the nation's small and feeble banking system. The bank would be chartered by the federal government and would have a monopoly of the government's own banking business, but much of its capital would come from private investors.

The funding and assumption of debts would require new sources of revenue for the national government. Hamilton recommended two kinds of taxes to complement the receipts anticipated from the sales of public land. One was an excise tax on alcoholic beverages, a tax that would be most burdensome to the whiskey distillers of the backcountry, especially those in Pennsylvania, Virginia, and North Carolina—small farmers who converted part of their corn and rye crops into whiskey. The other was a tariff on imports, which Hamilton saw not only as a way to raise money but as a way to protect domestic industries from foreign competition. In his famous "Report on Manufactures" of 1791, he outlined a plan for stimulating the growth of industry in the United States and spoke glowingly of the advantages to society of a healthy manufacturing sector.

The Federalists, in short, offered more than a vision of a stable new government. They offered a vision of the sort of nation America should become—a nation with a wealthy, enlightened ruling class, a vigorous, independent commercial economy, and a thriving manufacturing sector; a country able to play a prominent role in world economic affairs.

Enacting the Federalist Program

Few members of Congress objected to Hamilton's plan for funding the national debt, but many did oppose his proposal to exchange new bonds for old certificates of indebtedness on a dollar-for-dollar basis. Many of the original holders—farmers and merchants who had sold goods to the Continental army, soldiers who had received bonds as payment for their service—had been forced to sell during the hard times of the 1780s to speculators, who had bought them at a fraction of their face value. James Madison, now a representative from Virginia, argued for a plan by which the new bonds would be divided between the original purchasers and the speculators. But Hamilton's allies insisted that such a plan was both impractical and dangerous, that the honor of the government required a literal fulfillment of its earlier promises to pay whoever held the bonds. Congress finally passed the funding bill Hamilton wanted.

Hamilton's proposal that the federal government assume the state debts encountered greater difficulty. Its opponents argued that if the federal government took over the state debts, the states with few debts would have to pay taxes to service the states with large ones. Massachusetts, for example, owed much more money than did Virginia. Only by striking a bargain with the Virginians were Hamilton and his supporters able to win passage of the assumption bill.

The deal involved the location of the national capital. The Virginians wanted to create a new capital near them in the South. Hamilton and Jefferson met and agreed to exchange northern support for placing the capital in the South for Virginia's votes for the assumption bill. The bargain called for the construction of a new capital city on the banks of the Potomac River, which divided Maryland and Virginia, on land to be selected by George Washington. The government would move its operations there by the beginning of the new century.

Hamilton's bank bill produced the most heated debates. Madison, Jefferson, Randolph, and others argued that because the Constitution made no provision for a national bank (or for Congress's issuing of articles of incorporation), Congress had no authority to create one. But Congress agreed to Hamilton's bill despite these objections, and Washington, although he had some apparent reservations, signed it. The Bank of the United States began operations in 1791, under a twenty-year charter.

Hamilton also had his way with the excise tax, although protests from farmers later forced revisions to reduce the burden on the smaller distillers. He failed to win passage of a tariff as highly protective as he had hoped for, but the tariff law of 1792 did raise the rates somewhat.

Once enacted, Hamilton's program won the support of manufacturers, creditors, and other influential segments of the population, as he had hoped. But others found the Hamilton program less appealing. Small farmers, who formed the majority of the population, complained that they were being taxed excessively. They and others began to argue that the Federalist program served the interests not of the people but of small, wealthy elites. Out of this feeling an organized political opposition arose.

The Republican Opposition

The Constitution made no reference to political parties, and the omission was not an oversight. Most of the framers—and George Washington in particular—believed that organized parties were dangerous and to be avoided. Disagreement was inevitable on particular issues, but most of the founders believed that such disagreements need not and should not lead to the formation of permanent factions.

Yet not many years had passed after the ratification of the Constitution before Madison and others became convinced that Hamilton and his followers had become a dangerous, self-interested faction. The Federalists had used the powers of their offices to reward their supporters and win additional allies. They had encouraged the formation of local associations—largely aristocratic in nature—to strengthen their standing in local communities. They were doing many of the same things, their opponents believed, that the corrupt British governments of the early eighteenth century had done.

Because the Federalists appeared to their critics to be creating such a menacing and tyrannical structure of power, there was no alternative but to organize a vigorous opposition. The result was the emergence of an alternative political organization, whose members called themselves "Republicans." (These first Republicans are not institutionally related to the modern Republican Party, which was born in the 1850s.) By the late 1790s, the Republicans were going to even greater lengths than the Federalists to create vehicles of partisan influence. In every state they had formed committees, societies, and caucuses; Republican groups were cor-

responding with one another across state lines; they were banding together to influence state and local elections. And they were justifying their
actions by claiming, just as Hamilton and his supporters claimed, that they
and they alone represented the true interests of the nation. Neither side
was willing to admit that it was acting as a party, nor would either concede
the right of the other to exist. This institutionalized factionalism is known
to historians as the "first party system."

From the beginning, the preeminent figures among the Republicans
were Thomas Jefferson and James Madison. Jefferson, the more politically
magnetic of the two, became the most prominent spokesman for the
cause. He promoted a vision of an agrarian republic, in which most citizens would farm their own land. Jefferson did not scorn commercial or industrial activity. But he believed that the nation should be wary of too
much urbanization and industrialization.

Although both parties had supporters in all parts of the country and
among all classes, there were regional and economic differences. The
Federalists were most numerous in the commercial centers of the Northeast and in such southern seaports as Charleston; the Republicans were
most numerous in the rural areas of the South and the West. The difference in their philosophies was visible in, among other things, their reactions to the progress of the French Revolution. As that revolution grew
increasingly radical in the 1790s, with its attacks on organized religion,
the overthrow of the monarchy, and eventually the execution of the king
and queen, the Federalists expressed horror. But the Republicans applauded the democratic, antiaristocratic spirit they believed the French
Revolution displayed.

When the time came for the nation's second presidential election, in
1792, both Jefferson and Hamilton urged Washington to run for a second
term. The president reluctantly agreed. But while Washington had the respect of both factions, he was, in reality, more in sympathy with the Federalists than with the Republicans. And during his presidency, Hamilton
remained the dominant figure in government.

ESTABLISHING NATIONAL SOVEREIGNTY

The Federalists consolidated their position—and attracted wide public
support for the new national government—by acting effectively in two
areas in which the old Confederation had not always been successful: the
western territories and diplomacy.

A COMMENT ON THE WHISKEY REBELLION Although Thomas Jefferson and other Republicans claimed to welcome occasional popular uprisings, the Federalists were horrified by such insurgencies as Shays's Rebellion in Massachusetts and, later, the Whiskey Rebellion in Pennsylvania. This Federalist cartoon portrays the rebels as demons who pursue and eventually hang an unfortunate "exciseman" (tax collector) who has confiscated two kegs of rum.

Securing the West

Despite the Northwest Ordinance, the old Congress had largely failed to tie the outlying western areas of the country firmly to the national government. Farmers in western Massachusetts had rebelled; settlers in Vermont, Kentucky, and Tennessee had flirted with seceding from the Union. At first, the new government under the Constitution faced similar problems.

In 1794, farmers in western Pennsylvania raised a major challenge to federal authority when they refused to pay the new whiskey excise tax and began terrorizing tax collectors in the region. But the federal government did not leave settlement of the so-called Whiskey Rebellion to the authorities of Pennsylvania as Congress had left the task of quelling Shays's Rebellion to the authorities of Massachusetts. At Hamilton's urging, Washington called out the militias of three states and assembled an army of nearly 15,000—a larger force than he had commanded against the British during most of the Revolution—and he personally accompanied the troops into Pennsylvania. At the approach of the militiamen, the rebellion quickly collapsed.

The federal government won the allegiance of the whiskey rebels through intimidation. It won the loyalties of other western people by accepting new states as members of the Union. The last two of the original thirteen colonies joined the Union once the Bill of Rights had been appended to the Constitution—North Carolina in 1789 and Rhode Island in 1790. Vermont became the fourteenth state in 1791 after New York and New Hampshire agreed to give up their claims to it. Next came Kentucky, in 1792, when Virginia gave up its claim to that region. After North Carolina ceded its western lands to the Union, Tennessee became a state in 1796.

The new government faced a greater challenge in more distant areas of the Northwest and the Southwest. The ordinances of 1784–1787, establishing the terms of white settlement in the West, had produced a series of border conflicts with Indian tribes that were resisting white settlement in their lands. The new government inherited these clashes, which continued with few interruptions for nearly a decade.

These clashes revealed another issue the Constitution had done little to resolve: the place of the Indian nations within the new federal structure. The Constitution made almost no mention of Native Americans. It gave Congress power to "regulate Commerce . . . with the Indian tribes." And it bound the new government to respect treaties negotiated by the Confederation, most of which had been with the tribes. But none of this did very much to clarify the precise legal standing of Indians or Indian nations within the United States. The tribes received no direct representation in the new government. Above all, the Constitution did not address the major issue that would govern relations between whites and Indians: land. Indian nations lived within the boundaries of the United States, yet they claimed (and the white government at times agreed) that they had some measure of sovereignty over their own land. But neither the Constitution nor common law offered any clear guide to the rights of a "nation within a nation" or to the precise nature of tribal sovereignty, which ultimately depended on control of land.

Maintaining Neutrality

Not until 1791 did Great Britain send a minister to the United States, and then only because Madison and the Republicans were threatening to place special trade restrictions on British ships. A new crisis in Anglo-American relations emerged in 1793 when the new French government established after the revolution of 1789 went to war with Great Britain. Both the president and Congress took steps to establish American neutrality in the conflict, but that neutrality was severely tested.

Early in 1794, the Royal Navy began seizing hundreds of American ships engaged in trade in the French West Indies, outraging public opinion in the United States. Hamilton was deeply concerned. War would mean an end to imports from England, and most of the revenue for maintaining his financial system came from duties on those imports.

Hamilton and the Federalists did not trust the State Department, now in the hands of the ardently pro-French Edmund Randolph, to find a solution to the crisis. So they persuaded Washington to name a special commissioner to go to England and negotiate a solution: the staunch New York Federalist and chief justice of the Supreme Court, John Jay. Jay was instructed to secure compensation for the recent British assaults on American shipping, to demand withdrawal of British forces from their posts on the frontier of the United States, and to negotiate a commercial treaty with Britain compatible with America's 1778 treaty with France.

The long and complex treaty Jay negotiated in 1794 failed to achieve these goals. But it was not without merit. It settled the conflict with Britain, avoiding a likely war. It provided for undisputed American sovereignty over the entire Northwest. It produced a reasonably satisfactory commercial relationship with a nation whose trade was important to the United States. Nevertheless, when the terms became known in America, criticism was intense and Jay was burned in effigy in some places. Opponents of the treaty—who included almost all the Republicans and even many Federalists—went to great lengths to defeat it in the Senate, cheered on by agents of France. But in the end the Senate ratified what was by then known as Jay's Treaty.

Jay's Treaty paved the way for a settlement of important American disputes with Spain. Under Pinckney's Treaty (negotiated by Thomas Pinckney and signed in 1795), Spain recognized the right of Americans to navigate the Mississippi to its mouth and to deposit goods at New Orleans for reloading on oceangoing ships; agreed to fix the northern boundary of Florida where Americans always had insisted it should be, along the 31st parallel; and commanded its authorities to prevent the Indians in Florida from launching raids north across the border.

THE DOWNFALL OF THE FEDERALISTS

Since almost everyone in the 1790s agreed that there was no place in a stable republic for organized parties, the emergence of the Republicans as a powerful and apparently permanent opposition seemed to the Federalists a grave threat to national stability. And so when major international perils confronted the government in the 1790s, the temptation to move forcefully against this "illegitimate" opposition was strong.

The Election of 1796

George Washington refused to run for a third term as president in 1796, thus removing the last obstacle to the open expression of the partisan rivalries that had been building over the previous eight years. Jefferson was the obvious presidential candidate of the Republicans that year, but the Federalists faced a more difficult choice. Hamilton had created too many enemies to be a credible candidate. Vice President John Adams, who was directly associated with none of the controversial Federalist achievements, received the party's nomination for president at a caucus of the Federalists in Congress.

The Federalists were still clearly the dominant party. But without Washington to mediate, they fell victim to fierce factional rivalries. Adams defeated Jefferson by only three electoral votes and assumed the presidency as head of a divided party facing a powerful opposition. Jefferson became vice president as a result of finishing second. (Not until the adoption of the Twelfth Amendment in 1804 did electors vote separately for president and vice president.)

The Quasi War with France

American relations with Great Britain and Spain improved as a result of Jay's and Pinckney's Treaties. But the nation's relations with revolutionary France quickly deteriorated. French vessels captured American ships on the high seas and at times imprisoned the crews. The French government refused to receive Charles Cotesworth Pinckney when he arrived in Paris as the new American minister. In an effort to stabilize relations, Adams appointed a bipartisan commission to negotiate with France. When the Americans arrived in Paris in 1797, three agents of the French foreign minister, Prince Talleyrand, demanded a loan for France and a bribe for French officials before any negotiations could begin. Pinckney, a member of the commission, responded succinctly and angrily: "No! No! Not a sixpence!"

When Adams heard of the incident, he sent a message to Congress denouncing French insults and urging preparations for war. Before giving the commissioners' report to Congress, he deleted the names of the three French agents and designated them only as Messrs. X, Y, and Z. When the report was published, the "XYZ Affair," as it quickly became known, provoked widespread popular outrage at France's actions and strong popular support for the Federalists' response. For nearly two years, 1798 and 1799, the United States found itself engaged in an undeclared war with France.

Adams persuaded Congress to cut off all trade with France, to abrogate the treaties of 1778, and to authorize American vessels to capture French armed ships on the high seas. In 1798, Congress created the Department of the Navy and appropriated money for the construction of new warships. The navy soon won a number of duels and captured a total of eighty-five French ships, including armed merchantmen. The United States also began cooperating so closely with the British as to be virtually a cobelligerent in England's war with France. In response, the French began trying to conciliate the United States. Adams sent another commission to Paris in 1800, and the new French government (headed now by "First Consul" Napoleon Bonaparte) agreed to a treaty with the United States that canceled the old agreements of 1778 and established new commercial arrangements. As a result, the "quasi war" came to a reasonably peaceful end, and the United States freed itself from the entanglements and embarrassments of its alliance with France.

Repression and Protest

The conflict with France helped the Federalists increase their majorities in Congress in 1798. Armed with this new strength, they began to consider ways to silence the Republican opposition. The result was some of the most controversial legislation in American history: the Alien and Sedition Acts.

The Alien Act placed new obstacles in the way of foreigners who wished to become American citizens, and it strengthened the president's hand in dealing with aliens. The Sedition Act allowed the government to prosecute those who engaged in "sedition" against the government. In theory, only libelous or treasonous activities were subject to prosecution; but since such activities had no clear definition, the law, in effect, gave the government authority to stifle virtually any opposition. The Republicans interpreted the new laws as part of a Federalist campaign to destroy them and fought back.

President Adams signed the new laws but was cautious in implementing them. He did not deport any aliens, and he prevented the government from launching a broad crusade against the Republicans. But the legislation did have a significant repressive effect. The Alien Act discouraged immigration and encouraged some foreigners already in the country to leave. And the administration used the Sedition Act to arrest and convict ten men, most of them Republican newspaper editors whose only crime had been criticism of the Federalists in government.

Republican leaders began to look for ways to reverse the Alien and Sedition Acts. The Supreme Court had not yet established its right to nullify congressional legislation, so some Republicans looked to the state legislatures for help. They developed a theory to justify action by the states against the federal government in two sets of resolutions of 1798–1799, one written (anonymously) by Jefferson and adopted by the Kentucky legislature and the other drafted by Madison and approved by the Virginia legislature. The Virginia and Kentucky Resolutions, as they were known, used the ideas of John Locke and the Tenth Amendment to the Constitution to argue that the federal government had been formed by a "compact" or contract among the states and possessed only certain delegated powers. Whenever a party to the contract, a state, decided that the central government had exceeded those powers, it had the right to "nullify" the appropriate laws.

The Republicans did not win wide support for the nullification idea; only Virginia and Kentucky declared the congressional statutes void. They did, however, succeed in elevating their dispute with the Federalists to the level of a national crisis. By the late 1790s, the entire nation was as deeply and bitterly politicized as at any time in its history. State legislatures at times resembled battlegrounds. Even the United States Congress was plagued with violent disagreements. In one celebrated incident in the chamber of the House of Representatives, Matthew Lyon, a Republican from Vermont, responded to an insult from Roger Griswold, a Federalist from Connecticut, by spitting in Griswold's eye. Griswold attacked Lyon with his cane, Lyon fought back with a pair of fire tongs, and soon the two men were wrestling on the floor.

The "Revolution" of 1800

These bitter controversies shaped the presidential election of 1800. The presidential candidates were the same as four years earlier: Adams for the Federalists, Jefferson for the Republicans. But the campaign of 1800 was very different from the one preceding it. Indeed, it was probably the ugliest in American history. Adams and Jefferson themselves displayed reasonable dignity, but their supporters showed no such restraint. The Federalists accused Jefferson of being a dangerous radical and his followers of being wild men who, if they should come to power, would bring on a reign of terror

CONGRESSIONAL BRAWLERS, 1798 This savage cartoon was inspired by the celebrated fight on the floor of the House of Representatives between Matthew Lyon, a Republican representative from Vermont, and Roger Griswold, a Federalist from Connecticut. Griswold (at right) attacks Lyon with his cane, and Lyon retaliates with fire tongs. Other members of Congress are portrayed enjoying the battle.

comparable to that of the French Revolution. The Republicans portrayed Adams as a tyrant conspiring to become king, and they accused the Federalists of plotting to subvert human liberty and impose slavery on the people. There was considerable personal invective as well. (It was during this campaign that the story of Jefferson's alleged romantic involvement with Sally Hemmings, a slave woman on his plantation, was first widely aired.) The election was close, and the crucial contest was in New York. There, Aaron Burr mobilized an organization of Revolutionary War veterans, the Tammany Society, to serve as a Republican political machine. Through Tammany's efforts, the party carried the city by a large majority, and with it the state. Jefferson was, apparently, elected.

But an unexpected complication soon jeopardized the Republican victory. The Constitution called for each elector to "vote by ballot for two persons." The normal practice was that an elector would cast one vote for his party's presidential candidate and another for the vice presidential candidate. To avoid a tie, the Republicans had intended that one elector would refrain from voting for the party's vice-presidential candidate,

Aaron Burr. But the plan went awry. When the votes were counted, Jefferson and Burr each had 73. No candidate had a majority, and—in accordance with the Constitution—the House of Representatives had to choose between the two top candidates, Jefferson and Burr. Each state delegation would cast a single vote.

The new Congress, elected in 1800 with a Republican majority, was not to convene until after the inauguration of the president, so it was the Federalist Congress that had to decide the question. Some Federalists hoped to use the situation to salvage the election for their party; others wanted to strike a bargain with Burr and elect him. But after a long deadlock, several leading Federalists, most prominent among them Alexander Hamilton, concluded that Burr (whom many suspected of having engineered the deadlock in the first place) was too unreliable to trust with the presidency. On the thirty-sixth ballot, Jefferson was elected.

After the election of 1800, the only branch of the federal government left in Federalist hands was the judiciary. The Adams administration spent its last months in office taking steps to make the party's hold on the courts secure. With the Judiciary Act of 1801, passed by the lame duck Congress, the Federalists reduced the number of Supreme Court justiceships by one but greatly increased the number of federal judgeships as a whole. Adams quickly appointed Federalists to the newly created positions. Indeed, there were charges that he stayed up until midnight on his last day in office to finish signing the new judges' commissions. These officeholders became known as the "midnight appointments."

Even so, the Republicans viewed their victory as almost complete. The nation had, they believed, been saved from tyranny. A new era could now begin, one in which the true principles of America would once again govern the land. The exuberance with which the victors viewed the future— and the importance they ascribed to the defeat of the Federalists—was evident in the phrase Jefferson himself later used to describe his election. He called it the "Revolution of 1800."

CONCLUSION

The writing of the Constitution of 1787 was the single most important political event in the history of the United States, and a notable event in the political history of the modern world. In creating a "federal" system of dispersed authority—authority divided among national and state governments, authority divided among an executive, a legislature, and a judiciary—the young nation sought to balance its need for an effective central government against its fear of concentrated and despotic power. The ability of the delegates to the Constitutional Convention to compromise again and again to produce the ultimate structure gave evidence of the deep yearning among them for a stable political system. The same willingness to compromise allowed the greatest challenge to the ideals of the new democracy—slavery—to survive intact.

The writing and ratifying of the Constitution settled some questions about the shape of the new nation. The first twelve years under the government created by the Constitution solved others. And yet by the year 1800, a basic disagreement about the future of the nation—a disagreement personified by the differences between committed nationalist Alexander Hamilton and the self-proclaimed champion of democracy Thomas Jefferson—remained unresolved and was creating bitter divisions and conflicts within the political world. The election of Thomas Jefferson to the presidency that year opened a new chapter in the nation's public history. It also brought to a close, at least temporarily, savage political conflicts that had seemed to threaten the nation's future.

FOR FURTHER REFERENCE

Suggested Readings

Charles Beard, *An Economic Interpretation of the Constitution of the United States* (1913), a seminal work of modern American historical inquiry, offers a class-centered interpretation of the origins of the Constitution. Gordon Wood, *The Creation of the American Republic* (1969) is the leading analysis of the intellectual path from the Declaration of Independence to the American Constitution. Jack Rakove, *Original Meanings: Politics and Ideas in the Making of the Constitution* (1996) connects the politics of the 1780s with the political ideas embedded in the Constitution. Michael Kammen, *A Machine that Would Go of Itself: The Constitution in American Culture* (1986) discusses the ways in which different generations of Americans have viewed the Constitution. Max Farrand, ed., *Records of the Federal Convention of 1787*, 4 vols. (1911–1937) is an excellent documentary source. Stanley Elkins and Eric McKitrick, *The Age of Federalism* (1993) provides a lengthy overview of political and economic development in the 1790s. Joyce Appleby, *Capitalism and a New Social Order: The Republican Vision of the 1790s* (1984) highlights liberal and capitalist impulses unleashed after the ratification of the Constitution. Dumas Malone, *Jefferson and His Time*, 6 vols. (1948–1981) is a magisterial biography of one of the greatest of the nation's founders.

Films

(The best source for information on how to find these and other films is *Bowker's Complete Video Directory*—3 volumes.) *The American Story, No. 3: Creating a Republic; No. 4: Experiment in Government; No. 5: The Federalist Era* (1985) cover the years from the American Revolution to 1800. *The Constitution: An American Adventure* explores the development of the Constitution from colonial dissent in the 1760s through the Articles of Confederation. *The Background of the United States Constitution* (1982) explains the calling of the Constitutional Convention as well as the compromises hammered out to produce the Constitution and get it ratified. *The Constitution of the United States* (1982) is a dramatized version of the Constitutional Convention, seen through the eyes of James Madison. *George Washington—The Man Who Wouldn't Be King* (1992) explores the life of America's first president. *George Washington & the Whiskey Rebellion* (1975) illustrates an important episode in Washington's presidency, one of the first challenges to the authority of the federal government.

Internet Resources

Internet websites containing historical material relevant to the subjects discussed in this chapter can be reached through the McGraw-Hill history site at www.mhhe.com/socscience/history/usa/link/linktop.htm.

CHAPTER SEVEN

The Jeffersonian Era

The Rise of Cultural Nationalism ~ Stirrings of Industrialism
Jefferson the President ~ Doubling the National Domain
Expansion and War ~ The War of 1812

T HOMAS JEFFERSON AND his followers assumed control of the national government in 1801 as the champions of a distinctive vision of America. They favored a society of sturdy, independent farmers, happily free from the workshops, the industrial towns, and the city mobs of Europe. They celebrated localism and republican simplicity. Above all, they proposed a federal government of sharply limited power, with most public authority remaining at the level of the states.

Almost nothing worked out as they had planned, for during their years in power the young republic was developing in ways that made much of their vision obsolete. The American economy in the period of Republican ascendancy became steadily more diversified and complex, making the ideal of a simple, agrarian society impossible to maintain. American cultural life was dominated by a vigorous and ambitious nationalism reminiscent of (and often encouraged by) the Federalists. And Jefferson himself contributed to the changes by exercising strong national authority at times, and by arranging the greatest single increase in the size of the United States in its history.

THE RISE OF CULTURAL NATIONALISM

In many respects, American cultural life in the early nineteenth century reflected the Republican vision of the nation's future. Opportunities for education increased, the nation's literary and artistic life began to free itself from European influences, and American religion began to adjust to

TIME LINE				
1793	**1800**	**1801**	**1803**	**1804–1806**
Eli Whitney invents cotton gin	U.S. capital moves to Washington	Second Great Awakening begins Marshall chief justice of Supreme Court	Louisiana Purchase *Marbury* v. *Madison*	Lewis and Clark expedition
1804	**1807**	**1808**	**1809**	**1810**
Jefferson reelected	Embargo	Madison elected president	Non-Intercourse Act Tecumseh Confederacy formed	Macon's Bill No. 2
1811	**1812**		**1814**	**1815**
Battle of Tippecanoe	U.S. declares war on Great Britain Madison reelected		Hartford Convention Treaty of Ghent	Battle of New Orleans

the spread of Enlightenment rationalism. In other respects, however, the new culture was posing a serious challenge to Republican ideals.

Educational and Literary Nationalism

Central to the Republican vision of America was the concept of a virtuous and enlightened citizenry. Republicans believed, therefore, in the creation of a nationwide system of public schools in which all male citizens would receive free education. Such hopes were not fulfilled. As late as 1815, no state had actually created an effective system of free schools (although several had endorsed the idea). Instead, schooling remained primarily the responsibility of private institutions, most of which were open only to those who could afford to pay for them. In the South and in the mid-Atlantic states, most schools were run by religious groups. In New England, private academies were often more secular, many of them modeled on those founded by the Phillips family at Andover, Massachusetts, in 1778, and at Exeter, New Hampshire, three years later. Many were frankly aristocratic in outlook, training their students to become members of the nation's elite. There were a few educational institutions open to the poor, but not nearly enough to accommodate everyone, and the education they offered was usually clearly inferior to that provided for more prosperous students.

Private secondary schools such as those in New England generally accepted only male students; even many public schools excluded females from the classroom. Yet the late eighteenth and early nineteenth centuries did see some important advances in education for women. As Americans began to place a higher value on the importance of the "republican mother" who would help train the new generation, they began to ask how mothers could raise their children to be enlightened if the mothers themselves were uneducated. Such concerns helped speed the creation of female academies throughout the nation (usually for the daughters of affluent families). In 1789, Massachusetts required that its public schools serve females as well as males. Other states, although not all, soon followed.

Some women aspired to more. In 1784, Judith Sargent Murray published an essay defending the right of women to education, and defending it in terms very different from those used by most men. Men and women were equal in intellect and equal in potential, Murray argued. Women, therefore, should have precisely the same educational opportunities as men. What was more, they should have opportunities to earn their own livings and to establish roles for themselves in society apart from their husbands and families. Murray's ideas attracted relatively little support at the time from men or women.

Many early-nineteenth-century reformers believed in the power of education to reform and redeem "backward" people, and they took an interest, therefore, in Indian education. Because Jefferson and his followers liked to think of Native Americans as "noble savages" (uncivilized but not necessarily uncivilizable) they hoped that schooling the Indians in white culture would "uplift" the tribes. Missionaries and mission schools proliferated among the tribes. There were no comparable efforts to educate enslaved African Americans, largely because their owners preferred that they remain ignorant and thus presumably less likely to rebel.

Higher education similarly diverged from Republican ideals. The number of colleges and universities in America grew substantially, from nine at the time of the Revolution to twenty-two in 1800, and the number increased steadily thereafter. None of the new schools, however, was truly public. Even universities established by state legislatures (in Georgia, North Carolina, Vermont, Ohio, and South Carolina, for example) relied on private contributions and tuition fees to survive. Scarcely more than one white man in a thousand (and virtually no women, blacks, or Indians) had access to any college education, and those few who did attend universities were, almost without exception, members of prosperous, propertied families.

"DR. WILLIAM GLEASON" This 1780 painting by the American artist Winthrop Chandler shows a male physician treating a female patient. Obviously reluctant to see a woman reclining in her bed, he takes her pulse by holding the wrist she discreetly extends from behind a curtain.

Medicine and Science

Medicine and science were not always closely connected to one another in the early nineteenth century, but many physicians were working hard to strengthen the link. The University of Pennsylvania created the first American medical school early in the nineteenth century, under the leadership of Benjamin Rush. Most doctors, however, studied medicine by working with an established practitioner, who might or might not have had any scientific training himself. Some American physicians believed in applying new scientific methods to medicine, but they had to struggle against age-old prejudices and superstitions. Efforts to teach anatomy, for example, encountered strong public hostility because of the dissection of cadavers that the study required. Municipal authorities had virtually no understanding of medical science and almost no idea of what to do in the face of the severe epidemics that so often swept their populations; only slowly did they respond to the warnings of Rush and others that lack of adequate sanitation programs was to blame for much disease.

Individual patients often had more to fear from their doctors than from their illnesses. Even the leading advocates of scientific medicine often embraced useless and dangerous treatments. Benjamin Rush, for example, was an advocate of the new and supposedly scientific techniques of bleeding and purging. Many of his patients died. George Washington's death in 1799 was probably less a result of the minor throat infection that had afflicted him than of his physicians' efforts to cure him by bleeding and purging.

The medical profession also used its newfound commitment to the "scientific" method to justify expanding its control over kinds of care that had traditionally been outside its domain. Most childbirths, for example, had been attended by female midwives. In the early nineteenth century, physicians began to handle deliveries themselves and to demand restrictions on the role of midwives. Among the results of that change was a narrowing of opportunities for women (midwifery was an important female occupation) and a restriction of access to childbirth care for poor mothers (who could have afforded midwives, but who could not pay the higher physicians' fees).

Cultural Aspirations of the New Nation

Many Americans—Federalists and Republicans alike—dreamed of an American literary and artistic life that would rival the greatest achievements of Europe. The 1772 "Poem on the Rising Glory of America" predicted that America was destined to become the "seat of empire" and the "final stage" of civilization, with "glorious works of high invention and of wond'rous art." The Connecticut schoolmaster and lawyer Noah Webster (author of widely used American spellers and dictionaries) echoed such sentiments, arguing that the American schoolboy should be educated as a nationalist. "As soon as he opens his lips," Webster wrote, "he should rehearse the history of his own country; he should lisp the praise of liberty, and of those illustrious heroes and statesmen who have wrought a revolution in her favor."

American writers had great difficulty getting their work published. Even so, a growing number of native authors began working to create a strong American literature. Among the most ambitious was the Philadelphia writer Charles Brockden Brown. But his fascination with horror and deviance kept him from developing a popular audience. More successful was Washington Irving of New York, whose popular folk tales, recounting the adventures of such American rustics as Ichabod Crane and Rip Van Winkle, made him the widely acknowledged leader of American literary life in the early eighteenth century.

Religion and Revivalism

The American Revolution had weakened traditional forms of religious practice. It had detached established churches from government, and it had elevated ideas of individual liberty and reason that challenged many ecclesiastical traditions. By the 1790s, only a small proportion of white Americans (perhaps as few as 10 percent) were members of formal churches, and ministers were complaining about the "decay of vital piety."

Religious traditionalists were particularly alarmed about the emergence of new, "rational" religious doctrines—theologies that reflected modern, scientific attitudes and sharply de-emphasized the role of God in the world. "Deism," which had originated among Enlightenment philosophers in France, attracted such educated Americans as Jefferson and Franklin and by 1800 was reaching a moderately broad popular audience. Deists accepted the existence of God, but they considered Him a remote being who, after having created the universe, had withdrawn from direct involvement with the human race and its sins. Religious skepticism also produced the philosophies of "universalism" and "unitarianism." Disciples of these new ideas rejected the traditional Calvinist belief in predestination, arguing that salvation was available to all. They rejected, too, the idea of the Trinity. Jesus was only a great religious teacher, they claimed, not the son of God. But religious skepticism appeared more powerful than it actually was, in part because those who clung to more traditional faiths were for a time confused and disorganized, unable to react effectively. Beginning in 1801, however, traditional religion staged a dramatic comeback in the form of a wave of revivalism known as the Second Great Awakening.

The origins of the Awakening lay in the efforts of conservative theologians of the 1790s to fight the spread of religious rationalism and in the efforts of church establishments to revitalize their organizations. Presbyterians expanded their efforts on the western fringes of white settlement. The Methodists, whose denomination had been founded in England by John Wesley and had spread to America in the 1770s, sent itinerant preachers throughout the nation to win recruits for the new church, which soon became the fastest-growing denomination in America. Almost as successful were the Baptists, who were themselves relatively new to America; they found an especially fervent following in the South.

By 1800, the revivalist energies of all these denominations were combining to create the greatest surge of evangelical fervor since the first Great Awakening sixty years before. In only a few years, the revivalists mobilized a large proportion of the American people, and membership in those churches embracing revivalism—most prominently the Methodist, Baptist, and Presbyterian—was mushrooming. At Cane Ridge, Kentucky, in the summer of 1801, a group of evangelical ministers presided over the nation's first "camp meeting"—an extraordinary revival that lasted several days and impressed all who saw it with its size (some estimated that 25,000 people attended) and its fervor. Such events became common in subsequent years, as the Methodists in particular came to rely on them as a way to "harvest" new members.

The basic message of the Second Great Awakening was that individuals must readmit God and Christ into their daily lives; must embrace a fervent, active piety; and must reject the skeptical rationalism that threatened traditional beliefs. Yet the wave of revivalism did not restore the religion of the past. Few denominations any longer accepted the idea of predestination, and the belief that a person could affect his or her own chances for salvation, rather than encouraging irreligion as many had feared, added intensity to the individual's search for salvation. The Awakening, in short, combined a more active piety with a belief in a God whose grace could be attained through faith and good works.

One of the striking features of the Awakening was the preponderance of women, particularly young women, within it. Female converts far outnumbered males. That may have been in part because of the movement of industrial work out of the home (where women had often contributed to the family economy through spinning and weaving) and into the factory. That process, which was making rapid strides in the early nineteenth century, robbed women of one of their most important social roles. Religious enthusiasm provided, among other things, access to a new range of activities associated with the churches—charitable societies ministering to orphans and the poor, missionary organizations, and others—in which women came to play important roles.

THE CAMP MEETING Camp meetings became a popular feature of evangelical religion in America beginning around 1800. By the 1820s, there were about 1,000 such meetings a year, most of them in the South and the West. This lithograph, which dates from the 1830s, illustrates the central role of women in the religious revivals of the time.

In some areas of the country, revival meetings were open to people of all races. From these revivals emerged a group of black preachers who became important figures within the slave community. Some of them translated the apparently egalitarian religious message of the Awakening—that salvation was available to all—into a similarly egalitarian message for blacks in the present world. Out of black revival meetings in Virginia, for example, arose an elaborate plan in 1800 (devised by Gabriel Prosser, the brother of a black preacher) for a slave rebellion and an attack on Richmond. The plan was discovered and foiled in advance by whites, but revivalism continued in subsequent years to create occasional racial unrest in the South.

The spirit of revivalism was particularly strong in these years among Native Americans, although its origins and the forms it took were very different from those in white or black society. Presbyterian and Baptist missionaries were active among the southern tribes and sparked a wave of conversions. But the most important revivalism came from the efforts of a great Indian prophet: Handsome Lake, a Seneca whose seemingly miraculous "rebirth" after years of alcoholism helped give him a special stature within his tribe. Handsome Lake, like the earlier Indian prophet Neolin, who had been active in the 1760s, called for a revival of traditional Indian ways. That meant repudiating the individualism of white society and restoring the communal quality of the Indian world. Handsome Lake's message spread through the scattered Iroquois communities that had survived the military and political setbacks of previous decades and inspired many Indians to give up whiskey, gambling, and other destructive customs derived from white society. But Handsome Lake also encouraged Christian missionaries to become active within the tribes, and he urged Iroquois men to abandon their roles as hunters (partly because so much of their hunting land had been seized by whites) and become sedentary farmers instead. Iroquois women, who had traditionally done the farming, were to move into more domestic roles.

STIRRINGS OF INDUSTRIALISM

It was not only culturally and religiously that the nation was developing in ways unforeseen by Jefferson and his followers. Economically, the United States was taking the first, tentative steps toward a transformation that would ultimately shatter forever the vision of a simple, agrarian republic.

Technology in America

While Americans were engaged in a revolution to win their independence, an even more important revolution was in progress in England: the emergence of modern industrialism. Power-driven machines were taking the place of hand-operated tools and were permitting manufacturing to become more rapid and extensive—with profound social and economic consequences. Not since the agrarian revolution thousands of years earlier, when humans had turned from hunting to farming for sustenance, had there been an economic change of a magnitude comparable to the industrial revolution. Centuries of traditions, of social patterns, of cultural and religious assumptions were challenged and often shattered.

Nothing even remotely comparable to the English industrial revolution occurred in America in the first two decades of the nineteenth century. Yet even while Jeffersonians warned of the dangers of rapid economic change, they were witnessing a series of technological advances that would ultimately help ensure that the United States too would be transformed. Some of these technological advances were imported from

SLATER'S MILL   Slater served as an apprentice in England in the 1780s to Richard Arkwright, an inventor of machinery for the new cotton mills that were driving the English industrial revolution. In 1790 Slater, having immigrated to America, designed the first successful cotton-spinning mill in the United States at Pawtucket, Rhode Island. This drawing shows the Pawtucket bridge, falls, and mill as they appeared sometime between 1810 and 1819.

England. Despite efforts by the British government to prevent the export of textile machinery or the emigration of skilled mechanics, a number of immigrants with advanced knowledge of English technology arrived in the United States eager to introduce the new machines to America. Samuel Slater, for example, used the knowledge he had acquired before leaving England to build a spinning mill in Pawtucket, Rhode Island, for the Quaker merchant Moses Brown in 1790. It was generally recognized as the first modern factory in America.

America in the early nineteenth century also produced notable inventors of its own. In 1793, Eli Whitney, a New Englander who was working as a tutor on a Georgia plantation, invented a machine that performed the arduous task of removing the seeds from short-staple cotton quickly and efficiently. It was dubbed the cotton gin ("gin" was a derivative of "engine"). With the device a single operator could clean as much cotton in a few hours as a group of workers had once needed a whole day to do. The results were profound. Soon cotton growing spread throughout the South.

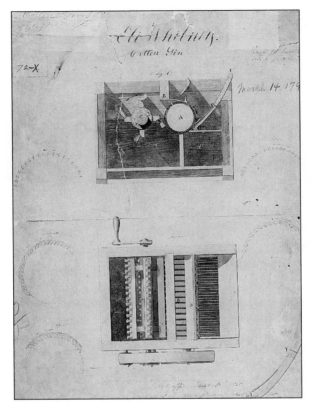

THE COTTON GIN Eli Whitney's cotton gin revolutionized the cotton economy
of the South by making the processing of short-staple cotton simple and
economical. These 1794 drawings are part of Whitney's application for a federal
patent on his device.

(Previously it had been restricted largely to the coast and the Sea Islands,
the only places where long-staple cotton—easily cleaned without the cotton gin—could be grown.) Within a decade, the total cotton crop increased eightfold. African-American slavery, which with the decline of tobacco production had seemed for a time to be a dwindling institution,
expanded and firmly fixed itself upon the South. The large supply of do-
mestically produced fiber also served as a strong incentive to entrepreneurs in New England and elsewhere to develop a native textile industry.

Whitney was an important figure in the history of American technology for another reason as well—as a major figure in introducing the concept of interchangeable parts to the United States. As machines such as

the cotton gin began to be widely used, it became increasingly important that owners of such machines have access to spare parts—and that the parts be made so that they would fit the machines properly. Whitney not only designed the cotton gin, therefore, but designed machine tools that could manufacture its component parts to exact specifications. Thus a cotton gin in Alabama would be identical to one in Georgia, and could use the same parts. The U.S. government later commissioned Whitney to manufacture 1,000 muskets for the army. Each part of the gun had to be interchangeable with the equivalent part in every other gun.

Interchangeability was of great importance in the United States because of the vast size of the nation, the great distances many people had to travel to reach towns or cities, and the relatively limited transportation systems available to them. Many people, farmers in particular, lived far from skilled toolmakers and other craftsmen. Interchangeable parts meant that a farmer could repair a machine himself rather than transport it over great distances to a machine shop or armory. But the interchangeability that Whitney championed was not easy to achieve. In theory, many parts were designed to be interchangeable. In reality, the actual manufacturing of such parts was for many years not nearly as precise as it was supposed to be. Farmers and others often had to do considerable fitting before the parts would work in their equipment. Not until later in the nineteenth century would machine tools be developed to the point that parts could be made truly interchangeable.

Transportation Innovations

One of the prerequisites for industrialization is a transportation system that allows the efficient movement of raw materials to factories and of finished goods to markets. The United States had no such system in the early years of the republic, and thus it had no domestic market extensive enough to justify large-scale production. But projects were under way that would ultimately remove the transportation obstacle.

One such project was the development of the steamboat. England had pioneered steam power, and even steam navigation, in the eighteenth century, and there had been experiments in America in the 1780s and 1790s in various forms of steam-powered transportation. John Fitch attached a small steam engine to a series of oars on a boat in 1787. Two years later, Oliver Evans received the first U.S. patent for a steam-powered boat. A major advance over these early efforts emerged out of the efforts of the inventor Robert Fulton and the promoter Robert R. Livingston, who made significant advances in steam-powered navigation that made possible the launching of a steamboat large enough to carry passengers. Their *Clermont*, equipped with paddle wheels and an English-built engine, sailed up the Hudson in the summer of 1807.

Meanwhile, what was to become known as the "turnpike era" had begun. There was no public sentiment on behalf of using government funds to build roads, so Americans turned to a method that had been introduced to England in the 1660s: allowing private companies to build roads and then to charge a fee to those who used them. In 1794, a corporation constructed a toll road running the sixty miles from Philadelphia to Lancaster, Pennsylvania, with a hard-packed surface of crushed stone, which provided a good year-round surface with effective drainage (but was very expensive to use). The Pennsylvania venture proved so successful that similar turnpikes (so named from the kind of tollgate frequently used) were laid out from other cities to neighboring towns.

The process of building the turnpikes was a difficult one. Companies had to survey their routes with many things in mind, particularly elevation. Horse-drawn vehicles had great difficulty traveling along roads with more than a five-degree incline, which required many roads to take very circuitous routes to avoid climbing straight up steep hills. Building roads over mountains was an almost insurmountable task, and no company was successful in doing so until governments began to participate in the financing of the projects.

Country and City

Despite all the changes, America remained in the early nineteenth century an overwhelmingly rural and agrarian nation. Only 3 percent of the population lived in towns of more than 8,000 in 1800. Even the nation's largest cities could not begin to compare, either in size or in cultural sophistication, with such European capitals as London and Paris (although Philadelphia, with 70,000 residents, New York, with 60,000, and others were becoming centers of commerce, learning, and urban culture comparable to many of the secondary cities of Europe).

People who lived in cities and towns lived differently from the vast majority of Americans who continued to work as farmers. Among other things, urban life produced affluence, and affluent people sought amenities that would not have entered the imaginings of all but the wealthiest farmers. They sought increasing elegance and refinement in their homes, their grounds, and their dress. They also looked for diversions—music, theater, dancing, and, for many people, one of the most popular entertainments of all, horse racing. It was natural that horse racing would appeal to Americans in this era, when horses were a daily part of life and virtually the only means of transportation other than walking for most people. Informal horse racing had begun as early as the 1620s, and the first formal race course opened near New York City in 1665. By the early nineteenth century, horse racing was a popular activity in most areas of the country, and many cities had heavily attended race tracks. Many of the best jockeys were African Americans (some of them young male slaves trained to race the masters' horses). The crowds that gathered at horse races were an early sign of the vast appetite for popular, public entertainments that would be an enduring part of American culture—and a powerful force unifying an otherwise fragmented nation.

It was still possible for some to believe in the early eighteenth century that this small, half-formed nation might not become a complex modern society. But the forces already at work would soon lastingly transform the United States. And Thomas Jefferson, for all his commitment to the agrarian ideal, found himself, as president, obliged to confront and accommodate them.

JEFFERSON THE PRESIDENT

Privately, Thomas Jefferson may well have considered his victory over John Adams in 1800 to be what he later termed it: a revolution "as real . . . as that of 1776." Publicly, however, he was restrained and conciliatory, attempting to minimize the differences between the two parties and calm the passions that the bitter campaign had aroused. There was no complete repudiation of Federalist policies, no true "revolution." Indeed, at times Jefferson seemed to outdo the Federalists at their own work—most notably in overseeing a remarkable expansion of the territory of the United States.

The Federal City and the "People's President"

The relative unimportance of the federal government during the Jeffersonian era was symbolized by the character of the newly founded national capital, the city of Washington. John Adams had moved to the new seat of government during the last year of his administration. And there were many at that time who envisioned that the raw, uncompleted town would soon emerge as a great and majestic city. The French architect Pierre

THOMAS JEFFERSON This 1805 portrait by the noted American painter Rembrandt Peale shows Jefferson at the beginning of his second term as president. It also conveys (through the simplicity of dress and the slightly unkempt hair) the image of democratic simplicity that Jefferson liked to project as the champion of the "common man."

L'Enfant had designed the capital on a grand scale. Many Americans believed Washington would become the Paris of the United States.

In reality, throughout Jefferson's presidency—indeed, throughout most of the nineteenth century—Washington remained little more than a straggling, provincial village. Although the population increased steadily from the 3,200 counted in the 1800 census, it never rivaled that of New York, Philadelphia, or the other major cities of the nation. The city remained a raw, inhospitable community, with few public buildings of any consequence. Members of Congress viewed Washington not as a home but as a place to visit briefly during sessions of the legislature and leave as quickly as possible. Most lived in a cluster of simple boardinghouses in the vicinity of the Capitol. It was not unusual for a member of Congress to resign his seat in the midst of a session to return home if he had an opportunity to accept the more prestigious post of member of his state legislature.

Jefferson was a wealthy and aristocratic planter by background, but as president he conveyed to the public an image of plain, almost crude disdain for pretension. He walked like an ordinary citizen to and from his inauguration at the Capitol, instead of riding in a coach at the head of a procession. In the presidential mansion, which had not yet acquired the name "White House," he disregarded the courtly etiquette of his predecessors. He did not always bother to dress up, prompting the British ambassador to complain on one occasion of being received by the president in clothes that were "indicative of utter slovenliness and indifference to appearances."

Yet Jefferson managed nevertheless to impress most of those who knew him. He was a brilliant conversationalist, a gifted writer, and one of the nation's most intelligent and creative men, with a wider range of interests and accomplishments than any major public figure in American history with the possible exception of Benjamin Franklin. In addition to politics and diplomacy, he was an active architect, educator, inventor, scientific farmer, and philosopher-scientist.

Jefferson was, above all, a shrewd and practical politician. He went to great lengths to eliminate the aura of majesty surrounding the presidency that he believed his predecessors had created. But he also worked hard to exert influence as the leader of his party, giving direction to Republicans in Congress by quiet and sometimes even devious means. Although the Republicans had objected strenuously to the efforts of their Federalist predecessors to build a network of influence through patronage, Jefferson used his powers of appointment as an effective political weapon. Like Washington before him, he believed that federal offices should be filled with men loyal to the principles and policies of the administration. By the end of his second term practically all federal jobs were held by loyal Republicans. Jefferson was a popular president during his first term and had little difficulty winning reelection against the Federalist Charles C. Pinckney in 1804. The Republican ticket carried even the New England states (except Connecticut), and Jefferson won by the overwhelming electoral majority of 162 to 14. Republican membership of both houses of Congress increased.

Dollars and Ships

Under Washington and Adams, the Republicans believed, the government had been needlessly extravagant. Yearly federal expenditures had nearly tripled between 1793 and 1800. The public debt had also risen, as Hamilton had intended. And an extensive system of internal taxation, including the hated whiskey excise tax, had been erected.

The Jefferson administration moved deliberately to reverse these trends. In 1802, the president persuaded Congress to abolish all internal taxes, leaving customs duties and the sale of western lands as the only sources of revenue for the government. Meanwhile, Secretary of the Treasury Albert Gallatin drastically reduced government spending, cutting the already small staffs of the executive departments to minuscule levels. Although Jefferson was unable entirely to retire the national debt as he had hoped, he did cut it almost in half (from $83 million to $45 million).

Jefferson also scaled down the armed forces. He reduced the already tiny army of 4,000 men to 2,500. He pared down the navy from twenty-five ships in commission to seven, cutting the number of officers and sailors accordingly. Anything but the smallest of standing armies, he argued, might menace civil liberties and civilian control of government. And a large navy, he feared, might be misused to promote overseas commerce, which Jefferson believed should remain secondary to agriculture. Yet Jefferson was not a pacifist. At the same time that he was reducing the size of the army and navy, he helped establish the United States Military Academy at West Point, founded in 1802. And when trouble started brewing overseas, he began again to build up the fleet. Such trouble appeared first in the Mediterranean, off the coast of northern Africa. For years the Barbary states of North Africa—Morocco, Algiers, Tunis, and Tripoli—had been demanding protection money, paid to avoid piracy, from all nations whose ships sailed the Mediterranean. Even Great Britain gave regular contributions to the pirates. During the 1780s and 1790s the United States, too, had agreed to treaties providing for annual tribute to the Barbary states, but Jefferson showed reluctance to continue this policy of appeasement.

In 1801, the pasha of Tripoli forced Jefferson's hand. Unhappy with American responses to his demands, he ordered the flagpole of the American consulate chopped down—a symbolic declaration of war. Jefferson responded cautiously and built up American naval forces in the area over the next several years. Finally, in 1805, he agreed to terms by which the United States ended the payment of tribute to Tripoli but paid a substantial (and humiliating) ransom for the release of American prisoners.

Conflict with the Courts

Having won control of the executive and legislative branches of government, the Republicans looked with suspicion on the judiciary, which remained largely in the hands of Federalist judges. Soon after Jefferson's first inauguration, his followers in Congress launched an attack on this last preserve of the opposition. Their first step was the repeal of the Judiciary Act of 1801, thus eliminating the judgeships to which Adams had made his "midnight appointments."

The debate over the courts led to one of the most important judicial decisions in the history of the nation. Federalists had long maintained that the Supreme Court had the authority to nullify acts of Congress (although the Constitution said nothing specifically to support the claim), and the Court itself had actually exercised the power of judicial review in 1796 when it upheld the validity of a law passed by Congress. But the Court's authority in this area would not be secure, it was clear, until it actually declared a congressional act unconstitutional. In 1803, in the case of *Marbury* v. *Madison*, it did so. William Marbury, one of Adams's "midnight appointments," had been named a justice of the peace in the District of Columbia. But his commission, although signed and sealed, had not been delivered to him before Adams left office. When Jefferson took office, his secretary of state, James Madison, refused to hand over the commission. Marbury asked the Supreme Court to direct Madison to perform his official duty. But the Court ruled that while Marbury had a right to his commission, the Court had no authority to order Madison to deliver it. On the surface, therefore, the decision was a victory for the administration. But of much greater importance than the relatively insignificant matter of Marbury's commission was the Court's reasoning in the decision.

The original Judiciary Act of 1789 had given the Court the power to compel executive officials to act in such matters as the delivery of commissions, and it was on that basis that Marbury had filed his suit. But the Court ruled that Congress had exceeded its authority, that the Constitution defined the powers of the judiciary, and that the legislature had no right to expand them. The relevant section of the 1789 act was, therefore, void. In seeming to deny its own authority, the Court was in fact radically enlarging it. The justices had repudiated a relatively minor power (the power to force the delivery of a commission) by asserting a vastly greater one (the power to nullify an act of Congress).

The chief justice of the United States at the time of the ruling (and until 1835) was John Marshall, one of the towering figures in the history of American law. A leading Federalist and prominent Virginia lawyer, he had served John Adams as secretary of state. (It was Marshall, ironically, who had neglected to deliver Marbury's commission in the closing hours of the administration.) In 1801, just before leaving office, Adams had appointed him chief justice, and almost immediately Marshall established himself as the dominant figure of the Court, shaping virtually all its most important rulings—including, of course, *Marbury* v. *Madison*. Through a succession of Republican presidents, he battled to give the federal government unity and strength. And in so doing, he established the judiciary as a coequal branch of government with the executive and the legislature—a position that the founders of the republic had never clearly indicated it should occupy.

DOUBLING THE NATIONAL DOMAIN

In the same year Jefferson was elected president of the United States, Napoleon Bonaparte made himself ruler of France with the title of first consul. In the year Jefferson was reelected, Napoleon named himself emperor. The two men had little in common. Yet for a time they were of great assistance to each other in international politics—until Napoleon's ambitions moved from Europe to America and created conflict and estrangement.

Jefferson and Napoleon

Having failed in a grandiose plan to seize India from the British Empire, Napoleon began to dream of restoring French power in the New World. The territory east of the Mississippi, which France had ceded to Great Britain in 1763, was now part of the United States and lost forever. But Napoleon hoped to regain the lands west of the Mississippi, which belonged to Spain. In 1800, under the secret Treaty of San Ildefonso, France regained title to Louisiana, which included almost the whole of the Mississippi Valley to the west of the river, plus New Orleans near the river's mouth. The Louisiana Territory would, Napoleon hoped, become the heart of a great French empire in America.

Jefferson was unaware at first of Napoleon's imperial ambitions in America, and for a time he pursued a foreign policy that reflected his well-known admiration for France. But he began to reassess American relations with the French when he heard rumors of the secret transfer of Louisiana. Particularly troubling to Jefferson was French control of New Orleans, the outlet through which the produce of the fast-growing western regions of the United States was shipped to the markets of the world. If France should actually take and hold New Orleans, Jefferson said, then "we must marry ourselves to the British fleet and nation."

Jefferson was even more alarmed when, in the fall of 1802, he learned that the Spanish intendant at New Orleans (who still governed the city, since the French had not yet taken formal possession of the region) had announced a disturbing new regulation. American ships sailing the Mississippi River had for many years been accustomed to depositing their cargoes in New Orleans for transfer to oceangoing vessels. The intendant now forbade the practice, even though Spain had guaranteed Americans that right in the Pinckney Treaty of 1795; the prohibition effectively closed the lower Mississippi to American shippers.

Westerners demanded that the federal government do something to re-open the river, and the president faced a dilemma. If he yielded to the frontier clamor and tried to change the policy by force, he would run the risk of a major war with France. If he ignored the westerners' demands, he might lose political support. But Jefferson saw another solution. He instructed Robert Livingston, the American ambassador in Paris, to negotiate for the purchase of New Orleans. Livingston, on his own authority, proposed that the French sell the United States the rest of Louisiana as well.

In the meantime, Jefferson persuaded Congress to appropriate funds for an expansion of the army and the construction of a river fleet, and he hinted that American forces might soon descend on New Orleans and that the United States might form an alliance with Great Britain if the problems with France were not resolved. Perhaps in response, Napoleon suddenly decided to offer the United States the entire Louisiana Territory.

Napoleon had good reasons for the decision. His plans for an empire in America had already gone seriously awry, partly because a yellow fever epidemic had wiped out much of the French army in the New World and partly because the expeditionary force he wished to send to reinforce the troops and take possession of Louisiana had been icebound in a Dutch harbor through the winter of 1802–1803. By the time the harbor thawed in the spring of 1803, Napoleon was preparing for a renewed war in Europe. He would not, he realized, have the resources to secure an empire in America.

The Louisiana Purchase

Faced with Napoleon's sudden proposal, Livingston and James Monroe, whom Jefferson had sent to Paris to assist in the negotiations, had to decide whether they should accept it even if they had no authorization from their government to do so. But fearful that Napoleon might withdraw the offer, they decided to proceed without further instructions from home. After some haggling over the price, Livingston and Monroe signed an agreement with Napoleon on April 30, 1803.

By the terms of the treaty, the United States was to pay a total of 80 million francs ($15 million) to the French government. The United States was also to grant certain exclusive commercial privileges to France in the port of New Orleans and was to incorporate the residents of Louisiana into the Union with the same rights and privileges as other citizens. The boundaries of the purchase were not clearly defined; the treaty simply specified that Louisiana would consist of the same territory France and Spain had claimed.

In Washington, the president was both pleased and embarrassed when he received the treaty. He was pleased with the terms of the bargain; but because he believed the Constitution should be strictly observed, he was uncertain about his authority to accept it, since the Constitution said nothing about the acquisition of new territory. But Jefferson's advisers persuaded him that his treaty-making power under the Constitution would justify the purchase of Louisiana, and Congress promptly approved the treaty and appropriated money to implement it. Finally, late in 1803, General James Wilkinson, commissioner of the United States and the commander of a small occupation force, took formal control of the territory on behalf of the United States. In New Orleans, beneath a bright December sun, the French tricolor was lowered and the American flag raised.

Before long, the Louisiana Territory was organized on the general pattern of the Northwest Territory, with the assumption that it would be divided eventually into states. The first of these was admitted to the Union as the state of Louisiana in 1812.

Exploring the West

Meanwhile, a series of explorations was revealing the geography of the far-flung new territory to white Americans. In 1803, even before Napoleon's offer to sell Louisiana, Jefferson helped plan an expedition that was to cross the continent to the Pacific Ocean, gather geographical facts, and investigate prospects for trade with the Indians. He named as its leader his private secretary and Virginia neighbor, the thirty-two-year-old Meriwether Lewis, a veteran of Indian wars who was skilled in the ways of the wilderness. Lewis chose as a colleague the twenty-eight-year-old William Clark, who—like George Rogers Clark, his older brother—was an experienced frontiersman and Indian fighter. In the spring of 1804, Lewis and Clark, with a company of four dozen men, started up the Missouri River from St. Louis. With the Shoshone woman Sacajawea as their interpreter, they eventually crossed the Rocky Mountains, descended

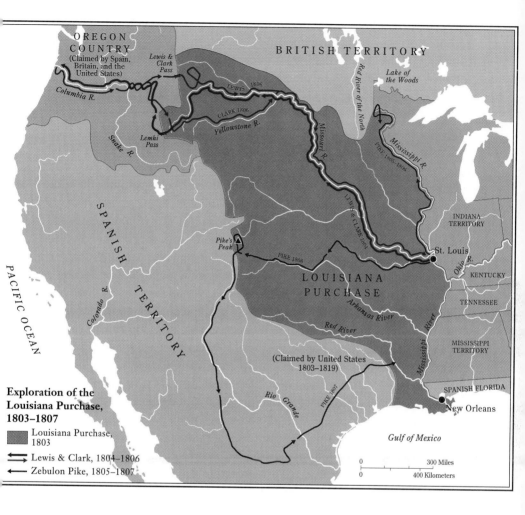

Exploration of the Louisiana Purchase, 1803–1807

■ Louisiana Purchase, 1803

⇔ Lewis & Clark, 1804–1806

◄— Zebulon Pike, 1805–1807

along the Snake and Columbia Rivers, and in the late autumn of 1805 camped on the Pacific coast. In September 1806, they were back in St. Louis with elaborate records of the geography and the Indian civilizations they had observed along the way.

While Lewis and Clark were on their journey, Jefferson dispatched other explorers to other parts of the Louisiana Territory. Lieutenant Zebulon Montgomery Pike, twenty-six years old, led an expedition in the fall of 1805 from St. Louis into the upper Mississippi Valley. In the summer of 1806, he set out again, proceeding up the valley of the Arkansas River and into what later became Colorado, where he encountered, but failed in his attempt to climb, the peak that now bears his name. His account of his western travels helped create an enduring (and inaccurate) impression among most Americans that the land between the Missouri and the Rockies was a desert that farmers could never cultivate and that would be left forever to the nomadic Indian tribes.

The Burr Conspiracy

Jefferson's triumphant reelection in 1804 suggested that most of the nation approved the new territorial acquisition. But some New England Federalists raged against it. They realized that the more the West grew and the more new states joined the Union, the less power the Federalists and their region would retain. In Massachusetts, a group of the most extreme Federalists, known as the Essex Junto, concluded that the only recourse for New England was to secede from the Union and form a separate "northern confederacy." If a northern confederacy was to have any hope for lasting success as a separate nation, the Federalists believed, it would have to include New York and New Jersey as well as New England. But the leading Federalist in New York, Alexander Hamilton, refused to support the secessionist scheme.

Federalists in New York then turned to Hamilton's greatest political rival: Vice President Aaron Burr, a politician without prospects in his own party, because Jefferson had never forgiven him for the 1800 election deadlock. Burr accepted a Federalist proposal that he become their candidate for governor of New York in 1804, and there were rumors (unsupported by any evidence) that he had also agreed to support the Federalist plans for secession. Hamilton accused Burr of plotting treason and made numerous private remarks, widely reported in the press, about Burr's "despicable" character. When Burr lost the election, he blamed his defeat on Hamilton's malevolence and challenged him to a duel. Hamilton feared that refusing Burr's challenge would brand him a coward. And so, on a July morning in 1804, the two men met at Weehawken, New Jersey. Hamilton was mortally wounded; he died the next day.

The resourceful and charismatic Burr was now a political outcast, who had to flee New York to avoid an indictment for murder. He found new outlets for his ambitions in the West. Even before the duel, he had begun corresponding with prominent white settlers in the Southwest, especially with General James Wilkinson, now governor of the Louisiana Territory. Burr and Wilkinson, it seems clear, hoped to lead an expedition that would capture Mexico from the Spanish. But there were also rumors that they wanted to separate the Southwest from the Union and create a western empire that Burr would rule. There is little evidence that these rumors were true.

Whether true or not, many of Burr's opponents chose to believe the rumors—including, ultimately, Jefferson himself. When Burr led a group of armed followers down the Ohio River by boat in 1806, disturbing reports flowed into Washington (the most alarming from Wilkinson, who had suddenly turned against Burr and who now informed the president that treason was afoot) that an attack on New Orleans was imminent. Jefferson ordered the arrest of Burr and his men as traitors. Burr was brought to Richmond for trial. Jefferson carefully managed the government's case from Washington. But Chief Justice Marshall, presiding over the case on circuit duty, limited the evidence the government could present and defined the charge in such a way that the jury had little choice but to acquit Burr.

The Burr conspiracy was in part the story of a single man's soaring ambitions and flamboyant personality. But it was also a symbol of the larger perils still facing the new nation. With a central government that remained deliberately weak, with vast tracts of land only nominally controlled by the United States, with ambitious political leaders willing, if necessary, to circumvent normal channels in their search for power, the legitimacy of the federal government—and indeed the existence of the United States as a stable and united nation—remained to be fully established.

EXPANSION AND WAR

Two very different conflicts were taking shape in the last years of Jefferson's presidency that would, together, draw the United States into a difficult and frustrating war. One was the continuing tension in Europe, which in 1803 escalated once again into a full-scale conflict (the Napoleonic Wars). As fighting between the British and the French increased, each side took steps to prevent the United States from trading with (and thus assisting) the other. The other conflict occurred in North America itself, a result of the ceaseless westward expansion of white settlement, which was now stretching to the Mississippi River and beyond, colliding again with a native population committed to protecting its lands from intruders. In both the North and the South, the threatened tribes mobilized to resist white encroachments. They began as well to forge connections with British forces in Canada and Spanish forces in Florida. The Indian conflict on land, therefore, became intertwined with the European conflict on the seas, and ultimately helped cause the War of 1812, an unpopular conflict with ambiguous results.

Conflict on the Seas

Politicians at the time, and historians since, have argued over whether the conflict in the West or the conflict on the seas was the real cause of the War of 1812. In fact, the war was a result of both.

In 1805, at the Battle of Trafalgar, a British fleet virtually destroyed what was left of the French navy. Because France could no longer challenge the British at sea, Napoleon now chose to pressure England in other ways. The result was what he called the Continental System, designed to close the European continent to British trade. Napoleon issued a series of decrees (one in Berlin in 1806 and another in Milan in 1807) barring British ships and neutral ships touching at British ports from landing their cargoes at any European port controlled by France or its allies. The British government replied to Napoleon's decrees by establishing— through a series of "orders in council"—a blockade of the European coast. The blockade required that any goods being shipped to Napoleon's Europe be carried either in British vessels or in neutral vessels stopping at British ports—precisely what Napoleon's policies forbade.

In the early nineteenth century, the United States had developed one of the most important merchant marines in the world, one that soon controlled a large proportion of the trade between Europe and the West Indies. But the events in Europe now challenged that control, because American ships were caught between Napoleon's Berlin and Milan decrees and Britain's orders in council. If they sailed directly for the European continent, they risked being captured by the British navy. If they sailed by way of a British port, they ran the risk of seizure by the French. Both of the warring powers were violating America's rights as a neutral nation. But most Americans considered the British, with their greater sea power, the worse offender—especially since British vessels frequently stopped American ships on the high seas and seized sailors off the decks, making them victims of "impressment."

Impressment

British sailors called their navy—with its floggings, its low pay, and its terrible shipboard conditions—a "floating hell." Few volunteered. Most had had to be "impressed" (forced) into the service. At every opportunity they deserted. By 1807, many of these deserters had emigrated to the United States and joined the American merchant marine or the American navy. To check this loss of manpower, the British claimed the right to stop and search

American merchantmen (although not naval vessels) and reimpress deserters. They did not claim the right to take native-born Americans, but they did insist on the right to seize naturalized Americans born on British soil. In practice, the British navy often made no careful distinctions, impressing British deserters and native-born Americans alike into their service.

In the summer of 1807, the British went to more provocative extremes in an incident involving a vessel of the American navy. Sailing from Norfolk, with several alleged deserters from the British navy among the crew, the American naval frigate *Chesapeake* was hailed by the British ship *Leopard*. When the American commander, James Barron, refused to allow the British to search the *Chesapeake*, the *Leopard* opened fire. Barron had no choice but to surrender, and a boarding party from the *Leopard* dragged four men off the American frigate.

When news of the *Chesapeake-Leopard* incident reached the United States, there was a great popular clamor for revenge. But Jefferson and Madison tried to maintain the peace. Jefferson expelled all British warships from American waters to lessen the likelihood of future incidents. Then he sent instructions to his minister in England, James Monroe, to demand from the British government an end to impressment. The British government disavowed the actions of the *Leopard's* commanding officer and recalled him; it offered compensation for those killed and wounded in the incident; and it promised to return three of the captured sailors (one of the original four had been hanged). But the British cabinet refused to renounce impressment and instead reasserted its right to recover deserting seamen.

"Peaceable Coercion"

In an effort to prevent future incidents that might bring the nation again to the brink of war, Jefferson persuaded Congress to pass a drastic measure late in 1807. It was known as the Embargo, and it prohibited American ships from leaving the United States for any foreign port anywhere in the world. (If it had specified only British and French ports, Jefferson reasoned, it could have been evaded with false clearance papers.)

The law was widely evaded, but it was effective enough to create a serious depression throughout most of the nation. Hardest hit were the merchants and shipowners of the Northeast, most of them Federalists. Their once-lucrative shipping business came to a virtual standstill. They became convinced that Jefferson had acted unconstitutionally.

The presidential election of 1808 came in the midst of this Embargo-induced depression. James Madison, Jefferson's secretary of state and political ally, was elected president, but the Federalist candidate, Charles Pinckney again, ran much more strongly than he had in 1804. The Federalists gained seats in Congress, although the Republicans still controlled both houses. The Embargo was clearly a growing political liability, and Jefferson decided to back down. A few days before leaving office, he approved a bill ending his experiment with what he called "peaceable coercion."

To replace the Embargo, Congress passed the Non-Intercourse Act just before Madison took office. It reopened trade with all nations but Great Britain and France. A year later, in 1810, the Non-Intercourse Act expired and was replaced by Macon's Bill No. 2, which reopened free commercial relations with Britain and France but authorized the president to prohibit commerce with either belligerent if it should continue violating neutral shipping after the other had stopped. Napoleon, in an effort to induce the United States to reimpose the Embargo against Britain, announced that France would no longer interfere with American shipping. Madison announced that an embargo against Great Britain alone would automatically go into effect early in 1811 unless Britain renounced its restrictions on American shipping.

In time, this new, limited embargo persuaded England to repeal its blockade of Europe. But the repeal came too late to prevent war. In any case, naval policies were only part of the reason for tensions between Britain and the United States.

The "Indian Problem" and the British

Given the ruthlessness with which white settlers in North America had dislodged Indian tribes to make room for expanding settlement, it was hardly surprising that ever since the Revolution most Indians had continued to look to England—which had historically attempted to limit western expansion—for protection. The British in Canada, for their part, had relied on the Indians as partners in the lucrative fur trade and as potential military allies. There had been relative peace in the Northwest for over a decade after Jay's Treaty and Anthony Wayne's victory over the tribes at Fallen Timbers in 1794. But the 1807 war crisis following the *Chesapeake-Leopard* incident revived the conflict between Indians and white settlers. Two important (and very different) men emerged to lead it: William Henry Harrison and Tecumseh.

The Virginia-born Harrison, already a veteran Indian fighter at age twenty-six, went to Washington as the congressional delegate from the

Northwest Territory in 1799. He was a committed advocate of growth and development in the western lands, and he was largely responsible for the passage in 1800 of the so-called Harrison Land Law, which enabled white settlers to acquire farms from the public domain on much easier terms than before.

In 1801, Jefferson appointed Harrison governor of Indiana Territory to administer the president's proposed solution to the "Indian problem." Jefferson offered the Indians a choice: they could convert themselves into settled farmers and become a part of white society, or they could migrate west of the Mississippi. In either case, they would have to give up their claims to their tribal lands in the Northwest.

Jefferson considered the assimilation policy a benign alternative to the continuing conflict between Indians and white settlers, a conflict he assumed the tribes were destined to lose. But to the tribes, the new policy seemed far from benign, especially given the bludgeonlike efficiency with which Harrison set out to implement it. He played one tribe against another and used threats, bribes, trickery, and whatever other tactics he felt would help him. By 1807, the United States had extracted treaty rights to eastern Michigan, southern Indiana, and most of Illinois from reluctant tribal leaders.

Meanwhile, in the Southwest, white Americans were taking millions of acres from other tribes in Georgia, Tennessee, and Mississippi. The Indians wanted desperately to resist, but the separate tribes were helpless by themselves against the power of the United States. They might have accepted their fate passively but for the emergence of two new factors.

One factor was the policy of British authorities in Canada. After the *Chesapeake* incident and the surge of anti-British feeling throughout the United States, the British colonial authorities began to expect an American invasion of Canada and took desperate measures for their own defense. Among those measures were efforts to renew friendship with the Indians and provide them with increased supplies.

Tecumseh and the Prophet

The second, and more important, factor intensifying the border conflict was the rise of two remarkable native leaders. One was Tenskwatawa, a charismatic religious leader and orator known as "the Prophet." He had experienced a mystical awakening in the process of recovering from alcoholism. Having freed himself from what he considered the evil effects of white culture, he began to speak to his people of the superior virtues of

Indian civilization and the sinfulness and corruption of the white world. In the process, he inspired a religious revival that spread through numerous tribes and helped unite them. The Prophet's headquarters at the meeting of Tippecanoe Creek and the Wabash River (known as Prophetstown) became a sacred place for people of many tribes and attracted thousands of Indians from throughout the Midwest. Out of their common religious experiences, they began to consider joint political and military efforts as well.

The Prophet's brother Tecumseh—"the Shooting Star," chief of the Shawnees—emerged as the leader of these more secular efforts. Tecumseh understood, as few other Indian leaders had, that only through united action could the tribes hope to resist the steady advance of white civilization. Beginning in 1809, he set out to unite all the tribes of the Mississippi Valley, north and south into what became known as the Tecumseh Confederacy. Together, he promised, they would halt white expansion, recover the whole Northwest, and make the Ohio River the boundary between the United States and Indian country. He maintained that Harrison and others, by negotiating treaties with individual tribes, had obtained no real title to land. The land belonged to all the tribes; none of them could rightfully cede any of it without the consent of the others. In 1811, Tecumseh left Prophetstown and traveled down the Mississippi to visit the tribes of the South and persuade them to join the alliance.

During Tecumseh's absence, Governor Harrison saw a chance to destroy the growing influence of the two Indian leaders. With 1,000 soldiers he camped near Prophetstown, and on November 7, 1811, he provoked an armed conflict. Although the white forces suffered losses as heavy as those of the natives, Harrison drove off the Indians and burned the town. The Battle of Tippecanoe (named for the creek near which it was fought) disillusioned many of the Prophet's followers, who had believed that his magic would protect them; and Tecumseh returned to find the confederacy in disarray. But there were still warriors eager for combat, and by spring of 1812 they were active along the frontier, from Michigan to Mississippi, raiding white settlements and terrifying settlers.

The bloodshed along the western borders was largely a result of the Indians' own initiative, but Britain's agents in Canada had encouraged and helped to supply the uprising. To Harrison and most white residents of the regions, there seemed only one way to make the West safe for Americans: to drive the British out of Canada and annex that province to the

United States—a goal that many westerners had long cherished for other reasons as well.

Florida and War Fever

While white "frontiersmen" in the North demanded the conquest of Canada, those in the South looked to the acquisition of Spanish Florida (a territory that included the present state of Florida and the southern areas of what are now Alabama, Mississippi, and Louisiana). The territory was a continuing threat to whites in the southern United States. Slaves escaped across the Florida border; Indians in Florida launched frequent raids north into white settlements along the border. But white southerners also coveted Florida because through it ran rivers that could provide residents of the Southwest with access to valuable ports on the Gulf of Mexico.

In 1810, American settlers in West Florida (the area presently part of Mississippi and Louisiana) seized the Spanish fort at Baton Rouge and asked the federal government to annex the territory to the United States. President Madison happily agreed and then began planning to get the rest of Florida, too. The desire for Florida became yet another motivation for war with Britain. Spain was Britain's ally, and a war with England might provide an excuse for taking Spanish as well as British territory.

By 1812, therefore, war fever was raging on both the northern and southern borders of the United States. The demands of the residents of these areas found substantial support in Washington among a group of determined young congressmen who soon earned the name "War Hawks."

In the congressional elections of 1810, voters elected a large number of representatives of both parties eager for war with Britain. These congressmen represented a new generation, aggressive and impatient. The most influential of them came from the new states in the West or from the backcountry of the old states in the South. Two of their leaders, both recently elected to the House of Representatives, were Henry Clay of Kentucky and John C. Calhoun of South Carolina, men of great intellect, magnetism, and ambition who would play a large role in national politics for nearly forty years. Both were supporters of war with Great Britain.

Clay was elected Speaker of the House in 1811, and he appointed Calhoun to the crucial Committee on Foreign Affairs. Both men began agitating for the conquest of Canada. Madison still preferred peace but was losing control of Congress. On June 18, 1812, he approved a declaration of war against Britain.

THE WAR OF 1812

Preoccupied with their struggle against Napoleon in Europe, the British were not eager for an open conflict with the United States. Even after the Americans declared war, Britain largely ignored them for a time. But in the fall of 1812, Napoleon launched a catastrophic campaign against Russia that left his army in disarray and his power in Europe diminished. By late 1813, with the French empire on its way to final defeat, Britain was able to turn its military attention to America.

Battles with the Tribes

Americans entered the War of 1812 with great enthusiasm, but events on the battlefield soon cooled their ardor. In the summer of 1812, American forces invaded Canada through Detroit. They soon had to retreat back to Detroit and in August surrendered the fort there. Other invasion efforts also failed. In the meantime, Fort Dearborn (later Chicago) fell before an Indian attack.

Things went only slightly better for the United States on the seas. At first, American frigates won some spectacular victories over British warships. But by 1813, the British navy was counterattacking effectively, driving the American frigates to cover and imposing a blockade on the United States.

The United States did, however, achieve significant early military successes on the Great Lakes. First, the Americans took command of Lake Ontario; this permitted them to raid and burn York (now Toronto), the capital of Canada. American forces then seized control of Lake Erie, mainly through the work of the young Oliver Hazard Perry, who engaged and dispersed a British fleet at Put-in Bay on September 10, 1813. This made possible, at last, an invasion of Canada by way of Detroit, which Americans could now reach easily by water. William Henry Harrison, the American commander in the West, pushed up the river Thames into upper Canada and on October 5, 1813, won a victory notable for the death of Tecumseh, who was serving as a brigadier general in the British army. The Battle of the Thames resulted in no lasting occupation of Canada, but it weakened and disheartened the Indians of the Northwest and greatly diminished their ability to defend their claims to the region.

In the meantime, another white military leader was striking an even harder blow at the Indians of the Southwest. The Creeks, aroused by Tecumseh on a southern visit and supplied by the Spaniards in Florida, had been attacking white settlers near the Florida border. Andrew Jackson, a

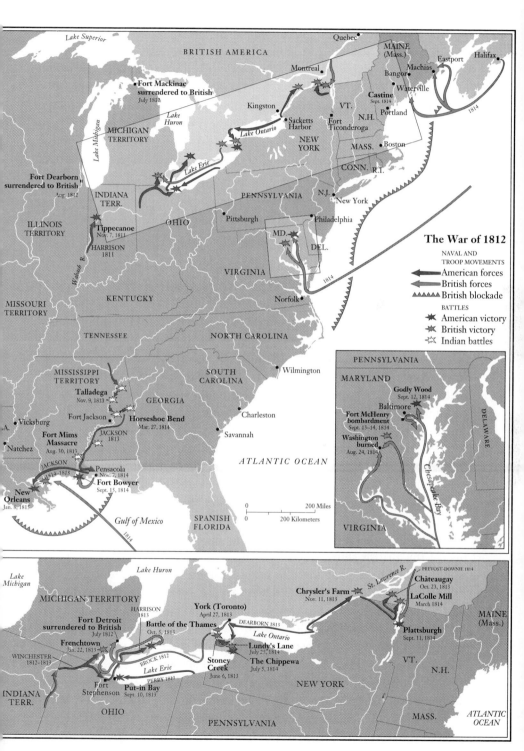

The War of 1812

NAVAL AND TROOP MOVEMENTS
→ American forces
→ British forces
▲▲▲ British blockade

BATTLES
✳ American victory
✳ British victory
☆ Indian battles

Fort Mackinac surrendered to British
July 1812

Fort Dearborn surrendered to British
Aug. 1812

Tippecanoe Nov. 7, 1811

HARRISON 1811

Talladega Nov. 9, 1813

Fort Jackson

Horseshoe Bend Mar. 27, 1814

JACKSON 1813

Fort Mims Massacre Aug. 30, 1813

JACKSON 1814-1815

Pensacola Nov. 7, 1814

Fort Bowyer Sept. 15, 1814

New Orleans Jan. 8, 1815

Castine Sept. 1814

Godly Wood Sept. 12, 1814

Baltimore

Fort McHenry bombardment Sept. 13-14, 1814

Washington burned Aug. 24, 1814

Chrysler's Farm Nov. 11, 1813

Châteaugay Oct. 23, 1813

LaColle Mill March 1814

PREVOST-DOWNIE 1814

Plattsburgh Sept. 11, 1814

York (Toronto) April 27, 1813

HARRISON 1813

Battle of the Thames Oct. 5, 1813

DEARBORN 1813

Fort Detroit surrendered to British July 1812

Frenchtown Jan. 22, 1813

WINCHESTER 1812-1813

BROCK 1812

Stoney Creek June 6, 1813

Lundy's Lane July 25, 1814

The Chippewa July 5, 1814

Fort Stephenson

Put-in Bay Sept. 10, 1813

PERRY 1813

211

wealthy Tennessee planter and a general in the state militia, temporarily abandoned plans for an invasion of Florida and set off in pursuit of the Creeks. On March 27, 1814, in the Battle of Horseshoe Bend, Jackson's men took terrible revenge on the Indians—slaughtering women and children along with warriors—and broke the resistance of the Creeks. The tribe agreed to cede most of its lands to the United States and retreated westward, farther into the interior. The battle also won Jackson a commission as major general in the United States Army, and in that capacity he led his men farther south into Florida. On November 7, 1814, he seized the Spanish fort at Pensacola.

Battles with the British

But the victories over the tribes were not enough to win the war. After the surrender of Napoleon in 1814, England prepared to invade the United States. A British armada sailed up the Patuxent River from Chesapeake Bay and landed an army that marched to nearby Bladensburg, on the outskirts of Washington, where it dispersed a poorly trained force of American militiamen. On August 24, 1814, the British troops entered Washington and put the government to flight. Then they set fire to several public buildings, including the White House, in retaliation for the earlier American burning of the Canadian capital at York. This was the low point of American fortunes in the war.

Leaving Washington in partial ruins, the invading army proceeded up the bay toward Baltimore. But Baltimore, guarded by Fort McHenry, was prepared. To block the approaching fleet, the American garrison had sunk several ships in the Patapsco River (the entry to Baltimore's harbor), thus forcing the British to bombard the fort from a distance. Through the night of September 13, Francis Scott Key (a Washington lawyer on board one of the British ships, where he was trying to secure the release of an American prisoner) watched the bombardment. The next morning, "by the dawn's early light," he could see the flag on the fort still flying; he recorded his pride in the moment by writing a poem—"The Star-Spangled Banner." The British withdrew from Baltimore, and Key's words were soon set to the tune of an old English drinking song. (In 1931 "The Star-Spangled Banner" became the official national anthem.)

Meanwhile, American forces repelled another British invasion in northern New York; at the Battle of Plattsburgh, on September 11, 1814, they turned back a much more numerous British naval and land force and secured the northern border of the United States. In the South, a formi-

THE BURNING OF WASHINGTON This dramatic engraving somewhat exaggerates the extent of the blazes in Washington when the British occupied the city in August 1814. But the invaders did set fire to the Capitol, the White House, and other public buildings in retaliation for the American burning of the Canadian capital at York.

dable array of battle-hardened British veterans, fresh from the campaign against the French in Spain, landed below New Orleans and prepared to advance north up the Mississippi. Awaiting the British was Andrew Jackson with a motley collection of Tennesseans, Kentuckians, Creoles, blacks, pirates, and regular army troops drawn up behind earthen breastworks. On January 8, 1815, the redcoats advanced on the American fortifications, but the exposed British forces were no match for Jackson's well-protected men. After the Americans had repulsed several waves of attackers, the British finally retreated, leaving behind 700 dead (including their commander, Sir Edward Pakenham), 1,400 wounded, and 500 prisoners. Jackson's losses: 8 killed, 13 wounded. Only later did news reach North America that the United States and Britain had signed a peace treaty several weeks before the Battle of New Orleans.

The Revolt of New England

With a few notable exceptions, such as the Battles of Put-in Bay and New Orleans, the military efforts of the United States between 1812 and 1815 consisted of a series of humiliating failures. As a result, the American government faced increasing popular opposition as the contest dragged on. In New England, opposition both to the war and to the Republican government that was waging it was so extreme that some Federalists celebrated British victories. In Congress, in the meantime, the Republicans had continual trouble with the Federalist opposition, led by a young congressman from New Hampshire, Daniel Webster, who missed no opportunity to embarrass the administration.

By now the Federalists were very much in the minority in the country as a whole, but they were still the majority party in New England. Some of them began to dream of creating a separate nation in that region, which they could dominate and in which they could escape what they saw as the tyranny of slaveholders and backwoodsmen. Talk of secession reached a climax in the winter of 1814–1815.

On December 15, 1814, delegates from the New England states met in Hartford, Connecticut, to discuss their grievances against the Madison administration. The would-be seceders at the Hartford Convention were outnumbered by a comparatively moderate majority. But while the convention's report only hinted at secession, it reasserted the right of nullification and proposed seven amendments to the Constitution (presumably as the condition of New England's remaining in the Union)—amendments designed to protect New England from the growing influence of the South and the West.

Because the war was going so badly, the New Englanders assumed that the Republicans would have to agree to their demands. Soon after the convention adjourned, however, the news of Jackson's victory at New Orleans reached the cities of the Northeast. A day or two later, reports of a peace treaty arrived from abroad. In the changed atmosphere these apparent triumphs produced, the Hartford Convention and the Federalist party came to seem futile, irrelevant, even treasonable.

The Peace Settlement

Serious negotiations between the United States and Britain began in August 1814, when American and British diplomats met in Ghent, Belgium. John Quincy Adams, Henry Clay, and Albert Gallatin led the American delegation. Although both sides began with extravagant demands, the final treaty did very little except end the fighting itself. The Americans gave up their demand for a British renunciation of impressment and for the cession of Canada to the United States. The British abandoned their call for creation of an Indian buffer state in the Northwest and made other, minor territorial concessions. The negotiators referred other disputes to arbitration. Hastily drawn up, the treaty was signed on Christmas Eve 1814.

Both sides had reason to accept this skimpy agreement. The British, exhausted and in debt from their prolonged conflict with Napoleon, were eager to settle the lesser dispute in North America. The Americans realized that with the defeat of Napoleon in Europe, the British would no longer have much incentive to interfere with American commerce. Indeed, by the end of 1815, impressment had all but ceased.

Other settlements followed the Treaty of Ghent and contributed to a long-term improvement in Anglo-American relations. A commercial treaty in 1815 gave Americans the right to trade freely with England and much of the British Empire. The Rush-Bagot agreement of 1817 provided for mutual disarmament on the Great Lakes; eventually (although not until 1872) the Canadian-American boundary became the longest "unguarded frontier" in the world.

For the other parties to the War of 1812—the Indian tribes east of the Mississippi—the conflict proved another disastrous blow to the capacity of Indians to resist white expansion. Tecumseh, their most important leader, was dead. The British, their most important allies, were gone from the Northwest. The intertribal alliance that Tecumseh and the Prophet had forged was in disarray. The end of the war served to spur white movement westward, into land the Indians were less than ever able to defend.

CONCLUSION

Thomas Jefferson called his election to the presidency the "Revolution of 1800," and his supporters believed that his victory would bring a dramatic change in the character of the nation—a retreat from Hamilton's dreams of a powerful, developing nation with great stature in the world; a return to an ideal of simple agrarian republic happily isolated from the corruption and intrigue of Europe.

But American society was changing rapidly in the early nineteenth century, making it virtually impossible for the Jeffersonian dream to prevail. The nation's population was expanding and diversifying. Its cities were growing, and its commercial life was becoming ever more important. In 1803, Jefferson himself made one of the most important contributions to the growth of the United States: the Louisiana Purchase, which dramatically expanded the physical boundaries of the nation—and which began extending white settlement deeper into the continent. In the process, it greatly widened the battles between Europeans and Native Americans.

The growing national pride and commercial ambitions of the United States gradually created another serious conflict with Great Britain: the War of 1812, a war that went badly for the Americans on the whole, but that was settled finally in 1814 on terms at least mildly favorable to the United States. By then, the bitter party rivalries that had characterized the first years of the republic had to some degree subsided, and the nation was poised to enter what became known as the "Era of Good Feelings." It was to be an era in which good feelings did not last for very long.

FOR FURTHER REFERENCE

Suggested Readings

Charles Mayfield, *The New Nation* (1981) is a useful survey of the period. Henry Adams, *History of the United States During the Administration of Jefferson and Adams*, 9 vols. (1889–1891) is one of the great literary achievements of early American historiography. Thomas C. Cochran, *Frontiers of Change: Early Industrialization in America* (1981) summarizes economic development in the early republic. Jeanne Boydston, *Home and Work: Housework, Wages, and the Ideology of Labor in the Early Republic* (1990) argues that the cultural status of women declined as the market revolution began to transform the American economy. Joseph J. Ellis, *American Sphinx: The Character of Thomas Jefferson* (1997) is an excellent inquiry into the roots of Jefferson's beliefs and actions. Drew McCoy, *The Elusive Republic: Political Economy in Jeffersonian America* (1980) traces the Jeffersonian struggle to keep the United States free from European-style corruption and decay. Paul Finkleman, *Slavery and the Founders: Race and Liberty in the Age of Jefferson* (1996) reflects on the problem of slavery in the early republic. James Henretta and Gregory Nobles, *The Evolution of American Society, 1700–1815* (rev. ed. 1987) examines the economic growth of the United States in the early nineteenth century. Richard White, *The Roots of Dependency* (1983) examines the tangled relationship between Native Americans and the white citizens of the early United States. J. C. A. Stagg, *Mr. Madison's War: Politics, Diplomacy, and Warfare in the Early American Republic, 1783–1830* (1983) argues that James Madison led the United States to war against Great Britain in order to preserve vital American commercial interests, but that he underestimated New England opposition to his policies.

Films

(The best source for information on how to find these and other films is *Bowker's Complete Video Directory*—3 volumes.) *An Age of Revolutions* (1978) traces early American diplomacy from the Revolution through the early federal period, including the Louisiana Purchase and the War of 1812. *The Louisiana Purchase: Moving West of the Mississippi* (1990) highlights the political events that led to the Louisiana Purchase and links the settlement of the region with the era of "Manifest Destiny." *The War of 1812* (1982) introduces students to an important but poorly understood event in American history. *The American Story, No. 6: Nationalism* and *No. 7: The Emerging Nation* (1985) detail American political and economic development after the War of 1812, through the Era of Good Feelings. *Sea of Honor: The U.S. Navy Story, Vol. 3: The War of 1812* explores one of the formative moments for the American military.

Internet Resources

Internet websites containing historical material relevant to the subjects discussed in this chapter can be reached through the McGraw-Hill history site at www.mhhe.com/socscience/history/usa/link/linktop.htm.

CHAPTER EIGHT

Varieties of American Nationalism

Stabilizing Economic Growth ∼ *Expanding Westward*
The "Era of Good Feelings" ∼ *Sectionalism and Nationalism*
The Revival of Opposition

IKE A "FIRE BELL in the night," as Thomas Jefferson put it, the issue of slavery arose after the War of 1812 to threaten the unity of the nation. The debate began when the territory of Missouri applied for admission to the Union, raising the question of whether it would be a free or a slaveholding state. But the larger issue, one that would arise again and again to plague the republic, was whether the vast new western regions of the United States would ultimately move into the orbit of the North or the South.

The Missouri crisis, which Congress settled by compromise in 1820, was significant because it was a sign of the sectional crises to come. But at the time, it was also significant because it stood in such sharp contrast to the rising American nationalism of the years following the war. Whatever forces might be working to pull the nation apart, stronger ones were acting for the moment to draw it together.

STABILIZING ECONOMIC GROWTH

The end of the War of 1812 allowed the United States to resume the economic growth and territorial expansion that had characterized the first decade of the nineteenth century. A vigorous postwar boom led to a disastrous bust in 1819. Brief though it was, the collapse was evidence that the United States continued to lack some of the basic institutions necessary to sustain long-term growth.

TIME LINE

1815		1816	1818	1819
U.S. takes western lands from Indians	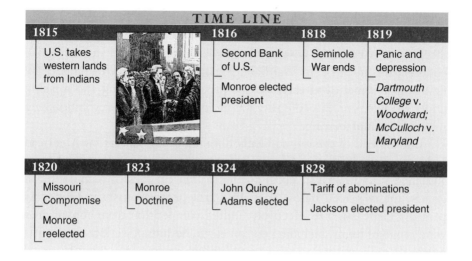	Second Bank of U.S. Monroe elected president	Seminole War ends	Panic and depression *Dartmouth College* v. *Woodward*; *McCulloch* v. *Maryland*

1820	1823	1824	1828
Missouri Compromise Monroe reelected	Monroe Doctrine	John Quincy Adams elected	Tariff of abominations Jackson elected president

The Government and Economic Growth

The War of 1812 may have stimulated the growth of manufactures. But it also produced chaos in shipping and banking, and it exposed dramatically the inadequacy of the existing transportation and financial systems. The aftermath of the war, therefore, saw the emergence of a series of political issues connected with national economic development.

The wartime experience underlined the need for another national bank. After the expiration of the first Bank's charter, a large number of state banks had issued vast quantities of bank notes, creating a confusing variety of currency of widely differing value in circulation at the same time. Honest business was difficult since it was difficult to tell what any bank note was really worth, and counterfeiting was easy. In response to these problems, Congress chartered a second Bank of the United States in 1816, much like its predecessor of 1791 but with more capital. The national bank could not forbid state banks from issuing notes, but its size and power enabled it to compel the state banks to issue only sound notes or risk being forced out of business.

Congress also acted to promote manufacturing, which the war (by cutting off imports) had already greatly stimulated. The American textile industry had experienced a particularly dramatic growth. Between 1807 and 1815, the total number of cotton spindles in the country increased more than fifteenfold, from 8,000 to 130,000. Until 1814, the textile factories—most of them in New England—produced only yarn and thread;

families operating hand looms at home did the actual weaving of cloth. Then the Boston merchant Francis Cabot Lowell, after examining textile machinery in England, developed a power loom better than its English counterpart. In 1813, in Waltham, Massachusetts, Lowell founded the first mill in America to carry on the processes of spinning and weaving under a single roof. His company was an important step in revolutionizing American manufacturing.

But the end of the war suddenly dimmed the prospects for American industry. British ships—determined to recapture their lost markets—swarmed into American ports and unloaded cargoes of manufactured goods, many priced below cost. In 1816, protectionists in Congress passed a tariff law that effectively limited competition from abroad on a wide range of items, including cotton cloth, despite objections from agricultural interests, who stood to pay higher prices for manufactured goods.

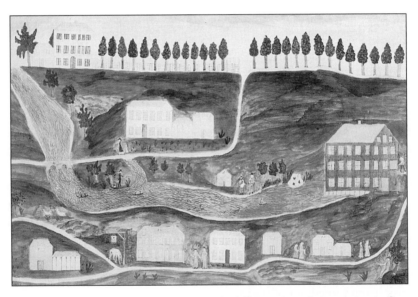

AN EARLY MILL IN NEW ENGLAND This early folk painting, dating around 1814, shows the small town of East Chelmford, Massachusetts—still primarily agrarian, with its rural houses, open fields, and grazing livestock, but with a small textile mill already operating along the stream, at right. A little more than a decade later, the town had been transformed into a major manufacturing center and renamed for the family that owned the mills: Lowell.

Transportation

The nation's most pressing economic need was for improvements in its transportation system that would give manufacturers access to raw materials and markets. An old debate resumed: Should the federal government help to finance roads and other "internal improvements"? The idea of using government funds to finance road building was not a new one. When Ohio entered the Union in 1803, the federal government agreed that part of the proceeds from the sale of public lands there should finance road construction. And in 1807, Congress enacted a law proposed by the Jefferson administration that permitted using revenues from Ohio land sales to finance a National Road from the Potomac River to the Ohio. By 1818, the highway ran as far as Wheeling, Virginia, on the Ohio River; and the Lancaster Pike, financed in part by the state of Pennsylvania, extended westward to Pittsburgh. The roads were heavily traveled and helped lower shipping costs across the mountains.

At the same time, on the rivers and the Great Lakes, steam-powered shipping was expanding rapidly. By 1816, river steamers were beginning to journey up and down the Mississippi to the Ohio River, and up the Ohio as far as Pittsburgh. Steamboats were soon carrying more cargo on the Mississippi than all the earlier forms of river transport—flatboats, barges, and others—combined. They stimulated the agricultural economy of the West and the South by providing access to markets at greatly reduced cost, and they enabled eastern manufacturers to send their finished goods west much more readily.

But despite the progress with steamboats and turnpikes, serious gaps in the nation's transportation network remained, as experience during the War of 1812 had shown. Once the British blockade had cut off Atlantic shipping, the coastal roads had become choked by the unaccustomed volume of north-south traffic. Merchants and consumers experienced long delays and serious shortages. Congress passed a bill introduced by Representative John C. Calhoun that allowed the use of government funds to finance internal improvements, but Madison, on his last day in office, vetoed it. He supported the purpose of the bill, he explained, but he believed that Congress lacked authority to fund the improvements without a constitutional amendment. For a time, state governments and private enterprise were left on their own to build the transportation network necessary for the growing American economy.

THE CLERMONT'S ENGINE Robert Fulton's Clermont became the first steamboat to travel from New York to Albany (in 32 hours) in 1809. Its great paddle was driven by a powerful piston, which was driven in turn by power generated by a steam boiler. This is Fulton's own drawing of the engine system.

EXPANDING WESTWARD

One reason for the growing interest in internal improvements was the sudden and dramatic surge in westward expansion in the years following the War of 1812. By the time of the census of 1820, white settlers had pushed well beyond the Mississippi River, and the population of the western regions was increasing more rapidly than that of the nation as a whole.

The Great Migration

The westward movement of the white American population was one of the most important developments of the century. There were several major reasons for this expansion.

One reason was population growth, which drove many white Americans out of the East. Between 1800 and 1820, the population nearly doubled—from 5.3 million to 9.6 million. Most Americans were still farmers, and the agricultural lands of the East were by now largely occupied or exhausted. In the South, the spread of the plantation system and its slave labor force limited opportunities for new settlers. Another reason was that the West itself was becoming increasingly attractive to white settlers. Land there was much more plentiful than it was in the East. And in the aftermath of the War of 1812, the federal government continued its policy of pushing the Indian tribes farther and farther west, making the fertile regions beyond the Mississippi safer for white settlement. Migrants from throughout the East flocked in increasing numbers to what was then known as the Old Northwest (now part of the Midwest), most of them via the Ohio and Monongahela Rivers. Once on the Ohio, most floated downstream on flatboats, then left the river (often at Cincinnati, which was becoming one of the region's—and the nation's—principal cities) and traveled overland with wagons, handcarts, packhorses, cattle, and hogs.

White Settlers in the Old Northwest

Having arrived at their destination, most settlers built lean-tos or cabins and then hewed clearings out of the forest and planted crops of corn to supplement the wild game they caught and the domestic animals they had brought with them. It was a rough and lonely existence. Men, women, and children worked side by side in the fields—and at times had virtually no contact for weeks or months with anyone outside their own families.

Life in the western territories was not, however, entirely solitary or individualistic. Migrants often journeyed westward in groups, stayed together, and built new communities with schools, churches, stores, and other institutions. The labor shortage in the interior led neighbors to develop systems of mutual aid. They gathered periodically to raise a barn, clear land, harvest crops, or make quilts.

Another common feature of life in the Northwest (and indeed in much of early-nineteenth-century America) was mobility. Individuals and families were constantly on the move, settling for a few years in one place and then selling their land (often at a significant profit, given the rapidly rising prices in the region) and resettling somewhere else. When new areas for settlement opened farther to the west, it was often the people already on the western edges of white settlement—rather than those who remained in the East—who flocked to them first.

The Plantation System in the Old Southwest

In the Old Southwest (now generally known as the Deep South), the new agricultural economy emerged along different lines. The market for cotton continued to grow, and the Southwest contained a broad zone where cotton could thrive. That zone included what was to become known as the Black Belt of central Alabama and Mississippi, a vast prairie with a dark, productive soil.

The first arrivals in the uncultivated regions of the Old Southwest were usually ordinary people like the settlers farther north, small farmers who made rough clearings in the forest. But wealthier planters soon followed. They bought up the cleared or partially cleared land, and the original settlers moved farther west and started over again. Success in the wilderness was by no means assured, even for the wealthiest settlers. But many planters soon expanded small clearings into vast cotton fields. They replaced the cabins of the early pioneers with more sumptuous log dwellings and ultimately with imposing mansions that demonstrated the rise of a newly wealthy class. They also built up large slave work forces.

The rapid growth of the Old Northwest and Southwest resulted in the admission of four new states to the Union in the immediate aftermath of the War of 1812: Indiana in 1816, Mississippi in 1817, Illinois in 1818, and Alabama in 1819.

Trade and Trapping in the Far West

Not many Anglo-Americans yet knew much about or were much interested in the far western areas of the continent. But a significant trade nevertheless began to develop between these western regions and the United States early in the nineteenth century, and it grew steadily for decades.

Mexico, which continued to control Texas, California, and much of the rest of the far Southwest, won its independence from Spain in 1821. Almost immediately, it opened its northern territories to trade with the United States, hoping to revive their stagnant economy. American traders poured into the region—overland into Texas and New Mexico, by sea into California. Merchants from the United States quickly displaced Indian and Mexican traders. In New Mexico, for example, the Missouri trader William Becknell began in 1821 to offer American manufactured goods for sale, priced considerably below the inferior Mexican goods that had dominated the market in the past. Mexico effectively lost its markets in its own colony as a steady traffic of commercial wagon trains began moving back and forth along the Santa Fe Trail between Missouri and New Mexico.

Becknell and those who followed him diverted an established trade from Mexico to the United States. But fur traders created a wholly new kind of commerce. After the War of 1812, John Jacob Astor's American Fur Company and others extended their operations from the Great Lakes area westward to the Rockies. At first, fur traders did most of their business by purchasing pelts from the Indians. But increasingly, white trappers entered the region and joined the Iroquois and other Indians in pursuit of beaver and other furs.

The trappers, or "mountain men," who began trading in and exploring the Far West were small in number. But they developed important relationships with the existing residents of the West—Indian and Mexican—and altered the character of society there. White trappers were mostly young, single men. Perhaps unsurprisingly, many of them entered into sexual relationships with Indian and Mexican women. They also recruited the women as helpers in the difficult work of preparing furs and skins for trading. Perhaps two-thirds of the white trappers married Indian or Hispanic women.

In 1822, Andrew and William Ashley founded the Rocky Mountain Fur Company and recruited white trappers to move permanently into the Rockies in search of furs, which were becoming scarce farther east. The Ashleys dispatched supplies annually to their trappers in exchange for furs and skins. The arrival of the supply train became the occasion for a gathering of scores

THE RENDEZVOUS The annual rendezvous of fur trappers and traders was a major event in the lives of the lonely men who made their livelihoods gathering furs. It was also a gathering of representatives of the many cultures that mingled in the Far West, among them Anglo-Americans, French Canadians, Indians, and Hispanics.

of mountain men, some of whom lived much of the year in considerable isolation.

But however isolated their daily lives, these mountain men were closely bound up with the expanding market economy of the United States. Some were employees of the Rocky Mountain Fur Company (or some other, similar business enterprise), earning a salary in return for providing a steady supply of furs. Others trapped on their own and simply sold their furs for cash, but they too depended on merchants from the East for their livelihoods. Whatever the character of the transactions, the bulk of the profits from the trade flowed to the merchants, not the trappers.

Eastern Images of the West

Americans in the East were only dimly aware of the world the trappers were entering and helping to reshape, and the trappers themselves, who did not often write of their lives or draw maps of the lands they explored, did little to enlighten others. More important in increasing eastern awareness of the West were explorers, many of them dispatched by the United States government with instructions to chart the territories they visited. In 1819 and 1820, with instructions from the War Department to find the source of the Red River, Stephen H. Long led nineteen soldiers on a journey up the Platte and South Platte Rivers through what is now Nebraska and eastern Colorado (where he discovered the peak that would be named for him), and then returned eastward along the Arkansas River through what is now Kansas. He failed to find the headwaters of the Red River. But he wrote an influential report on his trip, which echoed the dismissive conclusions of Zebulon Pike fifteen years before. The region "between the Missouri River and the Rocky Mountains," Long wrote, "is almost wholly unfit for cultivation, and of course uninhabitable by a people depending upon agriculture for their subsistence." On the published map of his expedition, he labeled the Great Plains the "Great American Desert."

THE "ERA OF GOOD FEELINGS"

The expansion of the economy, the growth of white settlement and trade in the West, the creation of new states—all reflected the rising spirit of nationalism that was permeating the United States in the years following the War of 1812. That spirit found reflection for a time in the character of national politics.

The End of the First Party System

Ever since 1800, the presidency seemed to have been the special possession of Virginians. After two terms in office Jefferson chose his secretary of state, James Madison of Virginia, to succeed him, and after two more terms, Madison secured the presidential nomination for his secretary of state, James Monroe, also of Virginia. Many in the North were expressing impatience with the so-called Virginia Dynasty, but the Republicans had no difficulty electing their candidate in the listless campaign of 1816. Monroe received 183 ballots in the electoral college; his Federalist opponent, Rufus King of New York, received only 34—from Massachusetts, Connecticut, and Delaware.

Monroe was sixty-one years old when he became president. In the course of his long career, he had served as a soldier in the Revolution, as a diplomat, and most recently as a cabinet officer. He entered office under what seemed to be remarkably favorable circumstances. With the decline of the Federalists, his party faced no serious opposition. With the conclusion of the War of 1812, the nation faced no important international threats. American politicians had dreamed since the first days of the republic of a time in which partisan divisions and factional disputes might come to an end. In the prosperous postwar years, Monroe attempted to use his office to realize that dream.

THE INAUGURATION OF JAMES MONROE, 1816 The ruins of part of the United States Capitol, burned by the British two years earlier late in the War of 1812, provided a bleak backdrop for James Monroe's first inauguration in 1816.

He made that clear, above all, in the selection of his cabinet. For secretary of state, he chose the New Englander and former Federalist John Quincy Adams. Jefferson, Madison, and Monroe had all served as secretary of state before becoming president; Adams, therefore, immediately became the heir apparent, suggesting that the "Virginia Dynasty" would soon come to an end. Speaker of the House Henry Clay declined an offer to be secretary of war, so Monroe named John C. Calhoun instead. In his other appointments, too, Monroe took pains to include both northerners and southerners, easterners and westerners, Federalists and Republicans.

Soon after his inauguration, Monroe did what no president since Washington had done: he made a good-will tour through the country. In New England, so recently the scene of rabid Federalist discontent, he was greeted everywhere with enthusiastic demonstrations. The *Columbian Centinel*, a Federalist newspaper in Boston, commenting on the "Presidential Jubilee" in that city, observed that an "era of good feelings" had arrived. And on the surface, at least, the years of Monroe's presidency did appear to be an "era of good feelings." In 1820, Monroe was reelected without opposition. For all practical purposes, the Federalist Party had now ceased to exist.

John Quincy Adams and Florida

Like his father, the second president of the United States, John Quincy Adams had spent much of his life in diplomatic service. And even before becoming secretary of state, he had become one of the great diplomats in American history. He was also a committed nationalist, and he considered his most important task to be the promotion of American expansion.

His first challenge was Florida. The United States had already annexed West Florida, but that claim was in dispute. Most Americans, moreover, still believed the nation should gain possession of the entire peninsula. In 1817, Adams began negotiations with the Spanish minister, Luis de Onís, in hopes of resolving the dispute and gaining the entire territory for the United States.

In the meantime, however, events were taking their own course in Florida itself. Andrew Jackson, now in command of American troops along the Florida frontier, had orders from Secretary of War Calhoun to "adopt the necessary measures" to stop continuing raids on American territory by Seminole Indians south of the border. Jackson used those orders as an excuse to invade Florida, seize the Spanish forts at St. Marks and Pensacola, and order the hanging of two British subjects on the charge of

SEMINOLE DANCE This 1838 drawing by a U.S. military officer portrays a dance by Seminole Indians near Fort Butler in Florida. It was made in the midst of the prolonged Second Seminole War, which ended in 1842 with the removal of most of the tribe from Florida to reservations west of the Mississippi.

supplying and inciting the Indians. The operation became known as the Seminole War.

Instead of condemning Jackson's raid, Adams urged the government to assume responsibility for it. The United States, he told the Spanish, had the right under international law to defend itself against threats from across its borders. Since Spain was unwilling or unable to curb those threats, America had simply done what was necessary. Jackson's raid demonstrated to the Spanish that the United States could easily take Florida by force. Adams implied that the nation might consider doing so.

Onís realized, therefore, that he had little choice but to come to terms with the Americans. Under the provisions of the Adams-Onís Treaty of 1819, Spain ceded all of Florida to the United States and gave up its claim to territory north of the 42nd parallel in the Pacific Northwest. In return, the American government gave up its claims to Texas.

The Panic of 1819

But the Monroe administration had little time to revel in its diplomatic successes, for the nation was falling victim to a serious economic crisis: the Panic of 1819. It followed a period of high foreign demand for American farm goods and thus of exceptionally high prices for American farmers (all as a result of the disruption of European agriculture caused by the Napoleonic Wars). The rising prices for farm goods had stimulated a land boom in the western United States. Fueled by speculative investments, land prices soared.

The availability of easy credit to settlers and speculators—from the government (under the land acts of 1800 and 1804), from state banks and wildcat banks, even for a time from the rechartered Bank of the United States—fueled the land boom. Beginning in 1819, however, new management at the national bank began tightening credit, calling in loans, and foreclosing mortgages. This precipitated a series of failures by state banks, and the result was a financial panic, which many Americans, particularly those in the West, blamed on the national bank. Thus began a process that would eventually make the Bank's existence one of the nation's most burning political issues. Six years of depression followed.

Some Americans saw the Panic of 1819 and the widespread distress that followed as a warning that rapid economic growth and territorial expansion would destabilize the nation and threaten its survival. But by 1820 most Americans were irrevocably committed to the idea of growth and expansion. Public debate in the future would revolve less around whether growth was good or bad than around how to encourage and control it.

SECTIONALISM AND NATIONALISM

For a brief but alarming moment in 1819–1820, the increasing differences between the North and the South threatened the unity of the United States—until the Missouri Compromise averted a sectional crisis for a time. The forces of nationalism continued to assert themselves, and the federal government began to assume the role of promoter of economic growth.

The Missouri Compromise

When Missouri applied for admission to the Union as a state in 1819, slavery was already well established there. Even so, Representative James Tallmadge, Jr. of New York proposed an amendment to the Missouri statehood bill that would prohibit the further introduction of slaves into

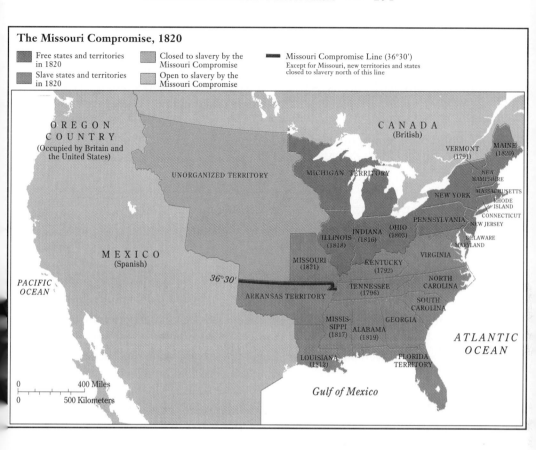

The Missouri Compromise, 1820

- Free states and territories in 1820
- Slave states and territories in 1820
- Closed to slavery by the Missouri Compromise
- Open to slavery by the Missouri Compromise
- Missouri Compromise Line (36°30')
  Except for Missouri, new territories and states closed to slavery north of this line

Missouri and provide for the gradual emancipation of those already there. The Tallmadge Amendment provoked a controversy that was to rage for the next two years.

Since the beginning of the republic, partly by chance and partly by design, new states had come into the Union more or less in pairs, one from the North, another from the South. In 1819, there were eleven free states and eleven slave states; the admission of Missouri would upset that balance and increase the political power of the North over the South. Hence the controversy over slavery and freedom in Missouri.

Complicating the Missouri question was the application of Maine (previously the northern part of Massachusetts) for admission as a new (and free) state. Speaker of the House Henry Clay informed northern members that if they blocked Missouri from entering the Union as a slave state, southerners would block the admission of Maine. But Maine ultimately offered a way out of the impasse, as the Senate agreed to combine the Maine and Missouri proposals into a single bill. Maine would be admitted as a free state, Missouri as a slave state. Then Senator Jesse B. Thomas of Illinois proposed an amendment prohibiting slavery in the rest of the Louisiana Purchase territory north of the southern boundary of Missouri (the 36° 30′ parallel). The Senate adopted the Thomas Amendment, and Speaker Clay, with great difficulty, guided the amended Maine-Missouri bill through the House.

Nationalists in both North and South hailed this settlement—which became known as the Missouri Compromise—as a happy resolution of a danger to the Union. But the debate over it had revealed a strong undercurrent of sectionalism that was competing with—although at the moment failing to derail—the powerful tides of nationalism.

Marshall and the Court

John Marshall served as chief justice of the United States for almost thirty-five years, from 1801 to 1835, and he dominated the Court more fully than anyone else before or since. More than anyone but the framers themselves, he molded the development of the Constitution: strengthening the judicial branch at the expense of the executive and legislative branches, increasing the power of the federal government at the expense of the states, and advancing the interests of the propertied and commercial classes.

Committed to promoting commerce, the Marshall Court staunchly defended the inviolability of contracts. In *Fletcher* v. *Peck* (1810), which arose out of a series of notorious land frauds in Georgia, the Court had to decide whether the Georgia legislature of 1796 could repeal the act of the previous legislature granting lands under shady circumstances to the Yazoo Land Companies. In a unanimous decision, Marshall held that a land grant was a valid contract and could not be repealed even if corruption was involved.

Dartmouth College v. *Woodward* (1819) further expanded the meaning of the contract clause of the Constitution. Having gained control of the New Hampshire state government, Republicans tried to revise Dartmouth College's charter (granted by King George III in 1769) to convert the private college into a state university. Daniel Webster, a Dartmouth graduate and brilliant orator, argued the college's case. The Dartmouth charter, he insisted, was a contract, protected by the same doctrine that the Court had already upheld in *Fletcher* v. *Peck*. Then, according to legend, he brought some of the justices to tears with an irrelevant passage that concluded: "It is, sir, . . . a small college. And yet there are those who love it." The Court ruled for Dartmouth, proclaiming that corporation charters such as

JOHN MARSHALL Marshall became Chief Justice of the United States Supreme Court in 1801 after establishing himself as one of the leaders of the Federalist Party. He served as Chief Justice for thirty-five years, longer than anyone else in American history. And despite the frequent opposition of a series of Republican presidents, he used his position to make the judiciary a vigorous instrument for asserting and strengthening American nationalism.

the one the colonial legislature had granted the college were contracts and thus inviolable. The decision placed important restrictions on the ability of state governments to control corporations.

In overturning the act of the legislature and the decisions of the New Hampshire courts, the justices also implicitly claimed for themselves the right to override the decisions of state courts. But advocates of states' rights, especially in the South, continued to challenge its right to do so. In *Cohens* v. *Virginia* (1821), Marshall explicitly affirmed the constitutionality of federal review of state court decisions. The states had given up part of their sovereignty in ratifying the Constitution, he explained, and their courts must submit to federal jurisdiction; otherwise, the federal government would be prostrated "at the feet of every state in the Union."

Meanwhile, in *McCulloch* v. *Maryland* (1819), Marshall confirmed the "implied powers" of Congress by upholding the constitutionality of the Bank of the United States. The Bank had become so unpopular in the South and the West that several of the states tried to drive branches out of business by outright prohibition or by confiscatory taxes. This case presented two constitutional questions to the Supreme Court: Could Congress charter a bank? And if so, could individual states ban it or tax it? Daniel Webster, one of the Bank's attorneys, argued that establishing such an institution came within the "necessary and proper" clause of the Constitution and that the power to tax involved a "power to destroy." If the states could tax the Bank at all, they could tax it to death. Marshall adopted Webster's words in deciding for the Bank.

In the case of *Gibbons* v. *Ogden* (1824), the Court strengthened Congress's power to regulate interstate commerce. The state of New York had granted the steamboat company of Robert Fulton and Robert Livingston the exclusive right to carry passengers on the Hudson River to New York City. Fulton and Livingston then gave Aaron Ogden the business of carrying passengers across the river between New York and New Jersey. But Thomas Gibbons, with a license granted under an act of Congress, began competing with Ogden for the ferry traffic. Ogden brought suit against him and won in the New York courts. Gibbons appealed to the Supreme Court. The most important question facing the justices was whether Congress's power to give Gibbons a license to operate his ferry superseded the state of New York's power to grant Ogden a monopoly. Marshall claimed that the power of Congress to regulate interstate commerce (which, he said, included navigation) was "complete in itself" and might be "exercised to its utmost extent." Ogden's state-granted monopoly, therefore, was void.

The decisions of the Marshall Court established the primacy of the federal government over the states in regulating the economy and opened the way for an increased federal role in promoting economic growth. They protected corporations and other private economic institutions from local government interference. They were, in short, highly nationalistic decisions, designed to promote the growth of a strong, unified, and economically developed United States.

The Court and the Tribes

The nationalist inclinations of the Marshall Court were visible as well in a series of decisions concerning the legal status of Indian tribes within the United States. But these decisions did not simply affirm the supremacy of the United States; they also carved out a distinctive position for Native Americans within the constitutional structure.

The first of the crucial Indian decisions was in the case of *Johnson* v. *McIntosh* (1823). Leaders of the Illinois and Pinakeshaw tribes had sold parcels of their land to a group of white settlers (including Johnson) but had later signed a treaty with the federal government ceding territory that included those same parcels to the United States. The government proceeded to grant homestead rights to new white settlers (among them McIntosh) on the land claimed by Johnson. The Court was asked to decide which claim had precedence. Marshall's ruling, not surprisingly, favored the United States. But in explaining it, he offered a preliminary definition of the place of Indians within the nation. The tribes had a basic right to their tribal lands, he said, that preceded all other American law. Individual American citizens could not buy or take land from the tribes; only the federal government—the supreme authority—could do that.

Even more important was the Court's 1832 decision in *Worcester* v. *Georgia*, in which the Court invalidated a Georgia law that attempted to regulate access by U.S. citizens to Cherokee country. Only the federal government could do that, Marshall claimed, thus taking another important step in consolidating federal authority over the states (and over the tribes). In doing so, he further defined the nature of the Indian nations. The tribes, he explained, were sovereign entities in much the same way Georgia was a sovereign entity—"distinct political communities, having territorial boundaries within which their authority is exclusive." In defending the power of the federal government, he was also affirming, indeed expanding, the rights of the tribes to remain free from the authority of state governments.

The Marshall decisions, therefore, did what the Constitution itself had not done: they defined a place for Indian tribes within the American political system. The tribes had basic property rights. They were sovereign entities not subject to the authority of state governments. But the federal government, like a "guardian" governing its "ward," had ultimate authority over tribal affairs—even if that authority was, according to the Court, limited by the government's obligation to protect Indian welfare. These provisions were seldom enough to defend Indians from the steady westward march of white civilization, but they formed the basis of what legal protections they had.

The Latin American Revolution and the Monroe Doctrine

Just as the Supreme Court was asserting American nationalism in the shaping of the country's economic life, so the Monroe administration was asserting nationalism in foreign policy. As always, American diplomacy was principally concerned with Europe. But in the 1820s, dealing with Europe forced the United States to develop a policy toward Latin America.

Americans looking southward in the years following the War of 1812 beheld a gigantic spectacle: the Spanish Empire in its death throes, a whole continent in revolt, new nations in the making. Already the United States had developed a profitable trade with Latin America and was rivaling Great Britain as the principal trading nation there. Many believed the success of the anti-Spanish revolutions would further strengthen America's position in the region.

In 1815, the United States proclaimed neutrality in the wars between Spain and its rebellious colonies, implying a partial recognition of the rebels' status as nations. Moreover, the United States sold ships and supplies to the revolutionaries, a clear indication that it was not genuinely neutral but was trying to help the insurgents. Finally, in 1822, President Monroe established diplomatic relations with five new nations—La Plata (later Argentina), Chile, Peru, Colombia, and Mexico—making the United States the first country to recognize them.

In 1823, Monroe went further and announced a policy that would ultimately be known (beginning some thirty years later) as the "Monroe Doctrine," even though it was primarily the work of John Quincy Adams. "The American continents," Monroe declared, ". . . are henceforth not to be considered as subjects for future colonization by any European powers." The United States would consider any foreign challenge to the sovereignty of existing American nations an unfriendly act. At the same time, he proclaimed, "Our policy in regard to Europe . . . is not to interfere in the internal concerns of any of its powers."

The Monroe Doctrine emerged directly out of America's relations with Europe in the 1820s. Many Americans feared that Spain's European allies (notably France) would assist Spain in an effort to retake its lost empire. Even more troubling to Adams (and many other Americans) was the fear that Great Britain had designs on Cuba. Adams wanted to keep Cuba in Spanish hands until it fell (as he believed it ultimately would) to the Americans.

The Monroe Doctrine had few immediate effects, but it was important as an expression of the growing spirit of nationalism in the United States in the 1820s. And it established the idea of the United States as the dominant power in the Western Hemisphere.

THE REVIVAL OF OPPOSITION

After 1816, the Federalist Party offered no presidential candidate and soon ceased to exist as a national political force. The Republican Party (which considered itself not a party at all but an organization representing the whole of the population) was the only organized force in national politics.

By the late 1820s, however, partisan divisions were emerging once again. In some respects, the division mirrored the schism that had produced the first party system in the 1790s. The Republicans had in many ways come to resemble the early Federalist regimes in their promotion of economic growth and centralization. And the opposition, like the opposition in the 1790s, objected to the federal government's expanding role in the economy. There was, however, a crucial difference. At the beginning of the century, the opponents of centralization had also often been opponents of economic growth. Now, in the 1820s, the controversy involved not whether but how the nation should continue to expand.

The "Corrupt Bargain"

Until 1820, when the Federalist Party effectively ceased operations and James Monroe ran for reelection unopposed, presidential candidates were nominated by caucuses of the two parties in Congress. But in 1824, "King Caucus" was overthrown. The Republican caucus nominated William H. Crawford of Georgia, the secretary of the treasury and the favorite of the extreme states' rights faction of the party. But other candidates received nominations from state legislatures and won endorsements from irregular mass meetings throughout the country.

One of them was Secretary of State John Quincy Adams, who held the office that was the traditional stepping-stone to the presidency. But as he himself ruefully understood, he was a man of cold and forbidding manners, with little popular appeal. Another contender was Henry Clay, the Speaker of the House. He had a devoted personal following and a definite and coherent program: the "American System," which proposed creating a great home market for factory and farm producers by raising the protective tariff, strengthening the national bank, and financing internal improvements. Andrew Jackson, the fourth major candidate, had no significant political record—even though he had served briefly as a representative in Congress and was now a new member of the United States Senate. But he was a military hero and had the help of shrewd political allies from his home state of Tennessee.

Jackson received more popular and electoral votes than any other candidate, but not a majority. He had 99 electoral votes to Adams's 84, Crawford's 41, and Clay's 37. The Twelfth Amendment to the Constitution (passed in the aftermath of the contested 1800 election) required the House of Representatives to choose among the three candidates with the largest numbers of electoral votes. Crawford was seriously ill and not a plausible candidate. Clay was out of the running, but he was in a strong position to influence the result. Jackson was Clay's most dangerous political rival in the West, so Clay supported Adams, in part because, alone among the candidates, he was an ardent nationalist and a likely supporter of the American System. With Clay's endorsement, Adams won election in the House.

The Jacksonians believed their large popular and electoral pluralities entitled their candidate to the presidency, and they were enraged when he lost. But they grew angrier still when Adams named Clay his secretary of state. The State Department was the well-established route to the presidency, and Adams thus appeared to be naming Clay as his own successor. The outrage the Jacksonians expressed at what they called a "corrupt bargain" haunted Adams throughout his presidency.

The Second President Adams

Throughout Adams's term in the White House, the political bitterness arising from the "corrupt bargain" charges thoroughly frustrated his policies. Adams proposed an ambitiously nationalist program reminiscent of Clay's American System. But Jacksonians in Congress blocked most of it.

Adams also experienced diplomatic frustrations. He appointed delegates to an international conference that the Venezuelan liberator, Simón Bolívar, had called in Panama in 1826. But Haiti was one of the participating nations, and southerners in Congress opposed the idea of white Americans mingling with the black delegates. Congress delayed approving the Panama mission so long that the American delegation did not arrive until after the conference was over.

Adams also lost a contest with the state of Georgia, which wished to remove the remaining Creek and Cherokee Indians from the state to gain additional soil for cotton planters. The United States government, in a 1791 treaty, had guaranteed that land to the Creeks; but in 1825, white Georgians had extracted a new treaty from William McIntosh, the leader of one faction in the tribe and a longtime advocate of Indian cooperation with the United States. Adams believed the new treaty had no legal force, since McIntosh clearly did not represent the wishes of the tribe; and he refused to enforce the treaty, setting up a direct conflict between the president and the state. The governor of Georgia defied the president and proceeded with plans for Indian removal. Adams found no way to stop him.

Even more damaging to the administration was its support for a new tariff on imported goods in 1828. This measure originated with the demands of Massachusetts and Rhode Island woolen manufacturers, who complained that the British were dumping textiles on the American market at artificially low prices. But to win support from middle and western states, the administration had to accept duties on other items. In the process, it antagonized the original New England supporters of the bill; the benefits of protecting their manufactured goods from foreign competition now had to be weighed against the prospects of having to pay more for raw materials. Adams signed the bill, earning the animosity of southerners, who cursed it as the "tariff of abominations."

Jackson Triumphant

By the time of the 1828 presidential election, a new two-party system had begun to emerge out of the divisions among the Republicans. On one side stood the supporters of John Quincy Adams, who called themselves the National Republicans and who supported the economic nationalism of the preceding years. Opposing them were the followers of Andrew Jackson, who took the name Democratic Republicans and who called for an assault on privilege and a widening of opportunity. Adams attracted the support of most of the remaining Federalists; Jackson appealed to a broad coalition that opposed the "economic aristocracy."

But issues seemed to count for little in the end, as the campaign degenerated into a war of personal invective. The Jacksonians charged that Adams as president had been guilty of gross waste and extravagance and had used public funds to buy gambling devices (a chess set and a billiard table) for the White House. Adams's supporters hurled even worse accusations at Jackson. They called him a murderer and distributed a "coffin handbill," which listed, within coffin-shaped outlines, the names of militiamen whom Jackson was said to have shot in cold blood during the War of 1812. (The men had been deserters who were legally executed after sentence by a court-martial.) And they called his wife a bigamist. Jackson had married his beloved Rachel at a time when the pair incorrectly believed her first husband had divorced her. (When Jackson's wife first read of the accusations against her shortly after the election, she collapsed, and a few weeks later, died; not without reason, Jackson blamed his opponents for her death.)

Jackson's victory was decisive, but sectional. He won 56 percent of the popular vote and an electoral majority of 178 votes to 83. Adams swept virtually all of New England and showed significant strength in the mid-Atlantic region. Nevertheless, the Jacksonians considered their victory as complete and as important as Jefferson's in 1800. Once again, the forces of privilege had been driven from Washington. Once again, a champion of democracy would occupy the White House and restore liberty to the people and to the economy. America had entered, some Jacksonians claimed, a new era of democracy, the "era of the common man."

CONCLUSION

In the aftermath of the War of 1812, a vigorous nationalism came increasingly to characterize the political and popular culture of the United States. In all regions of the country, white men and women celebrated the achievements of the early leaders of the republic, the genius of the Constitution, and the success of the nation in withstanding serious challenges both from without and within. Party divisions faded to the point that James Monroe, the fifth president, won reelection in 1820 without opposition.

But the broad nationalism of the so-called era of good feelings disguised some deep divisions within the United States. Indeed, the character of American nationalism differed substantially from one region, and one group, to another. Battles continued between those who favored a strong central government committed to advancing the economic development of the nation and those who wanted a decentralization of power to open opportunity to more people. Battles continued as well over the role of slavery in American life—and in particular over the place of slavery in the new western territories that the United States was rapidly populating (and wresting from the tribes). The Missouri Compromise of 1820 postponed the day of reckoning on that issue—but only for a time, as Andrew Jackson would discover soon after becoming president in 1829.

FOR FURTHER REFERENCE

Suggested Readings

Frederick Jackson Turner, *The Frontier in American History* (1920) is the classic statement of American exceptionalism. Turner argued that the western frontier endowed the United States with a distinctive, individualist and democratic national character. John Mack Faragher, *Women and Men on the Overland Trail* (1979) was an early and influential book in the "new western history" that challenged Turner. Robert V. Remini, *Andrew Jackson and the Course of American Empire: 1767–1821* (1977) emphasizes Andrew Jackson's importance in American territorial expansion in the South prior to 1821 and in the development of American nationalism. Morton J. Horwitz, *The Transformation of American Law, 1780–1865* (1977), an important work in American legal history, connects changes in the law to changes in the American economy. Ernest R.

May, *The Making of the Monroe Doctrine* (1975) describes the creation of a leading principle of American foreign policy.

Films

(The best source for information on how to find these and other films is *Bowker's Complete Video Directory*—3 volumes.) *Expansionism, Vol. 6* (1996) discusses American expansion from the Louisiana Purchase to the California gold rush. *Expansion & Growth: Nineteenth-Century America* explores similar themes. *Lewis & Clark*, an A&E Biography, traces the historic expedition that mapped the Louisiana Purchase. *Daniel Boone's Final Frontier* (1995) reenacts Daniel Boone's last years in the Louisiana Territory, based on the journals of Nathan and Jemima Boone. *Marbury v. Madison* (1977) dramatizes the 1803 Supreme Court case that established the legitimacy of judicial review. *John Marshall* (1983) focuses on the 1807 treason trial of Aaron Burr. *McCulloch v. Maryland* (1977) examines the case that helped to establish federal supremacy over the states.

Internet Resources

Internet websites containing historical material relevant to the subjects discussed in this chapter can be reached through the McGraw-Hill history site at www.mhhe.com/socscience/history/usa/link/linktop.htm

CHAPTER NINE

Jacksonian America

The Rise of Mass Politics ⌐ *"Our Federal Union"*
The Removal of the Indians ⌐ *Jackson and the Bank War*
The Emergence of the Second Party System ⌐ *Politics After Jackson*

ANY AMERICANS WERE growing apprehensive about the future of their republic in the 1820s and 1830s, as the nation expanded both economically and territorially. Some feared that the rapid growth of the United States would produce social chaos; they insisted that the country's first priority must be to establish order and a clear system of authority. Others argued that the greatest danger facing the nation was the growth of inequality and privilege; they believed that society's goal should be to eliminate the favored status of powerful elites and make opportunity more widely available. Advocates of this latter vision seized control of the federal government in 1829 with the inauguration of Andrew Jackson.

THE RISE OF MASS POLITICS

On March 4, 1829, thousands of Americans from all regions of the country—including many farmers, laborers, and other ordinary men and women—crowded before the United States Capitol to watch the inauguration of Andrew Jackson. After the ceremonies, the crowd poured into a public reception at the White House, where, in their eagerness to shake the new president's hand, they filled the state rooms to overflowing, trampled one another, soiled the carpets, and damaged the upholstery. "It was a proud day for the people," wrote Amos Kendall, one of Jackson's closest political associates. Supreme Court justice Joseph Story, a

TIME LINE

1830	1830–1838	1831	1832
Webster and Hayne debate	Indians expelled from Southeast	Anti-Mason Party holds first convention	Jackson vetoes recharter of Bank of U.S. Jackson reelected

1832–1833	1833	1835	1835–1842
Nullification crisis	Jackson removes deposits from Bank of U.S. Commercial panic	Taney named chief justice of Supreme Court	Seminole War

1836	1837–1844	1840	1841
Specie Circular Van Buren elected president	Panic and depression	William Henry Harrison elected president Independent Treasury Act	Harrison dies; Tyler becomes president

friend and colleague of John Marshall, looked on the inaugural levee, as it was called, and remarked with disgust: "The reign of King 'Mob' seems triumphant."

In fact, the "age of Jackson" was much less a triumph of the common people than Kendall hoped and Story feared. But it did mark a transformation of American politics that extended power widely to new groups. Once restricted to a relatively small elite of property owners, politics now became open to virtually all the nation's white male citizens. In a political sense at least, the era had some claim to the title the Jacksonians gave it: the "era of the common man."

The Expanding Electorate

Until the 1820s, relatively few Americans had been permitted to vote; most states restricted the franchise to white male property owners or taxpayers or both, effectively removing a great mass of the less affluent from

ANDREW JACKSON EN ROUTE TO WASHINGTON, 1829 Only a few weeks after Andrew Jackson's wife died (a result, he believed, of vicious attacks on her by his political enemies), the president-elect began a slow, triumphal procession from Tennessee to Washington, greeted by throngs of admirers in every town through which he passed.

the voting lists. But even before Jackson's election, the franchise began to expand. Change came first in Ohio and other new states of the West, which, on joining the Union, adopted constitutions that guaranteed all adult white males—not just property owners or taxpayers—the right to vote and permitted all voters the right to hold public office. Older states, concerned about the loss of their population to the West, began to drop or reduce their own property ownership or taxpaying requirements. Eventually, every state democratized its electorate to at least some degree.

The wave of state reforms was generally peaceful, but in Rhode Island democratization efforts created considerable instability. The Rhode Island constitution barred more than half the adult males in the state from voting in the 1830s. In 1840, the lawyer and activist Thomas L. Dorr and a group of his followers formed a "People's party," held a convention, drafted a new constitution, and submitted it to a popular vote. It was overwhelmingly approved, and the Dorrites began to set up a new government, with Dorr as governor. The existing legislature, however, rejected the legitimacy of Dorr's constitution. And so, in 1842, two governments were claiming to be the real power in Rhode Island. The old state government proclaimed that Dorr and his followers were rebels and began to imprison them. The Dorrites, meanwhile, made an ineffectual effort to capture the state arsenal. The Dorr Rebellion, as it was known, quickly failed; Dorr himself surrendered and was briefly imprisoned. But the episode helped spur the old guard to draft a new constitution that greatly expanded the suffrage.

The democratization process was far from complete. In much of the South, of course, no slaves could vote. In addition, southern election laws continued to favor the planters and politicians of the older counties and to limit the influence of white residents of more newly settled western areas. Free blacks could not vote anywhere in the South and hardly anywhere in the North. Pennsylvania, in fact, amended its state constitution in 1838 to strip blacks of the right to vote, which they had previously held. In no state could women vote. Nowhere was the ballot secret, and often it was cast as a spoken vote rather than a written one, which meant that voters could be, and often were, bribed or intimidated. Despite the persisting limitations, however, the number of voters increased much more rapidly than did the population as a whole.

One of the most striking political trends of the early nineteenth century was the change in the method of choosing presidential electors and the dramatic increase in popular participation in the process. In 1800, the legislatures had chosen the presidential electors in ten states, and the people in only six. By 1828, electors were chosen by popular vote in every state but South Carolina. In the presidential election of 1824, fewer than 27 percent of adult white males had voted. In the election of 1828, the figure was 58 percent; and in 1840, 80 percent.

The high level of voter participation was only in part the result of an expanded electorate. It was also the result of a growing popular interest in politics and a strengthening of party organization.

The Legitimization of Party

Although factional competition was part of American politics almost from the beginning of the republic, acceptance of the idea of party was not. But in the 1820s and 1830s, most Americans gradually came to consider permanent, institutionalized parties to be a desirable part of the political process, indeed essential to democracy.

The elevation of the idea of party occurred first at the state level, most prominently in New York. There, Martin Van Buren led a dissident political faction (known as the "Bucktails" or the "Albany Regency"). In the years after the War of 1812 this group began to challenge the established political elite—led by the aristocratic governor, De Witt Clinton—that had dominated the state for years. Refuting the traditional view of political parties as undemocratic, they argued that only an institutionalized party, based in the populace, could ensure genuine democracy. The alternative was the sort of closed elite that Clinton had created. For a party to survive, moreover, it must have a permanent opposition. Competing parties would force politicians to remain continually sensitive to the will of the people; they would check and balance each other in much the same way that the different branches of government checked and balanced one another.

By the late 1820s, this new idea of party had spread beyond New York. The election of Jackson in 1828, the result of a popular movement that stood apart from the usual political elites, seemed further to legitimize it. In the 1830s, finally, a fully formed two-party system began to operate at the national level, with each party committed to its own existence as an institution and willing to accept the legitimacy of its opposition. The anti-Jackson forces began to call themselves the Whigs. Jackson's followers called themselves Democrats, thus giving a permanent name to what is now the nation's oldest political party.

President of the Common Man

Andrew Jackson embraced a distinct and simple theory of democracy. Government, he said, should offer "equal protection and equal benefits" to all its white male citizens and favor no one region or class over another. In practice, that meant launching an assault on what Jackson and his associates considered the citadels of the eastern aristocracy and making an effort to extend opportunities to the rising classes of the West and the South.

Jackson's first target was the entrenched officeholders in the federal government, many of whom had been in place for a generation or more. Jackson bitterly denounced what he considered a class of permanent officeholders. Offices, he said, belonged to the people, not to a self-serving bureaucracy. Equally important, a large turnover in the bureaucracy would allow him to reward his own supporters with offices.

ELECTION SCENE Frequent and often boisterous campaign rallies were characteristic of electoral politics in the 1840s, when party loyalties were high and political passions intense—as this 1845 drawing by Alfred Jacob Miller of a rally in Catonsville, Maryland suggests.

One of Jackson's allies, William L. Marcy of New York, once explained, "To the victors belong the spoils"; and patronage, the process of giving out jobs as political rewards, became known as the "spoils system." Although Jackson removed no more than one-fifth of the existing federal officeholders, his embrace of the spoils system helped cement its place in party politics.

Jackson's supporters also worked to transform the process by which presidential candidates were selected. In 1832, the president's followers staged a national convention to renominate him. Through the convention, its founders believed, power in the party would arise directly from the people in a great democratic conclave rather than from such elite political institutions as the congressional caucus.

D E B A T I N G   T H E   P A S T

Jacksonian Democracy

T O MANY Americans in the 1820s and 1830s, Andrew Jackson was a champion of democracy, a symbol of the spirit of antielitism and egalitarianism that was sweeping American life. Historians, however, have disagreed sharply not only in their assessments of Jackson himself but in their portrayal of American society in his era.

The "progressive" historians of the early twentieth century tended to see Jacksonian politics as a forebear of their own battles against economic privilege and political corruption. Frederick Jackson Turner encouraged scholars to see Jacksonianism as the product of the democratic West: a protest by the people of the frontier against the conservative aristocracy of the East, which they believed restricted their own freedom and opportunity. Jackson represented those who wanted to make government responsive to the will of the people rather than to the power of special interests. The culmination of this progressive interpretation of Jacksonianism was the publication in 1945 of Arthur M. Schlesinger, Jr.'s *The Age of Jackson*. Schlesinger was less interested in the regional basis of Jacksonianism than the disciples of Turner had been. Jacksonian Democracy, he argued, was the effort "to control the power of the capitalist groups, mainly Eastern, for the benefit of non-capitalist groups, farmers and laboring men, East, West, and South." He portrayed Jacksonianism as an early version of modern reform efforts (in the progressive era and the New Deal) to "restrain the power of the business community."

Richard Hofstadter, in an influential 1948 essay, sharply disagreed. Jackson, he argued, was the spokesman of rising entrepreneurs—aspiring businessmen who saw the road to opportunity blocked by the monopolis-

tic power of Eastern aristocrats. The Jacksonians opposed special privileges only to the extent that those privileges blocked their own road to
success. They were less sympathetic to the aspirations of those below
them. Bray Hammond, writing in 1957, argued similarly that the Jacksonian cause was "one of enterpriser against capitalist," of rising elites against
entrenched ones. Other historians, exploring the ideological origins of the
movement, saw Jacksonianism less as a democratic reform movement than
as a nostalgic effort to restore a lost (and largely imagined) past. Marvin
Meyers's *The Jacksonian Persuasion* (1957) argued that Jackson and his followers looked with misgivings on the new industrial society emerging
around them and yearned instead for a restoration of the agrarian, republican virtues of an earlier time.

In the 1960s, historians began taking less interest in Jackson and his
supporters and more in the social and cultural bases of American politics
in the time of Jackson. Lee Benson's *The Concept of Jacksonian Democracy*
(1961) used quantitative techniques to demonstrate the role of religion
and ethnicity in shaping party divisions. Edward Pessen's *Jacksonian
America* (1969) portrayed America in the Jacksonian era as an increasingly
stratified, and increasingly unequal, society. This inclination to look
more closely at society than at formal "Jacksonianism" has continued into
the 1980s and 1990s. Sean Wilentz, in *Chants Democratic* (1984), examined the rise of a powerful class identification among workers in New
York, who were attracted less to Jackson than to an artisanal notion of
democracy.

Gradually, this attention to the nature of society has led to reassess-
ments of Jackson himself and the nature of his regime. In *Father and Children* (1975), Michael Rogin portrays Jackson as a leader determined to secure the supremacy of white men in the United States, a commitment
illustrated by his almost pathological violence toward Indians. Alexander
Saxton, in *The Rise and Fall of the White Republic* (1990) makes the related
argument that "Jacksonian Democracy" was explicitly a white man's
democracy that rested on the subjugation of slaves, women, and Native
Americans. But the portrayal of Jackson as a champion of the common
man has not vanished from scholarship entirely. The most renowned postwar biographer of Jackson, Robert V. Remini, argues that, despite the
flaws in his democratic vision, he was—within the context of his time—a
genuine "man of the people."

"OUR FEDERAL UNION"

Jackson's commitment to extending power beyond entrenched elites led him to want to reduce the functions of the federal government. A concentration of power in Washington would, he believed, restrict opportunity to people with political connections. But Jackson also believed in forceful presidential leadership and was strongly committed to the preservation of the Union. Thus at the same time that Jackson was promoting an economic program to reduce the power of the national government, he was asserting the supremacy of the Union in the face of a potent challenge. For no sooner had he entered office than his own vice president—John C. Calhoun—began to champion a controversial (and, in Jackson's view, dangerous) constitutional theory: nullification.

Calhoun and Nullification

Calhoun was forty-six years old in 1828, with a distinguished past and an apparently promising future. But the smoldering issue of the tariff created a dilemma for him. Once he had been an outspoken protectionist and had strongly supported the tariff of 1816. But by the late 1820s, many South Carolinians had come to believe that the "tariff of abominations" was responsible for the stagnation of their state's economy—even though the stagnation was largely a result of the exhaustion of South Carolina's farmland, which could no longer compete effectively with the newly opened and fertile lands of the Southwest. Some exasperated Carolinians were ready to consider a drastic remedy—secession.

Calhoun's future political hopes rested on how he met this challenge in his home state. He did so by developing a theory that he believed offered a more moderate alternative to secession: the theory of nullification. Drawing from the ideas of Madison and Jefferson and their Virginia and Kentucky Resolutions of 1798–1799 and citing the Tenth Amendment to the Constitution, Calhoun argued that since the federal government was a creation of the states, the states—not the courts or Congress—were the final arbiters of the constitutionality of federal laws. If a state concluded that Congress had passed an unconstitutional law, then it could hold a special convention and declare the federal law null and void within the state. The nullification doctrine—and the idea of using it to nullify the 1828 tariff—quickly attracted broad support in South Carolina. But it did nothing to help Calhoun's standing within the new administration, in part because he had a powerful rival in Martin Van Buren.

The Rise of Van Buren

Van Buren was about the same age as Calhoun and equally ambitious. He had won election to the governorship of New York in 1828 and then resigned in 1829 when Jackson appointed him secretary of state. Alone among the figures in the Jackson administration, Van Buren soon established himself as a member both of the official cabinet and of the president's unofficial circle of political allies, known as the "Kitchen Cabinet" (which included such Democratic newspaper editors as Isaac Hill of New Hampshire and Amos Kendall and Francis P. Blair of Kentucky). Van Buren's influence with the president was unmatched and grew stronger still as a result of a quarrel over etiquette that drove a wedge between the president and Calhoun.

Peggy O'Neale was the attractive daughter of a Washington tavern keeper with whom both Andrew Jackson and his friend John H. Eaton had taken lodgings while serving as senators from Tennessee. O'Neale was married, but rumors circulated in Washington in the mid-1820s that she and Senator Eaton were having an affair. O'Neale's husband died in 1828, and she and Eaton were soon married. A few weeks later, Jackson named Eaton secretary of war and thus made the new Mrs. Eaton a cabinet wife. The rest of the administration wives, led by Mrs. Calhoun, refused to receive her. Jackson (remembering the effects of public slander directed against his own late wife) was furious and demanded that the members of the cabinet accept her into their social world. Calhoun, under pressure from his wife, refused. Van Buren, a widower, befriended the Eatons and thus ingratiated himself with Jackson. By 1831, partly as a result of the Peggy Eaton affair, Jackson had chosen Van Buren to succeed him in the White House, apparently ending Calhoun's dreams of the presidency.

The Webster-Hayne Debate

In January 1830, as the controversy over nullification grew more intense, a great debate occurred in the United States Senate over another sectional controversy. In the midst of a routine debate over federal policy toward western lands, a senator from Connecticut suggested that all land sales and surveys be temporarily discontinued. Robert Y. Hayne, a young senator from South Carolina, responded, charging that slowing down the growth of the West was a way for the East to retain its political and economic power. Although he had no real interest in western lands, he hoped his stance would attract support from westerners in Congress for South

Carolina's drive to lower the tariff. Both the South and the West, he argued, were victims of the tyranny of the Northeast. He hinted that the two regions might combine to defend themselves against that tyranny.

Daniel Webster, now a senator from Massachusetts and a nationalistic Whig, answered Hayne the next day. He attacked Hayne, and through him Calhoun, for what he considered their challenge to the integrity of the Union—in effect, challenging Hayne to a debate not on public lands and the tariff but on the issue of states' rights versus national power. Hayne, coached by Calhoun, responded with a defense of the theory of nullification. Webster then spent two full afternoons delivering what became known as his "Second Reply to Hayne," a speech that northerners quoted and revered for years to come. He concluded with the ringing appeal: "Liberty and Union, now and for ever, one and inseparable!"

Both sides now waited to hear what President Jackson thought of the argument. The answer became clear at the annual Democratic Party banquet in honor of Thomas Jefferson. After dinner, guests delivered a series of toasts. The president arrived with a written text in which he had underscored certain words: "Our Federal Union—It must be preserved." While he spoke, he looked directly at Calhoun. The diminutive Van Buren, who stood on his chair to see better, thought he saw Calhoun's hand shake and a trickle of wine run down his glass as he responded to the president's toast with his own: "The Union, next to our liberty most dear." Sharp lines were being drawn.

The Nullification Crisis

In 1832, finally, the controversy over nullification produced a crisis when South Carolinians responded angrily to a congressional tariff bill that offered them no relief from the 1828 "tariff of abominations." Almost immediately, the legislature summoned a state convention, which voted to nullify the tariffs of 1828 and 1832 and to forbid the collection of duties within the state. At the same time, South Carolina elected Hayne to serve as governor and Calhoun (who resigned as vice president) to replace Hayne as senator.

Jackson insisted that nullification was treason and that those implementing it were traitors. He strengthened the federal forts in South Carolina and ordered a warship and several revenue ships to Charleston. When Congress convened early in 1833, Jackson proposed a force bill authorizing the president to use the military to see that acts of Congress were obeyed. Violence seemed a real possibility.

Calhoun faced a predicament as he took his place in the Senate. Not a single state had come to South Carolina's support. Even South Carolina itself was divided and could not hope to prevail in a showdown with the federal government. But the timely intervention of Henry Clay, newly elected to the Senate, averted a crisis. Clay devised a compromise by which the tariff would be lowered gradually so that, by 1842, it would reach approximately the same level as in 1816. The compromise and the force bill were passed on the same day, March 1, 1833. Jackson signed them both. In South Carolina, the convention reassembled and repealed its nullification of the tariffs. But unwilling to allow Congress to have the last word, the convention nullified the force act—a purely symbolic act, since the tariff toward which the force act was directed had already been repealed. Calhoun and his followers claimed a victory for nullification, which had, they insisted, forced the revision of the tariff. But the episode taught Calhoun and his allies that no state could defy the federal government alone.

THE REMOVAL OF THE INDIANS

Andrew Jackson's attitude toward the Indian tribes that remained in the eastern United States was simple and clear. He wanted them to move west, out of the way of expanding white settlement. Jackson harbored a deep hostility toward the Indians drawn from his earlier experiences leading military campaigns against the tribes. In embracing these prejudices, he was little different from most white Americans.

White Attitudes Toward the Tribes

In the eighteenth century, many whites had shared Thomas Jefferson's view of the Indians as "noble savages," peoples without real civilization but with an inherent dignity that made civilization possible among them. By the first decades of the nineteenth century, however, this vaguely philanthropic attitude was fading, particularly among the whites in the West. They were coming to view Native Americans simply as "savages," not only uncivilized but uncivilizable. That was one reason for the growing white commitment to removing the Indians from all the lands east of the Mississippi: the belief that whites could not be expected to live in close proximity to "savages." But white westerners also favored removal to put an end to violence and conflict in the western areas of white settlement. Most of all, however, they wanted valuable land that the tribes still possessed.

BLACK HAWK AND WHIRLING THUNDER After his defeat by white settlers in Illinois in 1832, the famed Sauk warrior Black Hawk and his son, Whirling Thunder, were captured and sent on a tour by Andrew Jackson, displayed to the public as trophies of war. They showed such dignity through the ordeal that much of the white public quickly began to sympathize with them. This portrait, by John Wesley Jarvis, was painted on the tour's final stop, in New York City. Black Hawk wears the European-style suit, while Whirling Thunder wears native costume to emphasize his commitment to his tribal roots. Soon thereafter, Black Hawk returned to his tribe, wrote a celebrated autobiography, and died in 1838.

Events in the Northwest added urgency to the issue of removal. In Illinois, an alliance of Sauk (or Sac) and Fox Indians under the fabled and now aged warrior Black Hawk fought white settlers in 1831–1832 in an effort to overturn what Black Hawk considered an illegal treaty ceding tribal lands in that state to the United States. The Black Hawk War was a major defeat for the Indians, and was notable for the viciousness of the white military efforts. White forces attacked the Indians even when they attempted to surrender, pursued them as they retreated, and slaughtered many of them. But its real impact was to reinforce the determination of whites to remove all the tribes to the West.

The "Five Civilized Tribes"

Even more troubling to the government in the 1830s were the remaining Indian tribes of the South. In western Georgia, Alabama, Mississippi, and Florida lived what were known as the "Five Civilized Tribes"—the Cherokee, Creek, Seminole, Chickasaw, and Choctaw—most of whom were part of settled agricultural societies. In 1830, both the federal government and several southern states were accelerating efforts to remove the tribes to the West. Most were too weak to resist, but some fought back.

The Cherokees tried to stop the state of Georgia from taking their lands through an appeal in the Supreme Court, and the Court's rulings in *Cherokee Nation* v. *Georgia* and *Worcester* v. *Georgia* supported the tribe's contention that the state had no authority to negotiate with tribal representatives. But Jackson repudiated the decisions, reportedly responding to news of the rulings with the contemptuous statement: "John Marshall has made his decision. Now let him enforce it." Then, in 1835, the United States government extracted a treaty from a minority faction of the Cherokees that ceded to Georgia the tribe's land in that state in return for $5 million and a reservation west of the Mississippi. The great majority of the 17,000 Cherokees did not recognize the treaty as legitimate and refused to leave their homes. But Jackson sent an army of 7,000 under General Winfield Scott to round them up and drive them westward.

Trails of Tears

About 1,000 Cherokee fled to North Carolina, where eventually the federal government provided them with a small reservation in the Smoky Mountains that survives today. But most of the rest made a long, forced trek to "Indian Territory" (formally created by the Indian Intercourse Act of 1834), what later became Oklahoma, beginning in the winter of 1838. Thousands, perhaps a quarter or more of the émigrés, perished before reaching their unwanted destination. In the harsh new reservations in which they were now forced to live, the survivors remembered the terrible journey as "The Trail Where They Cried," the Trail of Tears.

Between 1830 and 1838, virtually all the Five Civilized Tribes were expelled from the southern states and forced to travel along their own Trails of Tears to Indian Territory. The Choctaws of Mississippi and western Alabama were the first to make the trek, beginning in 1830. The army moved out the Creeks of eastern Alabama and western Georgia in 1836. The Chickasaws in northern Mississippi began the long march westward a year later, and the Cherokees, finally, a year after that.

Only the Seminoles in Florida were able to resist the pressures, and even their success was limited. Like other tribes, the Seminoles had

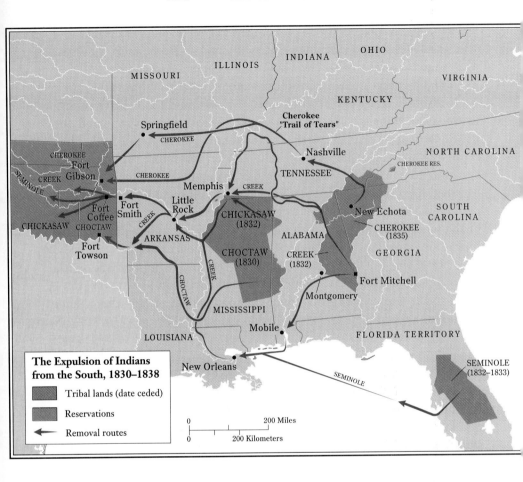

The Expulsion of Indians from the South, 1830–1838

■ Tribal lands (date ceded)

■ Reservations

← Removal routes

0   200 Miles
0   200 Kilometers

agreed under pressure to a settlement (the 1832–1833 treaties of Payne's Landing) by which they ceded their lands to the United States and agreed to move to Indian Territory within three years. Most did move west, but a substantial minority, under the leadership of the chieftain Osceola, balked and staged an uprising beginning in 1835 to defend their lands. (Joining the Indians in their struggle was a group of runaway black slaves, who had been living with the tribe.) The Seminole War dragged on for years. Jackson sent troops to Florida, but the Seminoles and their black allies were masters of guerrilla warfare in the junglelike Everglades. Finally, in 1842, the government abandoned the war. By then, many of the Seminoles had been either killed or forced westward. But the relocation of the Seminoles, unlike the relocation of most of the other tribes, was never complete.

The Meaning of Removal

By the end of the 1830s, virtually all the important Indian societies east of the Mississippi (with a few exceptions such as remnants of the Seminoles and Cherokees) had been removed to the West. The tribes had ceded over 100 million acres of eastern land to the federal government; they had received in return about $68 million and 32 million acres in the far less hospitable lands west of the Mississippi. There they lived, divided by tribe into a series of separate reservations, in a territory surrounded by a string of United States forts to keep them in (and to keep most whites out), in a region whose climate and topography bore little relation to anything they had known before. Eventually, even this forlorn enclave would face pressures from white civilization.

What were the alternatives to the removal of the eastern Indians? There was probably never any realistic possibility that the government could stop white expansion westward. White people had already been penetrating the West for nearly two centuries, and such penetrations were certain to continue. But there were, in theory at least, alternatives to the brutal removal policy. The West was filled with examples of white settlers and native tribes living side by side and creating a shared (if not necessarily equal) world. In the pueblos of New Mexico, in the fur trading posts of the Pacific Northwest, in parts of Texas and California, settlers from Mexico, Canada, and the United States had created societies in which Indians and whites were in intimate contact with each other. Even the Lewis and Clark expedition, during its famous explorations, had lived with western Indians on terms of such intimacy that many of its members contracted venereal disease from Indian sexual partners. Sometimes these close contacts between whites and Indians were beneficial to both sides, even reasonably equal. Often they were cruel and exploitive. But the early multiracial societies of the West did not separate whites and Indians. They demonstrated ways in which the two cultures could interact, each shaping the other.

By the mid-nineteenth century, however, white Americans had adopted a different model as they contemplated westward expansion. Much as the early British settlers along the Atlantic coast had established "plantations," from which natives were, in theory, to be excluded, so the western whites of later years believed that Indians could not be partners—either equal or subordinate—in the creation of new societies in the West. They were obstacles to be removed and, as far as possible, isolated.

JACKSON AND THE BANK WAR

Jackson was quite willing to use federal power against the Indian tribes. Where white Americans were concerned, however, he was more reluctant. An early example of that was his 1830 veto of a congressional measure providing a subsidy to the proposed Maysville Road in Kentucky. The bill was unconstitutional, Jackson argued, because the road in question lay entirely within Kentucky and was not, therefore, a part of "interstate commerce." But the bill was also unwise because it committed the government to what Jackson considered extravagant expenditures. A similar resistance to federal power lay behind the most celebrated episode of Jackson's presidency: the war against the Bank of the United States.

Biddle's Institution

The Bank of the United States had a monopoly on the deposits of the federal government, which owned one-fifth of the Bank's stock; it also did a tremendous business in general banking. It provided credit to growing enterprises; it issued bank notes that served as a dependable medium of exchange throughout the country; and it exercised a restraining effect on the less well-managed state banks. Nicholas Biddle, who ran the Bank from 1823 on from its imposing headquarters in Philadelphia, had done much to put the institution on a sound and prosperous basis. Nevertheless, many Americans—among them Andrew Jackson—were determined to destroy it.

Opposition to the Bank came from two very different groups: the "soft-money" faction and the "hard-money" faction. Advocates of soft money consisted largely of state bankers and their allies. They objected to the Bank of the United States because it restrained the state banks from issuing notes freely. The hard-money supporters believed that coin was the only safe currency, and they condemned all banks that issued bank notes, including the Bank of the United States. The soft-money advocates were believers in rapid economic growth and speculation; the hard-money forces embraced older ideas of "public virtue" and looked with suspicion on expansion and speculation. Jackson himself supported the hard-money position, but he was also sensitive to the complaints of his many soft-money supporters in the West and the South. He made it clear that he would not favor renewing the charter of the Bank of the United States, which was due to expire in 1836.

Biddle was a Philadelphia aristocrat, unaccustomed to politics. But in his efforts to save the Bank, he began granting banking favors to influential men. In particular, he relied on Daniel Webster, whom he named the Bank's legal counsel and director of the Boston branch. Webster was also a frequent, heavy borrower. He helped Biddle enlist the support of Henry Clay as well. Clay, Webster, and other advisers persuaded Biddle to apply to Congress for a recharter bill in 1832, four years ahead of the expiration date. Congress passed the recharter bill; Jackson vetoed it; and the Bank's supporters in Congress failed to override the veto. The Bank question then emerged as the paramount issue of the 1832 election, just as Clay had hoped.

In 1832, Clay ran for president as the unanimous choice of the National Republicans. But the "Bank War" failed to provide Clay with the winning issue for which he had hoped. Jackson, with Van Buren as his running mate, won an overwhelming victory with 55 percent of the popular vote and 219 electoral votes.

The "Monster" Destroyed

Jackson was now more determined than ever to destroy the "monster." He could not legally abolish the Bank before the expiration of its charter. But he weakened it by removing the government's deposits from it. His secretary of the treasury believed that such an action would destabilize the financial system and refused to give the order. Jackson fired him and appointed a replacement. When the new secretary similarly procrastinated, Jackson fired him, too, and named a third: Roger B. Taney, the attorney general, a close friend and loyal ally of the president.

Taney soon began taking the government's deposits out of the Bank of the United States and putting them in a number of state banks (which Jackson's enemies called "pet banks"). In response, Biddle called in loans and raised interest rates, explaining that without the government deposits the Bank's resources were stretched too thin. His actions precipitated a short recession, which Biddle thought would pressure Congress to recharter the Bank.

As financial conditions worsened in the winter of 1833–1834, supporters of the Bank organized meetings around the country and sent petitions to Washington urging a rechartering of the Bank. But the Jacksonians blamed the recession on Biddle and refused. The banker finally carried his contraction of credit too far and had to reverse himself to appease the business community. His hopes of winning a recharter of the Bank died in the process. Jackson had won a considerable political victory. But when the Bank of the United States died in 1836, the country lost an important financial institution and was left with a fragmented and chronically unstable banking system that would plague the economy for many years.

The Taney Court

In the aftermath of the Bank War, Jackson moved against the most powerful remaining institution of economic nationalism: the Supreme Court. In 1835, when John Marshall died, the president appointed as the new chief justice his trusted ally Roger B. Taney. Taney did not bring a sharp break in constitutional interpretation, but he did help modify Marshall's vigorous nationalism.

Perhaps the clearest indication of the new judicial climate was the celebrated case of *Charles River Bridge* v. *Warren Bridge* of 1837. The case involved a dispute between two Massachusetts companies over the right to build a bridge across the Charles River between Boston and Cambridge. One company had a longstanding charter from the state to operate a toll bridge, a charter that the firm claimed guaranteed it a monopoly of the bridge traffic. Another company had applied to the legislature for authorization to construct a second, competing bridge that would—since it would be toll-free—greatly reduce the value of the first company's charter. The first company contended that in granting the second charter, the legislature was engaging in a breach of contract; and it noted that the Marshall Court, in the *Dartmouth College* case and other decisions, had ruled that states had no right to abrogate contracts. But now Taney, speaking for the Democratic majority on the Court, supported the right of Massachusetts to award the second charter. The object of government, Taney maintained, was to promote the general happiness, an object that took precedence over the rights of property. A state, therefore, had the right to amend or abrogate a contract if such action was necessary to advance the well-being of the community. The decision reflected one of the cornerstones of the Jacksonian idea: that the key to democracy was an expansion of economic opportunity, which would not occur if older corporations could maintain monopolies and choke off competition from newer companies.

THE EMERGENCE OF THE SECOND PARTY SYSTEM

Jackson's forceful—some claimed tyrannical—tactics in crushing first the nullification movement and then the Bank of the United States helped galvanize a growing opposition coalition that by the mid-1830s was ready to assert itself in national politics. It began as a gathering of national political leaders opposed to Jackson's use of power. Denouncing the president as "King Andrew I," they began to refer to themselves as Whigs, after the party in England that traditionally worked to limit the power of the king. With the emergence of the Whigs, the nation once again had two competing political parties. What scholars now call the "second party system" had begun what would turn out to be its relatively brief life.

The Two Parties

The philosophy of the Democratic Party in the 1830s bore the stamp of Andrew Jackson. The federal government, the Democrats believed, should be limited in power, except to the degree that it worked to eliminate social and economic arrangements that entrenched privilege and stifled opportunity. The rights of states should be protected except to the extent that state governments interfered with social and economic mobility. Jacksonian Democrats celebrated "honest workers," "simple farmers," and "forthright businessmen" and contrasted them to the corrupt, monopolistic, aristocratic forces of established wealth. Democrats were more likely than Whigs to support territorial expansion, which would, they believed, widen opportunities for aspiring Americans. Among the most radical members of the party—the so-called Locofocos, mainly workingmen and small businessmen and professionals in the Northeast—sentiment was strong for a vigorous, perhaps even violent, assault on monopoly and privilege far in advance of anything Jackson himself ever contemplated.

The political philosophy that became known as Whiggery favored expanding the power of the federal government, encouraging industrial and commercial development, and knitting the country together into a consolidated economic system. Whigs were cautious about westward expansion, fearful that rapid territorial growth would produce instability. Their vision of America was of a nation embracing the industrial future and rising to greatness as a commercial and manufacturing power. And although Whigs insisted that their vision would result in increasing opportunities for all Americans, they tended to attribute particular value to the elites they considered the productive, modernizing forces in society—the entrepreneurs and institutions that most effectively promoted economic growth.

The Whigs were strongest among the more substantial merchants and manufacturers of the Northeast; the wealthier planters of the South (those who favored commercial development and the strengthening of ties with the North); and the ambitious farmers and rising commercial class of the West—usually migrants from the Northeast—who advocated internal improvements, expanding trade, and rapid economic progress. The Democrats drew more support from smaller merchants and the workingmen of the Northeast; from Southern planters suspicious of industrial growth; and from westerners—usually with Southern roots—who favored a predominantly agrarian economy and opposed the development of powerful economic institutions in their region. Whigs tended to be wealthier than Democrats, tended to have more aristocratic backgrounds, and tended to be more commercially ambitious. But Whigs and Democrats alike were more interested in winning elections than in maintaining philosophical purity. And both parties made adjustments from region to region in order to attract the largest possible number of voters, often at the sacrifice of party philosophy.

In New York, for example, the Whigs developed a popular following through a movement known as Anti-Masonry. The Anti-Mason Party had emerged in the 1820s in response to widespread resentment against the secret and exclusive, hence supposedly undemocratic, Society of Freemasons. Such resentment increased in 1826 when a former Mason, William Morgan, mysteriously disappeared from his home in Batavia, New York, shortly before he was scheduled to publish a book that would allegedly expose the secrets of Freemasonry. The assumption was widespread that Morgan had been abducted and murdered by the vengeful Masons. Whigs seized on the Anti-Mason frenzy to launch spirited attacks on Jackson and Van Buren (both Freemasons), implying that the Democrats were connected with the antidemocratic conspiracy. By embracing Anti-Masonry, Whigs were attacking the Democrats with the Democrats' own issues.

Religious and ethnic divisions also played an important role in determining the constituencies of the two parties. Irish and German Catholics, among the largest of the recent immigrant groups, tended to support the

Democrats, who appeared to share their own vague aversion to commercial development and entrepreneurial progress and who seemed to respect and protect their cultural values and habits. Evangelical Protestants gravitated toward the Whigs because they associated the party with constant development and improvement, goals their own religion embraced. They envisioned a society progressing steadily toward unity and order, and they looked on the new immigrant communities as a threat to that progress—as groups that needed to be disciplined and taught "American" ways.

The Whig Party was more successful at defining its positions and attracting a constituency than it was in uniting behind a national leader. No one person was ever able to command the loyalties of the party in the way Jackson commanded the loyalties of the Democrats. Instead, Whigs tended to divide their allegiance among three major figures: Henry Clay, Daniel Webster, and John C. Calhoun.

Clay won support from many of those who favored internal improvements and economic development, what he called the American System; such improvements were especially important to people living in the western states, where the absence of good transportation routes to the markets of the east often proved crippling to commerce. But Clay's image as a devious political operator and his identification with the West proved an insuperable liability. He ran for president three times and never won. Daniel Webster, the greatest orator of his era, won broad support among the Whigs with his passionate speeches in defense of the Constitution and the Union; but his close connection with the Bank of the United States and the protective tariff, his reliance on rich men for financial support, and his excessive fondness for brandy prevented him from developing enough of a national constituency to win him the office he so desperately wanted. John C. Calhoun, the third member of what became known as the Great Triumvirate, never considered himself a true Whig, and his identification with the nullification controversy in effect disqualified him from national leadership in any case. Yet, he sided with Clay and Webster on the issue of the national bank, and he shared with them a strong animosity toward Andrew Jackson.

The Whigs competed relatively evenly with the Democrats in congressional, state, and local races, but they managed to win only two presidential elections in the more than twenty years of their history. Their problems became particularly clear in 1836. The Democrats were united behind Andrew Jackson's personal choice for president, Martin Van Buren. The Whigs could not even agree on a single candidate. Instead, they ran several candidates, hoping to profit from the regional strength of each: Webster in New England; Hugh Lawson White of Tennessee in the South; and the former Indian fighter and hero of the War of 1812, William Henry Harrison of Ohio, in the middle states and the West. Whig leaders hoped they might separately draw enough votes from Van Buren to prevent his getting a majority and throw the election to the House of Representatives, where the Whigs might be better able to elect one of their candidates. In the end, however, the three Whigs were no match for the one Democrat. Van Buren won easily, with 170 electoral votes to 124 for all his opponents.

POLITICS AFTER JACKSON

Andrew Jackson retired from public life in 1837, the most beloved political figure of his age. Martin Van Buren was less fortunate. He could not match Jackson's personal magnetism, and his administration suffered from economic difficulties that hurt both him and his party.

The Panic of 1837

Van Buren's success in the 1836 election was a result in part of a nationwide economic boom that was then reaching its height. Canal and railroad builders were at a peak of activity. Prices were rising, and credit was plentiful. The land business, in particular, was booming. Between 1835 and 1837, the government sold nearly 40 million acres of public land, nearly three-fourths of it to speculators who purchased large tracts in hopes of reselling them at a profit. These land sales, along with revenues the government received from the tariff of 1833, created a series of substantial federal budget surpluses and made possible a steady reduction of the national debt (something Jackson had always advocated). From 1835 to 1837, the government for the first and only time in its history was out of debt, with a substantial surplus in the Treasury.

Congress and the administration now faced the question of what to do with the Treasury surplus. Support soon grew for returning the federal surplus to the states. An 1836 "distribution" act required the federal government to pay its surplus funds to the states each year in four quarterly installments as interest-free, unsecured loans. No one expected the "loans" to be repaid. The states spent the money quickly, mainly to promote the construction of highways, railroads, and canals. The distribution of the surplus thus gave further stimulus to the economic boom. At the same time, the withdrawal of federal funds strained the state (or "pet") banks in which they had been deposited by the government; the banks had to call in their own loans to make the transfer of funds to the state governments.

Congress did nothing to check the speculative fever, with which many congressmen themselves were badly infected. But Jackson, always suspicious of paper currency, feared that the government was selling land for state bank notes of questionable value. In 1836, not long before leaving office, he issued an executive order, the "specie circular." It provided that in payment for public lands, the government would accept only gold or silver coins or currency backed by gold or silver. The specie circular produced a financial panic that began in the first months of Van Buren's presidency. Hundreds of banks and hundreds of businesses failed. Unemployment grew. There were bread riots in some of the larger cities. Prices fell, especially the price of land. Many railroad and canal projects failed; several of the debt-burdened state governments ceased to pay interest on their bonds, and a few repudiated their debts, at least temporarily. It was the worst depression in American history to that point, and it lasted for five years. It was a political catastrophe for Van Buren and the Democrats.

The Van Buren Program

The Van Buren administration, which strongly opposed government intervention in the economy, did little to fight the depression. Some of the steps it took—borrowing money to pay government debts and accepting only specie for payment of taxes—may have made things worse. Other efforts failed in Congress: a "preemption" bill that would have given settlers the right to buy government land near them before it was opened for public sale, and another bill that would have lowered the price of land. Van Buren did succeed in establishing a ten-hour workday on all federal projects by issuing a presidential order, but he had few legislative achievements.

The most important and controversial measure in the president's program was a proposal for a new financial system to replace the Bank of the United States. Under Van Buren's plan, known as the "independent treasury" or "subtreasury" system, government funds would be placed in an independent treasury in Washington and in subtreasuries in other cities. No private banks would have the government's money or name to use as a basis for speculation; the government and the banks would be "divorced." Van Buren called a special session of Congress in 1837 to consider the proposal, which failed in the House. In 1840, the administration finally succeeded in driving the measure through both houses of Congress.

The Log Cabin Campaign

As the campaign of 1840 approached, the Whigs realized that they would have to settle on one candidate for president. In December 1839, they held their first nomination convention. Passing over Henry Clay, they chose William Henry Harrison—a descendant of the Virginia aristocracy who had spent his adult life in the Northwest. He was a renowned soldier and a popular national figure. The Democrats again nominated Van Buren.

The 1840 campaign was the first in which the new and popular "penny press" carried news of the candidates to large audiences of workers and tradespeople. Newspapers of the "penny press" were deliberately livelier and even more sensationalistic than the newspapers of the past, which had been almost entirely directed at the upper classes. The New York *Sun*, the first of the new breed, began publishing in 1833 and was from the beginning self-

THE NEW YORK *SUN* This 1834 front page of the *Sun*, which had begun publication a year earlier, contains advertisements, light stories, a description of a slave auction in Charleston, South Carolina, and homespun advice: "Life is short. The poor pittance of several years is not worth being a villain for."

consciously egalitarian, eager to tweak and embarrass the rich and powerful. It soon had the largest circulation in New York. Other, similar papers soon began appearing in other cities—reinforcing the increasingly democratic character of political culture and validating the inclination of both parties to try to appeal to ordinary voters as they planned their campaigns.

The campaign of 1840 also illustrated how fully the spirit of party competition had established itself in America. The Whigs—who had emerged as a party largely because of their opposition to Andrew Jackson's common-man democracy, who in most regions represented the

WHIG HEADQUARTERS The Whig Party managed in 1840 to disguise its relatively elitist roots by portraying its presidential candidate, the patrician General William Henry Harrison, as a product of a log cabin who enjoyed drinking hard cider from a jug. Pictures of log cabins abounded in Whig campaign posters, as seen in this drawing of a Harrison rally in Philadelphia.

more affluent elements of the population, who favored government policies that would aid business—presented themselves in 1840 as the party of the common people. So, of course, did the Democrats. Both parties used the same techniques of mass voter appeal, the same evocation of simple, rustic values. What mattered was not the philosophical purity of the party but its ability to win votes. The Whig campaign was particularly effective in portraying William Henry Harrison, a wealthy member of the frontier elite with a considerable estate, as a simple man of the people who loved log cabins and hard cider. The Democrats, already weakened by the depression, had no effective defense against such tactics. Harrison won the election with 234 electoral votes to 60 for Van Buren and with a popular majority of 53 percent.

The Frustration of the Whigs

But the Whigs found the four years after their resounding victory frustrating and divisive. In large part, that was because their appealing new president died of pneumonia one month after taking office. Vice President John Tyler of Virginia succeeded him. Control of the administration thus fell to a man with whom the Whig Party leadership had relatively weak ties.

Tyler was a former Democrat who had left the party in reaction to what he considered Jackson's excessively egalitarian program and his imperious methods. But his approach to public policy still showed signs of his Democratic past. The president did agree to bills abolishing Van Buren's independent-treasury system and raising tariff rates. But he refused to support Clay's attempt to recharter the Bank of the United States. And he vetoed several internal improvement bills sponsored by Clay and other congressional Whigs. Finally, a conference of congressional Whigs (many of whom referred scornfully to the new president as "His Accidency") read Tyler out of the party. Every cabinet member but Webster, who was serving as secretary of state, resigned; five former Democrats took their places. When Webster, too, left the cabinet, Tyler appointed Calhoun, who had rejoined the Democratic Party, to replace him.

A new political alignment was taking shape. Tyler and a small band of conservative southern Whigs were preparing to rejoin the Democrats. Into the common man's party of Jackson and Van Buren was arriving a faction with decidedly aristocratic political ideas, men who thought that government had an obligation to protect and even expand the institution of slavery and who believed in states' rights with almost fanatical devotion.

Whig Diplomacy

In the midst of these domestic controversies, a series of incidents brought Great Britain and the United States to the brink of war in the late 1830s.

Anti-British factions in Canada launched an unsuccessful rebellion against the colonial government there in 1837. When the insurrection failed, some of the rebels took refuge near the United States border and chartered an American steamship, the *Caroline*, to ship them supplies across the Niagara River from New York. British authorities in Canada seized the *Caroline* and burned it, killing one American in the process. The British government refused either to disavow the attack or to provide compensation for it, and resentment in the United States grew rapidly.

At the same time, tensions flared over the boundary between Canada and Maine, which had been in dispute since the treaty of 1783. In 1838, rival groups of Americans and Canadians, mostly lumberjacks, began moving into the Aroostook River region in the disputed area, precipitating a violent brawl between them that became known as the "Aroostook War." Several years later, there were yet more Anglo-American problems. In 1841, an American ship, the *Creole*, sailed from Virginia for New Orleans with more than 100 slaves aboard. En route the slaves mutinied, seized possession of the ship, and took it to the Bahamas. British officials there declared the slaves free, and the English government refused to overrule them. Many Americans, especially southerners, were furious.

At this critical juncture a new government eager to reduce tensions with the United States came to power in Great Britain. It sent Lord Ashburton, an admirer of America, to negotiate an agreement on the Maine boundary and other matters. The result was the Webster-Ashburton Treaty of 1842, under which the United States received slightly more than half the disputed area and agreed to a revised northern boundary as far west as the Rocky Mountains. Ashburton also eased the memory of the *Caroline* and *Creole* affairs by expressing regret and promising no future "officious interference" with American ships. The Webster-Ashburton Treaty was popular in America, and Anglo-American relations improved significantly as a result.

During the Tyler administration, the United States established its first diplomatic relations with China as part of an effort to win a share in the newly emerging China trade. In the Treaty of Wang Hya, concluded in 1844, American diplomats secured the same trading privileges as the English. In the next ten years, American trade with China steadily increased.

In their diplomatic efforts, at least, the Whigs were able to secure some important successes. But by the end of the Tyler administration, the party could look back on few other victories. In the election of 1844, the Whigs lost the White House. They were to win only one more national election in their history.

CONCLUSION

The election of Andrew Jackson to the presidency in 1828 marked not only the triumph of a particular vision of government and democracy. It represented as well the emergence of a new political world. Throughout the American nation, the laws governing political participation were loosening and the number of people permitted to vote (which eventually included most white males, but almost no one else) was increasing. Along with this expansion of the electorate was emerging a new spirit of party politics. Parties had once been reviled by American leaders as contributing to the spirit of faction. Now a new set of ideas was emerging that saw institutionalized parties not as a challenge, but as a contribution to democracy. Party competition would be a way of containing and muting disagreements that might otherwise run amok. It would be another of the healthy restraints—another part of the system of checks and balances—that made American government work.

Andrew Jackson was a party man, and he set out as president to entrench his party, the Democrats, in power. He was also a fierce defender of his region, the West, and a sharp critic of what he considered the strangehold of the aristocratic East on the nation's economic life. He sought to limit the role of the federal government in economic affairs, fearful that it would serve to entrench existing patterns of wealth and power. He worked to destroy the Bank of the United States, which he considered a corrupt vehicle of aristocratic influence. Jackson was, finally, a nationalist. And he confronted the greatest challenge to American unity yet to have emerged in the young nation—the nullification crisis of 1832–1833—with a strong assertion of the power and importance of the Union. These positions won him broad popularity and ensured his reelection in 1832 and the election of his designated successor, Martin Van Buren, in 1836.

But the Democrats were not the only ones to have learned the lessons of the age of parties. A new coalition of anti-Jacksonians, who called themselves the Whigs, launched a powerful new party that used much of the same anti-elitist rhetoric the Democrats had used to win support for their own much more nationalist program. Their emergence culminated in the campaign of 1840 with the election of the first Whig president.

FOR FURTHER REFERENCE

Suggested Readings

Harry L. Watson, *Liberty and Power: The Politics of Jacksonian America* (1990) and Charles Sellers, *The Market Revolution: Jacksonian America, 1815–1846* (1991) are good recent syntheses of the Jacksonian era. Arthur M. Schlesinger, Jr., *The Age of Jackson* (1945) is a classic study, which represents Jacksonian politics as an eastern, urban democratic movement. Bray Hammond, *Banks and Politics in America from the Revolution to the Civil War* (1957) challenged Schlesinger by arguing that the Bank War was essentially a struggle between different groups of capitalist elites. Daniel Walker Howe, *The Political Culture of the American Whigs* (1979) analyzes the careers of several leading Whig politicians, including the Whig triumvirate of Calhoun, Clay, and Webster. William V. Freehling, *Prelude to Civil War: The Nullification Controversy in South Carolina* (1966) argues that South Carolina planters' anxiety over the fate of slavery was at the heart of the nullification crisis. Francis P. Prucha, *American Indian Policy in the Formative Years* (1962) is an overview of early Indian policy by the leading scholar of the subject. Michael Rogin, *Fathers and Children: Andrew Jackson and the Destruction of American Indians* (1975) offers a more radical and idiosyncratic perspective on Jackson's career as an Indian-fighter using the methods of psychoanalysis. Sean Wilentz, *Chants Democratic: New York City and the Rise of the American Working Class, 1788–1850* (1984) is an important study of the working-class ideology during the Jacksonian period. Robert V. Remini, the leading modern biographer of Jackson, is the author of *Andrew Jackson and the Course of American Empire: 1767–1821* (1977); *Andrew Jackson and the Course of American Freedom: 1822–1832* (1981); *Andrew Jackson and the Course of American Democracy* (1984); and *The Life of Andrew Jackson* (1988).

Films

Andrew Jackson: A Man for the People is part of the Arts & Entertainment Network biography series. *The Jackson Years: The New Americans* (1971) dramatizes episodes in Jackson's life. *The Jackson Years: Toward Civil War* (1971) focuses on Jackson's dominant personality in an analysis of the major events of Jackson's presidential administration. *The Jacksonian Persuasion* uses the example of a country store in the West and Charleston, South Carolina, to illustrate themes in Jacksonian politics from Indian removal to nullification. *The American Story, No. 8: Expansion and Removal* (1985) examines the removal of Indians from their lands east of the Mississippi and the expansion of United States settlement to the west. *Trail of Tears* (1973) follows the forced removal of the Cherokee Indians to the West, and the subsequent Cherokee struggle to retain a sense of identity and heritage. See also *The Seminole* (1993).

Internet Resources

Internet websites containing historical material relevant to the subjects discussed in this chapter can be reached through the McGraw-Hill history site at www.mhhe.com/socscience/history/usa/link/linktop.htm.

CHAPTER TEN

America's Economic Revolution

The Changing American Population
Transportation and Commucications Revolutions
Commerce and Industry ～ *Men and Women at Work*
Patterns of Society ～ *The Agricultural North*

W HEN THE UNITED States entered the War of 1812, it was still an essentially agrarian nation. There were, to be sure, some substantial cities in America. There was also modest but growing manufacturing, mainly in the Northeast. But the overwhelming majority of Americans were farmers and tradespeople, working within an economy that was still mainly local.

By the time the Civil War began in 1861, the United States had transformed itself. Most Americans were still rural people. But even American farmers were, with few exceptions, now part of a national, and even international, market economy. Equally important, the United States had developed a major manufacturing sector and was beginning to challenge the industrial nations of Europe for supremacy. The nation had experienced the beginning of its industrial revolution.

THE CHANGING AMERICAN POPULATION

The American industrial revolution was a result of many factors: population growth, advances in transportation and communications, the growth of manufacturing technology, and the development of new systems of business organization. By 1860, the northern regions of the nation had acquired at least the beginnings of all those things.

272

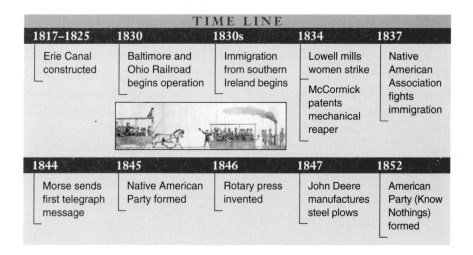

TIME LINE				
1817–1825	**1830**	**1830s**	**1834**	**1837**
Erie Canal constructed	Baltimore and Ohio Railroad begins operation	Immigration from southern Ireland begins	Lowell mills women strike McCormick patents mechanical reaper	Native American Association fights immigration
1844	**1845**	**1846**	**1847**	**1852**
Morse sends first telegraph message	Native American Party formed	Rotary press invented	John Deere manufactures steel plows	American Party (Know Nothings) formed

The American Population, 1820–1840

Three trends characterized the American population between 1820 and 1840, all of them contributing in various ways to economic growth. The population was increasing rapidly. Much of it was moving westward. And much of it was becoming concentrated in towns and cities, where the new residents provided a work force for industry.

The American population had stood at only 4 million in 1790. By 1820, it had reached 10 million; and by 1840, 17 million. The United States was growing much more rapidly in population than Britain or Europe. One reason for the growth was improvements in public health; the number and ferocity of epidemics (such as the great cholera plague of 1832) slowly declined, as did the mortality rate as a whole. But the population increase was also a result of a high birth rate. In 1840, white women bore an average of 6.14 children each.

The African-American population increased more slowly than the white population. After 1808, when the importation of slaves became illegal, the proportion of blacks to whites in the nation as a whole steadily declined. In 1820, there was one African American to every four whites; in 1840, one to every five. The slower increase of the black population was a result of its comparatively high death rate. Slave mothers had large families, but life was shorter for both slaves and free blacks than for whites—a result of the enforced poverty in which virtually all African Americans lived.

Immigration, choked off by wars in Europe and economic crises in America, contributed little to the American population in the first three decades of the nineteenth century. Of the total 1830 population of nearly 13 million, the foreign-born numbered fewer than 500,000. Soon, however, immigration began to grow once again. Reduced transportation costs and increasing economic opportunities in America helped stimulate the immigration boom, as did deteriorating economic conditions in some areas of Europe. The migrations introduced new groups to the United

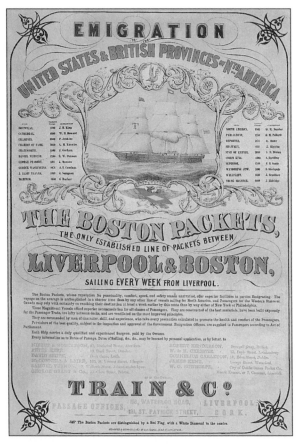

AN APPEAL TO EMIGRANTS This widely-distributed advertising card was one of many such appeals to potential English and Irish travelers to America in the 1830s and 1840s. Like many such companies, this shipping line tried to appeal both to affluent passengers (by boasting of "superior accommodations") and working-class people of modest means.

States. In particular, the number of immigrants arriving from the southern (Catholic) counties of Ireland began to grow.

Much of this new European immigration flowed into the rapidly growing cities of the Northeast. But urban growth was a result of substantial internal migration as well. As the agricultural regions of New England and other areas grew less profitable, more and more people picked up stakes and moved—some to promising agricultural regions in the West, but many to eastern cities. In 1790, one person in thirty had lived in a city (defined as a community of 8,000 or more); in 1820, one in twenty; and in 1840, one in twelve. The largest such cities were in the Northeast.

The rise of New York City was particularly dramatic. By 1810 it was the largest city in the United States, partly a result of its excellent natural harbor. It was also a result of the Erie Canal (completed in 1825), which gave the city unrivaled access to the interior. And it was a result, too, of liberal state laws that made the city attractive for both foreign and domestic commerce.

Immigration and Urban Growth, 1840–1860

The growth of cities accelerated dramatically between 1840 and 1860. The population of New York, for example, rose from 312,000 to 805,000. Philadelphia's population grew over the same twenty-year period from 220,000 to 565,000; Boston's, from 93,000 to 177,000. By 1860, 26 percent of the population of the free states was living in towns (places of 2,500 people or more) or cities, up from 14 percent in 1840. In the South, by contrast, the increase of urban residents was only from 6 percent in 1840 to 10 percent in 1860.

The booming agricultural economy of the western regions of the nation produced significant urban growth as well. Between 1820 and 1840, communities that had once been small villages or trading posts became major cities: St. Louis, Pittsburgh, Cincinnati, Louisville. Each of them benefited from a strategic position on the Mississippi River or one of its major tributaries. All of them became centers of the growing carrying trade that connected the farmers of the Midwest with New Orleans and, through it, the cities of the Northeast. After 1830, however, an increasing proportion of this shipping moved from the river to the Great Lakes and created major new urban centers that gradually superseded the river ports. Among them were Buffalo, Detroit, Milwaukee, Cleveland, and—most important in the end—Chicago.

The enlarged urban population was to a large degree a result of the flow of two major groups of people into cities: the native farmers of the Northeast, who were being forced off the land by competition from the West; and, even more significantly by the 1850s, immigrants from Europe. Only 500,000 foreigners had arrived in the United States in the depression years of the 1830s, but between 1840 and 1850, more than 1.5 million Europeans moved to America. In the 1850s, the number rose to 2.5 million. Almost half the residents of New York City in the 1850s were recent immigrants. In St. Louis, Chicago, and Milwaukee, the foreign-born outnumbered those of native birth. Few immigrants settled in the South. Only 500,000 lived in the slave states in 1860, a third of them in Missouri.

The newcomers came from many different countries, but the overwhelming majority came from Ireland and Germany, where widespread poverty and political upheavals were driving many people out. By 1860, there were more than 1.5 million Irish-born and approximately 1 million German-born people in the United States. Most of the Irish stayed in the eastern cities where they landed and became part of the unskilled labor force. The largest single group of Irish immigrants were young, single women, who worked in factories or in domestic service. Germans, who—unlike the Irish—usually arrived with at least some money and often came in family groups, generally moved on to the Northwest, where they became farmers or went into business in the western towns.

The Rise of Nativism

The new foreign-born population almost immediately became a major factor in American political life. Many politicians eagerly courted the support of the new arrivals. Others, however, viewed the growing foreign population with alarm. Some argued that the immigrants were racially inferior or that they corrupted politics by selling their votes. Others complained that because the foreign-born were willing to work for low wages, they were stealing jobs from the native work force. Protestants worried that the growing Irish population would increase the power of the Catholic Church in America. Older-stock Americans feared that immigrants would become a radical force in politics. Out of these fears and prejudices emerged a number of secret societies to combat the "alien menace."

The first was the Native American Association, founded in 1837, which in 1845 became the Native American Party. In 1850, it joined with other nativist groups to form the Supreme Order of the Star-Spangled Banner, whose demands included banning Catholics or aliens from holding public office, enacting more restrictive naturalization laws, and establishing literacy tests for voting. The order adopted a strict code of secrecy, which included a secret password, used in lodges across the country: "I know nothing." Ultimately, members of the movement came to be known as the "Know-Nothings."

After the 1852 elections, the Know-Nothings created a new political organization that they called the American Party. It scored an immediate and astonishing success in the elections of 1854. The Know-Nothings did well in Pennsylvania and New York and actually won control of the state government in Massachusetts. Outside the Northeast, however, their progress was more modest. After 1854, the strength of the Know-Nothings declined and the party soon disappeared.

TRANSPORTATION AND COMMUNICATIONS REVOLUTIONS

Just as the industrial revolution required an expanding population, it also required an efficient and effective system of transportation and communications. The first half of the nineteenth century saw dramatic changes in both.

The Canal Age

From 1790 until the 1820s, the so-called turnpike era, the United States had relied largely on roads for internal transportation. But roads alone were not adequate for the nation's expanding needs. And so, in the 1820s and 1830s, Americans began to turn to other means of transportation as well.

The larger rivers, especially the Mississippi and the Ohio, became increasingly important as steamboats replaced the slow barges that had previously dominated water traffic. The new riverboats carried the corn and wheat of northwestern farmers and the cotton and tobacco of southwestern planters to New Orleans. From New Orleans, oceangoing ships took the cargoes on to eastern ports.

But this roundabout river-sea route satisfied neither western farmers nor eastern merchants, who wanted a way to ship goods directly to the urban markets of the Atlantic coast. New highways across the mountains provided a partial solution to the problem. But the costs of hauling goods overland, although lower than before, were still too high for anything except the most compact and valuable merchandise. And so interest grew in

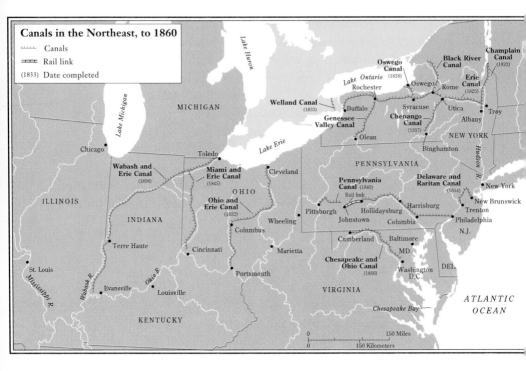

Canals in the Northeast, to 1860

building inland waterways. On a turnpike, four horses could haul one and a half tons eighteen miles in a day. But the same four horses could draw a boatload of a hundred tons twenty-four miles a day on a canal.

Canal building was too expensive for private enterprise, and the job of financing canals fell largely to the states. New York was the first to act. It had the natural advantage of a good land route between the Hudson River and Lake Erie through the only break in the Appalachian chain. But the engineering tasks were still imposing. The distance was more than 350 miles, several times as long as any of the existing canals in America. The route was interrupted by high ridges and thick woods. After a long public debate, canal advocates prevailed when De Witt Clinton, a late but ardent convert to the cause, became governor in 1817. Digging began on July 4, 1817.

The building of the Erie Canal was the greatest construction project Americans had ever undertaken. The canal itself was basically a simple ditch forty feet wide and four feet deep, with towpaths along the banks for the horses or mules that were to draw the canal boats. But its construction involved hundreds of difficult cuts and fills to enable the canal to pass through hills and over valleys, stone aqueducts to carry it across streams, and eighty-eight locks, of heavy masonry with great wooden gates, to permit ascents and descents. The Erie Canal was not just an engineering triumph but an immediate financial success. It opened in October 1825, amid elaborate ceremonies and celebrations, and traffic was soon so heavy that within about seven years tolls had repaid the entire cost of construction. By providing a route to the Great Lakes, the canal gave New York access to Chicago and the growing markets of the West and established the city as the greatest metropolitan center in the nation. The Erie Canal also contributed to the decline of agriculture in New England. Now that it was so much cheaper for western farmers to ship their crops east, people farming marginal land in the Northeast found themselves unable to compete.

The system of water transportation extended farther when the states of Ohio and Indiana, inspired by the success of the Erie Canal, provided water connections between Lake Erie and the Ohio River. These canals made it possible to ship goods by inland waterways all the way from New York to New Orleans, although it was still necessary to transfer cargoes several times between canal, lake, and river craft.

One of the immediate results of these new transportation routes was increased white settlement in the Northwest, because it was now easier for migrants to make the westward journey and to ship their goods back to eastern markets. Much of the western produce continued to go downriver to New Orleans, but an increasing proportion (including most of the wheat of the Northwest) went east to New York. And manufactured goods from throughout the East now moved in growing volume through New York and then to the West via the new water routes.

Rival cities along the Atlantic seaboard took alarm at the prospect of New York's acquiring access to (and control over) so vast a market, largely at their expense. But they had limited success in catching up. Boston, its way to the Hudson River blocked by the Berkshire Mountains, did not even try to connect itself to the West by canal. Philadelphia, Baltimore, Richmond, and Charleston all aspired to build water routes to the Ohio Valley, but never completed them.

Canals did not provide a satisfactory way to the West for any of New York's rivals. Some cities, however, saw opportunities in a different and newer means of transportation. Even before the canal age had reached its height, the era of the railroad was beginning.

The Early Railroads

Railroads played a relatively small role in the nation's transportation system in the 1820s and 1830s, but railroad pioneers laid the groundwork in those years for the great surge of railroad building in midcentury that would link the nation together as never before. Eventually, railroads became the primary transportation system for the United States, and they remained so until the construction of the interstate highway system in the mid-twentieth century. They also eventually became critical sites of development for innovations in technology and corporate organization.

Railroads emerged from a combination of technological and entrepreneurial innovations: the invention of tracks, the creation of steam-powered locomotives, and the development of trains as public carriers of passengers and freight. By 1804, both English and American inventors had experimented with steam engines for propelling land vehicles. In 1820, John Stevens ran a locomotive and cars around a circular track on his New Jersey estate. And in 1825, the Stockton and Darlington Railroad in England opened a short length of track and became the first line to carry general traffic.

American entrepreneurs, especially in those northeastern cities that sought better communication with the West, quickly grew interested in the English experiment. The first company to begin actual operations was the Baltimore and Ohio, which opened a thirteen-mile stretch of

RACING ON THE RAILROAD Peter Cooper designed and built the first steam-powered locomotives in America in 1830 for the Baltimore and Ohio railroad. On August 28 of that year, he raced his locomotive (the "Tom Thumb") against a horse-drawn railroad car. This sketch depicts the moment when Cooper's engine overtook the horse-car.

track in 1830. In New York, the Mohawk and Hudson began running trains along the sixteen miles between Schenectady and Albany in 1831. By 1836, more than a thousand miles of track had been laid in eleven states.

But there was not yet a true railroad system. Even the longest of the lines was comparatively short in the 1830s, and most of them served simply to connect water routes, not to link one railroad to another. When two lines did connect, the tracks often differed in gauge (width), so cars from one line could not fit onto the tracks of another. Schedules were erratic, and wrecks were frequent. But railroads made some important advances in the 1830s and 1840s. The introduction of heavier iron rails improved the roadbeds. Steam locomotives became more flexible and powerful. Redesigned passenger cars became stabler, more comfortable, and larger.

The Triumph of the Rails

After 1840, railroads gradually supplanted canals and all other forms of transport. In 1840, the total railroad trackage of the country was under 3,000 miles. By 1860, it was over 27,000 miles. The Northeast developed the most comprehensive and efficient system, with twice as much trackage per square mile as the Northwest and four times as much as the South. Railroads even crossed the Mississippi at several points by great iron bridges. Chicago eventually became the rail center of the West, served by fifteen lines and more than a hundred daily trains.

The emergence of the great train lines diverted traffic from the main water routes—the Erie Canal and the Mississippi River. By lessening the dependence of the West on the Mississippi, the railroads also helped weaken further the connection between the Northwest and the South.

Railroad construction required massive amounts of capital. Some of it came from private sources, but much of it came from government funding. State and local governments invested in railroads, but even greater assistance came from the federal government in the form of public land grants. By 1860, Congress had allotted over 30 million acres to eleven states to assist railroad construction.

It would be difficult to exaggerate the impact of the rails on the American economy, on American society, even on American culture. It was, some claimed, a "magic wand" that transformed everything in its path. It was, according to one writer, "the resistless chariot of civilization with

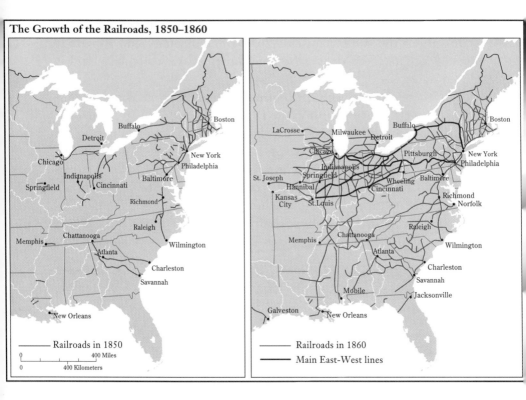

The Growth of the Railroads, 1850–1860

Railroads in 1850
0   400 Miles
0   400 Kilometers

Railroads in 1860
Main East-West lines

scythed axles mowing down ignorance and prejudice as it whirls along
. . . [driving] the shadows of the past . . . into the dim woods." Where
railroads went, towns, ranches, and farms grew up rapidly along their
routes. Areas once cut off from markets during winter and other spells of
bad weather found that the railroad could transport goods to and from
them at any time of year. Most of all, the railroads cut the time of shipment and travel. In the 1830s, traveling from New York to Chicago by
lake and canal took roughly three weeks. By railroad in the 1850s, the
same trip took less than two days. A team of horses could haul a wag-
onload of grain a dozen miles on a good day; a railroad could carry it hundreds of miles in the same amount of time.

The railroads were much more than a fast and economically attractive
form of transportation. As the nation's largest enterprises in the second
half of the nineteenth century, railroads were the breeding ground for several generations of technological advances; a key to the nation's economic
growth; and the birthplace of the modern corporate form of organization.

They also became a symbol to many Americans of the nation's technological prowess, and as such turned into something close to a national obsession. To many people, railroads were the most visible sign of the country's progress and greatness. Many Americans expressed great pride, for example, when Russia asked for help from railroad engineers in the United States when they built the rail line connecting Moscow and St. Petersburg in the 1840s.

The Telegraph

What the railroad was to transportation the telegraph was to communication—a dramatic advance over traditional methods and a symbol of national progress and technological expertise.

Before the invention of the telegraph, communication over great distances on land—a particular challenge in the increasingly vast United States—could be achieved only by direct, physical contact. That meant that virtually all long-distance communication relied on the mail, which traveled first on horseback and coach, and later by railroad. There were obvious disadvantages to this system, not the least of which was the difficulty in coordinating the necessarily precise schedules of railroads. By the 1830s, experiments with many methods of improving long-distance communication had been conducted, among them using the sun and reflective devices to send light signals as far as 187 miles (although only, of course, in sunny weather).

In 1832, Samuel F. B. Morse—a professor of art at New York University with an essentially amateur interest in science—began experimenting with a different system. Fascinated with the possibilities of electricity, which still had found few wide utilities despite the great enthusiasm that had greeted its discovery a half-century earlier, Morse set out to find a way to send signals along an electrical cable. Technology did not yet permit the use of electrical wiring to send reproductions of the human voice or any complex information. But Morse realized that electricity itself could serve as a communication device—that pulses of electricity could themselves become a kind of language. He experimented at first with a numerical code, in which each number would represent a word on a list available to recipients. Gradually, however, he became convinced of the need to find a more universal telegraphic "language," and he developed what became the Morse Code, in which alternating long and short bursts of electrical current would represent individual letters.

By 1835, Morse had developed his idea for telegraphic communication to the point that he was ready to promote it. Eight years later, Congress appropriated $30,000 for the construction of an experimental telegraph line between Baltimore and Washington; in May 1844, it was complete, and Morse succeeded in transmitting the news of James K. Polk's nomination for the presidency over the wires from Baltimore to Washington. By 1860, more than 50,000 miles of wire connected most parts of the country; a year later, the Pacific Telegraph, with 3,595 miles of wire, opened between New York and San Francisco. By then, nearly all the independent lines had joined in one organization, the Western Union Telegraph Company. The telegraph spread rapidly across Europe as well, and in 1866, the first transatlantic cable was laid across the Atlantic, permitting telegraphic communication between the United States and Europe.

One of the first beneficiaries of the telegraph was the growing system of rails in the United States. Telegraph wires often ran alongside railroad tracks, and telegraph offices were often located in railroad stations—which suggests how closely connected the two technologies were. The telegraph allowed railroad operators to communicate directly with stations in cities, small towns, and even rural hamlets—to alert them to schedule changes, warn them about delays and breakdowns, and convey other information about the movement of the trains. Among other things, this new form of communication helped prevent accidents on the rails by alerting stations to problems that in the past engineers had to discover for themselves.

New Forms of Journalism

Another beneficiary of the telegraph was American journalism, which used the wires to get news from around the country—and eventually, the world—that had once taken days, weeks, and even months to reach them, in the space of a few hours. Where once the exchange of national and international news relied on the cumbersome exchange of newspapers by mail, now it was possible for papers to share their reporting with one another. In 1846, newspaper publishers from around the nation formed the Associated Press to promote cooperative news gathering by wire.

Other technological advances spurred the development of the American press. In 1846, Richard Hoe invented the steam cylinder rotary press, making it possible to print newspapers much more rapidly and cheaply than had been possible in the past. Among other things, the rotary press spurred the dramatic growth of mass-circulation newspapers, such as the penny press, which had emerged over a decade earlier. The New York *Sun,* the most widely circulated paper in the nation, had 8,000 readers in 1834. By 1860, its succesful rival the *New York Herald*—benefitting from the speed and economies of production the rotary press made possible, had a circulation of 77,000.

COMMERCE AND INDUSTRY

By the middle years of the nineteenth century, aided by population growth and improvements in transportation and communications, the United States had developed the beginnings of a modern capitalist economy and an advanced industrial capacity. But the economy had developed along highly unequal lines—benefiting some classes and some regions far more than others.

The Expansion of Business, 1820–1840

American business grew rapidly in the 1820s and 1830s in part because of important innovations in business management. Individuals or limited partnerships continued to operate most businesses, and the dominating figures were still the great merchant capitalists, who generally had sole ownership of their enterprises. In some larger businesses, however, the individual merchant capitalist was giving way to the corporation. Corporations had the advantage of combining the resources of a large number of shareholders, and they began to develop particularly rapidly in the 1830s, when some legal obstacles to their formation were removed. Previously, a corporation could obtain a charter only by a special act of a state legislature; by the 1830s, states were beginning to pass general incorporation laws, under which a group could secure a charter merely by paying a fee. The laws also permitted a system of limited liability, in which individual stockholders risked losing only the value of their own investment if a corporation should fail; they were not liable (as they had been in the past) for the corporation's larger losses. These changes made possible the accumulation of much greater amounts of capital and hence made possible much larger manufacturing and business enterprises.

The Emergence of the Factory

The most profound economic development in mid-nineteenth-century America was the rise of the factory. Before the War of 1812, most of what manufacturing there was in the United States took place within households or in small, individually operated workshops. Early in the nineteenth century, however, New England textile manufacturers began using new machines driven by water power that allowed them to bring their operations together under a single roof. This "factory system," as it came to be known, spread rapidly in the 1820s and soon penetrated the shoe industry and other industries as well. Machine technology advanced more rapidly in the United States in the mid-nineteenth century than in any other country in the world. By the end of the 1830s, American technology had become so advanced—particularly in textile manufacturing—that industrialists in Britain and Europe were beginning to travel to the United States to learn new techniques, instead of the other way around.

Between 1840 and 1860, American industry—spurred on by the factory system—experienced particularly dramatic growth. In 1840, the total value of manufactured goods produced in the United States stood at $483 million; by 1860 it had climbed to nearly $2 billion. For the first time, the value of manufactured goods was roughly equal to that of agricultural products. More than half of the approximately 140,000 manufacturing establishments in the country in 1860 were located in the Northeast, and they included most of the larger enterprises. The Northeast thus produced more than two-thirds of the manufactured goods and employed nearly three-quarters of the men and women working in manufacturing.

Advances in Technology

Even the most highly developed industries were still relatively immature. American cotton manufacturers, for example, produced goods of coarse grade; fine items continued to come from England. But by the 1840s, significant advances were in progress.

Among the most important was in the manufacturing of machine tools—the tools used to make machinery parts. The government supported much of the research and development of machine tools, often in connection with supplying the military. For example, a government armory in Springfield, Massachusetts, developed two important tools—the turret lathe (used for cutting screws and other metal parts) and the universal milling machine (which replaced the hand chiseling of complicated parts and dies with a machine process that could ensure that all milling would be identical)—early in the nineteenth century. The precision grinding machine (which became critical to, among other things, the construction of sewing machines) was designed in the 1850s to help the United States Army produce standardized rifle parts. The federal armories such as those at Springfield and Harpers Ferry, Virginia, where these and other tools were developed, became the breeding ground for many technological discoveries, and a magnet for craftsmen and factory owners looking for ideas that could be of use to them. By the 1840s, the machine tools used in the factories of the Northeast were already better than those in most European factories.

One of the principal results of the creation of better machine tools was that the principle of interchangeable parts, which Eli Whitney and Simeon North had tried to introduce into gun factories they had designed decades earlier, now found its way into many industries. Eventually, interchangeability would revolutionize watch and clock making, the manufacturing of locomotives, the creation of steam engines, and the making of many farm tools. It would also help make possible such newer devices as bicycles, sewing machines, typewriters, cash registers, and eventually the automobile.

Industrialization was also profiting from the introduction of new sources of energy. Coal was replacing wood and water power as fuel for many factories. The production of coal, most of it mined around Pittsburgh in western Pennsylvania, leaped from 50,000 tons in 1820 to 14 million tons in 1860. The new power source made it possible to locate mills away from running streams and thus permitted industry to expand still more widely.

The great technological advances in American industry owed much to American inventors, as the patent records of the time make clear. In 1830, the number of inventions patented was 544; by 1850, the figure had risen to 993; and in 1860, it stood at 4,778. Several industries provide particularly vivid examples of how a technological innovation could produce a major economic change. In 1839, Charles Goodyear, a New England hardware merchant, discovered a method of vulcanizing rubber (treating it to give it greater strength and elasticity); by 1860, his process had found over 500 uses and had helped create a major American rubber

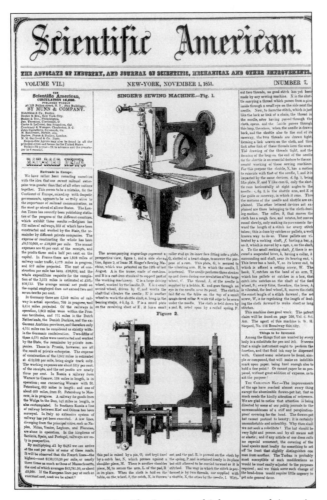

THE EARLY SEWING MACHINE *Scientific America*, which reported American scientific and technological achievements, was a popular journal in the mid-nineteenth century. Here it gives front-page attention to the design and construction of Isaac Singer's sewing machine, alongside articles trumpeting news of the progess of the railroads and urging the invention of a ballpoint pen.

industry. In 1846, Elias Howe of Massachusetts constructed a sewing machine; Isaac Singer made improvements on it, and the Howe-Singer machine was soon being used in the manufacture of ready-to-wear clothing. A few years later, during the Civil War, it would supply the Northern troops with uniforms.

Innovations in Corporate Organization

The merchant capitalists—entrepreneurs who were engaged primarily in foreign and domestic trade and who at times invested some of their profits in small-scale manufacturing ventures—remained figures of importance in the 1840s. In such cities as New York, Philadelphia, and Boston, influential mercantile groups operated shipping lines to southern ports—carrying off cotton, rice, and sugar—or dispatched fleets of trading vessels to the ports of Europe and Asia. Among their vessels were the famous clippers, the fastest (and most beautiful) sailing ships afloat. In their heyday in the late 1840s and early 1850s, the clippers could average 300 miles a day, which compared favorably with the best time of contemporary steamships.

But merchant capitalism was declining by the middle of the century. This was partly because British competitors were stealing much of America's export trade. But the more important reason for the decline was the discovery by the merchants themselves that there were greater opportunities for profit in manufacturing than in trade. That was one reason why industries developed first in the Northeast: an affluent merchant class already existed there and had the money and the will to finance them.

By the 1840s, the corporate form of organization was spreading rapidly, particularly in the textile industry. Ownership of American enterprise was gradually moving away from individuals and families and toward its highly dispersed modern form: many stockholders, each owning a relatively small proportion of the total. But whatever the form of business organization—and there continued to be many different forms—industrial capitalists soon became the new ruling class, the aristocrats of the Northeast, with far-reaching economic and political influence.

MEN AND WOMEN AT WORK

However advanced industrial firms became technologically and administratively, manufacturers still relied above all on a supply of labor. In the 1820s and 1830s, factory labor came primarily from the native-born population. After 1840, the growing immigrant population became the most important new source of workers.

Recruiting a Native Work Force

Recruiting a labor force was not an easy task in the early years of the factory system. Ninety percent of the American people in the 1820s still lived and worked on farms. Many of the relatively small number of urban residents were skilled artisans who owned and managed their own shops. The available unskilled workers were not numerous enough to form a reservoir from which the new industries could draw. But the transformation of American agriculture in the nineteenth century gradually created a supply of industrial workers. Dramatic improvements in agricultural production, particularly in the Midwest, meant that each region no longer had to feed itself; it could import the food it needed. As a result, some of the relatively unprofitable farming areas of the East began to decline, and rural people began leaving the land to work in the factories.

Two systems of recruitment emerged to bring this new labor supply to the expanding textile mills. One, common in the mid-Atlantic states (especially in New York and Philadelphia), brought whole families from the farm to work together in the mill—parents working alongside children, some of whom were no more than four or five years old. The second sys-

NEW ENGLAND TEXTILE WORKERS Women continued to constitute the majority of the work force in the cotton mills of New England even after the carefully monitored life of the "Lowell girls" became a thing of the past—as this 1868 engraving by Winslow Homer suggests.

tem, common in Massachusetts, enlisted young women, mostly farmers' daughters in their late teens and early twenties. It was known as the Lowell or Waltham system, after the towns in which it first emerged. Many of these women worked for several years in the factories, saved their wages, and then returned home to marry and raise children. Others married men they met in the factories or in town and remained part of the industrial world. Most eventually stopped working in the mills and took up domestic roles instead.

Labor conditions in these early years of the factory system, hard as they often were, remained significantly better than they would later become. The Lowell workers, for example, lived in clean boardinghouses and dormitories, which the factory owners maintained for them. They were well fed and carefully supervised. Employers quickly dismissed women suspected of immoral conduct. Wages for the Lowell workers were relatively generous by the standards of the time. The women even published a monthly magazine, the *Lowell Offering*.

Yet even these relatively well-treated workers found the transition from farm life to factory work difficult, even traumatic. Uprooted from everything familiar, forced to live among strangers in a regimented environment, many women had difficulty adjusting to the nature of factory work—the repetition of fixed tasks hour after hour, day after day. However uncomfortable women may have found factory work, they had few other options. Work in the mills was in many cases virtually the only alternative to returning to farms that could no longer support them.

The paternalistic factory system of Lowell did not, in any case, survive for long. In the competitive textile market as it developed in the 1830s and 1840s—a market prey to booms and busts—manufacturers found it difficult to maintain the high living standards and reasonably attractive working conditions with which they had begun. Wages declined; the hours of work lengthened; the conditions of the boardinghouses deteriorated as buildings decayed and overcrowding increased. In 1834, mill workers in Lowell organized a union—the Factory Girls Association—which staged a strike to protest a 25 percent wage cut. Two years later, the association struck again—against a rent increase in the boardinghouses. Both strikes failed, and a recession in 1837 virtually destroyed the organization. Eight years later the Lowell women, led by the militant Sarah Bagley, created the Female Labor Reform Association and began agitating for a ten-hour day and for improvements in conditions in the mills. The new association not only made demands of management; it turned to state government and asked for legislative investigation of conditions in the mills. By then, however, the character of the factory work force was changing again. Many mill girls were gradually moving into other occupations: teaching, domestic service, or marriage. And textile manufacturers were turning to a less demanding labor supply: immigrants.

The Immigrant Work Force

The increasing supply of immigrant workers after 1840 was a boon to manufacturers and other entrepreneurs. At last they had access to a cheap and plentiful source of labor. These new workers, because of their growing numbers and their unfamiliarity with their new country, had even less leverage than the women they at times displaced, and thus they often encountered far worse working conditions. Poorly paid construction gangs, made up increasingly of Irish immigrants, performed the heavy, unskilled work on turnpikes, canals, and railroads under often intolerable conditions. Many of them lived in flimsy shanties, in grim conditions that endangered the health of their families (and reinforced native prejudices toward the "shanty Irish"). Irish workers began to predominate in the New England textile mills as well in the 1840s, and their arrival accelerated the deterioration of working conditions there. Employers began paying piece rates rather than a daily wage and used other devices to speed up production and exploit the labor force more efficiently. The factories themselves were becoming large, noisy, unsanitary, and often dangerous places to work; the average workday was extending to twelve, often fourteen hours; and wages were declining. Women and children, whatever their skills, earned less than most men.

The Factory System and the Artisan Tradition

Mill workers were not the only group who suffered from the transition to the modern factory system. Factories were also displacing the trades of skilled artisans. The artisan tradition was as much a part of the older, republican vision of America as the tradition of sturdy yeoman farmers. Independent craftsmen clung to a vision of economic life that was in some ways very different from the one the new capitalist class was promoting. It was a vision based not just on the idea of individual, acquisitive success but also on a sense of a "moral community." Skilled artisans valued their independence; they also valued the stability and relative equality within their economic world.

The factory system threatened that world with obsolescence. Some artisans made successful transitions into small-scale industry. But others found themselves unable to compete with the new factory-made goods that sold for a fraction of the artisans' prices. In the face of this competition from industrial capitalists, skilled workers in cities such as Philadelphia, Baltimore, Boston, and New York formed societies for mutual aid. During the 1820s and 1830s, these craft societies began to combine on a

A TOLEWARE MAKER, C. 1850 By the middle of the nineteenth century, skilled artisans—such as this maker of handcrafted kitchenware—were rapidly being replaced by semiskilled workers producing similar goods in factories. The craftsman pictured here conveys some of the important elements of the vanishing artisanal world: formal dress in the workplace, to suggest his status as a highly skilled craftsman; pride in his workmanship; and a middle-class sensibility that, in the end, made it difficult for artisans to fight the forces driving them toward obsolescence.

citywide basis and set up central organizations known as trade unions. In 1834, delegates from six cities founded the National Trades' Union, and in 1836, printers and cordwainers (makers of high-quality shoes and boots) set up their own national craft unions.

This early craft union movement fared poorly. Hostile laws and hostile courts handicapped the unions. The Panic of 1837 and the depression that followed weakened the movement further. But the failure of these first organizations did not end the efforts by workers—artisans and factory operatives alike—to gain some control over their productive lives.

Fighting for Control

Workers at all levels of the emerging industrial economy made continuous efforts to improve their lots. They tried, with little success, to persuade state legislatures to pass laws setting a maximum workday and regulating child labor. The greatest legal victory of industrial workers came in Massachusetts in 1842, when the state supreme court, in *Commonwealth* v. *Hunt,* declared that unions were lawful organizations and that the strike was a lawful weapon. Other state courts gradually accepted the principles of the Massachusetts decision. But on the whole, the union movement of the 1830s and 1840s remained generally ineffective.

Virtually all the early craft unions excluded women, even though female workers were numerous in almost every industry. As a result, women began establishing their own protective unions by the 1850s, often with the support of middle-class female reformers. Like the male craft unions, the female protective unions had little power in dealing with employers. They did, however, serve an important role as mutual aid societies for women workers.

Many factors combined to inhibit the growth of effective labor resistance. Among the most important was the flood of immigrant laborers into the country. The newcomers were usually willing to work for lower wages than native workers; and because they were so numerous, manufacturers had little difficulty replacing disgruntled or striking workers with eager immigrants. Ethnic divisions and tensions—both between natives and immigrants and among the various immigrant groups themselves—often led workers to channel their resentments into internal bickering rather than into their shared grievances against employers. Another obstacle was the sheer strength of the industrial capitalists, who had not only economic but political and social power and could usually triumph over even the most militant challenges.

PATTERNS OF SOCIETY

The industrial revolution was making the United States—and particularly its more economically developed regions—dramatically wealthier by the year. It was also making society more unequal, and it was transforming social relationships at almost every level—from the workplace to the family.

The Rich and the Poor

The commercial and industrial growth of the United States greatly elevated the average income of the American people. But this increasing wealth was being distributed highly unequally. Substantial groups of the population, of course, shared hardly at all in the economic growth: slaves, Indians, landless farmers, and many of the unskilled workers on the fringes of the manufacturing system. But even among the rest of the population, disparities of income were increasingly marked. Among the American people overall in 1860, according to scholarly estimates, 5 percent of the families possessed more than 50 percent of the wealth. Merchants and industrialists were accumulating enormous fortunes; and because there was now a significant number of rich people living in cities, a distinctive culture of wealth began to emerge.

In large cities, people of great wealth gathered together in neighborhoods of astonishing opulence. They founded clubs and developed elaborate social rituals. They looked increasingly for ways to display their wealth—in the great mansions they built, the showy carriages in which they rode, the lavish household goods they accumulated, the clothes they wore, the elegant social establishments they patronized. New York, which had more wealthy families than anywhere else, developed a particularly elaborate high society. The construction of the city's great Central Park, which began in the 1850s, was in part a result of pressure from the members of high society, who wanted an elegant setting for their daily carriage rides.

There was also a significant population of genuinely destitute people emerging in the growing urban centers of the nation. These were people who were not merely poor, in the sense of having to struggle to sustain themselves—most Americans were poor in that sense. They were almost entirely without resources, often homeless, dependent on charity or crime or both for survival. Substantial numbers of people actually starved to death or died of exposure. Some of these "paupers," as contemporaries called them, were recent immigrants who had failed to find work or to adjust to life in the New World. Some were widows and orphans, stripped of the family structures that allowed most working-class Americans to survive. Some were people suffering from alcoholism or mental illness, unable to work. Others were victims of native prejudice—barred from all but the most menial employment because of race or ethnicity. The Irish were particular victims of such prejudice.

Among the worst victims were free blacks. African-American communities in antebellum northern cities were small by later standards, but most major urban areas had significant black populations. Some of these African Americans were descendants of families that had lived in the North for generations. Others were former slaves who had escaped or been released by their masters. In material terms, at least, life was not always much better for them in the North than it had been in slavery. Most had access to very menial jobs at best. In most parts of the North, blacks could not vote, could not attend public schools, indeed could not use any of the public services available to white residents. Even so, most blacks preferred life in the North, however arduous, to life in the South, because it permitted them at least some level of freedom.

Social Mobility

Despite the contrasts between conspicuous wealth and conspicuous poverty in antebellum America, there was relatively little overt class conflict. For one thing, life, in material terms at least, was better for most factory workers than it had been on the farms or in the European societies from which they had migrated. They ate better, they were often better clothed and housed, and they had greater access to consumer goods.

There was also a significant amount of mobility within the working class, which helped limit discontent. A few workers managed to move from poverty to riches by dint of work, ingenuity, and luck—a very small number, but enough to support the dreams of those who watched them. And a much larger number of workers managed to move at least one notch up the ladder—for example, becoming in the course of a lifetime a skilled, rather than an unskilled, laborer. Such people could envision their children and grandchildren moving up even further.

More important than social mobility was geographical mobility. Some workers saved money, bought land, and moved west to farm it. But few urban workers, and even fewer poor ones, could afford to make such a move. Much more common was the movement of laborers from one industrial town to another. These migratory workers were often the victims of layoffs, looking for better opportunities elsewhere. Their search may seldom have led to a marked improvement in their circumstances, but the rootlessness of this large segment of the work force—one of the most distressed segments—made effective organization and protest more difficult.

Middle-Class Life

For all the visibility of the very rich and the very poor in antebellum society, the fastest-growing group in America was the middle class. The expansion of the middle class was in part a result of the growth of the industrial economy, and the increasing commercial life that accompanied it. Economic development opened many more opportunities for people to own or work in businesses, to own shops, to engage in trade, to enter professions, and to administer organizations. In earlier times, when ownership of land had been the only real basis of wealth, society had been divided between people with little or no land (people Europeans generally called peasants) and a landed gentry (which in Europe usually became an inherited aristocracy). Once commerce and industry became a source of wealth, these rigid distinctions broke down; many people could become prosperous without owning land, but by providing valuable services to the new economy.

Middle-class life in the years before the Civil War rapidly established itself as the most influential cultural form of urban America. Middle-class families lived in solid and often substantial homes. Their houses lined city streets, larger in size and more elaborate in design than the cramped, functional rowhouses in working-class neighborhoods—but also far less lavish than the great houses of the very rich. Like the wealthy, middle-class people tended to own their homes. Workers and artisans were increasingly becoming renters—a relatively new phenomenon in American cities that spread widely in the early nineteenth century.

Middle-class women usually remained in the home and cared for their children and the household, although increasingly they were also able to hire servants—usually young, unmarried immigrant women who put in long hours of arduous work for very little money. One of the aspirations of middle-class women in an age when doing the family's laundry could take an entire day was to escape from some of the drudgery of housework.

New household inventions altered, and greatly improved, the character of life in middle-class homes. Perhaps the most important was the invention of the cast-iron stove, which began to replace fireplaces as the principal vehicle for cooking in the 1840s and also became an important source of heat. These wood- or coal-burning devices were hot, clumsy,

NATHAN HAWLEY AND FAMILY Nathan Hawley, seated at center in this 1801 painting, was typical of many early-nineteenth-century middle-class fathers in having a very large family. Nine members are visible here. Hawley at the time was the warden of the Albany County jail in New York, and the painting was by William Wilkie, one of the inmates there. The painting suggests that Hawley was a man of modest but not great means. His family is fashionably dressed, and there are paintings on the walls—signs of style and affluence. But the house is very simply furnished, without drapes for the windows, and with a simple painted floor cloth in the front room and a bare floor in the back.

and dirty by the standards of the twentieth century; but compared to the inconvenience and danger of cooking on an open hearth, they seemed a great luxury to nineteenth-century families. Stoves gave cooks more control over the preparation of food and allowed them to cook several things at once.

Middle-class diets were changing rapidly in the antebellum years, and not just because of the wider range of cooking the stove made possible. The expansion and diversification of American agriculture and the ability of farmers to ship goods to urban markets by rail from distant regions greatly increased the variety of food available in cities. Fruits and vegetables were difficult to ship over long distances in an age with little refrigeration, but families had access to a greater variety of meats, grains, and dairy products than they had had in the past. A few households acquired iceboxes in the years before the Civil War, and the sight of wagons delivering large chunks of ice to wealthy and middle-class homes began to become a familiar part of urban life. Iceboxes allowed some families to keep fresh meat and dairy products for as long as several days without spoilage. Most families, however, did not yet have any kind of refrigeration. For them, preserving food meant curing meat with salt and preserving fruits in sugar. Diets were generally much heavier and starchier than they are today, and middle-class people tended to be considerably stouter than would be considered healthy or fashionable in the twentieth century.

Middle-class homes came to differentiate themselves from those of workers and artisans in other ways as well. They were more elaborately decorated and furnished, with items made available for the first time through factory production of household goods. Houses that had once had bare walls and floors now had carpeting, wallpaper, and curtains. The spare, simple styles of eighteenth-century homes gave way to the much more elaborate, even baroque household styles of the Victorian era— styles increasingly characterized by crowded, even cluttered rooms, dark colors, lush fabrics, and heavy furniture and draperies. Middle-class homes also became larger. It became less common for children to share beds and for all members of families to sleep in the same room. Parlors and dining rooms separate from the kitchen—once a luxury reserved largely for the wealthy—became the norm now for the middle class as well. Some urban middle-class homes had indoor plumbing and indoor toilets by the 1850s—a significant advance over the outdoor wells and privies that had been virtually universal only a few years earlier (and that remained common among working-class people).

The Changing Family

The new industrializing society of the northern regions of the United States produced profound changes in the nature and function of the family. At the heart of the transformation was the movement of families from farms to urban areas, where jobs, not land, were the most valued commodities. The family patterns of the countryside, where powerful fathers controlled their children's futures by controlling the distribution of land to them, could not survive the move to a city or town. Sons and daughters in urban households were much more likely to leave the family in search of work than they had been in the rural world.

Another important change was the shift of income-earning work out of the home and into the shop, mill, or factory. In the early decades of the nineteenth century (and for many years before that), the family itself had been the principal unit of economic activity. Now most income earners left home each day to work elsewhere. A sharp distinction began to emerge between the public world of the workplace—the world of commerce and industry—and the private world of the family. The world of the family was now dominated not by production but by housekeeping, child rearing, and other primarily domestic concerns.

Accompanying (and perhaps in part caused by) the changing economic function of the family was a decline in the birth rate. In 1800, the average American woman could be expected to give birth to approximately seven children during her childbearing years. By 1860, the average woman bore five children. The birth rate fell most quickly in urban areas and among middle-class women.

The "Cult of Domesticity"

The growing separation between the public and private worlds, between the workplace and the home, helped cause increasingly sharp distinctions between the social roles of men and women. Those distinctions affected not only factory workers and farmers but members of the growing middle class as well.

Traditional inequalities remained. Women had many fewer legal and political rights than did men, and within the family they remained under the virtually absolute authority of their husbands. Women were seldom encouraged—and in most cases were effectively barred—from pursuing education above the primary level. Not until 1837 did any college or university accept women students: Oberlin in Ohio, which educated both women and men; and Mt. Holyoke in Massachusetts, founded by Mary Lyon as an academy for women. Not until much later in the century were there more than a handful of others.

However unequal the positions of men and women in the preindustrial era, those positions had generally been defined within the context of a household in which all members played important economic roles. In the middle-class family of the new industrial society, by contrast, the husband was assumed to be the principal, usually the only, income producer. The wife was now expected to remain in the home and to engage in largely domestic activities. The image of women changed from one of contributors to the family economy to one of guardians of the "domestic virtues." Middle-class women, no longer producers, now became more important as consumers. They learned to place a higher value on keeping a clean, comfortable, and well-appointed home; on entertaining; on dressing elegantly and stylishly.

Within their own separate sphere, middle-class women began to develop a distinctive female culture. A "lady's" literature began to emerge to meet the demands of middle-class women. There were romantic novels (many of them by female writers), which focused on the private sphere that middle-class women now inhabited. There were women's magazines, which focused on fashions, shopping, homemaking, and other purely domestic concerns.

This "cult of domesticity," as some scholars have called it, gave many women greater material comfort than they had enjoyed in the past and placed a higher value on their "female virtues" and on their roles as wives and mothers. At the same time, it left women increasingly detached from the public world, with few outlets for their interests and energies. Except for teaching and nursing—the favored occupations of unmarried middle-class women—work by women outside the household gradually came to be seen as a lower-class preserve.

Working-class women continued to work in factories and mills, but under conditions far worse than those that the original, more "respectable" women workers of Lowell and Waltham had experienced. Domestic service became another frequent source of female employment. Now that production had moved outside the household, women who needed to earn money had to move outside their own homes to do so.

Leisure Activities

Leisure time was scarce for all but the wealthiest Americans in the mid-nineteenth century. Most people worked long hours. Saturday was a normal working day. Vacations—paid or unpaid—were rare. For most people, Sunday was the only respite from work; and Sundays were generally reserved for religion and rest. For many working-class and middle-class people, therefore, holidays took on a special importance. That was one reason for the strikingly elaborate celebrations of the Fourth of July throughout the country in the nineteenth century. The celebrations were not just expressions of patriotism. They were a way of enjoying one of the few non-religious holidays from work available to most Americans.

In rural America, where most people still lived, the erratic pattern of farmwork gave many people some relief from the relentless working schedules of city residents. For urban people, however, leisure was something to be seized in what few free moments they had. Men gravitated to taverns for drinking, talking, and game-playing after work. Women gathered in one another's homes for conversation and card games, or to share work on such household tasks as sewing. For educated people, whose numbers were rapidly expanding, reading became one of the principal leisure activities. Newspapers and magazines proliferated rapidly, and books—novels, histories, autobiographies, biographies, travelogues, and others—became staples of affluent homes. Women were particularly avid readers, and women writers created a new genre of fiction specifically for females—the "sentimental novel," which often offered idealized visions of women's lives and romances.

There was also a vigorous culture of public leisure, even if many families had to struggle to find time to participate in it. In larger cities, theaters were becoming increasingly popular; and while some of them catered to particular social groups, others attracted audiences that crossed class lines. Wealthy people, middle-class people, workers and their families—all could sometimes be found together watching a performance. Much of the popular theater of the time consisted of melodrama based on popular novels or American myths. But much of it reflected the great love of Shakespeare that extended through all levels of the theater-going population.

By the 1830s, when theater was the single most popular entertainment in America, Shakespeare was the single most popular playwright. American performances of his work tended to be lively, irreverent, and highly inaccurate. Tragedies had happy endings. Texts included American dialect. Plays were abbreviated and sandwiched into programs containing other popular works. So familiar were many Shakespearean plots that parodies of them were staples of regional theater, through productions of such comedies as *Hamlet and Egglet* or *Julius Sneezer*. American audiences were noisy and rambunctious, and at times crowded onto the stage to participate in battle or crowd scenes. The love of Shakespeare among many ordinary people of all classes was so intense, and their loyalties to their favorite actors so strong, that in 1849 there was a major riot at New York's Astor Place Opera House when supporters of a popular American Shakespearean actor, Edwin Forrest, gathered to protest a visit from an eminent English Shakespearean, Charles Macready. More than twenty people died.

Minstrel shows—in which white actors wearing blackface mimicked (and ridiculed) African-American culture—became increasingly popular. Public sporting events—boxing, horse racing, cockfighting (already becoming controversial), and others—often attracted considerable audiences. Baseball—not yet organized into professional leagues—was beginning to attract large crowds when played in city parks or fields on the edges of towns. A particularly exciting event in many communities was the arrival of the circus—a traveling entertainment with roots in the middle ages that continued to entertain, delight, and bamboozle children and adults alike.

Popular tastes in public spectacle tended toward the bizarre and the fantastic. Most men and women lived in a constricted world of familiar things. Relatively few people traveled; and in the absence of film, radio, television, or even much photography, they hungered for visions of unusual phenomena that contrasted with their normal experiences. People going to the theater or the circus or the museum wanted to see things that amazed and even frightened them. Perhaps the most celebrated provider of such experiences was the famous and unscrupulous showman P. T. Barnum, who opened the American Museum in New York in 1842—not a showcase for art or nature, but a great freak show populated by midgets (the most famous named Tom Thumb), Siamese twins, magicians, and ventriloquists. Barnum was a genius in publicizing his ventures with garish posters and elaborate newspaper announcements. Later, in the 1870s, he launched the famous circus for which he is still best remembered. He was a pioneer in exploiting public tastes for the wild and exotic.

One of the ways Barnum tried to draw visitors to his museum was by engaging lecturers. He did so because he understood that the lecture was one of the most popular forms of entertainment in nineteenth-century America. Men and women flocked in enormous numbers to lyceums, churches, schools, and auditoriums to hear lecturers explain the latest advances in science, describe their visits to exotic places, provide vivid historical narratives, or rail against the evils of alcohol or slavery. Messages of social uplift and reform attracted rapt audiences, particularly among women eager for guidance as they adjusted to the often jarring changes in the character of family life in the industrializing world.

THE AGRICULTURAL NORTH

Even in the rapidly urbanizing and industrializing Northeast, and more so in what nineteenth-century Americans called the Northwest (what Americans today call the Midwest), most people remained tied to the agricultural world. But agriculture, like industry and commerce, was becoming increasingly a part of the new capitalist economy, linked to the national and international market.

Northeastern Agriculture

The story of agriculture in the Northeast after 1840 is one of decline and transformation. The reason for the decline was simple: the farmers of the section could no longer compete with the new and richer soil of the Northwest. In 1840, the leading wheat-growing states were New York, Pennsylvania, Ohio, and Virginia; in 1860 they were Illinois, Indiana, Wisconsin, Ohio, and Michigan. In raising corn, Illinois, Ohio, and Missouri supplanted New York, Pennsylvania, and Virginia. In 1840 the most important cattle-raising areas in the country were New York, Pennsylvania, and New England; but by the 1850s the leading cattle states were Illinois, Indiana, Ohio, and Iowa in the West and Texas in the South.

Some eastern farmers responded to these changes by moving west themselves and establishing new farms. Still others moved to mill towns and became laborers. Some farmers, however, remained on the land and turned to the task of supplying food to the growing cities of the East; they raised vegetables (truck farming) or fruit and sold their produce in nearby towns. New York, for example, led all other states in apple production. Supplying milk, butter, and cheese to local urban markets also attracted many farmers in central New York, southeastern Pennsylvania, and various parts of New England.

The Old Northwest

Life was different in the states of the Northwest in the mid-nineteenth century. There was some industry in this region (more than in the South), and in the two decades before the Civil War the section experienced steady industrial growth. There were flourishing industrial and commercial areas in and around Cleveland (on Lake Erie) and Cincinnati, the center of meatpacking in the Ohio Valley. Farther west, the rising city of Chicago, destined to become the great metropolis of the section, was emerging as the national center of the agricultural machinery and meatpacking industries. Most of the major industrial activities of the West either served agriculture (as in the case of farm machinery) or relied on agricultural products (as in flour milling, meatpacking, whiskey distilling, and the making of leather goods).

Some areas of the Northwest were not yet dominated by whites. Indians remained the most numerous inhabitants of large portions of the upper third of the Great Lakes states until after the Civil War. In those areas, hunting and fishing, along with some sedentary agriculture, remained the principal economic activities. But the tribes did not become integrated into the new commercialized economy that was emerging elsewhere in the Northwest.

For the white (and occasionally black) settlers who populated the lands farther south that they had by now largely wrested from the natives, the Northwest was primarily an agricultural region. Its rich and plentiful lands made farming a lucrative and expanding activity there, in contrast to the declining agrarian Northeast. Thus the typical citizen of the Northwest was not the industrial worker or poor, marginal farmer but the owner of a reasonably prosperous family farm. The average size of western farms was 200 acres, the great majority of them owned by the people who worked them.

Industrialization, in both the United States and Europe, provided the greatest boost to agriculture. With the growth of factories and cities in the Northeast, the domestic market for farm goods increased dramatically. The growing national and worldwide demand for farm products resulted in steadily rising farm prices. For most farmers, the 1840s and early 1850s were years of increasing prosperity.

The expansion of agricultural markets had profound effects on sectional alignments in the United States. The Northwest sold most of its products to the Northeast and became an important market for the products of eastern industry. A strong economic relationship was emerging between the two sections that was profitable to both—and that was increasing the isolation of the South within the Union.

By 1850, the growing western white population was moving into the prairie regions on both sides of the Mississippi: areas of Indiana, Michigan, Illinois, Missouri, Iowa, and Minnesota. These farmers cleared forest lands or made use of fields the Indians had cleared many years earlier. And they began to develop a timber industry to make use of the forests that remained. Wheat was the staple crop of the region, but other crops—corn, potatoes, and oats—and livestock were also important.

The Northwest also increased production by adopting new agricultural techniques that greatly reduced the labor necessary for producing a crop. Farmers began to cultivate new varieties of seed, notably Mediterranean wheat, which was hardier than the native type; and they imported better breeds of animals, such as hogs and sheep from England and Spain, to take the place of native stock. Most important were improved tools and farm machines. The cast-iron plow, an earlier innovation, remained popular because its parts could be replaced when broken. An even better tool appeared in 1847, when John Deere established at Moline, Illinois, a factory to manufacture plows with steel moldboards, which were more durable than those made of iron.

Two new machines heralded a coming revolution in grain production. The most important was the automatic reaper, the invention of Cyrus H. McCormick of Virginia. The reaper took the place of sickle, cradle, and hand labor. Pulled by a team of horses, it had a row of horizontal knives on one side for cutting wheat; the wheels drove a paddle that bent the stalks over the knives, which then fell onto a moving belt that carried it into the back of the vehicle. The reaper enabled a crew of six or seven men to harvest in a day as much wheat (or any other small grain) as fifteen men could harvest using the older methods. McCormick, who had patented his device in 1834, established a factory at Chicago, in the heart of the grain belt, in 1847. By 1860, more than 100,000 reapers were in use on western farms. Almost as important to the grain grower was the thresher—a machine that separated the grain from the wheat stalks. Threshers appeared in large numbers after 1840. Before that, farmers generally flailed grain by hand (seven bushels a day was a good average for a farm) or used farm animals to tread it (twenty bushels a day on the average). A threshing machine could thresh twenty-five bushels or more in an hour. The Jerome I. Case factory in Racine, Wisconsin, manufactured most of the threshers. (Modern "harvesters" later combined the functions of the reaper and the thresher.)

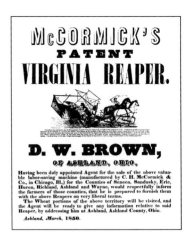

McCORMICK'S REAPER This 1850 advertisement for the automatic reaper created by Cyrus McCormick was aimed at farmers in Ohio and Illinois. But the reaper's greatest impact was to be in the vast grain-growing regions farther west, which were already attracting large numbers of white settlers and would attract many more in the decades to come.

The Northwest was the most self-consciously democratic section of the country. But its democracy was of a relatively conservative type—capitalistic, property-conscious, middle-class. Abraham Lincoln, an Illinois Whig, voiced the economic opinions of many of the people of his section. "I take it that it is best for all to leave each man free to acquire property as fast as he can," said Lincoln. "Some will get wealthy. I don't believe in a law to prevent a man from getting rich; it would do more harm than good. . . . When one starts poor, as most do in the race of life, free society is such that he knows he can better his condition; he knows that there is no fixed condition of labor for his whole life."

Rural Life

Life for farming people was very different from life for people in towns and cities. It also varied greatly from one farming region to another. In the more densely populated farm areas east of the Appalachians and in the easternmost areas of the Northwest, farmers were usually part of relatively vibrant communities and made extensive use of the institutions of those communities—the churches, schools, stores, and taverns. As white settlement moved further west, farmers became more isolated and had to struggle to find any occasions for contact with people outside their own families.

Although the extent of social interaction differed from one area to another, the forms of interaction—outside the South at least—were usually very similar. Religion drew farm communities together perhaps more than any other force, particularly since so many farm areas were populated by people of common ethnic (and therefore religious) backgrounds. Town or village churches were popular meeting places, both for services and for social events—most of them dominated by women. Even in areas with no organized churches, farm families—and, again, women in particular—gathered in one another's homes for prayer meetings, Bible readings, and other religious activities. Weddings, baptisms, and funerals also brought communities together in celebration or mourning.

But religion was only one of many reasons for interaction. Farm people joined together frequently to share tasks that a single family would have difficulty performing on their own; barn raisings were among the most frequent. On those occasions, families would gather and create a festive atmosphere of celebration. Women prepared large suppers while the men worked on the barn and the children played. Large numbers of families gathered together at harvest time as well to help bring in crops, husk corn, or thresh wheat. Women came together to share domestic tasks as well, holding "bees" in which groups of women joined together to make quilts, baked goods, preserves, and other products.

Rural life was not always as isolating as it was sometimes portrayed. But despite the many social gatherings farm families managed to create, they lived in a world with much less contact with popular culture and public social life than people who lived in towns and cities. Rural people, often even more than urban ones, treasured their links to the outside world—letters from relatives and friends in distant places, newspapers and magazines from cities they had never seen, catalogs advertising merchandise that their local stores never had. Yet many also valued their separation from urban culture and cherished the relative autonomy that a farm life gave them. One reason many rural Americans looked back nostalgically on country life once they moved to the city was that they sensed that in the urban world they did not have as much control over the patterns of their daily lives as they had once known.

CONCLUSION

Between the 1820s and the 1850s, the American economy experienced the beginnings of an industrial revolution—a change so profound that in the United States, as in Europe, it transformed almost every area of life in fundamental ways.

The American industrial revolution was a result of many things: population growth (through both natural increase and immigration), advances in transportation and communication, new technologies that spurred the development of factories capable of mass producing goods, the recruiting of a large industrial labor force, and the creation of corporate bodies capable of managing large enterprises. The new economy created great wealth, expanding the ranks of the wealthy and helping to create a large new middle class. It also created high levels of inequality.

Culture in the industrializing areas of the North changed, too, and there were important changes in the structure and behavior of the family, in the role of women, and in the way people used their leisure time and encountered popular culture. The changes were often alluring, often disorienting, and often both. They helped widen the gap in experience and understanding between the generation of the Revolution and the generation of the mid-nineteenth century. They also helped widen the gap between North and South.

FOR FURTHER REFERENCE

Suggested Readings

George R. Taylor, *The Transportation Revolution* (1951) is an authoritative account of economic development in the antebellum period. Charles G. Sellers, *The Market Revolution: Jacksonian America, 1815–1846* (1991) demonstrates the overwhelming impact of the market revolution on American social and political development, but from a pessimistic perspective. Daniel Feller, *The Jacksonian Promise: America, 1815–1840* (1995) challenges Sellers by suggesting a more optimistic portrait of the impact of economic change. Sean Wilentz, *Chants Democratic: New York City and the Rise of the American Working Class, 1788–1850* (1984) is an influential account of the impact of early industrialization on mostly male artisans in the most industrialized city of the era. David R. Roediger, *The Wages of Whiteness: Race and the Making of the American Working Class* (1991) is a provocative and controversial history of labor and race in early America. Alice Kessler-Harris, *Out to Work: A History of Wage-Earning Women in the United States* (1982), in contrast, reminds readers that women were a substantial part of the early wage labor force. Christine Stansell, *City of Women: Sex and Class in New York, 1789–1860* (1986) examines the social and cultural milieu in which women lived and worked. Mary Ryan, *Cradle of the Middle Class: The Family in Oneida County, New York, 1790–1865* (1981) demonstrates the relationship between the market revolution and the changing character of middle-class family structure. John Bodnar, *The Transplanted: A History of Immigrants in America* (1985) is an excellent survey.

Films

(The best source for information on how to find these and other films is *Bowker's Complete Video Directory*—3 volumes.) *The Industrial Revolution: Beginnings in the United States* (1968) traces the explosive growth of American industry beginning in the 1790s. *Samuel Slater & the Industrial Revolution* (1981) sketches the biography of a pioneer in early American textile manufacturing. *Irish Americans* (1993) celebrates the history and culture of Irish Americans. *Her Own Words: Pioneer Women's Diaries* (1986) brings to life the observations of pioneer women in the upper Midwest in the 1830s, 1840s, and 1850s. *In Search of the Oregon Trail* (1996) focuses on the role of women in the epic migration on the Oregon Trail. *California Gold: Stories of Two Women* (1985) traces the lives of two women who lived through the gold rush.

Internet Resources

Internet websites containing historical material relevant to the subjects discussed in this chapter can be reached through the McGraw-Hill history site at www.mhhe.com/socscience/history/usa/link/linktop.htm.

CHAPTER ELEVEN

Cotton, Slavery, and the Old South

The Cotton Economy ～ *Southern White Society*
The "Peculiar Institution" ～ *The Culture of Slavery*

T HE SOUTH, LIKE the North, experienced dramatic growth in the middle years of the nineteen century. Southerners fanned out into the Southwest and established new communities, new states, and new markets. The southern agricultural economy grew increasingly productive and increasingly prosperous. Trade in such staples as sugar, rice, tobacco, and above all cotton made the South a major force in international commerce and created substantial new wealth within the region. It also tied the South securely to the emerging capitalist world of the United States and its European trading partners.

Yet for all the changes, the South experienced a much less fundamental transformation in these years than did the North. It had begun the nineteenth century a primarily agricultural region; it remained overwhelmingly agrarian in 1860. It had begun the century with few important cities and little industry; and so it remained sixty years later. In 1800, a plantation system dependent on slave labor had dominated the southern economy; by 1860, that system had only strengthened its grip on the region. As one historian has written, "The South grew, but it did not develop." And as a result, it became increasingly unlike the North and increasingly sensitive to what it considered to be threats to its distinctive way of life.

THE COTTON ECONOMY

The most important economic development in the mid-nineteenth-century South was the shift of economic power from the "upper South," the original

310

TIME LINE				
1800	**1808**	**1820s**	**1822**	**1831**
Gabriel Prosser's unsuccessful slave revolt	Slave importation banned	Depression in tobacco prices begins High cotton production in Southwest	Denmark Vesey's conspiracy	Nat Turner slave rebellion
1833	**1837**	*1846*	**1849**	
John Randolph frees 400 slaves	Cotton prices plummet	*De Bow's Review* founded	Cotton Production boom	

southern states along the Atlantic coast, to the "lower South," the expanding agricultural regions in the new states of the Southwest. That shift reflected above all the growing dominance of cotton in the southern economy.

The Rise of King Cotton

Much of the upper South continued in the nineteenth century to rely, as it always had, on the cultivation of tobacco. But the market for that crop was notoriously unstable, and tobacco rapidly exhausted the land on which it grew. By the 1830s, therefore, many farmers in the old tobacco-growing regions of Virginia, Maryland, and North Carolina were shifting to other crops—notably wheat—while the center of tobacco cultivation was moving westward, into the Piedmont area.

The southern regions of the coastal South—South Carolina, Georgia, and parts of Florida—continued to rely on the cultivation of rice, a more stable and lucrative crop. But rice demanded substantial irrigation and needed an exceptionally long growing season (nine months), so cultivation of that staple remained restricted to a relatively small area. Sugar growers along the Gulf Coast, similarly, enjoyed a reasonably profitable market for their crop. But sugar cultivation required intensive (and debilitating) labor and a long growing time; only relatively wealthy planters could afford to engage in it. In addition, producers faced major competition from the great sugar plantations of the Caribbean. Sugar cultivation, therefore, did not spread much beyond a small area in southern Louisiana and eastern Texas. Long-staple (Sea Island) cotton was another lucrative crop, but like rice and sugar, it could grow only in a limited area—the coastal regions of the Southeast.

The decline of the tobacco economy in the upper South, and the inherent limits of the sugar, rice, and long-staple cotton economies farther south, might have forced the region to shift its attention in the nineteenth century to other, nonagricultural pursuits had it not been for the growing importance of a new product that soon overshadowed all else: short-staple cotton. This was a hardier and coarser strain of cotton that could grow successfully in a variety of climates and in a variety of soils. It was harder to process than the long-staple variety because its seeds were difficult to remove from the fiber. But the invention of the cotton gin (see p. 189) had largely solved that problem.

Demand for cotton increased rapidly in the nineteenth century with the growth of the textile industry in Britain in the 1820s and 1830s and in New England in the 1840s and 1850s. In response to that demand, beginning in the 1820s, cotton production spread rapidly. From the western areas of South Carolina and Georgia, production moved into Alabama and Mississippi and then into northern Louisiana, Texas, and Arkansas. By the 1850s, cotton had become the linchpin of the southern economy. In 1820, the South had produced only about 500,000 bales of cotton. By 1860 it was producing nearly 5 million bales a year. There were periodic booms and busts, but the cotton economy continued to grow, even if in fits and starts. By the time of the Civil War, cotton constituted nearly two-thirds of the total export trade of the United States. It was little wonder that southern politicians now proclaimed: "Cotton is king!"

Cotton production boomed in the relatively recently settled areas of what came to be known as the "lower South" (or, in a later era, the "Deep South"). Some began to call it the "Cotton Kingdom." The prospect of tremendous profits drew settlers to the lower South by the thousands. Some were wealthy planters from the older states who transferred their assets and slaves to new and larger plantations. Most were small slaveholders or slaveless farmers who hoped to move into the planter class.

A similar shift, if an involuntary one, occurred in the slave population. In the period from 1820 to 1860, the number of slaves in Alabama leaped from 41,000 to 435,000, and in Mississippi from 32,000 to 436,000. Between 1840 and 1860, according to some estimates, 410,000 slaves moved from the upper South to the cotton states—either accompanying masters who were themselves migrating to the Southwest or (more often) sold to planters already there. The sale of slaves to the Southwest became an important economic activity in the upper South

Slavery and Cotton: The South in 1820 and 1860

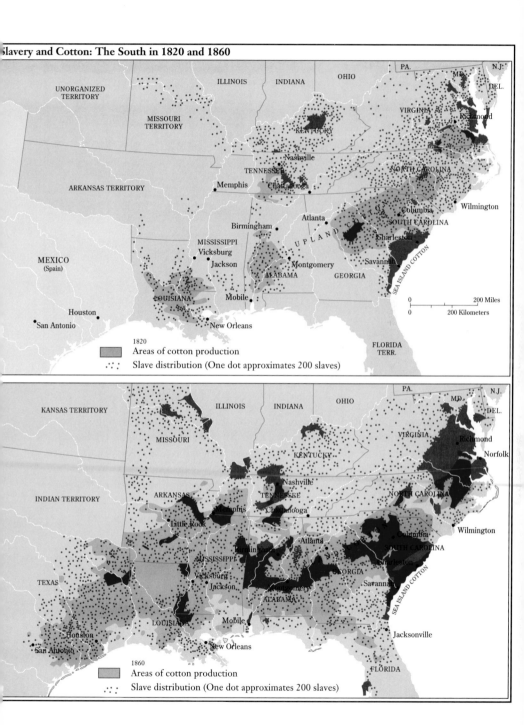

1820

- Areas of cotton production
- ⋰⋱ Slave distribution (One dot approximates 200 slaves)

1860

- Areas of cotton production
- ⋰⋱ Slave distribution (One dot approximates 200 slaves)

313

THE NEW ORLEANS COTTON EXCHANGE Edgar Degas, the great French impressionist, painted this scene of cotton traders examining samples in the New Orleans cotton exchange in 1873. By that time the cotton trade was producing less impressive profits than those that had made it the driving force of the booming southern economy of the 1850s. Degas's mother came from a Creole family of cotton brokers in New Orleans, and two of the artist's brothers (depicted here reading a newspaper and leaning against a window) joined the business in America.

and helped the troubled planters of that region compensate for the declining value of their crops.

Southern Trade and Industry

In the face of this booming agricultural expansion, other forms of economic activity developed slowly in the South. There was growing activity in flour milling and in textile and iron manufacturing, particularly in the upper South. The Tredegar Iron Works in Richmond, for example, compared favorably with the best iron mills in the Northeast. But indus-try remained an insignificant force in comparison with the agricultural economy. The total value of southern textile manufactures in 1860 was $4.5 million—a threefold increase over the value of those goods twenty years before, but only about 2 percent of the value of the cotton ex-ported that year.

The limited nonfarm commercial sector that did develop in the South was largely intended to serve the needs of the plantation econ-omy. Particularly important were the brokers, or "factors," who mar-keted the planters' crops. The South had only a very rudimentary finan-cial system, and the factors often also served the planters as bankers, providing them with credit. Other obstacles to economic development included the South's inadequate transportation system. In the North in the antebellum period, governments and entrepreneurs were investing enormous sums in roads, canals, and above all railroads to knit the re-gion together into an integrated market. In the South there were few such investments. Canals were almost nonexistent; most roads were crude and unsuitable for heavy transport; and railroads, although they expanded substantially in the 1840s and 1850s, failed to tie the region together effectively. The principal means of transportation was water. Planters generally shipped their crops to market along rivers or by sea; most manufacturing was in or near port towns.

The South was, therefore, becoming more and more dependent on the manufacturers, merchants, and professionals of the North. Some southerners began to advocate economic independence for the region, among them James B. D. De Bow of New Orleans, whose magazine *De Bow's Commercial Review*, published from 1846 to 1860, called for southern commercial and agricultural expansion and economic inde-pendence from the North. Yet even *De Bow's Commercial Review* was filled with advertisements from northern manufacturing firms; and its circulation was far smaller in the South than such northern magazines as *Harper's Weekly*.

Sources of Southern Difference

Despite this growing concern about what De Bow called the region's "colonial dependency," the South made few serious efforts to build an economy that might challenge that dependency. An important question about antebellum southern history, therefore, is why the region did so little

DE BOW'S COMMERCIAL REVIEW J. D. B. De Bow, owner and editor of the South's leading magazine, presented his *Review* as a commercial publication—designed for those committed to commerce. But it also contained essays and articles promoting the South's way of life and what many white southerners considered the region's distinctive (and superior) culture.

to develop a larger industrial and commercial economy of its own. Why did it remain so different from the North?

Part of the reason was the great profitability of the region's agricultural system, and particularly of cotton production. In the Northeast, many people had turned to manufacturing as the agricultural economy of the region declined. In the South, the agricultural economy was booming, and ambitious people eager to profit from the emerging capitalist economy had little incentive to look elsewhere. Another reason was that wealthy southerners had so much capital invested in their land and their slaves that they had little left for other investments. Some historians have suggested that the southern climate—with its long, hot, steamy summers—was less suitable for industrial development than the climate of the North.

But the southern failure to create a flourishing commercial or industrial economy was also in part the result of a set of values distinctive to the South. Many white southerners liked to think of themselves as representatives of a special way of life. Southerners were, they argued, people happily free from the base, acquisitive instincts of northerners; they were more concerned with a refined and gracious way of life than with rapid growth and development. But appealing as this image was to southern whites, it conformed to the reality of southern society in very limited ways.

SOUTHERN WHITE SOCIETY

Only a small minority of southern whites owned slaves. In 1860, when the white population was just above 8 million, the number of slaveholders was only 383,637. Even with all members of slaveowning families included in the figures, those living in slaveowning households still amounted to perhaps no more than one-quarter of the white population. And only a small proportion of this relatively small number of slaveowners owned slaves in substantial numbers.

The Planter Class

How, then, did the South come to be seen—both by the outside world and by many southerners themselves—as a society dominated by great plantations and wealthy landowning planters? In large part, it was because the planter aristocracy exercised power and influence far in excess of their numbers. They became a class to which all others deferred.

White southerners liked to compare their planter class to the old upper classes of England and Europe: true aristocracies, long entrenched, "cavaliers." In fact, most of the southern upper class was in most cases not at all similar to the landed aristocracies of the Old World. In some areas of the upper South—the tidewater region of Virginia, for example—some of the great aristocrats were indeed people whose families had occupied positions of wealth and power for generations. In most of the South, however, there was no longstanding landed aristocracy. As late as the 1850s, many of the great landowners in the lower South were still first-generation settlers, who had arrived with only modest resources, struggled for many years, and only relatively recently started to live in the comfort and luxury for which they became famous. Large areas of the South had been settled and cultivated for less than two decades at the time of the Civil War.

Nor was the world of the planter nearly as leisured and genteel as the "cavalier" myth would suggest. Growing staple crops was a business— often a big and highly profitable business. Planters were, in many respects, just as much competitive capitalists as the industrialists of the North whose lifestyles they claimed to hold in contempt. Even many affluent planters lived rather modestly, their wealth so heavily invested in land and slaves that there was little left for personal comfort. And white planters, including some substantial ones, tended to move frequently as new and presumably more productive areas opened up to cultivation.

Wealthy southern whites sustained their image of themselves as aristocrats in many ways. They adopted an elaborate code of "chivalry," which obligated white men to defend their "honor," often through dueling— which survived in the South long after it had largely vanished in the North. They avoided such "coarse" occupations as trade and commerce; those who did not become planters often gravitated toward the military. The aristocratic ideal also found reflection in the definition of a special role for southern white women.

The "Southern Lady"

In some respects, affluent white women in the South occupied roles very similar to those of middle-class white women in the North. Their lives generally centered in the home, where (according to the South's social ideal) they served as companions to and hostesses for their husbands and as nurturing mothers for their children. Even less frequently than in the North did "genteel" southern white women engage in public activities or find income-producing employment.

But the life of the "southern lady" was also in many ways very different from that of her northern counterpart. For one thing, the cult of honor in the region meant that southern white men gave particular importance to the defense of women. In practice, this generally meant that white men were even more dominant and white women even more subordinate in southern culture than they were in the North. George Fitzhugh, one of the South's most important social theorists, wrote in the 1850s: "Women, like children, have but one right, and that is the right to protection. The right to protection involves the obligation to obey."

More important in determining the role of southern white women, however, was that the vast majority of them lived on farms, relatively isolated from people outside their own families, with little access to the "public world" and thus few opportunities to look beyond their roles as wives and mothers. For many white women, living on farms of modest size meant a fuller engagement in the economic life of the family than was becoming typical for middle-class women in the North. These women engaged in spinning, weaving, and other production; they participated in agricultural tasks; they helped supervise the slave work force. On the larger plantations, however, even these limited roles were often considered unsuitable for white women, and the "plantation mistress" became, in some cases, more an ornament for her husband than an active part of the economy or the society. Southern white women also had less access to education than their northern counterparts. Nearly a quarter of all white women over twenty were completely illiterate; relatively few women had more than a rudimentary education. The few female "academies" in the South trained women primarily to be suitable wives.

Southern white women had other special burdens as well. The southern white birth rate remained nearly 20 percent higher than that of the nation as a whole, and infant mortality in the region remained higher than elsewhere. The slave labor system also had a mixed impact on white women. It helped spare many of them from certain kinds of arduous labor, but it also damaged their relationships with their husbands. Male slaveowners had frequent sexual relationships with the female slaves on their plantations; the children of those unions became part of the plantation labor force and served as a constant reminder to white women of their husbands' infidelities. Black women (and men) were obviously the most important victims of such practices, but white women suffered, too.

The Plain Folk

The typical white southerner was not a great planter and slaveholder but a modest yeoman farmer. Some of these "plain folk," as they became known, owned a few slaves, with whom they worked and lived more closely than did the larger planters. Most owned no slaves at all. Some plain folk, most of whom owned their own land, devoted themselves largely to subsistence farming; others grew cotton or other crops for the market, but usually could not produce enough to allow them to expand their operations or even get out of debt. Most yeomen knew that they had little prospect of substantially bettering their lot.

One reason was the southern educational system. For the sons of wealthy planters, the region provided ample opportunities to gain an education. In 1860 there were 260 southern colleges and universities, public and private, with 25,000 students enrolled in them—more than half the total number of students in the United States. But as in the rest of the United States, universities were only within the reach of the upper class. The elementary and secondary schools of the South were not only fewer than but also inferior to those of the Northeast (although not much worse than the crude schools of the Northwest). The South had more than 500,000 illiterate whites, or over half the country's total.

The subordination of the plain folk to the planter class raises an important question: Why did lower-class whites not oppose the aristocratic social system from which they benefited so little? Why did they not resent the system of slavery, from which they generally did not profit?

Some nonslaveowning whites did oppose the planter elite, but for the most part in limited ways and in relatively few, isolated areas. These were mainly the southern highlanders, the "hill people," who lived in the Appalachian ranges east of the Mississippi, in the Ozarks to the west of the river, and in other "hill country" or "backcountry" areas cut off from the more commercial world of the plantation system. Of all southern whites, they were the most isolated from the mainstream of the region's life. They practiced a simple form of subsistence agriculture and owned practically no slaves. They were, in most respects, unconnected to the new commercial economy that dominated the great cotton-planting region of the South.

Such whites frequently expressed animosity toward the planter aristocracy of the other regions of the South. The mountain region was the only part of the South to defy the trend toward sectional conformity, and it was the only part to resist the movement toward secession when it finally developed. Even during the Civil War itself, many refused to support the Confederacy; some went so far as to fight for the Union.

Far greater in number, however, were the nonslaveowning whites who lived in the midst of the plantation system. Many, perhaps most of them, accepted that system because they were tied to it in important ways. Small farmers depended on the local plantation aristocracy for many things: access to cotton gins, markets for their modest crops and their livestock, credit or other financial assistance in time of need. In many areas, moreover, the poorest resident of a county might easily be a cousin of the richest aristocrat. In the 1850s, the boom in the cotton economy allowed many small farmers to improve their economic fortunes. Some bought more land, became slaveowners, and moved into at least the fringes of plantation society. Others simply felt more secure in their positions as independent yeomen and hence more likely to embrace the fierce regional loyalty that was spreading throughout the white South in these years.

There were other white southerners, however, who shared almost not at all in the plantation economy and yet continued to accept its premises. These were the members of a degraded class—numbering perhaps a half-million in 1850—known variously as "crackers," "sand hillers," or "poor white trash." Occupying the infertile lands of the pine barrens, the red hills, and the swamps, they lived in genuine squalor. Many owned no land (or owned land on which virtually nothing could be grown) and supported themselves by foraging or hunting. Others worked at times as common laborers for their neighbors, although the slave system limited their opportunities to do so. Their degradation resulted partly from dietary deficiencies and disease. They resorted at times to eating clay (hence the tendency of more affluent whites to refer to them disparagingly as "clay eaters"), and they suffered from pellagra, hookworm, and malaria. Planters and small farmers alike held them in contempt. In some material respects, their plight was worse than that of the black slaves (who themselves often looked down on the poor whites).

Even among these southerners—the true outcasts of white society in the region—there was no real opposition to the plantation system or slavery. In part, undoubtedly, this was because these men and women were so benumbed by poverty that they had little strength to protest. But it resulted also from perhaps the single greatest unifying factor among the southern white population: their perception of race. However poor and miserable white southerners might be, they could still consider themselves members of a ruling race; they could still look down on the black population of the region and feel a bond with their fellow whites born of a determination to maintain their racial supremacy.

THE "PECULIAR INSTITUTION"

White southerners often referred to slavery as the "peculiar institution." By that they meant not that the institution was odd but that it was distinctive, special. American slavery was indeed distinctive. The South in the

RETURNING FROM THE COTTON FIELD In this photograph, South Carolina field workers return after a day of picking cotton, some of their harvest carried in bundles on their heads. A black slave driver leads the way.

mid-nineteenth century was the only area in the Western world—except for Brazil, Cuba, and Puerto Rico—where slavery still existed. Slavery, more than any other single factor, isolated the South from the rest of American society. And as that isolation increased, so did the commitment of southerners to defend the institution.

Within the South itself, the institution of slavery had paradoxical results. On the one hand, it isolated blacks from whites, drawing a sharp and inviolable racial line dividing one group of southerners from another. As a result, African Americans under slavery began to develop a society and culture of their own. On the other hand, slavery created a unique bond between blacks and whites—masters and slaves—in the South. The two groups may have maintained separate spheres, but each sphere was deeply influenced by, indeed dependent on, the other.

Varieties of Slavery

Slavery was an institution established and regulated in detail by law. The slave codes of the southern states forbade slaves to hold property, to leave their masters' premises without permission, to be out after dark, to congregate with other slaves except at church, to carry firearms, or to strike a white person even in self-defense. The codes prohibited whites from teaching slaves to read or write and denied slaves the right to testify in court against white people. The laws contained no provisions to legalize slave marriages or divorces. If an owner killed a slave while punishing him, the act was generally not considered a crime. Slaves, however, faced the death penalty for killing or even resisting a white person and for inciting revolt. The codes also contained extraordinarily rigid provisions for defining a person's race. Anyone with a trace (or often even a rumor) of African ancestry was defined as black.

Enforcement of the laws, however, was spotty and uneven. Some slaves did acquire property, did learn to read and write, and did assemble with other slaves, in spite of laws to the contrary. White owners handled most transgressions by their slaves and inflicted widely varying punishments. In other words, despite the rigid provisions of law, there was in reality considerable variety within the slave system. Some slaves lived in almost prisonlike conditions, rigidly and harshly controlled by their masters. Many (probably most) others enjoyed considerable flexibility and autonomy.

The nature of the relationship between masters and slaves depended in part on the size of the plantation. White farmers with few slaves generally supervised their workers directly and often worked closely alongside them. On such farms, blacks and whites developed a form of intimacy unknown on larger plantations. The paternal relationship between such masters and their slaves could, like relationships between fathers and children, be warm and benevolent. It could also be tyrannical and cruel. In general, African Americans themselves preferred to live on larger plantations, where they had more privacy and a chance for a social world of their own.

Although the majority of slaveowners were small farmers, the majority of slaves lived on plantations of medium or large size, with substantial slave work forces. Thus the relationship between master and slave was much less intimate for the typical slave than for the typical slaveowner. Substantial planters often hired overseers and even assistant overseers to represent them. "Head drivers," trusted and responsible slaves often assisted by several subdrivers, acted under the overseer as foremen.

Life Under Slavery

Slaves generally received an adequate yet simple diet, consisting mainly of cornmeal, salt pork, molasses, and on special occasions fresh meat or poultry. Many slaves cultivated gardens for their own use. Their masters provided them with cheap clothing and shoes. They lived in rough cabins, called slave quarters, usually clustered together in a complex near the master's house. The plantation mistress or a doctor retained by the owner provided some medical care, but slave women themselves—as "healers" and midwives, or simply as mothers—were the more important source.

Slaves worked hard, beginning with light tasks as children; their workdays were longest at harvest time. Slave women worked particularly hard. They generally labored in the fields with the men, and they also handled cooking, cleaning, and child rearing. Many slave families were divided. Husbands and fathers often lived on neighboring plantations; at times, one spouse (usually the male) would be sold to a plantation owner far away. As a result, black women often found themselves acting in effect as single parents. Within the slave family, therefore, women had special burdens but also a special authority.

Slaves were, as a group, much less healthy than southern whites. After 1808, when the importation of slaves became illegal, the proportion of blacks to whites in the nation as a whole steadily declined. The slower increase of the black population was a result of its comparatively high death rate. Slave mothers had large families, but the enforced poverty in which virtually all African Americans lived ensured that fewer of their children would survive to adulthood than the children of white parents. Even those who did survive typically died at a younger age than the average white person.

Household servants had a somewhat easier life—physically at least—than did field hands. On a small plantation, the same slaves might do both field work and housework. But on a large estate, there would generally be a separate domestic staff: nursemaids, housemaids, cooks, butlers, coachmen. These people lived close to the master and his family, eating the leftovers from the family table and in some cases even sleeping in the "big house." Between the blacks and whites of such households affectionate, almost familial relationships might develop. More often, however, house servants resented their isolation from their fellow slaves and the lack of privacy that came with living in such close proximity to the master's family. Among other things, that proximity meant that their transgressions were more visible than those of field hands, and so they received punishments more often than did other slaves. When emancipation came after the Civil War, it was often the house servants who were the first to leave the plantations of their former owners.

Female household servants were especially vulnerable to sexual abuse by their masters and white overseers, who often pressured them into sexual relationships and sometimes literally raped them. In addition to being subjected to unwanted sexual attention from white men, female slaves often received vindictive treatment from white women. Plantation mistresses naturally resented the sexual liaisons between their husbands and female slaves. Punishing their husbands was not usually possible, so they often punished the slaves instead—with arbitrary beatings, increased workloads, and various forms of psychological torment.

Slavery in the Cities

The conditions of slavery in the cities differed significantly from those in the countryside. On the relatively isolated plantations, slaves had little contact with free blacks and lower-class whites, and masters maintained a fairly direct and effective control; a deep and seemingly unbridgeable chasm yawned between slavery and freedom. In the city, however, a master often could not supervise his slaves closely and at the same time use them profitably. Even if they slept at night in carefully watched backyard barracks, they moved about during the day alone, performing errands of various kinds.

There was a considerable market in the South for common laborers, particularly since, unlike in the North, there were few European immigrants to perform menial chores. As a result, masters often hired out slaves for such tasks. Slaves on contract worked in mining and lumbering (often far from cities), but others worked on the docks and on construction sites, drove wagons, and performed other unskilled jobs in cities and towns. Slave women and children worked in the region's few textile mills. Particularly skilled workers such as blacksmiths or carpenters were also often hired out. After regular working hours, many of them fended for themselves; neither their owners nor their employers bothered to supervise them. Thus urban slaves gained numerous opportunities to mingle with free blacks and with whites. In the cities, the line between slavery and freedom was less distinct than on the plantation.

Free Blacks

There were about 250,000 free blacks in the slaveholding states by the start of the Civil War, more than half of them in Virginia and Maryland. In some cases, they were slaves who had somehow earned money with which they managed to buy their own and their families' freedom, usually by developing a skill they could market independently of their masters. It was most often urban blacks, with their greater freedom of movement and activity, who could take that route. One example was Elizabeth Keckley, a slave woman who bought freedom for herself and her son with proceeds from sewing. She later became a seamstress, personal servant, and companion to Mary Todd Lincoln in the White House. But few masters had any incentive, or inclination, to give up their slaves, so this route was open to relatively few people.

Some slaves were set free by a master who had moral qualms about slavery, or by a master's will after his death—for example, the more than 400 slaves belonging to John Randolph of Roanoke, freed in 1833. From the 1830s on, however, state laws governing slavery became more rigid. That was in part a response to the fears Nat Turner's revolt (see pp. 330-331) created among white southerners: free blacks, removed from close supervision by whites, might generate more violence and rebellion than would slaves. The new laws made it more and more difficult, and in some cases practically impossible, for owners to set free (or "manumit") their slaves.

A few free blacks (generally those on the northern fringes of the slave-holding regions) attained wealth and prominence. Some owned slaves themselves, usually relatives whom they had bought in order to ensure their ultimate emancipation. In a few cities—New Orleans, Natchez, and Charleston—free black communities managed to flourish relatively unmolested by whites and with some economic stability. Most southern free blacks, however, lived in abject poverty, under conditions even worse than those of blacks in the North. Yet, great as were the hardships of freedom, blacks usually preferred them to slavery.

Slave Resistance

Slaveowners, and many white Americans after emancipation, liked to argue that the slaves were generally content, "happy with their lot." That may have been true in some cases. But it is clear that the vast majority of southern blacks were not content with being slaves, that they yearned for freedom even though most realized there was little they could do to se-cure it. Evidence for that conclusion can be found, if nowhere else, in the reaction of slaves when emancipation finally came. Virtually all reacted to freedom with great joy; relatively few chose to remain in the service of the whites who had owned them before the Civil War.

Rather than contented acceptance, the dominant response of blacks to slavery was a complex one: a combination of adaptation and resistance. At the extremes, slavery could produce two very different reactions, each of which served as the basis for a powerful stereotype in white society. One extreme was what became known as the "Sambo"—the shuffling, grinning, head-scratching, deferential slave who acted out the role that he recog-nized the white world expected of him. More often than not, the "Sambo" pattern of behavior was a charade, a facade assumed in the presence of whites. The other extreme was the slave rebel—the African American who could not bring himself or herself to either acceptance or accommodation but remained forever rebellious.

Actual slave revolts were extremely rare, but the knowledge that they were possible struck terror into the hearts of white southerners everywhere. In 1800, Gabriel Prosser gathered 1,000 rebellious slaves outside Richmond; but two Africans gave the plot away, and the Virginia militia stymied the up-rising before it could begin. Prosser and thirty-five others were executed. In 1822, the Charleston free black Denmark Vesey and his followers—rumored to total 9,000—made preparations for revolt; but again word leaked out, and suppression and retribution followed. On a summer night in 1831, Nat Turner, a slave preacher, led a band of African Americans armed with guns and axes from house to house in Southampton County, Virginia. They killed sixty white men, women, and children before being overpowered by state and federal troops. More than a hundred blacks were executed in the after-math. Nat Turner's was the only actual slave insurrection in the nineteenth-century South, but fear of slave conspiracies and renewed violence pervaded the section as long as slavery lasted.

For the most part, however, resistance to slavery took other, less dras-tic forms. Some blacks attempted to resist by running away. A small num-ber managed to escape to the North or to Canada, especially after sympa-thetic whites and free blacks began organizing the so-called underground railroad to assist them in flight. But the odds against a successful escape, particularly from the Deep South, were very high. The hazards of distance and the slaves' ignorance of geography were serious obstacles. So were the white "slave patrols," which stopped wandering blacks on sight through-out the South demanding to see travel permits. Despite all the obstacles to

HARRIET TUBMAN WITH ESCAPED SLAVES Harriet Tubman (c. 1820–1913) was born into slavery in Maryland. In 1849, when her master died, she escaped to Philadelphia to avoid being sold out of state. Over the next ten years, she assisted first members of her own family and then up to 300 other slaves to escape from Maryland to freedom. During the Civil War, she served alternately as a nurse and as a spy for Union forces in South Carolina. She is shown here, on the left, with some of the slaves she helped to free.

success, however, blacks continued to run away from their masters in large numbers. Some did so repeatedly, undeterred by the whippings and other penalties inflicted on them when captured.

But perhaps the most important method of resistance was simply a pattern of everyday behavior by which blacks defied their masters. That whites so often considered blacks to be lazy and shiftless suggests one means of resistance: refusal to work hard. Some slaves stole from their masters or from neighboring whites. Some performed isolated acts of sabotage: losing or breaking tools (southern planters gradually began to buy unusually heavy hoes because so many of the lighter ones got broken) or performing tasks improperly. In extreme cases, blacks might make themselves useless by cutting off their fingers or even committing suicide. Or, despite the terrible consequences, a few turned on their masters and killed them. The extremes, however, were rare. For the most part, blacks resisted by building subtle methods of rebellion into their normal patterns of behavior.

THE CULTURE OF SLAVERY

Resistance was only part of the slave response to slavery. Another was an elaborate process of adaptation—a process that did not imply contentment with bondage but a recognition that there was no realistic alternative. One of the ways blacks adapted was by developing their own, separate culture, one that enabled them to sustain a sense of racial pride and unity.

Slave Religion

A separate slave religion was not supposed to exist. Almost all African Americans were Christians by the early nineteenth century. Some had converted voluntarily and some after coercion from their masters and Protestant missionaries who evangelized among them. Masters expected their slaves to worship under the supervision of white ministers. Indeed, autonomous black churches were banned by law, and many slaves became members of the same denominations as their owners—usually Baptist or Methodist.

Nevertheless, blacks throughout the South developed their own version of Christianity, at times incorporating into it such practices as voodoo or other polytheistic religious traditions of Africa. Or they simply bent religion to the special circumstances of bondage. Natural leaders emerging within the slave community rose to the rank of preacher.

African-American religion was more emotional than its white counterpart and reflected the influence of African customs and practices. Slave prayer meetings routinely involved fervent chanting, spontaneous exclamations from the congregation, and ecstatic conversion experiences. Black religion was also more joyful and affirming than that of many white denominations. And above all, African-American religion emphasized the dream of freedom and deliverance. In their prayers and songs and sermons, black Christians talked and sang of the day when the Lord would "call us home," "deliver us to freedom," "take us to the Promised Land." And while their white masters generally chose to interpret such language merely as the expression of hopes for life after death, many blacks themselves used the images of Christian salvation to express their own dream of freedom in the present world. Christian images, and biblical injunctions, were central to Gabriel Prosser, Denmark Vesey, Nat Turner, and others who planned or engaged in open resistance to slavery.

DEBATING THE PAST

The Character of Slavery

N
O ISSUE IN American history has produced a richer literature or a more spirited debate than the nature of plantation slavery. The debate began even before the Civil War, when abolitionists strove to expose slavery to the world as a brutal, dehumanizing institution, while Southern defenders of slavery tried to depict it as a benevolent, paternalistic system. That same debate continued for a time after the Civil War; but by the late nineteenth century, with white Americans eager for sectional conciliation, most Northern and Southern chroniclers of slavery began to accept a romanticized and unthreatening picture of the Old South and its peculiar institution.

The first major scholarly examination of slavery was fully within this romantic tradition. Ulrich B. Phillips's *American Negro Slavery* (1918) portrayed slavery as an essentially benign institution in which kindly masters looked after submissive, childlike, and generally contented African Americans. Phillips's apologia for slavery remained the authoritative work on the subject for nearly thirty years.

In the 1940s, as concern about racial injustice increasingly engaged the attention of white Americans, challenges to Phillips began to emerge. In 1941, for example, Melville J. Herskovits challenged Phillips's contention that black Americans retained little of their African cultural inheritance. In 1943, Herbert Aptheker published a chronicle of slave revolts as a way of challenging Phillips's claim that blacks were submissive and content.

A somewhat different challenge to Phillips emerged in the 1950s from historians who emphasized the brutality of the institution. Kenneth Stampp's *The Peculiar Institution* (1956) and, even more powerfully, Stanley Elkins's *Slavery* (1959) described a labor system that did serious physical and psychological damage to its victims. Stampp and Elkins portrayed slavery as something like a prison, in which men and women had virtually no space to develop their own social and cultural lives. Elkins compared the system to Nazi concentration camps during World War II and likened the childlike "Sambo" personality of slavery to the tragic distortions of character produced by the Holocaust.

In the early 1970s, an explosion of new scholarship on slavery shifted the emphasis away from the damage the system inflicted on African Americans and toward the striking success of the slaves themselves in building a culture of their own despite their enslavement. John Blassingame in 1973, echoing Herskovits's claims of thirty years earlier, argued that "the most remarkable aspect of the whole process of enslavement is the extent to which the American-born slaves were able to retain their ancestors' culture." Herbert Gutman, in *The Black Family in Slavery and Freedom* (1976), challenged the prevailing belief that slavery had weakened and even destroyed the African-American family. On the contrary, he argued, the black family survived slavery with impressive strength, although with some significant differences from the prevailing form of the white family. Eugene Genovese's *Roll, Fordan, Roll* (1974) revealed how African Americans manipulated the paternalist assumptions that lay at the heart of slavery to build a large cultural space of their own, within the system, where they could develop their own family life, social traditions, and religious patterns. That same year, Robert Fogel and Stanley Engerman published their controversial *Time on the Cross*, a highly quantitative study that supported some of the claims of Gutman and Genovese about black achievement but that went much further in portraying slavery as a successful and reasonably humane (if ultimately immoral) system. Slave workers, they argued, were better treated and lived in greater comfort than most Northern industrial workers of the same era. Their conclusions produced a storm of criticism.

Some of the most important recent scholarship on slavery extends the notion of slave autonomy to discussions of African-American women. Elizabeth Fox-Genovese's *Within the Plantation Household* (1988) examined the lives of both white and black women on the plantation. Rejecting the claims of some feminist historians that black and white women shared a common female identity born of their shared subordination to men, she portrayed slave women as defined by their dual roles as members of the plantation work force and anchors of the black family. Slave women, she argued, professed loyalty to their mistresses when forced to serve them as domestics; but their real loyalty remained to their own communities and families.

In cities and towns in the South, some African Americans had their own churches, where free blacks occasionally worshiped alongside slaves. In the countryside, however, slaves usually attended the same churches as their masters. Seating in such churches was usually segregated. Blacks sat in the rear or in balconies. They held their own services later, often in secret, usually at night.

Language and Music

In many areas, slaves retained a language of their own, sometimes incorporating African speech patterns into English. Having arrived in America speaking many different African languages, the first generations of slaves had as much difficulty communicating with one another as they did with white people. To overcome these barriers, they learned a simple, common language (known to linguists as "pidgin"). It retained some African words, but it drew primarily, if selectively, from English. And while slave language grew more sophisticated as blacks spent more time in America—and as new generations grew up never having known African tongues—some features of this early pidgin survived in black speech for many generations.

Music was especially important in slave society. In some ways, it was almost as important to African Americans as language. Again, the African heritage was an important influence. African music relied heavily on rhythm, and so did black music in America. Africans thought of music as an accompaniment to dance, and so did blacks in America. The banjo, an instrument original to Africa, became important to slave music. But most important were voices and song.

Field workers often used songs to pass the time in the fields; since they sang them in the presence of the whites, they usually attached relatively innocuous words to them. But African Americans also created more emotionally rich and politically challenging music in the relative privacy of their religious services. It was there that the tradition of the spiritual emerged in the early nineteenth century. Through the spiritual, Africans in America not only expressed their religious faith, but also lamented their bondage and expressed continuing hope for freedom. Similar sentiments surfaced throughout slave religion.

Slave songs were rarely written down and often seemed entirely spontaneous; but much slave music was really derived from African and Caribbean traditions passed on through generations. Performers also improvised variations on other songs they had heard. Slaves sang whether or not there were musical instruments to accompany them, but they often created instruments

THE OLD PLANTATION This painting, by an unidentified folk artist of the early nineteenth century, suggests the importance of music in the lives of plantation slaves in America. The banjo, which the black musician at right is playing, was originally an African instrument.

for themselves out of whatever materials were at hand. When the setting permitted it, African Americans danced to their music—dances very different from and much more spontaneous than the formal steps that nineteenth-century whites generally learned. They also used music to accompany another of their important cultural traditions: storytelling.

The Slave Family

The slave family was the other crucial institution of black culture in the South. Like religion, it suffered from legal restrictions—most notably the lack of legal marriage. Nevertheless, what we now call the "nuclear family" consistently emerged as the dominant kinship model among African Americans.

Such families did not always operate according to white customs. Black women generally began bearing children at younger ages than most whites, often as early as age fourteen or fifteen. Slave communities did not condemn premarital pregnancy in the way white society did, and black couples would often begin living together before marrying. It was customary, however, for couples to marry—in a ceremony involving formal vows—soon after conceiving a child. Many marriages occurred between slaves living on neighboring plantations. Husbands and wives sometimes visited each other with the permission of their masters, but often such visits had to be in secret, at night. Family ties were generally no less strong than those of whites, and many slave marriages lasted through long lifetimes.

When marriages did not survive, it was often because of circumstances over which blacks had no control. Up to a third of all black families were broken apart by the slave trade; an average slave might expect during a lifetime to see ten or more relatives sold. That accounted for some of the other distinctive characteristics of the black family. Extended kinship networks—which grew to include not only spouses and their children but aunts, uncles, grandparents, even distant cousins—were strong and important, and often helped compensate for the breakup of nuclear families. A slave forced suddenly to move to a new area, far from his or her family, might create fictional kinship ties and become "adopted" by a family in the new community. Even so, the impulse to maintain contact with a spouse and children remained strong long after the breakup of a family. One of the most frequent causes of flight from the plantation was a slave's desire to find a husband, wife, or child who had been sent elsewhere.

However much blacks resented their lack of freedom, they often found it difficult to maintain an entirely hostile attitude toward their owners. They depended on whites for the material means of existence—food, clothing, and shelter—and they relied on them as well for security and protection. There was, in short, a paternal relationship between slave and master—sometimes harsh, sometimes kindly, but always important. That paternalism, in fact, became (even if not always consciously) a vital instrument of white control. By creating a sense of mutual dependence, whites helped reduce resistance to an institution that, in essence, served only the interests of the ruling race.

CONCLUSION

While the North was creating a complex and rapidly developing commercial-industrial economy, the South was expanding its agrarian economy without making many fundamental changes in its character. Great migrations took many southern whites, and even more African-American slaves, into new agricultural areas in the Deep South, where they created a booming "cotton kingdom" that raised crops for export around the world. The cotton economy created many great fortunes, and some modest ones. It also entrenched the planter class as the dominant force within southern society—both as owners of vast numbers of slaves and as patrons, creditors, landlords, and marketers for the large number of poor whites who lived on the edge of the planter world.

The differences between the North and the South were a result of differences in natural resources, differences in social structure, differences in climate, and differences in culture. Above all, they were the result of the existence within the South of an unfree labor system that prevented the kind of social fluidity that an industrializing society usually requires.

FOR FURTHER REFERENCE

Suggested Readings

Frederick Douglass's *Narrative of the Life of Frederick Douglass*, first published in 1845, is an American classic. Peter Kolchin, *American Slavery, 1619–1877* (1993) is the most recent synthesis of the history of slavery in the United States from the settlement of Virginia through Reconstruction. James Oakes, *Slavery and Freedom* (1990) provides an overview of southern politics and society in the antebellum period. Eugene Genovese, *Roll, Jordan, Roll: The World the Slaves Made* (1974) argues that masters and slaves forged a system of mutual obligations within a fundamentally coercive social system. Genovese's *The Political Economy of Slavery* (1965) argues that slavery blocked southern economic development. Robert Fogel and Stanley Engerman, *Time on the Cross*, 2 vols. (1974) is a controversial quantitative study of slavery. Herbert Gutman, *The Black Family in Slavery and Freedom* (1976) is a sweeping and important history. Elizabeth Fox-Genovese, *Within the Plantation Household* (1988) argues against the idea that black and white women shared a community of interests on southern plantations. Charles Joyner, *Down by the Riverside: A South Carolina Slave Community* (1984) is an excellent study of slavery in a single community. Bertram Wyatt-Brown, *Southern Honor: Ethics and Behavior in the Old South* (1982) argues that concepts of honor lay at the core of southern white identity in the antebellum period. Suzanne Lebsock, *The Free Women of Petersburg: Status and Culture in a Southern Town* (1984) is an excellent local study of southern white women, and Anne Firor Scott, *The Southern Lady* (1970) is a pioneering general study. Steven Hahn, *The Roots of Southern Populism: Yeomen Farmers and the Transformation of the Georgia Upcountry, 1850–1890* (1983) argues that white farmers in upcountry regions of the antebellum South maintained economically self-sufficient communities on the periphery of the market.

Films

(The best source for information on how to find these and other films is *Bowker's Complete Video Directory*—3 volumes.) *The Antebellum South* (1987) is a brief introduction to the economic and political consequences of the rise of the cotton economy. *The Plantation South* portrays the development of the plantation system in antebellum southern society. *The African American Experience: 1500–1864* covers the role and contributions of black Americans from the earliest presence of Africans on American soil. See also *Black Americans of Achievement, No. 24: A History of Slavery in America* (1994). *African American Gender Roles* (1994) examines the gender patterns established in the slave community. *A Slave's Story: Running a Thousand Miles to Freedom* (1972) is based on the story of fugitive slaves William and Ellen Craft. *Virginia Plantations: Mount Vernon, Monticello & Other Great Houses of Old Virginia* (1986) is an introduction to the planter class through their architecture.

Internet Resources

Internet websites containing historical material relevant to the subjects discussed in this chapter can be reached through the McGraw-Hill history site at www.mhhe.com/socscience/history/usa/link/linktop.htm.

CHAPTER TWELVE

Antebellum Culture and Reform

The Romatic Impulse ~ *Remaking Society*
The Crusade Against Slavery

HE UNITED STATES in the mid-nineteenth century was growing rapidly in geographical extent, in the size and diversity of its population, and in the dimensions and complexity of its economy. And like any people faced with such rapid and fundamental change, Americans reacted with ambiguity. On one hand, they were excited by the new possibilities that economic growth was providing. On the other hand, they were painfully aware of the dislocations that it was creating: the challenges to traditional values and institutions, the social injustice and instability, the uncertainty about the future.

One result of these conflicting attitudes was the emergence of movements to "reform" the nation. Such movements were highly diverse, but most reflected one of two basic impulses, and at times elements of both. Some rested on an optimistic faith in human nature, a belief that within every individual resided a spirit that was basically good and that society should attempt to unleash. This assumption—which produced in both Europe and America a movement known as romanticism—stood in marked contrast to the traditional Calvinist assumption that human desires and instincts were sinful and needed to be repressed.

A second impulse was a desire for order and control. With their society changing so rapidly, with their traditional values and institutions being challenged and eroded, many Americans yearned above all for a restoration of stability and discipline to their nation. Often, this impulse embodied a conservative nostalgia for better, simpler times. But it also inspired efforts to create new institutions of social control, suited to the realities of the new age.

337

TIME LINE

1821	1826	1830	1831
New York constructs first penitentiary	Cooper's *The Last of the Mohicans*	Joseph Smith publishes the Book of Mormon	The *Liberator* begins publication

1833	1837	1840	1841	1845
American Antislavery Society founded	Horace Mann secretary of Massachusetts Board of Education	Liberty Party formed	Brook Farm founded	Frederick Douglass's autobiography

1848	1850	1851	1852	1854	1855
Women's rights convention at Seneca Falls, N.Y.	Hawthorne's *The Scarlet Letter*	Melville's *Moby Dick*	Beecher Stowe's *Uncle Tom's Cabin*	Thoreau's *Walden*	Whitman's *Leaves of Grass*
Oneida Community founded					

Reform efforts took many forms and could be found in every part of the nation. By the end of the 1840s, however, one issue—slavery—had come to overshadow all others. And one group of reformers—the abolitionists—had become the most influential of all. At that point, the reform impulse became another wedge between the North and the South.

THE ROMANTIC IMPULSE

"In the four quarters of the globe," wrote the English wit Sydney Smith in 1820, "who reads an American book? or goes to an American play? or looks at an American picture or statue?" The answer, he assumed, was obvious: no one.

American intellectuals were painfully aware of the low regard in which Europeans held their culture, and they tried in the middle decades of the nineteenth century to create an American artistic life that would express their own nation's special virtues. At the same time, many of the nation's cultural leaders were striving for another kind of liberation, which was—

ironically—largely an import from Europe: the spirit of romanticism. In literature, in philosophy, in art, even in politics and economics, American intellectuals were committing themselves to the liberation of the human spirit.

Nationalism and Romanticism in American Painting

When Sydney Smith asked in 1820 who looked at an American painting, he was expressing the almost universal belief among European artists that they—and they alone—stood at the center of the world of art. But in the United States, a great many people were, in fact, looking at American paintings in the antebellum era—and they were doing so not because the paintings introduced them to the great traditions of Europe, but because they believed Americans were creating important new artistic traditions of their own.

The most important and popular American paintings of the first half of the nineteenth century set out to evoke the wonder of the American landscape. American painters sought to capture the undiluted power of nature by portraying some of the nation's most spectacular and undeveloped areas. The first great school of American painters emerged in New York. Frederic Church, Thomas Cole, Thomas Doughty, and Asher Durand—who were, along with others, known as the Hudson River School—painted the spectacular vistas of the rugged and still largely untamed Hudson Valley. Like Emerson and Thoreau, whom many of the painters read and admired, they considered nature—far more than civilization—the best source of wisdom and fulfillment. In portraying the Hudson Valley, they seemed to announce that in America, unlike in Europe, "wild nature" still existed; and that America, therefore, was a nation of greater promise than the played-out lands of the Old World. And yet there was also a sense of nostalgia in many of the Hudson River paintings, an effort to preserve and cherish a kind of nature that many Americans feared was fast disappearing.

In later years, some of the Hudson River painters traveled further west, in search of even more profound spiritual experiences in an even more rugged and spectacular natural world. Their enormous canvases of great natural wonders—the Yosemite Valley, Yellowstone, the Rocky Mountains—touched a passionate chord among the public. Some of the most famous of their paintings—particularly the works of Albert Bierstadt and Thomas Moran—traveled around the country attracting enormous crowds.

KINDRED SPIRITS Thomas Cole was one of the early leaders of the Hudson River School of artists in New York, and he is shown here, in a painting by Asher Durand, standing in the wilderness of the Hudson Valley with the great New York poet and editor William Cullen Bryant, a hero of mid-nineteenth century intellectual life. Durand, who succeeded Cole as a leader of the Hudson Valley School, painted this scene not long after Cole's death. It was inspired by a moving eulogy Bryant had given at Cole's funeral, and Durand concluded that the two men were "kindred spirits" in their reverence for nature. Durand himself once wrote that "art must be a vision of God through nature."

An American Literature

The effort to create a distinctively American literature, which Washington Irving and others had begun in the first decades of the century, made considerable progress in the 1820s through the work of the first great American novelist: James Fenimore Cooper. What most distinguished his work was its evocation of the American West. Cooper had a lifelong fascination with the human relationship to nature and with the challenges (and dangers) of America's expansion westward. His most important novels—among them *The Last of the Mohicans* (1826) and *The Deerslayer* (1841)—explored the experience of rugged white frontiersmen with Indians, pioneers, violence, and the law. Cooper not only celebrated the American spirit and landscape; he also evoked the ideal of the independent individual with a natural inner goodness—an ideal that many Americans feared was in jeopardy in the expanding, industrializing world of the East.

Another later group of American writers displayed more clearly the appeal of romanticism to the nation's artists and intellectuals. In 1855, Walt Whitman published his first book of poems, *Leaves of Grass*, and established himself as one of the nation's most important writers. His poems celebrated democracy, the liberation of the individual spirit, and the pleasures of the flesh. Whitman helped liberate verse from traditional, restrictive conventions; he also expressed a yearning for emotional and physical release and personal fulfillment—a yearning perhaps rooted in part in his own experience as a homosexual living in a society profoundly intolerant of unconventional sexuality.

Less exuberant was Herman Melville, perhaps the greatest American writer of his era. The most important of his novels was *Moby Dick*, published in 1851—the story of Ahab, the powerful, driven captain of a whaling vessel, who was obsessed with his search for Moby Dick, the great white whale that had once maimed him. It was a story of courage and of the strength of human will. But it was also a tragedy of pride and revenge, and an uncomfortable metaphor for the harsh, individualistic, achievement-driven culture of nineteenth-century America.

Literature in the Antebellum South

Similarly bleak were the works of the southern writer Edgar Allan Poe, who produced stories and poems that were primarily sad and macabre. His first book, *Tamerlane and Other Poems* (1827), received little recognition. But later works, including his most famous poem, "The Raven" (1845), established him as a major, if controversial, literary figure. Poe evoked images of individuals rising above the narrow confines of intellect and exploring the deeper world of the spirit and the emotions. Yet that world, he seemed to say, contained much pain and horror. Other American writers were contemptuous of Poe's work and his message, but he was ultimately to have a profound effect on European poets such as Baudelaire.

Poe, however, was something of an exception in the world of southern literature. The South experienced a literary flowering of its own in the mid-nineteenth century, and it produced writers and artists who were, like their northern counterparts, concerned with defining the nature of American society and of the American nation. But white southerners tended to produce very different images of what that society was and should be.

Southern novelists of the 1830s (among them Beverly Tucker, William Alexander Caruthers, and John Pendleton Kennedy), some of them writers of great talent, many of them residents of Richmond, produced historical romances or romantic eulogies of the plantation system of the upper South. In the 1840s, the southern literary capital moved to Charleston, home of the most distinguished of the region's men of letters: William Gilmore Simms. For a time, his work expressed a broad nationalism that transcended his regional background; but by the 1840s he too had become a strong defender of southern institutions—especially slavery—against the encroachments of the North. There was, he believed, a unique quality to southern life that it was the duty of intellectuals to defend.

One group of southern writers, however, produced works that were more broadly American and less committed to a glorification of the peculiarities of southern life. These were writers from the fringes of plantation society, who depicted the world of the backwoods rural areas. Augustus B. Longstreet, Joseph G. Baldwin, Johnson J. Hooper, and others focused not on aristocratic "cavaliers," but on ordinary people and poor whites. Instead of romanticizing their subjects, they were deliberately and sometimes painfully realistic. And they seasoned their sketches with a robust, vulgar humor that was new to American literature. These southern realists established a tradition of American regional humor that was ultimately to find its most powerful voice in Mark Twain.

The Transcendentalists

One of the outstanding expressions of the romantic impulse in America came from a group of New England writers and philosophers known as the transcendentalists. Borrowing heavily from German and English writers and philosophers, the transcendentalists embraced a theory of the individual that rested on a distinction between what they called "reason" and "understanding"—words they used in ways that seem unfamiliar, even strange, to modern ears. Reason, as they defined it, had little to do with rationality. It was, rather, the individual's innate capacity to grasp beauty and truth by giving full expression to the instincts and emotions; and as such it was the highest human faculty. Understanding, by contrast, was the use of intellect in the narrow, artificial ways imposed by society; it involved the repression of instinct and the victory of externally imposed learning. Every person's goal, therefore, should be liberation from "understanding" and, instead, the cultivation of "reason." Each individual should strive to "transcend" the limits of the intellect and allow the emotions, the "soul," to create an "original relation to the Universe."

Transcendentalist philosophy emerged first in America among a small group of intellectuals centered in Concord, Massachusetts, and led by Ralph Waldo Emerson. A Unitarian minister in his youth, Emerson left the clergy in 1832 to devote himself to writing, teaching, and lecturing. In "Nature" (1836), Emerson wrote that in the quest for self-fulfillment, individuals should work for a communion with the natural world: "in the woods, we return to reason and faith. . . . Standing on the bare ground,—my head bathed by the blithe air, and uplifted into infinite space,—all mean egotism vanishes. . . . I am part and particle of God." In other essays, he was even more explicit in advocating a commitment of the individual to the full exploration of inner capacities. "Nothing is at last sacred," he wrote in "Self-Reliance" (1841), "but the integrity of your own mind."

Almost as influential as Emerson was another Concord transcendentalist, Henry David Thoreau. Thoreau went even further than his friend Emerson in repudiating the repressive forces of society, which produced, he said, "lives of quiet desperation." Each individual should work for self-realization by resisting pressures to conform to society's expectations and responding instead to his or her own instincts. Thoreau's own effort to free himself—immortalized in *Walden* (1854)—led him to build a small cabin in the Concord woods on the edge of Walden Pond, where he lived alone for two years as simply as he could, attempting to liberate himself from repressive convention and from what he considered society's excessive interest in material comforts. Thoreau's rejection of what he considered the artificial constraints of society extended to his relationship with government. In his 1849 essay "Resistance to Civil Government," he argued that a government that required an individual to violate his or her own morality had no legitimate authority. The proper response was "civil disobedience," or "passive resistance"—a public refusal to obey unjust laws.

Visions of Utopia

Although transcendentalism was at its heart an individualistic philosophy, it helped spawn one of the most famous of all nineteenth-century experiments in communal living: Brook Farm. The dream of the Boston transcendentalist George Ripley, Brook Farm was established in 1841 as an experimental community in West Roxbury, Massachusetts. There, according to Ripley, individuals would gather to create a new society that would permit every member to have full opportunity for self-realization. All residents would share equally in the labor of the community so that all could share in the leisure as well, which was essential for cultivation of the self. (Ripley was one of the first Americans to attribute positive connotations to the idea of leisure; most of his contemporaries equated it with laziness and sloth.) The tension between the ideal of individual freedom and the demands of a communal society took their toll on Brook Farm. Many residents became disenchanted and left. When a fire destroyed the central building of the community in 1847, the experiment dissolved.

Among the original residents of Brook Farm was the writer Nathaniel Hawthorne, who expressed his disillusionment with the experiment and, to some extent, with transcendentalism in a series of novels voicing some of the same concerns that his contemporary Herman Melville was articulating. In *The Blithedale Romance* (1852), he wrote scathingly of Brook Farm itself. In other novels—most notably *The Scarlet Letter* (1850) and *The House of the Seven Gables* (1851)—he wrote equally passionately about the price individuals pay for cutting themselves off from society. Egotism, he claimed (in an indirect challenge to the transcendentalist faith in the self), was the "serpent" that lay at the heart of human misery.

The failure of Brook Farm did not, however, prevent the formation of other experimental communities. The Scottish industrialist and philanthropist Robert Owen founded an experimental community in Indiana in 1825, which he named New Harmony. It was to be a "Village of Cooperation," in which every resident worked and lived in total equality. The community was an economic failure, but the vision that had inspired it continued to enchant some Americans. Dozens of other "Owenite" experiments began in other locations in the ensuing years.

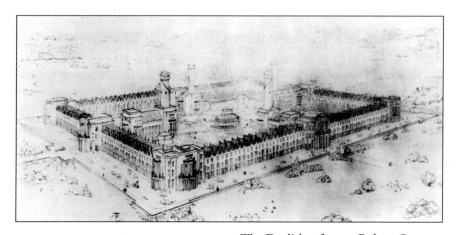

PLAN FOR THE COLONY AT NEW HARMONY The English reformer Robert Owen
came to America in the 1820s to create an experimental community in which to
test his own theories of cooperative living. This architect's drawing reveals the
grandiose plans Owen and his followers had for the colony, which was in Indiana
on the banks of the Wabash River on the site of an earlier social experiment by
German idealists. In this plan, which was never constructed, the architecture
reflects the sense of order and rationality Owen hoped to bring to the community.
The plan was designed "to form a new combination of circumstances, capable of
producing permanently greater physical, moral, and intellectual advantages . . .
than have ever yet been realized in any age or country."

Redefining Gender Roles

Many of the new utopian communities (and many of the new social
philosophies on which they rested) were centrally concerned with the relationship between men and women. Some experimented with a radical
redefinition of gender roles.

Such a redefinition was central to one of the most enduring of the
utopian colonies of the nineteenth century: the Oneida Community, established in 1848 in upstate New York by John Humphrey Noyes. The
Oneida "Perfectionists," as residents of the community called themselves,
rejected traditional notions of family and marriage. All residents, Noyes
declared, were "married" to all other residents; there were to be no permanent conjugal ties. But Oneida was not, as horrified critics often
claimed, an experiment in unrestrained "free love." It was a place where
the community carefully monitored sexual behavior; where women were
protected from unwanted childbearing; and where children were raised
communally, often seeing little of their own parents. The Oneidans took

pride in what they considered their liberation of women from the demands of male "lust" and from the traditional bonds of family.

The Shakers, too, made a redefinition of traditional gender roles central to their society. Founded by "Mother" Ann Lee in the 1770s, the society of the Shakers survived into the twentieth century. (A tiny remnant is left today.) But the Shakers attracted a particularly large following in the mid-nineteenth century and established more than twenty communities throughout the Northeast and Northwest in the 1840s. They derived their name from a unique religious ritual—a sort of dance, in which members of a congregation would "shake" themselves free of sin while performing a loud chant and an ecstatic dance.

The most distinctive feature of Shakerism, however, was its commitment to complete celibacy—which meant, of course, that no one could be born into Shakerism; all Shakers had to choose the faith voluntarily. Shakerism attracted about 6,000 members in the 1840s, more women than men. They lived in communities where contacts between men and women were strictly limited, and they endorsed the idea of sexual equality. Within Shaker society, women exercised the most power. Shakerism, one observer wrote in the 1840s, was a refuge from the "perversions of marriage" and "the gross abuses which drag it down."

The Shakers were not, however, motivated only by a desire to escape the burdens of traditional gender roles. They were trying as well to create a society separated and protected from the chaos and disorder that they believed had come to characterize American life as a whole. In that, they were much like other dissenting religious sects and other utopian communities of their time.

The Mormons

Perhaps the most important effort to create a new and more ordered society in America was that of the Church of Jesus Christ of Latter-day Saints, whose members are known as Mormons. Mormonism began in upstate New York as a result of the efforts of Joseph Smith, an energetic but economically unsuccessful man, who had spent most of his twenty-four years moving restlessly through New England and the Northeast. Then, in 1830, he published a remarkable document—the Book of Mormon—which he claimed was a translation of a set of golden tablets he had found in the hills of New York after a revelation by an angel of God. The Book of Mormon told the story of an ancient civilization in America, whose now vanished kingdom could become a model for a new holy community in the United States.

Gathering a small group of believers around him, Smith began in 1831 to seek a sanctuary for his new community of "saints," an effort that would continue, unhappily, for more than twenty years. Time and again, the Mormons attempted to establish their "New Jerusalem." Time and again, they met with persecution from surrounding communities suspicious of their radical religious doctrines—which included polygamy (the right of men to take several wives), a rigid form of social organization, and an intense secrecy that gave rise to wild rumors among their critics of conspiracy and depravity.

Driven from their original settlements in Independence, Missouri, and Kirtland, Ohio, the Mormons founded Nauvoo, Illinois, which in the early 1840s became an imposing and economically successful community. In 1844, however, Joseph Smith was arrested, charged with treason (for conspiring against the government to win foreign support for a new Mormon colony in the Southwest), and imprisoned in nearby Carthage, Illinois. There an angry mob attacked the jail, forced Smith from his cell, and shot and killed him. The Mormons then abandoned Nauvoo and, under the leadership of Smith's successor, Brigham Young, traveled across the desert—a society of 12,000 people, one of the largest group migrations in American history—and established a new settlement in Utah, the present Salt Lake City. There, at last, the Mormons were able to create a permanent settlement.

Like other experiments in social organization of the era, Mormonism reflected a belief in human perfectibility. God had once been a man, the church taught; and thus every man or woman could aspire to become, in effect, a god—as Joseph Smith had done. But the Mormons did not celebrate individual liberty. Instead, they created a highly organized, centrally directed, almost militarized social structure as a refuge against the disorder and uncertainty of the secular world. They placed particular emphasis on the structure of the family. The original Mormons were, for the most part, men and women who felt displaced in their rapidly changing society—economically marginal people left behind by the material growth and social progress of their era. In the new religion, they found security and order.

REMAKING SOCIETY

The reform impulse also helped create new movements to remake mainstream society—movements in which, to a striking degree, women formed both the rank and file and the leadership. By the 1830s, such movements had taken the form of organized reform societies.

Revivalism, Morality, and Order

The philosophy of reform arose in part from the optimistic vision of those such as the transcendentalists who preached the divinity of the individual. But another, and in many respects more important, source was Protestant revivalism—the movement that had begun with the Second Great Awakening early in the century and had, by the 1820s, evolved into a powerful force for social reform.

The New Light evangelicals—having rejected the Calvinist idea of predestination—embraced the optimistic belief that every individual was capable of salvation through his or her own efforts. Partly as a result, revivalism soon became not only a means of personal salvation but an effort to reform the larger society. In particular, revivalism produced a crusade against personal immorality. "The church," said Charles Grandison Finney, the leading revivalist of his time, "must take right ground on the subject of Temperance, the Moral Reform, and all the subjects of practical morality which come up for decision from time to time."

Evangelical Protestantism added major strength to one of the most influential reform movements of the era: the crusade against drunkenness. No social vice, temperance advocates argued, was more responsible for crime, disorder, and poverty than the excessive use of alcohol. Women, who were particularly active in the temperance movement, complained that men spent money their families needed on alcohol and that drunken husbands often beat and abused their wives. Temperance also appealed to those who were alarmed by immigration; drunkenness, many nativists believed, was responsible for violence and disorder in immigrant communities and temperance was a way to discipline them. By 1840, temperance had become a major national movement, with powerful organizations and more than a million followers who had signed a formal pledge to forgo hard liquor.

Health, Science, and Phrenology

For some Americans, the search for individual and social perfection led to an interest in new theories of health and knowledge. Threats to public health were critical to the sense of insecurity that underlay many reform movements, especially after the terrible cholera epidemics of the 1830s and 1840s. Cholera is a severe bacterial infection of the intestines, usually a result of consuming contaminated food or water. In the nineteenth century, before the emergence of the germ theory of disease (which eventually helped with prevention) and long before the discovery of antibiotics (which made possible a cure), fewer than half of those who contracted the

THE DRUNKARD'S PROGRESS This 1846 lithograph by Nathaniel Currier shows what temperance advocates argued was the inevitable consequence of alcohol consumption. Beginning with an apparently innocent "glass with a friend," the young man rises step by step to the summit of drunken revelry, then declines to desperation and suicide while his abandoned wife and child grieve.

disease normally survived. Thousands of people died of cholera during its occasional outbreaks, and in certain cities—New Orleans in 1833 and St. Louis in 1849—the effects were truly catastrophic. Nearly a quarter of the population of New Orleans died in the 1833 epidemic. Many municipalities, pressured by reformers, established city health boards to try to find solutions to the problems of epidemics. But the medical profession of the time, unaware of the nature of bacterial infections, had no answers, and the boards therefore found little to do.

Instead, many Americans turned to nonscientific theories for improving health. Affluent men and, especially, women flocked to health spas for the celebrated "water cure" (known to modern scientists as hydrotherapy), which purported to improve health through immersing people in hot or cold baths or wrapping them in wet sheets. Although the water cure in fact delivered few of the benefits its promoters promised, it did have some therapeutic value; some forms of hydrotherapy are still in use today. Other people adopted new dietary theories. Sylvester Graham, a Connecticut-born Presbyterian minister and committed reformer, won many followers with his prescriptions for eating fruits, vegetables, and bread made from coarsely ground flour—a prescription not unlike some dietary theories today— instead of meat. (The "Graham cracker" is made from a kind of flour named for him.) Graham accompanied his dietary prescriptions with moral warnings about the evils of excess and luxury.

Perhaps strangest of all to modern sensibilities was the widespread belief in the new "science" of phrenology, which appeared first in Germany and became popular in the United States beginning in the 1830s through the efforts of Orson and Lorenzo Fowler, publishers of the *Phrenology Almanac*.

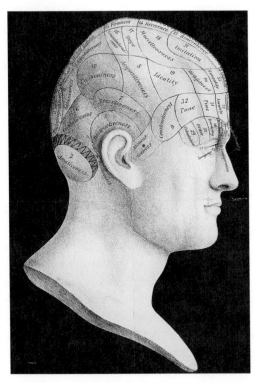

PHRENOLOGY This lithograph illustrates some of the ideas of the popular "science" of phrenology in the 1830s. Drawing from the ideas of the German writer Johann Gaspar Spurzheim, American phrenologists promoted the belief that a person's character and talents could be understood by the formation of his or her skull— that the brain was, in fact, a cluster of autonomous organs, each controlling some aspect of human thought or behavior. In this diagram, the areas of the brain that supposedly control "identity," "acquisitiveness," "secretiveness," "marvellousness," and "hope" are clearly identified. The theory has no scientific basis.

Phrenologists argued that the shape of an individual's skull was an important indicator of his or her character and intelligence. They made elaborate measurements of bumps and indentations to calculate the size (and, they claimed, the strength) of different areas of the brain. For a time, phrenology seemed to many Americans an important vehicle for improving society. It provided a way of measuring an individual's fitness for various positions in life and seemed to promise an end to the arbitrary process by which people matched their talents to occupations and responsibilities. The theory is now universally believed to have no scientific value at all.

Medical Science

In an age of rapid technological and scientific advances, the science of medicine sometimes seemed to lag behind. In part, that was because of the greater difficulty of experimentation in medicine, which required human subjects as compared to other areas of science and technology that relied on inanimate objects. In part, it was because of the character of the medical profession, which—in the absence of any significant regulation—attracted many poorly-educated people and many quacks, in addition to trained physicians. Efforts to regulate the profession were beaten back in the 1830s and 1840s by those who considered the licensing of physicians to be a form of undemocratic monopoly. The prestige of the profession, therefore, remained low, and it was for many people a career of last resort.

The biggest problem facing American medicine, however, was the absence of basic knowledge about disease. The great medical achievement of the eighteenth century—the development of a vaccination against smallpox by Edward Jenner—came from no broad theory of infection, but from a brilliant adaptation of folk practices among country people. The development of anesthetics came not from medical doctors at first, but from a New England dentist, William Morton, who was looking for ways to help his patients endure the extraction of teeth. Beginning in 1844, Morton began experimenting with using sulphuric ether. John Warren, a Boston surgeon, soon began using ether to sedate surgical patients. Even these advances met with stiff resistance from traditional physicians, some of whom continued to believe that all medical knowledge derived from timeless truths and ancient scholars and who mistrusted innovation and experimentation. Others rejected scientific advances because they became convinced of the power of new, unorthodox, and untested "medical" techniques popularized by entrepreneurs, many of them charlatans.

In the absence of any broad acceptance of scientific methods and experimental practice in medicine, it was very difficult for even the most talented doctors to make progress in treating disease. Indeed, almost no one had any idea at all how diseases were transmitted. Even so, halting progress toward the discovery of the germ theory did occur in antebellum America. In 1843, the Boston essayist, poet, and physician Oliver Wendell Holmes published his findings from a study of large numbers of cases of "puerperal fever" (septicemia in children) and concluded that the disease could be transmitted from one person to another. This discovery of contagion met with a storm of criticism, but was later vindicated by the clinical success of the Hungarian physician Ignaz Semmelweis, who noticed that the infection seemed to be spread by medical students who had been working with corpses. Once he began requiring students to wash their hands and disinfect their instruments, the infections virtually disappeared.

Education

One of the most important reform movements of the mid-nineteenth century was the effort to produce a system of universal public education. As of 1830, no state had such a system, although some—such as Massachusetts—were supporting limited versions. Soon after that, however, interest in public education began growing rapidly.

The greatest of the educational reformers was Horace Mann, the first secretary of the Massachusetts Board of Education, which was established in 1837. To Mann and his followers, education was the only way to "counterwork this tendency to the domination of capital and the servility of labor." It was also the only way to protect democracy, for an educated electorate was essential to the workings of a free political system. Mann reorganized the Massachusetts school system, lengthened the academic year (to six months), doubled teachers' salaries (although he did not eliminate the large disparities between the salaries of male and female teachers), broadened the curriculum, and introduced new methods of professional training for teachers. Other states followed similar courses: building new schools, creating teachers' colleges, and offering many children access to education for the first time. By the 1850s, the principle (although not yet the reality) of tax-supported elementary schools was established in every state.

Yet the quality of public education continued to vary widely. In some places—Massachusetts, for example—educators were generally capable men and women, often highly trained, who had an emerging sense of themselves as career professionals. In other areas, however, teachers were often barely literate, and funding for education was severely limited. In much of the West, where the population was highly dispersed, many children had no access to schools at all. In the South, all African Americans were barred from education (although approximately 10 percent of them managed to achieve literacy anyway), and only about a third of all white children of school age were actually enrolled in schools in 1860. In the North, 72 percent were enrolled, but even there, many students attended classes only briefly and casually.

The interest in education also was visible in the growing movement to educate American Indians in the antebellum period. Some reformers, even many who considered black people inferior and unredeemable, believed that Indians could be "civilized" if only they could be taught the ways of the white world. Efforts by missionaries and others to educate Indians and encourage them to assimilate were particularly prominent in such areas of the Far West as Oregon, where substantial numbers of whites were beginning to settle in the 1840s and where conflicts with the natives had not yet become acute. Nevertheless, the great majority of Native Americans remained outside the reach of educational reform, either by choice or by circumstance, or both.

Despite limitations and inequities, the achievements of the school reformers were impressive. By the beginning of the Civil War, the United States had one of the highest literacy rates of any nation of the world: 94 percent of the population of the North, 83 percent of the white population (and 58 percent of the total population) of the South.

Rehabilitation

The belief in the potential of the individual also sparked the creation of new institutions to help the disabled: institutions that formed part of a great network of charitable activities known as the Benevolent Empire. Among them was the Perkins School for the Blind in Boston, the first such school in America. Nothing better exemplified the romantic spirit of the era than the belief of those who founded Perkins that even society's supposedly most disadvantaged members—unsighted and otherwise handicapped people—could be helped to discover their own inner strength and wisdom.

More typical of educational reform, however, were efforts to use schools to impose a set of social values on children—values that reformers and others believed were appropriate for their new, industrializing society.

These values included thrift, order, discipline, punctuality, and respect for authority. Horace Mann, for example, spoke of the role of public schools in extending democracy and expanding individual opportunity. But he spoke, too, of their role in creating social order: "The unrestrained passions of men are not only homicidal, but suicidal. . . . Train up a child in the way he should go, and when he is old he will not depart from it."

Similar impulses produced another powerful movement of reform: the creation of "asylums" for criminals and the mentally ill. In advocating prison and hospital reform, Americans were reacting against one of society's most glaring ills: antiquated jails and mental institutions whose inmates lived in almost inhuman conditions. Beginning in the 1820s, many states built new penitentiaries and mental asylums. New York built the first penitentiary at Auburn in 1821. In Massachusetts, the reformer Dorothea Dix began a national movement for new methods of treating the mentally ill.

But the creation of asylums for social deviants was not simply an effort to curb the abuses of the old system. It was also an attempt to reform and rehabilitate the inmates. New forms of prison discipline were designed to rid criminals of the "laxness" that had presumably led them astray. Solitary confinement and the imposition of silence on work crews (both instituted in Pennsylvania and New York in the 1820s) were meant to give prisoners opportunities to meditate on their wrongdoings and develop "penitence" (hence the name "penitentiary").

Some of the same impulses that produced asylums underlay the emergence in the 1840s and 1850s of a new "reform" approach to the problems of Native Americans: the idea of the reservation. For several decades, the dominant thrust of the United States' policy toward the Indians in areas of white settlement had been relocation. The principal motive behind relocation was simple: getting the tribes out of the way of white civilization. But among some whites there had also been another, if secondary, intent: to move the Indians to a place where they would be protected from whites and allowed to develop to a point at which assimilation might be possible.

It was a small step from the idea of relocation to the idea of the reservation, the notion of creating an enclosed region in which Indians would live in isolation from white society. Just as prisons, asylums, and orphanages would provide society with an opportunity to train and uplift misfits and unfortunates within white society, so the reservations might provide a way to undertake what one official called "the great work of regenerating the Indian race."

The Rise of Feminism

Many of the women who became involved in reform movements in the 1820s and 1830s came to resent the social and legal restrictions that limited their participation. Out of their concerns emerged the first American feminist movement. Sarah and Angelina Grimké, sisters born in South Carolina who had become active and outspoken abolitionists, ignored attacks by men who claimed that their activism was inappropriate to their gender. "Men and women were created equal," they argued. "They are both moral and accountable beings, and whatever is right for man to do, is right for women to do." Other reformers—Catharine Beecher, Harriet Beecher Stowe (her sister), Lucretia Mott, Elizabeth Cady Stanton, and Dorothea Dix—similarly pressed at the boundaries of "acceptable" female behavior, chafing at the restrictions placed on women by men.

In 1840, American female delegates arrived at a world antislavery convention in London, only to be turned away by the men who controlled the proceedings. Angered at the rejection, several of the delegates—notably Lucretia Mott and Elizabeth Cady Stanton—became convinced that their first duty as reformers should now be to elevate the status of women. Over the next several years, Mott, Stanton, and others began drawing pointed parallels between the plight of women and the plight of slaves; and in 1848, in Seneca Falls, New York, they organized a convention to discuss the question of women's rights. Out of the meeting came the "Declaration of Sentiments and Resolutions" (patterned on the Declaration of Independence), which stated that "all men and women are created equal," that women no less than men are endowed with certain inalienable rights. In demanding the right to vote, they launched a movement for woman suffrage that would survive until the battle was finally won in 1920. The Seneca Falls document was at least equally important for its rejection of the whole notion that men and women should be assigned separate "spheres" in society.

Many of the women involved in these feminist efforts were Quakers. Quakerism had long embraced the ideal of sexual equality and had tolerated, indeed encouraged, the emergence of women as preachers and community leaders. Of the women who drafted the Declaration of Sentiments, all but Elizabeth Cady Stanton were Quakers. Stanton, joined two years later by Susan B. Anthony, led the movement to implement the Seneca Falls resolutions in the 1850s and beyond. Together, they ultimately transformed it into a powerful force for change.

Feminists benefited greatly from their association with other reform movements, most notably abolitionism, but they also suffered as a result. The demands of women were usually assigned—even by some women themselves—a secondary position to what many considered the far greater issue of the rights of slaves.

THE CRUSADE AGAINST SLAVERY

The antislavery movement was not new to the mid-nineteenth century. But only in 1830 did it begin to gather the force that would ultimately enable it to overshadow virtually all other efforts at social reform.

Early Opposition to Slavery

In the early years of the nineteenth century, those who opposed slavery were, for the most part, a calm and genteel lot, expressing moral disapproval but doing little else. To the extent that there was an organized antislavery movement, it centered on the concept of colonization—the effort to resettle American blacks in Africa or the Caribbean. In 1817, a group of prominent white Virginians organized the American Colonization Society (ACS), which tried to challenge slavery without challenging property rights or southern sensibilities. The ACS proposed a gradual freeing of slaves, with masters receiving compensation. The liberated blacks would then be transported out of the country and helped to establish a new society of their own. The ACS received some funding from private donors, some from Congress, some from the legislatures of Virginia and Maryland. And it arranged to have several groups of blacks transported out of the United States, some of them to the west coast of Africa, where in 1830 they established the nation of Liberia. (In 1846, Liberia became an independent black republic, with its capital, Monrovia, named for the American president who had presided over the initial settlement.)

But the ACS was in the end a negligible force. Neither private nor public funding was nearly enough to carry out the vast projects its supporters envisioned. There were far too many blacks in America in the nineteenth century to be transported to Africa by any conceivable program. And the ACS met resistance, in any case, from blacks themselves, many of whom were now three or more generations removed from Africa and, despite their loathing of slavery, had no wish to emigrate.

Garrison and Abolitionism

In 1830, with slavery spreading rapidly in the South and the antislavery movement seemingly on the verge of collapse, a new figure emerged to transform it: William Lloyd Garrison. Born in Massachusetts in 1805, Garrison was in the 1820s an assistant to the New Jersey Quaker Benjamin Lundy, who published the leading antislavery newspaper of the time. Garrison grew impatient with his employer's moderate tone and mild proposals for reform. In 1831, therefore, he returned to Boston to found his own weekly newspaper, the *Liberator*.

Garrison's philosophy was so simple that it was genuinely revolutionary. Opponents of slavery, he said, should not talk, as earlier reformers had done, about the evil influence of slavery on white society; they should talk about the damage the system did to blacks. And they should, therefore, reject "gradualism" and demand the immediate, unconditional, universal abolition of slavery and the extension to blacks of all the rights of American citizenship. Garrison wrote in a relentless, uncompromising tone. "I am aware," he wrote in the very first issue of the *Liberator*, "that many object to the severity of my language; but is there not cause for severity? I will be as harsh as truth, and as uncompromising as justice. . . . I am in earnest—I will not equivocate—I will not excuse—I will not retreat a single inch—and I will be heard."

Garrison soon attracted a large group of followers throughout the North, enough to enable him to found the New England Antislavery Society in 1832 and a year later, after a convention in Philadelphia, the American Antislavery Society. By 1835, there were more than 400 local societies; by 1838, there were 1,350, with more than 250,000 members.

Abolitionists were a part of the larger spirit of reform of their era. Like other reformers, they were calling for an unleashing of the individual human spirit, the elimination of artificial social barriers to fulfillment. Who, after all, needed help in realizing individual potential more than enslaved men and women?

Black Abolitionists

Abolitionism had a particular appeal to the free black population of the North, which in 1850 numbered about 250,000, mostly concentrated in cities. These free blacks lived in conditions of poverty and oppression at times worse than those of their slave counterparts in the South. For all their problems, however, northern blacks were fiercely proud of their freedom and sensitive to the plight of those members of their race who remained in bondage; and they were aware that their own position in society would remain precarious as long as slavery existed. Many in the 1830s came to support Garrison. But they also rallied to leaders of their own.

The greatest of the black abolitionists was Frederick Douglass, one of the most electrifying orators of his time. Born a slave in Maryland, Douglass escaped to Massachusetts in 1838, became an outspoken leader of antislavery sentiment, and spent two years lecturing in England, where members of that country's vigorous antislavery movement lionized him. On his return to the United States in 1847, Douglass purchased his freedom from his Maryland owner and founded an antislavery newspaper, the *North Star*, in Rochester, New York. He achieved wide renown as well for his autobiography, *Narrative of the Life of Frederick Douglass* (1845), in which he presented a damning picture of slavery. Douglass demanded not only freedom but full social and economic equality.

FREDERICK DOUGLASS Frederick Douglass was the most prominent African American of the nineteenth century. Born in Maryland to an unknown white father and a slave mother, he escaped from slavery into the North in 1838. He quickly became a leader in the abolitionist movement.

Anti-Abolitionism

The rise of abolitionism was a powerful force, but it provoked a powerful opposition as well. Almost all white southerners, of course, were bitterly hostile to the movement. But even in the North, abolitionists were a small, dissenting minority whom most whites viewed as dangerous radicals. Some feared that abolitionism would produce a destructive war between the sections. Others feared that it would lead to a great influx of free blacks into the North.

The result of such fears was an escalating wave of violence directed toward abolitionists in the 1830s. A mob in Philadelphia attacked the abolitionist headquarters there in 1834, burned it to the ground, and began a bloody race riot. Another mob seized Garrison on the streets of Boston in 1835 and threatened to hang him. He was saved from death only by being locked in jail. Elijah Lovejoy, the editor of an abolitionist newspaper in Alton, Illinois, was victimized repeatedly by mob violence and finally killed when he tried to defend his press from attack.

That so many men and women continued to embrace abolitionism in the face of such vicious opposition from within their own communities suggests that abolitionists were not people who made their political commitments lightly or casually. They were strong-willed, passionate crusaders who displayed not only enormous courage and moral strength but at times a fervency that many of their contemporaries (even some who shared their dislike of slavery) found deeply disturbing. The mobs were only the most violent expression of a hostility to abolitionism that many, perhaps most, other white Americans shared.

Abolitionism Divided

By the mid-1830s, the abolitionist crusade had begun to experience serious internal strains and divisions. One reason was the violence of the anti-abolitionists, which persuaded some members of the movement that a more moderate approach was necessary. Another reason was the growing radicalism of William Lloyd Garrison, who shocked even many of his own allies (including Frederick Douglass) by attacking not only slavery but the government itself. The Constitution, he said, was "a covenant with death and an agreement with hell." The nation's churches, he claimed, were bulwarks of slavery. In 1840, Garrison precipitated a formal division within the American Antislavery Society by insisting that women, who had always been central to the organization's work, be permitted to participate in the movement on terms of full equality. He continued after 1840 to arouse controversy with new and even more radical stands: an extreme pacifism that rejected even defensive wars; opposition to all forms of coercion—not just slavery, but prisons and asylums; and finally, in 1843, a call for northern disunion from the South. The nation could, he suggested, purge itself of the sin of slavery by expelling the slave states from the Union.

From 1840 on, therefore, abolitionism moved in many channels and spoke with many different voices. The Garrisonians, with their radical and uncompromising moral stance, remained influential. But others operated in more moderate ways, arguing that abolition could be accomplished only as the result of a long, patient, peaceful struggle— "immediate abolition gradually accomplished," as they called it. They appealed to the conscience of the slaveholders, attempting to convince them that their institution was sinful. When that produced no results, they turned to political action, seeking to induce the northern states and the federal government to aid the cause. They joined the Garrisonians in helping runaway slaves find refuge in the North or in Canada through what became known as the underground railroad (although their efforts were never as highly organized as the name suggests). After the Supreme Court (in *Prigg* v. *Pennsylvania*, 1842) ruled that states need not aid in enforcing the 1793 law requiring the return of fugitive slaves to their owners, abolitionists won passage in several northern states of "personal liberty laws," which forbade state officials to assist in the capture and return of runaways. The antislavery societies also petitioned Congress to abolish slavery in places where the federal government had jurisdiction—in the territories and in the District of Columbia—and to prohibit the interstate slave trade.

Antislavery sentiment underlay the formation in 1840 of the Liberty Party, which ran Kentucky antislavery leader James G. Birney for president. But this party and its successors never campaigned for outright abolition (an illustration of the important fact that "antislavery" and "abolitionism" were not always the same thing). They stood instead for "free soil," for keeping slavery out of the territories. Some free-soilers were concerned about the welfare of blacks; others were people who cared nothing about slavery but simply wanted to keep the West a country for whites. Garrison dismissed free-soilism as "white-manism." But the free-soil position would ultimately do what abolitionism never could: attract the support of large numbers, even a majority, of the white population of the North.

The frustrations of political abolitionism drove some critics of slavery to embrace more drastic measures. A few began to advocate violence; it was a group of prominent abolitionists in New England, for example, who funneled money and arms to John Brown for his bloody uprisings in Kansas and Virginia. Others attempted to arouse public anger through propaganda. The most powerful of all abolitionist propaganda was Harriet Beecher Stowe's novel *Uncle Tom's Cabin*, published as a book in 1852. It rocked the nation. It sold more than 300,000 copies within a year of publication and was later issued again and again, becoming one of the most remarkable best-sellers in American history. It succeeded in bringing the message of abolitionism to an enormous new audience—not only those who read the book but those who watched dramatizations of its story by countless theater companies across the nation. Reviled throughout the South, Stowe became a hero to many in the North. And in both regions, her novel helped inflame sectional tensions to a new level of passion. Few books in American history have had so great an impact on the course of public events.

UNCLE TOM'S CABIN This poster (advertising, among other things, a German edition of Harriet Beecher Stowe's novel) did not exaggerate when it described *Uncle Tom's Cabin* as "The Greatest Book of the Age." There were, to be sure, greater literary accomplishments; but no American book of the nineteenth century had so profound a political impact.

Even divided, therefore, abolitionism remained a powerful influence on the life of the nation. Only a relatively small number of people before the Civil War ever accepted the abolitionist position that slavery must be entirely eliminated in a single stroke. But the crusade that Garrison had launched, and that thousands of committed men and women kept alive for three decades, was a constant, visible reminder of how deeply the institution of slavery was dividing America.

CONCLUSION

The rapidly changing society of antebellum America intensified cultural nationalism and encouraged interest in a wide range of reforms. Writers, artists, intellectuals, and others drew heavily from new European notions of personal liberation and fulfillment—a set of ideas often known as romanticism. But they also strove to create a truly American cultrure, unbeholden to European models. The literary and artistic life of the nation expressed the rising interest in personal liberation—in giving individuals the freedom to explore their own souls and to find in nature a full expression of their divinity. It also called attention to some of the nation's glaring social problems.

Reformers, too, made use of the romantic belief in the divinity of the individual. They flocked to religious revivals, worked on behalf of such "moral" reforms as temperance, supported education, and articulated some of the first statements of modern feminism. Above all, in the North, they rallied against slavery. Out of this growing antislavery movement emerged a new and powerful phenomenon: abolitionism, which rejected moderate reform and insisted on nothing less than immediate emancipation of slaves. The abolitionist movement galvanized much of the North. It also contributed greatly to the growing schism between North and South.

FOR FURTHER REFERENCE

Suggested Readings

Ronald G. Walters, *American Reformers, 1815–1860* (1978) is a good overview of antebellum reform. David Reynolds, *Walt Whitman's America* (1995) is both a cultural biography of Whitman and an evocation of the society Whitman celebrated. Van Wyck Brooks, *The Flowering of New England: 1815–1865* (1936) is a classic study. Ann Douglas, *The Femi-*

nization of American Culture (1977) is a pioneering work in the history of gender and culture. Leo Marx, *The Machine in the Garden* (1964) is an influential study of ideas about technology in the era of industrialization. Paul Johnson, *A Shopkeeper's Millennium: Society and Revivals in Rochester, New York, 1815–1837* (1978) links revivalism in the "Burnt-Over District" to changing patterns of work and social control. Jon Butler, *Awash in a Sea of Faith: Christianizing the American People* (1990) is an important study of revivalism. Nancy F. Cott, *The Bonds of Womanhood: "Woman's Sphere" in New England, 1780–1835* (1977) argues that nineteenth century feminism emerged from the separation of home and work in the early nineteenth century. James Brewer Stewart, *Holy Warriors* (1976) is a good summary of the trajectory of abolitionism from the American Revolution through emancipation. Ronald G. Walters, *The Antislavery Appeal: American Abolitionists After 1830* (1976) emphasizes the religious motivations of antebellum abolitionism.

Films

(The best source for information on how to find these and other films is *Bowker's Complete Video Directory*—3 volumes.) *The American Story, No. 9: Social Reform* (1985) documents attempts by reformers to eliminate the disruptive effects of industrialization and to abolish slavery. *Walt Whitman: Poet for a New Age* (1971) reveals Whitman's faith in democracy, as well as his mystical ideas about life and death, personality, and love. *Thoreau's Walden* re-creates the two-year period when Henry David Thoreau lived alone at Walden Pond. *The Second Great Awakening* (1994) illuminates the resurgence of religious reform in the early nineteenth century. *Reforming the Republic* weaves together the urges for religious revivalism and reform in antebellum America. *The Abolitionists* (1987) discusses abolitionists such as Frederick Douglass and William Lloyd Garrison. *Frederick Douglass—An American Life* (1985) explores the life and times of one of the most famous fugitive slaves and black abolitionists. *Rebel Hearts* (1995) is a lively portrait of Sarah and Angelina Grimké, two important white women abolitionists. *Black Americans of Achievement, No. 8: Sojourner Truth*, and *Black Americans of Achievement, No. 9: Harriet Tubman* explore the lives of two very important black women abolitionists.

Internet Resources

Internet websites containing historical material relevant to the subjects discussed in this chapter can be reached through the McGraw-Hill history site at www.mhhe.com/socscience/history/usa/link/linktop.htm.

CHAPTER THIRTEEN

The Impending Crisis

Looking Westward ~ *Expansion and War*
The Sectional Debate ~ *The Crisis of the 1850s*

U NTIL THE 1840S, the tensions between North and South remained relatively contained. Had no new sectional issues arisen, it is possible that the two sections might have resolved their differences peaceably over time. But new issues did arise, centered around the expansion of slavery. From the North came the strident and increasingly powerful abolitionist movement. From the South came a newly militant defense of slavery and the way of life it supported. And from the West, more significantly, came a series of controversies that would ultimately tear the fragile Union apart.

LOOKING WESTWARD

More than a million square miles of new territory came under the control of the United States during the 1840s—the greatest wave of expansion since the Louisiana Purchase nearly forty years before. By the end of the decade, the nation possessed all the territory of the present-day United States except Alaska, Hawaii, and a few relatively small areas acquired later through border adjustments. Many factors accounted for this great new wave of expansion, but one of the most important was an ideology known as "Manifest Destiny."

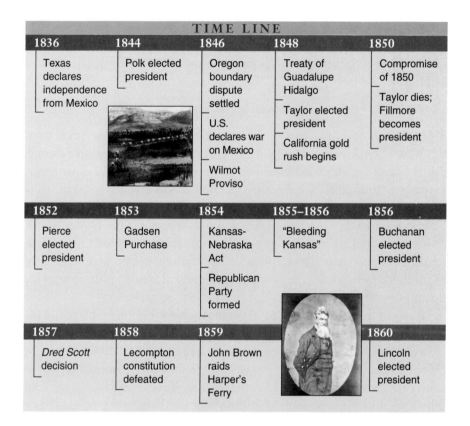

TIME LINE				
1836	**1844**	**1846**	**1848**	**1850**
Texas declares independence from Mexico	Polk elected president	Oregon boundary dispute settled U.S. declares war on Mexico Wilmot Proviso	Treaty of Guadalupe Hidalgo Taylor elected president California gold rush begins	Compromise of 1850 Taylor dies; Fillmore becomes president
1852	**1853**	**1854**	**1855–1856**	**1856**
Pierce elected president	Gadsen Purchase	Kansas-Nebraska Act Republican Party formed	"Bleeding Kansas"	Buchanan elected president
1857	**1858**	**1859**		**1860**
Dred Scott decision	Lecompton constitution defeated	John Brown raids Harper's Ferry		Lincoln elected president

Manifest Destiny

Manifest Destiny reflected both the burgeoning pride that characterized American nationalism in the mid-nineteenth century and the idealistic vision of social perfection that fueled so much of the reform energy of the time. It rested on the idea that America was destined—by God and by history—to expand its boundaries over a vast area.

By the 1840s, the idea of Manifest Destiny had spread throughout the nation, publicized by the new "penny press," which made newspapers available to a far greater proportion of the population than ever before, and fanned by the rhetoric of nationalist politicians. Some advocates of Manifest Destiny had relatively limited territorial goals; others envisioned a vast new "empire of liberty" that would include Canada, Mexico, Caribbean and Pacific islands, and ultimately, a few dreamed, much of the rest of the world. Henry Clay and others warned that territorial expansion would reopen the painful controversy over slavery. Their voices, however, could not compete with the enthusiasm over expansion in the 1840s, which began with the issues of Texas and Oregon.

Americans in Texas

Twice in the 1820s, the United States had offered to purchase Texas from the Republic of Mexico, only to meet with indignant Mexican refusals. But in 1824, the Mexican government launched an ill-advised experiment. Hoping to strengthen the economy of the sparsely-populated territory, it enacted a colonization law offering cheap land and a four-year exemption from taxes to any American willing to move into Texas. Thousands of Americans flocked into the region, the great majority of them white southerners and their slaves, intent on establishing cotton plantations. By 1830, there were about 7,000 Americans living in Texas, more than twice the number of Mexicans there.

Most of the settlers came to Texas through the efforts of American intermediaries, who received sizable land grants from Mexico in return for promising to bring new residents into the region. The most successful of them was Stephen F. Austin, a young immigrant from Missouri who established the first legal American settlement in Texas in 1822. Austin and others recruited many American immigrants to Texas; in the process, they created centers of power in the region that competed with the Mexican government. In 1830, after an unsuccessful effort by its own American *impresario* to establish Texas as an independent nation, the Mexcian government barred any further American immigration into the region. But Americans kept flowing into Texas anyway. By 1835 over 30,000 Americans, white and black, had settled there.

Friction between the American settlers and the Mexican government was already growing in the mid-1830s when instability in Mexico itself drove General Antonio López de Santa Anna to seize power as a dictator and create a new, more autocratic regime. He increased the powers of the national government at the expense of the state governments, a measure that Texans from the United States assumed Santa Anna was aiming specifically at them. Sporadic fighting between Americans and Mexicans in Texas began in 1835, and in 1836, the American settlers defiantly proclaimed their independence from Mexico.

Santa Anna led a large army into Texas, where the American settlers were divided into several squabbling factions. Mexican forces annihilated an American garrison at the Alamo mission in San Antonio after a famous,

if futile, defense by a group of Texas "patriots" that included, among others, the renowned frontiersman and former Tennessee congressman Davy
Crockett. Another garrison at Goliad suffered substantially the same fate
when the Mexicans executed most of the force after it had surrendered. By
the end of 1836, the rebellion appeared to have collapsed.

But General Sam Houston managed to keep a small force together.
And on April 21, 1836, at the Battle of San Jacinto (near the present-day
city of Houston), he defeated the Mexican army and took Santa Anna prisoner. Santa Anna, under pressure from his captors, signed a treaty giving
Texas independence.

A number of Mexican residents of Texas (*Tejanos*) had fought with the
Americans in the revolution. But soon after Texas won its independence,
their positions grew difficult. The Americans did not trust them, feared
that they were agents of the Mexican government, and in effect drove
many of them out of the new republic. Most of those who stayed had to
settle for a politically and economically subordinate status within the
fledgling republic.

One of the first acts of the new president of Texas, Sam Houston, was
to send a delegation to Washington with an offer to join the Union. But
President Jackson, fearing that adding a large new slave state to the Union
would increase sectional tensions, blocked annexation and even delayed recognizing the new republic until 1837. Presidents Martin Van Buren and
William Henry Harrison also avoided the issue during their terms of office.

Spurned by the United States, Texas cast out on its own. England and
France, concerned about the growing power of the United States, saw
Texas as a possible check on its growth and began forging ties with the
new republic. At that point, President Tyler persuaded Texas to apply for
statehood again in 1844. But Secretary of State Calhoun presented an annexation treaty to Congress as if its only purpose were to extend slavery,
and northern senators defeated it. The Texas question quickly became the
central issue in the election of 1844.

Oregon

Control of what was known as Oregon country, in the Pacific Northwest,
was another major political issue in the 1840s. Its half-million square
miles included the present states of Oregon, Washington, and Idaho, parts
of Montana and Wyoming, and half of British Columbia. Both Britain and
the United States claimed sovereignty in the region. Unable to resolve
their conflicting claims diplomatically, they agreed in an 1818 treaty to

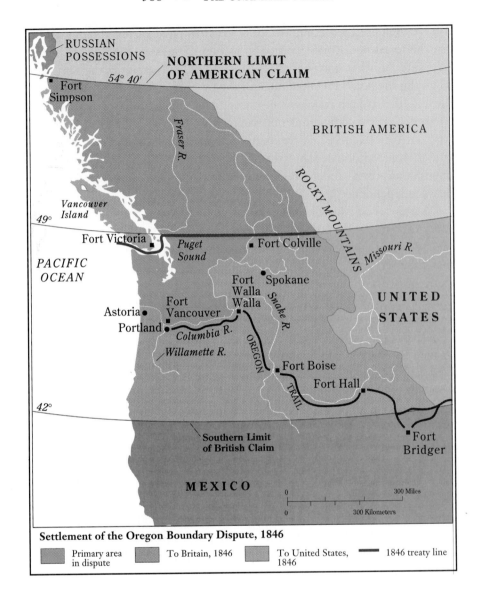

Settlement of the Oregon Boundary Dispute, 1846

Primary area in dispute	To Britain, 1846	To United States, 1846	▬ 1846 treaty line

allow citizens of each country equal access to the territory. This arrangement, known as "joint occupation," continued for twenty years.

In fact, at the time of the treaty neither Britain nor the United States had established much of a presence in Oregon country. White settlement in the region consisted largely of American and Canadian fur traders, and the most significant white settlements were scattered fur trading posts, the largest of which was John Jacob Astor's Astoria. But American interest in Oregon grew substantially in the 1820s and 1830s.

By the mid-1840s, white Americans substantially outnumbered the British in Oregon. They had also devastated much of the Indian population, in part through a measles epidemic that spread through the Cayuse. American settlements had spread up and down the Pacific coast, and the new settlers (along with advocates of Manifest Destiny in the East) were urging the United States government to take possession of the disputed Oregon Territory.

The Westward Migration

The migrations into Texas and Oregon were part of a larger movement that took hundreds of thousands of white and black Americans into the far western regions of the continent between 1840 and 1860. Southerners flocked mainly to Texas. But the largest number of migrants came from the Old Northwest (today's Midwest)—white men and women, and a few blacks, who undertook arduous journeys in search of new opportunities. Most traveled in family groups, until the early 1850s, when the great California gold rush attracted many single men (See pp. 379–380). Most were relatively young people. Few were wealthy, but many were relatively prosperous. Poor people who could not afford the trip on their own usually had to join other families or groups as laborers—men as farm or ranch hands, women as domestic servants, teachers, or, in some cases, prostitutes. Groups heading for areas where mining or lumbering was the principal economic activity consisted mostly of men. Those heading for farming regions traveled mainly as families.

Most migrants—about 300,000 between 1840 and 1860—traveled west along the great overland trails. They generally gathered in one of several major depots in Iowa and Missouri (Independence, St. Joseph, or Council Bluffs), joined a wagon train led by hired guides, and set off with their belongings piled in covered wagons, livestock trailing behind. The major route west was the 2,000-mile Oregon Trail, which stretched from Independence across the Great Plains and through the South Pass of the Rocky Mountains. From there, migrants moved north into Oregon or south (along the California trail) to the northern California coast. Other migrations moved along the Santa Fe Trail, southwest from Independence into New Mexico.

However they traveled, overland migrants faced an arduous journey—although the death rate for travelers was only slightly higher than the rate for the American population as a whole. Most journeys lasted five or six

Western Trails, to 1860

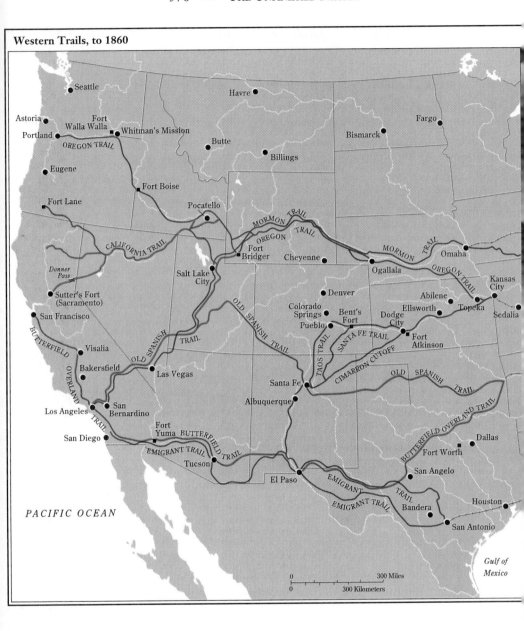

months (from May to November), and there was always pressure to get through the Rockies before the snows began, often not an easy task given the very slow pace of most wagon trains (about fifteen miles a day). There was also the danger of disease; many groups were decimated by cholera. Almost everyone, male or female, walked the great majority of the time, to

CROSSING THE PLAINS A long wagon train carries migrants across the Plains toward Montana in 1866. This photograph gives some indication of the rugged condition of even some of the most well-traveled trails.

lighten the load for the horses drawing the wagons. The women, who did the cooking and washing at the end of the day, generally worked harder than the men, who usually rested when the caravan halted.

Only a few expeditions experienced Indian attacks. In the twenty years before the Civil War, fewer than 400 migrants (slightly more than one-tenth of 1 percent) died in conflicts with the tribes. In fact, Indians were usually more helpful than dangerous to the white migrants. They often served as guides, and they traded horses, clothing, and fresh food with the travelers.

Despite the traditional image of westward migrants as rugged individualists, most travelers found the journey a very communal experience. That was partly because many expeditions consisted of groups of friends, neighbors, or relatives who had decided to pull up stakes and move west together. And it was partly because of the intensity of the journey: many weeks of difficult travel with no other human contact except, occasionally, with Indians. It was a rare expedition in which there were not some internal conflicts before the trip was over; but those who made the journey successfully generally learned the value of cooperation.

EXPANSION AND WAR

The growing number of white Americans in the lands west of the Mississippi put great pressure on the government in Washington to annex Texas, Oregon, and other territory. And in the 1840s, these expansionist pressures helped push the United States into a war that—however dubious its origins—became a triumph for the advocates of Manifest Destiny.

The Democrats and Expansion

In preparing for the election of 1844, the two leading candidates—Henry Clay and the Democrat and former president Martin Van Buren—both tried to avoid taking a stand on the controversial issue of the annexation of Texas. Sentiment for expansion was mild within the Whig Party, and Clay had no difficulty securing the nomination despite his noncommittal position. But many southern Democrats supported annexation, and the party passed over Van Buren to nominate a strong supporter of annexation, the previously unheralded James K. Polk.

Polk was not as obscure as his Whig critics claimed. He had represented Tennessee in the House of Representatives for fourteen years, four of them as Speaker, and had subsequently served as governor. But by 1844, he had been out of public office—and for the most part out of the public mind—for three years. What made his victory possible was his support for the position, expressed in the Democratic platform, "that the re-occupation of Oregon and the re-annexation of Texas at the earliest practicable period are great American measures." By combining the Oregon and Texas questions, the Democrats hoped to appeal to both northern and southern expansionists. Polk carried the election by 170 electoral votes to 105, although his popular majority was less than 40,000.

Polk entered office with a clear set of goals and with plans for attaining them. John Tyler accomplished the first of Polk's goals for him in the last days of his own presidency. Interpreting the election returns as a mandate for the annexation of Texas, the outgoing president won congressional approval for it in February 1845. That December, Texas became a state.

Polk himself resolved the Oregon question. The British minister in Washington brusquely rejected a compromise Polk offered that would establish the United States–Canadian border at the 49th parallel; he did not even refer the proposal to London. Incensed, Polk again asserted the American claim to all of Oregon. There was loose talk of war on both sides of the Atlantic—talk that in the United States often took the form of the bellicose slogan "Fifty-four forty or fight!" (a reference to where the Americans hoped to draw the northern boundary of their part of Oregon). But neither country really wanted war. Finally, the British government accepted Polk's original proposal to divide the territory at the 49th parallel. On June 15, 1846, the Senate approved a treaty that fixed the boundary at the 49th parallel, where it remains today.

The Southwest and California

One of the reasons the Senate and the president had agreed so readily to the British offer to settle the Oregon question was that new tensions were emerging in the Southwest—tensions that ultimately led to a war with Mexico. As soon as the United States admitted Texas to statehood in 1845, the Mexican government broke diplomatic relations with Washington. Mexican-American relations grew still worse when a dispute developed over the boundary between Texas and Mexico. Texans claimed the Rio Grande as their western and southern border, a claim that would have added much of what is now New Mexico to Texas. Mexico, although still not conceding the loss of Texas, argued nevertheless that the border had always been the Nueces River, to the north of the Rio Grande. Polk accepted the Texas claim, and in the summer of 1845 he sent a small army under General Zachary Taylor to Texas to protect it against a possible Mexican invasion.

Part of the area in dispute was New Mexico, whose Spanish and Indian residents lived in a multiracial society that had by the 1840s endured for nearly a century and a half. In the 1820s, the Mexican government had invited American traders into the region (just as it invited American settlers into Texas), hoping to speed development of the province. And New Mexico, like Texas, soon began to become more American than Mexican. A flourishing commerce soon developed between Santa Fe and Independence, Missouri.

Americans were also increasing their interest in an even more distant province of Mexico: California. In this vast region lived members of several western Indian tribes and perhaps 7,000 Mexicans, mostly descendants of Spanish colonists. Gradually, however, white Americans began to arrive: first maritime traders and captains of Pacific whaling ships, who stopped to barter goods or buy supplies; then merchants, who established stores, imported merchandise, and developed a profitable trade with the Mexicans and Indians; and finally pioneering farmers, who entered California from the east, by land, and settled in the Sacramento Valley. Some of these new settlers began to dream of bringing California into the United States.

President Polk soon came to share their dream and committed himself to acquiring both New Mexico and California for the United States. At the same time that he dispatched the troops under Taylor to Texas, he sent secret instructions to the commander of the Pacific naval squadron to seize the California ports if Mexico declared war. Representatives of the president quietly informed Americans in California that the United States would respond sympathetically to a revolt against Mexican authority there.

The Mexican War

Having appeared to prepare for war, Polk turned to diplomacy and dispatched a special minister, John Slidell, to try to buy off the Mexicans. But Mexican leaders rejected Slidell's offer to purchase the disputed territories. On January 13, 1846, as soon as he heard the news, Polk ordered Taylor's army in Texas to move across the Nueces River, where it had been stationed, to the Rio Grande. For months, the Mexicans refused to fight. But finally, according to disputed American accounts, some Mexican troops crossed the Rio Grande and attacked a unit of American soldiers. Polk now told Congress: "War exists by the act of Mexico herself." On May 13, 1846, Congress declared war by votes of 40 to 2 in the Senate and 174 to 14 in the House.

The war had many opponents in the United States. Whig critics charged from the beginning (and not without some justification) that Polk had deliberately maneuvered the country into the conflict and had staged the border incident that had precipitated the declaration. Many argued that the hostilities with Mexico were draining resources and attention away from the more important issue of the Pacific Northwest; and when the United States finally reached its agreement with Britain on the Oregon question, opponents claimed that Polk had settled for less than he should have because he was preoccupied with Mexico. Opposition intensified as the war continued and as the public became aware of the casualties and expense.

American forces did well against the Mexicans, but victory did not come as quickly as Polk had hoped. The president ordered Taylor to cross the Rio Grande, seize parts of northeastern Mexico, beginning with the city of Monterrey, and then march on to Mexico City itself. Taylor captured Monterrey in September 1846, but he let the Mexican garrison evacuate without pursuit. Polk now began to fear that Taylor lacked the tactical skill for the planned advance against Mexico City. He also feared that, if successful, Taylor would become a powerful political rival (as, in fact, he did).

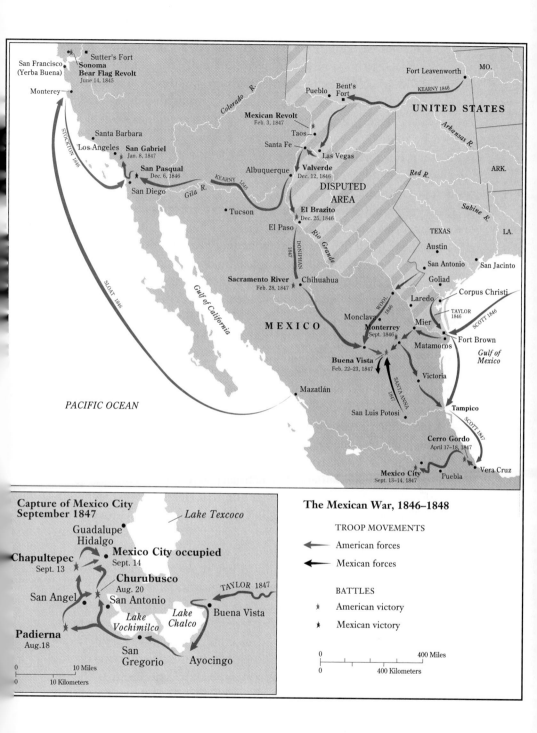

San Francisco
(Yerba Buena)

Sonoma
Bear Flag Revolt
June 14, 1845

Sutter's Fort

Monterey

STOCKTON 1846

Santa Barbara

Los Angeles
San Gabriel
Jan. 8, 1847

San Pasqual
Dec. 6, 1846

San Diego

SLOAT 1846

KEARNY 1846

Gila R.

Tucson

El Paso

Colorado R.

Pueblo

Bent's
Fort

Mexican Revolt
Feb. 3, 1847

Taos

Santa Fe

Las Vegas

Albuquerque

Valverde
Dec. 12, 1846

Fort Leavenworth

MO.

KEARNY 1846

UNITED STATES

Arkansas R.

ARK.

Red R.

DISPUTED
AREA

El Brazito
Dec. 25, 1846

Rio Grande

Sabine R.

TEXAS

LA.

Austin

1847

DONIPHAN

Sacramento River
Feb. 28, 1847

Chihuahua

Gulf of California

MEXICO

WOOL 1846

Monclava

San Antonio

Goliad

Laredo

San Jacinto

Corpus Christi

TAYLOR
1846

SCOTT 1846

Mier

Monterrey
Sept. 1846

Buena Vista
Feb. 22–23, 1847

Matamoros

Fort Brown

*Gulf of
Mexico*

SANTA ANNA 1847

Victoria

PACIFIC OCEAN

Mazatlán

San Luís Potosí

Tampico

SCOTT 1847

Cerro Gordo
April 17–18, 1847

Vera Cruz

Mexico City
Sept. 13–14, 1847

Puebla

Capture of Mexico City
September 1847

Lake Texcoco

Guadalupe
Hidalgo

Chapultepec
Sept. 13

Mexico City occupied
Sept. 14

Churubusco
Aug. 20

San Angel

San Antonio

*Lake
Vochimilco*

*Lake
Chalco*

TAYLOR 1847

Buena Vista

Padierna
Aug.18

San
Gregorio

Ayocingo

0   10 Miles

0   10 Kilometers

The Mexican War, 1846–1848

TROOP MOVEMENTS

← American forces

← Mexican forces

BATTLES

✴ American victory

✴ Mexican victory

0   400 Miles

0   400 Kilometers

In the meantime, Polk ordered other offensives against New Mexico and California. In the summer of 1846, a small army under Colonel Stephen W. Kearny captured Santa Fe with no opposition. Then Kearny proceeded to California, where he joined a conflict already in progress that was being staged jointly by American settlers, a well-armed exploring party led by John C. Frémont, and the American navy: the so-called Bear Flag Revolution. Kearny brought the disparate American forces together under his command, and by the autumn of 1846 he had completed the conquest of California.

The United States now controlled the two territories for which it had gone to war. But Mexico still refused to concede defeat. At this point, Polk and General Winfield Scott, the commanding general of the army and its finest soldier, launched a bold new campaign. Scott assembled an army at Tampico, which the navy transported down the Mexican coast to Veracruz. With an army that never numbered more than 14,000, Scott advanced 260 miles along the Mexican National Highway toward Mexico City, kept American casualties low, and never lost a battle before finally seizing the Mexican capital. A new Mexican government took power and announced its willingness to negotiate a peace treaty.

President Polk was now growing thoroughly unclear about his objectives. He continued to encourage those who demanded that the United States annex much of Mexico itself. At the same time, concerned about the approaching presidential election, he was growing anxious to get the war finished quickly. Polk had sent a special presidential envoy, Nicholas Trist, to negotiate a settlement. On February 2, 1848, he reached agreement with the new Mexican government on the Treaty of Guadalupe Hidalgo, by which Mexico agreed to cede California and New Mexico to the United States and acknowledge the Rio Grande as the boundary of Texas. In return, the United States promised to assume any financial claims its new citizens had against Mexico and to pay the Mexicans $15 million. Trist had obtained most of Polk's original demands, but he had not satisfied the new, more expansive dreams of acquiring additional territory in Mexico itself. Polk angrily claimed that Trist had violated his instructions, but he soon realized that he had no choice but to accept the treaty to silence a bitter battle growing between ardent expansionists demanding the annexation of "All Mexico!" and antislavery leaders charging that the expansionists were conspiring to extend slavery to new realms. The president submitted the Trist treaty to the Senate, which approved it by a vote of 38 to 14. The war was over, and America had gained a vast new territory. But it had also acquired a new set of troubling and divisive issues.

STEVEN KEARNY IN SANTA FE Colonel Stephen Kearny led a small U.S. military party to Santa Fe in 1846 and seized the town without opposition. In this 1909 drawing (which the artist Kenneth Chapman acknowledged was not entirely accurate), Kearny raises the American Flag over the "old palace" in Santa Fe. The image appeared on a U.S. postage stamp in 1946.

THE SECTIONAL DEBATE

James Polk tried to be a president whose policies transcended sectional divisions. But conciliating the sections was becoming an ever more difficult task, and Polk gradually earned the enmity of northerners and westerners alike, who believed his policies (and particularly his enthusiasm for territorial expansion in the Southwest) favored the South at their expense.

Slavery and the Territories

In August 1846, while the Mexican War was still in progress, Polk asked Congress to appropriate $2 million for purchasing peace with Mexico. Representative David Wilmot of Pennsylvania, an antislavery Democrat, introduced an amendment to the appropriation bill prohibiting slavery in any territory acquired from Mexico. The so-called Wilmot Proviso passed

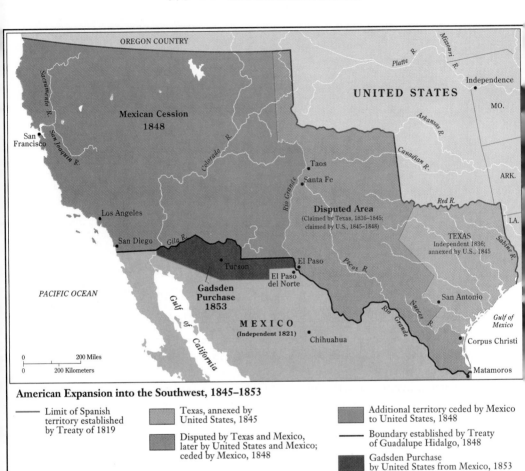

American Expansion into the Southwest, 1845–1853

—— Limit of Spanish territory established by Treaty of 1819	Texas, annexed by United States, 1845	Additional territory ceded by Mexico to United States, 1848
	Disputed by Texas and Mexico, later by United States and Mexico; ceded by Mexico, 1848	—— Boundary established by Treaty of Guadalupe Hidalgo, 1848
		Gadsden Purchase by United States from Mexico, 1853

the House but failed in the Senate. It would be called up, debated, and voted on repeatedly for years. Southern militants, in the meantime, contended that all Americans had equal rights in the new territories, including the right to move their slaves (which they considered property) into them.

As the sectional debate intensified, President Polk supported a proposal to extend the Missouri Compromise line through the new territories to the Pacific coast, banning slavery north of the line and permitting it south of the line. Others supported a plan, originally known as "squatter sovereignty" and later by the more dignified phrase "popular sovereignty," which would allow the people of each territory (acting through their legislature) to decide the status of slavery there. The debate over these various proposals dragged on for many months, and the issue remained unresolved when Polk left office in 1849.

The presidential campaign of 1848 dampened the controversy for a time as both Democrats and Whigs tried to avoid the slavery question. When Polk, in poor health, declined to run again, the Democrats nominated Lewis Cass of Michigan, a dull, aging party regular. The Whigs nominated General Zachary Taylor of Louisiana, hero of the Mexican War but a man with no political experience whatsoever. Opponents of slavery found the choice of candidates unsatisfying, and out of their discontent emerged the new Free-Soil Party, which drew from the existing Liberty Party and the antislavery wings of the Whig and Democratic Parties and which endorsed the Wilmot Proviso. Its candidate was former president Martin Van Buren.

Taylor won a narrow victory. But while Van Buren failed to carry a single state, he polled an impressive 291,000 votes (10 percent of the total), and the Free-Soilers elected ten members to Congress. The emergence of the Free-Soil Party as an important political force, like the emergence of the Know-Nothing and Liberty Parties before it, signaled the inability of the existing parties to contain the political passions slavery was creating. It was an important part of a process that would lead to the collapse of the second party system in the 1850s.

The California Gold Rush

By the time Taylor took office, the pressure to resolve the question of slavery in the far western territories had become more urgent as a result of dramatic events in California. In January 1848, a foreman working in a sawmill owned by John Sutter (one of California's leading ranchers) found traces of gold in the foothills of the Sierra Nevada. Within months, news of the discovery had spread throughout the nation and much of the world. Almost immediately, hundreds of thousands of people began flocking to California in a frantic search for gold. The non-Indian population of the territory increased nearly twentyfold in only four years.

The atmosphere in California at the peak of the gold rush was one of almost crazed excitement and greed. Most migrants to the Far West prepared carefully before making the journey. But the California migrants (known as "Forty-niners") threw caution to the winds. They abandoned farms, jobs, homes, families; they piled onto ships and flooded the overland trails—many carrying only what they could pack on their backs. The overwhelming majority of the Forty-niners (perhaps 95 percent) were men, and the society they created on their arrival in California was unusually fluid and volatile because of the almost total absence of women, children, or families.

The gold rush also attracted some of the first Chinese migrants to the western United States. News of the discoveries created great excitement in China, particularly in impoverished areas, where letters home from Chinese already in California and reports from American visitors spread the word. It was, of course, extremely difficult for a poor Chinese peasant to get to America; but many young, adventurous people (mostly men) decided to go anyway—in the belief that they could quickly become rich and then return to China. Emigration brokers loaned many migrants money for passage to California, which the migrants were to pay off out of their earnings there. The Chinese in California were free laborers and merchants, looking for gold or, more often, hoping to profit from other economic opportunities the gold boom was creating.

The gold rush was producing a serious labor shortage in California, as many male workers left their jobs and flocked to the gold fields. That created opportunities for many people who needed work (including Chinese immigrants). It also led to a frenzied exploitation of Indians that resembled slavery in all but name. A new state law permitted the arrest of "loitering" or orphaned Indians and their assignment to a term of "indentured" labor.

The gold rush was of critical importance to the growth of California, but not for the reasons most of the migrants hoped. There was substantial gold in the hills of the Sierra Nevada, and many people got rich from it. But only a tiny fraction of the Forty-niners ever found gold, or even managed to stake a claim to land on which they could look for gold. Some disappointed migrants returned home after a while. But many stayed in California and swelled both the agricultural and urban populations of the territory. By 1856, for example, San Francisco—whose population had been 1,000 before the gold rush (and at one point declined to about 100 as people left for the mines)—was the home of over 50,000 people. By the early 1850s, California, which had always had a diverse population, had become even more heterogeneous. The gold rush had attracted not just white Americans but Europeans, Chinese, South Americans, Mexicans, free blacks, and slaves who accompanied southern migrants. Conflicts over gold intersected with racial and ethnic tensions to make the territory an unusually turbulent place. The gold rush, therefore, became another factor putting pressure on the United States to resolve the status of the territories—and of slavery within them.

Rising Sectional Tensions

Zachary Taylor believed statehood could become the solution to the issue of slavery in the territories. As long as the new lands remained territories, the federal government was responsible for deciding the fate of slavery within them. But once they became states, he thought, their own governments would be able to settle the slavery question. At Taylor's urging, California quickly adopted a constitution that prohibited slavery, and in December 1849 Taylor asked Congress to admit California as a free state. New Mexico, he added, should also be granted statehood as soon as it was ready and should, like California, be permitted to decide for itself what it wanted to do about slavery.

Congress balked, in part because of several other controversies concerning slavery that were complicating the debate. One was the effort of antislavery forces to abolish slavery in the District of Columbia, a movement bitterly resisted by southerners. Another was the emergence of personal liberty laws in northern states, which barred courts and police officers from helping to return runaway slaves to their owners. In response, southerners demanded a stringent law that would require northern states to return fugitive slaves to their owners. But the biggest obstacle to the president's program was the white South's fear that two new free states would be added to the northern majority. The number of free and slave states was equal in 1849—fifteen each. But the admission of California would upset the balance; and New Mexico, Oregon, and Utah might upset it further, leaving the South in a minority in the Senate, as it already was in the House.

Tempers were now rising to dangerous levels. Even many otherwise moderate southern leaders were beginning to talk about secession from the Union. In the North, every state legislature but one adopted a resolution demanding the prohibition of slavery in the territories.

The Compromise of 1850

Faced with this mounting crisis, moderates and unionists spent the winter of 1849–1850 trying to frame a great compromise. The aging Henry Clay, who was spearheading the effort, believed that no compromise could last unless it settled all the issues in dispute between the sections. As a result, he took several measures that had been proposed separately, combined them into a single piece of legislation, and presented it to the Senate on January 29, 1850. Among the bill's provisions were the admission of California as a free state; the formation of territorial governments in the rest of the lands acquired from Mexico, without restrictions on slavery; the abolition of the slave trade, but not slavery itself, in the District of Columbia; and a new and more effective fugitive slave law. These resolutions launched a debate that raged for seven months—both in Congress and throughout the nation. The debate occurred in two phases, the differences between which revealed much about how American politics was changing in the 1850s.

In the first phase of the debate, the dominant voices in Congress were those of old men—national leaders who still remembered Jefferson, Adams, and other founders—who argued for or against the compromise on the basis of broad ideals. Clay himself, seventy-three years old in 1850, appealed to shared national sentiments of nationalism. Early in March, another of the older leaders—John C. Calhoun, sixty-eight years old and so ill that he had to sit grimly in his seat while a colleague read his speech for

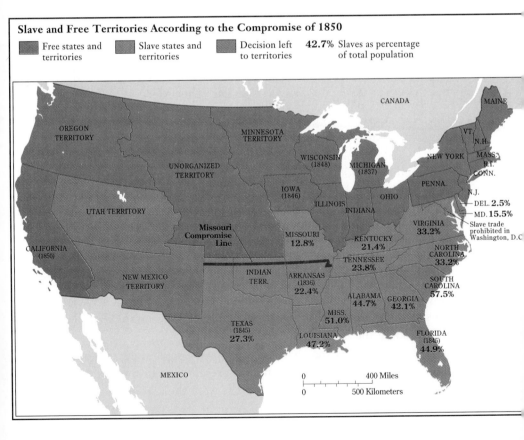

Slave and Free Territories According to the Compromise of 1850

Free states and territories

Slave states and territories

Decision left to territories

42.7% Slaves as percentage of total population

him—joined the debate. He insisted that the North grant the South equal rights in the territories, that it agree to observe the laws concerning fugitive slaves, that it cease attacking slavery, and that it amend the Constitution to create dual presidents, one from the North and one from the South, each with a veto. Calhoun was making radical demands that had no chance of passage. But like Clay, he was offering what he considered a comprehensive, permanent solution to the sectional problem that would, he believed, save the Union. After Calhoun came the third of the elder statesmen, sixty-eight-year-old Daniel Webster, one of the great orators of his time. Still nourishing presidential ambitions, he delivered an eloquent address in the Senate, trying to rally northern moderates to support Clay's compromise.

But in July, after six months of this impassioned, nationalistic debate, Congress defeated the Clay proposal. And with that, the controversy moved into its second phase, in which a very different cast of characters predominated. Clay, ill and tired, left Washington to spend the summer resting in the mountains. Calhoun had died even before the vote in July. And Webster accepted a new appointment as secretary of state, thus removing himself from the Senate and from the debate.

In place of these leaders, a new, younger group now emerged. One spokesman was William H. Seward, forty-nine years old, of New York, a wily political operator who staunchly opposed the proposed compromise. The ideals of Union were to him less important than the issue of eliminating slavery. Another was Jefferson Davis of Mississippi, forty-two years old, a representative of the new, cotton South. To him, the slavery issue was less one of principles and ideals than one of economic self-interest. Most important of all, there was Stephen A. Douglas, a thirty-seven-year-old Democratic senator from Illinois. A westerner from a rapidly growing state, he was an open spokesman for the economic needs of his section—and especially for the construction of railroads. His was a career devoted not to any broad national goals but frankly to sectional gain and personal self-promotion.

The new leaders of the Senate were able, as the old leaders had not been, to produce a compromise. One spur to the compromise was the disappearance of the most powerful obstacle to it: the president. Zachary Taylor had been adamant that only after California and possibly New Mexico were admitted as states could other measures be discussed. But on July 9, 1850, Taylor suddenly died—the victim of a violent stomach disorder. He was succeeded by Millard Fillmore of New York—a dull, handsome, dignified man who understood the political importance of flexibility. He supported the compromise and used his powers of persuasion to swing northern Whigs into line.

The new leaders also benefited from their own pragmatic tactics. Douglas's first step, after the departure of Clay, was to break up the "omnibus bill" that Clay had envisioned as a great, comprehensive solution to the sectional crisis and to introduce instead a series of separate measures to be voted on one by one. Thus representatives of different sections could support those elements of the compromise they liked and oppose those they did not. Douglas also gained support with complicated backroom deals linking the compromise to such nonideological matters as the sale of government bonds and the construction of railroads. As a result of his efforts, by mid-September Congress had enacted and the president had signed all the components of the compromise.

The Compromise of 1850, unlike the Missouri Compromise thirty years before, was not a product of widespread agreement on common national ideals. It was, rather, a victory of self-interest. Still, members of Congress hailed the measure as a triumph of statesmanship; and Millard Fillmore, signing it, called it a just settlement of the sectional problem, "in its character final and irrevocable."

THE CRISES OF THE 1850S

For a few years after the Compromise of 1850, the sectional conflict seemed briefly to be forgotten amid booming prosperity and growth. But the tensions between North and South remained, and the crisis continued to smolder until—in 1854—it once more burst into the open.

The Uneasy Truce

Both major parties endorsed the Compromise of 1850 in 1852, and both nominated presidential candidates unidentified with sectional passions. The Democrats chose the obscure New Hampshire politician Franklin Pierce and the Whigs the military hero General Winfield Scott, a man of entirely unknown political views. But the sectional question was a divisive influence in the election anyway, and the Whigs were the principal victims. They suffered massive defections from antislavery members angered by the party's evasiveness on the issue. Many of them flocked to the Free-Soil Party, whose antislavery presidential candidate, John P. Hale, repudiated the Compromise of 1850. The divisions among the Whigs helped produce a victory for the Democrats in 1852.

Franklin Pierce, a charming, amiable man of no particular distinction, attempted to maintain party—and national—harmony by avoiding divisive issues, and particularly by avoiding the issue of slavery. But it was an impossible task. Northern opposition to the Fugitive Slave Act intensified quickly after 1850, when southerners began appearing occasionally in northern states to pursue people they claimed were fugitives. Mobs formed in some northern cities to prevent enforcement of the law, and several northern states also passed their own laws barring the deportation of fugitive slaves. White southerners watched with growing anger and alarm as the one element of the Compromise of 1850 that they had considered a victory seemed to become meaningless as a result of northern defiance.

"Young America"

One of the ways Franklin Pierce hoped to dampen sectional controversy was through his support of a movement in the Democratic Party known as "Young America." Its adherents saw the expansion of American democracy throughout the world as a way to divert attention from the controversies over slavery. The great liberal and nationalist revolutions of 1848 in Europe stirred them to dream of a republican Europe with governments based on the model of the United States. They dreamed as well of expanding American commerce in the Pacific and acquiring new territories in the Western Hemisphere.

But efforts to extend the nation's domain could not avoid becoming entangled with the sectional crisis. Pierce had been pursuing unsuccessful diplomatic attempts to buy Cuba from Spain (efforts begun in 1848 by Polk). In 1854, however, a group of his envoys sent him a private document from Ostend, Belgium, making the case for seizing Cuba by force. When the Ostend Manifesto, as it became known, was leaked to the public, it enraged many antislavery northerners, who charged the administration with conspiring to bring a new slave state into the Union.

The South, for its part, opposed all efforts to acquire new territory that would not support a slave system. The kingdom of Hawaii agreed to join the United States in 1854, but the treaty died in the Senate because it contained a clause prohibiting slavery in the islands. A powerful movement to annex Canada to the United States—a movement that had the support of many Canadians eager for access to American markets—similarly foundered, at least in part because of slavery.

Slavery, Railroads, and the West

What fully revived the sectional crisis, however, was the same issue that had produced it in the first place: slavery in the territories. By the 1850s, the line of substantial white settlement had moved beyond the boundaries of Missouri, Iowa, and what is now Minnesota into a great expanse of plains, which many white Americans had once believed was unfit for cultivation. Now it was becoming apparent that large sections of this region were, in fact, suitable for farming. In the states of the Old Northwest, therefore, prospective settlers urged the government to open the area to them, provide territorial governments, and—despite the solemn assurance the United States had earlier given the Indians of the sanctity of their reservations—dislodge the tribes located there so as to make room for white settlers. There was relatively little opposition from any segment of white society to this proposed violation of Indian rights. But the interest in further settlement raised two issues that did prove highly divisive and that gradually became entwined with each other: railroads and slavery.

As the nation expanded westward, the problem of communication between the older states and the areas west of the Mississippi River became more and more critical. As a result, broad support began to emerge for building a transcontinental railroad. The problem was where to place it—and in particular, where to locate the railroad's eastern terminus, where the line could connect with the existing rail network east of the Mississippi. Northerners favored Chicago, the rapidly growing capital of the free states of the Northwest. Southerners supported St. Louis, Memphis, or New Orleans—all located in slave states. The transcontinental railroad, in other words, had become part of the struggle between the North and the South.

Pierce's secretary of war, Jefferson Davis of Mississippi, removed one obstacle to a southern route. Surveys indicated that a railroad with a southern terminus would have to pass through an area in Mexican territory. But in 1853 Davis sent James Gadsden, a southern railroad builder, to Mexico, where he persuaded the Mexican government to accept $10 million in exchange for a strip of land that today comprises part of Arizona and New Mexico. The so-called Gadsden Purchase only accentuated the sectional rivalry.

The Kansas-Nebraska Controversy

As a senator from Illinois, a resident of Chicago, and the acknowledged leader of northwestern Democrats, Stephen A. Douglas naturally wanted the transcontinental railroad for his own city and section. He also realized the strength of the principal argument against the northern route west of the Mississippi: that it would run mostly through country with a substantial Indian population. As a result, he introduced a bill in January 1854 to organize (and thus open to white settlement) a huge new territory, known as Nebraska, west of Iowa and Missouri.

Douglas knew the South would oppose his bill because it would prepare the way for a new free state; the proposed territory was in the area of the Louisiana Purchase north of the Missouri Compromise line (36°30′) and hence closed to slavery. In an effort to make the measure acceptable to southerners, Douglas inserted a provision that the status of slavery in the territory would be determined by the territorial legislature—that is, according to "popular sovereignty." In theory, the region could choose to open itself to slavery (although few believed it actually would). When southern Democrats demanded more, Douglas agreed to an additional clause explicitly repealing the Missouri Compromise. He also agreed to divide the area into two territories—Nebraska and Kansas—instead of one. The new, second territory (Kansas) was more likely to become a slave state. In its final form the measure was known as the Kansas-Nebraska Act. President Pierce supported the bill, and after a strenuous debate, it became law in May 1854 with the unanimous support of the South and the partial support of northern Democrats.

No piece of legislation in American history produced so many immediate, sweeping, and ominous consequences. It divided and destroyed the Whig Party, which disappeared almost entirely by 1856. It divided the northern Democrats (many of whom were appalled at the repeal of the Missouri Compromise, which they considered an almost sacred part of the fabric of the Union) and drove many of them from the party. Most important of all, it spurred the creation of a new party that was frankly sectional in composition and creed. People in both major parties who opposed Douglas's bill began to call themselves Anti-Nebraska Democrats and Anti-Nebraska Whigs. In 1854, they formed a new organization and named it the Republican Party. It instantly became a major force in American politics. In the elections of that year, the Republicans won enough seats in Congress to permit them, in combination with allies among the Know-Nothings, to organize the House of Representatives.

"Bleeding Kansas"

Events in Kansas itself in the next two years increased the political turmoil in the North. White settlers from both the North and the South began moving into the territory almost immediately after the passage of the Kansas-Nebraska Act. In the spring of 1855, elections were held for a territorial legislature. There were only about 1,500 legal voters in Kansas by then, but thousands of Missourians, some traveling in armed bands into Kansas, swelled the vote to over 6,000. The result was that pro-slavery forces elected a majority to the legislature, which immediately legalized slavery. Outraged free-staters elected their own delegates to a constitutional convention, which met at Topeka and adopted a constitution excluding slavery. They then chose their own governor and legislature and petitioned Congress for statehood. President Pierce denounced them as traitors and threw the full support of the federal government behind the pro-slavery territorial legislature. A few months later a pro-slavery federal marshal assembled a large posse, consisting mostly of Missourians, to arrest the free-state leaders, who had set up their headquarters in Lawrence. The posse sacked the town, burned the "governor's" house, and destroyed several printing presses. Retribution came quickly.

Among the most fervent abolitionists in Kansas was John Brown, a grim, fiercely committed zealot who considered himself an instrument of God's will to destroy slavery. He had moved to Kansas with his sons so that they could fight to make it a free state. After the events in Lawrence, he gathered six followers (including four of his sons) and in one night murdered five pro-slavery settlers, leaving their mutilated bodies to discourage other supporters of slavery from entering Kansas. This terrible episode, known as the Pottawatomie Massacre, led to more civil strife in Kansas—irregular, guerrilla warfare conducted by armed bands, some of them more interested in land claims or loot than in ideologies. Northerners and southerners alike came to believe that the events in Kansas illustrated (and were caused by) the aggressive designs of the other section. "Bleeding Kansas" became a symbol of the sectional controversy.

Another symbol soon appeared, in the United States Senate. In May 1856, Charles Sumner of Massachusetts—a militant and passionately doctrinaire opponent of slavery—rose to give a speech entitled "The Crime Against Kansas." In it, he gave particular attention to Senator Andrew P. Butler of South Carolina, an outspoken defender of slavery. The South Carolinian was, Sumner claimed, the "Don Quixote" of slavery, having "chosen a mistress . . . who, though ugly to others, is always lovely to

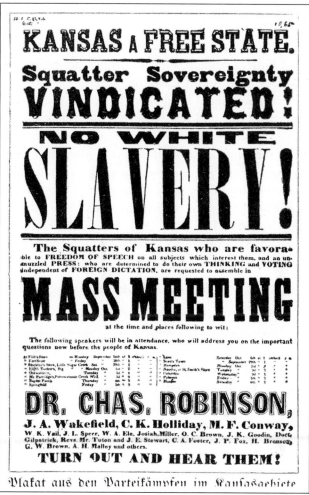

"BLEEDING KANSAS" The battle over the fate of slavery in Kansas was one of the most turbulent events of the 1850s. This 1855 poster invites antislavery forces to a meeting to protest the actions of the "bogus" pro-slavery territorial legislature, which had passed laws that, among other things, made it illegal to speak or write against slavery. "Squatter sovereignty" was another term for "popular sovereignty," the doctrine that gave residents of a prospective state the power to decide the fate of slavery there.

him, though polluted in the sight of the world, is chaste in his sight . . . the harlot slavery."

The pointedly sexual references and the general viciousness of the speech enraged Butler's nephew, Preston Brooks, a member of the House of Representatives from South Carolina. Several days after the speech, Brooks approached Sumner at his desk in the Senate chamber during a recess, raised a heavy cane, and began beating him repeatedly on the head and shoulders. Sumner, trapped in his chair, rose in agony with such strength that he tore the desk from the bolts holding it to the floor. Then he collapsed, bleeding and unconscious. So severe were his injuries that he was unable to return to the Senate for four years. Throughout the North, he became a hero—a martyr to the barbarism of the South. In the South, Preston Brooks became a hero, too. Censured by the House, he resigned his seat, returned to South Carolina, and stood successfully for reelection.

The Free-Soil Ideology

What had happened to produce such deep hostility between the two sections? In part, the tensions were reflections of the two sections' differing economic and territorial interests. But they were also reflections of a hardening of ideas in both North and South. As the nation expanded and political power grew more dispersed, each section became concerned with ensuring that its vision of America's future would be the dominant one.

In the North, assumptions about the proper structure of society came to center on the belief in "free soil" and "free labor." Although abolitionists generated some support for their argument that slavery was a moral evil and must be eliminated, most white northerners came to believe that the existence of slavery was dangerous not because of what it did to blacks but because of what it threatened to do to whites. At the heart of American democracy, they argued, was the right of all citizens to own property, to control their own labor, and to have access to opportunities for advancement.

According to this vision, the South was the antithesis of democracy—a closed, static society, in which slavery preserved an entrenched aristocracy and in which common whites had no opportunity to improve themselves. While the North was growing and prospering, the South was stagnating, rejecting the values of individualism and progress. The South was, northern free-laborites further maintained, engaged in a conspiracy to extend slavery throughout the nation and thus to destroy the openness of northern capitalism and replace it with the closed, aristocratic system of the South. The only solution to this "slave power conspiracy" was to fight the spread of slavery and extend the nation's democratic (i.e., free-labor) ideals to all sections of the country.

This ideology, which lay at the heart of the new Republican Party, also strengthened the commitment of Republicans to the Union. Since the idea of continued growth and progress was central to the free-labor vision, the prospect of dismemberment of the nation—a diminution of America's size and economic power—was unthinkable.

The Pro-Slavery Argument

In the South, in the meantime, a very different ideology—entirely incompatible with the free-labor ideology—was emerging out of a rapid hardening of position among southern whites on the issue of slavery. It was a result of many things: the Nat Turner uprising in 1831, which terrified southern whites and made them more determined than ever to make slavery secure; the expansion of the cotton economy into the Deep South, which made slavery unprecedentedly lucrative; and the growth of the Garrisonian abolitionist movement, with its strident attacks on southern society. The popularity of Harriet Beecher Stowe's *Uncle Tom's Cabin* was perhaps the most glaring evidence of the success of those attacks, but other abolitionist writings had been antagonizing white southerners for years.

In response to these pressures, a number of white southerners produced a new intellectual defense of slavery. Professor Thomas R. Dew of the College of William and Mary helped begin that effort in 1832. Twenty years later, apologists for slavery summarized their views in an anthology that gave their ideology its name: *The Pro-Slavery Argument*. John C. Calhoun stated the essence of the case in 1837: Southerners should stop apologizing for slavery as a necessary evil and defend it as "a good—a positive good." It was good for the slaves, the southern apologists argued, because they enjoyed better conditions than industrial workers in the North. Slavery was good for southern society as a whole because it was the only way the two races could live together in peace. It was good for the entire country because the southern economy, based on slavery, was the key to the prosperity of the nation.

Above all, southern apologists argued, slavery was good because it served as the basis for the southern way of life—a way of life superior to any other in the United States, perhaps in the world. White southerners looking at the North saw a spirit of greed, debauchery, and destructiveness. "The masses of the North are venal, corrupt, covetous, mean and selfish," wrote one southerner. Others wrote with horror of the factory system and the crowded, pestilential cities filled with unruly immigrants. But the South, they believed, was a stable, orderly society, operating at a slow and human pace. It was free from the feuds between capital and labor plaguing the North. It protected the welfare of its workers. And it allowed the aristocracy to enjoy a refined and accomplished cultural life. It was, in short, an ideal social order in which all elements of the population were secure and content.

The defense of slavery rested, too, on increasingly elaborate arguments about the biological inferiority of African Americans, who were, white Southerners claimed, inherently unfit to take care of themselves, let alone exercise the rights of citizenship. And just as abolitionist arguments drew strength from Protestant theology in the North, the pro-slavery defense mobilized the Protestant clergy in the South to give the institution a religious and biblical justification.

Buchanan and Depression

In this unpromising climate, the presidential campaign of 1856 began. Democratic Party leaders wanted a candidate who, unlike President Pierce, was not closely associated with the explosive question of "Bleeding Kansas." They chose James Buchanan of Pennsylvania, a reliable party stalwart who as minister to England had been safely out of the country during the recent controversies. The Republicans, participating in their first presidential contest, denounced the Kansas-Nebraska Act and the expansion of slavery but also endorsed a Whiggish program of internal improvements, thus combining the idealism of antislavery with the economic aspirations of the North. As eager as the Democrats to present a safe candidate, the Republicans nominated John C. Frémont, who had made a national reputation as an explorer of the Far West and who had no political record. The Native American, or Know-Nothing, Party was beginning to break apart, but it nominated former president Millard Fillmore, who also received the endorsement of a sad remnant of the Whig Party.

After a heated, even frenzied campaign, Buchanan won a narrow victory over Frémont and Fillmore. A slight shift of votes in Pennsylvania and Illinois would have elected the Republican candidate. Particularly ominous was that Frémont had attracted virtually no votes at all in the South while outpolling all other candidates in the North. At the time of his inauguration, Buchanan was, at age sixty-five, the oldest president, except for William Henry Harrison, ever to have taken office. Whether because of age and physical infirmities or because of a more fundamental weakness of character, he became a painfully timid and indecisive president at a critical moment in history.

In the year Buchanan took office, a financial panic struck the country, followed by a depression that lasted several years. In the North, the depression strengthened the Republican Party because distressed manufacturers, workers, and farmers came to believe that the hard times were the result of the unsound policies of southern-controlled Democratic administrations. They expressed their frustrations by moving into an alliance with antislavery elements and thus into the Republican Party.

The Dred Scott Decision

On March 6, 1857, the Supreme Court of the United States projected itself into the sectional controversy with one of the most controversial and notorious decisions in its history—its ruling in the case of *Dred Scott* v. *Sandford*, handed down two days after Buchanan was inaugurated. Dred Scott was a Missouri slave, once owned by an army surgeon who had taken Scott with him into Illinois and Wisconsin, where slavery was forbidden. In 1846, after the surgeon died, Scott sued his master's widow for freedom on the grounds that his residence in free territory had liberated him from slavery. The claim was well grounded in Missouri law, and in 1850 the circuit court in which Scott filed the suit declared him free. By now, John Sanford, the brother of the surgeon's widow, was claiming ownership of Scott, and he appealed the circuit court ruling to the state supreme court, which reversed the earlier decision. When Scott appealed to the federal courts, Sanford's attorneys claimed that Scott had no standing to sue because he was not a citizen, but private property.

The Supreme Court (which misspelled Sanford's name in its decision) was so divided that it was unable to issue a single ruling on the case. The thrust of the various rulings, however, was a stunning defeat for the antislavery movement. Chief Justice Roger Taney, who wrote one of the majority opinions, declared that Scott could not bring a suit in the federal courts because he was not a citizen. Blacks had no claim to citizenship, Taney argued, and in fact virtually no rights at all under the Constitution. Slaves were property, and the Fifth Amendment prohibited Congress from taking property without "due process of law." Consequently, Taney concluded, Congress possessed no authority to pass a law depriving persons of their slave property in the territories. The Missouri Compromise, therefore, had always been unconstitutional.

The ruling did nothing to challenge the right of an individual state to prohibit slavery within its borders, but the statement that the federal government was powerless to act on the issue was a drastic and startling one. Few judicial opinions have ever created as much controversy. Southern whites were elated: the highest tribunal in the land had sanctioned parts of the most extreme southern argument. In the North, the decision produced widespread dismay. Republicans threatened that when they won control of the national government, they would reverse the decision—by "packing" the Court with new members.

Deadlock over Kansas

President Buchanan timidly endorsed the *Dred Scott* decision. At the same time, he tried to resolve the controversy over Kansas by supporting its admission to the Union as a slave state. In response, the pro-slavery territorial legislature called an election for delegates to a constitutional convention. The free-state residents refused to participate, claiming that the legislature had discriminated against them in drawing district lines. As a result, the pro-slavery forces won control of the convention, which met in 1857 at Lecompton, framed a constitution legalizing slavery, and refused to give voters a chance to reject it. When an election for a new territorial legislature was called, the antislavery groups turned out to vote and won a majority. The new legislature promptly submitted the Lecompton constitution to the voters, who rejected it by more than 10,000 votes.

Both sides had resorted to fraud and violence, but it was clear nevertheless that a majority of the people of Kansas opposed slavery. Buchanan, however, pressured Congress to admit Kansas under the Lecompton constitution. Stephen A. Douglas and other western Democrats refused to support the president's proposal, which died in the House of Representatives. Finally, in April 1858, Congress approved a compromise: The Lecompton constitution would be submitted to the voters of Kansas again. If it was approved, Kansas would be admitted to the Union; if it was rejected, statehood would be postponed. Again, Kansas voters decisively rejected the Lecompton constitution. Not until the closing months of Buchanan's administration in 1861, after several southern states had already withdrawn from the Union, did Kansas enter the Union—as a free state.

The Emergence of Lincoln

Given the gravity of the sectional crisis, the congressional elections of 1858 took on a special importance. Of particular note was the United States Senate election in Illinois, which pitted Stephen A. Douglas, the most prominent northern Democrat, against Abraham Lincoln, who was largely unknown outside Illinois but who quickly emerged as one of the most skillful politicians in the Republican Party.

Lincoln was a successful lawyer who had long been involved in state politics. He had served several terms in the Illinois legislature and one undistinguished term in Congress. But he was not a national figure like Douglas, and so he tried to increase his visibility by engaging Douglas in a series of debates. The Lincoln-Douglas debates attracted enormous crowds and received wide attention. By the time they ended, Lincoln's increasingly eloquent and passionate attacks on slavery had made him nationally prominent.

At the heart of the debates was a basic difference on the issue of slavery. Douglas appeared to have no moral position on the issue and, Lincoln claimed, did not care whether slavery was "voted up, or voted down." Lincoln's opposition to slavery was more fundamental. If the nation could accept that blacks were not entitled to basic human rights, he argued, then it could accept that other groups—immigrant laborers, for example—could be deprived of rights, too. And if slavery were to extend into the western territories, he argued, opportunities for poor white laborers to better their lots there would be lost. The nation's future, he argued (reflecting the central idea of the Republican Party), rested on the spread of free labor.

Lincoln believed slavery was morally wrong, but he was not an abolitionist. That was in part because he could not envision an easy alternative to slavery in the areas where it already existed. He shared the prevailing view among northern whites that the black race was not prepared (and perhaps never would be) to live on equal terms with whites. He and his party would "arrest the further spread" of slavery—that is, prevent its expansion into the territories; they would not directly challenge it where it already existed, but would trust that the institution would gradually die out there of its own accord.

Douglas's position satisfied his followers sufficiently to win him reelection to the Senate, but it aroused little enthusiasm and did nothing to enhance his national political ambitions. Lincoln, by contrast, lost the election but emerged with a growing following both in and beyond the state. And outside Illinois, the elections went heavily against the Democrats, who lost ground in almost every northern state. The party retained control of the Senate but lost its majority in the House, with the result that the congressional sessions of 1858 and 1859 were bitterly deadlocked.

John Brown's Raid

The battles in Congress, however, were almost entirely overshadowed by a spectacular event that enraged and horrified the entire South and greatly hastened the rush toward disunion. In the fall of 1859, John Brown, the antislavery zealot whose bloody actions in Kansas had inflamed the crisis there, staged an even more dramatic episode, this time in the South itself. With private encouragement and financial aid from some prominent eastern abolitionists, he made elaborate plans to seize a mountain fortress in Virginia from which, he believed, he could foment a slave insurrection in the South. On October 16, he and a group of eighteen followers attacked and seized control of a United States arsenal in Harpers Ferry, Virginia. But the slave uprising Brown hoped to inspire did not occur, and he quickly found himself besieged in the arsenal by citizens, local militia companies, and before long United States troops under the command of Robert E. Lee. After ten of his men were killed, Brown surrendered. He was promptly tried in a Virginia court for treason against the state, found guilty, and sentenced to death. He and six of his followers were hanged.

JOHN BROWN Even in this formal photographic portrait (taken in 1859, the last year of his life), John Brown coveys the fierce sense of righteousness that fueled his extraordinary activities in the fight against slavery.

No other single event did more than the Harpers Ferry raid to convince white southerners that they could not live safely in the Union. John Brown's raid, many southerners believed (incorrectly) had the support of the Republican Party, and it suggested to them that the North was now committed to producing a slave insurrection.

The Election of Lincoln

The presidential election of 1860 had the most momentous consequences of any in American history. It was also among the most complex.

The Democratic Party was torn apart by a battle between southerners, who demanded a strong endorsement of slavery, and westerners, who supported the idea of popular sovereignty. The party convention met in April in Charleston, South Carolina. When the convention endorsed popular sovereignty, delegates from eight states in the lower South walked out. The remaining delegates could not agree on a presidential candidate and finally adjourned after agreeing to meet again in Baltimore in June. The decimated convention at Baltimore nominated Stephen Douglas for president. In the meantime, disenchanted southern Democrats met in Richmond and nominated John C. Breckinridge of Kentucky. Later, a group of conservative ex-Whigs met in Baltimore to form the Constitutional Union Party, with John Bell of Tennessee as their presidential candidate. They endorsed the Union and remained silent on slavery.

The Republican leaders, in the meantime, were trying to broaden their appeal so as to attract every major interest group in the North that feared the South was blocking its economic aspirations. The platform endorsed such traditional Whig measures as a high tariff, internal improvements, a homestead bill, and a Pacific railroad to be built with federal financial assistance. It supported the right of each state to decide the status of slavery within its borders. But it also insisted that neither Congress nor territorial legislatures could legalize slavery in the territories. The Republican convention chose Abraham Lincoln as the party's presidential nominee. Lincoln was appealing because of his growing reputation for eloquence, because of his firm but moderate position on slavery, and because his relative obscurity ensured that he would have none of the drawbacks of other, more prominent (and therefore more controversial) Republicans. He was a representative of the West, a considerable asset in a race against Douglas.

In the November election, Lincoln won the presidency with a majority of the electoral votes but only about two-fifths of the fragmented popular vote. The Republicans, moreover, failed to win a majority in Congress. Even

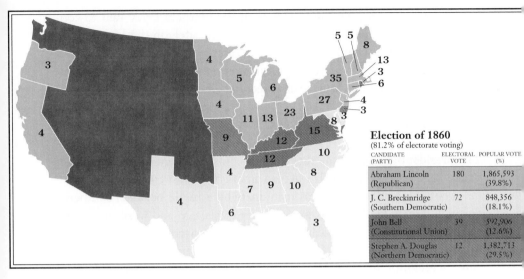

Election of 1860
(81.2% of electorate voting)

CANDIDATE (PARTY)	ELECTORAL VOTE	POPULAR VOTE (%)
Abraham Lincoln (Republican)	180	1,865,593 (39.8%)
J. C. Breckinridge (Southern Democratic)	72	848,356 (18.1%)
John Bell (Constitutional Union)	39	592,906 (12.6%)
Stephen A. Douglas (Northern Democratic)	12	1,382,713 (29.5%)

so, the election of Lincoln became the final signal to many white southerners that their position in the Union was hopeless. And within a few weeks of Lincoln's victory, the process of disunion began—a process that would quickly lead to a prolonged and bloody war between two groups of Americans, each heir to more than a century of struggling toward nationhood, each now convinced that it shared no common ground with the other.

CONCLUSION

In the decades following the War of 1812, a vigorous sense of nationalism pervaded much of American life, helping to smooth over the growing differences among the very different societies emerging in the regions of the United States. During the 1850s, however, the forces that had worked to hold the nation together in the past fell victim to new and much more divisive pressures that were working to split the nation apart.

Driving the sectional tensions of the 1850s was a battle over national policy toward the western territories, which were clamoring to become states of the Union—and over the place of slavery within them. Should slavery be permitted in the new states? And who should decide whether to permit it or not? There were strenuous efforts to craft compromises and solutions to this dilemma: the Compromise of 1850, the Kansas–Nebraska Act of 1854, and others. But despite these efforts, positions on slavery continued to harden in both the North and South until ultimately each region came to consider the other its enemy. Bitter battles in the territory of Kansas over whether to permit slavery there; growing agitation by abolitionists in the North and pro-slavery advocates in the South; the Supreme Court's controversial *Dred Scott* decision in 1857; the popularity of *Uncle Tom's Cabin* throughout the decade; and the emergence of a new political party—the Republican party—openly and centrally opposed to slavery: all worked to destroy the hopes for compromise and push the South toward secession.

In 1860, all pretense of common sentiment collapsed when no political party presented a presidential candidate capable of attracting national support. The Republicans nominated Abraham Lincoln of Illinois, a little-known politician recognized for his eloquent condemnations of slavery in a Senate race two years earlier. The Democratic party split apart, with its northern and southern wings each nominating different candidates. A third party, devoted to the Constitution and the Union, forlornly nominated a candidate of its own who found almost no constituency at all. Lincoln won the election easily, but with less than forty percent of the vote. And almost immediately after his victory, the states of the South began preparing to secede from the Union.

FOR FURTHER REFERENCE

Suggested Readings

David Potter, *The Impending Crisis* (1976) is an excellent summary of the decisive decade of the 1850s. Allan Nevins, *The Ordeal of the Union*, 2 vols. (1947), and *The Emergence of Lincoln*, 2 vols. (1950) comprise a classic narrative history of the coming of the Civil War. Anders Stephanson, *Manifest Destiny* (1995) briefly traces the origins of American expansion ideology. John M. Faragher, *Women and Men on the Overland Trail* (1979) is a good social history of the westward migration. David M. Pletcher, *The Diplomacy of Annexation: Texas, Oregon, and the Mexican War* (1973) is the standard work on war and diplomacy in the 1840s. William W. Freehling, *The Road to Disunion. Vol. 1: Secessionists at Bay, 1776–1854* (1990) explores the successful containment of sectionalism prior to the 1850s. Eric Foner, *Free Soil, Free Labor, Free Men* (1970) traces the emergence of the Republican Party. Michael Holt, *The Political Crisis of the 1850s* (1978) challenges Foner by emphasizing ethnic and religious alignment in northern politics. David Donald, *Charles Sumner and the Coming of the Civil War* (1960) is a superb biography of one of the most powerful and controversial figures in the early Republican party. Don E. Fehrenbacher, *The Dred Scott Case* (1978) explains the Supreme Court's most infamous decision.

Films

(The best source for information on how to find these and other films is *Bowker's Complete Video Directory*—3 volumes.) *The American Story, No. 10: Manifest Destiny* (1985) traces American industrial growth and commercial expansion through the Taylor, Fillmore, and Polk presidencies. *Manifest Destiny* examines the implications of this concept for war and diplomacy in the United States. *Texas & the Mexican Cession* (1990) brings to life the days of Davy Crockett and Sam Houston. *Uncle Tom's Cabin* (1987) is a recent adaptation of Harriet Beecher Stowe's influential and controversial novel. *The Background of the Civil War* (1981) introduces the differences between North and South that eventually led to war. *The Civil War: Union at Risk* (1989) presents the pre-Civil War differences between North and South and argues that the war was fought over Constitutional interpretation. *Abraham Lincoln: A New Birth of Freedom* (1992) features commentators from Mario Cuomo to Ted Koppel. *The Lincoln-Douglas Debates: The House Divides* (1989) examines the two barnstorming politicians' pivotal debates over the status of slavery in the western territories.

Internet Resources

Internet websites containing historical material relevant to the subjects discussed in this chapter can be reached through the McGraw-Hill history site at www.mhhe.com/socscience/history/usa/link/linktop.htm.

CHAPTER FOURTEEN

The Civil War

B Y THE END of 1860, the cords that had once bound the Union together seemed to have snapped. The almost mystical veneration of
the Constitution and the romantic vision of America's great national destiny
had now taken very different forms in the North and the South. The relatively stable second party system had collapsed, replaced by a new one that
accentuated rather than muted regional controversy. The federal government
was no longer the remote, unthreatening presence it once had been; the need
to resolve the status of the territories had made it necessary for Washington
to deal directly with sectional issues. The election of 1860 brought these tensions to a head and precipitated the most terrible war in the nation's history.

THE SECESSION CRISIS

Almost as soon as the news of Abraham Lincoln's election reached the
South, the militant leaders of the region began to demand an end to the
Union. Within weeks, the process of secession had begun.

The Withdrawal of the South

South Carolina, long the hotbed of southern separatism, seceded first, on De-
cember 20, 1860. By the time Lincoln took office, six other southern states—
Mississippi (January 9, 1861), Florida (January 10), Alabama (January 11),
Georgia (January 19), Louisiana (January 26), and Texas (February 1)—had

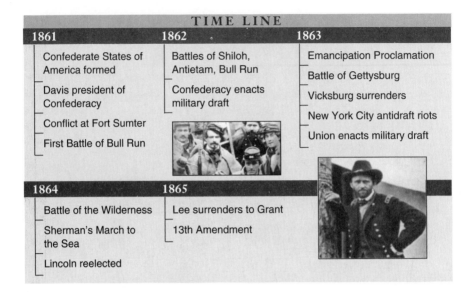

TIME LINE

1861	1862	1863
Confederate States of America formed	Battles of Shiloh, Antietam, Bull Run	Emancipation Proclamation
Davis president of Confederacy	Confederacy enacts military draft	Battle of Gettysburg
Conflict at Fort Sumter		Vicksburg surrenders
First Battle of Bull Run		New York City antidraft riots
		Union enacts military draft

1864	1865
Battle of the Wilderness	Lee surrenders to Grant
Sherman's March to the Sea	13th Amendment
Lincoln reelected	

withdrawn from the Union. In February 1861, representatives of the seven seceded states met at Montgomery, Alabama, and formed a new nation—the Confederate States of America. President James Buchanan told Congress in December 1860 that no state had the right to secede from the Union but that the federal government had no authority to stop a state if it did.

The seceding states immediately seized the federal property—forts, arsenals, government offices—within their boundaries. But they did not at first have sufficient military power to seize two fortified offshore military installations: Fort Sumter, on an island in the harbor of Charleston, South Carolina, garrisoned by a small force under Major Robert Anderson; and Fort Pickens, in the harbor of Pensacola, Florida. Buchanan, timid though he was on most matters, refused to yield Fort Sumter when South Carolina demanded it. Instead, in January 1861, he ordered an unarmed merchant ship to proceed to Fort Sumter with additional troops and supplies. Confederate guns turned it back. Still, neither section was yet ready to concede that war had begun. And in Washington, efforts began once more to forge a compromise.

The Failure of Compromise

Gradually, the compromise efforts came together around a proposal first submitted by Senator John J. Crittenden of Kentucky and known as the Crittenden Compromise. The heart of the plan was a proposal to reestablish the Missouri Compromise line and extend it westward, so that it would

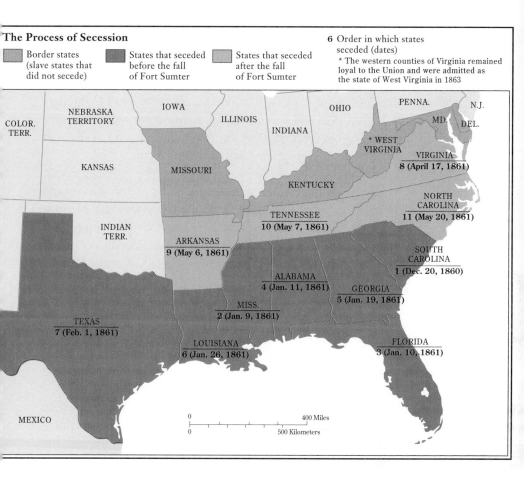

The Process of Secession

◾ Border states (slave states that did not secede)

◾ States that seceded before the fall of Fort Sumter

◾ States that seceded after the fall of Fort Sumter

6 Order in which states seceded (dates)
* The western counties of Virginia remained loyal to the Union and were admitted as the state of West Virginia in 1863

COLOR. TERR.

NEBRASKA TERRITORY

IOWA

ILLINOIS

OHIO

PENNA.

N.J.

MD.

DEL.

INDIANA

* WEST VIRGINIA

KANSAS

MISSOURI

KENTUCKY

VIRGINIA
8 (April 17, 1861)

NORTH CAROLINA
11 (May 20, 1861)

INDIAN TERR.

ARKANSAS
9 (May 6, 1861)

TENNESSEE
10 (May 7, 1861)

SOUTH CAROLINA
1 (Dec. 20, 1860)

ALABAMA
4 (Jan. 11, 1861)

GEORGIA
5 (Jan. 19, 1861)

MISS.
2 (Jan. 9, 1861)

TEXAS
7 (Feb. 1, 1861)

LOUISIANA
6 (Jan. 26, 1861)

FLORIDA
3 (Jan. 10, 1861)

MEXICO

0   400 Miles

0   500 Kilometers

divide all the present and future territory of the United States: slavery would be prohibited north of the line and permitted south of it. Southerners in the Senate seemed willing to accept the plan. But the compromise would have required the Republicans to abandon their most fundamental position—that slavery not be allowed to expand—and they rejected it.

And so nothing had been resolved when Abraham Lincoln arrived in Washington for his inauguration—entering the city in disguise on a night train to avoid assassination as he passed through the slave state of Maryland. In his inaugural address, Lincoln insisted acts of force or violence to support secession were insurrectionary and that the government would "hold, occupy, and possess" federal property in the seceded states—a clear reference to Fort Sumter.

But Union forces at Fort Sumter were running short of supplies; unless they received fresh provisions, they would have to evacuate the fort.

So Lincoln sent a relief expedition to the fort and informed the South Carolina authorities that he would send no troops or munitions unless the supply ships met with resistance. But the new Confederate government, rather than allowing the U.S. government to exercise authority in South Carolina, ordered General P. G. T. Beauregard, commander of Confederate forces at Charleston, to take the fort. When Anderson refused to give up, the Confederates bombarded it for two days, April 12–13, 1861. On April 14, Anderson surrendered. The Civil War had begun.

Almost immediately, Lincoln began mobilizing the North for war. Equally promptly, four more slave states seceded from the Union and joined the Confederacy: Virginia (April 17, 1861), Arkansas (May 6), Tennessee (May 7), and North Carolina (May 20). The four remaining slave states, Maryland, Delaware, Kentucky, and Missouri—under heavy political and even military pressure from Washington—remained in the Union.

The Opposing Sides

All the important material advantages for waging war lay with the North. Its population was more than twice as large as that of the South. It had an advanced industrial system and was able by 1862 to manufacture almost all its own war materials. The South had almost no industry at all.

In addition, the North had a much better transportation system than did the South, and in particular more and better railroads: twice as much trackage and a much better integrated system of lines. During the war, the already inferior Confederate railroad system steadily deteriorated and by the beginning of 1864 had almost collapsed.

But the South had advantages as well. The Southern armies were, for the most part, fighting a defensive war on familiar land with local support. The Northern armies, on the other hand, were fighting mostly within the South amid hostile local populations; they had to maintain long lines of communication and had access only to the South's own inadequate transportation system. The commitment of the white population of the South to the war was, with limited exceptions, clear and firm. In the North, opinion about the war was more divided, and support for it remained shaky until very near the end. A major Southern victory at any one of several crucial moments might have proved decisive by breaking the North's will to continue the struggle. Finally, the dependence of the English and French textile industries on American cotton inclined many leaders in those countries to favor the Confederacy; and Southerners hoped, with some reason, that one or both might intervene on their behalf.

THE MOBILIZATION OF THE NORTH

In the North, the war produced considerable discord, frustration, and suffering. But it also produced prosperity and economic growth by giving a major stimulus to both industry and agriculture. With the South now gone from Congress, the Republican Party had almost unchallenged supremacy. During the war, it enacted an aggressively nationalistic program to promote economic development.

Economic Nationalism

Two acts of 1862 assisted the rapid development of the West. The Homestead Act permitted any citizen or prospective citizen to purchase 160 acres of public land for a small fee after living on it for five years. The Morrill Act transferred substantial public acreage to the state governments, which could now sell the land and use the proceeds to finance public education. This act led to the creation of many new state colleges and universities, the so-called land-grant institutions. Congress also passed a series of tariff bills that by the end of the war had raised duties to the highest level in the nation's history—a great boon to domestic industries eager for protection from foreign competition, but a hardship for many farmers and other consumers.

Congress also moved to spur completion of a transcontinental railroad. It created two new federally chartered corporations: the Union Pacific Railroad Company, which was to build westward from Omaha, and the Central Pacific, which was to build eastward from California. The two projects were to meet in the middle and complete the link. The government provided free public lands and generous loans to the companies.

The National Bank Acts of 1863–1864 created a new national banking system. Existing or newly formed banks could join the system if they had enough capital and were willing to invest one-third of it in government securities. In return, they could issue United States Treasury notes as currency. The new system eliminated much (although not all) of the chaos and uncertainty in the nation's currency and created a uniform system of national bank notes.

More difficult than promoting economic growth was financing the war itself. The government tried to do so in three ways: levying taxes, issuing paper currency, and borrowing. Congress levied new taxes on almost all goods and services; and in 1861 the government levied an income

D E B A T I N G   T H E   P A S T

The Causes of the Civil War

BRAHAM LINCOLN, in his 1865 inaugural address, looked back at the beginning of the terrible war that was now nearing its end and said, "All knew [that slavery] was somehow the cause of the war." Few historians dispute that. But disagreement has been sharp over whether slavery was the only, or even the principal cause of the war, and on such other questions as whether or not the war was inevitable.

The debate began even before the war itself. In 1858, Senator William H. Seward of New York took note of the two competing explanations of the sectional tensions that were then inflaming the nation. On one side, he said, stood those who believed the conflicts to be "accidental, unnecessary, the work of interested or fanatical agitators." Opposing them stood those (among them Seward himself) who believed there to be "an irrepressible conflict between opposing and enduring forces." Without realizing it, Seward had identified a division of opinion that would survive among historians for more than a century.

The "irrepressible-conflict" argument dominated historical discussion of the war from the 1860s to the 1920s. War was inevitable, some historians claimed, because there was no room for compromise on the central issue of slavery. Others de-emphasized slavery and pointed to the economic differences between the agrarian South and the industrializing North. Charles and Mary Beard, for example, wrote in 1927 of the "inherent antagonisms" between the interests of planters and those of industrialists.

Each group was seeking to control the federal government to promote its own economic interests. Still others cited social and cultural differences between the two sections as the source of an irrepressible conflict. Slavery, the historian Allan Nevins argued, was only one factor in the cultural divergence that was making residents of the North and South "separate peoples." There were fundamental differences in "assumptions, tastes, and cultural aim" that made it virtually impossible for the two societies to live together in peace.

More recent proponents of irrepressible-conflict arguments similarly emphasize culture and ideology but define the concerns of the North and the South in different terms. Eric Foner, writing in 1970, argued that the moral concerns of abolitionists and the economic concerns of industrialists were less important in explaining Northern hostility to the South than was the broad-based "free-labor" ideology of the region. Northerners opposed slavery because they feared it might spread into their own region and threaten the position of free white laborers, hence their insistence that it not be allowed to expand into the West.

Other historians have argued that the war was not inevitable, beginning with a group of scholars in the 1920s known as the revisionists. James G. Randall and Avery Craven were the two leading proponents of the view that the differences between the North and the South were not so great as to require a war, that only a "blundering generation" of leaders caused the conflict. Michael Holt revived the revisionist argument in a 1978 book, in which he too emphasized the partisan ambitions of politicians who used sectional rivalries to advance their own aims. But Holt also helped introduce another element to the debate. He was, along with Paul Kleppner, Joel Silbey, and William Gienapp, one of the creators of an "ethnocultural" interpretation of the war, which emphasizes that the collapse of the party system—which was central to the coming of the conflict—was a result less of the debate over slavery than of such ethnocultural issues as temperance and nativism. These scholars would not entirely dispute Lincoln's claim that slavery was "somehow the cause of the war." But they do challenge the arguments of Eric Foner and others that the "free-labor ideal" of the North—and the challenge slavery and its possible expansion into the territories posed to that ideal—was the principal reason for the conflict.

tax for the first time, with rates that eventually rose to 10 percent on incomes above $5,000. But taxation raised only a small proportion of the funds necessary for financing the war, and strong popular resistance prevented the government from raising the rates.

At least equally controversial was the printing of paper currency, or "greenbacks." The new currency was backed not by gold or silver but simply by the good faith and credit of the government (much like today's currency). The value of the greenbacks fluctuated according to the fortunes of the Northern armies. Early in 1864, with the war effort bogged down, a greenback dollar was worth only 39 percent of a gold dollar. Even at the close of the war, with confidence high, it was worth only 67 percent of a gold dollar. The government used greenbacks sparingly.

By far the largest source of financing for the war, therefore, was loans. The Treasury persuaded ordinary citizens to buy over $400 million worth of bonds—the first example of mass financing of a war in American history. But public bond purchases constituted only a small part of the government's borrowing, which in the end totaled $2.6 billion, most of it from banks and large financial interests.

Raising the Union Armies

Over 2 million men served in the Union military forces during the Civil War. But at the beginning of 1861, the regular army of the United States consisted of only 16,000 troops, many of them stationed in the West to protect white settlers from Indians. So the Union, like the Confederacy, had to raise its army mostly from scratch. Lincoln called for an increase of 23,000 in the regular army, but the bulk of the fighting, he knew, would have to be done by volunteers in state militias. When Congress convened in July 1861, it authorized enlisting 500,000 volunteers for three-year (as opposed to the customary three-month) terms.

This voluntary system of recruitment produced adequate forces only briefly, during the first flush of enthusiasm for the war. By March 1863, Congress was forced to pass a national draft law. Virtually all young adult males were eligible to be drafted, although a man could escape service by hiring someone to go in his place or by paying the government a fee of $300. Only about 46,000 men were ever actually conscripted, but the draft greatly increased voluntary enlistments.

To many who were accustomed to a remote and inactive national government, conscription was strange and threatening. Opposition to the law was widespread, particularly among laborers, immigrants, and Democrats opposed to the war. Occasionally it erupted into violence. Demonstrators against the draft rioted in New York City for four days in July 1863. Over 100 people died. The rioters lynched several African Americans (whom many opponents of the war blamed for the conflict) and burned down black homes, businesses, and even an orphanage. It was the bloodiest riot in American history. Only the arrival of federal troops halted the violence.

Wartime Leadership and Politics

When Abraham Lincoln arrived in Washington early in 1861, many Republicans considered him a minor politician from the prairie who would be easily controlled by the real leaders of his party. The new president understood his own (and his party's) weaknesses, and he assembled a cabinet representing every faction of the Republican Party and every segment of Northern opinion—men of exceptional prestige, influence, and in some cases arrogance, several of whom believed that they, not Lincoln, should be president. But Lincoln was a man of great self-confidence, and he was not cowed by the distinguished figures around him. He moved boldly to use the war powers of the presidency, blithely ignoring inconvenient parts of the Constitution because, he said, it would be foolish to lose the whole by being afraid to disregard a part.

He sent troops into battle without asking Congress for a declaration of war, arguing that the conflict was a domestic insurrection and that no congressional authorization was necessary. He increased the size of the regular army without receiving legislative authority to do so. He unilaterally proclaimed a naval blockade of the South.

Lincoln's greatest political problem was the widespread popular opposition to the war, mobilized by those in the Democratic Party who were known as Peace Democrats (or, by their enemies, "Copperheads"). Lincoln used extraordinary methods to suppress them. He ordered military arrests of civilian dissenters and suspended the right of habeas corpus (the right of an arrested person to receive a speedy trial). At first, Lincoln used these methods only in sensitive areas such as the border states; but in 1862, he proclaimed that all persons who discouraged enlistments or engaged in disloyal practices were subject to martial law. In all, more than 13,000 persons were arrested and imprisoned for varying periods.

By the time of the presidential election of 1864, the North was in political turmoil. The Republicans had suffered heavy losses in 1862, and in response leaders of the party tried to create a broad coalition of all the groups that supported the war. They called the new organization the Union Party, but it was, in reality, little more than the Republican Party and a small faction of War Democrats. The Union Party nominated Lincoln for another term as president and Andrew Johnson of Tennessee, a War Democrat who had opposed his state's decision to secede, for the vice presidency.

The Democrats nominated George B. McClellan, a celebrated former Union general who had been relieved of his command by Lincoln, and adopted a platform denouncing the war and calling for a truce. McClellan repudiated that demand, but the Democrats were clearly the peace party in the campaign, trying to profit from growing war weariness and from the Union's discouraging military position in the summer of 1864. For a time, Lincoln's prospects for reelection seemed doubtful.

At this crucial moment, however, several Northern military victories, particularly the capture of Atlanta, Georgia, early in September, rejuvenated Northern morale and boosted Republican prospects. Lincoln won reelection comfortably, with 212 electoral votes to McClellan's 21. But Lincoln's lead in the popular vote was a more modest 10 percent.

The Politics of Emancipation

Despite their surface unity in supporting the war and their general agreement on most economic matters, the Republicans disagreed sharply with one another on the issue of slavery. Radicals—led in Congress by such men as Representative Thaddeus Stevens of Pennsylvania and Senators Charles Sumner of Massachusetts and Benjamin Wade of Ohio—wanted to use the war to abolish slavery immediately and completely. Conservatives favored a more cautious policy—in part so as to placate the border slave states that remained, precariously, within the Union. In the beginning, at least, the president seemed to share that caution.

Nevertheless, momentum began to gather behind Emancipation early in the war. In 1861, Congress passed the Confiscation Act, which declared that all slaves used for "insurrectionary" purposes (that is, in support of the Confederate military effort) would be considered freed. Subsequent laws in the spring of 1862 abolished slavery in the District of Columbia and in the western territories and provided for the compensation of owners. In July 1862, Radicals pushed through Congress the second Confiscation Act, which declared free the slaves of persons supporting the insurrection (whether or not the slaves themselves were doing so) and authorized the president to employ African Americans, including freed slaves, as soldiers.

As the war progressed, many in the North seemed slowly to accept emancipation as a central war aim; nothing less, they believed, would justify the enormous sacrifices the struggle had required. As a result, the Radicals gained increasing influence within the Republican Party—a development that did not go unnoticed by the president, who decided to seize the leadership of the rising antislavery sentiment himself.

On September 22, 1862, after the Union victory at the Battle of Antietam, the president announced his intention to use his war powers to issue an executive order freeing all slaves in the Confederacy. And on January 1, 1863, he formally signed the Emancipation Proclamation, which declared forever free the slaves inside the Confederacy. The proclamation did not apply to the border slave states, which had never seceded from the Union; nor did it affect those parts of the Confederacy already under Union control (Tennessee, western Virginia, and southern Louisiana). It applied, in short, only to slaves over which the Union had no control and thus had few immediate results. But the document was of great importance because it clearly and irrevocably established that the war was being fought not only to preserve the Union but also to eliminate slavery. Eventually, as federal armies occupied much of the South, the proclamation became a practical reality and led directly to the freeing of thousands of slaves. About 186,000 of them served in the Union forces.

Even in areas not directly affected by the proclamation, the antislavery impulse gained strength. By the end of the war, two Union slave states (Maryland and Missouri) and three Confederate states occupied by Union forces (Tennessee, Arkansas, and Louisiana) had abolished slavery. In 1865, finally, Congress approved and the states ratified the Thirteenth Amendment, which abolished slavery as an institution in all parts of the United States, not just the areas covered by the Emancipation Proclamation. After more than two centuries, legalized slavery finally ceased to exist in the United States.

African Americans and the Union Cause

About 186,000 emancipated blacks served as soldiers, sailors, and laborers for the Union forces, joining a significant number of free blacks from the North. The services of African Americans to the Union military were significant in many ways, not least because of the substantial obstacles many blacks had to surmount in order to enlist.

In the first months of the war, blacks were largely excluded from the military. A few black regiments eventually took shape in some of the Union-occupied areas of the Confederacy, largely because they were a ready source of manpower in these defeated regions. But once Lincoln issued the Emancipation Proclamation, black enlistment increased rapidly and the Union military began actively to recruit African-American soldiers and sailors in both the North and, where possible, the South.

Some of these men were organized into fighting units, of which the best known was probably the Fifty-fourth Massachusetts infantry which (like most black regiments) had a white commander: Robert Gould Shaw, a member of an aristocratic Boston family. Shaw and more than half his regiment died during a battle near Charleston, South Carolina, in the summer of 1863.

Most black soldiers, however, were assigned menial tasks behind the lines such as digging trenches and transporting water. Even though many fewer blacks than whites died in combat, the African-American mortality rate was actually higher than the rate for white soldiers because so many black soldiers died of disease from working long, arduous hours in unsanitary conditions. Conditions for blacks and whites were unequal in other ways as well. Black soldiers were paid a third less than were white soldiers (until Congress changed the law in mid-1864). Black fighting men captured by the Confederates were, unlike white prisoners, not returned to the North in exchange for Southern soldiers being returned to the South. They were sent back to their masters (if they were escaped slaves) or often executed. In 1864, Confederate soldiers killed over 260 black Union soldiers after capturing them in Tennessee.

AFRICAN-AMERICAN TROOPS Although most of the black soldiers who enlisted in the Union army during the Civil War performed noncombat jobs behind the lines, there were also black combat regiments—members of one of which are pictured here—that fought with great success and valor in critical battles.

The War and Economic Development

The Civil War did not, as some historians used to claim, transform the North from an agrarian to an industrial society. Industrialization was already far advanced when the war began, and in some areas, the war actually retarded growth by diverting labor and resources to military purposes.

On the whole, however, the war sped the economic development of the North. That was in part a result of the political dominance of the Republican Party and its promotion of nationalistic economic legislation. But it was also because the war itself required the expansion of certain sectors of the economy. Coal production increased by nearly 20 percent during the war. Railroad facilities improved—mainly through the adoption of a standard gauge (track width) on new lines. The loss of farm labor to the military forced many farmers to increase the mechanization of agriculture.

The war was a difficult experience for many American workers. Industrial laborers suffered a substantial loss of purchasing power, as prices in the North rose by more than 80 percent during the war while wages rose only about 40 percent. Wages remained low because liberalized immigration laws permitted a flood of new workers to enter the labor market and because the increasing mechanization of production eliminated the jobs of many skilled workers. One result was a substantial increase in union membership in some industries and the creation of several national unions for coal miners, railroad engineers, and others—organizations bitterly opposed and rigorously suppressed by employers.

Women, Nursing, and the War

The war thrust women into new and often unfamiliar roles. They took over positions vacated by men as teachers, salesclerks, office workers, and mill and factory hands. Above all, women entered nursing, a field previously dominated by men. The United States Sanitary Commission, an organization of civilian volunteers led by Dorothea Dix, mobilized large numbers of female nurses to serve in field hospitals. By the end of the war, women were the dominant force in nursing; by the end of the century, nursing had become an almost entirely female profession.

Female nurses encountered considerable resistance from male doctors, many of whom considered women too weak for medical work and many of whom thought it inappropriate for women to be taking care of male strangers. The Sanitary Commission countered such arguments by presenting nursing in domestic terms: as a profession that made use of the same maternal, nurturing roles women played as wives and mothers.

THE U.S. SANITARY COMMISSION Mathew Brady took this photograph of female nurses and Union soldiers standing before an infirmary at Brandy Station, Virginia, near Petersburg, in 1864. The infirmary was run by the U.S. Sanitary Commission, the government-supported nursing corps that became indispensable to the medical care of wounded soldiers during the Civil War.

Some women, especially those who had been committed to feminist causes earlier, came to see the war as an opportunity to win support for their own goals. Elizabeth Cady Stanton and Susan B. Anthony, who together founded the National Woman's Loyal League in 1863, worked simultaneously for the abolition of slavery and the awarding of suffrage to women.

THE MOBILIZATION OF THE SOUTH

Early in February 1861, representatives of the seven states that had seceded from the Union met at Montgomery, Alabama, to create a new Southern nation. When Virginia seceded several months later, the leaders of the Confederacy moved to Richmond—one of the few Southern cities large enough to house a government.

There were, of course, important differences between the new Confederate nation and the nation it had left. But there were also important similarities between the Union and the Confederacy, which became particularly clear as the two sides mobilized for war.

Confederate Government

The Confederate constitution was almost identical to the Constitution of the United States, with several significant exceptions. It explicitly acknowledged the sovereignty of the individual states (although not the right of secession). And it specifically sanctioned slavery and made its abolition (even by one of the states) practically impossible.

The constitutional convention at Montgomery named a provisional president and vice president: Jefferson Davis of Mississippi and Alexander H. Stephens of Georgia. They were later elected by the general public, without opposition, for six-year terms. Davis had been a moderate secessionist before the war. Stephens had argued against secession. The Confederate government, like the Union government, was dominated throughout the war by men of the political center.

Davis was an unsuccessful president. He was a reasonably able administrator, and encountered little interference from the generally tame members of his unstable cabinet. He served, in effect, as his own secretary of war. But he rarely provided genuinely national leadership. He spent too much time on routine items, and unlike Lincoln, he displayed a punctiliousness about legal and constitutional requirements inappropriate to the needs of a new nation at war. One shrewd Confederate official wrote: "All the revolutionary vigor is with the enemy. . . . With us timidity—hair splitting."

There were no formal political parties in the Confederacy, but its congressional and popular politics were badly divided nevertheless. Some white Southerners (and most blacks who were aware of the course of events) opposed secession and war altogether. Most white Southerners supported the war, but as in the North many were openly critical of the government and the military, particularly as the tide of battle turned against the South and the Confederate economy decayed.

States' rights had become such a cult among many white Southerners that they resisted virtually all efforts to exert national authority, even those necessary to win the war. States' rights enthusiasts restricted Davis's ability to impose martial law and suspend habeas corpus. They obstructed conscription. Governors such as Joseph Brown of Georgia and Zebulon M. Vance of North Carolina tried at times to keep their own troops apart from the Confederate forces and insisted on hoarding surplus supplies for their own state militias. But the national government was not impotent. It experimented, successfully for a time, with a "food draft," which permitted soldiers to feed themselves by seizing crops from farms in their path. The government impressed slaves, often over the objections of their owners, to work as laborers on military projects. The Confederacy seized control of the railroads and shipping; it imposed regulations on industry; it limited corporate profits. States' rights sentiment was a significant handicap, but the South nevertheless took dramatic steps in the direction of centralization—becoming in the process increasingly like the region whose institutions it was fighting to escape.

Money and Manpower

Financing the Confederate war effort was a monumental and ultimately impossible task. The Confederate congress tried at first to requisition funds from the individual states; but the states were as reluctant to tax their citizens as the congress was and usually failed to comply. In 1863, therefore, the congress enacted an income tax. But taxation produced only about 1 percent of the government's total income. Borrowing was not much more successful. The Confederate government issued bonds in such vast amounts that the public lost faith in them and stopped buying them, and efforts to borrow money in Europe using cotton as collateral fared no better.

As a result, the Confederacy had to pay for the war through the least stable, most destructive form of financing: paper currency, which it began issuing in 1861. By 1864, the Confederacy had issued the staggering total of $1.5 billion in paper money, more than three times what the Union had produced. The result was a disastrous inflation—a 9,000 percent increase in prices in the course of the war (in contrast to 80 percent in the North)—with devastating effects on Confederate morale.

Like the United States, the Confederacy first raised armies by calling for volunteers. And as in the North, by the end of 1861 voluntary enlistments were declining. In April 1862, therefore, the congress enacted the Conscription Act, which subjected all white males between the ages of eighteen and thirty-five to military service for three years. As in the North, a draftee could avoid service if he furnished a substitute. But since the price of substitutes was high, the provision aroused such opposition from poorer whites that it was repealed in 1863. Even more controversial were other provisions of the draft, especially the exemption of one white man on each plantation with twenty or more slaves.

Even so, conscription worked for a time, in part because enthusiasm for the war was intense and widespread among white men in most of the South. At the end of 1862, about 500,000 soldiers were in the Confederate army. That number did not include the many slave men and women recruited by the military to perform such services as cooking, laundry, and

CONFEDERATE VOLUNTEERS Smiling and apparently confident, young Southern soldiers pose for a photograph in 1861, shortly before the First Battle of Bull Run. The Civil War was one of the first military conflicts extensively chronicled by photographers.

manual labor, hence freeing additional white manpower for fighting. Small numbers of slaves and free blacks enlisted, apparently voluntarily, in the Confederate army, and a few participated in combat.

After 1862, however, conscription began producing fewer men, and by 1864 the Confederate government faced a critical manpower shortage. The nation was suffering from intense war weariness, and many had concluded that defeat was inevitable. Nothing could attract or retain an adequate army any longer. In 1864–1865, there were 100,000 desertions. In a frantic final attempt to raise men, the congress authorized the conscription of 300,000 slaves, but the war ended before the government could attempt this incongruous experiment.

Economic and Social Effects of the War

The war had a devastating effect on the South's economy. It cut off Southern planters and producers from markets in the North, and a Union blockade of Confederate ports made the sale of cotton overseas much more difficult. The war robbed those farms and industries that did not have large slave populations of a male work force. In the North, production of all goods increased during the war; in the South, it declined by more than a third. Above all, the fighting itself—almost all of which occurred inside the Confederacy—wreaked havoc on the Southern landscape, destroying farmland, towns, cities, and railroads.

As the war continued, the shortages, the inflation, and the carnage created increasing instability in Southern society. There were major food riots (some led by women) in cities in Georgia, North Carolina, and Alabama in 1863, as well as a large and violent demonstration in Richmond. Resistance to conscription, food impressment, and taxation increased throughout the Confederacy, as did hoarding and black-market commerce.

The war forced many women (and some men) to question the prevailing assumption of their society that females were not suited for the public sphere, since so many women had to perform untraditional, nondomestic tasks during the conflict. The war also decimated the male population and created a major gender imbalance in the region. After the war, women outnumbered men in most Southern states by significant margins. The result was a large number of unmarried or widowed women who, both during and after the war, had no choice but to find employment.

Even before emancipation, the war had far-reaching effects on the lives of slaves. Confederate leaders were more terrified of slave revolts during the war than they had been in peacetime, and they enforced slave codes with particular severity. Even so, many slaves—especially those near the front—escaped their masters and crossed Union lines.

STRATEGY AND DIPLOMACY

The social and economic circumstances of the North and the South helped shape the outcome of the war. But much rested on the military and diplomatic strategies that the two sides employed.

The Commanders

The most important Union military commander was Abraham Lincoln, whose previous military experience consisted only of brief service in his state militia. Lincoln made many mistakes, but he was on the whole a successful commander in chief because he realized that numbers and resources were on his side and because he knew how to exploit the North's material advantages. He realized, too, that the proper objective of his armies was the destruction of the Confederate armies and not the occupation of Southern territory. It was fortunate for the North that Lincoln had a good grasp of strategy, because many of his generals did not. The problem of finding adequate commanders for the troops in the field plagued him throughout the first three years of the war.

From 1861 to 1864, Lincoln tried time and again to find a chief of staff capable of orchestrating the Union war effort. He turned first to General Winfield Scott, the aging hero of the Mexican War. But Scott was unprepared for the magnitude of the new conflict and soon retired. Lincoln then appointed the young George B. McClellan, who was the commander of the Union forces in the East, the Army of the Potomac; but the proud, arrogant McClellan had a wholly inadequate grasp of strategy and in any case returned to the field in March 1862. For most of the rest of the year, Lincoln had no chief of staff at all. And when he eventually appointed General Henry W. Halleck to the post, he found him an ineffectual strategist who left all substantive decision making to the president or the generals in the field. Not until March 1864 did Lincoln finally find a general he trusted to command the war effort: Ulysses S. Grant, who shared Lincoln's belief in unremitting combat and in making enemy armies and resources, not enemy territory, the target of military efforts.

Lincoln's handling of the war effort faced constant scrutiny from the Committee on the Conduct of the War, a joint investigative committee of the two houses of Congress and the most powerful voice the legislative branch has ever had in formulating war policies. Established in December 1861 and chaired by Senator Benjamin E. Wade of Ohio, it complained constantly of the inadequate ruthlessness of Northern generals, which Radicals on the committee attributed (largely inaccurately) to a secret sympathy among the officers for slavery. The committee's efforts often seriously interfered with the conduct of the war.

Southern military leadership centered on President Davis, who unlike Lincoln was a trained professional soldier but who, also unlike Lincoln, failed ever to create an effective central command system. Early in 1862, Davis named General Robert E. Lee as his principal military adviser. But in fact, Davis had no intention of sharing control of strategy with anyone. After a few months, Lee left Richmond to command forces in the field, and for the next two years Davis planned strategy alone. In February 1864, he named General Braxton Bragg as a military adviser, but Bragg never provided much more than technical advice.

At lower levels of command, men of markedly similar backgrounds controlled the war in both the North and the South. Many of the professional officers on both sides were graduates of the United States Military Academy at West Point and the United States Naval Academy at Annapolis and thus had been trained in similar ways. Amateur officers played an important role in both armies as commanders of volunteer regiments. In both North and South, such men were usually economic or social leaders in their communities who appointed themselves officers and rounded up troops to lead. Sometimes this system produced officers of real ability; more often it did not.

The Role of Sea Power

The Union had an overwhelming advantage in naval power, and it gave its navy two important roles in the war. One was enforcing a blockade of the Southern coast. The other was assisting the Union armies in field operations.

The blockade of the South, which began in the first weeks of the war, kept most oceangoing ships out of Confederate ports, but for a time small blockade runners continued to slip through. Gradually, however, federal forces tightened the blockade by seizing the ports themselves. The last important port in Confederate hands—Wilmington, North Carolina—fell to the Union early in 1865.

The Confederates made a bold attempt to break the blockade with an ironclad warship, constructed by plating with iron a former United States frigate, the *Merrimac*, which the Union navy had scuttled in Norfolk harbor when Virginia seceded. On March 8, 1862, the refitted *Merrimac*, renamed the *Virginia*, left Norfolk to attack a blockading squadron of wooden ships at nearby Hampton Roads. It destroyed two of the ships and scattered the rest. But the Union government had already built ironclads of its own. And one of them, the *Monitor*, arrived off the coast of Virginia only a few hours after the *Virginia's* dramatic foray. The next day, it met the *Virginia* in the first battle ever between ironclad ships. Neither vessel was able to sink the other, but the *Monitor* put an end to the Virginia's raids and preserved the blockade.

The Union navy was particularly important in the western theater of the war—the vast region between the Appalachian Mountains and the Mississippi River—where the major rivers were navigable by large vessels. The navy transported supplies and troops and joined in attacking Confederate strong points. The South had no significant navy of its own and could defend against the Union gunboats only with ineffective fixed land fortifications.

Europe and the Disunited States

Judah P. Benjamin, the Confederate secretary of state for most of the war, was an intelligent but undynamic man who attended mostly to routine administrative tasks. William Seward, his counterpart in Washington, gradually became one of the outstanding American secretaries of state. He had invaluable assistance from Charles Francis Adams, the American minister to London, who had inherited the considerable diplomatic talents of his father, John Quincy Adams, and his grandfather, John Adams. The gap between the diplomatic skills of the Union and the Confederacy proved to be a decisive factor in the war.

At the beginning of the conflict, the sympathies of the ruling classes of England and France, the two nations whose support was most crucial to both sides, lay largely with the Confederacy. That was partly because the two nations imported much Southern cotton; but it was also because they were eager to weaken the United States, an increasingly powerful rival to them in world commerce. But France was unwilling to take sides in the conflict unless England did so first. And in England, the government was reluctant to act because there was powerful popular support for the Union—particularly from the large and influential English antislavery movement. After Lincoln issued the Emancipation Proclamation, antislavery groups worked particularly avidly for the Union. Southern leaders hoped to counter the strength of the British antislavery forces by arguing that access to Southern cotton was vital to the English and French textile industries, an approach known as "King Cotton diplomacy." But English manufacturers had a surplus of both raw cotton and finished goods on hand in 1861 and could withstand a temporary loss of access to American cotton. Later, as the supply of cotton began to diminish, both England and France managed to keep at least some of their mills open by importing cotton from Egypt, India, and other sources. Equally important, even the 500,000 English textile workers thrown out of jobs as a result of mill closings continued to support the North. In the end, therefore, no European nation offered diplomatic recognition to the Confederacy or intervened in the war. No nation wanted to antagonize the United States unless the Confederacy seemed likely to win, and the South never came close enough to victory to convince its potential allies to support it.

Even so, there was considerable tension, and on occasion near hostilities, between the United States and Britain. The Union government was angry when Great Britain, France, and other nations declared themselves neutral early in the war, thus implying that the two sides to the conflict had equal stature. Washington was insisting that the conflict was simply a domestic insurrection, not a war between two legitimate governments.

A more serious crisis, the so-called *Trent* affair, began in late 1861. Two Confederate diplomats, James M. Mason and John Slidell, had slipped through the then-ineffective Union blockade to Havana, Cuba, where they boarded an English steamer, the *Trent*, for England. Waiting in Cuban waters was the American frigate *San Jacinto*, commanded by the impetuous Charles Wilkes. Acting without authorization, Wilkes stopped the British vessel, arrested the diplomats, and carried them in triumph to Boston. The British government demanded the release of the prisoners, reparations, and an apology. Lincoln and Seward, aware that Wilkes had violated maritime law and unwilling to risk war with England, eventually released the diplomats with an indirect apology.

A second diplomatic crisis produced problems that lasted for years. Unable to construct large ships itself, the Confederacy bought six ships, known as commerce destroyers, from British shipyards. The best known of them were the *Alabama*, the *Florida*, and the *Shenandoah*. The United States protested that this sale of military equipment to a belligerent violated the laws of neutrality, and the protests became the basis, after the war, of a prolonged battle over damage claims (known as the *Alabama* claims) by the United States against Great Britain.

CAMPAIGNS AND BATTLES

In the absence of direct intervention by the European powers, the two contestants in North America were left to resolve the conflict between themselves. They did so in four long years of bloody combat that produced more carnage than any other war in American history, before or since. More than 618,000 Americans died in the course of the Civil War, far more than the 115,000 who perished in World War I or the 318,000 who died in World War II—more, indeed, than died in all other American wars prior to Vietnam combined. There were nearly 2,000 deaths for every 100,000 of population during the Civil War. In World War I, the comparable figure was only 109; in World War II, 241.

The Technology of War

Much of what happened on the battlefield in the Civil War was a result of new technologies that transformed the nature of combat. The Civil War has often been called the first "modern" war and the first "total" war. Such descriptions are imprecise and debatable. But it is certainly true that the great conflict between the North and the South was unlike any war fought before it. It is also clearly true that it suggested a great deal about what warfare would be like in the future.

The most obvious change in the character of warfare in the 1860s was the nature of the armaments that both sides used in battle. Among the most important was the introduction of repeating weapons. Samuel Colt had patented a repeating pistol (the revolver) in 1835, but more important for military purposes was the repeating rifle, introduced in 1860 by Oliver Winchester. Two years later, Richard Gatling perfected the revolving machine gun (although it was little used during the Civil War). Also important were greatly improved cannons and artillery, a result of advances in iron and steel technology of the previous decades.

These devastating advances in the effectiveness of arms and artillery changed the way soldiers in the field fought. It was now impossibly deadly to fight battles as they had been fought for centuries, with lines of infantry soldiers standing erect in the field firing volleys at their opponents until one side withdrew. Fighting in that way now produced almost inconceivable slaughter, and soldiers quickly learned that the proper position for combat was staying low to the ground and behind cover. For the first time in the history of organized warfare, therefore, infantry did not fight in formation, and the battlefield became a more chaotic place. Gradually, the deadliness of the new weapons encouraged armies on both sides to spend a great deal of time building elaborate fortifications and trenches to protect themselves from enemy fire. The sieges of Vicksburg and Petersburg, the defense of Richmond, and many other military events all produced the construction of vast fortifications around the cities and around the attacking armies. (They became the predecessors to the great network of trenches that became so central a part of World War I.)

Other weapons technologies were less central to the fighting of the war, but important nevertheless. There was sporadic use of the relatively new technology of hot-air balloons, employed intermittently to provide a view of enemy formations in the field. (During one battle, a Union balloonist took a telegraph line aloft with him in his balloon and tapped out messages about troop movements to the commanders below.) Iron-clad ships such as the *Merrimac* (or *Virginia)* and the *Monitor* suggested the dramatic changes that would soon overtake naval warfare, but did not have a great impact on the fighting of the Civil War. Torpedoes and submarine technology also made a fleeting appearance in the 1860s, showing the way to future innovations in warfare but not playing a major role in the Civil War.

Critical to the conduct of the war, however, were two other rela-tively new technologies: the railroad and the telegraph. The railroad was particularly important in a war in which millions of soldiers were being mobilized and transferred to the front, and in which a single field army could number as many as 250,000 men. Transporting such enor-mous numbers of soldiers, and the supplies necessary to sustain them, by land or by horse and wagon would have been almost impossible. Railroads made it possible for these large armies to be assembled and moved from place to place. However, they also limited the mobility of the armies. Railroad lines and stations are, of course, in fixed positions. Commanders, therefore, were forced to organize their campaigns at least in part around the location of the railroads rather than on the basis of the best topography or most direct land route to a destination. The dependence on the rails—and the resulting necessity of concentrating huge numbers of men in a few places—also encouraged commanders to prefer great battles with large armies rather than smaller engagements with fewer troops.

The impact of the telegraph on the war was limited both by the scarcity of qualified telegraph operators and by the difficulty of bringing telegraph wires into the fields where battles were being fought. Things improved somewhat after the new U.S. Military Telegraph Corps, headed by Thomas Scott and Andrew Carnegie, trained and employed over 1,200 operators. Gradually, too, both the Union and Confederate armies learned to string telegraph wires along the routes of their troops (who, once they were off the railroads, generally moved slowly, on foot or horseback), so that field commanders were able to stay in close touch with one another during battles. Both the North and the South sent spies behind enemy lines who tried to tap the telegraph lines of their op-ponents and send important information back about troop movements and formations.

The Opening Clashes, 1861

The Union and the Confederacy fought their first major battle of the war in northern Virginia. A Union army of over 30,000 men under the command of General Irvin McDowell was stationed just outside Washington. About thirty miles away, at Manassas, was a slightly smaller Confederate army under P. G. T. Beauregard. If the Northern army could destroy the Southern one, Union leaders believed, the war might end at once. In mid-July, McDowell marched his inexperienced troops toward Manassas. Beauregard moved his troops behind Bull Run, a small stream north of Manassas, and called for reinforcements, which reached him the day before the battle. The two armies were now approximately the same size.

On July 21, in the First Battle of Bull Run, or First Battle of Manassas, McDowell almost succeeded in dispersing the Confederate forces. But the Southerners managed to stop a last strong Union assault and then began a savage counterattack. The Union troops, exhausted after hours of hot, hard fighting, suddenly panicked. They broke ranks and retreated chaotically. McDowell was unable to reorganize them, and he had to order a retreat to Washington—a disorderly withdrawal complicated by the presence along the route of many civilians, who had ridden down from the capital, picnic baskets in hand, to watch the battle from nearby hills. The Confederates, as disorganized by victory as the Union forces were by defeat, did not pursue. The battle was a severe blow to Union morale and to the president's confidence in his officers.

Elsewhere, Union forces achieved some small but significant victories in 1861. Nathaniel Lyon, who commanded a small regular army force in St. Louis, moved his troops into southern Missouri to face secessionists trying to lead the state out of the Union. On August 10, at the Battle of Wilson's Creek, he was defeated and killed—but not before he had seriously weakened the striking power of the Confederates. Union forces were subsequently able to hold most of the state.

Meanwhile, a Union force under George B. McClellan moved east from Ohio into western Virginia. By the end of 1861, it had "liberated" the antisecession mountain people of the region, who created their own state government loyal to the Union; the state was admitted to the Union as West Virginia in 1863.

The Western Theater, 1862

After the battle at Bull Run, military operations in the East settled into a long and frustrating stalemate. The first decisive operations in 1862 occurred, therefore, in the western theater. Here the Union forces were trying to seize control of the southern part of the Mississippi River; this would divide the Confederacy and give the North easy transportation into the heart of the South. Northern soldiers advanced on the southern Mississippi from both the north and south, moving down the river from Kentucky and up from the Gulf of Mexico toward New Orleans.

In April, a Union squadron of ironclads and wooden vessels commanded by David G. Farragut gathered in the Gulf of Mexico, then smashed past weak Confederate forts near the mouth of the Mississippi, and from there sailed up to New Orleans. The city was virtually defenseless because the Confederate high command had expected the attack to come from the north. The surrender of New Orleans on April 25, 1862, was the first major Union victory and an important turning point in the war. From then on, the mouth of the Mississippi was closed to Confederate trade, and the South's largest city and most important banking center was in Union hands.

Farther north in the western theater, Confederate troops under the command of Albert Sidney Johnston were stretched out in a long defensive line around two forts in Tennessee, Fort Henry and Fort Donelson, on the Tennessee and Cumberland Rivers respectively. Early in 1862, Ulysses S. Grant attacked Fort Henry, whose defenders, awed by the ironclad riverboats accompanying the Union army, surrendered with almost no resistance on February 6. Grant then moved both his naval and ground forces to Fort Donelson, where the Confederates put up a stronger fight but finally, on February 16, had to surrender. Grant thus gained control of river communications and forced Confederate troops out of Kentucky and half of Tennessee.

With about 40,000 men, Grant now advanced south along the Tennessee River to seize control of vital Confederate railroad lines. At Shiloh, Tennessee, he met a force almost equal to his own, commanded by Albert Sidney Johnston and P. G. T. Beauregard. The result was the Battle of Shiloh, April 6–7. In the first day's fighting (during which Johnston was killed), the Southerners drove Grant back to the river. But the next day, reinforced by 25,000 fresh troops, Grant recovered the lost ground and forced Beauregard to withdraw. After the narrow Union victory at Shiloh, Northern forces occupied Corinth, Mississippi, the hub of several important railroads, and took control of the Mississippi River as far south as Memphis.

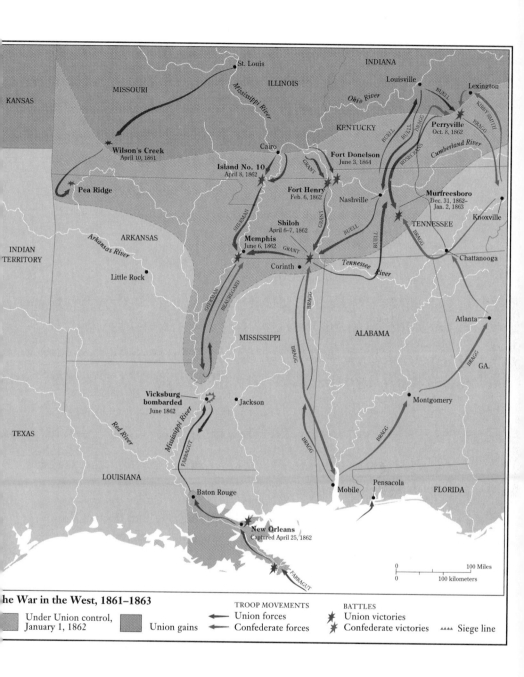

KANSAS

MISSOURI

St. Louis

ILLINOIS

INDIANA

Louisville

Lexington

Mississippi River

Ohio River

KENTUCKY

Perryville
Oct. 8, 1862

Cumberland River

Wilson's Creek
April 10, 1861

Cairo

Fort Donelson
June 3, 1864

Island No. 10
April 8, 1862

Pea Ridge

Fort Henry
Feb. 6, 1862

Nashville

Murfreesboro
Dec. 31, 1862–
Jan. 2, 1863

Knoxville

Arkansas River

ARKANSAS

Shiloh
April 6–7, 1862

Memphis
June 6, 1862

Corinth

TENNESSEE

Chattanooga

Little Rock

Tennessee River

INDIAN
TERRITORY

Atlanta

MISSISSIPPI

ALABAMA

GA.

Vicksburg
bombarded
June 1862

Jackson

Montgomery

TEXAS

Red River

Mississippi River

LOUISIANA

Baton Rouge

Mobile

Pensacola

FLORIDA

New Orleans
Captured April 25, 1862

| 0 | | 100 Miles |
| 0 | | 100 kilometers |

he War in the West, 1861–1863

Under Union control,
January 1, 1862

Union gains

TROOP MOVEMENTS

← Union forces

← Confederate forces

BATTLES

✳ Union victories

✳ Confederate victories

▲▲▲ Siege line

427

Braxton Bragg, now in command of the Confederate army in the West, gathered his forces at Chattanooga, in eastern Tennessee, where he faced a Union army (commanded first by Don Carlos Buell and then by William S. Rosecrans) trying to capture Chattanooga. The two armies maneuvered for advantage inconclusively in northern Tennessee and southern Kentucky for several months until they finally met, on December 31–January 2, in the Battle of Murfreesboro, or Stone's River. Bragg was forced to withdraw to the South in defeat.

By the end of 1862, therefore, Union forces had made considerable progress in the West. But the major conflict remained in the East, and the North was having much less success there.

The Virginia Front, 1862

George B. McClellan, commander of the Army of the Potomac and the most controversial general of the war, was a superb trainer of men; but he often seemed reluctant to commit his troops to battle. During the winter of 1861–1862, McClellan concentrated on training his army of 150,000 men near Washington. Finally, he designed a spring campaign to capture the Confederate capital at Richmond. But instead of heading overland directly toward Richmond, McClellan chose a complicated route that he thought would circumvent the Confederate defenses. The navy would carry his troops down the Potomac to a peninsula east of Richmond, between the York and James Rivers; the army would approach the city from there. The combined operations became known as the Peninsular campaign.

McClellan set off with 100,000 men, reluctantly leaving 30,000 members of his army behind, under General Irvin McDowell, to protect Washington. McClellan eventually persuaded Lincoln to send him the additional men. But before the president could do so, a Confederate army under Thomas J. ("Stonewall") Jackson staged a rapid march north through the Shenandoah Valley, as if preparing to cross the Potomac and attack Washington. Lincoln postponed sending reinforecments to McClellan, retaining McDowell's corps to head off Jackson. In the Valley campaign of May 4–June 9, 1862, Jackson defeated two separate Union forces and slipped away before McDowell could catch him.

Meanwhile, McClellan was battling Confederate troops under Joseph E. Johnston outside Richmond in the two-day Battle of Fair Oaks, or Seven Pines (May 31–June 1), and holding his ground. Johnston, badly wounded, was replaced by Robert E. Lee, who then recalled Stonewall Jackson from the Shenandoah Valley. With a combined force of 85,000 to

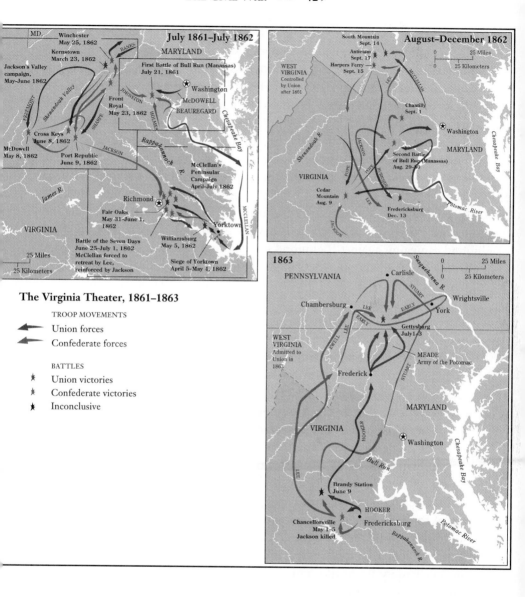

The Virginia Theater, 1861–1863

TROOP MOVEMENTS

Union forces

Confederate forces

BATTLES

* Union victories

* Confederate victories

* Inconclusive

face McClellan's 100,000, Lee launched a new offensive, known as the Battle of the Seven Days (June 25–July 1), in an effort to cut McClellan off from his base on the York River. But McClellan fought his way across the peninsula and set up a new base on the James. There, with naval support, the Army of the Potomac was safe.

McClellan was now only twenty-five miles from Richmond and in a good position to renew the campaign. But despite continuing pressure from Lincoln, he did not advance. Instead of replacing McClellan with a more aggressive commander, as many were urging him to do, the president finally ordered the army to move back to northern Virginia and join a smaller force under John Pope. The president hoped to begin a new offensive against Richmond on the direct overland route that he himself had always preferred. As the Army of the Potomac left the peninsula by water, Lee moved north with the Army of Northern Virginia to strike Pope before McClellan could join him. Pope was as rash as McClellan was cautious, and he attacked the approaching Confederates without waiting for the arrival of all of McClellan's troops. In the Second Battle of Bull Run, or Manassas (August 29–30), Lee threw back the assault and routed Pope's army, which fled to Washington. With hopes for an overland campaign against Richmond now in disarray, Lincoln removed Pope from command and put McClellan back in charge of all the federal forces in the region.

Lee soon went on the offensive again, heading north through western Maryland, and McClellan moved out to meet him. McClellan had the good luck to get a copy of Lee's orders, which revealed that a part of the Confederate army, under Stonewall Jackson, had separated from the rest to attack Harpers Ferry. But instead of attacking quickly before the Confederates could recombine, McClellan stalled and gave Lee time to pull most of his forces together behind Antietam Creek, near the town of Sharpsburg. There, on September 17, in the bloodiest engagement of the war, McClellan's 87,000-man army repeatedly attacked Lee's force of 50,000, with staggering casualties on both sides. In all, 6,000 men were killed, 17,000 wounded. Late in the day, just as the Confederate line seemed ready to break, the last of Jackson's troops arrived from Harpers Ferry to reinforce it. McClellan might have broken through with one more assault. Instead, he allowed Lee to retreat into Virginia. Technically, Antietam was a Union victory; but in reality, McClellan had squandered an opportunity to destroy much of the Confederate army. In November, Lincoln finally removed McClellan from command for good.

McClellan's replacement, Ambrose E. Burnside, was a short-lived mediocrity. He tried to move toward Richmond by crossing the Rappahannock River at Fredericksburg, the strongest defensive point on the river. There, on December 13, he launched a series of attacks against Lee, all of them bloody, all of them hopeless. After losing a large part of his army, he withdrew to the north bank of the Rappahannock. He was relieved at his own request. The year 1862 ended, therefore, with a series of frustrations for the Union.

SKIRMISH AT ANTIETAM The American public followed the course of the Civil War through newspaper reports and, at times, through published drawings of the battlefields by traveling artists who sketched important events for publication. Photographers chronicled the war as well. But cameras in the 1860s could not easily capture action scenes, and very few newspapers or magazines were technologically equipped to publish photographs. So drawings such as this one by A. R. Waud—of a Brooklyn, New York, regiment fighting Southern calavry at the battle of Antietam—were much in demand.

1863: Year of Decision

At the beginning of 1863, General Joseph Hooker was commanding the still-formidable Army of the Potomac, whose 120,000 troops remained north of the Rappahannock, opposite Fredericksburg. Taking part of his army, Hooker crossed the river above Fredericksburg and moved toward the town and Lee's army. But at the last minute, he drew back to a defensive position in a desolate area of brush and scrub trees known as the Wilderness. Lee had only half as many men as Hooker had, but he boldly divided his forces for a dual assault on the Union army. In the Battle of Chancellorsville, May 1–5, Stonewall Jackson attacked the Union right and Lee himself charged the front. Hooker barely managed to escape with his army. Lee had frustrated Union objectives, but he had not destroyed the Union army. And his ablest officer, Jackson, was fatally wounded in the course of the battle.

While the Union forces were suffering repeated frustrations in the East, they were winning some important victories in the West. In the spring of 1863, Ulysses S. Grant was driving at Vicksburg, Mississippi, one of the Confederacy's two remaining strongholds on the southern Mississippi River. Vicksburg was well protected on land and had good artillery coverage of the river itself. But in May, Grant boldly moved men and supplies—over land and by water—to an area south of the city, where the terrain was reasonably good. He then attacked Vicksburg from the rear. Six weeks later, on July 4, Vicksburg—whose residents were by then literally starving as a result of the prolonged siege—surrendered. At almost the same time, the other Confederate strong point on the river, Port Hudson, Louisiana, also surrendered to a Union force that had moved north from New Orleans. The Union had achieved one of its basic military aims: control of the whole length of the Mississippi. The Confederacy was split in two, with Louisiana, Arkansas, and Texas cut off from the other seceded states. The victories on the Mississippi were one of the great turning points of the war.

During an early stage of the siege of Vicksburg, Lee proposed an invasion of Pennsylvania, which would, he argued, divert Union troops north and remove the pressure on the lower Mississippi. Further, he argued, if he could win a major victory on Northern soil, England and France might come to the Confederacy's aid. The war-weary North might even quit the war before Vicksburg fell.

In June 1863, Lee moved up the Shenandoah Valley into Maryland and then entered Pennsylvania. The Union Army of the Potomac, commanded first by Hooker and then (after June 28) by George C. Meade, moved north, too, paralleling the Confederates' movement and staying between Lee and Washington. The two armies finally encountered one another at the small town of Gettysburg, Pennsylvania. There, on July 1–3, 1863, they fought the most celebrated battle of the war.

Meade's army established a strong, well-protected position on the hills south of the town. The confident and combative Lee attacked, even though his army of 75,000 was outnumbered by Meade's 90,000. His first assault on the Union forces on Cemetery Ridge failed. A day later, he ordered a second, larger effort. In what is remembered as Pickett's Charge, a force of 15,000 Confederate soldiers advanced for almost a mile across open country while being swept by Union fire. Only about 5,000 made it up the ridge, and this remnant finally had to surrender or retreat. By now, Lee had lost nearly a third of his army. On July 4, the same day as the surrender of Vicksburg, he withdrew from Gettysburg. The retreat was another major turning point in the war. Never again were the weakened Confederate forces able seriously to threaten Northern territory.

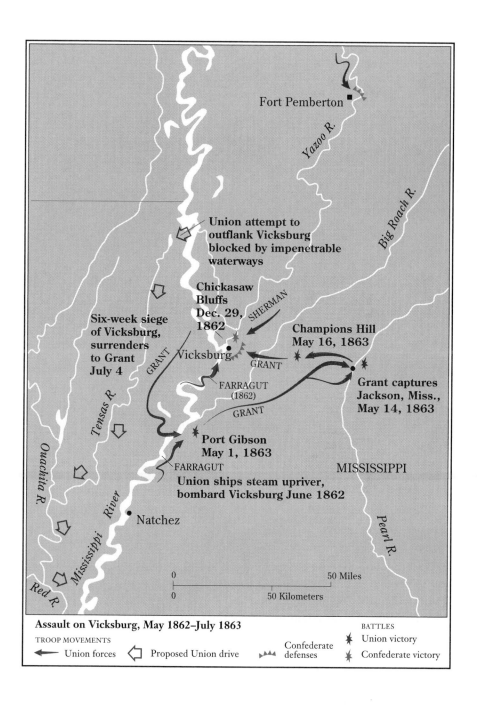

Fort Pemberton

Yazoo R.

Big Roach R.

Union attempt to outflank Vicksburg blocked by impenetrable waterways

Chickasaw Bluffs Dec. 29, 1862

SHERMAN

Champions Hill May 16, 1863

Six-week siege of Vicksburg, surrenders to Grant July 4

GRANT

Vicksburg

GRANT

Grant captures Jackson, Miss., May 14, 1863

FARRAGUT (1862)

Tensas R.

GRANT

Ouachita R.

Port Gibson May 1, 1863

FARRAGUT

Union ships steam upriver, bombard Vicksburg June 1862

MISSISSIPPI

Mississippi River

Natchez

Pearl R.

| 0 | | 50 Miles |
| 0 | | 50 Kilometers |

Red R.

Assault on Vicksburg, May 1862–July 1863

TROOP MOVEMENTS

← Union forces   ◁ Proposed Union drive   ▸▴▴ Confederate defenses

BATTLES

✳ Union victory

✸ Confederate victory

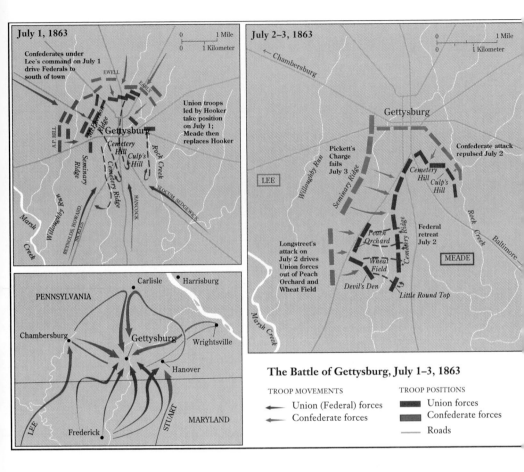

The Battle of Gettysburg, July 1–3, 1863

Before the end of the year, there was another important turning point, this one in Tennessee. After occupying Chattanooga on September 9, Union forces under William Rosecrans began an unwise pursuit of Bragg's retreating Confederate forces. The two armies engaged in western Georgia, in the Battle of Chickamauga (September 19–20), one of the few battles in which the Confederates enjoyed a numerical superiority (70,000 to 56,000). Union forces could not break the Confederate lines and retreated back to Chattanooga.

Bragg now began a siege of Chattanooga itself, seizing the heights nearby and cutting off fresh supplies to the Union forces. Grant came to the rescue. In the Battle of Chattanooga (November 23–25), the reinforced Union army drove the Confederates back into Georgia. Northern troops then occupied most of eastern Tennessee. Union forces had now achieved a second important objective: control of the Tennessee River. Four of the eleven Confederate states were now effectively cut off from the rest of the Southern nation.

ULYSSES S. GRANT One observer said of Grant (photographed here during the Wilderness campaign of 1864): "He habitually wears an expression as if he had determined to drive his head through a brick wall, and was about to do it." It was an apt metaphor for Grant's military philosophy, which relied on constant, unrelenting assault.

The Last Stage, 1864–1865

By the beginning of 1864, Ulysses S. Grant had become general in chief of all the Union armies. Grant was not a subtle, strategic or tactical general; he simply believed in using the North's great advantage in troops and material resources to overwhelm the South. He was not afraid to absorb massive casualties as long as he was inflicting similar or greater casualties on his opponents.

Grant planned two great offensives for 1864. In Virginia, the Army of the Potomac would advance toward Richmond and force Lee into a decisive battle. In Georgia, the western army, under William T. Sherman, would advance east toward Atlanta and destroy the remaining Confederate force, now under the command of Joseph E. Johnston.

The northern campaign began when the Army of the Potomac, 115,000 strong, plunged into the rough, wooded Wilderness area of northwestern Virginia in pursuit of Lee's 75,000-man army. After avoiding an engagement for several weeks, Lee turned Grant back in the Battle of the Wilderness (May 5–7), but without stopping to rest or reorganize, Grant resumed his march toward Richmond and met Lee again in the bloody, five-day Battle of Spotsylvania Court House, in which 12,000 Union troops and a large, but unknown, number of Confederates fell. Grant kept moving, but victory continued to elude him. Lee kept his army between Grant and the Confederate capital and on June 1–3 repulsed the Union forces again, just northeast of Richmond, at Cold Harbor. The month-long Wilderness campaign had cost Grant 55,000 men (killed, wounded, or captured) and had cost Lee 31,000. Richmond still had not fallen.

Grant now changed his strategy. He moved his army east of Richmond, bypassing the capital altogether, and headed south toward the railroad center at Petersburg. If he could seize Petersburg, he could cut off the capital's communications with the rest of the Confederacy. But Petersburg had strong defenses; and once Lee came to the city's relief, the assault became a prolonged siege, which lasted nine months.

In Georgia, meanwhile, Sherman was facing less ferocious resistance. With 90,000 men, he confronted Confederate forces of 60,000 under Johnston, who was unwilling to risk a direct engagement. As Sherman advanced, Johnston tried to delay him by maneuvering. The two armies fought only one real battle—Kennesaw Mountain, northwest of Atlanta, on June 27— where Johnston scored an impressive victory. Even so, he was unable to stop the Union advance toward Atlanta. Sherman took the city on September 2 and burned it. News of the victory electrified the North and helped unite the previously divided Republican Party behind President Lincoln.

Hood now tried unsuccessfully to draw Sherman out of Atlanta by moving back up through Tennessee and threatening an invasion of the North. Sherman sent Union troops to reinforce Nashville. In the Battle of Nashville on December 15–16, 1864, Northern forces practically destroyed what was left of Hood's army.

Meanwhile, Sherman had left Atlanta to begin his soon-to-be-famous "March to the Sea." Living off the land, destroying supplies it could not use, his army cut a sixty-mile-wide swath of desolation across Georgia. "War is all hell," Sherman had once said. By that he meant not that war is terrible, and to be avoided, but that it should be made as horrible and costly as possible for the opponent. He sought not only to deprive the Confederate army of war materials and railroad communications but also to break the will of the Southern people by burning towns and plantations along his route. By December 20, he had reached Savannah, which surrendered two days later. Early in 1865, Sherman continued his destructive march, moving northward through South Carolina. He was virtually unopposed until he was well inside North Carolina, where a small force under Johnston could do no more than cause a brief delay.

In April 1865, Grant's Army of the Potomac—still engaged in the prolonged siege at Petersburg—finally captured a vital railroad junction south-

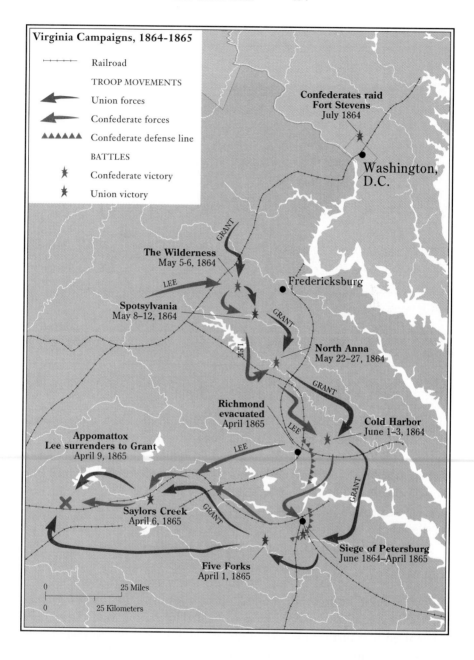

Virginia Campaigns, 1864–1865

┼┼┼┼┼	Railroad

TROOP MOVEMENTS

←	Union forces
←	Confederate forces
▲▲▲▲▲▲	Confederate defense line

BATTLES

✶	Confederate victory
✶	Union victory

**Confederates raid
Fort Stevens**
July 1864

**Washington,
D.C.**

GRANT

The Wilderness
May 5–6, 1864

LEE

Fredericksburg

Spotsylvania
May 8–12, 1864

GRANT

LEE

North Anna
May 22–27, 1864

GRANT

**Richmond
evacuated**
April 1865

LEE

Cold Harbor
June 1–3, 1864

**Appomattox
Lee surrenders to Grant**
April 9, 1865

LEE

Saylors Creek
April 6, 1865

GRANT

GRANT

Five Forks
April 1, 1865

Siege of Petersburg
June 1864–April 1865

0 _____ 25 Miles

0 _____ 25 Kilometers

west of the town. Without rail access to the South, cut off from other Confederate forces, plagued by heavy casualties and massive desertions, Lee informed the Confederate government that he could no longer defend Richmond. Within hours, Jefferson Davis, his cabinet, and as much of the white population as could find transportation fled along with Lee's soldiers. That

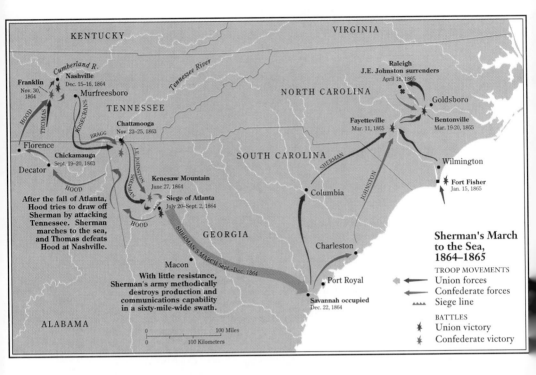

Sherman's March to the Sea, 1864–1865

TROOP MOVEMENTS
Union forces
Confederate forces
Siege line

BATTLES
Union victory
Confederate victory

night, mobs roamed the city, setting devastating fires. And the next morning, Northern forces (led by an African-American infantry brigade) entered the Confederate capital. With them was Abraham Lincoln, who walked through the streets of the burned-out city surrounded by black men and women cheering him as the "Messiah" and "Father Abraham." In one particularly stirring moment, the president turned to a former slave kneeling on the street before him and said: "Don't kneel to me. . . . You must kneel to God only, and thank Him for the liberty you will enjoy hereafter."

With the remnant of his army, now about 25,000 men, Lee began moving west in the forlorn hope of finding a way around the Union forces so that he could move south and link up with Johnston in North Carolina. But the Union army pursued him and blocked his escape route. Lee finally recognized that further bloodshed was futile. He arranged to meet Grant at a private home in the small town of Appomattox Courthouse, Virginia, where on April 9 he surrendered what was left of his forces. Nine days later, near Durham, North Carolina, Johnston surrendered to Sherman.

The long war was now effectively over. Jefferson Davis was finally captured in Georgia. A few Southern diehards continued to fight, but even their resistance collapsed before long. And well before the last shot was fired, the difficult process of reuniting the shattered nation had begun.

CONCLUSION

The American Civil War began with high hopes and high ideals on both sides. In the North and the South alike, thousands of men enthusiastically enlisted in local regiments and went off to war. Four years later, over 600,000 of them were dead and many more maimed and traumatized for life. A fight for "principles" and "ideals"—a fight few people had thought would last more than a few months—had become one of the longest wars, and by far the bloodiest war, in American history, before or since.

During the first two years of fighting, the Confederate forces seemed to have all the advantages. They were fighting on their own soil. Their troops seemed more committed to the cause than those of the North. Their commanders were exceptionally talented, while Union forces were, for a time, erratically led. Gradually, however, the Union's advantages began to assert themselves. The North had a stabler political system led by one of the greatest leaders in the nation's history (as opposed to the Confederacy's untested government led by a relatively weak president). It had a much larger population, a far more developed industrial economy, superior financial institutions, and a better railroad system. By the middle of 1863, the tide of the war had shifted; over the next two years, Union forces gradually wore down the Confederate armies before finally triumphing in 1865.

The war strengthened the North's economy, giving a spur to industry and railroad development. It greatly weakened the South's, by destroying millions of dollars of property and depleting the region's young male population. Southerners had gone to war in part because of their fears of growing northern dominance. The war itself, ironically, confirmed and strengthened that dominance. There was no doubt by 1865 that the future of the United States lay in the growth of industry and commerce, which would occur for many years primarily outside the South.

But most of all, the Civil War was a victory for the millions of African-American slaves, over whose plight the conflict had largely begun in the first place. The war produced Abraham Lincoln's epochal Emancipation Proclamation and, later, the Thirteenth Amendment to the Constitution, which abolished slavery altogether. It also encouraged hundreds of thousands of slaves literally to free themselves, to desert their masters and seek refuge behind Union lines—at times to fight in the Union armies. The future of the freed slaves was not to be an easy one, but three and a half million people who had once lived in bondage emerged from the war as free men and women.

FOR FURTHER REFERENCE

Suggested Readings

James McPherson, *Battle Cry of Freedom* (1988) is the standard text on the Civil War. Shelby Foote, *The Civil War: A Narrative*, 3 vols. (1958–1974) is an elegant and powerful military history of the war. Allan Nevins, *The War for the Union*, 4 vols. (1959–1971) and Bruce Catton, *This Hallowed Ground* (1956) are among many other powerful and popular general histories of the Civil War. David Donald, *Lincoln* (1995) is the best modern biography of Abraham Lincoln. James M. McPherson, *Abraham Lincoln and the Second American Revolution* (1990) offers provocative reflections on the life and significance of Lincoln. Douglas Southall Freeman, *Robert E. Lee*, 4 vols. (1934–1935) and William McFeely, *Grant* (1981) are the leading biographies of the two most important Civil War generals. Iver Bernstein, *The New York City Draft Riots* (1990) is a good study of one of the most dramatic nonmilitary events in the North during the Civil War. Emory Thomas, *The Confederate Nation* (1979) is a fine one-volume history of the Confederacy. Drew Gilpin Faust, *Mothers of Invention: Women of the Slaveholding South in the American Civil War* (1996), and C. Vann Woodward, ed., *Mary Chesnut's Civil War* (1982) are important sources for understanding the role and experiences of women in the Confederacy. Ira Berlin, et al., eds., *Free at Last: A Documentary History of Slavery, Freedom and the Civil War* (1992) is a superb compilation of primary sources from slaves and slaveowners relating to the demise of slavery during the Civil War years. Ira Berlin, et al., *Slaves No More: Three Essays on Emancipation and the Civil War* (1992), the companion volume to the documents in *Free at Last*, argues that slaves and freedmen played an active role in destroying slavery and redefining freedom. Catherine Clinton and Nina Silber, *Divided Houses* (1992) is a collection of essays demonstrating the importance of gender in the history of the Civil War.

Films

(The best source for information on how to find these and other films is *Bowker's Complete Video Directory*—3 volumes.) *The Civil War* (1989) is Ken Burns's award-winning, nine-volume epic documentary. *Civil War Journal*, hosted by Danny Glover, focuses on the private stories within the great conflict. *The American Story, No. 11: The Eve of Conflict, No. 12: The Blue and the Grey*, and *No. 13: The Road to Appomattox* (1985) explore the Civil War from Lincoln's election to the end of the war. *Civil War Legends* (1989) includes biographies of Robert E. Lee, Stonewall Jackson, Ulysses S. Grant, and Abraham Lincoln. *The Civil War: Anguish of Emancipation* (1972) reenacts the events confronting Abraham Lincoln as he prepared to issue the Emancipation Proclamation. *The Fifty-Fourth Massachusetts*, from the Arts & Entertainment Network Civil War Series, illuminates the history of Massachusetts's famous regiment of African-American soldiers. *Clara Barton* (1995) traces the life of a woman who became a nurse during the Civil War and was instrumental in establishing the American Red Cross.

Internet Resources

Internet websites containing historical material relevant to the subjects discussed in this chapter can be reached through the McGraw-Hill history site at www.mhhe.com/socscience/history/usa/link/linktop.htm.

CHAPTER FIFTEEN

Reconstruction and the New South

The Problems of Peacemaking ~ *Radical Reconstruction*
The South in Reconstruction ~ *The Grant Administration*
The Abandonment of Reconstruction ~ *The New South*

EW PERIODS IN the history of the United States have produced as much bitterness or created such enduring controversy as the era of Reconstruction—the years following the Civil War during which Americans attempted to reunite their shattered nation. To many white Southerners, Reconstruction was a vicious and destructive experience—a period when vindictive Northerners inflicted humiliation and revenge on the prostrate South. Northern defenders of Reconstruction, in contrast, argued that their policies were the only way to prevent unrepentant Confederates from restoring Southern society to what it had been before the war; without forceful federal intervention, there would be no way to forestall the reemergence of a backward aristocracy and the continued subjugation of former slaves.

To most African Americans at the time, and to many people of all races since, Reconstruction was notable for other reasons. Neither a vicious tyranny, as white Southerners charged, nor a thoroughgoing reform, as many Northerners claimed, it was, rather, a small but important first step in the effort to secure civil rights and economic power for the former slaves. Reconstruction did not provide African Americans with either the legal protections or the material resources to assure them anything like real equality. For the remainder of the nineteenth century, and through much of the twentieth, most black men and women who continued to live in what came to be known as the New South had little power to resist their oppression.

TIME LINE

1863	1864	1865	1866	1867
Lincoln announces Reconstruction plan	Lincoln vetoes Wade-Davis bill	Lincoln assassinated; Johnson becomes president Freedmen's Bureau established Joint Committee on Reconstruction established	Republicans gain in congressional elections	Congressional Reconstruction begins

1868	1869	1872	1873	1875
Grant elected president Johnson impeached and acquitted	Congress passes 15th Amendment	Grant reelected	Panic and depression	"Whiskey ring" scandal

1877	1883	1890s	1895	1896
Hayes wins disputed election Compromise of 1877 ends Reconstruction	Supreme Court upholds segregation	Jim Crow laws in South	Atlanta Compromise	Plessy v. Ferguson

And yet for all its shortcomings, Reconstruction did help African Americans create some new institutions and some important legal precedents that helped them survive and that ultimately, well into the twentieth century, became the basis of later efforts to win freedom and equality.

THE PROBLEMS OF PEACEMAKING

In 1865, when it became clear that the war was almost over, no one in Washington was certain about what to do. Abraham Lincoln could not negotiate a treaty with the defeated government; he continued to insist that the Confederate government had no legal right to exist. Yet neither could he simply readmit the Southern states into the Union as if nothing had happened.

The Aftermath of War and Emancipation

The South after the Civil War was a desolate place. Towns had been gutted, plantations burned, fields neglected, bridges and railroads destroyed. Many white Southerners—stripped of their slaves through emancipation and stripped of the capital they had invested in now worthless Confederate bonds and currency—had almost no personal property. More than 258,000 Confederate soldiers had died in the war, and thousands more returned home wounded or sick. Many families had to rebuild their lives without the help of adult males. Some white Southerners faced starvation and homelessness.

If conditions were bad for Southern whites, they were far worse for Southern blacks—the 4 million men and women now emerging from

CHARLESTON, 1865 Not until 1864 did substantial fighting and destruction begin to take place in the urban South. But in the last year of the war, several major cities (and many towns and smaller communities) experienced devastation at the hands of the Northern armies—among them Richmond, Atlanta, and (as seen here) Charleston.

bondage. As soon as the war ended, hundreds of thousands of them—young and old, many of them ill and feeble—left the plantations in search of a new life in freedom. But most had nowhere to go, and few had any possessions except the clothes they wore.

Competing Notions of Freedom

Despite the disarray of Southern society, almost everyone faced the future with some very clear aspirations. For blacks and whites alike, Reconstruction became a struggle to define the meaning of freedom. But the former slaves and the defeated whites had very different conceptions of what freedom meant.

For African Americans, freedom meant above all an end to slavery. But it also meant acquiring rights and protections that would enable them to live as free people, just as whites did. Some blacks believed the only way to secure freedom was to have the government take land away from white people, who owned virtually all of it, and give it to black people, who owned virtually none. Others asked only for legal equality, confident that they could advance successfully in American society once the formal obstacles to their advancement disappeared. But whatever their particular demands, virtually all former slaves were united in their desire for independence from white control. Throughout the post-Civil War South, African Americans separated themselves from white institutions—pulling out of white-controlled churches and establishing their own, creating clubs and societies for their own people, and in some cases starting their own schools.

For most white Southerners, freedom meant something very different. It meant the ability to control their own destinies without interference from the North or the federal government. And in the immediate aftermath of the war, they attempted to exercise this version of freedom by trying to restore their society to its antebellum form. When these white Southerners fought for what they considered freedom, they were fighting above all to preserve local and regional autonomy and white supremacy.

In the immediate aftermath of the war, the federal government's contribution to solving the question of the future of the South was modest. Federal troops remained in the South to preserve order and protect the freedmen. And in March 1865, Congress established the Freedmen's Bureau, an agency of the army directed by General Oliver O. Howard. The Freedmen's Bureau distributed food to millions of former slaves. It established schools, staffed by missionaries and teachers who had been sent to

A MONUMENT TO THE CONFEDERATE DEAD This monument in the town square of
Greenwood, South Carolina, was typical of many such memorials erected all across
the South in the aftermath of the Civil War. They served to commemorate the
soldiers who had died in the struggle, but also to remind white Southerners of what
was by the 1870s already widely known and romanticized as the "Lost Cause."

the South by Freedmen's Aid Societies and other private and church
groups in the North. It made a modest effort to settle blacks on lands of
their own. (The bureau also offered considerable assistance to poor whites,
many of whom were similarly destitute and homeless after the war.) But
the Freedmen's Bureau was not a permanent solution. It had authority to

operate for only one year, and it was, in any case, far too small to deal effectively with the enormous problems facing Southern society. By the time the war ended, other proposals for reconstructing the defeated South were emerging.

Plans for Reconstruction

Control of Reconstruction remained in the hands of the Republicans, who had substantial majorities in both houses of Congress and who were divided in their approach to the issue. Conservatives within the party insisted that the South accept the abolition of slavery, but they proposed few other conditions for the readmission of the seceded states. The Radicals, led by Representative Thaddeus Stevens of Pennsylvania and Senator Charles Sumner of Massachusetts, urged a much harsher course, including disfranchising large numbers of Southern whites, protecting black civil rights, and confiscating the property of wealthy white Southerners who had aided the Confederacy and distributing the land among the freedmen. There was also a group of Republican Moderates, who rejected the most stringent demands of the Radicals but supported extracting at least some concessions from the South on black rights.

President Lincoln's sympathies lay with the Moderates and Conservatives of his party. He favored a lenient Reconstruction policy, and he believed that Southern Unionists (mostly former Whigs) could become the nucleus of new, loyal state governments in the South. Lincoln announced his Reconstruction plan in December 1863, more than a year before the war ended. It offered a general amnesty to white Southerners—other than high officials of the Confederacy—who would pledge an oath of loyalty to the government and accept the elimination of slavery. When 10 percent of a state's total number of voters in 1860 took the oath, those loyal voters could set up a state government. Lincoln also proposed extending suffrage to those African Americans who were educated, owned property, and had served in the Union army. Three Southern states—Louisiana, Arkansas, and Tennessee, all under Union occupation—reestablished loyal governments under the Lincoln formula in 1864.

The Radical Republicans were outraged at the mildness of Lincoln's program and refused to admit representatives from the three "reconstructed" states to Congress. In July 1864, they pushed their own plan through Congress in the form of the Wade-Davis Bill. It called for the

ABRAHAM LINCOLN Lincoln was the subject of many photographic portraits, of which this one, by Mathew Brady, is among the most famous.

president to appoint a provisional governor for each conquered state. When a majority (not Lincoln's 10 percent) of the white males of a state pledged their allegiance to the Union, the governor could summon a state constitutional convention, whose delegates were to be elected by voters who had never borne arms against the United States (again, a major departure from Lincoln's plan). The new state constitutions would be required to abolish slavery, disfranchise Confederate civil and military leaders, and repudiate debts accumulated by the state governments during the war. Only then would Congress readmit the states to the Union. Like the president's proposal, the Wade-Davis Bill left the question of political rights for blacks up to the states.

Congress passed the bill a few days before it adjourned in 1864, and Lincoln disposed of it with a pocket veto. His action enraged the Radical leaders, and the pragmatic Lincoln realized he would have to accept at least some of the Radical demands. In the first weeks of 1865, he began to move toward a new approach to Reconstruction.

The Death of Lincoln

What plan he might have produced no one can say. On the night of April 14, 1865, Lincoln and his wife attended a play at Ford's Theater in Washington. As they sat in the presidential box, John Wilkes Booth, an actor fervently committed to the Southern cause, entered the box from the rear and shot Lincoln in the head. Early the next morning, the president died.

The circumstances of Lincoln's death earned him immediate martyrdom. They also produced something close to hysteria throughout the North, especially because it quickly became clear that Booth had been the leader of a conspiracy. One of his associates shot and wounded Secretary of State William Seward on the night of the assassination, and another abandoned at the last moment a scheme to murder Vice President Andrew Johnson. Booth himself escaped on horseback into the Maryland countryside, where, on April 26, he was cornered by Union troops and shot to death in a blazing barn. Eight other people were convicted by a military tribunal of participating in the conspiracy (at least two of them on the basis of virtually no evidence). Four were hanged.

To many Northerners, however, the murder of the president seemed evidence of an even greater conspiracy—one masterminded and directed by the unrepentant leaders of the defeated South. Militant Republicans exploited such suspicions relentlessly in the ensuing months, ensuring that Lincoln's death would help doom his plans for a relatively easy peace.

Johnson and "Restoration"

Leadership of the Moderates and Conservatives fell to Lincoln's successor, Andrew Johnson of Tennessee, who was not well suited, either by circumstance or personality, for the task. A Democrat until he had joined the Union ticket with Lincoln in 1864, he became president at a time of growing partisan passions. Johnson himself was an intemperate and tactless man, filled with resentments and insecurities.

Johnson revealed his plan for Reconstruction—or "Restoration," as he preferred to call it—soon after he took office, and he implemented it during the summer of 1865 when Congress was in recess. Like Lincoln, he offered some form of amnesty to Southerners who would take an oath of allegiance. In most other respects, however, his plan resembled the Wade-Davis Bill. The president appointed a provisional governor in each state

and charged him with inviting qualified voters to elect delegates to a constitutional convention. In order to win readmission to Congress, a state
had to revoke its ordinance of secession, abolish slavery and ratify the
Thirteenth Amendment, and repudiate Confederate and state war debts.

By the end of 1865, all the seceded states had formed new governments—some under Lincoln's plan, some under Johnson's—and awaited
congressional approval of them. But Radicals in Congress vowed not to
recognize the Johnson governments, just as they had previously refused to
recognize the Lincoln regimes, for, by now, Northern opinion had become more hostile toward the South than it had been a year earlier when
Congress had passed the Wade-Davis Bill. Delegates to the Southern conventions had angered much of the North by their apparent reluctance to
abolish slavery and by their refusal to grant suffrage to any blacks. Southern states had also seemed to defy the North by electing prominent Confederate leaders to represent them in Congress, among them Alexander
H. Stephens, former vice president of the Confederacy, who was selected
as a United States senator from Georgia.

RADICAL RECONSTRUCTION

Reconstruction under Johnson's plan—often known as "presidential Reconstruction"—continued only until Congress reconvened in December
1865. At that point, Congress refused to seat the representatives of the
"restored" states and created a new Joint Committee on Reconstruction to
frame a Reconstruction policy of its own. The period of "congressional"
or "Radical" Reconstruction had begun.

The Black Codes

Meanwhile, events in the South were driving Northern opinion in even
more radical directions. Throughout the South in 1865 and early 1866,
state legislatures were enacting sets of laws known as the Black Codes, designed to give whites substantial control over the former slaves. The codes
authorized local officials to apprehend unemployed blacks, fine them for
vagrancy, and hire them out to private employers to satisfy the fine. Some
of the codes forbade blacks to own or lease farms or to take any jobs other
than as plantation workers or domestic servants.

D E B A T I N G   T H E   P A S T

Reconstruction

D EBATE OVER THE nature of Reconstruction has been unusually intense, not only among historians but among much of the larger public as well. Indeed, few issues in American history have raised such deep and enduring passions.

Beginning in the late nineteenth century and continuing well into the twentieth, a relatively uniform and highly critical view of Reconstruction prevailed among historians—a reflection of a broad consensus among white Americans about the inferiority of blacks and of a yearning in both the North and the South for sectional reconciliation. William A. Dunning's *Reconstruction, Political and Economic* (1907) was the principal scholarly expression of this prevailing view. Dunning portrayed Reconstruction as a corrupt and oppressive outrage imposed on a prostrate South by a vindictive group of Northern Republican Radicals. Unscrupulous carpetbaggers flooded the South and plundered the region. Ignorant African Americans were thrust into political offices for which they were unfit. Reconstruction governments were awash in corruption and compiled enormous levels of debt. The Dunning interpretation dominated several generations of historical scholarship. It also helped shape such popular images of Reconstruction as those in the novel and film *Gone with the Wind*.

Among historians, at least, the Dunning interpretation gradually lost credibility in the face of a series of challenges. W. E. B. Du Bois, the great African-American scholar, offered one of the first alternative views in *Black Reconstruction* (1935). To Du Bois, Reconstruction was an effort by freed blacks (and their white allies) to create a more democratic society in the South, and it was responsible for many valuable social innovations. In the early 1960s, John Hope Franklin and Kenneth Stampp, building on a generation of work by other scholars, published new histories of Reconstruction that also radically revised the Dunning interpretation. Reconstruction, they argued, was a genuine, if flawed, effort to solve the problem of race in the South. The Reconstruction governments were not perfect, but they were bold experiments in interracial politics. Congressional Radicals were not saints, but they were genuinely concerned with protecting the rights of former slaves. Reconstruction had brought important, if temporary, progress to the South and had created no more corruption there than governments were creating in the North at the same time. What was tragic about Reconstruction, the revisionists claimed, was not what it did to Southern whites but what it failed to do for Southern blacks. It was, in the end, too weak and too short-lived to guarantee African Americans genuine equality.

In more recent years, some historians have begun to question the assessment of the first revisionists that, in the end, Reconstruction accomplished relatively little. Leon Litwack argued in *Been in the Storm So Long* (1979) that former slaves used the protections Reconstruction offered them to carve out a certain level of independence for themselves within Southern society: strengthening churches, reuniting families, and resisting the efforts of white planters to revive the gang labor system.

Eric Foner's *Reconstruction: America's Unfinished Revolution* (1988) also emphasized how far African Americans moved toward freedom and independence in a short time, how much of lasting value they were able to accomplish despite imposing obstacles, and how important they were in shaping the execution of Reconstruction policies. Reconstruction, he argues, "can only be judged a failure" as an effort to secure "blacks' rights as citizens and free laborers." But it "closed off even more oppressive alternatives. . . . The post-Reconstruction labor system embodied neither a return to the closely supervised gang labor of antebellum days, nor the complete dispossession and immobilization of the black labor force and coercive apprenticeship systems envisioned by white Southerners in 1865 and 1866. Nor were blacks, as in twentieth-century South Africa, barred from citizenship, herded into labor reserves, or prohibited by law from moving from one part of the country to another. . . . The doors of economic opportunity that had opened could never be completely closed."

Congress first responded to the Black Codes by passing an act extending the life of the Freedmen's Bureau and widening its powers so that it could nullify work agreements forced on freedmen under the Black Codes. Then, in April 1866, Congress passed the first Civil Rights Act, which declared blacks to be citizens of the United States and gave the federal government power to intervene in state affairs to protect the rights of citizens. Johnson vetoed both bills, but Congress overrode him on each of them.

The Fourteenth Amendment

In April 1866, the Joint Committee on Reconstruction proposed a new amendment to the Constitution, which Congress approved in early summer and sent to the states for ratification. Eventually, it became one of the most important of all the provisions in the Constitution.

The Fourteenth Amendment offered the first constitutional definition of American citizenship. Everyone born in the United States, and everyone naturalized, was automatically a citizen and entitled to all the "privileges and immunities" guaranteed by the Constitution, including equal protection of the laws by both the state and national governments. There could be no other requirements for citizenship. The amendment also imposed penalties—reduction of representation in Congress and in the electoral college—on states that denied suffrage to any adult male inhabitants. (The wording reflected the prevailing view in Congress and elsewhere that the franchise was properly restricted to men.) Finally, it prohibited former members of Congress or other former federal officials who had aided the Confederacy from holding any state or federal office unless two-thirds of Congress voted to pardon them.

Congressional Radicals offered to readmit to the Union any state whose legislature ratified the Fourteenth Amendment. Only Tennessee did so. All the other former Confederate states, along with Delaware and Kentucky, refused, leaving the amendment temporarily without the necessary approval of three-fourths of the states.

But by now, the Radicals were growing more confident and determined. Bloody race riots in New Orleans and other Southern cities—riots in which African Americans were the principal victims—were among the events that strengthened their hand. In the 1866 congressional elections, Johnson actively campaigned for Conservative candidates, but he did his own cause more harm than good with his intemperate speeches. The voters returned an overwhelming majority of Republicans, most of them Radicals, to Congress. In the Senate, there were now 42 Republicans to 11 Democrats; in the

House, 143 Republicans to 49 Democrats. (The South remained largely unrepresented in both chambers.) Congressional Republicans were now strong enough to enact a plan of their own even over the president's objections.

The Congressional Plan

The Radicals passed three Reconstruction bills early in 1867 and overrode Johnson's vetoes of all of them. These bills finally established, nearly two years after the end of the war, a coherent plan for Reconstruction.

A CELEBRATION OF RECONSTRUCTION The celebrated cartoonist Thomas Nast—best known for his savage caricatures of machine politicians in New York's Tammany Hall—drew this celebratory, and optimistic, image of Reconstruction not long after the end of the Civil War: a classical goddess restoring the former Confederate states to their rightful place within a symbolic fasces that represented union. In fact, the Reconstruction process proved much more difficult than this hopeful image suggested.

Under the congressional plan, Tennessee, which had ratified the Fourteenth Amendment, was promptly readmitted. But Congress rejected the Lincoln-Johnson governments of the other ten Confederate states and, instead, combined those states into five military districts. A military commander governed each district and had orders to register qualified voters (defined as all adult black males and those white males who had not participated in the rebellion). Once registered, voters would elect conventions to prepare new state constitutions, which had to include provisions for black suffrage. Once voters ratified the new constitutions, they could elect state governments. Congress had to approve a state's constitution, and the state legislature had to ratify the Fourteenth Amendment. Once that happened, and once enough states ratified the amendment to make it part of the Constitution, then the former Confederate states could be restored to the Union.

By 1868, seven of the ten former Confederate states (Arkansas, North Carolina, South Carolina, Louisiana, Alabama, Georgia, and Florida) had fulfilled these conditions (including ratification of the Fourteenth Amendment, which now became part of the Constitution) and were readmitted to the Union. Conservative whites held up the return of Virginia and Texas until 1869 and Mississippi until 1870. By then, Congress had added an additional requirement for readmission—ratification of another constitutional amendment, the Fifteenth, which forbade the states and the federal government to deny suffrage to any citizen on account of "race, color, or previous condition of servitude."

To stop the president from interfering with their plans, the congressional Radicals passed two remarkable laws of dubious constitutionality in 1867. One, the Tenure of Office Act, forbade the president to remove civil officials, including members of his own cabinet, without the consent of the Senate. The principal purpose of the law was to protect the job of Secretary of War Edwin M. Stanton, who was cooperating with the Radicals. The other law, the Command of the Army Act, prohibited the president from issuing military orders except through the commanding general of the army (General Grant), who could not be relieved or assigned elsewhere without the consent of the Senate.

The congressional Radicals also took action to stop the Supreme Court from interfering with their plans. In 1866, the Court had declared in the case of *Ex parte Milligan* that military tribunals were unconstitutional in places where civil courts were functioning, a decision that seemed to threaten the system of military government the Radicals were planning for the South. Radicals in Congress immediately proposed several bills that would require two-thirds of the justices to support any decision overruling a law of Congress, would deny the Court jurisdiction in Reconstruction cases, would reduce its membership to three, and would even abolish it. The justices apparently took notice. Over the next two years, the Court refused to accept jurisdiction in any cases involving Reconstruction (and the congressional bills concerning the Court never passed).

The Impeachment of the President

President Johnson had long since ceased to be a serious obstacle to the passage of Radical legislation, but he was still the official charged with administering the Reconstruction programs. As such, the Radicals believed, he remained a serious impediment to their plans. Early in 1867, they began looking for a way to impeach him and remove him from office. A search for grounds for impeachment began. Republicans found them, they believed, when Johnson dismissed Secretary of War Stanton despite Congress's refusal to agree, thus deliberately violating the Tenure of Office Act in hopes of testing the law before the courts. Elated Radicals in the House quickly impeached the president and sent the case to the Senate for trial.

The trial before the Senate lasted throughout April and May 1868. The Radicals put heavy pressure on all the Republican senators, but the Moderates (who were losing faith in the Radical program) vacillated. On the first three charges to come to a vote, seven Republicans joined the Democrats and independents to support acquittal. The vote was 35 to 19, one short of the constitutionally required two-thirds majority. After that, the Radicals dropped the impeachment effort.

THE SOUTH IN RECONSTRUCTION

Reconstruction may not have accomplished what its framers intended or what its defenders had hoped. But it did have profound effects on the South.

The Reconstruction Governments

Critics labeled Southern white Republicans with the derogatory terms "scalawags" and "carpetbaggers." Many of the "scalawags" were former Whigs who had never felt comfortable in the Democratic Party or farmers who lived in remote areas where there had been little or no slavery; most of these Republicans hoped the party's program of internal improvements would help end their economic isolation. The "carpetbaggers" were white men from the North, most of them veterans of the Union army who looked on the South as a new frontier, more promising than the West. They had settled there at war's end as hopeful planters, businessmen, or professionals.

The most numerous Republicans in the South were the black freedmen, most of whom had no previous experience in politics and tried, therefore, to build institutions through which they could learn to exercise their power. In several states, African-American voters held their own conventions to chart their future course. Freedmen had created their own churches after emancipation, withdrawing from the white-dominated congregations they had been compelled to attend under slavery. This religious independence also helped give them unity and self-confidence.

African Americans played a significant role in the politics of the Reconstruction South. They served as delegates to the constitutional conventions. They held public offices of practically every kind. Between 1869 and 1901, twenty blacks served in the United States House of Representatives, two in the Senate. They served, too, in state legislatures and in various other state offices. Southern whites complained loudly about "Negro rule" during Reconstruction, but no such thing ever actually existed in any of the states. In the South as a whole, the percentage of black officeholders was always far lower than the percentage of blacks in the population.

The record of the Reconstruction governments is mixed. Critics at the time and later denounced them for corruption and financial extravagance, and there is some truth to both charges. But the corruption in the South, real as it was, was hardly unique to the Reconstruction governments. Corruption had been rife in some antebellum and Confederate governments, and it was at least as rampant in the Northern states. And the large state expenditures of the Reconstruction years were huge only in comparison with the meager budgets of the antebellum era. They repre-

AFTER SLAVERY Although most freed slaves remained agricultural laborers after Emancipation, a considerable number moved off the land in search of new occupations and new homes. For many, that meant living for some time without stable employment or a permanent home. This photograph from the late 1860s shows a group of former slaves at a county almshouse in the South.

sented an effort to provide the South with desperately needed services that antebellum governments had never offered: public education, public works programs, poor relief, and other costly new commitments.

Education

Perhaps the most important of the accomplishments of the Reconstruction governments was a dramatic improvement in Southern education—an improvement that benefited both whites and blacks. In the first years of Reconstruction, much of the impetus for educational reform in the South came from outside groups—from the Freedmen's Bureau, from Northern private philanthropic organizations, from the many Northern white women who traveled to the South to teach in freedmen's schools—and from African Americans themselves. Over the opposition of many

Southern whites, who feared that education would give blacks "false notions of equality," these reformers established a large network of schools for former slaves—4,000 schools by 1870, staffed by 9,000 teachers (half of them black), teaching 200,000 students (about 12 percent of the total school-age population of the freedmen). In the 1870s, Reconstruction governments began to build a comprehensive public school system in the South. By 1876, more than half of all white children and about 40 percent of all black children were attending schools in the South (although almost all such schools were racially segregated). Several black "academies," offering more advanced education, also began operating. Gradually, these academies grew into an important network of black colleges and universities.

Landownership and Tenancy

The most ambitious goal of the Freedmen's Bureau, and of some Republican Radicals in Congress, was to reform landownership in the South. The effort failed. By June 1865, the bureau had settled nearly 10,000 black families on their own land—most of it drawn from abandoned plantations in areas occupied by the Union armies. By the end of that year, however, Southern plantation owners were returning and demanding the restoration of their property. President Johnson supported their demands, and the government eventually returned most of the confiscated lands to their original white owners. Congress never had much stomach for the idea of land redistribution, and the experiment quickly died.

Even so, the distribution of landownership in the South changed considerably in the postwar years. Among whites, there was a striking decline in landownership, from 80 percent before the war to 67 percent by the end of Reconstruction. Some whites lost their land because of unpaid debt or increased taxes; some left the marginal lands they had owned to move to more fertile areas, where they rented. Among blacks, during the same period, the proportion who owned land rose from virtually none to more than 20 percent.

Still, most blacks, and a growing minority of whites, did not own their own land during Reconstruction, and some who acquired land in the 1860s had lost it by the 1890s. Instead, they worked for others in one form or another. Many black agricultural laborers—perhaps 25 percent of the total—simply worked for wages. Most, however, became tenants of white landowners—that is, they worked their own plots of land and paid their landlords either a fixed rent or a share of their crop (hence the term "sharecropping"). The new system represented a repudiation by blacks of the gang-labor system of the antebellum plantation, in which slaves had lived and worked together under the direction of a master. As tenants and sharecroppers, blacks enjoyed at least a physical independence from their landlords and had the sense of working their own land, even if in most cases they could never hope to buy it. But tenantry also benefited landlords in some ways, relieving them of the cost of purchasing slaves and of responsibility for the physical well-being of their workers.

Incomes and Credit

In some respects, the postwar years were a period of remarkable economic progress for African Americans in the South. The per capita income of blacks (when the material benefits of slavery are counted as income) rose 46 percent between 1857 and 1879, while the per capita income of whites declined 35 percent. This represented one of the most significant redistributions of income in American history. African Americans were also able to work less than they had under slavery. Women and children were less likely to labor in the fields, and adult men tended to work shorter days. In all, the black labor force worked about one-third fewer hours during Reconstruction than it had been compelled to work under slavery—a reduction that brought the working schedule of blacks roughly into accord with that of white farm laborers.

But other developments were limiting these gains. While black share of profits was increasing, the total profits of Southern agriculture were declining—a result of the dislocations of the war and a reduction in the world market for cotton. Nor did the income redistribution of the postwar years lift many blacks out of poverty. Black per capita income rose from about one-quarter of white per capita income (which was itself low) to about one-half in the first few years after the war. After this initial increase, however, it rose hardly at all.

Blacks and poor whites alike often found themselves virtually imprisoned by the crop-lien system. Few of the traditional institutions of credit in the South—the "factors" and banks—returned after the war. In their stead emerged a new system of credit, centered in large part on local country stores—some of them owned by planters, others owned by independent merchants. Blacks and whites, landowners and tenants—all depended on these stores for such necessities as food, clothing, seed, and farm implements. And since farmers did not have the same steady cash flow as other workers, customers usually had to rely on credit from these merchants in order to purchase what they needed. Most local stores had no competition (and went to great lengths to ensure that things stayed that way). As a result, they were able to set interest rates as high as 50 or 60 percent. Farmers had to give the merchants a lien (or claim) on their crops as collateral for the loans (thus the term "crop-lien system," generally used to describe Southern farming in this period). Farmers who suffered a few bad years in a row, as many did, could become trapped in a cycle of debt from which they could never escape.

One effect of this burdensome credit system was that some blacks who had acquired land during the early years of Reconstruction gradually lost it as they fell into debt. So, to a lesser extent, did white small landowners. Another was that Southern farmers became almost wholly dependent on cash crops—and most of all on cotton—because only such marketable commodities seemed to offer any possibility of escape from debt. The relentless planting of cotton contributed to an exhaustion of the soil. The crop-lien system, in other words, was not only helping to impoverish small farmers; it was also contributing to a general decline in the Southern agricultural economy.

The African-American Family in Freedom

One of the most striking features of the black response to Reconstruction was the effort to build or rebuild family structures. A major reason for the rapid departure of so many blacks from plantations was the desire to find lost relatives and reunite families. Thousands of African Americans wandered through the South looking for husbands, wives, children, or other relatives from whom they had been separated. Former slaves rushed to have their marriages, previously without legal standing, sanctified by church and law.

Within the black family, the definition of male and female roles quickly came to resemble that within white families. Many women and children ceased working in the fields. Such work, they believed, was a badge of slavery. Instead, many women restricted themselves largely to domestic tasks—cooking, cleaning, gardening, raising children, attending

AFRICAN-AMERICAN WORK AFTER SLAVERY Black men and women engaged in a wide
range of economic activities in the aftermath of slavery. But discrimination by white
Southerners and the former slaves' own lack of education limited most of them to
relatively menial jobs. Many black women (including this former slave) earned money
for their families by working as "washer women," doing laundry for white people

to the needs of their husbands. Still, economic necessity often compelled
black women to engage in income-producing activities: working as domestic servants, taking in laundry, or helping their husbands in the fields.
By the end of Reconstruction, half of all black women over the age of sixteen were working for wages.

THE GRANT ADMINISTRATION

Exhausted by the political turmoil of the Johnson administration, American voters in 1868 yearned for a strong, stable figure to guide them through the troubled years of Reconstruction. They turned trustingly to General Ulysses S. Grant, the hero of the war and, by 1868, a revered national idol.

The Soldier President

Grant could have had the nomination of either party in 1868. But believing that Republican Reconstruction policies were more popular in the North, he accepted the Republican nomination. The Democrats nominated former governor Horatio Seymour of New York. The campaign was a bitter one, and Grant's triumph was surprisingly narrow. Without the 500,000 new black Republican voters in the South, he would have had a minority of the popular vote.

Grant entered the White House with no political experience, and his performance was clumsy and ineffectual from the start. Except for Hamilton Fish, whom Grant appointed secretary of state and who served for eight years with great distinction, most members of the cabinet were ill-equipped for their tasks. Grant relied chiefly, and increasingly, on established party leaders—the group most ardently devoted to patronage, and his administration used the spoils system even more blatantly than most of its predecessors, embittering reform-minded members of his party. Grant also alienated the many Northerners who were growing disillusioned with the Radical Reconstruction policies, which the president continued to support. Some Republicans suspected, correctly, that there was also corruption in the Grant administration itself.

By the end of Grant's first term, therefore, members of a substantial faction of the party—who referred to themselves as Liberal Republicans—had come to oppose what they called "Grantism." In 1872, hoping to prevent Grant's reelection, they bolted the party and nominated their own presidential candidate: Horace Greeley, veteran editor and publisher of the *New York Tribune*. The Democrats, somewhat reluctantly, named Greeley their candidate as well, hoping that the alliance with the Liberals would enable them to defeat Grant. But the effort was in vain. Grant won a substantial victory, polling 286 electoral votes to Greeley's 66, and nearly 56 percent of the popular total.

The Grant Scandals

During the 1872 campaign, the first of a series of political scandals came to light that would plague Grant and the Republicans for the next eight years. It involved the French-owned Crédit Mobilier construction company, which had helped build the Union Pacific Railroad. The heads of Crédit Mobilier had used their positions as Union Pacific stockholders to steer large fraudulent contracts to their construction company, thus bilking the Union Pacific (and the federal government, which provided large subsidies to the railroad) of millions. To prevent investigations, the directors had given Crédit Mobilier stock to key members of Congress. But in 1872, Congress did conduct an investigation, which revealed that some highly placed Republicans—including Schuyler Colfax, now Grant's vice president—had accepted stock.

One dreary episode followed another in Grant's second term. Benjamin H. Bristow, Grant's third Treasury secretary, discovered that some of his officials and a group of distillers operating as a "whiskey ring" were cheating the government out of taxes by filing false reports. Then a House investigation revealed that William W. Belknap, secretary of war, had accepted bribes to retain an Indian-post trader in office (the so-called Indian ring). Other, lesser scandals added to the growing impression that "Grantism" had brought rampant corruption to government.

The Greenback Question

Compounding Grant's, and the nation's, problems was a financial crisis, known as the Panic of 1873. It began with the failure of a leading investment banking firm, Jay Cooke and Company, which had invested too heavily in postwar railroad building. There had been panics before—in 1819, 1837, and 1857—but this was the worst one yet. The depression it produced lasted four years.

Debtors now pressured the government to redeem federal war bonds with greenbacks, paper currency of the sort printed during the Civil War, which would increase the amount of money in circulation. But Grant and most Republicans wanted a "sound" currency—based solidly on gold reserves—which would favor the interests of banks and other creditors. There was approximately $356 million in paper currency issued during the Civil War that was still in circulation. In 1873, the Treasury issued more in response to the panic. But in 1875, Republican leaders in Congress, in an effort to crush the greenback movement for good, passed the Specie Resumption Act. It provided that after January 1, 1879, the greenback dollars, whose value constantly fluctuated, would be redeemed by the government and replaced with new certificates, firmly pegged to the price of gold. The law satisfied creditors, who had worried that debts would be repaid in paper currency of uncertain value. But "resumption" made things more difficult for debtors, because the gold-based money supply could not easily expand.

In 1875, the "greenbackers," as the inflationists were called, formed their own political organization: the National Greenback Party. It was active in the next three presidential elections, but it failed to gain widespread support. It did, however, keep the money issue alive. The question of the proper composition of the currency was to remain one of the most controversial and enduring issues in late-nineteenth-century American politics.

Republican Diplomacy

The Johnson and Grant administrations achieved their greatest successes in foreign affairs. The accomplishments were the work not of the presidents themselves, who displayed little aptitude for diplomacy, but of two outstanding secretaries of state: William H. Seward, who had served Lincoln and who remained in office until 1869; and Hamilton Fish, who served throughout the two terms of the Grant administration.

An ardent expansionist, Seward acted with as much daring as the demands of Reconstruction politics and the Republican hatred of President Johnson would permit. Seward accepted a Russian offer to sell Alaska to the United States for $7.2 million, despite criticism from many who considered Alaska a frozen wasteland and derided it as "Seward's Folly." In 1867, Seward also engineered the American annexation of the tiny Midway Islands, west of Hawaii.

Hamilton Fish's first major challenge was resolving the longstanding controversy with England over the American claims that it had violated neutrality laws during the Civil War by permitting English shipyards to build ships (among them the *Alabama*) for the Confederacy. American demands that England pay for the damage these vessels had caused became known as the "*Alabama* claims." In 1871, after a number of failed efforts, Fish forged an agreement, the Treaty of Washington, which provided for international arbitration and in which Britain expressed regret for the escape of the *Alabama* from England.

THE ABANDONMENT OF RECONSTRUCTION

As the North grew increasingly preoccupied with its own political and economic problems, interest in Reconstruction began to wane. By the time Grant left office, Democrats had taken back (or, as white Southerners liked to put it, "redeemed") seven of the governments of the former Confederate states. For three other states—South Carolina, Louisiana, and Florida—the end of Reconstruction had to wait for the withdrawal of the last federal troops in 1877, a withdrawal that was the result of a long process of political bargaining and compromise at the national level.

The Southern States "Redeemed"

In the states where whites constituted a majority—the states of the upper South—overthrowing Republican control was relatively simple. By 1872, all but a handful of Southern whites had regained suffrage. Now a clear majority, they needed only to organize and elect their candidates.

In other states, where blacks were a majority or where the populations of the two races were almost equal, whites used intimidation and violence to undermine the Reconstruction regimes. Secret societies—the Ku Klux Klan, the Knights of the White Camellia, and others—used terrorism to frighten or physically bar blacks from voting or otherwise exercising citizenship. Paramilitary organizations—the Red Shirts and White Leagues—armed themselves to "police" elections and worked to force all white males to join the Democratic Party and to exclude all blacks from meaningful political activity. Strongest of all, however, was the simple weapon of economic pressure. Some planters refused to rent land to Republican blacks; storekeepers refused to extend them credit; employers refused to give them work.

The Republican Congress responded to this wave of repression with the Enforcement Acts of 1870 and 1871 (better know as the Ku Klux Klan Acts), which prohibited states from discriminating against voters on the basis of race and gave the national government the authority to supersede state courts and prosecute crimes by individuals under federal law—the first time the federal government had ever asserted that right. The laws also authorized the president to use federal troops to protect civil rights—a provision President Grant used in 1871 in nine counties of South Carolina. The Enforcement Acts, although seldom used, discouraged Klan violence, which declined by 1872.

Waning Northern Commitment

But this Northern commitment to civil rights in the South did not last very long. Southern blacks were gradually losing the support of many of their former advocates in the North. After the adoption of the Fifteenth Amendment in 1870, some reformers convinced themselves that their long campaign on behalf of black people was now over, that with the vote blacks ought to be able to take care of themselves. Former Radical leaders such as Charles Sumner and Horace Greeley now began calling themselves Liberals, cooperating with the Democrats, and denouncing what they viewed as black-and-carpetbag misgovernment. Within the South itself, many white Republicans now moved into the Democratic Party.

The Panic of 1873 further undermined support for Reconstruction. In the congressional elections of 1874, the Democrats won control of the House of Representatives for the first time since 1861. Grant took note of the changing temper of the North and reduced the use of military force to prop up the Republican regimes in the South.

By the end of 1876, only three states were left in the hands of the Republicans—South Carolina, Louisiana, and Florida. In the state elections that year, Democrats (after using terrorist tactics) claimed victory in all three. But the Republicans claimed victory as well and were able to remain in office because of the presence of federal troops. If the troops were to be withdrawn, the last of the Republican regimes would fall.

The Compromise of 1877

Grant had hoped to run for another term in 1876, but most Republican leaders—shaken by recent Democratic successes, afraid of the scandals with which Grant was associated, and worried about the president's failing health—resisted. Instead, they settled on Rutherford B. Hayes, a former Union army officer and congressman, three-time governor of Ohio, and a champion of civil service reform. The Democrats united behind Samuel J. Tilden, the reform governor of New York, who had been instrumental in overthrowing the corrupt Tweed Ring of New York City's Tammany Hall.

Although the campaign was a bitter one, there were few differences of principle between the candidates. The November election produced an apparent Democratic victory. Tilden carried the South and several large Northern states, and his popular margin over Hayes was nearly 300,000

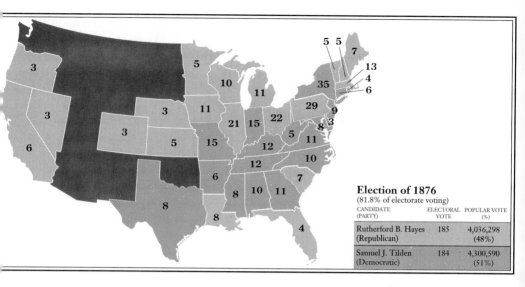

Election of 1876
(81.8% of electorate voting)

CANDIDATE (PARTY)	ELECTORAL VOTE	POPULAR VOTE (%)
Rutherford B. Hayes (Republican)	185	4,036,298 (48%)
Samuel J. Tilden (Democratic)	184	4,300,590 (51%)

votes. But disputed returns from Louisiana, South Carolina, Florida, and Oregon, whose electoral votes totaled 20, threw the election in doubt. Tilden had undisputed claim to 184 electoral votes, only one short of the majority. But Hayes could still win if he managed to receive all 20 disputed votes.

The Constitution had established no method to determine the validity of disputed returns. The decision clearly lay with Congress, but it was not clear with which house or through what method. (The Senate was Republican, and the House was Democratic.) Members of each party naturally supported a solution that would yield them the victory. Finally, late in January 1877, Congress tried to break the deadlock by creating a special electoral commission composed of five senators, five representatives, and five justices of the Supreme Court. The congressional delegation would consist of five Republicans and five Democrats. The Court delegation would include two Republicans, two Democrats, and the only independent, Justice David Davis. But when the Illinois legislature elected Davis to the United States Senate, the justice resigned from the commission. His seat went instead to a Republican justice. The commission voted along straight party lines, 8 to 7, awarding every disputed vote to Hayes. Congress accepted the verdict on March 2. Two days later, Hayes was inaugurated.

Behind the resolution of the deadlock, however, lay a series of elaborate compromises among leaders of both parties. When a Democratic filibuster threatened to derail the commission's report, Republican Senate leaders met secretly with Southern Democratic leaders to work out terms by which the Democrats would support Hayes. As the price of their cooperation, the Southern Democrats (among them some former Whigs) exacted several pledges from the Republicans: the appointment of at least one Southerner to the Hayes cabinet, control of federal patronage in their areas, generous internal improvements, federal aid for the Texas and Pacific Railroad, and withdrawal of the troops. Many powerful Southern Democrats believed that Republican programs of federal support for business and industry would help their region develop economically.

In his inaugural address, Hayes announced that the South's most pressing need was the restoration of "wise, honest, and peaceful local self-government," and he soon withdrew the troops and let white Democrats take over the remaining southern state governments. That produced charges that he was paying off the South for acquiescing in his election and strengthened the widespread characterization of him as "His Fraudulency." But the election had already created such bitterness that not even Hayes's promise to serve only one term could mollify his critics.

The president and his party hoped to build up a "new Republican" organization in the South drawn from Whiggish conservative white groups and committed to modest support for black rights. But all such efforts failed. Although many white Southern leaders sympathized with Republican economic policies, resentment of Reconstruction was so deep that supporting the party was politically impossible. The "solid" Democratic South, which would survive until the mid-twentieth century, was taking shape.

The Legacy of Reconstruction

Reconstruction made important contributions to the efforts of former slaves to achieve dignity and equality in American life. There was a significant redistribution of income, from which blacks benefited. There was a more limited but not unimportant redistribution of landownership, which enabled some former slaves to acquire property. Perhaps most important, there was a large, and largely successful, effort by

African Americans themselves to carve out a society and culture of their own within the American South, to create or strengthen their own institutions, and to convince themselves that they were, indeed, no longer slaves.

In addition, Reconstruction was not as disastrous an experience for Southern white elites as most believed at the time. Within little more than a decade after the end of a devastating war, the white South had regained control of its own institutions and, to a great extent, restored its traditional ruling class to power. Former Confederate leaders received no severe punishments. The federal government imposed no drastic economic reforms on the region, and indeed few lasting political changes of any kind other than the abolition of slavery. Not many conquered peoples have fared as well.

But Reconstruction was also notable for its limitations. For in those years the United States failed in its first serious effort to resolve its oldest and deepest social problem—the problem of race. What was more, the experience so disappointed, disillusioned, and embittered white Americans that it would be nearly a century before they would try again in any serious way to end racism.

Given the odds confronting them, however, African Americans had reason for considerable pride in the gains they were able to make during Reconstruction. And future generations could be grateful for two great charters of freedom—the Fourteenth and Fifteenth Amendments to the Constitution—which, although widely ignored at the time, would one day serve as the basis for a "Second Reconstruction" that would renew the drive to bring freedom to all Americans.

THE NEW SOUTH

The agreement between southern Democrats and northern Republicans that helped settle the disputed election of 1876 was supposed to be the first step toward developing a stable, permanent Republican Party in the South. In that respect, at least, it failed. In the years following the end of Reconstruction, white southerners established the Democratic Party as the only viable political organization for the region's whites. Even so, the South did change in the years after Reconstruction in some of the ways the framers of the Compromise of 1877 had hoped.

"IS THIS A REPUBLICAN FORM OF GOVERNMENT?" The New York artist and cartoonist Thomas Nast marked the end of Reconstruction in 1876 with this biting cartoon in *Harper's Weekly*, expressing his dismay at what he considered the nation's betrayal of the former slaves, who still had not received adequate guarantees of their rights. The caption of the carton continued: "Is *this* protecting life, liberty, or property? Is *this* equal protection of the laws?"

The "Redeemers"

Many white southerners rejoiced at the restoration of what they liked to call "home rule" after the last of the Reconstruction regimes fell in 1877. But in reality, political power in the region was soon more restricted than at any time since the Civil War. Once again, the South fell under the control of a powerful, conservative oligarchy, whose members were known variously as the "Redeemers" or the "Bourbons."

In some places, this post-Reconstruction ruling class was much the same as the ruling class of the antebellum period. In Alabama, for example, the old planter elite—despite challenges from new merchant and industrial forces—retained much of its former power and continued largely to dominate the state for decades. In other areas, however, the Redeemers constituted a genuinely new ruling class. They were merchants, industrialists, railroad developers, and financiers. Some of them were former planters, some of them northern immigrants who had been absorbed into the region's life, some of them ambitious, upwardly mobile white southerners from the region's lower social tiers. They combined a commitment to "home rule" and social conservatism with a commitment to economic development.

The various Bourbon governments of the New South behaved in many respects quite similarly. Virtually all the new Democratic regimes lowered taxes, reduced spending, and drastically diminished state services. One state after another eliminated or reduced its support for public school systems.

Industrialization and the "New South"

Many white southern leaders in the post-Reconstruction era hoped to see their region become the home of a vigorous industrial economy, a "New South." Henry Grady, editor of the *Atlanta Constitution*, and other New South advocates seldom challenged white supremacy, but they did advocate other important changes in southern values. Above all, they promoted the virtues of thrift, industry, and progress—qualities that prewar southerners had often denounced in northern society.

Southern industry did expand dramatically in the years after Reconstruction. Most visible was the growth in textile manufacturing, which increased ninefold in the last twenty years of the century. In the past, southern planters had usually shipped their cotton out of the region to manufacturers in the North or in Europe. Now textile factories appeared in the South itself—many of them drawn to the region from New England by the abundance of water power, the ready supply of cheap labor, the low taxes, and the accommodating conservative governments. The tobacco-processing industry, similarly, established an important foothold in the region. In the lower South, and particularly in Birmingham, Alabama, the iron (and, later, steel) industry grew rapidly. By 1890, the southern iron and steel industry represented nearly a fifth of the nation's total capacity.

Railroad development also increased substantially in the post-Reconstruction years—at a rate far greater than that of the nation at large.

Between 1880 and 1890, trackage in the South more than doubled. And in 1886, the South changed the gauge (width) of its trackage to correspond with the standards of the North. No longer would it be necessary for cargoes heading into the South to be transferred from one train to another at the borders of the region.

Yet southern industry developed within strict limits, and its effects on the region were never even remotely comparable to the effects of industrialization on the North. The southern share of national manufacturing doubled in the last twenty years of the century, but it was still only 10 percent of the total. The region's per capita income increased 21 percent in the same period, but average income in the South was still only 40 percent of that in the North; in 1860 it had been more than 60 percent. And even in those industries where development had been most rapid—textiles, iron, railroads—much of the capital had come from, and many of the profits thus flowed to, the North.

The growth of industry in the South required the region to recruit a substantial industrial work force for the first time. From the beginning, a high percentage of the factory workers (and an especially high percentage of textile workers) were women. Heavy male casualties in the Civil War had helped create a large population of unmarried women who desperately needed employment. Factories also hired entire families, many of whom moved into towns from failed farms. Hours were long (often as much as twelve hours a day), and wages were far below the northern equivalent; indeed, one of the greatest attractions of the South to industrialists was that employers were able to pay workers there as little as one-half what northern workers received. Life in most mill towns was rigidly controlled by the owners and managers of the factories. They rigorously suppressed attempts at protest or union organization. Company stores sold goods to workers at inflated prices and issued credit at exorbitant rates (much like country stores in agrarian areas), and mill owners ensured that no competing merchants were able to establish themselves in the community.

Some industries, such as textiles, offered virtually no opportunities to African-American workers. Others—tobacco, iron, and lumber, for example—did provide some employment for blacks, usually the most menial and lowest-paid positions. Some mill towns, therefore, were places where the black and white cultures came into close contact. This juxtaposition of cultures inhibited the growth of racial harmony and increased the determination of white leaders to take additional measures to protect white supremacy.

Tenants and Sharecroppers

Despite significant growth in southern industry, the region remained primarily agrarian. The most important economic reality in the post-Reconstruction South, therefore, was the impoverished state of agriculture. The 1870s and 1880s saw an acceleration of the process that had begun in the immediate postwar years: the imposition of systems of tenantry and debt peonage on much of the region; the reliance on a few cash crops rather than on a diversified agricultural system; and increasing absentee ownership of valuable farmlands. During Reconstruction, perhaps a third or more of the farmers in the South were tenants; by 1900 the figure had increased to 70 percent.

Tenantry, which now dominated Southern agriculture, took several forms. Farmers who owned tools, equipment, and farm animals—or who had the money to buy them—usually paid an annual cash rent for their land. But many farmers (including most black ones) had no money or equipment at all. Landlords would supply them with land, a crude house, a few tools, seed, and sometimes a mule. In return, the farmers would promise the landlord a large share of the annual crop. After paying their landlords and their local furnishing merchants (who were often the same people), these "sharecroppers" seldom had anything left to sell on their own.

African Americans and the New South

The "New South creed" was not the property of whites alone. Many African Americans were attracted to the vision of progress and self-improvement as well. Some blacks succeeded in elevating themselves into a distinct middle class—even if one far less prosperous than the white middle class. These were former slaves (and, as the decades passed, their offspring) who managed to acquire property, establish small businesses, or enter professions. This rising group of African Americans believed strongly that education was vital to the future of their people, and they expanded the network of black colleges and institutes that had taken root during Reconstruction into an important educational system.

TUSKEGEE INSTITUTE, 1881 From these modest beginnings, Booker T. Washington's Tuskegee Institute in Alabama became the preeminent academy offering technical and industrial training to black men. It deliberately de-emphasized the traditional liberal arts curricula of most colleges. Washington considered such training less important than developing practical skills.

The chief spokesman for this commitment to education, and for a time the most prominent spokesman for black people as a whole, was Booker T. Washington, founder and president of the Tuskegee Institute in Alabama. Born into slavery, Washington had worked his way out of poverty after acquiring an education (at Virginia's Hampton Institute). He urged other blacks to follow the same road to self-improvement.

Washington's message was both cautious and hopeful. African Americans should attend school, learn skills, and establish a solid footing in agriculture and the trades. Industrial, not classical, education should be their goal. Blacks should, moreover, refine their speech, improve their dress, and adopt habits of thrift and personal cleanliness; they should, in short, adopt the standards of the white middle class. Only thus, he claimed, could they win the respect of the white population, the prerequisite for any larger social gains.

In a famous speech in Georgia in 1895, Washington outlined a controversial philosophy of race relations that became widely known as the Atlanta Compromise. Blacks, he said, should forgo agitating for political rights and concentrate on self-improvement and preparation for equality. If blacks were ever to win the rights and privileges of citizenship, they must first show that they were "prepared for the exercise of these privileges." Washington offered a powerful challenge to those whites who wanted to discourage African Americans from acquiring an education or winning any economic gains. But his message was also intended to assure whites that blacks would not challenge the system of segregation, which southern governments were in the process of creating.

The Birth of Jim Crow

Few white southerners had ever accepted the idea of racial equality. That the former slaves acquired any legal and political rights at all after emancipation was in large part the result of their own efforts and critical federal support. That outside support all but vanished after 1877, when federal troops withdrew and the Supreme Court stripped the Fourteenth and Fifteenth Amendments of much of their significance. In the so-called civil rights cases of 1883, the Court ruled that the Fourteenth Amendment prohibited state governments from discriminating against people because of race but did not restrict private organizations or individuals from doing so. Thus railroads, hotels, theaters, and the like could legally practice segregation.

Eventually, the Court also validated state legislation that institutionalized the separation of the races. In *Plessy v. Ferguson* (1896), a case involving a Louisiana law that required separate seating arrangements for the races on railroads, the Court held that separate accommodations did not deprive blacks of equal rights if the accommodations were equal, a decision that survived for years as part of the legal basis of segregated schools. In *Cumming v. County Board of Education* (1899), the Court ruled that communities could establish schools for whites only, even if there were no comparable schools for blacks.

Even before these decisions, white southerners were working to separate the races to the greatest extent possible. They were particularly determined to strip African Americans of the right to vote. In some states, disfranchisement had begun almost as soon as Reconstruction ended. But in other areas, black voting continued for some time after Reconstruction—largely because conservative whites believed they could control the black electorate and use it to beat back the attempts of poor white farmers to take control of the Democratic Party.

In the 1890s, however, franchise restrictions became much more rigid. During those years, some small white farmers began to demand complete black disfranchisement—because they objected to the black vote being used against them by the Bourbons. At the same time, many members of the conservative elite began to fear that poor whites might unite politically with poor blacks to challenge them. They too began to support further franchise restrictions.

In devising laws to disfranchise black males (black females, like white women, had never voted), the southern states had to find ways to evade the Fifteenth Amendment, which prohibited states from denying anyone the right to vote because of race. Two devices emerged before 1900 to accomplish this goal. One was the poll tax or some form of property qualification; few blacks were prosperous enough to meet such requirements. Another was the "literacy" or "understanding" test, which required voters to demonstrate an ability to read and to interpret the Constitution. Even those African Americans who could read had a hard time passing the difficult test white officials gave them. The laws affected poor white voters as well as blacks. By the late 1890s, the black vote had decreased by 62 percent, the white vote by 26 percent. The Supreme Court proved as compliant in upholding the disfranchising laws as it was in dealing with the civil rights cases.

Laws restricting the franchise and segregating schools were only part of a network of state and local statutes—known as the Jim Crow laws—that by the first years of the twentieth century had institutionalized an elaborate system of segregation reaching into almost every area of southern life. Blacks and whites could not ride together in the same railroad cars, sit in the same waiting rooms, use the same washrooms, eat in the same restaurants, or sit in the same theaters. Blacks had no access to many public parks, beaches, or picnic areas; they could not be patients in many hospitals. Much of the new legal structure did no more than confirm what had already been widespread social practice in the South since well before the end of Reconstruction. But the Jim Crow laws also stripped blacks of many of the modest social, economic, and political gains they had made in the more fluid atmosphere of the late nineteenth century.

More than legal efforts were involved in this process. The 1890s witnessed a dramatic increase in white violence against blacks, which, along with the Jim Crow laws, served to inhibit black agitation for equal rights. The worst such violence—lynching of blacks by white mobs, either because the victims were accused of crimes or because they had seemed somehow to violate their proper station—reached appalling levels. In the nation as a whole in the 1890s, there was an average of 187 lynchings each year, more than 80 percent of them in the South. The vast majority of victims were black. Those involved in lynchings often saw their actions as a legitimate form of law enforcement, and some victims of lynchings had in fact committed crimes. But lynchings were also a means by which whites controlled the black population through terror and intimidation.

The rise of lynchings shocked the conscience of many white Americans in a way that other forms of racial injustice did not. In 1892 Ida B. Wells, a committed black journalist, launched what became an international antilynching movement with a series of impassioned articles after the lynching of three of her friends in Memphis, Tennessee, her home. The movement gradually gathered strength in the first years of the twentieth century, attracting substantial support from whites in both the North and South (particularly from white women). Its goal was a federal antilynching law, which would allow the national government to do what state and local governments in the South were generally unwilling to do: punish those responsible for lynchings.

But the substantial southern white opposition to lynchings stood as an exception to the general white support for suppression of African Americans. Indeed, just as in the antebellum period, the shared commitment to white supremacy helped dilute class animosities between poorer whites and the Bourbon oligarchies. Economic issues tended to play a secondary role to race in southern politics, distracting people from the glaring social inequalities that afflicted blacks and whites alike. The commitment to white supremacy, in short, was a burden for poor whites as well as for blacks.

CONCLUSION

Reconstruction, long remembered by many whites as a vindictive outrage or a tragic failure, was a profoundly important moment in American history. Despite the bitter political battles in Washington and throughout the South, culminating in the unsuccessful effort to remove President Andrew

Johnson from office, the most important result of the effort to reunite the nation after its long and bloody war was a reshaping of the lives of ordinary people in all regions of the nation.

In the North, Reconstruction solidified the power of the Republican Party and ensured that public policy would support the continued growth of an advanced industrial economy. The rapid expansion of the northern economy continued and accelerated, drawing more and more of its residents into a burgeoning commercial world.

In the South, Reconstruction did more than simply bring slavery to an end. It fundamentally rearranged the relationship between the region's white and black citizens. Only for a while did Reconstruction permit African Americans to participate actively and effectively in southern politics. After a few years of widespread black voting and significant black officeholding, the forces of white supremacy forced most African Americans to the margins of the southern political world, where they would mostly remain until the 1960s.

In other ways, the lives of southern blacks changed dramatically. Overwhelmingly, they left the plantations. Some sought work in towns and cities. Some left the region altogether. But the great majority began farming on small farms of their own—not as landowners, except in rare cases, but as tenants and sharecroppers on land owned by whites. The result was a form of economic bondage, driven by debt, only scarcely less oppressive than the legal bondage of slavery. Within this system, however, African Americans managed to carve out a much larger sphere of social and cultural activity than they had ever been able to create under slavery. Black churches proliferated in great numbers. African-American schools emerged in some communities, and black colleges began to operate in the region. Some former slaves owned businesses and flourished. In southern cities and towns, a fledgling black middle class began to emerge.

The system of tenantry, which emerged in the course of Reconstruction, continued after its end to dominate the southern economy. Strenuous efforts by "New South" advocates to advance industry and commerce in the region produced significant results in a few areas. But the South on the whole remained what it had always been: an overwhelmingly rural society with a sharply defined class structure. It was also a region with a deep commitment among its white citizens to the subordination of African Americans—a commitment solidified in the 1890s and the early twentieth century when white southerners erected an elaborate legal system of segregation (the "Jim Crow" laws). The promise of the great Reconstruction amendments to the Constitution—the Fourteenth and Fifteenth—remained largely unfulfilled in the South as the century drew to its close.

FOR FURTHER REFERENCE

Suggested Readings

Eric Foner, *Reconstruction: America's Unfinished Revolution, 1863–1877* (1988), the most important modern synthesis of Reconstruction scholarship, emphasizes the radicalism of Reconstruction and the agency of freedpeople in the process of political and economic renovation. Eric McKitrick, *Andrew Johnson and Reconstruction* (1960) is a classic study of the national political battles over Reconstruction. Leon Litwack, *Been in the Storm So Long: The Aftermath of Slavery* (1979) is an excellent examination of the immediate consequences of emancipation. Thomas Holt, *Black over White: Negro Political Leadership in South Carolina During Reconstruction* (1977) examines Reconstruction in the state where black political power reached its apex. Jacqueline Jones, *Soldiers of Light and Love: Northern Teachers and Georgia Blacks, 1865–1873* (1980) is a study of the interaction between northern white women and freedpeople. C. Vann Woodward, *Origins of the New South* (1951), still the leading work on the history of the South after Reconstruction after forty years, argues that a rising middle class defined the economic and political transformation of the New South. Jonathan Wiener, *Social Origins of the New South: Alabama, 1860–1885* (1978) offers an alternative view of the origins of the New South. Edward Ayers, *The Promise of the New South* (1992) offers a rich portrait of social and cultural life in the New South. Steven Hahn, *The Roots of Southern Populism: Yeoman Farmers and the Transformation of the Georgia Upcountry* (1983) argues that southern farmers experienced an erosion of autonomy in the years after the Civil War, and their increasing discontent with market relations helped produce the populist revolt of the 1890s. Roger L. Ransom and Richard Sutch, *One Kind of Freedom: The Economic Consequences of Emancipation* (1977) explores the emergence of the crop-lien system. C. Vann Woodward, *The Strange Career of Jim Crow* (rev. 1974) claims that segregation emerged only gradually across the South after Reconstruction. The "Woodward Thesis" has been challenged by, among others, Joel Williamson, *After Slavery: The Negro in South Carolina During Reconstruction* (1965); John W. Cell, *The Highest Stage of White Supremacy: The Origins of Segregation in South Africa and the American South* (1982); and Howard N. Rabinowitz, *Race Relations in the Urban South, 1865–1890* (1978). J. Morgan Kousser, *The Shaping of Southern Politics: Suffrage Restriction and the Establishment of the One-Party South, 1880–1910* (1974) is an important quantitative study of the effects of disfranchisement.

Films

(The best source for information on how to find these and other films is *Bowker's Complete Video Directory*—3 volumes.) *The American Story, No. 14: Reconstruction* and *No. 14: Rebuilding the Union* (1985) detail the effects of Lincoln's assassination and the course of Reconstruction under the Grant Administration. *Reconstructing the South*, featuring Eric Foner, highlights the difficult social, political, and economic adjustments of the postwar era. *Reconstruction & Segregation 1870–1910* (1996) follows race relations from the assassination of Lincoln through the rise of the Ku Klux Klan and the imposition of Jim Crow. *The Civil War: Promise of Reconstruction* (1972) focuses on the Port Royal "experiment" in South Carolina.

Internet Resources

Internet websites containing historical material relevant to the subjects discussed in this chapter can be reached through the McGraw-Hill history site at www.mhhe.com/socscience/history/usa/link/linktop.htm.

CHAPTER SIXTEEN

The Conquest of the Far West

HROUGH MUCH OF the first half of the nineteenth century, relatively few English-speaking Americans considered moving into the vast and presumably arid lands west of the Mississippi River. By the mid-1840s, however, migrants from the eastern regions of the nation had settled in the West in substantial numbers. Farmers, ranchers, and miners all found opportunity in the western lands. By the end of the Civil War, the West had become legendary in the eastern states. No longer the Great American Desert, it was now the "frontier": an empty land awaiting settlement and civilization; a place of wealth, adventure, opportunity, and untrammeled individualism.

In fact, the real West of the mid-nineteenth century bore little resemblance to its popular image. It was a diverse land, with many different regions, many different climates, many different stores of natural resources. And it was extensively populated, with a number of well-developed societies and cultures. The English-speaking migrants of the late nineteenth century did not find an empty, desolate land. They found Indians, Mexicans, French and British Canadians, Asians, and others, some of whose families had been living in the West for generations.

THE SOCIETIES OF THE FAR WEST

The Far West—the region beyond the Mississippi River into which millions of Anglo-Americans moved in the years after the Civil War—was in

TIME LINE

1862	1865–1867	1866	1869
Homestead Act	Sioux Wars	Western cattle bonanza begins	Transcontinental railroad completed

1873	1874	1876	1877	1882
Barbed wire invented	Black Hills gold rush	Battle of Little Bighorn	Desert Land Act	Chinese Exclusion Act

1885	1887	1889	1890	1893
Twain's *Huckleberry Finn*	Dawes Act	Oklahoma opened to white settlement	Battle of Wounded Knee	Turner's "Frontier Thesis"

fact many lands. It contained some of the most arid territory in the United States, and some of the wettest and lushest. It contained the flattest plains and the highest mountains. And it contained many peoples.

The Western Tribes

The largest and most important western population group before the great white migration from the East was the Indian tribes. Some were members of eastern tribes—Cherokee, Creek, and others—who had been forcibly resettled west of the Mississippi to "Indian Territory" (later Oklahoma) and elsewhere before the Civil War. But most were members of tribes indigenous to the West.

The western tribes had developed a number of patterns of civilization. More than 300,000 Indians (among them the Serrano, Chumash, Pomo, Maidu, Yurok, and Chinook) had lived on the Pacific coast before the arrival of Spanish settlers, supporting themselves through a combination of fishing, foraging, and simple agriculture. The Pueblos of the Southwest had long lived largely as farmers and had established permanent settlements there even before the Spanish arrived in the seventeenth century.

The most widespread Indian groups in the West were the Plains Indians. They were, in fact, made up of many different tribal and language groups. Some lived more or less sedentary lives as farmers. But many of the Plains tribes—including some of the most powerful tribes in the Sioux nation—subsisted largely through hunting buffalo. Riding small but powerful horses, the tribes moved through the grasslands following the herds. Permanent settlements were rare. When a band halted, it constructed tepees as temporary dwellings; when it departed, it left the landscape almost completely undisturbed. The buffalo, or bison, which the Indians so relentlessly pursued, provided the economic basis for the Plains Indians' way of life. The flesh of the large animal was their principal source of food, and its skin supplied materials for clothing, shoes, tepees, blankets, robes, and utensils. "Buffalo chips"—dried manure—provided fuel; buffalo bones became knives and arrow tips; buffalo tendons formed the strings of bows.

The Plains warriors proved to be the most formidable foes white settlers had encountered. But the various tribes (and often even of the bands within tribes) were usually unable to unite against white aggression. At times, tribal warriors faced white forces who were being assisted by guides and even fighters from other, usually rival, tribes. Some tribes, however, were able to overcome their divisions at times and unite effectively. By the mid-nineteenth century, for example, the Sioux, Arapaho, and Cheyenne had forged a powerful alliance that dominated the northern plains. That proved no protection, however, against the greatest danger to the tribes: ecological and economic decline. Indians were tragically vulnerable to eastern infectious diseases. Smallpox epidemics, for example, decimated the Pawnees in Nebraska in the 1840s and many of the California tribes in the early 1850s. And the tribes were, of course, at a considerable disadvantage in any long-term battle with an economically and industrially advanced people. They were, in the end, outmanned and outgunned.

Hispanic New Mexico

For centuries, much of the Far West had been part of, first, the Spanish Empire and, later, the Mexican Republic. When the United States acquired its new lands there in the 1840s, it acquired many Mexican residents at the same time.

In New Mexico, the centers of Spanish-speaking society were the farming and trading communities the Spanish had established in the seventeenth century. Descendants of the original Spanish settlers (and more recent migrants from Mexico) lived alongside the Pueblo Indians and some American traders and engaged primarily in cattle and sheep ranching. When the United States acquired title to New Mexico in the aftermath of the Mexican War, General Stephen Kearny—who had commanded the American troops in the region during the conflict—tried to establish a territorial government out of the approximately 1,000 Anglo-Americans in the region, ignoring the over 50,000 Hispanics. There were widespread fears among the Hispanics and Indians that the new American rulers of the region would confiscate their lands. In 1847, before the new government had established itself, Taos Indians rebelled; they killed the new governor and other Anglo-American officials before being subdued by United States Army forces. New Mexico remained under military rule for three years, until the United States finally organized a territorial government there in 1850. The United States Army finally did what the Hispanic residents had been unable to accomplish for 200 years: it broke the power of the Navajo, Apache, and other tribes in the region. The defeat of the tribes led to substantial Hispanic migration into other areas of the Southwest and as far north as Colorado.

The Anglo-American presence in the Southwest grew rapidly once the railroads established lines into the region in the 1880s and early 1890s. With the railroads came extensive new ranching, farming, and mining. The expansion of economic activity in the region attracted a new wave of Mexican immigrants as well—perhaps as many as 100,000 by 1900—who moved across the border (which was unregulated until World War I) in search of work. The English-speaking proprietors of the new enterprises restricted most Mexicans to the lowest-paying and least stable jobs.

Hispanic California and Texas

In California, Spanish settlement began in the eighteenth century with a string of Christian missions along the Pacific coast. The missionaries and the soldiers who accompanied them gathered most of the coastal Indians into their communities, some forcibly and some by persuasion. In the 1830s, after the new Mexican government began reducing the power of the church, the mission society largely collapsed. In its place emerged a secular Mexican aristocracy, which controlled a chain of large estates (some of them former missions) in the fertile lands west of the Sierra mountains. For them, the acquisition of California by the United States and the arrival of Anglo-Americans before and after the Civil War was disastrous. So vast were the numbers of English-speaking immigrants that the *californios* (as the Hispanic residents of the region were known) had little power to resist the onslaught. English-speaking prospectors organized to exclude them, sometimes violently, from the mines during the gold rush. Many *californios* also lost their lands—either through corrupt business deals or through outright seizure (sometimes with the help of the courts and often through simple occupation by squatters).

Increasingly, Mexicans and Mexican Americans became part of the lower end of the state's working class, clustered in *barrios* in Los Angeles or elsewhere or laboring as migrant farmworkers. Even small Hispanic landowners who managed to hang on to their farms found themselves unable to raise livestock, as the once-communal grazing lands fell under the control of powerful Anglo ranchers.

A similar pattern occurred in Texas after it joined the United States. Many Mexican landowners lost their land—some as a result of fraud and coercion, some because even the most substantial Mexican ranchers could not compete with the enormous Anglo-American ranching kingdoms that were emerging. In 1859, angry Mexicans, led by the rancher Juan Cortina, raided the jail in Brownsville and freed all the Mexican prisoners inside. But such resistance had little long-term effect. As in California, Mexicans in southern Texas (who constituted nearly three-quarters of the population there) became an increasingly impoverished working class relegated largely to unskilled farm or industrial labor.

The Chinese Migration

At the same time that ambitious or impoverished Europeans were crossing the Atlantic in search of opportunities in the New World, many Chinese were crossing the Pacific in hopes of better lives than they could expect in their own poverty-stricken land. Not all came to the United States. Many Chinese moved to Hawaii, Australia, Latin America, South Africa, and even the Caribbean—some as "coolies" (indentured servants whose condition was close to slavery).

A few Chinese traveled to the American West even before the gold rush, but after 1848 the flow increased dramatically. By 1880, more than 200,000 Chinese had settled in the United States, mostly in California, where they constituted nearly a tenth of the population. Almost all came as free laborers. For a time, white Americans welcomed the Chinese as a conscientious, hardworking people. Very quickly, however, white opinion turned hostile—in part because the Chinese were so industrious and successful that some white Americans began considering them rivals, even threats.

In the early 1850s, large numbers of Chinese immigrants joined the hunt for gold. Many of them were well-organized, hardworking prospectors, and for a time some of them enjoyed considerable success. But opportunities for Chinese to prosper in the mines were fleeting. In 1852, the California legislature began trying to exclude the Chinese from gold mining by enacting a "foreign miners" tax (which also helped exclude Mexicans). Gradually, the effect of the discriminatory laws, the hostility of white miners, and the declining profitability of the surface mines drove most Chinese out of prospecting.

As mining declined as a source of wealth and jobs for the Chinese, railroad employment grew. Beginning in 1865, over 12,000 Chinese found work building the transcontinental railroad. In fact, Chinese workers

CHINESE WORKERS ON THE UNION PACIFIC RAILROAD The Union Pacific Railroad, which moved east from California en route to its meeting with the Central Pacific in Utah, was one of the great engineering feats of the nineteenth century. It was also one of the largest employers of its day, and the captains of the project made heavy use of Chinese laborers—because they accepted low wages, because they worked reliably and hard, and because they seldom complained about the arduous conditions under which they were often forced to live.

formed 90 percent of the labor force of the Central Pacific and were mainly responsible for construction of the western part of the new road. The company preferred them to white laborers because they worked hard, made few demands, and accepted relatively low wages.

Work on the Central Pacific was arduous and often dangerous, and the company made few concessions to the difficult conditions. In the winter, many Chinese tunneled into snow banks at night to create warm sleeping areas for themselves, even though such tunnels frequently collapsed, suffocating those inside. In the spring of 1866, 5,000 Chinese railroad workers rebelled against the terrible conditions of their work and went on strike demanding higher wages and a shorter workday. The company isolated them, surrounded them with strikebreakers, and starved them into submission. The strike failed, and most of the workers returned to their jobs.

In 1869 the transcontinental railroad was completed, and thousands of Chinese lost their jobs. Some moved into agricultural work, usually in menial positions. Increasingly, however, the Chinese flocked to cities. By 1900, nearly half the Chinese population of California lived in urban areas. By far the largest single Chinese community was in San Francisco. Much of community life there, and in other "Chinatowns" throughout the West, revolved around organizations—usually formed by people from the same clan or community in China—that functioned as something like benevolent societies and filled many of the roles that political machines often served in immigrant communities in eastern cities. They were often led by prominent merchants. (In San Francisco, the leading merchants—known as the "Six Companies"—often worked together to advance their interests in the larger community of the city and state.) These organizations became, in effect, employment brokers, unions, arbitrators of disputes, defenders of the community against outside persecution, and dispensers of social services. They also organized the elaborate festivals and celebrations that were such a conspicuous and important part of life in Chinatowns.

Other Chinese organizations were secret societies, known as "tongs." And some of the tongs were violent criminal organizations, involved in the opium trade and prostitution. Few people outside the Chinese communities were aware of their existence, except when rival tongs engaged in violent conflict (or "tong wars"), as occurred frequently in San Francisco in the 1880s.

In San Francisco and other western cities, the Chinese usually occupied the lower rungs of the employment ladder. Many worked as common laborers, servants, and unskilled factory hands. Some established their own small businesses, especially laundries. They moved into this business not because of experience—there were few commercial laundries in China—but because laundries could be started with very little capital and required only limited command of English. By the 1890s, Chinese constituted over two-thirds of all the laundry workers in California, many of them in shops they themselves owned and ran.

During the earliest Chinese migrations to California, virtually all the relatively small number of women who made the journey did so because they had been sold into prostitution in China. As late as 1880, nearly half the Chinese women in California were prostitutes. Gradually, however, the number of Chinese women increased (both through immigration and birth), and Chinese men in America became more likely to seek companionship in families.

Anti-Chinese Sentiments

As Chinese communities grew larger and more conspicuous in western cities, anti-Chinese sentiment among white residents became increasingly strong. In fact, next to the Indians, the Chinese probably suffered more intense persecution from white Americans in the West than anyone else. Anti-Chinese activities, some of them violent, reflected the resentment of many white workers toward Chinese laborers for accepting low wages and thus undercutting union members. As the political value of attacking the Chinese grew in California, the Democratic Party took up the call. So did the Workingmen's Party of California—created in 1878 by Denis Kearney, an Irish immigrant—which gained significant political power in the state in large part on the basis of its hostility to the Chinese. By the mid-1880s, anti-Chinese agitation and violence had spread up and down the Pacific coast and into other areas of the West—combining economic and racist resentments.

In 1882, Congress responded to the political pressure and the growing violence by passing the Chinese Exclusion Act, which banned Chinese immigration into the United States for ten years and barred Chinese already in the country from becoming naturalized citizens. Congress renewed the law for another ten years in 1892 and made it permanent in 1902. It had a dramatic effect on the Chinese population, which declined by more than 40 percent in the forty years after the act's passage.

Migration from the East

The scale of the post–Civil War migration to the American West dwarfed everything that had preceded it. In previous decades, the settlers had come in thousands. Now they came in millions, spreading throughout the vast western territories—into empty and inhabited lands alike. Most of the new settlers were from the established Anglo-American societies of the eastern United States, but substantial numbers—over 2 million between 1870 and 1900—were foreign-born immigrants from Europe: Scandinavians, Germans, Irish, Russians, Czechs, and others.

They came to the West for many reasons. Settlers were attracted by gold and silver deposits, by the shortgrass pasture for cattle and sheep, and ultimately by the sod of the plains and the meadowlands of the mountains, which they discovered were suitable for farming or ranching. The completion of the great transcontinental railroad line in 1869, and the construction of the many subsidiary lines that spread out from it, encouraged settlement. So did the land policies of the federal government. The Homestead Act of 1862 permitted settlers to buy plots of 160 acres for a small fee if they occupied the land they purchased for five years and improved it.

Supporters of the Homestead Act believed it would create new markets and new outposts of commercial agriculture for the nation's growing economy. But a unit of 160 acres, while ample in much of the East, was too small for the grazing and grain farming of the Great Plains. Eventually, the federal government provided some relief. The Timber Culture Act (1873) permitted homesteaders to receive grants of 160 additional acres if they planted 40 acres of trees on them. The Desert Land Act (1877) provided that claimants could buy 640 acres at $1.25 an acre provided they irrigated part of their holdings within three years. These and other laws ultimately made it possible for individuals to acquire as much as 1,280 acres of land at little cost. Some enterprising settlers got much more through deception and fraud.

Political organization followed on the heels of settlement. By the close of the 1860s, territorial governments were in operation in the new provinces of Nevada, Colorado, Dakota, Arizona, Idaho, Montana, and Wyoming. Statehood rapidly followed. Nevada became a state in 1864, Nebraska in 1867, and Colorado in 1876. In 1889, North and South Dakota, Montana, and Washington won admission; Wyoming and Idaho entered the next year. Congress denied Utah statehood until its Mormon leaders

convinced the government in 1896 that polygamy (the practice of men taking several wives) had been abandoned. At the turn of the century, only Arizona, New Mexico, and Oklahoma—all with small white populations—
remained outside the Union.

THE CHANGING WESTERN ECONOMY

Among many other things, the great wave of Anglo-American settlement
transformed the economy of the Far West. The new American settlers
tied the West firmly to the growing industrial economy of the East (and to
much of the rest of the world).

Labor in the West

As commercial activity increased, many farmers, ranchers, and miners
found it necessary to recruit a paid labor force—not an easy task for people far away from major population centers and unable or unwilling to
hire Indian workers. The labor shortage of the region led to higher wages
for some workers than were typical in most areas of the East. But working
conditions were often arduous, and job security was almost nonexistent.
Once a railroad was built, a crop harvested, a herd sent to market, a mine
played out, hundreds and even thousands of workers could find themselves suddenly unemployed. Competition from Chinese immigrants,
whom employers could usually hire for considerably lower wages than
they had to pay whites, also forced some Anglo-Americans out of work.

Even more than in many parts of the East, the western working class
was highly multiracial. English-speaking whites worked alongside African
Americans and immigrants from southern and eastern Europe, as they did
in the East. Even more, they worked with Chinese, Filipinos, Mexicans,
and Indians. But the work force was highly stratified along racial lines. In
almost every area of the western economy, white workers (whatever their
ethnicity) occupied the upper tiers of employment: management and
skilled labor. The lower tiers—unskilled and often arduous work in the
mines, on the railroads, or in agriculture—consisted overwhelmingly of
nonwhites.

The western economy was, however, no more a single entity than the
economy of the East. In the late nineteenth century, the region produced
three major industries, each with a distinctive history and distinctive characteristics: mining, ranching, and commercial farming.

The Arrival of the Miners

The first economic boom in the Far West came in mining. The life span of the mining boom was relatively brief. It began in earnest around 1860 (although there had, of course, been some earlier booms, most notably in California), and it flourished until the 1890s. Then it abruptly declined.

News of a gold or silver strike in an area would start a stampede reminiscent of the California gold rush of 1849, followed by several stages of settlement. Individual prospectors would exploit the first shallow deposits of ore largely by hand, with pan and placer mining. After these surface deposits dwindled, corporations moved in to engage in lode or quartz mining, which dug deeper beneath the surface. Then, as those deposits dwindled, commercial mining either disappeared or continued on a restricted basis, and ranchers and farmers moved in and established a more permanent economy.

The first great mineral strikes (other than the California gold rush) occurred just before the Civil War. In 1858, gold was discovered in the Pike's Peak district of what would soon be the territory of Colorado; the

COLORADO BOOM TOWN After a prospector discovered silver nearby in 1890, miners flocked to the town of Creede, Colorado. For a time in the early 1890s, 150 to 300 people arrived there daily. Although the town was located in a canyon so narrow that there was room for only one street, buildings sprouted rapidly to serve the growing community. Like other such boom towns, however, Creede's prosperity was short-lived. In 1893 the price of silver collapsed, and by the end of the century, Creede was almost deserted.

following year, 50,000 prospectors stormed in from California, the Mississippi Valley, and the East. Denver and other mining camps blossomed into "cities" overnight. Almost as rapidly as it had developed, the boom ended. Later, the discovery of silver near Leadville supplied a new source of mineral wealth.

While the Colorado rush of 1859 was still in progress, news of another strike drew miners to Nevada. Gold had been found in the Washoe district. But even more plentiful and thus more valuable was the silver found in the great Comstock Lode (first discovered in 1858 by Henry Comstock) and other Washoe veins. The first prospectors to reach the Washoe fields came from California, and from the beginning, Californians dominated the settlement and development of Nevada. In a remote desert without railroad transportation, the territory produced no supplies of its own, and everything—from food and machinery to whiskey and prostitutes—had to be shipped from California to Virginia City, Carson City, and other roaring camp towns. When the first placer (or surface) deposits ran out, Californian and eastern capitalists bought the claims of the pioneer prospectors and began to use the more difficult process of quartz mining, which enabled them to retrieve silver from deeper veins. For a few years these outside owners reaped tremendous profits: from 1860 to 1880 the Nevada lodes yielded bullion worth $306 million. After that, the mines quickly played out.

The next important mineral discoveries came in 1874, when gold was found in the Black Hills of southwestern Dakota Territory. Prospectors swarmed into the area, then (and for years to come) accessible only by stagecoach. Like the others, the boom flared for a time, until surface resources faded and corporations took over from the miners. One enormous company, the Homestake, came to dominate the fields. The Dakotas, like other boom areas of the mineral empire, ultimately developed a largely agricultural economy.

Although the gold and silver discoveries generated the most popular excitement, in the long run other, less glamorous natural resources proved more important to the development of the West. The great Anaconda copper mine launched by William Clark in 1881 marked the beginning of an industry that would remain important to Montana for many decades. In other areas, mining operations had significant success with lead, tin, quartz, and zinc.

Men greatly outnumbered women in the mining towns, and younger men in particular had difficulty finding female companions of comparable age. Those women who did gravitate to the new communities often came with their husbands, and their activities were generally (although not always) confined to the same kinds of domestic tasks that eastern women performed. Single women, or women whose husbands were earning no money, did work for wages at times, as cooks, laundresses, and tavern keepers. And in the sexually imbalanced mining communities, there was always a ready market for prostitutes.

The thousands of people who flocked to the mining towns in search of quick wealth and failed to find it often remained as wage laborers in corporate mines after the boom period, working in almost uniformly terrible conditions. In the 1870s, before technological advances eliminated some of the dangers, one worker in every thirty was disabled in the mines, and one in every eighty was killed. That rate fell later in the nineteenth century, but mining remained one of the most dangerous and arduous working environments in the United States.

The Cattle Kingdom

A second important element of the changing economy of the Far West was cattle ranching. The open range—the vast grasslands of the public domain—provided a huge area on the Great Plains where cattle raisers could graze their herds free of charge and unrestricted by the boundaries of private farms. The railroads gave birth to the range-cattle industry by giving it access to markets. Eventually, the same railroads ended it by bringing farmers to the plains and thus destroying the open range.

The western cattle industry was Mexican and Texan by ancestry. Long before citizens of the United States entered the Southwest, Mexican ranchers had developed the techniques and equipment that the cattlemen and cowboys of the Great Plains later employed: branding (a device known in all frontier areas where stock was grazing in common areas), roundups, roping, and the gear of the herders—their lariats, saddles, leather chaps, and spurs. Americans in Texas adopted these methods and carried them to the northernmost ranges of the cattle kingdom. Texas also had the largest herds of cattle in the country. From Texas, too, came the small, muscular horses (broncos and mustangs) that enabled cowboys to control the herds.

At the end of the Civil War, an estimated 5 million cattle roamed the Texas ranges. Eastern markets were offering fat prices for steers in any condition, and the challenge facing the cattle industry was getting the animals from the range to the railroad centers. Early in 1866, some Texas cattle ranchers began driving their combined herds, some 260,000 head, north to

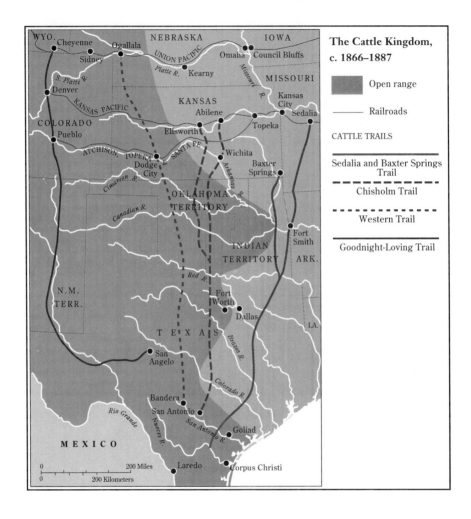

The Cattle Kingdom, c. 1866–1887

Open range

———— Railroads

CATTLE TRAILS

Sedalia and Baxter Springs Trail

Chisholm Trail

Western Trail

Goodnight-Loving Trail

Sedalia, Missouri, on the Missouri Pacific Railroad. The caravan suffered heavy losses. But the drive proved that cattle could be driven to distant markets and pastured along the trail, and that they would even gain weight during the journey. This earliest of the "long drives," in other words, established the first, tentative link between the isolated cattle breeders of west Texas and the booming urban markets of the East. It laid the groundwork for the explosion of the industry—for the creation of the "cattle kingdom."

With the precedent of the long drive established, the next step was to find an easier route through more accessible country. Market facilities grew up at Abilene, Kansas, on the Kansas Pacific Railroad, and for years the town reigned as the railhead of the cattle kingdom. But by the mid-

1870s, agricultural development in western Kansas was eating away at the open-range land. Cattlemen had to develop other trails and other market outlets. As the railroads began to reach farther west, Dodge City and Wichita in Kansas, Ogallala and Sidney in Nebraska, Cheyenne and Laramie in Wyoming, and Miles City and Glendive in Montana all began to rival Abilene as major centers of stock herding.

There had always been an element of risk and speculation in the open-range cattle business. At any time, "Texas fever"—a disease transmitted to cattle by parasite-carrying ticks—might decimate a herd. Rustlers and Indians frequently seized large numbers of animals. But as settlement of the plains increased, new forms of competition joined these traditional risks. Sheep breeders from California and Oregon brought their flocks onto the range to compete for grass. Farmers ("nesters") from the East threw fences around their claims, blocking trails and breaking up the open range. A series of "range wars"—between sheepmen and cattlemen, between ranchers and farmers—erupted out of the tensions between these competing groups. Some of the wars resulted in significant loss of life and extensive property damage.

Accounts of the lofty profits to be made in the cattle business—an investment of $5,000 would reportedly return $45,000 in four years—tempted eastern, English, and Scottish capital to the plains. Increasingly, the structure of the cattle economy became corporate; in one year, twenty corporations with a combined capital of $12 million were chartered in Wyoming. The result of this frenzied, speculative expansion was that the ranges, already severed and shrunk by the railroads and the farmers, became overstocked. There was not enough grass to support the crowding herds or sustain the long drives. Two severe winters, in 1885–1886 and 1886–1887, with a searing summer between them, stung and scorched the plains. Hundreds of thousands of cattle died; streams and grass dried up; princely ranches and costly investments disappeared in a season.

The open-range industry never recovered; the long drive finally disappeared for good. Railroads displaced the trail as the route to market for livestock. But established cattle ranches—with fenced-in grazing land and stocks of hay for winter feed—survived, grew, and prospered, eventually producing more beef than ever.

Although the cattle industry was overwhelmingly male in its early years, there were always a few women involved in ranching and driving. And as ranching became more sedentary, the presence of women greatly increased. By 1890, more than 250,000 women owned ranches or farms in the western states (many of them as proxies for their husbands or fathers, but some in their own right). Indeed, the region provided women with many opportunities that were closed to them in the East—including the opportunity to participate in politics. Wyoming was the first state in the Union to guarantee woman suffrage.

THE ROMANCE OF THE WEST

The West occupied a special place in the Anglo-American imagination in the nineteenth century. Although it was in fact a rapidly developing commercial region, many white Americans continued to consider it a romantic place, a wilderness where individuals could experience true freedom.

The Western Landscape

Part of the reason was the spectacular natural landscape of the West, so different from anything most Americans had known in the East. Painters of the new "Rocky Mountain School"—of whom the best known were Albert Bierstadt and Thomas Moran—celebrated the new West in grandiose canvases, some of which were taken on tours around the eastern and midwestern states and attracted enormous crowds, eager for a vision of the Great West.

Gradually, the interest in paintings of the West inspired a growing wave of tourism among people eager to see the natural wonders of the region. In the 1880s and 1890s, as railroads extended further into the region and as the Indian Wars subsided, resort hotels began to spring up near some of the most spectacular landscapes in the region.

The Cowboy Culture

Even more appealing than the landscape, perhaps, was the rugged, free-spirited lifestyle that many Americans associated with the West. Many nineteenth-century Americans came to romanticize, especially, the figure of the cowboy and transformed him remarkably quickly from the low-paid worker he actually was into a powerful and enduring figure of myth.

Western novels such as Owen Wister's *The Virginian* (1902) romanticized the cowboy's supposed freedom from traditional social constraints, his affinity with nature, even his supposed propensity for violence. Wister's character—one of the most enduring in popular American literature—was a semi-educated man whose natural decency, courage, and compassion made him a powerful symbol of the supposed virtues of the "frontier." But

The Virginian was only the most famous example of a type of literature that soon swept throughout the United States: novels and stories about the West, and about the lives of cowboys in particular, that appeared in boys' magazines, pulp novels, theater, and even serious literature. The cowboy had become perhaps the most widely admired popular hero in America.

One reason for that was the remarkable popularity of the Wild West shows that traveled throughout the United States and Europe in the late nineteenth and early twentieth centuries and presented entertaining and highly romanticized pictures of the West and the cowboy's life. The most successful were the shows of Buffalo Bill Cody, a former Pony Express rider and Indian fighter, and the hero of popular dime novels for children. Cody's Wild West show, which had dozens of imitators, exploited his own fame. But it was mainly popular for its romanticization of the West and of the life of the cowboy. It included re-enactments of Indian battles and displays of horsemanship and riflery (many of them by the famous sharpshooter Annie Oakley). Buffalo Bill and his imitators confirmed the popular image of the West as a place of romance and glamour and helped keep that image alive for later generations.

PROMOTING THE WEST Buffalo Bill's Wild West show was popular all over the United States, and indeed through much of the world. He was so familiar a figure that many of his posters contained only his picture with the words. "He is Coming." This more conventional poster announces a visit of the show to Brooklyn.

The Idea of the Frontier

Yet it was not simply the particular character of the new West that made it so important to the nation's imagination. It was also that many Americans considered it the last frontier. Since the earliest moments of European settlement in America, the image of uncharted territory to the west had always comforted and inspired those who dreamed of starting life anew. Now, with the last of that unsettled land being slowly absorbed into the nation's civilization, that image exercised a stronger pull than ever.

Mark Twain, one of the great American writers of the nineteenth century, gave voice to this romantic vision of the frontier in a series of brilliant novels and memoirs. In *The Adventures of Tom Sawyer* (1876) and *The Adventures of Huckleberry Finn* (1885), he produced characters who repudiated the constraints of organized society and attempted to escape into a more natural world. For Huck Finn, the vehicle of escape might be a small raft on the Mississippi, but the yearning for freedom reflected a larger vision of the West as the last refuge from the constraints of civilization.

The painter and sculptor Frederic Remington also captured the romance of the West and its image as an alternative to the settled civilization of the East. He portrayed the cowboy as a natural aristocrat, much like Wister's Virginian, living in a natural world in which all the normal supporting structures of "civilization" were missing. Remington became one of the most beloved and successful artists of the nineteenth century.

Theodore Roosevelt, like both Wister and Remington a man born and raised in the East, traveled to the Dakota badlands in the mid-1880s to help himself recover from the sudden death of his young wife. In the 1890s, he published a four-volume history, *The Winning of the West*, with a romanticized account of the spread of white civilization into the frontier.

The clearest and most influential statement of the romantic vision of the frontier came from the historian Frederick Jackson Turner, in a memorable paper he delivered to a meeting of the American Historical Association in Chicago entitled "The Significance of the Frontier in American History." In it he boldly claimed that "the existence of an area of free land [in the West], its continuous recession, and the advance of settlement westward, explain American development." This experience of expansion into the frontier had stimulated individualism, nationalism, and democracy. It had kept opportunities for advancement alive. It had made Americans the distinctive people that they were. "Now," Turner concluded portentously, "the frontier has gone and with its going has closed the first period of American history."

In accepting the idea of the "passing of the frontier," many Americans were acknowledging the end of one of their most cherished myths. As long as it had been possible for them to consider the West an empty, open land, it was possible to believe that there were constantly revitalizing opportunities in American life. Now there was a vague and ominous sense of opportunities foreclosed, of individuals losing their ability to control their own destinies.

THE DISPERSAL OF THE TRIBES

Having imagined the West as a "virgin land" awaiting civilization by white people, many Americans tried to force the region to match their image of it. That meant, above all, ensuring that the Indian tribes would not remain obstacles to the spread of white society.

White Tribal Policies

The traditional policy of the federal government was to regard the tribes simultaneously as independent nations (with which the United States could negotiate treaties) and as wards of the president (who would exercise paternalistic authority over the Indians). The concept of Indian sovereignty had supported the government's attempt before 1860 to erect a permanent frontier between whites and Indians and to reserve the region west of the bend of the Missouri River as a permanent Indian country separated from the rest of the United States. But the belief in tribal sovereignty, and the treaties or agreements with the Indians, were not strong enough to withstand the pressure of white settlers eager for access to Indian lands.

By the early 1850s, the idea of establishing one great enclave in which many tribes could live gave way, in the face of white demands for access to Indian Territory, to a new reservations policy known as "concentration." In 1851, the government assigned all the tribes their own defined reservations, confirmed by individual treaties—treaties often illegitimately negotiated with unauthorized "representatives" chosen by whites, people known sarcastically as "treaty chiefs." The new arrangement had many benefits for whites and few for the Indians. It divided the tribes from one another and made them easier to control. It allowed the government to force tribes into scattered locations and to take over the most desirable lands for white settlement. But it did not survive as the basis of Indian policy for long.

D E B A T I N G　　T H E　　P A S T

The Frontier and the West

T HE EMERGENCE OF the history of the American West as an important field of scholarship can be traced to the paper Frederick
Jackson Turner delivered at a meeting of the American Historical Association in 1893: "The Significance of the Frontier in American History." The
"Turner thesis," or "frontier thesis," as his argument became known,
shaped both popular and scholarly views of the West for two generations.

Turner stated his thesis simply. The settlement of the West by white
Americans—"the existence of an area of free land, its continuous recession, and the advance of American settlement westward"—was the central
story of the nation's history. The process of westward expansion had transformed a desolate and savage land into modern civilization. It had also
continually renewed American ideas of democracy and individualism.

In the first half of the twentieth century, virtually everyone who wrote
about the West echoed at least part of Turner's argument. Ray Allen
Billington's *Westward Expansion* (1949), the standard textbook in the field
for decades, was almost wholly consistent with the Turnerian model. In
The Great Plains (1931) and *The Great Frontier* (1952), Walter Prescott
Webb similarly emphasized the bravery and ingenuity of white settlers in
the Southwest.

Serious efforts to displace the Turner thesis as the explanation of western American history began after World War II. In *Virgin Land* (1950),
Henry Nash Smith examined many of the same heroic images of the West
that Turner and his disciples had presented; but he treated those images
less as descriptions of reality than as myths. Earl Pomeroy challenged
Turner's notion of the West as a place of individualism, innovation, and
democratic renewal. "Conservatism, inheritance, and continuity bulked at
least as large," he claimed. Howard Lamar, in *Dakota Territory, 1861–1889*
(1956) and *The Far Southwest* (1966), emphasized the highly diverse charac-

ters of different areas of the West and thus challenged the Turnerian idea that a single western environment shaped the western experience.

The western historians who began to emerge in the late 1970s launched an even more emphatic attack on the Turner thesis and the idea of the "frontier." Echoing the interest of other historians in issues of race, gender, ethnicity, and culture, "new" western historians such as Richard White, Patricia Nelson Limerick, William Cronon, Donald Worster, Peggy Pascoe, and many others challenged the Turnerians on a number of points.

Turner saw the nineteenth-century West as "free land" awaiting the expansion of Anglo-American settlement and American democracy. The "new western historians" have rejected the concept of an empty "frontier," emphasizing instead the elaborate and highly developed civilizations (Native American, Hispanic, mixed-blood, and others) that already existed in the region. White, English-speaking Americans, they have argued, did not so much settle the West as conquer it. And Anglo-Americans in the West continue to share the region not only with the Indians and Hispanics who preceded them there, but also with African Americans, Asians, Latin Americans, and others who flowed into the West at the same time they did.

The Turnerian West was a place of heroism, triumph, and above all progress, dominated by the feats of brave white men. The West the new historians describe is a less triumphant (and less masculine) place in which bravery and success coexist with oppression, greed, and failure; in which decaying ghost towns, bleak Indian reservations, impoverished barrios, and ecologically devastated landscapes are as characteristic of western development as great ranches, rich farms, and prosperous cities; and in which women are as important as men in shaping the societies that emerged.

To Turner and his disciples, the nineteenth-century West was a place where rugged individualism flourished and replenished American democracy. The new scholars consider that belief a self-serving myth. Western "pioneers" were never self-sufficient. The region was inextricably tied to a national and international capitalist economy. Westerners depended on government-subsidized railroads for access to markets, federal troops for protection from Indians, and (later) government-funded dams and canals for irrigating their fields and sustaining their towns.

And while Turner defined the West as a process—a process of settlement that came to an end with the "closing of the frontier" in the late nineteenth century—the new historians see the West as a region. Its history does not end in 1890. It continues into our own time.

In 1867, in the aftermath of a series of bloody conflicts, Congress established the Indian Peace Commission, composed of both soldiers and civilians, to recommend a new and presumably permanent Indian policy. The commission recommended replacing the "concentration" policy with a new one. The government would move all the Plains tribes into two large reservations—one in Indian Territory (Oklahoma), the other in the Dakotas. At a series of meetings with the tribes, government agents cajoled, bribed, and tricked representatives of the Arapaho, Cheyenne, Sioux, and other tribes into agreeing to treaties establishing the new reservations.

But this "solution" worked little better than previous ones. Part of the problem was the abysmal way in which corrupt or incompetent agents of the Bureau of Indian Affairs administered the reservations the government had established. White management of Indian matters was entrusted to the Bureau of Indian Affairs, located in the Department of the Interior. But the problem was also a result of the relentless slaughtering by whites of the buffalo herds that supported the tribes' way of life. After the Civil War, white demand for buffalo hides (especially in the East) became a national phenomenon. Professional and amateur hunters—even casual visitors shooting from passing trains—swarmed over the plains, killing the

BUFFALO HIDES The appetite for buffalo hides in the urban East grew rapidly in the late nineteenth century, creating an incentive for hunters to decimate the massive herds. This photograph shows 40,000 buffalo hides piled up in a yard in Dodge City, Kansas, in 1878. Within a few years after that, the buffalo herds were almost extinct.

huge animals. Some Indian tribes (notably the Blackfeet) also began killing large numbers of buffalo to sell in the booming new market. The southern herd was virtually exterminated by 1875, and within a few years the smaller northern herd had met the same fate. In 1865, there had been at least 15 million buffalo; a decade later, fewer than a thousand of the great beasts survived. By destroying the buffalo herds, whites were destroying the Indians' source of food and supplies and their ability to resist white advance.

The Indian Wars

There was almost incessant fighting between whites and Indians from the 1850s to the 1880s, as Indians struggled against the growing threats to their civilizations. Indian warriors, usually traveling in raiding parties of thirty to forty men, attacked wagon trains, stagecoaches, and isolated ranches, often in retaliation for earlier attacks on them by whites. As the United States Army became more deeply involved in the fighting, the tribes began to focus more of their attacks on white soldiers.

At times, this small-scale fighting escalated. During the Civil War, the eastern Sioux in Minnesota, cramped on a small reservation and exploited by corrupt white agents, suddenly rebelled. Led by Little Crow, they killed more than 700 whites before being subdued by a force of regulars and militiamen. Thirty-eight of the Indians were hanged, and the tribe was exiled to the Dakotas.

At the same time, fighting flared up in eastern Colorado, where the Arapaho and Cheyenne were coming into conflict with white miners settling in the region. Bands of Indians attacked stagecoach lines and settlements in an effort to regain territory they had lost. In response to these incidents, whites called up a large territorial militia, and the army issued dire threats of retribution. The governor urged all friendly Indians to congregate at army posts for protection before the army began its campaign. One Arapaho and Cheyenne band under Black Kettle, apparently in response to the invitation, camped near Fort Lyon on Sand Creek in November 1864. Some members of the party were warriors, but Black Kettle believed he was under official protection and exhibited no hostile intention. Nevertheless, Colonel J. M. Chivington, apparently encouraged by the army commander of the district, led a volunteer militia force—largely consisting of unemployed miners, many of whom were apparently drunk—to the unsuspecting camp and massacred 133 people, 105 of them women and children. Black Kettle himself escaped the Sand

Creek massacre. But four years later, in 1868, he and his Cheyennes, some of whom were now at war with the whites, were caught on the Washita River, near the Texas border, by Colonel George A. Custer. White troops killed the chief and his people.

At the end of the Civil War, white troops stepped up their wars against the western Indians on several fronts. The most serious and sustained conflict was in Montana, where the army was attempting to build a road, the Bozeman Trail, to connect Fort Laramie, Wyoming, to the new mining centers. The western Sioux resented this intrusion into the heart of their buffalo range. Led by one of their great chiefs, Red Cloud, they so harried the soldiers and the construction party—among other things, burning the forts that were supposed to guard the route—that the road could not be used.

But it was not only the United States military that harassed the tribes. It was also unofficial violence by white vigilantes who engaged in what became known as "Indian hunting." In California, in particular, tracking down and killing Indians became for some whites a kind of sport. Sometimes the killing was in response to Indian raids on white communities. But considerable numbers of whites were committed to the goal of literal "elimination" of the tribes whatever their behavior, a goal that rested on the belief in the essential inhumanity of Indians and the impossibility of white coexistence with them. In California, civilians killed close to 5,000 Indians between 1850 and 1880—one of many factors (disease and poverty being the more important) that reduced the Indian population of the state from 150,000 before the Civil War to 30,000 in 1870.

The treaties negotiated in 1867 brought a temporary lull to many of the conflicts. But new forces soon shattered the peace again. In the early 1870s, more waves of white settlers, mostly miners, began to penetrate some of the lands in Dakota Territory supposedly guaranteed to the tribes in 1867. Indian resistance flared anew, this time with even greater strength. In the northern plains, the Sioux rose up in 1875 and left their reservation. When white officials ordered them to return, bands of warriors gathered in Montana and united under two great leaders: Crazy Horse and Sitting Bull. Three army columns set out to round them up and force them back onto the reservation. With the expedition, as colonel of the famous Seventh Cavalry, was the colorful and controversial George A. Custer. At the Battle of the Little Bighorn in southern Montana in 1876—perhaps the most famous of all conflicts between whites and Indians—an unprecedentedly large army, perhaps 2,500 tribal warriors, surprised Custer and part of his regiment, surrounded them, and killed every man.

But the Indians did not have the political organization or the supplies to keep their troops united. Soon the warriors drifted off in bands to elude pursuit or search for food, and the army ran them down singly and returned them to Dakota. The power of the Sioux—and of their proud leaders, Crazy Horse and Sitting Bull—soon collapsed. They accepted defeat and life on reservations.

One of the most dramatic episodes in Indian history occurred in Idaho in 1877. The Nez Percé were a small and relatively peaceful tribe, some of whose members had managed to live unmolested in Oregon into the 1870s without ever signing a treaty with the United States. But under pressure from white settlers, the government forced them to move onto a reservation that another branch of the tribe had accepted by treaty in the 1850s. With no realistic prospect of resisting, the Indians began the journey to the reservation; but on the way, several younger Indians, drunk and angry, killed four white settlers.

The leader of the band, Chief Joseph, persuaded his followers to flee from the expected retribution. American troops pursued and attacked them, only to be driven off in a battle at White Bird Canyon. After that, the Nez Percé scattered in several directions and became part of a remarkable chase. Joseph moved with 200 warriors and 350 women, children, and old people in an effort to reach Canada and take refuge with the Sioux there. Pursued by four columns of American soldiers smarting from their defeat at White Bird Canyon, the Indians covered 1,321 miles in seventy-five days, repelling or evading the army time and again. They were finally caught just short of the Canadian boundary. Some escaped and slipped across the border; but Joseph and most of his followers, weary and discouraged, finally gave up. "Hear me, my chiefs," Joseph said after meeting with the American general Nelson Miles. "I am tired. My heart is sick and sad. From where the sun now stands, I will fight no more forever."

The last Indians to maintain organized resistance against the whites were the Chiricahua Apaches, who fought intermittently from the 1860s to the late 1880s. The two ablest chiefs of this fierce tribe were Mangas Colorados and Cochise. Mangas was murdered during the Civil War by white soldiers who tricked him into surrendering, and in 1872 Cochise agreed to peace in exchange for a reservation that included some of the tribe's traditional land. But Cochise died in 1874, and his successor, Geronimo—unwilling to bow to white pressures to assimilate—fought on for more than a decade longer, establishing bases in the mountains of Arizona and Mexico and leading warriors in intermittent raids against white outposts. With each raid, however, the number of warring Apaches dwindled, as some warriors died and others

THE SURRENDER OF GERONIMO The great Apache warrior Geronimo (front row, third from right) sits with members of his diminished band after surrendering to United States troops in 1886. The two men at front row, left, are Geronimo's half brothers. The young boy at front row, right, is his son.

drifted away to the reservation. By 1886, Geronimo's plight was hopeless. His band consisted of only about 30 people, including women and children, while his white pursuers numbered perhaps 10,000. Geronimo recognized the odds and surrendered, an event that marked the end of formal warfare between Indians and whites.

The Apache wars were the most violent of all the Indian conflicts, perhaps because the tribes were now the most desperate, and they produced brutality on both sides. But it was the whites who committed the most flagrant atrocities. That did not end with the conclusion of the Apache wars. Another tragic encounter occurred in 1890 as a result of a religious revival among the Sioux—a revival that itself symbolized the catastrophic effects of the white assaults on Indian civilization. As other tribes had done in trying times in the past, many of these Indians turned to a prophet who led them in a religious revival.

This time the prophet was Wovoka, a Paiute who inspired a fervent spiritual awakening that began in Nevada and spread quickly to the plains. The new revival emphasized the coming of a messiah, but its most conspicuous feature was a mass, emotional "Ghost Dance," which inspired ecstatic, mystical visions among many participants. Among these visions were images of a retreat of white people from the plains and a restoration of the great buffalo herds. White agents on the Sioux reservation watched the dances in bewilderment and fear; some believed they might be the preliminary to hostilities.

On December 29, 1890, the Seventh Cavalry (which had once been Custer's regiment) tried to round up a group of about 350 cold and starving Sioux at Wounded Knee, South Dakota. Fighting broke out in which about 40 white soldiers and up to 200 of the Indians, including women and children, died. An Indian may well have fired the first shot, but the battle soon turned into a one-sided massacre, as the white soldiers turned their new machine guns on the Indians and mowed them down in the snow.

The Dawes Act

Even before the Ghost Dance and the Wounded Knee tragedy, the federal government had moved to destroy forever the tribal structure that had always been the cornerstone of Indian culture. Reversing its policy of nearly fifty years of creating reservations in which the tribes would be isolated from white society, Congress abolished the practice by which tribes owned reservation lands communally. Some supporters of the new policy believed they were acting for the good of the Indians, whom they considered a "vanishing race" in need of rescue by white society. The action was designed to force Indians to become landowners and farmers, to abandon their collective society and culture and become part of white civilization.

The Dawes Severalty Act of 1887 (usually known simply as the Dawes Act) provided for the gradual elimination of most tribal ownership of land and the allotment of tracts to individual owners: 160 acres to the head of a family, 80 acres to a single adult or orphan, 40 acres to each dependent child. Adult owners were given United States citizenship, but unlike other citizens, they could not gain full title to their property for twenty-five years (supposedly to prevent them from selling the land to speculators). The act applied to most of the western tribes.

In applying the Dawes Act, the Bureau of Indian Affairs relentlessly promoted the idea of assimilation that lay behind it. Not only did agents of the bureau try to move Indian families onto their own plots of land; they also took many Indian children away from their families and sent them to boarding schools run by whites, where they believed the young people could be educated to abandon tribal ways. They moved as well to stop Indian religious rituals and encouraged the spread of Christianity and the creation of Christian churches on the reservations.

Few Indians were prepared for this wrenching change. In any case, white administration of the Dawes Act was so corrupt and inept that ultimately the government simply abandoned most efforts to enforce it. Much of the reservation land, therefore, was never distributed to individual owners. Congress attempted to speed assimilation with the Burke Act of 1906, but Indians continued to resist.

THE RISE AND DECLINE
OF THE WESTERN FARMER

The arrival of the miners, the empire building of the cattle ranchers, the dispersal of the Indian tribes—all served as a prelude to the decisive phase of white settlement of the Far West. Even before the Civil War, farmers had begun moving into the plains region, challenging the dominance of the ranchers and the Indians and occasionally coming into conflict with both. By the 1870s, what was once a trickle had become a deluge. Farmers poured into the plains and beyond, enclosed land that had once been hunting territory for Indians and open range for cattle, and established a new agricultural region.

For a time in the late 1870s and early 1880s, the new western farmers flourished, enjoying the fruits of an agricultural economic boom comparable in many ways to the booms that eastern industry periodically enjoyed. Beginning in the mid-1880s, however, the boom turned to bust, and the western agricultural economy began a long, steady decline.

Farming on the Plains

Many factors combined to produce the surge of western agricultural settlement, but the most important was the railroads. Before the Civil War, the Great Plains had been accessible only through a difficult journey by wagon. But beginning in the 1860s, a great new network of railroad lines developed, spearheaded by the transcontinental route Congress had authorized and subsidized in 1862. They made huge new areas of settlement accessible.

The building of the transcontinental line—completed in 1869 when the two lines met at Promontory Point, Utah—was a dramatic and monumental achievement. But while this first transcontinental line captured the public imagination, the construction of subsidiary lines in the following years proved of greater importance to the West. State governments, imitating Washington, subsidized railroad development by offering direct financial aid, favorable loans, and more than 50 million acres of land (on top of the 130 million acres the federal government had already provided). Although built and operated by private corporations, the railroads were in many respects public projects.

The railroads spurred agricultural settlement by making access to the Great Plains easier. But the railroad companies also actively promoted settlement, both to provide themselves with customers for their services and to increase the value of their vast landholdings. The companies set rates so low for settlers that almost anyone could afford the trip west. And they sold much of their land at very low prices and with liberal credit to prospective settlers.

Contributing further to the great surge of white agricultural expansion was a pronounced but temporary change in the climate of the Great Plains. For several years in succession, beginning in the 1870s, rainfall in the plains states was well above average. White Americans now rejected the old idea that the region was the Great American Desert. Some even claimed that cultivation of the plains actually encouraged rainfall.

Even under the most favorable conditions, farming on the plains presented special problems. First was the problem of fencing. Farmers had to enclose their land, if for no other reason than to protect it from the herds of the open-range cattlemen. But materials for traditional wood or stone fences were unavailable. In the mid-1870s, however, two Illinois farmers, Joseph H. Glidden and I. L. Ellwood, solved this problem by developing and marketing barbed wire, which became standard equipment on the plains and revolutionized fencing practices all over the country and the world.

The second problem was water. Water was scarce even when rainfall was above average. After 1887, a series of dry seasons began, and lands that had been fertile now returned to semidesert. Some farmers dealt with the problem by using deep wells pumped by steel windmills, by turning to what was called dryland farming (a system of tillage designed to conserve moisture in the soil by covering it with a dust blanket), or by planting drought-resistant crops. In many areas of the plains, however, only large-scale irrigation could save the endangered farms. But irrigation projects of the necessary magnitude required government assistance, and neither the federal nor the state governments were prepared to fund the projects.

Most of the people who moved into the region had previously been farmers in the Middle West, the East, or Europe. In the booming years of the early 1880s, with land values rising, the new farmers had no problem obtaining extensive and easy credit and had every reason to believe they would soon be able to retire their debts. But the arid years of the late 1880s—during which crop prices were falling while production was becoming more expensive—changed that prospect. Tens of thousands of farmers could not pay their debts and were forced to abandon their farms. There was, in effect, a reverse migration: white settlers moving back east, sometimes turning once-flourishing communities into desolate ghost towns. Those who remained continued to suffer from falling prices (for example, wheat, which had sold for $1.60 a bushel at the end of the Civil War, dropped to 49 cents in the 1890s) and persistent indebtedness.

Commercial Agriculture

American farming by the late nineteenth century no longer bore very much relation to the comforting image many Americans continued to cherish. The sturdy, independent farmer of popular myth was being replaced by the commercial farmer—attempting to do in the agricultural economy what industrialists were doing in the manufacturing economy.

Commercial farmers were not self-sufficient and made no effort to become so. They specialized in cash crops that were sold in national or world markets. They did not often make their own household supplies or grow their own food but bought them from merchants. This kind of farming, when it was successful, raised farmers' living standards. But it also made them dependent on bankers and interest rates, railroads and freight rates, national and European markets, world supply and demand. And unlike the capitalists of the industrial order, they could not regulate their production or influence the prices of what they sold.

Between 1865 and 1900, agriculture became an international business. Farm output increased dramatically, not only in the United States but in Brazil, Argentina, Canada, Australia, New Zealand, Russia, and elsewhere. At the same time, modern forms of communication and transportation—the telephone, the telegraph, steam navigation, railroads—were creating new markets around the world for agricultural goods. American commercial farmers, constantly opening new lands, produced much more than the domestic market could consume; they relied on the world market to absorb their surplus, but in that market they faced major competition. Cotton farmers depended on export sales for 70 percent of their annual income, wheat farmers for 30 to 40 percent; but the volatility of the international market put them at great risk. Beginning in the 1880s, worldwide overproduction led to a drop in prices for most agricultural goods and hence to great economic distress for many of the more than 6 million American farm families. By the 1890s, 27 percent of the farms in the country were mortgaged; by 1910, 33 percent. In 1880, 25 percent of all farms had been operated by tenants; by 1910, the proportion had grown to 37 percent. Commercial farming made some people fabulously wealthy. But the farm economy as a whole was suffering a significant decline relative to the rest of the nation.

The Farmers' Grievances

American farmers were painfully aware that something was wrong. But few yet understood the implications of national and world overproduction. Instead, they concentrated their attention and anger on more immediate, more comprehensible—and no less real—problems: inequitable freight rates, high interest charges, and an inadequate currency.

The farmers' first and most burning grievance was against the railroads. In many cases, the railroads charged higher rates for farm goods than for other goods, and higher rates in the South and West than in the Northeast. Railroads also controlled elevator and warehouse facilities in buying centers and charged arbitrary storage rates.

Farmers also resented the institutions controlling credit—banks, loan companies, insurance corporations. Since sources of credit in the West and South were few, farmers had to take loans on whatever terms they could get, often at interest rates of from 10 to 25 percent. Many farmers had to pay these loans back in years when prices were dropping and currency was becoming scarce. As a result, expansion of the currency became an increasingly important issue to farmers.

A third grievance concerned prices—both the prices farmers received for their products and the prices they paid for goods they bought. A farmer could plant a large crop at a moment when its price was high and find that by the time of the harvest the price had declined. Farmers' fortunes rose and fell in response to unpredictable forces. But many farmers became convinced (often with some reason) that "middlemen"—speculators, bankers, regional and local agents—were conspiring with one another to fix prices so as to benefit themselves at the growers' expense. Many farmers also came to believe (again, not entirely without reason) that manufacturers in the East were colluding to keep the prices of farm goods low and the prices of industrial goods high. Although farmers sold their crops in a competitive world market, they bought manufactured goods in a domestic market protected by tariffs and dominated by trusts and corporations.

The Agrarian Malaise

These economic difficulties produced a series of social and cultural resentments. In part, this was a result of the isolation of farm life. Farm families in some parts of the country—particularly in the prairie and plains regions, where large farms were scattered over vast areas—were virtually cut off from the outside world. During the winter months and spells of bad weather, the loneliness and boredom could become nearly unbearable. Many farmers lacked access to adequate education for their children, to proper medical facilities, to recreational or cultural activities, to virtually anything that might give them a sense of being members of a community. Older farmers felt the sting of watching their children leave the farm for the city. They felt the humiliation of being ridiculed as "hayseeds" by the new urban culture that was coming to dominate American life.

The result of this sense of isolation and obsolescence was a growing malaise among many farmers, a discontent that would help create a great national political movement in the 1890s. It found reflection, too, in the literature that emerged from rural America. Writers in the late nineteenth century might romanticize the rugged life of the cowboy and the western miner. For the farmer, however, the image was usually different. Hamlin Garland, for example, reflected the growing disillusionment in a series of novels and short stories. In the past, Garland wrote in the introduction to his novel *Jason Edwards* (1891), the agrarian frontier had seemed to be "the Golden West, the land of wealth and freedom and happiness. All of the associations called up by the spoken word, the West, were fabulous, mythic, hopeful." Now, however, the bright promise had faded. The trials of rural life were crushing the human spirit. "So this is the reality of the dream!" a character in *Jason Edwards* exclaims. "A shanty on a barren plain, hot and lone as a desert. My God!" Once, sturdy yeoman farmers had viewed themselves as the backbone of American life. Now they were becoming painfully aware that their position was declining in relation to the rising urban-industrial society to the east.

CONCLUSION

To many Americans in the late nineteenth century, the West seemed a place utterly unlike the rest of the United States—an untamed "frontier" in which hardy pioneers were creating a new society, in which sturdy individuals still had a chance to be heroes. The reality of the West in these years, however, was very different from this enduring image. White Americans were moving into the vast regions west of the Mississippi at a remarkable rate in the years after the Civil War, and many of them were indeed settling in lands far from any civilization they had ever known. But the West was not an empty place. It contained a large population of Indians, with whom the white settlers sometimes lived uneasily and sometimes battled, but almost always in the end pushed aside and (with help from the federal government) relocated onto lands whites did not want. There were significant numbers of Mexicans in some areas, small populations of Asians in others, and African Americans moving in from the South in search of land and freedom. The West was not a barren frontier, but a place of many cultures.

The West was also closely and increasingly tied to the emerging capitalist-industrial economy of the East. The miners who flooded into California, Colorado, Nevada, the Dakotas, and elsewhere were responding to the demand in the East for gold and silver, but even more for utilitarian minerals that had industrial uses, such as iron ore, copper, lead, zinc, and quartz. Cattle and sheep ranchers produced meat, wool, and leather for eastern consumers and manufacturers. Farmers grew crops for sale in national and international commodities markets. The West certainly looked different from the East, and its people lived their lives in surroundings very different from those of eastern cities. But the growth of the West was very much a part of the growth of the rest of the nation. And the culture of the West, despite the romantic images of pioneering individuals embraced by easterners and westerners alike, was at its heart as much a culture of economic growth and capitalist ambition as was the culture of the rest of the nation.

FOR FURTHER REFERENCE

Suggested Readings

Frederick Jackson Turner, *The Frontier in American History* (1920) is a classic argument on the centrality of the frontier experience to American democracy. Richard White, *"It's Your Misfortune and None of My Own": A History of the American West* (1991) is a substantial revision of myths about the West and an excellent general history of the region. Patricia Nelson Limerick's *The Legacy of Conquest: The Unbroken Past of the American West* (1987) argues the West was not a frontier but rather an inhabited place conquered by Anglo-Americans. Ronald Takaki, *Strangers from a Different Shore: A History of Asian Americans* (1989) surveys the Asian-American experience of immigrants to America's western shore. Sarah Deutsch, *No Separate Refuge: Culture, Class, and Gender on the Anglo-Hispanic Frontier in the Early Southwest, 1880–1940* (1987) and Mario T. Garcia, *Desert Immigrants: The Mexicans of El Paso, 1880–1920* (1981) are important studies of Latinos in the West. Frederick E. Hoxie, *A Final Promise: The Campaign to Assimilate the Indians, 1880–1920* (1984) is a good examination of the society of the tribes and the government policies that affected them after the end of the Indian Wars. John Mack Faragher, *Women and Men on the Overland Trail* (1979) is a good account of the social experience of westering migrants, and Peggy Pascoe, *Relations of Rescue: The Search for Female Moral Authority in the American West, 1874–1939* (1990) examines the female communities of the West. William Cronon, *Nature's Metropolis: Chicago and the Great West* (1991) examines the relationships among various environments and economies of the West. John Mack Faragher, *Daniel Boone* (1992) is a study of one of the West's most fabled figures. Richard Slotkin, *The Fatal Environment: The Myth of the Frontier in the Age of Industrialization* (1985) and *Gunfighter Nation* (1992) are provocative cultural studies of the idea of the West. Henry Nash Smith, *Virgin Land* (1950) is a classic study of the West in American culture.

Films

(The best source for information on how to find these and other films is *Bowker's Complete Video Directory*—3 volumes.) *The Gold Rush* (1996) is a stirring introduction to the California gold rush and its impact on indigenous cultures. The Anglo-American conquest of the West more generally is the subject of *The Way West* (1995). *Ishi: The Last Yahi* (1992) depicts the mass extermination of Native Americans in the United States between 1492 and 1910. *"The Buffalo Soldiers"* (1997) recounts the heroism and pathos of the black 9th and 10th Cavalry, called "buffalo soldiers" by their enemies.

Internet Resources

Internet websites containing historical material relevant to the subjects discussed in this chapter can be reached through the McGraw-Hill history site at www.mhhe.com/socscience/history/usa/link/linktop.htm.

CHAPTER SEVENTEEN

Industrial Supremacy

Sources of Industrial Growth ～ *Capitalism and Its Critics*
The Ordeal of the Worker

ITH A STRIDE that astonished statisticians, the conquering hosts of business enterprise swept over the continent; twenty-five years after the death of Lincoln, America had become, in the quantity and value of her products, the first manufacturing nation of the world. What England had accomplished in a hundred years, the United States had achieved in half the time." So wrote the historians Charles and Mary Beard in the 1920s, expressing the amazement many Americans felt when they considered the remarkable expansion of their industrial economy in the late nineteenth century.

In fact, America's rise to industrial supremacy was not as sudden as such observers suggested. The nation had been building a manufacturing economy since early in the nineteenth century; industry was well established before the Civil War. But Americans were clearly correct in observing that the accomplishments of the last three decades of the nineteenth century overshadowed all the earlier progress. Those years witnessed nothing less than the transformation of the nation.

The remarkable growth did much to increase the wealth and improve the lives of many Americans. But such benefits were very unequally shared. While industrial titans and a growing middle class were enjoying a prosperity without precedent in the nation's history, workers, farmers, and others were experiencing an often painful ordeal that slowly edged the United States toward a great economic and political crisis.

515

TIME LINE				
1859	**1866**	**1870**	**1873**	**1876**
First oil well drilled	National Labor Union founded First transatlantic cable	Rockefeller founds Standard Oil	Carnegie Steel founded Economic panic	Bell invents telephone

1877	**1879**	**1881**	**1886**	**1888**	**1892**
Nationwide railroad strike	Edison invents electric light bulb	American Federation of Labor founded	Haymarket bombing	Bellamy's *Looking Backward*	Homestead steel strike

1893	**1894**	**1901**	**1903**	**1914**	
Depression begins	Pullman strike	Morgan creates U.S. Steel	Wright brothers' airplane flight	Ford introduces factory assembly lines	

SOURCES OF INDUSTRIAL GROWTH

Many factors contributed to the growth of American industry: abundant raw materials; a large and growing labor supply; a surge in technological innovation; the emergence of a talented, ambitious, and often ruthless group of entrepreneurs; a federal government eager to assist the growth of business; and a great and expanding domestic market for the products of manufacturing.

Industrial Technologies

The rapid emergence of new technologies, together with the discovery of new materials and productive processes, was one of the principal sources of late-nineteenth-century industrial growth.

Some of the most important innovations were in communications. In 1866, Cyrus W. Field laid a transatlantic telegraph cable to Europe. During the next decade, Alexander Graham Bell developed the first telephone with commercial capacity; and by the 1890s, the American Telephone and Telegraph Company, which handled his interests, had installed nearly half

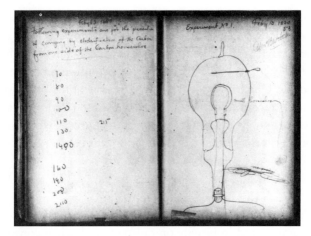

EDISON'S NOTEBOOK This page from one of Thomas Edison's notebooks shows
sketches of and notes on some of his early experiments with an incandescent
lamp—what we know as an electric lightbulb. Edison was not only the most
celebrated inventor of his day, but by the early twentieth century one of the
greatest popular heroes in American life in a time when scientific and
technological progress was considered the defining feature of the age.

a million telephones in American cities. By 1900 there were 1.35 million
telephones, and by 1920 13.3 million (see pp. 567–569). And the Italian
inventor Guglielmo Marconi was taking the first steps toward the development of radio in the 1890s; the technology he developed quickly found
its way to the United States. Other inventions that speeded the pace of
business organization were the typewriter (by Christopher L. Sholes in
1868), the cash register (by James Ritty in 1879), and the calculating or
adding machine (by William S. Burroughs in 1891).

Among the most revolutionary innovations was the introduction in
the 1870s of electricity as a source of light and power. Among the pioneers
of electric lighting were Charles F. Brush, who devised the arc lamp for
street illumination, and Thomas A. Edison, who invented the incandescent lamp (or lightbulb), which could be used for both street and home
lighting. Edison and others designed improved generators and built large
power plants to furnish electricity to whole cities. By the turn of the century, electric power was becoming commonplace in street railway systems,
in the elevators of urban skyscrapers, in factories, and increasingly in offices and homes.

Particularly important to trade and industry was the development of new, high-efficiency steam engines capable of powering larger ships at faster speeds than ever imagined in the past. The new high-speed freighters, for example, made it cheaper for Britain to buy wheat grown in Canada and the United States than to grow it at home. The introduction of refrigerated ships in the 1870s made it possible to transport meat from North America and even Australia and Asia to Europe, which also encouraged reductions in domestic food production there.

The Technology of Iron and Steel Production

Perhaps the most important technological development in a nation whose economy rested so heavily on railroads and urban construction was the revolutionizing of iron and steel production in the late nineteenth century. Iron production had developed slowly in the United States through most of the nineteenth century, mostly driven by the demand for iron rails for railroads; steel production had developed hardly at all by the end of the Civil War. In the 1870s and 1880s, however, iron production soared as railroads added 40,000 new miles of track, and steel production made great strides toward what would soon be its dominance in the metals industry.

The story of the rise of steel is, like so many other stories of economic development, a story of technological discovery. An Englishman, Henry Bessemer, and an American, William Kelly, had developed, almost simultaneously, a process for converting iron into the much more durable and versatile steel. (The process, which took Bessemer's name, consisted of blowing air through molten iron to burn out the impurities.) The Bessemer process also relied on the discovery by the British metallurgist Robert Mushet that ingredients could be added to the iron during conversion to transform it into steel. In 1868, the New Jersey ironmaster Abram S. Hewitt introduced from Europe another method of making steel—the open-hearth process, which ultimately largely supplanted the Bessemer process. These techniques made possible the production of steel in great quantities and large dimensions, for use in the manufacture of locomotives, steel rails, and girders for the construction of tall buildings.

The steel industry emerged first in western Pennsylvania and eastern Ohio. That was partly because iron ore could be found there in abundance and because there was already a flourishing iron industry there. It was also because the new forms of steel production created a demand for new kinds of fuel—and particularly for the anthracite (or hard) coal that was plentiful in Pennsylvania. Later, new techniques made it possible to use soft bituminous coal (easily mined in western Pennsylvania), which could then be converted to coke to fuel steel furnaces. As a result, Pittsburgh quickly became the center of the steel world. But the industry was growing so fast that new sources of ore were soon necessary. The upper peninsula of Michigan, the Mesabi Range in Minnesota, and the area around Birmingham, Alabama, became important ore-producing centers by the end of the century, and new centers of steel production grew up near them: Cleveland, Detroit, Chicago, and Birmingham, among others.

Until the Civil War, iron and steel furnaces were mostly made of stone and usually built against the side of a hill to reduce construction demands. In the 1870s and after, however, furnaces were redesigned as cylindrical iron shells lined with brick. These massive new furnaces were 75 feet tall and higher and could produce over 500 tons a week.

As the steel industry spread, new transportation systems emerged to serve it. The steel production in the Great Lakes region was possible only because of the availability of steam freighters capable of carrying ore on the lakes. The demand for vessels capable of transporting oil and the development of the new and more powerful steam engine encouraged, in turn, the design of larger and heavier freighters—such as the *R. J. Hackett*, launched in 1869, which could carry 1,200 tons of ore. Shippers used new steam engines to speed the unloading of ore, a task that previously had been performed, slowly and laboriously, by men and horses.

There was even a closer relationship between the emerging steel companies and the railroads. Steel manufacturers provided rails and parts for cars to the railroads; railroads were both markets for and transporters of manufactured steel. But the relationship soon became more intimate than that. The Pennsylvania Railroad, for example, literally created the Pennsylvania Steel Company, provided it with substantial initial capital, and ensured it a market for its products with an immediate contract for steel rails. That was only one of many cases in which railroad and steel companies effectively merged or formed intimate connections.

The steel industry's need for lubrication for its machines helped create another important new industry in the late nineteenth century—oil. (Not until later did oil become important primarily for its potential as a fuel.) The existence of petroleum reserves in western Pennsylvania had been common knowledge for some time. Not until the 1850s, however, after Pennsylvania businessman George Bissell showed that the substance could be burned in lamps and that it could also yield such products as paraffin, naphtha, and lubricating oil, was there any sense of its commercial value. Bissell raised money to begin drilling; and in 1859, Edwin L. Drake, one of Bissell's employees, established the first oil well near Titusville, Pennsylvania, which was soon producing 500 barrels of oil a month. Demand for petroleum grew quickly, and promoters soon developed other fields in Pennsylvania, Ohio, and West Virginia. By the 1870s, oil had advanced to fourth place among the nation's exports.

The Airplane and the Automobile

Among the technological innovations that was to have the farthest-reaching impact on the United States was the invention of the automobile. Two technologies were critical to its development. One was the creation of gasoline (or petrol), which was the result of an extraction process developed in the late nineteenth century in the United States by which lubricating oil and fuel oil were removed separately from crude oil. As early as the 1870s, designers in France, Germany, and Austria—inspired by the success of railroad engines—had begun to develop an "internal combustion engine," which used the expanding power of burning gas to drive pistons. A German, Nicolaus August Otto, created a gas-powered "four-stroke" engine in the mid-1860s, which was a precursor to automobile engines. But he did not develop a way to untether it from gas lines to be used portably in machines. One of Otto's former employees, Gottfried Daimler later perfected an engine that could be used in automobiles (including the famous early car that took Daimler's name).

The American automobile industry developed rapidly in the aftermath of these breakthroughs. Charles and Frank Duryea built the first gasoline-driven motor vehicle in America in 1903. Three years later, Henry Ford produced the first of the famous cars that would bear his name. By 1910, the industry had become a major force in the economy, and the automobile was beginning to reshape American social and cultural life, as well as the nation's landscape. In 1895, there were only four automobiles on the American highways. By 1917, there were nearly 5 million.

The search for a means of human flight was as old as civilization, and had been almost entirely futile until the late nineteenth century when engineers, scientists, and tinkerers in both the United States and Europe began to experiment with a wide range of aeronautic devices. Balloonists began to consider ways to make dirigibles useful vehicles of transportation. Others experimented with kites and gliders to see if they could somehow be used to propel humans through the air.

Among those testing gliders were two brothers in Ohio, Wilbur and Orville Wright, who owned a bicycle shop in which they began to construct a glider that could be propelled through the air by an internal-combustion engine (the same kind of engine that was propelling automobiles). Four years after they began their experiments, Orville made a celebrated test flight near Kitty Hawk, North Carolina, in which an airplane took off by itself and traveled 120 feet in 12 seconds under its own power before settling back to earth. By the fall of 1904, they had improved the plane to the point where they were able to fly over 23 miles, and in the following year they began to take a few passengers on their flights with them.

Although the first working airplane was built in the United States, aviation technology was slow to gain a foothold in America. Most of the early progress in airplane design occurred in France, where there was substantial government funding for research and development. The U.S. government created the National Advisory Committee on Aeronautics in 1915, twelve years after the Wright brothers' flight, and American airplanes became a significant presence in Europe during World War I. But the prospects for commercial flight seemed dim until the 1920s, when Charles Lindbergh's famous solo flight from New York to Paris electrified the nation and the world and helped make aviation a national obsession.

Research and Development

The rapid development of new industrial technologies, and the emergence of large integrated corporations taking advantage of those technologies, persuaded a growing number of business leaders of the need to sponsor their own research to allow them to keep up with the rapid changes in industry. General Electric, fearful of technological competition, created one of the first corporate laboratories in 1900. The emergence of corporate research and development laboratories coincided with a decline in government support for research. That helped corporations to attract skilled researchers who had found themselves without their traditional forms of support. It also decentralized the sources of research funding and ensured that inquiry would move in many different directions, and not just along paths determined by the government.

A rift began to emerge between scientists and engineers. Engineers— both inside and out of universities—became increasingly tied up with the research and development agendas of corporations and worked hard to be of practical use to the new economy. Many scientists continued to scorn this "commercialization" of knowledge and preferred to stick to basic research that had no immediate practical applications. Even so, American scientists were more closely connected to practical challenges than were their European counterparts, and some joined engineers in corporate research and development laboratories, which over time began to sponsor not just practical but also basic research.

The Science of Production

Central to the growth of the automobile and other industries were changes in the techniques of production. By the turn of the century, many industrialists were embracing the new principles of "scientific management," often known as "Taylorism" after its leading theoretician, Frederick Winslow Taylor. Taylor himself, and his many admirers, argued that scientific management made it possible to manage human labor to make it compatible with the demands of the machine age. But scientific management was also a way to increase the employer's control of the workplace, to make working people less independent. Taylor urged employers to reorganize the production process by subdividing tasks. This would speed up production; it would also make workers more interchangeable (less skilled, less in need of training) and thus diminish a manager's dependence on any particular employee. If properly managed by trained experts, he claimed, workers using modern machines could perform simple tasks at much greater speed, greatly increasing productive efficiency.

The most important change in production technology in the industrial era was the emergence of mass production and, along with it, the moving assembly line, which Henry Ford introduced in his automobile plants in 1914. The assembly line was both a particular place—a factory through which automobiles moved as they were being assembled by workers who specialized on particular tasks—and a concept. The concept stressed the complete interchangeability of parts, which was a central concept at Ford even before the assembly line was fully developed. General Motors adopted the same philosophy, and even proceeded to demonstrate it at a motor works in England in 1906—when three Cadillacs were dismantled, their engines disassembled, the pieces mixed up with one another, and then completely reassembled by several mechanics, who then turned on the engines and drove them onto a track. Automobile production relied on other technologies, too, in particular the intensive use of electricity—to drive the assembly line, to light the factories, and to run the critical ventilating systems to keep dust from interfering with the ma-

THE ASSEMBLY LINE Workers in the Ford Motor Company's plant in Highland Park, Michigan, guide auto bodies down a ramp onto chassis that have moved into position from below. This was the final stage of the assembly line, which Henry Ford pioneered and which by 1914 (when this photograph was taken) had become common in other industries as well.

chines. The revolutionary assembly-line technique cut the time for assembling a chassis from twelve and a half hours to one and a half hours. It enabled Ford to raise the wages and reduce the hours of his workers while cutting the base price of his Model T from $950 in 1914 to $290 in 1929. It became a standard for many other industries.

Railroad Expansion and the Corporation

But the principal agent of industrial development in the late nineteenth century was the expansion of the railroads. Railroads were now the nation's primary method of transportation and gave industrialists access to distant markets and distant sources of raw materials. They were the nation's largest businesses and created new forms of corporate organization

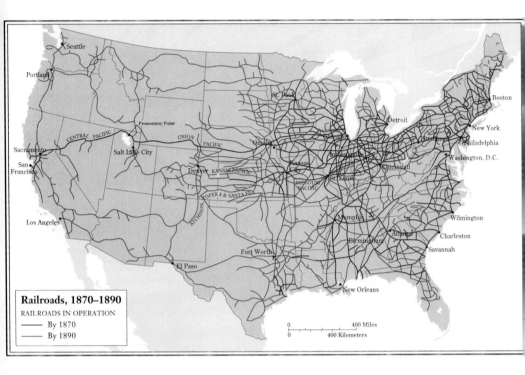

Railroads, 1870–1890
RAILROADS IN OPERATION
——— By 1870
——— By 1890

that served as models for other industries. And they were America's biggest investors, stimulating economic growth through their own enormous expenditures on construction and equipment.

Total railroad trackage increased dramatically in the last forty years of the nineteenth century: from 30,000 miles in 1860 to 193,000 in 1900. Subsidies from federal, state, and local governments (along with foreign loans and investments) were vital to this expansion, which required far more capital than private entrepreneurs could raise by themselves. Equally important was the emergence of great railroad combinations, many of them dominated by one or two individuals. The achievements (and excesses) of these tycoons—Cornelius Vanderbilt, James J. Hill, Collis R. Huntington, and others—became symbols to much of the nation of concentrated economic power. But railroad development was less significant for the individual barons it created than for its contribution to the growth of a new institution: the modern corporation.

There had been various forms of corporations in America since colonial times, but the modern corporation emerged as a major force only after the Civil War. By then, railroad magnates and other industrialists realized that their great ventures could not be financed by any single person, no matter how wealthy, or even by any single group of partners.

Under the laws of incorporation passed in many states in the 1830s and 1840s, business organizations could raise money by selling stock to members of the public; after the Civil War, one industry after another began doing so. What made the stocks more appealing than they had been in the past was that investors now had only "limited liability"—that is, they risked only the amount of their investments; they were not liable for any debts the corporation might accumulate beyond that point. The ability to sell stock to a broad public made it possible for entrepreneurs to gather vast sums of capital and undertake great projects.

The Pennsylvania and other railroads were among the first to adopt the new corporate form of organization. But incorporation quickly spread beyond the railroad industry. In steel, the central figure was Andrew Carnegie, a Scottish immigrant who had worked his way up from modest beginnings and in 1873 opened his own steelworks in Pittsburgh. Soon he dominated the industry. With his associate Henry Clay Frick, he bought up coal mines and leased part of the Mesabi iron range in Minnesota, operated a fleet of ore ships on the Great Lakes, and acquired railroads. Ultimately, he controlled the processing of his steel from mine to market. He financed his vast undertakings not only out of his own profits but out of the sale of stock. Then, in 1901, he sold out for $450 million to the banker J. Pierpont Morgan, who merged the Carnegie interests with others to create the giant United States Steel Corporation—a $14 billion enterprise that controlled almost two-thirds of the nation's steel production.

There were similar developments in other industries. Gustavus Swift developed a relatively small meatpacking company into a great national corporation. Isaac Singer patented a sewing machine in 1851 and created I. M. Singer and Company—one of the first modern manufacturing corporations.

Large, national business enterprises needed more systematic administrative structures than the limited, local ventures of the past. As a result, corporate leaders introduced a set of managerial techniques—the genesis of modern business administration—that relied on systematic division of responsibilities, a carefully designed hierarchy of control, careful cost-accounting procedures, and perhaps above all a new breed of business executive: the "middle manager," who formed a layer of command between workers and owners. Efficient administrative capabilities helped make possible another major feature of the modern corporation: consolidation.

Businessmen created large, consolidated organizations primarily through two methods. One was "horizontal integration"—the combining of a number of firms engaged in the same enterprise into a single corporation. The consolidation of many different railroad lines into one company was an example. Another method, which became popular in the 1890s, was "vertical integration"—the taking over of all the different businesses on which a company relied for its primary function. Carnegie Steel, which came to control not only steel mills but mines, railroads, and other enterprises, was an example of vertical integration.

The most celebrated corporate empire of the late nineteenth century was John D. Rockefeller's Standard Oil, a great combination created through both horizontal and vertical integration. Shortly after the Civil War, Rockefeller launched a refining company in Cleveland and immediately began trying to eliminate his competition. Allying himself with other wealthy capitalists, he proceeded methodically to buy out competing refineries. In 1870, he formed the Standard Oil Company of Ohio, which in a few years had acquired twenty of the twenty-five refineries in Cleveland, as well as plants in Pittsburgh, Philadelphia, New York, and Baltimore.

So far, Rockefeller had expanded only horizontally. But soon he began expanding vertically as well. He built his own barrel factories, terminal warehouses, and pipelines. Standard Oil owned its own freight cars and developed its own marketing organization. By the 1880s, Rockefeller had established such dominance within the petroleum industry that to much of the nation he served as the leading symbol of monopoly. He controlled access to 90 percent of the nation's refined oil.

Rockefeller and other industrialists saw consolidation as a way to cope with what they believed was the greatest curse of the modern economy: "cutthroat competition." Most businessmen claimed to believe in free enterprise and a competitive marketplace, but in fact they feared that substantial competition could spell instability and ruin for all. A successful enterprise, many capitalists believed (but did not say), was one that could eliminate or absorb its competitors.

As the movement toward combination accelerated, new vehicles emerged to facilitate it. The railroads began with so-called pool arrangements—informal agreements among various companies to stabilize rates and divide markets (arrangements that would, in later years, be known as cartels). But if even a few firms in an industry were unwilling to cooperate (as was almost always the case), the pool arrangements collapsed.

The failure of the pools led to new techniques of consolidation. At first, the most successful such technique was the creation of the "trust"—

pioneered by Standard Oil in the early 1880s and perfected by the banker J. P. Morgan. Over time, the word "trust" became a popular term for describing any great economic combination, but the trust was in fact a particular kind of organization. Under a trust agreement, stockholders in individual corporations transferred their stocks to a small group of trustees in exchange for shares in the trust itself. Owners of trust certificates often had no direct control over the decisions of the trustees; they simply received a share of the profits of the combination. The trustees themselves, on the other hand, might literally own only a few companies but could exercise effective control over many.

In 1889, the state of New Jersey helped produce a third form of consolidation by changing its laws of incorporation to permit companies to buy up other companies. Other states soon followed. That made the trust unnecessary and permitted actual corporate mergers. Rockefeller, for example, quickly relocated Standard Oil to New Jersey and created there what became known as a "holding company"—a central corporate body that would buy up the stock of various members of the Standard Oil trust and establish direct, formal ownership of the corporations in the trust.

By the end of the nineteenth century, as a result of corporate consolidation, 1 percent of the corporations in America were able to control more than 33 percent of the manufacturing. A system of economic organization was emerging that lodged enormous power in the hands of very few men—the great bankers of New York such as J. P. Morgan, industrial titans such as Rockefeller (who himself gained control of a major bank), and others.

The industrial giants of the era were clearly responsible for substantial economic growth. They were also creating the basis for one of the greatest public controversies of their era: a raging debate over concentrated economic and political power that continued well into the twentieth century.

CAPITALISM AND ITS CRITICS

The rise of big business was not without its critics. Farmers and workers saw in the growth of the new corporate power centers a threat to notions of a republican society in which wealth and authority were widely distributed. Middle-class critics pointed to the corruption that the new industrial titans seemed to produce in their own enterprises and in local, state, and national politics. The growing criticisms challenged the captains of industry to create a defense of the new corporate economy.

Survival of the Fittest

The new rationale for capitalism rested squarely on an older ideology of individualism. The new industrial economy, its defenders argued, was not shrinking opportunities for individual advancement. It was expanding those opportunities. It was providing every individual with a chance to succeed and attain great wealth.

There was an element of truth in such claims, but only a small element. Before the Civil War there had been few millionaires in America; by 1892 there were more than 4,000. Some of them—Carnegie, Rockefeller, and a few others—were in fact what almost all millionaires claimed to be: "self-made men." But most of the new business tycoons had begun their careers from positions of comfort, privilege, and wealth. Nor was their rise to power and prominence always a result simply of hard work and ingenuity, as they liked to claim. It was also a result of ruthlessness and, at times, rampant corruption.

Nevertheless, most tycoons continued to claim that they had attained their wealth and power through hard work, acquisitiveness, and thrift— the traditional virtues of Protestant America. Those who succeeded, they argued, deserved their success, and those who failed had earned their failure through their own laziness, stupidity, or carelessness. Such assumptions became the basis of a popular social theory of the late nineteenth century: Social Darwinism, the application of Charles Darwin's laws of evolution and natural selection among species to human society. Just as only the fittest survived in the process of evolution, the Social Darwinists argued, so in human society only the fittest individuals survived and flourished in the marketplace.

The English philosopher Herbert Spencer was the first and most important proponent of this theory. Society, he argued, benefited from the elimination of the unfit and the survival of the strong and talented. Spencer's teachings found prominent supporters among American intellectuals, most notably William Graham Sumner of Yale, who promoted similar ideas in lectures, articles, and a famous 1906 book, *Folkways*. Sumner did not agree with everything Spencer wrote, but he did share Spencer's belief that individuals must have absolute freedom to struggle, to compete, to succeed, or to fail.

Social Darwinism appealed to corporate leaders because it seemed to legitimize their success and confirm their virtues. It was not, however, an ideology that had very much to do with the realities of the corporate economy. At the same time that businessmen were celebrating the virtues of competition and the free market, they were making active efforts to protect themselves from competition and to replace the natural workings of the marketplace with control by great combinations. Vicious competitive battle—which Spencer and Sumner celebrated and called a source of healthy progress—was in fact the very thing that American businessmen most feared and tried to eliminate.

The Gospel of Wealth

Some businessmen attempted to temper the harsh philosophy of Social Darwinism with a gentler, if in some ways equally self-serving, idea: the "gospel of wealth." People of great wealth, advocates of this idea argued, had not only great power but great responsibilities. It was their duty to use their riches to advance social progress. Andrew Carnegie elaborated on the creed in his 1901 book, *The Gospel of Wealth*, in which he wrote that people of wealth should consider all revenues in excess of their own needs as "trust funds" to be used for the good of the community. Carnegie was only one of many great industrialists who devoted large parts of their fortunes to philanthropic works.

The notion of private wealth as a public blessing existed alongside another popular concept: the notion of great wealth as something available to all. Russell H. Conwell, a Baptist minister, became the most prominent spokesman for the idea by delivering one lecture, "Acres of Diamonds," more than 6,000 times between 1880 and 1900. Conwell told a series of stories, which he claimed were true, of individuals who had found opportunities for extraordinary wealth in their own backyards. (One such story involved a modest farmer who discovered a vast diamond mine in his own fields in the course of working his land.) Most of the millionaires in the country, Conwell claimed (inaccurately), had begun on the lowest rung of the economic ladder and had worked their way to success. Every industrious individual had the chance to do likewise.

Horatio Alger was the most famous promoter of the success story. Alger was originally a minister in a small town in Massachusetts but was driven from his pulpit as a result of a scandal connected to his active, but hidden, homosexuality. He moved to New York, where he wrote his celebrated novels: *Ragged Dick, Tom the Bootblack, Sink or Swim,* and many others, more than 100 in all, which together sold more than 100 million copies. The basic story was almost always the same: A young boy, perhaps an orphan, makes his perilous way through life on the

A NEWSBOY'S STORY Alger's novels were even more popular after his death in 1899 than they had been in his lifetime. This reprint of one of his many "rags-to-riches" stories—about a New York newsboy's rise to wealth and success—includes in the background a rendering of the Woolworth building, built in 1913 and one of the first and most celebrated skyscrapers of the early twentieth century.

rough streets of the city by selling newspapers or peddling matches. One day, his energy and determination catches the eye of a wealthy man, who gives him a chance to improve himself. Through honesty, charm, hard work, and aggressiveness, the boy rises in the world to become a successful man.

The purpose of writing, Alger claimed, was twofold. He wanted to "exert a salutary influence upon the class of whom [I] was writing, by setting before them inspiring examples of what energy, ambition, and an honest purpose may achieve." He also wanted to show his largely middle-class readers "the life and experiences of the friendless and vagrant children to be found in all our cities."

But Alger's intentions probably had little to do with the success of his books. Most Americans of the late nineteenth and early twentieth centuries were attracted to Alger because his stories helped them to believe in one of the most cherished of all our national myths: that it is possible for individuals to rise in the world with willpower and hard work, that anyone can become a "self-made man." Alger's admirers came to ignore his own misgivings about industrialism and to portray his books purely as a celebration of (and justification for) laissez-faire capitalism and the accumulation of wealth.

Alternative Visions

Alongside the celebrations of competition, the justifications for great wealth, and the legitimization of the existing order stood a group of alternative philosophies, challenging the corporate ethos and at times capitalism itself.

One such philosophy emerged in the work of the sociologist Lester Frank Ward. Ward was a Darwinist, but he rejected the application of Darwinian laws to human society. In *Dynamic Sociology* (1883) and other books, he argued that civilization was not governed by natural selection but by human intelligence, which was capable of shaping society as it wished. In contrast to Sumner, who believed that state intervention to remodel the environment was futile, Ward thought that an active government engaged in positive planning was society's best hope.

Other Americans skeptical of the laissez-faire ideas of the Social Darwinists adopted more radical approaches to reform. Some dissenters found a home in the Socialist Labor Party, founded in the 1870s and led for many years by Daniel De Leon, an immigrant from the West Indies. Although De Leon attracted a modest following in the industrial cities, the party never became a major political force and never polled more than 82,000 votes. A dissident faction of De Leon's party, eager to forge stronger ties with organized labor, broke away and in 1901 formed the more enduring American Socialist Party.

Other radicals gained a wider following. One of the most influential was the California writer and activist Henry George. His angrily eloquent *Progress and Poverty*, published in 1879, became one of the best-selling nonfiction works in American publishing history. George blamed social problems on the ability of a few monopolists to grow wealthy as a result of rising land values. An increase in the value of land, he claimed, was not a result of any effort by the owner. It was an "unearned increment," produced by the growth of society around the land. Such profits were rightfully the property of the community. And so George proposed a "single tax" on land, to replace all other taxes, which would return the increment to the people. The tax, he argued, would destroy monopolies, distribute wealth more equally, and eliminate poverty. Single-tax societies sprang up in many cities, and in 1886, George, with the support of labor and the socialists, narrowly missed being elected mayor of New York.

Rivaling George in popularity was Edward Bellamy, whose utopian novel *Looking Backward*, published in 1888, sold more than 1 million copies. It described the experiences of a young Bostonian who went into a hypnotic sleep in 1887 and awoke in the year 2000 to find a new social order in which want, politics, and vice were unknown. The new society had emerged through a peaceful, evolutionary process: the large trusts of the late nineteenth century had continued to grow in size and to combine with one another until ultimately they formed a single, great trust, controlled by the government, which distributed the abundance of the industrial economy equally among all the people. "Fraternal cooperation" had replaced competition. Class divisions had disappeared. Bellamy labeled the philosophy behind this vision "nationalism," and his work inspired the formation of more than 160 Nationalist Clubs to propagate his ideas.

The Problems of Monopoly

Relatively few Americans shared the views of those who questioned capitalism itself. But as time went on, a growing number of people were becoming deeply concerned about a particular, glaring aspect of capitalism: the growth of monopoly.

By the end of the century, a wide range of groups had begun to assail monopoly and economic concentration. Workers, farmers, consumers, small manufacturers, conservative bankers and financiers, advocates of radical change—all joined the attack. They blamed monopoly for creating artificially high prices. In the absence of competition, they argued, monopolistic industries could charge whatever prices they wished; railroads, in particular, charged very high rates along some routes because, in the absence of competition, they knew their customers had no choice but to pay them. Artificially high prices, moreover, contributed to the economy's instability, as production consistently outpaced demand. Beginning in 1873, the economy fluctuated erratically, producing severe recessions every five or six years, each worse than the last.

"MODERN COLOSSUS OF (RAIL) ROADS" Cornelius Vanderbilt, known as the "Commodore," accumulated one of America's great fortunes by consolidating several large railroad companies under his control in the 1860s. His name became a synonym not only for enormous wealth, but also (in the eyes of many Americans) for excessive corporate power—as suggested in this cartoon, showing him standing astride his empire and manipulating its parts.

THE ORDEAL OF THE WORKER

The American working class was both a beneficiary and a victim of the growth of industrial capitalism. Most workers in the late nineteenth century experienced a real rise in their standard of living. But they did so at the cost of arduous and often dangerous working conditions, diminishing control over their own work, and a growing sense of powerlessness.

The Immigrant Work Force

The industrial work force expanded dramatically in the late nineteenth century as demand for factory labor grew. The source of that expansion was a massive migration into industrial cities—immigration of two sorts. The first was the continuing flow of rural Americans into factory towns and cities—people disillusioned with or bankrupted by life on the farm and eager for new economic and social opportunities. The second was the great wave of immigration from abroad (primarily from Europe, but also from Asia, Canada, and other areas) in the decades following the Civil War—an influx greater than that of any previous era. The 25 million immigrants who arrived in the United States between 1865 and 1915 were more than four times the number who had arrived in the previous fifty years.

In the 1870s and 1880s, most of the immigrants came from the nation's traditional sources: England, Ireland, and northern Europe. By the end of the century, however, the major sources of immigrants had shifted, with large numbers of southern and eastern Europeans (Italians, Poles, Russians, Greeks, Slavs, and others) moving into the country and into the industrial work force.

The new immigrants were coming to America in part to escape poverty and oppression in their homelands. But they were also lured to the United States by expectations of new opportunities. Some such expectations were unrealistic, the result of false promises. Railroads tried to lure immigrants into their western landholdings by distributing misleading advertisements overseas. Industrial employers actively recruited immigrant workers under the Labor Contract Law, which—until its repeal in 1885—permitted them to pay for the passage of workers in advance and deduct the amount later from their wages. Even after the repeal of the law, employers continued to encourage the immigration of unskilled laborers, often with the assistance of foreign-born labor brokers, such as the Greek and Italian *padrones*, who recruited work gangs of their fellow nationals.

The arrival of these new groups introduced heightened ethnic tensions into the dynamics of the working class. Low-paid Poles, Greeks, and French Canadians began to displace higher-paid British and Irish workers in the textile factories of New England. Italians, Slavs, and Poles emerged as a major source of labor for the mining industry, traditionally dominated by native workers or northern European immigrants. Chinese and Mexicans competed with Anglo-Americans and African Americans in mining, farmwork, and factory labor in California, Colorado, and Texas.

Wages and Working Conditions

At the turn of the century, the average income of the American worker was $400 to $500 a year—below the $600 figure that many believed was the minimum required to maintain a reasonable level of comfort. Nor did workers have much job security. All were vulnerable to the boom-and-bust cycle of the industrial economy, and some lost their jobs because of technological advances or because of the cyclical or seasonal nature of their work. Even those who kept their jobs could find their wages suddenly and substantially cut in hard times. Few workers, in other words, were ever very far from poverty.

American laborers faced a wide array of other hardships as well. For first-generation workers accustomed to the patterns of agrarian life, there was a difficult adjustment to the nature of modern industrial labor: the performance of routine, repetitive tasks, often requiring little skill, on a strict and monotonous schedule. To skilled artisans whose once-valued tasks were now performed by machines, the new system was impersonal and demeaning. Factory laborers worked ten-hour days, six days a week; in the steel industry they worked twelve hours a day. Industrial accidents were frequent and severe.

Women and Children at Work

The decreasing need for skilled work in factories induced many employers to increase the use of women and children, whom they could hire for lower wages than adult males. By 1900, 20 percent of all manufacturing workers were women, and 20 percent of all women (well over 5 million) were wage earners. Women worked in all areas of industry, even in some of the most arduous jobs. Most women, however, worked in a few industries where unskilled and semiskilled machine labor (as opposed to heavy manual labor) prevailed. The textile industry remained the largest single industrial employer of women. (Domestic service remained the most common female occupation overall.) Women worked for wages well below the minimum necessary for survival (and well below the wages paid to men working the same jobs).

At least 1.7 million children under sixteen years of age were employed in factories and fields, more than twice the number of thirty years before; 10 percent of all girls aged ten to fifteen, and 20 percent of all boys, held jobs. Under public pressure, thirty-eight states passed child labor laws in

SPINDLE BOYS Young boys, some of them barefoot, clamber along the great textile machines in a Georgia cotton mill adjusting spindles. Many of them were the children of women who worked in the plants. The photograph is by Lewis Hine.

the late nineteenth century. But 60 percent of child workers were employed in agriculture, which was typically exempt from the laws. And even for children employed in factories, the laws merely set a minimum age of twelve years and a maximum workday of ten hours, standards that employers often ignored in any case.

Emerging Unionization

Laborers attempted to fight back against such conditions by adopting one of the same tactics their employers had used so effectively: creating large combinations—national unions. By the end of the century, however, their efforts had met with little success.

There had been craft unions in America, representing small groups of skilled workers, since well before the Civil War. Alone, however, individual unions could not hope to exert significant power in the economy. And during the turbulent recession years of the 1870s, unions faced the additional problem of widespread public hostility. When labor disputes with employers turned bitter and violent, as they occasionally did, much of the public instinctively blamed the workers (or the "radicals" and "anarchists" they believed were influencing the workers) for the trouble, rarely the employers. Particularly alarming to middle-class Americans was the emergence of the "Molly Maguires" in the anthracite coal region of western Pennsylvania. This militant labor organization sometimes used violence and even murder in its battle with coal operators. Much of the violence attributed to the Molly Maguires, however, was deliberately instigated by informers and agents employed by the mine owners, who wanted a pretext for ruthless measures to suppress unionization.

Excitement over the Molly Maguires paled beside the near hysteria that gripped the country during the railroad strike of 1877, which began when the eastern railroads announced a 10 percent wage cut. The strike soon expanded into something approaching a class war. Strikers disrupted rail service from Baltimore to St. Louis, destroyed equipment, and rioted in the streets of Pittsburgh and other cities. State militias were called out, and in July President Hayes ordered federal troops to suppress the disorders in West Virginia. In Baltimore, eleven demonstrators died and forty were wounded in a conflict between workers and militiamen. In Philadelphia, the state militia killed twenty people when the troops opened fire on thousands of workers and their families who were attempting to block the railroad crossings. In all, over 100 people died before the strike finally collapsed several weeks after it had begun. The great railroad strike was America's first major, national labor conflict, and it illustrated that disputes between labor and capital could no longer be localized in the increasingly national economy.

The Knights of Labor

The first major effort to create a genuinely national labor organization was the founding in 1869 of the Noble Order of the Knights of Labor, under the leadership of Uriah S. Stephens. Membership was open to all who "toiled," a definition that included all workers, most business and professional people, and virtually all women—whether they worked in factories, as domestic servants, or in their own homes. The only excluded groups were lawyers, bankers, liquor dealers, and professional gamblers. The Knights of Labor was loosely organized, without much central direction. Its program was similarly vague. Although its leaders championed an eight-hour workday and the abolition of child labor, they were more interested in long-range reform of the economy. The Knights hoped to replace the "wage system" with a new "cooperative system," in which workers would themselves control a large part of the economy.

For several years, the Knights remained a secret fraternal organization. But in the late 1870s, under the leadership of Terence V. Powderly, the order moved into the open and entered a period of spectacular expansion. By 1886, it claimed a total membership of over 700,000, including some militant elements that the moderate leadership could not always control. Local unions or assemblies associated with the Knights launched a series of railroad and other strikes in the 1880s in defiance of Powderly's wishes. Their failure helped discredit the organization. By 1890, the membership of the Knights had shrunk to 100,000. A few years later, the organization disappeared altogether.

The AFL

Even before the Knights began to decline, a rival association based on a very different organizational concept appeared. In 1881, representatives of a number of craft unions formed the Federation of Organized Trade and Labor Unions of the United States and Canada. Five years later, this body took the name it has borne ever since, the American Federation of Labor (AFL), and it soon became the most important labor group in the country.

Rejecting the Knights' idea of one big union for everybody, the Federation was an association of essentially autonomous craft unions that represented mainly skilled workers. Samuel Gompers, the powerful leader of the AFL, concentrated on labor's immediate objectives: wages, hours, and working conditions. While the AFL hoped to attain its ends by collective bargaining, it was ready to use strikes if necessary.

As one of its first objectives, the AFL demanded a national eight-hour workday and called for a general strike if the goal was not achieved by May 1, 1886. On that day, strikes and demonstrations for a shorter workday took place all over the country, most of them staged by AFL unions but a few by more radical groups.

In Chicago, a center of labor and radical strength, a strike was already in progress before at the McCormick Harvester Company. City police had been harassing the strikers, and labor and radical leaders called a protest meeting at Haymarket Square on May 1. When the police ordered the crowd to disperse, someone threw a bomb that killed seven policemen and injured sixty-seven others. The police, who had killed four strikers the day before, fired into the crowd and killed four more people. Conservative, property-conscious Americans—frightened and outraged—demanded retribution, even though no one knew who had thrown the bomb. Chicago officials finally rounded up eight anarchists and charged them with murder, on the grounds that their statements had incited whoever had hurled the bomb. All eight scapegoats were found guilty after a remarkably injudicious trial. Seven were sentenced to death. One of them committed suicide, four were executed, and two had their sentences commuted to life imprisonment.

To most middle-class Americans, the Haymarket bombing was an alarming symbol of social chaos and radicalism. "Anarchism" now became in the public mind a code word for terrorism and violence, even though most anarchists were relatively peaceful visionaries dreaming of a new social order. For the next thirty years, the specter of anarchism remained one of the most frightening concepts in the American imagination. It was a constant obstacle to the goals of the AFL and other labor organizations, and it did particular damage to the Knights of Labor. However much they tried to distance themselves from radicals, labor leaders were always vulnerable to accusations of anarchism, as the violent strikes of the 1890s occasionally illustrated.

The Homestead Strike

The Amalgamated Association of Iron and Steel Workers, which was affiliated with the American Federation of Labor, was the most powerful trade union in the country. Its members were skilled workers, in great demand by employers, and thus had long been able to exercise significant power in the workplace. In the mid-1880s, however, demand for skilled workers was in decline as new production methods changed the steel-making process. In the Carnegie system, which was coming to dominate the steel industry, the union was able to maintain a foothold in only one of the corporation's three major factories—the Homestead plant near Pittsburgh.

By 1890, Carnegie and his chief lieutenant, Henry Clay Frick, had decided that the Amalgamated "had to go." Over the next two years, they repeatedly cut wages at Homestead. At first, the union acquiesced, aware that it was not strong enough to wage a successful strike. But in 1892, when the company stopped even discussing its decisions with the union and gave it two days to accept another wage cut, the Amalgamated called for a strike.

BREAKING THE HOMESTEAD STRIKE, 1892 State militiamen enter Homestead, Pennsylvania, to put an end to the Amalgamated union's violent strike by opening the Carnegie-owned steel plant to strikebreaking workers. This double photograph forms a "stereograph," which, when viewed through a special lens (a "stereoscope"), gave the impression of a three-dimensional scene.

Frick abruptly shut down the plant and called in 300 guards from the Pinkerton Detective Agency to enable the company to hire nonunion workers. The hated Pinkertons were well-known strikebreakers, and their presence alone was often enough to incite workers to violence. The Pinkertons approached the plant by river, on barges, on July 6, 1892. The strikers poured gasoline on the water, set it on fire, and then met the Pinkertons at the docks with guns and dynamite. A pitched battle broke out. After several hours of fighting, which killed three guards and ten strikers and injured many others, the Pinkertons surrendered and were escorted roughly out of town.

But the workers' victory was temporary. The governor of Pennsylvania, at the company's request, sent the state's entire National Guard contingent, some 8,000 men, to Homestead. Production resumed, with strikebreakers now protected by troops. And public opinion turned against the strikers when a radical made an attempt to assassinate Frick. Slowly, workers drifted back to their jobs, and finally—four months after the strike began—the Amalgamated surrendered. By 1900, every major steel plant in the Northeast had broken with the Amalgamated, which now had virtually no power to resist. Its membership shrank from a high of 24,000 in 1891 (two-thirds of all eligible steelworkers) to fewer than 7,000 a decade later.

The Pullman Strike

A dispute of greater magnitude, if less violence, was the Pullman strike in 1894. The Pullman Palace Car Company manufactured sleeping and par-lor cars for railroads, which it built and repaired at a plant near Chicago. There the company constructed a 600-acre town, Pullman, and rented its trim, orderly houses to the employees. George M. Pullman, owner of the company, saw the town as a model—a solution to the problems of indus-trial workers; he referred to the workers as his "children." But many resi-dents chafed at the regimentation (and the high rents). In the winter of 1893–1894, the Pullman Company slashed wages by about 25 percent, cit-ing its own declining revenues in the depression, without reducing the rent it charged its employees. Workers went on strike and persuaded the militant American Railway Union, led by Eugene V. Debs, to support them by refusing to handle Pullman cars and equipment. Within a few days thousands of railroad workers in twenty-seven states and territories were on strike, and transportation from Chicago to the Pacific coast was paralyzed.

Unlike most elected politicians, the governor of Illinois, John Peter Altgeld, was a man with demonstrated sympathies for workers and their grievances. He refused to call out the militia to protect employers now. Bypassing Altgeld, railroad operators asked the federal government to send regular army troops to Illinois, using the pretext that the strike was preventing the movement of mail on the trains. In July 1894, President Grover Cleveland, over Altgeld's objections, ordered 2,000 troops to the Chicago area. A federal court issued an injunction forbidding the union to continue the strike. When Debs and his associates defied it, they were arrested and imprisoned. With federal troops protecting the hiring of new workers and with the union leaders in a federal jail, the strike quickly collapsed.

Sources of Labor Weakness

The last decades of the nineteenth century were years in which labor, despite militant organizing efforts that created one of the greatest waves of social conflict in American history, made few real gains. Industrial wages rose hardly at all. Labor leaders won a few legislative victories—the abolition of the Contract Labor Law, the establishment of an eight-hour day for government employees, compensation for some workers injured on the job, and others. But many such laws were not enforced. There were widespread strikes and protests, and many other working-class forms of resistance, large and small, but few real gains. The end of the century found most workers with less political power and less control of the workplace than they had had forty years before.

Workers failed to make greater gains for many reasons. The principal labor organizations represented only a small percentage of the industrial work force; the AFL, the most important, excluded unskilled workers, who were emerging as the core of the industrial work force, and along with them most women, blacks, and recent immigrants. Divisions within the work force contributed further to union weakness. Tensions among different ethnic and racial groups kept laborers divided.

Another source of labor weakness was the shifting nature of the work force. Many immigrant workers came to America intending to remain only briefly, to earn some money and then return home. The assumption that they had no long-range future in the country, even if that assumption was often inaccurate, eroded their willingness to organize. Other workers—natives and immigrants alike—were in constant motion, moving from one job to another, one town to another, seldom in a single place long enough to establish any institutional ties or exert any real power.

Above all, perhaps, workers made few gains in the late nineteenth century because of the strength of the forces arrayed against them. They faced corporate organizations of vast wealth and power, which were generally determined to crush any efforts by workers to challenge their prerogatives. And as the Homestead and Pullman strikes suggest, the corporations usually had the support of local, state, and federal authorities, who were willing to send in troops to "preserve order" and crush labor uprisings on demand.

Despite the creation of new labor unions, despite a wave of strikes and protests that in the 1880s and 1890s reached startling proportions, workers in the late nineteenth century failed on the whole to create successful organizations or to protect their interests in the way the large corporations managed to do. In the battle for power within the emerging industrial economy, almost all the advantages seemed to lie with capital.

CONCLUSION

In the four decades following the end of the Civil War, the United States propelled itself into the forefront of the industrializing nations of the world. Large areas of the nation remained overwhelmingly rural, to be sure, and the majority of the population was still engaged in activities closely tied to farming. Even so, America's economy, and along with it the nation's society and culture, were being profoundly transformed.

New technologies, new forms of corporate management, and new supplies of labor helped make possible the rapid growth of the nation's industries and the construction of its railroads. The factory system contributed to the growth of the nation's cities, and at times created entirely new ones. Immigration provided a steady supply of new workers for the growing industrial economy. The result was a steady and substantial increase in national wealth, rising living standards for much of the population, and the creation of great new fortunes.

But industrialization did not spread its fruits evenly. Large areas of the country, most notably the South, and large groups in the population, most notably minorities, women, and recent immigrants, profited relatively little from economic growth. Industrial workers experienced arduous conditions of labor and wages that rose much more slowly than the profits of the corporations for which they worked. Small merchants and manufacturers found themselves overmatched by great new combinations.

Industrialists strove to create a rationale for their power and to persuade the public that everyone had something to gain from it. But many Americans remained skeptical of modern capitalism, and some—workers struggling to form unions, reformers denouncing trusts, women fighting to win protections for female laborers, socialists envisioning a new world, and many others—created broad and powerful critiques of the new economic order. Industrialization brought both progress and pain to late-nineteenth-century America. Controversies over its effects defined the era and would continue to define the first decades of the twentieth century.

FOR FURTHER REFERENCE

Suggested Readings

Robert Wiebe's *The Search for Order, 1877–1920* (1968) is a classic analysis of America's evolution from a society of island communities to a national urban society. Alfred D. Chandler, Jr., describes the new business practices that made industrialization possible in *The Visible Hand: The Managerial Revolution in American Business* (1977) and *Scale and Scope: The Dynamics of Industrial Capitalism* (1990). Olivier Zunz offers a provocative analysis of the social underpinnings of the new corporate order in *Making America Corporate, 1870–1920* (1990) and *Why the American Century?* (1998). David Montgomery, *The Fall of the House of Labor: The Workplace, the State, and American Labor Activism, 1865–1925* (1987) analyzes the way industrialization shaped (and was shaped by) the workers, their expertise, and the strong cultural traditions of the shop floor. Alice Kessler-Harris documents the tremendous movement of women into the work force in the period in *Out to Work: A History of Wage-Earning Women in the United States* (1982). Daniel T. Rodgers, *The Work Ethic in Industrial America, 1850–1920* (1978) is an important intellectual history of the way in which Americans viewed the working class. John L. Thomas, *Alternative America: Henry George, Edward Bellamy, Henry Demarest Lloyd, and the Adversary Tradition* (1983) examines some important critics of corporate capitalism.

Films

(The best source for information on how to find these and other films is *Bowker's Complete Video Directory*—3 volumes.) *The Iron Road* (1990) is the story of the completion of the transcontinental railroad, which reduced the cross-country trip to just nine and a half days. *Andrew Carnegie and Business Ideology* (1981) features a biographical sketch of this leading industrialist and his role in the creation of a new business ideology in the last decades of the nineteenth century. *1877: The Grand Army of Starvation* (1985) portrays the incongruity of prosperity and poverty in industrializing America and the tremendous wave of strikes that scarred the year 1877.

Internet Resources

Internet websites containing historical material relevant to the subjects discussed in this chapter can be reached through the McGraw-Hill history site at www.mhhe.com/socscience/history/usa/link/linktop.htm.

CHAPTER EIGHTEEN

The Age of the City

T HE FACE OF American society changed in countless ways in response to the growth of industry and commerce. No change was
more profound, however, than the growing size and influence of cities.
Having begun its life as a primarily agrarian republic, the United States in
the late nineteenth century was becoming an urban nation—with a culture
increasingly shaped and dominated by its cities.

THE NEW URBAN GROWTH

The great movement of people from the countryside to the city was not
unique to the United States. But America, a society with little experience
of great cities, found urbanization particularly jarring. The urban population of America increased sevenfold in the half-century after the Civil
War. And in 1920, the census revealed that for the first time, a majority of
the American people lived in "urban" areas—defined as communities of
2,500 people or more. The United States was an agrarian society no more.

Natural increase accounted for only a small part of the urban growth.
Urban families experienced a high rate of infant mortality, a declining fer-
tility rate, and a high death rate from disease. Without immigration, cities
would have grown relatively slowly.

TIME LINE

1869	1870	1871	1872	1876	1882
First intercollegiate football game	NYC opens first elevated railroads	Boston and Chicago fires	Boss Tweed convicted	Baseball's National League founded	Congress restricts Chinese immigration

1884	1890		1891	1894	1895
First "skyscraper" in Chicago	Riis's *How the Other Half Lives*		Basketball invented	Immigration Restriction League formed	Crane's *The Red Badge of Courage*

1897	1901	1903	1906	1910
Boston opens first subway in America	Baseball's American League founded	First World Series	San Francisco earthquake and fire / Sinclair's *The Jungle*	NCAA founded

The Migrations

The late nineteenth century was an age of unprecedented geographical mobility, as Americans left the declining agricultural regions of the East at a dramatic rate. Some of those who left were moving to the newly developing farmlands of the West. But almost as many were moving to the cities of the East and the Midwest.

Among those leaving rural America for industrial cities in the 1880s were southern blacks. They were escaping the poverty, debt, violence, and oppression they faced in the rural South. They were also seeking new opportunities in cities—opportunities that were limited but usually an improvement over what they left behind. Factory jobs for blacks were rare and professional opportunities almost nonexistent. Urban blacks tended to work as cooks, janitors, and domestic servants, as well as in other service occupations. Because many such jobs were considered women's work, black women often outnumbered black men in the cities. By the end of the nineteenth century, there were substantial black communities (10,000 people or more) in over thirty cities.

The most important source of urban population growth in the late nineteenth century, however, was the arrival of great numbers of new immigrants from abroad. Some came from Canada, Latin America, and—

particularly on the West Coast—China and Japan. But the greatest number came from Europe. After 1880, the flow of new arrivals began to include large numbers of people from southern and eastern Europe. By the 1890s, more than half of all immigrants came from these regions, as opposed to fewer than 2 percent in the 1860s.

In earlier years, most new immigrants from Europe (particularly Germans and Scandinavians) had arrived with at least some money and education. Most of them arrived at one of the major port cities on the Atlantic coast (the greatest number in New York, through the famous immigrant depot on Ellis Island) and then headed west—either to be farmers or to work as businessmen, professionals, or skilled laborers in midwestern cities such as St. Louis, Cincinnati, and Milwaukee. But the new immigrants of the late nineteenth century generally lacked the capital to buy farmland and lacked the education to establish themselves in professions. So, like similarly poor Irish immigrants before the Civil War, they settled overwhelmingly in industrial cities, where they occupied largely unskilled jobs.

The Ethnic City

By 1890, most of the population of the major urban areas consisted of immigrants: 87 percent of the population in Chicago, 80 percent in New York, 84 percent in Milwaukee and Detroit. (London, the largest industrial city in Europe, had by contrast a population that was 94 percent native.)

Equally striking was the diversity of the new immigrant populations. In other countries experiencing heavy immigration in this period, most of the new arrivals were coming from one or two sources. But in the United States, no single national group dominated. In some towns, a dozen different ethnic groups might find themselves living in close proximity to one another.

Most of the new immigrants were rural people, and for many the adjustment to city life was painful. To help ease the transition, some national groups formed close-knit ethnic communities within the cities: neighborhoods (often called "immigrant ghettoes") that attempted to re-create in the New World many of the features of the Old. Ethnic neighborhoods offered newcomers much that was familiar. They could find newspapers and theaters in their native languages, stores selling their native foods, and church and fraternal organizations that provided links with their national pasts. Many immigrants also maintained close ties with their native countries. They stayed in touch with relatives who had remained behind. Some (perhaps as many as a third in the early years) returned to their homelands after a relatively short time; others helped bring the rest of their families to America.

The cultural cohesiveness of the ethnic communities clearly eased the pain of separation from the immigrants' native lands. What role it played in helping immigrants become absorbed into the economic life of America is a more difficult question to answer. Some ethnic groups (Jews and Germans in particular) advanced economically more rapidly than others (for example, the Irish). One explanation is that, by huddling together in ethnic neighborhoods, immigrant groups tended to reinforce the cultural values of their previous societies. When those values were particularly well suited to economic advancement—as was, for example, the high value Jews placed on education—ethnic identification may have helped members of a group to improve their lots. When other values predominated—maintaining community solidarity, strengthening family ties, preserving order—progress could be less rapid.

But other factors were at least as important in determining how well immigrants fared. Immigrants who aroused strong racial prejudice among native-born whites—most notably African Americans, Asians, and Mexicans—found it very difficult to advance whatever their talents. Those white immigrants who arrived with a valuable skill or with some capital did better than those who did not. And over time, those who lived in cities where people of their own nationality came to predominate—for example, the Irish in New York and Boston, or the Germans in Milwaukee—gained an advantage as they learned to exert their political power.

Assimilation and Exclusion

Despite the many differences among the various immigrant communities, virtually all groups had certain things in common. Most immigrants shared the experience of living in cities (and of adapting from a rural past to an urban present). Most were young; the majority of newcomers were between fifteen and forty-five years old. And in most communities of the foreign-born, the strength of ethnic ties had to compete against another powerful force: the desire for assimilation.

Many of the new arrivals had come to America with romantic visions of the New World. And however disillusioning they might find their first contact with the United States, they usually retained the dream of becoming true "Americans." Second-generation immigrants were particularly likely to attempt to break with the old ways. Some even looked with contempt on parents and grandparents who continued to defend traditional ethnic habits and values. Young women, in particular, sometimes rebelled against parents who tried to arrange (or prevent) marriages or who opposed women entering the workplace.

Native-born Americans encouraged immigrants to assimilate in countless ways. Public schools taught children in English, and employers often insisted that workers speak English on the job. Most stores sold mainly American products, forcing immigrants to adapt their diets, clothing, and lifestyles to American norms. Church leaders were often native-born Americans or more assimilated immigrants who encouraged their parishioners to adopt American ways. Some even embraced reforms to make their religion more compatible with the norms of the new country. Reform Judaism, imported from Germany in the late nineteenth century, was an effort by American Jewish leaders (as it had been by German ones) to make their faith less "foreign" to the dominant culture of a largely Christian nation.

The arrival of these vast numbers of new immigrants, and the way many of them clung to old ways and created distinctive communities, provoked fear and resentment among some native-born Americans in much the same way earlier arrivals had done. The rising nativism provoked political responses. In 1887, Henry Bowers, a self-educated lawyer preoccupied with what he considered the growing power of Catholics and foreigners, founded the American Protective Association, a group committed to stopping immigration. By 1894, membership in the organization reportedly reached 500,000, with chapters throughout the Northeast and Midwest. That same year, five Harvard alumni founded a more genteel organization—the Immigration Restriction League—in Boston. They proposed screening immigrants through literacy tests and other standards, to separate the "desirable" from the "undesirable."

The government responded to popular concern about immigration even earlier. In 1882 Congress, in response to strong anti-Asian sentiment in California and elsewhere, excluded the Chinese. In the same year, Congress denied entry to "undesirables"—convicts, paupers, the mentally incompetent—and placed a tax of 50 cents on each person admitted. Later legislation of the 1890s enlarged the list of those barred from immigrating and increased the tax.

But these laws kept out only a small number of aliens, and more ambitious restriction proposals made little progress in Congress. That was because immigration was providing a cheap and plentiful labor supply to the rapidly growing economy, and many argued that America's industrial (and indeed agricultural) development would be impossible without it.

THE URBAN LANDSCAPE

The city was a place of remarkable contrasts. It had homes of almost unimaginable size and grandeur and hovels of indescribable squalor. It had conveniences unknown to earlier generations and problems that seemed beyond the capacity of society to solve. Both the attractions and the problems were results of the stunning pace at which cities were growing.

The Creation of Public Space

In the eighteenth and early nineteenth centuries, cities had generally grown up haphazardly. By the mid-nineteenth century, however, reformers, planners, architects, and others began to call for a more ordered vision of the city. The result was the self-conscious creation of public spaces and public services.

Among the most important innovations of the mid-nineteenth century were great city parks, which reflected the desire of a growing number of urban leaders to provide an antidote to the congestion of the city landscape. Parks, they argued, would allow city residents a healthy, restorative escape from the strains of urban life by reacquainting them with the natural world. The most successful promoters of this notion of the park as refuge were the landscape designers Frederick Law Olmsted and Calvert Vaux, who teamed with one another in the late 1850s to design New York's Central Park. They deliberately created a public space that would look as little like the city as possible. Instead of the ordered, formal spaces common in some European cities, they created instead a space that seemed to be entirely natural. Central Park was from the start one of the most popular and admired public spaces in the world, and as a result Olmsted and Vaux were recruited to design other great parks and public spaces in other cities: Brooklyn, Boston, Philadelphia, Chicago, and Washington, D.C.

At the same time that cities were creating great parks, they were also creating great public buildings: libraries, art galleries, natural history museums, theaters, concert and opera halls. New York's Metropolitan Museum of Art was only the largest and best known of many great museums taking shape in the late nineteenth century; others were created in such cities as Boston, Chicago, Philadelphia, and Washington. In one city after another, new and lavish public libraries appeared as if to confirm the city's role as a center of learning and knowledge.

Wealthy residents of cities were the principal force behind the creation of the great art museums, concert halls, opera houses, and at times even parks. As their own material and social aspirations grew, they wanted the public life of the city to provide them with amenities to match their expectations. Becoming an important patron of a major cultural institution was an especially effective route to social distinction. But this philanthropy, whatever the motives behind it, also produced valuable assets for the city as a whole.

As both the size and the aspirations of the great cities increased, urban leaders launched monumental projects to remake the way their cities looked. Inspired by massive city rebuilding projects in Paris, London, Berlin, and other European cities, some American cities began to clear away older neighborhoods and streets and create grand, monumental avenues lined with new and more impressive buildings. A particularly important event in inspiring this effort to remake the city was the 1893 Columbian Exposition in Chicago, a world's fair constructed to honor the 400th anniversary of Columbus's first voyage to America. At the center of the wildly popular exposition was a cluster of neoclassical buildings—the "Great White City"—constructed in the fashionable "beaux-arts" style of the time, arranged symmetrically around a formal lagoon. It became the inspiration for what became known as the "city beautiful" movement, led by the architect of the Great White city, Daniel Burnham. The movement strove to impose a similar order and symmetry on the disordered life of cities around the country. "Make no little plans," Burnham liked to tell city planners. Those influenced by him aspired to remake cities all across the country—from Washington, D.C. to Chicago and San Francisco. Only rarely, however, were planners able to overcome the obstacles of private landowners and complicated urban politics to realize more than a small portion of their dreams. There were no reconstructions of American cities to match the elaborate nineteenth-century reshaping of Paris and London.

The effort to remake the city did not focus only on redesigning the existing landscapes. It occasionally led to the creation of entirely new ones. In Boston in the late 1850s, a large area of marshy tidal land was gradually filled in to create the neighborhood known as "Back Bay." The landfill project took more than forty years to complete and was one of the largest public works projects ever undertaken in America to that point. But Boston was not alone. Chicago reclaimed large areas from Lake Michigan as it expanded and at one point raised the street level for the entire city to help avoid the problems the marshy land created. In Washington, D.C., another marshy site, large areas were filled in and slated for development. In New York and other cities, the response to limited space was not so much creating new land as annexing adjacent territory. A great wave of annexations expanded the boundaries of many American cities in the 1890s and beyond.

The Search for Housing

One of the greatest urban problems was providing housing for the thousands of new residents who were pouring into the cities every day. For the prosperous, housing was seldom a worry. The availability of cheap labor and the increasing accessibility of tools and materials reduced the cost of building in the late nineteenth century and permitted anyone with even a moderate income to afford a house. Some of the richest urban residents lived in palatial mansions located in exclusive neighborhoods in the heart of the city—Fifth Avenue in New York, Back Bay and Beacon Hill in Boston, Society Hill in Philadelphia, Lake Shore Drive in Chicago, Nob Hill in San Francisco, and many others.

Many of the moderately well-to-do took advantage of less expensive land on the edges of the city and settled in new suburbs, linked to the downtowns by trains or streetcars. Chicago in the 1870s, for example, connected nearly 100 residential suburbs to the downtown by railroad. Boston, too, saw the development of some of the earliest suburbs, connected to the center of the city by streetcar. Real estate developers worked to create and promote suburban communities that would appeal to the nostalgia for the countryside that many city dwellers felt. Affluent suburbs in particular were notable for lawns, trees, and houses designed to look manorial. Even more modest communities strove to emphasize the opportunities suburbs provided for owning land.

Most urban residents, however, could not afford either to own a house in the city or to move to the suburbs. Instead, they stayed in the city centers and rented. Landlords tried to squeeze as many rent-paying residents as possible into the smallest available space. In Manhattan, for example, the average population density in 1894 was 143 people per acre—a rate higher than that of the most crowded cities of Europe (Paris had 127 per acre, Berlin 101) and far higher than that of any other American city then or since. In the cities of the South—Charleston, New Orleans, Richmond—poor blacks lived in crumbling former slave quarters. In Boston, immigrants moved into cheap three-story wooden houses ("triple deckers"). In Baltimore and Philadelphia, the new arrivals crowded into narrow brick row houses. And in New York and many other cities, they lived in tenements.

The word "tenement" had originally referred simply to a multiple-family rental building, but by the late nineteenth century it had become a term for slum dwellings only. The first tenements, built in 1850, had been hailed as a great improvement in housing for the poor. But most were, in fact, miserable places, with many windowless rooms, little or no plumbing or heating, and often a row of privies in the basement. Jacob Riis, a Danish immigrant and New York newspaper reporter and photographer, shocked many middle-class Americans with his sensational (and some claimed sensationalized) descriptions and pictures of tenement life in his 1890 book, *How the Other Half Lives*. But the solution reformers often adopted was simply to raze slum dwellings without building any new housing to replace them.

A TENEMENT LAUNDRY Immigrant families living in tenements, in New York and in many other cities, earned their livelihoods as they could. This woman, shown here with her children, was typical of many working-class mothers who found income-producing activities they could pursue in the home (in this case laundry). The room, dominated by large vats and piles of other people's laundry, is also the family's home, as the crib and religious pictures make clear.

Urban Technologies: Transportation and Construction

Urban growth posed monumental transportation challenges. Old downtown streets were inadequate for the heavy traffic that was beginning to travel over them. The numbers of people who needed to move every day from one part of the city to another mandated the development of mass transportation. Streetcars drawn on tracks by horses had been introduced into some cities even before the Civil War. But the horsecars were not fast enough, so many communities developed new forms of mass transit. In 1870, New York opened its first elevated railway, whose noisy, steam-powered trains, belching thick black smoke into the sky, moved rapidly above the city streets on massive iron structures. New York, Chicago, San Francisco, and other cities also experimented with cable cars, towed by continuously moving underground cables. Richmond, Virginia, introduced the first electric trolley line in 1888, and in 1897 Boston opened the first American subway. At the same time, cities were developing new techniques of road and bridge building. One of the great technological marvels of the 1880s was the completion of the Brooklyn Bridge in New York—a dramatic steel-cable suspension span designed by John A. Roebling.

Cities were growing upward as well as outward. In Chicago, the construction in 1884 of the first modern "skyscraper"—by later standards a relatively modest building, ten stories high—launched a new era in urban architecture. Critical to the creation of the skyscraper was a new technology of construction, which emerged as a result of several related developments. One was the creation of new kinds of steel girders, capable of supporting much greater tension than the metals of the past and thus capable of providing steel beams that could support very tall buildings. Still another was the invention and development of the passenger elevator, which made it possible for people to move through buildings too tall for stairways to be practical. And another was the search for ways to protect cities from the ravages of great fires, which caused such terrible destruction in wood-frame cities of the late nineteenth century. Steel-frame construction was, among other things, a way to make cities more fireproof. Once the technology existed to permit the construction of tall buildings, there were few obstacles to building taller and taller structures. The early Chicago skyscrapers paved the way for some of the great construction marvels of the later twentieth century: the Chrysler Building and the Empire State Building in New York, the Lasalle Building in Chicago, and ultimately the vast numbers of steel and glass skyscrapers of the post-1945 cities of America and the world.

STRAINS OF URBAN LIFE

The increasing congestion of the city and the absence of adequate public services produced serious hazards. Crime, fire, disease, and indigence all placed strains on the capacities of metropolitan institutions, and both governments and private agencies were for a time poorly equipped to respond to them.

Fire and Disease

One serious problem was fire. In one major city after another, fires destroyed large downtown areas. Chicago and Boston suffered "great fires" in 1871. Other cities—among them Baltimore and San Francisco, where a tremendous earthquake produced a catastrophic fire in 1906—experienced similar disasters. The great fires were terrible experiences, but they were also important events in the development of the cities involved. They encouraged the construction of fireproof buildings and the development of professional fire departments. They also forced cities to rebuild at a time when new technological and architectural innovations were available. Some of the high-rise downtowns of American cities arose out of the rubble of great fires.

An even greater hazard than fire was disease, especially in poor neighborhoods with inadequate sanitation facilities. But an epidemic that began in a poor neighborhood could (and often did) spread easily into other neighborhoods as well. Few municipal officials recognized the relationship of improper sewage disposal and water contamination to such epidemic diseases as typhoid fever and cholera; many cities lacked adequate systems for disposing of human waste until well into the twentieth century. Flush toilets and sewer systems began to appear in the 1870s, but they could not solve the problem as long as sewage continued to flow into open ditches or streams, polluting cities' water supplies.

Urban Poverty, Crime, and Violence

Above all, perhaps, the expansion of the city spawned widespread and often desperate poverty. Public agencies and private philanthropic organizations offered some relief. But they were generally poorly funded, and in any case dominated by middle-class people who believed that too much assistance would breed dependency and that poverty was the fault of the poor themselves. Most tried to restrict aid to the "deserving poor"—those who truly could not help themselves (at least according to the standards of the organizations themselves, which conducted elaborate "investigations" to separate the "deserving" from the "undeserving").

Other charitable societies—for example, the Salvation Army, which began operating in America in 1879, one year after it was founded in London—concentrated more on religious revivalism than on the relief of the homeless and hungry. Tensions often arose between native Protestant philanthropists and Catholic immigrants over religious doctrine and standards of morality. Middle-class faith in the idea of self-improvement led to a widespread inattention to the structural roots of urban poverty.

Middle-class people grew particularly alarmed over the rising number of poor children in the cities, some of them orphans or runaways, living alone or in small groups scrounging for food. These "street arabs," as they were often called, attracted more attention from reformers than any other group—although that attention produced no lasting solutions to their problems.

Poverty and crowding naturally bred crime and violence. The American murder rate rose rapidly in the late nineteenth century (even as such rates were declining in Europe), from 25 murders for every million people in 1880 to over 100 by the end of the century—matching the highest murder rate of the late twentieth century. That reflected in part a very high level of violence in some nonurban areas: the American South, where lynching and homicide were particularly high; and the West, where the rootlessness and instability of new communities (cow towns, mining camps, and the like) created much violence. But the cities contributed their share to the increase in crime as well. Native-born Americans liked to believe that crime was a result of the violent proclivities of immigrant groups, and they cited the rise of gangs and criminal organizations in various ethnic communities. But even in the cities, native-born Americans were as likely to commit crimes as immigrants. The rising crime rates encouraged many cities to develop larger and more professional police forces. But police forces themselves could spawn corruption and brutality, particularly since jobs on them were often filled through political patronage.

Some members of the middle class, fearful of urban insurrections, felt the need for even more substantial forms of protection. Urban national guard groups (many of them created and manned by middle-class elites) built imposing armories on the outskirts of affluent neighborhoods and stored large supplies of weapons and ammunition in preparation for uprisings that, in fact, virtually never occurred.

The city was a place of strong allure and great excitement. Yet it was also a place of alienating impersonality and, to some, a place of degradation and exploitation. Theodore Dreiser's novel *Sister Carrie* (1900) exposed one troubling aspect of urban life: the plight of single women (like Dreiser's heroine, Carrie) who moved from the countryside into the city and found themselves without any means of support. Carrie first took an exhausting and ill-paying job in a Chicago shoe factory; then she drifted into a life of "sin," exploited by predatory men. Many women were experiencing in reality the dilemmas Carrie experienced in fiction.

The Machine and the Boss

Newly arrived immigrants, many of whom could not speak English, were much in need of institutions to help them adjust to American urban life. For many residents of the inner cities, the principal source of assistance was the political "machine."

The urban machine owed its existence to the power vacuum that the chaotic growth of cities (and the very limited growth of governments) had created. It was also a product of the potential voting power of large immigrant communities. Out of that combination emerged a group of "urban" bosses, themselves often of foreign birth or parentage. Many were Irish, because they spoke English and because some had previous political experience from the long Irish struggle against the English at home.

The principal function of the political boss was simple: to win votes for his organization. That meant winning the loyalty of his constituents. To do so, a boss might provide them with occasional relief—a basket of groceries or a bag of coal. He might step in to save those arrested for petty crimes from jail. When he could, he found work for the unemployed. Above all, he rewarded many of his followers with patronage: with jobs in city government or in such city agencies as the police (which the machine's elected officials often controlled); with jobs building or operating the new transit systems; and with opportunities to rise in the political organization itself.

Machines were also vehicles for making money. Politicians enriched themselves and their allies through various forms of graft and corruption. Some of it might be fairly open—what George Washington Plunkitt of New York's Tammany Hall called "honest graft." For example, a politician might discover in advance where a new road or streetcar line was to be built, buy land near it, and sell it at a profit when property values rose as a result of the construction. There was also covert graft. Officials received kickbacks from contractors in exchange for contracts to build public projects, and they sold franchises for the operation of public utilities. The most famously corrupt city boss was William M. Tweed, boss of New York City's Tammany Hall in the 1860s and 1870s, whose extravagant use of public funds on projects that paid kickbacks to the organization landed him in jail in 1872.

The urban machine was not without competition. Reform groups frequently mobilized public outrage at the corruption of the bosses and often succeeded in driving machine politicians from office. But the reform organizations typically lacked the permanence of the machine, and more often than not, their power faded after a few years.

THE RISE OF MASS CONSUMPTION

For urban middle-class Americans, the last decades of the nineteenth century were a time of dramatic advances. Indeed, it was in those years that a distinctive middle-class culture began to exert a powerful influence over the whole of American life. Other groups in society advanced less rapidly, or not at all, but almost no one was unaffected by the rise of the new urban, consumer culture.

Patterns of Income and Consumption

Incomes were rising for almost everyone in the industrial era, although at highly uneven rates. The most conspicuous result of the new economy was the creation of vast fortunes, but perhaps the most important result for society as a whole was the growth and increasing prosperity of the middle class. The salaries of clerks, accountants, middle managers, and other "white-collar" workers rose by an average of a third between 1890 and 1910—and in some parts of the middle class, much higher. Doctors, lawyers, and other professionals, for example, experienced a particularly dramatic increase in both the prestige and the profitability of their professions. Working-class incomes rose in those years as well, although from a much lower base and often more slowly. The iron and steel industries saw workers' hourly wages increase by a third between 1890 and 1910; but industries with large female work forces—shoes, textiles, and paper—saw more modest increases, as did almost all industries in the South. Wages for African Americans, Mexicans, and Asians also rose more slowly than those for other workers.

Rising incomes created new markets for consumer goods. Affordable products and new merchandising techniques soon made many consumer goods available to this mass market for the first time. A good example of such changes was the emergence of ready-made clothing. In the early nineteenth century, most Americans had made their own clothing—usually from cloth they bought from merchants, at times from fabrics they spun and wove themselves. The invention of the sewing machine and the spur that the Civil War (and its demand for uniforms) gave to the manufacture of clothing helped create an enormous industry devoted to producing ready-made garments. By the end of the century, virtually all Americans bought their clothing from stores. Partly as a result, much larger numbers of people became concerned with personal style. Interest in women's fashion, for example, had once been a luxury reserved for the relatively affluent. Now middle-class and even working-class women could strive to develop a distinctive style of dress.

Buying and preparing food also became a critical part of the new consumerism. The development and mass production of tin cans in the 1880s created a large new industry devoted to packaging and selling canned food and condensed milk. Refrigerated railroad cars made it possible for perishables—meats, vegetables, dairy products, and other foodstuffs—to be transported over long distances without spoiling. Artificially frozen ice enabled many households to afford iceboxes. The changes brought improved diets and better health. Life expectancy rose six years in the first two decades of the twentieth century.

Chain Stores, Mail-Order Houses, and Department Stores

Changes in marketing also altered the way Americans bought goods. New "chain stores" could usually offer a wider array of goods at lower prices than the small local stores with which they competed. The Atlantic and Pacific Tea Company (the A & P) began a national network of grocery stores in the 1870s. F. W. Woolworth built a chain of dry goods stores. Sears and Roebuck established a large market for its mail-order merchandise by distributing an enormous catalog each year. Even people in remote rural areas could order its products.

In larger cities, the emergence of great department stores helped transform buying habits and turn shopping into a more alluring and glamorous activity. Marshall Field in Chicago created one of the first American department stores—a place deliberately designed to produce a sense of

THE DEPARTMENT STORE, C. 1892 This detail from an advertisement shows an interior cross section of the Abraham and Straus department store in Brooklyn, New York. Early department stores boasted not just of the variety of their merchandise but also of the almost magical consumer world they created.

wonder and excitement. Similar stores emerged in New York, Brooklyn, Boston, Philadelphia, and other cities.

Women as Consumers

The rise of mass consumption had particularly dramatic effects on American women, who were generally the primary consumers within families. Women's clothing styles changed much more rapidly and dramatically than men's, which encouraged more frequent purchases. Women generally bought and prepared food for their families, so the availability of new food products changed not only the way everyone ate, but also the way women shopped and cooked. Canning and refrigeration meant greater variety in the diet. It also meant that food did not always have to be eaten on the day it was purchased.

The consumer economy produced new employment opportunities for women as salesclerks in department stores and as waitresses in rapidly proliferating restaurants. And it spawned the creation of a new movement in which women were to play a vital role: the consumer protection movement. The National Consumers League, formed in the 1890s under the leadership of Florence Kelley, attempted to mobilize the power of women as consumers to force retailers and manufacturers to improve wages and working conditions.

LEISURE IN THE CONSUMER SOCIETY

Closely related to the growth of consumption was a growing interest in leisure time, which for many people was increasing rapidly. Members of the urban middle and professional classes had large blocks of time during which they were not at work—evenings, weekends, even paid vacations. Working hours in many factories declined, from an average of nearly seventy hours a week in 1860 to under sixty in 1900. Even farmers found that the mechanization of agriculture gave them more free time. The lives of many Americans were becoming more compartmentalized, with clear distinctions between work and leisure. The change produced a search for new forms of recreation and entertainment.

Redefining Leisure

It also produced a redefinition of the idea of "leisure." In earlier eras, relatively few Americans had considered leisure a valuable thing. On the contrary, many equated it with laziness or sloth. In the late nineteenth century, however, the beginnings of a redefinition of leisure appeared. With the rapid expansion of the economy and the increasing number of hours workers had away from work, it became possible to imagine leisure time as a normal part of the lives of many people. Industrial workers, in pursuit of shorter hours, adopted the slogan: "Eight hours for work, eight hours for rest, and eight hours for what we will." Others were equally adamant in claiming that leisure time was both a right and an important contribution to an individual's emotional and even spiritual health.

The economist Simon Patten was one of the first intellectuals to articulate this new view of leisure, which he tied closely to the rising interest in consumption. Patten, in *The Theory of Prosperity* (1902), *The New Basis of Civilization* (1910), and other works, challenged the centuries-old assumption that the normal condition of civilization was a scarcity of goods. In earlier times, Patten argued, fear of scarcity had caused people to place a high value on thrift, self-denial, and restraint. But in modern industrial societies, the problems of scarcity had been overcome. The new economies could create enough wealth to satisfy not just the needs, but also the desires, of all.

As Americans became more accustomed to leisure as a normal part of their lives, they not only made increased use of traditional forms of recreation and entertainment; they also began to look for new experiences with which to entertain themselves. In cities, in particular, the demand for popular entertainment produced a rich mix of spectacles, recreations, and other activities.

Mass entertainment occasionally bridged differences of class, race, or gender. But it could also be sharply divided. Saloons and some sporting events tended to be male preserves. Shopping (itself becoming a valued leisure-time activity) and going to tea rooms and luncheonettes was more characteristic of female leisure. Theaters, pubs, and clubs were often specific to particular ethnic communities or particular work groups. When the classes did meet in public spaces—as they did, for example, in city parks—there was often considerable conflict over what constituted appropriate public behavior. Elites in New York City, for example, tried to prohibit anything but quiet, "genteel" activities in Central Park, while working-class people wanted to use the public spaces for sports and entertainments.

Spectator Sports

Among the most important responses to the search for entertainment was the rise of organized spectator sports, and especially baseball, which by the end of the century was well on its way to becoming the "national pastime." A game much like baseball—known as "rounders" and derived from cricket—had enjoyed limited popularity in Great Britain in the early nineteenth century. Versions of the game began to appear in America in the early 1830s.

By the end of the Civil War, interest in the game had grown rapidly. More than 200 amateur or semiprofessional teams and clubs existed, many of which joined a national association and proclaimed a set of standard rules. As the game grew in popularity, it offered opportunities for profit. The first salaried team, the Cincinnati Red Stockings, was formed in 1869. Other cities soon fielded professional teams, and in 1876 the teams banded together in the National League. A rival league, the American Association, soon appeared. It eventually collapsed, but in 1901 the American League emerged to replace it. And in 1903, the first modern World Series was played, in which the American League Boston Red Sox beat the National League Pittsburgh Pirates. By then, baseball had become an important business and a great national preoccupation (at least among men), attracting paying crowds at times as large as 50,000.

Baseball had its greatest appeal to working-class males. The second most popular game, football, appealed at first to a more elite segment of the male population, in part because it originated in colleges and universities. The first intercollegiate football game in America occurred between Princeton and Rutgers in 1869, and soon the game began to become entrenched as part of collegiate life. Early intercollegiate football bore only an indirect relation to the modern game; it was more similar to what is now known as rugby. By the late 1870s, however, the game was becoming standardized and was taking on the outlines of its modern form.

Basketball was invented in 1891 at Springfield, Massachusetts, by Dr. James A. Naismith, a Canadian working as athletic director for a local college. Boxing, which had long been a disreputable activity concentrated primarily among the urban lower classes, became by the 1880s a more popular and, in some places, more reputable sport.

Participation in the major sports of the era was almost exclusively the province of men, but several sports emerged in which women became important participants. Golf and tennis both experienced a rapid increase in participation among relatively wealthy men and women. Bicycling and croquet also enjoyed widespread popularity in the 1890s among women as well as men. Women's colleges introduced their students to more strenuous sports as well—track, crew, swimming, and (beginning in the late 1890s) basketball—challenging the once-prevalent notion that vigorous exercise was dangerous to women.

Music and Theater

Other forms of popular entertainment developed in the cities in response to the large potential markets there. Many ethnic communities maintained their own theaters, catering to the tastes and experiences of immigrant audiences. Urban theaters also introduced new and distinctively American entertainment forms: the musical comedy, which evolved gradually from the comic operettas of Europe; and vaudeville, a form of theater adapted from French models, which remained the most popular urban entertainment in the first decades of the twentieth century. It consisted of a variety of acts (musicians, comedians, magicians, jugglers, and others) and was, at least in the beginning, inexpensive to produce. As the economic potential of vaudeville grew, some promoters—most prominently Florenz Ziegfeld of New York—staged much more elaborate spectacles.

Vaudeville was also one of the few entertainment media open to black performers. They brought to it elements of the minstrel shows they had earlier developed for black audiences in the late nineteenth century. Some minstrel singers (including the most famous, Al Jolson) were whites wearing heavy makeup (or "blackface"), but most were black. Entertainers of both races performed music based on the gospel and folk tunes of the plantation and on the jazz and ragtime of black urban communities. Performers of both races also tailored their acts to prevailing white prejudices, ridiculing blacks by acting out demeaning stereotypes.

The Movies

The most important form of mass entertainment (until the invention of radio and television), and the one that reached most widely across the nation, was the movies. Thomas Edison and others had created the technology of the motion picture in the 1880s. Soon after that, short films became available to individual viewers watching peepshows in pool halls, penny arcades, and amusement parks. Soon, larger projectors made it possible to project the images onto big screens, which permitted substantial audiences to see films in theaters. By 1900, Americans were becoming attracted in large numbers to these early movies—usually plotless films of trains or waterfalls or other spectacles designed mainly to show off the technology. The great D. W. Griffith carried the motion picture into a new era with his silent epics—*The Birth of a Nation* (1915), *Intolerance* (1916), and others—which introduced serious (if notoriously racist) plots and elaborate productions to filmmaking. Motion pictures were the first truly mass entertainment medium—one that reached all areas of the country and most groups in the population.

Patterns of Public and Private Leisure

Particularly striking about popular entertainment in the late nineteenth and early twentieth centuries was its public quality. Many Americans spent their leisure time in places where they would find not only entertainment but also other people. Thousands of working-class New Yorkers spent evenings in dance halls, vaudeville houses, and concert halls. More affluent New Yorkers enjoyed afternoons in Central Park, where a principal attraction was seeing other people (and being seen by them). Moviegoers were attracted not just by the movies themselves but by the energy of the audiences at the lavish "movie palaces" that began to appear in cities in the early twentieth century, just as sports fans were drawn by the crowds as well as by the games.

Perhaps the most striking example of popular, public entertainment was Coney Island, the famous and self-consciously fabulous amusement

A NICKELODEON, 1905 Before the rise of great movie palaces, urban families flocked to "nickelodeons," smaller theaters that charged five cents for admission and that showed many different films each day, including serials—dramas that drew audiences back into theaters day after day with new episodes of a running story.

park and resort on a popular beach in Brooklyn that became a magnet for visitors from around the nation and the world. The greatest of the Coney Island attractions, Luna Park, opened in 1903. It provided rides and stunts, and also lavish reproductions of exotic places and spectacular adventures: Japanese gardens, Venetian canals with gondoliers, a Chinese theater, a simulated trip to the moon, and re-enactments of such disasters as burning buildings, earthquakes, and even the volcanic eruption that destroyed Pompeii. A year later, a competing company opened Dreamland, which tried to outdo even Luna Park with a 375-foot tower (modeled on a famous building in Spanish Seville), a three-ring circus, chariot races, and a Lilliputian village from *Gulliver's Travels*. The popularity of Coney Island in these years was phenomenal. Thousands of people flocked to the large resort hotels that lined the beaches. Many thousands more made day trips out from the city by train and (after 1920) subway. In 1904, the average daily attendance at Luna Park alone was 90,000 people.

POSTCARD FROM LUNA PARK Visitors to Coney Island sent postcards to friends and relatives by the millions, and those cards were among the most effective promotional devices for the amusement parks. This one shows the brightly-lit entrance to Luna Park, Coney Island's most popular attraction for many years.

Coney Island gave people who had few opportunities for travel a simulated glimpse of exotic places and events that they would never be able to experience in reality. For immigrants, Coney Island provided a way of experiencing American mass culture on an equal footing with people from backgrounds different from their own. And almost everyone who found Coney Island appealing did so in part because it provided them with an escape from the genteel standards of behavior that governed so much of American life at the time. In the amusement parks of Coney Island, decorum was often forgotten, and people delighted in finding themselves in situations that in any other setting would have seemed embarrassing or improper: women's skirts blown above their heads with hot air; people pummeled with water and rubber paddles by clowns; hints of sexual freedom as strangers were forced to come into physical contact with one another on rides and amusements and as men and women revealed themselves to each other wearing bathing suits on the beach.

Not all popular entertainment, however, involved public events. Many Americans amused themselves privately by reading novels and poetry. The so-called dime novels, cheaply bound and widely circulated, became popular after the Civil War, with detective stories, tales of the "Wild West," sagas of scientific adventure (such as the Tom Swift stories), and novels of "moral uplift" (among them those of Horatio Alger). Publishers also distributed sentimental novels of romance, which developed a large audience among women, as did books about animals and about young children growing up. Louisa May Alcott's *Little Women*, most of whose readers were women, sold more than 2 million copies.

The Technologies of Mass Communication

Urban-industrial society created a vast market for news and information. As a result, American publishing and journalism experienced an important change in the decades following the Civil War. Between 1870 and 1910, the circulation of daily newspapers increased nearly ninefold (from under 3 million to more than 24 million), a rate three times as great as the rate of population increase. And while standards varied widely from one paper to another, American journalism was developing the beginnings of a professional identity. Salaries of reporters increased; many newspapers began separating the reporting of news from the expression of opinion; and newspapers themselves became important businesses.

The transformation of publishing and journalism was to a large degree a result of new technologies of communication. The emergence of national press services, for example, was a product of the telegraph, which made it possible to supply papers throughout the country with news and features from around the nation and the world (and which contributed, as a result, to a standardization of the product). By the turn of the century important newspaper chains had emerged as well, linked together by their own internal wire services. The most powerful was owned by William Randolph Hearst, who by 1914 controlled nine newspapers and two magazines. New printing technologies were making possible more elaborate layouts, the publication of color pictures, and, by the end of the century, the printing of photographs. These advances not only helped publishers make their own stories more vivid; they also made it possible for them to attract more advertisers, who could use the pages of newspapers and magazines to illustrate their wares more dramatically than ever before.

The Telephone

The most important new technology of communication in the late nine-teenth century, however, was the telephone, which Alexander Graham Bell had first demonstrated in 1876 (see p. 516). In its first years, the tele-phone was a relatively impractical tool. Those who subscribed to tele-phone service had to have direct wire links to everyone else they wished to call, which meant that no one could have access to more than a few, rela-tively nearby people. In 1878, the first "switchboard" opened in New Haven, Connecticut, opening the way for more practical uses of the tele-phone. Once there was a switchboard, a telephone subscriber needed only a line to the central telephone office from which connections could be made to any other subscriber. A new occupation—the "telephone opera-tor"—was born; and for many years, all telephone calls required a caller to speak directly with an operator. The Bell System, which controlled all American telephone service, hired young white women to work as opera-tors, hoping that a pleasant female voice would make the experience of using the telephone (and the inconvenience of the frequent technological problems that accompanied it) more appealing, or less irritating, to cus-tomers. Telephone signals were very weak at first, and callers could sel-dom reach anyone more than a few miles away. In an effort to increase the range of telephones, engineers created the "repeater," which periodically strengthened the signal as it moved over distances. The first repeater ap-peared in 1910, but only modestly improved performance. By 1914, how-ever, the repeaters had improved to the point that it was now practical to envision a transcontinental line.

In its early years, the telephone was an almost entirely commercial in-strument. Of the nearly 7,400 telephone customers in the New York-New Jersey area in 1891, 6,000 were businesses and organizations: hospitals, physicians, stores, professional offices, and the like. Even the residential telephones tended to belong to doctors or business managers.

The growing reach of the telephone in the early years of the twentieth century—when it began to become a staple of most middle-class homes and to connect people over long distances—made the Bell System (formally named American Telephone and Telegraph, or AT&T) one of the most pow-erful corporations in America and a genuine monopoly. Central to its success was an early decision by executives that the company would exclusively build and own all telephone instruments and then lease them to subscribers. That made it possible for AT&T to control both the equipment and the telephone service itself, and to exclude any competitors in either field. It also gave

AT&T effective control over the local telephone companies allied with it and made the nation's telephone system into an effective cartel.

HIGH CULTURE IN THE URBAN AGE

In addition to the important changes in popular culture that accompanied the rise of cities and industry, there were profound changes in the realm of "high culture"—in the ideas and activities of intellectuals and elites. The distinction between "highbrow" and "lowbrow" culture was largely new to the industrial era. In the early nineteenth century, most cultural activities had attracted people of widely varying backgrounds and targeted people of all classes. By the late nineteenth century, however, elites were developing a cultural and intellectual life quite separate from the popular amusements of the urban masses.

The Literature of Urban America

One of the strongest impulses in late-nineteenth- and early-twentieth-century American literature was the effort to re-create urban social reality. This trend toward realism found an early voice in Stephen Crane, who—although perhaps best known for his novel of the Civil War, *The Red Badge of Courage* (1895)—created a sensation in 1893 when he published *Maggie: A Girl of the Streets*, a grim picture of urban poverty and slum life. Theodore Dreiser, Frank Norris, and Upton Sinclair were similarly drawn to social issues as themes. Kate Chopin, a southern writer who explored the oppressive features of traditional marriage, encountered widespread public abuse (and in some places formal bans) after publication of her shocking novel, *The Awakening*, in 1899. It described a young wife and mother who abandoned her family in search of personal fulfillment. William Dean Howells, in *The Rise of Silas Lapham* and other works, described what he considered the shallowness and corruption in ordinary American lifestyles.

Other critics of American society responded to the new civilization not by attacking it but by withdrawing from it. The historian Henry Adams published an autobiography in 1906, *The Education of Henry Adams*, which portrayed a man disillusioned with and unable to relate to his society, even though he continued to live in it. The novelist Henry James lived the major part of his adult life in England and Europe and produced a series of coldly realistic novels—*The American* (1877), *Portrait of a Lady* (1881), *The Ambassadors* (1903), and others—that showed his ambivalence about the merits of both American and European civilization.

Art in the Age of the City

American art through most of the nineteenth century had been overshadowed by the art of Europe. By 1900, however, a number of American artists, although some continued to study and even live in Europe, broke from the Old World traditions and experimented with new styles. Winslow Homer was vigorously American in his paintings of New England maritime life and other native subjects. James McNeil Whistler was one of the first Western artists to appreciate the beauty of Japanese color prints and to introduce Oriental themes into American and European art.

By the first years of the new century, some American artists were turning decisively away from the traditional academic style (a style perhaps most identified in America by the brilliant portraitist John Singer Sargent). Instead, many younger painters were exploring the same grim aspects of modern life that were becoming the subject of American literature. Members of the so-called Ashcan School produced work startling in its naturalism and stark in its portrayal of the social realities of the era. John Sloan portrayed the dreariness of American urban slums; George Bellows caught the vigor and violence of his time in paintings and drawings of prizefights; Edward Hopper explored the starkness and loneliness of the modern city. The Ashcan artists were also among the first Americans to appreciate expressionism and abstraction; and they showed their interest in new forms in 1913 when they helped stage the famous "Armory Show" in New York City, which displayed works of the French postimpressionists and of some American moderns.

The Impact of Darwinism

Perhaps the most profound intellectual development in the late nineteenth century was the widespread acceptance of the theory of evolution, associated most prominently with the English naturalist Charles Darwin. Darwin argued that the human species had evolved from earlier forms of life (and most immediately from simian creatures similar to apes) through a process of "natural selection." History, Darwin suggested, was not the working out of a divine plan, as most Americans had always believed. It was a random process dominated by the fiercest or luckiest competitors.

The theory of evolution met widespread resistance at first from educators, theologians, and even many scientists. By the end of the century, however, the evolutionists had converted most members of the urban professional and educated classes. Even many middle-class Protestant reli-

EDWARD HOPPER, *AUTOMAT* Edward Hopper was one of a growing group of American painters in the early twentieth century who chose to chronicle not the world of wealth and power, the characteristic subject of earlier artists, but the harsh, gritty world of the modern city. Hopper's work was distinctive for its evocation of the loneliness of urban life. This 1927 painting of a scene in an "automat" in New York City is characteristic of his work.

gious leaders had accepted the doctrine, making significant alterations in theology to accommodate it. Unseen by most urban Americans at the time, however, the rise of Darwinism was contributing to a deep schism between the new, cosmopolitan culture of the city—which was receptive to new ideas such as evolution—and the more traditional, provincial culture of some rural areas—which remained wedded to fundamentalist religious beliefs and older values. Thus the late nineteenth century saw not only the rise of a liberal Protestantism in tune with new scientific discoveries but also the beginning of an organized Protestant fundamentalism, which would make its presence felt politically in the 1920s and beyond.

Darwinism helped spawn other new intellectual currents. There was the Social Darwinism of William Graham Sumner and others, which industrialists used so enthusiastically to justify their favored position in

American life. But there were also more sophisticated philosophies, among them a doctrine that became known as "pragmatism," which reflected Darwinism's rejection of inherited ideas and its emphasis on scientific research. William James, a Harvard psychologist (and brother of the novelist Henry James), was the most prominent publicist of the new theory, although earlier intellectuals such as Charles S. Peirce and later ones such as John Dewey were also important to its development and dissemination. According to the pragmatists, modern society should rely for guidance not on inherited ideals and moral principles but on the test of scientific inquiry. No idea or institution (not even religious faith) was valid, they claimed, unless it worked, unless it stood the test of experience.

A similar concern for scientific inquiry was influencing the social sciences and challenging traditional orthodoxies. Sociologists such as Edward A. Ross and Lester Frank Ward urged applying the scientific method to the solution of social and political problems. Historians such as Frederick Jackson Turner and Charles Beard argued that economic factors more than spiritual ideals had been the governing force in historical development. John Dewey proposed a new approach to education that placed less emphasis on the rote learning of traditional knowledge and more on a flexible, democratic approach to schooling, one that enabled students to acquire knowledge that would help them deal with the realities of their society.

The implications of Darwinism also promoted the growth of anthropology and encouraged some scholars to begin examining other cultures—most significantly, perhaps, the culture of American Indians—in new ways. Some white Americans began to look at Indian society as a coherent culture with its own norms and values that were worthy of respect and preservation, even though they were different from those of white society.

Toward Universal Schooling

The growing demand for specialized skills and scientific knowledge naturally created a growing, and changing, demand for education. The late nineteenth century, therefore, was a time of rapid expansion and reform of American schools and universities.

One example was the spread of free public primary and secondary education. In 1860, there were only 100 public high schools in the entire United States. By 1900, the number had reached 6,000 and by 1914 over 12,000. By 1900, compulsory school attendance laws were in effect in thirty-one states and territories. Education was still far from universal. Rural areas lagged far behind urban-industrial ones in funding public education. In the

South, many blacks had access to no schools at all. But for many white men and women, educational opportunities were expanding dramatically.

Educational reformers tried to extend educational opportunities to the Indian tribes as well, in an effort to "civilize" them and help them adapt to white society. In the 1870s, reformers recruited small groups of Indians to attend Hampton Institute (a primarily black college). In 1879 they organized the Carlisle Indian Industrial School in Pennsylvania. Like many black colleges, Carlisle emphasized the kind of practical "industrial" education that Booker T. Washington had urged on blacks. Ultimately, however, these reform efforts failed, partly because of inadequate funding and commitment and partly because the venture itself—the effort to remove Indians from their traditional surroundings and transform them into members of white society—was unpopular with its intended beneficiaries.

Universities and the Growth of Science and Technology

Colleges and universities were also proliferating rapidly in the late nineteenth century. They benefited particularly from the Morrill Land Grant Act of 1862, by which the federal government had donated public land to states for the establishment of colleges. After 1865, states in the South and West took particular advantage of the law. Sixty-nine "land-grant" institutions were established in the last decades of the century—among them the state university systems of California, Illinois, Minnesota, and Wisconsin. Other universities benefited from millions of dollars contributed by business and financial titans. Rockefeller, Carnegie, and others gave generously to such schools as Columbia, Chicago, Harvard, Northwestern, Princeton, Syracuse, and Yale. Other philanthropists founded new universities or reorganized older ones and perpetuated their family names—Vanderbilt, Johns Hopkins, Cornell, Duke, Tulane, and Stanford.

The growth of these and other universities was important not just for the educational opportunities they provided growing numbers of students. They also played a vital role in the economic development of the United States in the late nineteenth century and beyond. The land-grant institutions were specifically mandated to advance knowledge in "agriculture and mechanics." From the beginning, therefore, they were committed not to abstract knowledge, but to making discoveries that would be of practical use to farmers and manufacturers. As they evolved into great state universities, they retained that tradition and became the source of many of the great technological and scientific discoveries that helped American industry and commerce to advance. Private universities emerged that served many of the same purposes: the Massachusetts Institute of Technology, founded in 1865, which soon became the nation's premier engineering school and from the beginning had close relationships with industry; Johns Hopkins University in Baltimore, founded in 1876, which did much to advance medical scholarship; the Rockefeller Institute for Medical Research in New York (later Rockefeller University); the Carnegie Institution. By the early twentieth century, even much older and more traditional universities were beginning to form relationships with the private sector and the government, doing research that did not just advance knowledge for its own sake but that was directly applicable to practical problems of the time.

By contrast, most European universities had few if any connections to business, industry, or government. There were many great scientists and engineers in European academies, but they tended to consider practical application of scientific knowledge an activity for others, not worthy of true scholars. The United States economy profited enormously from the matrix of universities, government agencies, and private enterprise, which together made the American economy the most technologically and scientifically innovative in the world.

Medical Science

Both the culture of and the scientific basis for medical care was changing rapidly in the early twentieth century, driven in part by the new research universities and medical schools that were doing so much to produce new scientific knowledge. By the turn of the century, most doctors were beginning to accept the new medical assumption that there were underlying causes to particular symptoms—that a symptom was not itself a disease. They were also beginning to make use of new or improved technologies—the X-ray, improved microscopes, and other diagnostic devices in laboratories—that made it possible to classify, and distinguish among, different diseases. Laboratory tests could now identify infections such as typhoid and dysentery. That did not in itself help doctors treat diseases, but it was a critical first step toward finding effective treatment. At about the same time, pharmaceutical research was beginning to produce some important new medicines. Aspirin was first synthesized in 1899. Other researchers were beginning to experiment with chemicals that might destroy diseases in the blood, an effort that eventually led to the various forms of chemotherapy that are still widely used in treating cancer. In 1906, an American surgeon, G. W. Crile, became the first physician to use blood transfusion in treatment, which revolutionized surgery. In the past, patients often lost so much blood during operations that extensive surgery could be fatal for that reason alone. With transfusions, it became possible to conduct much longer and more elaborate operations.

The widespread acceptance by the end of the nineteenth century of the germ theory of disease not only had important implications for public health efforts, but also for medical practice. Physicians quickly discovered that exposure to germs did not by itself necessarily cause disease, and they began looking for the other factors that determined who got sick and who did not. Among the factors they eventually discovered were general health, previous medical history, diet and nutrition, and eventually genetic predisposition. The awareness of the importance of infection in spreading disease also encouraged doctors to sterilize their instruments, use surgical gloves, and otherwise purify the medical environment of patients.

By the early twentieth century, American physicians and surgeons were generally recognized as among the best in the world, and American medical education was beginning to attract students from many other countries. These improvements in medical knowledge and training, along with improvements in sanitation and public health, did much to reduce infection and mortality in most American communities and to decrease the incidence of such previously common and deadly diseases as cholera and typhoid.

Education for Women

The post–Civil War era saw an important expansion of educational opportunities for women, although such opportunities continued to lag far behind those available to men and were almost without exception denied to black women.

Most public high schools accepted women readily, but opportunities for higher education were fewer. At the end of the Civil War, only three American colleges were coeducational. In the years after the war, many of the land-grant colleges and universities in the Midwest and such private universities as Cornell and Wesleyan began to admit women along with men. But coeducation was less crucial to women's education in this period than was the creation of a network of women's colleges. Mount Holyoke in central Massachusetts had begun its life in 1836 as a "seminary" for women; it became a full-fledged college in the 1880s, at about the same time that entirely new female institutions were emerging: Vassar, Wellesley, Smith, Bryn Mawr, Wells, and Goucher. A few of the larger private universities created separate colleges for women on their campuses

(Barnard at Columbia and Radcliffe at Harvard, for example). Proponents of women's colleges saw the institutions as places where female students would not be treated as "second-class citizens" by predominantly male student bodies and faculties.

The female college was part of an important phenomenon in the history of modern American women: the emergence of distinctive women's communities outside the family. Most faculty members and many administrators were women (usually unmarried). And the life of the college produced a spirit of sorority and commitment among educated women that had important effects in later years, as women became the leaders of many reform activities. Most female college graduates ultimately married, but they married at a more advanced age than their noncollege counterparts. A significant minority, perhaps over 25 percent, did not marry at all, but devoted themselves to careers. The growth of female higher education clearly became for some women a liberating experience, persuading them that they had roles to perform in their rapidly changing urban-industrial society other than those of wives and mothers.

CONCLUSION

The extraordinary growth of American cities in the last decades of the nineteenth century led to both great achievements and enormous problems. Cities became centers of learning, art, and commerce. They produced great advances in technology, transportation, architecture, and communications. They provided their residents—and their many visitors—with varied and dazzling experiences, so much so that many people increasingly left the countryside to move to the city, and many more dreamed of doing so.

But cities were also places of congestion, filth, disease, and corruption. With populations expanding too rapidly for services to keep up, most American cities in this era struggled with makeshift government and makeshift techniques to solve the basic problems of providing water, disposing of sewage, building roads, running public transportation, fighting fire, stopping crime, and preventing or curing disease. City governments, many of them dominated by political machines and ruled by party bosses, were often models of inefficiency and corruption—although in their informal way they also provided substantial services to the working-class and immigrant constituencies who needed them most. Yet they also managed, despite the administrative limitations of most municipal governments, to oversee great public projects: the building of parks, museums, opera houses, and theaters, usually in partnership with private developers.

The city brought together races, ethnic groups, and classes of extraordinary variety—from the families of great wealth that the new industrial age was creating to the vast working class, much of it consisting of immigrants, that crowded into densely-packed neighborhoods sharply divided by nationality. The city also spawned new forms of popular culture. It created temples of consumerism: shops, boutiques, and above all the great department stores. And it created forums for public recreation and entertainment: parks, theaters, athletic fields, amusement parks, and later movie palaces.

Urban life created great anxiety among those who lived within the cities and among those who observed them from afar—so much so that in some cities middle-class people literally armed themselves to prepare for the insurrections they expected from the poor. But in fact, American cities adapted reasonably successfully over time to the great demands their growth made of them and learned to govern themselves if not entirely honestly and efficiently, at least adequately to allow them to survive and grow.

FOR FURTHER REFERENCE

Suggested Readings

Lewis Mumford, author of *The City in History* (1961), was America's foremost critic and chronicler of urbanization. John Bodnar provides a penetrating view of the lives of immigrants in his study, *The Transplanted: A History of Immigrants in America* (1985), which complements (and challenges) Oscar Handlin, *The Uprooted*, rev. ed. (1973), an influential study first published in the 1950s. John Higham, *Strangers in the Land: Patterns of American Nativism* (1955) is a classic study. The new urban mass culture of America's cities is the subject of William Leach, *Land of Desire: Merchants, Power, and the Rise of a New American Culture* (1993) and Kathy Peiss, *Cheap Amusements: Working Women and Leisure in Turn-of-the-Century New York* (1986). Stuart Blumin, *The Emergence of the Middle Class: Social Experience in the American City, 1760–1900* (1989) and Gunther Barth, *City People: The Rise of Modern City Culture in Nineteenth-Century America* (1980) are other important studies of urban culture. T. J. Jackson Lears, *No Place of Grace: Antimodernism and the Transformation of American Culture, 1880–1920* (1981) chronicles patterns of resistance to the new culture. Stephan Thernstrom, *Poverty and Progress* (1964) and *The Other Bostonians* (1973) are important studies of urban social mobility. Olivier Zunz, *The Changing Face of Inequality: Urbanization, Industrial Development, and Immigrants in Detroit, 1880–1920* (1982) examines the shifting fortunes of ethnic groups in an industrial city. Timothy J. Gilfoyle, *City of Eros: New York City, Prostitution, and the Commercialization of Sex, 1790–1920* (1992) examines gender relations and sexual commerce in developing New York. John F. Kasson,

Amusing the Millions: Coney Island at the Turn of the Century (1978) is an excellent short study of the nation's most famous urban, commercial amusement park, and Roy Rosenzweig and Elizabeth Blackmar, *The Park and the People: A History of Central Park* (1992) studies the creation of its most famous public park. Edwin G. Burrows and Mike Wallace, *Gotham: A History of New York City to 1898* (1998) is a sweeping history of the nation's largest city.

Films

(The best source for information on how to find these and other films is *Bowker's Complete Video Directory*—3 volumes.) *Journey to America* (1988) presents the personal stories of the men, women, and children who came to America between 1890 and 1920 in the largest single recorded migration in human history. The Irish mass migration to America is dramatically portrayed in *Out of Ireland: The Story of Irish Emigration to America* (1994). *The Great San Francisco Earthquake* (1997) features accounts of people who lived in San Francisco before and after it was destroyed by a devastating earthquake and fire in April 1906. *Coney Island* (1991), directed by Ric Burns, presents the colorful history of America's favorite seaside resort. *Baseball* (1994) is a sweeping narrative of the national pastime, its origins in the age of the city, and its wider social context of race relations, immigration, and popular culture.

Internet Resources

Internet websites containing historical material relevant to the subjects discussed in this chapter can be reached through the McGraw-Hill history site at www.mhhe.com/socscience/history/usa/link/linktop.htm.

CHAPTER NINETEEN

From Stalemate to Crisis

The Politics of Equilibrium ∼ *The Agrarian Revolt*
The Crisis of the 1890s

HE ENORMOUS CHANGES America was experiencing in the late nineteenth century strained not only the nation's traditional social arrangements but its political institutions as well. Industrialization and urbanization had produced considerable progress and substantial achievements. They had also created disorder and despair. Gradually, Americans began to look to government for leadership in their search for stability and social justice.

Yet American government during much of this period was ill equipped to deal with the new challenges confronting it. In the face of unprecedented dilemmas, it responded with apparent passivity and confusion. Its leaders, for the most part, seemed political mediocrities. Most of the issues with which it was concerned had little to do with the nation's most important problems.

THE POLITICS OF EQUILIBRIUM

To modern eyes, the nature of the American political system in the late nineteenth century appears in many ways paradoxical. The two political parties enjoyed a strength and stability during those years that neither was ever to know again. And yet the federal government, which the two parties were struggling to control, was doing relatively little of importance. In fact, most Americans in those years engaged in political activity not because of

TIME LINE

1867	1880	1881	1883
National Grange founded	Garfield elected president	Garfield assassinated Arthur becomes president	Pendleton Act

1884	1887	1888	1890
Cleveland elected president	Interstate Commerce Act	Benjamin Harrison elected president	Sherman Antitrust Act Sherman Silver Purchase Act McKinley Tariff

1892	1893	1894	1896	1900
Cleveland elected president People's Party formed	Economic depression begins Sherman Silver Purchase Act repealed	Coxey's Army	McKinley elected president	Gold Standard Act

an interest in particular issues but because of broad regional, ethnic, or religious sentiments.

The Party System

The most striking feature of the late-nineteenth-century party system was its remarkable stability. From the end of Reconstruction until the late 1890s, the electorate was divided almost precisely evenly between the Republicans and the Democrats. Loyalties fluctuated almost not at all. Sixteen states were solidly and consistently Republican, and fourteen states (most of them in the South) were solidly and consistently Democratic. Only five states (the most important of them New York and Ohio) were usually in doubt, and their voters generally decided the results of national elections, often on the basis of voter turnout. The Republican Party captured the presidency in all but two of the elections of the era, but the party was not really as dominant as those victories suggest. In the five presidential elections beginning in 1876, the average popular-vote margin separating the Democratic and Republican candidates was 1.5 percent. The congressional balance was similarly stable, with the Republicans generally controlling the Senate and the Democrats generally controlling the House.

As striking as the balance between the parties was the intensity of public loyalty to them. In most of the country, Americans viewed their party affiliations with a passion and enthusiasm that is difficult for later generations to understand. Voter turnout in presidential elections between 1860 and 1900 averaged over 78 percent of all eligible voters (as compared with only about 50 percent in the 1980s and 1990s). Even in nonpresidential years, from 60 to 80 percent of the voters turned out to cast ballots for congressional and local candidates. Large groups of potential voters were disfranchised in these years: women in most states; almost all blacks and many poor whites in the South. But for adult white males outside the South, there were few franchise restrictions. The remarkable turnout represented a genuinely mass-based politics.

What explains this extraordinary loyalty to the two political parties? It was not, certainly, that the parties took distinct positions on important public issues. They did so rarely. Party loyalties reflected other factors. Region was perhaps the most important. To white southerners, loyalty to the Democratic Party was a matter of unquestioned faith. It was the vehicle by which they had triumphed over Reconstruction, the vehicle by which they preserved white supremacy. To many northerners, white and black, Republican loyalties were equally intense. To them, the party of Lincoln remained what it had been during the Civil War: a bulwark against slavery and treason.

Religious and ethnic differences also shaped party loyalties. The Democratic Party attracted most of the Catholic voters, most of the recent immigrants, and most of the poorer workers—groups that often overlapped. The Republican Party appealed to northern Protestants, citizens of old stock, and much of the middle class—groups that also had considerable overlap. Among the few substantive issues on which the parties took clearly different stands were matters connected with immigrants. Republicans tended to support measures restricting immigration and to favor temperance legislation, which many believed would help discipline immigrant communities. Catholics and immigrants viewed such proposals as assaults on them and their cultures and opposed them; the Democratic Party followed their lead.

Party identification, then, was usually more a reflection of cultural inclinations than a calculation of economic interest. Individuals might affiliate with a party because their parents had done so, or because it was the party of their region, their church, or their ethnic group. Most clung to their party loyalties with great persistence and passion.

The National Government

One reason the two parties managed to avoid substantive issues was that the federal government (and to some degree state and local governments as well) did relatively little. The government in Washington was responsible for delivering the mails, for maintaining a national military, for conducting foreign policy, and for collecting tariffs and taxes. It had few other responsibilities and few institutions with which it could have undertaken additional responsibilities even if it had chosen to do so.

There was one significant exception. From the end of the Civil War to the early twentieth century, the federal government administered a system of annual pensions for Union Civil War veterans who had retired from work and for their widows. At its peak, this pension system was making payments to a majority of the male citizens (black and white) of the North and to many women as well. Some reformers hoped to make the system permanent and universal; they pressured the government to create a system of old-age pensions for all Americans. But their efforts failed, in part because the Civil War pension system was awash in party patronage and corruption. Other reformers—believers in "good government"—saw elimination of the pension system as a way to fight graft, corruption, and party rule. When the Civil War generation died out, the pension system died with it.

In most other respects, the United States in the late nineteenth century was a society without a modern, national government. The most powerful national political institutions were the two political parties (and the bosses and machines that dominated them) and the federal courts. The national leaders of both parties were primarily concerned not with policy but with office—with winning elections and controlling patronage.

Presidents and Patronage

The power of party bosses had an important effect on the power of the presidency. The office had great symbolic importance, but its occupants were unable to do very much except distribute government appointments. A new president and his tiny staff had to make almost 100,000 appointments (most of them in the post office, the only really large government agency); and even in that function, presidents had limited latitude, since they had to avoid offending the various factions within their own parties.

Sometimes that proved impossible, as the presidency of Rutherford B. Hayes (1877–1881) demonstrated. By the end of his term, two groups— the Stalwarts, led by Roscoe Conkling of New York, and the Half-Breeds, captained by James G. Blaine of Maine—were competing for control of the Republican Party and threatening to split it. The dispute between the Stalwarts and the Half-Breeds was characteristic of the political battles of the era in having little basis in substance. Rhetorically, the Stalwarts favored traditional, professional machine politics, while the Half-Breeds favored reform. In fact, both groups were mainly interested in a larger share of the patronage pie. Hayes tried to satisfy both and ended up satisfying neither.

The battle over patronage overshadowed all else during Hayes's unhappy presidency. His one important substantive initiative—an effort to create a civil service system—attracted no support from either party. And his early announcement that he would not seek reelection only weakened him further. (His popularity with politicians in Washington was not enhanced by the unwillingness of his wife, a temperance advocate widely known as "Lemonade Lucy," to permit alcoholic beverages to be served in the White House.) Hayes's presidency was a study in frustration.

The Republicans managed to retain the presidency in 1880 in part because they agreed on a ticket that included a Stalwart and a Half-Breed. After a long convention deadlock, they nominated James A. Garfield, a veteran congressman from Ohio and a Half-Breed, for president and Chester A. Arthur of New York, a Stalwart and Conkling henchman, for vice president. The Democrats nominated General Winfield Scott Hancock, a minor Civil War commander with no national following. Benefiting from the end of the recession of 1879, Garfield won a decisive electoral victory, although his popular-vote margin was very thin. The Republicans also captured both houses of Congress.

Garfield began his presidency by trying to defy the Stalwarts in his appointments and by showing support for civil service reform. He soon found himself embroiled in an ugly public quarrel with both Conkling and other Stalwarts. It was never resolved. On July 2, 1881, only four months after his inauguration, Garfield was shot twice while standing in the Washington railroad station by an apparently deranged gunman (and unsuccessful office seeker) who shouted, "I am a Stalwart and Arthur is president now!" Garfield lingered for nearly three months but finally died, a victim as much of inept medical treatment as of the wounds themselves.

Chester A. Arthur, who succeeded Garfield, had spent a political lifetime as a devoted, skilled, and open spoilsman and a close ally of Roscoe Conkling. But on becoming president, he tried—like Hayes and Garfield before him—to follow an independent course and even to promote reform, aware no doubt that the Garfield assassination had to some degree discredited the traditional spoils system. To the dismay of the Stalwarts, Arthur kept most of Garfield's appointees in office and supported civil service reform. In 1883, Congress passed the first national civil service measure, the Pendleton Act, which required that some federal jobs be filled by competitive written examinations rather than by patronage. Relatively few offices fell under civil service at first, but its reach extended steadily so that by the mid-twentieth century most federal employees were civil servants.

Cleveland, Harrison, and the Tariff

In the unsavory election of 1884, the Republican candidate for president was Senator James G. Blaine of Maine—known to his adoring admirers as "the Plumed Knight" but to thousands of other Americans as a symbol of seamy party politics. A group of disgruntled "liberal Republicans," known derisively by their critics as the "mugwumps," announced they would bolt the party and support an honest Democrat. Rising to the bait, the Democrats nominated Grover Cleveland, the "reform" governor of New York. He differed from Blaine on no substantive issues but had acquired a reputation as an enemy of corruption.

In a campaign filled with personal invective, what may have decided the election was the last-minute introduction of a religious controversy. Shortly before the election, a delegation of Protestant ministers called on Blaine in New York City; their spokesman, Dr. Samuel Burchard, referred to the Democrats as the party of "rum, Romanism, and rebellion." Blaine was slow to repudiate Burchard's indiscretion, and Democrats quickly spread the news that Blaine had tolerated a slander on the Catholic Church. Cleveland's narrow victory was probably a result of an unusually heavy Catholic vote for the Democrats in New York. Cleveland won 219 electoral votes to Blaine's 182; his popular margin was only 23,000.

Grover Cleveland was respected, if not often liked, for his stern and righteous opposition to politicians, grafters, pressure groups, and Tammany Hall. He had become famous as the "veto governor," as an official who was not afraid to say no. He was the embodiment of an era in which few Americans believed the federal government could, or should, do very much. Cleveland had always doubted the wisdom of protective tariffs (taxes on imported goods designed to protect domestic producers). The existing high rates, he believed, were responsible for the annual surplus in federal revenues, which was tempting Congress to pass "reckless" and "extravagant" legislation, which he frequently vetoed. In December 1887, therefore, he asked Congress to reduce the tariff rates. Democrats in the

REVOLT AMONG REPUBLICANS Many Republican reformers, believers in "good
government," were aghast when their party nominated James G. Blaine for
president in 1884. Blaine, a former Speaker of the House, U.S. senator, and
secretary of state, was the leader of the "Half-Breed" faction of the party, the
faction that claimed to support cautious reform. But he was controversial even
among reformers after a long career of wily political maneuvering and because
of the scandals that continually attached themselves to his name. This cartoon
by Joseph Keppler in the political magazine *Puck* shows Republican leaders
responding with horror to "the writing on the wall," and to the dire
consequences they believed would follow the nomination of Blaine. Blaine
himself, at left, hides behind the *New York Herald-Tribune*, the principal organ of
the reformers and a critic of Blaine.

House approved a tariff reduction, but Senate Republicans defiantly
passed a bill of their own actually raising the rates. The resulting deadlock
made the tariff an issue in the election of 1888.

The Democrats renominated Cleveland and supported tariff reductions.
The Republicans settled on former senator Benjamin Harrison of Indiana,
who was obscure but respectable (and the grandson of President William
Henry Harrison); and they endorsed protection. The campaign was the first
since the Civil War to involve a clear question of economic difference between the parties. It was also one of the most corrupt (and one of the closest)
elections in American history. Harrison won an electoral majority of 233 to
168, but Cleveland's popular vote exceeded Harrison's by 100,000.

New Public Issues

Benjamin Harrison's record as president was little more substantial than that of his grandfather, who had died a month after taking office. Harrison had few visible convictions, and he made no effort to influence Congress. And yet during Harrison's passive administration, public opinion was beginning to force the government to confront some of the pressing social and economic issues of the day. Most notably, perhaps, sentiment was rising in favor of legislation to curb the power of trusts.

By the mid-1880s, fifteen western and southern states had adopted laws prohibiting combinations that restrained competition. But corporations found it easy to escape limitations by incorporating in states such as New Jersey and Delaware that offered them special privileges. If antitrust legislation was to be effective, its supporters believed, it would have to come from the national government. Responding to growing popular demands, both houses of Congress passed the Sherman Antitrust Act in July 1890, almost without dissent. Most members of Congress saw the act as a largely symbolic measure, one that would help deflect public criticism but was not likely to have any real effect on corporate power. For over a decade after its passage, the Sherman Act—indifferently enforced and steadily weakened by the courts—had virtually no impact. As of 1901, the Justice Department had instituted many antitrust suits against unions, but only fourteen against business combinations; there had been few convictions.

The Republicans were more interested, however, in the issue they believed had won them the 1888 election: the tariff. Representative William McKinley of Ohio and Senator Nelson W. Aldrich of Rhode Island drafted the highest protective measure ever proposed to Congress. Known as the McKinley Tariff, it became law in October 1890. But Republican leaders apparently misinterpreted public sentiment, for the party suffered a stunning reversal in the 1890 congressional election. The Republicans' substantial Senate majority was slashed to 8; in the House, the party retained only 88 of the 323 seats. McKinley himself was among those who went down in defeat. Nor were the Republicans able to recover in the course of the next two years. In the presidential election of 1892, Benjamin Harrison once again supported protection; Grover Cleveland, renominated by the Democrats, once again opposed it. A new third party, the People's Party, with James B. Weaver as its candidate, advocated more substantial economic reform. Cleveland won 277 electoral votes to Harrison's 145 and had a popular margin of 380,000. Weaver showed some significant strength, but still ran far behind. For the first time since 1878, the Democrats won a majority of both houses of Congress.

The policies of Cleveland's second term were much like those of his first—devoted to minimal government and hostile to active efforts to deal with social or economic problems. Again, he supported a tariff reduction, which the House approved but the Senate weakened. Cleveland denounced the result but allowed it to become law as the Wilson-Gorman Tariff. It included only a few, very modest reductions.

But public pressure was growing in the 1880s for other reforms, among them regulation of the railroads. Farm organizations in the Midwest (most notably the Grangers) had persuaded several state legislatures to pass regulatory legislation in the early 1870s. But in 1886, the Supreme Court—in *Wabash, St. Louis, and Pacific Railway Co. v. Illinois*, known as the *Wabash* case—ruled one of the Granger Laws in Illinois unconstitutional. According to the Court, the law was an attempt to control interstate commerce and thus infringed on the exclusive power of Congress. Later, the courts limited the powers of the states to regulate commerce even within their own boundaries.

Effective railroad regulation, it was now clear, could come only from the federal government. Congress grudgingly responded to public pressure in 1887 with the Interstate Commerce Act, which banned discrimination in rates between long and short hauls, required that railroads publish their rate schedules and file them with the government, and declared that all interstate rail rates must be "reasonable and just"—although the act did not define what that meant. A five-person agency, the Interstate Commerce Commission (ICC), was to administer the act. But it had to rely on the courts to enforce its rulings. For almost twenty years after its passage, the Interstate Commerce Act—which was, like the Sherman Act, haphazardly enforced and narrowly interpreted by the courts—was without much practical effect.

THE AGRARIAN REVOLT

No group watched the performance of the federal government in the 1880s with more dismay than American farmers. The serious problems that afflicted them, and the absence of any effective government response to them, helped produce of one of the most powerful movements of political protest in American history: what became known as Populism.

The Grangers

Farmers had been making efforts to organize politically for several decades before the 1880s. The first major farm organization was the National Grange of the Patrons of Husbandry, founded in 1867. From it emerged a network of local organizations that tried to teach new scientific agricultural techniques to members. But when the depression of 1873 caused a sharp decline in farm prices, membership rapidly increased and the direction of the organization changed. Granges in the Midwest began to organize marketing cooperatives, which they hoped would give them more control over the prices of their goods. And they promoted political action to curb the monopolistic practices of the railroads and warehouses. At their peak, Grange supporters controlled the legislatures in most of the midwestern states. The result was the Granger Laws of the early 1870s, by which many states imposed strict regulations on railroad rates and practices. But the destruction of the new regulations by the courts, combined with the political inexperience of many Grange leaders and the return of prosperity in the late 1870s, produced a dramatic decline in the power of the association by the end of the decade.

The Alliances

The successor to the Granges began to emerge even before the Granger movement had faded. As early as 1875, farmers in parts of the South (most notably in Texas) were banding together in so-called Farmers' Alliances. By 1880, the Southern Alliance had more than 4 million members; and a comparable Northwestern Alliance was taking root in the plains states and the Midwest and developing ties with its southern counterpart.

Like the Granges, the Alliances formed cooperatives and other marketing mechanisms. They established stores, banks, processing plants, and other facilities for their members—to free them from dependence on the hated "furnishing merchants" who kept so many farmers in debt. Some Alliance leaders, however, saw the movement in larger terms: as an effort to build a new kind of society in which economic competition might give way to cooperation. Alliance lecturers traveled throughout rural areas lambasting the concentrated power of the great corporations and financial institutions.

Although the Alliances quickly became far more widespread than the Granges had ever been, they suffered from similar problems. Their cooperatives did not always work well, partly because the market forces operating against them were sometimes too strong to be overcome and partly because the cooperatives themselves were often mismanaged. These economic frustrations helped push the movement into a new phase at the end of the 1880s: the creation of a national political organization.

In 1889, the Southern and Northwestern Alliances, despite continuing differences between them, agreed to a loose merger. The next year the Alliances held a national convention at Ocala, Florida, and issued the so-called Ocala Demands, which were, in effect, a party platform. In the 1890 off-year elections, candidates supported by the Alliances won partial or complete control of the legislatures in twelve states. They also won six governorships, three seats in the Senate, and approximately fifty in the House of Representatives. Many of the successful Alliance candidates were simply Democrats who had benefited—often passively—from Alliance endorsements. But dissident farmers drew enough encouragement from the results to contemplate further political action, including forming a party of their own.

Alliance leaders discussed plans for a third party at meetings in Cincinnati in May 1891 and St. Louis in February 1892. Then, in July 1892, 1,300 exultant delegates poured into Omaha, Nebraska, to proclaim the creation of the new party, approve an official set of principles, and nominate candidates for the presidency and vice presidency. The new organization's official name was the People's Party, but the movement was more commonly referred to as Populism.

The election of 1892 demonstrated the potential power of the new movement. The Populist presidential candidate—James B. Weaver of Iowa, a former Greenbacker—polled more than 1 million votes, 8.5 percent of the total, and carried six mountain and plains states for 22 electoral votes. Nearly 1,500 Populist candidates won election to state legislatures and local offices. The party elected three governors, five senators, and ten congressmen. It could also claim the support of many Republicans and Democrats in Congress who had been elected by appealing to Populist sentiment.

The Populist Constituency

Already, however, there were signs of the limits of Populist strength. Populism had great appeal to farmers, and particularly to small farmers with little long-range economic security—people whose operations were only minimally mechanized, if at all, who relied on one crop, and who had little access to credit. But Populism failed to move much beyond that group. Its leaders made energetic efforts to include labor within the coalition. In addition to courting the Knights of Labor, the new party added a labor plank to its platform—calling for shorter hours for workers and restrictions on

D E B A T I N G   T H E   P A S T

Populism

T HE SCHOLARLY DEBATES over the nature of Populism have tended to reflect a larger debate over the nature of popular mass movements. To some historians, mass uprisings seem dangerous and potentially antidemocratic; and to them, the Populist movement has usually appeared ominous. To others, such insurgency is evidence of a healthy democratic resistance to oppression; and to them, Populism has generally seemed more appealing.

The latter view shaped the first, and for many years the only, general history of Populism: John D. Hicks's *The Populist Revolt* (1931). Reflecting the influence of Frederick Jackson Turner, Hicks portrayed Populism as an expression of the healthy, democratic sentiments of the West. (He paid relatively little attention to the South.) Populists were reacting rationally and constructively to the harsh impact of eastern industrial growth on agrarian society, and they were proposing potentially valuable reforms to restrict the power of the new financial titans. Populism was, he wrote, "the last phase of a long and perhaps a losing struggle—the struggle to save agricultural America from the devouring jaws of industrial America."

In the early 1950s, scholars sensitive to the nature of European fascism and contemporary communism took a more suspicious view of mass popular politics and a more hostile view of Populism. The leading figure in this reinterpretation was Richard Hofstadter. In *The Age of Reform* (1955), he conceded that the Populists had genuine grievances and advanced some sensible reforms. But he concentrated on revealing what he called the "soft" and "dark" sides of the movement. Populism, Hofstadter claimed, rested on a romanticized and obsolete vision of the role of farmers in American society. And it was permeated with bigotry and ignorance.

Hofstadter's harsh portrait inspired a series of spirited challenges. Norman Pollack, beginning in 1962, argued that the agrarian revolt rested not on nostalgic and romantic concepts but on a sophisticated and even radical vision of reform. A year later, Walter T. K. Nugent attempted to show that Populists were not bigoted, that they not only tolerated but welcomed Jews and other minorities into their party. And in 1976, Lawrence Goodwyn published *Democratic Promise*, the first full-scale history of the Populist movement since Hick's study forty-five years earlier. Goodwyn described Populism as a "cooperative crusade" battling against the "coercive potential of the emerging corporate state." Populism was offering a genuine alternative to the inequities of modern, corporate capitalism, and it was promoting that alternative by developing an intensely democratic popular movement.

At the same time that historians were debating the meaning of Populism, they were also arguing over who the Populists were. Hicks, Hofstadter, and Goodwyn, for all their many disagreements, shared a belief that Populists were victims of economic distress—usually one-crop farmers in economically marginal regions victimized by drought and debt. Others, however, have suggested that this description is, if not wrong, at least inadequate. Sheldon Hackney maintained in 1969 that Populists in Alabama were not only economically troubled but socially rootless, "only tenuously connected to society by economic function, by personal relationships, by stable community membership, by political participation, or by psychological identification with the South's distinctive myths." Peter Argersinger, Stanley Parsons, James Turner, and others have similarly suggested that Populists tended to be people who were socially and even geographically isolated. Steven Hahn's 1983 study *The Roots of Southern Populism* described the poor farmers of "upcountry" Georgia who became Populists as people almost entirely unconnected to the modern capitalist economy. They were reacting not simply to the distress of being "left behind," but also to a real economic threat to their way of life from the intrusion into their world of a new commercial order of which they were not a part and from which they were unlikely to benefit.

There has, finally, been continuing debate over the legacy of Populism. Michael Kazin, in *The Populist Persuasion* (1994), is one of a number of scholars who have argued that a Populist tradition has survived throughout much of the twentieth century, influencing movements as different as those led by Huey Long in the 1930s, George Wallace in the 1960s, and Ross Perot in the 1990s.

immigration, and denouncing the use of private detective agencies as strikebreakers in labor disputes. But Populism never attracted any substantial labor support, in part because the economic interests of labor and the interests of farmers were often at odds.

In the South in particular, white Populists struggled with the question of accepting African Americans in the party, since their numbers and their poverty made them potentially valuable allies. And indeed there was an important black component to the movement—a network of "Colored Alliances" that by 1890 numbered over 1.25 million members. But most white Populists were willing to accept the assistance of blacks only as long as it was clear that whites would remain indisputably in control. When southern conservatives began to attack the Populists for undermining white supremacy, the interracial character of the movement quickly faded.

Populist Ideas

The reform program of the Populists was spelled out first in the Ocala Demands of 1890 and then, even more clearly, in the Omaha platform of 1892. It proposed a system of "subtreasuries," which would replace and strengthen the cooperatives with which the Granges and Alliances had been experimenting for years. The national government would establish a network of warehouses, where farmers could deposit their crops. Using those crops as collateral, growers could then borrow money from the government at low rates of interest and wait for the price of their goods to go up before selling them. In addition, the Populists called for the abolition of national banks, which they believed were dangerous institutions of concentrated power; the end of absentee ownership of land; the direct election of United States senators (which would weaken the power of conservative state legislatures); and other devices to improve the ability of the people to influence the political process. They called as well for regulation and (after 1892) government ownership of railroads, telephones, and telegraphs. And they demanded a system of government-operated postal savings banks, a graduated income tax, the inflation of the currency, and, later, the remonetization of silver.

Some Populists were openly anti-Semitic. Others were anti-intellectual, antieastern, and antiurban. But bigotry was not the dominant force behind Populism. The movement was a serious and at times highly intelligent effort to find solutions to real problems. Populists emphatically rejected the laissez-faire orthodoxies of their time, the idea that the rights of ownership are absolute. Populism was less a critique of industrialization or

A POPULIST GATHERING Populism was a response to real economic and political grievances. But like most political movements of its time, it was also important as a cultural experience. For farmers in sparsely settled regions in particular, it provided an antidote to isolation and loneliness. This gathering of Populist farmers in Dickinson County, Kansas, shows how the political purposes of the movement were tightly bound up with its social purposes.

capitalism than a challenge, one of the most powerful such challenges of the era, to what the Populists considered the brutal and chaotic way in which the economy was developing. Progress and growth should continue, they urged, but should be strictly defined by the needs of individuals and communities.

THE CRISIS OF THE 1890S

The rising agrarian protest was only one of many indications of the national political crisis emerging in the 1890s. There was a severe depression, which began in 1893. There was widespread labor unrest and violence, culminating in the tumultuous strikes of 1894. There was the continuing failure of either major party to respond to the growing distress. And there was the rigid conservatism of Grover Cleveland, who took office for the second time just at the moment that the economy collapsed.

The Panic of 1893

The Panic of 1893 precipitated the most severe depression the nation had ever experienced. It began in March 1893, when the Philadelphia and Reading Railroads declared bankruptcy, unable to meet demands for payment by British banks from which they had borrowed large sums. Two months later, the National Cordage Company failed as well. Together, the two corporate failures triggered a collapse of the stock market. And since many of the major New York banks were heavy investors in the market, a wave of bank failures soon began. That caused a contraction of credit, which meant that many of the new, aggressive businesses that had recently begun operations soon went bankrupt because they were unable to secure the loans they needed.

The depression reflected, among other things, the degree to which all parts of the American economy were now interconnected, the degree to which failures in one area affected all other areas. And the depression showed how dependent the economy was on the health of the railroads, which remained the nation's most powerful corporate and financial institutions. When the railroads suffered, as they did beginning in 1893, everything suffered.

Once the panic began, its effects spread with startling speed. Within six months, more than 8,000 businesses, 156 railroads, and 400 banks failed. Already low agricultural prices tumbled further. Up to 1 million workers, 20 percent of the labor force, lost their jobs—the highest level of unemployment in American history to that point, a level comparable to that of the Great Depression of the 1930s. The depression was unprecedented not only in its severity but also in its persistence. Although there was slight improvement beginning in 1895, prosperity did not fully return until after 1898.

The depression produced widespread social unrest, not least among the enormous numbers of unemployed workers. In 1894, Jacob S. Coxey, an Ohio businessman and Populist, began advocating an inflation of the currency and a massive public works program to create jobs for the unemployed. When it became clear that his proposals were making no progress in Congress, Coxey organized a march of the unemployed (known as "Coxey's Army") to Washington to present his demands to the government. Congress took no action on the demands.

There were major labor upheavals as well during the decade—of which the Homestead and Pullman strikes were only the most prominent examples (see pp. 539–541). To many middle-class Americans, the worker

COXEY'S ARMY Jacob S. Coxey's "army" of the unemployed marches toward Washington in 1894 to demand relief from the federal government. Although several thousand people started out from various parts of the country to join the army, only about 400 actually reached the Capital. The protest disbanded after Coxey and several others were arrested for "trespassing" on the grounds of the United States Capitol.

unrest was a sign of dangerous social instability, even perhaps a revolution. Labor radicalism—some of it real, much of it imagined by the frightened middle class—was seldom far from the public mind, heightening the general sense of crisis.

The Silver Question

Debate over the causes of the depression centered increasingly on the currency. Populists, and many others, blamed the crisis on an inadequate supply of money. Conservatives blamed it on a lack of commitment to a "sound currency." The "money question," therefore, became one of the burning issues of the era.

The currency issue is a complicated and confusing one, and it has often been difficult for later generations to understand the enormous passions the controversy aroused. The heart of the debate was over what would form the basis of the dollar, what would lie behind it and give it value. Today, the value of the dollar rests on little more than public confidence in the government. But in the nineteenth century, most people assumed that currency was worthless if there was not something concrete behind it—precious metal (specie), which holders of paper money could collect if they presented their currency to a bank or to the Treasury.

During most of its existence as a nation, the United States had recognized two metals—gold and silver—as a basis for the dollar, a formula known as "bimetallism." In the 1870s, however, that had changed. The official ratio of the value of silver to the value of gold for purposes of creating currency (the "mint ratio") was 16 to 1: sixteen ounces of silver equaled one ounce of gold. But the actual commercial value of silver was much higher than that. Owners of silver could get more by selling it for manufacture into jewelry and other objects than they could by taking it to the mint for conversion to coins. So they stopped taking it to the mint, and the mint stopped coining silver.

In 1873, Congress passed a law that seemed simply to recognize the existing situation by officially discontinuing silver coinage. Few objected at the time. But later in the 1870s, the market value of silver fell well below the official mint ratio of 16 to 1. (Sixteen ounces of silver, in other words, were now worth less, not more, than one ounce of gold.) Silver was suddenly available for coinage again, and it soon became clear that Congress had foreclosed a potential method of expanding the currency. Before long, many Americans concluded that a conspiracy of big bankers had been responsible for the "demonetization" of silver, and they referred to the law as the "Crime of '73."

Two groups of Americans were especially determined to undo the "Crime of '73." One consisted of silver-mine owners and their allies, now understandably eager to have the government take their surplus silver and pay them much more than the market price. The other group consisted of discontented farmers, who wanted an increase in the quantity of money—an inflation of the currency—as a means of raising the prices of farm products and easing payment of the farmers' debts. The inflationists demanded that the government return at once to "free silver"—that is, to the "free and unlimited coinage of silver" at the old ratio of 16 to 1. Congress responded weakly to these demands with the Sherman Silver Purchase Act of 1890, which required the government to purchase (but not coin) silver and pay for it in gold. That provided some relief to silver miners, but it did nothing to expand the currency.

At the same time, the nation's gold reserves were steadily dropping. And the Panic of 1893 intensified the demands on those reserves. President Cleveland believed that the chief cause of the weakening gold reserves was the Sherman Silver Purchase Act. Early in his second administration, therefore, Congress responded to his request and repealed the act—although only after a bitter and divisive battle that helped create a permanent split in the Democratic Party. The president's gold policy had aligned the southern and western Democrats in a solid phalanx against him and his eastern followers. Only substantial Republican support had allowed the bill to pass.

"A Cross of Gold"

Republicans, watching the failure of Cleveland and the Democrats to deal effectively with the depression, were confident of success in 1896. Party leaders, led by the Ohio boss Marcus A. Hanna, settled on former congressman William McKinley, author of the 1890 tariff act and now governor of Ohio, as the party's presidential candidate. The tariff, they believed, should be the principal issue in the campaign. But their platform also opposed the free coinage of silver except by agreement with the leading commercial nations (which everyone realized was unlikely). Thirty-four delegates from the mountain and plains states walked out in protest and joined the Democratic Party.

The Democratic convention of 1896 was unusually tumultuous. Southern and western delegates, eager for a way to compete with the Populists, were determined to seize control of the party from conservative easterners and incorporate some Populist demands—among them free silver—into the Democratic platform. They wanted as well to nominate a pro-silver candidate. The divided platform committee presented two reports to the convention. The majority report, the work of westerners and southerners, called for tariff reduction, an income tax, "stricter control" of trusts and railroads, and—most prominently—free silver. The minority report, the product of the party's eastern wing, echoed the Republican platform by opposing the free coinage of silver except by international agreement. The debate over the two competing platforms dominated the convention.

Defenders of the gold standard seemed to prevail in the debate, until the final speech. Then William Jennings Bryan, a handsome, thirty-six-year-old congressman from Nebraska, already well known as an effective orator, mounted the podium to address the convention. His great voice echoed through the hall as he delivered a defense of free silver that became one of the most famous political speeches in American history. The closing passage sent his audience into something close to a frenzy: "If they dare to come out in the open and defend the gold standard as a good thing, we will

WILLIAM JENNINGS BRYAN Bryan addresses a crowd late in his career, displaying the flamboyant oratorical style that characterized his public life from the beginning. The poster at the lower left of the platform shows him as he appeared in the 1890s, when, as a young congressman from Nebraska, he became known as the "Boy Orator of the Platte" and the leader of the national free-silver movement.

fight them to the uttermost. Having behind us the producing masses of this nation and the world, supported by the commercial interests, the laboring interests and the toilers everywhere, we will answer their demand for a gold standard by saying to them: 'You shall not press down upon the brow of labor this crown of thorns; you shall not crucify mankind upon a cross of gold.' " It became known as the "Cross of Gold" speech.

In the glow of Bryan's speech, the convention voted to adopt the pro-silver platform. Perhaps more important, the agrarians embraced Bryan as their leader. The following day, Bryan (as he had eagerly, and not entirely secretly, hoped) was nominated for president on the fifth ballot. He remains the youngest man ever nominated for president by a major party.

The choice of Bryan and the nature of the Democratic platform created a quandary for the Populists. They had expected both major parties to adopt conservative programs and nominate conservative candidates, leaving the Populists to represent the growing forces of protest. But now the Democrats had stolen much of their thunder. The Populists faced the choice of naming their own candidate and splitting the protest vote or endorsing Bryan and losing their identity as a party. Many Populists argued that "fusion" with the Democrats—who had endorsed free silver but ignored the other, more important Populist demands—would destroy their party. But the majority concluded that there was no viable alternative. Amid considerable acrimony, the convention voted to support Bryan. In a feeble effort to maintain their independence, the Populists repudiated the Democratic nominee for vice president and chose their own, Tom Watson of Georgia.

The Conservative Victory

The campaign of 1896 produced desperation among conservatives. The business and financial community, frightened beyond reason at the prospect of a Bryan victory, contributed lavishly to the Republican campaign, which may have spent as much as $7 million, as compared with the Democrats' $300,000. From his home at Canton, Ohio, McKinley conducted a dignified "front-porch" campaign before pilgrimages of the Republican faithful, customary behavior in an age when many Americans considered it undignified for anyone to campaign too openly for the presidency.

Bryan showed no such restraint. He became the first presidential candidate in American history to stump the country systematically, to appear in

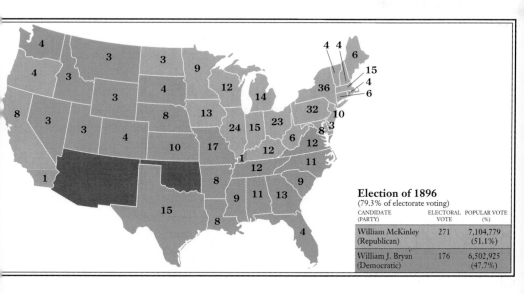

Election of 1896
(79.3% of electorate voting)

CANDIDATE (PARTY)	ELECTORAL VOTE	POPULAR VOTE (%)
William McKinley (Republican)	271	7,104,779 (51.1%)
William J. Bryan (Democratic)	176	6,502,925 (47.7%)

villages and hamlets—indeed, the first to say frankly to the voters that he wanted to be president. He traveled 18,000 miles (mostly in the West and South) and addressed an estimated 5 million people. His revivalistic, camp-meeting style pleased old-stock Protestants, but it alienated many of the immigrant Catholics and other ethnics who normally voted Democratic. Employers, meanwhile, warned workers that a Bryan victory would cost them their jobs, thus intimidating many traditional Democrats into supporting McKinley or not voting at all.

On election day, McKinley polled 271 electoral votes to Bryan's 176 and received 51.1 percent of the popular vote to Bryan's 47.7. Bryan carried only those areas of the South and West where miners or struggling staple farmers predominated. The Democratic program, like that of the Populists, had been too narrow to win a national election.

For the Populists and their allies, the election results were a disaster. They had gambled everything on their "fusion" with the Democratic Party and lost. Within months of the election, the People's Party began to dissolve.

McKinley and Prosperity

The administration of William McKinley, which began in the aftermath of turmoil, saw a return to relative calm. McKinley and his allies worked actively and energetically on only one issue, one on which they knew virtually all Republicans agreed: the need for higher tariff rates. Within weeks of McKinley's inauguration, the administration won approval of the Dingley Tariff, raising duties to the highest point in American history. The administration dealt more gingerly with the explosive silver question (an issue McKinley himself had never considered very important in any case). McKinley sent a commission to Europe to explore the possibility of a silver agreement with Great Britain and France. As he and everyone else anticipated, the effort produced no agreement. The Republicans then enacted the Currency, or Gold Standard, Act of 1900, which confirmed the nation's commitment to the gold standard.

And so the "battle of the standards" ended in victory for the forces of conservatism. Economic developments at the time seemed to vindicate them. Prosperity returned beginning in 1898. Foreign crop failures sent United States farm prices surging upward, and American business entered another cycle of booming expansion. Prosperity and the gold standard, it seemed, were closely allied.

But while the free-silver movement had failed, it had raised an important question for the American economy. In the quarter-century before 1900, the countries of the Western world had experienced a spectacular growth in productive facilities and population. Yet the supply of money had not kept pace with economic progress, because the supply was tied to gold and the amount of gold had remained practically constant. Had it not been for a dramatic increase in the gold supply in the late 1890s (a result of new techniques for extracting gold from low-content ores and the discovery of huge new gold deposits in Alaska, South Africa, and Australia), Populist predictions of financial disaster might in fact have proved correct. In 1898, two and a half times as much gold was produced as in 1890, and the currency supply was soon inflated far beyond anything Bryan and the free-silver forces had proposed.

By then, however, Bryan—like many other Americans—was becoming engaged with another major issue: the nation's growing involvement in world affairs and its increasing flirtation with imperialism.

CONCLUSION

For nearly three decades after the battles over Reconstruction, American politics remained locked in a rigid stalemate. The electorate was relatively evenly divided between the two major parties, which differed with one another on only a few issues. The national government, never fully dominated by either party, remained small and inconsequential. Except for Indian tribes, people engaged in international trade (who were thus subject to tariffs), and the many northern Civil War veterans who received federal pensions, few Americans had any direct contact with the government in Washington except to receive mail from the federal post office. A series of worthy and generally dull presidents presided over this political system as unwitting symbols of its stability and passivity.

Beneath the placid surface of national politics, however, great social issues were creating deep divisions in American life. Battles between employers and workers intensified. American farmers became increasingly resentful of their declining fortunes. Men and women throughout the country grew angry about corruption in government and excessive power in the hands of a few corporate leaders. When a great depression, the worst in the nation's history to that point, began in 1893, these social tensions exploded to the surface and reshaped national politics.

The most visible sign of the challenge to politics was the Populist movement, a great uprising of American farmers demanding far-reaching changes in the political, economic, and financial systems. The Populists created their own political party, showed impressive strength in several elections, and then—in 1896—joined with the Democrats to nominate the great Nebraska orator William Jennings Bryan for president. But the forces for insurgency were, in the end, no match for the forces of established institutions. After a campaign notable for its hysterical attacks on Bryan and on the issue with which he was identified ("free silver," making silver a basis for issuing currency in addition to gold), Bryan lost the election to William McKinley. Perhaps more important, the election became the occasion for a great electoral realignment that left the Republicans the clear majority party for the next three decades.

The Republican victory did not, however, end the battle over power and corruption in American life. It simply redirected it into other channels. The challenges to the old politics soon made themselves felt as more conventional reform movements that became known, collectively, as progressivism.

FOR FURTHER REFERENCE

Suggested Readings

Morton Keller, *Affairs of State: Public Life in Late Nineteenth-Century America* (1977) is an important study of politics and government after Reconstruction. Nell Irvin Painter's *Standing at Armageddon: The United States, 1877–1919* (1987) explores the multicultural dimensions of industrialization, emphasizing the particularly cataclysmic effect of industrialization on minority populations and on race relations. Martin J. Sklar, *The Corporate Reconstruction of American Capitalism, 1890–1916* (1988) provocatively describes the evolution of American business practice and, by extension, American politics and society. Two significant books charting the growing capacities of the American state during this period are Theda Skocpol, *Protecting Soldiers and Mothers: The Political Origins of Social Policy in the United States* (1992) and Stephen Skowronek, *Building a New American State: The Expansion of National Administrative Capacities, 1877–1920* (1982). Richard Hofstadter's *The Age of Reform: From Bryan to FDR* (1955) and Lawrence Goodwyn's *The Populist Moment* (1978), both classic studies, offer sharply contrasting characterizations of Populism. Other important studies of Populism include Steven Hahn, *The Roots of Southern Populism: Yeoman Farmers and the Transformation of the Georgia Upcountry, 1850–1890* (1983) and John D. Hicks, *The Populist Revolt* (1931).

Films

(The best source for information on how to find these and other films is *Bowker's Complete Video Directory*—3 volumes.) *The Wright Stuff* (1989) is the story of how Wilbur and Orville Wright, without college and scientific education or financial support, solved what for centuries had been one of the most baffling mysteries in science: manned flight. *The Populist Challenge* (1991) examines how political leaders, political parties, and the political system in general responded to industrialization and assesses the impact of the Populist challenge to the established political order.

Internet Resources

Internet websites containing historical material relevant to the subjects discussed in this chapter can be reached through the McGraw-Hill history site at www.mhhe.com/socscience/history/usa/link/linktop.htm.

CHAPTER TWENTY

The Imperial Republic

Stirrings of Imperialism ∽ *War with Spain*
The Republic as Empire

HE AMERICAN REPUBLIC had been an expansionist nation since the earliest days of its existence. Throughout the first half of the nineteenth century, as the population of the United States grew and pressed westward, the government, through purchase or conquest, had continually acquired new lands: the trans-Appalachian West, the Louisiana Territory, Florida, Texas, Oregon, California, New Mexico, Alaska. It was the nation's "Manifest Destiny," many Americans believed, to expand into new realms.

In the last years of the nineteenth century, with little room left for territorial growth on the North American continent, those who favored expansion set their eyes beyond the nation's shore. The United States began to consider joining England, France, Germany, and others in the great imperial drive that was, by the end of the century, to bring much of the nonindustrial world under the control of the industrial powers of the West.

STIRRINGS OF IMPERIALISM

For over two decades after the Civil War, the United States expanded geographically hardly at all. By the 1890s, however, some Americans were ready—indeed, eager—to resume the course of Manifest Destiny that had inspired their ancestors to wrest an empire from Mexico in the expansionist 1840s.

604

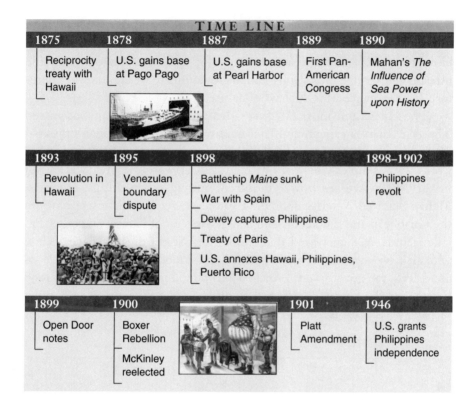

TIME LINE

1875	1878	1887	1889	1890
Reciprocity treaty with Hawaii	U.S. gains base at Pago Pago	U.S. gains base at Pearl Harbor	First Pan-American Congress	Mahan's *The Influence of Sea Power upon History*

1893	1895	1898	1898–1902
Revolution in Hawaii	Venezulan boundary dispute	Battleship *Maine* sunk War with Spain Dewey captures Philippines Treaty of Paris U.S. annexes Hawaii, Philippines, Puerto Rico	Philippines revolt

1899	1900	1901	1946
Open Door notes	Boxer Rebellion McKinley reelected	Platt Amendment	U.S. grants Philippines independence

The New Manifest Destiny

Several developments helped shift American attention to lands across the seas. The experience of subjugating the Indian tribes had established a precedent for exerting colonial control over dependent peoples. The supposed "closing of the frontier," widely heralded by Frederick Jackson Turner and others in the 1890s, produced fears that natural resources would soon dwindle and that alternative sources must be found abroad. The depression that began in 1893 encouraged some businessmen to look for new markets abroad. Americans were, moreover, well aware of the imperialist fever that was raging through Europe. It was leading the major powers to partition most of Africa among themselves and to turn covetous eyes on the Far East and the feeble Chinese Empire. Some Americans feared that their nation would soon be left out, that the Europeans would seize all these potential markets for themselves.

Scholars and others found a philosophic justification for expansionism in Charles Darwin's theories. They contended that nations or "races," like biological species, struggled constantly for existence and that only the fittest could survive. For strong nations to dominate weak ones was, therefore, in accordance with the laws of nature.

The ablest and most effective advocate of imperialism was Alfred Thayer Mahan, a captain and later admiral in the navy. Mahan's thesis—presented in *The Influence of Sea Power upon History* (1890) and other works—was simple: Countries with sea power were the great nations of history. Effective sea power required, among other things, colonies. Mahan believed America should, at the least, acquire defensive bases in the Caribbean and the Pacific and take possession of Hawaii and other Pacific islands. Mahan feared that the United States did not have a large enough navy to play the great role he envisioned. But during the 1870s and 1880s, the government launched a shipbuilding program that by 1898 had moved the United States to fifth place among the world's naval powers, and by 1900 to third.

LAUNCHING THE *MAINE*, 1889 The battleship *Maine* played a major role in American military history when it blew up in the harbor of Havana, Cuba, in 1898, and help precipitate the Spanish-American War. But it was also significant as part of the growing naval strength the United States was developing in the late nineteenth century. This engraving from *Harper's Weekly* portrays the launching of the *Maine* from the New York Navy Yard in November 1889.

Hemispheric Hegemony

James G. Blaine, who served as secretary of state in the Republican administrations of the 1880s, led the early efforts to expand American influence into Latin America, where, Blaine believed, the United States must look for markets for its surplus goods. In October 1889, he helped organize the first Pan-American Congress, which attracted delegates from nineteen nations. The delegates agreed to create the Pan-American Union, a weak international organization located in Washington that served as a clearinghouse for distributing information to the member nations. But they rejected Blaine's more substantive proposals: an inter-American customs union and arbitration procedures for hemispheric disputes.

The second Cleveland administration also took a lively interest in Latin America. In 1895, it supported Venezuela in a dispute with Great Britain over the boundary between Venezuela and British Guiana. When the British ignored American demands that the matter be submitted to arbitration, the Cleveland administration began threatening England with war. The British government finally realized that it had stumbled into a genuine diplomatic crisis and agreed to arbitration.

Hawaii and Samoa

The islands of Hawaii in the mid-Pacific had been an important way station for American ships in the China trade since the early nineteenth century. By the 1880s, officers of the expanding United States Navy were looking covetously at Pearl Harbor on the island of Oahu as a possible permanent base for American ships. Pressure for an increased American presence in Hawaii was emerging from another source as well: the growing number of Americans who had settled on the islands and who had gradually come to dominate their economic and political life.

In doing so, the Americans were wresting authority away from the leaders of an ancient civilization. Settled by Polynesian people beginning in about 1500 B.C., Hawaii had developed an agricultural and fishing society in which different islands (and different communities on the same islands), each with its own chieftain, lived more or less self-sufficiently. When the first Americans arrived in Hawaii in the 1790s on merchant ships from New England, there were perhaps a half-million people living there.

Battles among rival communities were frequent, as ambitious chieftains tried to consolidate power over their neighbors. In 1810, after a series of such battles, King Kamehameha I established his dominance over the other chieftains on Hawaii. He welcomed American traders and helped them develop a thriving trade between Hawaii and China, from which the natives profited along with the merchants. But Americans soon wanted more than trade. Missionaries began settling there in the early nineteenth century, and in the 1830s, William Hooper, a Boston trader, became the first of many Americans to buy land and establish a sugar plantation on the islands.

The arrival of these merchants, missionaries, and planters was devastating to native Hawaiian society. The newcomers inadvertently brought infectious diseases to which the Hawaiians, like the American Indians before them, were tragically vulnerable. By the mid-nineteenth century, more than half the native population had died. By the turn of the century, disease had cut the population by more than half again. But the Americans brought other incursions as well. Missionaries worked to replace native religion with Christianity. Other white settlers introduced liquor, firearms, and a commercial economy, all of which eroded the traditional character of Hawaiian society. By the 1840s, American planters had spread throughout the islands; and an American settler, G. P. Judd, had become prime minister of Hawaii under King Kamehameha III, who had agreed to establish a constitutional monarchy. Judd governed Hawaii for over a decade.

In 1887, the United States negotiated a treaty with Hawaii that permitted it to open a naval base at Pearl Harbor. By then, growing sugar for export to America had become the basis of the Hawaiian economy—as a result of an 1875 agreement allowing Hawaiian sugar to enter the United States duty-free. The American-dominated sugar plantation system displaced native Hawaiians from their lands and relied heavily for workers on Asian immigrants, whom the Americans considered more reliable and more docile than the natives. Indeed, finding adequate labor, and keeping it under control, was the principal concern of many planters. Some deliberately sought to create a mixed-race work force (Chinese, Japanese, native Hawaiian, Filipinos, Portuguese, and others) as a way to keep the workers divided and unlikely to challenge them.

Native Hawaiians did not accept these changes without protest. In 1891, they elevated a powerful nationalist to the throne: Queen Liliuokalani, who set out to challenge the growing American control of the islands. But her brief reign coincided with newly militant efforts by the Americans to seize power, efforts that came as a result of an act of Congress. In 1890, Congress had eliminated the 1875 exemption from tariffs for Hawaiian sugar planters. The result was devastating to the economy of the islands, and American planters concluded that the only way for them to recover was to become part of the United States (and hence exempt from its tariffs). In 1893 they staged a revolution and called on the United States for protection. After the American minister ordered marines from a warship in Honolulu harbor to go ashore to aid the rebels, the queen yielded her authority.

A provisional government, dominated by Americans (who constituted less than 5 percent of the population of the islands), immediately sent a delegation to Washington to negotiate a treaty of annexation. President Harrison signed an annexation agreement in February 1893, just before leaving office. But the Senate, controlled by Democrats after the 1892 election, refused to ratify the treaty, and Grover Cleveland, the new president, refused to support it. Debate over the annexation of Hawaii continued until 1898, when the Republicans, back in power, approved the agreement.

Three thousand miles south of Hawaii, the Samoan islands had also long served as a port for American ships in the Pacific trade. As American commerce with Asia increased, business groups in the United States regarded Samoa with new interest, and the American navy began eyeing the Samoan harbor at Pago Pago. In 1878, the Hayes administration extracted a treaty from Samoan leaders for an American naval station at Pago Pago. It bound the United States to arbitrate any differences between Samoa and other nations. Clearly, the United States now expected to have a voice in Samoan affairs.

But Great Britain and Germany were also interested in the islands, and they too secured treaty rights from the native princes. For the next ten years the three powers jockeyed for dominance in Samoa, playing off one native ruler against another and coming dangerously close to war. Finally, the three powers agreed to create a tripartite protectorate over Samoa, with the native chiefs exercising only nominal authority. The three-way arrangement failed to halt the intrigues and rivalries of its members, and in 1899, the United States and Germany divided the islands between them, compensating Britain with territories elsewhere in the Pacific. The United States retained the harbor at Pago Pago.

WAR WITH SPAIN

Imperial ambitions had thus begun to stir within the United States well before the late 1890s. But a war with Spain in 1898 turned those stirrings into overt expansionism. The war transformed America's relationship to the rest of the world, and it left the nation with a far-flung overseas empire.

Controversy over Cuba

The Spanish-American War emerged out of events in Cuba, which along with Puerto Rico represented virtually all that remained of Spain's once-extensive American empire. Cubans had been resisting Spanish rule intermittently since at least 1868, when they began a long but ultimately unsuccessful fight for independence. Many Americans had sympathized with the Cubans during that ten-year struggle, but the United States did not intervene.

In 1895, the Cubans rose up again. (Although their goal was an end to Spanish misrule, the island's problems were now in part a result of the Wilson-Gorman Tariff of 1894, whose high duties on sugar had badly damaged Cuba's important sugar economy by cutting off exports to the United States, the island's principal market.) This rebellion produced a ferocity on both sides that horrified Americans. The Cubans deliberately devastated the island to force the Spaniards to leave. The Spanish, commanded by General Valeriano Weyler (known in the American press as "Butcher" Weyler), confined civilians in certain areas to hastily prepared concentration camps, where they died by the thousands, victims of disease and malnutrition. The Spanish had used equally savage methods during the earlier struggle in Cuba without shocking American sensibilities. But the revolt of 1895 attracted unprecedented attention in the United States. That was partly because a growing population of Cuban émigrés in the United States—centered in Florida, New York, Philadelphia, and Trenton, New Jersey—gave extensive support to the Cuban Revolutionary Party (whose headquarters was in New York) and helped publicize its leader, José Martí, who was killed in Cuba in 1895. Later, Cuban Americans formed other clubs and associations to support the cause of *Cuba Libre* (Free Cuba).

But it was also because the events in Cuba were reported more fully and flamboyantly by American newspapers, and particularly by the new "yellow press" of William Randolph Hearst and Joseph Pulitzer, who were engaged in a ruthless circulation war with each other in New York City and elsewhere. The emergence of "yellow journalism" was one of the most striking phenomena in the growth of mass communications in the late nineteenth and early twentieth centuries. It was also a major factor in the march of the United States toward war with Spain. Pulitzer's *World*, which began publishing in New York in 1883, launched the age of yellow journalism—a term probably derived originally from the lavish use of color in the *World*, and the color yellow (an especially difficult one to print) in particular. But before long, the term came to be used to describe a sensationalist style of reporting and writing, and a self-conscious effort to reach a mass market. The success of the *World*, whose circulation reached 250,000 by 1886, spawned imitators in New York and elsewhere. Most prominent among them was Hearst's *New York Journal*, which cut its price to one cent after Hearst bought it in 1895 (Pulitzer quickly followed suit), copied many of the *World's* techniques, and within a year raised its circulation to 400,000. The competition between these two great "yellow" journals soon drove both to new levels of sensationalism. Their success drove newspapers in other cities around the nation to copy their techniques.

The civil war in Cuba gave both papers their best opportunities yet for combining sensational reporting with shameless appeals to patriotism and moral outrage. They avidly published exaggerated reports of Spanish atrocities against the Cuban rebels, fanning popular anger toward Spain. When the American battleship *Maine* mysteriously exploded in Havana harbor in 1898, both papers immediately blamed Spanish authorities (without any evidence). The *Journal* offered a $50,000 reward for information leading to the conviction of those responsible for the explosion, and it crowded all other stories off its front page ("There is no other news," Hearst told his editors) to make room for such screaming headlines as "THE WHOLE COUNTRY THRILLS WITH WAR FEVER" and "HAVANA POPULACE INSULTS THE MEMORY OF THE *MAINE* VICTIMS." In the three days following the *Maine* explosion, the *Journal* sold over 3 million copies, a new world's record for newspaper circulation. The *World* exploited the destruction of the *Maine* less successfully (although not for lack of trying), but it soon made up for it in its highly sensationalized coverage of the war itself. Hearst boasted at times that the conflict in Cuba was "the *Journal's* war" and even sent a cable to one of his reporters in Cuba saying: "You furnish the pictures, and I'll furnish the war."

Despite the mounting storm of indignation against Spain, President Cleveland refused to intervene in the conflict. But when McKinley became president in 1897, he formally protested Spain's "uncivilized and inhuman" conduct, causing the Spanish government (fearful of American intervention) to recall Weyler, modify the concentration policy, and grant the island a qualified autonomy. At the end of 1897, with the insurrection losing ground, it seemed that American involvement in the war might be averted.

But whatever chances there were for a peaceful settlement vanished as a result of two dramatic incidents in February 1898. The first occurred when a Cuban agent stole a private letter written by Dupuy de Lôme, the Spanish minister in Washington, and turned it over to the American press. It described McKinley as a weak man and "a bidder for the admiration of the crowd." This was no more than what many Americans, including some Republicans, were saying about their president (Assistant Secretary of the Navy Theodore Roosevelt once described McKinley as having "no more backbone than a chocolate eclair"). But coming from a foreigner, it created intense popular anger. Dupuy de Lôme promptly resigned.

While excitement over the de Lôme letter was still high, the American battleship *Maine* blew up in Havana harbor with a loss of more than 260 people. Many Americans assumed that the Spanish had sunk the ship, particularly when a naval court of inquiry reported that an external explosion by a submarine mine had caused the disaster. (Later evidence suggested that the disaster was actually the result of an accidental explosion inside one of the engine rooms.) War hysteria swept the country, and Congress unanimously appropriated $50 million for military preparations. "Remember the *Maine!*" became a national chant for revenge.

McKinley still hoped to avoid a conflict. But others in his administration (including Theodore Roosevelt) were clamoring for war. In March 1898, at McKinley's request, Spain agreed to stop the fighting and eliminate its concentration camps; but it refused to negotiate with the rebels and reserved the right to resume hostilities at its discretion. That satisfied neither public opinion nor Congress. A few days later, McKinley asked for and, on April 25, received a congressional declaration of war.

"A Splendid Little War"

Secretary of State John Hay called the Spanish-American conflict "a splendid little war," an opinion that most Americans—with the exception of many of the enlisted men who fought in it—seemed to share. Declared in April, it was over in August. That was in part because Cuban rebels had already greatly weakened the Spanish resistance, which made the American intervention in many respects little more than a "mopping up" exercise. Only 460 Americans were killed in battle or died of wounds, although some 5,200 perished of disease: malaria, dysentery, and typhoid, among others. Casualties among Cuban insurgents, who continued to bear the brunt of the struggle, were much higher.

Yet the American war effort was not without difficulties. United States soldiers faced serious supply problems: a shortage of modern rifles and ammunition, uniforms too heavy for the warm Caribbean weather, inadequate medical services, and skimpy, almost indigestible food. The regular army numbered only 28,000 troops and officers, most of whom had experience in quelling Indian outbreaks but none in larger-scale warfare. That meant that, as in the Civil War, the United States had to rely heavily on National Guard units, organized by local communities and commanded for the most part by local leaders without military experience. The entire mobilization process was an exercise in near chaos.

There were also racial conflicts. A significant proportion of the American invasion force consisted of black soldiers. Some were volunteer troops put together by black communities. Others were members of the four black regiments in the regular army, who had been stationed on the frontier to defend white settlements against Indians and were now transferred east to fight in Cuba. As the black soldiers traveled through the South toward the training camps, they chafed at the rigid segregation to which they were subjected and occasionally openly resisted the restrictions. Black soldiers in Georgia deliberately made use of a "whites only" park; in Florida, they beat a soda-fountain operator for refusing to serve them; in Tampa, white provocations and black retaliation led to a night-long riot that left thirty wounded.

Racial tensions continued in Cuba itself, where African Americans played crucial roles in some of the important battles of the war (including the famous charge at San Juan Hill) and won many medals. Nearly half the Cuban insurgents fighting with the Americans were black, but unlike their American counterparts they were fully integrated into the rebel army. (Indeed, one of the leading insurgent commanders, Antonio Maceo, was a black man.) The sight of black Cuban soldiers fighting alongside whites as equals gave African Americans a stronger sense of the injustice of their own position.

Seizing the Philippines

Assistant Secretary of the Navy Theodore Roosevelt was an ardent imperialist, an active proponent of war, and a man uninhibited by the fact that he was a relatively lowly figure in the military chain of command. As the tension with Spain rose, Roosevelt unilaterally strengthened the navy's Pacific squadron and instructed its commander, Commodore George Dewey, to attack Spanish naval forces in the Philippines, a colony of Spain, in the event of war.

Immediately after war was declared, Dewey sailed for the Philippines. On May 1, 1898, he steamed into Manila Bay and completely destroyed the aging Spanish fleet there. Only one American sailor died in the battle (of heatstroke), and George Dewey, immediately promoted to admiral, became the first hero of the war. Several months later, after the arrival of an American expeditionary force, the Spanish surrendered the city of Manila itself.

The Battle for Cuba

Cuba, however, remained the principal focus of American military efforts. At first, the American commanders planned a long period of training before actually sending troops into combat. But when a Spanish fleet under Admiral Pascual Cervera slipped past the American navy into Santiago harbor, on the southern coast of Cuba, plans changed quickly. The American Atlantic fleet quickly bottled Cervera up in the harbor. And the army's commanding general, Nelson A. Miles, hastily altered his strategy and ordered a force of 17,000 to leave Tampa in June to attack Santiago. Both the departure from Florida and the landing in Cuba were scenes of fantastic incompetence. It took five days for the relatively small army to get ashore, even though the enemy was offering no opposition.

General William R. Shafter, the American commander in Cuba, moved toward Santiago, which he planned to surround and capture. On the way he met and defeated Spanish forces at Las Guasimos and, a week later, in two simultaneous battles, El Caney and San Juan Hill. At the center of the fighting (and on the front pages of the newspapers) during all

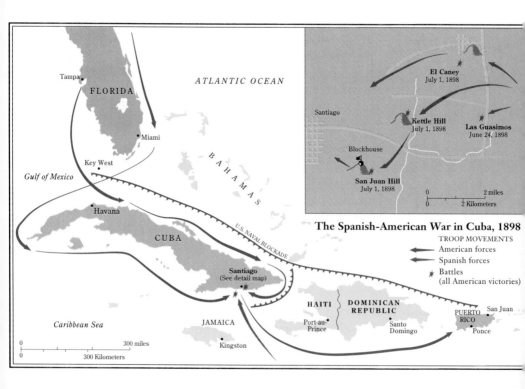

The Spanish-American War in Cuba, 1898

these engagements was a cavalry unit known as the Rough Riders. Nominally commanded by General Leonard Wood, its real leader was Colonel Theodore Roosevelt, who had resigned from the Navy Department to get into the war and who had struggled with an almost desperate fury to ensure that his regiment made it to the front before the fighting ended. Roosevelt rapidly emerged as a hero of the conflict. His fame rested in large part on his role in leading a bold, if perhaps reckless, charge up Kettle Hill (a charge that was a minor part of the larger battle for the adjacent San Juan Hill) directly into the face of Spanish guns. Roosevelt himself emerged unscathed, but nearly a hundred of his soldiers were killed or wounded. He remembered the battle as "the great day of my life."

Although Shafter was now in position to assault Santiago, his army was so weakened by sickness that he feared he could not go on. Disaster seemed imminent. But unknown to the Americans, the Spanish government had by now decided that Santiago was lost and had ordered Cervera to evacuate. On July 3, Cervera tried to escape the harbor. The waiting American

THE ROUGH RIDERS Theodore Roosevelt, center, poses with some of the Rough Riders after their famous charge in the Battle of San Juan Hill. The brigade had an unofficial anthem: "Rough, rough, we're the stuff. We want to fight, and we can't get enough."

squadron destroyed his entire fleet. On July 16, the commander of the Spanish ground forces in Santiago surrendered. At about the same time, an American army landed in Puerto Rico and occupied it against virtually no opposition. On August 12, the United States accepted an end to the war when Spain signed an armistice recognizing Cuban independence, ceding Puerto Rico to the United States, and accepting American occupation of Manila until the two nations reached a final agreement on the Philippines.

Puerto Rico and the United States

The annexation of Puerto Rico produced relatively little controversy in the United States—ironically, since of all the territory America acquired as a result of the Spanish-American War, Puerto Rico would be the most important to the nation's future.

The island of Puerto Rico had been a part of the Spanish Empire since Ponce de León arrived there in 1508, and it had contained Spanish settlements since the founding of San Juan in 1521. The native people of the island, the Arawaks, disappeared almost entirely as a result of infectious diseases, Spanish brutality, and poverty. Puerto Rican society developed, therefore, with a Spanish ruling class and a large African work force for the coffee and sugar plantations that came to dominate its economy.

Puerto Rican resistance to Spanish rule began to emerge in the nineteenth century, just as it had emerged in Cuba. Uprisings occurred intermittently beginning in the 1820s; the most important of them—the so-called Lares Rebellion—was, like the others, effectively crushed by the Spanish in 1868. But the growing resistance did prompt some reforms: the abolition of slavery in 1873, representation in the Spanish parliament, and other changes. Demands for independence continued to grow, and in 1898, in response to political pressure organized by Luis Muñoz Rivera, Spain granted the island a degree of independence. But before the changes had any chance to take effect, control of Puerto Rico shifted to the United States.

American military forces occupied the island during the war. They remained in control until 1900, when the Foraker Act ended military rule and established a formal colonial government. In 1917, under pressure to clarify the relationship between Puerto Rico and America, Congress passed the Jones Act, which declared Puerto Rico to be United States territory and made all Puerto Ricans American citizens.

The Puerto Rican sugar industry flourished as it took advantage of the American market that was now open to it without tariffs. As in Hawaii, Americans soon established large sugar plantations on the island and hired natives to work them. The growing emphasis on sugar as a cash crop and the transformation of many Puerto Rican farmers into paid laborers led to a reduction in the growing of food for the island and a higher reliance on imported goods. When international sugar prices were high, Puerto Rico did well. When they dropped, the island's economy sagged, pushing the many plantation workers—already desperately poor—into destitution. Many Puerto Ricans continued to agitate for independence. Others, however, began to envision closer relations with the United States, even statehood.

The Debate over the Philippines

If the annexation of Puerto Rico produced relatively little controversy, the annexation of the Philippines occasioned a long and impassioned debate. Controlling a nearby Caribbean island fit reasonably comfortably into America's sense of itself as the dominant power in the Western Hemisphere. Controlling a large and densely populated territory thousands of miles away seemed different and, to many Americans, more ominous.

McKinley claimed to be reluctant to support annexation. But, according to his own accounts, he emerged from an "agonizing night of prayer" convinced that there were no acceptable alternatives. Returning the Philippines to Spain would be "cowardly and dishonorable," he claimed. Turning the islands over to another imperialist power (France, Germany, or Britain) would be "bad business and discreditable." Granting them independence would be irresponsible; the Filipinos were "unfit for self government." The only solution was "to take them all and to educate the Filipinos, and uplift and Christianize them, and by God's grace do the very best we could by them." Growing popular support for annexation and the pressure of the imperialist leaders of his party undoubtedly helped him reach this decision of conscience.

The Treaty of Paris, signed in December 1898, brought a formal end to the Spanish-American War. It confirmed the terms of the armistice concerning Cuba, Puerto Rico, and Guam. American negotiators had startled the Spanish by demanding that they also cede the Philippines to the United States, but an offer of $20 million for the islands softened Spain's resistance. The negotiators accepted all the American terms.

In the United States Senate, however, resistance was fierce. During debate over ratification of the treaty, a powerful anti-imperialist movement arose throughout the country to oppose acquisition of the Philippines. Among the anti-imperialists were some of the nation's wealthiest and most influential figures: Andrew Carnegie, Mark Twain, Samuel

Gompers, Senator John Sherman, and others. Some believed simply that imperialism was immoral, a repudiation of America's commitment to human freedom. Some feared "polluting" the American population by introducing "inferior" Asian races into it. Industrial workers feared being undercut by a flood of cheap laborers from the new colonies. Conservatives feared that the large standing army and entangling foreign alliances they thought imperialism would require would threaten American liberties. Sugar growers and others feared unwelcome competition from the new territories. The Anti-Imperialist League, established by upper-class Bostonians, New Yorkers, and others late in 1898 to fight against annexation, attracted a widespread following in the Northeast and waged a vigorous campaign against ratification of the Paris treaty.

Favoring ratification was an equally varied group. There were the exuberant imperialists such as Theodore Roosevelt, who saw the acquisition of empire as a way to keep alive what they considered the healthy, restorative influence of the war. Some businessmen saw opportunities in the Philippines and believed annexation would position the United States to dominate the Asian trade. And most Republicans saw partisan advantages in acquiring valuable new territories through a war fought and won by a Republican administration. Perhaps the strongest argument in favor of annexation, however, was the apparent ease with which it could be accomplished. The United States, after all, already possessed the islands.

When anti-imperialists warned of the danger of acquiring heavily populated territories whose people might have to become citizens, the imperialists had a ready answer: The nation's longstanding policies toward Indians—treating them as dependents rather than as citizens—had created a precedent for annexing land without absorbing people. Senator Henry Cabot Lodge of Massachusetts, one of the leading imperialists in Congress, made the point explicitly:

> The other day . . . a great Democratic thinker announced that a Republic can have no subjects. He seems to have forgotten that this Republic not only has held subjects from the beginning, . . . but [that we have] acquired them by purchase. . . . [We] denied to the Indian tribes even the right to choose their allegiance, or to become citizens.

The fate of the treaty remained in doubt for weeks, until it received the unexpected support of William Jennings Bryan. Bryan was a fervent anti-imperialist who hoped to move the issue out of the Senate and make annexation the subject of a national referendum in 1900, when he expected to be the Democratic presidential candidate again. Bryan persuaded a number of anti-imperialist Democrats to support the treaty so as to set up the 1900 debate. The Senate ratified it finally on February 6, 1899.

But Bryan miscalculated. If the campaign of 1900 was in fact a debate on the Philippines, as Bryan tried to make it, the election proved beyond doubt that the nation had decided in favor of imperialism. Once again, Bryan ran against McKinley, and once again, McKinley won—even more decisively than in 1896. It was not only the issue of the colonies, however, that ensured McKinley's victory. The Republicans were the beneficiaries of growing national prosperity—and also of the colorful personality of their vice presidential candidate, Colonel Theodore Roosevelt, the hero of the Battle of San Juan Hill.

THE REPUBLIC AS EMPIRE

The new American empire was a small one by the standards of the great imperial powers of Europe. But it created large problems. It embroiled the United States in the politics of both Europe and the Far East in ways the nation had always tried to avoid in the past. It also drew Americans into a brutal war in the Philippines.

Governing the Colonies

Three of the new American dependencies—Hawaii, Alaska, and Puerto Rico—presented relatively few problems. They received territorial status (and their residents American citizenship) relatively quickly: Hawaii in 1900, Alaska in 1912, and Puerto Rico (in stages) by 1917. The navy took control of Guam and Tutuila. The United States had also acquired some of the smallest, least populated Pacific islands; it simply left them alone.

Cuba was a thornier problem. American military forces, commanded by General Leonard Wood, remained there until 1902 to prepare the is-land for independence. They built roads, schools, and hospitals; reorgan-ized the legal, financial, and administrative systems; and introduced med-ical and sanitation reforms. But when Cuba drew up a constitution that made no reference to the United States, Congress responded by passing the Platt Amendment in 1901 and pressuring Cuba into incorporating the amendment's terms into its constitution. The Platt Amendment barred

"MEASURING UNCLE SAM FOR A NEW SUIT" BY J. S. PUGHE, IN *PUCK* MAGAZINE, 1900
President William McKinley is approvingly depicted here as a tailor, measuring his
client for a suit large enough to accommodate the new possessions the United States
obtained in the aftermath of the Spanish-American War. The cartoon tries to link
this expansion with earlier, less controversial ones such as the Louisiana Purchase.

Cuba from making treaties with other nations (thus giving the United
States effective control of Cuban foreign policy); it gave the United States
the right to intervene in Cuba to preserve independence, life, and property; and it required Cuba to permit American naval stations on its territory. The amendment left Cuba with only nominal political independence. And American capital, which quickly took over the island's economy,
made the new nation an American economic appendage as well. American
investors poured into Cuba, buying up plantations, factories, railroads,
and refineries. Absentee American ownership of many of the island's most
important resources was the source of resentment and agitation for
decades. Resistance to "Yankee imperialism" produced intermittent revolts
against the Cuban government—revolts that at times prompted United
States military intervention. American troops occupied the island from
1906 to 1909 after one such rebellion; they returned again in 1912, to suppress a revolt by black plantation workers. As in Puerto Rico and Hawaii,
sugar production—spurred by access to the American market—increasingly dominated the island's economy and subjected it to the same cycle of
booms and busts that so plagued other sugar-producing appendages of the
United States economy.

The Philippine War

Americans did not like to think of themselves as imperial rulers in the European mold. Yet like other imperial powers, the United States soon discovered—as it had discovered at home in its relations with the Indians—that subjugating another people required more than ideals; it also required strength and at times brutality. That, at least, was the lesson of the American experience in the Philippines, where American forces soon became engaged in a long and bloody war with insurgent forces fighting for independence.

The conflict in the Philippines is the least remembered of all American wars. It was also one of the longest (it lasted from 1898 to 1902) and one of the most vicious. It involved 200,000 American troops and resulted in 4,300 American deaths, nearly ten times the number who had died in combat in the Spanish-American War. The number of Filipinos killed in the conflict is still in dispute, but it seems likely that at least 50,000 natives (and perhaps many more) died. The American occupiers faced guerrilla tactics in the Philippines very similar to those the Spanish occupiers had faced prior to 1898 in Cuba. And they soon found themselves drawn into the same pattern of brutality that had outraged so many Americans when Weyler had used them in the Caribbean.

The Filipinos had been rebelling against Spanish rule even before 1898. And as soon as they realized the Americans had come to stay, they rebelled against them as well. Ably led by Emilio Aguinaldo, who claimed to head the legitimate government of the nation, Filipinos harried the American army of occupation from island to island for more than three years. At first, American commanders believed the rebels had only a small popular following. But by early 1900, General Arthur MacArthur, an American commander in the islands (and the father of General Douglas MacArthur), was writing: "I have been reluctantly compelled to believe that the Filipino masses are loyal to Aguinaldo and the government which he heads."

To MacArthur and others, that was not a reason to moderate American tactics or conciliate the rebels. It was a reason to adopt more severe measures. Gradually, the American military effort became more systematically vicious and brutal. Captured Filipino guerrillas were treated not as prisoners of war but as murderers. Most were summarily executed. On some islands, entire communities were evacuated—the residents forced into concentration camps while American troops destroyed their villages, farms, crops, and livestock. A spirit of savagery grew among American soldiers, who came to view the Filipinos as almost subhuman and at times seemed to take pleasure in killing almost arbitrarily.

FILIPINO PRISONERS American troops guard captured Filipino guerrillas in Manila.
The suppression of the Filipino insurrection was a much longer and costlier military
undertaking than the Spanish-American War, by which the United States first
gained possession of the islands. By mid-1900 there were 70,000 American troops in
the Philippines, under the command of General Arthur MacArthur (whose son,
Douglas, won fame in the Philippines during World War II).

By 1902, reports of the brutality and of the American casualties had
soured the American public on the war. But by then, the rebellion had
largely exhausted itself and the occupiers had established control over
most of the islands. The key to their victory was the March 1901 capture
of Aguinaldo, who later signed a document in which he urged his followers to stop fighting and declared his own allegiance to the United States.
(Aguinaldo then retired from public life and lived quietly until 1964.)
Fighting continued intermittently until as late as 1906; but American possession of the Philippines was now secure.

In the summer of 1901, the military transferred authority over the islands to William Howard Taft, who became the first civilian governor. Taft

announced that the American mission in the Philippines was to prepare the islands for independence, and he gave the Filipinos broad local autonomy. The Americans also built roads, schools, bridges, and sewers; instituted major administrative and financial reforms; and established a public health system. Filipino self-rule slowly increased. But not until July 4, 1946, did the islands finally gain their independence.

The Open Door

The acquisition of the Philippines greatly increased the already strong American interest in Asia. Americans were particularly concerned about the future of China, with which the United States already had an important trading relationship and which was now so enfeebled that it provided a tempting target for exploitation by stronger countries. By 1900, England, France, Germany, Russia, and Japan were beginning to carve up China among themselves, pressuring the Chinese government for "concessions" that gave them effective economic control over various regions. In some cases, they simply seized Chinese territories and claimed them as their own "spheres of influence." Many Americans feared the process would soon cut them out of the China trade altogether.

Eager for a way to protect American interests in China without risking war, McKinley issued a statement in September 1898 saying the United States wanted access to China but no special advantages there: "Asking only the open door for ourselves, we are ready to accord the open door to others." Later, Secretary of State John Hay translated the president's words into policy when he addressed identical messages— which became known as the "Open Door notes"—to England, Germany, Russia, France, Japan, and Italy. He asked them to approve three principles: Each nation with a "sphere of influence" in China was to allow other nations to trade freely and equally in its sphere. The principles he outlined would allow the United States to trade with the Chinese without fear of interference and without having to become militarily involved in the region.

But the Open Door proposals were coolly received in Europe and Japan. Russia openly rejected them; the other powers claimed to accept them in principle but to be unable to act unless all the powers agreed. Hay, unperturbed, simply announced that all the powers had accepted the principles of the Open Door and that the United States expected them to observe those principles. But unless the United States was willing to resort to war, it could not prevent any nation that wanted to violate the Open Door from doing so.

No sooner had the diplomatic maneuvering over the Open Door ended than the Boxers, a secret Chinese martial-arts society, launched a revolt against foreigners in China. The climax of the Boxer Rebellion was a siege of the entire foreign diplomatic corps in the British embassy in Beijing (Peking). The imperial powers (including the United States) sent an international expeditionary force into China to rescue the diplomats. In August 1900, it fought its way into Beijing and broke the siege.

McKinley and Hay had agreed to American participation so as to secure a voice in the settlement of the uprising and to prevent the partition of China. Hay now won support for his Open Door approach from England and Germany and then induced the other participating powers to accept compensation from the Chinese for the damages the Boxer Rebellion had caused. Chinese territorial integrity survived at least in name, and the United States retained access to its lucrative trade.

A Modern Military System

The war with Spain had revealed glaring deficiencies in the American military system. Had the United States been fighting a more powerful nation, disaster might have resulted. After the war, McKinley appointed Elihu Root, an able New York corporate lawyer, as secretary of war to supervise a major overhaul of the armed forces. Between 1900 and 1903, Root created a new military system.

The Root reforms enlarged the maximum size of the regular army from 25,000 to 100,000. They established federal army standards for the National Guard, ensuring that never again would the nation fight a war with volunteer regiments trained and equipped differently from the regular army. They sparked the creation of a system of officer training schools, including the Army Staff College (later the Command and General Staff School) at Fort Leavenworth, Kansas, and the Army War College in Washington, D.C. And in 1903, they established a general staff (named the Joint Chiefs of Staff) to act as military advisers to the secretary of war. As a result of the new reforms, the United States entered the twentieth century with something resembling a modern military system. The country would make substantial use of it in the turbulent century to come.

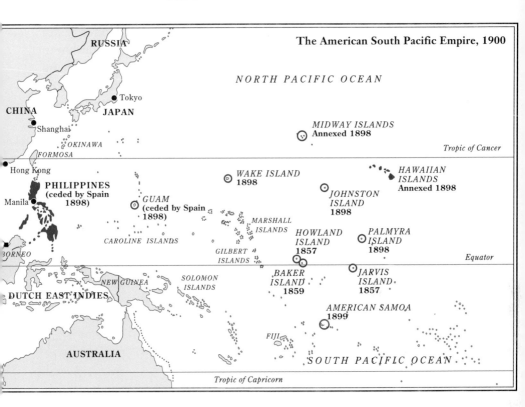

The American South Pacific Empire, 1900

NORTH PACIFIC OCEAN

RUSSIA

Tokyo

CHINA   JAPAN

Shanghai

OKINAWA

FORMOSA

Hong Kong

PHILIPPINES
(ceded by Spain
1898)

Manila

BORNEO

GUAM
(ceded by Spain
1898)

CAROLINE ISLANDS

MARSHALL
ISLANDS

GILBERT
ISLANDS

NEW GUINEA

SOLOMON
ISLANDS

DUTCH EAST INDIES

AUSTRALIA

MIDWAY ISLANDS
Annexed 1898

Tropic of Cancer

WAKE ISLAND
1898

HAWAIIAN
ISLANDS
Annexed 1898

JOHNSTON
ISLAND
1898

HOWLAND
ISLAND
1857

PALMYRA
ISLAND
1898

BAKER
ISLAND
1859

JARVIS
ISLAND
1857

Equator

AMERICAN SAMOA
1899

FIJI

SOUTH PACIFIC OCEAN

Tropic of Capricorn

CONCLUSION

After more than a century of continual national expansion on the North American continent, the United States joined the community of colonial nations in the 1890s and acquired a substantial empire far from its own shores. But the rise of American imperialism was a halting and contested process, whose purposes were never wholly clear.

In the beginning, America's new internationalism took the form of a supposedly humanitarian intervention in a civil war in Spanish Cuba. The American public, inflamed by lurid journalistic accounts of Spanish atrocities inflicted on innocent Cubans, helped push the United States into a short, victorious war with Spain, fought in theory to secure Cuban independence. But through the efforts of some committed internationalists in the McKinley administration, among them Theodore Roosevelt, the Spanish-American War was soon transformed from a fight to free Cuba into a fight to wrest important colonies from Spain. At its end, the United States found itself in possession of substantial new territories in the Caribbean (including Puerto Rico) and an important territory in the Pacific—the Philippines. A vigorous domestic anti-imperialist movement failed to stop the annexationist drive, and by 1899 the United States found itself in possession of colonies.

Taking the colonies proved easier than holding them. In the Philippines, American forces became bogged down in a four-year war with Filipino rebels, a war that dragged the American forces into the same kinds of brutal tactics that had so outraged Americans when the Spanish had used them in Cuba. The new colonial rulers soon pacified the Philippines, but not before souring much of the American public on the effort. In part as a result, the territories the United States acquired in the aftermath of the Spanish-American War marked not only the beginning but the end of American territorial imperialism.

FOR FURTHER REFERENCE

Suggested Readings

Walter LaFeber, *The New Empire: An Interpretation of American Expansion, 1860–1898* (1963) and Ernest May, *Imperial Democracy* (1961) are excellent introductions to the subject. David F. Healy, *U.S. Expansionism: Imperialist Urge in the 1890s* (1970) is a contrasting interpretation. Walter LaFeber, *The Cambridge History of American Foreign Relations, Vol. 2: The Search for Opportunity, 1865–1913* (1993) is an important general study. William Appleman Williams, *The Tragedy of American Diplomacy* rev. ed., 1972 is a classic revisionist work on the origins and tragic consequences of American imperialism. Anders Stephanson, *Manifest Destiny: American Expansionism and the Empire of Right* (1995) is a short and provocative history of Americans' ideology of expansionism. Robert L. Beisner's *Twelve Against Empire* (1968) chronicles the careers of the leading opponents of imperial expansion. Emily S. Rosenberg, *Spreading the American Dream: American Economic and Cultural Expansion, 1890–1945* (1982) is a provocative cultural interpretation. Gerald F. Linderman, *The Mirror of War: American Society and the Spanish-American War* (1974) is an interesting interpretation of the social meaning of the war. Stuart Creighton Miller, *"Benevolent Assimilation": The American Conquest of the Philippines, 1899–1903* (1982) is a disturbing account of the American war in the Philippines. Michael Hunt, *The Making of a Special Relationship: The United States and China to 1914* (1983) is a good introduction to the subject.

Films

(The best source for information on how to find these and other films is *Bowker's Complete Video Directory*—3 volumes.) *Savage Acts* (1995) focuses on the conquest of the

Philippines but places this episode in the broader context of American expansion that began with the first colonial settlements. *First in the Philippines* (1984) presents a more detailed portrait of American soldiers in the Philippines. For a stunning voyage through the Panama Canal and its history, see *A Man, A Plan, A Canal: Panama* (1987). *The Big Stick* (1991) analyzes the activist foreign policy of the United States during the early part of the twentieth century, particularly in reference to Latin America.

Internet Resources

Internet websites containing historical material relevant to the subjects discussed in this chapter can be reached through the McGraw-Hill history site at www.mhhe.com/socscience/history/usa/link/linktop.htm.

CHAPTER TWENTY-ONE

The Rise of Progressivism

The Progressive Impulse ~ *Women and Reform*
The Assault on the Parties ~ *Sources of Progressive Reform*
Crusades for Order and Reform

ELL BEFORE THE turn of the century, many Americans had become convinced that the rapid industrialization and urbanization of their society had created intolerable problems—that the nation's most pressing need was to impose order on the growing chaos and to curb industrial society's most glaring injustices. In the early years of the new century, that outlook acquired a name: progressivism.

Not even those who called themselves progressives could always agree on what the word "progressive" really meant. Indeed, more than one historian has suggested that the word ultimately came to mean so many different things to so many different people that it ceased to mean anything at all. Yet if progressivism was a phenomenon of great scope and diversity, it was also one that rested on an identifiable set of central assumptions. It was, first, an optimistic vision. Progressives believed, as their name implies, in the idea of progress. They believed that society was capable of improvement and that continued growth and advancement were the nation's destiny. But progressives believed, too, that growth and progress could not continue to occur recklessly, as they had in the late nineteenth century. The "natural laws" of the marketplace, and the doctrines of laissez faire and Social Darwinism that celebrated those laws, were not sufficient to create the order and stability that the growing society required. Purposeful human intervention was necessary to solve the nation's problems. Progressives did not always agree on the form that intervention should take, but most believed that government should play an important role in the process.

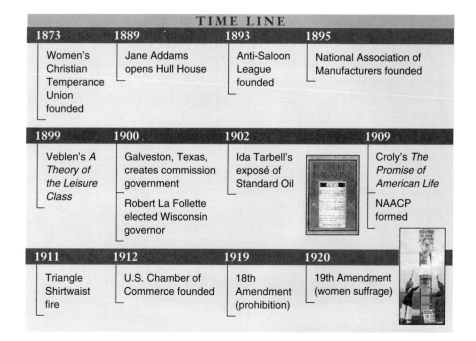

TIME LINE

1873	1889	1893	1895
Women's Christian Temperance Union founded	Jane Addams opens Hull House	Anti-Saloon League founded	National Association of Manufacturers founded

1899	1900	1902	1909
Veblen's *A Theory of the Leisure Class*	Galveston, Texas, creates commission government Robert La Follette elected Wisconsin governor	Ida Tarbell's exposé of Standard Oil	Croly's *The Promise of American Life* NAACP formed

1911	1912	1919	1920
Triangle Shirtwaist fire	U.S. Chamber of Commerce founded	18th Amendment (prohibition)	19th Amendment (women suffrage)

THE PROGRESSIVE IMPULSE

Beyond these central premises, progressivism flowed outward in a number of different directions. One powerful impulse was the spirit of "antimonopoly," the fear of concentrated power and the urge to limit and disperse authority and wealth. A second progressive impulse was a belief in the importance of social cohesion: the belief that individuals are not autonomous but part of a great web of social relationships, that the welfare of any single person is dependent on the welfare of society as a whole. And a third progressive impulse was a belief in organization and efficiency: the belief that social order was a result of intelligent social organization and rational procedures for guiding social and economic life. These varied reform impulses were not entirely incompatible with one another. Many progressives made use of all these ideas at times, and others as well, as they tried to restore order and stability to their turbulent society.

The Muckrakers and the Social Gospel

Among the first to articulate the new spirit of reform was a group of crusading journalists who in the late nineteenth and early twentieth centuries began to direct public attention toward social, economic, and political injustices. They became known as the "muckrakers" after Theodore Roosevelt accused one of them of raking up muck through his writings. They were committed to exposing scandal, corruption, and injustice to public view.

At first, their major targets were the trusts and particularly the railroads, which the muckrakers considered dangerously powerful and deeply corrupt. Exposés of the great corporate organizations began to appear as early as the 1860s, when Charles Francis Adams, Jr., and others uncovered corruption among the railroad barons. Decades later, Ida Tarbell produced a scorching study of the Standard Oil trust, keeping the issue of corporate power alive. By the turn of the century, however, many muckrakers were turning their attention to government and particularly to the urban political machines. The most influential, perhaps, was Lincoln Steffens, a reporter for *McClure's Magazine*. He created a series of portraits of "machine government" and "boss rule" in cities as diverse as St. Louis, Minneapolis, Cleveland, Cincinnati, Chicago, Philadelphia, and New York; his tone of studied moral outrage was reflected in the title of his series and of the book that emerged from it, *The Shame of the Cities*. His work helped arouse sentiment for urban political reform. The muckrakers reached the peak of their influence in the first decade of the twentieth century. They investigated governments, labor unions, and corporations. They explored the problems of child labor, immigrant ghettoes, prostitution, and family disorganization. They denounced waste and destruction of natural resources, the subjugation of women, even occasionally the oppression of blacks.

Many reformers became committed to the idea of what was known as "social justice." A clear expression of that concern was the rise within American religion of the "Social Gospel," the effort to make faith into a tool of social reform. The Salvation Army, which began in England but soon spread to the United States, was a Christian social welfare organization with a vaguely military structure. By 1900, it had recruited 3,000 "officers" and 20,000 "privates" and was offering both material aid and spiritual service to the urban poor. In addition, many ministers, priests, and rabbis left traditional parish work to serve in the troubled cities. Charles Sheldon's *In His Steps* (1898), the story of a young minister who abandoned a comfortable post to work among the needy, sold more than 15

MCCLURE'S MAGAZINE, MAY 1903 *McClure's* was the leading outlet for a form of journalism known as "muckraking," which exposed social and economic scandals in the hope of promoting reform. This issue contains articles by two of the leading muckrakers, Lincoln Steffens and Ida Tarbell.

million copies and established itself as the most successful novel of the era. The engagement of religion with reform helped bring to progressivism a powerful moral impulse and a concern for the plight of some of society's most impoverished and degraded people.

The Settlement House Movement

One of the strongest elements of progressive thought was the belief that the environment shaped individual development. Ignorance, poverty, even criminality, progressives argued, were not the result of inherent moral or genetic failings or of the workings of providence. They were, rather, the effects of an unhealthy environment. To elevate the distressed, therefore, required an improvement of the conditions in which the distressed lived.

Nothing produced more distress, many reformers believed, than the crowded immigrant neighborhoods of American cities. One response to the problems of such communities, borrowed from England, was the settlement house. The most famous was Hull House, which opened in 1889 in Chicago as a result of the efforts of Jane Addams. It became a model for more than 400 similar institutions throughout the nation. Staffed by members of the educated middle class, settlement houses sought to help immigrant families adapt to the language and customs of their new country. Settlement houses avoided the condescension and moral disapproval of earlier philanthropic efforts. But they generally embodied a belief that middle-class Americans had a responsibility to impart their own values to immigrants.

Central to the settlement houses were the efforts of educated women. Indeed, the movement became a training ground for many important female leaders of the twentieth century, among them Eleanor Roosevelt. The settlement houses also helped spawn another important institution of reform: the profession of social work—a profession in which women were to play an important role. The professional social worker combined a compassion for the poor with a commitment to the values of bureaucratic progressivism: scientific study, efficient organization, reliance on experts.

The Allure of Expertise

As the emergence of the social work profession suggests, progressives involved in humanitarian efforts often placed high value on knowledge and expertise. That belief found expression in many ways, among them through the writings of a new group of scholars and intellectuals who envisioned a new civilization in which the expertise of scientists and engineers would be put into the service of the economy and society. Among the most influential of these theorists was the social scientist Thorstein Veblen. Harshly critical of the industrial tycoons of the late nineteenth century—the "leisure class," as he satirically described them in his first major work, *A Theory of the Leisure Class* (1899)—Veblen proposed instead a new economic system in which power would reside in the hands of highly trained engineers. Only they, he argued, could fully understand the "machine process" by which modern society must be governed.

In practical terms, the impulse toward expertise and organization helped produce the idea of scientific management, or "Taylorism" (see p. 522). It encouraged the development of modern mass-production techniques and, above all, the assembly line. It inspired a revolution in American education and the creation of a new area of inquiry—social science, the use of scientific techniques in the study of society and its institutions. It also helped create a movement toward organization among the expanding new group of middle-class professionals.

The Professions

The late nineteenth century saw a dramatic expansion in the number of Americans engaged in administrative and professional tasks. Industries needed managers, technicians, and accountants as well as workers. Cities required commercial, medical, legal, and educational services. New technologies required scientists and engineers, who, in turn, required institutions and instructors to train them. By the turn of the century, the people performing these services had come to constitute a distinct social group—what some have called a new middle class.

By the early twentieth century, the millions of members of this new middle class were building organizations and establishing standards to secure their position in society. As one of their principal vehicles, they created the modern, organized professions. The idea of professionalism had been a frail one in America even as late as 1880. But as the demand for professional services increased, so did the pressures for reform.

Among the first to respond was the medical profession. Throughout the 1890s, doctors who considered themselves trained professionals began forming local associations and societies. In 1901, they reorganized the American Medical Association (AMA) into a national professional society. By 1920, nearly two-thirds of all American doctors were members. The AMA quickly called for strict, scientific standards for admission to the practice of medicine, with doctors themselves serving as protectors of the standards. State and local governments responded by creating medical schools in their universities and by passing new laws that required the licensing of all physicians and that restricted licenses to those practitioners approved by the profession.

There was similar movement in other professions. By 1916, lawyers in all forty-eight states had established professional bar associations, virtually all of which had succeeded in creating central examining boards, composed of lawyers, to regulate admission to the profession. Increasingly, aspiring lawyers found it necessary to enroll in graduate programs, and the nation's law schools accordingly expanded greatly, both in numbers and in the rigor of their curricula. Businessmen supported the creation of schools of business administration and established their own national organizations: the National Association of Manufacturers in 1895 and the United

States Chamber of Commerce in 1912. Even farmers, long the symbol of the romantic spirit of individualism, responded to the new order by forming, through the National Farm Bureau Federation, a network of agricultural organizations designed to spread scientific farming methods, teach sound marketing techniques, and lobby for the interests of their members.

Among the chief purposes of the new professionalism was guarding entry into the professions. This was only partly an effort to defend the professions from the untrained and incompetent. The admission requirements also protected those already in the professions from excessive competition and lent prestige and status to the professional label. Some professions used their entrance requirements to exclude blacks, women, immigrants, and other "undesirables" from their ranks. Others used them simply to keep the numbers down, to ensure that demand for the services of existing members would remain high.

Women and the Professions

American women found themselves excluded—both by custom and by active barriers of law and prejudice—from most of the emerging professions. But a substantial number of middle-class women—particularly those emerging from the new women's colleges and from the coeducational state universities—nevertheless entered professional careers.

A few women managed to establish themselves as physicians, lawyers, engineers, scientists, and corporate managers. Most, however, turned by necessity to those professions that society considered suitable for women. Settlement houses and social work provided two professional outlets that were widely considered appropriate for women. The most important, however, was teaching. Indeed, in the late nineteenth century, more than two-thirds of all grammar-school teachers were women, and perhaps 90 percent of all professional women were teachers. For educated black women, in particular, teaching was often the only professional opportunity they could hope to find. The segregated black schools of the South created a substantial market for African-American teachers.

Women also dominated other professional activities. Nursing had become primarily a women's field around the time of the Civil War, when it was still considered a menial occupation, akin to domestic service. But by the early twentieth century, it too was adopting professional standards. Women also found opportunities as librarians, another field beginning to define itself in professional terms. And many women entered academia—often studying at predominantly male institutions that permitted women

SETTLEMENT HOUSE WORKERS Nurses from the Henry Street settlement in New York leave their headquarters to begin their visits to the homes of poor immigrants in lower Manhattan. This photograph dates from the early 1900s.

to earn advanced degrees, among them the University of Chicago, MIT, and Columbia, and then finding professional opportunities in the new and expanding women's colleges.

The "women's professions" had much in common with other professions. But they also had distinctive qualities. Careers such as teaching, nursing, and library work were "helping" professions. They involved working primarily with other women or with children. They stood somehow outside the predominantly male business and professional worlds—the world of the market. Women's workplaces—schools, hospitals, and libraries—had a vaguely "domestic" or "feminine" image, which enabled men (and, indeed, most women) to reconcile the idea of female professional work with prevailing ideas about the proper role of women in society.

WOMEN AND REFORM

The prominent role of women in reform movements is one of the most striking features of progressivism. Women became important reformers even though they could not vote in most states, seldom held office, and had footholds in only a few professions. But their relative insulation from political and professional life in some ways enhanced their ability to wield influence, for it enabled them to tie their causes to the idea of a nonpartisan, nurturing culture uncontaminated by economic or political interests.

The "New Woman"

The phenomenon of the "new woman," widely remarked upon at the time, was a product of the social and economic changes of the era. By the end of the nineteenth century, almost all income-producing activity had moved out of the home and into the factory or the office. At the same time, many women were having fewer children, and their children were beginning school at earlier ages and spending more time there. For wives and mothers who did not work for wages, home and family were less all-consuming. Hence more and more women began looking for activities outside the home.

There were also more women who lived outside traditional families altogether. Approximately 10 percent of all American women in the last decades of the nineteenth century never married—a high proportion of them middle-class women—and single women were among the most prominent female reformers of the time. Some of these women lived alone. Others lived with other women, often in long-term relationships—some of them secretly romantic—that were known at the time as "Boston marriages." The divorce rate also rose rapidly in the late nineteenth century, from one divorce for every twenty-one marriages in 1880 to one in nine by 1916; women initiated the great majority of them.

Higher levels of education also contributed to the prominence of women in reform activities. The proliferation of women's colleges and of coeducational public universities in the late nineteenth century produced the first generation of women in which significant numbers had educations above the high-school level (see p. 575–576). The new colleges also helped create female communities, within which women could find support for their ambitions and companionship for their activities.

The Clubwomen

In the vanguard of many progressive social reforms was a large network of women's clubs, which proliferated rapidly beginning in the 1880s and 1890s. The women's clubs began largely as cultural organizations to provide middle- and upper-class women with an outlet for their intellectual energies. In 1892, when women formed the General Federation of Women's Clubs to coordinate the activities of local organizations, there were more than 100,000 members in nearly 500 clubs. By 1917, there were over 1 million members.

By the early twentieth century, the clubs were becoming less concerned with cultural activities and more concerned with making a contribution to social reform. Much of what they did was uncontroversial: planting trees; supporting schools, libraries, and settlement houses; building hospitals and parks. But many women's clubs also supported such controversial measures as child labor laws, worker compensation, pure food and drug legislation, occupational safety, reforms in Indian policy, and—beginning in 1914—woman suffrage. Because many club members were from wealthy families, some organizations had substantial funds at their disposal to make their influence felt.

Black women occasionally joined clubs dominated by whites. But African Americans also formed clubs of their own, some of which affiliated with the General Federation, but more of which became part of the independent National Association of Colored Women. They modeled themselves on their white counterparts, but some black clubs took positions on issues of particular concern to blacks. Some crusaded against lynching and called for congressional legislation to make lynching a federal crime. Others protested aspects of segregation.

The women's club movement raised few overt challenges to prevailing assumptions about the proper role of women in society. But, like the limited movement of women into professions, it did represent an important effort by women to extend their influence beyond the traditional female sphere within the home and the family. The club movement allowed women to define a space for themselves in the public world without openly challenging the existing, male-dominated order.

The importance of the club movement did not, however, lie simply in what it did for middle-class women. It lay also in what those women did for the working-class people they attempted to help. The women's club movement was an important force in winning passage of state (and ultimately federal) laws that regulated the conditions of woman and child labor, that established government inspection of workplaces, that regulated the food and drug industries, and that applied new standards to urban housing. In many of these efforts, the clubwomen formed alliances with other women's groups such as the Women's Trade Union League, founded in 1903 by female union members and upper-class reformers and committed to persuading women to join unions.

Woman Suffrage

Perhaps the largest single reform movement of the progressive era, indeed one of the largest in American history, was the fight for woman suffrage—a movement that attracted support from both women and men. It was the culmination of many decades of struggle by women to obtain basic politi-

SUFFRAGISTS Suffrage activists hang posters along the boardwalk in the beachfront town of Long Branch, New Jersey. Twenty-nine states had permitted women at least some access to the ballot before ratification of the Nineteenth Amendment in 1920. New Jersey was not one of them.

cal rights. But it was also the product of forces peculiar to the early twentieth century.

It is sometimes difficult for today's Americans to understand why the
suffrage (or right-to-vote) issue could have become the source of such enormous controversy in the early twentieth century. But at the time, suffrage
seemed to many of its critics a very radical demand—in part because of the
way some of its supporters promoted it. Throughout the late nineteenth
century, many suffrage advocates presented their views in terms of "natural
rights," arguing that women deserved the same rights as men—including,
first and foremost, the right to vote. Elizabeth Cady Stanton, for example,
wrote in 1892 of woman as "the arbiter of her own destiny . . . if we are to
consider her as a citizen, as a member of a great nation, she must have the
same rights as all other members." A woman's role as "mother, wife, sister,
daughter" was "incidental" to her larger role as a part of society.

This was an argument that boldly challenged the views of many men (and
even many women) who believed that society required a distinctive female
"sphere" in which women would serve first and foremost as wives and mothers. And so a powerful antisuffrage movement emerged, which challenged this
apparent threat to the existing social order. There were antisuffrage organizations, newspapers, and political crusades. Antisuffragists associated suffrage
with divorce, promiscuity, and neglect of children. Throughout much of the
late nineteenth century, they effectively blocked most efforts by women to gain
the vote.

The suffrage movement began to overcome this opposition and to win
some substantial victories in the first years of the twentieth century. That
was in part because suffragists were becoming better organized and more
politically sophisticated than their opponents. Under the leadership of
Anna Howard Shaw, a Boston social worker, and Carrie Chapman Catt, a
journalist from Iowa, the National American Woman Suffrage Association
grew from a membership of about 13,000 in 1893 to over 2 million in
1917. The involvement of such well-known and widely admired women as
Jane Addams gave added respectability to the cause.

But the movement also gained strength because many of its most
prominent leaders began to justify suffrage in less threatening ways. Suffrage, some supporters began to argue, would not challenge the "separate
sphere" in which women resided. It would allow women to bring their special and distinct virtues more widely to bear on society's problems. It was,
they claimed, precisely because women occupied a distinct sphere—because
as mothers and wives and homemakers they had special experiences and

special sensitivities to bring to public life—that woman suffrage could make such an important contribution to politics. In particular, many suffragists argued that enfranchising women would help the temperance movement by giving its largest group of supporters a political voice. Some suffrage advocates claimed that once women had the vote, war would become a thing of the past, since women would—through their maternal instincts and their calming, peaceful influence—help curb the natural belligerence of men. That was one reason why World War I gave the final, decisive push to the movement for suffrage.

The principal triumphs of the suffrage movement began in 1910. That year, Washington became the first state in fourteen years to extend suffrage to women. California joined it a year later, and in 1912 four other western states did the same. In 1913, Illinois became the first state east of the Mississippi to embrace woman suffrage. And in 1917 and 1918, New York and Michigan—two of the biggest states in the Union—gave women the vote. By 1919, thirty-nine states had granted women the right to vote in at least some elections; fifteen had allowed them full participation. In 1920, finally, suffragists won ratification of the Nineteenth Amendment, which guaranteed political rights to women throughout the nation.

To some feminists, however, the victory seemed incomplete. Alice Paul, the head of the militant National Woman's Party (founded in 1916), never accepted the relatively conservative "separate sphere" justification for suffrage. She argued that the Nineteenth Amendment alone would not be sufficient to protect women's rights. Women needed more: a constitutional amendment that would provide clear, legal protection for their rights and would prohibit all discrimination on the basis of sex. But for many years Alice Paul's argument found limited favor even among many of the most important leaders of the recently triumphant suffrage crusade.

THE ASSAULT ON THE PARTIES

Sooner or later, most progressive goals required the involvement of government. Only government, reformers agreed, could effectively counter the powerful private interests that threatened the nation. But American government at the dawn of the new century was, progressives believed, poorly adapted to perform their ambitious tasks. Before progressives could reform society effectively, they would first have to reform government itself. In the beginning, at least, many progressives believed that such reform should start with an assault on the domination of government and politics by the political parties, which they thought had become corrupt, undemocratic, and reactionary.

Early Attacks

Attacks on party dominance had been frequent in the late nineteenth century. Greenbackism and Populism, for example, had been efforts to break the hammerlock with which the Republicans and Democrats controlled public life. The Independent Republicans (or mugwumps) had attempted to challenge the grip of partisanship, and former mugwumps became important supporters of progressive political reform activity in the 1890s and later.

The early assaults enjoyed some success. In the 1880s and 1890s, for example, most states adopted the secret ballot. Prior to that, the political parties themselves had printed ballots (or "tickets") with only the party's candidates listed, which they distributed to their supporters, who then simply went to the polls to deposit the tickets in the ballot box. The old system had made it possible for bosses to monitor the voting behavior of their constituents; it had also made it very difficult for voters to "split" their tickets—to vote for candidates of different parties for different offices. The new ballot—printed by the government and distributed at the polls, where it was filled out and deposited in secret—helped chip away at the power of the parties over the voters. (It also excluded many illiterate and non-English-speaking voters.)

By the late 1890s, critics of the parties were expanding their goals. Party rule could be broken, they believed, in one of two ways. It could be broken by increasing the power of the people, by permitting them to circumvent partisan institutions and express their will directly at the polls. Or it could be broken by placing more power in the hands of nonpartisan, nonelective officials, insulated from political life. Reformers promoted measures that moved along both those paths.

Municipal Reform

Many progressives believed the impact of party rule was most damaging in the cities. Municipal government, therefore, became the first target of those working for political reform. Muckraking journalists such as Lincoln Steffens were especially successful in arousing public outrage at corruption and incompetence in city politics.

The muckrakers struck a responsive chord among a powerful group of urban middle-class progressives, who set out to destroy the power of machines. They faced formidable opposition. In addition to challenging the powerful city bosses and their entrenched political organizations, they attacked a large group of special interests: saloon owners, brothel keepers, businessmen who had established lucrative relationships with the urban machines and viewed reform as a threat to their profits, and many influential newspapers, which ridiculed the reformers as naive do-gooders. Finally, there was the great constituency of urban working people, many of them recent immigrants, for whom the machines were a source of needed jobs and services. Gradually, however, the reformers gained in political strength, and in the first years of the twentieth century, they began to score some important victories.

An early and influential success came in Galveston, Texas, where the old city government proved completely unable to deal with the effects of a destructive tidal wave in 1900. Capitalizing on public dismay, reformers (many of them local businessmen) won approval of a new city charter that replaced the mayor and council with an elected, nonpartisan commission. In 1907, Des Moines, Iowa, adopted its own version of the commission plan, and other cities followed.

Another approach to reform, similarly motivated by the desire to remove city government from the hands of the parties, was the city-manager plan (first adopted in Staunton, Virginia, in 1908), by which elected officials hired an outside expert—often a professionally trained business manager or engineer—to take charge of the government. The city manager would presumably remain untainted by the corrupting influence of politics. By the end of the progressive era, almost 400, mostly smaller cities were operating under commissions, and another 45 employed city managers.

In other cities, reformers organized to challenge the municipal electoral process or to change the distribution of powers within the existing government. Some cities made the election of mayors nonpartisan (so that the parties could not choose the candidates) or moved them to years when no presidential or congressional races were in progress (to reduce the influence of the large turnouts that party organizations produced on such occasions). Reformers tried to make city-council members run at large so as to limit the influence of ward leaders and district bosses. They tried to strengthen the power of the mayor at the expense of the city council, on the assumption that reformers were more likely to get a sympathetic mayor elected than to win control of the entire council.

Statehouse Progressivism

Other progressives turned to state government as an agent for reform. These state-level progressives, like their municipal counterparts, considered existing state governments unfit to provide reform. They looked with particular scorn on state legislatures, whose ill-paid, relatively undistinguished members were, they believed, generally incompetent, often corrupt, and almost always controlled by party bosses. Many reformers began looking for ways to circumvent the legislatures (and the party bosses who controlled them) by increasing the power of the electorate.

Two of the most important changes were innovations first proposed by Populists in the 1890s: the initiative and the referendum. The initiative allowed reformers to circumvent state legislatures altogether by submitting new legislation directly to the voters in general elections. The referendum provided a method by which actions of the legislature could be returned to the electorate for approval. By 1918, more than twenty states had enacted one or both of these reforms.

The direct primary and the recall were, similarly, efforts to limit the power of parties and improve the quality of elected officials. The primary election was an attempt to take the selection of candidates away from the bosses and give it to the people. (In the South, it was also a device for excluding African Americans from voting.) The recall gave voters the right to remove a public official from office through a special election, which could be called after a sufficient number of citizens had signed a petition. By 1915 every state in the nation had instituted primary elections for at least some offices. The recall encountered more strenuous opposition, but some states adopted it as well.

The most celebrated state-level reformer was Robert M. La Follette of Wisconsin. Elected governor in 1900, he helped turn his state into what reformers across the nation described as a "laboratory of progressivism." The Wisconsin progressives won approval of direct primaries, initiatives, and referendums. They regulated railroads and utilities. They passed laws to regulate the workplace and provide compensation for laborers injured on the job. They taxed inherited fortunes and nearly doubled state levies on railroads and other corporate interests. Ultimately, La Follette would find himself overshadowed by other national progressive leaders. In the early years of the century, however, few men were as effective in publicizing the message of reform.

ROBERT LA FOLLETTE CAMPAIGNING IN WISCONSIN After three terms as governor of Wisconsin, La Follette began a long career in the United States Senate in 1906, during which he worked uncompromisingly for advanced progressive reforms—so uncompromisingly, in fact, that he was often almost completely isolated. He entitled a chapter of his autobiography "Alone in the Senate." La Follette had a greater impact on his own state, whose politics he and his sons dominated for nearly forty years and where he was able to win passage of many reforms that the federal government resisted.

Parties and Interest Groups

The reformers did not, of course, eliminate parties from American political life. But they did diminish the parties' centrality. Evidence of that came from, among other things, the decline in voter turnout. In the late nineteenth century, up to 81 percent of eligible voters routinely turned out for national elections. In the early twentieth century, while turnout remained very high by today's standards, the figure declined markedly. In the presidential election of 1900, 73 percent of the electorate voted. By 1912, the figure had dropped to about 59 percent. Never again did voter turnout reach as high as 70 percent.

At the same time that parties were declining, other power centers were emerging to compete with them: what have become known as "interest groups": professional organizations, trade associations representing particular businesses and industries, labor organizations, farm lobbies, and many others. Social workers, the settlement house movement, women's clubs, and others learned to operate as interest groups to advance their demands. A new pattern of politics, in which many individual interests organized to influence government directly rather than operating through party structures, was emerging. It would become the characteristic form of American politics in the twentieth century.

SOURCES OF PROGRESSIVE REFORM

Middle-class reformers, most of them from the East, dominated the public image and much of the substance of progressivism in the late nineteenth and early twentieth centuries. But they were not alone in seeking to improve social conditions. Working-class Americans, African Americans, westerners, even party bosses also played crucial roles in advancing some of the important reforms of the era.

Labor, the Machine, and Reform

Although the American Federation of Labor, and its leader Samuel Gompers, remained largely aloof from many of the reform efforts of the time (reflecting Gompers's firm belief that workers could not rely on government to improve their lot), some unions nevertheless played important roles in reform battles. In San Francisco, for example, workers in the Building Trades Council spearheaded the formation of the new Union Labor Party, committed to a program of reform almost indistinguishable from that of middle-class and elite progressives in the city. Between 1911 and 1913, in significant part because of the new party's efforts, California passed a child labor law, a workmen's compensation law, and a limitation on working hours for women. Union pressures contributed to the passage of similar laws in many other states as well.

One result of the assault on the parties was a change in the party organizations themselves, which attempted to change so as to preserve their influence. Party bosses sometimes turned their machines into vehicles of social reform. One example was New York's Tammany Hall, the nation's oldest and most notorious city machine. Its astute leader, Charles Francis Murphy, began in the early years of the century to fuse the techniques of boss rule with some of the concerns of social reformers. Tammany used its political power on behalf of legislation to improve working conditions, protect child laborers, and eliminate the worst abuses of the industrial economy.

In 1911, a terrible fire swept through the factory of the Triangle Shirtwaist Company in New York's Union Square; 146 workers, most of them women, died. Many of them had been trapped inside the burning building because management had locked the emergency exits to prevent malingering. For the next three years, a state commission studied not only the background of the fire but the general condition of the industrial workplace. It was responding to intense public pressure from women's groups and New York City labor unions—and to less-public pressure from Tammany Hall. By 1914, the commission had issued a series of reports calling for major reforms in the conditions of modern labor. When its recommendations reached the New York legislature, its most effective supporters were not middle-class progressives but two Tammany Democrats from working-class backgrounds: Senator Robert F. Wagner and Assemblyman Alfred E. Smith. With the support of Murphy and the backing of other Tammany legislators, they steered through a series of pioneering labor laws that imposed strict regulations on factory owners and established effective mechanisms for enforcement.

Western Progressives

The American West produced some of the most notable progressive leaders of the time: Hiram Johnson of California, George Norris of Nebraska, William Borah of Idaho, and others—almost all of whom spent at least some of their political careers in the United States Senate. That was because for western states, the most important target of reform energies was not state or local governments, which had relatively little power, but the federal government, which exercised a kind of authority in the West that it had never possessed in the East.

Many of the most important issues to the future of the West required action above the state level. Disputes over water, for example, almost always involved rivers and streams that crossed state lines. More significant, perhaps, the federal government exercised enormous power over the lands and resources of the western states and provided substantial subsidies to the region in the form of land grants and support for railroad and water projects. Huge areas of the West remained (and still remain) public lands, controlled by Washington—a far greater proportion than in any states east of the Mississippi; and much of the growth of the West was (and continues to be) a result of federally funded dams and water projects.

Because so much authority in the region rested in federal bureaucracies that state and local governments could not control, political parties in most of the West were relatively weak. That was one reason why western states could move so quickly and decisively to embrace reforms that parties did not like: the initiative, the referendum, the recall, direct primaries. It is also why aspiring politicians were much quicker to look to Washington as a place from which they could influence the future of their region.

African Americans and Reform

The question of race received serious attention from relatively few white progressives, except among those white southerners who believed that the construction of legalized segregation was a progressive reform. But among African Americans themselves, the progressive era produced some significant challenges to existing racial norms.

African Americans faced greater obstacles than any other group in challenging their own oppressed status and seeking reform. That was one reason why so many had embraced the message of Booker T. Washington in the late nineteenth century, to "put down your bucket where you are," to work for immediate self-improvement rather than long-range social change. By the turn of the century, however, a powerful challenge was emerging—to the philosophy of Washington and, more important, to the entire structure of race relations. The chief spokesman for this new approach was W. E. B. Du Bois, a Harvard-trained sociologist and historian with a more expansive view than Washington of the future of his race.

In *The Souls of Black Folk* (1903), Du Bois launched an open attack on Washington's "Atlanta Compromise," which had urged blacks to postpone efforts to achieve political equality and concentrate on self-improvement. Du Bois accused Washington of encouraging white efforts to impose segregation and of unnecessarily limiting the aspirations of his race. Rather than content themselves with education at the trade and

W. E. B. DU BOIS AT HIS DESK Although W. E. B. Du Bois, unlike Booker T. Washington, never developed a large popular following, he was the acknowledged leader of the black elite in the late nineteenth and early twentieth centuries. He was the first African American to earn a doctorate at Harvard University, and he published a number of distinguished works of history and sociology during his long career. He also served as editor of *The Crisis*, the newspaper of the NAACP (which he had helped to found). He died in 1963, at the age of ninety-five.

agricultural schools, Du Bois advocated, talented blacks should accept nothing less than a full university education. They should aspire to the professions. They should, above all, fight for immediate progress on civil rights, not simply wait for them to be granted as a reward for patient striving. In 1905, Du Bois and a group of his supporters met at Niagara Falls—on the Canadian side of the border because no hotel on the American side of the Falls would have them—and launched what became known as the Niagara Movement. Four years later, after a race riot in Springfield, Illinois, they joined with white progressives sympathetic to their cause to form the National Association for the Advancement of Colored People (NAACP). In the years that followed, the new organization led the drive for equal rights, using as its principal weapon lawsuits in the federal courts.

CRUSADES FOR ORDER AND REFORM

Reformers directed many of their energies at the political process. But they also crusaded on behalf of what they considered moral issues. There were campaigns to eliminate alcohol from national life, to curb prostitution, to regulate divorce. There were efforts to restrict immigration and to curb the power of monopoly in the industrial economy. There were crusades to resolve what many considered longstanding injustices, of which the most prominent was the campaign for woman suffrage. Proponents of each of those reforms believed that success would help regenerate society as a whole.

The Temperance Crusade

Many progressives considered the elimination of alcohol from American life a necessary step in restoring order to society. Workers in settlement houses and social agencies abhorred the effects of drinking on working-class families: scarce wages vanished as workers spent hours in saloons; drunkenness spawned violence, and occasionally murder, within urban families. Women, in particular, saw alcohol as a source of some of the greatest problems of working-class wives and mothers, and hoped through temperance to reform abusive or irresponsible male behavior and thus improve women's lives. Employers complained that workers often missed time on the job because of drunkenness or, worse, came to the factory intoxicated and performed their tasks sloppily and dangerously. Critics of economic privilege denounced the liquor industry as one of the nation's most sinister trusts. And political reformers, who looked on the saloon (correctly) as one of the central institutions of the machine, saw an attack on drinking as part of an attack on the bosses. Out of such varied sentiments emerged the temperance movement.

Temperance had been a major reform movement before the Civil War, mobilizing large numbers of people (and particularly large numbers of women) in a crusade with strong religious overtones. Beginning in the 1870s, it experienced a major resurgence. As in the antebellum years, it was a movement led and supported primarily by women. In 1873, temperance advocates formed the Women's Christian Temperance Union (WCTU), led after 1879 by Frances Willard. By 1911, it had 245,000 members and had become the largest single women's organization in American history to that point. In 1893, the Anti-Saloon League joined the temperance movement

D E B A T I N G T H E P A S T

Progressivism

U NTIL THE EARLY 1950S, most historians seemed to agree on the central characteristics of early-twentieth-century progressivism. It was just what many progressives themselves had said it was: a movement by the "people" to curb the power of "special interests." More specifically, it was a protest by an aroused citizenry against the excessive power of urban bosses, corporate moguls, and corrupt elected officials.

In 1951, George Mowry began the process of challenging these assumptions by examining progressives in California and describing them as a small, privileged elite of business and professional figures: people who considered themselves the natural leaders of society and who were trying to recover their fading influence from the new capitalist institutions that had displaced them. Progressivism was not, in other words, a popular, democratic movement; it was the effort of a displaced elite to restore its authority. Richard Hofstadter expanded on this idea in *The Age of Reform* (1955) by describing reformers as people afflicted by "status anxiety," fading elites suffering not from economic but from psychological discontent.

The Mowry-Hofstadter argument soon encountered a range of challenges. In 1963, Gabriel Kolko published his influential study *The Triumph of Conservatism*, in which he rejected both the older "democratic" view of progressivism and the newer "status-anxiety" view. Progressive reform, he argued, was not an effort to protect the people from the corporations; it was, rather, a vehicle through which corporate leaders used the government to protect themselves from competition.

A more moderate reinterpretation came from historians embracing what would later be called the "organizational" approach to twentieth-century American history. First Samuel Hays, in *The Response to Industrial-*

ism (1957), and then Robert Wiebe, in *The Search for Order* (1967), portrayed progressivism as a broad effort by businessmen, professionals, and other middle-class people to bring order and efficiency to political and economic life. In the new industrial society, economic power was increasingly concentrated in large, national organizations, while social and political life remained centered primarily in local communities. Progressivism, Wiebe argued, was the effort of a "new middle class"—a class tied to the emerging national economy—to stabilize and enhance its position in society by bringing those two worlds together.

In the 1970s and 1980s, scholarship on progressivism moved in so many different directions that some historians came to despair of finding any consistent meaning in the term. Much of the new scholarship focused on discovering new groups among whom "progressive" ideas and efforts flourished. Historians found evidence of progressivism in the rising movement by consumers to define their interests; in the growth of reform movements among African Americans; in the changing nature of urban political machines; and in the political activism of working people and labor organizations.

Other scholars attempted to identify progressivism with broad changes in the structure and culture of politics. Richard McCormick, writing in 1981, argued that the crucial change in the "progressive era" was the decline of political parties and the corresponding rise of interest groups working for particular social and economic goals.

At the same time, many historians have focused on the role of women (and the vast network of voluntary associations they created in shaping and promoting progressive reform). Some progressive battles, such historians as Kathryn Sklar, Ruth Rosen, Elaine Tyler May, and Linda Gordon have argued, were part of an effort by women to protect their interests within the domestic sphere in the face of jarring challenges from the new industrial world. This protective urge drew women reformers to such issues as temperance, divorce, prostitution, and the regulation of female and child labor. Other women worked to expand their own roles in the public world, particularly through their support of suffrage. The gendered interests of women reformers are, many historians insist, critical to an understanding of progressivism.

The search for the "essence" of progressivism will undoubtedly continue. But the scholarship of recent decades suggests that the real answer to the nature of progressive reform may be a recognition of its enormous diversity.

and, along with the WCTU, began to press for a specific legislative solution: the legal abolition of saloons. Gradually, that demand grew to include the complete prohibition of the sale and manufacture of alcoholic beverages.

Despite substantial opposition from immigrant and working-class voters, pressure for prohibition grew steadily through the first decades of the new century. By 1916, nineteen states had passed prohibition laws. American entry into World War I, and the moral fervor it unleashed, provided the last push to the advocates of prohibition. In 1917, with the support of rural fundamentalists who opposed alcohol on moral and religious grounds, progressive advocates of prohibition steered through Congress a constitutional amendment embodying their demands. Two years later, after ratification by every state in the nation except Connecticut and Rhode Island (with large populations of Catholic immigrants opposed to prohibition), the Eighteenth Amendment became law, to take effect in January 1920.

Immigration Restriction

Virtually all reformers agreed that the growing immigrant population had created social problems, but there was wide disagreement on how best to respond. Some progressives believed that helping the new residents adapt to American society was the proper approach. Others argued that efforts at assimilation had failed and that the only solution was to limit the flow of new arrivals.

In the first decades of the century, the arguments of this second, more pessimistic, group gradually gained strength. New scholarly theories argued that the introduction of immigrants into American society was diluting the purity of the nation's racial stock. The spurious "science" of eugenics spread the belief that human inequalities were hereditary and that immigration was contributing to the multiplication of the unfit. A special federal commission of supposed experts, chaired by Senator William P. Dillingham of Vermont, issued an elaborate report filled with statistics and scholarly testimony. It argued that the newer immigrant groups—largely southern and eastern Europeans—had proved themselves less assimilable than earlier immigrants. Immigration, the report implied, should be restricted by nationality. Even many people who rejected racial arguments supported limiting immigration as a way to solve such urban problems as overcrowding, unemployment, strained social services, and social unrest.

The combination of these concerns gradually won for the nativists the support of some of the nation's leading public figures, among them

Theodore Roosevelt. Powerful opponents—employers who saw immigration as a source of cheap labor, immigrants themselves, and the immigrants' political representatives—managed to block the restriction movement for a time. But by the beginning of World War I (which itself effectively blocked immigration temporarily), the nativist tide was clearly rising.

The Dream of Socialism

At no time in the history of the United States to that point, and in few times after it, did radical critiques of the capitalist system attract more support than in the period between 1900 and 1914. Although never a force to rival, or even seriously threaten, the two major parties, the Socialist Party of America grew during the progressive era into a force of considerable strength. In the election of 1900, it had attracted the support of fewer than 100,000 voters; in 1912, its durable leader and perennial presidential candidate, Eugene V. Debs, received nearly 1 million ballots. Strongest in urban immigrant communities (particularly among Germans and Jews), it attracted the loyalties, too, of a substantial number of Protestant farmers in the South and Midwest. Socialists won election to over 1,000 state and local offices.

Virtually all socialists agreed on the need for basic structural changes in the economy, but they differed widely on the extent of those changes and the tactics necessary to achieve them. Some endorsed the radical goals of European Marxists (a complete end to capitalism and private property); others envisioned a more moderate reform that would allow small-scale private enterprise to survive but would nationalize major industries. Militant groups within the party favored direct, even revolutionary action. Most conspicuous was the radical labor union the Industrial Workers of the World (IWW), whose members were known to their opponents as "Wobblies." Under the leadership of William ("Big Bill") Haywood, the IWW advocated a single union for all workers. The Wobblies were widely believed to have been responsible for the dynamiting of railroad lines and power stations and other acts of terror, although their use of violence was greatly exaggerated by their opponents.

More moderate socialists, who advocated peaceful change through political struggle, dominated the party. They emphasized a gradual education of the public to the need for change and patient efforts within the system to achieve it. But by the end of World War I, because the party had refused to support the war effort and because of a growing wave of anti-radicalism, socialism was in decline as a significant political force.

Decentralization and Regulation

Many reformers agreed with the socialists that the greatest threat to the nation's economy was excessive centralization of power and concentration of wealth, but they retained a faith in the possibilities of reform within a capitalist system. Rather than nationalize basic industries, they hoped to restore the economy to a more human scale. They argued that the federal government should work to break up the largest combinations and enforce a balance between the need for bigness and the need for competition. This viewpoint came to be identified particularly closely with Louis D. Brandeis, a brilliant lawyer and later a justice of the Supreme Court, who spoke and wrote widely (most notably in his 1913 book, *Other People's Money*) about the "curse of bigness."

Other progressives were less enthusiastic about the virtues of competition. More important to them was efficiency, which they believed economic concentration encouraged. Government, they argued, should not fight "bigness," but should guard against abuses of power by large institutions. It should distinguish between "good trusts" and "bad trusts," encouraging the good while disciplining the bad. Since economic consolidation was destined to remain a permanent feature of American society, continuing oversight by a strong, modernized government, led by a strong president, was essential. One of the most important spokesmen for this emerging "nationalist" position was Herbert Croly, whose 1909 book, *The Promise of American Life*, became an influential progressive document. One of those who came to endorse that position (although not fully until after 1910) was Theodore Roosevelt, who became for a time the most powerful symbol of the reform impulse at the national level.

CONCLUSION

A powerful surge of reform efforts emerged in the last years of the nineteenth century and the first years of the twentieth—reforms intended to help the United States deal with the extraordinary changes and vexing problems that the rise of the modern industrial economy had caused. American reformers at the time thought of themselves as "progressives." But neither then nor since has there ever been wide agreement on what the term "progressive" meant in those years.

The reforms themselves were of a bewildering variety—efforts to improve the moral fabric of families and communities; efforts to make politics more efficient and less corrupt; efforts to tame or discipline the great industrial combinations of the time; efforts to empower some groups and restrict or control others. The ideas that lay behind these reforms were similarly various, and the constituencies supporting them included at times representatives of almost every group in the population. "Progressivism" was a remarkably heterogeneous movement, united—if it was united at all—by the common belief among reformers that progress was indeed possible, even necessary; and that laissez-faire orthodoxy was inadequate to the needs of the nation, that purposeful human intervention in the life of society and its economy was necessary. The reform crusades gained strength steadily from the 1880s onward, driven in large part by the energy and commitment of millions of women organized in clubs and other organizations. By the early years of the twentieth century, reform was beginning to transform the character of society and the nature of American politics.

FOR FURTHER REFERENCE

Suggested Readings

Richard Hofstadter's *The Age of Reform: From Bryan to FDR* (1955) is a classic, and now controversial, analysis of the partly psychological origins of the Populist and progressive movements. Robert Wiebe, *The Search for Order, 1877–1920* (1967) is an important organizational interpretation of the era. Gabriel Kolko makes a distinctly revisionist argument that business conservatism was at the heart of the progressive movement in *The Triumph of Conservatism* (1963). Alan Dawley, *Struggles for Justice: Social Responsibility and the Liberal State* (1991) is a sophisticated and synthetic account of progressive movements and their ideas. John Milton Cooper, *The Pivotal Decades: The United States, 1900–1920* (1990) is a good narrative history of the period. Arthur S. Link and Richard L. McCormick, *Progressivism* (1983) is an interesting, brief interpretation. For powerful insights into a leading progressive thinker, see Robert Westbrook's *John Dewey and American Democracy* (1991). Nancy Cott, *The Grounding of Modern Feminism* (1987) is an excellent study of the shifting roles and beliefs of women in the late nineteenth and early twentieth centuries. The impact of female reformers on the progressive movement and the nation's political culture as a whole is the subject of Kathryn Kish Sklar's *Florence Kelley and the Nation's Work: The Rise of Women's Political Culture, 1830–1900* (1995). Paula Giddings takes up the role of black women in *When and Where I Enter: The Impact of Black Women on Race and Sex in America* (1984). Glenda Elizabeth Gilmore, *Gender and Jim Crow: Women and the Politics of White Supremacy in North Carolina, 1896–1920* (1996) is a valuable examination of the origins of segregation. Louis Harlan, *Booker T. Washington: The Making of a Black Leader* (1956); *Booker T. Washington: The Wizard of Tuskegee, 1901–1915* (1983) is an outstanding biography, as is David L. Lewis, *W. E. B. Du Bois: Biography of a Race, 1868–1919* (1993). Thomas L. Haskell, *The Emergence of Professional Social Science* (1977) is an important study of the social sciences and of professionalism. Paul Starr, *The Social Transformation of American Medicine* (1982) is a pathbreaking study of the emergence of modern American health care. Morton J. Horwitz, *The Transformation of American Law, 1870–1960: The Crisis of Legal Orthodoxy* (1992) is an important study of the way in which the legal world responded to changes in the nation's economy and politics. Richard L. McCormick, *From Realignment to Reform: Political Change in New York State, 1893–1910* (1981); George E. Mowry, *California Progressives* (1951); and David P. Thelen, *The New Citizenship: Origins of Progressivism in Wisconsin* (1972) and *Robert M. La Follette and the Insurgent Spirit* (1976) are all important state studies of reform, which offer contrasting interpretations of the progressive idea.

Films

(The best source for information on how to find these and other films is *Bowker's Complete Video Directory*—3 volumes.) *The Progressive Impulse* (1991) examines the motives of the progressive reforms at the turn of the century. *One Woman, One Vote* (1995) highlights the victories and defeats of the suffrage movement from 1848 to 1920. *Booker T. Washington—The Life and Legacy* (1982) traces the life of this black leader, emphasizing his stewardship of the Tuskegee Institute.

Internet Resources

Internet websites containing historical material relevant to the subjects discussed in this chapter can be reached through the McGraw-Hill history site at www.mhhe.com/socscience/history/usa/link/linktop.htm.

CHAPTER TWENTY-TWO

The Battle for National Reform

Theodore Roosevelt and the Progressive Presidency
The Troubled Succession ∽ *Woodrow Wilson and the New Freedom*
The "Big Stick": America and the World, 1901–1917

EFFORTS TO REFORM the industrial economy encountered repeated frustrations at the state and local levels. The great combinations were national in scope, and reformers gradually concluded that only national action could effectively control their power. Beginning early in the twentieth century, they began to look to the federal government.

But as at the state and local levels, the national government—mired in partisan politics—seemed poorly suited to serve as an agent of reform. Progressives attempted to make it more responsive to their demands. Some reformers, for example, urged an end to the system by which state legislatures elected the members of the United States Senate; they proposed instead a direct popular election, which they believed would force the Senate to react more directly to public demands. The Seventeenth Amendment, passed by Congress in 1912 and ratified by the states in 1913, provided for that change.

But even a reformed Congress, progressives believed, could not be expected to provide the kind of coherent leadership their agenda required. Congress was too clumsy, too divided, too tied to local, parochial interests. If the federal government was truly to fulfill its mission, most reformers agreed, it would require leadership from the one office capable of providing "modern," "efficient" leadership: the presidency.

657

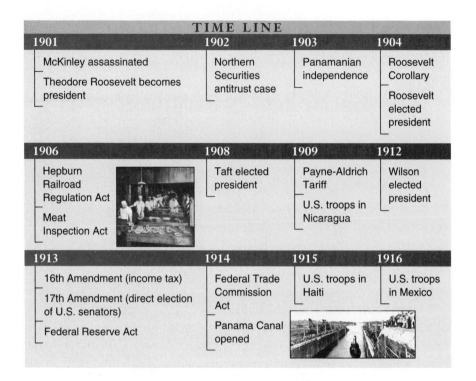

TIME LINE			
1901	**1902**	**1903**	**1904**
McKinley assassinated Theodore Roosevelt becomes president	Northern Securities antitrust case	Panamanian independence	Roosevelt Corollary Roosevelt elected president
1906	**1908**	**1909**	**1912**
Hepburn Railroad Regulation Act Meat Inspection Act	Taft elected president	Payne-Aldrich Tariff U.S. troops in Nicaragua	Wilson elected president
1913	**1914**	**1915**	**1916**
16th Amendment (income tax) 17th Amendment (direct election of U.S. senators) Federal Reserve Act	Federal Trade Commission Act Panama Canal opened	U.S. troops in Haiti	U.S. troops in Mexico

THEODORE ROOSEVELT AND THE PROGRESSIVE PRESIDENCY

To a generation of progressive reformers, Theodore Roosevelt was more than an admired public figure; he was an idol. No president before and few after attracted such attention and devotion. Yet for all his popularity among reformers, Roosevelt was in many respects decidedly conservative. He earned his extraordinary popularity less because of the extent of his reforms than because of his ebullient public personality and because he invested the presidency with something of its modern status as the center of national political life.

The Accidental President

When President William McKinley suddenly died in September 1901, the victim of an assassination, Roosevelt (who had been elected vice president less than a year before) was only forty-two years old, the youngest man ever to assume the presidency. Already, however, he had achieved a reputation within the Republican Party as something of a wild man. Mark Hanna, who had warned McKinley against selecting Roosevelt as his running mate, exclaimed, "Now look, that damned cowboy is president of the United States!" But Roosevelt as president never openly rebelled against the leaders of his party. He became, rather, a champion of cautious, moderate change.

Roosevelt envisioned the federal government not as the agent of any particular interest but as a mediator of the public good, with the president at its center. This attitude found expression in Roosevelt's policies toward the great industrial combinations. At the heart of Roosevelt's policy was his desire to win for government the power to investigate the activities of corporations and publicize the results. The pressure of educated public opinion, he believed, would alone eliminate most corporate abuses. Government could legislate solutions for those that remained.

Roosevelt engaged in a few highly publicized efforts to break up combinations, among them a 1902 suit against a great new railroad combination in the Northwest, the Northern Securities Company. But he was not a trust-buster at heart, and his occasional use of antitrust law did not mark any serious effort to reverse the prevailing trend toward economic concentration.

A similar commitment to establishing the government as an impartial regulatory mechanism shaped Roosevelt's policy toward labor. In the past, federal intervention in industrial disputes had almost always meant action on behalf of employers. Roosevelt was no champion of unions, but he was willing to consider labor's position as well. When a bitter 1902 strike by the United Mine Workers against the anthracite coal industry dragged on long enough to endanger coal supplies for the coming winter, Roosevelt asked both the operators and the miners to accept impartial federal arbitration; and he threatened to dispatch federal troops to seize the mines when the owners refused. They soon relented. Arbitrators awarded the strikers a 10 percent wage increase and a nine-hour day. On other occasions, he ordered federal troops to intervene in strikes on behalf of employers.

Reform was not Roosevelt's main priority during his first years as president. He was too concerned with winning an election in his own right, which meant not antagonizing the conservative Republican Old Guard. By early 1904, Roosevelt had all but neutralized his opposition within the party. He won its presidential nomination with ease. And in the general election, where he faced a pallid conservative Democrat, Alton B. Parker, he captured over 57 percent of the popular vote and lost no states outside the South.

The Square Deal

During the 1904 campaign, Roosevelt boasted that he had worked in the anthracite coal strike to provide everyone with a "square deal." In his second term, he set out to extend this square deal further, although some of his efforts were more symbolic than substantive. One of his first targets was the powerful railroad industry. The Interstate Commerce Act of 1887, establishing the Interstate Commerce Commission (ICC), had been an early effort to regulate the industry, but over the years the courts had sharply limited its influence. The Hepburn Railroad Regulation Act of 1906 sought to restore some regulatory authority to the government by giving the ICC authority to inspect the books of railroad companies, a relatively modest expansion of its power.

Roosevelt also pressured Congress to enact the Pure Food and Drug Act, which restricted the sale of dangerous or ineffective medicines but had very modest enforcement mechanisms. When Upton Sinclair's powerful novel *The Jungle* appeared in 1906, featuring appalling descriptions of conditions in the meatpacking industry, Roosevelt insisted on passage of the Meat Inspection Act, which ultimately helped eliminate many diseases once transmitted in impure meat. Starting in 1907, he proposed even more stringent measures: an eight-hour day for workers, broader compensation for victims of industrial accidents, inheritance and income taxes, regulation of the stock market, and others. But conservative opposition to his agenda was responsible for a widening gulf between the president and the conservative wing of his party.

Roosevelt's aggressive policies on behalf of conservation contributed to that gulf. A lifelong sportsman and naturalist, he had long been concerned about the unchecked exploitation of America's natural resources and its remaining wilderness. Using executive powers, he limited private development on millions of acres of undeveloped government land by adding them to the previously modest national forest system. When conservatives in Congress restricted his authority over public lands in 1907, Roosevelt and his chief forester, Gifford Pinchot, worked furiously before the bill became law to seize all the forests and many of the water power sites still in the public domain.

The Republican Old Guard may have opposed Roosevelt's efforts to extend government control over vast new lands. But they eagerly supported government assistance to economic development. In 1902, the president backed the Newlands Reclamation Act, which provided federal funds for the construction of dams, reservoirs, and canals in the West—projects to open new lands for cultivation and, years later, to provide cheap electric

MAKING SAUSAGES The shockingly unsanitary conditions by which meatpackers (such as those shown here in the Chicago stockyards) made sausages inspired Upton Sinclair's novel *The Jungle*, which in turn precipitated federal legislation, the Meat Inspection Act of 1906, establishing government inspection of meat products.

power. It was the beginning of many years of federal aid for irrigation and power development in the western states.

Despite the flurry of reforms Roosevelt was able to enact, the government still had relatively little control over the industrial economy. That became clear in 1907, when a serious recession began. Conservatives blamed Roosevelt's "mad" economic policies for the disaster. And while the president naturally (and correctly) disagreed, he nevertheless acted quickly to reassure business leaders that he would not interfere with their private recovery efforts.

The great financier J. P. Morgan helped construct a pool of the assets of several important New York banks to prop up shaky financial institutions. The key to the arrangement, Morgan told the president, was the purchase by U.S. Steel of the shares of the Tennessee Coal and Iron Company, currently held by a threatened New York bank. He would, he insisted, need assurances that the purchase would not prompt antitrust action. Roosevelt informally agreed, and the Morgan plan proceeded. Whether or not as a result, the panic soon subsided.

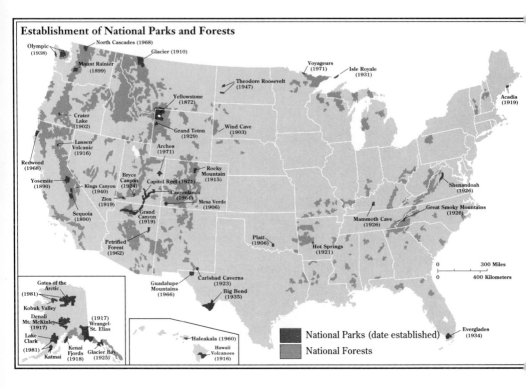

Establishment of National Parks and Forests

Roosevelt loved being president, and many people assumed he would run for the office again in 1908 despite the longstanding tradition of presidents serving no more than two terms. But the Panic of 1907 and Roosevelt's reform efforts had so alienated conservatives in his own party that he might have had difficulty winning the Republican nomination for another term despite his great popularity. In 1904, moreover, he had made a public promise to step down four years later. And so, after nearly eight energetic years in the White House, during which he had transformed the role of the presidency in American government, Theodore Roosevelt, fifty years old, retired from public life—briefly.

THE TROUBLED SUCCESSION

William Howard Taft, who assumed the presidency in 1909, had been Theodore Roosevelt's most trusted lieutenant and his hand-picked successor; progressive reformers believed him to be one of their own. But Taft had also been a restrained and moderate jurist, a man with a punctilious regard for legal process; conservatives expected him to abandon Roosevelt's aggressive use of presidential powers. By seeming acceptable to almost everyone, Taft easily won election to the White House in 1908. He received his party's nomination virtually uncontested. His victory in the general election in November—over William Jennings Bryan, running forlornly for the Democrats for the third time—was a foregone conclusion. Taft entered the White House on a wave of good feeling.

Four years later, however, Taft would leave office the most decisively defeated president of the twentieth century, his party deeply divided and the government in the hands of a Democratic administration for the first time in twenty years. Taft's failure was a result in part of his failure to match Roosevelt's personal dynamism. (Contributing to Taft's image as a less than vigorous man was his enormous weight, which at times rose to 350 pounds.) More significant, however, was that having come into office as the darling of progressives and conservatives alike, he soon found that he could not please both groups. Gradually he found himself pleasing the conservatives and alienating the progressives.

Taft and the Progressives

Taft's first problem arose in the opening months of the new administration, when he called Congress into special session to lower protective tariff rates, an old progressive demand. But the president made no effort to overcome the opposition of the congressional Old Guard, arguing that it would violate the constitutional doctrine of separation of powers if he were to intervene in legislative matters. The result was the feeble Payne-Aldrich Tariff, which reduced tariff rates scarcely at all and in some areas actually raised them. Progressives resented the president's passivity.

A sensational controversy broke out late in 1909 that helped destroy Taft's popularity with reformers for good. Many progressives had been unhappy when Taft replaced Roosevelt's secretary of the interior, James R. Garfield, an aggressive conservationist, with Richard A. Ballinger, a more conservative corporate lawyer. Suspicion of Ballinger grew when he attempted to invalidate Roosevelt's removal of nearly 1 million acres of forests and mineral reserves from the public lands available for private development.

In the midst of this mounting concern, Louis Glavis, an Interior Department investigator, charged the new secretary with having once connived to turn over valuable public coal lands in Alaska to a private syndicate for personal profit. Glavis took the evidence to Gifford Pinchot, still head of the Forest Service and a critic of Ballinger's policies. Pinchot took the charges to the president. Taft investigated them and decided they were groundless. But Pinchot was not satisfied, particularly after Taft fired Glavis for his part in the episode. He leaked the story to the press and asked Congress to investigate the scandal. The president discharged him for insubordination, and the congressional committee appointed to study the controversy, dominated by Old Guard Republicans, exonerated Ballinger. But progressives throughout the country supported Pinchot. The controversy aroused as much public passion as any dispute of its time; and when it was over, Taft had alienated the supporters of Roosevelt completely and, it seemed, irrevocably.

The Return of Roosevelt

During most of these controversies, Theodore Roosevelt was far away: on a long hunting safari in Africa and an extended tour of Europe. To the American public, however, Roosevelt remained a formidable presence. His return to New York in the spring of 1910 was a major public event. Roosevelt insisted that he had no plans to reenter politics, but within a month he announced that he would embark on a national speaking tour before the end of the summer. Furious with Taft, he was becoming convinced that he alone was capable of reuniting the Republican Party.

The real signal of Roosevelt's decision to assume leadership of Republican reformers came in a speech he gave on September 1, 1910, in Osawatomie, Kansas. In it he outlined a set of principles, which he labeled the "New Nationalism," that made clear he had moved a considerable way from the cautious conservatism of the first years of his presidency. He argued that social justice was possible only through the vigorous efforts of a strong federal government whose executive acted as the "steward of the public welfare." Those who thought primarily of property rights and personal profit "must now give way to the advocate of human welfare." He supported graduated income and inheritance taxes, workers' compensation for industrial accidents, regulation of the labor of women and children, tariff revision, and firmer regulation of corporations.

Spreading Insurgency

The congressional elections of 1910 provided further evidence of how far the progressive revolt had spread. In primary elections, conservative Republicans

ROOSEVELT AT OSAWATOMIE Roosevelt's famous speech at Osawatomie, Kansas, in 1910 was the most radical of his career and openly marked his break with the Taft administration and the Republican leadership.

suffered defeat after defeat while almost all the progressive incumbents were reelected. In the general election, the Democrats, who were now offering progressive candidates of their own, won control of the House of Representatives for the first time in sixteen years and gained strength in the Senate. Reform sentiment seemed clearly on the rise. But Roosevelt still denied any presidential ambitions and claimed that his real purpose was to pressure Taft to return to progressive policies. Two events, however, changed his mind. The first, on October 27, 1911, was the announcement by the administration of a suit against U.S. Steel, which charged, among other things, that the 1907 acquisition of the Tennessee Coal and Iron Company had been illegal. Roosevelt had approved that acquisition in the midst of the 1907 panic, and he was enraged by the implication that he had acted improperly.

Roosevelt was still reluctant to become a candidate for president, because Senator Robert La Follette, the great Wisconsin progressive, had been working since 1911 to secure the presidential nomination for himself. But La Follette's candidacy stumbled in February 1912 when, exhausted, and distraught over the illness of a daughter, he appeared to suffer a nervous breakdown during a speech in Philadelphia. Roosevelt announced his candidacy on February 22.

T. R. Versus Taft

La Follette retained some diehard support. But for all practical purposes, the campaign for the Republican nomination had now become a battle between Roosevelt, the champion of the progressives, and Taft, the candidate of the conservatives. Roosevelt scored overwhelming victories in all thirteen presidential primaries. Taft, however, remained the choice of most party leaders, who controlled the nominating process.

The battle for the nomination at the Chicago convention revolved around an unusually large number of contested delegates: 254 in all. Roosevelt needed fewer than half the disputed seats to clinch the nomination. But the Republican National Committee, controlled by the Old Guard, awarded all but 19 of them to Taft. At a rally the night before the convention opened, Roosevelt addressed 5,000 cheering supporters and announced that if the party refused to seat his delegates, he would continue his own candidacy outside the party. "We stand at Armageddon," he told the roaring crowd, "and we battle for the Lord." The next day, he led his supporters out of the convention, and out of the party. The convention then quietly nominated Taft on the first ballot.

Roosevelt summoned his supporters back to Chicago in August for another convention, this one to launch the new Progressive Party and nominate himself as its presidential candidate. Roosevelt approached the battle feeling, as he put it, "fit as a bull moose" (thus giving his new party an enduring nickname). But by then, he was aware that his cause was virtually hopeless. That was partly because many of the insurgents who had supported him during the primaries refused to follow him out of the Republican Party. It was also because of the man the Democrats had nominated for president.

WOODROW WILSON AND THE NEW FREEDOM

The 1912 presidential contest was not simply one between conservatives and reformers. It was also one between two brands of progressivism that reflected two different views of America's future. And it was one that matched the two most important national leaders of the early twentieth century in unequal contest.

Woodrow Wilson

Reform sentiment had been gaining strength within the Democratic as well as the Republican Party in the first years of the century. At the 1912 Democratic Convention in Baltimore in June, Champ Clark, the conservative Speaker of the House, was unable to assemble the two-thirds majority necessary for nomination because of progressive opposition. Finally, on the forty-sixth ballot, Woodrow Wilson, the governor of New Jersey and the only genuinely progressive candidate in the race, emerged as the party's nominee.

Wilson had risen to political prominence by an unusual path. He had been a professor of political science at Princeton until 1902, when he was named president of the university. Elected governor of New Jersey in 1910, he demonstrated a commitment to reform that he had already displayed as a university president, and during his two years in the statehouse, he earned a national reputation for winning passage of progressive legislation. As a presidential candidate in 1912, Wilson presented a progressive program that came to be called the "New Freedom." Wilson's New Freedom differed from Roosevelt's New Nationalism most clearly in its approach to economic policy and the trusts. Roosevelt believed in accepting economic concentration and using government to regulate and control it. Wilson seemed to side with those who (like Brandeis) believed that bigness was both unjust and inefficient, that the proper response to monopoly was not to regulate it but to destroy it.

The 1912 presidential campaign was something of an anticlimax. William Howard Taft, resigned to defeat, barely campaigned at all. Roosevelt campaigned energetically (until a gunshot wound from a would-be assassin forced him to the sidelines during the last weeks before the election), but he failed to draw any significant numbers of Democratic progressives away from Wilson. In November, Roosevelt and Taft split the Republican vote; Wilson held onto most Democrats and won. He polled only a plurality of the popular vote: 42 percent, compared with 27 percent for Roosevelt, 23 percent for Taft, and 6 percent for the socialist Eugene Debs. But in the electoral college, Wilson won 435 of the 531 votes. Roosevelt had carried only six states, Taft two, Debs none.

The Scholar as President

Wilson was a bold and forceful president. More than William Howard Taft, more even than Theodore Roosevelt, he concentrated the powers of

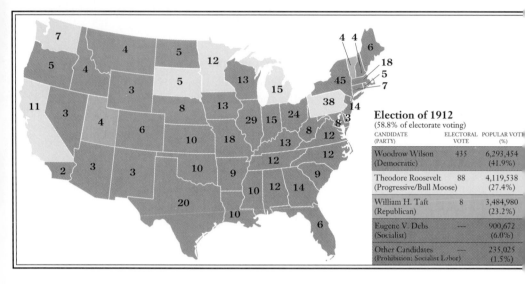

Election of 1912
(58.8% of electorate voting)

CANDIDATE (PARTY)	ELECTORAL VOTE	POPULAR VOTE (%)
Woodrow Wilson (Democratic)	435	6,293,454 (41.9%)
Theodore Roosevelt (Progressive/Bull Moose)	88	4,119,538 (27.4%)
William H. Taft (Republican)	8	3,484,980 (23.2%)
Eugene V. Debs (Socialist)	---	900,672 (6.0%)
Other Candidates (Prohibition; Socialist Labor)	---	235,025 (1.5%)

the executive branch in his own hands. He exerted firm control over his cabinet, and he delegated real authority only to those whose loyalty to him was beyond question. Perhaps the clearest indication of his style of leadership was the identity of his most powerful adviser: Colonel Edward M. House, an intelligent and ambitious Texan who held no office and whose only claim to authority was his personal intimacy with the president.

In legislative matters, Wilson skillfully used his position as party leader to weld together a coalition that would support his program. Democratic majorities in both houses of Congress made his task easier. Wilson's first triumph as president was the fulfillment of an old Democratic (and progressive) goal: a substantial lowering of the protective tariff. The Underwood-Simmons Tariff, passed in a special session of Congress that Wilson summoned shortly after his inauguration, provided cuts substantial enough, progressives believed, to introduce real competition into American markets and thus to help break the power of trusts. To make up for the loss of revenue under the new tariff, Congress approved a graduated income tax, which the recently adopted Sixteenth Amendment to the Constitution now permitted. This first modern income tax imposed a 1 percent tax on individuals and corporations earning over $4,000, with rates ranging up to 6 percent on incomes over $500,000.

Wilson held Congress in session through the summer to work on a major reform of the American banking system: the Federal Reserve Act, which Congress passed and which the president signed on December 23, 1913. It created twelve regional banks, each to be owned and controlled by the individual banks of its district. The regional Federal Reserve banks would hold a certain percentage of the assets of their member banks in reserve; they would use those reserves to support loans to private banks at an interest (or "discount") rate that the Federal Reserve system would set; they would issue a new type of paper currency—Federal Reserve notes— that would become the nation's basic medium of trade and would be backed by the government. Most important, perhaps, they would be able to shift funds quickly to troubled areas—to meet increased demands for credit or to protect imperiled banks. Supervising and regulating the entire system was a national Federal Reserve Board, whose members were appointed by the president. Nearly half the nation's banking resources were represented in the system within a year, and 80 percent by the late 1920s.

In 1914, turning to the central issue of his 1912 campaign, Wilson proposed two measures to deal with the problem of monopoly. In the process he revealed how his own approach to the issue was beginning to change. There was a proposal to create a federal agency through which the government would help business police itself—a regulatory commission of the type Roosevelt had advocated in 1912. There were also proposals to strengthen the government's ability actually to break up trusts—a decentralizing approach more characteristic of Wilson's 1912 campaign. The two measures took shape as the Federal Trade Commission Act and the Clayton Antitrust Act. The Federal Trade Commission Act created a regulatory agency that would help businesses determine in advance whether their actions would be acceptable to the government. The agency would also have authority to launch prosecutions against "unfair trade practices," which the law did not define, and it would have wide power to investigate corporate behavior. The act, in short, increased the government's regulatory authority significantly. Wilson signed it happily. But he seemed to lose interest in the Clayton Antitrust Bill and did little to protect it from conservative assaults, which greatly weakened it. The vigorous legal pursuit of monopoly that Wilson had promised in 1912 never materialized. The future, he had apparently decided, lay with government supervision.

Retreat and Advance

By the fall of 1914, Wilson believed that the program of the New Freedom was essentially complete and that agitation for reform would now subside. He refused to support the movement for national woman suffrage. Deferring to southern Democrats, and reflecting his own southern background, he condoned the reimposition of segregation in the agencies of the federal government (in contrast to Theodore Roosevelt, who had ordered the elimination of many such barriers). When congressional progressives attempted to enlist his support for new reform legislation, he dismissed their proposals as unconstitutional or unnecessary.

The congressional elections of 1914, however, shattered the president's complacency. Democrats suffered major losses in the House of Representatives, and voters who in 1912 had supported the Progressive Party began returning to the Republicans. Wilson would not be able to rely on a divided opposition when he ran for reelection in 1916. By the end of 1915, therefore, Wilson had begun to support a second flurry of reforms. In January 1916, he appointed Louis Brandeis to the Supreme Court, making him not only the first Jew but the most advanced progressive to serve there. Later, he supported a measure to make it easier for farmers to receive credit and one creating a system of workers' compensation for federal employees.

Wilson was sponsoring measures that expanded the role of the national government in important ways. In 1916, for example, Wilson supported the Keating-Owen Act, the first federal law regulating child labor. The measure prohibited the shipment of goods produced by underage children across state lines, thus giving an expanded importance to the constitutional clause assigning Congress the task of regulating interstate commerce. (It would be some years before the Supreme Court would uphold this interpretation of the clause; the Court invalidated the Keating-Owen Act in 1918.) The president similarly supported measures that used federal taxing authority as a vehicle for legislating social change. After the Court struck down Keating-Owen, a new law attempted to achieve the same goal by imposing a heavy tax on the products of child labor. (The Court later struck it down, too.) And the Smith-Lever Act of 1914 demonstrated another way in which the federal government could influence local behavior; it offered matching federal grants to states that agreed to support agricultural extension education.

THE "BIG STICK": AMERICA AND THE WORLD, 1901–1917

American foreign policy during the progressive years reflected many of the same impulses that were motivating domestic reform. But more than that, it reflected the nation's new sense of itself as a world power with far-flung economic and political interests.

Roosevelt and "Civilization"

Theodore Roosevelt was well suited, both by temperament and by ideology, for an activist foreign policy. He believed in the value and importance of using American power in the world (a conviction he once described by citing the proverb, "Speak softly, but carry a big stick"). But he had two different standards for using that power.

Roosevelt believed that an important distinction existed between the "civilized" and "uncivilized" nations of the world. "Civilized" nations, as he defined them, were predominantly white and Anglo-Saxon or Teutonic; "uncivilized" nations were generally nonwhite, Latin, or Slavic. But racism was only partly the basis of the distinction. Equally important was economic development. He believed, therefore, that Japan, a rapidly industrializing society, had earned admission to the ranks of the civilized.

Civilized nations were, by Roosevelt's definition, producers of industrial goods; uncivilized nations were suppliers of raw materials and markets. There was, he believed, an economic relationship between the two parts that was vital to both of them. A civilized society, therefore, had the right and duty to intervene in the affairs of a "backward" nation to preserve order and stability—for the sake of both nations. That belief was one important reason for Roosevelt's early support of the development of American sea power. By 1906, the American navy had attained a size and strength surpassed only by that of Great Britain (although Germany was fast gaining ground).

Protecting the "Open Door" in Asia

In 1904 the Japanese staged a surprise attack on the Russian fleet at Port Arthur in southern Manchuria, a province of China that both Russia and Japan hoped to control. Roosevelt, hoping to prevent either nation from becoming dominant there, agreed to a Japanese request to mediate an end to the conflict. Russia, faring badly in the war, had no choice but to agree. At a peace conference in Portsmouth, New Hampshire, in 1905, Roosevelt extracted from the embattled Russians a recognition of Japan's territorial gains and from the Japanese an agreement to cease the fighting and expand no further. At the same time, he negotiated a secret agreement with the Japanese to ensure that the United States could continue to trade freely in the region. Roosevelt won the Nobel Peace Prize in 1906 for his work in ending the Russo-Japanese War. But in the years that followed, relations between the United States and Japan steadily deteriorated. Having destroyed the Russian fleet at Port Arthur, Japan now emerged as the preeminent naval power in the Pacific and soon began to exclude American trade from many of the territories it controlled. Roosevelt took no direct action against Japan, but to be sure the Japanese government recognized the power of the United States, he sent sixteen battleships of the new American navy (known as the "Great White Fleet" because the ships were temporarily painted white for the voyage) on an unprecedented journey around the world that included a call on Japan—to remind the Japanese of the potential might of the United States.

The Iron-Fisted Neighbor

Roosevelt took a particular interest in events in what he (and most other Americans) considered the nation's special sphere of interest: Latin America. Unwilling to share trading rights, let alone military control, with any

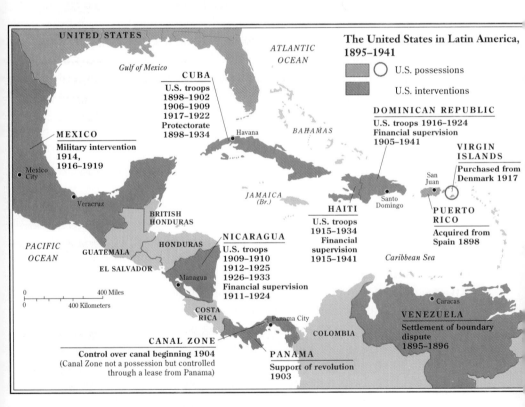

The United States in Latin America, 1895–1941

U.S. possessions

U.S. interventions

UNITED STATES

ATLANTIC OCEAN

Gulf of Mexico

CUBA
U.S. troops
1898–1902
1906–1909
1917–1922
Protectorate
1898–1934

Havana

BAHAMAS

MEXICO
Military intervention
1914,
1916–1919

Mexico City

Veracruz

DOMINICAN REPUBLIC
U.S. troops 1916–1924
Financial supervision
1905–1941

VIRGIN ISLANDS
Purchased from
Denmark 1917

San Juan

Santo Domingo

JAMAICA (Br.)

HAITI
U.S. troops
1915–1934
Financial supervision
1915–1941

PUERTO RICO
Acquired from
Spain 1898

BRITISH HONDURAS

NICARAGUA
U.S. troops
1909–1910
1912–1925
1926–1933
Financial supervision
1911–1924

HONDURAS

PACIFIC OCEAN

GUATEMALA

EL SALVADOR

Managua

Caribbean Sea

0 — 400 Miles
0 — 400 Kilometers

COSTA RICA

Panama City

Caracas

VENEZUELA
Settlement of boundary
dispute
1895–1896

COLOMBIA

CANAL ZONE
Control over canal beginning 1904
(Canal Zone not a possession but controlled
through a lease from Panama)

PANAMA
Support of revolution
1903

other nation, Roosevelt embarked on a series of ventures in the Caribbean and South America. He established a pattern of American intervention in the region that would long survive his presidency.

Crucial to Roosevelt's thinking was an incident early in his administration. In 1902, the financially troubled government of Venezuela began to renege on debts to European bankers. Naval forces of Britain, Italy, and Germany blockaded the Venezuelan coast in response. Then German ships began to bombard a Venezuelan port amid rumors that Germany planned to establish a permanent base in the region. Roosevelt used the threat of American naval power to pressure the German navy to withdraw.

The incident helped persuade Roosevelt that European intrusions into Latin America could result not only from aggression but from instability or irresponsibility (such as defaulting on debts) within the Latin American nations themselves. As a result, in 1904 he announced what came to be known as the "Roosevelt Corollary" to the Monroe Doctrine. The United States, he claimed, had the right not only to oppose European intervention in the Western Hemisphere but also to intervene itself in the domestic affairs of its neighbors if those neighbors proved unable to maintain order and national sovereignty on their own.

The immediate motivation for the Roosevelt Corollary, and the first opportunity for using it, was a crisis in the Dominican Republic. A revolution had toppled its corrupt and bankrupt government in 1903, but the new regime proved no better able than the old to make good on the country's $22 million in debts to European nations. Using the rationale provided by the Roosevelt Corollary, Roosevelt established, in effect, an American receivership, assuming control of Dominican customs and distributing 45 percent of the revenues to the Dominicans and the rest to foreign creditors. This arrangement lasted, in one form or another, for more than three decades.

In 1902, the United States granted political independence to Cuba, but only after the new government had agreed to the so-called Platt Amendment (named after Senator Thomas Platt of Pennsylvania) to its constitution. The amendment gave the United States the right to prevent any foreign power from intruding into the new nation. In 1906, when domestic uprisings seemed to threaten the internal stability of the island, American troops landed in Cuba, quelled the fighting, and remained there for three years.

The Panama Canal

The most celebrated accomplishment of Roosevelt's presidency was the construction of the Panama Canal, which linked the Atlantic and the Pacific by creating a channel through Central America. At first, Roosevelt and many others favored a route across Nicaragua, which would permit a sea-level canal requiring no locks. But they soon turned instead to the narrow Isthmus of Panama in Colombia, the site of an earlier, failed effort by a French company to construct a channel. Although the Panama route was not at sea level (and would thus require locks), it was shorter than the one in Nicaragua. And construction was already about 40 percent complete. When the French company lowered the price for its holdings from $109 million to $40 million, the United States chose Panama.

Roosevelt dispatched John Hay, his secretary of state, to negotiate an agreement with Colombian diplomats in Washington that would allow construction to begin without delay. Under heavy American pressure, the Colombian chargé d'affaires, Tomas Herrán, unwisely signed an agreement giving the United States perpetual rights to a six-mile-wide "canal zone" across Colombia; in return, the United States would pay Colombia $10 million and an annual rental of $250,000. The treaty produced outrage in the Colombian senate, which refused to ratify it. Colombia then sent a new

OPENING THE PANAMA CANAL The Panama Canal, the greatest engineering feat of the early twentieth century and one of the most notable achievements of Theodore Roosevelt's presidency, opened to shipping in 1914. This photograph shows the Tugboat *Gatun*, the first ship to travel through the canal to the Atlantic, in one of the canal's great locks.

representative to Washington with instructions to demand at least $20 million from the Americans plus a share of the payment to the French.

Roosevelt was furious and began to look for ways to circumvent the Colombian government. Philippe Bunau-Varilla, chief engineer of the French canal project, was a ready ally. In November 1903, he helped organize and finance a revolution in Panama. There had been many previous revolts, all of them failures, but this one had the support of the United States. Roosevelt landed troops from the USS *Nashville* in Panama to "maintain order." Their presence prevented Colombian forces from suppressing the rebellion, and three days later Roosevelt recognized Panama as an independent nation. The new Panamanian government quickly agreed to the terms the Colombian senate had rejected. Work on the canal proceeded rapidly, and it opened in 1914.

Taft and "Dollar Diplomacy"

Like his predecessor, William Howard Taft worked to advance the nation's economic interests overseas. But he showed little interest in Roosevelt's larger vision of world stability. Taft's secretary of state, the corporate attorney Philander C. Knox, worked aggressively to extend American investments into less-developed regions. Critics called his policies "Dollar Diplomacy."

It was particularly visible in American policy in the Caribbean. When a revolution broke out in Nicaragua in 1909, the administration quickly sided with the insurgents (who had been inspired to revolt by an American mining company) and sent American troops into the country to seize the customs houses. As soon as peace was restored, Knox encouraged American bankers to offer substantial loans to the new government, thus increasing Washington's financial leverage over the country. When the new pro-American government faced an insurrection less than two years later, Taft again landed American troops in Nicaragua, this time to protect the existing regime. The troops remained there for more than a decade.

Diplomacy and Morality

Woodrow Wilson entered the presidency with relatively little interest or experience in international affairs. Yet he faced international challenges of a scope and gravity unmatched by those of any president before him. Although the greatest test of Wilsonian diplomacy did not occur until World War I, many of the qualities that he would bring to that ordeal were evident in his foreign policy from his first moments in office, and particularly in his dealings with Latin America.

Having already seized control of the finances of the Dominican Republic in 1905, the United States established a military government there in 1916 when the Dominicans refused to accept a treaty that would have made the country a virtual American protectorate. The military occupation lasted eight years. In Haiti, which shares the island of Hispaniola with the Dominican Republic, Wilson landed the marines in 1915 to quell a revolution in the course of which a mob had murdered an unpopular president. American military forces remained in the country until 1934, and American officers drafted the new Haitian constitution adopted in 1918. When Wilson began to fear that the Danish West Indies might be about to fall into the hands of Germany, he bought the colony from Denmark and renamed it the Virgin Islands. Concerned about the possibility of European influence in Nicaragua, he signed a treaty with that country's government ensuring that no other nation would build a canal there and winning for the United States the right to intervene in Nicaragua's internal affairs to protect American interests. In all of these actions, Wilson was displaying an approach to Latin America very similar to the approaches of Roosevelt and Taft.

But Wilson's view of America's role in the Western Hemisphere (and the world) was not entirely similar to the views of his predecessors. That became clear in his dealings with Mexico. For many years, under the friendly auspices of the corrupt dictator Porfirio Díaz, American businessmen had been establishing an enormous economic presence in Mexico. In 1910, however, Díaz had been overthrown by the popular leader Francisco Madero, who promised democratic reform but who also seemed hostile to American businesses in Mexico. The United States quietly encouraged a reactionary general, Victoriano Huerta, to depose Madero early in 1913, and the Taft administration, in its last weeks in office, prepared to recognize the new Huerta regime and welcome back a receptive environment for American investments in Mexico. Before it could do so, however, the new government murdered Madero, and Woodrow Wilson took office in Washington. The new president instantly announced that he would never recognize Huerta's "government of butchers."

The conflict dragged on for years. At first, Wilson hoped that simply by refusing to recognize Huerta he could help topple the regime and bring to power the opposing Constitutionalists, led by Venustiano Carranza. But when Huerta, with the support of American business interests, established a full military dictatorship in October 1913, the president became more assertive. In April 1914, a minor naval incident provided the president with an excuse for open intervention. An officer in Huerta's army briefly arrested several American sailors from the U.S.S. *Dolphin* who had gone ashore in Tampico. The men were immediately released, but the American admiral—unsatisfied with the apology he received—demanded that the Huerta forces fire a twenty-one-gun salute to the American flag as a public display of penance. The Mexicans refused. Wilson used the trivial incident as a pretext for seizing the Mexican port of Veracruz.

Wilson had envisioned a bloodless action, but in a clash with Mexican troops in Veracruz, the Americans killed 126 of the defenders and suffered 19 casualties of their own. Now at the brink of war, Wilson began to look for a way out. His show of force, however, had helped strengthen the position of the Carranza faction, which captured Mexico City in August and forced Huerta to flee the country. At last, it seemed, the crisis might be over.

But Wilson was not yet satisfied. He reacted angrily when Carranza refused to accept American guidelines for the creation of a new government, and he briefly considered throwing his support to still another aspirant to leadership: Carranza's erstwhile lieutenant Pancho Villa, who was

PANCHO VILLA AND HIS SOLDIERS In 1913, when this photograph was taken, Pancho Villa (second from right) was still on good terms with the government of Woodrow Wilson, which viewed him as a fighter for democracy in Mexico. Three years later, Wilson declared Villa a "bandit" and sent American troops into Mexico in a futile effort to capture him.

now leading a rebel army of his own. When Villa's military position deteriorated, however, Wilson abandoned him and finally, in October 1915, granted preliminary recognition to the Carranza government. By now, however, he had created yet another crisis. Villa, angry at what he considered an American betrayal, retaliated in January 1916 by taking sixteen American mining engineers from a train in northern Mexico and shooting them. Two months later, he led his soldiers (or "bandits," as the United States called them) across the border into Columbus, New Mexico, where they killed seventeen more Americans.

With the permission of the Carranza government, Wilson ordered General John J. Pershing to lead an American expeditionary force across the Mexican border in pursuit of Villa. The American troops never found Villa, but they did engage in two ugly skirmishes with Carranza's army, in which forty Mexicans and twelve Americans died. Again, the United States and Mexico stood at the brink of war. But at the last minute, Wilson drew back. He quietly withdrew American troops from Mexico, and in March 1917, he at last granted formal recognition to the Carranza regime. By now, however, Wilson's attention was turning elsewhere—to the far greater international crisis engulfing the European continent and ultimately much of the world.

CONCLUSION

Driven by the great surge of reform energies emerging throughout the United States, American national politics in the early twentieth century itself became an important battleground for progressives. The rise of national reform was a result of many things, but two in particular.

First, many of the reform efforts that had been gaining strength outside of politics, or within states and localities, eventually discovered that success required the engagement of the federal government in their efforts. Progressives themselves increasingly turned to Washington as a potential ally in their efforts. Second, two national leaders helped transform both the image and the reality of the federal government from the inconspicuous ally of business interests it had been in the late nineteenth century into a visible and muscular vehicle of reform. Theodore Roosevelt's eight years as president transformed popular expectations of the office and launched a significant reform agenda. Woodrow Wilson, who defeated not only Roosevelt's ill-fated successor William Howard Taft in 1912, but also Roosevelt himself, running as a third-party challenger, became the most successful legislative president of the early twentieth century by winning passage of a broad and ambitious reform agenda of his own.

Roosevelt, Taft, and Wilson—despite considerable disagreements among them—also contributed to a continuation, and indeed an expansion, of America's active role in international affairs in the first years of the century, in part as an effort to abet the growth of American capitalism and in part as an attempt to impose American standards of morality and democracy on other parts of the world. Similar mixtures of ideals and self-interest would soon guide the United States into a great world war.

FOR FURTHER REFERENCE

Suggested Readings

John Milton Cooper, Jr., compares the lives and ideas of the progressive movement's leading politicians in *The Warrior and the Priest: Woodrow Wilson and Theodore Roosevelt* (1983). John Morton Blum, *The Republican Roosevelt* (1954) remains a valuable portrait of T. R. Donald E. Anderson, *William Howard Taft* (1973) is a useful study of this unhappy presidency. Arthur Link, *Woodrow Wilson and the Progressive Era, 1910–1917* (1954) is a classic general study by Wilson's most important biographer, who is also the author of *Woodrow Wilson*, 5 vols. (1947–1965). Samuel P. Hays, *The Gospel of Efficiency: The Progressive Conservation Movement, 1890–1920* (1962) makes a pioneering argument about the organizational imperatives behind the conservation movement. Howard K. Beale, *Theodore Roosevelt and the Rise of America to World Power* (1956) is a good general survey. Arthur Link, *Wilson the Diplomatist* (1957) and *Woodrow Wilson: Revolution, War, and Peace* (1979) are two overviews of Wilson's diplomacy, the second more sympathetic than the first. The effects of America's interventionist policies in Latin America are described in John Womack's arresting account of the revolution in Mexico, *Zapata and the Mexican Revolution* (1968).

Films

(The best source for information on how to find these and other films is *Bowker's Complete Video Directory*—3 volumes.) *The Indomitable Teddy Roosevelt* (1986) and *TR and His Times* (1985) are two biographical films about this dynamic president, historian, and outdoorsman. *The Battle for Wilderness* (1990) is an account of the conservation movement and two of its leaders, Gifford Pinchot and John Muir.

Internet Resources

Internet websites containing historical material relevant to the subjects discussed in this chapter can be reached through the McGraw-Hill history site at www.mhhe.com/socscience/history/usa/link/linktop.htm.

CHAPTER TWENTY-THREE

America and the Great War

T HE GREAT WAR, as it was known to a generation unaware that another, greater war would soon follow, began quietly in August 1914
when Austria-Hungary invaded the tiny Balkan nation of Serbia. Within
weeks, however, it had grown into a conflagration engaging the armies of
most of the major nations of Europe and shattering forever the delicate balance of power that had maintained a general peace on the Continent since
the early nineteenth century. Americans looked on with horror as the war became the most savage in history and as it dragged on, murderously and inconclusively, for two and a half years. But Americans also believed at first that
the conflict had little to do with them. They were wrong. After nearly three
years of attempting to affect the outcome of the conflict without becoming
embroiled in it, the United States formally entered the war in April 1917.

THE ROAD TO WAR

By 1914, the European nations had created an unusually precarious international system. It careened into war very quickly on the basis of what
most historians agree was a minor series of provocations.

The Collapse of the European Peace

The major powers of Europe were organized by 1914 in two great, competing alliances. The "Triple Entente," which during the war became

TIME LINE

1914	1915	1916	1917
World War I begins	*Lusitania* torpedoed	Wilson reelected	German unrestricted submarine warfare
	Wilson supports preparedness		U.S. enters World War I
			Selective Service Act
			War Industries Board created

1918	1919	1920	1927
Sedition Act	Senate rejects Treaty of Versailles	19th Amendment ratified	Sacco and Vanzetti executed
Wilson's Fourteen Points	Race riots in Chicago and other cities	Palmer Raids and Red Scare	
Armistice ends war		Harding elected president	
Paris Peace Conference	Steel strike and other labor actions		

known as the "Allies," linked Britain, France, and Russia. The "Triple Alliance," later called the "Central Powers," united Germany, the Austro-Hungarian Empire, and Italy. The chief rivalry, however, was not between the two alliances but between the great powers that dominated them: Great Britain and Germany.

The Anglo-German rivalry may have been the most important underlying source of the tensions that led to World War I, but it was not the immediate cause of its outbreak. The conflict emerged most directly out of a controversy involving nationalist movements within the Austro-Hungarian Empire. On June 28, 1914, the Archduke Franz Ferdinand, heir to the throne of the tottering empire, was assassinated while paying a state visit to Sarajevo. Sarajevo is the capital of Bosnia, then a province of Austria-Hungary, which Slavic nationalists wished to annex to neighboring Serbia; the archduke's assassin was a Serbian nationalist.

This local controversy quickly escalated through the workings of the system of alliances that the great powers had constructed. Germany supported Austria-Hungary's decision to launch a punitive assault on Serbia. The Serbians called on Russia to help with their defense. The Russians began mobilizing their army on July 30. Things quickly careened out of control. By August 3, Germany had declared war on both Russia and France and had invaded Belgium in preparation for a thrust across the French border. On August 4, Great Britain—ostensibly to honor its alliance with France, but more importantly to blunt the advance of its principal rival—declared war on Germany. Russia and the Austro-Hungarian Empire formally began hostilities on August 6. Within months, Italy, the Ottoman Empire (Turkey), and other, smaller nations all joined the fighting. By early 1915, virtually the entire European continent (and part of Asia) was embroiled in a major war.

Wilson's Neutrality

Wilson called on his fellow citizens in 1914 to remain "impartial in thought as well as deed." But that was impossible, for several reasons. For one thing, many Americans were not, in fact, genuinely impartial. Some sympathized with the German cause (German Americans, because of affection for Germany; Irish Americans, because of hatred of Britain). Many more (including Wilson himself) sympathized with Britain. Lurid reports of German atrocities in Belgium and France, skillfully exaggerated by British propagandists, strengthened the hostility of many Americans toward Germany.

Economic realities also made it impossible for the United States to deal with the belligerents on equal terms. The British had imposed a naval blockade on Germany to prevent munitions and supplies from reaching the enemy. As a neutral, the United States had the right, in theory, to trade with Germany. A truly neutral response to the blockade would be either to defy it or to stop trading with Britain as well. But while the United States could survive an interruption of its relatively modest trade with Germany and its allies, it could not easily weather an embargo on its much more extensive trade with Britain and France, particularly when war orders from them soared after 1914, helping produce a great economic boom in America. So America tacitly accepted the blockade of Germany and continued trading with Britain. By 1915, the United States had gradually transformed itself from a neutral power into the arsenal of the Allies.

The Germans, in the meantime, were resorting to a new and, in American eyes, barbaric tactic: submarine warfare. Unable to challenge

British domination on the ocean's surface, Germany began early in 1915 to use the newly improved submarine to try to stem the flow of supplies to England. Enemy vessels, the Germans announced, would be sunk on sight. Months later, on May 7, 1915, a German submarine sank the British passenger liner *Lusitania* without warning, causing the deaths of 1,198 people, 128 of them Americans. The ship was, it later became clear, carrying not only passengers but munitions; but most Americans considered the attack an unprovoked act on civilians.

Wilson angrily demanded that Germany promise not to repeat such outrages, and the Germans finally agreed to his demands. But early in 1916, in response to an announcement that the Allies were now arming merchant ships to sink submarines, Germany proclaimed that it would fire on such vessels without warning. A few weeks later, it attacked the unarmed French steamer *Sussex*, injuring several American passengers. Again, Wilson demanded that Germany abandon its "unlawful" tactics; again, the German government relented.

Preparedness Versus Pacifism

Despite the president's increasing bellicosity in 1916, he was still far from ready to commit the United States to war. One obstacle was American domestic politics. Facing a difficult battle for reelection, Wilson could not ignore the powerful factions that continued to oppose intervention.

The question of whether America should make military and economic preparations for war provided a preliminary issue over which pacifists and interventionists could debate. Wilson at first sided with the antipreparedness forces, denouncing the idea of an American military buildup as needless and provocative. As tensions between the United States and Germany grew, however, he changed his mind. In the fall of 1915, he endorsed an ambitious proposal by American military leaders for a large and rapid increase in the nation's armed forces. By midsummer 1916, armament for a possible conflict was well under way.

Still, the peace faction wielded considerable political strength, as became clear at the Democratic Convention in the summer of 1916. The convention became almost hysterically enthusiastic when the keynote speaker punctuated his list of the president's diplomatic achievements with the chant, "What did we do? What did we do? . . . We didn't go to war! We didn't go to war!" That speech helped produce one of the most prominent slogans of Wilson's reelection campaign: "He kept us out of war." During the campaign, Wilson did nothing to discourage those who argued that the Republican candidate, the progressive New York governor Charles Evans Hughes, was more likely than he to lead the nation into war. Wilson ultimately won reelection by fewer than 600,000 popular votes and only 23 electoral votes. The Democrats retained a precarious control over Congress.

A War for Democracy

The election was behind him. Tensions between the United States and Germany remained high. But Wilson still required a justification for American intervention that would unite public opinion and satisfy his own sense of morality. In the end, he created that rationale himself. The United States, Wilson insisted, had no material aims in the conflict. The nation was, rather, committed to using the war as a vehicle for constructing a new world order, one based on the same progressive ideals that had motivated a generation of reform efforts in America. In a speech before a joint session of Congress in January 1917, he presented a plan for a post-war order in which the United States would help maintain peace through a permanent league of nations—a "peace without victory." These were, Wilson believed, goals worth fighting for if there was sufficient provocation. That provocation came quickly.

In January, the military leaders of Germany decided on one last dramatic gamble to achieve victory: a series of major assaults on the enemy's lines in France. At the same time, they would begin unrestricted submarine warfare (against American as well as Allied ships) to cut Britain off from vital supplies. Then, on February 25, the British gave Wilson an intercepted telegram sent by the German foreign minister, Arthur Zimmermann, to the government of Mexico. It proposed that in the event of war between Germany and the United States, the Mexicans should join with Germany against the Americans. In return, they would regain their "lost provinces" in the north (Texas and much of the rest of the American Southwest) when the war was over. Widely publicized by British propagandists and in the American press, the Zimmermann telegram inflamed public opinion and helped build up popular sentiment for war. Wilson drew additional comfort from another event, in March 1917. A revolution in Russia toppled the reactionary

MARCHING FOR VICTORY One of the great tasks facing the United States government as it entered World War I in 1917 was to generate popular support for a war that most Americans had been reluctant to enter. The effort to do so produced some alarming violations of civil liberties. It also encouraged an enormous number of parades, rallies, and other popular demonstrations of support for the war. Here, President Wilson marches in a Red Cross parade in Washington shortly after the declaration of war.

czarist regime and replaced it with a new, republican government. The United States would now be spared the embarrassment of allying itself with a despotic monarchy.

On the rainy evening of April 2, two weeks after German submarines had torpedoed three American ships, Wilson appeared before a joint session of Congress and asked for a declaration of war. Even then, opposition remained. For four days, pacifists in Congress carried on their futile struggle. When the declaration of war finally passed on April 6, fifty representatives and six senators had voted against it.

"WAR WITHOUT STINT"

Armies on both sides in Europe were decimated and exhausted by the time of Woodrow Wilson's declaration of war. The Allies looked desperately to the United States for help in breaking the stalemate.

The Military Struggle

American intervention had its most immediate effect on the conflict at sea. By the spring of 1917, Great Britain was suffering such vast losses from attacks by German submarines—one of every four ships setting sail from British ports never returned—that its ability to continue receiving vital supplies from across the Atlantic was in jeopardy. Within weeks of joining the war the United States had begun to alter the balance. A fleet of American destroyers aided the British navy in its assault on the U-boats. Other American warships escorted merchant vessels across the Atlantic. Americans also helped plant antisubmarine mines in the North Sea. The results were dramatic. Sinkings of Allied ships had totaled nearly 900,000 tons in the month of April 1917; by December, the figure had dropped to 350,000; by October 1918, it had declined to 112,000.

Many Americans had hoped that providing naval assistance alone would be enough to turn the tide in the war, but it quickly became clear that a major commitment of American ground forces would be necessary as well to shore up the tottering Allies. Britain and France had few remaining reserves. By early 1918, Russia had withdrawn from the war altogether. After the Bolshevik Revolution in November 1917, a new communist government, led by V. I. Lenin, negotiated a hasty and costly peace with the Central Powers, thus freeing German troops to fight on the western front.

But the United States did not have a large enough standing army to provide the necessary ground forces in 1917. The president decided that only a national draft could provide the needed men. Despite protests, he won passage of the Selective Service Act in mid-May. The draft brought nearly 3 million men into the army; another 2 million joined various branches of the armed services voluntarily.

The engagement of these forces in combat was brief but intense. Not until the spring of 1918 were significant numbers of American troops available for battle. Eight months later, the war was over. Under the command of General John J. Pershing, the American troops joined the existing Allied

LONGPORT, FRANCE, 1918 American soldiers lead German prisoners of war through the streets of a French town shortly before the end of World War I. The devastation was typical of many areas of France where heavy fighting occurred.

forces in turning back a series of new German assaults. In early June, they assisted the French in repelling a bitter German offensive at Château-Thierry, near Paris. Six weeks later, the American Expeditionary Force (AEF) helped turn away another assault, at Rheims, farther south. By July 18, the German advance had been halted, and the Allies were beginning a successful offensive of their own. On September 26, an American fighting force of over 1 million soldiers advanced against the Germans in the Argonne Forest as part of a 200-mile attack that lasted nearly seven weeks. By the end of October, the force had helped push the Germans back toward their own border and had cut the enemy's major supply lines to the front.

Faced with an invasion of their own country, German military leaders now began to seek an armistice—an immediate cease-fire that would, they hoped, serve as a prelude to negotiations among the belligerents. Pershing wanted to drive on into Germany itself; but other Allied leaders, after first insisting on terms that made the agreement (in their eyes at least) little different from a surrender, accepted the German proposal. On November 11, 1918, more than four years after it began, the Great War shuddered to a close.

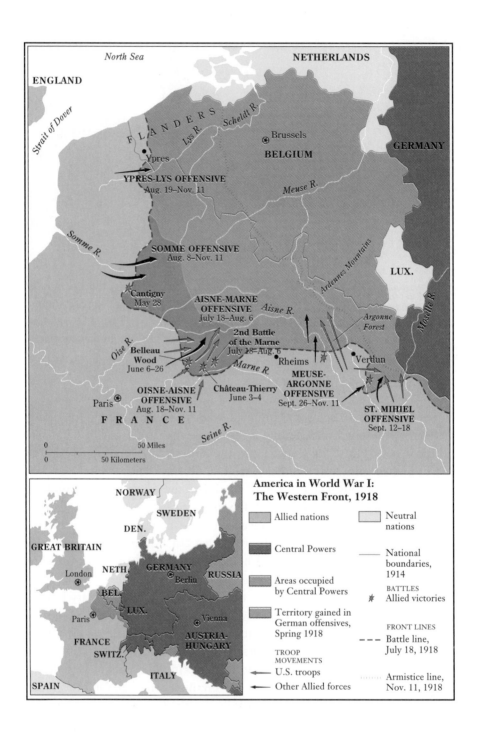

North Sea

NETHERLANDS

ENGLAND

F L A N D E R S

Lys R.

Scheldt R.

Brussels

BELGIUM

GERMANY

Strait of Dover

Ypres

YPRES-LYS OFFENSIVE
Aug. 19–Nov. 11

Meuse R.

Somme R.

SOMME OFFENSIVE
Aug. 8–Nov. 11

Ardennes Mountains

LUX.

Cantigny
May 28

AISNE-MARNE
OFFENSIVE
July 18–Aug. 6

Aisne R.

Argonne
Forest

Moselle R.

Oise R.

Belleau
Wood
June 6–26

2nd Battle
of the Marne
July 18–Aug. 6

Rheims

Marne R.

Verdun

OISNE-AISNE
OFFENSIVE
Aug. 18–Nov. 11

Château-Thierry
June 3–4

MEUSE-
ARGONNE
OFFENSIVE
Sept. 26–Nov. 11

ST. MIHIEL
OFFENSIVE
Sept. 12–18

Paris

F R A N C E

Seine R.

0   50 Miles

0   50 Kilometers

America in World War I:
The Western Front, 1918

NORWAY

SWEDEN

DEN.

GREAT BRITAIN

London

NETH.

GERMANY
Berlin

RUSSIA

BEL.

LUX.

Paris

Vienna

FRANCE

AUSTRIA-
HUNGARY

SWITZ.

ITALY

SPAIN

Allied nations

Central Powers

Areas occupied
by Central Powers

Territory gained in
German offensives,
Spring 1918

TROOP
MOVEMENTS

← U.S. troops

← Other Allied forces

Neutral
nations

National
boundaries,
1914

BATTLES
✳ Allied victories

FRONT LINES

– – – Battle line,
July 18, 1918

⋯⋯⋯ Armistice line,
Nov. 11, 1918

688

The New Technology of Warfare

World War I was a proving ground for a range of military and other technologies that came into use on a large scale for the first time during the fighting in France. The trench warfare that characterized the conflict was necessary because of the enormous destructive power of newly improved machine guns and higher-powered artillery. It was no longer feasible to send troops out into an open field, or even to allow them to camp in the open. The new weaponry would slaughter them in an instant. Trenches sheltered troops while allowing limited, and usually inconclusive, fighting. But technology overtook the trenches, too, as mobile weapons—tanks and flamethrowers—proved capable of piercing entrenched positions. Most terrible of all, perhaps, new chemical weapons—poisonous mustard gas, which required troops to carry gas masks at all times—made it possible to attack entrenched soldiers without direct combat.

The new forms of technological warfare required elaborate maintenance. Faster machine guns required more ammunition. Motorized vehicles required fuel and spare parts and mechanics capable of servicing them. The logistical difficulties of supplying so many supplies became a major factor in planning tactics and strategy. Once supplies were unloaded and stored, the process of repacking and moving them forward when troops broke through lines and advanced forward, was hopelessly time-consuming. Late in the war, when Allied armies were advancing toward Germany, they frequently had to stop for days at a time to wait for their equipment to catch up with them.

World War I was the first conflict in which airplanes played a significant role. The planes themselves were relatively simple and not very maneuverable; but anti-aircraft technology was not yet highly developed either, so their effectiveness was still considerable. Planes began to be constructed to serve various functions: bombers, fighters (planes that would engage in "dogfights" with other planes), and reconaissance aircraft.

The most "modern" part of the military during World War I was the navy. New battleships emerged—of which the British *Dreadnought* was perhaps the most visible example—that made use of new technologies such as turbine propulsion, hydraulic gun controls, electric light and power, wireless telegraphy, and advanced navigational aids. Submarines, which had made a brief appearance in the American Civil War, now became significant weapons (as the German U-boat campaign in 1915 and 1916 made clear). The new submarines were driven by diesel engines, which had the advantage of being more compact than a steam engine and

WARTIME TECHNOLOGY An American soldier mans one of the newly improved machine guns that became a staple of World War I combat, in a sandbagged bunker near the front in France.

whose fuel was less explosive than that of a gasoline engine. The diesel engine also had a much greater range than ships powered by other fuels.

The new technologies were to a large degree responsible for the most stunning and horrible characteristic of World War I—its appalling level of casualties. A million men representing the British Empire (Britain, Canada, Australia, India, and others) died. France lost 1.7 million men; Germany 2 million; the former Austro-Hungarian Empire 1.5 million; Italy 460,000; and Russia 1.7 million. The number of Turkish dead, which was surely large, was never counted. In Britain, one third of the men born between 1892 and 1895 died in the war. Similarly terrible percentages could be calculated for other warring nations. The United States, which entered the war near its end and became engaged only in the last successful offensives, suffered very light casualties in contrast—112,000 dead, half of them victims of influenza, not battle. But the American casualties were very high in the battles in which U.S. troops were centrally involved. One of the reasons that World War I became so reviled in the 1920s and 1930s, even by the victors, was that the enormous number of deaths—and the terrible grief those deaths created—afflicted all of Europe. But that did not stop the development of new and deadlier military technologies that, a generation later, would make World War II the source of even more terrible carnage.

Organizing the Economy for War

By the time the war ended, the federal government had appropriated $32 billion for expenses directly related to the conflict—a staggering sum at the time. The entire federal budget had seldom exceeded $1 billion before 1915, and the nation's entire gross national product had been only $35 billion as recently as 1910. To raise the money, the government relied on two

WOMEN WORKERS DURING WORLD WAR I With much of the male work force fighting overseas, women moved into occupations that in other times would have been considered unsuitable for them. One such occupation, pictured here, was delivering huge blocks of ice daily to households to be used (in this age before electric refrigeration) in wooden iceboxes.

devices. First, it launched a major drive to solicit loans from the American people by selling "Liberty Bonds" to the public. By 1920, the sale of bonds, accompanied by elaborate patriotic appeals, had produced $23 billion. At the same time, new taxes were bringing in an additional sum of nearly $10 billion—some from levies on the "excess profits" of corporations, much from new, steeply graduated income and inheritance taxes that ultimately rose as high as 70 percent in some brackets.

An even greater challenge was organizing the economy to meet war needs. In 1916, Wilson established the Council of National Defense, composed of members of his cabinet, and the Civilian Advisory Commission, which set up local defense councils in every state and locality. Economic mobilization, according to this first plan, was to rest on a large-scale dispersal of power to local communities.

But this early administrative structure soon proved completely unworkable, and members of the Council of National Defense urged a more centralized approach. Instead of dividing the economy geographically, they proposed dividing it functionally by organizing a series of planning bodies, each to supervise a specific sector of the economy. Thus one agency would control transportation, another agriculture, another manufacturing. The administrative structure that slowly emerged from such proposals was dominated by a series of "war boards," one to oversee the railroads (led by Secretary of the Treasury William McAdoo), one to supervise fuel supplies (largely coal), another to handle food (a board that helped elevate to prominence the brilliant young engineer and business executive Herbert Hoover). The boards were not without weaknesses, but they generally succeeded in meeting essential war needs without paralyzing the domestic economy.

At the center of the effort to rationalize the economy was the War Industries Board (WIB), an agency created in July 1917 to coordinate government purchases of military supplies. Casually organized at first, it stumbled badly until March 1918, when Wilson restructured it and placed it under the control of the Wall Street financier Bernard Baruch. From then on, the board wielded powers greater (in theory at least) than any government agency had ever possessed. Baruch decided which factories would convert to the production of which war materials, and he set prices for the goods they produced. When materials were scarce, Baruch decided to whom they should go. When corporations were competing for government contracts, he chose among them.

Many Americans saw the WIB as a model for rational organization of the economy. But the agency's reputation for efficiency was something of a myth. It was, in fact, plagued by mismanagement and inefficiency and was less responsible for the nation's ability to meet its war needs than was the sheer extent of American resources and productive capacities. Nor was the WIB in any real sense an example of state control of the economy. Baruch viewed himself, openly and explicitly, as a partner of business; and within the WIB, businessmen themselves—the so-called dollar-a-year men, who took paid leave from their corporate jobs and worked for the government for a token salary—supervised the affairs of the private economy.

This link between the public and the private sectors extended, although in very different form, to labor. The National War Labor Board, established in April 1918, served as the final mediator of labor disputes. It pressured industry to grant important concessions to workers: an eight-hour day, the maintenance of minimal living standards, equal pay for women doing equal work, recognition of the right of unions to organize and bargain collectively. In return, it insisted that workers forgo strikes and that employers not engage in lockouts. Membership in labor unions increased by more than 1.5 million between 1917 and 1919.

The Search for Social Unity

Government leaders were painfully aware that public sentiment about American involvement in the war had been divided before April 1917 and remained so even after the declaration of war. Many believed that a crucial prerequisite for victory was uniting public opinion behind the war effort. The government approached that task in several ways.

The most conspicuous of its efforts was a vast propaganda campaign aimed at drumming up enthusiasm for the conflict. It was orchestrated by the Committee on Public Information (CPI), under the direction of the Denver journalist George Creel. The CPI supervised the distribution of over 75 million pieces of printed material and controlled much of the information available for newspapers and magazines. Creel encouraged journalists to exercise "self-censorship" when reporting war news, and most journalists—fearful of more coercive measures—complied by covering the war largely as the government wished. The CPI attempted at first to distribute only the "facts," believing that the truth would speak for itself. By 1918, however, government-distributed posters and films were offering lurid (and exaggerated) portrayals of the savagery of the Germans.

The government also soon began efforts to suppress dissent. CPI-financed advertisements in magazines implored citizens to report to the authorities any evidence among their neighbors of disloyalty, pessimism, or yearning for peace. The Espionage Act of 1917 gave the government new tools with which to combat spying, sabotage, or obstruction of the war effort (crimes that were often broadly defined). More repressive were two measures of 1918: the Sabotage Act of April 20 and the Sedition Act of May 16. These bills expanded the meaning of the Espionage Act to make illegal any public expression of opposition to the war; in practice, they allowed officials to prosecute anyone who criticized the president or the government.

The most frequent targets of the new legislation (and one of the reasons for its enactment in the first place) were anticapitalist groups such as the Socialist Party and the Industrial Workers of the World (IWW). Unlike their counterparts in Europe, American socialists had not dropped their opposition to the war after their country had decided to join it. Many Americans had favored the repression of socialists and radicals even before the war; the wartime policies now made it possible to move against them with full legal sanction. Eugene V. Debs, the humane leader of the Socialist Party and an opponent of the war, was sentenced to ten years in prison in 1918. (A pardon by President Warren G. Harding ultimately won his release in 1921.) Big Bill Haywood and members of the IWW were especially energetically prosecuted. Only by fleeing to the Soviet Union did Haywood avoid a long imprisonment. In all, more than 11,500 people were arrested in 1918 for the crime of criticizing the government or the war.

State and local governments, corporations, universities, and private citizens contributed as well to the climate of repression. Vigilante mobs sprang up to "discipline" those who dared challenge the war. A cluster of citizens' groups emerged to mobilize "respectable" members of their communities to root out disloyalty. The greatest target of abuse was the German-American community. Its members had unwittingly contributed to their plight. In the first years of the war in Europe, some had openly advocated American assistance to the Central Powers, and many had opposed United States intervention on behalf of the Allies. But while most German Americans supported the American war effort once it began, public opinion turned bitterly hostile. A campaign to purge society of all things German quickly gathered speed, at times assuming ludicrous forms. Performances of German music were frequently banned. German books were removed from the shelves of libraries. Courses in the German language were dropped from school curricula. Germans were routinely fired from jobs in war industries, lest they "sabotage" important tasks. Some were fired from positions entirely unrelated to the war, among them Karl Muck, the German-born conductor of the Boston

Symphony Orchestra. Many Americans came to agree with the belief of the eminent psychologist G. Stanley Hall that "there is something fundamentally wrong with the Teutonic soul."

THE SEARCH FOR A NEW WORLD ORDER

Woodrow Wilson had led the nation into war promising a just and stable peace at its conclusion. Even before the armistice, he was preparing to lead the fight for what he considered a democratic postwar settlement—for a set of war aims resting on a vision of a new world order that became known as Wilsonian internationalism.

The Fourteen Points

On January 8, 1918, Wilson appeared before Congress to present the principles for which he claimed the nation was fighting. He grouped the war aims under fourteen headings, widely known as the Fourteen Points. They fell into three broad categories. First, Wilson's proposals contained a series of eight specific recommendations for adjusting postwar boundaries and for establishing new nations to replace the defunct Austro-Hungarian and Ottoman Empires. Those recommendations reflected his belief in the right of all peoples to self-determination. Second, there was a set of five general principles to govern international conduct in the future: freedom of the seas, open covenants instead of secret treaties, reductions in armaments, free trade, and impartial mediation of colonial claims. Finally, there was a proposal for a "League of Nations" that would help implement these new principles and territorial adjustments and resolve future controversies.

There were serious flaws in Wilson's proposals. For example, he provided no formula for deciding how to implement the "national self-determination" he promised for subjugated peoples. Nevertheless, Wilson's international vision quickly came to enchant not only much of his own generation (in both America and Europe) but members of generations to come. It reflected his belief, strongly rooted in the ideas of progressivism, that the world was as capable of just and efficient government as were individual nations—that once the international community accepted certain basic principles of conduct, and once it constructed modern institutions to implement them, the human race could live in peace.

Despite Wilson's confidence, there were ominous signs both at home and abroad that his path might be more difficult than he expected.

In Europe, leaders of the Allied powers were preparing to resist him even before the armistice was signed. Britain and France in particular, having suffered terrible losses and having developed great bitterness toward Germany as a result, were in no mood for a benign and generous peace. David Lloyd George, the British prime minister, had campaigned for reelection in 1918 by calling for the execution of Kaiser Wilhelm II.

At the same time, Wilson was encountering problems at home. In 1918, with the war almost over, Wilson unwisely appealed to the American voters to support his peace plans by electing Democrats to Congress in the November elections. Days later, the Republicans captured majorities in both houses. Domestic economic troubles, more than international issues, had been the most important factor in the voting; but because of the president's ill-timed appeal, the results damaged his ability to claim broad popular support for his peace plans.

The leaders of the Republican Party, in the meantime, were developing their own reasons for opposing Wilson. Many were angry that he had tried to make the 1918 balloting a referendum on his war aims, especially since many Republicans had been supporting the Fourteen Points. Wilson further antagonized them when he refused to appoint any important Republicans to the negotiating team that would represent the United States at the peace conference in Paris.

The Paris Peace Conference

Wilson arrived in Europe to a welcome such as few men in history have experienced. To the war-weary people of the Continent, he was nothing less than a savior, the man who would create a new and better world. When he entered Paris on December 13, 1918, he was greeted, some claimed, by the largest crowd in the history of France. The conference itself, however, proved less satisfying.

The principal figures in the negotiations were the leaders of the victorious Allied nations: David Lloyd George, the prime minister of Great Britain; Georges Clemenceau, the president of France; Vittorio Orlando, the prime minister of Italy; and Wilson, who hoped to dominate them all.

From the beginning, the atmosphere of idealism Wilson had sought to create competed with a spirit of national self-interest. There was also a pervasive sense of unease about the unstable situation in eastern Europe and the threat of communism. Russia, whose new Bolshevik government was still fighting "White" counterrevolutionaries, was unrepresented in Paris; but the radical threat it seemed to pose to Western governments was never far from the minds of the delegates. Wilson himself had sent American troops into Russia in 1918, allegedly to protect Czech forces trapped there. Many believed it was really to support the anti-Bolshevik forces in the civil war.

In this tense and often vindictive atmosphere, Wilson was unable to win approval of many of the broad principles he had espoused. He was also unable to prevent the other allies from imposing high reparations on the defeated Central Powers. Wilson did manage to win some important victories in Paris in setting boundaries and dealing with former colonies. But his most visible triumph, and the one of most importance to him, was the creation of a permanent international organization to oversee world affairs and prevent future wars. On January 25, 1919, the Allies voted to accept the "covenant" of the League of Nations. With that, Wilson believed, the peace treaty was transformed into a success.

The Ratification Battle

Wilson presented the Treaty of Versailles (which took its name from the former royal palace outside Paris where the final negotiating sessions had taken place) to the Senate on July 10, 1919. But members of the Senate had many objections to the treaty. Some—the so-called irreconcilables, many of them Western isolationists—opposed the agreement in principle. But many other opponents, with less fervent convictions, were principally concerned with constructing a winning issue for the Republicans in 1920. Most notable of these was Senator Henry Cabot Lodge of Massachusetts, the powerful chairman of the Foreign Relations Committee, who loathed the president. ("I never thought I could hate a man as I hate Wilson," Lodge once said.) He used every possible tactic to obstruct, delay, and amend the treaty.

Public sentiment clearly favored ratification, so at first Lodge could do little more than play for time. Gradually, however, Lodge's general opposition to the treaty crystallized into a series of "reservations"—amendments to the League covenant further limiting American obligations to the organization. Wilson might still have won approval at this point if he had agreed to some relatively minor changes in the language of the treaty. But the president refused to yield. When he realized the Senate would not budge, he decided to appeal to the public.

He embarked on a grueling, cross-country speaking tour to arouse public support for the treaty. For more than three weeks, he traveled over 8,000 miles by train, speaking as often as four times a day, resting hardly at all. Finally, he reached the end of his strength. After speaking at Pueblo, Colorado, on September 25, 1919, he collapsed with severe headaches.

Canceling the rest of his itinerary, he rushed back to Washington, where, a few days later, he suffered a major stroke. For two weeks, he was close to death; for six weeks more, he was so seriously ill that he could conduct virtually no public business. His wife and his doctor formed an almost impenetrable barrier around him, shielding the president from any official pressures that might impede his recovery and preventing the public from receiving any accurate information about the gravity of his condition.

Wilson ultimately recovered enough to resume a limited official schedule, but he was essentially an invalid for the remaining eighteen months of his presidency. His left side was partially paralyzed; more important, his mental and emotional state was unstable. His condition only intensified what had already been his strong tendency to view public issues in moral terms and to resist any attempts at compromise. When the Foreign Relations Committee finally sent the treaty to the Senate, recommending nearly fifty amendments and reservations, Wilson refused to consider any of them. The effort to win ratification failed.

In the aftermath of this defeat, Wilson became convinced that the 1920 national election would serve as a "solemn referendum" on the League. By now, however, public interest in the peace process had begun to fade—partly as a reaction against the bitterness of the ratification fight, but more in response to a series of other crises.

A SOCIETY IN TURMOIL

Even during the Paris Peace Conference, many Americans were concerned less about international matters than about turbulent events at home. Some of this unease was a legacy of the almost hysterical social atmosphere of the war years; some of it was a response to issues that surfaced after the armistice.

The Unstable Economy

The war ended sooner than almost anyone had anticipated, and without warning, without planning, the nation lurched into the difficult task of economic reconversion. At first, the boom continued, but accompanied by raging inflation, a result in part of the sudden abandonment of wartime price controls. Through most of 1919 and 1920, prices rose at an average of more than 15 percent a year. Finally, late in 1920, the economic bubble burst as many of the temporary forces that had created it disappeared and as inflation began killing the market for consumer goods. Between 1920 and 1921, the gross national product declined nearly 10 percent; 100,000 businesses went bankrupt; 453,000 farmers lost their land; and nearly 5 million Americans lost their jobs.

Well before this severe recession began, there was a dramatic increase in labor unrest. The raging inflation of 1919 wiped out the modest wage gains workers had achieved during the war; many laborers were worried about job security as hundreds of thousands of veterans returned to the work force; arduous working conditions—such as the twelve-hour day in the steel industry—continued to be a source of discontent. Employers aggravated the resentment by using the end of the war (and the end of government controls) to rescind benefits they had been forced to concede to workers in 1917 and 1918—most notably recognition of unions. The year 1919, therefore, saw an unprecedented wave of strikes—more than 3,600 in all, involving over 4 million workers. In January, a walkout by shipyard workers in Seattle, Washington, evolved into a general strike that brought the entire city to a virtual standstill. In September, there was a strike by the Boston police force, which was demanding recognition of its union in the wake of substantial layoffs and wage cuts. Seattle had remained generally calm; but with its police off the job, Boston erupted in violence and looting.

These and other strikes aroused widespread middle-class hostility to the unions, a hostility that played a part in defeating the greatest strike of 1919: a steel strike that began in September, when 350,000 steelworkers in several midwestern cities demanded an eight-hour day and recognition of their union. The steel strike was long and bitter and climaxed in a riot in Gary, Indiana, in which eighteen strikers were killed. Steel executives managed to keep most plants running with nonunion labor, and public opinion was so hostile to the strikers that the AFL timidly repudiated them. By January, the strike—like most of the others in 1919—had collapsed.

The Demands of African Americans

The black men who had served in the armed forces during the war (367,000 of them) came home in 1919 and marched down the main streets of the industrial cities with other returning troops. And then (in New York and other cities) they marched again through the streets of black neighborhoods such as Harlem, led by jazz bands, cheered by thousands of African Americans, who believed that the glory of black heroism in the war would make it impossible for white society ever again to treat African Americans as less than equal citizens.

In truth, the fact that black soldiers had fought in the war had almost no impact at all on white attitudes. But it did have a profound effect on black attitudes: it accentuated African-American bitterness—and increased determination of blacks to fight for their rights. Veterans expected a reward for their service. But for many other American blacks, the war raised expectations in other ways. Nearly half a million migrated from the rural South to industrial cities (often enticed by northern "labor agents," who offered them free transportation) in search of the factory jobs the war was rapidly generating. This was the beginning of what became known as the "Great Migration." Within a few years, the nation's racial demographics were transformed; suddenly there were large black communities crowding into northern cities, in some of which very few African Americans had lived in the past.

By 1919, however, the racial climate had become savage and murderous. In the South, there was a sudden increase in lynchings: more than seventy blacks, some of them war veterans, died at the hands of white mobs in 1919 alone. In the North, black factory workers faced widespread layoffs as returning white veterans displaced them from their jobs. Black veterans found no significant new opportunities. And as whites became convinced that black workers with lower wage demands were hurting them economically, animosity grew rapidly.

Wartime riots in East St. Louis and elsewhere were a prelude to a summer of much worse racial violence in 1919. In Chicago, a black teenager swimming in Lake Michigan on a hot July day happened to drift toward a white beach. Whites on shore allegedly stoned him unconscious; he sank and drowned. Angry blacks gathered in crowds and marched into white neighborhoods to retaliate; whites formed even larger crowds and roamed into black neighborhoods shooting, stabbing, and beating passersby and destroying homes and properties. For more than a week, Chicago was virtually at war. In the end, 38 people died—15 whites and 23 blacks—and 537 were injured; over 1,000 people were left homeless. The Chicago riot was the worst but not the only racial violence during the so-called red summer of 1919; in all, 120 people died in such racial outbreaks in the space of little more than three months.

Racial violence, and even racially motivated urban riots, were not new. But the 1919 riots were different in one respect: they did not just involve white people attacking blacks; they also involved blacks fighting back. The NAACP signaled this change by urging blacks not just to demand government protection but also to retaliate, to defend themselves. The poet Claude McKay, one of the major figures of what would shortly be known as the Harlem Renaissance, wrote a poem after the Chicago riot called "If We Must Die":

Like men we'll face the murderous cowardly pack.
Pressed to the wall, dying, but fighting back.

At the same time, a black Jamaican, Marcus Garvey, began to attract a
wide following in the United States, mostly among poor urban blacks,
with his ideology of black nationalism. Garvey encouraged African Americans to reject assimilation into white society and develop pride in their

MARCUS GARVEY, 1924 Garvey attracted a broad following in the early 1920s with his
message of black nationalism and self-help. He often dressed in semimilitary regalia
and organized meetings and parades with a vaguely martial tone. His influence
declined after he was convicted of fraud or misuse of funds he had raised to launch
an African-American steamship company. He served a short term in jail and in 1927
was deported to his native Jamaica, where he died in 1940 in relative obscurity.

own race and culture (which was, he claimed, superior to that of white society). His United Negro Improvement Association (UNIA) launched a chain of black-owned grocery stores and pressed for the creation of other black businesses. Eventually, Garvey began urging his supporters to leave America and return to Africa, where they could create a new society of their own. In the 1920s, the Garvey movement experienced explosive growth for a time. It began to decline, however, after Garvey was indicted in 1923 on charges of business fraud. He was deported to Jamaica two years later. But the allure of black nationalism, which he helped make visible to millions of African Americans, survived in black culture long after Garvey himself was gone.

The Red Scare

Much of the public considered the industrial warfare and the racial violence in 1919 a frightening omen of instability and radicalism. This was in part because other evidence emerging at the same time also seemed to suggest the existence of a radical menace. After the Russian Revolution of November 1917, communism was no longer simply a theory; it was now the basis of an important regime. Concerns about the communist threat grew in 1919 when the Soviet government announced the formation of the Communist International (or Comintern), whose purpose was to export revolution around the world.

In America, meanwhile, there was, in addition to the great number of imagined radicals, a modest number of real ones. These small groups of radicals were presumably responsible for a series of bombings in the spring of 1919 that produced great national alarm. In April, the post office intercepted several dozen parcels addressed to leading businessmen and politicians that were triggered to explode when opened. Two months later, eight bombs exploded in eight cities within minutes of one another, suggesting a nationwide conspiracy. One of them damaged the facade of United States Attorney General A. Mitchell Palmer's home in Washington.

In response to these and other provocations, what became known as the Red Scare began. Nearly thirty states enacted new peacetime sedition laws imposing harsh penalties on those who promoted revolution; some 300 people went to jail as a result. There were spontaneous acts of violence against supposed radicals in some communities, and more calculated efforts by universities and other institutions to expel radicals from their midst. But the greatest contribution to the Red Scare came from the federal government. On New Year's Day, 1920, Attorney General A. Mitchell

Palmer and his ambitious young assistant, J. Edgar Hoover, orchestrated a series of raids on alleged radical centers throughout the country and arrested more than 6,000 people. The Palmer Raids had been designed to uncover huge caches of weapons and explosives; they netted a total of three pistols. Most of those arrested were ultimately released, but about 500 who were not American citizens were summarily deported.

The ferocity of the Red Scare soon abated, but its effects lingered well into the 1920s, most notably in the celebrated case of Sacco and Vanzetti. In May of 1920, two Italian immigrants, Nicola Sacco and Bartolomeo Vanzetti, were charged with the murder of a paymaster in Braintree, Massachusetts. The case against them was weak and suffused with nativist prejudices and fears; but because both men were confessed anarchists, they faced a widespread public presumption of guilt. They were convicted and sentenced to death. Over the next several years, public support for Sacco and Vanzetti grew to formidable proportions. But all requests for a new trial or a pardon were denied. On August 23, 1927, amid widespread protests around the world, Sacco and Vanzetti, still proclaiming their innocence, died in the electric chair.

The Retreat from Idealism

On August 26, 1920, the Nineteenth Amendment, guaranteeing women the right to vote, became part of the Constitution. To the woman suffrage movement, this was the culmination of nearly a century of struggle. To many progressives, who had seen the inclusion of women in the electorate as a way of bolstering their political strength, it seemed to promise new support for reform. Yet the passage of the Nineteenth Amendment marked not the beginning of an era of progressive reform but the end of one.

Economic problems, labor unrest, racial tensions, and the intensity of the antiradicalism they helped create—all combined in the years immediately following the war to produce a general sense of disillusionment. That became particularly apparent in the election of 1920. Woodrow Wilson wanted the campaign to be a referendum on the League of Nations, and the Democratic candidates, Governor James M. Cox of Ohio and Assistant Secretary of the Navy Franklin D. Roosevelt, dutifully tried to keep Wilson's ideals alive. The Republican presidential nominee, however, offered a different vision. He was Warren Gamaliel Harding, an obscure Ohio senator whom party leaders had chosen as their nominee confident that he would do their bidding once in office. Harding offered no ideals, only a vague promise of a return, as he later phrased it, to "normalcy." He won in a landslide. The

Republican ticket received 61 percent of the popular vote and carried every state outside the South. The party made major gains in Congress as well. To many Americans it seemed that, for better or worse, a new era had begun.

CONCLUSION

The greatest and most terrible war in human history was also an important moment in the rise of the United States to global preeminence. The powers of Europe emerged from more than four years of carnage with their societies and economies in disarray. The United States emerged from its own, much briefer, involvement in the war poised to become the most important political and economic force in the world.

For a time after the outbreak of war in Europe in 1914, most Americans—President Wilson among them—wanted nothing so much as to stay out of the conflict. Gradually, however, as the war dragged on and on and the tactics of Britain and Germany began to impinge on American trade and on freedom of the seas, the United States found itself drawn slowly into the conflict. In April 1917, finally, Congress agreed (although not without considerable dissent) to the President's request that the United States enter the war as an ally of Britain.

American forces quickly broke the stalemate that had bogged the European forces down in years of inconclusive trench warfare. Within a few months of the arrival of substantial numbers of American troops in Europe, Germany agreed to an armistice and the war shuddered to a close. American casualties, although not inconsiderable, were negligible compared to the millions suffered by the European combatants. In the meantime, the American economy experienced an enormous industrial boom as a result of the war.

The social experience of the war in the United States was, on the whole, dismaying to reformers. Although the war enhanced some reform efforts—most notably prohibition and woman suffrage—it also introduced an atmosphere of intolerance and repression into American life, an atmosphere assisted by policies of the federal government designed to suppress dissent. The aftermath of the war was even more disheartening to progressives, both because of a brief but highly destabilizing recession and because of a wave of repression directed against labor, radicals, African Americans, and immigrants in 1919 and 1920.

At the same time, Woodrow Wilson's bold and idealistic dream of a peace based on the principles of democracy and justice suffered a painful death. The Treaty of Versailles, which he helped to draft, was itself far from what Wilson had hoped. It did, however, contain a provision for a League of Nations, which Wilson believed could transform the international order. But the League quickly became controversial in the United States; and despite strenuous efforts by the President—efforts that hastened his own physical collapse—the treaty was defeated in the Senate. In the aftermath of that traumatic battle, the American people turned away from Wilson and his ideals and prepared for a very different era.

FOR FURTHER REFERENCE

Suggested Readings

Ernest R. May, *The World War and American Isolation* (1959) is an authoritative account of America's slow and controversial entry into the Great War. Frank Freidel provides a sweeping account of the American soldier's battlefield experience during WWI in *Over There: The Story of America's First Great Overseas Crusade* (1964). David Kennedy, *Over Here: The First World War and American Society* (1980) is an important study of the domestic impact of the war. Robert D. Cuff, *The War Industries Board: Business-Government Relations During World War I* (1973) is an excellent institutional and economic history of American mobilization for war. John Keegan, *The First World War* (1998) is a superb military history of the conflict and includes a good account of the American role in the war. Thomas Knock, *To End All Wars: Woodrow Wilson and the Quest for a New World Order* (1992) is a valuable recent study of the battle for the peace. George F. Kennan, *Russia Leaves the War* (1956) is a classic study of the impact of the Bolshevik revolution on World War I. Arno Mayer, *Wilson vs. Lenin* (1959) and *Politics and Diplomacy of Peacemaking: Containment and Counterrevolution* (1965) are two important revisionist accounts of the peacemaking process. America's stormy debate over immigration and national identity before, during, and after World War I is best captured by John Higham in *Strangers in the Land: Patterns of American Nativism* (1955). William M. Tuttle, Jr., in *Race Riot: Chicago in the Red Summer of 1919* (1970), recounts the terrible riots of 1919 that showed America violently divided along racial and ideological lines.

Films

(The best source for information on how to find these and other films is *Bowker's Complete Video Directory*—3 volumes.) *The Killing Floor* (1984) uses scenes from Chicago's packing houses to illuminate larger themes of class and race in the difficult peace of 1919. *The Great War—1918* (1997) chronicles the story of American soldiers in the closing battle of World War I through the letters and diaries of fighting men.

Internet Resources

Internet websites containing historical material relevant to the subjects discussed in this chapter can be reached through the McGraw-Hill history site at www.mhhe.com/socscience/history/usa/link/linktop.htm.

CHAPTER TWENTY-FOUR

The New Era

The New Economy ∼ *The New Culture*
A Conflict of Cultures ∼ *Republican Government*

THE 1920S ARE OFTEN remembered as an era of affluence, conservatism, and cultural frivolity: the Roaring Twenties, the age of what Warren G. Harding once called "normalcy." In reality, however, the decade was a time of significant, even dramatic social, economic, and political change. It was an era in which the American economy not only enjoyed spectacular growth but developed new forms of organization. It was a time in which American popular culture reshaped itself to reflect the increasingly urban, industrial, consumer-oriented society of the United States. And it was a decade in which American government, for all its apparent conservatism, experimented with new approaches to public policy that helped pave the way for the important period of reform that was to follow. That was why contemporaries liked to refer to the 1920s as the "New Era"—an age in which America was becoming a modern nation.

At the same time, however, the decade saw the rise of a series of spirited and at times effective rebellions against the modern developments that were transforming American life. The intense cultural conflicts that characterized the 1920s were evidence of how much of American society remained unreconciled to the modernizing currents of the New Era.

THE NEW ECONOMY

After the recession of 1921–1922, the United States began a long period of almost uninterrupted prosperity and economic expansion. Less visible

706

TIME LINE

1914–1920	1920	1922	1923
Great Migration of blacks to the North	Prohibition begins Harding elected president	Lewis's *Babbitt*	Harding dies; Coolidge becomes president Harding administration scandals revealed

1924	1925	1927	1928
National Origins Act passed Coolidge elected president Ku Klux Klan membership peaks	Fitzgerald's *The Great Gatsby* Scopes trial	Lindbergh's solo transatlantic flight First sound motion picture, *The Jazz Singer*	Hoover elected president

at the time, but equally significant, was the survival (and even the growth) of severe inequalities and imbalances.

Technology, Organization, and Economic Growth

No one could deny the remarkable, some believed miraculous, feats of the American economy in the 1920s. The nation's manufacturing output rose by more than 60 percent during the decade. Per capita income grew by a third. Inflation was negligible. A mild recession in 1923 interrupted the pattern of growth; but when it subsided early in 1924, the economy expanded with even greater vigor than before.

The economic boom was a result of many things, but one of the most important causes was technology, and the great industrial expansion it made possible. The automobile industry, as a result of the development of the assembly line and other innovations, now became one of the most important industries in the nation. It stimulated growth in other, related industries as well. Auto manufacturers purchased the products of steel, rubber, glass, and tool companies. Auto owners bought gasoline from the oil corporations. Road construction in response to the proliferation of motor vehicles became an important industry. The increased mobility that the automobile made possible increased the demand for suburban housing, fueling a boom in the construction industry.

Other new industries benefiting from technological innovations contributed as well to the economic growth. Radio began to become a popular technology even before commercial broadcasting began in 1920. Early radio had been able to broadcast little beside pulses, which meant that radio communication could occur only through the Morse Code. But with the discovery of the theory of modulation, pioneered by the Canadian scientist Reginal Fessenden, it became possible to transmit speech and music. (Modulation also eventually made possible the transmission of video signals and later helped create radar and television.) Many people built their own radio sets at home for very little money, benefiting from the discovery that inexpensive crystals could receive signals over long distances (but not very well over short ones). These "short wave" radios, which allowed individual owners to establish contact with each other, marked the beginning of an enduring passion among millions of people around the world, who talked with one another over what later became known to many people as "ham radio." Once commercial broadcasting began, families flocked to buy more conventional radio sets, which could receive high-quality signals over short and medium distances. They were powered by vacuum tubes that were much more reliable than earlier models. By 1925, there were two million sets in American homes, and by the end of the 1920s almost every family had one.

Commercial aviation developed slowly in the 1920s, beginning with the use of planes to deliver mail. On the whole, airplanes remained curiosities and sources of entertainment. But technological advances—the development of the radial engine and the creation of pressurized cabins—were laying the groundwork for the great increase in commercial travel in the 1930s and beyond. Trains became faster and more efficient as well with the development of the diesel-electric engine. Electronics, home appliances, plastics and synthetic fibers such as nylon (both pioneered by researchers at DuPont), aluminum, magnesium, oil, electric power, and other industries fueled by technological advances—all grew dramatically and spurred the economic boom. Telephones continued to proliferate. By the late 1930s, there were approximately 25 million telephones in the United States, approximately one for every six people.

The seeds of future widespread technologies were also visible in the 1920s and 1930s. In both England and America, scientists and engineers were working to transform primitive calculating machines into devices capable of performing more complicated tasks. By the early 1930s, researchers at MIT, led by Vannevar Bush, had created an instrument capable of performing a variety of complicated tasks—the first analog computer, which became the starting point for dramatic progress over the next several decades. A few years later, Howard Aiken, with financial assistance from Harvard and MIT, built a much more complex computer with memory, capable of multiplying eleven-digit numbers in three seconds.

Genetic research had begun in Austria in the mid-nineteenth century through the work of Gregor Mendel, a Catholic monk who performed experiments on the hybridization of vegetables in the garden of his monastery. His findings attracted little attention during his lifetime, but in the early twentieth century they were discovered by several investigators and helped shape modern genetic research. Among the American pioneers was Thomas Hunt Morgan of Columbia University and later Cal Tech, whose experiments with fruit flies revealed how several genes could be transmitted together (as opposed to Mendel's belief that they could only be transferred separately). He also revealed the way in which genes were arranged along the chromosome. His work helped open the path to understanding how genes could recombine—a critical discovery that led to more advanced experiments in hybridization and genetics.

Large sectors of American business were accelerating their drive toward national organization and consolidation. Certain industries—notably those dependent on large-scale mass production, such as steel and automobiles—seemed naturally to move toward concentrating production in a few large firms. Others—industries less dependent on technology and less susceptible to great economies of scale—proved resistant to consolidation, despite the efforts of many businessmen to promote it.

The strenuous efforts by industrialists throughout the economy to find ways to curb competition reflected a strong fear of overcapacity. Even in the booming 1920s, industrialists remembered how too-rapid expansion and overproduction had helped produce recessions in 1893, 1907, and 1920. The great, unrealized dream of the New Era was to find a way to stabilize the economy so that such collapses would never occur again.

Workers in an Age of Capital

Despite the remarkable economic growth, more than two-thirds of the American people in 1929 lived at no better than what one major study described as the "minimum comfort level." Half of those were at or below the level of "subsistence and poverty." Large segments of society, unable to organize, were without power to protect their economic interests.

American labor experienced both the successes and the failures of the 1920s as much as any other group. On the one hand, most workers saw

THE STEAMFITTER Lewis Hine was among the first American photographers to recognize his craft as an art. In this carefully posed photograph from the mid-1920s, Hine made a point that many other artists were making in other media: The rise of the machine could serve human beings, but might also bend them to its own needs.

their standard of living rise during the decade; many enjoyed greatly improved working conditions and other benefits. Some employers in the 1920s, eager to avoid disruptive labor unrest and forestall the growth of unions, adopted paternalistic techniques that came to be known as "welfare capitalism." Henry Ford, for example, shortened the workweek, raised wages, and instituted paid vacations. By 1926, nearly 3 million industrial workers were eligible for at least modest pensions on retirement. When labor grievances surfaced despite these efforts, workers could voice them through the so-called company unions that were emerging in many industries—workers' councils and shop committees, organized by the corporations themselves. But welfare capitalism, in the end, gave workers no real control over their own fates. Company unions were feeble vehicles. And welfare capitalism survived only as long as industry prospered. After 1929, with the economy in crisis, the entire system collapsed.

Welfare capitalism affected only a relatively small number of workers in any case. Most laborers worked for employers interested primarily in keeping their labor costs low. Workers as a whole, therefore, received wage increases that were proportionately far below the growth of the economy as a whole. Unskilled workers, in particular, saw their wages increase hardly at all—by only a little over 2 percent between 1920 and 1926. At the end of the decade, the average annual income of a worker remained below $1,500 a year, when $1,800 was considered necessary to maintain a minimally decent standard of living. Only by relying on the earnings of several family members at once could many working-class families make ends meet.

The New Era was a bleak time for labor organization, in part because many unions themselves were relatively conservative and failed to adapt to the realities of the modern economy. The American Federation of Labor (led by the cautious William Green) remained wedded to the concept of the craft union, in which workers were organized on the basis of particular skills. The AFL sought peaceful cooperation with employers, without strikes. In the meantime, the number of unskilled industrial workers, many of them recent immigrants from southern or eastern Europe, was rising rapidly. They received little attention from the craft unions.

But whatever the weaknesses of the unions, the strength of the corporations was the principal reason for the absence of effective labor organization in the 1920s. After the turmoil of 1919, corporate leaders worked hard to spread the doctrine that unionism was somehow subversive, that a crucial element of democratic capitalism was the protection of the "open shop" (a shop in which no worker could be required to join a union). The crusade for the open shop, euphemistically titled the "American Plan," became a pretext for a harsh campaign of union-busting across the country. As a result, union membership fell from more than 5 million in 1920 to under 3 million in 1929.

Women and Minorities in the Work Force

A growing proportion of the work force consisted of women, who were concentrated in what have since become known as "pink-collar" jobs—low-paying service occupations with many of the same problems as manufacturing employment. Large numbers of women worked as secretaries, sales-clerks, and telephone operators and in other nonmanual service capacities. Because technically such positions were not industrial jobs, the AFL and other labor organizations were uninterested in organizing these workers.

Similarly, the half-million African Americans who had migrated from the rural South into the cities during the Great Migration after 1914 had few opportunities for union representation. The skilled crafts represented in the AFL often worked actively to exclude blacks from their trades and organizations. Most blacks, however, worked in jobs in which the AFL took no interest at all—as janitors, dishwashers, garbage collectors, domestics, and other service capacities. A. Philip Randolph's Brotherhood of Sleeping Car Porters was one of the few important unions dominated and led by African Americans.

In the West and the Southwest, the ranks of the unskilled included considerable numbers of Asians and Hispanics, few of them organized, most actively excluded from white-dominated unions. In the wake of the Chinese Exclusion Acts, Japanese immigrants increasingly took the place of the Chinese in menial jobs in California, despite the continuing hostility of the white population. They worked on railroads, construction sites, and farms and in many other low-paying workplaces. Some Japanese managed to escape the ranks of the unskilled by forming their own small businesses or setting themselves up as truck farmers; and many of the Issei (Japanese immigrants) and Nisei (their American-born children) enjoyed significant economic success—so much so that California passed laws in 1913 and 1920 to make it more difficult for them to buy land. Other Asians—most notably Filipinos—also swelled the unskilled work force and generated considerable hostility. Anti-Filipino riots in California beginning in 1929 helped produce legislation in 1934 virtually eliminating immigration from the Philippines.

Mexican immigrants formed a major part of the unskilled work force throughout the Southwest and California. Nearly half a million Mexicans entered the United States in the 1920s, more than any other national group, increasing the total Mexican population to over a million. Most lived in California, Texas, Arizona, and New Mexico; and by 1930, most lived in cities. Large Mexican barrios—usually raw urban communities, often without even such basic services as plumbing and sewerage—grew up in Los Angeles, El Paso, San Antonio, Denver, and many other cities and towns. Some of the residents found work locally in factories and shops; others traveled to mines or did migratory labor on farms but returned to the cities between jobs. Mexican workers, too, faced hostility and discrimination from the Anglo population of the region, but there were few efforts actually to exclude them. Employers in the relatively underpopulated West needed this ready pool of low-paid, unskilled, and unorganized workers.

Agricultural Technology and the Plight of the Farmer

Like industry, American agriculture in the 1920s was embracing new technologies for increasing production. The number of tractors on American farms, for example, quadrupled during the 1920s, especially after they began to be powered by internal combustion engines (like automobiles) rather than by the cumbersome steam engines of the past. They helped to open 35 million new acres to cultivation. Increasingly sophisticated combines and harvesters were proliferating, helping to make it possible to produce more crops with fewer workers.

Agricultural researchers were already at work on other advances that would later transform food production in America and around the world: the invention of hybrid corn (made possible by advances in genetic research), which became available to farmers in 1921 but was not grown in great quantities for a decade or more; and the creation of chemical fertilizers and pesticides, which also began to have limited use in the 1920s but which proliferated quickly in the 1930s and 1940s.

The new technologies greatly increased agricultural productivity, both in the United States and in other parts of the world. But the demand for agricultural goods was not rising as fast as production. The results were substantial surpluses, a disastrous decline in food prices, and a severe drop in farmers' income beginning early in the 1920s. More than 3 million people left agriculture altogether in the course of the decade. Of those who remained, many lost ownership of their lands and had to rent instead from banks or other landlords.

In response, some farmers began to demand relief in the form of government price supports. One price-raising scheme in particular came to dominate agrarian demands: the idea of "parity." Parity was a complicated formula for setting an adequate price for farm goods and ensuring that farmers would earn back at least their production costs no matter how the national or world agricultural market might fluctuate. Champions of parity urged high tariffs against foreign agricultural goods and a government commitment to buy surplus domestic crops at parity and sell them abroad at whatever the market would bring.

The legislative expression of the demand for parity was the McNary-Haugen Bill, named after its two principal sponsors in Congress and introduced repeatedly between 1924 and 1928. In 1926 and again in 1928, Congress (where farm interests enjoyed disproportionate influence) approved a bill requiring parity for grain, cotton, tobacco, and rice, but President Coolidge vetoed it both times.

THE NEW CULTURE

The increasingly urban and consumer-oriented culture of the 1920s helped Americans in all regions to live their lives and perceive their world in increasingly similar ways. That same culture exposed them to a new set of values that reflected both the prosperity and complexity of the modern economy. But different parts of American society experienced the new culture in very different ways.

Consumerism and Communications

The United States of the 1920s was a consumer society—a society in which increasing numbers of men and women could afford more than simply what was necessary to survive. Many more people than ever before could buy items not just because of need but for convenience and pleasure. Middle-class families purchased electric refrigerators, washing machines, and vacuum cleaners. People wore wristwatches and smoked cigarettes. Women purchased cosmetics and mass-produced fashions. Above all, Americans bought automobiles. By the end of the decade, there were more than 30 million cars on American roads.

No group was more aware of the emergence of consumerism (or more responsible for creating it) than the advertising industry. The first advertising and public relations firms (N. W. Ayer and J. Walter Thompson) had appeared well before World War I, but in the 1920s, partly as a result of techniques pioneered by wartime propaganda, advertising came of age. Publicists no longer simply conveyed information; they sought to identify products with a particular lifestyle. They also encouraged the public to absorb the values of promotion and salesmanship and to admire those who were effective "boosters" and publicists. One of the most successful books of the 1920s was *The Man Nobody Knows*, by advertising executive Bruce Barton. It portrayed Jesus Christ as not only a religious prophet but also a "super salesman." Barton's message, a message apparently in tune with the new spirit of the consumer culture, was that Jesus had been a man concerned with living a full and rewarding life in this world and that twentieth-century men and women should be concerned with doing the same.

The advertising industry could never have had the impact it did without the emergence of new vehicles of communication that made it

THE ELECTRIC REFRIGERATOR The development of new appliances for the home was an important part of the boom in the production and sale of consumer goods in the 1920s. Executives of the Delcom Light Company, a subsidiary of General Motors, pose here in front of the first Frigidaire electric refrigerator as it is readied for shipping from Dayton, Ohio, in 1921.

possible to reach large audiences quickly and easily. Newspapers were being absorbed into national chains. Mass-circulation magazines—*Time, Collier's, Ladies' Home Journal,* the *Saturday Evening Post, Reader's Digest,* and others—attracted broad, national audiences. The movies were becoming an ever more popular and powerful form of mass communication; over 100 million people saw films in 1930, as compared with 40 million in 1922.

The most important communications vehicle, however, was the only one truly new to the 1920s: radio. The first commercial radio station in America, KDKA in Pittsburgh, began broadcasting in 1920, and the first national radio network, the National Broadcasting Company, was formed in 1927.

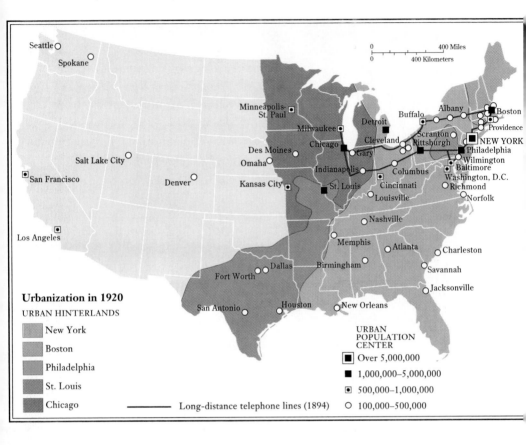

Urbanization in 1920

URBAN HINTERLANDS

New York
Boston
Philadelphia
St. Louis
Chicago

——— Long-distance telephone lines (1894)

URBAN POPULATION CENTER

■ Over 5,000,000
■ 1,000,000–5,000,000
▣ 500,000–1,000,000
○ 100,000–500,000

Psychology and Psychiatry

The increasing affluence and the growing consumerism of the 1920s produced new psychological challenges to individuals whose parents and grandparents had generally lived in a simpler and more formally structured society. The rise of anxiety and alienation as characteristic ailments of the consumer age coincided with the rise of new theories of psychology and psychiatry. Together these two phenomena helped entrench and expand important emerging fields in medicine and science.

Psychiatry had been spreading in the United States since the early twentieth century, driven in part by the growing awareness of the theories of Sigmund Freud and Carl Jung. Although Freud and Jung differed sharply on many points, they both helped legitimize the idea of exploring the unconscious as a way of discovering the roots of mental problems. Psychoanalysis, which Freud pioneered and Jung also advanced, began to attract American adherents as early as 1912 and spread significantly in the 1920s.

Competing with Freudian psychology were the ideas of behavioralism, associated most prominently with John Watson of Johns Hopkins University. Watson challenged the Freudian belief in introspection and the exploration of the unconscious. Instead, he argued that mental ailments, like physical ones, should be treated by observation and treatment of symptoms—of behavior. The point of therapy was to modify behavior—to discourage undesirable behavior and reinforce "acceptable" actions. Although many psychiatrists dismissed behavioralism and its associated therapies as treating symptoms rather than causes, it demonstrated significant success in treating such disorders as alcoholism, drug addiction, and phobias.

Although psychoanalysis and other forms of therapy could be performed by psychologists without medical training, the biggest growth in psychiatry was as a field of medicine—indeed, along with surgery, one of the first areas of medical specialization. At first, medical psychiatrists worked mostly in mental institutions. But as mental hospitals evolved from places where patients came for treatment and then were discharged to places where chronically ill people (many of them aged) resided indefinitely, psychiatrists began to move into other venues—into conventional hospitals and most notably into private practice. Psychiatry began to expand its claims and to offer services not just to the mentally ill, but to otherwise stable individuals experiencing difficulties with everyday life. A new theory of "dynamic" psychiatry emerged early in the twentieth century; and by the 1920s, it had helped psychiatrists to offer therapy for ordinary anxieties, not just severe mental disturbance.

Psychology and psychiatry were, from the beginning, fields in which women played a much larger role than in most areas of medicine. That was in part because training in psychology was considered valuable for occupations in which women had been traditionally dominant—teaching, social work, nursing. Many women who received early training in psychology later went on to graduate school in the field; and women who had medical training often found it easier to establish themselves in psychiatry than in other, more traditionally male-dominated areas of medicine.

Women in the New Era

College-educated women were no longer pioneers in the 1920s. There were now two and even three generations of graduates of women's or coeducational colleges and universities, and some were making their presence felt in professional areas that in the past women had rarely penetrated. The "new professional woman" was a vivid and widely publicized image in the

1920s. In reality, however, most employed women were nonprofessional, lower-class workers. Middle-class women, in the meantime, remained largely in the home—or worked in distinctively female professions such as teaching and nursing.

Yet the 1920s constituted a new era for middle-class women nonetheless. In particular, the decade saw a redefinition of motherhood. Shortly after World War I, an influential group of psychologists—the "behaviorists," led by John B. Watson—began to challenge the long-held assumption that women had an instinctive capacity for motherhood. Maternal affection was not, they claimed, sufficient preparation for child rearing. Instead, mothers should rely on the advice and assistance of experts and professionals: doctors, nurses, and trained educators in nursery schools and kindergartens.

For many middle-class women, these changes devalued what had been an important and consuming activity. Many attempted to compensate by devoting new attention to their roles as wives and companions. A woman's relationship with her husband assumed a greatly enhanced importance. And many women now openly considered their sexual relationships with their husbands not simply as a means of procreation, as earlier generations had been taught to do, but an important and pleasurable experience in its own right, as the culmination of romantic love.

One result was growing interest in birth control. The pioneer of the American birth-control movement, Margaret Sanger, began her career as a promoter of the diaphragm and other birth-control devices out of a concern for working-class women; she believed that large families were among the major causes of poverty and distress in poor communities. By the 1920s (partly because she had limited success in persuading working-class women to accept her teachings), she was becoming more concerned with and more effective in persuading middle-class women to see the benefits of birth control. Nevertheless, some birth-control devices remained illegal in many states (and abortion remained illegal nearly everywhere).

Some women concluded that in the New Era it was no longer necessary to maintain a rigid, Victorian female "respectability." They could smoke, drink, dance, wear seductive clothes and makeup, and attend lively parties. Those assumptions became the basis of the "flapper"—the modern woman whose liberated lifestyle found expression in dress, hairstyle, speech, and behavior. The flapper lifestyle had a particular impact on lower-middle-class and working-class single women, who were flocking to new jobs in industry and the service sector. (The young, middle-class, "Bohemian" women most often associated with the flapper image were, in fact, imitating a style that emerged among this larger group.) At night, such women flocked to clubs and dance halls in search of excitement and companionship.

Despite all the changes, most women remained highly dependent on men—both in the workplace and in the home—and relatively powerless when men exploited that dependence. The National Woman's Party, under the leadership of Alice Paul, attempted to fight that powerlessness through its campaign for the Equal Rights Amendment, although it found little support in Congress (and met continued resistance from other feminist groups). Responding to the suffrage victory, women organized the League of Women Voters and the women's auxiliaries of both the Democratic and Republican Parties. Female-dominated consumer groups grew rapidly and increased the range and energy of their efforts.

Women activists won a brief triumph in 1921 when they helped secure passage of a measure in keeping with the traditional feminist goal of securing "protective" legislation for women: the Sheppard-Towner Act. It provided federal funds to states to establish prenatal and child health-care programs. From the start, however, it produced controversy. Alice Paul and her supporters opposed the measure, complaining that it classified all women as mothers. More important, the American Medical Association fought Sheppard-Towner, warning that it would introduce untrained outsiders into the health-care field. In 1929, Congress terminated the program.

The Disenchanted

Many artists and intellectuals coming of age in the 1920s were experiencing a disenchantment with modern America so fundamental that they were often able to view it only with contempt. One result of this alienation was a series of savage critiques of modern society by a wide range of writers, some of whom were known as the "debunkers." Among them was the Baltimore journalist H. L. Mencken, who delighted in ridiculing religion, politics, the arts, even democracy itself. Sinclair Lewis, the first American to win a Nobel Prize in literature, published a series of savage novels—*Main Street* (1920), *Babbitt* (1922), *Arrowsmith* (1925), and others—in which he lashed out at one aspect of modern bourgeois society after another. Intellectuals of the 1920s claimed to reject the "success ethic" that they believed dominated American life. The novelist F. Scott Fitzgerald, for example, attacked the American obsession with material success in *The Great Gatsby* (1925). The roster of important American writers active in the

1920s may have no equal in any other period. It included Fitzgerald, Lewis, Ernest Hemingway, Thomas Wolfe, John Dos Passos, Ezra Pound, T. S. Eliot, Gertrude Stein, Edna Ferber, William Faulkner, and Eugene O'Neill.

It also included a remarkable group of black artists. In New York City, a new generation of African-American intellectuals created a flourishing artistic life widely described as the "Harlem Renaissance." The Harlem poets, novelists, and artists drew heavily from their African roots in an effort to prove the richness of their own racial heritage and to provide a basis for a cultural and political challenge to racial injustice. The poet Langston Hughes captured much of the spirit of the movement in a single sentence: "I am a Negro—and beautiful." Other black writers in Harlem and elsewhere—James Weldon Johnson, Countee Cullen, Zora Neale Hurston, Claude McKay, Alain Locke—as well as black artists and musicians helped to establish a thriving, and at times highly politicized, culture rooted in the historical legacy of their race.

A CONFLICT OF CULTURES

The modern, secular culture of the 1920s did not go unchallenged. It grew up alongside an older, more traditional culture, with which it continually and often bitterly competed.

Prohibition

When the prohibition of the sale and manufacture of alcohol went into effect in January 1920, it had the support of most members of the middle class and most of those who considered themselves progressives. Within a year, however, it had become clear that the "noble experiment," as its defenders called it, was not working well. Prohibition did substantially reduce drinking in most parts of the country. But it also produced conspicuous and growing violations that made the law an almost immediate source of disillusionment and controversy. Before long, it was almost as easy to acquire illegal alcohol in many parts of the country as it had once been to acquire legal alcohol. And since an enormous, lucrative industry was now barred to legitimate businessmen, organized-crime figures took it over.

Many middle-class progressives who had originally supported prohibition soon soured on the experiment. But an enormous constituency of provincial, largely rural, Protestant Americans continued vehemently to defend it. To them, prohibition had always meant more than stopping drinking. It represented the effort of an older America to defend traditional notions of morality and to maintain its dominance in a society in which they were becoming relatively less powerful. Drinking, which they associated with the modern city and with Catholic immigrants, became a symbol of the new culture they believed was displacing them.

As the decade proceeded, opponents of prohibition (or "wets," as they came to be known) gained steadily in influence. Not until 1933, however, when the Great Depression added weight to their appeals, were they finally able to effectively challenge the "drys" and win repeal of the Eighteenth Amendment.

Nativism and the Klan

The fear of immigrants that many prohibitionists expressed found other expressions as well. Agitation for a curb on foreign immigration to the United States had begun in the nineteenth century, and as with prohibition, it had gathered strength in the years before the war largely because of the support of middle-class progressives. In the years immediately following the war, when immigration began to be associated with radicalism, popular sentiment on behalf of restriction grew rapidly.

In 1921, Congress passed an emergency immigration act, establishing a quota system by which annual immigration from any country could not exceed 3 percent of the number of persons of that nationality who had been in the United States in 1910. The new law cut immigration from 800,000 to 300,000 in any single year, but the nativists remained unsatisfied. The National Origins Act of 1924 banned immigration from east Asia entirely, a measure clearly directed against Japan, since Chinese immigration was already illegal. It also reduced the quota for Europeans from 3 to 2 percent. The quota would be based, moreover, not on the 1910 census, but on the census of 1890, a year in which there had been far fewer southern and eastern Europeans in the country. What immigration there was, in other words, would heavily favor northwestern Europeans. Five years later, a further restriction set a rigid limit of 150,000 immigrants a year. In the years that followed, immigration officials seldom permitted even half that number actually to enter the country.

But the nativism of the 1920s extended well beyond restricting immigration. To defenders of an older, more provincial America, the growth of large communities of foreign peoples, alien in their speech, their habits, and their values, came to seem a direct threat to their own embattled way of life.

Among other things, this provincial nativism helped instigate the rebirth of the Ku Klux Klan as a major force in American society. The first Klan, founded during Reconstruction, had died in the 1870s. But in 1915, a new group of white southerners met on Stone Mountain near Atlanta and established a modern version of the society. Nativist passions had swelled in Georgia and elsewhere in response to the case of Leo Frank, a Jewish factory manager in Atlanta convicted in 1914 (on very flimsy evidence) of murdering a female employee; a mob stormed Frank's jail and lynched him. The premiere (also in Atlanta) of D. W. Griffith's film *The Birth of a Nation*, which glorified the early Klan, also helped inspire white southerners to join a new one.

At first the new Klan, like the old, was largely concerned with intimidating blacks. After World War I, however, concern about blacks gradually became secondary to concern about Catholics, Jews, and foreigners. At that point, membership in the Klan expanded rapidly and dramatically, not just in the small towns and rural areas of the South but in industrial cities in the North and Midwest. By 1924, there were reportedly 4 million members, and the largest state Klan was not in the South but in Indiana. Beginning in 1925, a series of scandals involving the organization's leaders precipitated a slow but steady decline in the Klan's influence.

Most Klan units (or "klaverns") tried to present their members as patriots and defenders of morality, and some did nothing more menacing than stage occasional parades and rallies. Often, however, the Klan also operated as a brutal, even violent, opponent of "alien" groups and as a defender of traditional, fundamentalist morality. Klansmen systematically terrorized blacks, Jews, Catholics, and foreigners. At times, they did so violently, through public whipping, tarring and feathering, arson, and lynching. What the Klan feared, however, was not simply "foreign" or "racially impure" groups; it feared anyone who posed a challenge to traditional values. Klansmen persecuted not only immigrants and blacks but those white Protestants they considered guilty of irreligion, sexual promiscuity, or drunkenness.

Religious Fundamentalism

Another cultural controversy of the 1920s was the result of a bitter conflict over the place of religion in contemporary society. By 1921, American Protestantism was already divided into two warring camps. On one side stood the modernists: mostly urban, middle-class people who were attempting to adapt religion to the teachings of modern science and to the realities of their modern, secular society. On the other side stood the fundamentalists: provincial, largely (although far from exclusively) rural men and women fighting to preserve traditional faith and to maintain the centrality of religion in American life. The fundamentalists insisted the Bible was to be interpreted literally. Above all, they opposed the teachings of Charles Darwin, who had openly challenged the biblical story of the Creation.

By the mid-1920s, to the great alarm of modernists, fundamentalism was gaining political strength in some states with its demands for legislation to forbid the teaching of evolution in public schools. In Tennessee in March 1925, the legislature actually adopted a measure making it illegal for any public school teacher "to teach any theory that denies the story of the divine creation of man as taught in the Bible."

When the fledgling American Civil Liberties Union (ACLU) offered free counsel to any Tennessee educator willing to defy the law and become the defendant in a test case, a twenty-four-year-old biology teacher in the town of Dayton, John T. Scopes, agreed to have himself arrested. And when the ACLU decided to send the famous attorney Clarence Darrow to defend Scopes, the aging William Jennings Bryan (now an important fundamentalist spokesman) announced that he would travel to Dayton to assist the prosecution. Journalists from across the country flocked to Tennessee to cover the trial, which opened in a circuslike atmosphere. Scopes had, of course, clearly violated the law; and a verdict of guilty was a foregone conclusion, especially when the judge refused to permit "expert" testimony by evolution scholars. Scopes was fined $100, and the case was ultimately dismissed in a higher court because of a technicality. Nevertheless, Darrow scored an important victory for the modernists by calling Bryan himself to the stand to testify as an "expert on the Bible." In the course of the cross-examination, which was broadcast by radio to much of the nation, Darrow made Bryan's stubborn defense of biblical truths appear foolish and finally tricked Bryan into admitting the possibility that not all religious dogma was subject to only one interpretation.

The Scopes trial put fundamentalists on the defensive and discouraged many of them from participating openly in politics. But it did not resolve the conflict between fundamentalists and modernists. Four other states soon proceeded to pass antievolution laws of their own, and the issue continued to smolder for decades.

The Democrats' Ordeal

The anguish of provincial Americans attempting to defend an embattled way of life proved particularly troubling to the Democratic Party during the 1920s as a result of tensions between its urban and rural factions.

DARROW AND BRYAN IN DAYTON Although the Scopes trial was chiefly significant for the issues it raised, it attracted national attention in 1925 at least as much because of its two celebrated attorneys: Clarence Darrow, the best-known defense attorney in America and a personification of the modern, skeptical, secular intellect; and William Jennings Bryan, the great political leader who had become, in the last years of his life, an ardent defender of Christian fundamentalism.

More than the Republicans, the Democrats consisted of a diverse coalition of interest groups, linked to the party largely by local tradition. Among those interest groups were prohibitionists, Klansmen, and fundamentalists on one side and Catholics, urban workers, and immigrants on the other.

At the 1924 Democratic National Convention in New York, a bitter conflict broke out over the platform when the party's urban wing attempted to win approval of planks calling for the repeal of prohibition and a denunciation of the Klan. Both planks narrowly failed. More serious was a deadlock in the balloting for a presidential candidate. Urban Democrats supported Alfred E. Smith, the Irish Catholic Tammanyite who had risen to become a progressive governor of New York; rural Democrats backed William McAdoo, Woodrow Wilson's Treasury secretary (and son-in-law), later to become a senator from California, who had skillfully positioned himself to win the support of southern and western delegates suspicious of

Tammany Hall and modern urban life. For 103 ballots, the convention dragged on, until finally both Smith and McAdoo withdrew and the party settled on a compromise: the corporate lawyer John W. Davis.

A similar schism plagued the Democrats again in 1928, when Al Smith finally secured his party's nomination for president after another acrimonious but less prolonged battle. He was not, however, able to unite his divided party—in part because of widespread anti-Catholic sentiment, especially in the South. He was the first Democrat since the Civil War not to carry the entire South. Outside the South, he carried no states at all except Massachusetts and Rhode Island. Smith's opponent, and the victor in the presidential election, was a man who perhaps more than any other personified the modern, prosperous, middle-class society of the New Era: Herbert Hoover.

REPUBLICAN GOVERNMENT

For twelve years, beginning in 1921, both the presidency and the Congress rested in the hands of the Republican Party—a party in which the power of reformers had greatly dwindled. For most of those years, the federal government enjoyed a warm and supportive relationship with the American business community. Yet the government of the New Era was more than the passive, pliant instrument that critics often described. It attempted to serve in many respects as an active agent of economic change.

Harding and Coolidge

Nothing seemed more clearly to illustrate the unadventurous character of 1920s politics than the characters of the two men who served as president during most of the decade: Warren G. Harding and Calvin Coolidge.

Harding was elected to the presidency in 1920, having spent many years in public life doing little of note. An undistinguished senator from Ohio, he had received the Republican presidential nomination as a result of an agreement among leaders of his party, who considered him, as one noted, a "good second-rater." Harding appointed capable men to the most important cabinet offices, and he attempted to stabilize the nation's troubled foreign policy. But even as he attempted to rise to his office, he seemed baffled by his responsibilities, as if he recognized his own unfitness. "I am a man of limited talents from a small town," he reportedly told friends on one occasion. "I don't seem to grasp that I am President."

Harding's intellectual limits were compounded by personal weaknesses: his penchant for gambling, illegal alcohol, and attractive women.

Harding lacked the strength to abandon the party hacks who had helped create his political success. One of them, Harry Daugherty, the Ohio party boss principally responsible for his meteoric political ascent, he appointed attorney general. Another, New Mexico Senator Albert B. Fall, he made secretary of the interior. Members of the so-called Ohio Gang filled important offices throughout the administration. Unknown to the public (and perhaps also to Harding), Daugherty, Fall, and others were engaged in fraud and corruption. The most spectacular scandal involved the rich naval oil reserves at Teapot Dome, Wyoming, and Elk Hills, California. At the urging of Fall, Harding transferred control of those reserves from the Navy Department to the Interior Department. Fall then secretly leased them to two wealthy businessmen and received in return nearly half a million dollars in "loans" to ease his private financial troubles. Fall was ultimately convicted of bribery and sentenced to a year in prison; Harry Daugherty barely avoided a similar fate for his part in another scandal.

In the summer of 1923, only months before Senate investigations and press revelations brought the scandals to light, a tired and depressed Harding left Washington for a speaking tour in the West. In Seattle late in July, he suffered severe pain, which his doctors wrongly diagnosed as food poisoning. A few days later, in San Francisco, he died. He had suffered two major heart attacks.

In many ways, Calvin Coolidge, who succeeded Harding in the presidency, was utterly different from his predecessor. Where Harding was genial, garrulous, and debauched, Coolidge was dour, silent, even puritanical. And while Harding was, if not perhaps personally corrupt, then at least tolerant of corruption in others, Coolidge seemed honest beyond reproach. In other ways, however, Harding and Coolidge were similar figures. Both took an essentially passive approach to their office.

Like Harding, Coolidge had risen to the presidency on the basis of few substantive accomplishments. Elected governor of Massachusetts in 1919, he had won national attention with his laconic response to the Boston police strike that year: "There is no right to strike against the public safety." That was enough to make him his party's vice presidential nominee in 1920. Three years later, after Harding's death, he took the oath of office from his father, a justice of the peace, by the light of a kerosene lamp.

If anything, Coolidge was even less active as president than Harding, partly as a result of his conviction that government should interfere as little as possible in the life of the nation. In 1924, he received his party's presidential nomination virtually unopposed. Running against John W. Davis, he won a comfortable victory: 54 percent of the popular vote and 382 of the 531 electoral votes. Robert La Follette, the candidate of the reincarnated Progressive Party, received 16 percent of the popular vote but carried only his home state of Wisconsin. Coolidge probably could have won renomination and reelection in 1928. Instead, in characteristically laconic fashion, he walked into a press room one day and handed each reporter a slip of paper containing a single sentence: "I do not choose to run for president in 1928."

Government and Business

The story of Harding and Coolidge themselves, however, is only a part—and by no means the most important part—of the story of their administrations. However passive the New Era presidents may have been, much of the federal government was working effectively and efficiently during the 1920s to adapt public policy to the widely accepted goal of the time: helping business and industry operate with maximum efficiency and productivity. The close relationship between the private sector and the federal government that had been forged during World War I continued. Secretary of the Treasury Andrew Mellon, a wealthy steel and aluminum tycoon, devoted himself to working for substantial reductions in taxes on corporate profits and personal incomes and inheritances. Largely because of his efforts, Congress cut them all by more than half. Mellon also worked closely with President Coolidge after 1924 on a series of measures to trim dramatically the already modest federal budget. The administration even managed to retire half the nation's World War I debt.

The most prominent member of the cabinet was Commerce Secretary Herbert Hoover, who considered himself, and was considered by others, a notable progressive. During his eight years in the Commerce Department, Hoover constantly encouraged voluntary cooperation in the private sector as the best avenue to stability. But the idea of voluntarism did not require that the government remain passive; on the contrary, public institutions, Hoover believed, had a duty to play an active role in creating the new, cooperative order. Above all, Hoover became the champion of the concept of business "associationalism"—a concept that envisioned the creation of national organizations of businessmen in particular industries. Through these trade associations, private entrepreneurs could, Hoover believed, stabilize their industries and promote efficiency in production and marketing.

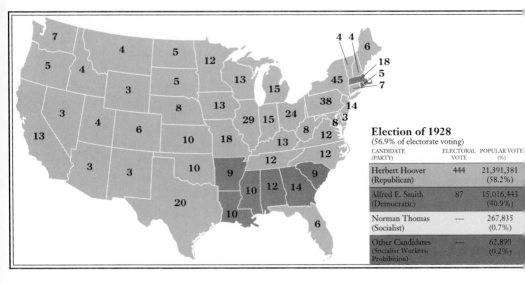

Election of 1928
(56.9% of electorate voting)

CANDIDATE (PARTY)	ELECTORAL VOTE	POPULAR VOTE (%)
Herbert Hoover (Republican)	444	21,391,381 (58.2%)
Alfred E. Smith (Democratic)	87	15,016,443 (40.9%)
Norman Thomas (Socialist)	---	267,835 (0.7%)
Other Candidates (Socialist Workers; Prohibition)	---	62,890 (0.2%)

Some progressives derived encouragement from the election of Herbert Hoover—widely regarded as the most progressive member of the Harding and Coolidge administrations—to the presidency in 1928. Hoover easily defeated Al Smith, the Democratic candidate. And he entered office promising bold new efforts to solve the nation's remaining economic problems. But Hoover had few opportunities to prove himself. Less than a year after his inauguration, the nation plunged into the severest and most prolonged economic crisis in its history—a crisis that brought many of the optimistic assumptions of the New Era crashing down and launched the nation into a period of unprecedented social innovation and reform.

CONCLUSION

The remarkable prosperity of the 1920s—a prosperity without parallel in the previous history of the United States—shaped much of what exuberant contemporaries liked to call the "New Era." In the years after World War I, America built a vibrant and extensive national culture. Its middle class moved increasingly into the embrace of the growing consumer culture. Its politics reorganized itself around the needs of a booming, interdependent industrial economy—rejecting many of the reform crusades of the previous generation, but also creating new institutions to help promote economic growth and stability.

Beneath the glittering surface of the New Era, however, were roiling controversies and timeless injustices clamoring for redress. Although the prosperity of the 1920s was more widely spread than at any time in the nation's industrial history, more than half the population failed to achieve any real benefits from the growth. A new, optimistic, secular culture was attracting millions of urban, middle-class people. But many other Americans looked at it with alarm and fought against it with great fervor. The unprepossessing conservative presidents of the era suggested a time with few political challenges, but in fact few eras in modern American history have seen so much political and cultural conflict.

The 1920s ended in a catastrophic economic crash that has colored the image of those years ever since. The crises of the 1930s should not obscure the real achievements of the New Era economy. Neither, however, should the prosperity of the 1920s obscure the inequity and instability in those years that helped produce the difficult years to come.

FOR FURTHER REFERENCE

Suggested Readings

Frederick Lewis Allen, *Only Yesterday* (1931) is a classic popular history of the 1920s. Michael Parrish, *Anxious Decades: America in Prosperity and Depression, 1920–1941* (1992) is a good recent survey. Ellis Hawley, *The Great War and the Search for a Modern Order* (1979) offers a good view of the institutional changes in American life in the 1920s. William E. Leuchtenburg, *The Perils of Prosperity* (1956, rev. ed. 1994) reveals the class divisions and culture dislocation that accompanied economic prosperity in the 1920s. David Brody, *Steelworkers in America* (1960) and *Workers in Industrial America* (1980) are important studies of labor after World War I. Jackson Lears, *Fables of Abundance: A Cultural History of Advertising in America* (1994) and Roland Marchand, *Advertising the American Dream* (1985) are both valuable inquiries into the important role of advertising in American culture. Robert Lynd and Helen Lynd, *Middletown* (1929) is a classic sociological study of how an American city encountered the new consumer economy and culture in the 1920s. Ann Douglas, *Terrible Honesty: Mongrel Manhattan in the 1920s* (1995) examines the cultural and political history of the New Era in New York City. George Chauncey, *Gay New York: Gender, Urban Culture, and the Making of the Gay Male World, 1890–1940* (1994) is an excellent work in a relatively new field of history. The decline of the feminist movement in the 1920s is explored in Nancy Cott, *The Grounding of American Feminism* (1987). Nathan I. Huggins chronicles the cultural and political efflorescence of black Harlem during these years in *Harlem Renaissance* (1971). George M. Marsden, *Fundamentalism and American Culture* (1980) is a good study of some of the religious controversies of the 1920s, and Leonard Moore, *Citizen*

Klansmen: The Ku Klux Klan in Indiana, 1921–1928 (1991) is a challenging view of the Klan. David Burner, *The Politics of Provincialism* (1967) is a good study of the ordeal of the Democratic Party in the 1920s. Morton Keller, *Regulating a New Economy: Public Policy and Economic Change in America, 1900–1933* (1990) and *Regulating a New Society: Public Policy and Social Change in America, 1900–1933* (1994) are important studies of New Era public policy.

Films

(The best source for information on how to find these and other films is *Bowker's Complete Video Directory*—3 volumes.) *Alfred Sloan & Corporate Bureaucracy* and *Herbert Hoover and Political Capitalism* (1981) are two selections from the American Business History Series that sketch the lives of key New Era business figures and through them provide an introduction to the changing American economic structure. The moving story of the southern West Virginia "mine war" of 1920–1921 has been artfully captured in *Matewan* (1987). *Coney Island* (1990) re-creates the drama and fantasy of Coney Island and explains its significance in the development of modern American consumer culture. *That Rhythm, Those Blues* (1997) documents the one-night stands, makeshift housing, and poor transportation that were all a step toward the big time at the famed Apollo Theatre on Harlem's 125th Street. *Mr. Sears' Catalogue* (1997) explores how the Sears' catalog became a symbol for the natural ambitions and dreams of a sprawling, fast developing America.

Internet Resources

Internet websites containing historical material relevant to the subjects discussed in this chapter can be reached through the McGraw-Hill history site at www.mhhe.com/socscience/history/usa/link/linktop.htm.

CHAPTER TWENTY-FIVE

The Great Depression

The Coming of the Depression ∼ *The American People in Hard Times*
The Depression and American Culture ∼ *The Ordeal of Herbert Hoover*

E IN AMERICA TODAY," Herbert Hoover proclaimed in August
1928, not long before his election to the presidency, "are nearer
to the final triumph over poverty than ever before in the history of any
land. The poorhouse is vanishing from among us." Only fifteen months
later, those words would return to haunt him, as the nation plunged into
the severest and most prolonged economic depression in its history—a depression that continued in one form or another for a full decade, not only
in the United States but throughout much of the world.

THE COMING OF THE DEPRESSION

The sudden financial collapse in 1929 came as an especially severe shock
because it followed so closely a period in which the New Era seemed to be
performing another series of economic miracles—miracles that seemed
especially evident in the remarkable performance of the stock market.

In February 1928, stock prices began a steady ascent that continued,
with only a few temporary lapses, for a year and a half. Between May 1928
and September 1929, the average price of stocks rose over 40 percent.
The stocks of the major industrials—the stocks that were used to determine the Dow Jones Industrial Average—doubled in value in that same
period. Trading mushroomed from 2 or 3 million shares a day to over
5 million, and at times to as many as 10 or 12 million. There was, in short,

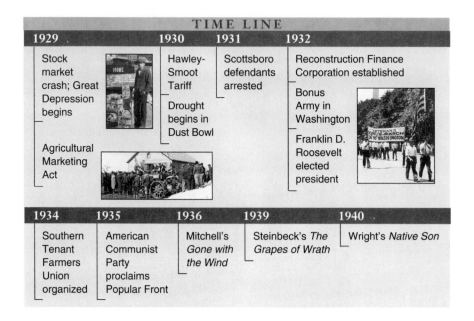

TIME LINE

1929	1930	1931	1932
Stock market crash; Great Depression begins	Hawley-Smoot Tariff	Scottsboro defendants arrested	Reconstruction Finance Corporation established
	Drought begins in Dust Bowl		Bonus Army in Washington
Agricultural Marketing Act			Franklin D. Roosevelt elected president

1934	1935	1936	1939	1940
Southern Tenant Farmers Union organized	American Communist Party proclaims Popular Front	Mitchell's *Gone with the Wind*	Steinbeck's *The Grapes of Wrath*	Wright's *Native Son*

a widespread speculative fever that grew steadily more intense, particularly once brokerage firms began encouraging the mania by offering absurdly easy credit to those buying stocks.

The Great Crash

In the autumn of 1929, the market began to fall apart. On October 29, "Black Tuesday," after a week of steadily rising instability, all efforts to save the market failed. Sixteen million shares of stock were traded; the industrial index dropped 43 points (or nearly 10 percent), wiping out all the gains of the previous year; stocks in many companies became virtually worthless. Within a month stocks had lost half their September value, and despite occasional, short-lived rallies, they continued to decline for several years after that. In July 1932, the industrial index—which had stood at 452 in September 1929—bottomed out at 58. The market did not fully recover for over a decade.

Popular folklore has established the stock market crash as the beginning, and even the cause, of the Great Depression. But although October 1929 might have been the most visible early sign of the crisis, the Depression had earlier beginnings and more important causes.

Causes of the Depression

Economists, historians, and others have argued for decades about the causes of the Great Depression. But most agree on several things. They agree, first, that what is remarkable about the crisis is not that it occurred, but that it was so severe and that it lasted so long. Most observers agree, too, that a number of different factors account for the severity of the crisis, even if there is considerable disagreement about which was the most important.

One of those factors was a lack of diversification in the American economy in the 1920s. Prosperity had depended excessively on a few basic industries, notably construction and automobiles. In the late 1920s, those industries began to decline. Expenditures on construction fell from $11 billion to under $9 billion between 1926 and 1929. Automobile sales fell by more than a third in the first nine months of 1929. Newer industries were emerging to take up the slack—among them petroleum, chemicals, and plastics—but had not yet developed enough strength to compensate for the decline in other sectors.

A second important factor was the maldistribution of purchasing power and, as a result, a weakness in consumer demand. As industrial and agricultural production increased, the proportion of the profits going to farmers, workers, and other potential consumers was too small to create an adequate market for the goods the economy was producing. Even in 1929, after nearly a decade of economic growth, more than half the families in America lived on the edge of or below the minimum subsistence level—too poor to buy the goods the industrial economy was producing.

A third major problem was the credit structure of the economy. Farmers were deeply in debt, and crop prices were too low to allow them to pay off what they owed. Small banks, especially those tied to the agricultural economy, were in constant trouble in the 1920s as their customers defaulted on loans; many of them failed. Large banks were in trouble, too. Although most American bankers were very conservative, some of the nation's biggest banks were investing recklessly in the stock market or making unwise loans. When the market crashed and the loans went bad, some banks failed and others made the crisis worse by contracting the already scarce credit and calling in loans that borrowers could not pay.

A fourth factor contributing to the Depression was America's position in international trade. Late in the 1920s, European demand for American goods began to decline. That was partly because European industry and agriculture were becoming more productive and partly because some European nations were having financial difficulties of their own and could not afford to buy goods from overseas. But it was also because the European economy was being destabilized by the international debt structure that had emerged in the aftermath of World War I.

The international debt structure, therefore, was a fifth factor contributing to the Depression. When the war came to an end in 1918, all the European nations that had been allied with the United States owed large sums of money to American banks, sums much too large to be repaid out of their shattered economies. That was one reason why the Allies had insisted (over Woodrow Wilson's objections) on reparation payments from Germany and Austria. Reparations, they believed, would provide them with a way to pay off their own debts. But Germany and Austria were themselves in economic trouble after the war; they were no more able to pay the reparations than the Allies were able to pay their debts.

The American government refused to forgive or reduce the debts. Instead, American banks began making large loans to European governments, which used them to pay off their earlier loans. Thus debts (and reparations) were being paid only by piling up new and greater debts. At the same time, American protective tariffs—many raised to their highest level ever by the Hawley-Smoot Tariff of 1930—were making it difficult for Europeans to sell their goods in American markets. Without any source of foreign exchange with which to repay their loans, they began to default. The collapse of the international credit structure was one of the reasons the Depression spread to Europe (and grew much worse in America) after 1931.

Progress of the Depression

The stock market crash of 1929 did not so much cause the Depression, then, as help trigger a chain of events that exposed larger weaknesses in the American economy. During the next three years, the crisis grew steadily worse.

The most serious problem at first was the collapse of much of the banking system. Over 9,000 American banks either went bankrupt or closed their doors to avoid bankruptcy between 1930 and 1933. Depositors lost over $2.5 billion in deposits. Partly as a result of these banking closures, the nation's money supply shrank by perhaps a third or more between 1930 and 1933. The declining money supply meant a decline in purchasing power, and thus deflation. Manufacturers and merchants

D E B A T I N G   T H E   P A S T

Causes of the Great Depression

W HAT WERE THE CAUSES of the Great Depression? Economists and historians have debated this question since the economic collapse began and still have not reached anything close to agreement on it. In the process, however, they have illustrated several very different theories about how a modern economy works.

During the Depression itself, different groups offered interpretations of the crisis that fit comfortably with their own self-interests. Some corporate leaders claimed that the Depression was the result of a lack of "business confidence," that businessmen were reluctant to invest because they feared government regulation and high taxes. The Hoover administration, unable to solve the crisis with the tools it considered acceptable, blamed international economic forces and sought, therefore, to stabilize world currencies and debt structures. New Dealers, determined to find a domestic solution to the crisis and ideologically inclined to place limits on corporate power, argued that the Depression was a crisis of "underconsumption," that low wages and high prices had made it too difficult to buy the products of the industrial economy; and that a lack of demand had led to the economic collapse. Other groups offered equally self-serving explanations.

(continued on next page)

Scholars in the years since the Great Depression have also created interpretations that fit their view of how the economy works and what public policies are appropriate for it. One of the first important postwar interpretations came from the economists Milton Friedman and Anna Schwartz, in their *Monetary History of the United States* (1963). In a chapter entitled "The Great Contraction," they argued for what has become known as the "monetary" interpretation. The Depression, they claimed, was a result of a drastic contraction of the currency (a result of mistaken decisions by the Federal Reserve Board, which raised interest rates when it should have lowered them). These deflationary measures turned an ordinary recession into the Great Depression. The monetary argument fits comfortably with the ideas that Milton Friedman, in particular, has advocated for many years: that sound monetary policy is the best way to solve economic problems—as opposed to fiscal policies, such as taxation and spending.

A second, very different argument is known as the "spending" interpretation, an interpretation supported by many liberal, Keynesian economists. It is identified with, among others, the economist Peter Temin, and his book *Did Monetary Forces Cause the Great Depression?* (1976). Temin's answer to his own question is "no." The cause of the crisis was not monetary contraction (although the contraction made it worse), but a drop in investment and consumer spending, which preceded the decline in the money supply and helped to cause it. Here again, there are obvious political implications. If a decline in spending was the cause of the Depression, then the proper response was an effort to stimulate demand—raising government spending, increasing purchasing power, redistributing wealth. The New Deal never ended the Depression because it did not spend enough. World War II did end it because it pumped so much public money into the economy. This is a liberal, Keynesian explanation, just as the "monetary hypothesis" is a more conservative explanation.

Another important explanation comes from the historian Michael Bernstein. In *The Great Depression* (1987) he avoids trying to explain why the economic downturn occurred and asks, instead, why it lasted so long. The reason the recession of 1929 became the Depression of the 1930s, he argues, was the timing of the collapse. The recession began as an ordinary cyclical downturn. Had it begun a few years earlier, the basic strength of the automobile and construction industries in the 1920s would have led to a reasonably speedy recovery. Had it begun a few years later, a group of newer, emerging industries would have helped produce a recovery in a reasonably short time. But the recession began in 1929, too late for the automobile and construction industries to help (since they had already experienced a serious, long-term relative decline) and too soon for emerging new industries—aviation, petrochemicals and plastics, aluminum, electronics and electrical appliances, processed foods, and others—to help, since they were still in their infancies.

The political implications of this argument are less obvious than those of some other interpretations. But one possible conclusion is that if economic growth depends on the successful development of new industries to replace declining ones, then the most sensible economic policy for government is to target investment and other policies toward the growth of new economic sectors. One of the reasons World War II was so important to the long-term recovery of the U.S. economy, Bernstein's argument suggests, was not just that it pumped money into the economy, but that much of that money contributed to developing new industries that would help sustain prosperity after the war. This is, in other words, an explanation of the Depression that seems to support some of the economic ideas that have become popular in the 1980s and 1990s calling for a more direct government role in stimulating the growth of new industries.

In the end, however, no single explanation of the Great Depression has ever seemed adequate to most scholars. The event, the economist Robert Lucas once argued, is simply "inexplicable" by any rational calculation. There is no one, wholly persuasive answer—at least no answer that an economist or historian has produced—to the question of what caused it.

began reducing prices, cutting back on production, and laying off workers. Some economists argue that a severe depression could have been avoided if the Federal Reserve system had acted responsibly. But late in 1931, in a misguided effort to build international confidence in the dollar, it raised interest rates, which contracted the money supply even further and hastened the demise of many banks and corporations.

The American gross national product plummeted from over $104 billion in 1929 to $76.4 billion in 1932—a 25 percent decline in three years. In 1929, Americans had spent $16.2 billion to promote capital growth; in 1933, they invested only a third of a billion. By 1932, according to the relatively crude estimates of the time, 25 percent of the American work force was unemployed. (Some believe the figure was even higher.) For the rest of the decade, unemployment averaged nearly 20 percent, never dropping below 15 percent. Up to another one-third of the work force was "underemployed"—experiencing major reductions in wages, hours, or both.

THE AMERICAN PEOPLE IN HARD TIMES

Someone asked the British economist John Maynard Keynes in the 1930s whether he was aware of any historical era comparable to the Great Depression. "Yes," Keynes replied. "It was called the Dark Ages, and it lasted 400 years." The Depression did not last 400 years. It did, however, bring unprecedented despair to the economies of the United States and much of the Western world. And it had far-reaching effects on American society and culture.

Unemployment and Relief

In the industrial Northeast and Midwest, cities were becoming virtually paralyzed by unemployment. Cleveland, Ohio, for example, had an unemployment rate of 50 percent in 1932; Akron, 60 percent; Toledo, 80 percent. Unemployed workers walked through the streets day after day looking for jobs that did not exist. An increasing number of families were turning to state and local public relief systems, just to be able to eat. But those systems, which in the 1920s had served only a small number of indigents, were totally unequipped to handle the new demands being placed on them. In many cities, therefore, relief simply collapsed. Private charities attempted to supplement the public relief efforts, but the problem was far beyond their capabilities as well.

In rural areas conditions were in many ways worse. Farm income declined by 60 percent between 1929 and 1932. A third of all American farmers lost their land. In addition, a large area of agricultural settlement in the Great Plains was suffering from a catastrophic natural disaster: one of the worst droughts in the history of the nation. Beginning in 1930, the region, which came to be known as the "Dust Bowl" and which stretched north from Texas into the Dakotas, experienced a steady decline in rainfall and an accompanying increase in heat. The drought continued for a decade, turning what had once been fertile farm regions into virtual deserts. It is a measure of how productive American farmers were and how depressed the market for agricultural goods had become that even with these disastrous conditions, the farm economy continued through the 1930s to produce far more than American or world consumers could afford to buy.

Many farmers, like many urban unemployed, left their homes in search of work. In the South, in particular, many dispossessed farmers—black and white—simply wandered from town to town, hoping to find jobs or handouts. Hundreds of thousands of families from the Dust Bowl (often known as "Okies," since many came from Oklahoma) traveled to California and other states, where they found conditions little better than

SELLING APPLES, NEW YORK CITY In the fall of 1931 and again in the fall of 1932, large numbers of unemployed took to selling apples on the streets of major cities and became in the process a popular symbol of economic despair.

AUCTIONING OFF A FARM Farm auctions such as this one, photographed in 1940 near Hastings, Nebraska, by the Farm Security Administration photographer Arthur Rothstein, were common sights in rural America during the Great Depression. Even after New Deal farm programs improved the fortunes of the agricultural economy as a whole, many small farmers continued to face debts they could not pay and hence foreclosure on their lands.

those they had left. Owning no land of their own, many worked as agricultural migrants, traveling from farm to farm picking fruit and other crops at starvation wages.

African Americans and the Depression

Most African Americans had not shared very much in the prosperity of the previous decade. But they did share the hardships of the Great Depression. They experienced more unemployment, homelessness, malnutrition, and disease than they had in the past, and more than most whites experienced.

As the Depression began, over half of all black Americans still lived in the South. Most were farmers. The collapse of prices for cotton and other staple crops left some with no income at all. Many left the land altogether—either by choice or because they had been evicted by landlords who no longer found the sharecropping system profitable. Some migrated to southern cities. But there, unemployed whites believed they had first claim to what work there was, and some now began to take positions as janitors, street cleaners, and domestic servants, displacing the blacks who formerly occupied those jobs. By 1932, over half the blacks in the South were without employment. And what limited relief there was went almost invariably to whites first.

Unsurprisingly, therefore, many black southerners—perhaps 400,000 in all—left the South in the 1930s and journeyed to the cities of the North. There they generally found less blatant discrimination. But conditions were in most respects little better than those in the South. In New York, black unemployment was nearly 50 percent. In other cities, it was higher. Two million African Americans—half the total black population of the country—were on some form of relief by 1932.

Traditional patterns of segregation and disfranchisement in the South survived the Depression largely unchallenged. But a few particularly notorious examples of racism did attract the attention of the nation. The most celebrated was the Scottsboro case. In March 1931, nine black teenagers were taken off a freight train in northern Alabama (in a small town near Scottsboro) and arrested for vagrancy and disorder. Later, two white women who had also been riding the train accused them of rape. In fact, there was overwhelming evidence, medical and otherwise, that the women had not been raped at all; they may have made their accusations out of fear of being arrested themselves. Nevertheless, an all-white jury in Alabama quickly convicted all nine of the "Scottsboro boys" (as they were known to both friends and foes) and sentenced eight of them to death.

The Supreme Court overturned the convictions in 1932, and a series of new trials began that gradually attracted national attention. The International Labor Defense, an organization associated with the Communist Party, came to the aid of the accused youths and began to publicize the case. Although the white southern juries who sat on the case never acquitted any of the defendants, all of the accused eventually gained their freedom—although the last of the Scottsboro defendants did not leave prison until 1950.

Hispanics and Asians in Depression America

Similar patterns of discrimination confronted many Mexicans and Mexican Americans. The Hispanic population of the United States had been growing steadily since early in the century, largely in California and other areas of the Southwest through massive immigration from Mexico (which was specifically excluded from the immigration restriction laws of the

1920s). Chicanos (as Mexican Americans are sometimes known) filled many of the same menial jobs there that blacks had traditionally filled in other regions. Some farmed small, marginal tracts. Some became agricultural migrants, traveling from region to region harvesting fruit, lettuce, and other crops. It had always been a precarious existence, and the Depression made things significantly worse. Unemployed whites in the Southwest demanded jobs held by Hispanics, jobs that whites had previously considered beneath them. Thus Mexican unemployment rose quickly to levels far higher than those for whites. Some officials arbitrarily removed Mexicans from relief rolls or simply rounded them up and transported them across the border. Perhaps half a million Chicanos left the United States for Mexico in the first years of the Depression.

There were, occasionally, signs of organized resistance by Mexican Americans themselves, most notably in California, where some formed a union of migrant farmworkers. But harsh repression by local growers and the public authorities allied with them prevented such organizations from having much impact. As a result, many Hispanics, like many African-American farmworkers, began to migrate to cities such as Los Angeles, where they lived in a poverty comparable to that of urban blacks in the South and Northeast.

For Asian Americans, too, the Depression reinforced longstanding patterns of discrimination and economic marginalization. In California, where the largest Japanese-American and Chinese-American populations were, even educated Asians had always found it difficult, if not impossible, to move into mainstream professions. Japanese-American college graduates often found themselves working in family fruit stands; 20 percent of all people of Japanese descent in Los Angeles worked at such stands at the end of the 1930s. For those who found jobs (usually poorly paid) in the industrial or service economy, employment was precarious; like blacks and Hispanics, Asians often lost jobs to white Americans desperate for work—jobs that a few years earlier the whites would not have considered accepting. Japanese farmworkers, like Chicano farmworkers, suffered from the increasing competition for even these low-paying jobs from white migrants from the Great Plains.

Chinese Americans fared no better. The overwhelming majority worked, as they had for many years, in Chinese-owned laundries and restaurants. Those who moved outside the Asian community could rarely find jobs above the entry level. Chinese women, for example, might find work as stock girls in department stores but almost never as salesclerks. Educated Chinese men and women could hope for virtually no professional opportunities outside the world of the Chinatowns.

Women and Families in the Great Depression

The economic crisis served in many ways to strengthen the widespread belief that a woman's proper place was in the home. Most men and many women believed that with employment so scarce, what work there was should go to men. There was a particularly strong belief that no woman whose husband was employed should accept a job. Indeed, from 1932 until 1937, it was illegal for more than one member of a family to hold a federal civil service job.

But the widespread assumption that married women, at least, should not work outside the home did not stop them from doing so. Both single and married women worked in the 1930s, despite public condemnation of the practice, because they or their families needed the money. By the end of the Depression, 25 percent more women were working than had been doing so at the beginning. This occurred despite considerable obstacles. Professional opportunities for women declined because unemployed men began moving into professions that had previously been considered women's fields, such as teaching and social work. Female industrial workers were more likely to be laid off or to experience wage reductions than their male counterparts. But white women also had certain advantages in the workplace. The nonprofessional jobs that women traditionally held—salesclerks, stenographers, and other service positions—were less likely to disappear than the predominantly male jobs in heavy industry.

Black women suffered massive unemployment, particularly in the South, because of a great reduction of domestic service jobs. As many as half of all black working women lost their jobs in the 1930s. Even so, at the end of the 1930s, 38 percent of black women were employed, as compared with 24 percent of white women. That was because black women—both married and unmarried—had always been more likely to work than white women, less out of preference than out of economic necessity.

The economic hardships of the Depression years placed great strains on American families. Middle-class families that had become accustomed in the 1920s to a steadily increasing standard of living now found themselves plunged suddenly into uncertainty, because of unemployment or the reduction of incomes among those who remained employed. Some working-class families had achieved a precarious prosperity in the 1920s as well, but saw their gains disappear in the 1930s. Such circumstances caused many families to change the way they lived. Some women returned to sewing clothes for themselves and their families and to preserving their own food. Others engaged in home businesses such as taking in laundry or boarders. Many households expanded to take in relatives (grandparents, grandchildren, and others) who needed assistance.

But the Depression also worked to erode the strength of many family units. There was a decline in the divorce rate, but largely because divorce was now too expensive for some. More common was the informal breakup of families, particularly the desertion of families by unemployed men trying to escape the humiliation of being unable to earn a living. The marriage rate and the birth rate both declined for the first time since the early nineteenth century.

THE DEPRESSION AND AMERICAN CULTURE

The Great Depression was a traumatic experience for millions of Americans, and it shook the confidence of many people in themselves, in their nation, and sometimes in both. Out of the crisis emerged probing criticisms of American life. But the Depression also produced powerful confirmations of more traditional values and reinforced many traditional goals. There was not one Depression culture, but many.

Depression Values

Prosperity and industrial growth had done much to shape American values in the 1920s. Mainstream culture, at least, had celebrated affluence and consumerism and had stressed the importance of personal gratification through both. Many Americans assumed, therefore, that the experience of hard times would have profound effects on the nation's social values. In general, however, American social values seemed to change relatively little in response to the Depression. Instead, many people responded to hard times by redoubling their commitment to familiar ideas and goals.

No assumption would seem to have been more vulnerable to erosion during the Depression than the belief that the individual was in control of his or her own fate, that anyone displaying sufficient talent and industry could become a success. And in some respects, the economic crisis did work to undermine the traditional "success ethic" in America. Many people began to look to government for assistance; many learned to blame corporate moguls, international bankers, "economic royalists," and others for their distress. Yet the Depression did not destroy the success ethic.

The survival of the ideals of work and individual responsibility was evident in many ways, not least in the reactions of those most traumatized by the Depression: conscientious working people who suddenly found themselves without employment. Some expressed anger and struck out at the economic system. Many, however, seemed to blame themselves. Many of the unemployed tended to hide themselves, unwilling to display to the world what they considered their own personal failure. At the same time, millions responded eagerly to reassurances that they could, through their own efforts, restore themselves to prosperity and success. Dale Carnegie's *How to Win Friends and Influence People* (1936), a self-help manual preaching individual initiative, was one of the best-selling books of the decade.

Artists and Intellectuals in the Great Depression

Not all Americans, of course, responded to the crisis of the Depression so passively. Among the many people who saw the hard times as evidence of deep-rooted social injustice were many artists and intellectuals. Some of them engaged in a broad effort to dramatize the problem of rural poverty and to use it as an indictment of the failures of the economic system. Among those involved in this venture was a group of documentary photographers, many of them employed by the federal Farm Security Administration in the late 1930s, who traveled through the South recording the nature of agricultural life. Men such as Roy Stryker, Walker Evans, Arthur Rothstein, and Ben Shahn and women such as Margaret Bourke-White and Dorothea Lange produced memorable studies of farm families and their surroundings, studies designed to show the savage impact of a hostile environment on its victims. Many writers, similarly, devoted themselves to exposés of social injustice. Erskine Caldwell's *Tobacco Road* (1932), which later became a long-running play, was an exposé of poverty in the rural South. Richard Wright, a major African-American novelist, exposed the plight of residents of the urban ghetto in *Native Son* (1940).

But the cultural products of the 1930s that attracted the widest popular audiences were those that diverted attention away from the Depression. And they came to Americans primarily through the two most powerful instruments of popular culture in the 1930s—radio and the movies.

Radio

Almost every American family had a radio in the 1930s. In cities and towns, radio consoles were as familiar a part of the furnishing of parlors and kitchens as tables and chairs. Even in remote rural areas without access to electricity, many families purchased radios and hooked them up to car batteries when they wished to listen.

Listening to radio is generally considered a private experience—something people do alone, or with their families, in their homes, rather than out in public with others. But in some communities, radio was often a community experience. Young people would place radios on their front porches and invite friends by to sit, talk, or dance. In poor urban neighborhoods, many people who could not afford other kinds of social activities would gather on a street or in a backyard to listen to sporting events or concerts. Within families, the radio often drew parents and children together to listen to favorite programs.

What did Americans hear on the radio? Although radio stations occasionally carried socially and politically provocative programs, the staple of broadcasting was escapism: comedies such as *Amos 'n Andy* (with its humorous if demeaning picture of urban blacks); adventures such as *Superman*, *Dick Tracy*, and *The Lone Ranger;* and other entertainment programs. Radio brought a new kind of comedy—previously limited to vaudeville or to ethnic theaters—to a wide audience. Jack Benny, George Burns and Gracie Allen, and other masters of elaborately-timed jokes and repartee began to develop broad followings (that they would later take with them to television). Soap operas, also later to become staples of television programming, were enormously popular as well in the 1930s, especially with women who were alone in the house during the day. (That was why they became known as soap operas; soap companies—whose advertising was targeted at women—generally sponsored them.)

Radio provided Americans with their first direct access to important public events, and radio news and sports divisions grew rapidly to meet the demand. Some of the most dramatic moments of the 1930s were a result of radio coverage of celebrated events: the World Series, major college football games, the Academy Awards, political conventions, presidential inaugurations. When the German dirigible the *Hindenburg* crashed in flames in Lakehurst, New Jersey, in 1937 after a transoceanic voyage, it produced an enormous national reaction largely because of the live radio account by a broadcaster overcome with emotion who cried out, as he watched the terrible crash, "Oh the humanity! Oh the humanity!" The actor/director Orson Welles created another memorable event on Halloween night, 1938, when he broadcast a radio play about aliens whose spaceship landed in central New Jersey and who had set off toward New York armed with terrible weapons. The play took the form of a news broadcast, and it created panic among millions of people who believed for a while that the events it described were real.

The Movies

In the first years of the Depression, movie attendance dropped significantly. By the mid-1930s, however, most Americans had resumed their moviegoing habits—in part because movies were a less expensive entertainment option than many other possibilities, and in part because the movies themselves (all of them now with sound, and by the end of the decade many of them in color) were becoming more appealing.

In many ways, movies were as safely conventional in the 1930s as they had been in the late 1920s. Hollywood continued to exercise tight control over its products in the 1930s through its resilient censor Will Hays, who ensured that most movies carried no sensational or controversial messages. The studio system—through which a few large movie companies exercised iron control over actors, writers, and directors, and through which a few great moguls such as Louis B. Mayer or Jack Warner could single-handedly decide the fate of most projects—also worked to ensure that Hollywood films avoided controversy.

Neither the censor nor the studio system, however, could (or wished to) prevent films from exploring social questions altogether. A few films, such as King Vidor's *Our Daily Bread* (1932) and John Ford's adaptation of *The Grapes of Wrath* (1940), did explore political themes. Gangster movies such as *Little Caesar* (1930) and *The Public Enemy* (1931) portrayed a dark, gritty, violent world with which few Americans were familiar, but their desperate stories were popular nevertheless with those engaged in their own difficult struggles; and they made stars out of such otherwise unlikely actors as James Cagney and Edward G. Robinson.

But the most effective presentation of a social message, even if a muted one, came from the brilliant Italian-born director Frank Capra, whose remarkable comedies became some of the most important cultural products of the 1930s. Capra had a deep and somewhat romanticized love for his adopted country, and he translated that love into a vaguely populistic admiration for ordinary people. He contrasted the decency of small-town America and the common man with what he considered the grasping opportunism of the city and the greedy capitalist marketplace. In *Mr. Deeds Goes to Town* (1936), a simple man from a small town inherits a large fortune, moves to the city, and—not liking the greed and dishonesty he finds there—gives the money away and moves back home. In *Mr. Smith Goes to Washington* (1939), a decent man from a western state is elected to the United States Senate, refuses to join in the self-interested politics of Washington, and dramatically exposes the corruption and selfishness of

MR. DEEDS GOES TO TOWN Gary Cooper, playing the newly wealthy Longfellow Deeds, leaves the friendly, virtuous small town of Mandrake Falls en route to New York to receive the fortune he has inherited. Capra's evocation of the warmth and generosity of Mandrake Falls was part of his effort to contrast the decent America of ordinary people with the grasping and corrupt America of the wealthy and the city.

his colleagues. "I would sing the songs of the working stiffs, of the short-changed Joes, the born poor, the afflicted," he once wrote. "I would fight their causes on the screens of the world." His films, outstandingly popular in the 1930s, helped audiences find solace in a vision of an imagined American past—in the warmth and goodness of idealized small towns and the decency of ordinary people.

More often, however, the commercial films of the 1930s, like most radio programs, were deliberately and explicitly escapist: lavish musicals such as *Gold Diggers of 1933* (whose theme song was "We're in the Money"), "screwball" comedies (such as Capra's *It Happened One Night*, produced before his "social" comedies), or the many films of the Marx Brothers—films designed to divert audiences from their troubles and, often, indulge their fantasies about quick and easy wealth.

The 1930s saw the beginning of Walt Disney's long reign as the champion of animation and children's entertainment. After producing cartoon shorts for theaters in the late 1920s, many of them starring the newly-created character of Mickey Mouse, who made his debut in the 1928 cartoon *Steamboat Willie*, Disney began to produce feature-length animated films, starting in 1937 with *Snow White*. Other enormously popular films of the 1930s were adaptations of popular novels: *The Wizard of Oz* and *Gone with the Wind*, both released in 1939.

Hollywood did little to challenge the conventions of popular culture on issues of gender and race. Women in movies were portrayed overwhelmingly as wives and mothers, or if not, as sexually attractive people engaged in elaborate flirtations (although seldom more than that) with men. Mae West portrayed herself in a series of successful films as an overtly sexual woman manipulating men through her attractiveness (although in her own life West was a successful, wealthy, and independent producer of films, her own and others). Few films included important African-American characters. Most of the black men and women who did appear in movies were portrayed as servants or farmhands.

Popular Literature and Journalism

The social and political strains of the Great Depression found voice much more successfully in print than they did on the airwaves or the screen. Much literature and journalism in the 1930s dealt directly or indirectly with the tremendous disillusionment, and the increasing radicalism, of the time.

Not all literature, of course, was challenging or controversial. The most popular books and magazines of the time, in fact, were as escapist and romantic as the most popular radio shows and movies. Two of the best-selling novels of the decade were romantic sagas set in earlier eras: Margaret Mitchell's *Gone with the Wind* (1936) and Hervey Allen's *Anthony Adverse* (1933). Leading magazines focused more on fashions, stunts, scenery, and the arts than on the social conditions of the nation. The enormously popular new photographic journal *Life*, which began publication in 1936 and quickly became one of the most successful magazines in American history, had the largest readership of any publication in the United States (with the exception of the *Reader's Digest*). It devoted some attention to politics and to the economic conditions of the Depression, more in fact than did many of its competitors. But it was best known for stunning photographs of sporting and theater events, natural landscapes, and impressive public projects. Its first cover was a striking picture by Margaret Bourke-White of a New Deal hydroelectric project. One of its most popular features was "*Life* Goes to a Party," which took the chatty social columns of daily newspapers and turned them into glossy photo-graphic glimpses of the rich and famous.

Other Depression writing, however, was frankly and openly challeng-ing to the dominant values of American popular culture. In the first years of the Depression, some of the most significant literature offered corro-sive portraits of the harshness and emptiness of American life: John Dos Passos's *U.S.A.* trilogy (1930–1936), which attacked what he considered the materialistic madness of American culture; Nathanael West's *Miss Lonelyhearts* (1933), the story of an advice columnist overwhelmed by the sadness he encounters in the lives of those who consult him; Jack Conroy's *The Disinherited* (1933), a harsh portrait of the lives of coalminers; and James T. Farrell's *Studs Lonigan* (1932), a portrait of a lost, hardened working-class youth.

The Popular Front and the Left

In the later 1930s, much of the political literature adopted a more opti-mistic, although often no less radical, approach to society. This was in part a result of the rise of the Popular Front, a broad coalition of "antifascist" groups on the left, of which the most important was the American Com-munist Party. The party had long been a harsh and unrelenting critic of American capitalism and the government it claimed was controlled by it. But in 1935, under instructions from the Soviet Union, the party softened its attitude toward Franklin Roosevelt (whom Stalin now saw as a poten-tial ally in the coming battle against Hitler) and formed loose alliances with many other "progressive" groups. The party began to praise the New Deal and John L. Lewis, a powerful (and strongly anticommunist) labor leader, and it adopted the slogan "Communism is twentieth-century Americanism." In its heyday, the Popular Front did much to enhance the reputation and influence of the Communist Party, whose formal member-ship grew to perhaps 100,000 in the mid-1930s, the highest it had ever been or ever would be again. But it also helped mobilize writers, artists, and intellectuals—many of them unconnected with (and many of them uninterested in) the party—behind a critical, democratic sensibility.

For intellectuals, the Popular Front offered an escape from the lonely and difficult stance of detachment and alienation many had embraced in the 1920s. The importance to many American intellectuals of the Spanish Civil War of the mid-1930s was a good example of how the left helped give meaning and purpose to individual lives. The war in Spain pitted the fascists of Francisco Franco (who was receiving support from Hitler and

Mussolini) against the existing republican government. It attracted a substantial group of young Americans—more than 3,000 in all—who formed the Abraham Lincoln Brigade and traveled to Spain to join in the fight against the fascists. About a third of its members died in combat; but those who survived remembered the experience with pride, as one of the great moments of their lives. The American Communist Party was instrumental in creating the Lincoln Brigade, and directed many of its activities.

The party was active as well in organizing the unemployed in the early 1930s and staged a hunger march in Washington, D.C., in 1931. Party members were among the most effective union organizers in some industries. And the party was virtually alone among political organizations in taking a firm stand in favor of racial justice; its active defense of the Scottsboro defendants was but one example of its efforts to ally itself with the aspirations of African Americans. It also helped organize a union of black sharecroppers in Alabama, which resisted—in several instances violently—efforts of white landowners and authorities to displace them from their farms.

The American Communist Party was not, however, the open, patriotic organization it tried to appear. It was always under the close and rigid supervision of the Soviet Union. Its leaders took their orders from the Comintern in Moscow. Most members obediently followed the "party line" (although there were many areas in which Communists were active for which there was no party line, areas in which members acted independently). The subordination of the party leadership to the Soviet Union was most clearly demonstrated in 1939, when Stalin signed a nonaggression pact with Nazi Germany. Moscow then sent orders to the American Communist Party to abandon the Popular Front and return to its old stance of harsh criticism of American liberals; and Communist Party leaders in the United States immediately obeyed—although thousands of disillusioned members left the party as a result.

The Socialist Party of America, now under the leadership of Norman Thomas, also cited the economic crisis as evidence of the failure of capitalism and sought vigorously to win public support for its own political program. Among other things, it attempted to mobilize support among the rural poor. The Southern Tenant Farmers Union, supported by the party and organized by a young socialist, H. L. Mitchell, attempted to create a biracial coalition of sharecroppers, tenant farmers, and others to demand economic reform. Neither the STFU nor the party itself, however, made any real progress toward establishing socialism as a major force in American politics. By 1936, in fact, membership in the Socialist Party had fallen below 20,000.

Antiradicalism was a powerful force in the 1930s, just as it had been during and after World War I and would be again in the 1940s and 1950s. Hostility toward the Communist Party, in particular, was intense at many levels of government. Congressional committees chaired by Hamilton Fish of New York and Martin Dies of Texas investigated communist influence wherever they could find it (or imagine it). State and local governments harried and sometimes imprisoned communist organizers. White southerners tried to drive communist organizers out of the countryside, just as growers in California and elsewhere tried (unsuccessfully) to keep communists from organizing Mexican-American and other workers.

Even so, at few times before (and few since) in American history did being part of the left seem so respectable and even conventional among workers, intellectuals, and others. Thus the 1930s witnessed an impressive, if temporary, widening of the ideological range of mainstream art and politics. The New Deal, for example, sponsored artistic work through the Works Projects Administration that was frankly challenging to the capitalist norms of the 1920s. The filmmaker Pare Lorentz, with funding from New Deal agencies, made a series of powerful documentaries—*The Plow that Broke the Plains* (1936), *The River* (1937)—that combined a celebration of New Deal programs with a harsh critique of the exploitation of people and the environment that industrial capitalism had produced.

A less confrontational grappling with the social misery of the 1930s was a remarkable book by the novelist James Agee and the photographer Walker Evans, *Let Us Now Praise Famous Men* (1941). Agee and Walker had traveled to rural Alabama in the mid-1930s on an assignment from *Fortune* magazine, a business-oriented periodical published by Henry Luce (who was also the founder and publisher of *Time* and *Life*). Luce had asked Agee and Walker to produce an article about sharecropping and rural poverty. The long, rambling, highly emotional text that Agee produced, accompanied by extraordinary photographs of three families of white southern sharecroppers, was too long and too unconventional for *Fortune*. But the book that eventually appeared, although it attracted little attention at the time, is an enduring portrait of a distressed area of what Agee called "human existence," but also a passionate tribute to the strength and even nobility of the struggling people he had come to know.

Perhaps the most successful chronicler of social conditions in the 1930s was the novelist John Steinbeck, particularly in his celebrated novel *The Grapes of Wrath*, published in 1939. In telling the story of the Joad family, migrants from the Dust Bowl to California who encounter an unending string of calamities and failures, he offered a harsh portrait of the exploitive features of agrarian life in the West, but also a tribute to the endurance of his main characters—and to the spirit of community they represent.

THE ORDEAL OF HERBERT HOOVER

Herbert Hoover began his presidency in March 1929 believing, like most Americans, that the nation faced a bright and prosperous future. For the first six months of his administration, he attempted to expand the policies he had advocated during his eight years as secretary of commerce, policies that would, he believed, complete a stable system of cooperative individualism and sustain a successful economy. The economic crisis that began before the year was out forced the president to deal with a new set of problems, but for most of the rest of his term, he continued to rely on the principles that had always governed his public life.

The Hoover Program

Hoover's first response to the Depression was to attempt to restore public confidence in the economy. "The fundamental business of this country, that is, production and distribution of commodities," he said in 1930, "is on a sound and prosperous basis." He then summoned leaders of business, labor, and agriculture to the White House and urged them to adopt a program of voluntary cooperation for recovery. He implored businessmen not to cut production or lay off workers; he talked labor leaders into forgoing demands for higher wages or better hours. But by mid-1931, economic conditions had deteriorated so much that the structure of voluntary cooperation he had erected collapsed.

Hoover also attempted to use government spending as a tool for fighting the Depression. The president proposed to Congress an increase of $423 million—a significant sum by the standards of the time—in federal public works programs, and he exhorted state and local governments to fund public construction. But the spending was not nearly enough in the face of such devastating problems. And when economic conditions worsened, he became less willing to increase spending, worrying instead about keeping the budget balanced. In 1932, at the depth of the Depression, he proposed a tax increase to help the government avoid a deficit.

Even before the stock market crash, Hoover had begun to construct a program to assist the already troubled agricultural economy. In April 1929, he proposed the Agricultural Marketing Act, which established the first major government program to help farmers maintain prices. A federally sponsored Farm Board would make loans to national marketing cooperatives or establish corporations to buy surpluses and thus raise prices. At the same time, Hoover attempted to protect American farmers from international competition by raising agricultural tariffs. The Hawley-Smoot Tariff of 1930 contained increased protection on seventy-five farm products. But neither the Agricultural Marketing Act nor the Hawley-Smoot Tariff ultimately helped American farmers significantly.

By the spring of 1931, Herbert Hoover's political position had deteriorated considerably. In the 1930 congressional elections, Democrats won control of the House and made substantial inroads in the Senate by promising increased government assistance to the economy. Many Americans held the president personally to blame for the crisis and began calling the shantytowns that unemployed people established on the outskirts of cities "Hoovervilles." Democrats urged the president to support more vigorous programs of relief and public spending. Hoover, instead, seized on a slight improvement in economic conditions early in 1931 as proof that his policies were working.

The international financial panic of the spring of 1931 destroyed the illusion that the economic crisis was coming to an end. Throughout the 1920s, European nations had depended on loans from American banks to allow them to make payments on their debts. After 1929, when they could no longer get such loans, the financial fabric of several European nations began to unravel. In May 1931, the largest bank in Austria collapsed. Over the next several months, panic gripped the financial institutions of neighboring countries. The American economy rapidly declined to new lows.

By the time Congress convened in December 1931, conditions had grown so desperate that Hoover supported a series of measures designed to keep endangered banks afloat and protect homeowners from foreclosure on their mortgages. More important was a bill passed in January 1932 establishing the Reconstruction Finance Corporation (RFC), a government agency whose purpose was to provide federal loans to troubled banks, railroads, and other businesses. It even made funds available to local governments to support public works projects and assist relief efforts. Unlike some earlier Hoover programs, it operated on a large scale. In 1932, the RFC had a budget of $1.5 billion for public works alone.

Nevertheless, the new agency failed to deal directly or forcefully enough with the real problems of the economy to produce any significant recovery. The RFC lent funds only to financial institutions with sufficient collateral; much of its money went to large banks and corporations. At

Hoover's insistence, it helped finance only those public works projects that promised ultimately to pay for themselves (toll bridges, public housing, and others). Above all, the RFC did not have enough money to make any real impact on the Depression, and it did not even spend all the money it had. Of the $300 million available to support local relief efforts, the RFC lent out only $30 million in 1932. Of the $1.5 billion public works budget, it released only about 20 percent.

Popular Protest

For the first several years of the Depression, most Americans were either too stunned or too confused to raise any effective protest. By the middle of 1932, however, dissident voices began to be heard.

In the summer of 1932, a group of unhappy farm owners gathered in Des Moines, Iowa, to establish a new organization: the Farmers' Holiday Association, which endorsed the withholding of farm products from the market—in effect a farmers' strike. The strike began in August in western Iowa, spread briefly to a few neighboring areas, and succeeded in blockading several markets, but in the end it dissolved in failure.

A more celebrated protest movement emerged from American veterans. In 1924, Congress had approved the payment of a $1,000 bonus to all those who had served in World War I, the money to be paid beginning in 1945. By 1932, however, many veterans were demanding that the bonus be paid immediately. Hoover, concerned about balancing the budget, rejected their appeal. In June, more than 20,000 veterans, members of the self-proclaimed Bonus Expeditionary Force, or "Bonus Army," marched into Washington, built crude camps around the city, and promised to stay until Congress approved legislation to pay the bonus. Some of the veterans departed in July, after Congress had voted down their proposal. Many, however, remained where they were.

Their continued presence in Washington embarrassed President Hoover. Finally, in mid-July, he ordered police to clear the marchers out of several abandoned federal buildings in which they had been staying. A few marchers threw rocks at the police, and someone opened fire; two veterans fell dead. Hoover called the incident evidence of uncontrolled violence and radicalism, and he ordered the United States Army to assist the police in clearing out the buildings.

General Douglas MacArthur, the army chief of staff, carried out the mission himself (with the assistance of his aide, Dwight D. Eisenhower) and greatly exceeded the president's orders. He led the Third Cavalry (under

THE BONUS MARCH The 1932 march on Washington by the so-called Bonus Army ended in violent disarray. But it began in high spirits and something close to military precision—as this march along Independence Avenue suggests.

the command of George S. Patton), two infantry regiments, a machine-gun detachment, and six tanks down Pennsylvania Avenue in pursuit of the Bonus Army. The veterans fled in terror. MacArthur followed them across the Anacostia River, where he ordered the soldiers to burn their tent city to the ground. More than 100 marchers were injured.

The incident served as perhaps the final blow to Hoover's already battered political standing. Hoover's own cold and gloomy personality reinforced the public image of him as aloof and unsympathetic to distressed people. The Great Engineer, the personification of the optimistic days of the 1920s, had become a symbol of the nation's failure to deal effectively with its startling reversal of fortune.

The Election of 1932

As the 1932 presidential election approached, few people doubted the outcome. The Republican Party dutifully renominated Herbert Hoover for a second term of office, but the gloomy atmosphere of the convention made it clear that few delegates believed he could win. The Democrats, in the

ROOSEVELT AND SMITH Franklin Roosevelt, the 1932 Democratic presidential nominee, and Al Smith, the 1928 candidate, appear together at a rally for Roosevelt at the Brooklyn Academy of Music in the fall of 1932. The two men had once been close political allies; but by 1932, they were already at odds. Not long after Roosevelt became president, Smith turned against him publicly and remained an outspoken critic.

meantime, gathered jubilantly in Chicago to nominate the governor of New York, Franklin Delano Roosevelt.

Roosevelt had been a well-known figure in the party for many years already. A Hudson Valley aristocrat, a distant cousin of Theodore Roosevelt (a connection strengthened by his marriage in 1904 to the president's niece, Eleanor), and a handsome, charming young man, he progressed rapidly: from a seat in the New York State legislature to a position as assistant secretary of the navy under Woodrow Wilson during World War I to his party's vice presidential nomination in 1920 on the ill-fated ticket with James M. Cox. Less than a year later, he was stricken with polio. Although he never regained use of his legs (and could walk only by using crutches and braces), he built up sufficient physical strength to return to politics in 1928. When Al Smith received the Democratic nomination for president that year, Roosevelt was elected to succeed him as governor. In 1930, he easily won reelection.

Roosevelt worked no miracles in New York, but he did initiate enough positive programs of government assistance to be able to present himself as a more energetic and imaginative leader than Hoover. In national politics, he avoided such divisive cultural issues as religion and prohibition and emphasized the economic grievances that most Democrats shared. He was able as a result to assemble a broad coalition within the party and win his party's nomination. In a dramatic break with tradition, he flew to Chicago to address the convention in person and accept the nomination. In the course of his acceptance speech, Roosevelt aroused the delegates with his ringing promise: "I pledge you, I pledge myself, to a new deal for the American people," giving his future program a name that would long endure. Neither then nor in the subsequent campaign did Roosevelt give much indication of what that program would be. But Herbert Hoover's unpopularity virtually ensured Roosevelt's election.

In November, to the surprise of no one, Roosevelt won by a landslide. He received 57.4 percent of the popular vote to Hoover's 39.7. In the electoral college, the result was even more overwhelming. Hoover carried Pennsylvania, Connecticut, Vermont, New Hampshire, and Maine. Roosevelt won everything else. Democrats won majorities in both houses of Congress. It was a broad and convincing mandate, but it was not yet clear what Roosevelt intended to do with it.

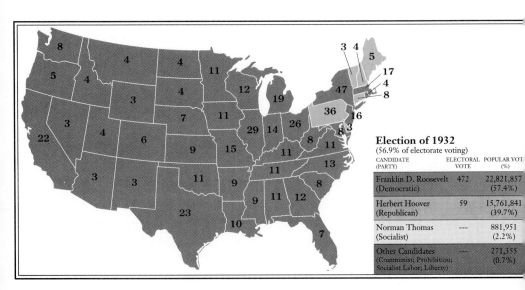

Election of 1932
(56.9% of electorate voting)

CANDIDATE (PARTY)	ELECTORAL VOTE	POPULAR VOTE (%)
Franklin D. Roosevelt (Democratic)	472	22,821,857 (57.4%)
Herbert Hoover (Republican)	59	15,761,841 (39.7%)
Norman Thomas (Socialist)	---	881,951 (2.2%)
Other Candidates (Communist; Prohibition; Socialist Labor; Liberty)	---	271,355 (0.7%)

The "Interregnum"

The period between the election and the inauguration (which in the early 1930s lasted more than four months) was a season of growing economic crisis. Presidents-elect traditionally do not involve themselves directly in government. But in a series of brittle exchanges with Roosevelt in the months following the election, Hoover tried to exact from the president-elect a pledge to maintain policies of economic orthodoxy. Roosevelt genially refused.

In February, only a month before the inauguration, a new crisis developed when the collapse of the American banking system suddenly and rapidly accelerated. Public confidence in the banks was ebbing; depositors were withdrawing their money in panic; and one bank after another was closing its doors and declaring bankruptcy. Hoover again asked Roosevelt to give prompt public assurances that there would be no tinkering with the currency, no heavy borrowing, no unbalancing of the budget. Roosevelt again refused.

March 4, 1933, was, therefore, a day of both economic crisis and considerable personal bitterness. On that morning, Herbert Hoover, convinced that the United States was headed for disaster, rode glumly down Pennsylvania Avenue with a beaming, buoyant Franklin Roosevelt, who would shortly be sworn in as the thirty-second president of the United States.

CONCLUSION

The Great Depression, which began so unexpectedly and spread so widely, changed many things in American life. It created unemployment on a scale never before experienced in the nation's history. It put enormous pressures on families, on communities, on state and local governments, and ultimately on Washington—which during the innovative but ultimately failed presidency of Herbert Hoover was unable to produce policies capable of dealing effectively with the crisis. In the nation's politics and culture, there were strong currents of radicalism and protest; and many middle-class Americans came to fear (and many less affluent people to hope) that a revolution might be approaching.

In reality, while the Great Depression shook much of American society and culture, it actually toppled very little. The capitalism system survived, damaged for a time but never truly threatened. The values of materialism and personal responsibility were shaken, but never overturned.

The American people in the 1930s were more receptive than they had been in the 1920s to evocations of community, generosity, and the dignity of common people. They were more open to experiments in government and business and even private lives than they had been in earlier years. But for most Americans, belief in the "American way of life"—a phrase that became widely resonant in the 1930s for the first time—remained strong throughout the long years of economic despair.

FOR FURTHER REFERENCE

Suggested Readings

Joan Hoff Wilson, *Herbert Hoover: Forgotten Progressive* (1975) argues that President Hoover was in many ways a surprisingly progressive thinker about the American social order. Donald Worster scathingly indicts agricultural capitalism for its destruction of the plains environment and ultimately the lives of the farmers themselves in *Dust Bowl: The Southern Plains in the 1930s* (1979). In *The Great Depression: Delayed Recovery and Economic Change in America, 1929–1939* (1987), Michael Bernstein argues that we should ask not so much why the economy crashed in 1929 but rather why the expected recovery from the crash was so disastrously delayed. Richard Pells, *Radical Visions and American Dreams: Culture and Social Thought in the Depression Years* (1973) is an important survey of the cultural and intellectual history of the 1930s. Susan Ware analyzes the effect of the Great Depression on women in *Holding Their Own: American Women in the 1930s* (1982). The Communist Party's most popular period in the United States is the subject of Harvey Klehr's *The Heyday of American Communism: The Depression Decade* (1984) and, from a quite different viewpoint, Robin D. G. Kelley, *Hammer and Hoe: Alabama Communists During the Great Depression* (1990).

Films

(The best source for information on how to find these and other films is *Bowker's Complete Video Directory*—3 volumes.) *The Great Depression* (1993) delves deeply into the imagery and underlying social and economic realities of the depression decade. *One Third of a Nation* (1997) is a Federal Theater Project play in their "Living Newspaper Project" intended to dramatize the problem of housing during the Depression and provoke social change. *Union Maids* (1997) is a vivid history of women organizing in the 1930s. *The Lemon Grove Incident* (1985) provides a rare glimpse of Mexican-American civil rights activism over school integration in the early 1930s.

Internet Resources

Internet websites containing historical material relevant to the subjects discussed in this chapter can be reached through the McGraw-Hill history site at www.mhhe.com/socscience/history/usa/link/linktop.htm.

CHAPTER TWENTY-SIX

The New Deal

Launching the New Deal ~ *The New Deal in Transition*
The New Deal in Disarray ~ *Limits and Legacies of the New Deal*

RANKLIN ROOSEVELT SERVED longer as president than anyone else before or since, and during his twelve years in office he became more central to the life of the nation than any chief executive had ever been. Most important, his administration constructed a series of programs that permanently altered the federal government and its relationship to society.

By the end of the 1930s, the New Deal (as the Roosevelt administration was called) had not ended the Great Depression; only World War II did that. But it had created many of the broad outlines of the political world we know today.

LAUNCHING THE NEW DEAL

Roosevelt's first task upon taking office was to alleviate the panic that was threatening to create chaos in the financial system. He did so in part by force of personality and in part by constructing very rapidly an ambitious and diverse program of legislation.

Restoring Confidence

Much of Roosevelt's early success was a result of his ebullient personality. He was the first president to make regular use of the radio; and his

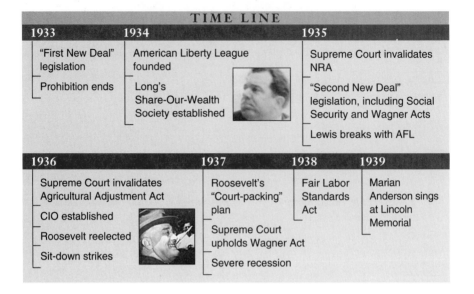

TIME LINE

1933	1934	1935
"First New Deal" legislation	American Liberty League founded	Supreme Court invalidates NRA
Prohibition ends	Long's Share-Our-Wealth Society established	"Second New Deal" legislation, including Social Security and Wagner Acts
		Lewis breaks with AFL

1936	1937	1938	1939
Supreme Court invalidates Agricultural Adjustment Act	Roosevelt's "Court-packing" plan	Fair Labor Standards Act	Marian Anderson sings at Lincoln Memorial
CIO established	Supreme Court upholds Wagner Act		
Roosevelt reelected			
Sit-down strikes	Severe recession		

friendly "fireside chats," during which he explained his programs and plans to the people, helped build public confidence in the administration. Roosevelt held frequent informal press conferences and won both the respect and the friendship of most reporters.

But Roosevelt could not rely on image alone. On March 6, two days after taking office, he issued a proclamation closing all American banks for four days until Congress could meet in special session to consider banking reform legislation. So great was the panic about bank failures that the "bank holiday," as the president euphemistically described it, created a general sense of relief and hope.

Three days later, Roosevelt sent to Congress the Emergency Banking Act, a generally conservative bill (much of it drafted by holdovers from the Hoover administration) designed primarily to protect the larger banks from being dragged down by the weakness of smaller ones. The bill provided for Treasury Department inspection of all banks before they would be allowed to reopen, for federal assistance to some troubled institutions, and for a thorough reorganization of those banks in the greatest difficulty. A confused and frightened Congress passed the bill within a few hours of its introduction. Whatever else the new law accomplished, it helped dispel the panic. Three-quarters of the banks in the Federal Reserve system reopened within the next three days, and $1 billion in hoarded currency and gold flowed back into them within a month. The immediate banking crisis was over.

THE ROOSEVELT SMILE The battered hat, the uptilted cigarette holder, the jaunty smile—all were hallmarks of Franklin Roosevelt's ebullient public personality. In part, at least, the president's hearty optimism was a deliberate pose, adopted to distract attention from the paralysis that had denied him the use of his legs since 1921.

On the morning after passage of the Emergency Banking Act, Roosevelt sent to Congress another measure—the Economy Act—designed to convince the public (and especially the business community) that the federal government was in safe, responsible hands. The act proposed to balance the federal budget by cutting the salaries of government employees and reducing pensions to veterans by as much as 15 percent. Like the banking bill, this one passed through Congress almost instantly—despite heated protests from some congressional progressives. Later that spring, Roosevelt signed the Glass-Steagall Act of June 1933, which gave the government authority to curb irresponsible speculation by banks. More important, perhaps, it established the Federal Deposit Insurance Corporation, which guaranteed all bank deposits up to $2,500. In other words, even if a bank should fail, small depositors would be able to recover their money. (Later, in 1935, Congress passed a major banking act that transferred much of the authority once wielded by the regional Federal Reserve banks to the Federal Reserve Board in Washington.)

To restore confidence in the stock market, Congress passed the so-called Truth in Securities Act of 1933, requiring corporations issuing new securities to provide full and accurate information about them to the public. Another act, of June 1934, established the Securities and Exchange Commission (SEC) to police the stock market.

Roosevelt also moved in his first days in office to put to rest one of the divisive issues of the 1920s. He supported and then signed a bill to legalize the manufacture and sale of beer with a 3.2 percent alcohol content—an interim measure pending the repeal of prohibition, for which a constitutional amendment (the Twenty-first) was already in process. The amendment was ratified later in 1933.

Agricultural Adjustment

These initial actions were largely stopgaps, to buy time for more comprehensive programs. The first was the Agricultural Adjustment Act, which Congress passed in May 1933. Its most important feature was its provision for reducing crop production to end agricultural surpluses and halt the downward spiral of farm prices.

Under the provisions of the act, producers of seven basic commodities (wheat, cotton, corn, hogs, rice, tobacco, and dairy products) would decide on production limits for their crops. The government, through the Agricultural Adjustment Administration (AAA), would then tell individual farmers how much they should produce and would pay them subsidies for leaving some of their land idle. A tax on food processing (for example, the milling of wheat) would provide the funds for the new payments. Farm prices were to be subsidized up to the point of parity.

The AAA helped bring about a rise in prices for farm commodities in the years after 1933. Gross farm income increased by half in the first three years of the New Deal, and the agricultural economy as a whole emerged from the 1930s much more stable and prosperous than it had been in many years. The AAA did, however, favor larger farmers over smaller ones, particularly since local administration of its programs often fell into the hands of the most powerful producers in a community. By distributing payments to landowners, not those who worked the land, the government did little to discourage planters who were reducing their acreage from evicting tenants and sharecroppers and firing field hands.

In January 1936, the Supreme Court struck down the crucial provisions of the Agricultural Adjustment Act, arguing that the government had no constitutional authority to require farmers to limit production. But within a few weeks the administration had secured passage of new legislation (the Soil Conservation and Domestic Allotment Act), which permitted the government to pay farmers to reduce production so as to "conserve soil," prevent erosion, and accomplish other secondary goals. The Court did not interfere with the new laws.

The administration launched several efforts to assist poor farmers as well. The Resettlement Administration, established in 1935, and its successor, the Farm Security Administration, created in 1937, provided loans to help farmers cultivating submarginal soil to relocate to better lands. But the programs never moved more than a few thousand farmers. More effective was the Rural Electrification Administration, created in 1935, which worked to make electric power available for the first time to thousands of farmers through utility cooperatives.

Industrial Recovery

Ever since 1931, leaders of the United States Chamber of Commerce and many others had been urging the government to adopt an antideflation scheme that would permit trade associations to cooperate in stabilizing prices within their industries. Existing antitrust laws clearly forbade such practices, and Herbert Hoover had refused to endorse suspension of the laws. The Roosevelt administration was more receptive. In exchange for relaxing antitrust provisions, however, New Dealers insisted on other provisions. Business leaders would have to make important concessions to labor—recognize the workers' right to bargain collectively through unions—to ensure that the incomes of workers would rise along with prices. And to help create jobs and increase consumer buying power, the administration added a major program of public works spending. The result of these and many other impulses was the National Industrial Recovery Act, which Congress passed in June 1933.

At first, the new program appeared to work miracles. At its center was a new federal agency, the National Recovery Administration (NRA), under the direction of the flamboyant and energetic Hugh S. Johnson. Johnson called on every business establishment in the nation to accept a temporary "blanket code": a minimum wage of between 30 and 40 cents an hour, a maximum workweek of thirty-five to forty hours, and the abolition of child labor. Adherence to the code, he claimed, would raise consumer purchasing power and increase employment. At the same time, Johnson negotiated another, more specific set of codes with leaders of the nation's major industries. These industrial codes set floors below which no company would

THE BLUE EAGLE The leaders of the National Recovery Administration, one of the first great New Deal experiments, believed that public support for the project was as important as the particular policies it pursued. As a result, they encouraged even the smallest businesses to sign an NRA "code" and to display the agency's symbol—a blue eagle above the phrase "We Do Our Part"—in their windows. The owners of this tailor shop proudly complied.

lower prices or wages in its search for a competitive advantage, and they included provisions for maintaining employment and production. He quickly won agreements from almost every major industry in the country.

From the beginning, however, the NRA encountered serious difficulties. The codes themselves were hastily and often poorly written. Administering them was beyond the capacities of federal officials with no prior experience in running so vast a program. Large producers consistently dominated the code-writing process and ensured that the new regulations would work to their advantage and to the disadvantage of smaller firms. And the codes at times did more than simply set floors under prices; they actively and artificially raised them—sometimes to levels higher than the market could sustain.

Other NRA goals did not progress as quickly as the efforts to raise prices. Section 7(a) of the National Industrial Recovery Act promised workers the right to form unions and engage in collective bargaining and encouraged many workers to join unions for the first time. But Section 7(a) contained no enforcement mechanisms. Hence recognition of unions by employers (and thus the significant wage increases the unions were committed to winning) did not follow. The Public Works Administration (PWA), established to administer the National Industrial Recovery Act's spending programs, only gradually allowed the $3.3 billion in public works funds to trickle out. Not until 1938 was the PWA budget pumping an appreciable amount of money into the economy.

Perhaps the clearest evidence of the NRA's failure was that industrial production actually declined in the months after the agency's establishment—from an index of 101 in July 1933 to 71 in November—despite the rise in prices that the codes had helped to create. By the spring of 1934, the NRA was besieged by criticism, and businessmen were flaunting many of its provisions. That fall, Roosevelt pressured Johnson to resign and established a new board of directors to oversee the NRA. Then in 1935, the Supreme Court intervened.

In 1935, a case came before the Court involving alleged NRA code violations by the Schechter brothers, who operated a wholesale poultry business confined to Brooklyn, New York. The Court ruled unanimously that the Schechters were not engaged in interstate commerce (and thus not subject to federal regulation) and, further, that Congress had unconstitutionally delegated legislative power to the president to draft the NRA codes. The justices struck down the legislation establishing the agency. Roosevelt denounced the justices for their "horse-and-buggy" interpretation of the interstate commerce clause. He was rightly concerned, for the reasoning in the Schechter case threatened many other New Deal programs as well. But the Court's destruction of the NRA itself gave the New Deal a convenient excuse for ending a failed experiment.

Regional Planning

The AAA and the NRA largely reflected the beliefs of New Dealers who favored economic planning but wanted private interests (farmers or business leaders) to dominate the planning process. Other reformers believed that the government itself should be the chief planning agent in the economy. Their most conspicuous success, and one of the most celebrated accomplishments of the New Deal, was an unprecedented experiment in regional planning: the Tennessee Valley Authority (TVA).

The TVA had its roots in a political controversy of the 1920s. Progressive reformers had agitated for years for public development of the nation's water resources as a source of cheap electric power. In particular, they had urged completion of a great dam at Muscle Shoals on the Tennessee River in Alabama—a dam begun during World War I but left unfinished when the war ended. But opposition from the utilities companies had been too powerful to overcome.

In 1932, however, one of the great utility empires—that of the electricity magnate Samuel Insull—collapsed spectacularly, amid widely publicized exposés of corruption. Hostility to the utilities soon grew so intense that the companies were no longer able to block the public power movement. The result was legislation supported by the president and enacted by Congress in May 1933 creating the Tennessee Valley Authority. The TVA was authorized to complete the dam at Muscle Shoals and build others in the region, and to generate and sell electricity from them to the public at reasonable rates. It was also intended to be an agent for a comprehensive redevelopment of the entire region: for stopping the disastrous flooding that had plagued the Tennessee Valley for centuries, for encouraging the development of local industries, for supervising a substantial program of reforestation, and for helping farmers improve productivity.

Opposition by conservatives within the administration ultimately blocked many of the ambitious social planning projects proposed by the more visionary TVA administrators, but the Authority revitalized the region in numerous ways. It improved water transportation. It virtually eliminated flooding in the region. It provided electricity to thousands who had never before had it. Throughout the country, largely because of the "yardstick" provided by the TVA's cheap production of electricity, private power rates declined. Even so, the Tennessee Valley remained a generally impoverished region despite the TVA's efforts. And like many other New Deal programs, it made no serious effort to challenge local customs and racial prejudices.

The Growth of Federal Relief

The Roosevelt administration did not consider relief to the unemployed its most important task, but it recognized the necessity of doing something to help impoverished Americans survive until the government could revive the economy to the point where relief might not be necessary. Among Roosevelt's first acts as president was the establishment of the Federal Emergency Relief Administration (FERA), which provided cash grants to states to prop up bankrupt relief agencies. To administer the program, he chose the director of the New York State relief agency, Harry Hopkins, who disbursed the FERA grants widely and rapidly. But both Hopkins and Roosevelt had misgivings about establishing a government "dole."

They felt somewhat more comfortable with another form of government assistance: work relief. Thus when it became clear that the FERA grants were not enough, the administration established a second program: the Civil Works Administration (CWA). Between November 1933 and April 1934, it put more than 4 million people to work on temporary projects. Some of the projects were of lasting value, such as the construction of roads, schools, and parks; others were little more than make-work. To Hopkins, however, the important thing was pumping money into an economy badly in need of it and providing assistance to people with nowhere else to turn.

Roosevelt's favorite relief project was the Civilian Conservation Corps (CCC). Established in the first weeks of the new administration, the CCC was designed to provide employment to the millions of young men who could find no jobs in the cities. The CCC created camps in national parks and forests and in other rural and wilderness settings. There young men (women were excluded from the program) worked in a semimilitary environment on such projects as planting trees, building reservoirs, developing parks, and improving agricultural irrigation. CCC camps were segregated by race. The vast majority of them were restricted to whites, but a few were reserved for blacks, Mexicans, and Indians.

Mortgage relief was a pressing need for millions of farm owners and homeowners. The Farm Credit Administration, which within two years refinanced one-fifth of all farm mortgages in the United States, was one response to that problem. The Frazier-Lemke Farm Bankruptcy Act of 1933 was another. It enabled some farmers to regain their land even after the foreclosure of their mortgages. Despite such efforts, however, 25 percent of all American farm owners had lost their land by 1934. Homeowners were similarly troubled, and in June 1933 the administration established the Home Owners' Loan Corporation, which by 1936 had refinanced the mortgages of more than 1 million householders. A year later, Congress established the Federal Housing Administration to insure mortgages for new construction and home repairs.

D E B A T I N G   T H E   P A S T

The New Deal

CONTEMPORARIES OF FRANKLIN ROOSEVELT debated the impact of the New Deal with ferocious intensity: conservatives complaining of a menacing tyranny of the state, liberals celebrating the New Deal's progressive achievements, people on the left charging that the reforms of the 1930s were largely cosmetic and ignored the nation's fundamental problems. Although the conservative critique has found relatively little scholarly expression since Roosevelt's death, the liberal and left positions continued for many years to shape the way historians described the Roosevelt administration.

The dominant view from the beginning was an approving liberal interpretation, and its most important early voice was that of Arthur M. Schlesinger, Jr. He argued in the three volumes of *The Age of Roosevelt* (1957–1960) that the New Deal marked a continuation of the long struggle between public power and private interests, a struggle Roosevelt had moved to a new level as the unconstrained influence of business elites finally encountered an effective challenge. Workers, farmers, consumers and others now had much more protection than they had enjoyed in the past.

At almost the same time, however, other historians were offering more qualified assessments of the New Deal, although they remained securely within the liberal framework. Richard Hofstadter argued in 1955 that the New Deal was a "drastic new departure . . . different from anything that had yet happened in the United States"; that it gave American liberalism a "social-democratic tinge that had never before been present in American reform movements"; but that its highly pragmatic approach lacked a central, guiding philosophy. James MacGregor Burns argued in 1956 that Roosevelt failed to make full use of his potential as a leader and had accommodated himself unnecessarily to existing patterns of power.

William Leuchtenburg's *Franklin D. Roosevelt and the New Deal* (1963) was the first systematic "revisionist" interpretation. Leuchtenburg was a sympathetic critic, arguing that most of the limitations of the New Deal were the result of political and ideological constraints over which Roosevelt had little control. But he challenged the views of earlier scholars who had proclaimed the New Deal a "revolution" in social policy. Leuchtenburg could muster only enough enthusiasm to call it a "halfway revolution," one that helped some previously disadvantaged groups (most notably farmers and workers) but that did little or nothing for many others (blacks, sharecroppers, the urban poor).

Harsher criticisms soon emerged. Barton Bernstein in a 1968 essay compiled a dreary chronicle of missed opportunities and inadequate responses to problems and concluded that the New Deal had saved capitalism, but at the expense of the least powerful. Ronald Radosh, Paul Conkin, and, more recently, Thomas Ferguson and Colin Gordon expanded on these criticisms; the New Deal, they contended, was part of the twentieth-century tradition of "corporate liberalism"—a tradition in which reform is closely wedded to the needs and interests of capitalism.

Most scholars in the 1980s and 1990s, however, seemed largely to have accepted the revised liberal view: that the New Deal was a significant (and most agree valuable) chapter in the history of reform, but one that worked within rigid, occasionally crippling limits. Much of the recent work on the New Deal, therefore, has focused on the constraints it faced. Some scholars (notably the sociologist Theda Skocpol) have emphasized the issue of "state capacity"—the absence of a government bureaucracy with sufficient strength and expertise to shape or administer many programs. James T. Patterson, Barry Karl, Mark Leff, and others have emphasized the political constraints the New Deal encountered—the conservative inhibitions about government that remained strong in Congress and among the public. Frank Freidel, Ellis Hawley, Herbert Stein, and many others point as well to the ideological constraints affecting Franklin Roosevelt and his supporters, the limits of their own understanding of their time. Alan Brinkley, in *The End of Reform* (1995), described an ideological shift within New Deal liberalism that marginalized older concerns about wealth and monopoly power.

The phrase "New Deal liberalism" has come in the postwar era to seem synonymous with modern ideas of aggressive federal management of the economy, elaborate welfare systems, a powerful bureaucracy, and large-scale government spending. But many historians of the New Deal would argue that the modern idea of New Deal liberalism bears only a limited relationship to the ideas that New Dealers themselves embraced.

THE NEW DEAL IN TRANSITION

Seldom has an American president enjoyed such remarkable popularity as Franklin Roosevelt did during his first two years in office. But by early 1935, with no end to the Depression yet in sight, the New Deal found itself the target of fierce public criticism. In the spring of 1935, partly in response to these growing attacks, Roosevelt launched an ambitious new program of legislation that has often been called the "Second New Deal."

Critics of the New Deal

Some of the most strident attacks on the New Deal came from critics on the right. Roosevelt had tried for a time to conciliate conservatives and business leaders. By the end of 1934, however, it was clear that the American right in general, and much of the corporate world in particular, had become irreconcilably hostile to the New Deal. In August 1934, a group of the most fervent (and wealthiest) Roosevelt opponents, led by members of the Du Pont family, formed the American Liberty League, designed specifically to arouse public opposition to the New Deal's "dictatorial" policies and its supposed attacks on free enterprise. But the new organization was never able to expand its constituency much beyond the northern industrialists who had founded it.

Roosevelt's critics on the far left also managed to produce alarm among some supporters of the administration, but like the conservatives, they proved to have only limited strength. The Communist Party, the Socialist Party, and other radical and semiradical organizations were at times harshly critical of the New Deal. But they too failed ever to attract genuine mass support.

More menacing to the New Deal than either the far right or the far left was a group of dissident political movements that defied easy ideological classification. Some gained substantial public support within particular states and regions. And three men succeeded in mobilizing genuinely national followings. Dr. Francis E. Townsend, an elderly California physician, rose from obscurity to lead a movement of more than 5 million members with his plan for federal pensions for the elderly. According to the Townsend Plan, all Americans over the age of sixty would receive monthly government pensions of $200, provided they retired (thus freeing jobs for younger, unemployed Americans) and spent the money in full each month (which would pump needed funds into the economy). By 1935, the Townsend Plan had attracted the support of many older men and women. And while the plan itself made little progress in Congress, the public sentiment behind it helped build support for the Social Security system, which Congress did approve in 1935.

Father Charles E. Coughlin, a Catholic priest in the Detroit suburb of Royal Oak, Michigan, achieved even greater renown through his weekly sermons broadcast nationally over the radio. He proposed a series of monetary reforms—remonetization of silver, issuing of greenbacks, and nationalization of the banking system—that he insisted would restore prosperity and ensure economic justice. At first a warm supporter of Franklin Roosevelt, by late 1934 Coughlin had become disheartened by what he claimed was the president's failure to deal harshly enough with the "money powers." In the spring of 1935, he established his own political organization, the National Union for Social Justice. He was widely believed to have one of the largest regular radio audiences of anyone in America.

Most alarming of all to the administration was the growing national popularity of Senator Huey P. Long of Louisiana. Long had risen to power in his home state through his strident attacks on the banks, oil companies, and utilities and on the conservative political oligarchy allied with them. Elected governor in 1928, he launched an assault on his opponents so thorough and forceful that they were soon left with virtually no political power whatsoever. Many claimed that he had, in effect, become a dictator. But he also maintained the overwhelming support of the Louisiana electorate, in part because of his flamboyant personality and in part because of his solid record of conventional progressive accomplishments: building roads, schools, and hospitals; revising the tax codes; distributing free textbooks; lowering utility rates. Barred by law from succeeding himself as governor, he ran in 1930 for a seat in the United States Senate and won easily.

Long, like Coughlin, supported Franklin Roosevelt for president in 1932. But within six months of Roosevelt's inauguration he had broken with the president. As an alternative to the New Deal, he advocated a drastic program of wealth redistribution, a program he ultimately named the Share-Our-Wealth Plan. The government, he claimed, could end the Depression easily by using the tax system to confiscate the surplus riches of the wealthiest men and women in America and distribute these surpluses to the rest of the population. That would, he claimed, allow the

HUEY LONG Few public speakers could arouse a crowd more effectively than Huey Long of Louisiana, known to many as "the Kingfish" (a nickname borrowed from the popular radio show *Amos 'n Andy*). It was Long's effective use of radio, however, that contributed most directly to his spreading national popularity in the early 1930s.

government to guarantee every family a minimum "homestead" of $5,000 and an annual wage of $2,500. In 1934, Long established his own national organization: the Share-Our-Wealth Society, which soon attracted a large following through much of the nation. A poll by the Democratic National Committee in the spring of 1935 disclosed that Long might attract more than 10 percent of the vote if he ran as a third-party candidate, possibly enough to tip a close election to the Republicans.

Members of the Roosevelt administration considered dissident movements—and the broad popular discontent they represented—a genuine threat to the president. An increasing number of advisers were warning Roosevelt that he would have to do something dramatic to counter their strength.

The "Second New Deal"

Roosevelt launched the so-called Second New Deal in the spring of 1935 in response both to the growing political pressures and to the continuing economic crisis. The new proposals represented, if not a new direction, at least a shift in the emphasis of New Deal policy. Perhaps the most conspicuous change was in the administration's attitude toward big business. Symbolically at least, the president was now willing to attack corporate interests openly. In March, for example, he proposed to Congress an act designed to break up the great utility holding companies, and he spoke harshly of monopolistic control of their industry. The Holding Company Act of 1935 was the result, although furious lobbying by the utilities led to amendments that sharply limited its effects.

Equally alarming to affluent Americans was a series of tax reforms proposed by the president in 1935, a program conservatives quickly labeled a "soak-the-rich" scheme. Apparently designed to undercut the appeal of Huey Long's Share-Our-Wealth Plan, the Roosevelt proposals called for establishing the highest and most progressive peacetime tax rates in history—although the actual impact of these rates was limited.

The Supreme Court decision in 1935 to strike down the National Industrial Recovery Act also invalidated Section 7(a) of the act, which had guaranteed workers the right to organize and bargain collectively. A group of progressives in Congress led by Senator Robert E. Wagner of New York introduced what became the National Labor Relations Act of 1935. The new law, popularly known as the Wagner Act, provided workers with a crucial enforcement mechanism missing from the 1933 law: the National Labor Relations Board (NLRB), which would have power to compel employers to recognize and bargain with legitimate unions. The president was not entirely happy with the bill, but he signed it anyway. That was in large part because American workers themselves had by 1935 become so important and vigorous a force that Roosevelt realized his own political future would depend in part on responding to their demands.

Labor Militancy

The emergence of a powerful trade union movement in the 1930s was one of the most important social and political developments of the decade. It occurred partly in response to government efforts to enhance the power of unions, but it was also a result of the increased militancy of American workers and their leaders. During the 1920s, most workers had displayed relatively little militancy in challenging employers or demanding recognition of their unions. In the 1930s, however, many of the factors that had impeded militancy vanished or grew weaker. Business leaders and industrialists lost (at least temporarily) the ability to control government policies. Equally important, new and more militant labor organizations emerged to challenge the established, relatively conservative unions.

The growing militancy first became obvious in 1934, when newly organized workers (many of them inspired by the collective bargaining provisions of the National Industrial Recovery Act) demonstrated an assertiveness and at times radicalism seldom seen in recent years. Despite the new militancy, however, it was clear that without stronger legal protection, most organizing drives would end in frustration. Once the Wagner Act became law, the search for more effective forms of organization rapidly gained strength in labor ranks.

The American Federation of Labor remained committed to the idea of the craft union: organizing workers on the basis of their skills. But that concept had little to offer unskilled laborers, who now constituted the bulk of the industrial work force. During the 1930s, therefore, a newer concept of labor organization challenged the craft union ideal: industrial unionism. Advocates of this approach argued that all workers in a particular industry should be organized in a single union, regardless of what functions the workers performed. All autoworkers should be in a single automobile union; all steelworkers should be in a single steel union. United in this way, workers would greatly increase their power.

Leaders of the AFL craft unions for the most part opposed the new concept. But industrial unionism found a number of important advocates, most prominent among them John L. Lewis, the talented, flamboyant, and eloquent leader of the United Mine Workers. At first, Lewis and his allies attempted to work within the AFL, but friction between the new industrial organizations Lewis was promoting and the older craft unions grew rapidly. At the 1935 AFL convention, Lewis became embroiled in a series of angry confrontations (and one celebrated fistfight) with craft union leaders before finally walking out. A few weeks later, he created the Committee on Industrial Organization. When the AFL expelled the new committee and all the industrial unions it represented, Lewis renamed the committee the Congress of Industrial Organizations (CIO), established it in 1936 as an organization directly rivaling the AFL, and became its first president.

The CIO expanded the constituency of the labor movement. It was more receptive to women and to blacks than the AFL had been, in part because women and blacks were more likely to be relegated to unskilled jobs and in part because CIO organizing drives targeted previously unorganized industries (textiles, laundries, tobacco factories, and others) where women and minorities constituted much of the work force. The CIO was also a more militant organization than the AFL. By the time of the 1936 schism, it was already engaged in major organizing battles in the automobile and steel industries.

Organizing Battles

Out of several competing auto unions, the United Auto Workers (UAW) was gradually emerging preeminent in the early and mid-1930s. But although it was gaining recruits, it was making little progress in winning recognition from the corporations. In December 1936, however, autoworkers employed a controversial and effective new technique for challenging corporate opposition: the sit-down strike. Employees in several General Motors plants in Detroit simply sat down inside the plants, refusing either to work or to leave, thus preventing the company from using strikebreakers. The tactic spread to other locations, and by February 1937 strikers had occupied seventeen GM plants. The strikers ignored court orders and local police efforts to force them to vacate the buildings. When Michigan's governor, Frank Murphy, a liberal Democrat, refused to call up the National Guard to clear out the strikers, and when the federal government also refused to intervene on behalf of employers, General Motors relented. In February 1937 it became the first major manufacturer to recognize the UAW; other automobile companies soon did the same. The sit-down strike proved effective for rubber workers and others as well, but it survived only briefly as a labor technique. Its apparent illegality aroused so much public opposition that labor leaders soon abandoned it.

In the steel industry, the battle for unionization was less easily won. In 1936, the Steel Workers' Organizing Committee (SWOC; later the United Steelworkers of America) began a major organizing drive involving thousands of workers and frequent, at times bitter, strikes. In March 1937, to the surprise of almost everyone, United States Steel, the giant of the industry, recognized the union rather than risk a costly strike at a time when it sensed itself on the verge of recovery from the Depression. But the smaller companies (known collectively as "Little Steel") were less accommodating.

On Memorial Day 1937, a group of striking workers from Republic Steel gathered with their families for a picnic and demonstration in South Chicago. When they attempted to march peacefully (and legally) toward the steel plant, police opened fire on them. Ten demonstrators were killed; another ninety were wounded. Despite a public outcry against the "Memorial Day Massacre," the harsh tactics of Little Steel companies succeeded. The 1937 strike failed.

But the victory of Little Steel was one of the last gasps of the kind of brutal strikebreaking that had proved so effective in the past. In 1937 alone, there were 4,720 strikes—over 80 percent of them settled in favor of the unions. By the end of the year, more than 8 million workers were members of unions recognized as official bargaining units by employers (as compared with 3 million in 1932). By 1941, that number had expanded to 10 million and included the workers of Little Steel, whose employers had finally recognized the SWOC.

Social Security

From the first moments of the New Deal, important members of the administration, most notably Secretary of Labor Frances Perkins, had been lobbying for a system of federally sponsored social insurance for the elderly and the unemployed. In 1935, Roosevelt gave public support to what became the Social Security Act, which Congress passed the same year. It established several distinct programs. For the elderly, there were two types of assistance. Those who were presently destitute could receive up to $15 a month in federal assistance. More important for the future, many Americans presently working were incorporated into a pension system, to which they and their employers would contribute by paying a payroll tax; it would provide them with an income on retirement. Pension payments would not begin until 1942 and even then would provide only $10 to $85 a month to recipients. And broad categories of workers (including domestic servants and agricultural laborers, occupations with disproportionate numbers of blacks and women) were excluded from the program. But the act was a crucial first step in building the nation's most important social program for the elderly.

In addition, the Social Security Act created a system of unemployment insurance, which employers alone would finance and which made it possible for workers laid off from their jobs to receive temporary government assistance. It also established a system of federal aid to people with disabilities and a program of aid to dependent children.

The framers of the Social Security Act wanted to create a system of "insurance," not "welfare." And the largest programs (old-age pensions and unemployment insurance) were in many ways similar to private insurance programs, with contributions from participants and benefits available to all. But the act also provided considerable direct assistance based on need—to the elderly poor, to those with disabilities, to dependent children and their mothers. These groups were widely perceived to be small and genuinely unable to support themselves. But in later generations the programs for these groups would expand until they assumed dimensions that the planners of Social Security had neither foreseen nor desired.

New Directions in Relief

Social Security was designed primarily to fulfill long-range goals. But millions of unemployed Americans had immediate needs. To help them, the Roosevelt administration established in 1935 the Works Progress Administration (WPA). Like the Civil Works Administration and other earlier efforts, the WPA established a system of work relief for the unemployed. But it was much bigger than the earlier agencies, both in the size of its budget ($5 billion at first) and in the energy and imagination of its operations.

Under the direction of Harry Hopkins, the WPA was responsible for building or renovating 110,000 public buildings (schools, post offices, government office buildings) and for constructing almost 600 airports, more than 500,000 miles of roads, and over 100,000 bridges. In the process, the WPA kept an average of 2.1 million workers employed and pumped needed money into the economy.

The WPA also displayed remarkable flexibility and imagination in offering assistance to those whose occupations did not fit into any traditional category of relief. The Federal Writers Project of the WPA, for example, gave unemployed writers a chance to do their work and receive a government salary. The Federal Arts Project, similarly, helped painters, sculptors, and others to continue their careers. The Federal Music Project and the Federal Theater Project oversaw the production of concerts and plays, creating work for unemployed musicians, actors, and directors. Other relief agencies emerged alongside the WPA. The National Youth Administration (NYA) provided work and scholarship assistance to high-school and college-age men and women. The Emergency Housing Division of the Public Works Administration began federal sponsorship of public housing.

WPA MURAL ART The Federal Arts Project of the Works Progress Administration commissioned an impressive series of public murals from the artists it employed. Many of these murals adorned post offices, libraries, and other public buildings constructed by the WPA. William Gropper's *Construction of a Dam*, a detail of which is seen here, is typical of much of the mural art of the 1930s in its celebration of the workingman. Workers are depicted in heroic poses, laboring in unison to complete a great public project.

Men and women alike were in distress in the 1930s (as in all difficult times). But the new welfare system dealt with members of the two sexes in very different ways. For men, the government concentrated mainly on work relief—on such programs as the CCC, the CWA, and the WPA, all of which were overwhelmingly male. The principal government aid to women was not work relief but cash assistance—most notably through the Aid to Dependent Children program of Social Security, which was designed largely to assist single mothers. This disparity in treatment reflected a widespread assumption that men constituted the bulk of the paid work force and that women needed to be treated within the context of the family. In fact, millions of women were already employed by the 1930s.

The 1936 "Referendum"

For a time in 1935 there had seemed reason to question the president's prospects for reelection. But by the middle of 1936—with the economy visibly reviving—there could be little doubt that he would win a second term. The Republican Party nominated the moderate governor of Kansas, Alf M. Landon, who waged a generally pallid campaign. Roosevelt's dissident challengers now appeared powerless. One reason was the violent death of their most effective leader, Huey Long, who was assassinated in Louisiana in September 1935. Another reason was the ill-fated alliance among Father Coughlin, Dr. Townsend, and Gerald L. K. Smith (an intemperate henchman of Huey Long), who joined forces that summer to establish a new political movement—the Union Party, which nominated an undistinguished North Dakota congressman, William Lemke, for president.

The result was the greatest landslide in American history to that point. Roosevelt polled just under 61 percent of the vote to Landon's 36 percent and carried every state except Maine and Vermont. The Democrats increased their already large majorities in both houses of Congress. The Union Party received fewer than 900,000 votes.

The election results demonstrated the party realignment that the New Deal had produced. The Democrats now controlled a broad coalition of western and southern farmers, the urban working classes, the poor and unemployed, and the black communities of northern cities, as well as traditional progressives and committed new liberals—a coalition that constituted a substantial majority of the electorate. It would be decades before the Republican Party could again create a lasting majority coalition of its own.

THE NEW DEAL IN DISARRAY

Roosevelt emerged from the 1936 election at the zenith of his popularity. Within months, however, the New Deal was mired in serious new difficulties—a result of continuing opposition, the president's own political errors, and major economic setbacks.

The Court Fight

The 1936 mandate, Franklin Roosevelt believed, made it possible for him to do something about the problem of the Supreme Court. No program of reform, he had become convinced, could long survive the conservative justices, who had already struck down the NRA and the AAA and threatened to invalidate even more legislation.

In February 1937, Roosevelt sent a surprise message to Capitol Hill proposing a general overhaul of the federal court system; included among the many provisions was one to add up to six new justices to the Supreme Court. The courts were "overworked," he claimed, and needed additional manpower and younger blood to enable them to cope with their increasing burdens. But Roosevelt's real purpose was to give himself the opportunity to appoint new, liberal justices and change the ideological balance of the Court.

Conservatives were outraged at the "Court-packing plan," and even many Roosevelt supporters were disturbed by what they considered evidence of the president's hunger for power. Still, Roosevelt might well have persuaded Congress to approve at least a compromise measure had not the Supreme Court itself intervened. Of the nine justices, three reliably supported the New Deal, and four reliably opposed it. Of the remaining two, Chief Justice Charles Evans Hughes often sided with the progressives and Associate Justice Owen J. Roberts usually voted with the conservatives. On March 29, 1937, Roberts, Hughes, and the three progressive justices voted together to uphold a state minimum-wage law—in the case of *West Coast Hotel* v. *Parrish*—thus reversing a 5-to-4 decision of the previous year invalidating a similar law. Two weeks later, again by a 5-to-4 margin, the Court upheld the Wagner Act, and in May it validated the Social Security Act. Whether or not for that reason, the Court's newly moderate position made the Court-packing bill seem unnecessary. Congress ultimately defeated it.

On one level, the affair was a significant victory for Franklin Roosevelt. The Court was no longer an obstacle to New Deal reforms, particularly after the older justices began to retire, to be replaced by Roosevelt appointees. But the Court-packing episode did lasting political damage to the administration. From 1937 on, southern Democrats and other conservatives voted against Roosevelt's measures much more often than they had in the past.

Retrenchment and Recession

By the summer of 1937, the national income, which had dropped from $82 billion in 1929 to $40 billion in 1932, had risen to nearly $72 billion. Other economic indices showed similar advances. Roosevelt seized on these improvements as an excuse to try to balance the federal budget, convinced by Treasury secretary Henry Morgenthau and many economists that the real danger now was no longer depression but inflation. Between January and August 1937, for example, he cut the WPA in half, laying off 1.5 million relief workers. A few weeks later, the fragile boom collapsed. The index of industrial production dropped from 117 in August 1937 to 76 in May 1938. Four million additional workers lost their jobs. Economic conditions were soon almost as bad as they had been in the bleak days of 1932–1933.

The recession of 1937, known to the president's critics as the "Roosevelt recession," was a result of many factors. But to many observers at the time (including, apparently, the president himself), it seemed to be a direct result of the administration's unwise decision to reduce spending. And so in April 1938, the president asked Congress for an emergency appropriation of $5 billion for public works and relief programs, and government funds soon began pouring into the economy once again. Within a few months, another tentative recovery seemed to be under way, and the advocates of spending pointed to it as proof of the validity of their approach.

At about the same time, at the urging of a group of younger, antimonopolist liberals in the administration, Roosevelt sent a stinging message to Congress, vehemently denouncing what he called an "unjustifiable concentration of economic power" and asking for the creation of a commission to examine that concentration with an eye to major reforms in the antitrust laws. In response, Congress established the Temporary National Economic Committee (TNEC), whose members included representatives of both houses of Congress and officials from several executive agencies. Also that spring, Roosevelt appointed a new head of the antitrust division of the Justice Department: Thurman Arnold, a Yale Law School professor who soon proved to be the most vigorous director ever to serve in that office.

Later in 1938, the administration successfully supported one of its most ambitious pieces of labor legislation, the Fair Labor Standards Act, which for the first time established a national minimum wage and a forty-hour work week, and which also placed strict limits on child labor.

Despite these achievements, however, by the end of 1938 the New Deal had essentially come to an end. Congressional opposition now made it difficult for the president to enact any major new programs. But more important, perhaps, the threat of world crisis hung heavy in the political atmosphere, and Roosevelt was gradually growing more concerned with persuading a reluctant nation to prepare for war than with pursuing new avenues of reform.

LIMITS AND LEGACIES OF THE NEW DEAL

The New Deal made major changes in American government, some of them still controversial today. It also left important problems unaddressed.

African Americans and the New Deal

One group the New Deal did relatively little to assist was African Americans. The administration was not hostile to black aspirations. On the contrary, the New Deal was probably more sympathetic to them than any previous government of the twentieth century had been. Eleanor Roosevelt spoke throughout the 1930s on behalf of racial justice and put continuing pressure on her husband and others in the federal government to ease discrimination against blacks. The president himself appointed a number of blacks to significant second-level positions in his administration, creating an informal network of officeholders that became known as

ELEANOR ROOSEVELT AND MARY MCLEOD BETHUNE Mrs. Roosevelt was a leading champion of racial equality within her husband's administration, and her commitment had an important impact on the behavior of the government even though she held no official post. She is seen here meeting in 1937 with Aubrey Williams, executive director of the National Youth Administration, and Mary McLeod Bethune, the agency's Director of Negro Affairs.

the "Black Cabinet." Eleanor Roosevelt, Interior secretary Harold Ickes, and WPA director Harry Hopkins all made efforts to ensure that New Deal relief programs did not exclude blacks, and by 1935 an estimated 30 percent of all African Americans were receiving some form of government assistance. One result was a historic change in black electoral behavior. As late as 1932, most American blacks were voting Republican, as they had been doing since the Civil War. By 1936, more than 90 percent of them were voting Democratic—the beginnings of a political alliance that would endure for many decades.

Blacks supported Franklin Roosevelt because they knew he was not their enemy. But they had few illusions that the New Deal represented a major turning point in American race relations. The president was, for example, never willing to risk losing the support of southern Democrats by supporting legislation to make lynching a federal crime or to ban the poll tax, one of the most potent tools by which white southerners kept blacks from voting.

New Deal relief agencies did not challenge, and indeed reinforced, existing patterns of discrimination. The Civilian Conservation Corps established separate black camps. The NRA codes tolerated paying blacks less than whites doing the same jobs. African Americans were largely excluded from employment in the TVA. The WPA routinely relegated black and Hispanic workers to the least-skilled and lowest-paying jobs; when funding ebbed, African Americans, like women, were among the first to be dismissed.

The New Deal was not hostile to black Americans, and it made some contributions to their progress. But it refused to make the issue of race a significant part of its agenda.

The New Deal and the "Indian Problem"

New Deal policy toward the Indian tribes marked a significant break from the approach in the years before Roosevelt, largely because of the efforts of the extraordinary commissioner of Indian affairs in the 1930s, John Collier. Collier was greatly influenced by the work of twentieth-century anthropologists who advanced the idea of cultural relativism—the theory that every culture should be accepted and respected on its own terms and that no culture is inherently superior to another.

Collier favored legislation that would, he hoped, reverse the pressures on Native Americans to assimilate and allow them to remain Indians. He effectively promoted legislation—which became the Indian Reorganization Act of 1934—to advance his goals. Among other things, it restored to the tribes the right to own land collectively (reversing the allotment policy adopted in 1887, which encouraged the breaking up of tribal lands into individually owned plots) and to elect tribal governments. In the thirteen years after passage of the 1934 bill, tribal land increased by nearly 4 million acres, and Indian agricultural income increased dramatically (from under $2 million in 1934 to over $49 million in 1947). Even with the redistribution of lands under the 1934 act, however, Indians continued to possess, for the most part, only territory whites did not want—much of it arid, some of it desert. And as a group, they continued to constitute the poorest segment of the population.

Women and the New Deal

Symbolically, at least, the New Deal marked a breakthrough in the role of women in public life. Roosevelt appointed the first female member of the cabinet in the nation's history, Secretary of Labor Frances Perkins. He also named more than 100 other women to positions at lower levels of the federal bureaucracy. But New Deal support for women operated within limits. Even many of the women in the administration were concerned not so much about achieving gender equality as about obtaining special protections for women.

The New Deal generally supported the widespread belief among men (and even among many women) that in hard times women should withdraw from the workplace to open up more jobs for men. Frances Perkins, for example, spoke out against what she called the "pin-money worker"—the married woman working to earn extra money for the household. New Deal relief agencies offered relatively little employment for women. The Social Security program excluded domestic servants, waitresses, and other predominantly female occupations.

As with African Americans, so also with women: The New Deal was not actively hostile to feminist aspirations; in many ways, it was unprecedentedly supportive. It did, however, accept prevailing cultural norms. There was not yet sufficient political pressure from women themselves to persuade the administration to do otherwise. Indeed, some of the most important supporters of policies that reinforced traditional gender roles (such as Social Security) were themselves women.

The New Deal and the West

One part of American society that did receive special attention from the New Deal was the American West, which benefited disproportionately from federal relief and public works programs. The West received more government funds per capita through New Deal relief programs than any other region.

Just as in the South, locally administered relief programs did not challenge prevailing racial norms; so in the West, New Deal programs sustained existing racial and ethnic prejudices. In several states, relief agencies paid different groups at different rates: white Anglos received the most generous aid; blacks, Indians, and Mexican Americans received lower levels of support. In the CCC camps in New Mexico, Hispanics and Anglos sometimes worked in the same camps, but there were frequent tensions and occasional conflicts between them.

But the main reason for the New Deal's particular impact on the West was that conditions in the region made the government's programs especially important. Federal agricultural programs had an enormous impact on the West because farming remained so much more central to the economy of the region than it did in much of the East. The largest New Deal public works programs—the great dams and power stations—were mainly in the West, both because the best locations for such facilities were there and because the West had the most need for new sources of water and power. The Grand Coulee Dam on the Columbia River was the largest public works project in American history to that point, and it provided cheap electric power for much of the Northwest. Its construction, and the construction of other, smaller dams and water projects, created a basis for economic development in the region.

Without this enormous public investment by the federal government, much of the economic growth that transformed the West after World War II would have been much more difficult, if not impossible, to achieve. For generations after the Great Depression, the federal government maintained a much greater and more visible bureaucratic presence in the West than in any other region.

The New Deal and the Economy

The most frequent criticisms of the New Deal involve its failure genuinely to revive or reform the American economy. New Dealers never fully recognized the value of government spending as a vehicle for recovery, and their efforts along other lines never succeeded in ending the Depression. The economic boom sparked by World War II, not the New Deal, finally ended the crisis. Nor did the New Deal substantially alter the distribution of power within American capitalism, and it had only a small impact on the distribution of wealth among the American people.

Nevertheless, the New Deal did have a number of important and lasting effects on both the behavior and the structure of the American economy. It helped elevate new groups—workers, farmers, and others—to positions from which they could at times effectively challenge the power of the corporations. It increased the regulatory functions of the federal government in ways that helped stabilize previously troubled areas of the economy: the stock market, the banking system, and others. And the administration helped establish the basis for new forms of federal fiscal policy, which in the postwar years would give the government tools for promoting and regulating economic growth.

The New Deal also created the rudiments of the American welfare state, through its many relief programs and above all through the Social Security system. The conservative inhibitions New Dealers brought to this task ensured that the welfare system that ultimately emerged would be limited in its impact (at least in comparison with the systems of other industrial nations), would reinforce some traditional patterns of gender and racial discrimination, and would be expensive and cumbersome to administer. But for all its limits, the new system marked a historic break with the nation's traditional reluctance to offer any public assistance whatsoever to its neediest citizens.

The New Deal and American Politics

Finally, the New Deal had a dramatic effect on the character of American politics. It took a weak and divided Democratic Party, which had been a minority force in American politics for many decades, and turned it into a mighty coalition that would dominate national party competition for more than thirty years. It turned the attention of many voters away from some of the cultural issues that had preoccupied them in the 1920s and awakened in them an interest in economic matters of direct importance to their lives.

CONCLUSION

The New Deal was the most dramatic and important moment in the modern history of American government. From the time of Franklin Roosevelt's inauguration in 1933 to the beginning of World War II eight years later, the federal government engaged in a broad and diverse series of experiments designed to relieve the distress of unemployment and poverty;

to reform the economy to prevent future crises; and to bring the Great Depression itself to an end. It had only partial success in all those efforts.

Unemployment and poverty remained high throughout the New Deal, although many federal programs provided assistance to millions of people who would otherwise have had none. The structure of the American economy remained essentially the same as it had been in earlier years, although there were by the end of the New Deal some important new regulatory agencies in Washington—and an important new role for organized labor, enforced by a new federal law. Nothing the New Deal did ended the Great Depression, but some of its policies kept it from getting worse—and some of them pointed the way toward more effective economic policies in the future.

Perhaps the most important legacy of the New Deal was to create a sense of possibilities among many Americans, to persuade them that the fortunes of individuals need not be left entirely to chance or to the workings of an unregulated market. Many Americans emerged from the 1930s convinced that individuals deserved some protections from the unpredictability and instability of the modern economy, and that the New Deal—for all its limitations—had demonstrated the value of enlisting government in the effort to provide those protections. The New Deal itself did not always fulfill the expectations it raised, but those expectations survived for generations to become the basis of new liberal crusades in the postwar era.

FOR FURTHER REFERENCE

Suggested Readings

William E. Leuchtenburg, *Franklin D. Roosevelt and the New Deal* (1963) remains the best short history of New Deal politics. David Kennedy, *Freedom from Fear* (1999) is an important new narrative history of the New Deal years. Anthony J. Badger, *The New Deal* (1989) is another valuable introduction. Arthur M. Schlesinger, Jr., *The Age of Roosevelt*, 3 vols. (1957–1960) is an eloquent classic study of the New Deal through 1936. Frank Freidel, *Franklin D. Roosevelt: A Rendezvous with Destiny* (1990) is a thorough one-volume biography. Ellis Hawley, *The New Deal and the Problem of Monopoly* (1967) is a classic examination of the economic policies of the Roosevelt administration in its first five years. Alan Brinkley, *The End of Reform: New Deal Liberalism in Recession and War* (1995) examines the transformation of liberalism after 1937. Linda Gordon, *Pitied But Not Entitled: Single Mothers and the History of Welfare* (1994) is a pioneering work on women as the recipients and also the authors of government welfare policies. The efforts of Chicago workers to protest, articulate, and organize for a new deal is the subject of Lizabeth Cohen, *Making a New Deal: Industrial Workers in Chicago, 1919–1939* (1990). Bruce Shulman, *From Cotton Belt to Sunbelt* (1991) explores the New Deal's effort to transform the region Roosevelt and others considered the nation's number one economic problem, the American South. Harvard Sitkoff, *A New Deal for Blacks* (1978) considers the New Deal's limited effort to confront the economic and social problems of African Americans. Alan Brinkley, *Voices of Protest: Huey Long, Father Coughlin, and the Great Depression* (1982) examines the careers of two important dissident leaders in the 1930s.

Films

(The best source for information on how to find these and other films is *Bowker's Complete Video Directory*—3 volumes.) *FDR* (1994) gives viewers a view of both the private and public life of Franklin D. Roosevelt. One of the president's most vocal and powerful critics is featured in another film entitled *Huey Long* (1986). The history of the New Deal's biggest public works project, the Tennessee Valley Authority, has been captured in *The Electric Valley* (1983). *Let Us Now Praise Famous Men Revisited* (1988) mixes images and passages from the 1941 classic photographic work with interviews with the surviving subjects. *The World of Tomorrow* (1984) is a documentary on the 1939 World's Fair.

Internet Resources

Internet websites containing historical material relevant to the subjects discussed in this chapter can be reached through the McGraw-Hill history site at www.mhhe.com/socscience/history/usa/link/linktop.htm.

CHAPTER TWENTY-SEVEN

The Global Crisis, 1921–1941

The Diplomacy of the New Era ∼ *Isolationism and Internationalism*
From Neutrality to Intervention

HENRY CABOT LODGE of Massachusetts, chairman of the Senate Foreign Relations Committee and one of the most powerful figures in the Republican Party, led the fight against ratification of the Treaty of Versailles in 1918 and 1919. In part because of his efforts, the treaty was defeated. The United States declined to join the League of Nations; and American foreign policy embarked on an independent course that for the next two decades would attempt, but ultimately fail, to expand American influence and maintain international stability without committing the United States to any lasting relationships with other nations.

Lodge was not an isolationist. He recognized that America had emerged from World War I the most powerful nation in the world. He believed the United States should exert its influence internationally. But he believed, too, that America's expanded role in the world should reflect the nation's own interests and its own special virtues; the United States should remain unfettered with obligations to anyone else. He said in 1919:

> We are a great moral asset of Christian civilization. . . . How did we get there? By our own efforts. Nobody led us, nobody guided us, nobody controlled us. . . . I would keep America as she has been—not isolated, not prevent her from joining other nations for . . . great purposes—but I wish her to be master of her own fate.

TIME LINE

1924	1928	1931	1933	1937
Dawes Plan	Kellogg-Briand Pact	Japan invades Manchuria	U.S. recognizes Soviet Union Good Neighbor Policy	Roosevelt's "quarantine" speech

1938	1939	1940	1941	
Munich Conference	Nazi-Soviet nonaggression pact World War II begins	Tripartite Pact America First Committee founded Roosevelt reelected Destroyers-for-bases deal	Lend-lease plan Atlantic Charter Japan attacks Pearl Harbor U.S. enters World War II	

In the end, the limited American internationalism of the interwar years proved insufficient to protect the interests of the United States, to create global stability, or to keep the nation from becoming involved in the most catastrophic war in human history.

THE DIPLOMACY OF THE NEW ERA

Critics of American foreign policy in the 1920s often described it with a single word: isolationism. But in reality, the United States played a more active role in world affairs in the 1920s than it had at almost any previous time in its history.

Replacing the League

By the time the Harding administration took office in 1921, American membership in the League of Nations was no longer a realistic possibility. But Secretary of State Charles Evans Hughes wanted to find something with which to replace the League as a guarantor of world peace and stability. He embarked on a series of efforts to build safeguards against future wars, but ones that would not hamper American freedom of action in the world.

The most important of such efforts was the Washington Conference of 1921—an attempt to prevent a destabilizing naval armaments race among the United States, Britain, and Japan. Hughes proposed a plan for dramatic reductions in the fleets of all three nations and a ten-year moratorium on the construction of large warships. To the surprise of almost everyone, the conference ultimately agreed to accept most of Hughes's terms. The Five-Power Pact of February 1922 established limits for total naval tonnage and a ratio of armaments among the signatories. For every 5 tons of American and British warships, Japan would maintain 3 and France and Italy 1.75 each.

When the French foreign minister, Aristide Briand, asked the United States in 1927 to join an alliance against Germany, Secretary of State Frank Kellogg (who had replaced Hughes in 1925) proposed instead a multilateral treaty outlawing war as an instrument of national policy. Fourteen nations signed the agreement in Paris on August 27, 1928, amid wide international acclaim. Forty-eight other nations later joined the Kellogg-Briand Pact. It contained no instruments of enforcement.

Debts and Diplomacy

The first responsibility of diplomacy, Hughes, Kellogg, and others agreed, was to ensure that American overseas trade faced no obstacles. Preventing a dangerous and expensive armaments race and reducing the possibility of war were two steps to that end. So were new financial arrangements to deal with international debts. The Allied powers of Europe were struggling to repay $11 billion in loans they had contracted with the United States during and shortly after the war. At the same time, Germany was attempting to pay the reparations levied by the Allies. With the financial structure of Europe on the brink of collapse as a result, the United States stepped in with a solution.

Charles G. Dawes, an American banker, negotiated an agreement in 1924 among France, Britain, Germany, and the United States under which American banks would provide enormous loans to the Germans, enabling them to meet their reparations payments; in return, Britain and France would agree to reduce the amount of those payments. Under the Dawes Plan, the United States would lend money to Germany, which would use that money to pay reparations to France and England, which would in turn use those funds (as well as large loans they themselves were receiving from American banks) to repay war debts to the United States. The flow was able to continue only by virtue of the enormous debts Germany and the

A FORD PLANT IN RUSSIA The success of Henry Ford in creating affordable, mass-produced automobiles made him famous around the world, and particularly popular in the Soviet Union in the 1920s and early 1930s, as the communist regime strove to push the nation into the industrial future. Russians called the system of large-scale factory production "Fordism," and they welcomed assistance from the Ford Motor Company itself, which sent engineers and workers over to Russia to help build large automobile plants such as this one.

other European nations were acquiring to American banks and corporations. The American economic involvement in Europe continued to expand until the worldwide depression shattered the system in 1931.

The government felt even fewer reservations about assisting American economic expansion in Latin America. During the 1920s, American military forces maintained a presence in Nicaragua, Panama, and several other countries in the region, while United States investments in Latin America more than doubled. American banks were offering large loans to Latin American governments, just as they were in Europe; and just as in Europe, the Latin Americans were having difficulty earning the money to repay them in the face of the formidable United States tariff barrier.

Hoover and the World Crisis

After the relatively placid international climate of the 1920s, the diplomatic challenges facing the Hoover administration must have seemed bewildering. The world financial crisis that had begun in 1929 and greatly intensified after 1931 was producing a rising nationalism in Europe, toppling some existing political leaders and replacing them with powerful, belligerent governments committed to expansion as a solution to their economic problems. An expansionist government in Japan was creating similar problems in Asia. Hoover was confronted with the beginning of a process that would ultimately lead to war.

In Latin America, Hoover tried to repair some of the damage earlier American policies had created. He made a ten-week good-will tour through the region before his inauguration. Once in office, he generally abstained from intervening in the internal affairs of neighboring nations and moved to withdraw American troops from Nicaragua and Haiti. When economic distress led to the collapse of several Latin American regimes, Hoover announced a new policy: America would grant diplomatic recognition to any sitting government in the region without questioning the means it had used to obtain power. He even repudiated the Roosevelt Corollary to the Monroe Doctrine by refusing to permit American intervention when several Latin American countries defaulted on debt obligations to the United States in October 1931.

In Europe, the administration enjoyed few successes in its efforts to promote economic stability. When Hoover's proposed moratorium on debts failed to attract broad support or produce financial stability, he refused to cancel all war debts to the United States as many economists advised him to do. Several European nations promptly went into default. Efforts to extend the 1921 limits on naval construction fell victim to French and British fears of German and Japanese militarism.

The ineffectiveness of American diplomacy in Europe was particularly troubling in light of the new governments on the Continent. Benito Mussolini's Fascist Party had been in control of Italy since the early 1920s and had become increasingly nationalistic and militaristic. Still more ominous was the growing power of the National Socialist (or Nazi) Party in Germany. By the late 1920s, the Weimar Republic, the nation's government since the end of World War I, had been largely discredited by, among other things, a ruinous inflation. Adolf Hitler, the leader of the Nazis, was growing rapidly in popular favor and would take power in 1933. Hitler believed in the genetic superiority of the Aryan (German) people and in extending German territory to provide *Lebensraum* (living space) for the German "master race." He also displayed a pathological anti-Semitism and a passionate militarism.

More immediately alarming to the Hoover administration was a major crisis in Asia—another early step toward World War II. The Japanese, suffering from an economic depression of their own, were concerned

HITLER AND MUSSOLINI The German and Italian dictators, shown here reviewing troops together in Berlin in the mid-1930s, acted publicly as if they were equals. Privately, however, Hitler viewed Mussolini with contempt, and the Italian dictator complained frequently of being treated as a junior partner by his ally.

about the increasing power of the Soviet Union and of Chiang Kai-shek's nationalist China. In particular, they were alarmed at Chiang's insistence on expanding his government's power in Manchuria, which remained officially a part of China but over which the Japanese had maintained informal economic control since 1905. In 1931, Japan's military leaders staged what was, in effect, a coup and took control of the government in Tokyo. Weeks later, they launched an invasion of northern Manchuria. They had conquered the region by the end of the year. Hoover permitted Secretary of State Henry Stimson to issue stern warnings to the Japanese but barred him from cooperating with the League of Nations to impose economic sanctions against them. Early in 1932, Japan expanded its aggression further into China, attacking the city of Shanghai and killing thousands of civilians.

ISOLATIONISM AND INTERNATIONALISM

The administration of Franklin Roosevelt faced a dual challenge as it entered office in 1933. It had to deal with the worst economic crisis in the nation's history, and it had to deal as well with the effects of a decaying international structure.

Depression Diplomacy

Perhaps Roosevelt's sharpest break with the policies of his predecessor was on the question of American economic relations with Europe. Hoover had argued that only by resolving the question of war debts and reinforcing the gold standard could the American economy hope to recover. He had, therefore, agreed to participate in the World Economic Conference, to be held in London in June 1933, to attempt to resolve these issues. By the time the conference assembled, however, Roosevelt had already become convinced that the gold value of the dollar had to be allowed to fall in order for American goods to be able to compete in world markets. Shortly after the conference convened, he released what became known as the "bombshell message," repudiating the orthodox views of most of the delegates and rejecting any agreement on currency stabilization. The conference quickly dissolved without reaching agreement.

At the same time, Roosevelt abandoned the commitments of the Hoover administration to settle the issue of war debts through international agreement. In April 1934 he signed a bill that prohibited American banks from making loans to any nation in default on its debts. The legislation ended the old, circular system by which debt payments continued only by virtue of increasing American loans; within months, war-debt payments from every nation except Finland stopped for good.

Sixteen years after the Bolshevik Revolution of 1917, the American government still had not officially recognized the government of the Soviet Union. But a growing number of influential Americans were urging a change in policy—largely because the Soviet Union appeared to be a possible source of trade. The Russians, for their part, were hoping for American cooperation in containing Japan. In November 1933, the United States and the Soviet Union agreed to open formal diplomatic relations.

Despite this promising beginning, however, relations with the Soviet Union soon soured once again. American trade failed to establish a foothold in Russia, disappointing hopes in the United States; and the American government did little to reassure the Soviets that it was interested in stopping

Japanese expansion in Asia, dousing expectations in Russia. By the end of 1934, the Soviet Union and the United States were once again viewing each other with considerable mistrust.

The United States succeeded during the 1930s in increasing both its exports to and its imports from Latin America by over 100 percent. At the same time, the Roosevelt administration was taking a new approach toward Latin America, an approach which became known as the "Good Neighbor Policy" and which expanded on the changes the Hoover administration had made. At the Inter-American Conference in Montevideo, Uruguay, in December 1933, Secretary of State Cordell Hull signed a formal convention declaring: "No state has the right to intervene in the internal or external affairs of another." By repudiating military intervention, Roosevelt, like Hoover, eased tensions between the United States and its neighbors considerably. But the Good Neighbor Policy did little to stem the growing American domination of the Latin American economy.

The Rise of Isolationism

With the international system of the 1920s now decayed beyond repair, the United States faced a choice between more active efforts to stabilize the world and more energetic attempts to isolate itself from it. Most Americans unhesitatingly chose the latter. Support for isolationism emerged from many quarters. Some Wilsonian internationalists had grown disillusioned with the League of Nations and its inability to stop Japanese aggression in Asia. Other Americans were listening to the argument that powerful business interests—Wall Street, munitions makers, and others—had tricked the United States into participating in World War I. An investigation by a Senate committee chaired by Senator Gerald Nye of North Dakota claimed to have produced evidence of exorbitant profiteering and tax evasion by many corporations during the war, and it suggested that bankers had pressured Wilson to intervene in the war so as to protect their loans abroad. (Few historians now lend much credence to these charges.)

Roosevelt himself was sympathetic to some of the isolationist arguments. But he continued to hope for at least a modest American role in maintaining world peace. In 1935, he proposed to the Senate a treaty to make the United States a member of the World Court—a largely symbolic gesture. Isolationists such as Father Coughlin and William Randolph Hearst aroused popular opposition to the agreement, and the Senate voted it down.

In the summer of 1935, it became clear that Mussolini's Italy was preparing to invade Ethiopia. Fearing the invasion would provoke a new

European war, American legislators began to design legal safeguards to prevent the United States from being dragged into the conflict. The result was the Neutrality Act of 1935, followed by additional acts in 1936 and 1937. The 1935 law established a mandatory arms embargo against both sides in any military conflict and directed the president to warn American citizens against traveling on the ships of warring nations. Thus, isolationists believed, the "protection of neutral rights" could not again become an excuse for American intervention in war. The 1936 Neutrality Act renewed these provisions, and the 1937 law added new ones, establishing the so-called cash-and-carry policy, by which belligerents could purchase only nonmilitary goods from the United States and could do so only by paying cash and shipping their purchases themselves.

Isolationist sentiment showed its strength again in 1936–1937 in response to the civil war in Spain. The Falangists of General Francisco Franco, a group much like the Italian fascists, revolted in July 1936 against the existing republican government. Hitler and Mussolini supported Franco, both vocally and with weapons and supplies. Some individual Americans traveled to Spain to assist the republican cause, but the United States government joined with Britain and France in an agreement to offer no assistance to either side.

In the summer of 1937, Japan intensified its six-year-old assault on Manchuria and attacked China's five northern provinces. Roosevelt responded in a speech in Chicago in October 1937. He warned of the dangers of the Japanese actions and argued that aggressors should be "quarantined" by the international community to prevent the contagion of war from spreading. He was deliberately vague about what such a "quarantine" would mean. Even so, public response to the speech was disturbingly hostile, and Roosevelt drew back. On December 12, 1937, Japanese aviators bombed and sank the United States gunboat *Panay*, almost certainly deliberately, as it sailed the Yangtze River in China. But so reluctant was the Roosevelt administration to antagonize the isolationists that the United States eagerly seized on Japanese claims that the bombing had been an accident, accepted Japan's apologies, and overlooked the attack.

The Failure of Munich

In 1936, Hitler had moved the revived German army into the Rhineland, rearming an area that had been off-limits to German troops since World War I. In March 1938, German forces marched without opposition into Austria, and Hitler proclaimed a union (or *Anschluss*) between Austria, his

THE BLITZ, LONDON The German Luftwaffe terrorized London and other British cities in 1940–1941 and again late in the war by bombing civilian areas indiscriminately in an effort to break the spirit of the English people. The effort failed, and the fortitude of the British did much to arouse support for their cause in the United States.

native land, and Germany, his adopted one. Neither in America nor in most of Europe was there much more than a murmur of opposition.

The Austrian invasion, however, soon created another crisis, for Germany had by now occupied territory surrounding three sides of western Czechoslovakia, a region Hitler dreamed of annexing. In September 1938, he demanded that Czechoslovakia cede him part of that region, the Sudetenland, an area in which many ethnic Germans lived. Although Czechoslovakia was prepared to fight to stop Hitler, it needed assistance from other nations. But most Western governments, including the United States, were willing to pay almost any price to settle the crisis peacefully. On September 29, Hitler met with the leaders of France and Great Britain at Munich in an effort to resolve the crisis. The French and British agreed to accept the German demands in Czechoslovakia in return for Hitler's promise to expand no farther.

The Munich agreement, which Roosevelt applauded at the time, was the most prominent element of a policy that came to be known as "appeasement" and that came to be identified (not altogether fairly) largely with British Prime Minister Neville Chamberlain. Whoever was to blame, the policy was a failure. In March 1939, Hitler occupied the remaining areas of Czechoslovakia, violating the Munich agreement unashamedly. And in April, he began issuing threats against Poland.

At that point, both Britain and France gave assurances to the Polish government that they would come to its assistance in case of an invasion; they even tried, too late, to draw the Soviet Union into a mutual defense agreement. But Stalin, who had not even been invited to the Munich Conference, had already decided he could expect no protection from the West. He signed a nonaggression pact with Hitler in August 1939, freeing the Germans for the moment from the danger of a two-front war. Shortly after that, Hitler staged an incident on the Polish border to allow him to claim that Germany had been attacked, and on September 1, 1939, he launched a full-scale invasion of Poland. Britain and France, true to their pledges, declared war on Germany two days later. World War II had begun.

FROM NEUTRALITY TO INTERVENTION

"This nation will remain a neutral nation," the president declared shortly after the hostilities began in Europe, "but I cannot ask that every American remain neutral in thought as well." There was never any question that both he and the majority of the American people favored Britain, France, and the other Allied nations in the contest. The question was how much the United States was prepared to do to assist them.

Neutrality Tested

At the very least, Roosevelt believed, the United States should make armaments available to the Allied armies to help them counter the military advantage the large German munitions industry gave Hitler. In September 1939, he asked Congress to revise the Neutrality Acts and lift the arms embargo against any nation engaged in war. Powerful isolationist opposition forced Congress to maintain the prohibition on American ships entering war zones. But the 1939 law did permit belligerents to purchase arms on the same cash-and-carry basis that the earlier Neutrality Acts had established for the sale of nonmilitary materials.

For a time, it was possible to believe that little more would be necessary. After the German armies quickly subdued Poland, the war in Europe settled into a long, quiet lull that lasted through the winter and spring—a "phony war," some called it. (In the meantime, the Soviet Union overran the small Baltic republics of Latvia, Estonia, and Lithuania and then, in late November, established effective control over Finland. The United States responded with nothing more than an ineffective "moral embargo" on the shipment of armaments to Russia.)

Whatever illusions Americans had harbored about the war in western Europe were shattered in the spring of 1940 when Germany launched a massive invasion to the west—first attacking Denmark and Norway, sweeping next across the Netherlands and Belgium, and driving finally deep into the heart of France. Allied efforts proved futile against the Nazi blitzkrieg. One western European stronghold after another fell into German hands. On June 10, Mussolini invaded France from the south as Hitler was attacking from the north. On June 22, finally, France fell, and Nazi troops marched into Paris. A new French regime assembled in Vichy, largely controlled by the German occupiers; and in all Europe, only the shattered remnants of the British and French armies, rescued from the beaches of Dunkirk, remained to oppose the Axis forces.

On May 16, in the midst of the offensive, Roosevelt asked Congress for an additional $1 billion for defense and received it quickly. That was one day after Winston Churchill, the new British prime minister, had sent Roosevelt the first of many long lists of requests for armaments, without which, he insisted, England could not long survive. Some Americans (including the United States ambassador to London, Joseph P. Kennedy) argued that the British plight was already hopeless, that any aid to the English was a wasted effort. But the president was determined to make war materials available to Britain. He even circumvented the cash-and-carry provisions of the Neutrality Acts by giving England fifty American destroyers (most of them left over from World War I) in return for the right to build American bases on British territory in the Western Hemisphere, and he returned to the factories a number of new airplanes purchased by the American military so that the British could buy them instead.

Roosevelt was able to take such steps in part because of a major shift in American public opinion. By July 1940, more than 66 percent of the public (according to opinion polls) believed that Germany posed a direct threat to the United States. Congress was, therefore, more willing to permit expanded American assistance to the Allies. Congress was also becoming more concerned about the need for internal preparations for war, and in September it approved the Burke-Wadsworth Act, inaugurating the first peacetime military draft in American history.

But the isolationists were far from finished. A powerful new isolationist lobby—the America First Committee, whose members included such prominent Americans as Charles Lindbergh and Senators Gerald Nye and Burton Wheeler—joined the debate over American policy toward the war. The lobby had at least the indirect support of a large proportion of the Republican Party. The debate was a bitter one. Through the summer and fall of 1940, moreover, it was complicated by a presidential campaign.

The Campaign of 1940

The biggest political question of 1940 was whether Franklin Roosevelt would break with tradition and run for an unprecedented third term. The president himself did not reveal his own wishes. But by refusing to withdraw from the contest, he made it impossible for any rival Democrat to establish a claim to the nomination. And when, just before the Democratic Convention in July, he let it be known that he would accept a "draft" from his party, the issue was virtually settled. The Democrats quickly renominated him and even reluctantly swallowed his choice for vice president: Agriculture secretary Henry A. Wallace, a man too liberal and too controversial for the taste of many party leaders.

The Republicans, again uncertain how to oppose Roosevelt effectively, nominated for president a politically inexperienced Indiana businessman, Wendell Willkie, who benefited from a powerful grassroots movement. Both the candidate and the party platform took positions little different from Roosevelt's: they would keep the country out of war but would extend generous assistance to the Allies. Willkie was an appealing figure and a vigorous campaigner, and he managed to evoke more public enthusiasm than any Republican candidate in decades. The election was closer than in either 1932 or 1936, but Roosevelt still won decisively. He received 55 percent of the popular vote to Willkie's 45 percent, and he won 449 electoral votes to Willkie's 82.

Neutrality Abandoned

In the last months of 1940, with the election behind him and with the situation in Europe deteriorating, Roosevelt began to make subtle but profound changes in the American role in the war. Great Britain was virtually bankrupt and could no longer meet the cash-and-carry requirements imposed by the Neutrality Acts. The president, therefore, proposed a new system for supplying Britain: "lend-lease." It would allow the government not only to sell but also to lend or lease armaments to any nation deemed "pivotal to the defense of the United States." In other words, America could funnel weapons to England on the basis of no more than Britain's promise to return them when the war was over. Isolationists attacked the measure bitterly, but Congress enacted the bill by wide margins.

With lend-lease established, Roosevelt soon faced another serious problem. Attacks by German submarines had made shipping lanes in the Atlantic extremely dangerous. The British navy was losing ships more rapidly than it could replace them and was finding it difficult to transport materials across the Atlantic from America. Secretary of War Henry Stimson (who had been Hoover's secretary of state and who returned to the cabinet at Roosevelt's request in 1940) argued that the United States should itself convoy vessels to England; but Roosevelt took a more limited approach. He argued that the western Atlantic was a neutral zone and the responsibility of the American nations. By July 1941, therefore, American ships were patrolling the ocean as far east as Iceland.

At first Germany did little to challenge these obviously hostile American actions. By September 1941, however, the situation had changed. Nazi forces had invaded the Soviet Union in June of that year. When the Soviets did not surrender, as many had predicted they would, Roosevelt persuaded Congress to extend lend-lease privileges to them. Now American industry was providing vital assistance to Hitler's foes on two fronts, and the American navy was protecting the flow of those goods to Europe. In September, Nazi submarines began a concerted campaign against American vessels. Roosevelt ordered American ships to fire on German submarines "on sight." In October, Nazi submarines hit two American destroyers and sank one of them, the *Reuben James*, killing many American sailors. Congress now voted to allow the United States to arm its merchant vessels and to sail all the way into belligerent ports. The United States had, in effect, launched a naval war against Germany.

In August 1941, Roosevelt met with Churchill aboard a British vessel off the coast of Newfoundland. The president made no military commitments, but he did join with the prime minister in releasing a document that became known as the Atlantic Charter, in which the two nations set out "certain common principles" on which to base "a better future for the world." It called openly for "the final destruction of the Nazi tyranny" and for a new world order in which every nation controlled its own destiny. It was, in effect, a statement of war aims.

The Road to Pearl Harbor

Japan, in the meantime, was taking advantage of events in Europe to extend its empire in the Pacific. In September 1940, the Japanese signed the Tripartite Pact, a loose defensive alliance with Germany and Italy (although in reality, the European Axis powers never developed a very strong relationship with Japan). In July 1941, imperial troops moved into Indochina and seized the capital of Vietnam, a colony of France. The United States, having broken Japanese codes, knew Japan's next target was to be the Dutch East Indies; and when Tokyo failed to respond to Roosevelt's stern warnings, the president froze all Japanese assets in the United States, severely limiting Japan's ability to purchase needed American supplies.

Tokyo now faced a choice. Either it would have to repair relations with the United States to restore the flow of supplies or it would have to find those supplies elsewhere, most notably by seizing British and Dutch possessions in the Pacific. In October, militants in Tokyo forced the moderate prime minister out of office and replaced him with the leader of the war party, General Hideki Tojo. There seemed little alternative now to war.

For several weeks, the Tojo government maintained a pretense of wanting to continue negotiations. But Tokyo had already decided it would not yield on the question of China, and Washington had made clear that it would accept nothing less. By late November, the State Department had given up on the possibility of a peaceful settlement. American intelligence, meanwhile, had decoded Japanese messages that made clear a Japanese attack was imminent. But Washington did not know where the attack would take place. Most officials continued to believe that the Japanese would move first not against American territory but against British or Dutch possessions to the south. A combination of confusion and miscalculation caused the government to overlook indications that Japan intended a direct attack on American forces.

At 7:55 A.M. on Sunday, December 7, 1941, a wave of Japanese bombers attacked the United States naval base at Pearl Harbor in Hawaii. A second wave came an hour later. Within two hours, the United States lost 8 battleships, 3 cruisers, 4 other vessels, 188 airplanes, and several vital shore installations. More than 2,400 soldiers and sailors died, and another 1,000 were injured. The Japanese suffered only light losses.

American forces were now greatly diminished in the Pacific (although by a fortunate accident, no American aircraft carriers—the heart of the Pacific fleet—had been at Pearl Harbor on December 7). Nevertheless,

PEARL HARBOR Virtually no one in authority in Hawaii or Washington imagined that the Japanese were capable of launching an attack on a place as far from Japan as Pearl Harbor. That is one reason why intelligence experts failed to predict the attack, despite the many clues they received from deciphering secret Japanese messages. It also helps to explain why so many ships remained bunched together helplessly in the harbor, easy prey to the Japanese bombers.

the raid on Hawaii unified the American people behind war. On December 8, after a stirring speech by the president, the Senate voted unanimously and the House voted 388 to 1 to approve a declaration of war against Japan. Three days later, Germany and Italy, Japan's European allies, declared war on the United States; on the same day, December 11, Congress reciprocated without a dissenting vote.

CONCLUSION

American foreign policy in the years after World War I attempted something that ultimately proved impossible. The United States was determined to be a major power in the world, to extend its trade broadly around the globe, and to influence other nations in ways Americans believed would be beneficial to their own, and the world's, interests. But the United States was also determined to do nothing that would limit its own freedom of action. It would not join the League of Nations. It would not join the World Court. It would not form alliances with other nations. It would operate powerfully—and alone.

But ominous forces were at work in the world that would gradually push the United States into greater engagement with other nations. The economic disarray that the Great Depression created all around the globe, the rise of totalitarian regimes, the expansionist ambitions of powerful new leaders: all worked to destroy the uneasy stability of the post–World War I international system. America's own interests, economic and otherwise, were now imperiled. And America's go-it-alone foreign policy seemed powerless to change the course of events.

Franklin Roosevelt tried throughout the later years of the 1930s to push the American people slowly into a greater involvement in international affairs. In particular, he tried to nudge the United States toward taking a more forceful stand against dictatorship and aggression. A powerful isolationist movement helped stymie him for a time, even after war broke out in Europe. Gradually, however, public opinion shifted toward support of the Allies (Britain, France, and Russia) and against the Axis (Germany, Italy, and Japan). The nation began to mobilize for war, to supply ships and munitions to Britain, even to engage in naval combat with German forces in the Atlantic. Finally, on December 7, 1941, the surprise Japanese attack on the American base at Pearl Harbor in Hawaii eliminated the last elements of uncertainty and drove the United States—now united behind the war effort—into the greatest and most terrible conflict in human history.

FOR FURTHER REFERENCE

Suggested Readings

Robert Dallek's *Franklin D. Roosevelt and American Foreign Policy, 1932–1945* (1979) is a comprehensive study of Roosevelt's foreign policy. Akira Iriye, *The Cambridge History of American Foreign Relations, Vol. 3: The Globalizing of America, 1913–1945* (1993). In *Inevitable Revolutions* (1983), Walter LaFeber recounts America's quixotic attempts to halt revolutionary movements throughout the world. Wayne S. Cole, *Roosevelt and the Isolationists, 1932–1945* (1983) is a solid overview of isolationism. James MacGregor Burns, *Roosevelt: The Soldier of Freedom* (1970) and Warren F. Kimball, *The Juggler:*

Franklin Roosevelt as Wartime Statesman (1991) are two thoughtful studies of the president. Joseph Lasch's *Roosevelt and Churchill* (1976) explores the dynamic relationship between the wartime leaders. Gordon Prange, *At Dawn We Slept* (1981) examines the controversial attack on Pearl Harbor from both the Japanese and American sides.

Films

(The best source for information on how to find these and other films is *Bowker's Complete Video Directory*—3 volumes.) *The Arsenal of Democracy* (1993) describes the economic revival of Depression America as it transformed itself into an arsenal for World War II combatants. *The Darkest Hour, 1939–1941* (1986) recounts Hitler's invasion of Poland, Britain and France's declaration of war against Germany, the Japanese alliance with Germany, and finally the December 7, 1941, attack on Pearl Harbor.

Internet Resources

Internet websites containing historical material relevant to the subjects discussed in this chapter can be reached through the McGraw-Hill history site at www.mhhe.com/socscience/history/usa/link/linktop.htm.

CHAPTER TWENTY-EIGHT

America in a World at War

HE ATTACK ON Pearl Harbor had thrust the United States into the greatest and most terrible war in the history of humanity. World War I had been extraordinarily bloody and had destroyed centuries-old European social and political institutions. But World War II surpassed it in carnage and horror, not only in Europe but around much of the rest of the globe. In the end, it changed the world as profoundly as any event of the twentieth century, perhaps of any century.

World War II also transformed the United States in profound, if not always readily visible, ways. The story of American involvement in the war, therefore, is the story of the creation of a new world, both abroad and at home.

WAR ON TWO FRONTS

Whatever political disagreements and social tensions there may have been among the American people during World War II, there was striking unity of opinion about the conflict itself. But both unity and confidence faced severe tests in the first, troubled months of 1942.

Containing the Japanese

Ten hours after the strike at Pearl Harbor, Japanese airplanes attacked the American airfields at Manila in the Philippines, destroying much of

TIME LINE			
1942	**1943**	**1944**	**1945**
Battle of Midway	Americans capture Guadalcanal	Allies invade Normandy	Roosevelt dies; Truman becomes president
Campaign in Northern Africa		Roosevelt reelected	
Japanese Americans interned	Allied invasion of Italy	Americans capture Philippines	Germany surrenders
Manhattan Project begins			U.S. drops atomic bombs on Hiroshima, Nagasaki
CORE founded			Japan surrenders
	Soviet victory at Stalingrad		

America's remaining air power in the Pacific. Three days later Guam, an American possession, fell to Japan; Wake Island and Hong Kong followed. The great British fortress of Singapore in Malaya surrendered in February 1942, the Dutch East Indies in March, Burma in April. In the Philippines, exhausted Filipino and American troops gave up their defense of the islands on May 6.

American strategists planned two broad offensives to turn the tide against the Japanese. One, under the command of General Douglas MacArthur, would move north from Australia, through New Guinea, and eventually to the Philippines. The other, under Admiral Chester Nimitz, would move west from Hawaii toward major Japanese island outposts in the central Pacific. Ultimately, strategists predicted, the two offensives would come together to invade Japan itself.

The Allies achieved their first important victory in the Battle of the Coral Sea, just northwest of Australia, on May 7–8, 1942, when American forces turned back the previously unstoppable Japanese navy. A month later, there was an even more important turning point northwest of Hawaii. An enormous battle raged for four days, June 3–6, 1942, near the small American outpost at Midway Island, at the end of which the United States, despite great losses, was clearly victorious. The American navy destroyed four Japanese aircraft carriers and lost only one of its own; the action regained control of the central Pacific for the United States.

The Americans took the offensive for the first time several months later in the southern Solomon Islands, to the east of New Guinea. In Au-

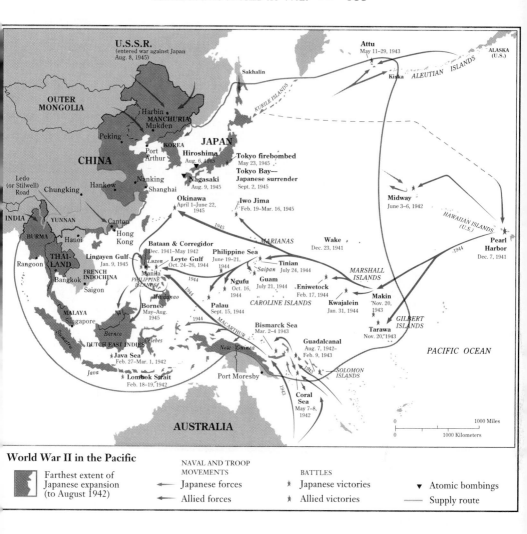

World War II in the Pacific

Farthest extent of
Japanese expansion
(to August 1942)

NAVAL AND TROOP
MOVEMENTS
← Japanese forces
← Allied forces

BATTLES
* Japanese victories
* Allied victories

▼ Atomic bombings
〜〜〜 Supply route

gust 1942, American forces assaulted three of the islands: Gavutu, Tulagi, and Guadalcanal. A struggle of terrible ferocity developed at Guadalcanal and continued for six months, inflicting heavy losses on both sides. In the end, however, the Japanese were forced to abandon the island—and with it their last chance of launching an effective offensive to the south. In both the southern and the central Pacific, therefore, the initiative had shifted to the United States by mid-1943. The Japanese advance had been halted. The Americans, with aid from the Australians and the New Zealanders, now began the slow, arduous process of moving toward the Philippines and Japan itself.

GUADALCANAL The battle of Guadalcanal, in the Solomon Islands, was the scene of some of the bloodiest and most protracted combat of the Pacific war. United States Marines are shown here charging ashore in August 1942, in the first stages of what became a six-month campaign.

Holding Off the Germans

In the European war, the United States was fighting in cooperation with, among others, Britain and the exiled "Free French" forces in the west; and it was trying also to conciliate its new ally, the Soviet Union, which was now fighting Hitler in the east. The army chief of staff, General George C. Marshall, supported a plan for a major Allied invasion of France across the English Channel in the spring of 1943, and he placed a previously little-known general, Dwight D. Eisenhower, in charge of planning the operation. But the American plan faced challenges from the other Allies. The Soviet Union, which was absorbing the brunt of the German war effort (as it would through most of the conflict), wanted the Allied invasion to begin at the earliest possible moment. The British, on the other hand, wanted first to launch a series of Allied offensives around the edges of the Nazi empire—in northern Africa and southern Europe—before undertaking the major invasion of France.

Roosevelt was torn, but he ultimately decided to support the British plan—in part because he was eager to get American forces into combat quickly and feared that a cross-Channel invasion would take a long time to prepare. At the end of October 1942, the British opened a counter-offensive against General Erwin Rommel and the Nazi forces in North Africa which were threatening the Suez Canal. In a major battle at El Alamein, they forced the Germans to retreat from Egypt. On November 8, Anglo-American forces landed at Oran and Algiers in Algeria and at Casablanca in Morocco—areas under the Nazi-controlled French government at Vichy—and began moving east toward Rommel. The Germans threw the full weight of their forces in Africa against the inexperienced Americans and inflicted a serious defeat on them at the Kasserine Pass in Tunisia. General George S. Patton, however, regrouped the American troops and began an effective counteroffensive. With the help of Allied air and naval power and of British forces attacking from the east under Field Marshall Bernard Montgomery (the hero of El Alamein), the American offensive finally drove the last Germans from Africa in May 1943.

The North African campaign had tied up a large proportion of Allied resources. That was one reason why the planned May 1943 cross-Channel invasion of France had to be postponed, despite angry complaints from the Soviet Union. By now, however, the threat of a Soviet collapse seemed much diminished, for during the winter of 1942–1943, the Red Army had successfully held off a major German assault at Stalingrad in southern Russia. Hitler had committed such enormous forces to the battle, and had suffered such appalling losses, that he could not continue his eastern offensive.

The Soviet successes persuaded Roosevelt to agree, in a January 1943 meeting with Churchill in Casablanca, to a British plan for an Allied invasion of Sicily. Churchill argued that the operation in Sicily might knock Italy out of the war and tie up German divisions that might otherwise be stationed in France. On the night of July 9, 1943, American and British armies landed in southeast Sicily; thirty-eight days later, they had conquered the island and were moving onto the Italian mainland. In the face of these setbacks, Mussolini's government collapsed and the dictator himself fled north toward Germany. (He was later captured by Italian insurgents and hung.) Although Mussolini's successor, Pietro Badoglio, quickly committed Italy to the Allies, Germany moved eight divisions into the country and established a powerful defensive line south of Rome. The Allied offensive on the Italian peninsula, which began on September 3, 1943,

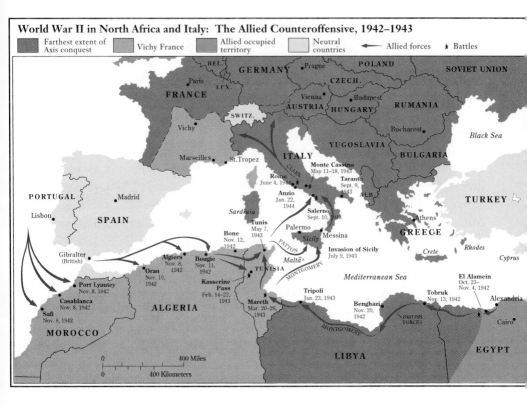

World War II in North Africa and Italy: The Allied Counteroffensive, 1942–1943

Farthest extent of Axis conquest | Vichy France | Allied occupied territory | Neutral countries | ← Allied forces | ⋆ Battles

soon bogged down. Not until May 1944 did the Allies break through the German defenses to resume their northward advance. On June 4, 1944, they captured Rome.

The invasion of Italy contributed to the Allied war effort in several important ways. But it contributed to postponing the invasion of France by as much as a year, deeply embittering the Soviet Union and giving the Soviets time to begin moving toward the countries of eastern Europe.

America and the Holocaust

In the midst of this intensive fighting, the leaders of the American government found themselves confronted with one of history's great tragedies: the Nazi campaign to exterminate the Jews of Europe—the Holocaust. As early as 1942, high officials in Washington had incontrovertible evidence that Hitler's forces were rounding up Jews and others (including Poles, homosexuals, and communists) from all over Europe, transporting them to concentration camps in eastern Germany and Poland, and systematically murdering them. (The death toll would ultimately reach 6 million Jews and at least 4 million others.) News of the atrocities was reaching the public as well, and pressure began to build for an Allied effort to end the killing or at least to rescue some of the surviving Jews.

The American government consistently resisted almost all such entreaties. Although by mid-1944 Allied bombers were flying missions within a few miles of the most notorious death camp, at Auschwitz in Poland, the War Department rejected pleas that the planes try to destroy the crematoria at the camp as militarily unfeasible. American officials also refused requests that the Allies try to destroy railroad lines leading to the camp. And the United States resisted pleas that it admit large numbers of the Jewish refugees attempting to escape Europe.

After 1941, there was probably little American leaders could have done, other than defeat Germany in the war, to save most of Hitler's victims. But more forceful action by the United States (and Britain, which was even less amenable to Jewish requests for assistance) might well have saved at least some lives. That they did not take such action, it seems clear in retrospect, constituted a considerable moral failure. But policymakers found it possible to justify ignoring pleas to help the Jews by insisting that they needed to focus exclusively on the larger goal of winning the war. Any diversion of energy and attention to other purposes, they apparently believed, would distract them from the overriding goal of victory.

THE AMERICAN ECONOMY IN WARTIME

Not since the Civil War had the United States been involved in so prolonged and consuming a military experience as World War II. American armed forces engaged in combat around the globe for nearly four years. American society, in the meantime, experienced changes that reached into virtually every corner of the nation.

Prosperity and the Rights of Labor

World War II had its most profound impact on American domestic life by ending the Great Depression at last. By the middle of 1941, the economic problems of the 1930s—unemployment, deflation, industrial sluggishness— had virtually vanished before the great wave of wartime industrial expansion.

The most important agent of the new prosperity was government spending, which after 1939 was pumping more money into the economy each year than all the New Deal relief agencies combined had done. In 1939, the federal budget had been $9 billion; by 1945, it had risen to $100 billion. Largely as a result, the gross national product soared: from $91 billion in 1939 to $166 billion in 1945. Personal incomes in some regions grew by as much as 100 percent or more. The demands of wartime production created a shortage of consumer goods, so many wage earners diverted much of their new affluence into savings, which would later help keep the economic boom alive in the postwar years.

The impact of government spending was perhaps most dramatic in the West. The West Coast, naturally, became the launching point for most of the naval war against Japan, and the government created large manufacturing facilities in California and elsewhere to serve the needs of its military. Altogether, the government made almost $40 billion worth of capital investments (factories, military and transportation facilities, highways, power plants) in the West during the war, more than in any other region. By the end of the war, the Pacific Coast had become the center of the growing American aircraft industry. New yards in southern California, Washington State, and elsewhere made the West a center of the shipbuilding industry. Los Angeles, formerly a medium-sized city notable chiefly for its film industry, now became a major industrial center as well.

Instead of the massive unemployment that had been the most troubling feature of the Depression economy, the war created a serious labor shortage. The armed forces took over 15 million men and women out of the civilian work force at the same time that the demand for labor was rising rapidly. Nevertheless, the civilian work force increased by almost 20 percent during the war—largely through the employment of many people previously considered inappropriate for the work force: the very young, the elderly, minorities, and, most important, several million women.

The war gave an enormous boost to union membership, which rose from about 10.5 million in 1941 to over 3 million in 1945. But it also created important new restrictions on unions. The government, struggling to keep production up and inflation down, managed to win two important concessions from union leaders. One was the "no-strike" pledge, by which unions agreed not to stop production in wartime. Another was the so-called Little Steel formula, which set a 15 percent limit on wage increases. In return, the government gave labor a "maintenance-of-membership" agreement, which ensured that the thousands of new workers pouring into unionized defense plants would be automatically enrolled in the unions.

Despite the no-strike pledge, there were nearly 15,000 work stoppages during the war, mostly wildcat strikes (strikes unauthorized by the union leadership), many for higher wages, many protesting harsh working conditions and high levels of stress, and some protesting the racial integration of the work force. When the United Mine Workers defied the government by striking in May 1943, Congress reacted by passing, over Roosevelt's veto, the Smith-Connally Act (the War Labor Disputes Act), which required that unions wait thirty days before striking and which empowered the president to seize a struck war plant. In the meantime, public animosity toward labor rose rapidly, and many states passed laws to limit union power.

Stabilizing the Boom and Mobilizing Production

The fear of deflation, the central concern of the 1930s, gave way during the war to a fear of inflation, particularly after prices rose 25 percent in the two years before Pearl Harbor. In October 1942, Congress passed the Anti-Inflation Act, which gave the administration authority to freeze agricultural prices, wages, salaries, and rents throughout the country. Enforcement of these provisions was the task of the Office of Price Administration (OPA), led first by Leon Henderson and then by Chester Bowles. The OPA was successful enough that inflation was a much less serious problem during World War II than it had been during World War I. Even so, the agency was never popular. Black-marketing and overcharging grew in proportions far beyond OPA policing capacity.

From 1941 to 1945, the federal government spent a total of $321 billion— twice as much as it had spent in the entire 150 years of its existence to that point, and ten times as much as the cost of World War I. The national debt rose from $49 billion in 1941 to $259 billion in 1945. The government borrowed about half the revenues it needed by selling $100 billion worth of bonds. Much of the rest it raised by radically increasing income-tax rates, through the Revenue Act of 1942. To simplify collection, Congress enacted a withholding system of payroll deductions in 1943.

The search for an effective mechanism to mobilize the economy for war began as early as 1939 and continued for nearly four years. One failed agency after another attempted to bring order to the mobilization effort. Finally, in January 1942, the president responded to widespread criticism by creating the War Production Board (WPB), under the direction of former Sears Roebuck executive Donald Nelson. In theory, the WPB was to be a "superagency," with broad powers over the economy. In fact, it never had as much authority as its World War I equivalent, the War Industries Board.

Throughout its troubled history, the WPB was never able to win complete control over military purchases; the army and navy often circumvented the board. It was never able to satisfy the complaints of small business, which charged (correctly) that most contracts were going to large corporations. Gradually, the president transferred much of the WPB's authority to a new office located within the White House: the Office of War Mobilization (OWM). But the OWM was only slightly more successful than the WPB.

Despite the administrative problems, however, the war economy managed to meet almost all of the nation's critical war needs. By the beginning of 1944, American factories were, in fact, producing more than the government needed. Their output was twice that of all the Axis countries combined.

Wartime Science and Technology

More than any previous American war, World War II was a watershed for technological and scientific innovation. That was partly because the American government—in its urgent efforts to overcome the effects of the 1920s and 1930s, during which few new military technologies had been developed—poured substantial funds into research and development beginning in 1940. In that year the government created the National Defense Research Committee, headed by the MIT scientist Vannevar Bush, who had been a pioneer in the early development of the computer. (It later became the Office of Scientific Research and Development.) By the end of the war, the new agency had spent more that $100 million on research, more than four times the amount spent by the government on military research and development in the previous forty years.

In the first years of the war, all the technological advantages seemed to lie with the Germans and Japanese. Germany had made great advances in tanks and other mechanized armor in the 1930s, particularly during the Spanish Civil War, when it had helped arm Franco's fascist forces. It used its armor effectively during its blitzkrieg in Europe in 1940 and again in North Africa in 1942. German submarine technology was significantly advanced compared to British and American capabilities in 1940, and German U-boats were, for a time, devastatingly effective in disrupting Allied shipping. Japan had developed extraordinary capacity in its naval-air technology. Its highly sophisticated fighter planes, launched from distant aircraft carriers, conducted the successful raid on Pearl Harbor in December 1941.

BOMBING AXIS FACTORIES The Boeing B-17 bomber was one of the great technological innovations of wartime aviation. It allowed Allied pilots to fly much further into ememy territory on bombing missions. Here, B-17s bomb factories in Austria in 1944.

But Britain and America had advantages of their own, which quickly helped redress these imbalances. American techniques of mass production—the great automotive assembly lines in particular—were converted efficiently to military production in 1941 and 1942 and soon began producing airplanes, ships, tanks, and other armaments in much greater numbers than the Germans and Japanese could produce. Allied scientists and engineers moved quickly as well to improve Anglo-American aviation and naval technology, and particularly to improve the performance of submarines and tanks. By late 1942, Allied weaponry was at least as advanced, and coming to be more plentiful, than that of the enemy.

In addition, each technological innovation by the enemy produced a corresponding innovation to limit the damage of the new techniques. American and British physicists made rapid advances in improving radar and sonar technology—taking advantage of advances in radio technology in the 1920s and beyond—which helped Allied naval forces decimate German U-boats in 1943 and effectively end their effectiveness in the naval war. Particularly important was the creation in 1940 of "centimetric radar," which used narrow beams of short wavelength that made radar more efficient and effective than ever before—as the British navy discovered in April 1941 when the instruments on one of its ships detected a surfaced submarine 10 miles away at night and, on another occasion, spotted a periscope at three-quarters of a mile range. With earlier technologies, both things would have been undetectable. This new radar could also be effectively miniaturized, which was critical to its use on airplanes and submarines in particular. It required only a small rotating aerial, and it used newly advanced cavity magnetron valves of great power. These innovations put the Allies far in advance of Germany and Japan in radar technology. The Allies also learned early how to detect and disable German naval mines; and when the Germans tried to counter this progress by introducing an "acoustic" mine, which detonated when a ship came near it, not necessarily just on contact, the Allies developed acoustical countermeasures of their own, which transmitted sounds through the water to detonate mines before ships came near them.

Anglo-American antiaircraft technology—both on land and on sea—also improved, although never to the point where it could stop bombing raids altogether. Germany made substantial advances in the development of rocket technology in the early years of the war, and it managed to launch some rocket-propelled bombs (the V1s and V2s) across the English Channel, aimed at London. The psychological effects of the rockets on the British people were considerable. But the Germans were never able to create a production technology capable of building enough such rockets to make a real difference in the balance of military power.

Beginning in 1942, British and American forces seized the advantage in the air war by producing new and powerful four-engine bombers in great numbers—among them the British Lancaster B1 and the American Boeing B17F, capable of flying a bomb load of 6,000 pounds for 1,300 miles, and capable of reaching 37,500 feet. Because they were able to fly higher and longer than the German equivalents, they were able to conduct extensive bombing missions over Germany (and later Japan) with much less danger of being shot down. But the success of the bombers rested heavily as well on new electronic devices capable of guiding their bombs to their targets. The Gee navigation system, which was also valuable to the navy, used electronic pulses to help pilots plot their exact location, something that in the past only a highly-skilled navigator could do, and then only in good weather. In March 1942, eighty Allied bombers fitted with Gee systems staged a devastatingly effective bombing raid on German industrial and military installations in the Ruhr Valley. In the past, studies had shown that night-bombing raids were at best 30 percent accurate. The Gee system doubled the accuracy rate. Also effective was the Oboe system, a radio device that sent a sonic message to airplanes to tell them when they were within 20 yards of their targets, first introduced in December 1942.

The area in which the Allies had perhaps the greatest advantages in technology and knowledge was the gathering of intelligence, much of it through Britain's top-secret Ultra project. Some of the advantages the Allies enjoyed came from successful efforts to capture or steal German and Japanese intelligence devices. More important, however, were the efforts of cryptologists to puzzle out the enemy's systems, and advances in computer technology that helped the Allies decipher coded messages sent by the Japanese and the Germans. Much of Germany's coded communication made use of the so-called Enigma machine, which was effective because it constantly changed the coding systems it used. In the first months of the war, Polish intelligence had developed an electro-mechanical computer, which it called the "Bombe," which could decipher some Enigma messages. After the fall of Poland, British scientists, led by the brilliant computer pioneer Alan Turing, took the Bombe, which was too slow to keep up with the increasingly frequent changes of coding the Germans were using, and greatly improved it. Among other things, they developed a punched-hole technology related to the punch cards that were for a time so central to computer technology of the postwar era. On April 15, 1940, the new, improved, high-speed Bombe broke the coding of a series of German messages within hours (not days, as had previously been the case). A few weeks later, it began decrypting German messages at the rate of 1,000 a day, providing the British (and later the Americans) with a constant flow of information about enemy operations that continued—completely unknown to the Germans—until the end of the war. Later in the war, British scientists working for the intelligence services built the first real programmable, digital computer—the Colossus II, which became operational less than a week before the beginning of the Normandy invasion and which was able to decipher an enormous number of intercepted German messages almost instantly.

The United States also had some important intelligence breakthroughs, including, in 1941, a dramatic success by the American Magic operation (the counterpart to the British Ultra) in breaking a Japanese coding system not unlike the German Enigma, a mechanical device known to the Allies as Purple. The result was that Americans had access to intercepted information that, if properly interpreted, could have alerted them to the Japanese raid on Pearl Harbor in December 1941. But because such a raid had seemed entirely inconceivable to most American officials prior to its occurrence, those who received the information failed to understand or disseminate it in time.

RACE AND GENDER IN WARTIME AMERICA

In most ways, the war loosened traditional barriers that had restricted the lives of minorities and women. There was too much demand for fighting men, too much demand for labor, and too much fluidity and mobility in society for rigid, traditional barriers to survive intact. Many barriers remained when the war came to an end, and many barriers that were weakened by the war grew stronger again—at least for a while—in peacetime. But for many women and minorities, the war was a time of considerable economic and even social progress—with the important exception of Japanese Americans.

African Americans and the War

In the summer of 1941, A. Philip Randolph, president of the Brotherhood of Sleeping Car Porters, an important union with a primarily black membership, began to insist that the government require companies receiving defense contracts to integrate their work forces. To mobilize support for the demand, Randolph planned a massive march on Washington. Roosevelt finally persuaded Randolph to cancel the march in return for a promise to establish what became the Fair Employment Practices Commission (FEPC) to investigate discrimination against blacks in war industries.

The need for labor in war plants greatly increased the migration of blacks from the rural areas of the South into industrial cities. The migration bettered the economic condition of many African Americans, but it also created urban tensions and occasionally violence. The most serious conflict occurred in Detroit in 1943, when racial friction in the city produced a major riot in which thirty-four people died, twenty-five of them blacks.

Despite such tensions, the leading black organizations redoubled their efforts during the war to challenge the system of segregation. The Congress of Racial Equality (CORE), organized in 1942, mobilized mass popular resistance to discrimination in a way that the older, more conservative organizations had never done. Randolph, Bayard Rustin, James Farmer, and other, younger black leaders helped organize sit-ins and demonstrations in segregated theaters and restaurants.

Pressure for change was also growing within the military. The armed forces maintained their traditional practice of limiting blacks to the most menial assignments, keeping them in segregated training camps and units, and barring them entirely from the Marine Corps and the Army Air Force. But there were signs of change. By the end of the war, the number of black servicemen had increased sevenfold, to 700,000; some training camps were being at least partially integrated; blacks were being allowed to serve on ships with white sailors; and more black units were being sent into combat. The changes did not come easily. In some of the partially integrated army bases—Fort Dix, New Jersey, for example—riots occasionally broke out when blacks protested having to serve in segregated divisions.

Native Americans and the War

Approximately 25,000 Indians performed military service during World War II. Many Native Americans served in combat. Others (mostly Navajos) became "code-talkers," working in military communications and speaking their own language (which enemy forces would be unlikely to understand) over the radio and the telephones. The war had important effects on the Indians who served in the military. It brought them into intimate contact (often for the first time) with white society, and it awakened among some of them a taste for the material benefits of life in capitalist America that they would retain after the war. Some never returned to the reservations, but chose to remain in the non-Indian world and assimilate to its ways.

The war had important effects, too, on those Native Americans who stayed on the reservations. Little war work reached the tribes. Government subsidies dwindled. Talented young people left the reservations to serve in the military or work in war production, creating manpower shortages in some tribes. The wartime emphasis on national unity undermined support for the revitalization of tribal autonomy that the Indian Reorganization Act of 1934 had launched. New pressures emerged to eliminate the reservation system and require the tribes to assimilate into white society—pressures so severe that John Collier, the energetic director of the Bureau of Indian Affairs who had done so much to promote the reinvigoration of the reservations, resigned in 1945.

Mexican-American War Workers

Large numbers of Mexican workers entered the United States during the war in response to labor shortages on the Pacific coast and in the Southwest. The American and Mexican governments agreed in 1942 to a program by which *braceros* (contract laborers) would be admitted to the United States for a limited time. Some worked as migrant farm laborers, but many Mexicans were able for the first time to find significant numbers of factory jobs. They formed the second-largest group of migrants (after blacks) to American cities in the 1940s. They were concentrated mainly in the West, but there were significant Mexican communities in Chicago, Detroit, and other industrial cities.

The sudden expansion of Mexican-American neighborhoods created tensions and occasionally conflict in some American cities. White residents of Los Angeles became alarmed at the activities of Mexican-American teenagers, many of whom were joining street gangs (*pachucos*). The youths were particularly distinctive because of their style of dress, which some whites considered outrageous. They wore long, loose jackets with padded shoulders, baggy pants tied at the ankles, long watch chains, broad-brimmed hats, and greased, ducktail hairstyles. The outfit was known as a "zoot suit." In June 1943, animosity toward the "zoot-suiters" produced a four-day riot in Los Angeles, during which white sailors stationed at a base in Long Beach invaded Mexican-American communities and attacked zoot-suiters (in response to alleged zoot-suiter attacks on servicemen). The police did little to restrain the sailors, who grabbed Hispanic teenagers, tore off and burned their clothes, cut off their ducktails, and beat them. When Mexicans tried to fight back, the police moved in and arrested them. In the aftermath of the "zoot-suit riots," Los Angeles passed a law prohibiting the wearing of zoot suits.

The Internment of Japanese Americans

Although World War II, unlike World War I, produced little popular animosity toward Germans, it created considerable animosity toward the Japanese. After the attack on Pearl Harbor, government propaganda and popular culture combined to create an image of the Japanese as a devious, malign, and savage people.

Predictably, this racial animosity soon extended to Americans of Japanese descent. There were not many Japanese Americans in the United States—about 127,000, most of them concentrated in a few areas in Cali-

ZOOT-SUITER The baggy pants, the long, loose jacket, the big collar, the exaggerated watch chain, the slicked-back hair—all were features of the outfit known as the zoot suit, which was popular among young Mexican Americans in Los Angeles and elsewhere. The "zoot-suit riots" in Los Angeles in June 1943 were a product of the suspicion with which Anglos (in this case servicemen stationed nearby) looked at the culture of the Chicano communities that were growing rapidly throughout the Southwest.

fornia. About a third of them were unnaturalized, first-generation immigrants (Issei); two-thirds were naturalized or native-born citizens of the United States (Nisei). Because they generally kept to themselves and preserved traditional Japanese cultural patterns, it was easy for some to imagine that the Japanese Americans were engaged in conspiracies on behalf of their ancestral homeland. (There is no evidence to suggest that they actually were.)

Finally, in February 1942, in response to pressure from military officials and political leaders on the West Coast and recommendations from the War Department, the president authorized the army to "intern" the Japanese Americans. More than 100,000 people (Issei and Nisei alike) were rounded up, told to dispose of their property however they could (which often meant simply abandoning it), and taken to what the government euphemistically called "relocation centers." In fact, they were facilities little different from prisons, many of them located in the western mountains and desert. As a result of prejudice and rumor, a group of innocent, hardworking people (many of them citizens of the United States) were forced to spend up to three years in grim, debilitating isolation, barred from lucrative employment, provided with only minimal medical care, and deprived of decent schools for their children. (In Hawaii, by contrast, residents of Japanese descent encountered little harassment, perhaps because they were more numerous and more crucial to the economy of the islands.) The Supreme Court upheld the evacuation in a 1944 decision; and although most of the Japanese Americans were released later that year, they were largely unable to win any compensation for their losses until Congress finally acted to redress the wrongs in the late 1980s.

Chinese Americans and the War

At the same time that the conflict with Japan undermined the position of Japanese Americans, the American alliance with China during World War II significantly enhanced both the legal and social status of Chinese Americans. In 1943, partly to improve relations with the government of China, Congress finally repealed the Chinese Exclusion Acts, which had barred almost all Chinese immigration since 1892. The new quota for Chinese immigrants was minuscule (105 a year), but a substantial number of Chinese women managed to gain entry into the country through other provisions covering war brides and fiancées. Over 4,000 Chinese women entered the United States in the first three years after the war. Permanent residents of the United States of Chinese descent were finally permitted to become citizens.

Racial animosity toward the Chinese did not disappear, but it did decline—in part because government propaganda and popular culture both began presenting positive images of the Chinese (partly to contrast them with the Japanese); in part because Chinese Americans (like African Americans and other previously marginal groups) began taking jobs in war plants and other booming areas suffering from labor shortages and hence moving out of the relatively isolated world of the Chinatowns. A higher proportion of Chinese Americans (22 percent of all adult males) were drafted than of any other national group, and the entire Chinese community in most cities worked hard and conspicuously for the war effort.

Women and Children in Wartime

The number of women in the work force increased by nearly 60 percent during the war, as many women took industrial jobs to replace male workers serving in the military. And these wage-earning women were more likely to be married and were, on the whole, older than most of those who had entered the work force in the past.

Many factory owners continued to categorize jobs by gender, reserving the most lucrative positions for men. (Female work, like male work, was also categorized by race: black women were usually assigned more menial tasks, and paid at a lower rate, than their white counterparts.) But

WOMEN WORKERS DURING WORLD WAR II Women—including many who had never worked for pay before—took over a broad range of traditionally male industrial jobs during World War II, replacing men serving in the armed forces. Some did so as a patriotic duty, some because they needed the money. But most also came to enjoy the independence paid employment provided, one reason why the number of women in the work force did not decline dramatically after the war.

some women began now to take on heavy industrial jobs that had long been considered "men's work." The famous wartime image of "Rosie the Riveter" symbolized the new importance of the female industrial worker. Women joined unions in substantial numbers, and they helped erode at least some of the prejudice, including the prejudice against mothers working, that had previously kept many of them from paid employment.

In the end, however, most women workers during the war were employed not in factories but in service-sector jobs. Above all, they worked for the government, whose bureaucratic needs expanded dramatically alongside its military and industrial needs. Even within the military, which enlisted substantial numbers of women as WAACs (army) and WAVEs (navy), most female work was clerical.

The new opportunities for employment produced new problems. Many mothers whose husbands were in the military had to combine working with caring for their children. The scarcity of child-care facilities or other community services meant that some women had no choice but to leave young children—often known as "latchkey children" or "eight-hour orphans"—at home alone (or sometimes locked in cars in factory parking lots) while they worked.

Perhaps in part because of the family dislocations the war produced, juvenile crime rose markedly in the war years. Young boys were arrested at rapidly increasing rates for car theft and other burglary, vandalism, and vagrancy. The arrest rate for prostitutes, many of whom were teenage girls, rose too, as did the incidence of venereal disease. For many children, however, the distinctive experience of the war years was not crime but work. More than a third of all teenagers between the ages of fourteen and eighteen were employed late in the war, causing some reduction in high-school enrollments.

The return of prosperity helped increase the marriage rate and lower the age at which people married, but many marriages were unable to survive the pressures of wartime separation. The divorce rate rose rapidly. The rise in the birth rate that accompanied the increase in marriages was the first sign of what would become the great postwar "baby boom."

ANXIETY AND AFFLUENCE
IN WARTIME CULTURE

The war created considerable anxiety in American lives. Families worried about loved ones at the front and, as the war continued, many mourned relatives who had died in combat. Women struggled to support families in the absence of husbands and fathers, who had been the principal bread-winners in peacetime. Businesses and communities struggled with short-ages of goods and shortages of labor. People living on the two coasts, in particular, worried about enemy invasions and sabotage.

But the abundance of the war years also created a striking buoyancy in American life. Suddenly people had money to spend again and—despite the many shortages—at least some things to spend it on. In fact, con-sumerism became, as it had in the 1920s, one of the most powerful forces in American culture and, for many, one of the features of American life that the war was being fought to defend. Advertisers, and at times even the gov-ernment, exhorted Americans to support the war effort to ensure a future of material comfort and consumer choice for themselves and their chil-dren. "Your people are giving their lives in useless sacrifice," the *Saturday Evening Post* wrote in a mock letter to the leaders of wartime Japan. "Ours are fighting for a glorious future of mass distribution and ownership."

Wartime Entertainment and Leisure

The book, theater, and movie industries did record business during the war. Audiences equal to about half the nation's population attended movies each week, often to watch heroic war films (including some—such as *Mission to Moscow*—that glorified America's murderous wartime ally, Josef Stalin). Magazines, particularly pictorial ones such as *Life*, reached the peak of their popularity, satisfying the seemingly insatiable hunger of readers for pictures and stories about the war. Radio ownership and listen-ership also increased, for the same reason.

Fuel rationing and rubber shortages limited travel by car, but many people traveled nevertheless—by train or bus, or to places relatively close to their homes. Resort hotels, casinos, and racetracks were jammed with customers. More often, however, people sought entertainment in their own communities. Dance halls were packed with young people drawn to the seductive music of bands; soldiers and sailors home on leave, or await-ing shipment abroad, were especially attracted to the dances and the big bands, which became to many of them a symbol of the life they were leav-ing and that they believed they were fighting to defend.

By far the most popular music in dance halls, and on radio, was the relatively new jazz form known as swing, which, like many other forms of popular music, had emerged from the African-American musical world. The black musician Fletcher Henderson began experimenting with swing in Harlem in the 1920s; he called it "hot jazz." In 1934, he began working with the white jazz musician Benny Goodman, arranging numbers for Goodman's own band. And in 1935, when Goodman played several of Henderson's arrangements to a wildly enthusiastic crowd of dancers in the Palomar Ballroom in Los Angeles, the "swing era"—the era of the new music's popularity among a broad, multiracial public—began. After his success at the Palomar, Goodman—soon to be known as the "King of Swing"—began playing more and more often on the radio, spreading the popularity of the music. And soon new big bands were springing up, both black and white, seizing the style, modifying it at times, and spreading it further: Count Basie, Tommy Dorsey, Artie Shaw, Duke Ellington, and, perhaps the performer etched most vividly in the memory of fighting men during World War II, Glenn Miller, whose early death while traveling to entertain troops made him something of a national hero.

During the heyday of swing, band leaders were among the most recognized and popular figures in American popular culture, rivaling movie stars in their celebrity. Swing dominated the radio. It drew huge audiences to dance halls. It sold more records than any other kind of music. And it became one of the first forms of popular music to challenge racial taboos. Benny Goodman hired the black pianist Teddy Wilson to play with his band in 1935; other white bandleaders followed.

Women and Men in the Armed Services

For men at the front, the image of home was a powerful antidote to the rigors of wartime. In the minds of many soldiers and sailors, especially those who were away from America for long periods, that image became increasingly romanticized. They dreamed of music, food, movies, and other material comforts. Many dreamed of women—wives and girlfriends, but also movie stars and others, who became the source of one of the most popular icons of the front: the pinup. Sailors pasted pinups inside their lockers. Infantrymen carried them (along with pictures of wives, mothers, and girlfriends) in their knapsacks. Fighter pilots gave their planes female names and painted bathing beauties on their nosecones. The most popular "pinup girl" was the actress Betty Grable. Her picture found its way into the hands of over 5 million fighting men by the end of the war. Grable was popular not just because she was sexually attractive, but also because she played roles in her films that made her a symbol of the wholesome, innocent girlfriend or wife many servicemen dreamed of finding on their return.

For the servicemen who remained in America during the war, and for soldiers and sailors in cities far from home in particular, the company of friendly, "wholesome" women was, the military believed, critical to sustaining morale. The branches of the United Servicemen's Organization (known as USOs) recruited thousands of young women to serve as hostesses in their clubs. They were expected to dress nicely, dance well, and chat happily with lonely men. Other women joined "dance brigades" and traveled by bus to military bases for social evenings with servicemen. They too were expected to be pretty, to dress attractively, and to interact comfortably with men they had never met before and would likely never see again. The "USO girls" and the members of the dance brigades were forbidden to have any contact with men except at parties at the clubs or during dances. Clearly such regulations were often violated. But while the military took elaborate measures to root out gay men and lesbians from their ranks—vigilantly searching for evidence of homosexuality and unceremoniously dismissing gay people with undesirable discharges—the services quietly tolerated illicit heterosexual relationships, which they believed were both natural and, for many men, necessary.

As during World War I, the armed services virtually took over many American colleges and universities. Emptied of male students and professors (and many females as well), who left to join the war effort, they turned themselves into training camps for military officers—helped by lavish funding from the federal government.

Retreat from Reform

Late in 1943, Franklin Roosevelt publicly suggested that "Dr. New Deal," as he called it, had served its purpose and should now give way to "Dr. Win-the-War." The statement reflected the president's own genuine shift in concern: victory was now more important than reform. But it reflected, too, the political reality that had emerged during the first two years of war.

The greatest assault on New Deal reforms came from conservatives in Congress, who seized on the war as an excuse to do what many had wanted to do in peacetime: dismantle many of the achievements of the New Deal. They were assisted by the end of mass unemployment, which decreased the need for such relief programs as the Civilian Conservation Corps and the Works Progress Administration (both of which Congress abolished). They were assisted, too, by their own increasing numbers. In the congressional elections of 1942, Republicans gained 47 seats in the House and 10 in the Senate.

Republicans approached the 1944 election determined to exploit what they believed was resentment of wartime regimentation and unhappiness with Democratic reform. They nominated as their candidate the young and vigorous governor of New York, Thomas E. Dewey. Roosevelt was unopposed within his party, but Democratic leaders pressured him to abandon Vice President Henry Wallace, an advanced New Dealer and hero of the CIO, and replace him with a more moderate figure. Roosevelt reluctantly acquiesced in the selection of Senator Harry S. Truman of Missouri, who had won acclaim as chairman of the Senate War Investigating Committee (known as the Truman Committee). It had compiled an impressive record uncovering waste and corruption in wartime production.

The election revolved around domestic economic issues and, indirectly, the president's health. The president was, in fact, gravely ill, suffering from, among other things, arteriosclerosis. But the campaign seemed momentarily to revive him. He made several strenuous public appearances late in October, which dispelled popular doubts about his health and ensured his reelection. He captured 53.5 percent of the popular vote to Dewey's 46 percent. He won 432 electoral votes to Dewey's 99. Democrats lost 1 seat in the Senate, gained 20 in the House, and maintained control of both.

THE DEFEAT OF THE AXIS

By the middle of 1943, America and its allies had succeeded in stopping the Axis advance both in Europe and in the Pacific. In the next two years, the Allies themselves seized the offensive and launched a series of powerful drives that rapidly led the way to victory.

The Liberation of France

By early 1944, American and British bombers were attacking German industrial installations and other targets almost around the clock, drastically cutting production and impeding transportation. Especially devastating was the massive bombing of such German cities as Leipzig, Dresden, and Berlin. A February 1945 incendiary raid on Dresden created a great firestorm that destroyed three-fourths of the previously undamaged city and killed approximately 135,000 people, almost all civilians. The morality of such attacks has been much debated in the years since the war; but at the time, few Americans questioned the claims of military leaders that the bombing cleared the way for the great Allied invasion of France in the late spring and the subsequent invasion of Germany.

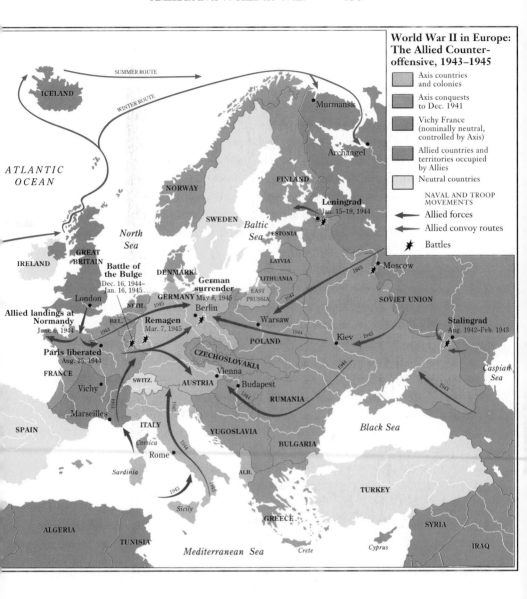

World War II in Europe: The Allied Counter-offensive, 1943–1945

Axis countries and colonies

Axis conquests to Dec. 1941

Vichy France (nominally neutral, controlled by Axis)

Allied countries and territories occupied by Allies

Neutral countries

NAVAL AND TROOP MOVEMENTS

Allied forces

Allied convoy routes

Battles

An enormous offensive force had been gathering in England for two years before the spring of 1944: almost 3 million troops, and perhaps the greatest array of naval vessels and armaments ever assembled in one place. On the morning of June 6, 1944, this vast invasion force moved into action. The landing came not at the narrowest part of the English Channel, where the Germans had expected and prepared for it, but along sixty miles of the Cotentin Peninsula on the coast of Normandy. While airplanes and battleships offshore bombarded the Nazi defenses, 4,000 vessels landed troops and supplies on the beaches. (Three divisions of paratroopers had been dropped behind the German lines the night before.) Fighting was intense along the beach, but the superior manpower and equipment of the Allied forces gradually prevailed. Within a week, the German forces had been dislodged from virtually the entire Normandy coast.

For the next month, further progress remained slow. But in late July in the Battle of Saint-Lô, General Omar Bradley's First Army smashed through the German lines. George S. Patton's Third Army, spearheaded by heavy tank attacks, then moved through the hole Bradley had created and began a drive into the heart of France. On August 25, Free French forces arrived in Paris and liberated the city from four years of German occupation. By mid-September the Allied armies had driven the Germans almost entirely out of France and Belgium.

The great Allied drive came to a halt, however, at the Rhine River against a firm line of Nazi defenses. In mid-December, German forces struck in desperation along fifty miles of front in the Ardennes Forest. In the Battle of the Bulge (named for a large bulge that appeared in the American lines as the Germans pressed forward), they drove fifty-five miles toward Antwerp before they were finally stopped at Bastogne. It was the last major battle on the western front.

While the western Allies were fighting their way through France, Soviet forces were sweeping westward into central Europe and the Balkans. In late January 1945, the Russians launched a great offensive toward the Oder River, inside Germany. By early spring, they were ready to launch a final assault against Berlin. General Omar Bradley, in the meantime, was pushing toward the Rhine from the west. Early in March, his forces captured the city of Cologne, on the river's west bank. The next day, he discovered and seized an undamaged bridge over the river at Remagen; Allied troops were soon pouring across the Rhine. In the following weeks the British commander, Montgomery, with a million troops, pushed into Germany in the north while Bradley's army, sweeping through central Germany, completed the encirclement of 300,000 German soldiers in the Ruhr.

The German resistance was now broken on both fronts. American forces were moving eastward faster than they had anticipated and could have beaten the Russians to Berlin and Prague. The American and British high commands decided, instead, to halt the advance along the Elbe River in central Germany to await the Russians. That decision enabled the Soviets to occupy eastern Germany and Czechoslovakia.

A VICTORY CELEBRATION IN SAN FRANCISCO Soldiers and sailors in San Francisco react jubilantly to the news that the war in Europe has ended. But the news they were celebrating was, in fact, one of the many false rumors of surrender circulating in the spring of 1945. The actual V-E Day occurred several weeks later.

On April 30, with Soviet forces on the outskirts of Berlin, Adolf Hitler killed himself in his bunker in the capital. And on May 8, 1945, the remaining German forces surrendered unconditionally.

The Pacific Offensive

In February 1944, American naval forces under Admiral Chester Nimitz won a series of victories in the Marshall Islands and cracked the outer perimeter of the Japanese Empire. Within a month, the navy had destroyed other vital Japanese bastions. American submarines, in the meantime, were decimating Japanese shipping and crippling Japan's domestic economy.

A more frustrating struggle was in progress in the meantime on the Asian mainland. In 1942, the Japanese had forced General Joseph H. Stilwell of the United States out of Burma and had moved their own troops as far west as the mountains bordering on India. For a time, Stilwell supplied the isolated Chinese forces still fighting Japan with an aerial ferry over the Himalayas. In 1943, finally, he led Chinese, Indian, and a few American troops back through northern Burma, constructing a road and pipeline across the mountains into China (the Burma Road, also known as the Ledo Road or Stilwell Road); the road opened in the fall of 1944.

By then, however, the Japanese had launched a major counteroffensive and had driven so deep into the Chinese interior that they threatened the terminus of the Burma Road and the center of Chinese government at Chungking. The Japanese offensive precipitated a long-simmering feud between General Stilwell and Premier Chiang Kai-shek of China. Stilwell was indignant because Chiang was using many of his troops to maintain an armed frontier against the Chinese communists and would not deploy those troops against the Japanese.

The decisive battles of the war against Japan, however, occurred in the Pacific. In mid-June 1944, an enormous American armada struck the heavily fortified Mariana Islands and, after some of the bloodiest operations of the war, captured Tinian, Guam, and Saipan, 1,350 miles from Tokyo. In September, American forces landed on the western Carolines. And on October 20, General MacArthur's troops landed on Leyte Island in the Philippines. The Japanese now employed virtually their entire fleet against the Allied invaders in three major encounters—which together constituted the decisive Battle of Leyte Gulf, the largest naval engagement in history. American forces held off the Japanese onslaught and sank four Japanese carriers, all but destroying Japan's capacity to continue a serious naval war. Nevertheless, as American forces advanced closer to the Japanese mainland early in 1945, the imperial forces seemed only to increase their resistance. In February 1945, American marines seized the tiny volcanic island of Iwo Jima, only 750 miles from Tokyo, but only after the costliest battle in the history of the Marine Corps.

The battle for Okinawa, an island only 370 miles south of Japan, was further evidence of the strength of the Japanese resistance in these last desperate days. Week after week, the Japanese sent kamikaze (suicide) planes against American and British ships, sacrificing 3,500 of them while inflicting great damage. Japanese troops on shore launched desperate nighttime attacks on the American lines. The United States and its allies suffered nearly 50,000 casualties before finally capturing Okinawa in late June 1945. Over 100,000 Japanese died in the siege.

It seemed likely that the same kind of bitter fighting would await the Americans when they invaded Japan. But there were also some signs early in 1945 that such an invasion might not be necessary. The Japanese had almost no ships or planes left with which to fight. The firebombing of Tokyo in March, in which American bombers dropped napalm on the city and created a firestorm in which over 80,000 people died, further weakened the Japanese will to resist. Moderate Japanese leaders, who had long since concluded the war was lost, were looking for ways to bring the fighting to an end, although they continued to face powerful opposition from military leaders. Whether the moderates could ultimately have prevailed is a question about which historians and others continue to disagree. In any case, their efforts became superfluous in August 1945, when the United States made use of a terrible new weapon it had been developing throughout the war.

The Manhattan Project and Atomic Warfare

Reports had reached the United States in 1939 that Nazi scientists had taken the first step toward the creation of an atomic bomb, a weapon more powerful than any ever previously devised. The United States and Britain immediately began a race to develop the weapon before the Germans did.

The search for the new weapon emerged from theories developed by atomic physicists, beginning early in the century, and particularly from some of the founding ideas of modern science developed by Albert Einstein. Einstein's famous theory of relativity had revealed the relationships between mass and energy. More precisely, he had argued that, in theory at least, matter could be converted into a tremendous force of energy. It was Einstein himself, who was by then living in the United States, who warned Franklin Roosevelt that the Germans were developing atomic weapons and that the United States must begin trying to do the same. The effort to build atomic weapons centered on the use of uranium, whose atomic structure made possible the creation of a nuclear chain reaction. A nuclear chain reaction occurs when the atomic nuclei in radioactive matter are split (a process known as nuclear fission) by neutrons. Each fission creates new neutrons that produce fissions in additional atoms at an ever increasing and self-sustaining pace.

The construction of atomic weapons had become feasible by the 1940s because of the discovery of the radioactivity of uranium in the

D E B A T I N G   T H E   P A S T

The Decision to Drop the Atomic Bomb

HERE HAS BEEN continuing disagreement since 1945 among historians—and among many others—about how to explain and evaluate President Truman's decision to use the atomic bomb in the war against Japan.

Truman himself, both at the time and in his 1955 memoirs, and many of his contemporaries insisted that the decision was a simple and straightforward one. The alternative to using atomic weapons, he claimed, was an American invasion of mainland Japan that might have cost as many as a million lives. That view has received considerable support from historians. Herbert Feis argued in *The Atomic Bomb and the End of World War II* (1966) that Truman made his decision on purely military grounds—to ensure a speedy American victory. David McCullough, the author of an enormously popular biography of Truman published in 1992, also accepted Truman's own account of his actions largely uncritically, as did Alonzo L. Hamby in

1930s by Enrico Fermi in Italy. In 1939, the great Danish physicist Niels Bohr, sent news of German experiments in radioactivity to the United States, where experiments began in many places. In 1940, scientists at Columbia began chain-reaction experiments with uranium and produced persuasive evidence of the feasibility of using uranium as fuel for a weapon. The Columbia experiments stalled in 1941, and the work moved to Berkeley and the University of Chicago, where Enrico Fermi (who had

Man of the People (1995), an important scholarly study of Truman. "One consideration weighed most heavily on Truman," Hamby concluded. "The longer the war lasted, the more Americans killed."

Others have strongly disagreed. As early as 1948, a British physicist, P. M. S. Blackett, wrote in *Fear, War, and the Bomb* that the destruction of Hiroshima and Nagasaki was "not so much the last military act of the second World War as the first major operation of the cold diplomatic war with Russia." The most important critic of Truman's decision is the historian Gar Alperovitz, the author of two influential books on the subject: *Atomic Diplomacy: Hiroshima and Potsdam* (1965) and *The Decision to Use the Atomic Bomb* (1995). Alperovitz dismissed the argument that the bomb was used to shorten the war and save lives. Japan was likely to have surrendered soon even if the bomb had not been used, he claimed. Instead, he argued, the United States used the bomb less to influence Japan than to intimidate the Soviet Union, "to make Russia more manageable in Europe."

John W. Dower's *War Without Mercy* (1986) contributed, by implication at least, to another controversial explanation of the American decision: racism. The Japanese, many Americans came to believe during the war, were almost a subhuman species. Even many of Truman's harshest critics, however, note that it is, as Alperovitz has written, "all but impossible to find specific evidence that racism was an important factor in the decision to attack Hiroshima and Nagasaki."

The debate over the decision to drop the atomic bomb is an unusually emotional one, and it has inspired bitter professional and personal attacks on advocates of almost every position. It illustrates clearly how history has often been, and remains, a powerful force in the way societies define themselves.

emigrated to the United States in 1938) achieved the first controlled fission chain reaction in December 1942.

By then, the army had taken control of the research and appointed General Leslie Groves to reorganize the project—which soon became known as the Manhattan Project, because it was devised in the Manhattan Engineer District Office of the Army Corps of Engineers. Over the next three years, the government secretly poured nearly $2 billion into the

Manhattan Project—a massive scientific and technological effort conducted at hidden laboratories in Oak Ridge, Tennessee; Los Alamos, New Mexico; Hanford, Washington; and other sites. Scientists in Oak Ridge, who were charged with finding a way to create a nuclear chain reaction that could be feasibly replicated within the confined space of a bomb, began experimenting with plutonium—a derivative of uranium first discovered by scientists at Berkeley. Plutonium proved capable of providing a practical fuel for the weapon. Scientists in Los Alamos, under the direction of J. Robert Oppenheimer, were charged with the construction of the actual atomic bomb.

By 1944, the government was secretly funneling over $1 billion a year to the Manhattan Project, and despite many unforeseen problems, the scientists pushed ahead much faster than anyone had predicted. Even so, the war in Europe ended before they were ready to test the first weapon. Just before dawn on July 16, 1945, in the desert near Alamogordo, New Mexico, the scientists gathered to witness the first atomic explosion in history: the detonation of a plutonium-fueled bomb that scientists had named Trinity. The explosion—a blinding flash of light, probably brighter than any ever seen on earth, followed by a huge, billowing mushroom cloud—created a vast crater in the barren desert.

News of the explosion reached President Harry S. Truman (who had taken office in April on the death of Roosevelt) in Potsdam, Germany, where he was attending a conference of Allied leaders. He issued an ultimatum to the Japanese (signed jointly by the British) demanding that they surrender by August 3 or face utter devastation. When the Japanese failed to meet the deadline, Truman ordered the air force to use the new atomic weapons against Japan.

Controversy has continued for decades over whether Truman's decision to use the bomb was justified and what his motives were. Some have argued that the atomic attack was unnecessary—that had the United States agreed to the survival of the emperor (which it ultimately did agree to in any case), or had it waited only a few more weeks, the Japanese would have surrendered. Others argue that nothing less than the atomic bombs could have persuaded the Japanese to surrender without a costly American invasion. Some critics of the decision, including some of the scientists involved in the Manhattan Project, have argued that whatever the Japanese intentions, the United States, as a matter of morality, should not have used the terrible new weapon.

The nation's military and political leaders, however, showed little concern about such matters. Truman, who had not even known of the existence of the Manhattan Project until he became president, was, apparently, making what he believed to be a simple military decision. A weapon was available that would end the war quickly; he could see no reason not to use it.

On August 6, 1945, an American B-29, the *Enola Gay*, dropped an atomic weapon on the Japanese industrial center at Hiroshima. With a single bomb, the United States completely incinerated a four-square-mile area at the center of the previously undamaged city. More than 80,000 civilians died, according to later American estimates. Many more survived to suffer the crippling effects of radioactive fallout or to pass those effects on to their children in the form of birth defects.

The Japanese government, stunned by the attack, was at first unable to agree on a response. Two days later, on August 8, the Soviet Union declared war on Japan. And the following day, another American plane dropped another atomic weapon—this time on the city of Nagasaki—inflicting 100,000 deaths and horrible damage on yet another unfortunate community. Finally, the emperor intervened to break the stalemate in the cabinet, and on August 14 the government announced that it was ready to give up. On September 2, 1945, on board the American battleship *Missouri*, anchored in Tokyo Bay, Japanese officials signed the articles of surrender.

The greatest war in the history of mankind had come to an end, and the United States had emerged from it not only victorious but in a position

HIROSHIMA Long after the city was destroyed by the first atomic bomb ever used in warfare, Hiroshima remained a ghostly landscape—an incongruous backdrop for a Japanese couple strolling along the street.

of unprecedented power, influence, and prestige. It was a victory, however, that few could greet with unambiguous joy. Fourteen million combatants had died in the struggle. Many more civilians had perished. The United States had suffered only light casualties in comparison with some other nations (and particularly in comparison with Russia and Germany), but the cost had still been high: 322,000 dead, another 800,000 injured. And despite the sacrifices, the world continued to face an uncertain future, menaced by the threat of nuclear warfare and by an emerging antagonism between the world's two strongest nations—the United States and the Soviet Union—that would darken the peace for many decades to come.

CONCLUSION

The United States played a critical, indeed decisive, role in the war against Germany and Italy; and it defeated Imperial Japan in the Pacific largely alone. But America's contributions to and sacrifices in the war paled next to those of its most important allies. Britain, France, and above all the Soviet Union paid a staggering price—in lives, treasure, and social unity—that had no counterpart in the United States. Most American citizens experienced a booming prosperity and only modest privations during the four years of American involvement in the conflict. There were, of course, jarring social changes during the war that even prosperity could not entirely offset: shortages, restrictions, regulations, family dislocations, and perhaps most of all the absence of millions of men, and considerable numbers of women, who went overseas to fight.

American fighting men and women, of course, had very different experiences from those of the people who remained at home. They endured tremendous hardships, substantial casualties, and great loneliness. They fought effectively and bravely. They helped liberate North Africa and Italy from German occupation. And in June 1944, finally, they joined British, French, and other forces in a great and successful invasion of France, which led less than a year later to the destruction of the Nazi regime and the end of the European war. In the Pacific, they turned back the Japanese offensive through a series of difficult naval and land battles. Ultimately, however, it was not the American army and navy that brought the war against Japan to a close. It was the unleashing of the most destructive weapon mankind had ever created—the atomic bomb—on the people of Japan that finally persuaded the leaders of that nation to surrender.

FOR FURTHER REFERENCE

Suggested Readings

David Kennedy, *Freedom from Fear* (1999) includes a thorough account of the war years. John Morton Blum, *V Was for Victory: Politics and American Culture During World War II* (1976) and Richard Polenberg, *War and Society* (1972) are valuable studies of the home front during World War II. Studs Terkel, *"The Good War": An Oral History of World War II* (1984) is a powerful oral history. Alan Brinkley, *The End of Reform: New Deal Liberalism in Recession and War* (1995) examines wartime politics and the political economy. Doris Kearns Goodwin, *No Ordinary Time: Franklin and Eleanor Roosevelt: The Home Front in World War II* (1994) is an engaging portrait of the Roosevelts during the war. Susan Hartmann examines the transformation in women's work and family roles during and after the war in her book, *The Homefront and Beyond: American Women in the 1940s* (1982). Maurice Isserman, *Which Side Were You On? The American Communist Party During World War II* (1982) portrays the dramatic shifts in Communist Party strategy and status during WWII. Racial hatred of Asians, especially the Japanese, played a disturbing role in America's military strategy in the Pacific according to John W. Dower, *War Without Mercy: Race and Power in the Pacific War* (1986). Peter Irons, *Justice at War* (1983) examines the internment of Japanese Americans. John Keegan, *Six Armies in Normandy: From D-Day to the Liberation of Paris, June 6–August 25, 1944* (1982) is a superb account of the Normandy invasion. David S. Wyman, *The Abandonment of the Jews: America and the Holocaust, 1941–1945* (1984) is a disturbing account of U.S. policy. Richard Rhodes, *The Making of the Atomic Bomb* (1987) is an excellent account of one of the great scientific projects of the century. Gar Alperovitz, *The Decision to Use the Atomic Bomb and the Architecture of an American Myth* (1995) is an exhaustive and highly critical account of why the United States used atomic weapons in 1945, which disagrees sharply with such earlier studies as Herbert Feis, *The Atomic Bomb and the End of World War II* (1966). John Hersey's *Hiroshima* (1946) reconstructs in minute detail the terrifying experience of the American atomic bomb attack on that Japanese city.

Films

(The best source for information on how to find these and other films is *Bowker's Complete Video Directory*—3 volumes.) *The Homefront* (1985) portrays World War II as a watershed event in American domestic life. *Without Due Process* (1991) provides a clear, vivid overview of the internment of Japanese Americans during World War II. *America & the Holocaust: Deceit and Indifference* (1994) weaves together interviews, official photos, documents, and archival film to trace the complex social and political factors that shaped America's response to the Holocaust. *D-Day* (1994) is a chronicle of the invasion of Europe at Normandy on June 6 by the Allied forces.

Internet Resources

Internet websites containing historical material relevant to the subjects discussed in this chapter can be reached through the McGraw-Hill history site at www.mhhe.com/socscience/history/usa/link/linktop.htm.

CHAPTER TWENTY-NINE

The Cold War

VEN BEFORE WORLD WAR II ended, there were signs of tension between the United States and the Soviet Union. Once the hostilities were over, those tensions quickly grew to create what became known as the "Cold War"—a tense and dangerous rivalry between the two former allies that would cast its shadow over international affairs for decades. The Cold War also had profound effects on American domestic life, ultimately producing the most corrosive outbreak of antiradical hysteria of the century.

ORIGINS OF THE COLD WAR

No issue in twentieth-century American history has aroused more debate than the question of the origins of the Cold War (see "Debating the Past," pp. 856–857). Some have claimed that Soviet duplicity and expansionism created the international tensions, others that American provocations and global ambitions were at least equally to blame.

Sources of Soviet-American Tension

At the heart of the rivalry between the United States and the Soviet Union in the 1940s was a fundamental difference in the ways the great powers envisioned the postwar world. One vision, first openly outlined in

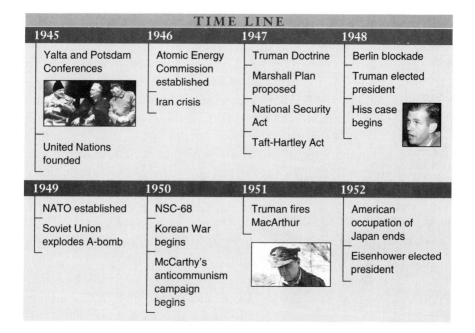

TIME LINE

1945	1946	1947	1948
Yalta and Potsdam Conferences	Atomic Energy Commission established	Truman Doctrine	Berlin blockade
	Iran crisis	Marshall Plan proposed	Truman elected president
		National Security Act	Hiss case begins
United Nations founded		Taft-Hartley Act	

1949	1950	1951	1952
NATO established	NSC-68	Truman fires MacArthur	American occupation of Japan ends
Soviet Union explodes A-bomb	Korean War begins		Eisenhower elected president
	McCarthy's anticommunism campaign begins		

the Atlantic Charter in 1941, was of a world in which nations abandoned their traditional beliefs in military alliances and spheres of influence and governed their relations with one another through democratic processes, with an international organization serving as the arbiter of disputes and the protector of every nation's right of self-determination. That vision appealed to many Americans, including Franklin Roosevelt.

The other vision was that of the Soviet Union and to some extent, it gradually became clear, of Great Britain. Both Stalin and Churchill had signed the Atlantic Charter. But Britain had always been uneasy about the implications of the self-determination ideal for its own enormous empire. And the Soviet Union was determined to create a secure sphere for itself in Central and Eastern Europe as protection against possible future aggression from the West. Both Churchill and Stalin, therefore, tended to envision a postwar structure in which the great powers would control areas of strategic interest to them, in which something vaguely similar to the traditional European balance of power would reemerge. Gradually, the differences between these two positions would turn the peacemaking process into a form of warfare.

Wartime Diplomacy

Serious strains had already begun to develop in the alliance with the Soviet Union in January 1943, when Roosevelt and Churchill met in Casablanca, Morocco, to discuss Allied strategy. (Stalin had declined Roosevelt's invitation to attend.) The two leaders could not accept Stalin's most important demand—the immediate opening of a second front in western Europe. But they tried to reassure Stalin by announcing that they would accept nothing less than the unconditional surrender of the Axis powers, thus indicating that they would not negotiate a separate peace with Hitler and leave the Soviets to fight on alone.

In November 1943, Roosevelt and Churchill traveled to Teheran, Iran, for their first meeting with Stalin. By now, however, Roosevelt's most effective bargaining tool—Stalin's need for American assistance in his struggle against Germany—had been largely removed. The German advance against Russia had been halted; Soviet forces were now launching their own westward offensive. Nevertheless, the Teheran Conference seemed in most respects a success. Roosevelt and Stalin established a cordial personal relationship. Stalin agreed to an American request that the Soviet Union enter the war in the Pacific soon after the end of hostilities in Europe. Roosevelt, in turn, promised that an Anglo-American second front would be established within six months.

On other matters, however, the origins of future disagreements were already visible. Most important was the question of the future of Poland. Roosevelt and Churchill were willing to agree to a movement of the Soviet border westward, allowing Stalin to annex some historically Polish territory. But on the nature of the postwar government in the portion of Poland that would remain independent, there were sharp differences. Roosevelt and Churchill supported the claims of the Polish government-in-exile that had been functioning in London since 1940; Stalin wished to install another, pro-communist exiled government that had spent the war in Lublin, in the Soviet Union. The three leaders avoided a bitter conclusion to the Teheran Conference only by leaving the issue unresolved.

Yalta

More than a year later, in February 1945, Roosevelt joined Churchill and Stalin for a great peace conference in the Soviet city of Yalta. On a number of issues, the Big Three reached agreements. In return for Stalin's renewed promise to enter the Pacific war, Roosevelt agreed that the Soviet

YALTA, 1945 Churchill (*left*) and Stalin (*right*) were shocked at the physical appearance of Franklin Roosevelt (*center*) when he arrived for their critical meeting at Yalta. Roosevelt had enough energy to perform capably at the conference, but he was in fact gravely ill. Two months later, not long after he gave Congress what turned out to be an unrealistically optimistic report of the prospects for postwar peace, he died.

Union should receive some of the territory in the Pacific that Russia had lost in the 1904 Russo-Japanese War.

The negotiators also agreed to a plan for a new international organization, a plan that had been hammered out the previous summer at a conference in Washington, D.C., at the Dumbarton Oaks estate. The new United Nations would contain a General Assembly, in which every member would be represented, and a Security Council, with permanent representatives of the five major powers (the United States, Britain, France, the Soviet Union, and China), each of which would have veto power. The Security Council would also have temporary delegates from several other nations. These agreements became the basis of the United Nations charter, drafted at a conference of fifty nations beginning April 25, 1945, in San Francisco. The United States Senate ratified the charter in July by a vote of 80 to 2 (a striking contrast to the slow and painful defeat it had administered to the charter of the League of Nations twenty-five years before).

On other issues, however, the Yalta Conference produced no real accord. Basic disagreement remained about the postwar Polish government. Stalin, whose armies now occupied Poland, had already installed a government composed of the pro-communist "Lublin" Poles. Roosevelt and Churchill insisted that the pro-Western "London" Poles must be allowed a place in the Warsaw regime. Roosevelt envisioned a government based on free, democratic elections—which both he and Stalin recognized the pro-Western forces would win. Stalin agreed only to a vague compromise by which an unspecified number of pro-Western Poles would be granted a place in the government. He reluctantly consented to hold "free and unfettered elections" in Poland on an unspecified future date. They did not take place for more than forty years.

Nor was there agreement about the future of Germany. Roosevelt seemed to want a reconstructed and reunited Germany. Stalin wanted to impose heavy reparations on Germany and to ensure a permanent dismemberment of the nation. The final agreement was, like the Polish accord, vague and unstable. The decision on reparations would be referred to a future commission. The United States, Great Britain, France, and the Soviet Union would each control its own "zone of occupation" in Germany—the zones to be determined by the position of troops at the end of the war. Berlin, the German capital, was already well inside the Soviet zone, but because of its symbolic importance it would itself be divided into four sectors, one for each nation to occupy. At an unspecified date, Germany would be reunited; but there was no agreement on how the reunification would occur. As for the rest of Europe, the conference produced a murky accord on the establishment of governments "broadly representative of all democratic elements" and "responsible to the will of the people."

The Yalta accords, in other words, were less a settlement of postwar issues than a set of loose principles that sidestepped the most difficult questions. Roosevelt, Churchill, and Stalin returned home from the conference each apparently convinced that he had signed an important agreement. But the Soviet interpretation of the accords differed so sharply from the Anglo-American interpretation that the illusion endured only briefly. In the weeks following the Yalta Conference, Roosevelt watched with growing alarm as the Soviet Union moved systematically to establish pro-communist governments in one Central or Eastern European nation after another and as Stalin refused to make the changes in Poland that the president believed he had promised.

But Roosevelt did not abandon hope. Still believing the differences could be settled, he left Washington early in the spring for a vacation at his retreat in Warm Springs, Georgia. There, on April 12, 1945, he suffered a sudden, massive stroke and died.

THE COLLAPSE OF THE PEACE

Harry S. Truman, who succeeded Roosevelt in the presidency, had almost no familiarity with international issues. Nor did he share Roosevelt's apparent faith in the flexibility of the Soviet Union. Roosevelt had apparently believed that Stalin was, essentially, a reasonable man with whom an ultimate accord might be reached. Truman, in contrast, sided with those in the government (and there were many) who considered the Soviet Union fundamentally untrustworthy and viewed Stalin himself with suspicion and even loathing.

The Failure of Potsdam

Truman had been in office only a few days before he decided to "get tough" with the Soviet Union. Stalin had made what the new president considered solemn agreements with the United States at Yalta. The United States should insist that the Soviets honor them. Truman met on April 23 with Soviet Foreign Minister Molotov and sharply chastised him for violations of the Yalta accords.

In fact, Truman had only limited leverage by which to compel the Soviet Union to carry out its agreements. Russian forces already occupied Poland and much of the rest of Central and Eastern Europe. Germany was already divided among the conquering nations. The United States was still engaged in a war in the Pacific and was neither able nor willing to enter into a second conflict in Europe. Truman insisted that the United States should be able to get "85 percent" of what it wanted, but he was ultimately forced to settle for much less.

He conceded first on Poland. When Stalin made a few minor concessions to the pro-Western exiles, Truman recognized the Warsaw government, hoping that noncommunist forces might gradually expand their influence there. Until the 1980s, they did not. Other questions remained, above all the question of Germany. To settle them, Truman met in July at Potsdam, in Russian-occupied Germany, with Churchill (who, after elections in Britain in the midst of the talks, was replaced as prime minister by Clement Attlee) and Stalin. Truman reluctantly accepted the adjustments of the Polish-German border that Stalin had long demanded; he refused, however, to permit the Russians to claim any reparations from the American, French, and British zones of Germany. This stance effectively confirmed that Germany would remain divided, with the western zones united into one nation, friendly to the United States, and the Russian zone surviving as another nation, with a pro-Soviet, communist government.

The China Problem

Central to American hopes for an open, peaceful world "policed" by the great powers was a strong, independent China. But even before the war ended, the American government was aware that those hopes faced a major, perhaps insurmountable obstacle: the Chinese government of Chiang Kai-shek. Chiang was generally friendly to the United States, but his government was corrupt and incompetent with feeble popular support. Chiang himself lived in a world of almost surreal isolation, unable or unwilling to face the problems that were threatening to engulf him. Ever since 1927, the nationalist government he headed had been engaged in a prolonged and bitter rivalry with the communist armies of Mao Zedong. So successful had the communist challenge grown that Mao was in control of one-fourth of the population by 1945.

Some Americans urged the government to try to find a "third force" to support as an alternative to either Chiang or Mao. A few argued that the United States should try to reach some accommodation with Mao. Truman, however, decided reluctantly that he had no choice but to continue supporting Chiang. For the next several years, as the long struggle between the nationalists and the communists erupted into a full-scale civil war, the United States continued to pump money and weapons to Chiang, even as it was becoming clear that the cause was lost. But Truman was not prepared to intervene militarily to save the nationalist regime.

Instead, the American government was beginning to consider an alternative to China as the strong, pro-Western force in Asia: a revived Japan. Abandoning the strict occupation policies of the first years after the war (when General Douglas MacArthur had governed the nation), the United States lifted all restrictions on industrial development and encouraged rapid economic growth in Japan. The vision of an open, united world was giving way in Asia, as it was in Europe, to an acceptance of a divided world with a strong, pro-American sphere of influence.

The Containment Doctrine

By the end of 1945, the Grand Alliance was a shambles. With its passing went any realistic hope of a postwar world constructed according to the Atlantic Charter ideals Roosevelt and others had supported. Instead, a new American policy was slowly emerging. It became known as containment. Rather than attempting to create a unified, "open" world, the United States and its allies would work to "contain" the threat of further Soviet expansion.

The new doctrine emerged in part as a response to events in Europe in 1946. In Turkey, Stalin was trying to win control over the vital sea lanes to the Mediterranean. In Greece, communist forces were threatening the pro-Western government; the British had announced they could no longer provide assistance. Faced with these challenges, Truman decided to enunciate a firm new policy. In doing so, he drew from the ideas of the influential American diplomat George F. Kennan, who had warned not long after the war that in the Soviet Union the United States faced "a political force committed fanatically to the belief that with the U.S. there can be no permanent modus vivendi," and that the only answer was "a long-term, patient but firm and vigilant containment of Russian expansive tendencies." On March 12, 1947, Truman appeared before Congress and used Kennan's warnings as the basis of what became known as the Truman Doctrine. "I believe," he argued, "that it must be the policy of the United States to support free peoples who are resisting attempted subjugation by armed minorities or by outside pressures." In the same speech he requested $400 million—part of it to bolster the armed forces of Greece and Turkey, another part to provide economic assistance to Greece. Congress quickly approved the measure.

The American commitment ultimately helped ease Soviet pressure on Turkey and helped the Greek government defeat the communist insurgents. More important, it established a basis for American foreign policy that would survive for more than thirty years.

The Marshall Plan

An integral part of the containment policy was a proposal to aid in the economic reconstruction of Western Europe. There were many motives: humanitarian concern for the European people; a fear that Europe would remain an economic drain on the United States if it could not quickly rebuild and begin to feed itself; a desire for a strong European market for American goods. But above all, American policymakers believed that unless something could be done to strengthen the shaky pro-American governments in Western Europe, those governments might fall under the control of rapidly growing domestic communist parties.

In June 1947, therefore, Secretary of State George C. Marshall announced a plan to provide economic assistance to all European nations (including the Soviet Union) that would join in drafting a program for recovery. Although Russia and its Eastern satellites quickly and predictably

THE MARSHALL PLAN, 1950 Workers in West Berlin rebuild the war-damaged city with the aid of money funneled to them from the United States through the European Recovery Program, better known as the Marshall Plan. This photograph shows repair work in progress on Titania Palace, Berlin's biggest concert hall.

rejected the plan, sixteen Western European nations eagerly participated. Whatever domestic opposition there was in the United States largely vanished after a sudden coup in Czechoslovakia in February 1948 that established a Soviet-dominated communist government there. In April, Congress approved the creation of the Economic Cooperation Administration, the agency that would administer the Marshall Plan, as it became known. Over the next three years, the Marshall Plan channeled over $12 billion of American aid into Europe, helping to spark a substantial economic revival. By the end of 1950, European industrial production had risen 64 percent, communist strength in the member nations had declined, and opportunities for American trade had revived.

Mobilization at Home

That the United States had fully accepted a continuing commitment to the containment policy became clear in 1947 and 1948 through a series of measures designed to maintain American military power at near wartime levels. In 1948, at the president's request, Congress approved a new military draft and revived the Selective Service System. In the meantime, the United States, having failed to reach agreement with the Soviet Union on international control of nuclear weapons, redoubled its own efforts in atomic research, elevating nuclear weaponry to a central place in its military arsenal. The Atomic Energy Commission, established in 1946, became the supervisory body charged with overseeing all nuclear research, civilian and military alike. And in 1950, the Truman administration approved the development of the new hydrogen bomb, a nuclear weapon far more powerful than the bombs the United States had used in 1945.

Particularly important was the National Security Act of 1947, which reshaped the nation's major military and diplomatic institutions. A new Department of Defense would oversee all branches of the armed services, combining functions previously performed separately by the War and Navy departments. A National Security Council (NSC), operating out of the White House, would govern foreign and military policy. A Central Intelligence Agency (CIA) would replace the wartime Office of Strategic Services and would be responsible for collecting information through both open and covert methods; as the Cold War continued, the CIA would also engage secretly in political and military operations on behalf of American goals. The National Security Act, in other words, gave the president expanded powers with which to pursue the nation's international goals.

The Road to NATO

At about the same time, the United States was moving to strengthen the military capabilities of Western Europe. Convinced that a reconstructed Germany was essential to the hopes of the West, Truman reached an agreement with England and France to merge the three western zones of occupation into a new West German republic (which would include the American, British, and French sectors of Berlin, even though that city lay well within the Soviet zone). Stalin responded quickly. On June 24, 1948, he imposed a tight blockade around the western sectors of Berlin. If Germany was to be officially divided, he was implying, then the country's

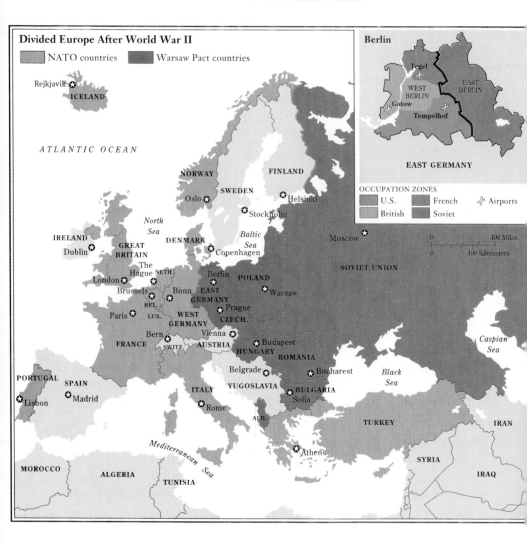

Divided Europe After World War II

- NATO countries
- Warsaw Pact countries

ATLANTIC OCEAN

ICELAND
Rejkjavik

NORWAY
Oslo
SWEDEN
FINLAND
Helsinki
Stockholm

North Sea
Baltic Sea

IRELAND
Dublin
GREAT BRITAIN
DENMARK
Copenhagen
London
The Hague NETH.
Brussels
BEL.
Bonn
Berlin
POLAND
Warsaw
EAST GERMANY
Prague
CZECH.
Paris
LUX.
WEST GERMANY
Bern
SWITZ.
Vienna
AUSTRIA
Budapest
HUNGARY
ROMANIA
FRANCE
ITALY
Belgrade
YUGOSLAVIA
Bucharest
BULGARIA
Sofia
PORTUGAL
SPAIN
Madrid
Lisbon
Rome
ALB.
Athens
MOROCCO
ALGERIA
TUNISIA
Mediterranean Sea

Moscow
SOVIET UNION
Caspian Sea
Black Sea
TURKEY
IRAN
SYRIA
IRAQ

Berlin

Tegel
WEST BERLIN
EAST BERLIN
Gatow
Tempelhof

EAST GERMANY

OCCUPATION ZONES
- U.S.
- British
- French
- Soviet
- Airports

0   400 Miles
0   400 Kilometers

Western government would have to abandon its outpost in the heart of the Soviet-controlled eastern zone. Truman refused to do so. Unwilling to risk war through a military challenge to the blockade, he ordered a massive airlift to supply the city with food, fuel, and other needed goods. The airlift continued for more than ten months, transporting nearly 2.5 million tons of material, keeping a city of 2 million people alive, and transforming West Berlin into a symbol of the West's resolve to resist communist expansion. In the spring of 1949, Stalin lifted the now ineffective blockade. And in October, the division of Germany into two nations—the Federal Republic in the west and the Democratic Republic in the East—became official.

The crisis in Berlin accelerated the consolidation of what was already in effect an alliance among the United States and the countries of Western Europe. On April 4, 1949, twelve nations signed an agreement establishing the North Atlantic Treaty Organization (NATO) and declaring that an armed attack against one member would be considered an attack against all. The NATO countries would, moreover, maintain a standing military force in Europe to defend against what many believed was the threat of a Soviet invasion. The formation of NATO eventually spurred the Soviet Union to create an alliance of its own with the communist governments in Eastern Europe—an alliance formalized in 1955 by the Warsaw Pact.

Reevaluating Cold War Policy

A series of events in 1949 propelled the Cold War in new directions. An announcement in September that the Soviet Union had successfully exploded its first atomic weapon, years earlier than predicted, shocked and frightened many Americans. So did the collapse of Chiang Kai-shek's nationalist government in China, which occurred with startling speed in the last months of 1949. Chiang fled with his political allies and the remnants of his army to the offshore island of Formosa (Taiwan), and the entire Chinese mainland came under the control of a communist government that many Americans believed to be an extension of the Soviet Union. The United States refused to recognize the new communist regime, and instead devoted increased attention to the revitalization of Japan as a buffer against Asian communism, ending the American occupation in 1952.

In this atmosphere of escalating crisis, Truman called for a thorough review of American foreign policy. The result was a National Security Council report, issued in 1950 and commonly known as NSC-68, which outlined a shift in the American position. The first statements of the containment doctrine—the writings of George Kennan, the Truman Doctrine speech—had made at least some distinctions between areas of vital interest to the United States and areas of less importance to the nation's foreign policy and called on America to share the burden of containment with its allies. But the April 1950 document argued that the United States could no longer rely on other nations to take the initiative in resisting communism. It must itself establish firm and active leadership of the noncommunist world. And it must move to stop communist expansion virtually anywhere it occurred, regardless of the intrinsic strategic or economic value of the lands in question. Among other things, the report called for a major expansion of American military power, with a defense budget almost four times the previously projected figure.

D E B A T I N G   T H E   P A S T

The Cold War

OR MORE THAN a decade after the beginning of the Cold War, few historians saw any reason to challenge the official American interpretation of its origins. The breakdown of relations between the United States and the Soviet Union was, most agreed, a direct result of Soviet expansionism and of Stalin's violation of the wartime agreements forged at Yalta and Potsdam. The Soviet imposition of communist regimes in Eastern Europe was part of a larger ideological design to spread communism throughout the world. American policy was the logical and necessary response: a firm commitment to oppose Soviet expansionism and to keep American forces in a continual state of readiness.

Disillusionment with the official justifications for the Cold War began to find expression even in the late 1950s, when anticommunist sentiment in America remained strong and pervasive. William Appleman Williams's *The Tragedy of American Diplomacy* (1959) insisted that the Cold War was simply the most recent version of a consistent American effort in the twentieth century to preserve an "open door" for American trade in world markets. The confrontation with the Soviet Union, he argued, was less a response to Soviet aggressive designs than an expression of the American belief in the necessity of capitalist expansion.

As the Vietnam War grew larger and more unpopular in the 1960s, the scholarly critique of the Cold War quickly gained intensity. Walter LaFeber's *America, Russia, and the Cold War*, first published in 1967, maintained that America's supposedly idealistic internationalism at the close of the war was in reality an effort to ensure a postwar order shaped in the American image—with every nation open to American influence (and to American trade). That was why the United States was so apt to misinterpret Soviet policy, much of which reflected a perfectly reasonable commitment to ensure the security of the Soviet Union itself, as part of a larger aggressive design.

The revisionist interpretations of the Cold War ultimately produced a reaction of their own: what has come to be known as "postrevisionist" scholarship. The most important works in this school have attempted to strike a balance between orthodoxy and revisionism and to identify areas of blame and patterns of misconceptions on both sides of the conflict. An important early statement of this approach was John Lewis Gaddis, *The United States and the Cold War, 1941–1947* (1972), which argued that "neither side can bear sole responsibility for the onset of the Cold War." Both sides had limited options, given their own political constraints and their own preconceptions. Other postrevisionist works—by Thomas G. Paterson, Melvyn Leffler, William Taubman, and others—have elaborated on ways in which the United States and the Soviet Union acted in response to genuine, if not necessarily accurate, beliefs about the intentions of the other. "The United States and the Soviet Union were doomed to be antagonists," Ernest May wrote in 1984. "There probably was never any real possibility that the post-1945 relationship could be anything but hostility verging on conflict."

The collapse of Soviet communism and the dissolution of the Soviet empire will undoubtedly stimulate new interpretations of the Cold War and will (by facilitating the opening of Soviet archives) cast new light on many contested issues. For the moment, however, the dominant scholarly view is one that de-emphasizes the question of who is to blame and emphasizes the ways in which both sides learned to manage a conflict that neither could easily have avoided.

HARRY AND BESS TRUMAN AT HOME Senator Harry Truman and his wife Bess pose for photographers in the kitchen of their Washington apartment, suggesting the "common man" image that Truman retained throughout his public life. The picture was taken shortly before the 1944 Democratic National Convention, which would nominate Truman for vice president. Less than a year later, the Trumans would be living in the White House.

AMERICA AFTER THE WAR

The crises overseas were not the only frustrations the American people encountered after the war. The nation also faced serious, if short-lived, economic difficulties in adapting to the peace. And it suffered from an exceptionally heated political climate that produced a new wave of insecurity and repression.

The Problems of Reconversion

Despite widespread predictions that the end of the war would return America to depression conditions, economic growth continued after 1945. Pent-up consumer demand from workers who had accumulated substantial savings during the war helped spur the boom. So did a $6 billion tax cut. The Servicemen's Readjustment Act of 1944, better known as the GI Bill of Rights, provided housing, education, and job training subsidies to veterans and increased spending even further.

This flood of consumer demand ensured that there would be no new depression, but it contributed to more than two years of serious inflation, during which prices rose at rates of 14 to 15 percent annually. Compounding the economic difficulties was a sharp rise in labor unrest, driven in part by the impact of inflation. By the end of 1945, there had already been major strikes in the automobile, electrical, and steel industries. In April 1946, John L. Lewis led the United Mine Workers out on strike, shutting down the coal fields for forty days. Fears grew rapidly that without vital coal supplies, the entire nation might virtually grind to a halt. Truman finally forced coal production to resume by ordering government seizure of the mines. But in the process, he pressured mine owners to grant the union most of its demands, which he had earlier denounced as inflationary. Almost simultaneously, the nation's railroads suffered a total shutdown—the first in the nation's history—as two major unions walked out on strike. By threatening to use the army to run the trains, Truman pressured the strikers back to work after only a few days.

Reconversion was particularly difficult for the millions of women and minorities who had entered the work force during the war. With veterans returning home and looking for jobs in the industrial economy, employers tended to push women, blacks, Hispanics, and others out of the plants to make room for white males. Some of the war workers, particularly women, left the work force voluntarily, out of a desire to return to their former domestic lives. But as many as 80 percent of women workers, and virtually all black and Hispanic males, wanted to continue working. The postwar inflation, the pressure to meet the growing expectations of a high-consumption society, the rising divorce rate (which left many women responsible for their own economic well-being)—all combined to create a high demand for paid employment among women. As they found themselves excluded from industrial jobs, therefore, women workers moved increasingly into other areas of the economy (above all, the service sector).

The Fair Deal Rejected

Days after the Japanese surrender, Truman submitted to Congress a twenty-one-point domestic program outlining what he later named the "Fair Deal." It called for expansion of Social Security benefits, the raising of the legal minimum wage from 40 to 65 cents an hour, a program to ensure full employment through aggressive use of federal spending and investment, a permanent Fair Employment Practices Act, public housing and slum clearance, long-range environmental and public works planning, and government promotion of scientific research. Weeks later he added other proposals: federal aid to education, government health insurance and prepaid medical care, funding for the St. Lawrence Seaway, and nationalization of atomic energy. The president was declaring an end to the wartime moratorium on liberal reform.

But the Fair Deal programs fell victim to the same public and congressional conservatism that had crippled the last years of the New Deal. Indeed, that conservatism seemed to be intensifying, as the November 1946 congressional elections suggested. Using the simple but devastating slogan "Had Enough?" the Republican Party won control of both houses of Congress. The new Republican Congress quickly moved to reduce government spending and chip away at New Deal reforms. Its most notable action, perhaps, was its assault on the Wagner Act of 1935, in the form of the Labor-Management Relations Act of 1947, better known as the Taft-Hartley Act. It made illegal the closed shop (a workplace in which no one can be hired without first being a member of a union). And although it continued to permit the creation of union shops (in which workers must join a union after being hired), it permitted states to pass "right-to-work" laws prohibiting even that. The Taft-Hartley Act also empowered the president to call for a ten-week "cooling-off" period before a strike by issuing an injunction against any work stoppage that endangered national safety or health. Outraged workers and union leaders denounced the measure as a "slave labor bill." Truman vetoed it. But both houses easily overruled him the same day. The Taft-Hartley Act did not destroy the labor movement, as many union leaders had predicted. But it did damage weaker unions in relatively lightly organized industries such as chemicals and textiles, and it made much more difficult the organizing of workers who had never been union members at all, especially in the South and the West.

The Election of 1948

Truman and his advisers believed that the American public was not ready to abandon the achievements of the New Deal, despite the 1946 election results. As they planned their strategy for the 1948 campaign, therefore, they placed their hopes in an appeal to enduring Democratic loyalties. Throughout 1948, Truman proposed one reform measure after another (including, on February 2, the first major civil rights bill of the century).

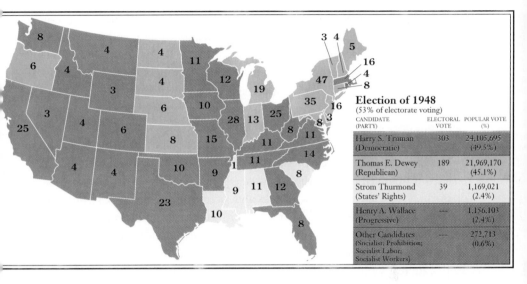

Election of 1948
(53% of electorate voting)

CANDIDATE (PARTY)	ELECTORAL VOTE	POPULAR VOTE (%)
Harry S. Truman (Democratic)	303	24,105,695 (49.5%)
Thomas E. Dewey (Republican)	189	21,969,170 (45.1%)
Strom Thurmond (States' Rights)	39	1,169,021 (2.4%)
Henry A. Wallace (Progressive)	---	1,156,103 (2.4%)
Other Candidates (Socialist; Prohibition; Socialist Labor; Socialist Workers)	---	272,713 (0.6%)

To no one's surprise, Congress ignored or defeated them all. The president was building campaign issues for the fall.

There remained, however, the problem of Truman's personal unpopularity—the assumption among much of the electorate that he lacked stature and that his administration was weak and inept—and the deep divisions within the Democratic Party. At the Democratic Convention that summer, two factions abandoned the party altogether. Southern conservatives were angered by Truman's proposed civil rights bill and by the approval at the convention of a civil rights plank in the platform (engineered by Hubert Humphrey, the reform mayor of Minneapolis). They walked out and formed the States' Rights (or "Dixiecrat") Party, with Governor Strom Thurmond of South Carolina as its nominee. At the same time, some members of the party's left wing joined the new Progressive Party, whose candidate was Henry A. Wallace. Wallace supporters objected to what they considered the slow and ineffective domestic policies of the Truman administration, but they resented even more the president's confrontational stance toward the Soviet Union.

Many Democratic liberals who were unhappy with Truman were unwilling to leave the party. The Americans for Democratic Action (ADA), a coalition of liberals, tried to entice Dwight D. Eisenhower, the popular war hero, to contest the nomination. Only after Eisenhower had refused did liberals concede the nomination to Truman. The Republicans, in the meantime, had once again nominated Governor Thomas E. Dewey of

New York, whose substantial reelection victory in 1946 had made him one of the nation's leading political figures. Austere, dignified, and competent, he seemed to offer an unbeatable alternative to the president.

Only Truman, it seemed, believed he could win. As the campaign gathered momentum, he became ever more aggressive, turning the fire away from himself and toward Dewey and the "do-nothing, good-for-nothing" Republican Congress, which was, he told the voters, responsible for fueling inflation and abandoning workers and common people. To dramatize his point, he called Congress into special session in July to give it a chance, he said, to enact the liberal measures the Republicans had recently written into their platform. Congress met for two weeks and, predictably, did almost nothing.

The president traveled nearly 32,000 miles and made 356 speeches, delivering blunt, extemporaneous attacks on the Republicans. On election night, to the surprise of almost everyone, he won a narrow but decisive and dramatic victory: 49.5 percent of the popular vote to Dewey's 45.1 percent (with the two splinter parties dividing the small remainder evenly between them), and an electoral margin of 303 to 189. Democrats, in the meantime, had regained both houses of Congress by substantial margins.

The Fair Deal Revived

Despite the Democratic victories, the Eighty-first Congress was little more hospitable to Truman's Fair Deal reform than its Republican predecessor had been. Truman did win some important victories, to be sure. Congress raised the legal minimum wage from 40 cents to 75 cents an hour. It approved an important expansion of the Social Security system, increasing benefits by 75 percent and extending them to 10 million additional people. And it passed the National Housing Act of 1949, which provided for the construction of 810,000 units of low-income housing accompanied by long-term rent subsidies.

But on other issues—national health insurance and aid to education among them—Truman made little progress. Nor was he able to persuade Congress to accept the civil rights legislation he proposed in 1949, legislation that would have made lynching a federal crime, provided federal protection of black voting rights, abolished the poll tax, and established a new Fair Employment Practices Commission to curb discrimination in hiring. Southern Democrats filibustered to kill the bill.

Truman did proceed on his own to battle several forms of racial discrimination. He ordered an end to discrimination in the hiring of government employees. He began to dismantle segregation within the armed forces. And he allowed the Justice Department to become actively involved in court battles against discriminatory statutes. The Supreme Court, in the meantime, signaled its own growing awareness of the issue by ruling, in *Shelley v. Kraemer* (1948), that the courts could not be used to enforce private "covenants" meant to bar blacks from residential neighborhoods.

THE KOREAN WAR

On June 24, 1950, the armies of communist North Korea swept across their southern border and invaded the pro-Western half of the Korean peninsula to the south. Within days, they had occupied much of South Korea, including Seoul, its capital. Almost immediately, the United States committed itself to the conflict. It was the first American military engagement of the Cold War.

The Divided Peninsula

The Korean conflict was the result of several years of tension within the peninsula. When World War II ended, both the United States and the Soviet Union had troops in Korea fighting the Japanese; neither army was willing to leave. Instead, they divided the nation, supposedly temporarily, along the 38TH parallel. The Russians finally departed in 1949, leaving behind a communist government in the north with a strong, Soviet-equipped army. The Americans left a few months later, handing control to the pro-Western government of Syngman Rhee, who was anticommunist but only nominally democratic. He had a relatively small military, which he used primarily to suppress internal opposition.

The relative weakness of the south offered a strong temptation to nationalists in the North Korean government who wanted to reunite the country. The temptation grew stronger when the American government implied that it did not consider South Korea within its own "defense perimeter." The role of the Soviet Union remains unclear; there is some reason to believe that the North Koreans acted without Stalin's approval. But the Soviets supported the offensive once it began.

The Truman administration responded quickly to the invasion. On June 27, 1950, the president ordered limited American military assistance

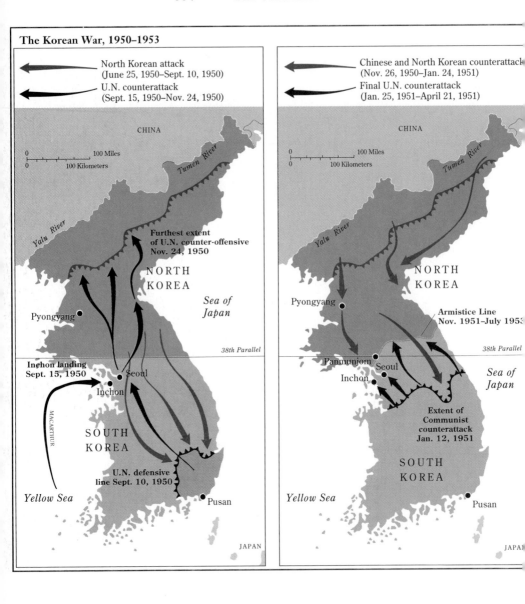

The Korean War, 1950–1953

North Korean attack
(June 25, 1950–Sept. 10, 1950)

U.N. counterattack
(Sept. 15, 1950–Nov. 24, 1950)

Chinese and North Korean counterattack
(Nov. 26, 1950–Jan. 24, 1951)

Final U.N. counterattack
(Jan. 25, 1951–April 21, 1951)

CHINA

0   100 Miles
0   100 Kilometers

Tumen River

Yalu River

Furthest extent
of U.N. counter-offensive
Nov. 24, 1950

NORTH
KOREA

Sea of
Japan

Pyongyang

38th Parallel

Inchon landing
Sept. 15, 1950

Seoul

Inchon

MACARTHUR

SOUTH
KOREA

U.N. defensive
line Sept. 10, 1950

Yellow Sea

Pusan

JAPAN

CHINA

0   100 Miles
0   100 Kilometers

Tumen River

Yalu River

NORTH
KOREA

Pyongyang

Armistice Line
Nov. 1951–July 1953

38th Parallel

Panmunjom

Seoul

Inchon

Sea of
Japan

Extent of
Communist
counterattack
Jan. 12, 1951

SOUTH
KOREA

Yellow Sea

Pusan

JAPAN

to South Korea, and on the same day he appealed to the United Nations to intervene. The Soviet Union was boycotting the Security Council at the time (to protest the council's refusal to recognize the new communist government of China) and was thus unable to exercise its veto power. As a result, American delegates were able to win UN agreement to a resolution calling for international assistance to the Rhee government. On June 30, the United States ordered its own ground forces into Korea, and Truman

MACARTHUR IN KOREA, 1950 General Douglas MacArthur visits Marines along the fighting front in Korea in September 1950. Revered by those who fought under him, MacArthur was nevertheless a persistent irritant to policymakers in Washington with his demands for widening the conflict—demands that grew more frequent and more public when the Chinese entered the war about two months after this photograph was taken.

appointed General Douglas MacArthur to command the UN operations there. (Several other nations provided assistance and troops, but the "UN" armies were, in fact, overwhelmingly American.)

After a surprise American invasion at Inchon in September had routed the North Korean forces from the south and sent them fleeing back across the 38TH parallel, Truman gave MacArthur permission to pursue the communists into their own territory. His aim was to create "a unified, independent and democratic Korea." He was moving beyond simple containment and envisioning a rollback of communist power.

From Invasion to Stalemate

For several weeks, MacArthur's invasion of North Korea proceeded smoothly. On October 19, the capital, Pyongyang, fell to the UN forces. Victory seemed near—until the Chinese government, alarmed by the movement of American forces toward its border, intervened. By November 4, eight divisions of the Chinese army had entered the war. The UN offensive stalled and then collapsed. Through December 1950, outnumbered American forces fought a bitter, losing battle against the Chinese divisions, retreating at almost every juncture. Within weeks, communist forces had pushed the Americans back below the 38TH parallel once again and had recaptured the South Korean capital of Seoul. By mid-January 1951 the rout had ceased; and by March the UN armies had managed to regain much of the territory they had recently lost, taking back Seoul and pushing the communists north of the 38TH parallel for the second time. With that, the war degenerated into a protracted stalemate.

From the start, Truman had been determined to avoid a direct conflict with China, which he feared might lead to a new world war. Once China entered the war, he began seeking a negotiated solution to the struggle; and for the next two years, he insisted that there be no wider war. But General MacArthur thought otherwise. The United States was really fighting the Chinese, MacArthur argued. It should, therefore, attack China itself, if not through an actual invasion, then at least by bombing communist forces massing north of the Chinese border. In March 1951, he indicated his unhappiness in a public letter to House Republican leader Joseph W. Martin that concluded: "There is no substitute for victory." His position had wide popular support.

The Martin letter came after nine months during which MacArthur had resisted Truman's decisions. More than once, the president had warned the general to keep his objections to himself. The release of the Martin letter, therefore, struck the president as intolerable insubordination. On April 11, 1951, he relieved MacArthur of his command.

There was a storm of public outrage. Sixty-nine percent of the American people supported MacArthur, a Gallup poll reported. When the general returned to the United States later in 1951, he was greeted with wild enthusiasm. Public criticism of Truman finally abated somewhat when a number of prominent military figures, including General Omar Bradley, publicly supported the president's decision. But substantial hostility toward Truman remained.

In the meantime, the Korean stalemate continued. Negotiations between the opposing forces began at Panmunjom in July 1951, but the talks—and the war—dragged on until 1953.

Limited Mobilization

Just as the war in Korea produced only a limited American military commitment abroad, so it created only a limited economic mobilization at home. Still, the government did try to control the wartime economy in several important ways.

First, Truman set up the Office of Defense Mobilization to fight inflation by holding down prices and discouraging high union wage demands. When these cautious regulatory efforts failed, the president took more drastic action. Railroad workers walked off the job in 1951, and Truman, who considered the workers' demands inflationary, ordered the government to seize control of the railroads. In 1952, during a nationwide steel strike, Truman seized the steel mills, citing his powers as commander in chief. But in a 6-to-3 decision, the Supreme Court ruled that the president had exceeded his authority, and Truman was forced to relent.

The Korean War gave a significant boost to economic growth by pumping new government funds into the economy at a point when many believed it was about to decline. But the war had other, less welcome effects. It came at a time of rising insecurity about America's position in the world and intensified anxiety about communism. As the long stalemate continued, producing 140,000 American dead and wounded, frustration turned to anger. The United States, which had recently won the greatest war in history, seemed unable to conclude what many Americans considered a minor border skirmish in a small country. Many began to believe that something must be deeply wrong—not only in Korea but within the United States as well. Such fears contributed to the rise of the second major campaign of the century against domestic communism.

THE CRUSADE AGAINST SUBVERSION

Why did the American people develop a growing fear of internal communist subversion—a fear that by the early 1950s had reached the point of near hysteria? There are many possible answers, but no single definitive explanation.

One factor was obvious. Communism was not an imagined enemy in the 1950s. It had tangible shape, in Josef Stalin and the Soviet Union. Adding to the concern were the setbacks America had encountered in its battle against communism: the Korean stalemate, the "loss" of China, the Soviet development of an atomic bomb. Searching for someone to blame, many were attracted to the idea of a communist conspiracy within American borders. But there were other factors as well, rooted in events in American domestic politics.

HUAC and Alger Hiss

Much of the anticommunist furor emerged out of the search by the Republican Party for an issue with which to attack the Democrats, and out of the efforts of the Democrats to take that issue away from them. Beginning in 1947, the House Un-American Activities Committee (HUAC) held widely publicized investigations to prove that, under Democratic rule, the government had tolerated (if not actually encouraged) communist subversion. The committee turned first to the movie industry, arguing that com-

ALGER HISS No single figure did more to polarize opinion about the dangers of domestic communism than Alger Hiss, the respected diplomat accused in 1948 of having been a spy in the 1930s for the Soviet Union and later convicted of perjury for testifying falsely before a congressional committee. Even half a century later, opinions remain sharply divided about Hiss's guilt.

munists had infiltrated Hollywood and tainted American films with pro-paganda. Writers and producers, some of them former communists, were called to testify; and when some of them ("the Hollywood Ten") refused to answer questions about their own political beliefs and those of their colleagues, they were sent to jail for contempt. Others were barred from employment in the industry when Hollywood, attempting to protect its public image, adopted a "blacklist" of those of "suspicious loyalty."

More alarming to the public was HUAC's investigation into charges of disloyalty leveled against a former high-ranking member of the State Department: Alger Hiss. In 1948, Whittaker Chambers, a self-avowed former communist agent, now a conservative editor at *Time* magazine, told the committee that Hiss had passed classified State Department doc-uments to him in 1937 and 1938. When Hiss sued him for slander, Cham-bers produced microfilms of the documents (called the "pumpkin papers," because Chambers had kept them hidden in a pumpkin in his vegetable garden). Hiss could not be tried for espionage because of the statute of limitations (which protects individuals from prosecution for most crimes after seven years have passed). But largely because of the relentless efforts of Richard M. Nixon, a freshman Republican congressman from Califor-nia and a member of HUAC, Hiss was convicted of perjury and served several years in prison. The Hiss case not only discredited a prominent young diplomat; it cast suspicion on a generation of liberal Democrats and made it possible for the public to believe that communists had actually in-filtrated the government. It also transformed Nixon into a national figure and helped him win a seat in the United States Senate in 1950.

The Federal Loyalty Program and the Rosenberg Case

Partly to protect itself against Republican attacks, partly to encourage support for the president's foreign policy initiatives, the Truman adminis-tration in 1947 initiated a widely publicized program to review the "loy-alty" of federal employees. By 1951, more than 2,000 government em-ployees had resigned under pressure and 212 had been dismissed.

The employee loyalty program became a signal throughout the execu-tive branch to launch a major assault on subversion. The attorney general established a widely cited list of supposedly subversive organizations. The director of the Federal Bureau of Investigation (FBI), J. Edgar Hoover, in-vestigated and harassed alleged radicals. In 1950, Congress passed the Mc-Carran Internal Security Act, which, among other restrictions on "subver-sive" activity, required that all communist organizations register with the government and publish their records. Truman vetoed the bill. Congress easily overrode his veto.

The successful Soviet detonation of an atomic bomb in 1949, earlier than generally expected, suggested to some people that there had been a conspiracy to pass American atomic secrets to the Russians. In 1950, Klaus Fuchs, a young British scientist, seemed to confirm those fears when he testified that he had delivered to the Russians details of the manufacture of the bomb. The case ultimately settled on an obscure New York couple, Julius and Ethel Rosenberg, members of the Communist Party. The government claimed the Rosenbergs had received secret information from Ethel's brother, a machinist on the Manhattan Project in New Mexico, and had passed it on to the Soviet Union through other agents (including Fuchs). The Rosenbergs were convicted and, on April 5, 1951, sentenced to death. After two years of appeals and public protests, they died in the electric chair on June 19, 1953, proclaiming their innocence to the end.

All these factors—the HUAC investigations, the Hiss trial, the loyalty investigations, the McCarran Act, the Rosenberg case—combined with other concerns by the early 1950s to create a fear of communist subversion that seemed to grip the entire country. State and local governments, the judiciary, schools and universities, labor unions—all sought to purge themselves of real or imagined subversives. A pervasive fear settled on much of the country—not only the fear of communist infiltration but the fear of being suspected of communism. It was a climate that made possible the rise of an extraordinary public figure.

McCarthyism

Joseph McCarthy was an undistinguished, first-term Republican senator from Wisconsin when, in February 1950, he suddenly burst into national prominence. In the midst of a speech in Wheeling, West Virginia, he lifted up a sheet of paper and claimed to "hold in my hand" a list of 205 known communists currently working in the American State Department. No person of comparable stature had ever made so bold a charge against the federal government; and in the weeks to come, as McCarthy repeated and expanded on his accusations, he emerged as the nation's most prominent leader of the crusade against domestic subversion.

Within weeks of his charges against the State Department, McCarthy was leveling accusations at other agencies. After 1952, with the Republicans in control of the Senate and McCarthy the chairman of a special subcommittee, he conducted highly publicized investigations of alleged subversion in many areas of the government. McCarthy never produced conclusive evidence that any federal employee was a communist. But a growing constituency adored him nevertheless for his coarse, "fearless" assaults on a government establishment that many considered arrogant, effete, even traitorous. Republicans, in particular, rallied to his claims that the Democrats had been responsible for "twenty years of treason" and that only a change of parties could rid the country of subversion. McCarthy, in short, provided his followers with an issue into which they could channel a wide range of resentments: fear of communism, animosity toward the country's "eastern establishment," and frustrated partisan ambitions. For a time, McCarthy intimidated all but a few people from opposing him. Even the highly popular Dwight D. Eisenhower, running for president in 1952, did not speak out against him, although he disliked McCarthy's tactics and was outraged at, among other things, McCarthy's attacks on General George Marshall.

The Republican Revival

Public frustration over the stalemate in Korea and popular fears of internal subversion combined to make 1952 a bad year for the Democratic Party. Truman, now deeply unpopular, wisely withdrew from the presidential contest. The party united instead behind Governor Adlai E. Stevenson of Illinois. Stevenson's dignity, wit, and eloquence made him a beloved figure to many liberals and intellectuals. But those same qualities seemed only to fuel Republican charges that Stevenson lacked the strength or the will to combat communism sufficiently.

Stevenson's greatest problem, however, was the Republican candidate opposing him. Rejecting the efforts of conservatives to nominate Robert Taft or Douglas MacArthur, the Republicans turned to a man who had no previous identification with the party: General Dwight D. Eisenhower—military hero, commander of NATO, president of Columbia University in New York—who won nomination on the first ballot. He chose as his running mate the young California senator who had gained national prominence through his crusade against Alger Hiss: Richard M. Nixon.

In the fall campaign, Eisenhower attracted support through his geniality and his statesmanlike pledges to settle the Korean conflict. Nixon (after surviving early accusations of financial improprieties, which he effectively neutralized in a famous television address, the "Checkers speech") exploited the issue of domestic anticommunism by attacking the

Democrats for "cowardice" and "appeasement." The response at the polls was overwhelming. Eisenhower won both a popular and an electoral landslide: 55 percent of the popular vote to Stevenson's 44 percent, 442 electoral votes to Stevenson's 89. Republicans gained control of both houses of Congress for the first time since 1946. The election of 1952 ended twenty years of Democratic dominance. And while it might not have seemed so at the time, it also signaled the end of some of the worst turbulence of the postwar era.

CONCLUSION

Even during World War II itself, when the United States and the Soviet Union were allies, it was evident to leaders in both nations that America and Russia had quite different visions of what the postwar world should look like. Very quickly after the war ended, those differences became visible to almost everyone, and the once fruitful relationship between the world's two greatest powers quickly soured. Americans came to believe that the Soviet Union was an expansionist tyranny little different from Hitler's Germany, and that Josef Stalin, the Soviet leader, was bent on world conquest. Soviets came to believe that the United States was trying to protect its own dominance in the world by encircling the Soviet Union and trying to limit its ability to operate as a great power. The result of these tensions was what became known by the end of the 1940s as the Cold War.

Actual conflicts in the early years of the Cold War were relatively few. Instead, the United States engaged in a series of policies designed to prevent both war and Soviet aggression. It helped rebuild the shattered nations of Western Europe with substantial economic aid, through the Marshall Plan, to stabilize those nations and prevent them from becoming communist. America announced a new foreign policy—known as containment—that committed it to an effort to keep the Soviet Union from expanding its influence further into the world. The United States and Western Europe formed a strong and enduring alliance, NATO, to defend Europe against possible Soviet advances.

In 1950, however, the armed forces of communist North Korea launched an invasion of the noncommunist South; and to most Americans—including, most importantly, President Truman—the conflict quickly came to be seen as a test of American resolve in the Cold War. The Korean War was long, costly, and unpopular, with many military setbacks and frustrations. In the end, however, the United States—working through the United Nations—managed to drive the North Koreans out of the south and stabilize the original division of the peninsula.

The Korean War had other effects on the domestic life of the United States. It hardened American foreign policy into a much more rigidly anticommunist form. It undermined the Truman administration, and the Democratic Party, and helped strengthen conservatives and Republicans. It greatly strengthened an already powerful crusade against communists, and those believed to be communists, within the United States—a crusade often known as McCarthyism, because of the notoriety of Senator Joseph McCarthy of Wisconsin, the most celebrated leader of the effort.

America after World War II was indisputably the wealthiest and most powerful nation in the world. But in the harsh climate of the Cold War, neither wealth nor power could prevent deep anxieties and bitter divisions.

FOR FURTHER REFERENCE

Suggested Readings

Two books by John Lewis Gaddis, *Strategies of Containment* (1982) and *The United States and the Origins of the Cold War, 1941–1947* (1972) provide a sound introduction to Cold War history. Walter LaFeber, *America, Russia, and the Cold War, 1945–1967* (rev. ed. 1980) is a classic survey of American-Soviet relations. Melvyn P. Leffler, *A Preponderance of Power: National Security, the Truman Administration, and the Cold War* (1992) is a superb, densely researched history of the policies of the 1940s. Warren I. Cohen, *The Cambridge History of American Foreign Relations, Vol. 4: America in the Age of Soviet Power, 1945–1991* (1991) is a good general history. Michael Hogan, *The Marshall Plan* (1987) is a provocative interpretation of one of the pillars of American foreign policy in the 1940s. David McCullough, *Truman* (1992) is an elegant, sympathetic biography. Alonzo Hamby, *Man of the People: A Life of Harry S. Truman* (1995) is a fine scholarly one. Bruce Cumings, *The Origins of the Korean War* (1980) is an important study of America's first armed conflict of the Cold War. Ellen Schrecker, *Many Are the Crimes* (1998) is an important interpretation of McCarthyism. Richard Fried, *Nightmare in Red* (1990) is a good introduction to the Red Scare. David M. Oshinsky, *A Conspiracy So Immense: The World of Joe McCarthy* (1983) is an excellent biography. Richard Pells, *The Liberal Mind in a Conservative Age: American Intellectuals in the 1940s and 1950s* (1985) is a valuable overview of postwar intellectual life.

Films

(The best source for information on how to find these and other films is *Bowker's Complete Video Directory*—3 volumes.) *The Spy in the Sky* (1996) tells the story of a team of engineers and pilots racing to design, perfect, and deploy the high-flying U2 spy plane in the 1950s. *The Age of Anxiety: 1952–1958* (1986) chronicles Eisenhower's election, the end of the Korean war, the death of Stalin, and the beginning of the arms race. *Truman* (1997) is an excellent documentary about the 33rd president.

Internet Resources

Internet websites containing historical material relevant to the subjects discussed in this chapter can be reached through the McGraw-Hill history site at www.mhhe.com/socscience/history/usa/link/linktop.htm.

CHAPTER THIRTY

The Affluent Society

The Economic "Miracle" ∽ *The Explosion of Science and Technology*
People of Plenty ∽ *The Other America*
The Rise of the Civil Rights Movement ∽ *Eisenhower Republicanism*
Eisenhower, Dulles, and the Cold War

I F AMERICA EXPERIENCED a golden age in the 1950s and early 1960s, as many Americans believed at the time and many continue to believe today, it was largely a result of two developments. One was a booming national prosperity, which profoundly altered the social, economic, and even physical landscape of the United States, as well as the way many Americans thought about their lives and their world. The other was the continuing struggle against communism, a struggle that created considerable anxiety but that also encouraged Americans to look even more approvingly at their own society. But if these powerful forces created a widespread sense of national purpose and self-satisfaction, they also helped blind many Americans to serious problems plaguing large groups of the population.

THE ECONOMIC "MIRACLE"

Perhaps the most striking feature of American society in the 1950s and early 1960s was the booming, almost miraculous economic growth that made even the heady 1920s seem pale by comparison. It was a better-balanced and more widely distributed prosperity than that of thirty years earlier. It was not, however, as universal as some Americans liked to believe.

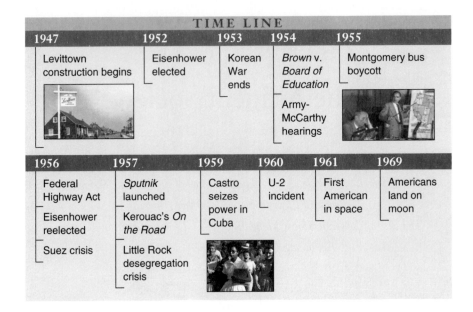

TIME LINE

1947	1952	1953	1954	1955
Levittown construction begins	Eisenhower elected	Korean War ends	*Brown* v. *Board of Education* Army-McCarthy hearings	Montgomery bus boycott

1956	1957	1959	1960	1961	1969
Federal Highway Act Eisenhower reelected Suez crisis	*Sputnik* launched Kerouac's *On the Road* Little Rock desegregation crisis	Castro seizes power in Cuba	U-2 incident	First American in space	Americans land on moon

Economic Growth

By 1949, despite the continuing problems of postwar reconversion, an economic expansion had begun that would continue with only brief interruptions for almost twenty years. Between 1945 and 1960, the gross national product grew by 250 percent, from $200 billion to over $500 billion. Unemployment, which during the Depression had averaged between 15 and 25 percent, remained at about 5 percent or lower throughout the 1950s and early 1960s. Inflation, in the meantime, hovered around 3 percent a year or less.

The causes of this growth were varied. Government spending, which had ended the Depression in the 1940s, continued to stimulate growth through public funding of schools, housing, veterans' benefits, welfare, and interstate highways. Above all, there was military spending. Economic growth was at its peak during the first half of the 1950s, when military spending was highest because of the Korean War. In the late 1950s, with spending on armaments in decline, the rate of growth declined by half.

The national birth rate reversed a long pattern of decline with the so-called baby boom, which had begun during the war and peaked in 1957.

THE BABY BOOM IN THE SUBURBS Mothers of young children cluster outside a shopping center in Levittown, New York in the spring of 1949, during the early years of the postwar baby boom. The rapid population growth the baby boom produced, and the massive movement of middle-class families into suburbs that accompanied it, were among the most important demographic trends of the postwar era.

The nation's population rose almost 20 percent in the decade, from 150 million in 1950 to 179 million in 1960. The baby boom meant increased consumer demand and expanding economic growth.

The rapid expansion of suburbs—whose population grew 47 percent in the 1950s—helped stimulate growth in several important sectors of the economy. The number of privately owned cars (more essential for suburban than for urban living) more than doubled in a decade, sparking a great boom in the automobile industry. Demand for new homes helped sustain a vigorous housing industry. The construction of roads, which was both a cause and a result of the growth of suburbs, stimulated the economy as well.

These and other forces helped the American economy to grow nearly ten times as fast as the population in the thirty years after the war. And while that growth was far from equally distributed, it affected most of society. The average American in 1960 had over 20 percent more purchasing power than in 1945, and more than twice as much as during the prosperous 1920s. The American people had achieved the highest standard of living of any society in the history of the world.

The Rise of the Modern West

No region of the country experienced more dramatic changes as a result of the new economic growth than the American West. Its population expanded dramatically; its cities boomed; its industrial economy flourished. Before World War II, most of the West had been, economically at least, an appendage of the great industrial economy of the East. By the 1960s, some parts of the West were among the most important (and populous) industrial and cultural centers of the nation in their own right.

As during World War II, much of the growth of the West was a result of federal spending and investment—on the dams, power stations, highways, and other infrastructure projects that made economic development possible; and on the military contracts that continued to flow disproportionately to factories in California and Texas, many of them built with government funds during the war. But other factors played a role as well. The growing number of automobiles created new demands for petroleum and contributed to the rapid growth of oil fields in Texas and Colorado and of the metropolitan centers serving them: Houston, Dallas, and Denver. State governments in the West invested heavily in their universities. The University of Texas and University of California systems, in particular, became among the nation's largest and best; as centers of research, they helped attract technology-intensive industries to the region. Climate also contributed. Southern California, Nevada, and Arizona, in particular, attracted many migrants from the East because of their warm, dry climates. The growth of Los Angeles after World War II was a remarkable phenomenon: more than 10 percent of all new businesses in the United States between 1945 and 1950 began in Los Angeles. Its population rose by over 50 percent between 1940 and 1960.

Capital and Labor

Corporations enjoying booming growth were reluctant to allow strikes to interfere with their operations; and since the most important labor unions were now so large and entrenched that they could not easily be suppressed or intimidated, leaders of large businesses made important concessions to them. By the mid-1950s, factory wages in all industries had risen substantially, to an average of $80 per week.

The economic successes of the 1950s helped pave the way for a reunification of the labor movement. In December 1955, the American Federation of Labor and the Congress of Industrial Organizations ended their twenty-year rivalry and merged to create the AFL-CIO, under the leadership of George Meany.

But success also bred stagnation and corruption in some union bureaucracies. In 1957, the powerful Teamsters Union became the subject of a congressional investigation, and its president, David Beck, was charged with the misappropriation of union funds. Beck ultimately stepped down to be replaced by Jimmy Hoffa, whom government investigators pursued for nearly a decade before finally winning a conviction against him (for tax evasion) in 1967. The United Mine Workers, similarly, became tainted by violence and charges of corruption.

THE EXPLOSION OF SCIENCE AND TECHNOLOGY

In 1961, *Time* magazine selected as its "man of the year" not a specific person but "the American Scientist." The choice was an indication of the widespread fascination with which Americans in the age of atomic weapons viewed science and technology. But it was also a sign of the remarkable, and remarkably rapid, scientific and technological advances in many areas during the postwar years.

Medical Breakthroughs

The twentieth century saw more progress in the development of medical science than had occurred in all the centuries before it. A very large proportion of that progress occurred during and after World War II. Particularly important was the development of new antibacterial drugs capable of fighting infections that in the past had been all but untreatable.

The development of antibiotics had its origins in the discoveries of Louis Pasteur and Jules-Francois Joubert. Working in France in the 1870s, they produced the first conclusive evidence that virulent bacterial infections could be defeated by other, more ordinary bacteria. Using their discoveries, the English physician Joseph Lister revealed the value of anti-septic solutions to prevent infection during surgery.

But the practical use of antibacterial agents to combat disease did not begin until many decades later. In the 1930s, scientists in Germany, France, and England demonstrated the power of so-called sulfa drugs—drugs derived from an antibacterial agent known as sulfanilamide—which could be used effectively to treat streptococcal blood infections. New sulfa drugs were soon being developed at an astonishing rate, and were frequently improved, with dramatic results in treating what had once been a major cause of death.

In 1928, in the meantime, Alexander Fleming, an English medical researcher, accidentally discovered the antibacterial properties of an organism that he named penicillin. There was little progress in using penicillin to treat human illness, however, until a group of researchers at Oxford University, directed by Howard Florey and Ernest Chain, learned how to produce stable, potent penicillin in sizable enough quantities to make it a practical weapon against bacterial disease. The first human trials of the new drug, in 1941, were dramatically successful, but progress toward the mass availability of penicillin was stalled in England because of World War II. American laboratories took the next crucial steps in developing methods for the mass production and commercial distribution of penicillin, which became widely available to doctors and hospitals around the world by 1948. Since then, a wide range of new antibiotics of highly specific character have been developed so that bacterial infections are now among the most successfully treated of all human illnesses.

There was also dramatic progress in immunization—the development of vaccines that can protect humans from contracting both bacterial and viral diseases. The first great triumph was the development of the small-pox vaccine by the English researcher Edward Jenner in the late eighteenth century. A vaccine effective against typhoid was developed by an English bacteriologist, Almorth Wright, in 1897, and was in wide use by World War I. Vaccination against tetanus became widespread just before and during World War II. Medical scientists also developed a vaccine, BCG, against another major killer, tuberculosis, in the 1920s; but controversy over its safety stalled its adoption, especially in the United States, for many years. It was not widely used in the United States until after World War II, when it largely eliminated tuberculosis—until a limited recurrence began in the 1990s.

Viruses are much more difficult to prevent and treat than bacterial infections, and progress toward vaccines against viral infections—except for smallpox—was relatively slow. Not until the 1930s, when scientists discovered how to grow viruses in laboratories in tissue cultures, could researchers study them with any real effectiveness. Gradually, they discovered how to produce forms of a virus incapable of causing disease but capable of triggering antibodies in vaccinated people that would protect them for contracting the disease. An effective vaccine against yellow fever was developed in the late 1930s, and one against influenza—one of the great killers of the first half of the twentieth century—appeared in 1945.

A particularly dramatic postwar triumph was the development of a vaccine against polio. In 1954, the American scientist Jonas Salk introduced an effective vaccine against the disease that had killed and crippled thousands of children and adults (among them Franklin Roosevelt). It was provided free to the public by the federal government beginning in 1955. After 1960, an oral vaccine developed by Albert Sabin—usually administered in a sugar cube—made widespread vaccination even easier. By the early 1960s, these vaccines had virtually eliminated polio from American life and much of the rest of the world.

As a result of these and many other medical advances, both infant mortality and the death rate among young children declined significantly in the first twenty-five years after the war (although not by as much as in Western Europe). Average life expectancy in that same period rose by five years, to seventy-one.

Pesticides

At the same time that medical researchers were finding cures for and vaccines against infectious diseases, other scientists were developing new kinds of chemical pesticides, which they hoped would protect crops from destruction by insects and protect humans from such insect-carried diseases as typhus and malaria. Perhaps the most famous of the new pesticides was dichlorodiphenyltrichloroethane, generally known as DDT, a compound discovered in 1939 by a Swiss chemist named Paul Muller. He had discovered that although DDT seemed harmless to human beings and other mammals, it was extremely toxic to insects. American scientists learned of Muller's discovery in 1942, just as the army was grappling with the insect-borne tropical diseases—especially malaraia and typhus—that threatened American soldiers.

Under these circumstances, DDT seemed a godsend. It was first used on a large scale in Italy in 1943–1944 during a typhus outbreak, which it

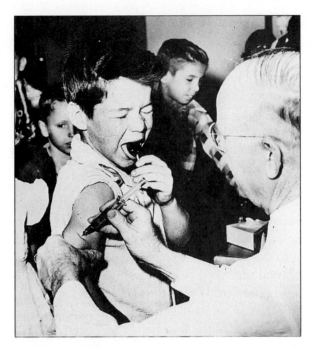

GETTING VACCINATED AGAINST POLIO Polio had been intermittently epidemic among American children for half a century until Jonas Salk developed an effective vaccine in the early 1950s. After successful tests, it was made available to the public in 1955; and that same year, Congress passed the Poliomyelitis Vaccination Act, which provided funds for vaccinating schoolchildren for free. Massive vaccination programs quickly followed, one of them shown in this photograph, and continued into the 1960s—when another, even more effective, vaccine developed by Albert Sabin largely replaced the Salk vaccine. In 1955, the last year before vaccination, there were 37,771 cases of polio reported in the United States. By 1957, the number had dropped to about 5,700; and by 1971, to 21. Today, as a result of the vaccines, polio is virtually unknown in much of the world.

quickly helped end. Soon it was being sprayed in mosquito-infested areas of Pacific islands where American troops were fighting the Japanese. No soldiers suffered any apparent ill effects from the sprayings, and the incidence of malaria dropped precipitously. DDT quickly gained a reputation as a miraculous tool for controlling insects, and it undoubtedly saved thousands of lives. Only later did it become evident that DDT had long-term toxic effects on animals and humans.

Postwar Electronic Research

The 1940s and 1950s saw dramatic new developments in electronic technology. Researchers in the 1940s produced the first commercially viable televisions and created a technology that made it possible to broadcast programming over large areas. Later, in the late 1950s, scientists at RCA's David Sarnoff Laboratories in New Jersey developed the technology for color television, which first became widely available in the early 1960s.

In 1948 Bell Labs, the research arm of AT&T, produced the first transistor, a solid-state device capable of amplifying electrical signals, which was much smaller and more efficient than the cumbersome vacuum tubes that had powered most electronic equipment in the past. Transistors made possible the miniaturization of many devices (radios, televisions, audio equipment, hearing aids) and were also important in aviation, weaponry, and satellites. They contributed as well to another major breakthrough in electronics: the development of integrated circuitry in the late 1950s.

Integrated circuits combined a number of once-separate electronic elements (transistors, resistors, diodes, and others) and embedded them into a single, microscopically small device. They made it possible to create increasingly complex electronic devices requiring complicated circuitry that would have been impractical to produce through other means. Most of all, integrated circuits helped advance the development of the computer.

Postwar Computer Technology

Prior to the 1950s, computers had been constructed mainly to perform complicated mathematical tasks, such as those required to break military codes. In the 1950s, they began to perform commercial functions for the first time, as data-processing devices used by businesses and other organizations.

The first significant computer of the 1950s was the Universal Automatic Computer (or UNIVAC), which was developed initially for the U.S. Bureau of the Census by the Remington Rand Company. It was the first computer able to handle both alphabetical and numerical information easily. It used tape storage and could perform calculations and other functions much faster than its predecessor, the ENIAC, developed in 1946 by the same researchers at the University of Pennsylvania who were responsible for the UNIVAC. Searching for a larger market than the census for their very expensive new device, Remington Rand arranged to use a UNIVAC to predict the results of the 1952 election for CBS television news. It would, they believed, produce valuable publicity for the machine. Analyzing early voting results, the UNIVAC accurately predicted an enormous landslide victory for Eisenhower over Stevenson. Few Americans had ever heard of a computer before that night, and the UNIVAC's television debut became, therefore, a critical breakthrough in public awareness of computer technology.

Remington Rand had limited success in marketing the UNIVAC, but in the mid-1950s the International Business Machines Company (IBM) introduced its first major data-processing computers and began to find a wide market for them among businesses in the United States and abroad. These early successes, combined with the enormous amount of money IBM invested in research and development, made the company the worldwide leader in computers for many years.

Bombs, Rockets, and Missiles

In 1952, the United States successfully detonated the first hydrogen bomb. (The Soviet Union tested its first H-bomb a year later.) Unlike the plutonium and uranium bombs developed during World War II, the hydrogen bomb derives its power not from fission (the splitting of atoms) but fusion (the joining together of lighter atomic elements with heavier ones). It is capable of producing explosions of vastly greater power than the earlier fission bombs.

The development of the hydrogen bomb gave considerable impetus to a stalled scientific project in both the United States and the Soviet Union—the effort to develop unmanned rockets and missiles capable of traveling the new weapons—not suitable for delivery by airplanes—to their targets. Both nations began to put tremendous resources into their development. The United States, in particular, benefited from the emigration to America of some of the German scientists who had helped develop rocketry for Germany during World War II.

In the United States, early missile research was conducted almost entirely by the Air Force, and there were significant early successes in developing rockets capable of traveling several hundred miles. But American and Soviet leaders were both struggling to build longer-range missiles that could cross oceans and continents—intercontinental ballistic missiles, or ICBMs, capable of traveling through space to distant targets. American scientists experimented in the 1950s first with the Atlas and then the Titan ICBM. There were some early successes, but there were also many setbacks, particularly because of the difficulty of massing sufficient, stable fuel to provide the tremendous power needed to launch missiles beyond the atmosphere. By 1958, scientists had created a solid fuel to replace the volatile liquid fuels of the early missiles; and they had also produced miniaturized guidance systems capable of ensuring that missiles could travel to reasonably precise destinations. Within a few years, a new generation of missile, known as the Minuteman, became the basis of the American atomic weapons arsenal. It was capable of traveling several thousand miles. American scientists also developed a nuclear missile capable of being carried and fired by submarines—the Polaris, which is launched from below the surface of the ocean by compressed air and fires its engines only once it is above the surface. A Polaris was first successfully fired from underwater in 1960.

The Space Program

The American space program eventually developed a rationale of its own. In the beginning, however, it was a byproduct of the rivalry with the Soviet Union and the effort to develop effective military uses for weapons. Its origins can perhaps be traced most directly to a dramatic event in 1957, when the Soviet Union announced that it had launched an earth-orbiting satellite—*Sputnik*—into outer space. The United States had yet to perform any similar feats, and the American government (and much of American society) reacted to the announcement with alarm, as if the Soviet achievement was also a massive American failure. Federal policy began encouraging (and funding) strenuous efforts to improve scientific education in the schools, to create more research laboratories, and, above all, to speed the development of America's own exploration of outer space. The United States launched its own first satellite, *Explorer I*, in January 1958.

The centerpiece of space exploration, however, soon became the manned space program, established in 1958 through the creation of a new agency, the National Aeronautics and Space Administration (NASA) and through the selection of the first American space pilots, or "astronauts." They quickly became the nation's most revered heroes. NASA's initial effort, the Mercury Project, was designed to launch manned vehicles into space to orbit the earth. On May 5, 1961, Alan Shepard became the first American launched into space. But his short, suborbital flight came several months after a Soviet "cosmonaut," Yuri Gagarin, had made a flight in which he had actually orbited the earth. On February 2, 1962, John Glenn (later a United States senator) became the first American to orbit the globe. (Thirty-six years later, at the age of seventy-seven, Glenn traveled in space again, as a member of the crew of a space shuttle mission—the oldest man ever to have done so.) NASA later introduced the Gemini program, whose spacecraft could carry two astronauts at once.

Mercury and Gemini were followed by the Apollo program, whose purpose was to land men on the moon. It had some catastrophic setbacks, most notably a fire in January 1967 that killed three astronauts as they sat in a capsule on the launch pad during a training session in Cape Canaveral, Florida. But on July 20, 1969, Neil Armstrong, Edwin Aldrin, and Michael Collins successfully traveled in a space capsule into orbit around the moon. Armstrong and Aldrin then detached a smaller craft from the capsule, landed on the surface of the moon, and became the first men to walk on a body other than earth. Six more lunar missions followed, the last in 1972. Not long after that, however, the government began to cut the funding for missions, and popular enthusiasm for the program began to wane.

The future of the manned space program did not lie primarily in efforts to reach distant planets, as originally envisioned. Instead, the program became a more modest effort to make travel in near-space easier and more practical through the development of the "space shuttle," an airplane-like device launched by a missile but capable both of navigating in space and landing on earth much like a conventional aircraft. The first space shuttle was successfully launched in 1982. The explosion of one shuttle, *Challenger*, in January 1986 shortly after takeoff, killing all seven astronauts, stalled the program for two years. But missions resumed in the late 1980s and have continued ever since, driven in part by commercial purposes. The space shuttle has been used to launch and repair communications satellites, to insert the Hubble Space Telescope into orbit in 1990 (and later to repair its flawed lens), and to service the orbiting Spacelab.

The space program, like the military development of missiles, gave a tremendous boost to the American aeronautics industry and was responsible for the development of many technologies that proved valuable in other areas.

PEOPLE OF PLENTY

Among the most striking social developments of the immediate postwar era was the rapid extension of a middle-class lifestyle and outlook to an expanding portion of the population. The American middle class was becoming a larger, more powerful, and more self-conscious force than it had ever been before. The new prosperity inspired some Americans to see abundance, and middle-class aspirations, as the key to understanding the American past and the American character. David Potter, a leading historian of the era, published an influential examination of "economic abundance and American character" in 1954. He called it *People of Plenty*. For the American middle class in the 1950s, at least, it seemed an appropriate label.

The Consumer Culture

At the center of middle-class culture in the 1950s was a growing absorption with consumer goods. That was a result of increased prosperity, of the increasing variety and availability of products, and of the adeptness of advertisers in creating a demand for those products. It was also a result of the growth of consumer credit, which increased by 800 percent between 1945 and 1957 through the development of credit cards, revolving charge accounts, and easy-payment plans. Prosperity fueled such longtime consumer crazes as the automobile, and Detroit responded to the boom with ever-flashier styling and accessories. Consumers also responded eagerly to the development of such new products as dishwashers, garbage disposals, television, hi-fis, and stereos. To a striking degree, the prosperity of the 1950s and 1960s was consumer driven (as opposed to investment driven).

Because consumer goods were so often marketed (and advertised) nationally, the 1950s were notable for the rapid spread of great national consumer crazes. For example, children, adolescents, and even some adults became entranced in the late 1950s with the hula hoop—a large plastic ring kept spinning around the waist. The popularity of the Walt Disney-produced children's television show *The Mickey Mouse Club* created a national demand for related products such as Mickey Mouse watches and hats. It also helped produce the stunning success of Disneyland, an amusement park near Los Angeles that re-created many of the characters and events of Disney entertainment programs. The Disney

THE MICKEY MOUSE CLUB In an early example of the highly integrated marketing for which it is now famous, the Walt Disney Corporation created this successful television program for children in the mid-1950s. It coincided with, and helped to promote, the 1955 opening of Disneyland—the company's enormously profitable theme park near Los Angeles.

technique of turning an entertainment success into an effective tool for marketing consumer goods was not an isolated event. Many other entertainers and producers took note and did the same.

The Suburban Nation

A third of the nation's population lived in suburbs by 1960. The growth of suburbs was a result not only of increased affluence but of important innovations in home building, which made single-family houses affordable to millions of new people. The most famous of the suburban developers, William Levitt, came to symbolize the new suburban growth with his use of mass-production techniques to construct large housing developments, the first of which was on Long Island, near New York City. The houses sold for under $10,000. Many other relatively inexpensive suburban developments soon began appearing throughout the country.

LEVITTOWN BEFORE THE TREES A section of the Levittown on Long Island in New York, photographed in July 1948, a few months after the first families moved in. The Levitt family pioneered techniques in constructing mass-produced housing that made possible the proliferation of similar inexpensive suburbs in many areas of the country.

Why did so many Americans want to move to the suburbs? One reason was the enormous importance postwar Americans placed on family life after five years of war during which families had often been separated or otherwise disrupted. Suburbs provided families with larger homes than they could find (or afford) in the cities, and thus made it easier to raise larger numbers of children. They provided privacy. They also provided a sense of security from the noise and dangers of urban living. They offered space for the new consumer goods—the appliances, cars, boats, outdoor furniture, and other products that many middle-class Americans craved.

Another factor motivating white Americans to move to the suburbs was race. Most suburbs were restricted to white inhabitants—both because relatively few blacks could afford to live in them and because formal and informal barriers kept even prosperous blacks out of all but a few. In an era when the black population of most cities was rapidly growing, many white families fled to the suburbs to escape the integration of urban neighborhoods and schools.

The Suburban Family

For professional men (who tended to work in the city, at some distance from their homes), suburban life generally meant a rigid division between their working and personal worlds. For many middle-class women, it meant an increased isolation from the workplace. The enormous cultural emphasis on family life in the 1950s strengthened popular prejudices against women entering the professions or occupying any paid job at all. Many middle-class husbands considered it demeaning for their wives to be employed. And many women themselves shied away from the workplace when they could afford to, in part because of prevailing ideas about motherhood (popularized by such widely consulted books as Dr. Benjamin Spock's *Baby and Child Care*, first published in 1946) that advised women to stay at home with their children.

Affluent women, then, faced heavy pressures—both externally and internally imposed—to remain in the home and concentrate on raising their children. Some women, however, had to balance these pressures against other, contradictory ones. As expectations of material comfort rose, many middle-class families needed a second income to maintain the standard of living they desired. As a result, the number of married women working outside the home actually increased in the postwar years—even as the social pressure for them to stay out of the workplace grew. By 1960, nearly a third of all married women were part of the paid work force.

The Birth of Television

Television was the result of a series of dramatic scientific and technological discoveries, but its impact was largely social and cultural. It quickly became perhaps the most powerful medium of mass communication in history, and it was central to the culture of the postwar era. Experiments in broadcasting pictures (along with sound) had begun as early as the 1920s, but commercial television began only shortly after World War II. Its growth was phenomenally rapid. In 1946, there were only 17,000 sets in the country; by 1957, there were 40 million television sets in use—almost as many sets as there were families. More people had television sets, according to one report, than had refrigerators (a statistic strikingly similar to one in the 1920s that had revealed more people owning radios than bathtubs).

The television industry emerged directly out of the radio industry, and all three of the major networks—The National Broadcasting Company, the Columbia Broadcasting System, and the American Broadcasting Company—had started as radio companies. Like radio, the television business was driven by advertising. The need to attract advertisers determined most programming decisions; and in the early days of television, sponsors often played a direct, powerful, and continuing role in determining the content of the programs they chose to sponsor. Many early television shows bore the names of the corporations that were paying for them: the GE Television Theater, the Chrysler Playhouse, the Camel News Caravan, and others. Some daytime serials (known as "soap operas," because their sponsors were almost always companies making household goods targeted at women) were actually written and produced by Procter & Gamble and other companies.

The impact of television on American life was rapid, pervasive, and profound. By the late 1950s, television news had replaced newspapers, magazines, and radios as the nation's most important vehicle of information. Television advertising helped create a vast market for new fashions and products. Televised athletic events gradually made college and professional sports one of the most important sources of entertainment (and one of the biggest businesses) in America. Television entertainment programming—almost all of it controlled by the three national networks and their corporate sponsors—replaced movies and radio as the principal source of diversion for American families.

Much of the programming of the 1950s and early 1960s created a common image of American life—an image that was predominantly white, middle class, and suburban, and that was epitomized by such popular situation comedies as *Ozzie and Harriet* and *Leave It to Beaver.* Programming also reinforced the concept of gender roles that most men (and many women) unthinkingly embraced. Most situation comedies, in particular, showed families in which, as the title of one of the most popular put it, *Father Knows Best,* and in which most women were mothers and housewives striving to serve their children and please their husbands.

But television also conveyed other images: the gritty, urban working-class families in Jackie Gleason's *The Honeymooners;* the childless show-business family of the early *I Love Lucy;* the unmarried professional women in *Our Miss Brooks* and *My Little Margie;* the hapless African Americans in *Amos 'n Andy.* Television not only sought to create an idealized image of a homogeneous suburban America. It also sought to convey experiences at odds with that image—but to convey them in warm, unthreatening terms, taking social diversity and cultural conflict and domesticating them, turning them into something benign and even comic.

Yet television also, inadvertently, created conditions that could accentuate social conflict. Even those unable to share in the affluence of the era could, through television, acquire a vivid picture of how the rest of their society lived. Thus at the same time that television was reinforcing the homogeneity of the white middle class, it was also contributing to the sense of alienation and powerlessness among groups excluded from the world it portrayed. And television news conveyed with unprecedented power the social upheavals that gradually spread beginning in the late 1950s, and in conveying them helped make more such upheavals likely.

Organized Society and Its Detractors

Large-scale organizations and bureaucracies increased their influence over American life in the postwar era, as they had been doing for many decades before. White-collar workers came to outnumber blue-collar laborers for the first time, and an increasing proportion of them worked in corporate settings with rigid hierarchical structures. Industrial workers also confronted large bureaucracies both in the workplace and in their own unions.

As in earlier eras, Americans reacted to these developments with ambivalence, often hostility. The debilitating impact of bureaucratic life on the individual slowly became one of the central themes of popular and scholarly debate. William H. Whyte, Jr., produced one of the most widely discussed books of the decade: *The Organization Man* (1956), which attempted to describe the special mentality of the worker in a large, bureaucratic setting. Self-reliance, Whyte claimed, was losing place to the ability to "get along" and "work as a team" as the most valuable trait in the modern character. The sociologist David Riesman made similar observations in *The Lonely Crowd* (1950), in which he argued that the traditional "inner-directed man," who judged himself on the basis of his own values and the esteem of his family, was giving way to a new "other-directed man," more concerned with winning the approval of the larger organization or community.

Novelists, too, expressed misgivings in their work about the enormity and impersonality of modern society. Saul Bellow produced a series of novels—*The Adventures of Augie March* (1953), *Seize the Day* (1956), *Herzog* (1964), and many others—that chronicled the difficulties American Jewish men had in finding fulfillment in modern urban America. J. D. Salinger wrote in *The Catcher in the Rye* (1951) of a prep-school student, Holden Caulfield, who was unable to find any area of society—school, family, friends, city—in which he could feel secure or committed.

The Beats and the Restless Culture of Youth

The most derisive critics of bureaucracy, and of middle-class society generally, were a group of young poets, writers, and artists known as the "beats" (or, by disapproving critics, as "beatniks"). They wrote harsh critiques of what they considered the sterility and conformity of American life, the meaninglessness of American politics, and the banality of popular culture. Allen Ginsberg's dark, bitter poem *Howl* (1955) decried the "Robot apartments! invincible suburbs! skeleton treasuries! blind capitals! demonic industries!" of modern life. Jack Kerouac produced what may have been the most popular document of the Beat Generation in his novel *On the Road* (1957), an account of a cross-country automobile trip that depicted the rootless, iconoclastic lifestyle of Kerouac and his friends.

The beats were the most visible evidence of a widespread restiveness among young Americans in the 1950s. In part, that restlessness was a result of prosperity itself—of a growing sense among young people of limitless possibilities, and of the declining power of such traditional values as thrift, discipline, and self-restraint. Young middle-class Americans were growing up in a culture that encouraged them to expect wholly fulfilling lives; but of course they were living in a world in which almost all of them experienced obstacles to complete fulfillment.

Youth in the 1950s never staged rebellions as widespread or as bitter as those of the 1960s, but their restiveness was visible nevertheless. The phenomenon of "juvenile delinquency" attracted tremendous public attention, and in both politics and popular culture there were dire warnings about the growing criminality of American youth. The 1955 film *Blackboard Jungle*, for example, was a frightening depiction of crime and violence in city schools. Scholarly studies, presidential commissions, and journalistic exposés all contributed to the sense of alarm about the spread of delinquency—although in fact youth crime did not dramatically increase in the 1950s.

Also disturbing to many older Americans was the style of youth culture. Many young people began to wear clothes and adopt hairstyles that mimicked popular images of juvenile criminal gangs. The culture of alienation that the beats so vividly represented had counterparts even in ordinary middle-class behavior: teenage rebelliousness toward parents, youthful fascination with fast cars and motorcycles, and an increasing visibility of teenage sex, assisted by the greater availability of birth-control devices and the spreading automobile culture that came to dominate the social lives of teenagers in much of the nation. The popularity of James Dean, in such movies as *Rebel Without a Cause* (1955), *East of Eden* (1955), and *Giant* (1956), was a particularly vivid sign of this aspect of youth culture in the 1950s. Both in the roles he played (moody, alienated teenagers and young men with a streak of self-destructive violence) and in the way he lived his own life (he died in 1955, at the age of 24, in a motorcycle accident), Dean became an icon of the unfocused rebelliousness of American youth in his time.

Rock 'n' Roll

One of the most powerful signs of the restiveness of American youth was the enormous popularity of rock 'n' roll—and of the greatest early rock star, Elvis Presley. Presley became a symbol of a youthful determination to push at the borders of the conventional and acceptable. Presley's sultry good looks, his self-conscious effort to dress in the vaguely rebellious style of urban gangs (motorcycle jackets and slicked-back hair, even though Presley himself was a product of the rural South), and, most of all, the open sexuality of his music and his public performances—all made him wildly popular among young Americans in the 1950s. His first great hit, "Heartbreak Hotel," established him as a national phenomenon in 1956, and he remained a powerful figure in American popular culture until—and indeed beyond—his death in 1977.

Presley's music, like that of most early white rock musicians, drew heavily from black rhythm and blues traditions, which appealed to some white youths in the early 1950s because of their pulsing, sensual rhythms and their hard-edged lyrics. Sam Phillips, a local record promoter who had recorded some of the important black rhythm and blues musicians of his time (among them B. B. King), reportedly said in the early 1950s: "If I could find a white man with a Negro sound, I could make a billion dollars." Soon after that, he found Presley. But there were others as well—among them Buddy Holly and Bill Haley (whose 1955 song "Rock Around the Clock"—used in the film *Blackboard Jungle*—served to announce the arrival of rock 'n' roll to millions of young people)—who were closely connected to African-American musical traditions. Rock drew from other sources too: from country western music (another strong influence on Presley), from gospel music, even from jazz. But nothing was so important to it as its roots in rhythm and blues.

The rise of such white rock musicians as Presley was a result in part (as Phillips's comment suggests) of the limited willingness of white audiences to accept black musicians. But the 1950s did see a growth in the popularity

ELVIS IN CONCERT Elvis Presley ended his career performing before wealthy audiences in Las Vegas, wearing garish sequined suits. But in the early years of his career, as this concert in the late 1950s suggests, both he and his fans were younger—and the connection between them was immediate and intense.

of African-American bands and singers among both black and white audiences. Chuck Berry, Little Richard, B. B. King, Chubby Checker, the Temptations, and others—many of them recorded by the black producer Berry Gordy, the founder and president of Motown Records in Detroit—never rivaled Presley in their popularity among white youths but did develop significant multiracial audiences of their own.

The rapid rise and enormous popularity of rock owed a great deal to innovations in radio and television programming. By the 1950s, radio stations no longer felt obliged to present mostly live programming—especially once television took over many of the entertainment functions radio had once performed. Instead, many radio stations devoted themselves almost entirely to playing recorded music. Early in the 1950s, a new breed of radio announcers, known as "disk jockeys," began to create programming aimed specifically at young fans of rock music; and when those programs became wildly successful, other stations followed suit. *American Bandstand*, which began airing in 1957, was a televised showcase for rock 'n' roll hits in which a live audience danced to recorded music. The program helped spread the popularity of rock—and made its host, Dick Clark, one of the best-known figures among young Americans.

Radio and television were important to the recording industry, of course, because they encouraged the sale of records, which was increasing rapidly in the mid- and late 1950s, especially in the inexpensive and popular 45 rpm format—small disks that contained one song on each side. Also important were juke boxes, which played individual songs on 45s and which proliferated in soda fountains, diners, bars, and almost every other place where young people were likely to congregate. It usually cost five cents to play a song on the juke box, and teenagers tended to make use of them whenever they could—thus promoting rock music further. Sales of records increased threefold—from $182 million to $521 million—between 1954 and 1960. The popularity of rock music was the driving force behind that increase. So eager were record promoters to get their songs on the air that they routinely made secret payments to station owners and disk jockeys to encourage them to showcase their artists. These payments, which became known as "payola," produced a briefly sensational series of scandals when they were exposed in the late 1950s and early 1960s.

Rock music began in the 1950s to do what jazz and swing had done in the 1920s, 1930s, and 1940s—to define both youth culture as a whole and the experiences of a generation. People who grew up in the 1950s defined their era, and to some degree themselves, by the music they knew as teenagers and young people, just as people who grew up in later decades defined their experiences in part by their own generations' versions of rock. Rock music in the 1950s worked, therefore, both to transform popular music in America and to give at least indirect voice to some of the anxieties and pent-up impulses of young people.

THE OTHER AMERICA

It was relatively easy for white, middle-class Americans in the 1950s to believe that the world they knew—a world of economic growth, personal affluence, and cultural homogeneity—was the world virtually all Americans knew, that the values and assumptions they shared were ones that most other Americans shared, too. But such beliefs were false. Even within the middle class, there was considerable restiveness—among women, intellectuals, young people, and others who found the middle-class consumer culture somehow unsatisfying, even stultifying. More importantly, large groups of Americans remained outside the circle of abundance and shared neither in the affluence of the middle class nor in many of its values.

On the Margins of the Affluent Society

In 1962, the socialist writer Michael Harrington published a celebrated book called *The Other America*, in which he chronicled the continuing existence of poverty in the United States. The conditions he described were not new. Only the attention he was bringing to them was.

The great economic expansion of the postwar years reduced poverty dramatically but did not eliminate it. In 1960, at any given moment, more than a fifth of all American families (over 30 million people) continued to live below what the government defined as the poverty line (down from a third of all families fifteen years before). Many millions more lived just above the official poverty line, but with incomes that gave them little comfort and no security.

Most of the poor—up to 80 percent—experienced poverty intermittently and temporarily. But approximately 20 percent of the poor were people for whom poverty was a continuous, debilitating reality from which there was no easy escape. That included approximately half the nation's elderly and a significant proportion of African Americans and Hispanics. Native Americans constituted the single poorest group in the country.

This "hard-core" poverty rebuked the assumptions of those who argued that economic growth would eventually lead everyone into prosperity—that, as many claimed, "a rising tide lifts all boats." It was a poverty that the growing prosperity of the postwar era seemed to affect hardly at all, a poverty, as Harrington observed, that appeared "impervious to hope."

Rural Poverty

Among those on the margins of the affluent society were many rural Americans. In 1948, farmers had received 8.9 percent of the national income; in 1956, they received only 4.1 percent. In part, this decline reflected the steadily shrinking farm population; in 1956 alone, nearly 10 percent of the rural population moved into or was absorbed by cities. But it also reflected declining farm prices. Because of enormous surpluses in basic staples, prices fell 33 percent in those years, even though national income as a whole rose 50 percent at the same time.

Not all farmers were poor. But the agrarian economy did produce substantial numbers of genuinely impoverished people. Black sharecroppers and tenant farmers continued to live at or below subsistence levels throughout the rural South—in part because of the mechanization of cotton picking beginning in 1944, in part because of the development of synthetic fibers that reduced demand for cotton generally. (Two-thirds of the cotton acreage of the South went out of production between 1930 and 1960.) Migrant farmworkers, a group concentrated especially in the West and Southwest and containing many Mexican-American and Asian-American workers, lived in similarly dire circumstances. In rural areas without much commercial agriculture—such as the Appalachian region in the East, where the decline of the coal economy reduced the one significant source of support for the region—whole communities lived in desperate poverty, increasingly cut off from the market economy. All these groups were vulnerable to malnutrition and even starvation.

The Inner Cities

As prospering white families moved from cities to suburbs in vast numbers, more and more inner-city neighborhoods became repositories for the poor, "ghettoes" from which there was no easy escape. The growth of these neighborhoods owed much to a vast migration of African Americans out of the countryside (where the cotton economy was in decline) and into industrial cities. Not all these black migrants were poor, and many found in the city some of the same routes to economic progress that many whites were finding. But African Americans were substantially more likely to live in poverty than most other groups, in part because of the persistence of historic patterns of discrimination that denied them any real opportunities.

More than 3 million black men and women moved from the South to northern cities between 1940 and 1960, many more than had made the same journey in the Great Migration during and after World War I. Chicago, Detroit, Cleveland, New York, and other eastern and midwestern industrial cities experienced a major expansion of their black populations— both in absolute numbers and, even more, as a percentage of the whole, since so many whites were leaving at the same time.

Similar migrations from Mexico and Puerto Rico expanded poor Hispanic neighborhoods in many American cities at the same time. Between 1940 and 1960, nearly a million Puerto Ricans moved into American cities (the largest group to New York). Mexican workers crossed the border into Texas and California and swelled the already substantial Latino communities of such cities as San Antonio, Houston, San Diego, and Los Angeles (which by 1960 had the largest Mexican-American population of any city, approximately 500,000 people).

Why these inner-city communities, populated largely by racial and ethnic minorities, remained so poor in the midst of growing affluence has been the subject of considerable, and very heated, debate. But it is indisputable that inner cities were filling up with poor minority residents at the same time that the unskilled industrial jobs they were seeking were diminishing. Employers were moving factories and mills from old industrial cities to new locations in suburbs, smaller cities, and even abroad—places where the cost of labor or of other things were lower. Even in the factories that remained, automation was reducing the number of unskilled jobs. The economic opportunities that had helped earlier immigrant groups to rise up from poverty were unavailable to many of the postwar migrants. Nor can there be any doubt that historic patterns of racial discrimination in hiring, education, and housing doomed many members of these communities to continuing, and in some cases increasing, poverty.

One result of inner-city poverty was a rising rate of juvenile crime. Indeed, "juvenile delinquency" was one of the few results of poverty that middle-class Americans discussed and worried about with any consistency. A 1955 book, *One Million Delinquents*, called juvenile crime a "national epidemic" and described a troubling subculture of inner-city youth—embittered, rebellious adolescents with no hope of advancement and no sense of having a stake in the structure of their society.

THE RISE OF THE CIVIL RIGHTS MOVEMENT

After decades of skirmishes, an open battle began in the 1950s against racial segregation and discrimination, a battle that would prove to be one of the longest and most difficult social struggles of the century. White Americans played an important role in the civil rights movement. But pressure from African Americans themselves was the crucial element in raising the issue of race to prominence.

The Brown *Decision and "Massive Resistance"*

On May 17, 1954, the Supreme Court announced one of the most important decisions in its history in the case of *Brown* v. *Board of Education of Topeka*. In considering the legal segregation of a Kansas public school system, the Court rejected its own 1896 *Plessy* v. *Ferguson* decision, which had ruled that communities could provide African Americans with separate facilities as long as the facilities were equal to those of whites. The *Brown* decision unequivocally declared the segregation of public schools on the basis of race unconstitutional. The justices argued that school segregation inflicted unacceptable damage on those it affected, regardless of the relative quality of the separate schools. Chief Justice Earl Warren explained the unanimous opinion of his colleagues: "We conclude that in the field of public education the doctrine of 'separate but equal' has no place. Separate educational facilities are inherently unequal." The following year, the Court issued another decision (known as *Brown II*) to provide rules for implementing the 1954 order. It ruled that communities must work to desegregate their schools "with all deliberate speed," but it set no timetable and left specific decisions up to lower courts.

In some communities, for example, Washington, D.C., compliance came relatively quickly and quietly. More often, however, strong local opposition (what came to be known in the South as "massive resistance") produced long delays and bitter conflicts. More than 100 southern members of Congress signed a "manifesto" in 1956 denouncing the *Brown* decision and urging their constituents to defy it. Southern governors, mayors, local school boards, and nongovernmental pressure groups (including hundreds of White Citizens' Councils) all worked to obstruct desegregation. By the fall of 1957, only 684 of 3,000 affected school districts in the South had even begun to desegregate their schools.

The Eisenhower administration was not eager to join the battle over desegregation. But in September 1957, it faced a case of direct state defiance of federal authority and felt compelled to act. Federal courts had or-

LITTLE ROCK An African-American student passes by jeering whites in Arkansas on her way to Little Rock High School, newly integrated by federal court order. The black students later admitted that they had been terrified during the first difficult weeks of integration. But in public, most of them acted with remarkable calm and dignity.

dered the desegregation of Central High School in Little Rock, Arkansas. An angry white mob tried to block implementation of the order by blockading the entrances to the school, and Governor Orval Faubus refused to do anything to stop the obstruction. President Eisenhower finally responded by sending federal troops to Little Rock to keep the peace and ensure that the court orders would be obeyed. Only then did Central High School admit its first black students.

The Expanding Movement

The *Brown* decision helped spark a growing number of popular challenges to other forms of segregation in the South. On December 1, 1955, Rosa Parks, an African-American woman, was arrested in Montgomery, Alabama, when she refused to give up her seat on a Montgomery bus to a white passenger (as required by the Jim Crow laws that regulated race relations in the city and throughout most of the South). Parks, an active civil rights leader in the community, had apparently decided spontaneously to resist the order to move. The arrest of this admired woman produced outrage in the city's African-American community, which organized a boycott of the bus system to demand an end to segregated seating.

Once launched, the boycott was almost completely effective. It put economic pressure not only on the bus company but on many Montgomery merchants, because the bus boycotters found it difficult to get to downtown stores and shopped instead in their own neighborhoods. Even so, the boycott might well have failed had it not been for a Supreme Court decision late in 1956, inspired in part by the protest, that declared segregation in public transportation to be illegal. The buses in Montgomery abandoned their discriminatory seating policies, and the boycott came to a close.

Perhaps the most important accomplishments of the Montgomery boycott were the legitimization of a new form of racial protest and the elevation to prominence of a new figure in the movement for civil rights. The man chosen to lead the boycott movement once it was launched was a local Baptist pastor, Martin Luther King, Jr., the son of a prominent Atlanta minister, a powerful orator, and a gifted leader. King's approach to black protest was based on the doctrine of nonviolence—that is, of nonviolent resistance to injustice even in the face of direct attack. And he produced an approach to racial struggle that captured the moral high ground for his supporters. For the next thirteen years—as leader of the Southern Christian Leadership Conference (SCLC), an interracial group he founded shortly after the bus boycott—he was the most influential and most widely admired black leader in the country. The popular movement he came to represent soon spread throughout the South and throughout the country.

Causes of the Civil Rights Movement

Why did a civil rights movement begin to emerge at this particular moment? The injustices it challenged and the goals it promoted were hardly new; in theory, African Americans could have launched the same movement fifty or a hundred years earlier, or decades later. Why did they do so in the 1950s and 1960s?

Several factors contributed to the rise of African-American protest in these years. The legacy of World War II was one of the most important. Millions of black men and women had served in the military or worked in war plants during the war and had derived from the experience a broader view of the world, and of their place in it, than they had been able to develop in their relatively isolated lives prior to the 1940s.

Another factor was the growth of an urban black middle class, which had been developing for decades but which began to flourish after the war. Much of the impetus for the civil rights movement came from the leaders of urban black communities—ministers, educators, professionals—and much of it came as well from students at black colleges and universities, which had expanded significantly in the previous decades. Men and women with education and a stake in society were often more aware of the obstacles to their advancement than poorer and more oppressed people, to whom the possibility of advancement may have seemed too remote even to consider. And urban blacks had considerably more freedom to associate with one another and to develop independent institutions than did rural blacks, who were often under the very direct supervision of white landowners.

Television and other forms of popular culture were another factor in the rising consciousness of racism among blacks. More than any previous generation, postwar blacks had constant, vivid reminders of how the white majority lived—of the world from which they were effectively excluded. Television also conveyed the activities of demonstrators to a national audience, ensuring that activism in one community would inspire similar protests in others.

In addition to the forces that were inspiring African Americans to mobilize, other forces were at work mobilizing many white Americans to support the movement once it began. One was the Cold War, which made racial injustice an embarrassment to Americans trying to present their nation as a model to the world. Another was the political mobilization of northern blacks, who were now a substantial voting bloc within the Democratic Party; politicians from northern industrial states could not ignore their views. Labor unions with substantial black memberships also played an important part in supporting (and funding) the civil rights movement.

This great and largely spontaneous social movement emerged, in short, out of an unpredictable combination of broad social changes and specific local grievances. Whatever its causes, it quickly took on a momentum that, by the early 1960s, had made it one of the most powerful forces in America.

EISENHOWER REPUBLICANISM

Dwight D. Eisenhower was the least experienced politician to serve in the White House in the twentieth century. He was also among the most popular and politically successful presidents of the postwar era. At home, he pursued essentially moderate policies, avoiding most new initiatives but accepting the work of earlier reformers. Abroad, he continued and even intensified American commitments to oppose communism but brought to some of those commitments a measure of restraint that his successors did not always match.

"What Was Good for . . . General Motors"

The first Republican administration in twenty years staffed itself with men drawn from the same quarter as those who had staffed Republican administrations in the 1920s: the business community. But by the 1950s, many business leaders had acquired a social and political outlook very different from that of their predecessors of earlier decades. Above all, many of the nation's leading business executives and financiers had reconciled themselves to at least the broad outlines of the Keynesian welfare state the New Deal had launched. Indeed, some corporate leaders had come to see it as something that actually benefited them—by helping maintain social order, by increasing mass purchasing power, and by stabilizing labor relations.

To his cabinet, Eisenhower appointed wealthy corporate lawyers and business executives who were not apologetic about their backgrounds. Charles Wilson, president of General Motors, assured senators considering his nomination for secretary of defense that he foresaw no conflict of interest because he was certain that "what was good for our country was good for General Motors, and vice versa."

Eisenhower's consistent inclination was to limit federal activities and encourage private enterprise. He supported the private rather than public development of natural resources. To the chagrin of farmers, he lowered federal support for farm prices. He also removed the last limited wage and price controls maintained by the Truman administration. He opposed the creation of new social service programs such as national health insurance. He strove constantly to reduce federal expenditures (even during the recession of 1958) and balance the budget. He ended 1960, his last full year in office, with a $1 billion budget surplus.

The Survival of the Welfare State

The president took few new initiatives in domestic policy, but he resisted pressure from the right wing of his party to dismantle those welfare policies of the New Deal that had survived the conservative assaults of the war years and after. Indeed, during his term, he agreed to extend the Social Security system to an additional 10 million people and unemployment compensation to an additional 4 million, and he agreed to increase the minimum hourly wage from 75 cents to $1. Perhaps the most significant legislative accomplishment of the Eisenhower administration was the Federal Highway Act of 1956, which authorized $25 billion for a ten-year project that built over 40,000 miles of interstate highways—the largest public works project in American history. The program was to be funded through a highway "trust fund," whose revenues would come from new taxes on the purchase of fuel, automobiles, trucks, and tires.

In 1956, Eisenhower ran for a second term, even though he had suffered a serious heart attack the previous year. With Adlai Stevenson opposing him once again, he won by another, even greater landslide, receiving nearly 57 percent of the popular vote and 457 electoral votes to Stevenson's 73. Democrats retained the control of both houses of Congress they had won back in 1954. And in 1958—during a serious recession—they increased that control by substantial margins.

The Decline of McCarthyism

The Eisenhower administration did little in its first years in office to discourage the anticommunist furor that had gripped the nation. By 1954, however, the crusade against subversion was beginning to produce significant popular opposition—an indication that the anticommunist passion of several years earlier was beginning to abate. The clearest signal of that change was the political demise of Senator Joseph McCarthy.

During the first year of the Eisenhower administration, McCarthy continued to operate with impunity. But in January 1954 he overreached himself when he attacked Secretary of the Army Robert Stevens and the

THE ARMY-MCCARTHY HEARINGS Senator Joseph McCarthy uses a map to show the supposed distribution of communists throughout the United States during the televised 1954 Senate hearings to mediate the dispute between McCarthy and the U.S. Army. Joseph Welch, chief counsel for the army, remains conspicuously unimpressed.

armed services in general. At that point, the administration and influential members of Congress organized a special investigation of the charges, which became known as the Army-McCarthy hearings. They were among the first congressional hearings to be nationally televised. The result was devastating to McCarthy. Watching McCarthy in action—bullying witnesses, hurling groundless (and often cruel) accusations, evading issues—much of the public began to see him as a villain, and even a buffoon. In December 1954, the Senate voted 67 to 22 to condemn him for "conduct unbecoming a senator." Three years later, with little public support left, he died—a victim, apparently, of complications arising from alcoholism.

EISENHOWER, DULLES, AND THE COLD WAR

The threat of nuclear war with the Soviet Union created a sense of high anxiety in international relations in the 1950s. But the nuclear threat had another effect as well. With the potential devastation of an atomic war so enormous, both superpowers began to edge away from direct confrontations. The attention of both the United States and the Soviet Union began to turn to the rapidly escalating instability in the nations of the Third World.

Dulles and "Massive Retaliation"

Eisenhower's secretary of state, and (except for the president himself) the dominant figure in the nation's foreign policy in the 1950s, was John Foster Dulles, an aristocratic corporate lawyer with a stern moral revulsion to communism. He entered office denouncing the containment policies of the Truman years as excessively passive, arguing that the United States should pursue an active program of "liberation," which would lead to a "rollback" of communist expansion. Once in power, however, he had to defer to the more moderate views of the president himself.

The most prominent of Dulles's innovations was the policy of "massive retaliation," which Dulles announced early in 1954. The United States would, he explained, respond to communist threats to its allies not by using conventional forces in local conflicts (a policy that had led to so much frustration in Korea) but by relying on "the deterrent of massive retaliatory power" (by which he clearly meant nuclear weapons). In part, the new doctrines reflected Dulles's inclination for tense confrontations, an approach he once defined as "brinksmanship"—pushing the Soviet Union to the brink of war in order to exact concessions. But the real force behind the massive-retaliation policy was economics. With pressure growing both in and out of government for a reduction in American military expenditures, an increasing reliance on atomic weapons seemed to promise, as some advocates put it, "more bang for the buck."

France, America, and Vietnam

What had been the most troubling foreign policy concern of the Truman years—the war in Korea—plagued the Eisenhower administration only briefly. On July 27, 1953, negotiators at Panmunjom finally signed an agreement ending the hostilities. Each antagonist was to withdraw its troops a mile and a half from the existing battle line, which ran roughly along the 38th parallel, the prewar border between North and South Korea. A conference in Geneva was to consider means by which to reunite the nation peacefully— although in fact the 1954 meeting produced no agreement and left the cease-fire line as the apparently permanent border between the two countries.

Almost simultaneously, however, the United States was being drawn into a long, bitter struggle in Southeast Asia. Ever since 1945, France had been attempting to restore its authority over Vietnam, its one-time colony, which it had been forced to abandon to the Japanese toward the end of World War II. Opposing the French, however, were the powerful nationalist forces of

Ho Chi Minh, determined to win independence for their nation. Ho had hoped for American support in 1945, on the basis of the anticolonial rhetoric of the Atlantic Charter and Franklin Roosevelt's speeches, and also because he had received support from American intelligence forces during World War II while he was fighting the Japanese. But he was then, as he had been for many years, not only a committed nationalist but a committed communist. The Truman administration ignored him and supported the French, one of America's most important Cold War allies.

By 1954, Ho was receiving aid from communist China and the Soviet Union. America, in the meantime, had been paying most of the costs of France's ineffective military campaign in Vietnam since 1950. Early in 1954, 12,000 French troops became surrounded in a disastrous siege at the village of Dien Bien Phu. Only American intervention, it was clear, could prevent the total collapse of the French military effort. Yet despite the urgings of Secretary of State Dulles, Vice President Nixon, and others, Eisenhower refused to permit direct American military intervention in Vietnam, claiming that neither Congress nor America's other allies would support such action.

Without American aid, the French defense of Dien Bien Phu finally collapsed on May 7, 1954, and France quickly agreed to a settlement of the conflict at the same international conference in Geneva that summer that was considering the Korean settlement. The Geneva accords on Vietnam of July 1954, to which the United States was not a direct party, established a supposedly temporary division of Vietnam along the 17TH parallel. The north would be governed by Ho Chi Minh, the south by a pro-Western regime. Democratic elections would be the basis for uniting the nation in 1956. The agreement marked the end of the French commitment to Vietnam and the beginning of an expanded American presence there. The United States helped establish a pro-American government in the south, headed by Ngo Dinh Diem, a member of his country's Roman Catholic minority. Diem, it was clear, would not permit the 1956 elections, which he knew he would lose. He felt secure in his refusal because the United States had promised to provide him with ample military assistance against any attack from the north.

Cold War Crises

American foreign policy in the 1950s rested on a reasonably consistent foundation: the containment policy, as revised by the Eisenhower administration. But the nation's leaders spent much of their time reacting to both real and imagined crises in far-flung areas of the world. Among them were a series of crises in the Middle East, a region in which the United States had been little involved until after World War II.

On May 14, 1948, after years of Zionist efforts and a dramatic decision by the new United Nations, the nation of Israel proclaimed its independence. President Truman recognized the new Jewish homeland the next day. But the creation of Israel, while it resolved some conflicts, created others. Palestinian Arabs, unwilling to accept being displaced from what they considered their own country, joined with Israel's Arab neighbors and fought determinedly against the new state in 1948—the first of several Arab-Israeli wars.

Committed as the American government was to Israel, it was also concerned about the stability and friendliness of the Arab regimes in the oil-rich Middle East, in which American petroleum companies had major investments. Thus the United States reacted with alarm as it watched Mohammed Mossadegh, the nationalist prime minister of Iran, begin to resist the presence of Western corporations in his nation in the early 1950s. In 1953, the American CIA joined forces with conservative Iranian military leaders to engineer a coup that drove Mossadegh from office. To replace him, the CIA helped elevate the young Shah of Iran, Mohammed Reza Pahlevi, from his position as token constitutional monarch to that of virtually absolute ruler. The Shah remained closely tied to the United States for the next twenty-five years.

American policy was less effective in dealing with the nationalist government of Egypt, under the leadership of General Gamal Abdel Nasser, which began to develop a trade relationship with the Soviet Union in the early 1950s. In 1956, to punish Nasser for his friendliness toward the communists, Dulles withdrew American offers to assist in building the great Aswan Dam across the Nile. A week later, Nasser retaliated by seizing control of the Suez Canal from the British, saying that he would use the income from it to build the dam himself.

On October 29, 1956, Israeli forces attacked Egypt. The next day the British and French landed troops in the Suez to drive the Egyptians from the canal. Dulles and Eisenhower feared that the Suez crisis would drive the Arab states toward the Soviet Union and precipitate a new world war. By refusing to support the invasion, and by joining in a United Nations denunciation of it, the United States helped pressure the French and British to withdraw and helped persuade Israel to agree to a truce with Egypt.

Cold War concerns affected American relations in Latin America as well. In 1954, the Eisenhower administration ordered the CIA to help topple the new, leftist government of Jacobo Arbenz Guzmán in

Guatemala, a regime that Dulles (responding to the entreaties of the United Fruit Company, a major investor in Guatemala fearful of Arbenz) argued was potentially communist.

No nation in the region had been more closely tied to America than Cuba. Its leader, Fulgencio Batista, had ruled as a military dictator since 1952, when with American assistance he had toppled a more moderate government. Cuba's relatively prosperous economy had become a virtual fiefdom of American corporations, which controlled almost all the island's natural resources and had cornered over half the vital sugar crop. American organized-crime syndicates controlled much of Havana's lucrative hotel and nightlife business. In 1957, a popular movement of resistance to the Batista regime began to gather strength under the leadership of Fidel Castro. On January 1, 1959, with Batista having fled to exile in Spain, Castro marched into Havana and established a new government.

Castro soon began implementing drastic policies of land reform and expropriating foreign-owned businesses and resources. Cuban-American relations deteriorated rapidly as a result. When Castro began accepting assistance from the Soviet Union in 1960, the United States cut back the "quota" by which Cuba could export sugar to America at a favored price. Early in 1961, as one of its last acts, the Eisenhower administration severed diplomatic relations with Castro. Isolated by the United States, Castro soon cemented an alliance with the Soviet Union.

Europe and the Soviet Union

Although the problems of the Third World were moving slowly toward the center of American foreign policy, the direct relationship with the Soviet Union and the effort to resist communist expansion in Europe remained the principal concerns of the Eisenhower administration. In 1955, Eisenhower and other NATO leaders met with the Soviet premier, Nikolai Bulganin, at a cordial summit conference in Geneva. But when a subsequent conference of foreign ministers met to try to resolve specific issues, they could find no basis for agreement. Relations between the Soviet Union and the West soured further in 1956 in response to the Hungarian Revolution. Hungarian dissidents had launched a popular uprising in November to demand democratic reforms. Before the month was out, Soviet tanks and troops entered Budapest to crush the uprising and restore an orthodox, pro-Soviet regime. The Eisenhower administration refused to intervene. But the suppression of the uprising convinced many American leaders that Soviet policies had not softened.

The U-2 Crisis

In November 1958, Nikita Khrushchev, who had succeeded Bulganin as Soviet premier and Communist Party chief earlier that year, renewed the demands of his predecessors that the NATO powers abandon West Berlin. When the United States and its allies predictably refused, Khrushchev suggested that he and Eisenhower discuss the issue personally, both in visits to each other's countries and at a summit meeting in Paris in 1960. The United States agreed. Khrushchev's 1959 visit to America produced a cool but polite public response. Plans proceeded for the summit conference and for Eisenhower's visit to Moscow shortly thereafter. Only days before the scheduled beginning of the Paris meeting, however, the Soviet Union announced that it had shot down an American U-2, a high-altitude spy plane, over Russian territory. Its pilot, Francis Gary Powers, was in captivity. Khrushchev lashed out angrily at the American incursion into Soviet air space, breaking up the Paris summit almost before it could begin and withdrawing his invitation to Eisenhower to visit the Soviet Union.

The events of 1960 provided a somber backdrop for the end of the Eisenhower administration. After eight years in office, Eisenhower had failed to eliminate, and in some respects had actually increased, the tensions between the United States and the Soviet Union. Yet Eisenhower had brought to the Cold War his own sense of the limits of American power. He had resisted military intervention in Vietnam. And he had placed a measure of restraint on those who urged the creation of an enormous American military establishment. In his farewell address in January 1961, he warned of the "unwarranted influence" of a vast "military-industrial complex." His caution, in both domestic and international affairs, stood in marked contrast to the attitudes of his successors, who argued that the United States must act more boldly and aggressively on behalf of its goals at home and abroad.

CONCLUSION

The booming economic growth of the 1950s—and the anxiety over the Cold War that formed a backdrop to it—shaped the politics and the culture of the decade. For most Americans, the 1950s were years of increasing personal prosperity. Sales of private homes increased dramatically; suburbs grew precipitously; young families had children at an astounding rate—creating what came to be known as the postwar "baby boom." After the end of the divisive Korean War, the nation's politics entered a period of relative calm, symbolized by the genial presence in the White House of Dwight D. Eisenhower, who provided moderate and undemanding leadership through most of the decade.

The nation's culture, too, helped create a broad sense of stability and calm. Television, which emerged in the 1950s as the most powerful medium of mass culture, presented largely uncontroversial programming dominated by middle-class images and traditional values. Movies, theater, popular magazines, and newspapers all contributed to a broad sense of well-being.

But the 1950s were not, in the end, as calm and contented as the politics and popular culture of the time suggested. A powerful youth culture emerged in these years that displayed a considerable level of restiveness and even disillusionment. African Americans began to escalate their protests against segregation and inequality. The continuing existence of widespread poverty among large groups of Americans attracted increasing attention as the decade progressed. These pulsing anxieties, combined with frustration over the continuing tensions of the Cold War, produced by the late 1950s a growing sense of impatience with the calm, placid public culture of the time. That was one reason for the growing desire for action and innovation as the 1960s began.

FOR FURTHER REFERENCE

Suggested Readings

James T. Patterson, *Grand Expectations: Postwar America, 1945–1974* (1996) is an important general history of the postwar era. John P. Diggins, *The Proud Decades* (1989) and Godfrey Hodgson, *America in Our Time* (1976) are other important surveys. Kenneth T. Jackson, *The Crabgrass Frontier: The Suburbanization of the United States* (1985) is a classic history of a major social movement. Elaine Tyler May, *Homeward Bound: American Families in the Cold War* (1988) is a challenging cultural history of the postwar family. Paul Boyer, *By the Bomb's Early Light* (1986) is a study of the impact of the atomic bomb on American culture. Stephen Ambrose, *Eisenhower the President* (1984) is a good biography, and Fred Greenstein, *The Hidden-hand Presidency* (1982) is a revisionist interpretation. Taylor Branch, *Parting the Waters: America in the King Years* (1988) is a superb narrative of the early years of the civil rights movement, and Richard Kluger, *Simple Justice* (1975) is a classic history of the *Brown* decision. John Egerton, *Speak Now Against the Day: The Generation Before the Civil Rights Movement in the South* (1994) is a fine history of the struggles over white supremacy in the pre-civil rights era.

Films

(The best source for information on how to find these and other films is *Bowker's Complete Video Directory*—3 volumes.) *A. Philip Randolph: For Jobs and Freedom* (1995) narrates the life and times of this preeminent labor and civil rights leader. *Goin' to Chicago* (1994) brings the black migration from South to North to life with interviews with African-American migrants in the 1930s through the 1940s. The stunning effect of the first Soviet satellite launch in 1957 is vividly and imaginatively portrayed in *The Satellite Sky* (1990). *Eisenhower* (1993) is an extensive portrait of the president and Supreme Commander of Allied Forces in WWII, offering a fresh reassessment of his legacy. *An Age of Conformity* (1991) describes domestic life in the 1940s and 1950s, exploring the reasons for general economic, political, and social/cultural conformity and, interestingly, the origins of the civil rights movement.

Internet Resources

Internet websites containing historical material relevant to the subjects discussed in this chapter can be reached through the McGraw-Hill history site at www.mhhe.com/socscience/history/usa/link/linktop.htm.

CHAPTER THIRTY-ONE

The Ordeal of Liberalism

Expanding the Liberal State ∽ The Battle for Racial Equality
"Flexible Response" and the Cold War ∽ Vietnam
The Traumas of 1968

B Y THE LATE 1950s, a growing restlessness was becoming visible beneath the apparently placid surface of American society. Anxiety about America's position in the world, growing pressures from African Americans and other minorities, the increasing visibility of poverty, the rising frustrations of women, and other long-suppressed discontents were beginning to make themselves felt in the nation's public life. Ultimately, that restlessness would make the 1960s one of the most turbulent and divisive eras of the twentieth century. But at first, it contributed to a bold and confident effort by political leaders to attack social and international problems within the framework of conventional liberal politics.

EXPANDING THE LIBERAL STATE

Those who yearned for a more active government in the late 1950s and who accused the Eisenhower administration of allowing the nation to "drift" hoped for vigorous new leadership. The two men who served in the White House through most of the 1960s—John Kennedy and Lyndon Johnson—seemed for a time to be the embodiment of these liberal hopes.

John Kennedy

The campaign of 1960 produced two young candidates who claimed to offer the nation active leadership. The Republican nomination went al-

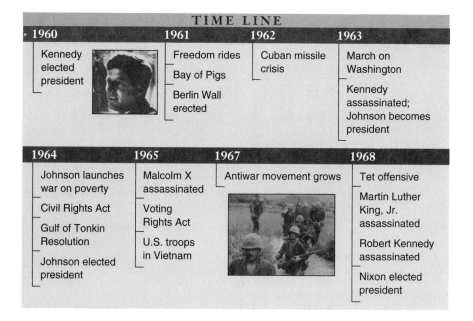

TIME LINE			
1960	**1961**	**1962**	**1963**
Kennedy elected president	Freedom rides Bay of Pigs Berlin Wall erected	Cuban missile crisis	March on Washington Kennedy assassinated; Johnson becomes president
1964	**1965**	**1967**	**1968**
Johnson launches war on poverty Civil Rights Act Gulf of Tonkin Resolution Johnson elected president	Malcolm X assassinated Voting Rights Act U.S. troops in Vietnam	Antiwar movement grows	Tet offensive Martin Luther King, Jr. assassinated Robert Kennedy assassinated Nixon elected president

most uncontested to Vice President Richard Nixon, who promised moderate reform. The Democrats, in the meantime, emerged from a spirited primary campaign united, somewhat uneasily, behind John Fitzgerald Kennedy, an attractive and articulate senator from Massachusetts who had narrowly missed being the party's vice presidential candidate in 1956.

John Kennedy was the son of the wealthy, powerful, and highly controversial Joseph P. Kennedy, former American ambassador to Britain. But while he had grown up in a world of ease and privilege, he became a spokesman for energy and sacrifice. He premised his campaign, he said, "on the single assumption that the American people are uneasy at the present drift in our national course." But his appealing public image was at least as important as his political positions in attracting popular support. He overcame doubts about his youth (he turned forty-three in 1960) and religion (he was Catholic) to win with a tiny plurality of the popular vote (49.9 percent to Nixon's 49.6 percent) and only a slightly more comfortable electoral majority (303 to 219).

Kennedy had campaigned promising a set of domestic reforms more ambitious than any since the New Deal, a program he described as the "New Frontier." But his thin popular mandate and a Congress dominated by a coalition of Republicans and conservative Democrats frustrated many

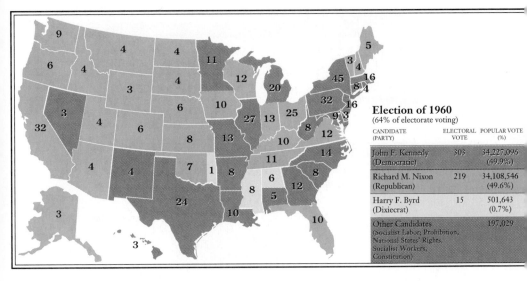

Election of 1960
(64% of electorate voting)

CANDIDATE (PARTY)	ELECTORAL VOTE	POPULAR VOTE (%)
John F. Kennedy (Democratic)	303	34,227,096 (49.9%)
Richard M. Nixon (Republican)	219	34,108,546 (49.6%)
Harry F. Byrd (Dixiecrat)	15	501,643 (0.7%)
Other Candidates (Socialist Labor, Prohibition, National States' Rights, Socialist Workers, Constitution)		197,029

of his hopes. Kennedy did manage to win approval of tariff reductions his administration had negotiated, and he began to build an ambitious legislative agenda that he hoped he might eventually see enacted—including a call for a significant tax cut to promote economic growth.

More than any other president of the century (except perhaps the two Roosevelts and, later, Ronald Reagan), Kennedy made his own personality an integral part of his presidency and a central focus of national attention. Nothing illustrated that more clearly than the popular reaction to the tragedy of November 22, 1963. Kennedy had traveled to Texas with his wife and Vice President Lyndon Johnson for a series of political appearances. While the presidential motorcade rode slowly through the streets of Dallas, shots rang out. Two bullets struck the president—one in the throat, the other in the head. He was sped to a nearby hospital, where minutes later he was pronounced dead. Lee Harvey Oswald, who appeared to be a confused and embittered Marxist, was arrested for the crime later that day, and then mysteriously murdered by a Dallas nightclub owner, Jack Ruby, two days later as he was being moved from one jail to another. Most Americans at the time accepted the conclusions of a federal commission, chaired by Chief Justice Earl Warren, appointed by President Johnson to investigate the assassination. The commission found that both Oswald and Ruby had acted alone, that there was no larger conspiracy. In later years, however, many Americans came to believe that the Warren Commission report had ignored evidence of a wider conspiracy behind the murders. Controversy over the truth about the assassination continues today.

JOHN KENNEDY The new president and his wife, Jacqueline, attend one of the five balls in Washington marking Kennedy's inauguration in 1961.

Lyndon Johnson

The Kennedy assassination was a national trauma—a defining event for almost everyone old enough to be aware of it. At the time, however, much of the nation took comfort in the personality and performance of Kennedy's successor in the White House, Lyndon Baines Johnson. Johnson was a native of the poor "hill country" of west Texas and had risen to become majority leader of the U.S. Senate by dint of extraordinary, even obsessive effort and ambition. Having failed to win the Democratic nomination for president in 1960, he surprised many who knew him by agreeing to accept the second position on the ticket with Kennedy. The events in Dallas thrust him into the White House.

Johnson's rough-edged, even crude personality could hardly have been more different from Kennedy's. But like Kennedy, Johnson was a man who believed in the active use of power. Between 1963 and 1966, he compiled the most impressive legislative record of any president since Franklin Roosevelt. He was aided by the tidal wave of emotion that followed the death of President Kennedy, which helped win support for many New Frontier proposals. But Johnson also constructed a remarkable reform program of his own, one that he ultimately labeled the "Great Society." And he won approval of much of it through the same sort of skillful lobbying in Congress that had made him an effective majority leader.

Johnson envisioned himself as a great "coalition builder." He wanted the support of everyone, and for a time he very nearly got it. His first year in office was, by necessity, dominated by the campaign for reelection. There was little doubt that he would win—particularly after the Republican Party fell under the sway of its right wing and nominated the conservative Senator Barry Goldwater of Arizona. In the November 1964 election, the president received a larger plurality, over 61 percent, than any candidate before or since. Goldwater managed to carry only his home state of Arizona and five states in the Deep South. Record Democratic majorities in both houses of Congress, many of whose members had been swept into office only because of the margin of Johnson's victory, ensured that the president would be able to fulfill many of his goals.

The Assault on Poverty

For the first time since the 1930s, the federal government took steps in the 1960s to create important new social welfare programs. The most important of these, perhaps, was Medicare: a program to provide federal aid to the elderly for medical expenses. Its enactment in 1965 came at the end of a bitter, twenty-year debate between those who believed in the concept of national health assistance and those who denounced it as "socialized medicine." But the program as it went into effect pacified many critics. For one thing, it avoided the stigma of "welfare" by making Medicare benefits available to all elderly Americans, regardless of need (just as Social Security had done with pensions). That created a large middle-class constituency for the program. The program also defused the opposition of the medical community by allowing doctors serving Medicare patients to practice privately and to charge their normal fees; Medicare simply shifted responsibility for paying those fees from the patient to the government. In 1966, Johnson steered to passage the Medicaid program, which extended federal medical assistance to welfare recipients and other indigent people of all ages.

Medicare and Medicaid were early steps in a much larger assault on poverty—one that Kennedy had been planning in the last months of his life and that Johnson launched only weeks after taking office. The center-piece of this "war on poverty," as Johnson called it, was the Office of Economic Opportunity (OEO), which created an array of new educational, employment, housing, and health-care programs. But the OEO was con-troversial from the start, in part because of its commitment to the idea of "Community Action."

Community Action was an effort to involve members of poor commu-nities themselves in the planning and administration of the programs de-signed to help them. The Community Action programs provided jobs for many poor people and gave them valuable experience in administrative and political work. Many men and women who went on to significant ca-reers in politics or community organizing, including many black and His-panic politicians, as well as many Indians, got their start in Community Action programs. But despite its achievements, the Community Action approach proved impossible to sustain, both because of administrative fail-ures and because the apparent excesses of a few agencies damaged the popular image of the Community Action programs, and indeed the war on poverty, as a whole.

The OEO spent nearly $3 billion during its first two years of exis-tence, and it helped reduce poverty in some areas. But it fell far short of eliminating poverty altogether. That was in part because of the weak-nesses of the programs themselves and in part because funding for them, inadequate from the beginning, dwindled as the years passed and a costly war in Southeast Asia became the nation's first priority.

Cities, Schools, and Immigration

Closely tied to the antipoverty program were federal efforts to promote the revitalization of decaying cities and to strengthen the nation's schools. The Housing Act of 1961 offered $4.9 billion in federal grants to cities for the preservation of open spaces, the development of mass-transit systems, and the subsidization of middle-income housing. In 1966, Johnson established a new cabinet agency, the Department of Housing and Urban Development (whose first secretary, Robert Weaver, was the first African American ever to serve in the cabinet). Johnson also inaugurated the Model Cities program, which offered federal subsidies for urban redevelopment pilot programs.

Kennedy had long fought for federal aid to public education, but he had failed to overcome two important obstacles: Many Americans feared that aid to education was the first step toward federal control of the schools, and Catholics insisted that federal assistance must extend to parochial as well as public schools. Johnson managed to circumvent both objections with the Elementary and Secondary Education Act of 1965 and a series of subsequent measures. The bills extended aid to both private and parochial schools and based the aid on the economic conditions of the students, not on the needs of the schools themselves. Total federal expenditures for education and technical training rose from $5 billion to $12 billion between 1964 and 1967.

The Johnson administration also supported the Immigration Act of 1965, one of the most important pieces of legislation of the 1960s. The law maintained a strict limit on the number of newcomers admitted to the country each year (170,000), but it eliminated the "national origins" system established in the 1920s, which gave preference to immigrants from northern Europe over those from other parts of the world. It continued to restrict immigration from some parts of Latin America, but it allowed people from all parts of Europe, Asia, and Africa to enter the United States on an equal basis. By the early 1970s, the character of American immigration had changed, with members of new national groups—and particularly large groups of Asians—entering the United States and changing the character of the American population.

Legacies of the Great Society

Taken together, the Great Society reforms meant a significant increase in federal spending. For a time, rising tax revenues from the growing economy nearly compensated for the new expenditures. In 1964, Johnson managed to win passage of the $11.5 billion tax cut that Kennedy had first proposed in 1962. The cut increased the federal deficit, but substantial economic growth over the next several years made up for much of the revenue initially lost. As Great Society programs began to multiply, however, and particularly as they began to compete with the escalating costs of America's military ventures, the federal budget rapidly outpaced increases in revenues. In 1961, the federal government had spent $94.4 billion. By 1970, that sum had risen to $196.6 billion.

The high costs of the Great Society programs, the failures of many of them, and the inability of the government to find the revenues to pay for them contributed to a growing disillusionment in later years with the idea of federal efforts to solve social problems. By the 1980s, many Americans had become convinced that the Great Society experiments had not worked and that, indeed, government programs to solve social problems could not work. But the Great Society, despite many failures, was also responsible for some significant achievements. It significantly reduced hunger in America. It made medical care available to millions of elderly and poor people who would otherwise have had great difficulty affording it. It contributed to the greatest reduction in poverty in American history. In 1959, according to the most widely accepted estimates, 21 percent of the American people lived below the officially established poverty line. By 1969, only 12 percent remained below that line. The improvements affected blacks and whites in about the same proportion: 56 percent of the black population had lived in poverty in 1959, while only 32 percent did so ten years later—a 42 percent reduction; 18 percent of all whites had been poor in 1959, but only 10 percent were poor a decade later—a 44 percent reduction. Much of that progress was a result of economic growth, but some of it was a result of Great Society programs.

THE BATTLE FOR RACIAL EQUALITY

The nation's most important domestic initiative in the 1960s was the effort to provide justice and equality to African Americans. It was the most difficult commitment, the one that produced the severest strains on American society. But it was one that could not be avoided. African Americans were themselves ensuring that the nation would have to deal with the problem of race.

Expanding Protests

John Kennedy had long been sympathetic to the cause of racial justice, but he was hardly a committed crusader. Like presidents before him, he feared alienating southern Democratic voters and powerful southern Democrats in Congress. His administration hoped to contain the racial problem by expanding enforcement of existing laws and supporting litigation to overturn existing segregation statutes.

But the pressure for change was growing uncontainable even before Kennedy took office. In February 1960, black college students in Greensboro, North Carolina, staged a sit-in at a segregated Woolworth's lunch counter; and in the following months, such demonstrations spread throughout the South, forcing many merchants to integrate their facilities. In the fall of 1960, some of those who had participated in the sit-ins formed the Student Nonviolent Coordinating Committee (SNCC)—a student branch of Martin Luther King, Jr.'s Southern Christian Leadership Council; the SNCC worked to keep the spirit of resistance alive.

In 1961, an interracial group of students, working with the Congress of Racial Equality (CORE), began what they called "freedom rides." Traveling by bus throughout the South, they tried to force the desegregation of bus stations. They were met in some places with such savage violence on the part of whites that the president finally dispatched federal marshals to help keep the peace and ordered the integration of all bus and train stations.

Events in the Deep South in 1963 helped bring the growing movement to something of a climax. In April, Martin Luther King, Jr., helped launch a series of nonviolent demonstrations in Birmingham, Alabama, a city unsurpassed in the strength of its commitment to segregation. Police Commissioner Eugene "Bull" Connor personally supervised a brutal effort to break up the peaceful marches, arresting hundreds of demonstrators and using attack dogs, tear gas, electric cattle prods, and fire hoses—at times even against small children—in full view of television cameras. Two months later, Governor George Wallace stood in the doorway of a building at the University of Alabama to prevent the court-ordered enrollment of several black students. Only after the arrival of federal marshals did he give way. The same night, NAACP official Medgar Evers was murdered in Mississippi.

A National Commitment

The events in Alabama and Mississippi were a warning to the president that he could no longer avoid the issue of race. In an important television address the night of the University of Alabama confrontation, Kennedy spoke eloquently of the "moral issue" facing the nation. Days later, he introduced a series of new legislative proposals prohibiting segregation in "public accommodations" (stores, restaurants, theaters, hotels), barring discrimination in employment, and increasing the power of the government to file suits on behalf of school integration.

THE MARCH ON WASHINGTON, 1963 Martin Luther King, Jr., waves to the vast crowd spreading out from the Lincoln Memorial shortly after delivering his famous "I Have a Dream" speech—the centerpiece of the March on Washington. Initially envisioned as a broad and militant protest against discrimination, it became in the end a moderate, interracial demonstration of support for the civil rights bill President Kennedy had recently proposed to Congress, which passed in 1964.

To generate support for the legislation, and to dramatize the power of the growing movement, more than 200,000 demonstrators marched down the Mall in Washington, D.C., in August 1963 and gathered before the Lincoln Memorial for the largest civil rights demonstration in the nation's history. Martin Luther King, Jr., in one of the greatest speeches of his distinguished oratorical career, aroused the crowd with a litany of images prefaced again and again by the phrase "I have a dream."

The assassination of President Kennedy three months later gave new impetus to the battle for civil rights legislation. The ambitious measure that Kennedy had proposed in June 1963 was stalled in the Senate after having passed through the House of Representatives with relative ease. Early in 1964, after Johnson had applied both public and private pressure, supporters of the measure finally mustered the two-thirds majority necessary to close debate and end a filibuster by southern senators; and the Senate passed the most comprehensive civil rights bill in the history of the nation.

The Battle for Voting Rights

Having won a significant victory in one area, the civil rights movement shifted its focus to another: voting rights. During the summer of 1964, thousands of civil rights workers, black and white, northern and southern, spread out through the South, but primarily into Mississippi, to work on behalf of black voter registration and participation. The campaign was known as "Freedom Summer," and it produced a violent response from some southern whites. Three of the first freedom workers to arrive in the South—two whites, Andrew Goodman and Michael Schwerner, and one black, James Chaney—were murdered. Local law enforcement officials were involved in the crime.

The "Freedom Summer" also produced the Mississippi Freedom Democratic Party (MFDP), an integrated alternative to the regular state party organization. Under the leadership of Fannie Lou Hamer and others, the MFDP challenged the regular party's right to its seats at the Democratic National Convention that summer. President Johnson, with King's help, managed to broker a compromise by which members of the MFDP could be seated as observers, with promises of party reforms later on, while the regular party retained its official standing. Many MFDP members rejected the agreement and left the convention embittered.

A year later, in March 1965, King helped organize a major demonstration in Selma, Alabama, to press the demand for the right of blacks to register to vote. Selma sheriff Jim Clark led local police in a brutal attack on the demonstrators—which, as in Birmingham, was televised nationally. Two northern whites participating in the Selma march were murdered in the course of the effort there. The widespread national outrage that followed the events in Alabama helped push Lyndon Johnson to propose and win passage of the Civil Rights Act of 1965, better known as the Voting Rights Act, which provided federal protection to African Americans attempting to exercise their right to vote. But important as such gains were, they failed to satisfy the rapidly rising expectations of American blacks as the focus of the movement began to move from political to economic issues.

The Changing Movement

For decades, the nation's African-American population had been undergoing a major demographic shift. By 1966, 69 percent of American blacks were living in metropolitan areas and 45 percent were living outside the South. Although the economic condition of most Americans was improving, in many poor urban black communities things were getting significantly worse. More than half of all nonwhite Americans lived in poverty at the beginning of the 1960s.

By the mid-1960s, therefore, the issue of race was moving out of the South and into the rest of the nation. The legal battle for racial justice was moving beyond the issue of formal, legal segregation to an attack on the informal practices that often sustained discrimination. That carried the fight into northern cities, which had no Jim Crow laws but much segregation. Many African-American leaders (and their white supporters) soon began demanding that the battle against job discrimination move to a new level. They argued that the only way for employers to prove that they were not discriminating against African Americans was for them to demonstrate that they were hiring minorities. If necessary, they should adopt positive measures to recruit minorities. Lyndon Johnson gave his support to the concept of "affirmative action" in 1965. Over the next decade, affirmative action guidelines gradually extended to virtually all institutions doing business with or receiving funds from the federal government (including schools and universities)—and to many others as well.

A symbol of the movement's new direction, and of the problems it would cause, was a major campaign in the summer of 1966 in Chicago, in which King played a prominent role. Organizers of the Chicago campaign hoped to direct national attention to housing and employment discrimination in northern industrial cities in much the same way that similar campaigns had exposed legal racism in the South. But the Chicago campaign evoked vicious and at times violent opposition from white residents of that city and failed to attract wide attention or support in the way events in the South had done.

Urban Violence

Well before the Chicago campaign, the problem of urban poverty had thrust itself into national prominence when riots broke out in black neighborhoods in major cities. There were a few scattered disturbances in the summer of 1964, most notably in New York City's Harlem. The most serious race riot since the end of World War II occurred the following summer in the Watts section of Los Angeles. In the midst of a traffic arrest, a white police officer struck a protesting black bystander with his club. The incident triggered a storm of anger and a week of violence. Thirty-four people died during the uprising, which was eventually quelled by the National Guard. In the summer of 1966, there were forty-three additional outbreaks, the most serious of them in Chicago and Cleveland. And in the summer of 1967, there were eight major riots, including the largest of them all—a racial clash in Detroit in which forty-three people died.

Televised reports of the violence alarmed millions of Americans and created both a new sense of urgency and a growing sense of doubt among some whites who had embraced the cause of racial justice only a few years before. A special Commission on Civil Disorders, created by the president in response to the riots, issued a celebrated report in the spring of 1968 recommending massive spending to eliminate the abysmal conditions of the ghettoes. To many white Americans, however, the lesson of the riots was the need for stern measures to stop violence and lawlessness.

Black Power

Disillusioned with the ideal of peaceful change through cooperation with whites, an increasing number of African Americans were turning to a new approach to the racial issue: the philosophy of "black power." Black power meant many different things. But in all its forms, it suggested a shift away from the goal of assimilation and toward increased awareness of racial distinctiveness.

Perhaps the most enduring impact of the black-power ideology was a social and psychological one: instilling racial pride in African Americans. But black power took political forms as well, and it created a deep schism within the civil rights movement. Traditional black organizations that emphasized cooperation with sympathetic whites—groups such as the NAACP, the Urban League, and King's Southern Christian Leadership Conference—now faced competition from more radical groups. The Student Nonviolent Coordinating Committee and the Congress of Racial Equality had both begun as relatively moderate, interracial organizations. By the mid-1960s, however, these and other groups were calling for more radical and occasionally even violent action against the racism of white society and were openly rejecting the approaches of older, more established black leaders.

The most radical expressions of the black-power idea came from such revolutionary organizations as the Black Panthers, based in Oakland, California, and the separatist group, the Nation of Islam, which denounced whites as "devils" and appealed to blacks to embrace the Islamic faith and work for complete racial separation. The most celebrated of the Black Muslims, as whites often termed them, was Malcolm Little, who had adopted the name Malcolm X ("X" to denote his lost African surname). He died in 1965 when black gunmen, presumably under orders from rivals within the Nation of Islam, assassinated him. But he remained a major figure in many black communities long after his death—as important to and revered by as many African Americans as Martin Luther King, Jr.

"FLEXIBLE RESPONSE" AND THE COLD WAR

In international affairs as much as in domestic reform, the optimistic liberalism of the Kennedy and Johnson administrations dictated a more active and aggressive approach to dealing with the nation's problems than that of the 1950s.

Diversifying Foreign Policy

The Kennedy administration entered office convinced that the United States needed to be able to counter communist aggression in more flexible ways than the atomic-weapons-oriented defense strategy of the Eisenhower years permitted. In particular, Kennedy was unsatisfied with the nation's ability to meet communist threats in "emerging areas" of the Third World—the areas in which, Kennedy believed, the real struggle against communism would be waged in the future. He gave enthusiastic support to the expansion of the Special Forces (or "Green Berets," as they were soon known)—soldiers trained specifically to fight guerrilla conflicts and other limited wars.

Kennedy also favored expanding American influence through peaceful means. To repair the badly deteriorating relationship with Latin America, he proposed an "Alliance for Progress": a series of projects for peaceful development and stabilization of the nations of that region. Kennedy also inaugurated the Agency for International Development (AID) to coordinate foreign aid. And he established what became one of his most popular innovations: the Peace Corps, which sent young American volunteers abroad to work in developing areas.

Among the first foreign policy ventures of the Kennedy administration was a disastrous assault on the Castro government in Cuba. The Eisenhower administration had started the project; and by the time Kennedy took office, the CIA had been working for months to train a small army of anti-Castro Cuban exiles in Central America. On April 17, 1961, with the approval of the new president, 2,000 of the armed exiles landed at the Bay of Pigs in Cuba, expecting first American air support and then a spontaneous uprising by the Cuban people on their behalf. They received neither. At the last minute, as it became clear that things

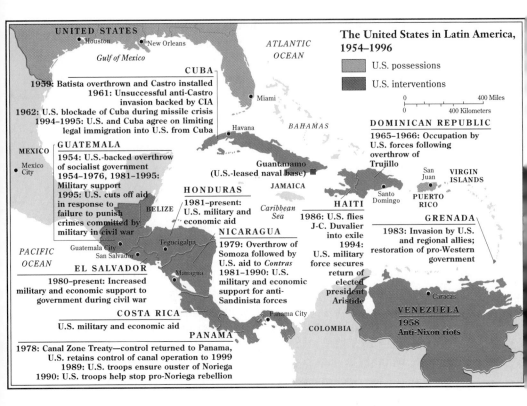

The United States in Latin America, 1954–1996

U.S. possessions
U.S. interventions

0   400 Miles
0   400 Kilometers

UNITED STATES
Houston   New Orleans

Gulf of Mexico

ATLANTIC OCEAN

Miami

CUBA
1959: Batista overthrown and Castro installed
1961: Unsuccessful anti-Castro invasion backed by CIA
1962: U.S. blockade of Cuba during missile crisis
1994–1995: U.S. and Cuba agree on limiting legal immigration into U.S. from Cuba

Havana

BAHAMAS

MEXICO
Mexico City

GUATEMALA
1954: U.S.-backed overthrow of socialist government
1954–1976, 1981–1995: Military support
1995: U.S. cuts off aid in response to failure to punish crimes committed by military in civil war

Guantánamo (U.S.-leased naval base)

JAMAICA

Caribbean Sea

DOMINICAN REPUBLIC
1965–1966: Occupation by U.S. forces following overthrow of Trujillo

San Juan   VIRGIN ISLANDS

Santo Domingo   PUERTO RICO

HAITI
1986: U.S. flies J-C. Duvalier into exile
1994: U.S. military force secures return of elected president Aristide

GRENADA
1983: Invasion by U.S. and regional allies; restoration of pro-Western government

HONDURAS
1981–present: U.S. military and economic aid

BELIZE

Tegucigalpa

PACIFIC OCEAN

Guatemala City
San Salvador

EL SALVADOR
1980–present: Increased military and economic support to government during civil war

Managua

NICARAGUA
1979: Overthrow of Somoza followed by U.S. aid to Contras
1981–1990: U.S. military and economic support for anti-Sandinista forces

COSTA RICA
U.S. military and economic aid

Panama City

PANAMA
1978: Canal Zone Treaty—control returned to Panama, U.S. retains control of canal operation to 1999
1989: U.S. troops ensure ouster of Noriega
1990: U.S. troops help stop pro-Noriega rebellion

COLOMBIA

Caracas

VENEZUELA
1958 Anti-Nixon riots

were going badly, Kennedy withdrew the air support, fearful of involving the United States too directly in the invasion. The expected uprising did not occur. Instead, well-armed Castro forces easily crushed the invaders, and within two days the entire mission had collapsed.

Confrontations with the Soviet Union

In the grim aftermath of the Bay of Pigs, Kennedy traveled to Vienna in June 1961 for his first meeting with Soviet Premier Nikita Khrushchev. Their frosty exchange of views did little to reduce tensions between the two nations—nor did Khrushchev's veiled threat of war unless the United States ceased to support a noncommunist West Berlin in the heart of East Germany.

Khrushchev was particularly unhappy about the mass exodus of residents of East Germany to the West through the easily traversed border in the center of Berlin. But he ultimately found a method short of war to stop it. Before dawn on August 13, 1961, the East German government, complying with directives from Moscow, constructed a wall between East and West Berlin. Guards fired on those who continued to try to escape. For nearly thirty years, the Berlin Wall served as the most potent physical symbol of the conflict between the communist and noncommunist worlds.

The rising tensions culminated the following October in the most dangerous and dramatic crisis of the Cold War. During the summer of 1962, American intelligence agencies had become aware of the arrival of a new wave of Soviet technicians and equipment in Cuba and of military construction in progress. On October 14, aerial reconnaissance photos produced clear evidence that the Soviets were constructing sites on the island for offensive nuclear weapons. To the Soviets, placing missiles in Cuba probably seemed a reasonable—and relatively inexpensive—way to counter the presence of American missiles in Turkey (and a way to deter any future American invasion of Cuba). But to Kennedy and most other Americans, the missile sites represented an act of aggression by the Soviets toward the United States. Almost immediately, the president decided that the weapons could not be allowed to remain. On October 22, he ordered a naval and air blockade around Cuba, a "quarantine" against all offensive weapons. Preparations were under way for an American air attack on the missile sites when, late in the evening of October 26, Kennedy received a message from Khrushchev implying that the Soviet Union would remove the missile bases in exchange for an American pledge not to invade Cuba. Ignoring other, tougher Soviet messages, the president agreed. The crisis was over.

Johnson and the World

Lyndon Johnson entered the presidency lacking even John Kennedy's limited prior experience with international affairs. He was eager, therefore, not only to continue the policies of his predecessor but to prove quickly that he too was a strong and forceful leader.

An internal rebellion in the Dominican Republic gave him an early opportunity to do so. A 1961 assassination had toppled the repressive dictatorship of General Rafael Trujillo, and for the next four years various factions in the country had struggled for dominance. In the spring of 1965, a conservative military regime began to collapse in the face of a revolt by a broad range of groups on behalf of the left-wing nationalist Juan Bosch. Arguing (without any evidence) that Bosch planned to establish a pro-Castro, communist regime, Johnson dispatched 30,000 American troops to quell the disorder. Only after a conservative candidate defeated Bosch in a 1966 election were the forces withdrawn.

From Johnson's first moments in office, however, his foreign policy was almost totally dominated by the bitter civil war in Vietnam and by the expanding involvement of the United States there.

VIETNAM

George Kennan, who helped devise the containment doctrine in the name of which America went to war in Vietnam, once called the conflict "the most disastrous of all America's undertakings over the whole 200 years of its history." In retrospect, few would now wholly disagree. Yet at first, the conflict in Vietnam seemed simply one more Third World struggle on the periphery of the Cold War.

America and Diem

Having thrown its support to the new leader of South Vietnam, Ngo Dinh Diem, in the aftermath of the Geneva accords, and having supported Diem in his refusal to hold the elections in 1956 that the accords had required, the United States found itself drawn steadily deeper into the unstable politics of this fractious new nation.

Although Diem was an aristocratic Catholic from central Vietnam, an outsider in the south, he was also a nationalist, uncontaminated by collaboration with the French. And he was, for a time, apparently successful. With the help of the American CIA, Diem waged an effective campaign against some of the powerful religious sects and the South Vietnamese mafia, which had challenged the authority of the central government. As a result, the United States came to regard Diem as a powerful and impressive alternative to Ho Chi Minh. America poured military and economic aid into South Vietnam. By 1956, it was the second-largest recipient of American military aid in the world, after Korea.

Diem's early successes in suppressing the sects in Vietnam led him in 1959 to begin a similar campaign to eliminate the supporters of Ho Chi Minh, the Vietminh, who had stayed behind in the south after the partition. That campaign persuaded Ho to resume the armed struggle for national unification. In 1959, the Vietminh cadres in the south created the National Liberation Front (NLF), known to many Americans as the Viet Cong—an organization closely allied with the North Vietnamese government. In 1960, under orders from Hanoi, and with both material and manpower support from North Vietnam, the NLF began military operations in

CHINA

NORTH VIETNAM

Lao Cai

Than Uyen

Yen Bay

Dienbienphu

Hanoi ✪

Haiphong

Red River Delta

BURMA

Gulf of Tonkin

Hainan

Pak Seng

PLAIN OF JARS

Luang Prabang

Ban Ban

Vang Vieng

Vinh

L A O S

Vientiane ✪

Udon Thani

Dong Hoi

Vinh Linh

Phanom

DMZ (Demilitarized Zone)

Mekong R.

Khesanh

Hue

QUANG TRI PROVINCE

Phu Bai

THAILAND

Da Nang

Hoi An

Tamky

South China Sea

Takhli

Don Muang

Lop Buri

Ratchasima

Udon Ratchathani

Chulai

My Lai

Quang Ngai

Dak To

Kontum

PLATEAU OF KONTUM

Ankhe

Pleiku

Quinhon

FRIENDSHIP HIGHWAY

Bangkok ✪

Angkor Wat

Battambang

Tonle Sap

CAMBODIA

PLATEAU OF DARLAC

Ban Me Thout

Sattahip

Kompong Chom

Da Lat

Nhatrang

Camranh Bay

Phanrang

Gulf of Thailand

Phnom Penh ✪

Prey Veng

Bo Duc

1970: U.S. and South Vietnam troops entered Viet Cong strongholds inside Cambodia

Tay Ninh

SOUTH VIETNAM

Ben Cat

Bienhua

Sihanoukville

Tan Son Nhut Airbase

Saigon ✪

Rach Gia

Cantho

Vung Tau

MEKONG DELTA

Quan Long

CA MAU PENINSULA

Con Son

The War in Vietnam and Indochina, 1964–1975

☐ U.S. bases

⇦ U.S. and South Vietnam invasion of Cambodia

➤ Ho Chi Minh Trail (communist supply route)

0   100 Miles

0   100 Kilometers

the south. This marked the beginning of the Second Indochina War. (The first was the struggle against the French, which had ended in 1954.)

By 1961, NLF forces had established effective control over many areas of the countryside. Diem was also by now losing the support of many other groups in South Vietnam, and he was even losing support within his own military. In 1963, the Diem regime precipitated a major crisis by trying to discipline and repress the South Vietnamese Buddhists in an effort to make Catholicism the dominant religion of the country. The Buddhists began to stage enormous antigovernment demonstrations, during which several monks doused themselves with gasoline, sat cross-legged in the streets of downtown Saigon, and set themselves on fire—in view of photographers and television cameras.

American officials pressured Diem to reform his now tottering government, but the president made no significant concessions. As a result, in the fall of 1963, Kennedy gave his tacit approval to a plot by a group of South Vietnamese generals to topple Diem. In early November 1963, the generals staged the coup, assassinated Diem and his brother and principal adviser, Ngo Dinh Nhu (killings the United States had not wanted or expected), and established the first of a series of new governments, which were, for over three years, even less stable than the one they had overthrown. A few weeks after the coup, John Kennedy too was dead.

From Aid to Intervention

Lyndon Johnson, therefore, inherited what was already a substantial American commitment to the survival of an anticommunist South Vietnam. During his first months in office, he expanded the American involvement in Vietnam only slightly, sending an additional 5,000 military advisers there and preparing to send 5,000 more. Then, early in August 1964, the president announced that American destroyers on patrol in international waters in the Gulf of Tonkin had been attacked by North Vietnamese torpedo boats. Later information raised serious doubts as to whether the administration reported the attacks accurately. At the time, however, virtually no one questioned Johnson's portrayal of the incident as a serious act of aggression or his insistence that the United States must respond. By a vote of 416 to 0 in the House and 88 to 2 in the Senate, Congress hurriedly passed the Gulf of Tonkin Resolution, which authorized the president to "take all necessary measures" to protect American forces and "prevent further aggression" in Southeast Asia. The resolution became, in Johnson's view at least, an open-ended legal authorization for escalation of the conflict.

ON PATROL IN VIETNAM, JUNE 1965 Several weeks before President Johnson
announced that American ground troops would enter the Vietnam War, United
States soldiers were already engaged in combat. These marines, patrolling the
area around the American base at Da Nang, were ambushed by communist
guerrillas moments after this photograph was taken. One marine was killed and
three were wounded.

With the South Vietnamese leadership still in disarray and the communist military pressure on the south growing stronger, more and more of
the burden of opposition to the Viet Cong fell on the United States. In
February 1965, after communist forces attacked an American military base
at Pleiku, Johnson ordered American bombings of the north, in an attempt
to destroy the depots and transportation lines responsible for the flow of
North Vietnamese soldiers and supplies into South Vietnam. The bombing
continued intermittently until 1972. A month later, in March 1965, two
battalions of American marines landed at Da Nang in South Vietnam.
There were now more than 100,000 American troops in Vietnam.

Four months later, the president finally admitted that the character of
the war had changed. American soldiers would now, he announced, begin

playing an active combat role in the conflict. By the end of the year, there were more than 180,000 American combat troops in Vietnam; in 1966, that number doubled; and by the end of 1967, there were over 500,000 American soldiers there. In the meantime, the air war had intensified until the tonnage of bombs dropped ultimately exceeded that in all theaters during World War II. And American casualties were mounting. By the spring of 1966, more than 4,000 Americans had been killed.

The Quagmire

For more than seven years, American combat forces remained bogged down in a war that the United States was never able either to win or fully to understand. Combating a foe whose strength lay less in weaponry than in its infiltration of the population, the United States responded with heavy-handed technological warfare designed for conventional battles against conventional armies.

Central to the American war effort was the strategy known to the military as "attrition," one premised on the belief that the United States could inflict more damage on the enemy than the enemy could absorb. But the attrition strategy failed because the North Vietnamese were willing to commit many more soldiers and resources to the conflict than the United States had expected.

It failed, too, because the United States was wrong in expecting its bombing of the north to eliminate the communists' war-making capacity. American bombers attacked almost every identifiable strategic target in North Vietnam as well as jungle areas in Cambodia and Laos thought to shelter the "Ho Chi Minh Trail," by which Hanoi sent troops and supplies into the south. But North Vietnam was not a modern industrial society, and it had relatively few of the sort of targets against which bombing is effective. The North Vietnamese responded to the bombing with great ingenuity: creating a network of underground tunnels, shops, and factories; securing substantial aid from the Soviet Union and China; and continually moving the Ho Chi Minh Trail to make it elusive to American bombers. Far from breaking the north's resolve, the bombing seemed actually to strengthen popular commitment to the war.

Another important part of the American strategy was the "pacification" program, whose purpose was to push the Viet Cong from particular regions and then "pacify" those regions by winning the "hearts and minds" of the people. Routing the Viet Cong was often possible, but the subsequent pacification was more difficult. Gradually, the pacification program gave way to the more heavy-handed relocation strategy, through which American troops uprooted villagers from their homes, sent them fleeing to refugee camps or into the cities (producing by 1967 more than 3 million refugees), and then destroyed the vacated villages and surrounding countryside.

As the war dragged on and victory remained elusive, some American officers and officials began to urge the president to expand the military efforts. But the Johnson administration resisted—in part because it was beginning to encounter obstacles and frustrations at home.

The War at Home

Few Americans, and even fewer influential ones, had protested the American involvement in Vietnam as late as the end of 1965. But as the war dragged on inconclusively, political support for it began to erode.

By the end of 1967, American students opposed to the war had become a significant political force. Enormous peace marches in New York, Washington, D.C., and other cities drew broad public attention to the antiwar movement. In the meantime, a growing number of journalists, particularly reporters who had spent time in Vietnam, helped sustain the movement with their frank revelations about the brutality and apparent futility of the war.

The growing chorus of popular protest helped stimulate opposition to the war from within the government. Senator J. William Fulbright of Arkansas, chairman of the powerful Senate Foreign Relations Committee, turned against the war and in January 1966 began to stage highly publicized and occasionally televised congressional hearings to air criticisms of it. Other members of Congress joined Fulbright in opposing Johnson's policies—including, in 1967, Robert F. Kennedy, brother of the slain president, now a senator from New York. Even within the administration, the consensus seemed to be crumbling. Robert McNamara, who had done much to help extend the American involvement in Vietnam, quietly left the government, disillusioned, in 1968. His successor as secretary of defense, Clark Clifford, became a quiet but powerful voice within the administration on behalf of a cautious scaling down of the commitment.

In the meantime, the American economy was beginning to suffer. Johnson's commitment to fighting the war while continuing his Great Society reforms helped cause a rise in inflation, from the 2 percent level it had occupied through most of the early 1960s to 3 percent in 1967, 4 percent in 1968, and 6 percent in 1969. In August 1967, Johnson asked Congress for a

D E B A T I N G　　T H E　　P A S T

The Vietnam Commitment

he debate over why the United States became involved in the conflict in Vietnam (which is only one of many debates about the meaning of the war) has centered on two different, if related, questions. One is an effort to assess the broad objectives Americans believed they were pursuing in Vietnam. The other is an effort to explain how and why policymakers made the specific decisions that led the United States to a military commitment in Indochina.

Scholars and writers such as Norman Podhoretz, Guenter Lewy, and R. B. Smith, echoing elements of the official government explanation of American intervention in the war in the 1960s, have argued that the communist aggression in Vietnam was part of a Chinese and Soviet design to spread revolution throughout Asia. America, therefore, was not only protecting Vietnam, although that was an important part of its mission; it was also defending the rest of Asia, which would soon be threatened by communism if Vietnam fell. The intervention in Vietnam was a rational and even necessary expression of America's legitimate security interests and its belief in democracy.

Most scholars, however, have been more skeptical. Historians on the left argue that America's intervention in Vietnam was a form of imperialism—part of a larger effort by the United States after World War II to impose a particular political and economic order on the world. "The Vietnam War," Gabriel Kolko wrote in 1985, "was for the United States the culmination of its frustrating postwar effort to merge its arms and politics to halt and reverse the emergence of states and social systems opposed to the international order Washington sought to establish." Others argued that the United States fought in Vietnam to serve the American economic interests that had a stake in the region or in the arms production the war stimulated. More moderate critics blame the Vietnam intervention on the myopia of a foreign policy elite unwilling to question its own unreflective commitment to containing communism everywhere and unable to distinguish between international aggression and domestic insurgency.

Those who have looked less at the nation's broad objectives than at the workings of the policymaking process have also produced competing explanations. David Halberstam's *The Best and the Brightest* (1972) argued that

> policymakers deluded themselves into thinking they could achieve their goals in Vietnam by ignoring, suppressing, or dismissing information that should have suggested that they were wrong; because of arrogance or ideological rigidity, they simply refused to consider that victory was beyond their grasp.

Larry Berman, writing in 1982, offered a somewhat different view. Neither Johnson nor his advisers were unaware of the obstacles to success in Vietnam. Almost everyone suspected that victory would be difficult, even impossible, to attain. The president was not misled or misinformed. But Johnson committed troops to the war anyway, because he feared that allowing Vietnam to fall would ruin him politically and destroy his hopes for building his "Great Society" at home. Leslie Gelb and Richard Betts made a related argument in 1979. Vietnam, they claimed, was the logical, perhaps inevitable result of a political and bureaucratic order shaped by the ideology of the Cold War. However costly the intervention in Vietnam, policymakers concluded, the costs of not intervening and allowing South Vietnam to fall always seemed higher. The war escalated in the 1960s not because American aims changed but because the situation in Vietnam deteriorated to the point where nothing short of intervention would prevent defeat. Only when the national and international political situation itself shifted in the late 1960s and early 1970s—only when it became clear that the political costs of staying in Vietnam were higher than the political costs of getting out—was it possible for the United States to begin disengaging.

tax increase to avoid even more ruinous inflation. In return, congressional conservatives demanded and received a $6 billion reduction in the funding for Great Society programs.

THE TRAUMAS OF 1968

By the end of 1967, the twin crises of the war in Vietnam and the deteriorating racial situation at home had produced great social and political tensions. In the course of 1968, those tensions seemed suddenly to burst to the surface and threaten national chaos.

The Tet Offensive

On January 31, 1968, the first day of the Vietnamese New Year (Tet), communist forces launched an enormous, concerted attack on American strongholds throughout South Vietnam. A few cities, most notably Hue, fell temporarily to the communists. Others suffered major disruptions. But what made the Tet offensive so shocking to the American people, who saw vivid reports of it on television, was the sight of communist forces in the heart of Saigon, setting off bombs, shooting down South Vietnamese officials and troops, and holding down fortified areas (including, briefly, the grounds of the American embassy). The Tet offensive also suggested to the American public something of the brutality of the fighting in Vietnam. In the midst of the fighting, television cameras recorded the sight of a South Vietnamese officer shooting a captured and defenseless young Viet Cong soldier in the head in the streets of Saigon.

American forces soon dislodged the Viet Cong from most of the positions they had seized, and the Tet offensive inflicted enormous casualties on the communists. Indeed, the Tet defeats permanently depleted the ranks of the NLF and forced North Vietnamese troops to take on a much larger share of the subsequent fighting. But all that had little impact on American opinion. Tet may have been a military victory for the United States, but it was a political defeat for the administration.

In the following weeks, opposition to the war grew substantially. Leading newspapers and magazines, television commentators, and mainstream politicians began taking public stands in favor of de-escalation of the conflict. Within weeks of the Tet offensive, public opposition to the war had almost doubled. And Johnson's personal popularity rating had slid to 35 percent, the lowest of any president since Harry Truman.

The Political Challenge

Beginning in the summer of 1967, dissident Democrats tried to mobilize support behind an antiwar candidate who would challenge Lyndon Johnson in the 1968 primaries. When Robert Kennedy turned them down, they recruited Senator Eugene McCarthy of Minnesota. A brilliantly orchestrated campaign by young volunteers in the New Hampshire primary produced a startling showing by McCarthy in March; he nearly defeated the president.

A few days later, Robert Kennedy entered the campaign, embittering many McCarthy supporters but bringing his own substantial strength among blacks, poor people, and workers to the antiwar cause. Polls showed the president trailing badly in the next scheduled primary, in Wisconsin. On March 31, 1968, Johnson went on television to announce a limited halt in the bombing of North Vietnam—his first major concession to the antiwar forces—and, much more surprising, his withdrawal from the presidential contest.

Robert Kennedy quickly established himself as the champion of the Democratic primaries, winning one election after another. In the meantime, however, Vice President Hubert Humphrey, with the support of

JOHNSON AND HUMPHREY, MARCH 27, 1968 Four days before announcing he would not run for reelection, a grim and tired Lyndon Johnson, accompanied by Vice President Hubert Humphrey, receives a briefing on the military situation in Vietnam.

President Johnson, entered the contest and began to attract the support of party leaders and of the many delegations that were selected not by popular primaries but by state party organizations. He soon appeared to be the front-runner in the race.

The King Assassination

On April 4, Martin Luther King, Jr., who had traveled to Memphis, Tennessee, to lend his support to striking black sanitation workers in the city, was shot and killed while standing on the balcony of his motel. The assassin, James Earl Ray, who was captured two months later in London, had no apparent motive. Subsequent evidence suggested that he had been hired by others to do the killing, but he himself never revealed the identity of his employers.

King's tragic death produced a great outpouring of grief. Among African Americans, it also produced anger. In the days after the assassination, major riots broke out in more than sixty American cities. Forty-three people died.

The Kennedy Assassination and Chicago

Late in the night of June 6, Robert Kennedy appeared in the ballroom of a Los Angeles hotel to acknowledge his victory in that day's California primary. As he left the ballroom after his victory statement, Sirhan Sirhan, a young Palestinian apparently enraged by pro-Israeli remarks Kennedy had recently made, emerged from a crowd and shot him in the head. Early the next morning, Kennedy died. The shock of this second tragedy in two months cast a pall over the remainder of the presidential campaign.

When the Democrats finally gathered in Chicago in August, for a convention in which Hubert Humphrey was now the only real contender, even the most optimistic observers were predicting turbulence. Inside the hall, delegates bitterly debated an antiwar plank in the party platform that both Kennedy and McCarthy supporters favored. Miles away, in a downtown park, thousands of antiwar protesters were staging demonstrations. On the third night of the convention, as the delegates were beginning their balloting on the now virtually inevitable nomination of Hubert Humphrey, demonstrators and police clashed in a bloody riot in the streets of Chicago. Hundreds of protesters were injured as police attempted to disperse them with tear gas and billy clubs. Aware that the violence was being televised to the nation, the demonstrators taunted the authorities with the chant, "The whole world is watching!" And Hubert Humphrey, who had spent years dreaming of becoming his party's candidate for president, received a nomination that night which appeared at the time to be almost worthless.

The Conservative Response

The turbulent events of 1968 persuaded some observers that American society was in the throes of revolutionary change. In fact, however, the response of most Americans to the turmoil was a conservative one.

The most visible sign of the conservative backlash was the surprising success of the campaign of George Wallace for the presidency. Wallace had established himself in 1963 as one of the leading spokesmen for the defense of segregation when, as governor of Alabama, he had attempted to block the admission of black students to the University of Alabama. In 1968, he became a third-party candidate for president, basing his campaign on a host of conservative grievances. He denounced the forced busing of students, the proliferation of government regulations and social programs, and the permissiveness of authorities toward crime, race riots, and antiwar demonstrations. There was never any serious chance that Wallace would win the election, but his standing in the polls rose at times to over 20 percent.

A more effective effort to mobilize the conservative middle in favor of order and stability was under way within the Republican Party. Richard Nixon, whose political career had seemed at an end after his losses in the presidential race of 1960 and a California gubernatorial campaign two years later, reemerged as the preeminent spokesman for what he sometimes called the "silent majority." Nixon recognized that many Americans were tired of hearing about their obligations to the poor, tired of hearing about the sacrifices necessary to achieve racial justice, tired of judicial reforms that seemed designed to help criminals. By offering a vision of stability, law and order, government retrenchment, and "peace with honor" in Vietnam, he easily captured the nomination of his party for the presidency. And despite a last-minute surge by Humphrey, he hung on to eke out a victory almost as narrow as his defeat in 1960. He received 43.4 percent of the popular vote to Humphrey's 42.7 percent (a margin of only about 500,000 votes), and 301 electoral votes to Humphrey's 191. George Wallace, who like most third-party candidates faded in the last weeks of the campaign, still managed to poll 13.5 percent of the popular vote and to carry five southern states with a total of 46 electoral ballots. Nixon had

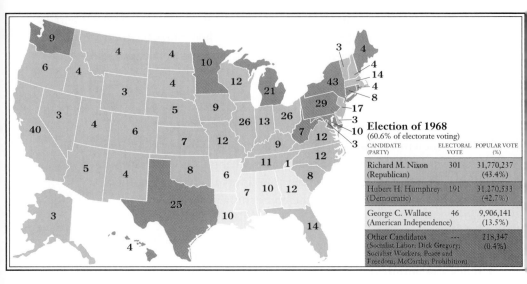

Election of 1968
(60.6% of electorate voting)

CANDIDATE (PARTY)	ELECTORAL VOTE	POPULAR VOTE (%)
Richard M. Nixon (Republican)	301	31,770,237 (43.4%)
Hubert H. Humphrey (Democratic)	191	31,270,533 (42.7%)
George C. Wallace (American Independence)	46	9,906,141 (13.5%)
Other Candidates (Socialist Labor; Dick Gregory; Socialist Workers; Peace and Freedom; McCarthy; Prohibition)	---	218,347 (0.4%)

hardly won a decisive personal mandate. But the election made clear that a majority of the American electorate was more interested in restoring stability than in promoting social change.

CONCLUSION

Perhaps no decade of the twentieth century has created more powerful and enduring images in America than the 1960s. It began with the election—and then the traumatic assassination—of an attractive and energetic young president, John Kennedy, who captured the imagination of millions and seemed to symbolize the rising idealism of the time. It produced a dramatic period of political innovation, christened the Great Society by President Lyndon Johnson, which greatly expanded the size and functions of the federal government and its responsibility for the welfare of the nation's citizens. It saw the emergence of a sustained, national, and enormously powerful civil rights movement that won a series of important legal victories, including two civil rights acts that dismantled the Jim Crow system so painstakingly constructed in the late nineteenth and early twentieth centuries.

The very spirit of dynamism and optimism that made the early 1960s so productive also helped bring to the surface problems and grievances that had no easy solutions. The civil rights movement ended legalized seg-regation and disfranchisement, but it also awakened expectations of social and economic equality that laws alone could not provide and that re-mained in many respects unfulfilled. The peaceful, interracial crusade of the early 1960s gradually turned into a much more militant, confronta-tional, and increasingly separatist movement toward the decade's end. The idealism among white youths that began the 1960s, and played an impor-tant role in the political success of John Kennedy, evolved into an angry rebellion against many aspects of American culture and politics and pro-duced a large upsurge of student protest that rocked the nation at the decade's end. Perhaps most of all, a small and largely unnoticed Cold War commitment to defend South Vietnam against communist aggression from the north led to a large and disastrous American military commit-ment that destroyed the presidency of Lyndon Johnson, shook the faith of millions in their leaders and their political system, sent thousands of young men to their deaths, and showed no signs of producing a victory. A decade that began with high hopes and soaring ideals ended with ugly and at times violent division, and deep disillusionment.

FOR FURTHER REFERENCE

Suggested Readings

Allen J. Matusow, *The Unraveling of America: A History of Liberalism in the 1960s* (1984) is a provocative history of this turbulent decade. Arthur M. Schlesinger, Jr., *A Thou-sand Days* (1965) is a celebrated and celebratory memoir of the Kennedy years. Garry Wills, *The Kennedy Imprisonment* (1982) is an important demystification. Robert Dallek, *Lone Star Rising: Lyndon Johnson and His Times, 1908–1960* (1991) and *Flawed Giant: Lyndon B. Johnson, 1960–1973* (1998) are important biographies. Taylor Branch, *Parting the Waters: America in the King Years* (1988) and *Pillar of Fire: America in the King Years, 1963–1965* (1998) are compelling narrative histories of the civil rights movement. William Chafe, *Civilities and Civil Rights: Greensboro, North Carolina, and the Black Struggle for Freedom* (1980) is an excellent local study of the movement in the South, and the white reaction to it. Nicholas Lemann, *The Promised Land: The Great Black Migration and How It Changed America* (1991) is a provocative study of the post-war African-American migration to northern cities, and of the Great Society's re-sponse to it. Robert D. Schulzinger, *A Time for War: The United States and Vietnam, 1945–1975* (1997) is a good general history of the war. Neil Sheehan, *A Bright Shining Lie: John Paul Vann and America in Vietnam* (1988) is a compelling picture of the war as experienced by a significant military figure of the 1960s. Christian G. Appy, *Working-Class War: American Combat Soldiers and Vietnam* (1993) argues that class determined who fought in Vietnam and who did not. Larry Berman, *Planning a Tragedy* (1982) and

Lyndon Johnson's War (1989); Leslie Gelb and Richard Betts, *The Irony of Vietnam: The System Worked* (1979); and David Halberstam, *The Best and the Brightest* (1972) are all important interpretations of why American leaders chose to intervene in Vietnam. Dan T. Carter, *The Politics of Rage: George Wallace, The Origins of the New Conservatism, and the Transformation of American Politics* (1995) is a good study of the career of George Wallace. David Farber, *Chicago '68* (1988) examines the turbulent Democratic Convention and, through it, the passions that shaped a traumatic year in recent American history.

Films

(The best source for information on how to find these and other films is *Bowker's Complete Video Directory*—3 volumes.) *Berkeley in the Sixties* (1990) portrays the tumultuous student politics at the University of California, Berkeley, and through them larger themes of the decade. *Eye's on the Prize: The American Civil Rights Struggle, 1954–1965* (1986–1987) is a six-part series on the history of the civil rights movement. *Malcolm X: Make it Plain* (1994) is the definitive film biography of Malcolm X. *The Kennedys* (1992) presents the lives of President John F. Kennedy and various members of his powerful political family. *LBJ* (1991) is a biographical treatment of President Lyndon Johnson. *America's War on Poverty* (1995) is a five-part series on the Kennedy and Johnson administrations' most dramatic welfare initiative.

Internet Resources

Internet websites containing historical material relevant to the subjects discussed in this chapter can be reached through the McGraw-Hill history site at www.mhhe.com/socscience/history/usa/link/linktop.htm.

CHAPTER THIRTY-TWO

The Crisis of Authority

The Youth Culture ∼ *The Mobilization of Minorities*
The New Feminism ∼ *Nixon, Kissinger, and the War*
Nixon, Kissinger, and the World
Politics and Economics in the Nixon Years ∼ *The Watergate Crisis*

T HE ELECTION OF Richard Nixon in 1968 was the result of more than the unpopularity of Lyndon Johnson and the war. It was the result, too, of a broad popular reaction against what many Americans considered a dangerous assault on the foundations of their society and culture. In Richard Nixon such Americans found a man who seemed perfectly to match their mood. Himself a product of a hardworking, middle-class family, he projected an image of stern dedication to traditional values. Yet the presidency of Richard Nixon, far from returning calm and stability to American politics, coincided with, and helped to produce, more years of crisis.

THE YOUTH CULTURE

Perhaps most alarming to many conservatives in the 1960s and 1970s was a pattern of social and cultural protest by younger Americans, who were giving vent to two related impulses. One was the impulse, emerging from the political left, to create a great new community of "the people," which would rise up to break the power of elites and force the nation to end the war, pursue racial and economic justice, and transform its political life. The other, at least equally powerful impulse was related to, but not entirely compatible with, the first: the vision of personal "liberation." It found expression in part through the efforts of many groups—African Americans, Indians, Hispanics, women, gay people, and others—to define

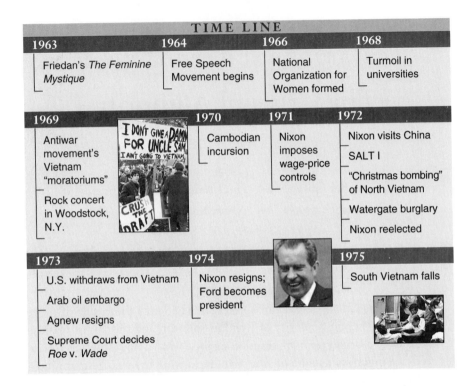

TIME LINE

1963	1964	1966	1968
Friedan's *The Feminine Mystique*	Free Speech Movement begins	National Organization for Women formed	Turmoil in universities

1969	1970	1971	1972
Antiwar movement's Vietnam "moratoriums" Rock concert in Woodstock, N.Y.	Cambodian incursion	Nixon imposes wage-price controls	Nixon visits China SALT I "Christmas bombing" of North Vietnam Watergate burglary Nixon reelected

1973	1974	1975
U.S. withdraws from Vietnam Arab oil embargo Agnew resigns Supreme Court decides *Roe* v. *Wade*	Nixon resigns; Ford becomes president	South Vietnam falls

and assert themselves and make demands on the larger society. It also found expression through the efforts of individuals to create a new culture—one that would allow them to escape from what some considered the dehumanizing pressures of the modern "technocracy."

The New Left

Among the products of the racial crisis and the war in Vietnam was a radicalization of many American students, who in the course of the 1960s formed what became known as the New Left. The New Left emerged from many sources, but from nothing so much as the civil rights movement, in which many idealistic young white Americans had become involved in the early 1960s. Within a few years, some white civil rights activists were beginning to consider broader political commitments. In 1962, a group of students (most of them white) gathered in Michigan to form an organization to give voice to their demands: Students for a Democratic Society (SDS). Their declaration of beliefs, the Port Huron

Statement, expressed their disillusionment with the society they had inherited and their determination to build a new politics. In the following years, SDS became the leading organization of student radicalism.

Since most members of the New Left were students, much of their radicalism centered for a time on issues related to the modern university. A 1964 dispute at the University of California at Berkeley over the rights of students to engage in political activities on campus—the Free Speech Movement—was the first outburst of what was to be nearly a decade of campus turmoil. Students at Berkeley and elsewhere protested the impersonal character of the modern university, and they denounced the role of educational institutions in sustaining what they considered corrupt or immoral public policies. The antiwar movement greatly inflamed and expanded the challenge to the universities; and beginning in 1968, campus demonstrations, riots, and building seizures became almost commonplace. At Columbia University in New York, students seized the offices of the president and other members of the administration and occupied them for several days until local police forcibly ejected them. Over the next several years, hardly any major university was immune to some level of disruption. Small groups of especially dogmatic radicals—among them the "Weathermen," an offshoot of SDS—were responsible for a few cases of arson and bombing that destroyed campus buildings and claimed several lives.

Not many people ever accepted the radical political philosophy that lay at the heart of the New Left. But many supported the position of SDS and other groups on particular issues, and above all on the Vietnam War. Between 1967 and 1969, student activists organized some of the largest political demonstrations in American history—in Washington, D.C., and around the country—to protest the war. They helped thrust the issue of Vietnam into the center of American politics.

Closely related to opposition to the war—and another issue that helped fuel the antiwar movement—was opposition to the military draft. The gradual abolition of many traditional deferments—for graduate students, teachers, husbands, fathers, and others—swelled the ranks of those faced with conscription (and thus likely to oppose it). Many draft-age Americans simply refused induction, accepting what were occasionally long terms in jail as a result. Thousands of others fled to Canada, Sweden, and elsewhere (where they were joined by many deserters from the armed forces) to escape conscription. Not until 1977, when President Jimmy Carter issued a general pardon to draft resisters and a far more limited amnesty for deserters, did the Vietnam exiles begin to return to the country in substantial numbers.

THE WAR AT HOME Demonstrators gather on the Mall in Washington in the fall of 1967 for one of the first of the great antiwar demonstrations of the late 1960s. Over time, the antiwar movement helped erode the national consensus on the conflict in Vietnam. But the principal basis for opposing the war was never the moral or economic arguments of the left; it was simply the frustration among many Americans of seeing a war continuing too long and too inconclusively.

The Counterculture

Closely related to the New Left was a new youth culture openly scornful of the values and conventions of middle-class society. The most visible characteristic of the counterculture, as it became known, was a change in personal styles. As if to display their contempt for conventional standards, young Americans flaunted long hair, shabby or flamboyant clothing, and a rebellious disdain for traditional speech and decorum. Central to the counterculture were drugs: marijuana smoking—which after 1966 became almost as common a youthful diversion as beer drinking had once been—and the use of other, more potent hallucinogens, such as LSD. There was also a new, more permissive view of sex.

The counterculture's iconoclasm and hedonism sometimes obscured the philosophy behind it, which offered a fundamental challenge to the American middle-class mainstream. Like the New Left, with which it in many ways overlapped, the counterculture challenged the structure of modern American society, attacking its banality, its hollowness, its artificiality, its isolation from nature. The most committed adherents of the counterculture—the hippies, who came to dominate the Haight-Ashbury neighborhood of San Francisco and other places, and the social dropouts, many of whom retreated to rural communes—rejected modern society altogether and attempted to find refuge in a simpler, more "natural" existence. But even those whose commitment to the counterculture was less intense shared a commitment to the idea of personal fulfillment through rejecting the inhibitions and conventions of middle-class culture and giving fuller expression to personal instinct and desire. The first responsibility of the individual, the counterculture seemed to suggest, is cultivation of the self, the unleashing of one's own full potential for pleasure and fulfillment.

The counterculture was in many ways only an exaggerated expression of impulses that were coursing through the larger society. A new set of social norms emerged among many young people (and some adults) whose links to the counterculture were otherwise negligible. Long hair and freakish clothing became the badge not only of hippies and radicals but of an entire generation. The use of marijuana, the freer attitudes toward sex, the iconoclastic (and often obscene) language—all spread far beyond the realm of the true devotees of the counterculture.

Perhaps the most pervasive element of the new youth society was one that even the least radical members of the generation embraced: rock music. Early in the 1960s, its influence began to spread, a result in large part of the phenomenal popularity of the Beatles, the English group whose first visit to the United States in 1964 created a remarkable sensation, "Beatlemania." For a time, most rock musicians—like most popular musicians before them—concentrated largely on uncontroversial romantic themes. One of the first great hits of the Beatles was a song with the innocuous title "I Want to Hold Your Hand." By the late 1960s, however, rock had begun to reflect many of the new iconoclastic values of its time. The Beatles, for example, abandoned their once simple and

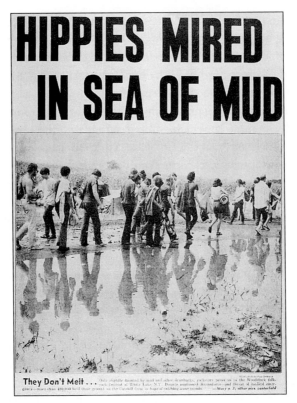

HIPPIES MIRED IN SEA OF MUD

They Don't Melt . . . Only slightly damped by mud and other drawbacks, rocksters press on to the Woodstock folk-rock festival at White Lake, N.Y. Despite unplanned discomforts—and threat of medical emergency—more than 400,000 held their ground on the Catskill farm in hopes of catching some sounds. —*Story p. 3; other pics. centerfold*

REPORTING WOODSTOCK The *New York Daily News*, whose largely working-class readership was not notably sympathetic toward the young people at Woodstock, ran this slightly derisive front-page story on the concert as heavy rains turned the concert site into a sea of mud. ["They Don't Melt," the caption said.]

seemingly innocent style for a new, experimental, even mystical approach that reflected the growing popular fascination with drugs and Eastern religions. Other groups, such as the Rolling Stones, turned even more openly to themes of anger, frustration, and rebelliousness. Many popular musicians used their music to express explicit political radicalism as well—especially some of the leading folk singers of the era, such as Bob Dylan and Joan Baez. Rock's driving rhythms, its undisguised sensuality, its often harsh and angry tone—all made it an appropriate vehicle for expressing the themes of the social and political unrest of the late 1960s.

A powerful symbol of the fusion of rock music and the counterculture was the great music festival at Woodstock, New York, in the summer of

1969, where 400,000 people gathered on a farm for nearly a week. Despite heavy rain, mud, inadequate facilities, and impossible crowding, the crowd remained peaceful and harmonious. Champions of the counterculture spoke rhapsodically at the time of how Woodstock represented the birth of a new youth nation, the "Woodstock nation." The Beat poet Allen Ginsberg, revered by many enthusiasts of the counterculture and himself a champion of the "new consciousness," wrote an ecstatic poem proclaiming that at Woodstock "a new kind of man has come to his bliss/to end the cold war he has borne/against his own kind of flesh." Four months later, however, another great rock concert—at the Altamont racetrack near San Francisco, featuring the Rolling Stones and attended by 300,000 people—exposed a darker side of the youth culture. Altamont became a brutal and violent event at which four people died, several accidentally or from drug overdoses, but one because of injuries received at the hands of members of the Hell's Angels motorcycle gang, who were serving as security guards at the concert and who brutally beat and stabbed a number of people.

Virtually no Americans could avoid seeing how rapidly the norms of their society were changing in the late 1960s. Those who attended movies saw a gradual disappearance of the banal, conventional messages that had dominated films since the 1920s. Instead, they saw explorations of political issues, of new sexual mores, of violence, of social conflict. Television too began to turn (even if more slowly than the other media) to programming that reflected social and cultural conflict—as exemplified by the enormously popular *All in the Family*, whose protagonist, Archie Bunker, was a lower-middle-class bigot.

THE MOBILIZATION OF MINORITIES

The growth of African-American protest, and of a significant white response to it, both preceded the political and cultural upheavals of the 1960s and helped to produce them. It also encouraged other minorities to assert themselves and demand redress of their grievances. For Indians, Hispanic Americans, gay men and lesbians, and others, the late 1960s and 1970s were a time of growing self-expression and political activism.

Seeds of Indian Militancy

Few minorities had deeper or more justifiable grievances against the prevailing culture than American Indians—or Native Americans, as some began defiantly to call themselves in the 1960s. Indians were the least prosperous, least healthy, and least stable group in the nation. And while black Americans attracted the attention (for good or for ill) of many whites, Indians for many years had remained largely ignored.

For much of the postwar era, federal policy toward the tribes had been shaped by a determination to incorporate Indians into mainstream American society whether Indians wanted to assimilate or not. Two laws passed in 1953 established the basis of a new policy, which became known as "termination." Through termination, the federal government withdrew all official recognition of the tribes as legal entities, administratively separate from state governments, and made them subject to the same local jurisdictions as white residents. At the same time, the government encouraged Indians to assimilate into the white world and worked to funnel Native Americans into cities, where, presumably, they would adapt themselves to the larger society and lose their cultural distinctiveness.

Despite some individual successes, the new policies were a disastrous failure on the whole. Indians themselves fought so bitterly against them that in 1958 the Eisenhower administration barred further "terminations" without the consent of the affected tribes. In the meantime, the struggle against termination had mobilized a new generation of Indian militants and had breathed life into the principal Native American organization, the National Congress of American Indians, which had been created in 1944.

The Democratic administrations of the 1960s made no effort to revive termination. Instead, they made modest efforts to restore at least some degree of tribal autonomy. The funneling of OEO money to tribal organizations through the Community Action program was one prominent example. In the meantime, the tribes themselves were beginning to fight for self-determination. The new militancy benefited from the rapid increase in the Indian population, which was growing much faster than that of the rest of the nation (nearly doubling between 1950 and 1970 to a total of about 800,000).

The Indian Civil Rights Movement

In 1961, more than 400 members of 67 tribes gathered in Chicago to discuss ways of bringing all Indians together in an effort to redress common wrongs. The manifesto they issued, the Declaration of Indian Purpose, stressed the "right to choose our own way of life" and the "responsibility of preserving our precious heritage."

The 1961 meeting was only one example of a growing Indian self-consciousness. The National Indian Youth Council, created in the aftermath of the 1961 Chicago meeting, promoted the idea of Indian national-ism and intertribal unity. In 1968, a group of young, militant Indians es-tablished the American Indian Movement (AIM), which drew its greatest support from those Indians who lived in urban areas but which established a significant presence on the reservations as well.

The new activism had some immediate political results. In 1968, Con-gress passed the Indian Civil Rights Act, which guaranteed reservation In-dians many of the protections accorded other citizens by the Bill of Rights, but which also recognized the legitimacy of tribal laws within the reservations. But leaders of AIM and other insurgent groups were not sat-isfied and turned increasingly to direct action. In 1968, Indian fishermen, citing old treaty rights, clashed with Washington State officials on the Co-lumbia River and in Puget Sound. The following year, members of several tribes occupied the abandoned federal prison on Alcatraz Island in San Francisco Bay, claiming the site "by right of discovery."

In response to the growing pressure, the new Nixon administration appointed Louis Bruce, a Mohawk-Sioux, to the position of commissioner

WOUNDED KNEE In 1890, Wounded Knee, South Dakota, had been the site of a bloody conflict between white troops and Sioux Indians, a conflict that turned into a notorious massacre in which over 300 Indians died. In 1973, the American Indian Movement chose the same place as a site for a militant protest against conditions on the Pine Ridge Indian reservation.

of Indian affairs in 1969; and in 1970 the president promised both increased tribal self-determination and an increase in federal aid. But the
protests continued. In November 1972, nearly a thousand demonstrators,
most of them Lakota Sioux, forcibly occupied the building of the Bureau
of Indian Affairs in Washington for six days. A more celebrated protest
occurred later that winter at Wounded Knee, South Dakota, the site of
the 1890 massacre of Sioux by federal troops. In February 1973, members
of AIM seized and occupied the town of Wounded Knee for two months,
demanding radical changes in the administration of the reservation and
insisting that the government honor its long-forgotten treaty obligations.
A brief clash between the occupiers and federal forces left one Indian dead
and another wounded. Shortly thereafter the siege came to an end.

The Indian civil rights movement, like other civil rights movements
of the same time, fell far short of winning full justice and equality for Native Americans. But it helped the tribes win a series of new legal rights and
protections that, together, gave them a stronger position than they had
enjoyed at any previous time in the twentieth century.

Latino Activism

More numerous and more visible than Indians were Hispanic Americans
(sometimes known as Latinos), the fastest-growing minority group in the
United States. Large numbers of Mexicans had entered the country during World War II in response to the wartime labor shortage, and many
had remained in the cities of the Southwest and the Pacific Coast. By
1960, Los Angeles had a bigger Mexican population than any place except
Mexico City.

But the greatest expansion in the Hispanic population of the United
States was yet to come. In 1960, the census reported slightly more than
3 million Latinos living in the United States. By 1970, that number had
grown to 9 million and by 1990 to 20 million. Hispanics constituted
more than a third of all legal immigrants to the United States after 1960.
There was also an uncounted but very large number of illegal Latino immigrants in those years (estimates ranged from 7 million to 12 million).

Large numbers of Puerto Ricans (who were entitled to American citizenship by birth) migrated to eastern urban areas, particularly New York,
where they formed one of the poorest communities in the city. South
Florida's substantial Cuban population began with a wave of middle-class
refugees fleeing the Castro regime in the early 1960s. These first Cuban
migrants quickly established themselves as a successful and highly assimi-

lated part of Miami's middle class. In 1980, a second, much poorer wave of Cuban immigrants—the so-called Marielietos, named for the port from which they left Cuba—arrived in Florida when Castro temporarily relaxed exit restrictions. Later in the 1980s, large numbers of immigrants (both legal and illegal) began to arrive from Central and South America—from Guatemala, Nicaragua, El Salvador, Peru, and other countries.

Like blacks and Indians, many Hispanic Americans responded to the highly charged climate of the 1960s by strengthening their ethnic identification and by organizing for political and economic power. Affluent Hispanics in Miami filled influential positions in the professions and local government; in the Southwest, Latino voters elected Mexican Americans to seats in Congress and to governorships. A Mexican-American political organization, La Raza Unida, exercised influence in southern California and elsewhere in the Southwest in the 1970s and beyond.

One of the most visible efforts to organize Hispanics occurred in California, where an Arizona-born farmworker of Mexican descent, César Chávez, created an effective union of itinerant farmworkers: the United Farm Workers (UFW), a largely Mexican organization. For most Hispanics, however, the path to economic and political power was more difficult. Partly because of language barriers, partly because of ineffective organization, and partly because of discrimination, Mexican Americans and others were slow to develop political influence in proportion to their numbers. In the meantime, Hispanics formed one of the poorest segments of the United States population.

Gay Liberation

The last important liberation movement to emerge in the 1960s, and the most unsettling to some Americans, was the effort by gay men and lesbians to win political and economic rights and social acceptance. Homosexuality has been a generally unacknowledged reality throughout American history. Nonheterosexual men and women were forced for generations either to suppress their sexual preferences, to exercise them surreptitiously, or to live within isolated and often persecuted communities. But by the late 1960s, the liberating impulses that had affected other groups helped mobilize gay men and lesbians to fight for their own rights.

On June 27, 1969, police officers raided the Stonewall Inn, a gay nightclub in New York City's Greenwich Village, and began arresting patrons simply for frequenting the place. The raid was not unusual, but the response was. Gay onlookers taunted the police and then attacked them.

Someone started a blaze in the Stonewall Inn itself, almost trapping the policemen inside. Rioting continued throughout Greenwich Village (the center of New York's gay community) through much of the night.

The "Stonewall Riot" marked the beginning of the gay liberation movement—one of the most controversial challenges to traditional values and assumptions of its time. New organizations—among them the Gay Liberation Front, founded in New York in 1969—sprang up around the country. Public discussion and media coverage of homosexuality, long subject to an unofficial taboo, quickly and dramatically increased. Gay activists were having some success in challenging the longstanding assumption that homosexuality was aberrant behavior; many were arguing that no sexual preference was any more normal than another.

Most of all, however, the gay liberation movement transformed the outlook of many gay men and lesbians themselves. It helped them to "come out," to express their preferences openly and unapologetically, and to demand from society a recognition that gay relationships could be as significant and worthy of respect as heterosexual ones. By the early 1980s, the gay liberation movement had made remarkable strides. Even the ravages of the AIDS epidemic, which, in the beginning at least, affected the gay community more disastrously than it affected any other group, failed to halt the growth of gay liberation. In many ways, it strengthened it.

By the early 1990s, gay men and lesbians were achieving many of the same milestones that other oppressed minorities had attained in earlier decades. Openly gay politicians won election to public office. Universities established gay and lesbian studies programs. Laws prohibiting discrimination on the basis of sexual preference made slow, halting progress at the state and local levels. But gay liberation produced a powerful backlash as well, as became evident in 1993 when President Bill Clinton's effort to end the ban on gay men and lesbians serving in the military met a storm of criticism from members of Congress and within the military itself. At the same time, voters in some cities and states were approving referendum questions on their ballots outlawing civil rights protections for gay men and lesbians.

THE NEW FEMINISM

Women constitute over 50 percent of the United States population. But during the 1960s and 1970s, many women began to identify with minority groups as they renewed demands for a liberation of their own.

The Rebirth

The 1963 publication of Betty Friedan's *The Feminine Mystique* is often cited as the first event of contemporary women's liberation. Friedan, who had been a writer for women's magazines in the 1950s, traveled around the country interviewing the women who had graduated with her from Smith College in 1947. Most of these women were living out the dream that postwar American society had created for them: they were affluent wives and mothers living in comfortable suburbs. And yet many of them were deeply frustrated and unhappy, with no outlets for their intelligence, talent, and education. By chronicling their unhappiness and frustration, Friedan's book had a powerful impact. But it did not so much cause the revival of feminism as help give voice to a movement that was already stirring.

By the time *The Feminine Mystique* appeared, John Kennedy had established the President's Commission on the Status of Women, which brought national attention to sexual discrimination. Also in 1963, the Kennedy administration helped win passage of the Equal Pay Act, which barred the pervasive practice of paying women less than men for the same work. A year later, Congress incorporated into the Civil Rights Act of 1964 an amendment—Title VII—that extended to women many of the same legal protections against discrimination that were being extended to blacks.

In 1966, Friedan joined with other feminists to create the National Organization for Women (NOW), which was to become the nation's largest and most influential feminist organization. NOW reflected the varying constituencies of the emerging feminist movement. It responded to the complaints of the women Friedan's book had examined—affluent suburbanites with no outlet for their interests—by demanding greater educational opportunities for women and denouncing the domestic ideal and the traditional concept of marriage. But the heart of the movement, at least in the beginning, was an effort to address the needs of women in the workplace. NOW denounced the exclusion of women from and discrimination against women within professions, politics, and countless other areas of American life.

Women's Liberation

By the late 1960s, new and more radical feminist demands were also attracting a large following, especially among younger, white, educated women. Many of them drew inspiration from the New Left and the counterculture. Some were involved in the civil rights movement, others in the antiwar crusade. Many had found that even within those movements, they faced discrimination and exclusion and were subordinated to male leaders.

In its most radical form, the new feminism rejected the whole notion of marriage, family, and even heterosexual intercourse (a vehicle, some women claimed, of male domination). Not many women, not even many feminists, embraced such extremes. But by the early 1970s large numbers of women were coming to see themselves as an exploited group banding together against oppression and developing a culture of their own. The women's liberation movement inspired the creation of grassroots organizations and activities through which women not only challenged sexism and discrimination but created communities of their own. In cities and towns across the country, feminists opened women's bookstores, bars, and coffee shops. They founded feminist newspapers and magazines. They created women's health clinics, centers to assist victims of rape and abuse, day-care centers, and, particularly after 1973, abortion clinics.

Expanding Achievements

By the early 1970s, the public and private achievements of the women's movement were already substantial. In 1971, the government extended its affirmative action guidelines to include women—linking sexism with racism as an officially acknowledged social problem. Women were making rapid progress, in the meantime, in their efforts to move into the economic and political mainstream. The nation's major all-male educational institutions began to open their doors to women. (Princeton and Yale did so in 1969, and most others soon did the same.)

Women were also becoming an important force in business and the professions. Nearly half of all married women held jobs by the mid-1970s, and almost 90 percent of all women with college degrees worked. The two-career family, in which both the husband and the wife maintained active professional lives, was becoming a widely accepted middle-class norm. (It had been common within the working class for decades.) There were also important symbolic changes, such as the refusal of many women to adopt their husbands' names when they married and the use of the term "Ms." in place of "Mrs." or "Miss" to signal the irrelevance of a woman's marital status in the professional world.

In politics, women began to compete effectively with men for both elected and appointive positions in the 1970s. By the mid-1980s, women were serving in both houses of Congress, on the Supreme Court, in numerous federal cabinet positions, as governors of several states, and in many other political positions. In 1981, Ronald Reagan named the first female Supreme Court justice, Sandra Day O'Connor; in 1993, Bill Clinton named the second, Ruth Bader Ginsburg. In 1984, the Democratic Party chose a woman, Representative Geraldine Ferraro of New York, as its vice presidential candidate. In academia, women were expanding their presence in traditional scholarly fields; they were also creating new fields—women's and gender studies, which in the 1980s and 1990s were among the fastest-growing areas of American scholarship.

In 1972, Congress approved the Equal Rights Amendment (ERA) to the Constitution, which some feminists had been promoting since the 1920s, and sent it to the states. For a while ratification seemed almost certain. By the late 1970s, however, the momentum behind the amendment had died. The ERA was in trouble not because of indifference but because of a rising chorus of objections to it from people (including many antifeminist women) who feared that it would disrupt traditional social patterns. In 1982, the amendment finally died when the ten years allotted for ratification expired.

The Abortion Controversy

A major element of American feminism since the 1920s has been the effort by women to win greater control of their own sexual and reproductive lives. In its least controversial form, this impulse helped produce an increasing awareness in the 1960s and 1970s of the problems of rape, sexual abuse, and wife beating. There continued to be some controversy over the dissemination of contraceptives and birth-control information, but that issue, at least, seemed to have lost much of the explosive character it had once possessed. A related issue, however, stimulated as much popular passion as any question of its time: abortion.

Abortion had once been legal in much of the United States, but by the beginning of the twentieth century it was banned by statute in most of the country and remained so into the 1960s (although many abortions continued to be performed quietly, and often dangerously, out of sight of the law). The women's movement created strong new pressures on behalf of the legalization of abortion. Several states had abandoned restrictions on abortion by the end of the 1960s. And in 1973, the Supreme Court's decision in *Roe* v. *Wade*, based on a new theory of a constitutional "right to privacy" first recognized by the Court only a few years earlier, invalidated all laws prohibiting abortion during the "first trimester"—the first three months of pregnancy. But even then, the issue was far from settled.

In many ways, feminism was much like other "liberation" movements of the 1960s and 1970s. But it differed from them in one fundamental respect: its success. The women's movement may not have fulfilled all its goals. But it achieved fundamental and permanent changes in the position of women in American life, and it promised to do much more.

NIXON, KISSINGER, AND THE WAR

Richard Nixon assumed office in 1969 committed not only to restoring stability at home but to creating a new and more stable order in the world. Central to Nixon's hopes for international stability was a resolution of the stalemate in Vietnam. Yet the new president felt no freer than his predecessor to abandon the American commitment there.

Vietnamization

Despite Nixon's own deep interest in international affairs, he brought with him into government a man who at times seemed to overshadow the president himself in the conduct of diplomacy: Henry Kissinger, a Harvard professor whom Nixon appointed as his special assistant for national security affairs. Kissinger quickly established dominance over Secretary of State William Rogers and Secretary of Defense Melvin Laird, who were both more experienced in public life. Together, Nixon and Kissinger set out to find an acceptable solution to the stalemate in Vietnam.

The new Vietnam policy moved along several fronts. One was an effort to limit domestic opposition to the war by "Vietnamizing" the conflict—that is, training and equipping the South Vietnamese military to assume the burden of combat in place of American forces. In the fall of 1969, Nixon announced the withdrawal of 60,000 American ground troops from Vietnam, the first reduction in United States troop strength since the beginning of the war. The withdrawals continued steadily for more than three years, so that by the fall of 1972 relatively few American soldiers remained in Indochina. From a peak of more than 540,000 in 1969, the number had dwindled to about 60,000.

Vietnamization (and the decreased draft calls it produced) did help quiet domestic opposition to the war for a time. It did nothing, however, to break the stalemate in the negotiations with the North Vietnamese in Paris. The new administration quickly decided that new military pressures would be necessary to do that.

Escalation

By the end of 1969, Nixon and Kissinger had decided that the most effective way to tip the military balance in America's favor was to destroy the bases in Cambodia and Laos from which the American military believed the North Vietnamese were launching many of their attacks. Very early in his presidency, Nixon ordered the air force to begin bombing Cambodian and Laotian territory to destroy the enemy sanctuaries. He kept the raids secret from Congress and the public. In the spring of 1970, conservative military leaders overthrew the neutral government of Cambodia and established a new, pro-American regime under General Lon Nol. Lon Nol quickly gave his approval to American incursions into his territory; and on April 30, Nixon went on television to announce that he was ordering American troops across the border into Cambodia to clean out the bases that the enemy had been using for its attacks on South Vietnam.

Literally overnight, the Cambodian invasion restored the dwindling antiwar movement to vigorous life. The first days of May saw the most widespread and vocal antiwar demonstrations ever. A mood of crisis was already mounting when, on May 4, four college students were killed and nine others injured after members of the National Guard opened fire on antiwar demonstrators at Kent State University in Ohio. Ten days later, police killed two African-American students at Jackson State University in Mississippi during a demonstration there.

The clamor against the war spread into the government and the press. Congress angrily repealed the Gulf of Tonkin Resolution in December. Then, in June 1971, first the *New York Times* and later other newspapers began publishing excerpts from a secret study of the war prepared by the Defense Department during the Johnson administration. The so-called Pentagon Papers, leaked to the press by former Defense official Daniel Ellsberg, confirmed what many had long believed: the government had been dishonest, both in reporting the military progress of the war and in explaining its own motives for American involvement. The administration went to court to suppress the documents, but the Supreme Court ruled that the press had the right to publish them.

There were by now signs of decay within the American military itself. Morale and discipline among American troops in Vietnam, who had been fighting a savage and inconclusive war for more than five years, were rapidly deteriorating. The 1971 trial and conviction of Lieutenant William Calley, who was charged with overseeing a massacre of more than 100 unarmed South Vietnamese civilians in 1968 near the village of My Lai, attracted wide

962 ~ THE UNFINISHED NATION

public attention to the dehumanizing impact of the war on those who fought it—and to the terrible consequences that dehumanization imposed on the Vietnamese people. Less publicized were other, more widespread problems among American troops in Vietnam: desertion, drug addiction, racial bias, refusal to obey orders, even the killing of unpopular officers by enlisted men.

The continuing carnage, the increasing savagery, and the social distress at home had largely destroyed public support for the war. By 1971, nearly two-thirds of those interviewed in public opinion polls were urging American withdrawal from Vietnam. President Nixon, however, was determined to resist, and if possible destroy, his critics, convinced that a defeat in Vietnam would cause unacceptable damage to the nation's (and his own) credibility. The FBI, the CIA, the White House itself, and other federal agencies increased their efforts to discredit and harass antiwar and radical groups, often through illegal means.

In Indochina, meanwhile, the fighting raged on. In February 1971, the president ordered the air force to assist the South Vietnamese army in an invasion of Laos—a test, as he saw it, of his Vietnamization program. Within weeks, the South Vietnamese scrambled back across the border in defeat. American bombing in Vietnam and Cambodia increased, despite its apparent ineffectiveness. In March 1972, the North Vietnamese mounted their biggest offensive since 1968 (the so-called Easter offensive). American and South Vietnamese forces managed to halt the communist advance, but it was clear that without American support the South Vietnamese would not have succeeded. At the same time, Nixon ordered American planes to bomb targets near Hanoi, the capital of North Vietnam, and Haiphong, its principal port, and called for the mining of seven North Vietnamese harbors (including Haiphong).

"Peace with Honor"

As the 1972 presidential election approached, the administration stepped up its effort to produce a breakthrough in negotiations with the North Vietnamese. In April 1972, the president dropped his longtime insistence on the removal of North Vietnamese troops from the south before any American withdrawal. Meanwhile, Henry Kissinger met privately in Paris with the North Vietnamese foreign secretary, Le Duc Tho, to work out terms for a cease-fire. On October 26, only days before the presidential election, Kissinger announced that "peace is at hand."

Several weeks later (after the election), negotiations broke down once again. Although both the American and the North Vietnamese governments were ready to accept the Kissinger-Tho plan for a cease-fire, President Nguyen Van Thieu of South Vietnam balked, still insisting on a full withdrawal of North Vietnamese forces from the south. Kissinger tried to win additional concessions from the communists to meet Thieu's objections, but on December 16 talks broke off.

The next day, December 17, American B-52s began the heaviest and most destructive air raids of the entire war on Hanoi, Haiphong, and other North Vietnamese targets. Civilian casualties were high, and fifteen American B-52s were shot down by the North Vietnamese; in the entire war to that point, the United States had lost only one of the giant bombers. On December 30, Nixon terminated the "Christmas bombing." The United States and the North Vietnamese returned to the conference table; and on January 27, 1973, they signed an "agreement on ending the war and restoring peace in Vietnam." Nixon claimed that the Christmas bombing had forced the North Vietnamese to relent. At least equally important, however, was the enormous American pressure on Thieu to accept the cease-fire.

The terms of the Paris accords were little different from those Kissinger and Tho had accepted in principle a few months before. There would be an immediate cease-fire. The North Vietnamese would release several hundred American prisoners of war, whose fate had become an emotional issue of great importance within the United States. The Thieu regime would survive for the moment, but North Vietnamese forces already in the south would remain there. An undefined committee would work out a permanent settlement.

Defeat in Indochina

American forces were hardly out of Indochina before the Paris accords began to collapse. In March 1975, finally, the North Vietnamese launched a full-scale offensive against the now greatly weakened forces of the south. Thieu appealed to Washington for assistance. The president (now Gerald Ford) appealed to Congress for additional funding; Congress refused. Late in April 1975, communist forces marched into Saigon, shortly after officials of the Thieu regime and the staff of the American embassy had fled the country in humiliating disarray. The communist forces quickly occupied the capital, renamed it Ho Chi Minh City, and began the process of reuniting Vietnam under the harsh rule of Hanoi. At about the same time, the Lon Nol regime in Cambodia fell to the murderous forces of the Khmer Rouge—whose brutal policies led to the death of more than a third of the country's people over the next several years.

THE FALL OF SAIGON The chaotic evacuation of Americans from Saigon in the spring of 1975, only hours before victorious North Vietnamese troops entered the city, was a humiliating spectacle. Desperate South Vietnamese soldiers and officials fought with American soldiers and diplomats for space on the few airplanes and helicopters available.

Such were the dismal results of more than a decade of direct American military involvement in Vietnam. More than 1.2 million Vietnamese soldiers had died in combat, along with countless civilians throughout the region. A beautiful land had been ravaged, its agrarian economy left in ruins; until an economic revival began in the early 1990s, Vietnam remained one of the poorest and most politically oppressive nations in the world. The United States had paid a heavy price as well. The war had cost the nation almost $150 billion in direct costs and much more indirectly. It had resulted in the deaths of over 57,000 young Americans and the injury of 300,000 more. And the nation had suffered a blow to its confidence and self-esteem from which it would not soon recover.

NIXON, KISSINGER, AND THE WORLD

The continuing war in Vietnam provided an unhappy backdrop to what Nixon considered his larger mission in world affairs: the construction of a new international order. The president had become convinced that the old assumptions of a "bipolar" world—in which the United States and the Soviet Union were the only real great powers—were now obsolete. America must adapt to the new "multipolar" international structure, in which China, Japan, and Western Europe were becoming major, independent forces. Nixon and Kissinger believed it was possible to construct something like the "balance of power" that had permitted nineteenth-century Europe to enjoy nearly a century of relative stability. To do so, however, required a major change in several longstanding assumptions of American foreign policy.

The China Initiative and Soviet-American Détente

For more than twenty years, ever since the fall of Chiang Kai-shek in 1949, the United States had treated China, the second-largest nation on earth, as if it did not exist. Instead, America recognized the forlorn regime-in-exile on Taiwan as the legitimate government of mainland China. Nixon and Kissinger wanted to forge a new relationship with the Chinese communists—in part to strengthen them as a counterbalance to the Soviet Union. The Chinese, for their part, were eager to forestall the possibility of a Soviet-American alliance against China and to end China's own isolation from the international arena.

In July 1971, Nixon sent Henry Kissinger on a secret mission to Beijing. When Kissinger returned, the president made the startling announcement that he would visit China himself within the next few months. That fall, with American approval, the United Nations admitted the communist government of China and expelled the representatives of the Taiwan regime. Finally, in February 1972, Nixon paid a formal visit to China and, in a single stroke, erased much of the deep animosity between the United States and the Chinese communists. Nixon did not yet formally recognize the communist regime, but in 1972 the United States and China began low-level diplomatic relations.

The initiatives in China coincided with (and probably assisted) an effort by the Nixon administration to improve relations with the Soviet Union. In 1969, American and Soviet diplomats met in Helsinki, Finland, to begin talks on limiting nuclear weapons. In 1972, they produced the first Strategic Arms Limitation Treaty (SALT I), which froze the arsenals of some nuclear missiles (ICBMs) on both sides at present levels. In May of that year, the president traveled to Moscow to sign the agreement. The next year, the Soviet premier, Leonid Brezhnev, visited Washington.

DÉTENTE AT HIGH TIDE The visit of Soviet premier Leonid Brezhnev to Washington in 1973 was a high-water mark in the search for détente between the two nations. Here, Brezhnev and Nixon share friendly words on the White House balcony.

Dealing with the Third World

The policies of rapprochement with communist China and détente with the Soviet Union reflected Nixon's and Kissinger's belief in the importance of stable relationships among the great powers. But great-power relationships could not alone ensure international stability, for the Third World remained the most volatile and dangerous source of international tension.

Central to the Nixon-Kissinger policy toward the Third World was the effort to maintain the status quo without involving the United States too deeply in local disputes. In 1969 and 1970, the president described what became known as the Nixon Doctrine, by which the United States would "participate in the defense and development of allies and friends" but would leave the "basic responsibility" for the future of those "friends" to the nations themselves. In practice, the Nixon Doctrine meant a declining American interest in contributing to Third World development; a growing contempt for the United Nations, where underdeveloped nations were gaining influence through their sheer numbers; and increasing support to authoritarian regimes attempting to withstand radical challenges from within.

In 1970, for example, the CIA poured substantial funds into Chile to help support the established government against a communist challenge. When the Marxist candidate for president, Salvador Allende, came to power through an open election despite U.S. efforts, the United States began funneling more money to opposition forces in Chile to help destabilize the new government. In 1973, a military junta seized power from Allende, who was subsequently murdered. The United States developed a friendly relationship with the new, repressive military government of General Augusto Pinochet.

In the Middle East, conditions grew more volatile in the aftermath of the 1967 war, in which Israel had occupied substantial new territories, dislodging many Palestinian Arabs from their homes. The refugees were a source of considerable instability in Jordan, Lebanon, and the other surrounding countries into which they moved. In October 1973, on the Jewish high holy day of Yom Kippur, Egyptian and Syrian forces attacked Israel. For ten days, the Israelis struggled to recover from the surprise attack; finally, they launched an effective counteroffensive against Egyptian forces in the Sinai. At that point, the United States intervened, placing heavy pressure on Israel to accept a cease-fire rather than press its advantage.

The imposed settlement of the Yom Kippur War demonstrated the growing dependence of the United States and its allies on Arab oil. Permitting Israel to continue its drive into Egypt might have jeopardized the ability of the United States to purchase needed petroleum from the Arab states. A brief but painful embargo by the Arab governments on the sale of oil to America in 1973 provided an ominous warning of the costs of losing access to the region's resources. The lesson of the Yom Kippur War, therefore, was that the United States could not ignore the interests of the Arab nations in its efforts on behalf of Israel.

A larger lesson of 1973 was that the nations of the Third World could no longer be expected to act as passive, cooperative "client states." And the United States could not depend on cheap, easy access to raw materials as it had in the past.

POLITICS AND ECONOMICS
IN THE NIXON YEARS

Nixon ran for president in 1968 promising a return to more conservative social and economic policies and a restoration of law and order. Once in office, however, his domestic policies often continued and even expanded the liberal initiatives of the previous two administrations.

Domestic Initiatives

Many of Nixon's domestic policies were a response to what he believed to be the demands of his constituency—conservative, middle-class people, the "silent majority" who he believed wanted to reduce federal interference in local affairs. He tried, unsuccessfully, to persuade Congress to pass legislation prohibiting school desegregation through the use of forced busing. He forbade the Department of Health, Education, and Welfare to cut off federal funds from school districts that had failed to comply with court orders to integrate. At the same time, he began to reduce or dismantle many of the social programs of the Great Society and the New Frontier. In 1973, he abolished the Office of Economic Opportunity, the centerpiece of the antipoverty program of the Johnson years.

Yet Nixon's domestic policies had progressive and creative elements as well. He signed legislation creating the Environmental Protection Agency and establishing the most stringent environmental regulations in the nation's history. He ordered the first affirmative action program for workers on federally funded projects. One of the administration's boldest efforts was an attempt to overhaul the nation's welfare system. Nixon proposed replacing the existing system, which almost everyone agreed was cumbersome, expensive, and inefficient, with what he called the Family Assistance Plan (FAP). It would in effect have created a guaranteed annual income for all Americans: $1,600 in federal grants, which could be supplemented by outside earnings up to $4,000. The FAP won approval in the House in 1970, but the bill failed in the Senate. Nixon also became the first president since Truman to propose a plan for national health insurance, which likewise made no progress in Congress.

From the Warren Court to the Nixon Court

Of all the liberal institutions that aroused the enmity of the conservative "silent majority" in the 1950s and 1960s, none evoked more anger and bitterness than the Supreme Court under Chief Justice Earl Warren. Not only did the Warren Court's rulings on racial matters disrupt traditional social patterns in both the North and the South, but its staunch defense of civil liberties directly contributed, in the eyes of many Americans, to the increase in crime, disorder, and moral decay. In *Engel* v. *Fitak* (1962), the Court ruled that prayers in public schools were unconstitutional, sparking outrage among religious fundamentalists and others. In *Roth* v. *United States* (1957), the Court had sharply limited the authority of local governments to curb pornography. In a series of other decisions, the Court greatly strengthened the civil rights of criminal defendants and, many Americans believed, greatly weakened the power of law enforcement officials to do their jobs. For example, in *Gideon* v. *Wainwright* (1963), the Court ruled that every felony defendant was entitled to a lawyer regardless of his or her ability to pay. In *Escobedo* v. *Illinois* (1964), it ruled that a defendant must be allowed access to a lawyer before questioning by police. In *Miranda* v. *Arizona* (1966), the Court confirmed the obligation of authorities to inform a criminal suspect of his or her rights. By 1968, the Warren Court had become the target of Americans of all kinds who felt the balance of power in the United States had shifted too far toward the poor, the dispossessed, and the criminal at the expense of the middle class.

Nixon was determined to use his judicial appointments to give the Court a more conservative cast. When Chief Justice Earl Warren retired early in 1969, Nixon replaced him with a federal appeals court judge of known conservative leanings, Warren Burger. At about the same time, Associate Justice Abe Fortas resigned his seat after the disclosure of a series of alleged financial improprieties. To replace him, Nixon named Clement F. Haynsworth, a respected federal circuit court judge from South Carolina. But Haynsworth came under fire from Senate liberals, black organizations, and labor unions for his conservative record on civil rights. The Senate rejected him. Nixon's next choice was G. Harrold Carswell, a judge of the Florida federal appeals court almost entirely lacking in distinction and widely considered unfit for the Supreme Court. The Senate rejected his nomination, too.

Nixon angrily denounced the votes. But he was careful thereafter to choose men of standing within the legal community to fill vacancies on the Supreme Court: Harry Blackmun, a moderate jurist from Minnesota; Lewis F. Powell, Jr., a respected lawyer from Virginia; and William Rehnquist, a member of the Nixon Justice Department.

The new Court, however, fell short of what the president and many conservatives had expected. Rather than retreating from its commitment to social reform, the Court in many areas actually moved further toward it. In *Swann* v. *Charlotte-Mecklenburg Board of Education* (1971), it ruled in favor of the use of forced busing to achieve racial balance in schools. Not even the intense and occasionally violent opposition of local communities as diverse as Boston and Louisville, Kentucky, was able to weaken the judicial commitment to integration. In *Furman* v. *Georgia* (1972), the Court overturned existing capital punishment statutes and established strict new guidelines for such laws in the future. In *Roe* v. *Wade* (1973), one of the most controversial decisions in the Court's modern history, it struck down laws forbidding abortions.

In other decisions, however, the Burger Court did demonstrate a more conservative temperament than the Warren Court had shown. Although the justices approved busing as a tool for achieving integration, they rejected, in *Milliken* v. *Bradley* (1974), a plan to transfer students across district lines (in this case, between Detroit and its suburbs) to achieve racial balance. While the Court upheld the principle of affirmative action in its celebrated 1978 decision in *Bakke* v. *Board of Regents of California*, it established restrictive new guidelines for such programs in the future. In *Stone* v. *Powell* (1976), the Court agreed to certain limits on the right of a defendant to appeal a state conviction to the federal judiciary.

The Election of 1972

However unsuccessful the Nixon administration may have been in achieving some of its specific goals, Nixon entered the presidential race in 1972 with a substantial reserve of strength. His energetic reelection committee had collected enormous sums of money to support the campaign. The president himself used the powers of incumbency to strengthen his political standing in strategic areas. And Nixon's foreign policy successes, especially his trip to China, increased his stature in the eyes of the nation.

Nixon was most fortunate in 1972, however, in his opposition. George Wallace, partly at Nixon's urging, entered the Democratic primaries and helped divide the party until a would-be assassin shot the Alabama governor during a rally at a Maryland shopping center in May. Paralyzed from the waist down, Wallace was unable to continue campaigning. In the meantime, the most liberal factions of the party were succeeding in establishing their candidate, Senator George S. McGovern of South Dakota, as the front-runner for the nomination. An outspoken critic of the war and a forceful advocate of advanced liberal positions on many social and economic issues, McGovern profited greatly from party reforms (which he himself had helped to draft) that gave increased influence to women, blacks, and young people in the selection of the Democratic ticket. But in the process, the McGovern campaign came to be associated with aspects of the turbulent 1960s that many middle-class Americans were eager to reject.

On election day, Nixon won reelection by one of the largest margins in history: 60.7 percent of the popular vote compared with 37.5 percent for the forlorn McGovern, and an electoral margin of 520 to 17. The Democratic candidate had carried only Massachusetts and the District of Columbia. But serious problems, some beyond the president's control and some of his own making, were already lurking in the wings.

The Troubled Economy

Although it was political scandal that would ultimately destroy the Nixon presidency, the most important national crisis of the early 1970s was the beginning of a long-term transformation of the American economy. For three decades, that economy had been the envy of the world. In fact, however, America's prosperity rested in part on several artificial conditions that were rapidly disappearing by the late 1960s.

The most immediate change was the end of the nation's easy access to cheap raw materials, a change that became a major cause of the serious inflation that plagued the economy through much of the 1970s. Large increases in federal deficit spending in the 1960s were responsible for some of the inflation. But at least equally important was the rising price of energy.

More than any nation on earth, the United States based its economy on the easy availability of cheap and plentiful fuels to meet the nation's enormous demand for energy. Domestic petroleum reserves were no longer sufficient to meet this demand, and the nation was growing increasingly dependent on imports from the Middle East and Africa.

For many years, the Organization of Petroleum Exporting Countries (OPEC) had operated as an informal bargaining unit for the sale of oil by Third World nations but had seldom managed to exercise any real strength. But in the early 1970s, OPEC began to assert itself, to use its oil both as an economic tool and as a political weapon. In 1973, in the midst of the Yom Kippur War, Arab members of OPEC announced that they would no longer ship petroleum to nations supporting Israel—that is, to the United States and its allies in Western Europe. At about the same time, the OPEC nations agreed to raise their prices 500 percent (from $3 to $15 a barrel). These twin shocks produced momentary economic chaos in the West. The United States suffered its first fuel shortage since World

War II. And although the crisis eased a few months later, the price of energy continued to skyrocket.

The energy crisis eventually subsided, but another, longer-term change in the American economy was the transformation of the nation's manufacturing sector. Ever since World War II, American industry had enjoyed relatively little competition from the rest of the world in its search for export markets and even less competition in its domination of the American domestic market. By the end of the 1960s, however, both Western Europe and Japan had recovered from the damage their manufacturing sectors had absorbed during World War II; by the early 1970s, they were providing stiff competition to American firms in the sale of automobiles, steel, and many other products both in world markets and within the United States. Many American corporations responded to these new conditions with confusion and bewilderment, and some failed altogether. Others restructured themselves to become more competitive again in world markets. In the process, they closed many older plants and eliminated hundreds of thousands of once-lucrative manufacturing jobs. The high-wage, high-employment industrial economy that had been a central fact of American life since the 1940s was gradually disappearing.

The Nixon Response

Nixon's initial answer to these mounting economic problems was a conventional anti-inflationary one. He reduced spending and raised taxes, producing a modest budget surplus in 1969. But when those policies proved difficult to sustain, Nixon turned increasingly to control of the currency. Placing conservative economists at the head of the Federal Reserve Board, he ensured sharply higher interest rates and a contraction of the money supply. Even so, the cost of living rose a cumulative 15 percent during Nixon's first two and a half years in office. Economic growth, in the meantime, declined. The United States was encountering a new and puzzling dilemma: "stagflation," a combination of rising prices and general economic stagnation.

In the summer of 1971, Nixon imposed a ninety-day freeze on all wages and prices at their existing levels. Then, in November, he launched Phase II of his economic plan: mandatory guidelines for wage and price increases, to be administered by a federal agency. Inflation subsided temporarily, but the recession continued. Fearful that the recession would be more damaging than inflation in an election year, the administration reversed itself late in 1971: interest rates were allowed to drop sharply, and government spending increased—producing the largest budget deficit since World War II. The new tactics helped revive the economy in the short term, but inflation rose substantially. In 1973, prices rose 9 percent; in 1974, after the Arab oil embargo and the OPEC price increases, they rose 12 percent—the highest rate since shortly after World War II. The new energy crisis, in the meantime, was quickly becoming a national preoccupation. But while Nixon talked often about the need to achieve "energy independence," he offered few concrete proposals.

THE WATERGATE CRISIS

Although economic problems greatly concerned the American people in the 1970s, another stunning development almost entirely preoccupied the nation beginning early in 1973: the fall of Richard Nixon. The president's demise was a result in part of his own personality. Defensive, secretive, resentful of his critics, he brought to his office an element of mean-spiritedness that helped undermine even his most important accomplishments. But the larger explanation for the crisis lay in Nixon's view of American society and the world, and of his own role in both. The president believed the United States faced grave dangers from the radicals and dissidents who were challenging his policies. He came increasingly to consider any challenge to his policies a threat to "national security." By identifying his own political fortunes with those of the nation, Nixon was creating a climate in which he and those who served him could justify almost any tactics to stifle dissent and undermine opposition.

The Scandals

Nixon's approach to his office was in part a culmination of long-term changes in the presidency. Public expectations of the president had increased dramatically in the years since World War II, yet the constraints on the authority of the office had grown as well. In response, a succession of presidents had sought new methods for exercising power, often stretching the law, occasionally breaking it.

Nixon not only continued but greatly accelerated these trends. Facing a Democratic Congress hostile to his goals, he attempted to find ways to circumvent the legislature whenever possible. Saddled with a federal bureaucracy unresponsive to his wishes, he constructed a hierarchy of command in which virtually all executive power became concentrated in the

White House. Unknown to all but a few intimates, he also became mired in a pattern of illegalities and abuses of power that late in 1972 began to break through to the surface.

Early on the morning of June 17, 1972, police arrested five men who had broken into the offices of the Democratic National Committee in the Watergate office building in Washington, D.C. Two others were seized a short time later and charged with supervising the break-in. When reporters for the *Washington Post* began researching the backgrounds of the culprits, they discovered that among those involved in the burglary were former employees of the Committee for the Re-Election of the President (CRP). One of them had worked in the White House itself. They had, moreover, been paid for the break-in from a secret fund of the reelection committee, a fund controlled by, among others, members of the White House staff.

Public interest in the disclosures grew slowly in the last months of 1972. Early in 1973, however, the Watergate burglars went on trial; and under prodding from federal judge John J. Sirica, one of the defendants, James W. McCord, agreed to cooperate both with the grand jury and with a special Senate investigating committee recently established under Senator Sam J. Ervin of North Carolina. McCord's testimony opened a floodgate of confessions, and for months a parade of White House and campaign officials exposed one illegality after another. Foremost among them was a member of the inner circle of the White House, John Dean, counsel to the president, who leveled allegations against Nixon himself.

Two different sets of scandals emerged from the investigations. One was a general pattern of abuses of power involving both the White House and the Nixon campaign committee, which included, but was not limited to, the Watergate break-in. The other scandal, and the one that became the major focus of public attention for nearly two years, was the way in which the administration tried to manage the investigations of the Watergate break-in and other abuses—a pattern of behavior that became known as the "cover-up." There was never any conclusive evidence that the president had planned or approved the burglary in advance. But there was mounting evidence that he had been involved in illegal efforts to obstruct investigations of and withhold information about the episode. As interest in the case grew to something approaching a national obsession, the investigation focused increasingly on a single question: in the words of Senator Howard Baker of Tennessee, a member of the Ervin Committee, "What did the President know and when did he know it?"

Nixon accepted the departure of those members of his administration implicated in the scandals. But the president continued to insist on his own innocence. There the matter might have rested had it not been for the disclosure during the Senate hearings of a White House taping system that had recorded virtually every conversation in the president's office during the period in question. All those investigating the scandals sought access to the tapes; Nixon, pleading "executive privilege," refused to release them. A special prosecutor appointed by the president to handle the Watergate cases, Harvard law professor Archibald Cox, took Nixon to court in October 1973 in an effort to force him to relinquish the recordings. Nixon, now clearly growing desperate, fired Cox and suffered the humiliation of watching both Attorney General Elliot Richardson and his deputy resign in protest. This "Saturday night massacre" made the president's predicament much worse. Not only did public pressure force him to appoint a new special prosecutor, Texas attorney Leon Jaworski, who proved just as determined as Cox to subpoena the tapes; but the episode precipitated an investigation by the House of Representatives into the possibility of impeachment.

The Fall of Richard Nixon

Nixon's situation deteriorated further in the following months. Late in 1973, Vice President Spiro Agnew became embroiled in a scandal of his own when evidence surfaced that he had accepted bribes and kickbacks while serving as governor of Maryland and even as vice president. In return for a Justice Department agreement not to press the case, Agnew pleaded no contest to a lesser charge of income-tax evasion and resigned from the government. With the controversial Agnew no longer in line to succeed to the presidency, the prospect of removing Nixon from the White House became less worrisome to his opponents. The new vice president (the first appointed under the terms of the Twenty-fifth Amendment, which had been adopted in 1967) was House Minority Leader Gerald Ford, an amiable and popular Michigan congressman.

The impeachment investigation quickly gathered momentum. In April 1974, in an effort to head off further subpoenas of the tapes, the president released transcripts of a number of relevant conversations, claiming that they proved his innocence. Investigators and much of the public felt otherwise. Even these edited tapes seemed to suggest Nixon's complicity in the cover-up. In July, the crisis reached a climax. First the Supreme Court ruled unanimously, in *United States* v. *Richard M. Nixon*, that the president must relinquish the tapes to Special Prosecutor Jaworski. Days later, the House Judiciary Committee voted to recommend three articles of impeachment.

D E B A T I N G   T H E   P A S T

Watergate

wenty-five years after Watergate—the most famous political scandal in American history—historians and others continue to argue about its causes and significance. Their interpretations tend to fall into several broad categories.

One argument emphasizes the evolution of the institution of the presidency over time and sees Watergate as the result of a much larger pattern of presidential usurpations of power that stretched back at least several decades. Arthur Schlesinger, Jr., helped develop this argument in his 1973 book *The Imperial Presidency*, which argued that the belief of a succession of presidents in the urgency of the Cold War, and in their duty to take whatever measures might be necessary to combat it, led them gradually to usurp more and more power from Congress, from the courts, and from the public. Gradually, presidents began to look for ways to circumvent constraints not just in foreign policy, but in domestic matters as well. Nixon's actions in the Watergate crisis were, in other words, a culmination of this long and steady expansion of covert presidential power. Jonathan Schell, in *The Time of Illusion* (1975), offered a variation of this argument, tying the crisis of the presidency to the pressure that nuclear weapons placed on presidents to protect the nation's—and their own—"credibility."

A second explanation of Watergate emphasizes the difficult social and political environment of the late 1960s and early 1970s. Nixon entered office, according to this view, facing an unprecedentedly radical opposition that would stop at nothing to discredit the war and destroy his authority. He found himself, therefore, drawn into taking similarly desperate measures of his own to defend himself from these extraordinary challenges. Nixon made this argument himself in his 1975 memoirs:

> Now that this season of mindless terror has fortunately passed, it is difficult—perhaps impossible—to convey a sense of the pressures that were influencing my actions and reactions during this period, but it was this epidemic of unprecedented domestic terrorism that prompted our efforts to discover the best means by which to deal with this new phenomenon of highly organized and highly skilled revolutionaries dedicated to the violent destruction of our democratic system.

The historian Herbert Parmet echoed parts of this argument in *Richard Nixon and His America* (1990). Stephen Ambrose offered a more muted version of the same view in *Richard Nixon* (1989).

Most of those who have written about Watergate, however, search for the explanation not in institutional or social forces, but in the personalities of the people involved, and most notably in the personality of Richard Nixon. Even many of those who have developed structural explanations (Schlesinger, Schell, and Ambrose, for example) return eventually to Nixon himself as the most important explanation for Watergate. Others begin there, perhaps most notably Stanley I. Kutler, in *The Wars of Watergate* (1990) and, more recently, *Abuse of Power* (1997), in which he presents extensive excerpts from conversations about Watergate taped in the Nixon White House. Kutler emphasizes Nixon's lifelong resort to vicious political tactics and his longstanding belief that he was a special target of unscrupulous enemies and had to "get" them before they got him. Watergate was rooted, Kutler argues, "in the personality and history of Nixon himself." A "corrosive hatred," he claims, "decisively shaped Nixon's own behavior, his career, and eventually his historical standing."

Even without additional evidence, Nixon might well have been impeached by the full House and convicted by the Senate. Early in August, however, he provided at last the "smoking gun"—the concrete proof of his guilt—that his defenders had long contended was missing from the case against him. Among the tapes that the Supreme Court compelled Nixon to relinquish were several that offered apparently incontrovertible evidence of his involvement in the Watergate cover-up. Only three days after the burglary, the recordings disclosed, the president had ordered the FBI to stop investigating the break-in. Impeachment and conviction now seemed inevitable.

For several days, Nixon brooded in the White House, on the verge, some claimed, of a breakdown. Finally, on August 8, 1974, he announced his resignation—the first president in American history ever to do so. At noon the next day, while Nixon and his family were flying west to their home in California, Gerald Ford took the oath of office as president.

Many Americans expressed relief and exhilaration that, as the new president put it, "our long national nightmare is over." They were relieved to be rid of Richard Nixon, who had lost the great popularity that had won him his landslide reelection victory only two years before. And they were exhilarated that, as some boasted, "the system had worked." But the wave of good feeling could not obscure the deeper and more lasting damage of the Watergate crisis. In a society in which distrust of leaders and institutions of authority was already widespread, the fall of Richard Nixon confirmed for many Americans their most cynical assumptions about the character of American public life.

CONCLUSION

The victory of Richard Nixon in the 1968 presidential election represented a popular repudiation of turbulence and radicalism. It was a call for a restoration of order and stability. But order and stability were not the dominant characteristics of Nixon's troubled years in office. Nixon entered office, rather, when the forces of the left and the counterculture were approaching the peak of their influence. American culture and society in the late 1960s and early 1970s were shaped decisively by, and were deeply divided over, the challenges of young people to the norms by which most Americans had lived. They were also the years in which a host of new liberation movements joined the drive for racial equality, and when, above all, women mobilized effectively and powerfully to demand changes in the way their society treated gender differences.

Nixon had run for office attacking the failure of his predecessor to end the war in Vietnam. But for four years under his presidency, the war—and the protests against it—continued and even in some respects escalated. The division of opinion over the war was as deep as any of the many other divisions in national life. It continued to poison the nation's politics and social fabric until the American role in the conflict finally shuddered to a humiliating close in 1973.

But much of the controversy and division in the 1970s was a product of the Nixon presidency itself. Nixon was in many ways a dynamic and even visionary leader, who proposed (but rarely succeeded in enacting) some important domestic reforms and who made important changes in American foreign policy, most notably making overtures to communist China and forging détente with the Soviet Union. He was also, however, a devious, secretive, and embittered man whose White House became engaged in a series of covert activities—many of them connected with the president's reelection campaign in 1972—that produced the most dramatic political scandal in American history. Watergate, as it was called, preoccupied much of the nation for nearly two years beginning in 1972; and ultimately, in the summer of 1974, the scandal forced Richard Nixon—who had been reelected to office only two years before by one of the largest majorities in modern history—to become the first president in American history to resign. He was a victim in part of the passions and divisions of his time and of the Vietnam War, which he had inherited but had not been able quickly to end. He was a victim as well of his own insecurities and resentments. Whatever the causes of his fall, however, the greatest cost of Watergate was not what it did to Nixon himself, but how it damaged the faith of the American people in their leaders and their government. That faith would remain weak through the remainder of the century.

FOR FURTHER REFERENCE

Suggested Readings

John Morton Blum, *Years of Discord: American Politics and Society, 1961–1974* (1991) is a good overview. James Miller, *"Democracy in the Streets": From Port Huron to the Siege of Chicago* (1987) is a perceptive history of the New Left through its leading organization, SDS. Kristin Luker, *Abortion and the Politics of Motherhood* (1984) is an excellent account of this central battle over the nature of feminism. Ronald Takaki, *Strangers from a Distant Shore: A History of Asian Americans* (1989), and *A Different Mirror: A History of Multicultural America* (1993) explore some of the struggles over ethnic and racial difference in the postwar era (and other periods). Stephen Ambrose, *Nixon: The Triumph of a Politician, 1962–1972* (1989), and *Nixon, Ruin and Recovery, 1973–1990* (1992) provide a thorough, if critical, chronicle of this important presidency. Joan Hoff, *Nixon Reconsidered* (1994) is a more sympathetic account of Nixon's presidency before Watergate. Stanley J. Kutler, *The Wars of Watergate* (1990) is a scholarly study of the great scandal. Jonathan Schell, *The Time of Illusion* (1975) and J. Anthony Lukas, *Nightmare: The Underside of the Nixon Years* (1976) are perceptive contemporary accounts.

Films

(The best source for information on how to find these and other films is *Bowker's Complete Video Directory*—3 volumes.) *Chicago 1968* (1995) is a complex and riveting portrait of the dramatic events around the Democratic National Convention of 1968. The three-part series *America in 1968* (1979) examines the political, cultural, and international events of that pivotal year. *Nixon* (1990) is a three-hour film biography of one of the most powerful and controversial figures in modern American history. *Watergate* (1994) portrays the unmaking of the Nixon presidency, including recent interviews with major participants. *Contrary Warriors: A Story of the Crow Tribe* (1985) successfully combines a modern-day history of the Crow Indians, a biography of the tribe's oldest living member, and a portrait of a contemporary Crow community. *In the Spirit of Crazy Horse* (1990) relates the history of the Lakota Indians on the centennial of the Wounded Knee massacre. *Chicano! History of the Mexican-American Civil Rights Movement* (1996) is a four-part series on their movement from the pivotal 1967 struggle to regain ownership of land grants to the 1970 Chicano Moratorium in East Los Angeles.

Internet Resources

Internet websites containing historical material relevant to the subjects discussed in this chapter can be reached through the McGraw-Hill history site at www.mhhe.com/socscience/history/usa/link/linktop.htm.

CHAPTER THIRTY-THREE

The "Age of Limits"

Politics and Diplomacy After Watergate
The Rise of the American Right ～ *The "Reagan Revolution"*

T|HE FRUSTRATIONS OF the early 1970s—the defeat in Vietnam, the Watergate crisis, the decay of the American economy—inflicted damaging blows to the confident, optimistic nationalism that had characterized so much of the postwar era. At first some Americans responded to these problems by announcing the arrival of an "age of limits," in which America would have to learn to live with increasingly constricted expectations. By the end of the decade, however, the contours of another response to the challenges had become visible in both American culture and American politics. It was a response that combined a conservative retreat from some of the heady visions of the 1960s with a reinforced commitment to the idea of economic growth, international power, and American exceptionalism.

POLITICS AND DIPLOMACY AFTER WATERGATE

In the aftermath of Richard Nixon's ignominious departure from office, many wondered whether faith in the presidency, and in the government as a whole, could easily be restored. The administrations of the two presidents who succeeded Nixon did little to answer those questions.

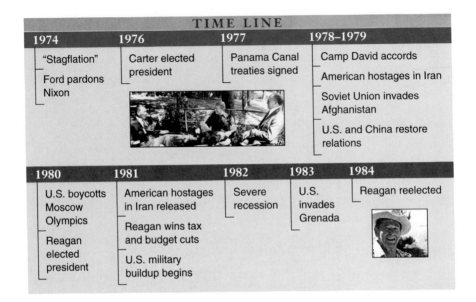

TIME LINE

1974	1976	1977	1978–1979
"Stagflation" Ford pardons Nixon	Carter elected president	Panama Canal treaties signed	Camp David accords American hostages in Iran Soviet Union invades Afghanistan U.S. and China restore relations

1980	1981	1982	1983	1984
U.S. boycotts Moscow Olympics Reagan elected president	American hostages in Iran released Reagan wins tax and budget cuts U.S. military buildup begins	Severe recession	U.S. invades Grenada	Reagan reelected

The Ford Custodianship

Gerald Ford inherited the presidency under unenviable circumstances. He had to try to rebuild confidence in government after the Watergate scandals. And he had to try to restore prosperity in the face of unprecedented domestic and international challenges to the American economy. He enjoyed some success in the first of these efforts but very little in the second.

The new president's effort to establish himself as a symbol of political integrity suffered a setback only a month after he took office, when he granted Richard Nixon "a full, free, and absolute pardon" for any crimes he may have committed during his presidency. Ford explained that he was attempting to spare the nation the ordeal of years of litigation and to spare Nixon himself any further suffering. But much of the public suspected a secret deal with the former president. The pardon caused a decline in Ford's popularity from which he never fully recovered. Nevertheless, most Americans considered Ford a decent man; his honesty and amiability did much to reduce the bitterness and acrimony of the Watergate years.

The Ford administration enjoyed less success in its effort to solve the problems of the American economy. In his attempts to curb inflation, the president rejected the idea of wage and price controls and called instead for largely ineffective voluntary efforts. After supporting high interest rates, opposing increased federal spending (through liberal use of his veto power), and resisting pressures for a tax reduction, Ford had to deal with a serious recession in 1974 and 1975. Central to the economic problems were the continuing rises in the price of energy. The OPEC cartel raised the price of oil by 400 percent in 1974 alone. Even so, American dependence on OPEC supplies continued to grow—one of the principal reasons why inflation reached 11 percent in 1976.

At first it seemed that the foreign policy of the new administration would differ little from that of its predecessor. The new president retained Henry Kissinger, whom Nixon had appointed secretary of state in 1973, and continued the general policies of the Nixon years. Late in 1974, Ford met with Leonid Brezhnev at Vladivostok in Siberia and signed an arms control accord that was to serve as the basis for SALT II, thus achieving a goal the Nixon administration had long sought. The following summer, after a European security conference in Helsinki, Finland, the Soviet Union and Western nations agreed to ratify the borders that had divided Europe since 1945; and the Soviets pledged to increase respect for human rights within their own country. In the Middle East, in the meantime, Henry Kissinger helped produce a new accord by which Israel agreed to return large portions of the occupied Sinai to Egypt; the two nations pledged not to resolve future differences by force.

Nevertheless, as the 1976 presidential election approached, Ford's policies were coming under attack from both the right and the left. In the Republican primary campaign, Ford faced a powerful challenge from former California governor Ronald Reagan, leader of the party's conservative wing, who spoke for many on the right who were unhappy with any conciliation of communists. The president only barely survived the assault to win his party's nomination. The Democrats, in the meantime, were gradually uniting behind a new and, before 1976, almost entirely unknown candidate: Jimmy Carter, a former governor of Georgia who organized a brilliant primary campaign and appealed to the general unhappiness with Washington by offering honesty, piety, and an outsider's skepticism of the federal government. And while Carter's mammoth lead dwindled to almost nothing by election day, unhappiness with the economy and a general disenchantment with Ford enabled the Democrat to hold on for a narrow victory. Carter emerged with 50 percent of the popular vote to Ford's 47.9 percent and 297 electoral votes to Ford's 240.

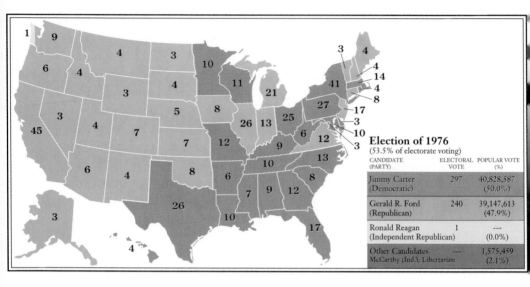

Election of 1976
(53.5% of electorate voting)

CANDIDATE (PARTY)	ELECTORAL VOTE	POPULAR VOTE (%)
Jimmy Carter (Democratic)	297	40,828,587 (50.0%)
Gerald R. Ford (Republican)	240	39,147,613 (47.9%)
Ronald Reagan (Independent Republican)	1	— (0.0%)
Other Candidates McCarthy (Ind.), Libertarian	—	1,575,459 (2.1%)

The Trials of Jimmy Carter

Like Ford, Jimmy Carter assumed the presidency at a moment when the nation faced problems of staggering complexity and difficulty. Perhaps no leader could have thrived in such inhospitable circumstances. But Carter seemed at times to make his predicament worse by a style of leadership that many considered self-righteous and inflexible. He left office in 1981 as one of the least popular presidents of the century.

Carter had campaigned for the presidency as an "outsider," representing Americans suspicious of entrenched bureaucracies and complacent public officials. He carried much of that suspiciousness with him to Washington. He surrounded himself in the White House with a group of close-knit associates from Georgia, and in the beginning, at least, he seemed deliberately to spurn assistance from more experienced political figures.

Carter devoted much of his time to the problems of energy and the economy. Entering office in the midst of a recession, he moved first to reduce unemployment by raising public spending and cutting federal taxes. Unemployment declined, but inflation soared—less because of Carter's fiscal policies than because of the escalating cost of oil. During Carter's last two years in office, prices rose at an annual rate of well over 10 percent. Like Nixon and Ford before him, Carter responded with a combination of tight money and calls for voluntary restraint. He appointed first G. William Miller and then Paul Volcker, conservative economists, to head the Federal Reserve Board, thus ensuring a policy of high interest rates and reduced money supplies. By 1980, interest rates had risen to the highest levels in American history; at times, they exceeded 20 percent.

The problem of energy also grew steadily more troublesome in the Carter years. In the summer of 1979, instability in the Middle East produced a second major fuel shortage in the United States. In the midst of the crisis, OPEC announced another major price increase, clouding the economic picture still further. Faced with increasing pressure to act (and with public opinion polls showing his approval rating at a dismal 26 percent), Carter delivered a remarkable television address. It included a series of proposals for resolving the energy crisis. But it was most notable for Carter's bleak assessment of the national condition: his complaints about a "crisis of confidence" that had struck "at the very heart and soul of our national will." The address became known as the "malaise" speech (although Carter himself had never used that word), and it helped fuel attacks that the president was trying to blame his own problems on the American people. Carter's sudden firing of several members of his cabinet a few days later deepened his political problems.

Human Rights and National Interests

Among Jimmy Carter's most frequent campaign promises was a pledge to build a new basis for American foreign policy, one in which the defense of "human rights" would replace the pursuit of "selfish interests." Carter spoke out sharply and often about violations of human rights in many countries (including, most prominently, the Soviet Union). Beyond that general commitment, the Carter administration focused on several more traditional concerns. Carter completed negotiations begun several years earlier on a pair of treaties to turn over control of the Panama Canal to the government of Panama. Domestic opposition to the treaties was intense, especially among conservatives who viewed the new arrangements as part of a general American retreat from international power. But the administration argued that relinquishing the canal was the best way to improve relations with Latin America and avoid violence in Panama. After an acrimonious debate, the Senate ratified the treaties by 68 to 32, only one vote more than the necessary two-thirds majority.

Far more popular, within the United States at least, was Carter's success in arranging a peace treaty between Egypt and Israel—the crowning

FORGING THE CAMP DAVID ACCORDS Probably the greatest achievement of Jimmy
Carter's generally frustrating presidency was his success in guiding Israel and
Egypt toward a peaceful settlement of their longstanding grievances. While
hosting Israeli Prime Minister Menachem Begin *(right)* and Egyptian president
Anwar Sadat *(left)* at his Camp David retreat in September 1978, he helped the
two leaders reach a historic agreement.

achievement of his presidency. Middle East negotiations had seemed
hopelessly stalled when a dramatic breakthrough occurred in November
1977. The Egyptian president, Anwar Sadat, accepted an invitation from
Prime Minister Menachem Begin to visit Israel. In Tel Aviv, Sadat announced that Egypt was now willing to accept the state of Israel as a legitimate political entity.

When talks between Israeli and Egyptian negotiators stalled, Carter
invited Sadat and Begin to a summit conference at Camp David in September 1978, holding them there for two weeks while he and others
helped mediate the disputes between them. On September 17, Carter escorted the two leaders into the White House to announce agreement on a
framework for an Egyptian-Israeli peace treaty. On March 26, 1979, after
additional negotiations, Begin and Sadat returned together to the White
House to sign a formal peace treaty between their two nations.

Carter responded eagerly to the overtures of Deng Xiaoping, the new
Chinese leader who was attempting to open his nation to the outside

world. On December 15, 1978, Washington and Beijing announced the establishment of formal diplomatic relations between the two nations. A few months later, Carter traveled to Vienna to meet with Brezhnev to finish drafting the new SALT II arms control agreement. The treaty set limits on the number of long-range missiles, bombers, and nuclear warheads on each side. Almost immediately, however, SALT II met with fierce conservative opposition in the United States. Central to the arguments against the treaty was a fundamental distrust of the Soviet Union that nearly a decade of détente had failed to destroy. By the fall of 1979, with the Senate scheduled to begin debate over the treaty shortly, ratification was already in jeopardy. Events in the following months provided a final blow, both to the treaty and to the larger framework of détente.

The Year of the Hostages

Ever since the early 1950s, the United States had provided political support and, more recently, massive military assistance to the government of the Shah of Iran, hoping to make his nation a bulwark against Soviet expansion in the Middle East. By 1979, however, the Shah was in deep trouble with his own people. Iranians resented the repressive, authoritarian tactics through which the Shah had maintained his autocratic rule. At the same time, Islamic clergy (and much of the fiercely religious populace) opposed his efforts to modernize and westernize a fundamentalist society. The combination of resentments produced a powerful revolutionary movement. In January 1979, the Shah fled the country. By late 1979, what official power there was in Iran was in the hands of a zealous religious leader, the Ayatollah Ruhollah Khomeini, whose hatred of the West in general and the United States in particular was intense. In late October 1979, the deposed Shah arrived in New York to be treated for cancer. Days later, on November 4, an armed mob invaded the American embassy in Teheran, seized the diplomats and military personnel inside, and demanded the return of the Shah to Iran in exchange for their freedom. Fifty-three Americans remained hostages in the embassy for over a year. Coming after years of what many Americans considered international humiliations and defeats, the hostage seizure released a deep well of anger and emotion.

Only weeks after the hostage seizure, on December 27, 1979, Soviet troops invaded Afghanistan, the mountainous nation bordering the Soviet Union and Iran. The Soviet Union had, in fact, been a power in Afghanistan for years, and the dominant force since April 1978, when a coup had established a Marxist government there with close ties to the

THE HOSTAGES ON DISPLAY The holding hostage of American diplomats in Iran for over a year beginning in November 1979 was always as much an effort to generate publicity as a real negotiating tactic. Anti-Western Iranians wasted few opportunities to display their grievances against the United States for its long support of the Shah, and they were eager to present the hostages themselves as evidence of their ability to humble the mighty United States. Here a number of the fifty-three hostages sit on display under signs written in English for the American television audience.

Kremlin. The Soviet invasion was at least in part a Russian attempt to secure the status quo against a growing rebel movement. But President Carter, and many other Western observers, charged that the invasion was a Russian "stepping stone to their possible control over much of the world's oil supplies." Carter angrily imposed a series of economic sanctions on the Russians, canceled American participation in the 1980 summer Olympic Games in Moscow, and announced the withdrawal of SALT II from Senate consideration.

The combination of domestic economic troubles and international crises created widespread anxiety, frustration, and anger in the United States—damaging President Carter's already low standing with the public, and giving added strength to an alternative political force that had already made great strides.

THE RISE OF THE AMERICAN RIGHT

The jarring public events of the 1960s and 1970s, and the broader changes in the character of America's economy, society, and culture, disillusioned many liberals, perplexed the already weakened left, and provided the right with its most important opportunity in generations to seize a position of authority in American life.

The Sunbelt and Its Politics

One of the major demographic events of the 1970s was the emergence of what became known as the "Sunbelt," a group of regions that included some of the most dynamically growing parts of the country. The Sunbelt included the Southeast (particularly Florida), the Southwest (particularly Texas), and above all, California, which became the nation's most populous state in 1964. By 1980, more people lived in the Sunbelt than lived in the industrial regions of the North and East.

Among other things, the rise of the Sunbelt helped produce a change in the political climate. The strong populist traditions in the South and the West—and the high emphasis on individual liberty in particular—were capable of producing progressive and even radical politics; but more often in the late twentieth century, they produced a strong opposition to the growth of government, and to government regulations in particular. Many federal regulations and restrictions—environmental laws, land-use restrictions, even the fifty-five-mile-per-hour speed limit created during the energy crisis to force motorists to conserve fuel—affected the West more than any other region.

The so-called Sagebrush Rebellion, which emerged in parts of the West in the late 1970s, mobilized conservative opposition to environmental laws and restrictions on development. It also sought to portray the West (which in reality had benefited more than any other region from federal investment) as a victim of government control. Its members complained about the very large amounts of land the federal government owned in many western states and demanded that they be opened for development.

The South as a whole was considerably more conservative than other parts of the nation, and its growth served to increase the power of the right in the 1960s and 1970s. The West had not, on the whole, been more conservative than other regions historically; but in the postwar period, the West produced some of the most numerous and powerful conservative movements in the nation—particularly in southern California, where Orange County (a large suburban area south of Los Angeles) emerged as one of the most important centers of right-wing politics in the country.

Religious Revivalism

The United States experienced the beginning of a major religious revival in the 1970s that continued in various forms through the 1990s. Some of the new religious enthusiasm found expression in the rise of cults and pseudo-faiths: the Church of Scientology; the Unification Church of the Reverend Sun Myung Moon; and the tragic People's Temple, whose members committed mass suicide in their jungle retreat in Guyana in 1978. But the most important impulse of the religious revival was the growth of evangelical Christianity. Evangelicalism is the basis of many forms of Christian faith, but Evangelicals have in common a belief in personal conversion through direct communication with God.

Earlier in the century, many (although never all) evangelicals had been relatively poor rural people. But the great capitalist expansion after World War II had lifted many of these people out of poverty and into the middle class, where they were more visible and more assertive. Over 70 million Americans now described themselves as "born-again" Christians—men and women who had established a "direct personal relationship with Jesus." Christian evangelicals owned their own newspapers, magazines, radio stations, and television networks. They operated their own schools and universities. One of them occupied the White House itself—Jimmy Carter, who during the 1976 campaign had talked proudly of his own "conversion experience" and who continued openly to proclaim his "born-again" Christian faith during his years in office.

For Jimmy Carter and for some others, evangelical Christianity had formed the basis for a commitment to racial justice and world peace. But many Evangelicals in the 1970s became active on the political and cultural right. They were alarmed by what they considered the spread of immorality and disorder in American life; and they were concerned about the way a secular and, as they saw it, godless culture was intruding into their communities and families—through popular culture, through the schools, and through government policies. Particularly alarming to them were Supreme Court decisions eliminating prayer from schools and, later, guaranteeing women the right to an abortion.

By the late 1970s, the "Christian right" had become a visible and increasingly powerful political force. Jerry Falwell, a fundamentalist minister in Virginia with a substantial television audience, launched a movement he called the Moral Majority, which attacked the rise of "secular humanism" in American culture. Pat Robertson, a Pentecostal minister with his own television network, became a perennial force in presidential politics within the Republican Party in the 1990s. Falwell, Robertson, and other right-wing evangelicals denounced abortion, divorce, feminism, and homosexuality; defended unrestricted free enterprise; and supported a strong American posture in the world. Some evangelicals reopened issues that had long seemed closed. For example, some conservative Evangelicals denied the scientific doctrine of evolution and instead urged the teaching in schools of the biblical story of the Creation. Others advocated various forms of censorship of books, films, plays, and other works of art whose content they considered immoral.

The Emergence of the New Right

Conservative evangelical Christians were an important part, but only a part, of what became known as the New Right—a diverse but powerful movement that enjoyed rapid growth in the 1970s and early 1980s. It had begun to take shape after the 1964 election, in which Barry Goldwater had suffered his shattering defeat. Richard Viguerie, a remarkable conservative activist and organizer, took a list of 12,000 contributors to the Goldwater campaign and used it to develop a formidable conservative communications and fund-raising organization. By the mid-1970s, he had gathered a list of 4 million contributors and 15 million supporters. Gradually these direct-mail operations helped create a much larger conservative infrastructure, designed to match and even exceed what the right saw as the powerful liberal infrastructure. By the late 1970s, there were right-wing think tanks, consulting firms, lobbyists, foundations, and scholarly centers. Another factor in the revival of the right was the emergence of credible leadership. Chief among this new generation of conservative leaders was Ronald Reagan, once a moderately successful film actor, who had become deeply involved in right-wing politics in California and, in 1966, won election as governor of the state. His engaging, self-assured demeanor and his smooth, eloquent speeches in defense of individual freedom and private enterprise won him increasing national recognition.

The presidency of Gerald Ford also played an important role in the rise of the right, by destroying the fragile equilibrium that had enabled the right wing and the moderate wing of the Republican Party to coexist. Ford appointed as vice president Nelson Rockefeller, the liberal Republican governor of New York and an heir to one of America's great fortunes; many conservatives had been demonizing Rockefeller and his family for more than twenty years. Ford proposed an amnesty program for draft re- sisters, embraced and even extended the hated Nixon-Kissinger policies of détente, presided over the fall of Vietnam, and agreed to cede the Panama Canal to Panama. When Reagan challenged Ford in the 1976 Republican primaries, the president survived, barely, only by dropping Nelson Rocke- feller from the ticket and agreeing to a platform largely written by one of Reagan's principal allies, Senator Jesse Helms of North Carolina. Reagan hailed that platform by saying that the party "must raise a banner of no pale pastels, but bold colors which make it unmistakably clear where we stand on all the issues troubling the people."

The Tax Revolt

At least equally important to the success of the New Right was a new and potent conservative issue: the tax revolt. It had its public beginnings in 1978, when Howard Jarvis, a conservative activist, launched a successful tax revolt in California with Proposition 13, a referendum question on the state ballot rolling back property-tax rates. Similar antitax movements soon began in other states and eventually spread to national politics.

For more than thirty years after the New Deal, Republican conserva- tives had struggled to halt and even reverse the growth of government. But during most of those years, as right-wing politicians from Robert Taft to Barry Goldwater discovered, attacking government programs did not succeed in attracting majority support. Every government program had a political constituency, and the biggest and most expensive programs had the broadest support. Proposition 13 and similar initiatives gave members of the right a better way to undermine government than by attacking spe- cific programs: attacking taxes. By separating the issue of taxes from the issue of what taxes supported, the right found a way to achieve the most controversial elements of its own agenda (eroding the government's ability to launch new ventures and even to sustain old ones) without openly an- tagonizing the millions of voters who supported specific programs. Virtu- ally no one liked to pay taxes, and as the economy grew weaker and the relative burden of paying taxes grew heavier, that resentment naturally rose. By exploiting that resentment, the right expanded its constituency far beyond anything it had known before. The 1980 presidential election propelled it to a historic victory.

The Campaign of 1980

By the time of the crises in Iran and Afghanistan, Jimmy Carter was in desperate political trouble. His standing in popularity polls was lower than that of any president in history. Senator Edward Kennedy, younger brother of John and Robert Kennedy, was preparing to challenge him in the primaries. For a short while, the seizure of the hostages and the stern American response to the Soviet invasion revived Carter's candidacy. But as the hostage crisis dragged on, public impatience grew. Kennedy won a series of victories over the president in the later primaries. And while Carter managed in the end to stave off Kennedy's challenge and win his party's nomination, it was an unhappy Democratic Convention that heard the president's listless call to arms.

The Republican Party, in the meantime, had rallied enthusiastically behind Ronald Reagan, a man whom, not many years before, many Americans had considered a frightening reactionary. But he now emerged not just as a poised and articulate campaigner but as a spokesman for the public's growing discontent with its leadership and its government.

On election day 1980, the anniversary of the seizure of the hostages in Iran, Reagan swept to victory with 51 percent of the vote to 41 percent for Jimmy Carter and 7 percent for John Anderson—a moderate Republican congressman from Illinois who had mounted an independent campaign.

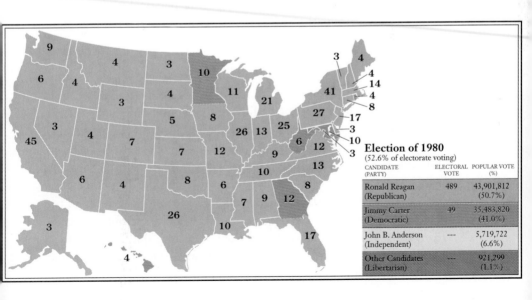

Election of 1980
(52.6% of electorate voting)

CANDIDATE (PARTY)	ELECTORAL VOTE	POPULAR VOTE (%)
Ronald Reagan (Republican)	489	43,901,812 (50.7%)
Jimmy Carter (Democratic)	49	35,483,820 (41.0%)
John B. Anderson (Independent)	---	5,719,722 (6.6%)
Other Candidates (Libertarian)	---	921,299 (1.1%)

Carter carried only five states and the District of Columbia, for a total of 49 electoral votes to Reagan's 489. The Republican Party won control of the Senate for the first time since 1952; and although the Democrats retained a narrow majority in the House, the lower chamber also seemed firmly in the hands of conservatives.

On the day of Reagan's inauguration, the American hostages in Iran were released after their 444-day ordeal, as a result of negotiations Jimmy Carter had concluded in the last hours of his presidency. Americans welcomed the hostages home with demonstrations of euphoria and patriotism not seen since the end of World War II. But while the celebration in 1945 had marked a great American triumph, the euphoria in 1981 marked something quite different—a troubled nation grasping for reassurance. Ronald Reagan set out to provide it.

THE "REAGAN REVOLUTION"

Reagan assumed the presidency in January 1981 promising a change in government more profound than any since the New Deal of fifty years before. His eight years in office produced a significant shift in public policy, but they brought nothing so fundamental as many of his supporters had hoped or his opponents had feared. There was, however, no ambiguity about his administration's purely political achievements. Ronald Reagan succeeded brilliantly in making his own engaging personality the central fact of American politics in the 1980s.

Reagan in the White House

Even many people who disagreed with the president's policies found themselves drawn to his attractive and carefully honed public image. Reagan was a master of television and a gifted public speaker. He was the oldest man ever to serve as president, but he seemed vigorous, resilient, even youthful. When he was wounded in an assassination attempt in 1981, he joked with doctors on his way into surgery and appeared to bounce back from the ordeal with remarkable speed. Four years later, he seemed to rebound from cancer surgery with similar zest. He had few visible insecurities. Even when things went wrong, as they often did, the blame seemed seldom to attach to Reagan himself (inspiring some Democrats to begin referring to him as "the Teflon president").

THE REAGANS IN SANTA BARBARA In the weeks before the 1980 Republican Convention, at which he was nominated for the presidency, Ronald Reagan and his wife Nancy spent time relaxing, very publicly, at their ranch near Santa Barbara, California. Reagan returned often to his ranch during his presidency and, indeed, spent more days vacationing than any president in decades.

Reagan was not much involved in the day-to-day affairs of running the government; he surrounded himself with tough, energetic administrators who insulated him from many of the pressures of the office and apparently relied on him largely for general guidance, not specific decisions. But Reagan did make active use of his office to generate support for his administration's programs, by appealing repeatedly to the public over television and by fusing his proposals with a highly nationalistic rhetoric.

"Supply-Side" Economics

Reagan's 1980 campaign for the presidency had promised, among other things, to restore the economy to health by a bold experiment that became known as "supply-side" economics or, to some, "Reaganomics." Supply-side economics operated from the assumption that the woes of the

American economy were in large part a result of excessive taxation, which left inadequate capital available to investors to stimulate growth. The solution, therefore, was to reduce taxes, with particularly generous benefits to corporations and wealthy individuals, in order to encourage new investments. The result would be a general economic revival that would help everyone. Because a tax cut would reduce government revenues (at least at first), it would also be necessary to reduce government expenses. Another cornerstone of the Reagan economic program, therefore, was a dramatic cut in the federal budget, which would, the administration promised, bring it into balance within a few years.

In its first months in office, accordingly, the new administration hastily assembled a legislative program based on the supply-side idea. It proposed $40 billion in budget cuts and managed to win congressional approval of almost all of them. In addition, the president proposed a bold, three-year rate reduction on both individual and corporate taxes. In the summer of 1981, Congress passed it too. Not since Lyndon Johnson had a president compiled so impressive a legislative record in his first months in office.

By early 1982, the nation had sunk into the most severe recession since the 1930s. The Reagan economic program was not directly to blame for the problems, but critics claimed that the administration's policies were doing nothing to improve the situation. In fact, however, the economy recovered more rapidly and impressively than almost anyone had expected. By the middle of 1983, unemployment (which had reached nearly 11 percent in 1982, the highest level in over forty years) had fallen to 8.2 percent. The gross national product had grown 3.6 percent, the largest increase since the mid-1970s. Inflation had fallen below 5 percent. The economy continued to grow, and both inflation and unemployment remained low (at least by the new and more pessimistic standards the nation seemed now to have accepted) through most of the decade.

The recovery was a result of many things. Years of tight money policies by the Federal Reserve Board had helped lower inflation. A worldwide "energy glut," the apparent collapse of the OPEC cartel, and the deregulation of natural-gas production had produced at least a temporary end to the inflationary pressures of spiraling fuel costs. And staggering federal budget deficits were pumping billions of dollars into the flagging economy but also, many warned, threatening ultimately to destroy the recovery they were helping to create.

The Fiscal Crisis

By the mid-1980s, the growing fiscal crisis had become one of the central issues in American politics. Having entered office promising a balanced budget within four years, Reagan presided over record budget deficits and accumulated more debt in his eight years in office than the American government had accumulated in its entire previous history. Before the 1980s, the highest single-year budget deficit in American history had been $66 billion (in 1976). Throughout the 1980s, the annual budget deficit consistently exceeded $100 billion (and in 1986 peaked at $221 billion). The national debt rose from $907 billion in 1980 to nearly $3 trillion by 1990.

The enormous deficits had many causes, some of them stretching back over decades of American public policy decisions. In particular, the budget suffered from enormous increases in the costs of "entitlement" programs (especially Social Security and Medicare), a result of the aging of the population and dramatic increases in the cost of health care. But some of the causes of the deficit lay in the policies of the Reagan administration. The 1981 tax cuts, the largest in American history, sharply eroded the revenue base of the federal government and accounted for a large percentage of the deficit. The massive increase in military spending (a proposed $1.6 trillion over five years) on which the Reagan administration insisted added more to the federal budget than its cuts in domestic spending removed.

In the face of these deficits, the administration refused to consider raising income taxes (although it did agree to a major increase in the Social Security tax). It would not agree to reductions in military spending. It was not willing to take the unpopular steps necessary to reduce the costs of entitlement programs, and it could do nothing to reduce interest payments on the massive (and growing) debt. Its answer to the fiscal crisis, therefore, was further cuts in "discretionary" domestic spending, which included many programs aimed at the poorest (and politically weakest) Americans. There were reductions in funding for food stamps; a major cut in federal subsidies for low-income housing; strict new limitations on Medicare and Medicaid payments; reductions in student loans, school lunches, and other educational programs; and an end to many forms of federal assistance to the states and cities—which helped precipitate years of local fiscal crises as well.

By the end of Reagan's third year in office, funding for domestic programs had been cut nearly as far as Congress (and, apparently, the public) was willing to tolerate. Congress responded with the Gramm-Rudman-Hollings Act, passed late in 1985, which mandated major deficit reductions over five years and provided for automatic budget cuts in all areas of government spending should the president and Congress fail to agree on an alternative solution. Under Gramm-Rudman-Hollings, the budget deficit did decline for several years. But much of that decline was a result of a substantial surplus in the Social Security trust fund (which the sharply increased Social Security taxes had produced), not of any larger fiscal successes. In the late 1980s, deficits began to rise again.

Reagan and the World

Reagan encountered a similar combination of triumphs and difficulties in international affairs. Determined to restore American pride and prestige in the world, he argued that the United States should once again become active and assertive in opposing communism and supporting friendly governments whatever their internal policies.

Relations with the Soviet Union, which had been steadily deteriorating in the last years of the Carter administration, grew still more chilly in the first years of the Reagan presidency. The president spoke harshly of the Soviet regime (which he once called the "evil empire"), accusing it of sponsoring world terrorism and declaring that any armaments negotiations must be linked to negotiations on Soviet behavior in other areas. Relations with the Russians deteriorated further after the government of Poland (under strong pressure from Moscow) imposed martial law on the country in the winter of 1981 to crush a growing challenge from an independent labor organization, Solidarity.

Although the president had long denounced the SALT II arms control treaty as unfavorable to the United States, he continued to honor its provisions. But the Reagan administration at first made little progress toward arms control in other areas, despite the growing political power of a popular antinuclear movement in both Europe and the United States. In fact, the president proposed the most ambitious new military program in many years: the Strategic Defense Initiative (SDI), widely known as "Star Wars" (after a popular science-fiction movie). Reagan claimed that SDI, through the use of lasers and satellites, could provide an effective shield against incoming missiles and thus make nuclear war obsolete. The Soviet Union claimed that the new program would elevate the arms race to new and more dangerous levels and insisted that any arms control agreement begin with an American abandonment of SDI.

At the same time, the Reagan administration began, rhetorically at least, to support opponents of communism anywhere in the world, whether or not the regimes they were challenging were directly allied to the Soviet Union. This policy became known as the Reagan Doctrine, and it meant, above all, a new American activism in the Third World. The most conspicuous examples of the new activism came in Latin America. In October 1983, the administration sent American soldiers and marines to the tiny Caribbean island of Grenada to oust an anti-American Marxist regime that was forging a relationship with the Soviet Union. In El Salvador, where first a repressive military regime and later a moderate civilian one were engaged in murderous struggles with left-wing revolutionaries (who were supported, according to the Reagan administration, by Cuba and the Soviet Union), the president provided increased military and economic assistance. In neighboring Nicaragua, a pro-American dictatorship had fallen to the revolutionary "Sandinistas" in 1979; the new government had grown increasingly anti-American (and increasingly Marxist) throughout the early 1980s. The administration gave both rhetorical and material support to the so-called contras, a guerrilla movement drawn from several antigovernment groups and fighting (without great success) to topple the Sandinista regime. Indeed, support of the contras became a mission of special importance to the president, and later the source of some of his greatest difficulties.

In other parts of the world, the administration's bellicose rhetoric seemed to hide an instinctive restraint. In June 1982, the Israeli army launched an invasion of Lebanon in an effort to drive guerrillas of the Palestinian Liberation Organization from the country. The United States supported the Israelis rhetorically but also worked to permit PLO forces to leave Lebanon peacefully. An American peacekeeping force entered Beirut to supervise the evacuation. American marines then remained in the city, apparently to protect the fragile Lebanese government, which was embroiled in a vicious civil war. Now identified with one faction in the struggle, Americans themselves became the targets; a 1983 terrorist bombing of a United States military barracks in Beirut left 241 marines dead. Rather than become more deeply involved in the Lebanese struggle, Reagan withdrew the American forces.

The Election of 1984

Reagan approached the campaign of 1984 at the head of a united Republican Party firmly committed to his candidacy. The Democrats, as had become their custom, followed a more fractious course. In the end, however, former vice president Walter Mondale withstood a series of vigorous challenges to capture the nomination. He brought momentary excitement to the Democratic Convention in San Francisco that summer by selecting a woman, Representative Geraldine Ferraro of New York, to be his running mate and the first female candidate ever to appear on a major-party national ticket.

The Republican Party, in the meantime, rallied comfortably behind its revered leader, whose triumphant campaign that fall scarcely took note of his opponents. Reagan's victory in 1984 was decisive. He won approximately 59 percent of the vote, and he carried every state except Mondale's native Minnesota and the District of Columbia. But Reagan was stronger than his party. Democrats gained a seat in the Senate and maintained only slightly reduced control of the House of Representatives.

CONCLUSION

America in the late 1970s was, by the standards of its own recent history, an unusually troubled nation: numbed by the Watergate scandals, the collapse of Vietnam, and perhaps most of all the nation's increasing economic difficulties. The unhappy presidencies of Gerald Ford and Jimmy Carter provided little relief from these accumulating problems and anxieties. Indeed, in the last year of the Carter presidency, the nation's prospects seemed particularly grim in light of growing economic difficulties, a traumatic seizure of American hostages in Iran, and a Soviet invasion of Afghanistan.

In the midst of these problems, American conservatives were slowly and steadily preparing for an impressive revival. A coalition of disparate but impassioned groups on the right—including a large movement known as the "New Right" with vaguely populist impulses—gained strength from the nation's troubles and from their own success in winning popularity for a broad-ranging revolt against taxes. Their efforts culminated in the election of 1980, when Ronald Reagan became the most conservative man in at least sixty years to be elected president of the United States.

Reagan's first term was a dramatic contrast to the troubled presidencies that had preceded it. He won substantial victories in Congress (cutting taxes, reducing spending on domestic programs, building up the military). Perhaps equally important, he made his own engaging personality one of the central political forces in national life.

The triumphant reelection of Ronald Reagan was the high-water mark up to that point of conservative, and Republican, fortunes in the postwar era. It reflected satisfaction with the impressive performance of the economy under the Republican economic program, and pride in the new assertiveness the United States was showing in the world. To many Reagan supporters, the 1984 election seemed to be the dawn of a new conservative era. Few anticipated that it also coincided with the beginning of a revolutionary change in the world order, and the United States' place in it. The election of 1984 was less the first marker of a new era than the last of the old one. It was the final campaign of the Cold War.

FOR FURTHER REFERENCE

Suggested Readings

Steven Gillon, *The Democrats' Dilemma: Walter Mondale and the Liberal Legacy* (1992) is a good discussion of the travails of the Democrats in the 1970s. Jerome L. Himmelstein, *To the Right: The Transformation of American Conservatism* (1990) is a good introduction to the subject. Sidney Blumenthal, *The Rise of the Counter-Establishment* (1986) traces the emergence of a right-wing infrastructure. Garry Wills, *Reagan's America* (1987) is an interesting, critical interpretation. Lou Cannon, *President Reagan: The Role of a Lifetime* (1990) is a good, straightforward account by a journalist who covered the Reagan White House. Hedrick Smith, *The Power Game* (1988) is a sweeping portrait of the culture of political Washington during the Reagan years.

Films

(The best source for information on how to find these and other films is *Bowker's Complete Video Directory*—3 volumes.) *Rachel Carson's Silent Spring* (1993) is a retrospective on perhaps the signal statement of the modern environmental movement. *The Conservative Resurgence* (1991) examines the reasons for the growing conservative trend in American politics during the late 1970s and 1980s.

Internet Resources

Internet websites containing historical material relevant to the subjects discussed in this chapter can be reached through the McGraw-Hill history site at www.mhhe.com/socscience/history/usa/link/linktop.htm.

Modern Times

O N NOVEMBER 8, 1989, East German soldiers stood guard at the Berlin Wall—keeping westerners out and easterners in—as they had done every day for more than twenty-eight years. The next day they were gone. Within hours, thousands of citizens of both sides of the divided city were swarming over the wall in celebration. Within weeks, bulldozers were tearing it down. Within a year, East and West Germany—divided by the Cold War for forty-five years—had reunited.

The breaching of the Berlin Wall and the reunification of Germany were among the most dramatic of a series of changes between 1986 and 1991 that radically transformed the world order. The Cold War, which as late as 1985 had seemed a permanent fact of international life, came to an end. A new world order, the outlines of which were only dimly visible, was in the process of being born.

America in the late 1980s and early 1990s was also encountering a series of other important social and economic changes, many of them unrelated to the Cold War. As the end of the twentieth century approached, most Americans were uncertain whether the changes would bring a better, safer world or a harsher and more dangerous one.

AMERICA AND THE WANING
OF THE COLD WAR

Many factors contributed to the collapse of the Soviet empire. The long, stalemated war in Afghanistan proved at least as disastrous to the Soviet

TIME LINE

1977	1979	1981	1985	1986
Apple introduces first personal computer	Three Mile Island nuclear accident	AIDS first reported in U.S.	Reagan and Gorbachev meet Crack cocaine appears in U.S. cities	U.S. bombs Libya Iran-contra scandal revealed

1987	1988	1989		1990
Gorbachev visits U.S. Stock market falls	Bush elected president	Berlin Wall dismantled Communist regimes collapse American troops in Panama Human Genome project launched		Iraq invades Kuwait

1991	1992		1993	1994
Collapse of Soviet regime Persian Gulf War	Los Angeles race riots Clinton elected president		North American Free Trade Agreement ratified	Health care reform fails Republicans capture Congress

1995	1996	1997	1998	1999
Government shutdown Crime rates decline O.J. Simpson trial	Welfare reform passed Clinton re-elected	Microsoft antitrust suit begins Balanced budget agreement	Lewinsky scandal breaks Democrats gain in congressional elections Clinton impeached by House	Clinton aquitted by Senate

Union as the Vietnam War had been to America. The government in Moscow had failed to address a long-term economic decline in the Soviet republics and the Eastern-bloc nations. Restiveness with the heavy-handed policies of communist police states was growing throughout much of the Soviet empire. But the most visible factor at the time was the emergence of Mikhail Gorbachev, who succeeded to the leadership of the Soviet Union in 1985 and, to the surprise of almost everyone (probably including himself), very quickly became the most revolutionary figure in world politics in at least four decades.

SMASHING THE WALL Once it became clear in November 1989 that the East German government was no longer defending the wall that had divided Berlin for nearly thirty years, Germans on both sides of the divide swarmed over it in celebration. Here, a West German takes a sledgehammer to the already battered wall as East German border guards passively look on.

The Fall of the Soviet Union

Gorbachev quickly transformed Soviet politics with two dramatic new initiatives. The first he called *glasnost* (openness): the dismantling of many of the repressive mechanisms that had been conspicuous features of Soviet life for over half a century. The other policy Gorbachev called *perestroika* (reform): an effort to restructure the rigid and unproductive Soviet economy by introducing, among other things, such elements of capitalism as private ownership and the profit motive. He also began to transform Soviet foreign policy.

The severe economic problems at home evidently convinced Gorbachev that the Soviet Union could no longer sustain its extended commitments around the world. As early as 1987, he began reducing Soviet influence in Eastern Europe. And in 1989, in the space of a few months, every communist state in Europe—Poland, Hungary, Czechoslovakia, Bulgaria, Romania, East Germany, Yugoslavia, and Albania—either overthrew its government or forced it to transform itself into an essentially noncommunist (and in some cases, actively anticommunist) regime. The Communist Parties of Eastern Europe collapsed or redefined themselves into more conventional left-leaning social democratic parties. Gorbachev and the Soviet Union actively encouraged the changes.

The challenges to communism were not successful everywhere. In May 1989, students in China launched a mass movement calling for greater democratization. But in June, hard-line leaders seized control of the government and sent military forces to crush the uprising. The result was a bloody massacre on June 3, 1989, in Tiananmen Square in Beijing, in which a still-unknown number of demonstrators died. The assault crushed the democracy movement and restored the hard-liners to power. It did not, however, stop China's efforts to modernize and even westernize its economy.

But China was an exception to the worldwide movement toward democratization, which even extended to parts of the world far removed from the Soviet empire. Early in 1990, the government of South Africa, long an international pariah for its rigid enforcement of "apartheid" (a system designed to protect white supremacy), began a cautious retreat from its traditional policies. Among other things, it legalized the chief black party in the nation, the African National Congress (ANC), which had been banned for decades; and on February 11, 1990, it released from prison the leader of the ANC, and a revered hero to black South Africans, Nelson Mandela, who had been in jail for twenty-seven years. Over the next several years, the South African government repealed its apartheid laws. And in 1994, there were national elections in which all South Africans could participate. As a result, Nelson Mandela became the first black president of South Africa.

In 1991, communism began to collapse at the site of its birth: the Soviet Union itself. An unsuccessful coup by hard-line Soviet leaders on August 19 precipitated a dramatic unraveling of communist power. Within days, the coup itself collapsed in the face of resistance from the public and, more important, crucial elements within the military. Mikhail Gorbachev returned to power, but it soon became evident that the legitimacy of both the Communist Party and the central Soviet government had been fatally injured. By the end of August, many of the republics of the Soviet Union had declared independence; the Soviet government was clearly powerless to stop the fragmentation. Gorbachev himself finally resigned as leader of the now virtually powerless Communist Party and Soviet government, and the Soviet Union ceased to exist.

Reagan and Gorbachev

The last years of the Reagan administration coincided with the first years of the Gorbachev regime; and while Reagan was skeptical of Gorbachev at first, he gradually became convinced that the Soviet leader was sincere in his desire for reform. At a summit meeting with Reagan in Reykjavik, Iceland, in 1986, Gorbachev proposed reducing the nuclear arsenals of both sides by 50 percent or more, although continuing disputes over Reagan's commitment to the SDI program prevented agreements. But in 1988, after Reagan and Gorbachev exchanged cordial visits to each other's capitals, the two superpowers signed a treaty eliminating American and Soviet intermediate-range nuclear forces (INF) from Europe—the most significant arms control agreement of the nuclear age. At about the same time, Gorbachev ended the Soviet Union's long and frustrating military involvement in Afghanistan.

The Fading of the Reagan Revolution

For a time, the dramatic changes around the world and Reagan's personal popularity deflected attention from a series of scandals that might well have destroyed another administration. There were revelations of illegality, corruption, and ethical lapses in the Environmental Protection Agency, the CIA, the Department of Defense, the Department of Labor, the Department of Justice, and the Department of Housing and Urban Development. A more serious scandal emerged within the savings and loan industry, which the Reagan administration had helped deregulate in the early 1980s. Many savings banks had responded by rapidly, often recklessly, and sometimes corruptly, expanding. By the end of the decade the industry was in chaos, and the government was forced to step in to prevent a complete collapse. Government insurance covered the assets of most savings and loan depositors; the cost of the debacle to the public eventually ran to more than half a trillion dollars.

But the most politically damaging scandal of the Reagan years came to light in November 1986, when the White House conceded that it had sold weapons to the revolutionary government of Iran as part of a largely unsuccessful effort to secure the release of several Americans being held hostage by radical Islamic groups in the Middle East. Even more damaging was the revelation that some of the money from the arms deal with Iran had been covertly and illegally funneled into a fund to aid the contras in Nicaragua.

In the months that followed, aggressive reporting and a highly publicized series of congressional hearings exposed a widespread pattern of covert activities orchestrated by the White House and dedicated to advancing the administration's foreign policy aims through secret and at times illegal means. The principal figure in this covert world appeared at first to be an obscure marine lieutenant colonel assigned to the staff of the National Security Council, Oliver North. But gradually it became clear that North was acting in concert with other, more powerful figures in the administration. The Iran-contra scandal, as it became known, did serious damage to the Reagan presidency—even though the investigations were never able decisively to tie the president himself to the most serious violations of the law.

The Election of 1988

The fraying of the Reagan administration helped the Democrats regain control of the United States Senate in 1986 and fueled hopes in the party for a presidential victory in 1988. Even so, several of the most popular figures in the Democratic Party refused to run, and the nomination finally went to a previously little-known figure: Michael Dukakis, a three-term governor of Massachusetts. Dukakis was a dry, even dull campaigner. But Democrats were optimistic about their prospects in 1988, largely because their opponent, Vice President George Bush, had failed to spark any real public enthusiasm. He entered the last months of the campaign well behind Dukakis.

Beginning at the Republican Convention, however, Bush staged a remarkable turnaround by making his campaign a long, relentless attack on Dukakis, tying him to all the unpopular social and cultural stances Americans had come to identify with "liberals." Indeed, the Bush campaign was almost certainly the most negative of the twentieth century. It was also, apparently, one of the most effective, although the listless, indecisive character of the Dukakis effort contributed to the Republican cause as well. Bush won a substantial victory in November: 54 percent of the popular vote to Dukakis's 46 percent, and 426 electoral votes to Dukakis's 112. But Bush carried few Republicans into office with him; the Democrats retained secure majorities in both houses of Congress.

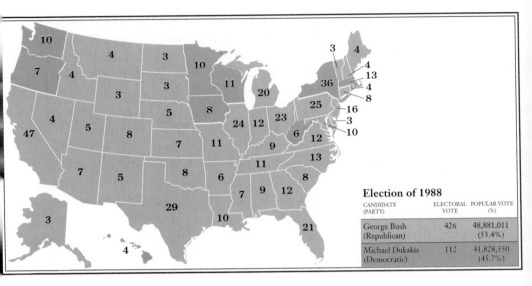

Election of 1988

CANDIDATE (PARTY)	ELECTORAL VOTE	POPULAR VOTE (%)
George Bush (Republican)	426	48,881,011 (53.4%)
Michael Dukakis (Democratic)	112	41,828,350 (45.7%)

The Bush Presidency

The Bush presidency was notable for the dramatic developments in international affairs with which it coincided and at times helped to advance, and for the absence of important initiatives or ideas on domestic issues.

The broad popularity Bush enjoyed during his first three years in office was partly a result of his subdued, unthreatening public image. But it was primarily because of the wonder and excitement with which Americans viewed the dramatic events in the rest of the world. Bush moved cautiously at first in dealing with the changes in the Soviet Union. But like Reagan, he eventually cooperated with Gorbachev and reached a series of significant agreements with the Soviet Union in its waning years. In the three years after the INF agreement in 1988, the United States and the Soviet Union moved rapidly toward even more far-reaching arms reduction agreements.

On domestic issues, the Bush administration was less successful—partly because the president himself seemed to have little interest in promoting a domestic agenda and partly because he faced serious obstacles. His administration inherited a staggering burden of debt and a federal deficit that had been out of control for nearly a decade. Any domestic agenda that required significant federal spending was, therefore, incompatible with the president's pledge to reduce the deficit and his 1988 campaign promise of "no new taxes." Bush faced a Democratic Congress with an agenda very different from his own. And he was constantly concerned

BUSH AND GORBACHEV When Bush became president in 1989, the Cold War with the Soviet Union—although much less intense than it had been several years earlier—was still in progress. By the time he left office in 1993, the Cold War was over; the once "captive nations" of eastern Europe were free of Soviet domination; and the Soviet Union itself had unravelled and dissoved. Much of the impetus for these changes originated with the last Soviet leader, Mikhail Gorbachev, whose efforts at reform unleashed forces he ultimately could not control. But before he lost power, he negotiated a series of historic agreements with the United States—some of them through summit meetings such as this one in Washingon in 1990.

about the right wing of his own party and, in his eagerness to ingratiate himself with it, took divisive positions on such cultural issues as abortion and affirmative action that further damaged his ability to work with the Democratic Congress.

Despite this political stalemate, Congress and the White House managed on occasion to agree on significant measures. They cooperated in producing the plan to salvage the floundering savings and loan industry. In 1990, the president bowed to congressional pressure and agreed to a significant tax increase as part of a multiyear "budget package" designed to reduce the deficit—thus violating his own 1988 campaign pledge of "no new taxes." In 1991, after almost two years of acrimonious debate, the president and Congress agreed on a civil rights bill to combat job discrimination.

But the most serious domestic problem facing the Bush administration was one for which neither the president nor Congress had any answer: a recession that began late in 1990 and slowly increased its grip on the national economy in 1991 and 1992. Because of the enormous level of debt that corporations (and individuals) had accumulated in the 1980s, the recession caused an unusual number of bankruptcies. It also increased the fear and frustration among middle- and working-class Americans and put pressure on the government to address such problems as the rising cost of health care.

The Gulf War

The events of 1989–1991 had left the United States in the unanticipated position of being the only real superpower in the world. The Bush administration, therefore, had to consider what to do with America's formidable political and military power in a world in which the major justification for that power—the Soviet threat—was now gone.

The events of 1989–1991 suggested two possible answers, both of which had some effect on policy. One was that the United States would reduce its military strength dramatically and concentrate its energies and resources on pressing domestic problems. There was, in fact, considerable movement in that direction both in Congress and within the administration. The other was that America would continue to use its power actively, not to fight communism but to defend its regional and economic interests. In 1989, that led the administration to order an invasion of Panama, which overthrew the unpopular military leader Manuel Noriega (under indictment in the United States for drug trafficking) and replaced him with an elected, pro-American regime. And in 1990, that same impulse drew the United States into the turbulent politics of the Middle East.

On August 2, 1990, the armed forces of Iraq invaded and quickly overwhelmed their small, oil-rich neighbor, the emirate of Kuwait. Saddam Hussein, the militaristic leader of Iraq, soon announced that he was annexing Kuwait and set out to entrench his forces there. After some initial indecision, the Bush administration agreed to lead other nations in a campaign to force Iraq out of Kuwait—through the pressure of economic sanctions if possible, through military force if necessary. Within a few weeks, Bush had persuaded virtually every important government in the world, including the Soviet Union and almost all the Arab and Islamic states, to join in a United Nations–sanctioned trade embargo of Iraq.

At the same time, the United States and its allies (including the British, French, Egyptians, and Saudis) began deploying a massive military force along the border between Kuwait and Saudi Arabia, a force that ultimately reached 690,000 troops (425,000 of them American). On November 29, the United Nations, at the request of the United States, voted to authorize military action to expel Iraq from Kuwait if Iraq did not leave by January 15, 1991. On January 12, both houses of Congress voted to authorize the use of force against Iraq. And on January 16, American and allied air forces began a massive bombardment of Iraqi forces in Kuwait and of military and industrial installations in Iraq itself.

The allied bombing continued for six weeks. On February 23, allied (primarily American) forces under the command of General Norman Schwarzkopf began a major ground offensive—not primarily against the heavily entrenched Iraqi forces along the Kuwait border, as expected, but to the north of them into Iraq itself. The allied armies encountered almost no resistance and suffered only light casualties (141 fatalities). Estimates of Iraqi deaths in the war were 100,000 or more. On February 28, Iraq announced its acceptance of allied terms for a cease-fire, and the brief Persian Gulf War came to an end.

The quick and (for America) relatively painless victory over Iraq was highly popular in the United States. But the tyrannical regime of Saddam Hussein survived, in a weakened form but showing few signs of retreat from its militaristic ambitions. It would plague the United States again.

The Election of 1992

President Bush's popularity reached a record high in the immediate aftermath of the Gulf War. But the glow of that victory faded quickly as the recession worsened in late 1991, and as the administration declined to propose any policies for combating it.

Because the early maneuvering for the 1992 presidential election occurred when President Bush's popularity remained high, many leading Democrats declined to run. That gave Bill Clinton, the young five-term governor of Arkansas, an opportunity to emerge early as the front-runner, as a result of a skillful campaign that emphasized broad economic issues instead of the racial and cultural questions that had so divided the Democrats in the past. Clinton survived a bruising primary campaign and a series of damaging personal controversies to win his party's nomination. And George Bush withstood an embarrassing primary challenge from the conservative journalist Pat Buchanan to become the Republican nominee again.

Complicating the campaign was the emergence of Ross Perot, a blunt, forthright Texas billionaire who became an independent candidate by tapping

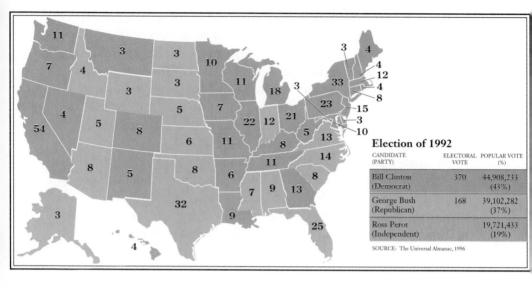

Election of 1992

CANDIDATE (PARTY)	ELECTORAL VOTE	POPULAR VOTE (%)
Bill Clinton (Democrat)	370	44,908,233 (43%)
George Bush (Republican)	168	39,102,282 (37%)
Ross Perot (Independent)		19,721,433 (19%)

SOURCE: The Universal Almanac, 1996

popular resentment of the federal bureaucracy and by promising tough, uncompromising leadership to deal with the fiscal crisis and other problems of government. At several moments in the spring, Perot led both Bush and Clinton in public opinion polls. In July, as he began to face hostile scrutiny from the media, he abruptly withdrew from the race. But early in October, he reentered and soon regained much (although never all) of his early support.

After a campaign in which the economy and the president's unpopularity were the principal issues, Clinton won a clear, but hardly overwhelming, victory over Bush and Perot. He received 43 percent of the vote in the three-way race, to the president's 38 percent and Perot's 19 percent (the best showing for a third-party or independent candidate since Theodore Roosevelt in 1912). Clinton won 370 electoral votes to Bush's 168; Perot won none. Democrats retained control of both houses of Congress.

PARTISAN STRUGGLES

Bill Clinton was the first Democratic president since Jimmy Carter, and the first liberal activist to be president since Lyndon Johnson. He entered office carrying the extravagant expectations of liberals who had spent a generation in exile and with a domestic agenda more ambitious than that of any president since Johnson. But Clinton also had significant political weaknesses. Having won the votes of well under half the electorate, he enjoyed no powerful mandate. Democratic majorities in Congress were frail, and Democrats in any case had grown unaccustomed to bowing to presidential leadership. The Republican leadership in Congress was highly adversarial and opposed the president with unusual unanimity on many issues. A tendency toward reckless personal behavior, both before and during his presidency, caused him continuing problems and gave his many enemies repeated opportunities to discredit him. The Clinton years, therefore, became a time of unusually intense and bitter partisan struggles.

Launching the Clinton Presidency

The new administration compounded its problems with a series of missteps and misfortunes in its first months. The president's effort to end the longtime ban on gay men and women serving in the military met with ferocious resistance from the armed forces themselves and from many conservatives in both parties. He was forced to settle for a pallid compromise. Several of his early appointments became so controversial he had to withdraw them. A longtime friend of the president, Vince Foster, serving in the office of the White House counsel, committed suicide in the summer of 1993. His death helped spark an escalating inquiry into some banking and real estate ventures involving the president and his wife in the early 1980s; and the actions of some administration officials in handling Foster's papers after his death raised suspicions that the White House was attempting to interfere with the investigation into what became known as the Whitewater affair. An independent counsel began examining these issues in 1993.

Despite its many problems, the Clinton administration could boast of some significant achievements in its first year. The president narrowly won approval of a budget that marked a significant turn away from the policies of the Reagan-Bush years. It included a substantial tax increase on the wealthiest Americans, a significant reduction in many areas of government spending, and a major expansion of tax credits to low-income working people, designed to help lift many struggling families out of poverty. After a long and difficult battle against, among others, Ross Perot, the AFL-CIO, and most Democrats in Congress, he won approval of the North American Free Trade Agreement, which eliminated most trade barriers among the United States, Canada, and Mexico.

But the administration's substantial achievements were overshadowed by a large failure. The president's most important and ambitious initiative—the project that he hoped would define his presidency—was a major reform of the nation's health-care system. Early in 1993, he appointed a task force chaired by his wife, Hillary Rodham Clinton, which proposed a sweeping reform designed to guarantee coverage to every American and hold down the costs of medical care. The Clinton plan relied heavily on existing institutions, most notably private insurance companies; and some critics from the left complained that the new system would be too closely tied to an undependable market. But the most substantial opposition came from those who believed the reform would transfer too much power to the government; and that opposition—combined with the determination of Republican leaders to deny the president any kind of victory on this potent issue—doomed the plan. In September 1994, after a series of compromises failed to attract majorities, Congress abandoned the health-care reform effort.

The foreign policy of the Clinton administration was at first cautious and even tentative—a reflection, perhaps, of the president's relative inexperience in international affairs, but also of the rapidly changing character of international politics. That was particularly clear in the administration's handling of one of the most troubling international questions of the early 1990s. Yugoslavia, a nation created after World War I out of a group of small Balkan countries that had once been part of the Austro-Hungarian Empire, dissolved again into several different nations in the wake of the collapse of its communist government in 1989. Bosnia was among the new nations, and it quickly became embroiled in a bloody civil war between its two major ethnic groups: one Muslim, the other Serbian and Christian, backed by the neighboring Serbian republic. All efforts by the other European nations and the United States to negotiate an end to the struggle failed until 1995, when the American negotiator Richard Holbrooke finally brought the warring parties together and crafted an agreement to partition Bosnia. The United States was among the nations to send peacekeeping troops to Bosnia to police the fragile settlement, which—despite many pessimistic predictions—was still largely in place three years later, although terrible new conflicts had by then emerged in Kosovo and other areas of the Balkans.

The Republican Resurgence

The trials of the Clinton administration, and the failure of health-care reform in particular, proved enormously damaging to the Democratic Party as it faced the congressional elections of 1994. Few doubted that the Republicans would make significant gains that year, but almost everyone was

CLINTON AND THE NEW CONGRESSIONAL LEADERSHIP In the aftermath of the dramatic Republican victories in the 1994 congressional elections, President Clinton vowed to cooperate with the new leaders of the House and Senate. He meets here, on January 5, 1995, with speaker of the House Newt Gingrich, who spearheaded the campaign that put Congress in Republican hands for the first time in forty years, and Senate Majority Leader Robert Dole, who was already preparing to challenge President Clinton in the 1996 election.

surprised by the dimensions of their victory. For the first time in forty years, Republicans gained control of both houses of Congress.

Several months before the election, the House Republican leader, Newt Gingrich of Georgia, released a set of campaign promises signed by almost all Republican candidates for the House and called the "Contract with America." It called for tax reductions, dramatic changes in federal spending to produce a balanced budget, and a host of other promises consistent with the long-time goals of the Republican Party's conservative wing. Opinion polls suggested that few voters in 1994 were aware of the "Contract" at the time they voted. But Gingrich and the new Republican congressional leadership nevertheless interpreted the election results as a mandate for their program.

Throughout 1995, the Republican Congress worked at a sometimes feverish pace to construct one of the most ambitious and even radical legislative programs in modern times. They proposed a series of measures to transfer important powers from the federal government to the states. They proposed dramatic reductions in federal spending, including a major restructuring of the once-sacrosanct Medicare program to reduce costs. They attempted to scale back a wide range of federal regulatory functions. In all these efforts, they could count on an unprecedentedly disciplined Republican majority in the House and an only slightly less united Republican majority in the Senate. The Republican agenda, if it had been successfully enacted, would have represented the most substantial shift in the distribution of public authority since the 1930s.

President Clinton responded to the 1994 election results by shifting his own agenda conspicuously to the center and calling for his own plan to cut taxes and balance the budget. Indeed, the gap between the Democratic White House and the Republican Congress on many major issues was relatively small. But because the legislative politics of 1995 was becoming part of the presidential politics of 1996, compromise between the president and Congress became very difficult. In November 1995 and again in January 1996, the federal government literally shut down for several days because the president and Congress could not agree on a budget. Republican leaders refused to pass a "continuing resolution" (to allow government operations to continue during negotiations) in hopes of pressuring the president to agree to their terms. That proved to be an epic political blunder. Public opinion turned quickly and powerfully against the Republican leadership, and against much of its agenda. Gingrich quickly became one of the most unpopular political leaders in the nation, while President Clinton slowly improved his standing in the polls.

The Election of 1996

By the time the 1996 presidential campaign began in earnest, President Clinton—who had seemed so disastrously wounded after the 1994 elections and whom many Republican leaders had come to consider almost irrelevant—was in a commanding position to win reelection. Unopposed for the Democratic nomination, he faced a Republican opponent—Senator Robert Dole of Kansas—who inspired little enthusiasm even within his own party. Clinton's revival was in part a result of his adroitness in taking centrist positions that undermined the Republicans on one issue after another, and in championing traditional Democratic issues—such as raising the minimum wage—that were broadly popular. Clinton benefited even more from the disastrous errors by congressional Republicans in 1995 and early 1996. Indeed, Clinton often seemed to be campaigning more against Newt Gingrich than against his actual opponent. But his greatest strength came from the remarkable success of the American economy and the

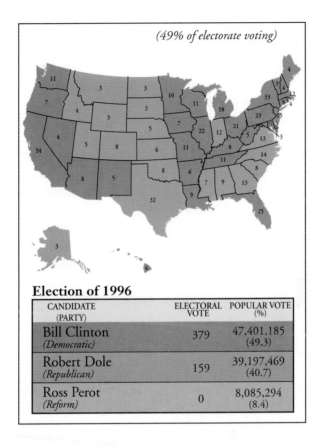

(49% of electorate voting)

Election of 1996

CANDIDATE (PARTY)	ELECTORAL VOTE	POPULAR VOTE (%)
Bill Clinton *(Democratic)*	379	47,401,185 (49.3)
Robert Dole *(Republican)*	159	39,197,469 (40.7)
Ross Perot *(Reform)*	0	8,085,294 (8.4)

marked reduction in the federal deficit that had occurred during his presidency. Like Reagan in 1984, he could campaign as the champion of peace, prosperity, and national well-being.

As the election approached, both Democrats and Republicans grew uneasy about the failure of the 104TH Congress to pass any significant measures. In a flurry of activity in the spring and summer of 1996, the Congress passed several important bills. It raised the minimum wage for the first time in more than a decade. It passed a law that required insurance companies to allow workers to retain their health insurance when they left their jobs and that forbade the companies from denying coverage to people with "pre-existing conditions" (people who were already ill when they applied for coverage). Most dramatically of all, the Congress passed a welfare reform bill, which President Clinton somewhat uneasily signed, that marked the most important change in aid to the poor since the Social Security Act of 1935. It ended the fifty-year federal guarantee of assistance to families with dependent children and turned most of the responsibility for allocating federal welfare funds (now greatly reduced) to the states. A strong economy in the first few years after the bill passed helped protect most welfare recipients from drastic hardships. The real test of the effects of the reform awaited a recession.

Clinton's buoyant campaign flagged slightly in the last weeks before the election in the face of allegations of improper or illegal fund-raising techniques by the Democrats. But the president nevertheless won a substantial victory. He received just over 49 percent of the popular vote to Dole's 41 percent; Ross Perot, running now as the candidate of what he called the Reform Party, generated much less enthusiasm than he had in 1992 but still received over 8 percent of the vote. Clinton won 379 electoral votes to Dole's 159; Perot again won none. But the president's victory did not have much effect on other Democrats, who made only modest gains over their disastrous showing in 1994 and failed to regain either house of Congress.

Clinton Triumphant and Embattled

Bill Clinton was the first Democratic president to win two terms as president since Franklin Roosevelt, and he began his second administration with what appeared to be serene confidence. Facing a somewhat chastened but still hostile Republican Congress, he proposed a relatively modest domestic agenda, consisting primarily of tax cuts and tax credits targeted at middle-class Americans and designed to help them educate their children. He also negotiated effectively with the Republican leadership on a plan for a balanced budget, which passed with much fanfare late in 1997. By the end of 1998, the federal budget—transformed both by a series of changes in fiscal policy and by the long-term strength of the economy—was generating its first surplus in thirty years. The president was only partially responsible for this remarkable change. But he received significant popular credit nevertheless and finished his fifth year in office more popular than he had ever been before.

That popularity would be important to him in the year that followed, when the most serious crisis of his presidency suddenly erupted. Clinton had been bedeviled by scandals almost from his first weeks in office: the investigations into Whitewater and related issues; charges of corruption leveled against members of his cabinet and his staff; harsh accusations of corruption in financing his 1996 campaign, which produced highly touted but ultimately inconclusive congressional investigations in 1997; and a civil suit for sexual harassment filed against the president early in his first term by a former state employee in Arkansas, Paula Jones, who charged that Clinton, while governor, had made unwanted sexual advances toward her.

In early 1998, inquiries associated with the Paula Jones case led to charges that the president had had a sexual relationship with a young White House intern, Monica Lewinsky, that he had lied about it in his deposition before Jones's attorneys, and that he had encouraged Lewinsky to do the same. Those revelations produced a new investigation by the independent counsel in the Whitewater case, Kenneth Starr, a former judge and official in the Reagan Justice Department.

Starr had been investigating the Whitewater matter for nearly four years without any significant results. But he suddenly resurfaced as a major threat to the president with a vigorous effort to prove that the president had lied under oath and had advised others to lie as well. Clinton forcefully denied the charges, and the public strongly backed him. His popularity soared to record levels—a 79 percent approval rating in one poll, and it remained over sixty percent throughout the year that followed. After a few weeks of frenzied speculation, the Lewinsky matter seemed to lose steam. In the meantime, a federal judge dismissed the Paula Jones case, which had launched the scandal.

But the Lewinsky scandal revived again with great force in August 1998, when Lewinsky struck a deal with the independent counsel and testified about her relationship with Clinton. Starr then subpoenaed Clinton himself, who—faced with the prospect of speaking to a grand jury—finally admitted that he and Lewinsky had had what he called an "improper relationship." A few weeks later, Starr submitted a lengthy and at times salacious report to Congress on the results of his investigation, recommending that Congress impeach the president.

The prospect of impeachment became an issue in the 1998 congressional elections. Republicans believed that the Clinton scandals would help them make substantial gains; Democrats, on the other hand, gambled that the public's strong opposition to impeachment would damage the Republicans. The Democrats were right. The Republicans actually lost ten seats in the House, cutting their already thin majority to five, and gained no seats in the Senate. Once again, the president seemed to have escaped his difficulties as a result of strong popular support.

SUPPORTING CLINTON President Clinton's greatest asset during his ordeal of scandal and impeachment in 1998 and early 1999, was the enormous popularity he continued to enjoy. He had particlarly strong support from African-Americans and other minorities. This demonstration of over 1000 people in support of the president outside the U.S. Capitol on December 17, 1998—during the House deliberations in impeachment—was organized by the Rainbow Coalition.

Impeachment

But Clinton and his supporters underestimated the determination of Republican conservatives to pursue the case, apparently without regard to public opinion. House leaders resisted all calls for dismissal of the charges or compromise. First the House Judiciary Committee and then, on December 19, 1998, the full House, both voting on strictly partisan lines, approved two counts of impeachment: lying to the grand jury and obstructing justice. The matter then moved to the Senate, where a trial of the president—the first since the trial of Andrew Johnson in 1868—began in early January. Even then, public opinion continued strongly to favor Clinton.

The Senate trial continued for several weeks without generating any significant public support, or even much public attention. The Senate, unlike the House, attempted to avoid partisan rancor, with only partial success. The trial ended with a decisive acquittal of the president. Neither of the charges attracted even a majority of the votes, let alone the two-thirds necessary for conviction. More than a year after it had began, the Lewinsky scandal came to an at least temporary end although it continued to reverberate in the media for many months more.

The investigation into the president's sexual behavior, and the political battle that followed it, illustrated two significant changes in the character of American public life. One was the increasing role of scandal in American politics, driven by an increasingly sensationalist media culture, the legal device of independent counsels, and the intensely adversarial quality of partisan politics. The other was the blurring of the distinction between public and private behavior, which made almost every facet of a politician's life a target of inquiry and exposure. This new political culture was in part a result of the increasing public cynicism about politics, politicians, and government. It was also a cause of that cynicism.

THE GLOBAL ECONOMY

American public life changed dramatically in the 1980s and 1990s, in part because of the end of the Cold War, but also because of dramatic, and sometimes jarring changes in the character and behavior of the American economy. Foremost among these changes was the dramatic transformation of the American economy, a transformation that had begun in earnest in the early 1970s and that continued unabated in the mid-1990s. The new economy was driven above all by dazzling new miracles of technology that transformed the lives of almost everyone.

The Personal Computer

The most visible element of the technological revolution to most Americans was the dramatic growth in the use of computers in almost every area of life. By the 1990s, most Americans were doing their banking by computer. Most retail transactions were conducted by computerized credit mechanisms. Most businesses, schools, and other institutions were using computerized record-keeping. Many areas of manufacturing were revolutionized by computer-driven product design and factory robotics. Scientific and technological research in almost all areas was transformed by computerized methods.

Among the most significant innovations was the development of the microprocessor, first introduced in 1971 by Intel, which represented a notable advance in the technology of integrated circuitry. A microprocessor miniaturized the central processing unit of a computer, making it possible for a small machine to perform calculations that in the past only very large machines could do. Considerable technological innovation was needed before the microprocessor could actually become the basis of what was at first known as a "minicomputer" and then a personal computer. But in 1977, Apple launched its Apple II personal computer, the first such machine to be widely available to the public. Several years later, IBM entered the personal computer market with the first "PC." IBM had engaged a small software development company, Microsoft, to design an operating system for their new computer. Microsoft produced a program known as MS-DOS (DOS for "disk operating system"). No PC could operate without it. The PC, and its software, made its debut in August 1981 and immediately became enormously successful. Three years later, Apple introduced its Macintosh computer, which marked another major innovation in computer technology, among other things because its software—very different from DOS—was much easier to use than that of the PC. But Apple could not match IBM's marketing power, and by the mid-1980s the PC had clearly established its dominance in the booming personal computer market—a dominance enhanced by the introduction of a new software package to replace DOS in 1985: Windows, also developed by Microsoft, which borrowed many concepts (most notably the Graphical User Interface, or GUI) from the Apple operating system. IBM, however, was not in the end the principal beneficiary of the dominance of its own system, as other companies began marketing their own IBM-compatible personal computers, usually at a lower price than IBM's, and seizing an increasing share of the market.

Personal computers very quickly established a presence in many areas of American life: homes, schools, businesses, universities, hospitals, government agencies, newsrooms. Computerized word processing programs replaced typewriters. Computerized spreadsheets revolutionized bookkeeping. Computerized data processing made obsolete much traditional information storage, such as filing. Some computer enthusiasts talked about the approach of a "paperless" office, in which all information or communication would be stored and distributed through computers. That day was slow to arrive. But the emergence of ever smaller and more powerful computers—laptops, notebooks, and palm-sized devices—greatly extended the reach of computer-related technology. At the same time, however, computer scientists were creating extraordinarily powerful new forms of networking; and many were predicting that before long the stand-alone personal computer would be obsolete, that the future lay in linking many computers together into powerful networks.

The computer revolution created thousands of new, lucrative businesses: computer manufacturers themselves (IBM, Apple, Compaq, Dell, Gateway, Sun, Digital, and many others); makers of the tiny silicon chips that ran the computers and allowed smaller and smaller machines to become more and more powerful (most notably Intel); and makers of software—chief among them Microsoft, the most powerful new corporation to arise in American life in generations. In the 1990s, Microsoft had a virtual monopoly on the operating systems for most personal computers in the world. It had also moved into new areas: creating other kinds of software (word processing, spreadsheets, databases, communications, personal finance, and many others) and producing software and content for the Internet. In 1997, after many abortive efforts, the Justice Department filed a series of antitrust suits against the giant corporation. In the meantime, Microsoft remained one of the most profitable corporations in the country.

But if Microsoft was the most conspicuous success story of the computer age, it was only one of many. Whole regions—the so-called Silicon Valley in northern California; areas around Boston, Austin, Texas, and Seattle, Washington; even areas in downtown New York City—became centers of booming economic activity servicing the new computer age.

The Internet

Out of the computer revolution emerged another dramatic source of information and communication: the Internet. The Internet is, in essence, a vast, geographically far-flung network of computers that allows people connected to the network to communicate with others all over the world. It had its beginning in 1963, in the U.S. government's Advanced Research Projects Agency (ARPA), which funneled federal funds into scientific research projects, many of them defense-related. In the early 1960s, J. C. R. Licklider, the head of ARPA's Information Processing Technique Office, was working on a project he called Libraries of the Future, through which he hoped to make vast amounts of information available electronically to people in far-flung areas. In 1963, he launched a program to link together computers over large distances. It was known as the Arpanet. For several years, the Arpanet served mainly as a way for people to make use of what were then relatively scarce computer facilities without having to go to the site of the computer. Gradually, however, both the size and the uses of the network expanded.

This expansion was facilitated in part by two important new technologies. One was a system developed in the early 1960s at the RAND

THE "NET" By the mid-1990s, the Internet—a communications system that made available vast amounts of information and entertainment through a worldwide computer network—had become something like an obsession to many Americans. Many predicted that the Internet would soon become one of the nation's primary forms of communication. Already by the mid-1990s, many people were using e-mail (electronic mail) transmitted through the Internet more often than they were using the telephone or the postal system. Access to the Internet was available at first only to employees of large institutions that had their own computer networks. But commercial services such as America Online—whose "home page" appears here—soon began to offer connections to individual consumers through their telephone lines.

Corporation in the United States and the National Physical Laboratory in England. It was known as "store-and-forward packet switching," and it made possible the transmission of large quantities of data between computers without directly wiring the computers together. There could be a central communications backbone through which messages and information could be routed to individual computers, much as the telegraph and telephone system used centralized carriers that eventually branched off into local connections. The other technological breakthrough was the development of computer software that would allow individual computers to handle the traffic over the network—what became known as the Interface Message Processor.

By 1971, twenty-three computers were linked together in the Arpanet, which served mostly research labs and universities. Gradually, interest in the system began to spread, and with it the number of computers connected to it. In the early 1980s, the Defense Department, an early partner in the development of the Arpanet, withdrew from the project for security reasons. The network, soon renamed the Internet, was then free to develop independently. It did so rapidly, especially after the invention of technologies that made possible electronic mail (or e-mail) and the emergence of the personal computer, which vastly increased the number of potential users of the Internet. As late as 1984, there remained fewer than a thousand host computers connected to the Internet. A decade later, there were over 6 million, and the number was growing rapidly. And since each host computer serviced many individual users on PCs and local networks, the number of actual users of the Internet was incalculable.

As the amount of information on the Internet unexpectedly proliferated, without any central direction, new forms of software emerged to make it possible for individual users to navigate through the vast number of Internet sites. In 1989, a laboratory in Geneva introduced the World Wide Web, through which individual users could publish information for the Internet, which helped establish an orderly system for both the distribution and retrieval of electronic information.

The Internet is still a relatively young communications medium, and its likely impact on society is not yet fully understood. Already, however, it has revolutionized many areas of life. E-mail has replaced conventional mail, telephone calls, and even face-to-face conversation for millions of people. Newspapers, magazines, and other publications have begun to publish on the Internet. It has become a powerful marketing tool, through which people can purchase items as small as books and as large as automobiles. It is a site for vast amounts of documentary material for researchers, reporters, students and others. And it is, finally, a highly democratic medium—through which virtually anyone with access to a personal computer can establish a website and present information in a form that is available to virtually anyone in the world who chooses to look at it.

Breakthroughs in Genetics

Aided in part by computer technology, there was explosive growth in another area of scientific research: genetics. Early discoveries in genetics by Gregor Mendel, Thomas Hunt Morgan, and others laid the groundwork for more dramatic breakthroughs—the discovery of DNA by the British scientists Oswald Avery, Colin MacLeod, and Maclyn McCarty in 1944; and in 1953, the dramatic discovery by the American biochemist James Watson and the

British biophysicist Francis Crick of the double-helix structure of DNA, and thus of the key to identifying genetic codes. From these discoveries emerged the new science—and ultimately the new industry—of genetic engineering, through which new medical treatments and new techniques for hybridization of plants and animals have already become possible.

Little by little, scientists began to identify specific genes in humans and other living things that determine particular traits, and to learn how to alter or reproduce them. But the identification of genes was painfully slow; and in 1989, the federal government appropriated $3 billion to fund the National Center for the Human Genome, to accelerate the mapping of human genes. The Human Genome Project set out to identify all of the more than 100,000 genes by 2005. But new technologies for research, and competition from other projects (some of them funded by pharmaceutical companies) drove the project forward faster than expected. In 1998, the genome project announced that it would finish its work in 2003.

In the meantime, DNA research had already attracted considerable public attention. In 1997, scientists in Scotland announced that they had cloned a sheep—which they named Dolly—using a cell from an adult ewe; in other words, the genetic structure of the newborn Dolly was identical to that of the sheep from which the cell was taken. The DNA structure of an individual, scientists have discovered, is as unique and as identifiable as a fingerprint. DNA testing, therefore, makes it possible to identify individuals through their blood or semen and played a major role first in the O. J. Simpson trial in 1995 and then in the 1998 investigation into President Clinton's relationship with Monica Lewinsky. Also in 1998, DNA testing appeared to establish with certainty that Thomas Jefferson had fathered a child with his slave Sally Hemings, by finding genetic similarities between descendants of both, thus resolving a political and scholarly dispute stretching back nearly 200 years. Genetic research has already spawned important new areas of medical treatment—and has helped the relatively new biotechnology industry to grow into one of the nation's most important economic sectors. Eventually, scientists expect the research to open up vast new areas for medical treatment—and also controversial new possibilities for genetically designing foods, animals, and even humans.

The Two-Tiered Economy

The new technologies helped revive the American economy from the sluggishness that had characterized it in the 1970s and early 1980s. Economic growth, beginning in the mid-1980s, remained remarkably robust into the late 1990s, except for a brief recession in 1991–1992. The value of stocks increased dramatically during a prolonged stock market boom that by 1998 had lasted, with only a few significant downturns, for nearly fifteen years. National income rose steadily.

But the benefits of the new economy were less widely shared than those of earlier boom times. The increasing abundance created enormous new wealth that enriched those talented, or lucky, enough to profit from the areas of booming growth. The rewards for education—particularly in such areas as science and engineering—increased enormously. In 1995, the average annual income of a person with less than a high-school education was $14,000. For a high-school graduate, that number rose to $21,400. But a college graduate's average salary was $37,000, and the average salary of someone with an advanced degree was $56,700—four times the level of those who did not graduate from high school. Between 1980 and the mid-1990s, the average family incomes of the wealthiest 20 percent of the population grew by nearly 20 percent (to over $100,000 a year); the average family income of the next 20 percent of the population grew by more than 8 percent.

But for others, the new economy produced no reward. It produced instead enormous disparities in income, wealth, and opportunity that contributed to deep and increasingly corrosive divisions in American society. The jarring changes in America's relationship to the world economy that had begun in the 1970s—the loss of cheap and easy access to raw materials, the penetration of the American market by foreign competitors, the restructuring of American heavy industry so that it produced fewer jobs and paid lower wages—continued and in some respects accelerated through the last decades of the century. For families and individuals outside the circle of knowledgeable people benefiting from the new technologies, the results of these contractions were often devastating.

Poverty in America had declined steadily and at times dramatically in the years after World War II, so that by the end of the 1970s the percentage of people living in poverty had declined to 12 percent (from about 20 percent in preceding decades). But the decline in poverty did not continue. In the 1980s, the poverty rate rose again, at times as high as 18 percent. By the late 1990s, it had dropped to under 13 percent again, but that was about the same as it had been twenty years before.

Globalization

Perhaps the most important economic change, and certainly the one whose impact was the most difficult to gauge, was what became known as the "globalization" of the economy. The great prosperity of the 1950s and 1960s had rested on, among other things, the relative insulation of the United States from the pressures of international competition. As late as 1970, international trade still played a relatively small role in the American economy as a whole, which thrived on the basis of the huge domestic market in North America.

By the end of the 1970s, however, the world had intruded on the American economy in profound ways, and that intrusion increased unabated for the next twenty years. Exports rose from just under $43 billion in 1970 to nearly $513 billion in 1994. But imports rose even more dramatically: from just over $40 billion in 1970 to over $663 billion in 1994. Most American products now faced foreign competition inside the United States. America had made 76 percent of the world's automobiles in 1950 and 48 percent in 1960. By 1990, that share had dropped to 20 percent; in the late 1990s, even after a substantial revival of the automobile industry, the American share had risen only to 25 percent. The first American trade imbalance in the postwar era occurred in 1971; only twice since then, in 1973 and 1975, has the balance been favorable.

Globalization brought many benefits for the American consumer: new and more varied products, and lower prices for many of them. Most economists, and most national leaders, welcomed the process and worked to encourage it through lowering trade barriers. The North American Free Trade Agreement (NAFTA), ratified by the U.S. Senate in 1993, and the General Agreement on Trade and Tariffs (GATT), ratified a year later, were the boldest of a long series of treaties designed to lower trade barriers stretching back to the 1960s. But globalization had many costs as well. It was particularly hard on industrial workers, who saw industrial jobs disappear as American companies lost market share to foreign competitors. American workers also lost jobs as American companies began exporting work—building plants in Mexico, Asia, and other lower-wage countries to avoid having to pay the high wages workers had won in America.

A CHANGING SOCIETY

The changes in the economy were one of many factors producing major changes in the character of American society. By the end of the twentieth century, the American population was growing larger, older, and more racially and geographically diverse.

The Graying of America

One of the most fundamental features of American life in the late twentieth century was the aging of the American population. After decades of steady growth, the nation's birth rate began to decline in the 1970s and remained low through the 1980s and 1990s. In 1970, there were 18.4 births for every 1,000 people in the population. By 1996, the rate had dropped to 14.8 births. The declining birth rate and a significant rise in life expectancy produced a substantial increase in the proportion of elderly citizens. Over 13 percent of the population was more than sixty-five years old by 1997, as compared with 8 percent in 1970. That figure was projected to rise to over 20 percent by the end of the century. The median age in 1996 was 34.9 years, as compared with 28.0 in 1970.

The aging of the population had important, if not entirely predictable, implications. It was, for example, a cause of the increasing costliness of Social Security pensions. It meant rapidly increasing health costs, both for the federal Medicare system and for private hospitals and insurance companies, and was one of the principal reasons for the anxiety about health-care costs that played such a crucial role in the politics of the early 1990s. It also ensured that the elderly, who already formed one of the most powerful interest groups in America, would remain politically formidable well into the twenty-first century.

New Patterns of Immigration and Ethnicity

Perhaps the most important demographic change in America in the last thirty years of the twentieth century was the enormous change in both the extent and the character of immigration. The nation's immigration quotas expanded significantly in those years (partly to accommodate refugees from Southeast Asia and other nations), allowing more newcomers to enter the United States legally than at any point since the beginning of the twentieth century. In 1996, nearly 25 million Americans—over 9 percent of the total population—consisted of immigrants (people born outside the United States).

Equally striking was the character of the new immigration. The Immigration Reform Act of 1965 (see p. 919) had eliminated quotas based on national origin; from then on, newcomers from regions other than Latin America were generally admitted on a first-come, first-served basis. In 1965, 90 percent of the immigrants to the United States came from Europe. By the mid-1980s, only 10 percent of the new arrivals were Europeans, although that figure rose in the 1990s as emigrants from Russia and eastern Europe—now free to leave their countries—came in increasing numbers. The extent and character of the new immigration was causing a dramatic change in the composition of the American population. Already by the late 1990s, people of white European background constituted under 80 percent of the population (as opposed to 90 percent a half-century before).

Particularly important to the new immigration were two groups: Latinos (people from Spanish-speaking nations, particularly Mexico) and Asians. Both had been significant segments of the American population for many decades—Latinos since the very beginning of the nation's history, Asians since the waves of Chinese and Japanese immigration in the nineteenth century. But both groups experienced enormous, indeed unprecedented, growth after 1965. People from Latin America constituted more than a third of the total number of legal immigrants to the United States in every year since 1965—and a much larger proportion of the total number of illegal immigrants. Mexico alone accounted for one-fourth of all the immigrants living in the United States in 1996. In California and the Southwest, in particular, Mexicans became an increasingly important presence. There were also substantial Latino populations in Illinois, New York, and Florida. High birth rates within Latino communities already in the United States further increased their numbers. In the 1980 census, 6 percent of the population (about 14 million) was listed as being of Hispanic origin. By 1997, census figures showed an increase to 11 percent—or 29 million people.

In the 1980s and 1990s, Asian immigrants arrived in even greater numbers than Latinos, constituting more than 40 percent of the total of legal newcomers. They swelled the already substantial Chinese and Japanese communities in California and elsewhere. And they created substantial new communities of immigrants from Vietnam, Thailand, Cambodia, Laos, the Philippines, Korea, and India. By 1997, there were more than 10 million Asian Americans in the United States (4 percent of the population), more than twice the number of fifteen years before. Like Latinos they were concentrated mainly in large cities and in the West. Many of the new Asian immigrants were refugees, including Vietnamese driven from their homes in the aftermath of the disastrous war in which the United States had so long been involved.

The Black Middle Class

The civil rights movement and the other liberal efforts of the 1960s had two very different effects on African Americans. On the one hand, there were increased opportunities for advancement available to those in a position to take advantage of them. On the other hand, as the industrial economy declined and government services dwindled, there was a growing sense of helplessness and despair among the large groups of nonwhites who continued to find themselves barred from upward mobility.

For the black middle class, which by the late 1990s constituted over half of the African-American population of America, progress was remarkable in the thirty years since the high point of the civil rights movement. Disparities between black and white professionals did not vanish, but they diminished substantially. African-American families moved into more affluent urban communities and, in many cases, into suburbs—at times as neighbors of whites, more often into predominantly black communities. The number of African Americans attending college rose by 350 percent in the decade following the passage of the civil rights acts (in contrast to a 150 percent increase among whites); African Americans made up 12 percent of the college population in the 1990s (up from 5 percent twenty-five years earlier). The percentage of black high-school graduates going on to college was by then virtually the same as that of white high-school graduates (although a far smaller proportion of blacks than whites managed to complete high school). And African Americans were making rapid strides in many professions from which, a generation earlier, they had been barred or within which they had been segregated. In increasing numbers, they were becoming partners in major law firms and joining the staffs of major hospitals and the faculties of major universities. Nearly half of all employed blacks in the United States had skilled white-collar jobs. There were few areas of American life from which blacks were any longer entirely excluded. Middle-class blacks, in other words, had realized great gains from the legislation of the 1960s, from the changing national mood on race, from the creation of controversial affirmative action programs, and from their own strenuous efforts.

Poor and Working-Class African Americans

But the rise of the black middle class also accentuated (and perhaps even helped cause) the increasingly desperate plight of other African Americans, whom the economic growth and the liberal programs of the 1960s and beyond had never reached. These impoverished people made up more than a fourth of the nation's black population. most of them lived in isolated, decaying, and desperately poor inner-city neighborhoods, from which more successful blacks had departed. This growing "under-class" made up about a third of the nation's black population. As more successful blacks moved out of the inner cities, the poor were left virtually alone in their decaying neighborhoods. Fewer than half of young inner-city blacks finished high school; more than 60 percent were unemployed. The black family structure suffered as well from the dislocations of urban poverty. There was a radical increase in the number of single-parent, female-headed black households. In 1970, 59 percent of all black children under 18 lived with both their parents (already down from 70 percent a decade earlier). In 1995, only 33 percent of black children lived in such households, while 76 percent of white children did.

Nonwhites were disadvantaged by many factors in the changing social and economic climate of the 1980s and 1990s. Among them was a growing impatience with affirmative action and other programs designed to advance their fortunes. They suffered as well from a steady decline in the number of unskilled jobs in the economy. They suffered from the deterioration of public education and of other social services, which made it more difficult for them to find opportunities for advancement. And they suffered, in some cases, from a sense of futility and despair, born of years of entrapment in brutal urban ghettoes.

The anger and despair such conditions were creating among inner-city residents became clear in many ways, including in the most popular new black musical form of the 1980s and 1990s, rap. Rap music emerged out of the street life of the inner city and the hip-hop culture that was born there. Hip-hop created many of the patterns of dress and behavior that became common among inner-city youths: the popularity of athletic clothes, hats, and shoes; the practice of young men giving themselves "street names"; and—in the 1980s at least—graffiti and break dancing. In the 1990s, break dancing lost its popularity, clothes became baggier, hats became larger, and the most popular element of hip-hop culture was rap, which had by then been developing for nearly twenty years. It came most directly from New York City's South Bronx, where some of the popular DJs set up equipment in the street and gave performances of their own over the music they played—with spoken rhymes, jazzy phrases, and pointed comments about the audience, the neighborhood, and themselves. Gradually, the DJs began to bring "rappers"—young men who took the DJ style and developed it into a much more elaborate form of performance—into the shows. As rap grew more popular in the inner city, record promoters began signing some of its new stars. Rap has taken many forms and conveyed many messages. But at its heart, it is primarily a product of the young male culture of the inner city. Some of the most

LOS ANGELES, APRIL 1992 An aerial view of a section of south central Los Angeles in the immediate aftermath of the great riot of 1992. The decision of an all-white jury to acquit Los Angeles police officers accused of brutalizing a black suspect (a beating recorded by a bystander on video tape) created widespread outrage and crystallized the frustration that residents of this poor, crime-plagued community had been feeling for years.

successful rap has conveyed the frustration and anger that these men have felt about their lives.

That anger and frustration became visible even more graphically in the summer of 1992 in Los Angeles. The previous year, a bystander had videotaped several Los Angeles police officers beating an apparently help-less black man whom they had captured after an auto chase. Broadcast re-peatedly around the country, the tape evoked outrage among whites and blacks alike. But an all-white jury in a suburban community just outside Los Angeles acquitted the officers when they were tried for assault. Black residents of South Central Los Angeles, one of the poorest communities in the city, erupted in anger—precipitating the largest racial disturbance of the twentieth century. There was widespread looting and arson. More than fifty people died.

What Americans had long called "race relations," the way in which white and black Americans viewed each other, grew increasingly sour in these difficult years. White impatience with black demands grew, as did a willingness to listen to old and long-discredited arguments about genetic differences between the races. A controversial book by two white social scientists, *The Bell Curve*, published in 1994, helped reopen this bitter debate about the innate capacities of members of different races. Many African Americans, for their part, developed an intensified mistrust of the institutions of white society—of the government, the corporations, the universities, and perhaps above all the system of law enforcement.

Nowhere was this mutual suspicion more evident than in the celebrated trial of the former football star O. J. Simpson, who was accused of murdering his former wife and a young man in Los Angeles in 1994. The long and costly "O. J. trial" was an enormous media sensation for over a year. Throughout the proceedings, opinions about Simpson's guilt broke down strikingly along racial lines. A vast majority of whites believed that he was guilty, and a vast majority of blacks believed he was innocent. Simpson's acquittal in the fall of 1995, after a trial in which the defense tried to portray him as a victim of police racism, caused great celebrations in many black communities and a quiet disgust among many whites.

Modern Plagues: Drugs and AIDS

The new immigrants of the 1980s and 1990s arrived in cities being ravaged by two new and deadly epidemics. One was a dramatic increase in drug use, which penetrated nearly every community in the nation. The enormous demand for drugs, and particularly for "crack" cocaine, spawned what was in effect a multibillion-dollar industry; and those reaping the enormous profits of the illegal trade fought strenuously and often savagely to protect their positions. Political figures of both parties spoke heatedly about the need for a "war on drugs"; but in the absence of significant funding for such programs, government efforts appeared to be having little effect. Drug use declined significantly among middle-class people beginning in the late 1980s, but the epidemic showed no signs of abating in the poor urban neighborhoods where it was doing the most severe damage.

The drug epidemic was directly related to another scourge of the 1980s and 1990s: the epidemic spread of a new and lethal disease first documented in 1981 and soon named AIDS (acquired immune deficiency syndrome). AIDS is the product of the HIV virus, which is transmitted by the exchange of bodily fluids (blood or semen). The virus gradually destroys the body's immune system and makes its victims highly vulnerable to a

IGNORANCE = FEAR The artist Keith Haring (whose work was inspired in large part by urban graffiti) created this striking poster in 1989, the year before he himself died of AIDS, to generate support for the battle against the disease. "ACT UP," the organization that distributed it, was among the most militant groups in demanding more rapid efforts to search for a cure.

number of diseases (particularly to various forms of cancer and pneumonia) to which they would otherwise have a natural resistance. Those infected with the virus (i.e., HIV positive) can live for a long time without developing AIDS, but for many years those who became ill were virtually certain to die. The first American victims of AIDS, (and in the early 1990s the group among whom cases remained the most numerous) were homosexual men. But by the late 1980s, as the gay community began to take preventive measures, the most rapid increase in the spread of the disease occurred among heterosexuals, many of them intravenous drug users, who spread the virus by sharing contaminated hypodermic needles. In 1996, U.S. government agencies estimated that about 780,000 Americans were infected with the HIV virus and that another 362,000 had already died from the disease. Worldwide, the figure was approximately 22 million infected people. Governments and private groups, in the meantime, began promoting AIDS awareness in increasingly visible and graphic ways—urging young people, in particular, to avoid "unsafe sex" through abstinence or the use of latex condoms.

In the mid-1990s, AIDS researchers, after years of frustration, began discovering effective treatments for the disease. By taking a combination of powerful drugs, among them a group known as protease inhibitors, on a rigorous schedule, even people with relatively advanced cases of AIDS experienced dramatic improvement—so much so that in many cases there were no measurable quantities of the virus left in their bloodstreams. Although the long-term effectiveness of the new drugs was not yet demonstrated, they did give promise for the first time of dramatically extending the lives of people with AIDS, perhaps to normal life spans. The drugs were not a cure for AIDS; people who stopped taking them experienced a rapid return of the disease. Nor were they effective in all cases. In addition, the drugs were very expensive and difficult to administer; poorer AIDS patients often could not obtain access to them, and they remained almost unknown in less affluent parts of the world where the epidemic was rampant. Nevertheless, the new medications restored hundreds of thousands of desperately ill people to health and gave them something perhaps equally important that they had not had before: hope.

The Decline in Crime

One of the most striking social developments of the late 1990s was also one of the least expected: a dramatic reduction in crime rates across most of the United States. The rising incidence of violent crime had been one of the most disturbing facts of American life for two generations—and a central fact of national politics since at least the 1960s. But beginning in the mid-1990s, crime began to fall—in many cities, quite dramatically.

There was no agreement about the causes of this unexpected reduction. Prosperity and declining unemployment were certainly factors. So were new, sophisticated police techniques that helped deter many crimes and that led to the arrest of many criminals who would previously have escaped capture. New incarceration policies—longer, tougher sentences and fewer paroles and early releases for violent criminals—led to a radical increase in the prison population and, consequently, a reduction in the number of criminals at liberty to commit crimes.

Whatever the reason, the decline in crime—when combined with the booming prosperity of the 1990s, which (however unequally distributed) affected most Americans at least to some degree—helped produce an unusual level of social contentment, as recorded in public opinion surveys, in the late 1990s. In stark contrast to the late 1970s, and even the 1980s, most Americans expressed general contentment with the state of their society and optimism about the future.

A CONTESTED CULTURE

But American life, no matter what the level of contentment, is never without controversy. And few things created more controversy and anxiety in the 1980s and 1990s than the battles over the character of American culture. That culture had changed dramatically in many ways since World War II. It had seen a profound redefinition of the roles of women. It had produced a mobilization of many minorities and an at least partial inclusion of them into mainstream culture. It had experienced a sexual revolution. It had become much less restrained in its depiction of sex, violence, and dissent. American culture was more diverse, more open, less restrained, and more contentious than it had been in the past. One result of these changes was a series of new controversies and new issues.

Battles over Feminism and Abortion

Among the principal goals of the New Right as it became more powerful and assertive in the 1980s and 1990s, and as it focused on cultural changes it did not like, was to challenge feminism and its achievements. Leaders of the New Right had campaigned successfully against the proposed Equal Rights Amendment to the Constitution. And they played a central role in the most divisive issue of the late 1980s and early 1990s: the controversy over abortion rights.

For those who favored allowing women to choose to terminate unwanted pregnancies, the Supreme Court's decision in *Roe v. Wade* (1973) had seemed to settle the question. By the 1980s, abortion was the most commonly performed surgical procedure in the country. But at the same time, opposition to abortion was creating a powerful grassroots movement. The right-to-life movement, as it called itself, found its most fervent supporters among Catholics; and indeed, the Catholic Church itself lent its institutional authority to the battle against legalized abortion. Religious doctrine also motivated the anti-abortion stance of Mormons, fundamentalist Christians, and other groups. The opposition of some other anti-abortion activists had less to do with religion than with their commitment to traditional notions of family and gender relations. To them, abortion was a particularly offensive part of a much larger assault by feminists on the role of women as wives and mothers. It was also, many foes contended, a form of murder. Fetuses, they claimed, were human beings who had a "right to life" from the moment of conception.

Although the right-to-life movement was persistent in its demand for a reversal of *Roe* v. *Wade* or, barring that, a constitutional amendment banning abortion, it also attacked abortion in more limited ways, at its most vulnerable points. In the 1970s, Congress and many state legislatures began barring the use of public funds to pay for abortions, thus making them almost inaccessible for many poor women. The Reagan and Bush administrations imposed further restrictions on federal funding and even on the right of doctors in federally funded clinics to give patients any information on abortion. Extremists in the right-to-life movement began picketing, occupying, and at times bombing abortion clinics. Several anti-abortion activists murdered doctors who performed abortions; other physicians were subject to campaigns of terrorism and harassment—part of an effort to force them to abandon serving women who wanted abortions.

The changing composition of the Supreme Court in the 1980s and early 1990s (when five new conservative justices were named by Presidents Reagan and Bush) renewed the right-to-life movement's hopes for a reversal of *Roe* v. *Wade*. In *Webster* v. *Reproductive Health Services* (1989), the Court upheld a Missouri law that forbade any institution receiving state funds from performing abortions, whether or not those funds were used to finance the abortions. But the Court stopped short of overturning its 1973 decision.

Through much of the 1970s and 1980s, defenders of abortion had remained confident that *Roe* v. *Wade* protected their right to choose abortion and that the anti-abortion movement was unlikely to prevail. But the changing judicial climate of the late 1980s mobilized defenders of abortion as never before. They called themselves the "pro-choice" movement, because they were defending not so much abortion itself as every woman's right to choose whether and when to bear a child. It quickly became clear that the pro-choice movement was in many parts of the country at least as strong as, and in some areas much stronger than, the right-to-life movement. With the election of President Clinton in 1992, the immediate threat to *Roe* v. *Wade* seemed to fade. In his first week in office, he overturned several of the restrictions on federally funded abortions imposed by Reagan and Bush. And during his first two years in office, Clinton named two pro-choice justices to the Court—Ruth Bader Ginsburg and Stephen Breyer. Clinton's reelection in 1996 was, among other things, evidence that the pro-choice movement maintained considerable political strength. But abortion rights remained highly vulnerable, given the intensity of feeling among those who opposed them.

At times the pro-choice campaign overshadowed other efforts by feminists to protect and expand the rights of women. But such efforts continued. Women's organizations and many individual women worked strenuously in the 1980s and 1990s to improve access to child care for poor women, and to win the right to caregiver leaves for parents, which a law passed by Congress and signed by President Clinton in 1993 helped secure. They also worked to raise awareness of sexual harassment in the work-place, with considerable success. Colleges, universities, the military, government agencies, even many corporations established strict new standards of behavior for their employees in dealing with members of the opposite sex and created grievance procedures for those who believed they had been harassed.

Both the achievements and the limits of their progress on this issue were evident in the sensational controversy in 1991 over Judge Clarence Thomas, President Bush's nominee for a seat on the Supreme Court. Late in the confirmation proceedings, accusations of sexual harassment from Anita Hill, a law professor and former employee of Thomas, became public. Hill's testimony before the Senate Judiciary Committee dramatically polarized both the Senate and the nation. Feminists and others tended to believe the accusations and hailed the accuser for drawing national attention to the issue of harassment; but many Americans (and most members of the virtually all-male Senate) apparently did not believe her—or at least concluded that the alleged activities should not disqualify Thomas from serving on the Court. Thomas was ultimately confirmed by a narrow margin.

The Changing Left and the New Environmentalism

The New Left of the 1960s and early 1970s did not disappear after the end of the war in Vietnam, but it faded rapidly. Many of the students who had fought in its battles grew up, left school, and entered conventional careers. Some radical leaders, disillusioned by the unresponsiveness of American society to their demands, resignedly gave up the struggle and chose instead to work "within the system." Marxist critiques continued to flourish in academic circles, but to much of the public they came to appear dated and irrelevant—particularly as, beginning in 1989, Marxist governments collapsed in disrepute.

Yet a left of sorts did survive, giving evidence in the process of how greatly the nation's political climate had changed. Where 1960s activists had rallied to protest racism, poverty, and war, their counterparts in the 1980s and 1990s more often worked to organize communities to fight for local concerns. A great resurgence of grassroots organizing in many parts

D E B A T I N G   T H E   P A S T

Women's History

T he revival of feminism as a powerful social and political force in the 1960s and 1970s brought with it a dramatic rise of interest in, and a transformation of, women's history. Both men and women have been writing histories of women for centuries, but during much of the twentieth century, women's history remained in the shadows of other fields. However, as modern feminism began to sweep across society in the 1960s and 1970s, interest in women's history revived as well. For a time, the new women's history replicated the pattern of earlier studies of women. Much of the early work was in the "contributionist" tradition, revealing ways in which women had contributed more to American history than scholars had previously recognized. Other work stressed ways in which women had been victimized by their subordination to men and by their powerlessness within the industrial economy.

Increasingly, however, women's history began to emphasize the nature of gender itself. Some scholars emphasized the artificiality of gender distinctions. The difference between women and men in the public world, they argued, was socially constructed, not inherent in the biological differences

of the country was, in part, testament to the legacy of the New Left. Most of all, activists in the 1980s and 1990s organized to stop the proliferation of nuclear weapons and power plants, to save the wilderness, to protect endangered species, to limit reckless economic development, and to otherwise protect the environment.

between the sexes, and thus—in the public world at least—unimportant. Much of the history of women was, therefore, the history of how men (with the unwitting help of many women) had created and maintained a set of fictions about women's capacities that late-twentieth-century women were now attempting to shatter.

By the early 1980s, however, some feminists were beginning to make a very different argument: that there were basic differences between women and men—not just biological differences, but differences in values, sensibilities, and culture. These differences were not evidence of women's incapacities. Instead, feminist historians argued, they were evidence of an alternative female culture capable of challenging (and improving) the male-dominated world. Historians of women, therefore, began exploring areas of female experience that revealed the special character of women's culture and values: family, housework, motherhood, women's clubs and organizations, female literature, the social lives of working-class women, women's sexuality, and many other subjects that suggested "difference" more than "contributions" or "victimization." Partly in response, some historians began to make the same argument about men—that understanding "masculinity" and its role in shaping men's lives is as important as understanding notions of "femininity" in explaining the history of women.

The notion of gender as a source of social and cultural difference was responsible for the most powerful challenge women's history raised to the way in which scholars viewed the past. Gender, women's historians argued, is a critical element of the explanation for many kinds of historical experiences, not just women's experiences. Historians in all fields need to incorporate gender into their categories of analysis and make it stand alongside such other categories as race, class, ethnicity, religion, and region as a major element of any historical explanation.

Public concerns about the environment had arisen intermittently since the beginning of the industrial era. A signal event in increasing that concern was the publication in 1962 of Rachel Carson's *Silent Spring*. Carson was already one of the nation's most popular nature writers when a friend in New England alerted her to some previously unnoticed effects of the popular pesticide DDT. It was, according to Carson's friend, killing songbirds in the areas in which it was sprayed. As Carson investigated further, she discovered evidence that DDT also inhibited the reproductive capacities of larger creatures, and, most disturbing of all, stored itself in the fatty tissues of animals where it could be passed on to other animals and to humans. In *Silent Spring*, the book she wrote in response to her growing concern, she warned that the indiscriminate use of pesticides was wreaking havoc with the web of life, destroying wildlife populations and threatening human health. She wrote of a landscape in which sickness and death threatened animals and people alike, in which "a strange stillness" had replaced the familiar songs of birds. *Silent Spring* became one of the most controversial books of the 1960s. It sold nearly half a million copies within six months of its publication and was discussed everywhere. In response to the passions it aroused, the United States finally banned the sale and use of DDT in 1972.

Several highly visible environmental catastrophes in the 1960s and 1970s greatly increased the environmental concerns that Carson had helped to arouse. Among them were a major oil spill off Santa Barbara, California, in 1969; the discovery of large deposits of improperly disposed toxic waste in a residential community in upstate New York in 1978; and a frightening accident at the nuclear power plant on Three Mile Island, Pennsylvania in 1979. These and other revelations of the extent to which human progress threatened the natural world helped produce a major popular movement.

In the spring of 1970, a nationwide "Earth Day" signaled the beginning of the environmental movement. It differed markedly from the "conservation" movements of earlier years. Modern environmentalists shared the concerns of such earlier figures as John Muir and Gifford Pinchot about preserving some areas of the wilderness and carefully managing the exploitation of resources. But the new activists went much further, basing their positions on the developing field of ecology, the study of the interconnections among all components of an environment. Toxic waste, air and water pollution, the destruction of forests, the extinction of species—these were not separate, isolated problems. All elements of the earth's environment were intimately and delicately linked, ecologists claimed. Damaging any one of those elements risked damaging all the others. Only by adopting a new social ethic, in which economic growth became less important than ecological health, or a new economics, in which environmental costs were factored into economic analyses, could the human race hope to survive in a healthy world.

In the decades after the first Earth Day, environmental issues gained increasing attention and support. Although the federal government generally displayed limited interest in the subject, environmentalists won a series of significant battles, mostly at the local level. They blocked the construction of roads, airports, and other projects (including American development of the supersonic transport airplane, or SST) that they claimed would be ecologically dangerous.

As the environmental movement gained power and public support, government felt obliged to respond. A flurry of legislation in the early 1970s created the Environmental Protection Agency and set federal standards for clean air and water, for preserving endangered species, and for restricting the use of pesticides. Over time, this legislation helped produce a dramatic improvement in some areas: less smog in industrial cities; greatly reduced pollution in many lakes, streams, and rivers; a decline in the amounts of toxic waste dumped onto the landscape. There was less progress in dealing with some of the most ominous environmental hazards. By the end of the 1970s, many scientists were warning that the release of certain industrial pollutants (most notably chlorofluorocarbons) into the atmosphere was depleting the ozone layer of the earth's atmosphere, which protects the globe from the sun's most dangerous rays. They warned, too, of the related danger of global warming, a rise in the earth's temperature as a result of emissions from the burning of fossil fuels (coal and oil). These problems—and such others as the pollution of the oceans and the destruction of rain forests—required international solutions, which were much more difficult to produce. International conferences—in Montreal in 1987 and in Brazil in 1992 (the celebrated "Earth Summit")—produced some broad agreements on several global environmental problems. But there was no way to enforce compliance with them; and the United States government, during the Bush administration, publicly rejected some of the accords.

The concern for the environment, the opposition to nuclear power, the resistance to economic development—all were reflections of a more fundamental characteristic of the post-Vietnam left. In a sharp break from the nation's long commitment to growth and progress, many dissidents argued that only by limiting growth and curbing traditional forms of progress could society hope to survive. Some of these critics of the "idea of progress" expressed a gloomy resignation, urging a lowering of social expectations and predicting an inevitable deterioration in the quality of life. Other advocates of restraint believed that change did not require decline: human beings could live more comfortably and more happily if they learned to respect the limits imposed on them by their environment. But in either case, such arguments evoked strong opposition from conservatives and others, who ridiculed the no-growth ideology as an expression of defeatism and despair. Ronald Reagan, in particular, made an attack on the idea of "limits" central to his political success.

The rising popularity of environmental issues reflected another important shift both in the character of the American left and in the tone of American public life generally. Through much of the first half of the twentieth century, American politics had been preoccupied with debates over economic power and disparities of wealth. In the late twentieth century, even though inequality in the distribution of wealth and power was reaching unprecedented levels, such debates had largely ceased. There were, of course, economic implications to environmentalism and other no-growth efforts. But what drove such movements was less a concern about class than a concern about the quality of individual and community life.

The Fragmentation of Mass Culture

One of the most powerful cultural trends throughout much of the twentieth century was the growing power and the increasing standardization of mass culture. The institutions of the media—news, entertainment, advertising, and others—grew steadily more powerful. Almost without exception, they also strove to attract the largest possible audience or market. In doing so, they attempted to standardize their products so that they would be familiar and accessible to everyone. This standardization began with mass merchandising in the late nineteenth century; it accelerated in the early twentieth century with the rise of Hollywood movies, national radio networks, and powerful, mass-circulation magazines; it became dramatically more important in the 1950s, with the rise of network television. It was reinforced by the philosophy of the advertising industry to promote most products for the largest possible audience.

Beginning in the 1970s, and accelerating in the 1980s and 1990s, the character of mass culture changed in some important ways. There was, of course, continued standardization in many areas. McDonald's, Burger King, and other fast-food chains became the most widely-known restaurants in America (and indeed the world). Huge retail chains—K-Mart, Bradlees, Wal-Mart, Barnes & Noble, Blockbuster, the Gap, and others—dominated retail sales in many communities. The most popular Hollywood films attracted larger audiences than ever before; and the most powerful media companies—most notably, Disney—produced merchandise that made their film and television characters familiar to almost everyone in the world. But there was also a very different trend at work at the same time: a tendency in both retailing and entertainment to appeal less to mass markets and more to specific segments of the market.

This segmentation was first visible in new ideas about advertising that became powerful in the 1970s, ideas known as "targeting." Instead of finding promotional techniques to appeal to everyone, advertisers sought to identify a product with a particular "segment" of the market (men, women, young people, old people, health-conscious people, the rich, people of modest means, children) and create advertisements designed to appeal to it. As if in response, the television networks began to produce programming that focused on particular segments of the audience. Some programs were aimed at women, some at African Americans, some at affluent, urban middle-class viewers, some at more rural and provincial people. Fewer and fewer programs had a truly "mass" audience; more and more aimed at a particular group within that audience.

Even more important was the rapid proliferation of media outlets. As late as the 1970s, American television audiences overwhelmingly watched programs on the three major networks: NBC, CBS, and ABC. In the 1980s, that began to change. One reason was the proliferation of video cassette recorders (VCRs), which were in 70 percent of all homes by 1990. Instead of watching network television, viewers could now rent or buy videotapes and watch movies or other programming of their own choosing—available in enormous variety at thousands of video stores all across the country. Another reason was the increasing availability of cable and satellite television, which allowed homes to receive many more channels than ever before. The percent of television viewers watching the major networks declined steadily in the 1980s. New networks (Fox and Warner Brothers), along with specialized sports, movie, shopping, music, weather, and other channels, began to compete with the traditional leaders, distributing their programming over a combination of broadcast and cable channels. And many people turned away from television altogether and began to explore the powerful new medium of the Internet.

As audiences fragmented among many different stations and media, the phenomenon of the national "shared experience" declined as well. Network news, once the most important source for the vast majority of information, experienced a dramatic decline in viewership; many people now got their news from a variety of cable stations, from the increasingly powerful vehicle of talk radio, or from the new national newspaper *USA Today*. Young people found their own media world in MTV and other cable stations that focused on rock music and other elements of youth culture.

Hollywood continued to turn out hugely expensive "blockbusters" in a search for a mass audience. But many filmgoers turned instead to smaller independent films, which targeted particular segments of the population.

The "Culture Wars"

As American culture became more segmented, it also became more contentious. That contentiousness was reinforced by the decline of class-based controversies in American public life, and an increasing attention to cultural battles in their place. Indeed, few issues attracted more attention in the 1990s than the battle over what became known as "multiculturalism." Multiculturalism meant different things to different people, but at its core it was an effort to legitimize the cultural pluralism of the rapidly diversifying American population. That meant acknowledging that "American culture," which had long been defined primarily by white males of European descent, also included other traditions: female, African-American, Indian, and increasingly in the late twentieth century, Hispanic and Asian. Although such demands were often controversial, especially when they became the basis of assaults on traditional academic curricula, much greater acrimony emerged out of efforts by some revisionists to portray traditional Western culture as inherently racist and imperialistic.

A prolonged, if somewhat muted, dispute over how to commemorate the 500TH anniversary of Columbus's first voyage to the New World illustrated how sharply ideas of multiculturalism had changed the way Americans discussed their past. In 1892, the Columbian anniversary had been the occasion of boisterous national celebration—and a great World's Fair in Chicago. In 1992, it produced agonizing debates over the impact of the European discovery on native peoples; and the only World's Fairs were in Italy and Spain.

Debates over multiculturalism and related issues helped produce an increasingly strained climate in academia and in the larger American intellectual world. People on the left complained that the ascendancy of conservative politics placed new and intolerable limits on freedom of expression, as efforts to restrict NEA grants to controversial artists suggested. Many on the right complained equally vigorously of a tyranny of "political correctness," by which feminists, cultural radicals, and others introduced a new form of intolerance to public discourse in the name of defending the rights of women and minorities.

The controversies surrounding multiculturalism and "political correctness" were illustrations of a painful change in the character of American society. Traditional patterns of authority faced challenges from women, minorities, and others. The liberal belief in tolerance and assimilation was fraying in the face of the growing cultural separatism of some ethnic and racial groups. But multiculturalism, in many of its forms, was also a way of broadening the definition of American culture to include all the nation's diverse peoples. It was an expression of confidence in society's ability to tolerate and understand its many differences.

CONCLUSION

Americans reached the end of the twentieth century afflicted with many anxieties, doubts, and resentments. Faith in the nation's institutions—most notably, government—was at its lowest point in many decades. Confidence in the nation's leaders had dramatically eroded in the wake of the tawdry scandals and vicious partisanship of the Clinton years. Ugly battles over differing standards of morality and different cultural styles disturbed many communities. Vague resentments over the increasingly unequal patterns of income and wealth in the new economy, which few Americans seemed able to translate into a coherent economic agenda, increased the nation's unease.

And yet the United States at the end of the century, despite its many problems, was a remarkably successful society. It had made dramatic strides in improving the lives of its citizens and in dealing with many of its social problems since the end of World War II. It approached the century's end with the strongest economy in the world; with violent crime—one of its most corrosive problems for more than a generation—in a marked decline; and with its power and stature in the world unrivaled.

The American people have rarely, if ever, been wholly content about the condition of their nation. But they have also been extraordinarily resilient, and through much of their history most Americans have believed that if they tried hard enough, they could improve their world. As the United States moved rapidly into a new century and a new age, its people continued to search—as they had since the nation's beginnings—to fulfill its promise as a great democratic experiment in both diversity and union.

FOR FURTHER REFERENCE

Suggested Readings

John Lewis Gaddis, *The United States and the End of the Cold War* (1992) and *We Now Know: Rethinking Cold War History* (1997) are early examinations of the transformation of the world order. E. J. Dionne, *Why Americans Hate Politics* (1991) is a perceptive discussion of the political discontents of the 1980s and early 1990s. Thomas Byrne Edsall and Mary D. Edsall, *Chain Reaction: The Impact of Race, Rights, and Taxes on American Politics* (1991) is an alternative interpretation of the changes in American politics, focusing primarily on the impact of race. Lawrence Walsh, *Iran-Contra: The Final Report* (1994) is the independent counsel's account of his investigations into the scandals that plagued Reagan's second term. Herbert Parmet, *George Bush: The Life of a Lone Star Yankee* (1997) is the first serious biography of the 41ST president. David Marannis, *First in His Class: A Biography of Bill Clinton* (1995) traces Clinton's pre-presidential career. Theda Skocpol, *Boomerang: Clinton's Health Security Effort and the Turn Against Government in U.S. Politics* (1996) is an account of one of the major setbacks of Clinton's first term. Michael A. Bernstein and David E. Adler, *Understanding American Economic Decline* (1994) is an important collection of essays on the changes in the American economy since the 1970s. *Computer: A History of the Information Machine,* by Martin Campbell-Kelly and William Aspray (1996) is an introduction to the development of one of the critical technologies of the late twentieth century. Randy Shilts, *And the Band Played On: Politics, People, and the AIDS Epidemic* (1987) is a provocative discussion of the early years of AIDS in America. Andrew Hacker, *Two Nations: Black and White, Separate, Hostile, Unequal* (1992) and Michael Katz, *The Undeserving Poor: From the War on Poverty to the War on Welfare* (1989) are two contrasting arguments about the nature of African-American life and inner-city poverty. William Julius Wilson, *The Truly Disadvantaged* (1987) and *When Work Disappears* (1996) are important studies of the inner-city poor from one of America's leading sociologists. David A. Hollinger, *Postethnic America: Beyond Multiculturalism* (1995) is an intelligent and spirited comment on the debates over multiculturalism.

Films

(The best source for information on how to find these and other films is *Bowker's Complete Video Directory*—3 volumes.) *The Fall of Communism* (1997), assembled by the ABC News Team Staff, narrates the transition to democracy in one communist country after another. *The Fall of the Berlin Wall* (1990) collects footage of the dismantling of the symbolic center of the "iron curtain." That the "new world order" after the end of the Cold War would not necessarily be a peaceful order is clear from the early documentary entitled *The Gulf War: Frontline* (1997).

Internet Resources

Internet websites containing historical material relevant to the subjects discussed in this chapter can be reached through the McGraw-Hill history site at www.mhhe.com/socscience/history/usa/link/linktop.htm.

APPENDIXES

CANADA

Lake of the Woods

national Falls

Lake Superior

Duluth

MINNESOTA

Sault Ste. Marie

MICHIGAN

St. Paul

Minneapolis

WISCONSIN

Green Bay

Lake Michigan

Lake Huron

St. Lawrence River

MAINE

Bangor

Augusta

VERMONT

Montpelier   NEW   Portland
              HAMPSHIRE
                    Concord
                    Portsmouth

Springfield   Boston

Lake Ontario

Schenectady

MASSACHUSETTS

Milwaukee

Grand
Rapids   Lansing

Bay City

Flint

Sterling
Heights

Rochester   Syracuse   Albany

Buffalo   NEW YORK

Providence

RHODE ISLAND

Madison   Kalamazoo   Livonia   Detroit

Lake
Erie   Erie

White Plains   Hartford

Paterson   Scranton

CONNECTICUT

New Haven

Iowa City   Waterloo

IOWA

Rockford   Chicago

Ann Arbor   Cleveland

Stamford

Newark   New York

Cedar   Aurora   Gary   South
Des   Rapids   Bend   Toledo   Akron   Youngstown
Moines   Davenport

Fort Wayne

OHIO

PENNSYLVANIA

Allentown   Trenton

NEW JERSEY

Harrisburg   Philadelphia

Omaha

Peoria

Muncie

Columbus

Pittsburgh

Baltimore   Dover

ILLINOIS   INDIANA

Dayton

Washington, D.C.

DELAWARE

Annapolis

St. Joseph   Springfield

Indianapolis

Cincinnati

WEST
VIRGINIA

Alexandria

MARYLAND

Kansas City

VIRGINIA

Chesapeake Bay

Independence

St. Louis

Louisville   Frankfort

Charleston

Richmond

Newport News

Jefferson
City

Evansville

Lexington/
Fayette

Lynchburg

Hampton
Norfolk

Roanoke   Portsmouth   Chesapeake

ATLANTIC

MISSOURI

KENTUCKY

OCEAN

Springfield

Durham

Greensboro   Raleigh

Cape Hatteras

Nashville/
Davidson   Knoxville   NORTH CAROLINA

ARKANSAS

TENNESSEE

Charlotte

Fort
Smith

Chattanooga

Greenville

Wilmington

Cape Fear

Little
Rock

Huntsville

Columbia

Texarkana

Atlanta

SOUTH   Myrtle Beach

Monroe

MISSISSIPPI   ALABAMA

Birmingham   Augusta

CAROLINA

Charleston

Shreveport

Vicksburg

Selma

Macon

Columbus

LOUISIANA

Jackson

Montgomery   GEORGIA

Savannah

Albany

Mobile

Jacksonville

Baton Rouge

Pensacola

Tallahassee   St. Augustine

Beaumont

Houston
Pasadena

Lake
Charles   Lafayette   New Orleans

FLORIDA

Daytona Beach

Cape
Canaveral

Galveston

Orlando

Tampa

St. Petersburg

Lake
Okeechobee

Sarasota

Fort Myers   Fort
                Lauderdale

Hollywood

Hialeah   Miami

Gulf of Mexico

Key West

0   300 Miles
0   400 Kilometers

A–3

United States Territorial Expansion, 1783–1898

(1859) Date of statehood

The United States in 1783

Louisiana Purchase, 1803

1819 Treaty with Spain defined border of Oregon and Louisiana

West Florida annexation, 1810, 1813

Florida: East Florida cession by Spain, 1819;

Texas Annexation, 1845

Texas boundary claimed by U.S., 1845–1848

Oregon Country, 1846

Mexican Cession, 1848

Gadsden Purchase 1853

Alaska Purchase, 1867

Hawaii Annexation, 1898

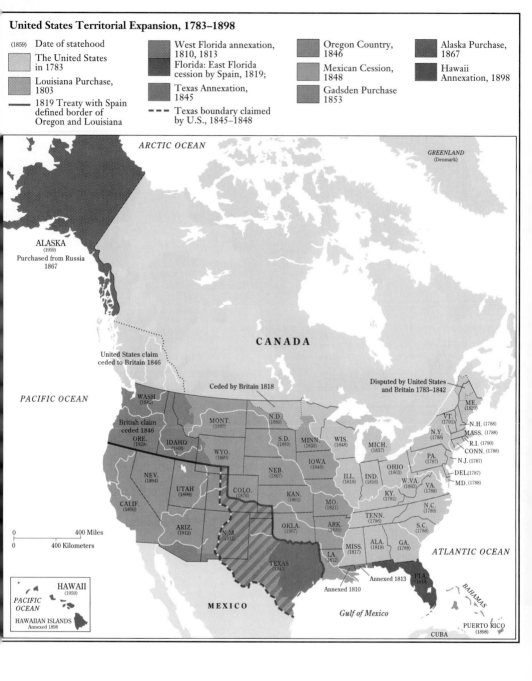

ARCTIC OCEAN

GREENLAND (Denmark)

ALASKA (1959)
Purchased from Russia 1867

PACIFIC OCEAN

CANADA

United States claim ceded to Britain 1846

Ceded by Britain 1818

Disputed by United States and Britain 1783–1842

British claim ceded 1846

WASH. (1889)

MONT. (1889)

N.D. (1889)

ME (1820)

VT. (1791)

N.H. (1788)

MASS. (1788)

R.I. (1790)

CONN. (1788)

ORE. (1859)

IDAHO (1890)

S.D. (1889)

MINN. (1858)

WIS. (1848)

MICH. (1837)

N.Y. (1788)

PA. (1787)

N.J. (1787)

NEV. (1864)

WYO. (1890)

NEB. (1867)

IOWA (1846)

ILL. (1818)

IND. (1816)

OHIO (1803)

W.VA. (1863)

VA. (1788)

DEL. (1787)

MD. (1788)

UTAH (1896)

COLO. (1876)

KAN. (1861)

MO. (1821)

KY. (1792)

N.C. (1789)

CALIF. (1850)

ARIZ. (1912)

N.M. (1912)

OKLA. (1907)

ARK. (1836)

TENN. (1796)

S.C. (1788)

0   400 Miles

0   400 Kilometers

TEXAS (1845)

LA. (1812)

MISS. (1817)

ALA. (1819)

GA. (1788)

FLA. (1845)

ATLANTIC OCEAN

BAHAMAS

Annexed 1813

Annexed 1810

Gulf of Mexico

MEXICO

HAWAII (1959)

PACIFIC OCEAN

HAWAIIAN ISLANDS
Annexed 1898

PUERTO RICO (1898)

CUBA

Documents and Tables

THE DECLARATION OF INDEPENDENCE

In Congress, July 4, 1776,

THE UNANIMOUS DECLARATION OF THE THIRTEEN UNITED STATES OF AMERICA

When, in the course of human events, it becomes necessary for one people to dissolve the political bands which have connected them with another, and to assume, among the powers of the earth, the separate and equal station to which the laws of nature and of nature's God entitle them, a decent respect to the opinions of mankind requires that they should declare the causes which impel them to the separation.

We hold these truths to be self-evident, that all men are created equal; that they are endowed by their Creator with certain unalienable rights; that among these, are life, liberty, and the pursuit of happiness. That, to secure these rights, governments are instituted among men, deriving their just powers from the consent of the governed; that, whenever any form of government becomes destructive of these ends, it is the right of the people to alter or to abolish it, and to institute a new government, laying its foundation on such principles, and organizing its powers in such form, as to them shall seem most likely to effect their safety and happiness. Prudence, indeed, will dictate that governments long established, should not be changed for light and transient causes; and, accordingly, all experience hath shown, that mankind are more disposed to suffer, while evils are sufferable, than to right themselves by abolishing the forms to which they are accustomed. But, when a long train of abuses and usurpations, pursuing invariably the same object, evinces a design to reduce them under absolute despotism, it is their right, it is their duty, to throw off such government and to provide new guards for their future security. Such has been the patient sufferance of these colonies, and such is now the necessity which constrains them to alter their former systems of government. The history of the present King of Great Britain is a history of repeated injuries and usurpations, all having, in direct object, the establishment of an absolute tyranny over these States. To prove this, let facts be submitted to a candid world:

He has refused his assent to laws the most wholesome and necessary for the public good.

He has forbidden his governors to pass laws of immediate and pressing importance, unless suspended in their operation till his assent should be obtained; and, when so suspended, he has utterly neglected to attend to them.

He has refused to pass other laws for the accommodation of large districts of people, unless those people would relinquish the right of representation in the legislature; a right inestimable to them, and formidable to tyrants only.

He has called together legislative bodies at places unusual, uncomfortable, and distant from the depository of their public records, for the sole purpose of fatiguing them into compliance with his measures.

He has dissolved representative houses repeatedly for opposing, with manly firmness, his invasions on the rights of the people.

He has refused, for a long time after such dissolutions, to cause others to be elected; whereby the legislative powers, incapable of annihilation, have returned to the people at large for their exercise; the state remaining, in the meantime, exposed to all the danger of invasion from without, and convulsions within.

He has endeavored to prevent the population of these States; for that purpose, obstructing the laws for naturalization of foreigners, refusing to pass others to encourage their migration hither, and raising the conditions of new appropriations of lands.

He has obstructed the administration of justice, by refusing his assent to laws for establishing judiciary powers.

He has made judges dependent on his will alone, for the tenure of their offices, and the amount and payment of their salaries.

He has erected a multitude of new offices, and sent hither swarms of officers to harass our people, and eat out their substance.

He has kept among us, in time of peace, standing armies, without the consent of our legislatures.

He has affected to render the military independent of, and superior to, the civil power.

He has combined, with others, to subject us to a jurisdiction foreign to our Constitution, and unacknowledged by our laws; giving his assent to their acts of pretended legislation:

For quartering large bodies of armed troops among us:

For protecting them by a mock trial, from punishment, for any murders which they should commit on the inhabitants of these States:

For cutting off our trade with all parts of the world:

For imposing taxes on us without our consent:

For depriving us, in many cases, of the benefit of trial by jury:

For transporting us beyond seas to be tried for pretended offences:

For abolishing the free system of English laws in a neighboring province, establishing therein an arbitrary government, and enlarging its boundaries, so as to render it at once an example and fit instrument for introducing the same absolute rule into these colonies:

For taking away our charters, abolishing our most valuable laws, and altering, fundamentally, the powers of our governments:

For suspending our own legislatures, and declaring themselves invested with power to legislate for us in all cases whatsoever.

He has abdicated government here, by declaring us out of his protection, and waging war against us.

He has plundered our seas, ravaged our coasts, burnt our towns, and destroyed the lives of our people.

He is, at this time, transporting large armies of foreign mercenaries to complete the works of death, desolation, and tyranny, already begun, with circumstances of cruelty and perfidy scarcely paralleled in the most barbarous ages, and totally unworthy the head of a civilized nation.

He has constrained our fellow citizens, taken captive on the high seas, to bear arms against their country, to become the executioners of their friends, and brethren, or to fall themselves by their hands.

He has excited domestic insurrections amongst us, and has endeavored to bring on the inhabitants of our frontiers, the merciless Indian savages, whose known rule of warfare is an undistinguished destruction of all ages, sexes, and conditions.

In every stage of these oppressions, we have petitioned for redress, in the most humble terms; our repeated petitions have been answered only by repeated injury. A prince, whose character is thus marked by every act which may define a tyrant, is unfit to be the ruler of a free people.

Nor have we been wanting in attention to our British brethren. We have warned them, from time to time, of attempts made by their legislature to extend an unwarrantable jurisdiction over us. We have reminded them of the circumstances of our emigration and settlement here. We have appealed to their native justice and magnanimity, and we have conjured them, by the ties of our common kindred, to disavow these usurpations, which would inevitably interrupt our connections and correspondence. They, too, have been deaf to the voice of justice and consanguinity. We must, therefore, acquiesce in the necessity which denounces our separation, and hold them as we hold the rest of mankind, enemies in war, in peace, friends.

We, therefore, the representatives of the United States of America, in general Congress assembled, appealing to the Supreme Judge of the world for the rectitude of our intentions, do, in the name, and by the authority of the good people of these colonies, solemnly publish and declare, that these united colonies are, and of right ought to be, free and independent states: that they are absolved from all allegiance to the British Crown, and that all political connection between them and the state of Great Britain is, and ought to be, totally dissolved; and that, as free and independent states, they have full power to levy war, conclude peace, contract alliances, establish commerce, and to do all other acts and things which independent states may of right do. And, for the support of this declaration, with a firm reliance on the protection of Divine Providence, we mutually pledge to each other our lives, our fortunes, and our sacred honor.

The foregoing Declaration was, by order of Congress, engrossed, and signed by the following members:

John Hancock

New Hampshire	*Massachusetts Bay*	*Rhode Island*
Josiah Bartlett	Samuel Adams	Stephen Hopkins
William Whipple	John Adams	William Ellery
Matthew Thornton	Robert Treat Paine	
	Elbridge Gerry	

Connecticut
Roger Sherman
Samuel Huntington
William Williams
Oliver Wolcott

New York
William Floyd
Philip Livingston
Francis Lewis
Lewis Morris

New Jersey
Richard Stockton
John Witherspoon
Francis Hopkinson
John Hart
Abraham Clark

Pennsylvania
Robert Morris
Benjamin Rush
Benjamin Franklin
John Morton
George Clymer
James Smith
George Taylor
James Wilson
George Ross

Delaware
Caesar Rodney
George Read
Thomas M'Kean

Maryland
Samuel Chase
William Paca
Thomas Stone
Charles Carroll,
  of Carrollton

Virginia
George Wythe
Richard Henry Lee
Thomas Jefferson
Benjamin Harrison
Thomas Nelson, Jr.
Francis Lightfoot Lee
Carter Braxton

North Carolina
William Hooper
Joseph Hewes
John Penn

South Carolina
Edward Rutledge
Thomas Heyward, Jr.
Thomas Lynch, Jr.
Arthur Middleton

Georgia
Button Gwinnett
Lyman Hall
George Walton

Resolved, That copies of the Declaration be sent to the several assemblies, conventions, and committees, or councils of safety, and to the several commanding officers of the continental troops; that it be proclaimed in each of the United States, at the head of the army.

THE CONSTITUTION
OF THE UNITED STATES[1]

We the People of the United States, in Order to form a more perfect Union, establish Justice, insure domestic Tranquility, provide for the common defence, promote the general Welfare, and secure the Blessings of Liberty to ourselves and our Posterity, do ordain and establish this CONSTITUTION for the United States of America.

Article I

Section 1.
All legislative Powers herein granted shall be vested in a Congress of the United States, which shall consist of a Senate and House of Representatives.

Section 2.
The House of Representatives shall be composed of Members chosen every second Year by the People of the several States, and the Electors in each State shall have the Qualifications requisite for Electors of the most numerous Branch of the State Legislature.

No Person shall be a Representative who shall not have attained to the Age of twenty-five Years, and been seven Years a Citizen of the United States, and who shall not, when elected, be an Inhabitant of that State in which he shall be chosen.

[Representatives and direct Taxes[2] shall be apportioned among the several States which may be included within this Union, according to their respective Numbers, which shall be determined by adding to the whole Number of free Persons, including those bound to Service for a Term of Years, and excluding Indians not taxed, three fifths of all other Persons.][3] The actual Enumeration shall be made within three Years after the first Meeting of the Congress of the United States, and within every subsequent Term of ten Years, in such Manner as they shall by Law direct. The Number of Representatives shall not exceed one for every thirty Thousand, but each State shall have at Least one Representative; and until such enumeration shall be made, the State of New Hampshire shall be entitled to chuse three, Massachusetts eight, Rhode-Island and Providence Plantations one, Connecticut five, New York six, New Jersey four, Pennsylvania eight, Delaware one,

---

[1] This version, which follows the original Constitution in capitalization and spelling, was published by the United States Department of the Interior, Office of Education, in 1935.

[2] Altered by the Sixteenth Amendment.

[3] Negated by the Fourteenth Amendment.

Maryland six, Virginia ten, North Carolina five, South Carolina five, and Georgia three.

When vacancies happen in the Representation from any State, the Executive Authority thereof shall issue Writs of Election to fill such Vacancies.

The House of Representatives shall chuse their Speaker and other Officers; and shall have the sole Power of Impeachment.

Section 3.

The Senate of the United States shall be composed of two Senators from each State, chosen by the Legislature thereof, for six Years; and each Senator shall have one Vote.

Immediately after they shall be assembled in Consequence of the first Election, they shall be divided as equally as may be into three Classes. The Seats of the Senators of the first Class shall be vacated at the Expiration of the second Year, of the second Class at the Expiration of the fourth Year, and of the third Class at the Expiration of the sixth Year, so that one-third may be chosen every second Year; and if Vacancies happen by Resignation, or otherwise, during the Recess of the Legislature of any State, the Executive thereof may make temporary Appointments until the next Meeting of the Legislature, which shall then fill such Vacancies.

No Person shall be a Senator who shall not have attained to the Age of thirty Years, and been nine Years a Citizen of the United States, and who shall not, when elected, be an Inhabitant of that State for which he shall be chosen.

The Vice President of the United States shall be President of the Senate, but shall have no vote, unless they be equally divided.

The Senate shall chuse their other Officers, and also a President pro tempore, in the absence of the Vice President, or when he shall exercise the Office of President of the United States.

The Senate shall have the sole Power to try all Impeachments. When sitting for that purpose they shall be on Oath or Affirmation. When the President of the United States is tried, the Chief Justice shall preside: And no person shall be convicted without the Concurrence of two thirds of the Members present.

Judgment in Cases of Impeachment shall not extend further than to removal from Office, and disqualification to hold and enjoy any Office of honor, Trust, or Profit under the United States: but the Party convicted shall nevertheless be liable and subject to Indictment, Trial, Judgment, and Punishment, according to Law.

Section 4.

The Times, Places and Manner of holding Elections for Senators and Representatives, shall be prescribed in each State by the Legislature thereof; but the Congress may at any time by Law make or alter such Regulations, except as to the Places of Chusing Senators.

The Congress shall assemble at least once in every Year, and such Meeting shall be on the first Monday in December, unless they shall by Law appoint a different Day.

Section 5.

Each House shall be the Judge of the Elections, Returns and Qualifications of its own Members, and a Majority of each shall constitute a Quorum to do Business; but a smaller number may adjourn from day to day, and may be authorized to compel the Attendance of absent Members, in such Manner, and under such Penalties, as each House may provide.

Each House may determine the Rules of its Proceedings, punish its Members for disorderly Behaviour, and, with the Concurrence of two thirds, expel a Member.

Each House shall keep a Journal of its Proceedings, and from time to time publish the same, excepting such Parts as may in their Judgment require Secrecy; and the Yeas and Nays of the Members of either House on any question shall, at the Desire of one fifth of those Present, be entered on the Journal.

Neither House, during the Session of Congress, shall, without the Consent of the other, adjourn for more than three days, nor to any other Place than that in which the two Houses shall be sitting.

Section 6.

The Senators and Representatives shall receive a Compensation for their Services, to be ascertained by Law, and paid out of the Treasury of the United States. They shall in all Cases, except Treason, Felony, and Breach of the Peace, be privileged from Arrest during their Attendance at the Session of their respective Houses, and in going to and returning from the same; and for any Speech or Debate in either House, they shall not be questioned in any other Place.

No Senator or Representative shall, during the Time for which he was elected, be appointed to any civil Office under the Authority of the United States, which shall have been created, or the Emoluments whereof shall have been increased, during such time; and no Person holding any Office under the United States shall be a Member of either House during his continuance in Office.

Section 7.

All Bills for raising Revenue shall originate in the House of Representatives; but the Senate may propose or concur with Amendments as on other bills.

Every Bill which shall have passed the House of Representatives and the Senate, shall, before it become a Law, be presented to the President of the United States; If he approve he shall sign it, but if not he shall return it, with his Objections, to that House in which it shall have originated, who shall enter the Objections at large on their Journal, and proceed to reconsider it. If after such Reconsideration two thirds of that House shall agree to pass the bill, it shall be sent, together with the objections, to the other House, by which it shall likewise be reconsidered, and if approved by two thirds of that House, it shall become a Law. But in all such Cases the Votes of both Houses shall be determined by Yeas and Nays, and the Names of the Persons voting for and against the Bill shall be entered on the Journal of each House respectively. If any Bill shall not be returned by the President within ten Days (Sundays excepted) after it shall have been presented to him, the Same shall be a Law, in like Manner as if he had signed it, unless the Congress by their Adjournment prevent its Return, in which Case it shall not be a Law.

Every Order, Resolution, or Vote to which the Concurrence of the Senate and House of Representatives may be necessary (except on a question of Adjournment) shall be presented to the President of the United States; and before the Same shall take Effect, shall be approved by him, or being disapproved by him, shall be repassed by two thirds of the Senate and House of Representatives, according to the Rules and Limitations prescribed in the Case of a Bill.

Section 8.
The Congress shall have Power To lay and collect Taxes, Duties, Imposts and Excises, to pay the Debts and provide for the common Defence and general Welfare of the United States; but all Duties, Imposts and Excises shall be uniform throughout the United States;

To borrow money on the credit of the United States;

To regulate Commerce with foreign Nations, and among the several States, and with the Indian Tribes;

To establish an uniform rule of Naturalization, and uniform Laws on the subject of Bankruptcies throughout the United States;

To coin Money, regulate the Value thereof, and of foreign Coin, and fix the Standard of Weights and Measures;

To provide for the Punishment of counterfeiting the Securities and current Coin of the United States;

To establish Post Offices and post Roads;

To promote the Progress of Science and useful Arts, by securing for limited Times to Authors and Inventors the exclusive Right to their respective Writings and Discoveries;

To constitute Tribunals inferior to the Supreme Court;

To define and punish Piracies and Felonies committed on the high Seas, and Offenses against the Law of Nations;

To declare War, grant Letters of Marque and Reprisal, and make Rules concerning Captures on Land and Water;

To raise and support Armies, but no Appropriation of Money to that Use shall be for a longer Term than two Years;

To provide and maintain a Navy;

To make Rules for the Government and Regulation of the land and naval forces;

To provide for calling forth the Militia to execute the Laws of the Union, suppress Insurrections and repel Invasions;

To provide for organizing, arming, and disciplining the Militia, and for governing such Part of them as may be employed in the Service of the United States, reserving to the States respectively, the Appointment of the Officers, and the Authority of training the Militia according to the discipline prescribed by Congress;

To exercise exclusive Legislation in all Cases whatsoever, over such District (not exceeding ten Miles square) as may, by Cession of particular States, and the acceptance of Congress, become the Seat of the Government of the United States, and to exercise like Authority over all Places purchased by the Consent of the Legislature of the State in which the Same shall be, for the Erection of Forts, Magazines, Arsenals, Dock-yards, and other needful Buildings;—And

To make all Laws which shall be necessary and proper for carrying into Execution the foregoing Powers, and all other Powers vested by this Constitution in the Government of the United States, or in any Department or Officer thereof.

Section 9.

The Migration or Importation of such Persons as any of the States now existing shall think proper to admit, shall not be prohibited by the Congress prior to the Year one thousand eight hundred and eight, but a tax or duty may be imposed on such Importation, not exceeding ten dollars for each Person.

The privilege of the Writ of Habeas Corpus shall not be suspended, unless when in Cases of Rebellion or Invasion the public Safety may require it.

No bill of Attainder or ex post facto Law shall be passed.

No capitation, or other direct, Tax shall be laid unless in Proportion to the Census or Enumeration herein before directed to be taken.

No Tax or Duty shall be laid on Articles exported from any State.

No Preference shall be given by any Regulation of Commerce or Revenue to the Ports of one State over those of another: nor shall Vessels bound to, or from, one State, be obliged to enter, clear, or pay Duties in another.

No Money shall be drawn from the Treasury, but in Consequence of Appropriations made by Law; and a regular Statement and Account of the Receipts and Expenditures of all public Money shall be published from time to time.

No Title of Nobility shall be granted by the United States: And no Person holding any Office of Profit or Trust under them, shall, without the Consent of the Congress, accept of any present, Emolument, Office, or Title, of any kind whatever, from any King, Prince, or foreign State.

Section 10.

No State shall enter into any Treaty, Alliance, or Confederation; grant Letters of Marque and Reprisal; coin Money; emit Bills of Credit; make any Thing but gold and silver Coin a Tender in Payment of Debts; pass any Bill of Attainder, ex post facto Law, or Law impairing the Obligation of Contracts, or grant any Title of Nobility.

No State shall, without the Consent of the Congress, lay any Imposts or Duties on Imports or Exports, except what may be absolutely necessary for executing its inspection Laws; and the net Produce of all Duties and Imposts, laid by any State on Imports or Exports, shall be for the use of the Treasury of the United States; and all such Laws shall be subject to the Revision and Control of the Congress.

No state shall, without the Consent of Congress, lay any duty of Tonnage, keep Troops, or Ships of War in time of Peace, enter into any Agreement or Compact with another State, or with a foreign Power, or engage in War, unless actually invaded, or in such imminent Danger as will not admit of delay.

Article II

Section 1.

The executive Power shall be vested in a President of the United States of America. He shall hold his Office during the Term of four years, and, together with the Vice President, chosen for the same Term, be elected, as follows:

Each State shall appoint, in such Manner as the Legislature thereof may direct, a Number of Electors, equal to the whole Number of Senators and Representatives to which the State may be entitled in the Congress: but no Senator or Representative, or Person holding an Office of Trust or Profit under the United States, shall be appointed an Elector.

[The Electors shall meet in their respective States, and vote by Ballot for two persons, of whom one at least shall not be an Inhabitant of the same State with themselves. And they shall make a List of all the Persons voted for, and of the Number of Votes for each; which List they shall sign and certify, and transmit sealed to the Seat of the Government of the United States, directed to the President of the Senate. The President of the Senate shall, in the Presence of the Senate and House of Representatives, open all the Certificates, and the Votes shall then be counted. The Person having the greatest Number of Votes shall be the President, if such Number be a Majority of the whole Number of Electors appointed; and if there be more than one who have such Majority, and have an equal Number of Votes, then the House of Representatives shall immediately chuse by Ballot one of them for President; and if no Person have a Majority, then from the five highest on the List the said House shall in like Manner chuse the President. But in chusing the President, the Votes shall be taken by States, the Representation from each State having one Vote; a quorum for this Purpose shall consist of a Member or Members from two-thirds of the States, and a Majority of all the States shall be necessary to a Choice. In every Case, after the Choice of the President, the Person having the greatest Number of Votes of the Electors shall be the Vice President. But if there should remain two or more who have equal votes, the Senate shall chuse from them by Ballot the Vice President.][4]

The Congress may determine the Time of chusing the Electors, and the Day on which they shall give their Votes; which Day shall be the same throughout the United States.

No person except a natural-born Citizen, or a Citizen of the United States, at the time of the Adoption of this Constitution, shall be eligible to the Office of President; neither shall any Person be eligible to that Office who shall not have attained to the Age of thirty-five years, and been fourteen Years a Resident within the United States.

In Case of the Removal of the President from Office, or of his Death, Resignation, or Inability to discharge the Powers and Duties of the said Office, the same

---

[4] Revised by the Twelfth Amendment.

shall devolve on the Vice President, and the Congress may by Law provide for the Case of Removal, Death, Resignation, or Inability, both of the President and Vice President, declaring what Officer shall then act as President, and such Officer shall act accordingly, until the disability be removed, or a President shall be elected.

The President shall, at stated Times, receive for his Services a Compensation, which shall neither be increased nor diminished during the Period for which he shall have been elected, and he shall not receive within that Period any other Emolument from the United States, or any of them.

Before he enter on the execution of his Office, he shall take the following Oath or Affirmation:—"I do solemnly swear (or affirm) that I will faithfully execute the Office of President of the United States, and will, to the best of my Ability, preserve, protect, and defend the Constitution of the United States."

Section 2.

The President shall be Commander in Chief of the Army and Navy of the United States, and of the Militia of the several States, when called into the actual Service of the United States; he may require the Opinion, in writing, of the principal Officer in each of the executive Departments, upon any subject relating to the Duties of their respective Offices, and he shall have Power to Grant Reprieves and Pardons for Offenses against the United States, except in Cases of Impeachment.

He shall have Power, by and with the Advice and Consent of the Senate, to make Treaties, provided two-thirds of the Senators present concur; and he shall nominate, and by and with the Advice and Consent of the Senate, shall appoint Ambassadors, other public Ministers and Consuls, Judges of the supreme Court, and all other Officers of the United States, whose Appointments are not herein otherwise provided for, and which shall be established by Law: but the Congress may by Law vest the Appointment of such inferior Officers, as they think proper, in the President alone, in the Courts of Law, or in the Heads of Departments.

The President shall have Power to fill up all Vacancies that may happen during the Recess of the Senate, by granting Commissions which shall expire at the End of their next Session.

Section 3.

He shall from time to time give to the Congress Information of the State of the Union, and recommend to their Consideration such Measures as he shall judge necessary and expedient; he may, on extraordinary occasions, convene both Houses, or either of them, and in Case of Disagreement between them, with respect to the Time of Adjournment, he may adjourn them to such Time as he shall think proper; he shall receive Ambassadors and other public Ministers; he shall take care that the Laws be faithfully executed, and shall Commission all the Officers of the United States.

Section 4.

The President, Vice President and all civil Officers of the United States, shall be removed from Office on Impeachment for, and Conviction of, Treason, Bribery, or other high Crimes and Misdemeanors.

Article III

Section 1.

The judicial Power of the United States, shall be vested in one supreme Court, and in such inferior Courts as the Congress may from time to time ordain and establish. The Judges, both of the supreme and inferior Courts, shall hold their Offices during good Behaviour, and shall, at stated Times, receive for their Services, a Compensation, which shall not be diminished during their Continuance in Office.

Section 2.

The judicial Power shall extend to all Cases, in Law and Equity, arising under this Constitution, the Laws of the United States, and Treaties made, or which shall be made, under their Authority;—to all Cases affecting ambassadors, other public ministers and consuls;—to all cases of admiralty and maritime Jurisdiction;—to Controversies to which the United States shall be a Party;—to Controversies between two or more States;—between a State and Citizens of another State;[5]—between Citizens of different States—between Citizens of the same State claiming Lands under Grants of different States, and between a State, or the Citizens thereof, and foreign States, Citizens, or Subjects.

In all Cases affecting Ambassadors, other public Ministers and Consuls, and those in which a State shall be Party, the supreme Court shall have original Jurisdiction. In all the other Cases before mentioned, the supreme Court shall have appellate Jurisdiction, both as to Law and Fact, with such Exceptions, and under such Regulations as the Congress shall make.

The trial of all Crimes, except in Cases of Impeachment, shall be by Jury; and such Trial shall be held in the State where the said Crimes shall have been committed; but when not committed within any State, the Trial shall be at such Place or Places as the Congress may by Law have directed.

Section 3.

Treason against the United States, shall consist only in levying War against them, or in adhering to their Enemies, giving them Aid and Comfort. No Person shall be convicted of Treason unless on the Testimony of two Witnesses to the same overt Act, or on Confession in open Court.

The Congress shall have power to declare the Punishment of Treason, but no Attainder of Treason shall work Corruption of Blood, or Forfeiture except during the Life of the Person attained.

---

[5] Qualified by the Eleventh Amendment.

Article IV

Section 1.
Full Faith and Credit shall be given in each State to the public Acts, Records, and judicial Proceedings of every other State. And the Congress may by general Laws prescribe the Manner in which such Acts, Records and Proceedings shall be proved, and the Effect thereof.

Section 2.
The Citizens of each State shall be entitled to all Privileges and Immunities of Citizens in the several States.

A Person charged in any State with Treason, Felony, or other Crime, who shall flee from Justice, and be found in another State, shall on demand of the executive Authority of the State from which he fled, be delivered up, to be removed to the State having Jurisdiction of the crime.

No Person held to Service or Labour in one State, under the Laws thereof, escaping into another, shall, in Consequence of any Law or Regulation therein, be discharged from such Service or Labour, but shall be delivered up on Claim of the Party to whom such Service or Labour may be due.

Section 3.
New States may be admitted by the Congress into this Union; but no new State shall be formed or erected within the Jurisdiction of any other State; nor any State be formed by the Junction of two or more States, or parts of States, without the Consent of the Legislatures of the States concerned as well as of the Congress.

The Congress shall have Power to dispose of and make all needful Rules and Regulations respecting the Territory or other Property belonging to the United States; and nothing in this Constitution shall be so construed as to Prejudice any Claims of the United States, or of any particular State.

Section 4.
The United States shall guarantee to every State in this Union a Republican Form of Government, and shall protect each of them against Invasion; and on Application of the Legislature, or of the Executive (when the Legislature cannot be convened) against domestic Violence.

Article V

The Congress, whenever two-thirds of both Houses shall deem it necessary, shall propose Amendments to this Constitution, or, on the Application of the Legislatures of two-thirds of the several States, shall call a Convention for proposing Amendments, which, in either Case, shall be valid to all Intents and Purposes, as part of this Constitution, when ratified by the Legislatures of three-fourths of the several States, or by Conventions in three-fourths thereof, as the one or the other Mode of Ratification may be proposed by the Congress; Provided that no Amendment which may be made prior to the Year One thousand eight hundred and eight shall in any Manner affect the first and fourth Clauses in the Ninth Section of the first Article; and that no State, without its Consent, shall be deprived of its equal Suffrage in the Senate.

Article VI

All Debts contracted and Engagements entered into, before the Adoption of this Constitution, shall be as valid against the United States under this Constitution, as under the Confederation.

This Constitution, and the Laws of the United States which shall be made in Pursuance thereof; and all Treaties made, or which shall be made, under the Authority of the United States, shall be the supreme Law of the Land; and the Judges in every State shall be bound thereby, any Thing in the Constitution or Laws of any State to the Contrary notwithstanding.

The Senators and Representatives before mentioned, and the Members of the several State Legislatures, and all executive and judicial Officers, both of the United States and of the several States, shall be bound by Oath or Affirmation to support this Constitution; but no religious Tests shall ever be required as a qualification to any Office or public Trust under the United States.

Article VII

The Ratification of the Conventions of nine States shall be sufficient for the Establishment of this Constitution between the States so ratifying the same.

Done in Convention by the Unanimous Consent of the States present the Seventeenth Day of September in the Year of our Lord one thousand seven hundred and Eighty seven, and of the Independence of the United States of America the Twelfth. In Witness whereof We have hereunto subscribed our Names.[6]

George Washington
President and deputy from Virginia

New Hampshire	*Pennsylvania*	*Virginia*
John Langdon	Benjamin Franklin	John Blair
Nicholas Gilman	Thomas Mifflin	James Madison, Jr.
	Robert Morris	
Massachusetts	George Clymer	*North Carolina*
Nathaniel Gorham	Thomas FitzSimons	William Blount
Rufus King	Jared Ingersoll	Richard Dobbs
	James Wilson	Spaight
	Gouverneur Morris	Hugh Williamson

[6] These are the full names of the signers, which in some cases are not the signatures on the document.

Connecticut
William Samuel Johnson
Roger Sherman

New York
Alexander Hamilton

New Jersey
William Livingston
David Brearley
William Paterson
Jonathan Dayton

Delaware
George Read
Gunning Bedford, Jr.
John Dickinson
Richard Bassett
Jacob Broom

Maryland
James McHenry
Daniel of
    St. Thomas Jenifer
Daniel Carroll

South Carolina
John Rutledge
Charles Cotesworth
    Pinckney
Charles Pinckney
Pierce Butler

Georgia
William Few
Abraham Baldwin

Articles in Addition to, and Amendment of, the Constitution of the United States of America, Proposed by Congress, and Ratified by the Legislatures of the Several States, Pursuant to the Fifth Article of the Original Constitution.[7]

[Article I]

Congress shall make no law respecting an establishment of religion, or prohibiting the free exercise thereof; or abridging the freedom of speech, or of the press; or the right of the people peaceably to assemble, and to petition the Government for a redress of grievances.

[Article II]

A well regulated Militia, being necessary to the security of a free State, the right of the people to keep and bear Arms shall not be infringed.

[Article III]

No Soldier shall, in time of peace, be quartered in any house, without the consent of the Owner, nor in time of war, but in a manner to be prescribed by law.

[Article IV]

The right of the people to be secure in their persons, houses, papers, and effects, against unreasonable searches and seizures, shall not be violated, and no Warrants shall issue, but upon probable cause, supported by Oath or affirmation, and particularly describing the place to be searched, and the persons or things to be seized.

---

[7] This heading appears only in the joint resolution submitting the first ten amendments.

[Article V]

No person shall be held to answer for a capital or otherwise infamous crime, unless on a presentment or indictment of a Grand Jury, except in cases arising in the land or naval forces, or in the Militia, when in actual service in time of War or public danger; nor shall any person be subject for the same offence to be twice put in jeopardy of life or limb; nor shall be compelled in any criminal case to be a witness against himself, nor be deprived of life, liberty, or property, without due process of law; nor shall private property be taken for public use, without just compensation.

[Article VI]

In all criminal prosecutions, the accused shall enjoy the right to a speedy and public trial, by an impartial jury of the State and district wherein the crime shall have been committed, which district shall have been previously ascertained by law, and to be informed of the nature and cause of the accusation; to be confronted with the witnesses against him; to have compulsory process for obtaining witnesses in his favour, and to have the Assistance of Counsel for his defense.

[Article VII]

In suits at common law, where the value in controversy shall exceed twenty dollars, the right of trial by jury shall be preserved, and no fact tried by a jury, shall be otherwise reexamined in any Court of the United States, than according to the rules of the common law.

[Article VIII]

Excessive bail shall not be required, nor excessive fines imposed, nor cruel and unusual punishments inflicted.

[Article IX]

The enumeration of the Constitution, of certain rights, shall not be construed to deny or disparage others retained by the people.

[Article X]

The powers not delegated to the United States by the Constitution, nor prohibited by it to the States, are reserved to the States respectively, or to the people.
  [Amendments I–X, in force 1791.]

[Article XI][8]

The Judicial power of the United States shall not be construed to extend to any suit in law or equity, commenced or prosecuted against one of the United States by Citizens of another State, or by Citizens or Subjects of any Foreign State.

[Article XII][9]

The Electors shall meet in their respective States and vote by ballot for President and Vice-President, one of whom, at least, shall not be an inhabitant of the same State with themselves; they shall name in their ballots the person voted for as President, and in distinct ballots the person voted for as Vice-President, and they shall make distinct lists of all persons voted for as President, and of all persons voted for as Vice-President, and of the number of votes for each, which lists they shall sign and certify, and transmit sealed to the seat of the government of the United States, directed to the President of the Senate;—The President of the Senate shall, in the presence of the Senate and House of Representatives, open all the certificates and the votes shall then be counted;—The person having the greatest number of votes for President, shall be the President, if such number be a majority of the whole number of Electors appointed; and if no person have such majority, then from the persons having the highest numbers not exceeding three on the list of those voted for as President, the House of Representatives shall choose immediately, by ballot, the President. But in choosing the President, the votes shall be taken by states, the representation from each state having one vote; a quorum for this purpose shall consist of a member or members from two-thirds of the states, and a majority of all the states shall be necessary to a choice. And if the House of Representatives shall not choose a President whenever the right of choice shall devolve upon them, before the fourth day of March next following, then the Vice-President shall act as President, as in the case of the death or other constitutional disability of the President.—The person having the greatest number of votes as Vice-President, shall be the Vice-President, if such number be a majority of the whole number of Electors appointed, and if no person have a majority, then from the two highest numbers on the list, the Senate shall choose the Vice-President; a quorum for the purpose shall consist of two-thirds of the whole number of Senators, and a majority of the whole number shall be necessary to a choice. But no person constitutionally ineligible to the office of President shall be eligible to that of Vice-President of the United States.

---

[8] Adopted in 1798.
[9] Adopted in 1804.

[Article XIII][10]

Section 1.
Neither slavery nor involuntary servitude, except as a punishment for crime whereof the party shall have been duly convicted, shall exist within the United States, or any place subject to their jurisdiction.

Section 2.
Congress shall have power to enforce this article by appropriate legislation.

[Article XIV][11]

Section 1.
All persons born or naturalized in the United States, and subject to the jurisdiction thereof, are citizens of the United States and of the State wherein they reside. No State shall make or enforce any law which shall abridge the privileges or immunities of citizens of the United States; nor shall any State deprive any person of life, liberty, or property, without due process of law; nor deny to any person within its jurisdiction the equal protection of the laws.

Section 2.
Representatives shall be apportioned among the several States according to their respective numbers, counting the whole number of persons in each State, excluding Indians not taxed. But when the right to vote at any election for the choice of electors for President and Vice-President of the United States, Representatives in Congress, the Executive and Judicial officers of a State, or the members of the Legislature thereof, is denied to any of the male inhabitants of such State, being twenty-one years of age, and citizens of the United States, or in any way abridged, except for participation in rebellion, or other crime, the basis of representation therein shall be reduced in the proportion which the number of such male citizens shall bear to the whole number of male citizens twenty-one years of age in such State.

Section 3.
No person shall be a Senator or Representative in Congress, or elector of President and Vice-President, or hold any office, civil or military, under the United States, or under any State, who, having previously taken an oath, as a member of Congress, or as an officer of the United States, or as a member of any State legislature, or as

[10] Adopted in 1865.
[11] Adopted in 1868.

an executive or judicial officer of any State, to support the Constitution of the United States, shall have engaged in insurrection or rebellion against the same, or given aid or comfort to the enemies thereof. But Congress may by a vote of two-thirds of each House, remove such disability.

Section 4.
The validity of the public debt of the United States, authorized by law, including debts incurred for payment of pensions and bounties for services in suppressing insurrection or rebellion, shall not be questioned. But neither the United States nor any State shall assume or pay any debts or obligation incurred in aid of insurrection or rebellion against the United States, or any claim for the loss or emancipation of any slave; but all such debts, obligations, and claims shall be held illegal and void.

Section 5.
The Congress shall have the power to enforce, by appropriate legislation, the provisions of this article.

[Article XV][12]

Section 1.
The right of citizens of the United States to vote shall not be denied or abridged by the United States or by any State on account of race, color, or previous condition of servitude—

Section 2.
The Congress shall have power to enforce this article by appropriate legislation.

[Article XVI][13]

The Congress shall have power to lay and collect taxes on incomes, from whatever source derived, without apportionment among the several States, and without regard to any census or enumeration.

[Article XVII][14]

The Senate of the United States shall be composed of two Senators from each State, elected by the people thereof, for six years; and each Senator shall have one vote. The electors in each State shall have the qualifications requisite for electors of the most numerous branch of the State legislatures.

[12] Adopted in 1870.
[13] Adopted in 1913.
[14] Adopted in 1913.

When vacancies happen in the representation of any State in the Senate, the executive authority of such State shall issue writs of election to fill such vacancies: *Provided,* That the legislature of any State may empower the executive thereof to make temporary appointments until the people fill the vacancies by election as the legislature may direct.

This amendment shall not be so construed as to affect the election or term of any Senator chosen before it becomes valid as part of the Constitution.

[Article XVIII][15]

Section 1.
After one year from the ratification of this article the manufacture, sale, or transportation of intoxicating liquors within, the importation thereof into, or the exportation thereof from the United States and all territory subject to the jurisdiction thereof for beverage purposes is hereby prohibited.

Section 2.
The Congress and the several States shall have concurrent power to enforce this article by appropriate legislation.

Section 3.
This article shall be inoperative unless it shall have been ratified as an amendment to the Constitution by the legislatures of the several States, as provided in the Constitution, within seven years from the date of the submission hereof to the States by the Congress.

[Article XIX][16]

The right of citizens of the United States to vote shall not be denied or abridged by the United States or by any State on account of sex.

Congress shall have power to enforce this article by appropriate legislation.

[Article XX][17]

Section 1.
The terms of the President and Vice-President shall end at noon on the 20th day of January, and the terms of Senators and Representatives at noon on the 3d day of January, of the years in which such terms would have ended if this article had not been ratified; and the terms of their successors shall then begin.

[15] Adopted in 1918.
[16] Adopted in 1920.
[17] Adopted in 1933.

Section 2.
The Congress shall assemble at least once in every year, and such meeting shall begin at noon on the 3d day of January, unless they shall by law appoint a different day.

Section 3.
If, at the time fixed for the beginning of the term of the President, the President elect shall have died, the Vice-President elect shall become President. If a President shall not have been chosen before the time fixed for the beginning of his term or if the President elect shall have failed to qualify, then the Vice-President elect shall act as President until a President shall have qualified; and the Congress may by law provide for the case wherein neither a President elect nor a Vice-President elect shall have qualified, declaring who shall then act as President, or the manner in which one who is to act shall be selected, and such person shall act accordingly until a President or Vice-President shall have qualified.

Section 4.
The Congress may by law provide for the case of the death of any of the persons from whom the House of Representatives may choose a President whenever the right of choice shall have devolved upon them, and for the case of the death of any of the persons from whom the Senate may choose a Vice-President whenever the right of choice shall have devolved upon them.

Section 5.
Sections 1 and 2 shall take effect on the 15th day of October following the ratification of this article.

Section 6.
This article shall be inoperative unless it shall have been ratified as an amendment to the Constitution by the legislatures of three-fourths of the several States within seven years from the date of its submission.

[Article XXI][18]

Section 1.
The eighteenth article of amendment to the Constitution of the United States is hereby repealed.

Section 2.
The transportation or importation into any State, Territory, or possession of the United States for delivery or use therein of intoxicating liquors, in violation of the laws thereof, is hereby prohibited.

[18] Adopted in 1933.

Section 3.

This article shall be inoperative unless it shall have been ratified as an amendment to the Constitution by conventions in the several States, as provided in the Constitution, within seven years from the date of the submission hereof to the States by the Congress.

[Article XXII][19]

No person shall be elected to the office of the President more than twice, and no person who has held the office of President, or acted as President, for more than two years of a term to which some other person was elected President shall be elected to the office of the President more than once.

But this Article shall not apply to any person holding the office of President when this Article was proposed by the Congress, and shall not prevent any person who may be holding the office of President, or acting as President, during the term within which this Article becomes operative from holding the office of President or acting as President during the remainder of such term.

This article shall be inoperative unless it shall have been ratified as an amendment to the Constitution by the legislatures of three-fourths of the several states within seven years from the date of its submission to the states by the Congress.

[Article XXIII][20]

Section 1.

The District constituting the seat of Government of the United States shall appoint in such manner as the Congress may direct:

A number of electors of President and Vice-President equal to the whole number of Senators and Representatives in Congress to which the District would be entitled if it were a State, but in no event more than the least populous State; they shall be in addition to those appointed by the States, but they shall be considered, for the purposes of the election of President and Vice-President, to be electors appointed by a State; and they shall meet in the District and perform such duties as provided by the twelfth article of amendment.

Section 2.

The Congress shall have power to enforce this article by appropriate legislation.

[19] Adopted in 1961.
[20] Adopted in 1961.

[Article XXIV][21]

Section 1.
The right of citizens of the United States to vote in any primary or other election for President or Vice President, for electors for President or Vice President, or for Senator or Representative in Congress, shall not be denied or abridged by the United States or any state by reason of failure to pay any poll tax or other tax.

Section 2.
The Congress shall have the power to enforce this article by appropriate legislation.

[Article XXV][22]

Section 1.
In case of the removal of the President from office or of his death or resignation, the Vice President shall become President.

Section 2.
Whenever there is a vacancy in the office of the Vice President, the President shall nominate a Vice President who shall take office upon confirmation by a majority vote of both Houses of Congress.

Section 3.
Whenever the President transmits to the President Pro Tempore of the Senate and the Speaker of the House of Representatives his written declaration that he is unable to discharge the powers and duties of his office, and until he transmits to them a written declaration to the contrary, such powers and duties shall be discharged by the Vice President as Acting President.

Section 4.
Whenever the Vice President and a majority of either the principal officers of the executive departments or of such other body as Congress may by law provide, transmit to the President Pro Tempore of the Senate and the Speaker of the House of Representatives their written declaration that the President is unable to discharge the powers and duties of his office, the Vice President shall immediately assume the powers and duties of the office as Acting President.

Thereafter, when the President transmits to the President Pro Tempore of the Senate and the Speaker of the House of Representatives his written declaration that no inability exists, he shall resume the powers and duties of his office unless the Vice President and a majority of either the principal officers of the executive departments or of such other body as Congress may by law provide, transmit within four days to

[21] Adopted in 1964.
[22] Adopted in 1967.

the President Pro Tempore of the Senate and the Speaker of the House of Representatives their written declaration that the President is unable to discharge the powers and duties of his office. Thereupon Congress shall decide the issue, assembling within forty-eight hours for that purpose if not in session. If the Congress, within twenty-one days after receipt of the latter written declaration, or, if Congress is not in session, within twenty-one days after Congress is required to assemble, determines by two-thirds vote of both Houses that the President is unable to discharge the powers and duties of his office, the Vice President shall continue to discharge the same as Acting President; otherwise, the President shall resume the powers and duties of his office.

[Article XXVI][23]

Section 1.
The right of citizens of the United States, who are eighteen years of age or older, to vote shall not be denied or abridged by the United States or by any State on account of age.

Section 2.
The Congress shall have power to enforce this article by appropriate legislation.

[Article XXVII][24]

No law varying the compensation for the services of the Senators and Representatives shall take effect until an election of Representatives shall have intervened.

[23] Adopted in 1971.
[24] Adopted in 1992.

Year	Candidates	Parties	Popular Vote	Percentage of Popular Vote	Electoral Vote	Percentage of Voter Participation
1789	**GEORGE WASHINGTON (Va.)***				69	
	John Adams				34	
	Others				35	
1792	**GEORGE WASHINGTON (Va.)**				132	
	John Adams				77	
	George Clinton				50	
	Others				5	
1796	**JOHN ADAMS (Mass.)**	Federalist			71	
	Thomas Jefferson	Democratic-Republican			68	
	Thomas Pinckney	Federalist			59	
	Aaron Burr	Dem.-Rep.			30	
	Others				48	
1800	**THOMAS JEFFERSON (Va.)**	Dem.-Rep.			73	
	Aaron Burr	Dem.-Rep.			73	
	John Adams	Federalist			65	
	C. C. Pinckney	Federalist			64	
	John Jay	Federalist			1	
1804	**THOMAS JEFFERSON (Va.)**	Dem.-Rep.			162	
	C. C. Pinckney	Federalist			14	

Year	Candidate	Party	Popular Vote	%	Electoral Vote	% Participation
1808	**JAMES MADISON (Va.)**	Dem.-Rep.			122	
	C. C. Pinckney	Federalist			47	
	George Clinton	Dem.-Rep.			6	
1812	**JAMES MADISON (Va.)**	Dem.-Rep.			128	
	De Witt Clinton	Federalist			89	
1816	**JAMES MONROE (Va.)**	Dem.-Rep.			183	
	Rufus King	Federalist			34	
1820	**JAMES MONROE (Va.)**	Dem.-Rep.			231	
	John Quincy Adams	Dem.-Rep.			1	
1824	**JOHN Q. ADAMS (Mass.)**	Dem.-Rep.	108,740	30.5	84	26.9
	Andrew Jackson	Dem.-Rep.	153,544	43.1	99	
	William H. Crawford	Dem.-Rep.	46,618	13.1	41	
	Henry Clay	Dem.-Rep.	47,136	13.2	37	
1828	**ANDREW JACKSON (Tenn.)**	Democratic	647,286	56.0	178	57.6
	John Quincy Adams	National Republican	508,064	44.0	83	
1832	**ANDREW JACKSON (Tenn.)**	Democratic	687,502	55.0	219	55.4
	Henry Clay	National Republican	530,189	42.4	49	
	John Floyd	Independent			11	
	William Wirt	Anti-Mason	33,108	2.6	7	
1836	**MARTIN VAN BUREN (N.Y.)**	Democratic	765,483	50.9	170	57.8
	W. H. Harrison	Whig			73	
	Hugh L. White	Whig	739,795	49.1	26	
	Daniel Webster	Whig			14	
	W. P. Magnum	Independent			11	

* State of residence at time of election.

(continued)

PRESIDENTIAL ELECTIONS (cont.)

Year	Candidates	Parties	Popular Vote	Percentage of Popular Vote	Electoral Vote	Percentage of Voter Participation
1840	WILLIAM H. HARRISON (Ohio)	Whig	1,274,624	53.1	234	80.2
	Martin Van Buren	Democratic	1,127,781	46.9	60	
	J. G. Birney	Liberty	7,069		—	
1844	JAMES K. POLK (Tenn.)	Democratic	1,338,464	49.6	170	78.9
	Henry Clay	Whig	1,300,097	48.1	105	
	J. G. Birney	Liberty	62,300	2.3	—	
1848	ZACHARY TAYLOR (La.)	Whig	1,360,967	47.4	163	72.7
	Lewis Cass	Democratic	1,222,342	42.5	127	
	Martin Van Buren	Free-Soil	291,263	10.1	—	
1852	FRANKLIN PIERCE (N.H.)	Democratic	1,601,117	50.9	254	69.6
	Winfield Scott	Whig	1,385,453	44.1	42	
	John P. Hale	Free-Soil	155,825	5.0	—	
1856	JAMES BUCHANAN (Pa.)	Democratic	1,832,955	45.3	174	78.9
	John C. Frémont	Republican	1,339,932	33.1	114	
	Millard Fillmore	American	871,731	21.6	8	
1860	ABRAHAM LINCOLN (Ill.)	Republican	1,865,593	39.8	180	81.2
	Stephen A. Douglas	Democratic	1,382,713	29.5	12	
	John C. Breckinridge	Democratic	848,356	18.1	72	
	John Bell	Union	592,906	12.6	39	
1864	ABRAHAM LINCOLN (Ill.)	Republican	2,213,655	55.0	212	73.8
	George B. McClellan	Democratic	1,805,237	45.0	21	

Year	Candidate	Party	Popular Vote	%	Electoral Vote	Turnout %
1868	**ULYSSES S. GRANT (Ill.)**	Republican	3,012,833	52.7	214	78.1
	Horatio Seymour	Democratic	2,703,249	47.3	80	
1872	**ULYSSES S. GRANT (Ill.)**	Republican	3,597,132	55.6	286	71.3
	Horace Greeley	Democratic; Liberal Republican	2,834,125	43.9	66	
1876	**RUTHERFORD B. HAYES (Ohio)**	Republican	4,036,298	48.0	185	81.8
	Samuel J. Tilden	Democratic	4,300,590	51.0	184	
1880	**JAMES A. GARFIELD (Ohio)**	Republican	4,454,416	48.5	214	79.4
	Winfield S. Hancock	Democratic	4,444,952	48.1	155	
1884	**GROVER CLEVELAND (N.Y.)**	Democratic	4,874,986	48.5	219	77.5
	James G. Blaine	Republican	4,851,981	48.2	182	
1888	**BENJAMIN HARRISON (Ind.)**	Republican	5,439,853	47.9	233	79.3
	Grover Cleveland	Democratic	5,540,309	48.6	168	
1892	**GROVER CLEVELAND (N.Y.)**	Democratic	5,556,918	46.1	277	74.7
	Benjamin Harrison	Republican	5,176,108	43.0	145	
	James B. Weaver	People's	1,041,028	8.5	22	
1896	**WILLIAM McKINLEY (Ohio)**	Republican	7,104,779	51.1	271	79.3
	William J. Bryan	Democratic-People's	6,502,925	47.7	176	
1900	**WILLIAM McKINLEY (Ohio)**	Republican	7,207,923	51.7	292	73.2
	William J. Bryan	Dem.-Populist	6,358,133	45.5	155	
1904	**THEODORE ROOSEVELT (N.Y.)**	Republican	7,623,486	57.9	336	65.2
	Alton B. Parker	Democratic	5,077,911	37.6	140	
	Eugene V. Debs	Socialist	402,283	3.0	—	

(continued)

PRESIDENTIAL ELECTIONS (cont.)

Year	Candidates	Parties	Popular Vote	Percentage of Popular Vote	Electoral Vote	Percentage of Voter Participation
1908	WILLIAM H. TAFT (Ohio)	Republican	7,678,908	51.6	321	65.4
	William J. Bryan	Democratic	6,409,104	43.1	162	
	Eugene V. Debs	Socialist	420,793	2.8	—	
1912	WOODROW WILSON (N.J.)	Democratic	6,293,454	41.9	435	58.8
	Theodore Roosevelt	Progressive	4,119,538	27.4	88	
	William H. Taft	Republican	3,484,980	23.2	8	
	Eugene V. Debs	Socialist	900,672	6.0	—	
1916	WOODROW WILSON (N.J.)	Democratic	9,129,606	49.4	277	61.6
	Charles E. Hughes	Republican	8,538,221	46.2	254	
	A. L. Benson	Socialist	585,113	3.2	—	
1920	WARREN G. HARDING (Ohio)	Republican	16,152,200	60.4	404	49.2
	James M. Cox	Democratic	9,147,353	34.2	127	
	Eugene V. Debs	Socialist	919,799	3.4	—	
1924	CALVIN COOLIDGE (Mass.)	Republican	15,725,016	54.0	382	48.9
	John W. Davis	Democratic	8,386,503	28.8	136	
	Robert M. LaFollette	Progressive	4,822,856	16.6	13	
1928	HERBERT HOOVER (Calif.)	Republican	21,391,381	58.2	444	56.9
	Alfred E. Smith	Democratic	15,016,443	40.9	87	
	Norman Thomas	Socialist	267,835	0.7	—	
1932	FRANKLIN D. ROOSEVELT (N.Y.)	Democratic	22,821,857	57.4	472	56.9
	Herbert Hoover	Republican	15,761,841	39.7	59	
	Norman Thomas	Socialist	881,951	2.2	—	

Year	Candidate	Party	Popular Vote	Percentage	Electoral Vote	Percentage of Voter Participation
1936	**FRANKLIN D. ROOSEVELT (N.Y.)**	Democratic	27,751,597	60.8	523	61.0
	Alfred M. Landon	Republican	16,679,583	36.5	8	
	William Lemke	Union	882,479	1.9	—	
1940	**FRANKLIN D. ROOSEVELT (N.Y.)**	Democratic	27,244,160	54.8	449	62.5
	Wendell L. Willkie	Republican	22,305,198	44.8	82	
1944	**FRANKLIN D. ROOSEVELT (N.Y.)**	Democratic	25,602,504	53.5	432	55.9
	Thomas E. Dewey	Republican	22,006,285	46.0	99	
1948	**HARRY S. TRUMAN (Mo.)**	Democratic	24,105,695	49.5	304	53.0
	Thomas E. Dewey	Republican	21,969,170	45.1	189	
	J. Strom Thurmond	State-Rights Democratic	1,169,021	2.4	38	
	Henry A. Wallace	Progressive	1,156,103	2.4	—	
1952	**DWIGHT D. EISENHOWER (N.Y.)**	Republican	33,936,252	55.1	442	63.3
	Adlai E. Stevenson	Democratic	27,314,992	44.4	89	
1956	**DWIGHT D. EISENHOWER (N.Y.)**	Republican	35,575,420	57.6	457	60.6
	Adlai E. Stevenson	Democratic	26,033,066	42.1	73	
	Other	—	—		1	
1960	**JOHN F. KENNEDY (Mass.)**	Democratic	34,227,096	49.9	303	62.8
	Richard M. Nixon	Republican	34,108,546	49.6	219	
	Other	—	—		15	
1964	**LYNDON B. JOHNSON (Tex.)**	Democratic	43,126,506	61.1	486	61.7
	Barry M. Goldwater	Republican	27,176,799	38.5	52	
1968	**RICHARD M. NIXON (N.Y.)**	Republican	31,770,237	43.4	301	60.6
	Hubert H. Humphrey	Democratic	31,270,533	42.7	191	
	George Wallace	American Independent	9,906,141	13.5	46	

(continued)

PRESIDENTIAL ELECTIONS (cont.)

Year	Candidates	Parties	Popular Vote	Percentage of Popular Vote	Electoral Vote	Percentage of Voter Participation
1972	**RICHARD M. NIXON (N.Y.)**	Republican	47,169,911	60.7	520	55.2
	George S. McGovern	Democratic	29,170,383	37.5	17	
	Other	—	—		1	
1976	**JIMMY CARTER (Ga.)**	Democratic	40,828,587	50.0	297	53.5
	Gerald R. Ford	Republican	39,147,613	47.9	241	
	Other	—	1,575,459	2.1	—	
1980	**RONALD REAGAN (Calif.)**	Republican	43,901,812	50.7	489	52.6
	Jimmy Carter	Democratic	35,483,820	41.0	49	
	John B. Anderson	Independent	5,719,722	6.6	—	
	Ed Clark	Libertarian	921,188	1.1	—	
1984	**RONALD REAGAN (Calif.)**	Republican	54,455,075	59.0	525	53.3
	Walter Mondale	Democratic	37,577,185	41.0	13	
1988	**GEORGE BUSH (Tex.)**	Republican	47,946,422	54.0	426	50.2
	Michael S. Dukakis	Democratic	41,016,429	46.0	112	
1992	**WILLIAM J. CLINTON (Ark.)**	Democratic	43,728,375	43.0	370	55.0
	George Bush	Republican	38,167,416	38.0	168	
	Ross Perot	Independent	19,237,247	19.0	0	
1996	**WILLIAM J. CLINTON (Ark.)**	Democratic	47,401,185	49.3	379	49.0
	Robert Dole	Republican	39,197,469	40.7	159	
	Ross Perot	Reform	8,085,294	8.4	—	

POPULATION OF THE UNITED STATES, 1790-1998

Year	Population	Percent Increase	Population per Square Mile	Percent Urban/ Rural	Percent White/ Nonwhite	Median Age
1790	3,929,214		4.5	5.1/94.9	80.7/19.3	NA
1800	5,308,483	35.1	6.1	6.1/93.9	81.1/18.9	NA
1810	7,239,881	36.4	4.3	7.3/92.7	81.0/19.0	NA
1820	9,638,453	33.1	5.5	7.2/92.8	81.6/18.4	16.7
1830	12,866,020	33.5	7.4	8.8/91.2	81.9/18.1	17.2
1840	17,069,453	32.7	9.8	10.8/89.2	83.2/16.8	17.8
1850	23,191,876	35.9	7.9	15.3/84.7	84.3/15.7	18.9
1860	31,443,321	35.6	10.6	19.8/80.2	85.6/14.4	19.4
1870	39,818,449	26.6	13.4	25.7/74.3	86.2/13.8	20.2
1880	50,155,783	26.0	16.9	28.2/71.8	86.5/13.5	20.9
1890	62,947,714	25.5	21.2	35.1/64.9	87.5/12.5	22.0
1900	75,994,575	20.7	25.6	39.6/60.4	87.9/12.1	22.9
1910	91,972,266	21.0	31.0	45.6/54.4	88.9/11.1	24.1
1920	105,710,620	14.9	35.6	51.2/48.8	89.7/10.3	25.3
1930	122,775,046	16.1	41.2	56.1/43.9	89.8/10.2	26.4
1940	131,669,275	7.2	44.2	56.5/43.5	89.8/10.2	29.0
1950	150,697,361	14.5	50.7	64.0/36.0	89.5/10.5	30.2
1960	179,323,175	18.5	50.6	69.9/30.1	88.6/11.4	29.5
1970	203,302,031	13.4	57.4	73.5/26.5	87.6/12.4	28.0
1980	226,545,805	11.4	64.0	73.7/26.3	86.0/14.0	30.0
1990	248,709,873	9.9	70.3	77.5/22.5	80.3/19.7	32.9
1998	270,312,000	8.6	76	80/20	82.6/17.4	35.3

NA = Not available.

EMPLOYMENT, 1870–1998

Year	Number of Workers (in millions)	Male/Female Employment Ratio	Percentage of Workers in Unions
1870	12.5	85/15	—
1880	17.4	85/15	—
1890	23.3	83/17	—
1900	29.1	82/18	3
1910	38.2	79/21	6
1920	41.6	79/21	12
1930	48.8	78/22	7
1940	53.0	76/24	27
1950	59.6	72/28	25
1960	69.9	68/32	26
1970	82.1	63/37	25
1980	108.5	58/42	23
1985	108.9	57/43	19
1988	114.9	55/45	17
1990	124.8	54/46	16
1998	137.7	54/46	13.9

Production, Trade, and Federal Spending/Debt, 1790–1998

Year	Gross National Product (GNP) (in billions $)	Balance of Trade (in millions $)	Federal Budget (in billions $)	Federal Surplus/Deficit (in billions $)	Federal Debt (in billions $)
1790	—	-3	.004	+0.00015	.076
1800	—	-20	.011	+0.0006	.083
1810	—	-18	.008	+0.0012	.053
1820	—	-4	.018	-0.0004	.091
1830	—	+3	.015	+0.100	.049
1840	—	+25	.024	-0.005	.004
1850	—	-26	.040	+0.004	.064
1860	—	-38	.063	-0.01	.065
1870	7.4	-11	.310	+0.10	2.4
1880	11.2	+92	.268	+0.07	2.1
1890	13.1	+87	.318	+0.09	1.2
1900	18.7	+569	.521	+0.05	1.2
1910	35.3	+273	.694	-0.02	1.1
1920	91.5	+2,880	6.357	+0.3	24.3
1930	90.7	+513	3.320	+0.7	16.3
1940	100.0	-3,403	9.6	-2.7	43.0
1950	286.5	+1,691	43.1	-2.2	257.4
1960	506.5	+4,556	92.2	+0.3	286.3
1970	992.7	+2,511	196.6	+2.8	371.0
1980	2,631.7	+24,088	579.6	-59.5	914.3
1990	5,465.1	-100,997.1	1,251.8	-220.3	3,223.3
1998	8,509.0	-231,000	1,653.0	69.0	5,479.0

Illustration Credits

Chapter 1, page 2: New York Public Library; **p. 4:** Smithsonian Institution; **p. 13:** Oroñoz-Nieto; **p. 24:** New York Public Library.
Chapter 2, page 28: New York Public Library; **pp. 29, 48:** New York Public Library, Rare Books Division.
Chapter 3, pages 61, 66: National Maritime Museum, Greenwich, England; **p. 73:** American Heritage Publishing Co./A Division of Forbes, Inc.; **p. 81:** Courtesy Peabody Essex Museum, Salem, MA; **p. 87:** Princeton University Library, Sinclair Hamilton Collection, Visual Materials Division, Department of Rare Books and Special Collections; **p. 90:** Library Company of Philadelphia.
Chapter 4, page 95: The Metropolitan Museum of Art, Gift of Mrs. Russell Sage, 1909 (10.125.103); **p. 100:** Corbis-Bettmann; **p. 110:** The Metropolitan Museum of Art, Gift of Mrs. Russell Sage, 1909 (10.125.103); **p. 114:** The Connecticut Historical Society, Hartford, Connecticut; **p. 117:** Library of Congress.
Chapter 5, page 123(left): The National Portrait Gallery, Smithsonian Institution/Art Resource, NY; **pp. 123(right), 128:** Anne S.K. Brown Military Collection, Brown University Library; **p. 151:** The National Portrait Gallery, Smithsonian Institution/Art Resource, NY.
Chapter 6, page 156(left): New York Public Library; **p.156(right):** Atwater Kent Museum; **p. 158:** New York Public Library; **p. 163:** North Wind Picture Archives; **p. 170:** Atwater Kent Museum; **p. 176:** New York Public Library.
Chapter 7, page 181(left): Monticello/Thomas Jefferson Memorial Foundation, Inc./National Portrait Gallery; **p. 181(right):** Library of Congress; **p. 183:** Ohio Historical Society; **p. 187:** Lithograph by Kennedy and Lucas, after A. Rider, © The New-York Historical Society; **p. 189:** Rhode Island Historical Society; **p. 190:** National Archives and Records Administration; **p. 194:** Monticello/Thomas Jefferson Memorial Foundation, Inc./National Portrait Gallery; **p. 213:** Library of Congress.
Chapter 8, page 219: Corbis-Bettmann; **p. 220:** Abby Aldrich Rockefeller Folk Art Center, Williamsburg, VA; **p. 222:** © The New-York Historical Society; **p. 225:** The Denver Public Library, Western History Collection; **p. 227:** Corbis-Bettmann; **p. 229:** This item is reproduced by permission of The Huntington Library, San Marino, California; **p. 233:** Collection of the Architect of the Capitol/Library of Congress.
Chapter 9, page 243: © The New-York Historical Society; **p. 244:** Library of Congress; **p. 247:** M. and M. Karolik Collection, Museum of Fine Arts, Boston; **p. 254:** Corbis-Bettmann; **p. 266:** © The New-York Historical Society; **p. 267:** Corbis-Bettmann.
Chapter 10, page 273: Museum of the City of New York; **p. 274:** Bostonian Society; **p. 280:** Museum of the City of New York; **p. 288:** Fair Street Pictures; **p. 290:** Library of Congress; **p. 293:** Collection of Zelda P. Mackay, San Francisco, CA; **p. 298:** Albany Institute of History and Art; **p. 306:** International Harvester.
Chapter 11, page 311: © The New-York Historical Society; **p. 314:** Giraudon/Art Resource, NY; **p. 316:** Department of Archives and History, Jackson, MI. Courtesy, New York Public Library; **p. 322:** © The New-York Historical Society; **p. 328:** Sophia Smith Collection, Smith College; **p. 333:** Abby Aldrich Rockefeller Folk Art Center, Williamsburg, VA.
Chapter 12, page 338: Library of Congress; **p. 340:** New York Public Library, Special Collections; **pp. 345, 349, 350, 358:** Library of Congress; **p. 361:** © The New-York Historical Society.
Chapter 13, page 365(left): © The New-York Historical Society; **p. 365(right):** Library of Congress; **p. 371,** © The New-York Historical Society; **p. 377:** Museum of New Mexico; **p. 389:** Corbis-Bettmann; **p. 396:** Library of Congress.
Chapter 14, page 402(left): Cook Collection, Valentine Museum; **pp. 402(right), 412:** Library of Congress; **p. 414:** Corbis-Bettmann; **p. 417:** Cook Collection, Valentine Museum; **p. 431:** Corbis-Bettmann; **p. 435,** Library of Congress.
Chapter 15, page 442(left): Library of Congress; **p. 442(middle):** Corbis-Bettmann; **p. 442(right):** North Wind Picture Archives; **p. 445:** The Museum of the Confederacy, Richmond, Virginia; **p. 447,** Library of Congress; **p. 453:** North Wind Picture Archives; **p. 457:** Corbis-Bettmann; **p. 461:** Historic New Orleans Collection; **p. 470:** The Newberry Library, Chicago, Illinois; **p. 474:** Corbis-Bettmann.

Chapter 16, page 482 (top): Union Pacific Museum Collection; **p. 482 (bottom):** Smithsonian Institution, National Anthropological Archives, Bureau of American Ethnology Collection; **p. 486:** Union Pacific Museum collection; **p. 491:** Henry Ford Museum & Greenfield Village; **p. 497:** Culver, Inc.; **p. 502:** Corbis-Bettmann; **p. 506:** Smithsonian Institution, National Anthropological Archives, Bureau of American Ethnology Collection.
Chapter 17, page 516: Henry Ford Museum & Greenfield Village; **p. 517:** U.S. Department of the Interior, National Park Service, Edison National Historic Site; **p. 523:** From the Collections of Henry Ford Museum & Greenfield Village; **p. 530:** Private Collection; **p. 533:** Culver, Inc.; **p. 536:** Corbis-Bettmann; **p. 540:** Carnegie Library of Pittsburgh.
Chapter 18, pages 546, 553: Corbis-Bettmann; **p. 560:** © The New-York Historical Society; **p. 565:** Brown Brothers; **p. 566:** Corbis-Bettmann; **p. 571:** Purchased with funds from the Edmundson Art Foundation, Inc., Des Moines Art Center Permanent Collections, 1958.2.
Chapter 19, page 580: Culver, Inc.; **p. 585:** New York Public Library; **p. 593:** Kansas State Historical Society; **p. 595:** Culver, Inc.; **p. 598:** Smithsonian Institution.
Chapter 20, page 605 (top): Naval Historical Center; **p. 605 (middle):** Theodore Roosevelt Association; **p. 605 (bottom):** Culver, Inc.; **p. 606:** Naval Historical Center; **p. 615:** Theodore Roosevelt Association; **p. 620:** Culver, Inc.; **p.622:** Library of Congress.
Chapter 21, pages 629 (both), 631: Culver, Inc.; **p. 635:** Corbis-Bettmann; **p. 638:** Culver, Inc.; **p. 644:** State Historical Society of Wisconsin; **p. 648:** Photographs and Prints Division, Schomburg Center for Research in Black Culture, The New York Public Library, Astor, Lenox, and Tilden Foundations.
Chapter 22, page 658 (top): Culver, Inc.; **p. 658 (bottom):** Historical Pictures / Stock Montage, Inc.; **p. 661:** Culver, Inc.; **p. 665:** Brown Brothers; **p. 674:** Historical Pictures / Stock Montage, Inc.; **p. 677:** Corbis-Bettmann.
Chapter 23, pages 681, 685: Corbis-Bettmann; **p. 687:** UPI/Corbis-Bettmann; **p. 690:** Corbis-Bettmann/Hulton-Deutsch Collection; **p. 691:** National Archives and Records Administration; **p. 701:** James Van Der Zee.
Chapter 24, page 707: UPI/Corbis-Bettmann; **p. 710:** Courtesy George Eastman House; **p. 715:** Corbis-Bettmann; **p. 724:** UPI/Corbis-Bettmann.
Chapter 25, page 732 (top left): Culver, Inc., **p. 732 (top right):** UPI/Corbis-Bettmann; **p. 732 (bottom left):** Photo by Arthur Rothstein for USDA Farm Security Administration/Library of Congress; **p. 739:** Culver, Inc.; **p. 740:** Photo by Arthur Rothstein for USDA Farm Security Administration/Library of Congress; **p. 748:** Photofest; **p. 756:** UPI/Corbis-Bettmann; **p. 757:** Franklin Delano Roosevelt Library.
Chapter 26, page 762 (top): Culver, Inc.; **pp. 762 (bottom), 763:** AP/Wide World; **p. 766:** UPI/Corbis-Bettmann; **p. 774:** Culver, Inc.; **p. 780:** U.S. Department of the Interior, National Park Service; **p. 784:** UPI/Corbis-Bettmann.
Chapter 27, page 792 (left): Culver, Inc.; **p. 792 (right):** Department of the Navy, NCCOSC; **p. 794:** UPI/Corbis-Bettmann; **p. 796:** Culver, Inc.; **p. 800:** Brown Brothers; **p. 806:** Department of the Navy, NCCOSC.
Chapter 28, pages 810, 812: UPI/Corbis-Bettmann; **p. 819:** Archive Photos/American Stock; **p. 825:** UPI/Corbis-Bettmann; **p. 827:** Corbis-Bettmann; **pp. 835, 841:** UPI/Corbis-Bettmann.
Chapter 29, page 845 (top left): Corbis-Bettmann, **p. 845 (top right and bottom right):** UPI/Corbis-Bettmann ; **p. 847:** Corbis-Bettmann; **pp. 852, 858, 865, 868:** UPI/Corbis-Bettmann.
Chapter 30, page 876 (top left): Culver, Inc.; **p. 876 (top right and bottom):** UPI/Corbis-Bettmann; **p. 877:** UPI/Corbis-Bettmann; **p. 882:** Archive Photos; **p. 888:** © Walt Disney Productions, Archive Photos; **p. 889:** Culver, Inc.; **p. 895:** Corbis-Bettmann; **pp. 901, 906:** UPI/Corbis-Bettmann.
Chapter 31, page 915 (top): Paul Schutzer, Life Magazine, © 1961 Time Warner, Inc.; **p. 915 (bottom):** UPI/Corbis-Bettmann Archive; **p. 917:** Paul Schutzer, Life Magazine, © 1961 Time Warner, Inc.; **pp. 923, 933:** UPI/Corbis-Bettmann Archive; **p. 939:** Corbis-Bettmann Archive.
Chapter 32, page 946 (left): Leif Skoogfors/Woodfin Camp & Associates; **p. 946 (middle):** J.P. Laffont/Sygma; **p. 946 (bottom):** UPI/Corbis-Bettmann; **p. 948:** Leif Skoogfors/Woodfin Camp & Associates; **p. 950:** © New York Daily News, L.P. Reprinted with Permission. Archive Photos/Blank Archive; **pp. 953, 964:** UPI/Corbis-Bettmann; **p. 966:** J.P. Laffont/Sygma.
Chapter 33, page 982 (both): UPI/Corbis-Bettmann; **pp. 986, 988, 995:** UPI/Corbis-Bettmann.
Chapter 34, pages 1003 (both), 1004: Reuters/Corbis-Bettmann Archive; **p. 1009:** Archive/Ron Sachs/Consolidated News Pictures; **p. 1015:** Reuters/Corbis-Bettmann; **p. 1020:** Corbis-Bettmann/AFP; **p. 1024:** Courtesy America Online; **p. 1033:** Reuters/Corbis-Bettmann; **p. 1035:** © The Estate of Keith Haring.

Index

Note: Page numbers followed by the letter *i* refer to illustrations and by the letter *m* to maps.

Little Turtle (Miami), 150
Little Women (Alcott), 567
Litwack, Leon, 451
Livestock industry, and economy of Far
West, 493–96
Livingston, Robert R., 191–92, 199, 234
Locke, Alain, 720
Locke, John, 50, 111, 124, 175
Lodge, Henry Cabot, 618, 697, 791
Log Cabin, election of 1840 and image of,
266–68
Lôme, Dupuy de, 611
London, and World War II, *800i*
London Company, 28–30, 43
Lonely Crowd, The (Riesman, 1950), 892
Long, Huey P., 591, 773–74, 781
Long, Stephen H., 226
Longstreet, Augustus B., 342
Lon Nol, Gen., 961
Looking Backward (Bellamy, 1888), 532
Lords of Trade, 56
Lorenz, Pare, 752
Los Angeles, California: South Central riots
of 1992, 1033; Watts riots in 1964, 925;
World War II and growth of, 816, 824,
878. *See also* California
Louisbourg, Nova Scotia, 98, 101
Louisiana, 401–2, 432. *See also* New Orleans
Louisiana Purchase, 198–200, *201m*
Lovejoy, Elijah, 359
Lowell, Francis Cabot, 220
Lowell system, 291
Loyalists, and American Revolution, 137–38
Lublin government, of Poland, 848
Lucas, Robert, 737
Luce, Henry, 752
Lumber industry, 305
Lundy, Benjamin, 357
Lusitania (ship), 683
Luther, Martin, 20
Lynching, 477, 556, 637, 700, 785
Lyon, Mary, 300
Lyon, Matthew, 175, *176i*
Lyon, Nathaniel, 425

MacArthur, Gen. Arthur, 621
MacArthur, Gen. Douglas: Great Depression
and veterans' protests, 755–56; Korean
War, 865, 866; occupation government in
Japan, 850; World War II, 810, 836
Maceo, Antonio, 613
Machine tools, 286–87
MacLeod, Colin, 1025
Macon's Bill No. 2 (1810), 206
Macready, Charles, 302
Madero, Francisco, 676
Madison, James: Bill of Rights, 164;
Confederation Congress and taxation, 151;
Constitutional Convention, 156, 157, 159,
160; Federalists and, 162; *Marbury v.
Madison*, 197; national debt, 167; as
president, 205–206, 221; Republicans and,
169; War of 1812, 205, 209
Magazines, 301, 315, 567, 715, 749, 829
Magellan, Ferdinand, 11
Maggie: A Girl of the Street (Dreiser, 1893), 569
Mahan, Alfred Thayer, 606

Maine: Aroostook War, 269; settlement of,
46; statehood, 231–32
Maine (battleship), *606i*, 611, 612
Maize. *See* Corn
Malaria, 28, 30, 73, 881, 882
Malcolm X, 926–27
Mali, empire of, 17, 18
Mandela, Nelson, 1005
Mangas Colorado (Apache), 505
Manhattan Project, 837
Manifest Destiny, 365–66, 605–6
Mann, Horace, 352, 354
Man Nobody Knows, The (Barton, 1920s), 714
Man of the People (Truman, 1995), 839
Manufacturing: government promotion of
after War of 1812, 219–20; growth of from
1840 to 1860, 286; interchangeability of
parts, 191, 287; mass production, 522; New
South, 472; personal computers in 1980s
and 1990s, 1022, 1023; transformation of
in 1970s, 972. *See also* Business; Factory;
Industry
Mao Zedong, 850
Marbury, William, 197
Marbury v. Madison (1803), 197
March on Washington (1963), 923
"March to the Sea," 436, *438m*
Marconi, Guglielmo, 517
Marcy, William L., 247
Mariana Islands, 836
Marielietos, 955
Marine Corps: African-Americans and World
War II, 823; Battle of Iwo Jima, 836. *See
also* Military
Marion, Francis, 134
Marketing, and consumer culture in late
1800s, 559–60. *See also* Advertising
Marriage: African-Americans and
Reconstruction, 460; higher education for
women and, 576; indentured servants in
Chesapeake colonies and, 64; New
England colonies and, 65; "New Woman"
and progressivism, 636; slavery and, 78–79,
333–34; World War II, 828. *See also*
Divorce; Family; Women
Marshall, Gen. George C., 812, 851–52, 871
Marshall, John, 197–98, 203, 232–34, 243
Marshall Plan, 851–52
Martí, José, 610
Martial law, and Civil War, 409
Martin, Joseph W., 866
Marx Brothers, 748
Marxism, 653, 1039
Mary, Queen of England, 21, 57
Maryland: Catholic Church, 36, 57–58,
83–84; early colonies of, 35–36; Glorious
Revolution, 57–58
Mason, James M., 422
Masons, and Society of Freemasons, 262
Massachusetts: American Revolution, 116,
118–20; Dominion of New England, 56,
57; education, 88, 182, 352–53; ironworks,
74; Massachusetts Bay experiment, 43–44;
mental hospitals, 354; Shays' Rebellion,
151–52; state government, 143; tavern
culture of revolutionary, 114; textile
industry, *220i*. *See also* Boston

Pinup girls, 830
Pitcairn, Major Thomas, 120
Pitcher, Molly, 139
Pitt, William, 99, 100, 108
Pittsburgh, Pennsylvania, 519
Pizarro, Francisco, 13
Plain folk, of antebellum South, 319–21
Plains Indians, 483
Plantations
—antebellum South: early Virginia and tobacco cultivation, 31; Old Southwest and system of, 224; slavery and, 78–79, 323–24; white society and, 317–18, 319, 320–21
—sugar and imperialism: Cuba, 620; Hawaii, 608; Puerto Rico, 616–17
Platt, Thomas, 673
Platt Amendment (1901), 619–20, 673
Plattsburgh, Battle of (1814), 212
Plessy v. Ferguson (1896), 475, 900
Plows, 305
Plow that Broke the Plains, The (film, 1936), 752
Plunkett, George Washington, 557
Plymouth, Massachusetts, 25, 41–43, 44
Pocahontas, 33
Podhoretz, Norman, 936
Poe, Edgar Allen, 341
Poetry: of antebellum South, 341; Whitman and, 341
Poland: German invasion in 1939, 801, 802; Potsdam accords, 849; Soviet Union and martial law in 1980s, 998; Teheran Conference, 846; World War II and Holocaust, 815; Yalta Conference, 847–48. *See also* Eastern Europe
Polaris submarines, 885
Police, 556, 699
Polio, 881, *882i*
Poliomyelitis Vaccination Act (1955), *882i*
"Political correctness," 1046, 1047
Political parties: Constitution and, 168–69; end of first system of, 227–28; legitimization of in 1830s, 245–46; progressivism, 640–45; revival of after 1816, 236–40; second party system and Jackson administration, 261–64; system of in late 1800s, 580–81. *See also* Democratic Party; Politics; Republican Party; Whig Party
Politics: agrarian revolt of late 1800s, 587–93; American Revolution, 152; in Colonial America, 90–91; crisis of 1890s, 593–601; Eisenhower and Republicanism, 904–6; emancipation and Civil War, 410–11; equilibrium in late 1800s, 579–87; Grant scandals, 463; Jacksonian era and rise of mass, 242–47; leadership and Civil War, 409–10; machines and bosses of late 1800s, 557–58; New Deal, 772–74, 788; Nixon years, 968–73; Popular Front and Left, 750–53; post-World War II period, 858–63; repression and Alien and Sedition Acts, 174–75; Sunbelt and rise of right in 1970s, 989–90; territorial governments in Far West, 489–90; Van Buren administration, 264–70; women in 1970s

and 1980s, 958–59; World War II, 831–32. *See also* Democratic Party; Elections; Government; Political parties; Republican Party
Polk, James K., 372, 373, 374–76, 378
Poll tax, 476
Polo, Marco, 8
Polynesians, 607
Pomeroy, Earl, 500
Pontiac (Ottawa), 103
Poor Richard's Almanac (Franklin), 86
Pope, John, 430
Popular culture: Great Depression, 749, 750; image of Far West, 497; nationalism, 240. *See also* Mass culture
Popular Front, 750–53
Popular sovereignty, 378, 387, *389i*
Population: aging of in 1990s, 1029; California in 1850s, 380; of Colonial America, 60–67, 70–71; demographic change in cities of 1950s, 899; distribution of in 1996, *A2–A3m*; growth from 1950 to 1960, 877, 878; increase from 1790 to 1996, *A37*; industrialization and growth of urban, 192; Industrial Revolution and changes in, 272–77; of New York in 1685, 52; slavery in antebellum South, 312, *313m*, 324; Spanish colonization of New Mexico and, 15; urban in late 1800s, 545; of Virginia colonies, 37; westward expansion and increase in, 222–23. *See also* Death rate; Immigration; Life expectancy; Migrations
—Europe: growth of in 1400s, 8, 19
—Native Americans: before European contact, 1, 2, 6–7, 25; Cahokia and, 3; European diseases and, 15, 25, 369; increase of in 1960s, 952
Populism: agrarian revolt of late 1800s, 587–93; election of 1896, 598–99
Populist Persuasion, The (Kazin, 1994), 591
Populist Revolt, The (Hicks, 1931), 590
Port Hudson, Louisiana, 432
Port Huron statement (1962), 946–47
Portrait of a Lady (James, 1881), 569
Port Royal (Carolinas), 50
Portugal, 9, 11, 18, 25
Postcards, *566i*
Postrevisionist history, and Cold War, 857
Potsdam accords (1945), 849
Pottawatomie Massacre (Kansas, 1855), 388
Potter, David, 887
Pound, Ezra, 720
Poverty: affluent society of 1950s and early 1960s, 897–99; African-Americans in 1980s and 1990s, 1031–34; in cities of colonial period, 82; in cities of 1850s, 295–96; in cities of late 1800s, 555–57; class system of antebellum South, 321; as motive for English colonization, 20; technological progress in colonial period and, 75–76; two-tiered economy of 1980s and 1990s, 1027; War on Poverty in 1960s, 918–19
Powderly, Terence V., 538
Powell, Lewis F., Jr., 969
Powers, Francis Gary, 911